PSYCHOLOGY

PSYCHOLOGY

THE STUDY OF HUMAN EXPERIENCE ■ THIRD EDITION

ROBERT ORNSTEIN
Visiting Professor at Stanford University

LAURA CARSTENSEN
Stanford University

with the assistance of
SHELLEY PATNOE
San Jose State University

HARCOURT BRACE JOVANOVICH, PUBLISHERS

San Diego   New York   Chicago   Austin   Washington, D.C.
London   Sydney   Tokyo   Toronto

PREFACE

sychology: The Study of Human Experience has introduced thousands of students to psychology. Like the previous editions, the purpose of the Third Edition is twofold: to present psychology as a unified science of the person, drawing contributions from different theoretical orientations; and to present the highest level of scientific information in a stimulating manner and at an accessible reading level.

The science of psychology examines how we develop, age, sense, perceive, learn, remember, think, engage in complex and intimate relationships, and how our brain, nervous system, and endocrine systems have evolved to suit our needs. It explores dreams, intelligence, emotions, motives, and creativity. Psychological research has helped us learn, for example, how to solve problems, what actions we can take to improve health, why we act as we do, and how we can understand and help others.

The Third Edition has been revised, reorganized, and updated throughout. It also boasts a broadened expertise and perspective, thanks to the contributions of many outstanding psychologists, yet it maintains a single, engaging voice. Most notably, Laura Carstensen of Stanford University, a clinical psychologist by training, is now coauthor. Her contributions to this edition are the work on gender throughout the text and the revisions of Chapters 2, 15, 16, and 21. Shelley Patnoe of San Jose State University contributed drafts of Chapters 14 and 17. Although these chapters aren't completely new, her teaching and writing experience has made these areas come alive for the student. Additional contributors to portions or all of individual chapters are mentioned in the summaries of the revised chapters, below.

To illustrate the social, biological, and cultural forces that act on people, we decided to highlight gender differences throughout the book. In many ways, we could just as easily have chosen class or ethnicity, but gender influences each of us in profound ways. Chapter 1 introduces biological, social, cognitive, and psychodynamic theories about gender differences. In boxes entitled "Being Female, Being Male," which are scattered throughout the book, we consider sex differences in the brain, in cognitive abilities (including the question of whether males are any better than females at math), in nonverbal behavior, in depression, and in the division of labor.

In addition to the new gender section, Chapter 1, "The Study of Human Experience," contains a new introduction to Freud and presents the SQ3R study method. Chapter 2, "Human Development," briefly discusses the history of developmental psychology and gives special attention to language development, the influence of day care, the interface between physical and cognitive development, and parenting. The chapter is quite different from the previous edition because the book now expresses a life-span orientation. Theories of adult development in this chapter carry the reader through late middle age. Old age and death are addressed specifically in Chapter 21, to close both this book and the book of human experience.

Chapter 3, "The Brain and Nervous System," is greatly updated, presenting recent discoveries on left-handedness, split-brain patients, and sex differences. Chapter 4, "Genetics and Evolution," is retitled and condensed. Chapter 5, "Sensory Experience," is refitted and contains both rewritten discussions of Fechner's Law, Steven's Power Law, and Weber's Law as well as new material on the psychological aspects of color perception, the visual pathways and the subjective dimensions of sound.

Chapter 6, "Perceiving the World," contains reworked discussions on brightness perception, size constancy, the development of perception, and a new section on Triesman's work on feature-object detection. Stephen LaBerge, of Stanford University, contributed generously to Chapter 7, "Consciousness and the Nature of the Mind," including material on his specialty, dreams. The drugs and sleep sections also are completely rewritten, and new material addresses experiences of dying, dissociation of conscoiusness, self-awareness, the conscious preparation for action, and Libet's work. Chapter 8, "The Basics of Learning," is almost entirely rewritten. Under the guidance of Stephen LaBerge, additions to the chapter include timing and its effect on operant conditioning, operant conditioning techniques in the classroom and in psychotherapy, the cognitive learning approach, and inborn potentials.

Chapter 9, "Remembering and Forgetting," integrates earlier discussions of different types of memory with the amnesia studies of Squire et al. and with Thompson's work on memory. Also added is Mishkin's work on coding of memory. Chapter 10, "Thinking and Language," is now briefer and more simplified. It contains new work by Tversky and Kahnemann and discusses neural networks. Tom Malone, of MIT's Sloane School, contributed material on computers and the mind, on artificial intelligence, and on how to organize work. Chapter 11, "The Measurement of Intelligence," features enhanced discussion of the inheritance of intellectual abilities.

Chapter 12, "Emotions and Happiness," is heavily revised to include updated information on emotions and the right hemisphere, the work of Ledoux et al. on dissonance between emotions and cognition, Zajonc's and new work on posing facial expressions, and a major section on happiness. Chapter 13, "Needs and Goals," is more accessible and contains many new real-life examples. Chapter 14, "Personality," contains new treatments of

Freud, Jung, and the importance of the unconscious, and it studies individual differences and action identification. Also new is work on temperament, the self, Q-sort, and social learning theory, as well as work by Hogan on human nature in the evolutionary context.

Chapter 15, "Psychological Disorders," reflects the changes in terminology and classification of the revised edition of the *Diagnostic and Statistical Manual (DSM-III-R)* of the American Psychiatric Association. The chapter expands upon the genetic transmission of disorders and, consistent with the life-span focus of the text, addresses age-related disorders like childhood autism and Alzheimer's disease. Chapter 16, "Psychotherapies," provides the historical context for psychotherapy and critiques it from a behavioral viewpoint. The chapter describes different theoretical orientations and summarizes their reliability and validity.

Chapter 17, "Social Psychology," includes new material on observing others, subtle influences on thought and action, the sunny side of social influence, and helping others. Chapter 18, "Human Intimacy," is new. It addresses attraction, Sternberg's theory of love, companionate love, loving styles, and sex and orgasms.

Charles Swencionis of Ferkhauf Graduate School, CUNY, and head of the health psychology program at Albert Einstein College of Medicine, contributed the first draft of new Chapter 19, "Health Psychology." This chapter presents new studies on stress, and it discusses how people act as patients and how mental factors can influence resistance to disease. It also considers behavioral medicine and treatment of stress-related disorders, addiction, and heart disease, and it contains an important discussion of AIDS. Chapter 20, "Adapting to the Modern World," is retitled and reorganized. It features a new section on designing machines for human use and an enhanced discussion of Zuboff's work.

Chapter 21, "Old Age," is virtually new, challenging many assumptions and myths about old age and presenting vital old age as something that is not only possible but also quite common. This chapter summarizes and integrates the human experiences addressed in the previous chapters. It begins with a review of biological aging and then considers psychological and social aging, pointing out how biology and psychology are inextricably tied.

Scattered throughout the text are advice and aside boxes based on current psychological research. Topics include how to study, how to enhance life's pleasures, how to improve memory, how to organize your desk, how to increase happiness, how to build confidence, how to choose a therapist, and how to counter social influence, as well as advice on sex, on getting feelings off your chest, on why education is important to health, and on growing old well. In all these boxes we use current research such as Pennebaker's recent work on confession and health benefits. These are presented as extra topics, to intrigue students about the value of psychology and to enhance their lives.

Once again we would like to thank our collaborators, especially Shelley Patnoe. Of course, a book like this can't be created without the help of many other people, since so much research must be organized, checked, and evaluated. We thank them here. Shane De Haven kept the book going, flowing through the zillion versions without a murmur. Linda Garfield, MD, rewrote the genetics section that in the Second Edition had been written by geneticist Anne Bowcock. Christina Lepnis added real-life material throughout, especially to the section on motives. Lynne Levitan drafted many treatments of research, performed original research, read proofs, and saved sanity on many occasions, especially when the work flooded unexpectedly. Denise Nessel contributed material to the chapter on learning, and Valerie Stone and Amanda Woodward contributed to the gender and development material.

We had great help at Harcourt Brace Jovanovich as well. Sarah Helyar Smith, manuscript editor, guided the book through the maze of editing and production to its finish; Nancy Lombardi, production editor, trafficked the proof and kept track of all the loose ends; Linda Wooton Miller, designer, created the handsome interior and exterior designs; Rebecca Lytle, art editor, selected the photographs and coordinated the line art; and Mandy Van Dusen, production manager, kept the myriad proof on track with the compositor and printer. Finally, we'd like to thank our exceptional acquisitions editor, Marc Boggs, who kept us on track for years after taking over the book almost a decade ago. Marc's help with both revisions is as much responsible for the shape and success of the book as anything the nominal authors did. He has now ascended to a new job and is reportedly knocking them out in his new position; we will miss him greatly.

Robert Ornstein
Laura Carstensen

ACKNOWLEDGMENTS

We wish to thank the following reviewers for critiquing the drafts of this Third Edition.

Harry Avis
Sierra College

Michael Brown
Pacific Lutheran University

Dennis Clare
College of San Mateo

Sharon Derry
Florida State University

John H. Flowers
University of Nebraska, Lincoln

George Fuller von Bozzay
Biofeedback Institute and
City College of San Francisco

Richard Harris
Kansas State University

Nancy Kalish
California State University, Sacramento

John P. Keith
Clark County Community College

Phil Law
DeAnza College

Delbert S. McHenry, Jr.
Seattle Pacific University

David Miller
Daytona Beach Community College

Teri Nicoll-Johnson
Modesto Junior College

Robert Numan
University of Santa Clara

Henry Peterson
Chico State University

David Phillips
Santa Monica College

Elane Rehr
Diablo Valley College

Frank M. Rosekrans
Eastern Washington University

Joyce R. Schaeuble
Sacramento City College

C. R. Snyder
University of Kansas

David Tiberi
Pasadena City College

Jose Vidal
Evergreen Valley College

Donald Yellin
Washburn University

CONTENTS

II
THE BIOLOGICAL WORLD 91

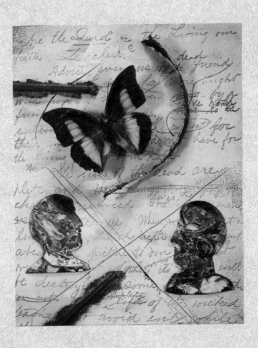

PSYCHOLOGY

1

THE STUDY OF HUMAN EXPERIENCE

You are the star of your own life. You are always on stage, always present. And like each of us, you may well have your ideas about who you are and what makes you and other people tick. However, all individuals' experiences are limited: you, like almost everyone, grow up in but one family, in one area, at one time, and in one place. You are only one of more than five billion people on this Earth, a combination of thousands of your parent's genes and millions of events in your environment. So you can't know how other people grow up, how they're taught, how they develop, and why they learn to think differently from you.

It takes a science to measure brain activity and relate it to immediate experience. It takes research and study to understand people's experiences, such as what we laugh at; how our schooling affects our lives; how we sense the reds of a sunset; how we see objects as the same size and shape, even as they move away, into the distance; how special people overcome obstacles and create inventions; how mothers provide the environment for children to thrive; and what makes us cry. That science, which studies the human experience—yours, mine, and others—how we are alike and how we differ, is psychology.

Psychology is a complete science of human experience and behavior. It examines the brain and nervous system, mental functioning, behavior, stresses, and mental disorders as well as creativity and triumphs.

HOW SCIENTIFIC PSYCHOLOGY DIFFERS FROM EVERYDAY PSYCHOLOGY

Most of us act like psychologists each day as we try to understand ourselves and others. We ask ourselves, "Why do I make so many mistakes?" and "How intelligent am I?" Some of the questions we have are more universal: "Is personality formed in the first years of life?" "Is an aggressive person always aggressive?"

The difference between everyday psychologists and the scientific ones is a matter of degree. In ordinary life we often cannot control what happens, and so our conclusions are imprecise. In science, many researchers may study the same problem for years, painstakingly checking their deductions.

Daily life is full of quick responses to specific situations. We may like or dislike someone on a whim or on the flimsiest evidence. But in scientific psychology, judgments are slow, measured, and tentative. And so the knowledge of psychology changes slowly; it is the most conservative and stable form of knowledge.

THE AIMS AND VIRTUES OF SCIENCE

Normal women and men, not inhuman calculating machines, create science. And they do it the way they do everything else: they make guesses and mistakes, argue, try out ideas to see what works, and discard what does not. Science may seem complex, but it is basically quite simple. Scientific methods are extensions and refinements of procedures that we use every day to answer questions about ourselves and about the world we live in. Individual scientists make the same mistakes everyone else does (Kahneman et al., 1986). But science differs from ordinary inquiry in that it is a systematic and formal process of gathering information; it has rules for testing ideas, interpreting results, and correcting mistakes.

ORDER, UNITY, AND SIMPLICITY

The world often seems mixed up: things happen all at once, and we have to make sense out of the confusion. The first assumption of science is that there is *order* in the world, and the second is that there is *unity* in it. Einstein (1956) neatly summarized these assumptions when he wrote "The great aim of science is to cover the greatest number of phenomena with the fewest number of ideas." Relying on the basic premises of order, unity, and simplicity of science, each generation of scientists can begin where the last left off. A text such as this contains information on the human brain, mental operations, development, social behavior, and therapies that were unknown to the most learned investigator of the 1940s. As Isaac Newton remarked on his accomplishments, "If I have seen farther than others, it is because I have stood on the shoulders of giants."

REPEATABILITY

In communicating results, scientists expose the scaffolding that supports their discoveries—what they were trying to do, how they did it, how they interpreted the results. A scientific discovery has to be as repeatable as a recipe. For instance, Aserinsky and Kleitman first discovered in 1953 that people dream every night. They published their findings in a scientific journal, and their findings have been repeated, or **replicated,** in many labs around the world.

Because you read about advancements, psychology may seem a certain, even boring, step-by-step process, everything neatly in place. But for every solution, for every successful experiment, there have been scores of blind alleys, straight out mistakes, and failures. And science, though it strives to be objective and unbiased in *understanding,* is not cool and detached in *operation.*

For example, there is great disagreement on such issues as the role of race in intelligence, on whether intelligence itself can be measured, on how important the early years of childhood are to adult life, on whether or not sex differences are biologically determined.

SCIENTIFIC IDEAS AND TESTS

Ordinary guesses are vague, and we do not always have all the information, so confirmation is haphazard. Scientific psychology is more specific: ideas are defined and tested by observation, demonstration, and experiment.

The **method of observation** uses the real world as its laboratory: researchers record but do not interfere with natural occurrences. **Demonstrations** are the most compelling method: psychology researchers present a phenomenon to their subjects so they experience it. The **experimental method** is the most creative. The experimenter intervenes, arranges a situation, controls all the parts of an experience, and records the results. While observation is most representative of life, experiments are precise and repeatable.

OBSERVATION

Observation is sometimes the only way to understand a phenomenon. If you want to discover, for example, how city life affects human experience, you may observe people in crowded cities. One study observed that people walk faster in cities than in the country. The larger the city, the faster people walk (Freedman, Sears, & Carlsmith, 1984). The faster walk of city dwellers may mean they are in a hurry or that they notice less of what is going on around them, or both. This is one reason why people are less likely to stop and help in cities, which we will see later in the discussion of the Good Samaritan experiment.

Formal observations are made in three ways: (1): case histories, (2) measurements and tests, and (3) questionnaires in which feelings and opinions may be reported.

CASE HISTORIES   A **case history** is an elaborate form of observation, in which a subject is studied in depth. The case of Nadia gave observers a rare glimpse into the world of an autistic child and clues to the operation of an otherwise impenetrable mind. Autism is a childhood disorder in which children seem lost in fantasy. Autistic children create and inhabit a world of their own and are usually inaccessible through the normal channels of communication, such as speech or gestures. For years researchers and therapists could find no way to reach them. In some rare cases, though, children have found a way to break through the barrier and communicate. Nadia did so in drawings (see Figure 1-1), which have been extremely helpful to psychologists to reach and help these children (Selfe, 1977).

MEASUREMENTS   Measurement is as central to psychology as it is to all science; it enables psychologists to make *quantitative* as well as *qualitative* distinctions. A qualitative distinction would be X is an aggressive person, Y is not. A

FIGURE 1-1
Art and Autism: A Case History

Nadia's precocious artistic ability (this drawing was done when she was only 5½ years old) showed that she could perceive and conceptualize complex ideas and images her autism prevented her from formulating verbally.
(Selfe, 1977)

5

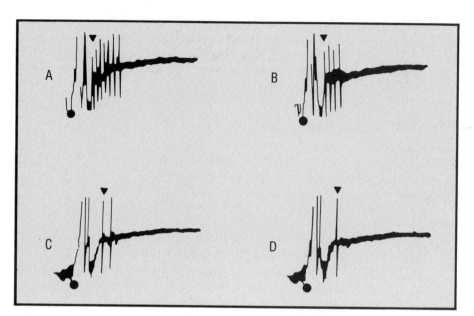

FIGURE 1-2
Measuring Habituation

The brain's ability to "tune out" background noises is called habituation. It can be measured by noting the decreasing firing rate, as shown here, of a neuron under constant stimulation.
(Groves & Thompson, 1973)

quantitative distinction would tell us *how much more* aggressive X is than Y, and in which situations.

Some measurements concern subtle physiological processes. When you walk into a room you may hear a clock ticking or a fan whirring, but after a while you do not notice these noises; you seem to tune them out. Psychologists can measure the changing response of the brain to recurring external noises: they can tell when it begins to ignore the noises and other continuously present stimuli. When we first hear a click, the brain responds one way. A few minutes later the same noise causes a different reaction (see Figure 1-2). The brain ceases to respond to the continuous presence of the click. This tuning out process, called *habituation*, is the simplest form of learning (Thompson, 1986).

TESTS Tests can be used to measure psychological abilities, such as intelligence, verbal and spatial ability, and the ability to get along well with others. The SAT you took to get into college was devised by educators and psychologists to measure your verbal and mathematical abilities in order to predict how well you would do at college. Each college has its own expectations of students and tries to select students who will fulfill those expectations. SAT scores are a form of guide used in the selection process. The SAT score is not merely the number of items answered correctly. It is a comparison: your test results are compared with a standard set of scores of high school seniors.

Like the measurement of the brain's electrical activity, test scores indicate the presence of an ability or quality. Achievement tests measure academic progress. An aptitude test may help you select a career. Personality tests measure such qualities as sociability, helpfulness, and leadership. Personality tests might be useful to an employer who may be looking for a manager for a sensitive position and wants someone who can get along with people and also shows qualities of leadership and initiative. Personality tests are also used by psychotherapists to measure the depth of their client's feelings and attitudes.

QUESTIONNAIRES   If you want to know how people feel about something, the most direct way to find out is to ask them. A **questionnaire** is a formal way of asking specific questions. Charles Tart (1971), for instance, wanted to find out about the general experience of marijuana intoxication and asked people to report what happened to them; then he compared the reports to see which experiences were universally shared. The effects reported were as follows:

■ Low level of intoxication: people are less noisy at parties than when drunk; they hear more subtle changes in sounds.

■ Moderately intoxicated: people are less noisy, experience new qualities of taste, enjoy eating a lot, experience insights about self, and need for sex goes up.

■ Strong intoxication: people are easily distracted, more here and now, feel emotions more strongly, new qualities to sexual orgasm, and forget start of conversation.

In a questionnaire, people report in a controlled manner. Researchers want to know only about the factors they are studying, so a questionnaire ensures that they will get the information they need. A survey or poll is a large-scale form of questionnaire. The information provided on a questionnaire becomes the data that scientists analyze and interpret. The questions may require only yes or no answers, such as Have you ever been in an automobile accident? Or people may be asked to rank their opinions or feelings, such as How do you think the president is doing?

THE EXPERIMENTAL METHOD

Experiments allow the scientist to *intervene* in a situation, to *control* its components. The essence of a good experiment is selection: what to include and what to exclude. In life, things happen in unplanned combinations and all at once. We cannot, in our ordinary experience, always tell what caused someone to act in a certain manner or have an instant replay to observe more carefully.

HYPOTHESES   The first step in an experiment is the development of the **hypothesis,** a specific statement about what will happen if certain events take place. Then the experimenter begins to act like a playwright, setting the stage, outlining the plot, and assembling the characters. But unlike the playwright, the experimenter does not decide *what* will happen. Rather, he or she sets events in motion and records what unfolds.

VARIABLES   Life is chaotic; things change or vary all the time. In an experiment most conditions are constant. Those few things that change in an experiment are thus called the **variables.** There are two kinds of variables: those the experimenter *changes*, called **independent variables**—for instance, an experimenter may vary the number of hours that an animal is deprived of food—and those the experimenter *measures*, called **dependent variables,** which in this case might be how much the animal eats.

THE SAMPLE: EXPERIMENTAL AND CONTROL GROUPS   The people or animals that are part of the psychology experiment are called **subjects.** The subjects must be selected to

Look at the three people in Figure 1-3. Which one is the largest? Now take out a ruler and measure them. They are the same! These figures *appear* to be different sizes because the converging lines give the impression of depth. The drawing is composed of two main elements: the people and the lines. Without the lines, the people appear as they are, the same size.

If you had merely read the boring textbook sentence "The rules of perspective, which allow us generally to make accurate guesses about an object's relative size and distance can also trick perceptions," you might not be convinced or even interested. However, you can see the results immediately, so this *demonstration* is more compelling.

**FIGURE 1-3
Demonstration of the
Rules of Perspective**

Notice how the figure on the right appears to be larger than the one on the left, even though they are the same size.
(Metzger, 1975)

represent accurately the entire population under study. The group of subjects is called the **sample.** The appropriate number of subjects necessary for the study, the *sample size*, varies depending on what is being studied. The smaller the differences from individual to individual on the specific measure, the smaller the sample size has to be. To study the effect of light on pupil dilation, a few subjects, perhaps fewer than 10, are enough, because the purely physical aspects of vision are fundamentally the same for all human beings.

Although eyes are similar, opinions are not. In an experiment to determine something such as the most popular television shows or voter preferences in election polls, a sample of about 1,200 people is used. Here individuality, personal preference, prejudices, background, and geography play an important role. The sample has to be large enough to average out the individual differences.

The sample is usually divided into two groups: the **experimental group** and the **control group.** The experimental group is one the researcher intervenes with, the one studied to judge the effect of the independent variable, which is changed and manipulated. The control group is similar to the experimental group in every respect *except* the independent variable. The control group shows what would have happened had the researcher not intervened. When the experiment is over, the two outcomes are compared.

Suppose a psychologist wants to know if a certain psychotherapy is effective. The findings are that, two years after treatment, 75 percent of the people who had undergone psychotherapy are improved. Looks good. Could the psychologist then report in a scientific journal that the therapy is effective? Not yet, because (and here is a big difference between life and science) he or she does not know what would have happened to these people if they had not received psychotherapeutic treatment, and in life we never do.

In this case, a control group would have to be included. The group would be similar to those who underwent therapy but for one reason or another were unable to obtain it. Suppose that after the same two years, *95* percent of the control group—those who had not undergone therapy—had improved. That figure would certainly change the psychologist's opinion on the benefits of psychotherapy! It would mean that psychotherapy is *less* effective than doing nothing! Or if only 35 percent of the control group improved, the psychologist would conclude that the therapy is effective, and would have a good idea just how effective. Note that in these two examples the *results* of the psychotherapy are the same, but the scientific judgment of its effectiveness depends on what would have happened if there were no therapy.

In experiments, the control group represents what would have happened anyway. The presence of the control group is one more way to ensure sound and measured judgements; it is the standard for scientific comparison.

THINKING LIKE A PSYCHOLOGIST

Let's look at the development of one study, which is composed of several experiments. Recall that the experimenter's job is to select a very few variables to alter and to observe, and that the procedures for doing an experiment derive from normal common sense.

Which factors make one person sexually attracted to another? The complete answer is quite complex: it includes the backgrounds of the persons, their expectations, whether one or the other person is already involved in a relationship. However, to think like an experimental psychologist, you might try to isolate one part of the puzzle. One major factor may be the circumstances of a meeting. In films or novels it is the daring hero, the one who takes chances, who always gets the girl. In fact, more people fall in love and get married in disasters and wartime than during times of quiescence. People go to horror movies, drive like maniacs, and ride on roller coasters on dates. These situations have in common the element of danger, and danger is sexually arousing (see Figure 1-4). Could a dangerous *location* contribute to sexual arousal? This is the primary question that a classic study sought to answer.

FIGURE 1-4
Does Danger Contribute to Sexual Arousal?

Psychological experiments have been conducted to determine whether or not dangerous situations play a role in sexual arousal.

9

What happens when people are put in exciting circumstances? The initial experiment involved attraction on a wobbly bridge (Dutton & Aron, 1974). A woman interviews two groups of men, each on a different bridge in Vancouver: one bridge is safe; the other, very precarious. One bridge is a solid wood structure 10 feet above a stream. This is the control bridge. The other is the Capilano Suspension Bridge, which is 450 feet long, 5 feet wide, and sways and wobbles over a 230-foot drop to rapids and rocks. This is the experimental bridge.

The experimenters compared meeting people of the opposite sex in both dangerous and safe circumstances. Men who were crossing one of the bridges were met by an attractive woman interviewer. To each man on both the experimental and control bridges she was asked to make up a story, saying she was researching the effects of scenic attraction on creative expression. She then asked the man to write a brief story based on a picture she showed him of a young woman covering her face with one hand while reaching out with the other.

When he finished, she gave the man her name and number and invited him to call her if he wanted more information about the experiment. If there were fewer calls from the men who went to the solid control bridge than from those who went to the wobbly experimental bridge, we might conclude that the arousing circumstances figured in sexual attraction. The stories were also scored for sexual imagery.

The *independent variables* were the two bridges. The *dependent variables* were the number of phone calls and the men's scores for sexual imagery. The hypothesis was that men on the experimental bridge would be more sexually aroused than men on the control bridge. Therefore, they should (1) telephone the assistant more often than the controls and (2) write stories with more sexual imagery.

The results showed that 12.5 percent of the men who were sent to the secure bridge called the woman for more information, whereas 50 percent of the men who were sent to the wobbly bridge called. Those who met the woman on the wobbly bridge also wrote stories with far more sexual imagery than did those on the secure bridge.

Therefore we *could* conclude that these results support the hypothesis that dangerous circumstances can lead to arousal and to increased sexual attraction. However, psychologists are rarely convinced by one study. To think like an experimental psychologist, we must consider whether the results could come about in another way, because in most studies, there are other possible interpretations of the findings.

Consider another interpretation of the results of this study: it could be that the men who *chose* to cross on the wobbly bridge were more daring than the ones who chose to cross on the secure control bridge. If so, these men might well have been more daring, too, about calling up a strange woman for a date than were the possibly more timid control bridge travelers, and the wobbly bridge travelers might also be more sexually daring. Therefore, the results might be due to existing differences in the *men* who cross on the bridge, not the *effect* of crossing a dangerous bridge. So, another experiment is necessary to find the most accurate interpretation of the results.

To rule out differences in the two groups of men, the sample in the second experiment was composed *entirely* of men who crossed the wobbly bridge, but they were divided into "aroused" and "nonaroused" groups. The aroused group was interviewed as before, just as they crossed the bridge. The nonaroused group was interviewed at least 10 minutes after they crossed the bridge, by which time the exciting effects of the bridge would have worn off.

If the original results were due to *differences* in the men who crossed the bridge, we would expect both groups in this second experiment to be *equally* attracted to the woman. If the original results were due to the arousal of crossing the bridge, then we should expect that the group interviewed *on* the bridge would be *more* attracted to the woman. The results showed the latter to be the case, and this provides further evidence for the idea that general arousal can lead to sexual arousal.

The results of the second experiment make the conclusion clearer. But, again, an experimental psychologist would then wonder whether this result applies to a limited situation or whether it is more general. That is, is this finding true only under certain conditions (such as a damsel in distress on a wobbly bridge), is it just a curiosity, or is the relationship between excitement and attraction more basic?

A third experiment was run, this time in the laboratory. A man sat in a room and was told that he was participating in a study to measure the effect of pain on learning. A woman entered and was introduced as the other subject in the experiment. Actually she was a confederate of the experimenters. The pair was told if they gave an incorrect answer on their test, they would receive an electric shock. Some of the men were told that they would receive a mild shock, others were told that they would receive a severe shock, and the experimenter would be measuring which shock level was the more effective learning tool. Now, again thinking like a psychologist, how would you make sure that brave men might choose the severe shock and be likely to call the woman, too?

Before the tests and shocks were to begin, each subject was sent to a different room and asked to fill out a questionnaire on their feelings and reactions at that time, since, the experimenters explained, "they often influence performance on the learning task." *This was the critical part of the experiment.* There were, actually, no tests or shocks. The first part of the questionnaire measured anxiety. As you might expect, the subjects who expected to receive a strong shock reported much more anxiety than those who anticipated a weak shock. The second part of the questionnaire related directly to arousal and sexual attraction. The men who expected severe shocks and were anxious about them also expressed more attraction for the woman than did the calmer men expecting a mild shock.

This series of experiments contributes a little evidence that a man who meets a woman in a dangerous or anxiety-producing circumstance is *more likely* to interpret the feeling of arousal as attraction to the other person. In this experiment we go from an everyday observation—that exciting people and situations are attractive—to a slightly more comprehensive understanding of the experience of sexual attraction.

We know a *little* more about how to think like a psychologist. Of course, this experiment would need to be replicated and many similar studies done before we could conclude that arousal has a general effect on sexual attraction. Then, of course, there would be many other new questions. Some of them will be treated later on in the book.

SOME PROBLEMS OF EXPERIMENTS

Even with all the rules of doing an experiment, there is the possibility that the experimenter may subtly and unconsciously influence or *bias* the results. Researchers so often find what they are looking for that psychologist Robert Rosenthal thought that something subtle and unconscious was occurring. He ran a now-classic experiment that clearly demonstrated the presence of this so-called **experimenter bias:** A group of students were told to run rats through a maze. Half were told that their rats were bred to be especially smart, called (in the trade) *maze bright,* and the other group was told that their rats were *maze dull.* In fact, there was no difference: the rats were selected at random; both groups were equal in ability. The independent variable was the expectation of the students. That expectation turned out to be an important difference: the "maze bright" rats learned the maze faster than their supposedly "dull" counterparts (Rosenthal, 1986).

There are two methods psychologists use to minimize the problem of experimenter bias. One is **replication.** Every experiment *may* be confirmed in the laboratory of others. The new investigator may have a different bias— perhaps even the desire to disprove the finding.

The second method is the **double-blind procedure.** The subject of an experiment is usually kept in the dark about the object of an experiment to be kept from skewing the results. A double-blind procedure keeps the experiment-er in the dark, or blind, as well—unaware of which is the experimental and which is the control group until after the experiment is over and the results have been tabulated. For example, suppose you invent a new sleeping pill, "Snooz-ie," and you want to test its effect. If the drug works and is a commercial success, you stand to make a lot of money. Suppose further that you give one group Snoozie and the other a sugar pill. Then you interview both groups on the drug's effects. If the people who took the pill knew that the pill was supposed to make them drowsy, they might report feeling that way. Subjects in experiments generally try to be cooperative, and the expectation of the feeling might lead to the feeling.

Similarly, if you *know* who has taken Snoozie and who has taken the sugar pill, you might influence the results by your questions during the interview: "Don't you feel sightly sleepy? Not even a teensy-weensy bit?" But if you do not know who took which pill, you cannot influence the results with questions. In the Dutton and Aron experiment, the attractive female *confederate* (the one who asked the questions) was kept in the dark about the real purpose of the experiment.

WHAT DOES *STATISTICS* MEAN?

Psychologists use the methods of demonstration, observation, and experiment to gather data. Once the evidence is in hand, the next step is to *evaluate* and

Most scientific conclusions are not about individuals; rather, they are about average differences. These differences, while important, need to be understood: they mean that *on average* one group scored higher, was more attracted, made more mistakes, or did something differently from the average of another group. This is fine as far as it goes, but sometimes average differences have a way of becoming thought of as true of all of those in one group or another.

Let's take a non-psychological example to explore this. Males run faster than females. True? Yes on average. All world records for running, at any distance, are held by males. The average marathon winner of the male race finishes 20 minutes ahead of the female winner. The same is true of many different distances.

Does this mean that a female will always be slow? Consider it this way: when we discuss group differences, we refer to the average of a large range of observations. Here it is male and female running, but it could be height, intelligence scores on a test, compliance to a directive, and the like.

Now look at it from the point of view of a fast female runner, say the women's marathon winner. She runs faster than 99 percent of all men! So the differences that scientific psychologists report are averages, and there is much variation in the individual results. In fact, most differences in the results of psychology experiments are much less than the difference in running speed suggested here.

---

interpret it. **Statistics** is the formal set of rules to evaluate evidence. It enables scientific judgments to be more precise and quantitative than ordinary judgments. If a study shows a difference between the groups, as we saw in the wobbly bridge experiment, we need to know if it is a *significant difference*.

Suppose you are interested in improving the mathematical skills of third graders. You have two gadgets designed to encourage the learning process, and you want to see which works better. One is a computer that flashes and wiggles when the child gives a correct answer. The other is a set of mathematical instruments that make noise and project the problems on the ceiling.

You have three groups of children, so you give the computer to the first group, the mechanical toy to the second, and nothing to the third, which will serve as the control group. You find that both toy groups show a 15 percent improvement in learning over their previous work and over the control group. Would you say that both methods are equally effective? At first glance, it seems so, but a statistical analysis shows that they are *not*.

Take a closer look at the evidence. In the first group, all the children using the computer made some improvement. The computer's effect on learning, as the statistical test showed, is constant and meaningful. But in the second group, 4 out of the 10 children were helped by the mechanical toy, but 6 out of the 10 children either showed no improvement or worsened. Both gadgets were not equally effective as a learning tool, even though the *average* difference is the same. A good psychologist would continue to work, however, to find out *why* the mechanical instrument toy provided such different results for different children.

MEAN AND MEDIAN

There are two forms of measurement that scientists use to analyze data: the mean and the median. The **mean** is the arithmetic average. The **median** is the middle figure of the results listed in numerical order.

13

In the table below, which is the more well-to-do street? The average, or mean, income is the same for both streets, $22,500.

Avenue A (in thousands of dollars)
 10, 10, 15, 15, 15, 17.5, 20, 20, 25, 25, 75

Avenue B
 15, 15, 20, 20, 20, 22.5, 24, 25, 27, 29, 30

But in this case 10 of the 11 families in Avenue B had higher incomes than their corresponding families in Avenue A. In this case the more accurate measure is the median. For Avenue A, it is $17,500; for B it is $22,500. That figure better reflects the consistent difference in income for the residents of the two streets. The median is used when an extreme value might unduly influence the average, as when a high scorer on a test might affect the average or, as in this case, one family's income might elevate the average of the incomes of the rest of the families on the avenue.

CORRELATION

Is there any *relationship* between a person's high school SAT score and college grades? or between years of drinking and decline of intelligence? or between a father's intelligence and his son's? We cannot do experiments to find out, but we can measure the relationship. When the relationship of two things is important to measure, psychologists compute a statistic called a **correlation.** The correlation is an important tool, for there are many studies that do not allow experimentation. Suppose you want to determine how much brain damage affects speech. Obviously, you could not produce brain damage in your subjects for this purpose, but you could study people who already have brain damage to determine the relationship of the amount of damage to speech impairment.

THE NATURAL EXPERIMENT   Sometimes things happen in life that cannot be duplicated but that can provide important evidence, and the correlation method can be used in these *natural experiments* to interpret the results. To find out which is the more important factor in human intelligence, *heredity* or the *environment* in which a person grows up, the most obvious thing to do would be to find a pair of identical twins (who are as close genetically as two human beings can possibly be), separate them at birth, let one child grow up in an intellectually enriched environment and the other in a similarly deprived one, then observe what happens. As a deliberate experiment, this is unthinkable: no one would manipulate people's lives for the sake of psychological knowledge, but a psychologist might use correlation to study circumstances where this occurs.

Sandra Scarr and associates studied groups of adopted children whose occupations, IQs, and interests of the natural parents were known and who were raised by couples with children of their own. Scarr et al. then compared the IQs and interests of adopted children reared in families with natural children, using correlations (see Figure 1-5). They found startling evidence that

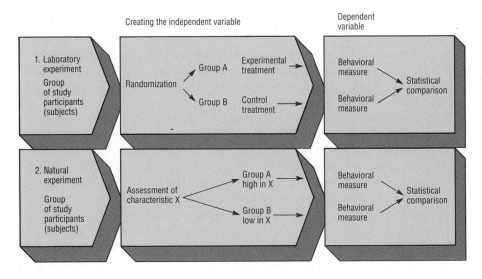

Creating the independent variable

Dependent variable

FIGURE 1-5
Laboratory Experiments and Natural Experiments

This flow chart shows that the principal difference between the two types of experiments is that in a natural experiment—such as the one conducted by Scarr and associates—the creation of the independent variable involves assesment of specified characteristics like occupations, IQs, and interests.

IQ and even interests seem to be inherited (Scarr & Carter-Saltzmann, 1983).

Is there a relationship between high school and college grades? First we plot one person's high school grades on one axis of a graph and college grades on the other. If the college grades are relatively low and the high school grades are high, the graph will look approximately like Figure 1-6A. If the high school grades are low and the college grades are high, it will look something like Figure 1-6B. If both are high, the graph will look like Figure 1-6C. If both are low, it will look like Figure 1-6D. Then we plot the grades of a very large sample of students on the graph.

If everyone who did well in high school got high grades in college, and everyone who did poorly in high school got low grades in college, that would be

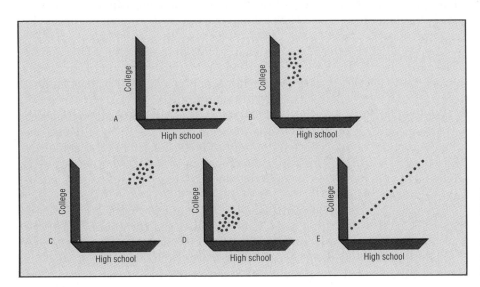

FIGURE 1-6
Correlation

Plotting data on scatter diagrams is one way to reveal possible correlations between sets of data.

15

a perfect correlation. The relationships displayed in Figures 1-6A to 1-6D are high correlations, not perfect ones. A perfect correlation would indicate a perfect relationship: Whenever X happens, Y happens; the more X, the more Y. On the graph a perfect correlation would look like Figure 1-6E. This 100 percent relationship is written in statistics as a correlation of 1.0, either positive or negative. Such a relationship is almost never found.

"No correlation" means there is no relation between X and Y (e.g., grades in high school and eye color). This lack of relationship is written 0.0. Most correlations fall somewhere between these two figures. There has to be a certain degree of relationship, usually at least 0.2, to be considered important. The relationship may be positive or negative. A *positive correlation* means the more of X, the more of Y. A *negative correlation* means the more X happens, the less Y happens (e.g., the more food you eat, the less weight you lose). A negative correlation is distinguished from a positive correlation by a minus sign in front of the figure, as in −0.4. A positive correlation would be written simply 0.4.

SELECTED MOMENTS FROM THE HISTORY OF PSYCHOLOGY

Psychology is a recent addition to the sciences. Whereas now there are more than 60,000 psychologists in the United States, in 1900 there were about 125. Psychology borders on and draws from many different disciplines—from biology and genetics to philosophy and sociology—since psychologists may probe a gene, a social group, a child's thoughts, or a politician's popularity.

It is a fertile science, and its sources are abundant. For centuries, inquiry regarding the mind, behavior, and human nature was the dominion of philosophical schools. But after the Renaissance, many thinkers speculated that direct observation of human conduct, as well as inspection of the structure of the human brain and body, might illuminate the perennial questions of philosophy: Is thinking innate or learned? Do human beings apprehend reality directly through their senses? How is knowledge gained? Is thought affected by others?

The beginnings of the modern attempt to find in the structure of the human nervous system the answers to many long-standing philosophical questions began with René Descartes (1596–1650). After a great deal of deliberation, Descartes came to believe that much human knowledge was innate, that it existed within the structure of the brain and nervous system. He then proposed that an inherent set of abilities exists through which the "Mind" directs the automaton of the body. He even proposed a physical location for this interaction—the *pineal* of the brain, for it is one organ of the brain whose structure is single rather than dual. Descartes set the modern study of mind-brain relationships in motion.

The British *empiricists* held that the human mind was not as prepared for such knowledge as Descartes proposed, but rather gained it through associations. *Association* is one of psychology's oldest principles. It refers to the link in the mind between two or more experiences. The exploration began with the Greek philosophers and was revived in the seventeenth century. John Locke, David Hume, and John Stuart Mill believed that the association of ideas (that is, of sensations or thoughts) connects experience. Ideas become associated when they occur close to each other in space or in time. John Locke (1670) explained:

> A man has suffered pain or sickness in a place; he saw his friend die in such a room, though these have in nature nothing to do with one another, yet when the idea of the place occurs to mind, it brings (the impressions being once made) that of pain and displeasure with it, he confounds them in his mind and can as little bear the one as the other.

The empiricists, who have been quite influential in science's view of the human mind, believed that all knowledge came from experience. They assumed that the mind was a

> white paper void of all characters, without any ideas—How comes it to be furnished? Whence comes it by that vast store which the busy and boundless fancy of man has painted on it with an almost endless variety? Whence has all the *materials* of reason and knowledge? To this I answer, in one word, from EXPERIENCE. (Locke, 1670)

This was Locke's colorful account, not looking to the structure of the nervous system, but to the world in which the person lives. These different proposals spawned later schools of psychology, notably the behaviorist and the physiological approach. The behaviorists are the heirs to Locke and the empiricists.

In the late nineteenth century when the field of psychology began to take shape, the predominant consideration was the mind. Researchers used the technique of **introspection,** observing how their own minds worked and dissecting the content of their own experiences. The problem was that the investigators could not agree; each person's experiences were different. John B. Watson (1914) proposed that introspection was therefore useless if psychology was to become a science and that the study of observable *behavior* was a more defensible subject for psychology. *Behaviorism,* an approach that deals with association, maintains that our knowledge is largely learned and comes from experience.

Other sciences inspired psychology. For almost all of human history, human beings assumed that they were at the center of the universe. After all, anyone can see that the Sun goes around the Earth. But Copernicus showed that this was not so, that the Earth was but one planet around its Sun and there were many more suns as well. Humanity was not special.

The next great blow came from a young British naturalist named Charles Darwin (1809–1882) who showed that human beings evolved along with the rest of life on earth and were descended from a common ancestor. Before the advent of modern science, it was generally believed that all creatures were individually created to suit their special environments. By the nineteenth century, the commonly held scientific view was that all animals did change and had developed from earlier forms of life. Darwin proposed a theory of how this change, or adaptation, occurs, called *natural selection.* Darwin's theory, combined with modern genetics, is the basis of the modern *theory of evolution,* now the generally accepted explanation of how organisms change through time. (See Chapter 4, section on Process of Adaptation and Evolution.)

Charles Darwin's theory of natural selection, which he published in *On the Origin of Species* in 1859, marked the beginning of the modern era in biology and

WILLIAM JAMES
(1842–1910)

WILHELM WUNDT
(1832–1920)

JOHN B. WATSON
(1878–1958)

greatly influenced psychology: Sigmund Freud's psychoanalysis, Jean Piaget's work on child development (Darwin wrote the first "baby biography"), and the study of emotions were all consequences of evolutionary thinking. Since human beings and other animals descended from a common ancestor, psychologists reasoned, then much wisdom could be gained from studying animals. So *comparative psychology* (the study of different organisms) and *ethology* (the study of animals in their natural habitat) owe their debt to Darwin, too.

Psychology owes its systematic beginnings to two men: William James (1842–1910) and Wilhelm Wundt (1832–1920). James, the first great synthesizer of psychology, wrote *The Principles of Psychology* in 1890, taking 20 years to do it. It remains one of the most eloquent descriptions of the science of psychology. The tradition of scientific investigation is due largely to Wundt, who established the first psychology laboratory. Modern psychologists combine a general understanding of their subject with the analysis of scientific data.

Today, many of these distinct early strands weave together: although Descartes may have been wrong in detail, the search for the machinery of the mind is one of the most important components of psychology; although Locke may have overstated the case, teaching by association is the main method of instruction; laboratory, clinical, and speculative insights routinely give rise to new treatments and studies. Every psychologist draws from the scientific study of behavior, physiology, perception, psychotherapy, and the like. Human experience and behavior is distressingly complex, and its determinants— biology, society, personal interactions, learning, associations, and difficulties— are combined in our modern understanding.

The present distinctions between types of psychologists concern mainly what they study and which method they use, rather than which doctrine they hold or what school they belong to. Psychologists study associations, but assume that the organism (whether a person or an animal) has built-in capabilities. Psychotherapists may approach a problem through talking or through biology. Social psychologists may base their analyses on the structure of thought or on society.

BEHAVIORISM: WHAT PEOPLE DO

Behaviorists assume that people do what they do because of conditions (or "prerequisite circumstances") in their environment. Behaviorists reason that if the conditions change, behavior can also change. Therefore, people can better themselves by altering their environment. As John B. Watson, the father of behaviorism, declared,

> Give me a dozen healthy infants, well-formed, and my own specified world to bring them up in and I'll guarantee to take any one at random and train him to become any type of specialist I might select—doctor, lawyer, artist, merchant-chief, and yes, even beggar-man and thief, regardless of his talents, penchants, tendencies, abilities, vocations, and race of his ancestors. (1925)

Or, more simply, "Control the conditions and you will see the order", the influential behaviorist B. F. Skinner wrote (1972). Thus, behaviorists often modify the conditions and observe the variations in behavior that follow.

Behavioral experiments have taught animals to choose between difficult alternatives and to perform complicated tricks. Following a complicated series of learning trials, pigeons can even become quality control inspectors (see Figure 1-7). Every psychologist has been influenced by behaviorism, and **behaviorism** has led to important discoveries about learning and remembering, how people act alone, with other people, and in society at large.

Consider this important issue: Why do people act violently? Some classic investigations have concentrated on the effect of television on violent behavior. A child of 10 has seen thousands of acts of violence on television, such as robberies, rapes, murders, and fights. Do these "conditions," or exposures to violent acts, affect how aggressive a child will be? A study of the behavior of people in different circumstances is the best way to find out.

Some psychologists propose that watching "fictional" violence may be constructive, because the viewer experiences a **catharsis**—that is, watching violence allows a viewer to discharge fierce feelings and thus to be *less* likely to act aggressively. Other psychologists believe that people learn by observation and imitation; they propose that the *more* violence a child sees, the *more* likely he or she is to act violently.

In an important study, children of several ages were shown films of adults (and other children) hitting dolls and other people. After the movie the children's behavior was monitored (see Figure 1-8). Children who watched violence afterward acted *more* aggressively (see Chapter 8 for a discussion of learning by observation).

FIGURE 1-7
Conditioned Behavior

The scientific alteration of the conditions in their environment can shape the responses of animals so they learn various new ways of behaving. A rat being trained in a "Skinner box."

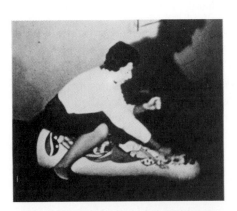

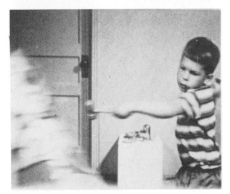

FIGURE 1-8
Imitating Violent Behavior

Hitting and kicking an inflated doll were among the ways nursery school children like this little girl and boy responded to seeing a film showing adults and other children acting violently.

THE BIOLOGICAL APPROACH

People come into the world with an amazing inheritance—a complex brain and nervous system. Studies of the structure and functions of the brain, the biological approach, give psychologists clues about how the intricate systems operate. In 1942, Wilder Penfield, a neurosurgeon, made a startling discovery while working on a patient who had a brain tumor. To study which parts of the brain were active, he stimulated the brain at different locations with a mild electrical current (see Figure 1-9). Penfield probed in one spot and got no response; he probed in another spot, and the patient's fingers twitched. He probed in still another location and here is the rest of the record (the numbers correspond to those in Figure 1-9):

11—"I heard something, I do not know what it was."

11—(Probe repeated without warning the patient) "Yes, Sir, I think I heard a mother calling her little boy somewhere. It seemed to be something that happened years ago." When asked to explain, she said, "It was somebody in the neighborhood where I live." Then she added that she herself "was somewhere close enough to hear."

12—"Yes, I heard voices down along the river somewhere—a man's voice and a woman's voice calling. . . . I think I saw the river."

15—"Just a tiny flash of a feeling of familiarity and a feeling that I knew everything that was going to happen in the near future."

17c— . . . "Oh! I had the same very, very familiar memory, in an office somewhere. I could see the desks. I was there and someone was calling to me, a man leaning on a desk with a pencil in his hand." I warned her I was going to stimulate, but I did not do so. "Nothing."

18a—(Stimulation without warning) "I had a little memory—a scene in a play—they were talking and I could see it—I was just seeing it in my memory." (Penfield, 1975)

Each time Penfield inserted the electrode into a particular spot, a similar experience was stimulated. Penfield writes: "I was more astonished each time my electrode brought forth such a response. How could it be? This had to do with the mind. I called such responses 'experiential'" (1975).

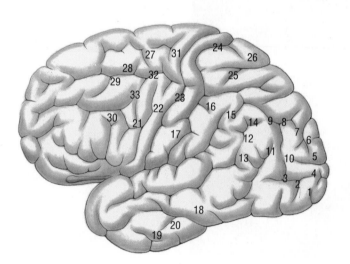

FIGURE 1-9
Electrical Stimulation of the Brain

The numbers indicate the locations at which Penfield stimulated the brain with his electrode.
(Penfield, 1975)

So, disturbances of the *brain's* electrical activity can influence the *mind* dramatically. There are other ways this comes about: injuries to the brain, surgery, and drugs that affect the chemistry of the brain all have striking effects on the mind. The biological underpinnings of experience are an increasingly important part of psychology, a part that has developed greatly since the 1950s, but one which has a long history (Ornstein & Sobel, 1987).

THE COGNITIVE APPROACH

The word *cognitive* comes from the Latin verb *cognoscere*, meaning "to know," so the central object of study in **cognitive psychology** is the mind. But the mind is *not* a tangible organ like the brain. Rather, it is the intangible product of the brain that involves many activities, such as thinking, memory, language, and consciousness.

Cognitive psychologists attempt to observe, as directly as possible, the operations of the mind. One question that would interest a cognitive psychologist is "How many things can a person do at once?" The common wisdom is that "you can't do two things at once." But is that "wisdom" true?

Ulric Neisser decided to see if it were possible for a person to do two extremely complex activities at once, specifically reading on one subject while writing on another. Two students, Diane and John, were enlisted as subjects. They read short stories while copying down a list of words that was being dictated to them rapidly. At first Diane and John found the task impossible. They read slowly and when they were tested later for story comprehension, they did poorly. But after six weeks of training, they could perform both tasks easily (see Figure 1-10).

Later the demonstration was extended. While Diane and John were reading, they took dictation, not simply of words, but of whole sentences. Again, it was

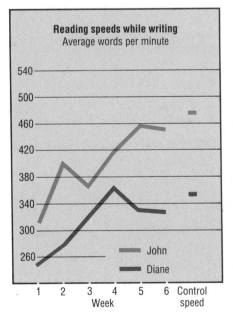

FIGURE 1-10
Learning To Do Two Things at Once
John and Diane steadily improved their ability to read while writing. After a few weeks their reading speeds were close to their normal rates, as this record of their progress in the experiment shows.
(Hirst et al., 1978)

difficult at first, but within weeks they were reading one subject and writing on another at the same time, at normal speed and with normal comprehension (Hirst, Neisser, & Spelke, 1978). It is thus possible to learn to increase mental capacity and to divide attention.

Cognitive psychologists also examine mental limitations. Suppose you were buying a toaster, and it cost $30 at the store you were in. Then you discovered that it was $20 at a store 20 minutes away. Would you make the trip? Most people say they would. Suppose, again, that you were going to buy a car that costs $14,320. You discover that another dealer (20 minutes away) is selling the same car for $14,310. Would you go? Most likely not.

The situation is actually the same. In *both* instances you are being asked to drive 20 minutes to save $10. The savings is the same; the drive is the same. But the $10 *seems* like a lot compared with the $30 for the toaster, and almost nothing compared with the price of the car (Kahneman, Slovic, & Tversky, 1982). We judge things by *comparing* them with others, not as they actually are.

MENTAL ERRORS

Psychologists analyze mental errors to diagnose the workings of normal thought. One common type of error is called a **capture error.** For example, you may have planned to stop at a fish store on your way home, but you find instead that you have driven past it and have just driven into your driveway. Another example is "I was using a copying machine and I was counting the pages. I found myself counting: 1, 2, 3, 4, 5, 6, 7, 8, 9, 10, *Jack, Queen, King*" (Norman, 1983). In both cases the intended action was replaced by the normal operation of mind, which presumably was stronger than the chosen action. While some psychologists assume that anything one does has a hidden meaning, these capture errors show that there may sometimes be a simpler explanation of why, when you move houses in a city, you automatically drive back to the old home for the first few days. It does not necessarily mean that you wish to return there.

COGNITION IN CONTEMPORARY SOCIETY

One of the discoveries made by modern psychology is that we do not perceive the world as it really is. In the summer of 1986, for instance, hundreds of thousands of American tourists stayed away from Europe because of the perceived threat of terrorism; up until that time, 25 Americans had been killed in various acts of terror all over Europe. Certainly no one would like to get gunned down in an airport shootout, but was staying away from Europe effective? Consider this set of statistics from *Newsweek* of June 2, 1986:

- 43,500 killed in automobile accidents in the U.S. (1985)
- 1,384 murdered in New York City (1985)
- 36 murdered in Honolulu (1985)
- 150 died in their own bathtubs (1984)
- 1,063 killed in boating accidents (1984)
- 3,100 died choking on food (1984)

Certain events, because of their new and surprising nature, become automatically emphasized in the mind (Ehrlich & Ornstein, 1988).

In early 1986 the space shuttle exploded, and the loss of seven lives captured the attention of the world. Again ignored are the hundreds who die dull deaths daily, deaths that could easily be prevented.

A single murder, that of hostage Leon Klinghoffer in 1985, commanded the front pages of almost every newspaper in the Western world. Extreme political demands can be made based on the importance that individuals, the media, and governments give to such actions. The threat of terrorism made millions of Americans change their travel plans in the summer of 1986. But more people are murdered every two hours in the USA than had been killed *in toto* by terrorists through the summer of 1986.

Late in 1985 there was a threat to consumers of drugs bought over the counter as two tainted Tylenol capsules commanded national attention, as such a sudden danger would. However, the danger, which killed no one, is still remembered. But *three hundred daily murders* in the USA, committed before the tamperings, and continuing each day after the tamperings, remain almost unnoticed.

The nature of human cognition makes terrorism very effective as an attention grabber. Terrorism taps into the nervous system program which originated to register short-term changes in a steady state. When a noise continues on, the nervous system stops responding to it; we habituate. When a new noise appears, automatic emphasis is given: an increased response. A sudden threat, even insignificant, is thus registered intensely. A continuing threat, just like a continuing noise, becomes part of the background; we habituate to threats as we do to sounds. This analysis, which draws together social and cognitive psychology, will be examined in Chapter 18.

THE SOCIAL ENVIRONMENT

Suppose you heard a scream from the room next door. Would you help? If you were alone, chances are that you would help, but if you were with six other people who did not help, chances are that you would not (Darley & Latane, 1968)! Human beings are quite dependent on each other: other people *intensify* actions: runners are faster when they run with others, people behave more aggressively in crowds than when alone. The investigation of how other people and our environment affect us is the social environment perspective.

Some social psychological studies are stimulated by life events. In 1964, for instance, a young woman named Kitty Genovese was mugged and stabbed to death in New York City. The murder of a woman is, unfortunately, not unusual, but what made this case horribly remarkable was that Kitty Genovese screamed repeatedly and was heard by at least 38 people who watched the crime from the safety of their homes. No one tried to help her; no one even called the police. This apathy shocked psychologists, who initiated many studies of what makes a person stop to help.

In one such study, which has come to be known as the *Good Samaritan experiment*, a divinity student would be told to give a sermon (Darley & Batson, 1973). On the way to the sermon, he would find a man (who was actually one of

What Makes a Person Stop to Help?

Psychologists study the social environment to discover factors accounting for bystander apathy, bystander intervention, and similar behavior that can affect our lives.

the psychologists) slumped and groaning in a doorway. Would the student/subject stop to help, and if so, under what conditions?

Sixty divinity students were divided into three groups: one-third were told that they were late and had to hurry; one-third were told to go to the building, but not necessarily to hurry; and one-third were told there was a delay and to take their time. All the students were assigned a topic for their sermon. Half were to talk on the biblical parable of the Good Samaritan, and half were assigned a nonreligious topic. The experimenters wanted to know if either the pressure of time or what they were thinking about influenced helping behavior.

Only 40 percent of the divinity students stopped to help; 60 percent did not. The pressure of time seems to have more of an influence on behavior than what they had just read or were just about to say (See Figure 1-11). Of the students

**FIGURE 1-11
Experimental Conditions in the Good Samaritan Experiment**

The experiment demonstrated that people are less likely to stop and help if they are in a hurry.
(Darley & Batson, 1973)

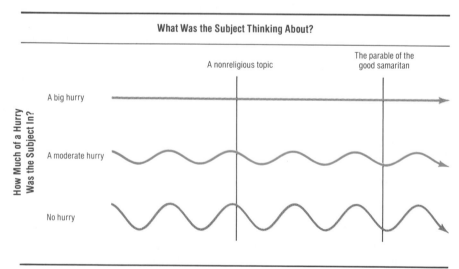

who were in no hurry, 63 percent stopped; only 10 percent of the rushed students did; 53 percent of those thinking about the Good Samaritan paused. The results showed that if people are in a hurry, they are not likely to stop to help.

Two other perspectives yield much data: the clinical approach, which analyzes disorders, and the humanistic approach, which studies the positive attributes of people.

THE CLINICAL APPROACH

Observing a person who is unable to perform a function can offer information on how that function usually operates. Here are several examples:

BIOLOGICAL MALFUNCTION

A man is interviewed in a hospital. His interviewer asks: "Can you tell me what work you have been doing?" He answers: "If you had said that, poomer, near the fortunate, tamppoo all around the fourth of marz. Oh, I get all confused!" (Gardner, 1975).

This man has a variety of *aphasia*, loss of language, caused by damage to part of the brain. If people with damage to the front of the left hemisphere of the brain have specific difficulties with language, we presume it has an important role in normal language.

PSYCHOANALYSIS

Devised by Sigmund Freud at the end of the 19th century, **psychoanalysis** is perhaps the most influential modern viewpoint on the mind. It proposes that the mind is layered, with a conscious mind riding atop an unconscious one. Unconscious attitudes deeply influence consciousness in this view, and so the roots of difficulties in adulthood may be found in experiences long hidden from mind, especially traumatic events in childhood. Later on in this chapter, for instance, we consider the psychoanalytic viewpoint of female-male differences, and we consider this important viewpoint in our discussions of development, consciousness, personality, and other areas.

MULTIPLE PERSONALITIES

In a college town in the Midwest a young man named Billy Milligan was arrested for raping a woman. The psychologist interviewing him asked for his social security number.

"He shrugged. 'I don't know.'"

The psychologist read his number to him.

... "That's not my number, it must be Billy's"

... "Well aren't you Billy?"

"I'm *David*."

"Well, where's Billy?"

"He's asleep."

"Asleep where?"

"He pointed to his chest. 'In here, he's asleep.'"

. . . "I have to talk to Billy."

"Well, *Arthur* won't let you. Billy's asleep. Arthur won't wake him up, 'cause if he does, Billy'll kill himself." (Keyes, 1982)

One might dismiss all these different "people" inside as a criminal's quite elaborate ruse to avoid conviction, but the Ohio authorities finally did not. Although Billy Milligan committed the crime, the court decided that another "person" inside himself was responsible and Billy as a whole could not be punished for the crime of one of his parts. A program of treatment to attempt to fuse the different personalities was prescribed. It was successful. While they are exotic and controversial, multiple personalities shed light on the many diverse systems, "minds", "traits" or "selves" that live within one person.

HEALTH, THE MIND, AND THE BRAIN

Recently there has been great excitement concerning discoveries about how mental events affect the body. This *health psychology* promises to become a major way in which psychological knowledge can be used to improve the lives of many (and possibly lengthen them). Many of the indicators of the role of the brain and nervous system in health are found in reactions to daily events.

One pioneering study took place in the 1970s. A telephone call comes late at night: "This is the police. I am sorry to have to inform you that your husband has died in a train wreck." It is a story we read almost every day in the newspapers. We know what happens after a train wreck. The dead are pulled away, and their mangled bodies are identified and buried. The train wreck also disorganizes the lives of many others. Close members of the family and friends grieve. They feel the pain of the loss and must now learn to live without their husband or wife, father or mother.

The train wreck wrecks the lives of those killed and of others. But an unexpected loss from an accident like this also wrecks the immune system of those who feel the loss! The discovery of the link between a shocking tragedy and subtle, internal changes in susceptibility to disease began with a newspaper story that was similar to many we see each week:

SYDNEY, AUSTRALIA [REUTERS]. A train heading for Melbourne derailed at a crossing killing 33 and injuring scores of passengers. The cause of the accident is not yet known but is under intense investigation.

After the Melbourne train wreck, many of the spouses suffered greatly, almost all grieved for their loss. Many were offered counseling services and the help of sympathetic friends to help them adjust. But there was a difference: many of those so affected were studied to determine how the stress of their grief affected the functioning of their immune system.

A group of psychiatrists and immunologists in New South Wales followed the lives of the spouses and their families. They charted the transient changes in family members' immune responses after the event. R. W. Barthrop and colleagues (1978) took blood samples from 26 of the spouses of those killed in the train wreck. The samples showed that, within three weeks of the accident, the immune systems of the grieving spouses had been weakened.

The blood samples showed lower levels of activity of those cells in the blood which attack foreign bodies—the lymphocytes. This study was the first to show, in human beings, a measurable depression of immune function following severe psychological stress in a real-life setting. The findings may also contribute to understanding the tremendous increase in illness and death which often follows loss of a spouse (Barthrop et al., 1978; Ornstein & Sobel, 1987). These studies and others have sparked the field of "psychoimmunology," the assessment of the effect of mental events on the immune system of the body.

THE HUMANISTIC APPROACH

The study of disorders yields much information on the workings of the normal mind. But to achieve a full understanding of the nature of the human mind and experience we must also know the extent of its capabilities. We might ask ourselves, "What am I really good at? What is the best I can do?"

This emphasis upon the important positive aspects of human experience is the humanistic approach. Abraham Maslow, its founder and leading theorist, believed that human beings have an inherent inclination toward growth and development, toward improvement in health, creativity, achievement, love, and understanding (Frager & Fadiman, 1987).

Maslow presumed that we all have within us genuine "potentials" and, given the opportunity, we strive to make those potentials actual—a process called self-actualization. Maslow studied people who seemed to develop their potential to its fullest, such as scientific geniuses like Einstein and world leaders like Gandhi.

> If we want to answer the question how tall can the human species grow, then obviously it is well to pick out the ones who are already tallest and study them. If we want to know how fast a human being can run, then it is no use to average out the speed of a "good sample" of the population: it is far better to collect Olympic gold medal winners and see how well they can do. If we want to know the possibilities for spiritual growth, value growth, or moral development in human beings, then I maintain that we can learn most by studying our most moral, ethical or saintly people.
>
> On the whole I think it fair to say that human history is a record of the ways in which human nature has been sold short. The highest possibilities of human nature have practically always been underrated. Even when "good specimens," the saints and sages and great leaders of history, have been available for study, the temptation too often has been to consider them not human but supernaturally endowed. (Maslow, 1970)

Humanistic psychologists also treat people with difficulties, emphasizing their positive elements and the possibilities for growth and development.

Psychology, the science of human experience, thus involves specific perspectives, methods of study, and statistical rules of interpretation. The *perspectives* psychology studies encompass are biology, mind, behavior and social environment, and the full range of disorders (the clinical perspective), and of great achievements (the humanistic perspective). These orientations can be further simplified into the biological, the clinical-psychodynamic, and the social-cognitive. We shall consider these major divisions in a moment.

Psychologists use numerous methods to go beyond ordinary experience. These methods may be systematic observation, including measurements and tests, demonstrations like illusions, and experiments such as the study at the wobbly bridge. However, these perspectives merge in today's science into three general lines of work: the clinical, including that influenced by psychoanalysis, the biological, including evolutionary, the cognitive environmental perspective, and the behavioral. Throughout the book we shall follow these perspectives as they affect us, but we will take one major example, the nature of sexuality, and follow what the biological, cognitive, and clinical perspectives, among others, contribute to our knowledge of how, when, where, and if, men and women differ on important characteristics.

BEING FEMALE, BEING MALE: AN INTRODUCTION

Scientists seek to identify universal laws that govern the actions of the subjects or issues they study. Physicists try to comprehend basic laws of nature. Astronomers attempt to understand the heavens. Psychologists aim to explain and predict human thought and behavior. There is a certain irony in the behavioral sciences because the scientist is both the researcher and the subject matter. Even though we might gain an insight into a problem from our own experience, just as often we are limited by our own human nature; we selectively remember information that confirms our expectations and neglect contradictory information; we remember the exceptional case more vividly than the typical one. These very human features of cognition serve adaptive functions at times. However, they are not so adaptive in the laboratory.

Historically, psychologists have been middle-class, Caucasian males. So have the participants in psychological studies. (One text on the history of psychology was aptly titled *Even the Rat Was White*.) Subsequently, most of the existing theories of behavior were developed by men, based on studies of men. There is nothing inherently wrong with understanding white men, but there is something wrong with assuming that findings about white men can be generalized to all humans. Race, class, and gender exert powerful influences on our thinking and our actions. Ignoring these influences can only lead to erroneous conclusions, even conclusions about white males. We warn you from the onset that the theories you read about in this text will reflect these biases. Obviously we cannot rewrite the field. But we can point out some issues along the way.

One way to do this is to focus on gender throughout the text. Class and race have powerful influences on behavior and in many ways are analogous to the influence of gender. In part because being male or female affects each of us profoundly, and in part because psychologists have learned a great deal about it during the past two decades, we have decided to point out the influence of gender as an illustration of the profound influence of social, biological, and cultural factors on emotion, cognition, and behavior.

Some terms require clarification. **Sex** is a biological fact: just as we have brown eyes or blue eyes and are either a boy or a girl. Sex is determined by our genetic make-up. **Gender,** in contrast, is a cultural construction. Every known culture has different roles for males and females. **Gender identity** refers to our sense of self as a male or a female.

Gender differences present a marvelously complicated challenge for psychologists. There is little doubt that both biology and socialization influence gender. Unlike race and class, in which biological differences are negligible, sex ensures some obvious biological features. The greatest difference between the sexes is that women can bear children and men cannot. Other biological differences are that, on average, men are taller and stronger than women. Women, on average, have better fine motor coordination than men. All in all, with the exception of childbearing, the differences are not large, and there is overlap in both directions; some females are stronger than some males, and some males have better fine motor dexterity than some females. Some scholars feel that males' greater aggressiveness is also biologically determined. But the social and cultural influences on behavior are enormous. Teasing apart the reasons for the differences we observe between girls and boys and men and women is no simple task.

A number of theories have been offered over the years to explain gender differences. Some theories place heavy emphasis on biology; others hold social factors as central. Below we describe three theoretical positions that have influenced psychological conceptualizations of gender. These are not exhaustive, of course, but do give you a sense of the great diversity of positions on gender difference.

BIOLOGICAL THEORIES

Biological theories of gender are premised on the belief that physical differences are the basis for males' and females' social roles. There are many biological theories of gender differences. Some focus on anatomical differences between males and females; others suggest that hormonal differences lead to gendered behavior. Evolutionary psychologists, also biological in emphasis, reason that gender differences emerged because of our ancestors' adaptiveness. In each theory, the different female and male behaviors should lead to increased reproductive potential, even though the male and female strategies may not be alike.

The hormonal theories hold that hormones particularly influence sexual and aggressive behavior. Essentially, animal research shows that when female offspring are exposed to the male hormone testosterone in utero, they display male sexual behaviors (such as mounting), not female sexual behaviors (such as arching the back and presenting the rear-end to the male), and they are more aggressive than males. Even when masculinized females later receive estrogen or progesterone (the female hormones), they continue to display masculine behaviors because their brains have been organized in such a way as to limit the effects of the female hormones. The reverse holds for males. When males are not exposed to testosterone in utero, they display female sexual behaviors and low levels of aggression.

Do these effects hold in humans? For obvious ethical reasons, we cannot conduct human **experiments** to study the effects of in utero exposure to hormones. As a result we are much more limited in our knowledge about humans. A general rule of thumb is that lower species are more invariable in sex-linked behavior than higher species (Hines, 1982). Guinea pig males, for example, almost always mount the females, whereas humans show great diversity in sexual behavior. So even when we find evidence for hormonal effects on behavior in other species, we do not know how much they affect human behavior.

Evolutionary theories of gender difference are based on the premise that the central task of both males and females is to pass along as many of their genes to successive generations as possible. Because males produce essentially unlimited sperm, their reproductive strategies are different from those of females, who are limited in the number of offspring they can produce in a lifetime. Many theorists, then, hold that there is a tendency in males to impregnate as many females as possible. Because females are limited in the number of offspring they can have, the best strategy for them is do whatever they can to ensure that their offspring survive to reproductive age. In contrast to males who mate with a large number of potentially child-bearing females, females fare better when they select a good provider—that is, a mate with good genes, or the most dominant male because he can help ensure the survival of her offspring. A recent cross-cultural study by David Buss (1989) found support for this theory by showing that women prefer mates who are powerful and wealthy, whereas males value youth and attractiveness in women.

SOCIAL LEARNING AND COGNITIVE THEORIES

Neither social learning theorists nor cognitive psychologists view gender acquisition as the result of biological destiny. Social learning theorists conceptualize gender as the product of social experience: girls and boys have to learn to act like girls and boys (Mischel, 1970). How do they do this? Children imitate role models. Because societies value gender distinctions, girls are rewarded for behavior regarded as feminine, and boys are rewarded for behavior regarded as masculine.

Cognitive models of gender differences focus on the psychological mechanisms that allow children to acquire gender roles. Before children can acquire gender identity, they must know which sex they belong to and that sex is a constant—that is, people do not change sex as they change age (Kohlberg, 1966). Children identify their own sex at roughly 18 months, but their gender constancy (knowing which gender they are) is actually weak until the age of 3 or 4. It is precisely this age when gender differences emerge in children. Cognitive theorists believe that children acquire gender identity before they identify with one parent or another. Identification can proceed only after children categorize themselves as male or female. Thus, in cognitive models, children's first step is to identify their sex. Only then can they begin the process of acquiring behaviors that are consistent with the *social* definitions of male or female, also termed **gender roles.**

Gender-schema theory (Bem, 1981) holds that from the time children identify their sex, they process information within an ever-evolving gender schema. A **schema** is a network of associations that we use to assimilate new information. Because gender is relevant so early in life, it is a fundamental part of our self-concept, and we learn new information differentially depending on our sex.

Other psychologists (Maccoby, 1988) believe that social differences in gender emerge during early and middle childhood as a function of sex-segregated social groupings. As soon as children identify their sex, they begin to show strong preferences for same-sex play partners. Maccoby points out that this is not due to adult pressures; in fact, in the absence of adults, segregation is more complete. Socialization proceeds differently for male and female groups. Boys are more likely to engage in rough-and-tumble play, whereas girls are more likely to play verbal games. Sex-segregation continues until adolescence. At this point mixed-sex groupings reappear, but the sexes have developed distinct interaction styles. Males rely on dominance to get their way, and females rely on verbal persuasiveness.

PSYCHOANALYTIC THEORY

Freudian theory is a stage theory of psychosexual development. The theory holds that children proceed through a fixed series of stages from birth to about the age of 6. Each of the stages involves the resolution of a central conflict. In contrast to the cognitive theorists, Freud believed that the process of moving through the stage sequence results in the formation of personality and the acquisition of gender. According to the theory, males and females at birth are highly similar. In fact, Freud argued that there were no differences psychologically until children entered the phallic stage of development at the age of 3 or 4. At this point, boys develop an overpowering sexual desire to possess their mothers. Simultaneously they realize that their fathers are mighty opponents and so fear castration by their fathers. The one way that they can secure their yearning for the mother is to identify with the father. By identifying with him, boys are able to possess their mothers indirectly. Through this identification, they acquire masculine characteristics, including the need for dominance and control.

For girls, gender identity proceeds somewhat differently, according to Freudian theory. By the age of 3 or 4, a girl realizes that she does not have a penis and feels cheated and envious. She holds her mother responsible for the loss and transforms her desire for a penis into a desire to become impregnated by the father. Instead of fearing castration, she comes to fear the loss of love from her mother. To resolve the conflict, she identifies with the mother. Freud believed that because the acquisition of gender in females is more passive than in males, feminine characteristics inherently involve passivity. And because impregnation involves a "beating by a penis," masochism (pleasure in pain) is fundamental to the female personality. As you can imagine, this is a very controversial approach, but it is one of the most influential theories of the twentieth century. Throughout the text, in areas where appropriate, we'll see how it has fared.

Psychology tells a story, and that story follows the course of our lives—where we come from; how each person grows from an infant to an adult; how people learn, think, remember; what consciousness is like; how we argue with and love other people; how groups affect us; and how we develop as we get older. This book follows that story, our story.

Think of our lives as a series of concentric circles: at the beginning is biology (see the innermost, first circle of Figure 1-12), followed by the normal processes of socialization and development out of which develops the mind (second circle). Then comes our life with other individuals: how we communicate, how we express our feelings, how we get into trouble (third circle). Finally, there is the "world" of society and of our adult life (fourth circle). Each stage is more complex and filled with more challenges than the last.

The second chapter, Part One, covers the developing person, from birth to adulthood. Part Two is the biological world and it begins with the most complex phenomenon in the universe, the human brain and goes on to consider how human beings first evolved, in East Africa, over 4 million years ago. This section ends with the outposts of the brain, our senses.

Part 3 examines the mental world. It begins with perception, how we organize the world, and continues with the study of how our consciousness changes and how we can change consciousness. The part continues with the basic processes of learning to associate things in the world with things in the mind, and then goes on to the mystery of how we remember. It ends with a

FIGURE 1-12
The Organization of This Book and of Human Experience

Our study of psychology —like the course of our individual lives—starts with the biological world before moving on to the mental world, the world of the individual, and the social world of the adult. Each stage augments and amplifies the others.

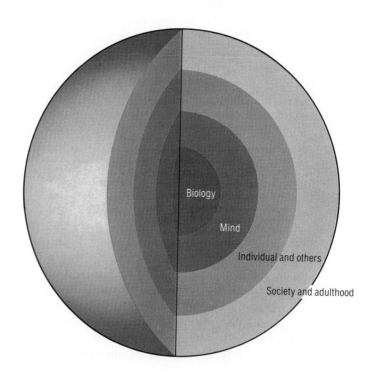

32

It is important in studying psychology (or other subjects) to use "psychology" to help you understand. This book is organized to assist you in this process: it presents ideas from different perspectives so you will be able to comprehend the entire field, and it organizes the different areas of psychology into principles. But you have to go further and learn to organize information in *your* own way. Here are a few study suggestions on how to understand psychology from a wide range of perspectives and meet your instructor's expectations and demands. See also the box on the SQ3R study method.

STRATEGY 1: SURVEY

Try to orient yourself to the field of psychology early in the course. Skim through several recent professional journals (available in the school library) to get an overview of the subject. (The *American Psychologist* and the *Psychological Review* are good places to start.) Try a few articles in the more popular magazines like *Psychology Today* and *Scientific American* to give you background information. Becoming familiar with the discipline will prepare you for the contents of the field and the emphases of the instructor, and you'll find much of interest, too!

STRATEGY 2: ACQUAINT YOURSELF WITH SPECIFIC RESEARCH IN THE FIELD

As a science, psychology is in its infancy. Psychologists have filled scientific journals with findings that relate to conditioning, learning, brain physiology, perception, and many other topics. But psychological theory and research should be thought of and approached as an exploration of how mind, consciousness, behavior, and environment interrelate. Acquaint yourself with some research in the professional journals, but at the same time develop a critical and open mind about their findings and conclusions.

STUDYING AND UNDERSTANDING PSYCHOLOGY

STRATEGY 3: STUDY HABITS

No extraordinary techniques are required to play the study game. Motivation and discipline are as necessary to studying psychology as they are with any other course. Good attendance, attentiveness in class, careful note taking, completing assignments on time, asking pertinent questions, and studying hard are important ingredients for being a successful student. Holding high standards for yourself is also important. But an additional step is required. Through outside reading you should eventually recognize that the importance of psychology extends beyond what is learned within a classroom setting.

STRATEGY 4: INTERPRETATION

Critical thinking is especially useful when interpreting research studies. Instructors, of course, will stamp their personal styles on the presentation of these findings (and what they mean) to students. But it is not necessary to accept unquestioningly conclusions based on psychological research. In fact, you can learn to develop rival hypotheses when you suspect a research design is flawed. Learn about findings, but do not always regard them as incontrovertible facts that need to be fixated in memory (unless temporarily, as for an exam).

STRATEGY 5: ASSOCIATION

And remember that the final product of your learning will reside in your memory. We will consider what makes us remember well in Chapter 9, but here are some things to keep in mind before you get there.

The more we associate something new with something we already know, the better we remember. We also remember meaningful events, things that tell us about ourselves. Psychology, then, is almost designed to be easy to study, because what you learn about growing up, the brain, our life with other people, and disorders all relate to you. When you read this book, try and relate the discoveries to yourself or to people you know.

chapter on thinking, how we create and make mistakes, and one on intelligence, asking can we assess intelligence, and can we increase it?

Part 4 considers the world of the self, beginning with our feelings and our relations with other people. The first chapters are on our emotions and our motives—*why* we do what we do. Then we deal with a most complex subject: what an individual's personality is really like. If you have ever tried to understand another person (let alone yourself) you will not be surprised to find that the answer is puzzling. The next chapter deals with the abnormal, with

You'll find that your ability to study progresses with active use. The more ways you try to understand information, the more you will remember, not just on the exam, but in your life! One study method is called **SQ3R,** which stands for "Survey, Question, Read, Recite, Review." We present it here for your use:

1. *Survey* each chapter before reading it—that is, review the outline, the general headings, and the chapter summary—to get an idea of what will be covered. In this book, the chapter outline and introduction at the beginning of each chapter provide an overall context, introducing important concepts and previewing topics covered in the chapter. The chapter summary also provides schemata for improving your understanding. If the chapter is lengthy or complex, break it down into manageable segments and follow the SQ3R procedure for each segment.

SQ3R

2. *Question* the material *before* you read it. Ask such questions as, "I wonder what this means?" and "Is this related to what I read in an earlier chapter?" Such questioning ignites your curiosity and demands answers. Your active questioning will lead to an active search for answers.

3. *Read* the material now that you have created a framework for encoding the information in the chapter.

4. *Recite* what you have learned from your reading. Try to answer the questions you asked before reading. Make sure you understand important concepts and facts featured in the introduction and the summary.

5. *Review* the material after you have retained the important information. Implicit in the SQ3R method are *rehearsal* and *relearning.* The greater the familiarity you have or the number of associations you make with the material, the better your retention and retrieval will be.

such disorders as when sadness becomes debilitating depression, when withdrawal becomes catatonia. The last chapter in Part 4 covers the psychotherapies, the attempts to relieve these disorders.

The final part, on the social world of the adult, is still more complex: it addresses our life in current society. The first chapter deals with the effect other people have on us, in small groups, in crowds, and in cities. The next one discusses more intimate social events: friendship, love, and sex. Then we consider one of the most important new areas of psychology: health. Here, many of the principles of the book are applied to resisting and avoiding disease as well as promoting healing. Next is another new area: the problems of adapting to the modern world. Many of our major social problems, such as crowding, overpopulation, and pollution, are unprecedented in human history. How can we call on our understanding of the mind to help us adapt? The final chapter deals with the process of growing up that lies ahead: job, marriage, family, aging, and, finally, death.

So, our story actually begins *before* our birth and ends after our death. In it we can obtain a few glimpses of why we are the way we are, and what we can become. There are a few myths dispelled, such as blacks and whites do not differ as much as some may think. Some obvious facts are analyzed closely—for example, why we will assist our own families at the expense of others, why we have great difficulty losing weight, and why emotions are universal. Some surprising findings show the importance of psychological factors in health. We know, for instance, that cigarette smoking is dangerous to health but do not realize that the effects on the heart of a divorce are equal to those of smoking two packs a day. Also, just watching a comedian has immediate effects on our immune systems.

1. Psychology is the science of human experience and behavior. It includes the study of the brain and nervous system, mental life, behavior, mental disorders, and human potentials. A science of psychology is needed to understand the human mind because each of us is only one in 5 billion people.

2. Scientific psychology provides more comprehensive, objective knowledge than everyday psychology. The findings of scientific psychology are relevant to most people. For example, people who never recall dreams might conclude that they do not dream. However, researchers have demonstrated that all humans dream every night.

3. Science is a systematic and formal process of gathering information. The goal of science is to find the order and unity in the world. Scientific results have to be replicable to be accepted as true. All scientific findings are subject to correction. Science uses several methods to study the world. Among these are *observation, case histories, measurements, tests,* and *questionnaires.*

4. The *experimental method* permits scientists to control the situation they are studying. The scientist develops a *hypothesis,* then chooses *independent variables* to manipulate. The results are found by measuring the *dependent variables.* Experiments are conducted on samples of the population under scrutiny. The sample is usually divided into an *experimental* and a *control group.*

5. Experimenters can bias the results of their experiments, sometimes unconsciously. To avoid this problem, researchers employ the *double-blind experimental procedure* and have their results confirmed by other scientists.

6. *Statistics* is the formal set of rules for evaluating the results of experiments. For a result to be meaningful, the differences found must attain statistical *significance.* Two important measures used in statistics are the *mean* and the *median.* Tests of *correlation* can show relationships between *variables,* even when experimental manipulation is not possible.

7. *Descartes* set the stage for the development of Western psychology by proposing that human knowledge was innate to the brain and nervous system. The British *empiricists* believed that all knowledge comes from *associations* developed through experience. *Darwin* expanded the field by showing that humans evolved from animals and, therefore, that animal behavior was relevant to human behavior. The systematic study of psychology began with *William James* and *Wilhelm Wundt.* James wrote *The Principles of Psychology,* and Wundt established the first psychology laboratory.

8. *Behaviorists* assume that people's behavior results from conditions in their *environment.* They believe that when conditions change, behavior changes. Behaviorists study psychology by manipulating the environment of an organism and observing the organism's resultant behavior. Behaviorists have contributed greatly to our understanding of learning and behavior.

9. The *biological* approach to psychology seeks to find the biological underpinnings of experience. Changes in the brain's *chemical* and *electrical* activity caused by injury, surgery, or drugs can dramatically influence the mind.

10. *Cognitive* psychology focuses on the operations of the mind. It looks for the *mechanisms, potentials,* and *limitations* of mental processes. One of the general findings of cognitive psychology is that people do not perceive the world as it really is.

11. *Social* psychologists study *interactions* between people and how people influence each other. Disturbing events, such as the murder of Kitty Genovese, witnessed by 38 people who did not help her, inspire social psychologists to examine the motivations behind human social behavior.

12. The *clinical* approach to psychology attempts to understand the functions of the mind by studying dysfunctions. Mental *dysfunctions* can be studied on a biological level or through Freudian psychoanalysis. The phenomenon of multiple personality illuminates something about the structure of the normal mind. Recent discoveries have shown that mental health affects physical health, spawning the field of *psychoimmunology.*

13. *Humanistic* psychology emphasizes the positive aspects of human experience. *Abraham Maslow,* the founder of humanistic psychology, believed that humans inherently incline toward growth and development. Maslow presumed that all people have potentials which they can reach through *self-actualization.*

14. Historically, psychological findings are based on studies of white men by white men. Therefore, they may not accurately describe nonwhites or women. Gender difference presents a challenge to psychologists. Several theories, from the fields of psychodynamics, biology, and social and cognitive psychology, propose explanations for gender differences.

TERMS AND CONCEPTS

behaviorism
capture error
case history
catharsis
cognitive psychology
control group
correlation
demonstration
dependent variable
double blind procedure
experiment
experimental group
experimental method
experimenter bias
gender
gender identity
gender role
humanistic approach

hypothesis
independent variable
introspection
mean
median
method of observation
psychoanalysis
questionnaire
replicability
sample
schema
self-actualization
sex
social environment perspective
SQ3R study method
statistics
subject
variable

Benderly, B. L. (1987). *The myth of two minds: What gender means and doesn't mean.* New York: Doubleday.

A discussion of the relationship of gender to physical, intellectual, sexual, and social dimensions of men and women.

Cialdini, R. (1988). *Influence.* Chicago: Scott, Foresman.

The most readable account of the social psychological perspective. Excellent introduction.

Erdelyi, M. H. (1985). *Psychoanalysis: Freud's cognitive psychology.* New York: Freeman.

An attempt to give Freud's ideas a contemporary treatment, written in fairly plain language.

Gardner, H. (1985). *The mind's new science.* New York: Basic Books.

How cognitive psychology came into being.

Huck, S. W., & Sandler, H. W. (1979). *Rival hypotheses: Alternative interpretations of data-based conclusions.* New York: Harper & Row.

Pennebaker, J. (1990). *Confiding secrets: The healing power of self-disclosure.* New York: Morrow.

An excellent story of how one researcher has made one of psychology's major discoveries.

Shah, I. (1988). *Caravan of dreams.* London: Octagon Press.

A modern account, in story and tale, of a different perspective on psychology.

SUGGESTIONS FOR FURTHER READING

"SONG"

I
THE WORLD OF THE DEVELOPING PERSON

In the beginning, each of us is a cell so small that we are invisible to the naked eye. Yet a miracle happens: the cell divides and divides, organs emerge, and a person is formed. From this beginning, formed by the physical joining of mother and father, breeds an organism more complex than any other in the world. The developing person grows in a sequence so specific that it even has different designations at different times: the ovum becomes an embryo and then a fetus; the infant becomes a toddler; the child an adolescent; the youth an adult; the middle-aged person an elderly one. This part of the book begins, simply, at the beginning of life. It considers what is inside us at birth and how our innate, inherent behaviors shape and are shaped by the worlds we grow up in—the worlds of our family, friendships, school, work, marriage, and parenthood. Once we become parents, we continue to grow as individuals, but we also complete a cycle by creating life anew.

2
HUMAN DEVELOPMENT: BIRTH TO ADULTHOOD

The most dazzling human biological achievement begins when a male's sperm unites with a female's ovum (Figure 2-1). During the next nine months, the fertilized cell divides again and again forming the brain, internal organs, muscles, skin, and bones. Only about 50 doublings of that first cell beget a baby! Scientists do not know why some cells become "brain" and others "tongue."

What we do know is that a speck starting so small that it is barely detectable under a microscope bursts upon the scene in 40 weeks in the form of a seven-pound baby. Even though life inside the womb is the period of the most rapid growth, development has just begun. From conception to adulthood an individual changes form so drastically and so often that it almost seems to be a succession of very different organisms: ovum, embryo, fetus, newborn, infant, child, adolescent, and adult.

Although babies are helpless and immature at birth, the seeds of adult abilities are present from the beginning. Those seeds begin to sprout and bear fruit. Growth and development is a process of widening capacities. A helpless baby blossoms into an adult capable of an extraordinary range of motor abilities, from running to writing. Mentally, a newborn, who can only recognize its mother's odor and face and barely track a moving light, blooms into an adult who can invent and imagine things never before dreamed of.

From the moment the umbilical cord is cut, the infant's social world begins to expand beyond the mother and includes other important figures. Children form attachments with the father and primary family members; later attachments are formed with friends, the community and work. As a child grows, life becomes determined less by biology and more by the family, friends, and choices. Two 6-month-old babies look and behave quite similarly. But it would be absurd to make the same claim about two 60 year olds. In fact, aging itself is sometimes referred to as the process of differentiation; throughout adulthood, people become more and more individualistic (Whitbourne & Weinstock, 1979).

Does human development ever stop? When most of us think about developmental psychology, we conjure up images of toddlers learning to walk and forming their first sentences. We think of grade school children starting school and learning to build friendships. Indeed, research on development has focused primarily on infancy and childhood. But life-span psychologists argue that human development is a life-long process that continues until death. Parenting, careers, and even wrestling with physical decline bring about human growth.

This chapter explores human development, the progression of a single cell to the self in adulthood. The thought processes begun in infancy continue as the child matures, becoming the basis for perception, cognition, and reasoning in adulthood. Chapter 21 completes the life cycle with a discussion of old age.

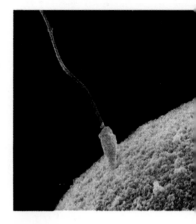

FIGURE 2-1
The Moment of Conception

HISTORICAL NOTE

We live in a youth-oriented era. Magazines, television shows, and books educate us about child development. Young parents benefit from an enormous literature on infancy; most people have at least heard of Dr. Spock. But historically, widespread attention to children has not been the case. The very idea of childhood as a period that is *qualitatively* distinct from adulthood is relatively new. Prior to the nineteenth century, children were typically viewed as small, inexperienced adults. Most children were put to work, usually assisting their parents, by the age of 5.

In the United States, during the heavy industrialization of the late nineteenth and early twentieth centuries, many children were sent to work in factories. In 1912, the government, concerned about the welfare of children in the work force, established the Federal Children's Bureau to monitor and explore the special needs of children (Horn, 1989). Laws to abolish child labor finally were enacted in 1936. About that time, major universities began to create child study centers, and within two decades the scientific investigation of child development was recognized as a legitimate science.

Today we know that children are far from being small adults. They see the world very differently from adults. How much do tiny infants understand about their physical and social worlds? How do friendships at age 3 differ from friendships at age 10? How do children acquire gender? These are but a few of the questions that developmental psychologists pursue. In the following pages we outline the story of development from conception to adulthood.

IMPORTANT TERMS AND CONCEPTS

There are several important terms and concepts that pervade the developmental psychology literature. Below we review a few of the most common:

Reflexes are automatic (unlearned) responses to environmental stimulation and are present at birth. Reflexive behaviors include sucking and grasping. No doubt, they have evolved due to their survival value.

Maturation is the emergence of individual characteristics through normal growth processes. **Physical maturation** is controlled by the information contained in the genes and is assumed to be relatively unaffected by experience. It follows a universal pattern: children all over the world learn to sit up before they walk, have milk teeth before permanent teeth, and mature sexually in their early teenage years.

Psychological maturation is the development of mental abilities that result from the normal growth of the brain and nervous system. Due to the long period of immaturity, experiences such as language, family, and culture can have profound effects on psychological maturation (Kagan, 1984).

Adaptation refers to the changes an individual makes to adjust to environment conditions. Chapter 3 will show how our earliest ancestors, through successive physical adaptations over thousands of years, evolved to meet the demands of a changing world. Although changes occur much more rapidly in an individual's development (years rather than millennia), the changes require continual adaptation.

In ordinary speech *egocentric* is a term that means self-absorbed or self-centered. In general, the term has negative connotations. But in developmental psychology, **egocentrism** is a technical term used to describe cognitive orientation. Newborns are highly egocentric; they do not recognize that other people exist outside of themselves, not to mention that others may hold different perspectives on the world. Young infants operate on the assumption that others perceive objects and situations as they do. Gradually, the child comes to understand that other people are distinct entities who see the world from different perspectives. By adolescence, the child can even understand that conflicting views can be valid simultaneously. In general, egocentrism diminishes with age, although there are situations in later childhood and even in adulthood in which egocentrism reappears.

Critical periods are times in life when specific environmental or biological events must occur or development will fail to proceed normally. Critical periods can refer to physical or behavioral development. Language acquisition is most often cited as evidence for critical periods in human behavior (Lenneberg, 1967).

THE NEWBORN

LIFE BEFORE BIRTH

The mother and the unborn child are the closest human relationship, a single biological unit for nine months. For the child, physical development is the most rapid and most vulnerable in the 40 weeks inside the mother's womb. There are three distinct periods **in utero** (in the womb): the germinal period, the embryonic period, and the fetal period. The **germinal period** begins at the moment of fertilization and ends about a week later when the fertilized egg, repeatedly dividing, has moved down the fallopian tube and implants itself in the uterus.

The **embryonic period** lasts from implantation until about the eighth week of pregnancy. It is the critical stage of development for the nervous system. In about the ninth week, the **fetal period** begins with the baby's first independent reaction to the world: the fetus responds to upsets by flexing its torso and extending its head.

During gestation the fetus is protected from many outside influences—but not completely. There are critical periods during prenatal development. If a woman contracts rubella (German measles) during her first two months of pregnancy, the unborn child runs a high risk of being severely retarded or deformed. If the same woman contracts rubella during her final weeks of pregnancy, the child will be unaffected. Exposure to alcohol, nicotine, heroin, cocaine, and many other drugs can also adversely affect the fetus's later physical and intellectual development.

Not all outside influences are harmful to the fetus. A number of researchers are beginning to investigate learning in the womb. Fetal education programs are even beginning to crop up that urge parents to give their children an academic head start before birth! Scientists view these programs with great skepticism, but they are actively pursuing answers to interesting questions about prenatal social and environmental influence. Recent research suggests that the fetus hears muffled speech after six months of gestation. It appears that the fetus is attuned to rhythm and melodic qualities of sound. In one study, when expectant mothers hummed "Mary Had a Little Lamb" three times a day during pregnancy, their babies, after birth, were more likely to be calmed by the tune when they cried (Field et al., 1986). Scientists have also observed prenatal responses to touch and light (MacFarlane, 1977).

THE FIRST TWO WEEKS OF LIFE

Babies are born with a number of reflexes that help them face new experiences such as sounds, hot and cold temperatures, movements, and pain. Babies are ready for these changes; they turn toward interesting noises and away from unpleasant events (Newman & Newman, 1987). Newborns know how to signal distress: they cry. A baby's cry gets the attention of the caretaker, usually the mother, who provides comfort.

Only two hours after birth, newborns can follow a slowly moving light in front of their eyes. If a nipple or a finger is put into their mouths, they begin to suck on it. This sucking response is a reflex, with important survival value: it allows them to obtain food. If their cheek or the corner of their mouth is gently stroked, they will turn their heads in that direction; this is called the *rooting reflex,* and it is an attempt to find their mother's nipple (Figure 2-2).

Many of these inborn responses are the building blocks of sophisticated motor skills, such as walking and speech. Trevarthen (1981) recorded the unforced lip movements of newborns and found that they were the same as those required for adult speech. In the first few months of life, an infant makes most of the sounds of every known language (Miller, 1981).

FIGURE 2-2
A newborn's survival depends on its ability to drink, so sucking is the strongest of its reflexes.

COGNITION

What does an infant know? William James (1890) wrote that the experience of the newborn is a "blooming, buzzing confusion." Jean Piaget (1952) character-ized it as a transitory world: "There are no permanent objects, only perceptual pictures which appear, dissolve and sometimes reappear."

These portrayals are somewhat accurate. Because the sensory systems are relatively well developed at birth (Coren et al., 1988), the newborn's world probably consists of a sequence of sounds, lights, and other sensations. Research has shown that the infant world is not so much confused as it is *simpler* and more *selective* than the adult world. Newborns are biologically unprepared to function in the adult world on their own, but they *are* prepared to function in their *limited* world. Their extreme egocentrism, for example, can be thought of as adaptive: an extremely narrow perspective is important for survival. That is, although infant thought is limited, it seems selectively attuned to aspects of the environment that are crucial to survival and development.

Newborns notice objects that are *very close* to them, things that are a part of their very small world. Later on, the newborns' world expands, and so do their thoughts and perspective. They become less egocentric. At birth newborns can focus up to only 10 inches away, about the distance from the breast to the mother's face. Later on, their range of vision expands. Newborns can distin-guish between figures and ground, have some depth perception, and can respond to different smells (Haith, 1980).

PREFERENCES IN PERCEPTION

From birth, babies are more interested in faces than other forms. Robert Fantz (1961) showed newborns a set of six discs (Figure 2-3). The babies looked longer

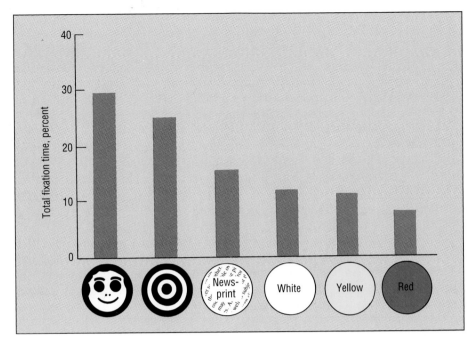

FIGURE 2-3
Visual Preference of
Newborns
In experiments exposing
infants to various visual
stimuli, newborns as young
as 10 hours old to 5 days old
looked longer at the disc with
the black-and-white face than
at simpler discs showing a
bull's-eye, newsprint, or solid
colors.
(Fantz, 1961)

at patterned discs than at single-color discs, and they looked the longest at the picture of a face. At first, babies seem to look primarily at the areas of most contour and change—that is, at the edges of objects. By six weeks they look at people's mouths, especially at their mother's mouth when she is talking (Bower, 1978). This inborn preference exists because being attracted to human beings is vital to their survival.

Babies seem to be born with a set of rules to look at the world by: (1) if awake and alert, they open their eyes; (2) if they find darkness, they search the environment; (3) if they find light but not edges, they begin a broad uncontrolled search of the environment; and (4) if they find an edge, they look near the edge and beyond it (Haith, 1980). It seems likely that the infant is born with a predisposition to search out new features of the environment.

PHYSICAL GROWTH IN THE EARLY YEARS

THE SEQUENCE OF MOTOR DEVELOPMENT

Figure 2-4 and Table 2-1 show when children achieve important motor skills. An infant may skip one or another stage in the sequence (for example, some babies never crawl), but the order in which these skills appear is the same for all children. No baby walks before sitting up or standing. Each element in the sequence builds to the next. Although there is some variation in the age at which any one of the particular skills may appear, there are limits: no baby walks at 6 months or sits up at 3 weeks.

FIGURE 2-4
The Achievement of
Motor Skills
Not all children achieve
these motor skills at
exactly these ages. But
this sequence is most
often observed, as are
the milestones of language
development described
in Table 2-1.
(Shirley, 1933/1960)

ADJUSTMENTS TO GROWTH

The first two years are marked by such rapid physical growth that the child must constantly adapt to a changing body. Children at 2 are almost twice as tall as they were at birth and are half their adult height. An infant's experience may be a gradual version of Alice's experience in Wonderland when she took the drink that suddenly made her tall. She constantly had to adjust her relationship to such familiar objects as tables and chairs.

Physical development has everything to do with psychological development. To lift a cup to your mouth, you must know not only where the cup is and how to move it toward you, but also where you are—where your arm is, how long it is, how far to stretch it, and where your mouth is. Growth affects all

TABLE 2-1
Developmental Milestones in Motor and Language Development

Age	Motor Development	Vocalization and Language
12 weeks	Supports head when in prone position; weight is on elbows; hands mostly open; no grasp reflex.	Markedly less crying than at 8 weeks; when talked to and nodded at, smiles, followed by squealing-gurgling sounds usually called *cooing,* which is vowellike in character and pitch-modulated; sustains cooing for 15–20 seconds.
16 weeks	Plays with a rattle placed in hands (by shaking it and staring at it); head self-supported; tonic neck reflex subsiding.	Responds to human sounds definitely; turns head; eyes seem to search for speaker; occasionally some chuckling sounds.
20 weeks	Sits with props.	The vowel-like sounds begin to be inter-spersed with more consonant sounds; labial fricatives, spirants, and nasals are common; acoustically, all vocalizations are very different from the sounds of the mature language of the environment.
6 months	Sitting: bends forward and uses hands for support; can bear weight when put into standing position, but cannot yet stand holding on; reaching: unilateral grasp; no thumb opposition yet; releases cube when given another.	Cooing changes into babbling resembling one-syllable utterances; neither vowels nor consonants have very fixed recurrences; most common utterances sound somewhat like *ma, mu, da,* or *di.*
8 months	Stands holding on; grasps with thumb opposition; picks up pellet with thumb and fingertips.	Reduplication (or more continuous repeti-tions) becomes frequent; intonation patterns become distinct; utterances can signal emphasis and emotions.
10 months	Creeps efficiently; takes side steps, holding on; pulls to standing position.	Vocalizations are mixed with sound-play such as gurgling or bubble blowing; appears to wish to imitate sounds, but the imitations are never quite successful; begins to differentiate between words heard by making differential adjustments.
12 months	Walks when held by one hand; walks on feet and hands, knees in air; mouthing of objects almost stopped; seats self on floor.	Identical sound sequences are replicated with higher relative frequency of occurrence, and words ("mamma" or "dadda") are emerging; definite signs of understanding some words and simple commands ("Show me your eyes").
18 months	Grasp, prehension, and release fully developed; gait stiff, propulsive, and precipitated; sits on child's chair with only fair aim; creeps downstairs backward; has difficulty building tower of three cubes.	Has a definite repertoire of words—more than 3, but less than 50; still much babbling but now of several syllables with intricate intonation pattern; no attempt at communicating information and no frustration for not being understood; words may include items such as "Thank you" or "Come here," but there is little ability to join any of the lexical items into spontaneous two-item phrases; understanding is progressing rapidly.
24 months	Runs, but falls in sudden turns; can quickly alternate between sitting and standing; climbs stairs up or down.	Vocabulary of more than 50 items (some children seem to be able to name everything in environment); begins spontaneously to join vocabulary items into two-word phrases; all phrases appear to be own creations; definite increase in communicative behavior and interest in language.

Note: These skills are given for the age at which *almost all* children will have accomplished them.
SOURCE: Lenneberg, 1967

47

sensory systems. As the head grows, the eyes grow farther apart, which makes it difficult to judge accurately the distance between yourself and an object (Bower, 1981).

Imagine the social implications of being unable to sit up, not to mention walking or crawling. Very young infants are unable to negotiate social interactions. Virtually anyone who wishes to interact with the infant can do so. Then somewhere between 6 and 8 months the child begins to locomote and a whole new world opens up for the child. For the first time, infants can initiate and terminate social situations. Moreover, they can actively explore their environment. Cognitive development soars once locomotion begins. While it is impossible to tease apart cause and effect during this period of rapid development, the interrelatedness of physical and cognitive development is undeniable.

Piaget (1951, 1954) believed that self-produced movement was fundamental to the child's understanding of space, objects, causality, and even the self. Joseph Campos and his colleagues have systematically researched the role that voluntary locomotion plays in facilitating understanding (Bertenthal & Campos, 1989; Bertenthal, Campos & Barrett, 1984; Kermoian & Campos, 1988). When infants crawl, and later walk, they come into contact with new experiences and cognitive challenges. They now see that a chair looks different depending on the perspective, and that moving faster or slower brings objects into close view at different speeds. Using imaginative experimental devices, such as toys that allow premotor babies to locomote, Campos has shown that cognitive gains reliably follow physical gains (Campos & Bertenthal, 1989).

COGNITIVE DEVELOPMENT

A father reads a book to his 2-year-old child and his 2-week-old child. The 2-year-old laughs, helps turn the pages, points to things and identifies them, asks questions, and asks for the book to be read again. The newborn coos, looks around the room, and dozes off. The infant seems oblivious to the surroundings. The 2-year-old and the newborn are closer in age than the 2-year-old is to the father, yet in terms of cognitive abilities, the 2-year-old and the father are more nearly alike. They share the same world, one which the newborn has not yet

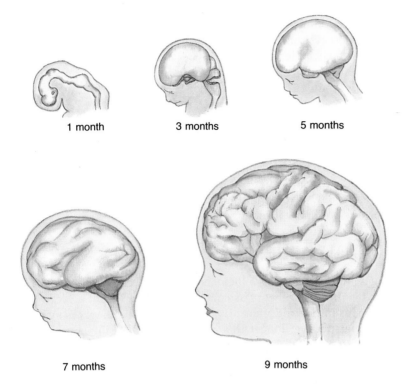

1 month   3 months   5 months

7 months   9 months

FIGURE 2-5
Embryonic Growth of the Human Brain

Note that the characteristic convolutions of the brain's surface do not appear until about mid-pregnancy. The brain grows amazingly fast: it is calculated that neurons are regenerated in the embryonic brain at a rate of 250,000 per minute!
(Adapted from "The Development of the Brain," by W. Maxwell Cowan. Copyright 1979 by SCIENTIFIC AMERICAN, Inc. All rights reserved.)

entered. The 2-year-old has attachments to people, can organize activities around a goal, and is concerned with competence.

During the early years a child gradually becomes more organized and more able to focus and direct attention for longer periods. Children who are 3 years of age and younger focus attention on an exciting event or object and are easily distracted by the next exciting event; they attend to irrelevant events. And they are easily fooled by deceptive appearances (Flavell, 1985). Halloween, for example, may frighten a 3-year-old because he may not understand that when his sister puts on a mask she is not really a witch. By 6 years of age, children have a more stable grasp of reality, and better control of attention, becoming less distractible by outside stimuli.

From one month after conception to birth, the human brain grows at an amazing rate and is fully developed at birth (Figure 2-5). By about 5 years of age the brain is about 95 percent of adult size. The maturation and growth of the brain and nervous system allow better coordination and motor control, including the fine control needed to draw, color, and write and the hand-eye coordination needed to catch balls and thread needles.

By 7 years of age, children have made great cognitive leaps. They know right from left, their memories have improved dramatically, and they can distinguish between the written letters *p* and *q*, and *b* and *d*. A 5-year-old uses simple reasoning, but is not very good at making and carrying out plans. A 7-year-old uses complex reasoning, plans, and works to get the right answer.

How does the infant move out of the world of "blooming, buzzing confusion" and enter the well-organized, predictable adult world? What mechanisms are at work? Does the child blossom from an innate program, or does she acquire sophisticated cognitive processes through learning and exposure to her environment? There are no simple answers. Theoretical approaches vary tremendously from those that emphasize biological maturation to those that emphasize social learning.

There is no doubt that biological maturation plays an essential role in child development. Maturation and growth of the brain and nervous system allow better coordination and motor control, including the fine control needed to draw, color, and write and the eye-hand coordination needed to catch balls and thread needles. But a child cannot catch a ball or thread a needle without practice. Below we review Piaget's stage theory of cognitive development. Many developmental psychologists take issue with Piaget's approach (we will review some of the criticisms later in the chapter), but his theory transformed psychologists' view of the child and laid the groundwork for developmental psychology as we know it today.

PIAGETIAN THEORY: ASSUMPTIONS AND TERMS

Jean Piaget (1896–1980) was a biologist turned psychologist. It is impossible to do full justice here to a theory as comprehensive as Piaget's. Nevertheless, we will outline his important premises and concepts. The theory is influenced by a Darwinian perspective; Piaget thought that mental abilities are adaptive and can be understood by studying how the child's mind becomes assembled during development.

Piaget assumed that *knowledge guides action.* The world we experience becomes more complex and detailed as we develop new mental structures. He also felt that *knowledge develops through experience and action.* Babies find out about the world by exploring things with their mouths; young children use their hands and their senses.

Also, in Piaget's view, the complexity of mental structures was strongly influenced by chronological age. The difference between a child at 3 and one at 10 is not merely that the older child has more information, but that the older child has a more complex and capable mind. This growth of capacity, or *mental structures*, is cognitive development.

SCHEMA Piaget assumed that the unit of mental life is the **schema. Schemata** (plural of schema) are the knowledge of how things are organized and relate to each other. Knowing that the general sequence of movements used in picking up a ball is similar to that used in picking up a pencil might be a general schema for "picking things up." A schema may also organize parts of an object onto a whole—for example, knowing that a nose, two eyes, and a mouth arranged in a certain way constitute a "face." A face schema would explain why babies prefer to look at the elements of an organized face rather than a disorganized one (Figure 2-6). Further, a schema may relate perceptions to actions; a baby smiles when it sees another face smile.

ASSIMILATION AND ACCOMMODATION Schemata *change* and grow by the processes of **assimilation** and **accommodation.** When children encounter a new event, they attempt to **assimilate** it into their existing knowledge structure, the schema. For instance, a toddler learns that the family pet is called "dog." During a walk the

JEAN PIAGET
(1896–1980)

child sees a German shepherd and says "dog"; collies, Chihuahuas, and poodles are all assimilated into this schema. But the child may also say "dog" when seeing a cat or a cow. This suggests that the schema was "all animals are dogs."

When young children cannot assimilate new events into existing schemata, they must change their thinking to **accommodate** the new information. This process usually involves changing or expanding the existing schemata. A child's parent may say, "That's wrong. There are many different kinds of animals. Only some are dogs." Then the schema "all animals are dogs" changes and expands to include the new knowledge. Each time children accommodate the schemata to new information, their intellectual worlds expand. Schemata, which shape experience, become more comprehensive and adaptive as the children mature.

OPERATIONS As children learn about the world, they join schemata to form repeated mental routines, called **operations.** Operations are rules for transforming and manipulating information. Operations are *reversible.* Consider the simple arithmetic operation, "If you add 2 of anything to 2 of anything, you will have 4 of anything." The reverse is, "If you have 4 of anything and take 2 away, you will have 2." This operation reflects a basic fact about the physical world, that quantities change when combined with other quantities.

Children's operations grow more complex as their cognition develops. Piaget proposed that children gain concepts by *performing operations* on things. As simple as 2 plus 2 equals 4 is, it is nevertheless an abstract mental concept, the understanding of which requires much repeated experience with counting things. Thus, physical manipulation of the environment leads to knowledge. Piaget developed many experiments to ascertain the level of a child's use of operations.

FIGURE 2-6
Innate Form Preferences
By turning their heads to look at the "face" with the features in the right places rather than at the other "faces," babies less than 1 day old showed an innate preference that could indicate they were born with a "face" schema.

STAGES OF COGNITIVE DEVELOPMENT

Piaget assumed that all children, regardless of culture, go through the same four stages of cognitive development: *sensorimotor, preoperational, concrete operational,* and *formal operational.*

SENSORIMOTOR STAGE (BIRTH TO 2 YEARS) In the **sensorimotor stage** children learn primarily through motor and sensory play. Babies are born with reflexes, innate motor programs, which develop in the first 18 to 24 months into complex and controlled movements. During this time, they develop a practical intelligence of their effect on the world. They may find that crying brings mother or that splashing in the bathtub makes all the bath toys move around. At around 18 months children begin to develop a sense of self and begin to be capable of **representational** or **symbolic thought.**

An important form of symbolic thought is the use of language. By 2 years of age, a toddler has a vocabulary of about 200 words, which he or she uses effectively in two-word sentences. Another indication of representational thought is metaphoric play, such as pretending to stroke a cat or pretending to be an elephant.

One of the most important attainments of the early phase of this sensorimotor stage is **object permanence:** babies discover that an object continues to exist even when they cannot see it. If you hide an object that a 5- to 7-month-old

FIGURE 2-7
Object Permanence

Because this infant does not yet have the concept of object permanence, it acts as if an object merely hidden from view has ceased to exist.

infant is reaching for behind a screen or under a cloth, the child will stop reaching (Figure 2-7). At 8 months the baby will look behind the screen or under the cloth. This new ability to search and find is a great advance, an important cognitive step. Peekaboo, basically a game of object permanence, is a favorite game for children 8 months and older.

Piaget first identified the concept of object permanence when he showed his 7-month-old daughter his watch on a chain and she reached for it. When he put his watch back in his pocket, she acted as if the watch had disappeared into thin air. But at 8 months, the child began to reach for and search in his pocket. She now knew the watch still existed, even though she could not see it.

FIGURE 2-8
Cognitive Development Revealed by Children's Art

Children's cognitive development is apparent in drawings like these. The simple face (A) drawn by a 3-year-old lacks the action and relatively complex composition of the work (B) by a 6-year-old. And although the sports picture (C) by a 9-year-old is exciting and evocative, it is crude compared to the drawing (D) by a 12-year-old. Artistic skill, like cognitive ability, emerges in stages.

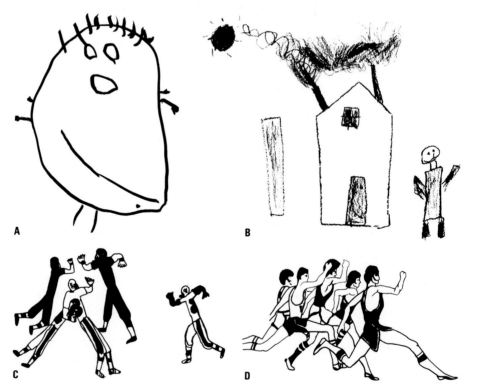

A

B

C

D

PREOPERATIONAL STAGE (2 TO 7 YEARS) In the **preoperational stage,** children use symbols; they can *represent* objects in drawings and words (Figure 2-8). Schemata that children were just beginning to arrange in the sensorimotor stage become more coordinated in the preoperational stage, but are not yet fully organized. Children at this stage are quite fluent in the use of language but rely primarily on their senses—on what they see or hear, rather than on what they know or imagine. They are unable to use *mental operations*—to reason, to deduce, to wonder about what *might* be.

Piaget extensively studied children in this stage, specifically on the basic operation called conservation. **Conservation** is an understanding that an object is the same even if it appears in different forms. Piaget contended that before the age of 6 or 7, the child has not formed the conservation rule. If you give one 3-year-old a sandwich cut into quarters and another 3-year-old a sandwich cut in half, the child with the two pieces may complain that he has less than the child with four pieces.

In Piaget's conservation of volume experiments, the experimenter shows the child two tumblers, one short and squat and the other tall and thin. He fills the short, squat one with water and then pours the water from that tumbler into the other (Figure 2-9). He asks the child, who has watched this whole procedure, if the same amount of water is in both tumblers. Because of the difference in shapes, the water is closer to the top of the long, thin tumbler. It appears to be full, unlike the short, squat one. Because of this a young child will usually say "no." An older child, however, understands the basic principle of constancy: "If you started out with the same amount of water, then it must be the same in each container." Piaget would conclude that the younger child is influenced more by appearances: information directly obtained through the senses dominates over reasoning.

CONCRETE OPERATIONS (7 TO 12 YEARS) In the **concrete operational stage** of cognitive development, thinking is no longer dominated by sensory information. Children begin to reason abstractly and can complete a task and understand such basic characteristics as number, weight, and order.

The child becomes more organized and able to plan and consequently can focus and direct attention for longer periods. There are large differences

FIGURE 2-9
Conservation of Volume

Around age 6 or 7 children start to understand the concept of conservation. Without it, they do not realize that equal amounts of a liquid in different-shaped containers are still equal, or that equal amounts of clay rolled into different shapes remain equal. Piaget repeatedly demonstrated that lack of this concept characterized preoperational children.

COMMUNICATING EMOTIONS

The earliest communication between parent and child is on an emotional plane. Around the world mothers use unique vocal patterns when talking to their babies (Fernald, 1984; Fernald & Simon, 1984). This form of speech, called **motherese,** is characterized by exaggerated intonation that highlights the emotional content of speech. A simple form of speech, motherese gets the baby's attention and regulates the child's emotional state. If a baby cries, for example, the mother might make her voice soothing as she says "Don't cry." In this case, it is the melody of her speech, rather than the linguistic message it carries, that is effective in calming the child. In addition to regulating emotion, such exaggerated intonational melodies may enable the infant to share emotions with the mother and thus pave the way for communication.

We communicate not only through words but also through facial and vocal expressions. A mother seeing her 8-month-old baby hovering near a flight of stairs, does not say calmly, "Don't go down the stairs, dear." Rather, she raises her eyebrows and opens

THE STORY OF COMMUNICATION AND LANGUAGE

her mouth, indicating fear. Preverbal infants recognize distinct facial expressions of their mothers and respond to them. The process is called **social referencing.** If babies are uncertain about the safety of a situation, they will look to their mothers to obtain additional information. If the mothers look frightened, the children will retreat; if the mothers smile, the infants will proceed (Campos & Stenberg, 1981).

LANGUAGE

Infants seem to communicate from the moment they are born. Initially communication occurs only because adults interpret infants' behavior. A cry signals discomfort; a gaze indicates interest. Communication is not the newborn's intent, even though parents often talk to their babies as if it were. Whatever the explicit purpose, these early verbal interchanges lay the groundwork for conversational speech (Dore, 1985).

Recognizable speech does not appear until somewhere around 12 to 18 months of age, but babies progress through essential and highly predictable stages of preverbal development (Clark & Clark, 1977). From birth, infants display preferences for the human voice over nonhuman sounds, and they respond vocally to speech emitted from people around them. Infants first coo and gurgle, especially in response to familiar people. When the parent coos, the 2- to 3-month-old child reciprocates. By 4 to 8 months, infants begin to babble, which allows them to practice sounds. During this stage infants vocalize a wide range of sounds, including some that are not used in the language they will eventually learn. Toward the end of the first year, jargoning or "pretend speech" begins—that is, vocalizing strings of syllables along with the intonation used in speech.

Babies' vocabularies first consist of object labels, like "dog," "car," or "duck" and social routine words like "bye bye." The number of words they know grows slowly but steadily (about one or two words a month) from as early as 10

between the ways preoperational and concrete operational children direct attention (Newman & Newman, 1987). Younger children direct attention to whichever event or object is most exciting to them and are thus easily distracted. A 7-year-old's attention is more focused, more under control; he or she is less distracted by novel stimuli and is more interested in information relevant to a *plan.*

FORMAL OPERATIONS (12 YEARS TO ADULT) Higher order thinking begins in the **formal operational stage.** Adolescents are capable of thinking abstractly and thinking through situations logically and systematically. They can follow a complex scientific experiment from start to finish and can sometimes formulate hypotheses and test them. For the first time, children are able to envision things as they *might be* instead of as they *are.* Their new capacity of conjectural thought launches them into the adult world. However, this is a somewhat idealized description, since not all adults possess this capacity, and it is not evident in all of the various skills of adulthood.

months. Then suddenly, at about 18 months, their vocabulary virtually explodes; their word learning becomes very rapid. In one well-documented case, for instance, a baby learned 45 words in one week (Dromi, 1987). Around the age of 2, children go beyond two-word utterances, like "See boy" and "No eat," to using longer and more syntactically complex speech. By age 3, speech is characterized by sentences like "Why did he go?" and "It's your turn." Children continue to master the more complex aspects of grammar as they grow (see Bowerman, 1988; Karmiloff-Smith, 1979).

Scholars continue to debate the degree to which language is learned or innate. Learning theorists argue that language is acquired according to the same principles of learning other behaviors (Skinner, 1957; Mower, 1950). They use the example of infants' initial ability to make sounds common to all known languages, and then as they learn the language of their culture, to retain some speech sounds while they drop others out of their vocal repertoires. We can see this specialization of speech sounds in the various dialects of the United States. Children raised in the Southern states learn to pronounce words very differently from children raised in New York City. And deaf children begin life cooing and babbling like hearing infants, but instead of a word explosion, they cease to vocalize much after 12 months. Instead they use their hands more in gestural communication (Bonvillian, Orlansky, & Novack, 1983).

Hearing spoken language is clearly necessary for the normal development of speech. But a gradual learning process does not explain the whole story. Children learn language and syntax much more quickly than would be predicted by learning curves. They make highly consistent grammatical errors, like "breaked" or "sitted," that they have never heard spoken before. Moreover, the information children get from listening to adults is insufficient for them to understand language's complexities. Parents, for example, don't conditionally reinforce certain vocalizations; rather they reinforce any and all vocalizations their children make.

Children's readiness for language learning, as well as the ability to generate sentences never before heard, suggests that there is an innate capacity for language learning (Chomsky, 1965, 1975). Vocabulary may be acquired via exposure to spoken language, but there appears to be a readiness to learn language from birth. Interestingly, the capacity for language acquisition changes with age. The older people are when they start to learn a first language, the harder it is to learn. After a certain age, successfully acquiring a first language may be impossible. Some researchers argue that the cognitive or linguistic biases children display do not limit language learning. On the contrary, they allow them to learn language (Clark, 1987; Markman, 1989).

Language and expression allow us to communicate. It is arguably our most remarkable developmental achievement. We can convey our feelings and inquire into the thoughts and wishes of others in a way unmatched by any other species. The process of language acquisition provides an excellent example of the interplay between our social environment and our innate capabilities.

EGOCENTRISM AND DECENTRATION

Important indicators of cognitive development, according to Piaget, are **egocentrism** and **decentration.** At each stage, children become more aware of the world outside and less focused on themselves. Infants are totally egocentric: they know no differences between themselves and other people or objects in the world. Between 18 and 24 months, children become aware that they are single individuals among many. They decenter—that is, they move away from thinking they are the center of the world and grow increasingly concerned with life outside themselves. Decentration continues throughout development in the following stages:

1. The sensorimotor phase of life is totally egocentric: "The world is me." It is not that the baby experiences itself as the center of the world, rather that it *is* the world. In this phase of life, babies appear to be unable to tell the difference between themselves and any external object. During the first two

months of life, for example, infants cry when they hear another infant cry, suggesting that the boundary between self and other is not clear (Sagi & Hoffman, 1976).

2. As they grow, children discover that there is a world apart from them. At first they think the world revolves around them and their families. In the preoperational stage children are aware of other people and things, but they cannot see or imagine the world from any viewpoint but their own: "The world is as I see it." If children see that mother is sad, they may bring her a toy to cheer her up because that is what cheers *them* up.

3. In the concrete operational stage, children recognize that there are ways of looking at things other than their own, but they think *their* way is the only *valid* one: "I have the right view of the world."

4. In the formal operational stage, adolescents are able to consider several different perspectives of the world, realizing that others are equally valid.

Most adults perceive that they are but one among many. As Billie Jean King, the tennis star, said after entering her final Wimbledon tournament, "When you're young, you think you're the center of the universe. When you're older, you realize that you're just a little speck" (*Time*, July 11, 1983). We become progressively less egocentric as we develop.

REVIEW AND CRITICISM OF PIAGET'S THEORY

Jean Piaget was one of the first to construct a comprehensive theory of how children acquire knowledge through the development of specific mental structures. But, as with many pioneering theories, Piaget's has limitations.

Piaget often seemed to underestimate the reasoning abilities of children and to overestimate their verbal abilities. Piaget's preoperational child is incapable of conservation and is unable to see things from another point of view. This assertion, however, depends on Piaget's particular experiments.

Consider the conservation experiments. Since young children are easily distracted, perhaps too much information confuses them. Bruner (1978) performed the same conservation experiment as Piaget but with one difference: before he emptied liquid from one tumbler into the other, Bruner placed a screen between the tumblers and the child to block the child's view. When he asked, "Is there the same amount of water now?" the 4-year-olds, unable to *see* the pouring of water into the tumblers, answered "yes."

When there is no information overload, children can understand constancy, even at this early stage. Other investigators have changed the experimental situation so the tasks are more fully explained. In these cases, children as young as 3 years are able to solve conservation problems and to see things from another point of view (see Kagan, 1984).

Object permanence also can be demonstrated earlier than Piaget reported. Spelke and her colleagues (in press) have studied perception in prereaching infants by focusing on the expression of surprise on the infant's face when a partly occluded object is revealed to be unusual.

Stages of cognitive development are not as fixed as Piaget assumed. Although development does seem to proceed generally the way Piaget proposed—that is, formal operations come later than sensorimotor, and the ability to think abstractly comes after the ability to perform operations—the idea of discrete stages of thought may be too rigid (Flavell, 1981).

According to Piaget, each stage of cognition builds upon an earlier stage, in the way a house is constructed: first the foundation is laid, then the walls, and finally the roof. Thus, the formal operational child experiences a dramatic transformation of her cognitive abilities, leaving the previous stage behind. However, children differ from one another, and life experiences may hasten or slow the appearance of one or another component of a stage (Brainerd et al., 1985). Not all of a child's cognitive abilities develop at the same time, and *some develop independently of one another* (Flavell, 1981; Gelman & Baillargeon, 1983).

Whether development is continuous or discrete and in stages according to Piaget depends upon the point of view. From one viewpoint, abilities required, for example, to ride a bike, develop at different rates: leg strength to pedal, eye-to-hand coordination, balance. However, *when these skills operate in unison, the child is at a different stage:* the child can now bicycle to school, to the store, and to a friend's house and can do many things that he or she could not do before. Similarly, the development of abstract thought enables the child to entertain fanciful ideas and to explore others' thoughts, which he or she had been unable to do previously.

Piaget's stages are useful as *descriptions* of the thinking of an "ideal" child at different points of development, but they are not accurate *explanations* of the course of intellectual growth (Gelman & Galistel, 1986). Piaget focuses too much on the cognitive aspects of development. He sees the child as a miniature scientist and logician, perhaps one in Piaget's own mold. This concentration leads to a neglect of other significant components such as social relationships, personality, emotions, fantasy, creativity, intuition, and other important aspects of experience.

It is only natural that many of Piaget's conceptions would prove too rigid and some ideas too narrowly based. But it is to his breadth of vision that we owe the most complete description of intellectual growth from birth to adolescence.

MORAL DEVELOPMENT: KOHLBERG'S THEORY

Morality is the knowledge of what is right and wrong. The development of a child's morals depends on the stage of thought. Piaget (1932) reasoned that moral judgments reflect a child's cognitive abilities at different stages. By observing children's games and recording their reactions to stories about children breaking windows and stealing apples, he described stages of moral development related to cognitive stages.

Lawrence Kohlberg, like Piaget, also assumes that moral reasoning is based on cognitive abilities. Kohlberg's theory of moral development, however, is of a process that continues throughout adolescence and adulthood. Kohlberg's focus is on people's *reasons* for doing what they think is right and on how moral reasoning and behavior shift as schemata become more complex. Kohlberg believes there are three basic levels of moral reasoning, each of which has two stages (Colby & Kohlberg, 1986):

- **Level I—Premoral**

  Stage 1 Obey rules to avoid punishment (punishment and obedience orientation).

  Stage 2 Conform to obtain rewards, to have favors returned.

- **Level II—Conventional morality**

  Stage 3 Conform to avoid disapproval or dislike by others ("good boy" morality, approval by others).

  Stage 4 Conform to avoid censure by legitimate authorities and resultant guilt (authorities maintain morality); obedience to laws.

- **Level III—Postconventional morality**

  Stage 5 Conform to maintain the respect of the impartial spectator judging in terms of community welfare (the morality of social contract, of individual rights, and of democratically accepted law).

  Stage 6 Conform to avoid self-condemnation (morality of individual principles of conscience).

These three levels represent a progression of *sociomoral perspective.* The development of this perspective in an individual is illustrated by one of Kohlberg's long-term subjects, "Joe" (Kohlberg, 1969). Joe was asked at ages 10, 17, and 24 the same question: "Why shouldn't you steal from a store?" His replies show the changes in his moral reasoning.

At age 10 he replied

> It is not good to steal from the store. It's against the law. Somebody might see you and call the police.

The reason not to steal is that you might get caught; the law can be enforced by the police. Joe's motivation is to avoid punishment. This level of moral reasoning is **premoral:** Joe considers only his own interests.

At age 17 he responded

> It is a matter of law. It's one of our rules that we're trying to help protect everyone, protect property, not just to protect a store. It's something that's needed in our society. If we didn't have these laws, people would steal, they wouldn't have to work for a living and our whole society would get out of kilter.

At this stage the concept of law is extended: not so much as rules *against* as rules *for* something. Law is made for the good of society. Joe thinks the law should be maintained. His perspective is **conventional.** He has gone beyond individual considerations and takes the view of society as a whole.

At age 24 Joe responded this way to the questioner:

A: It is violating another person's rights, in this case to property.

Q: Does the law enter in?

A: Well, the law in most cases is based on what is morally right, so it's not a separate subject, it's a consideration.

Q: What does "morality" or "morally right" mean to you?

A: Recognizing the rights of other individuals, first to life, and then to do as he pleases as long as it doesn't interfere with someone else's rights.

Joe's perspective has again widened. Stealing is wrong because it violates the *moral rights* of individuals. Property rights are universal human rights, and the purpose of society is to secure these rights for the individuals who live in it. This is the final, **postconventional** level.

CRITICISM OF KOHLBERG'S THEORY

Kohlberg's theory is complex, as is his way of assessing the stages of morality. Both of these characteristics have been at the center of controversies, and Kohlberg, in response, has made numerous changes to his theory and assessments.

Some critics point out that Kohlberg's stages are very Western in their emphasis on democracy and individual judgment. His stages might not hold true in a culture that places less emphasis on individual rights. Others argue that Kohlberg's measurements are not very reliable and do not work in the way his theory says (Kurtines & Grief, 1974).

Kohlberg and Nisan (1982), however, analyzed the sequence of moral development in youths in Turkey, with the "moral dilemmas" adapted to the Turkish setting. They found the same sequence of moral development, especially in the urban youths, as found in the studies in the West. This validates somewhat the conception that a sociomoral progression, if not universal, is at least possible in many different cultures (see Colby & Kohlberg, 1986).

Still other critics say that the stages of moral development are not fixed and can be greatly modified by experience at both young (Bandura & McDonald, 1963) and older ages (Prentice, 1972). Also, a person at a certain level of moral development may exhibit several different kinds of action (Colby & Kohlberg, 1986; Kurtines & Grief, 1974).

In recent years Kohlberg's model has also been criticized for being sexist. Gilligan (1982) alleges that the stages of morality described by Kohlberg are descriptive only of a male concept of development. Indeed, his original model was developed with an all-male sample. Gilligan believes that this bias resulted in values such as caring and responsibility for others (values regarded more traditionally as feminine) being assigned lower moral value by Kohlberg. Something about the notion that women are more concerned about interpersonal relationships than men rings true, but empirical evidence for Gilligan's position is lacking. Most studies do not show a gender difference in morality, and when they do it is quite small. At this point, it is premature to conclude that females and males differ significantly in their moral reasoning (Greeno & Maccoby, 1986).

MORAL BEHAVIOR

Does *knowing* what is right and wrong ensure moral *behavior?* Some psychologists feel that the correlation between what people think and what they do, between moral principles and moral actions, may not always be strong (Mischel, 1981). Numerous studies have tried to link moral judgment and moral behavior. The results have been mixed, but the bulk of evidence indicates that individuals at higher levels of development, assessed by Kohlberg's scales, appear to *behave* more "morally" than those at lower levels and tend to be more honest and altruistic, at least in their moral judgments. Juvenile delinquents are more likely to be at lower stages of moral development than nondelinquents. Thus, there seems to be a *general* progression in moral understanding close to the one Kohlberg describes (Blasi, 1980).

PSYCHOSOCIAL DEVELOPMENT

At age 2, children walk and talk and have begun to become part of society. But what children say, what they do, how they play, and how they think of themselves varies. **Psychosocial development** is the maturation of an individual's personality and response to various groups, such as family, school, community, and nation.

ATTACHMENT

As children mature, their social world expands from only their parents to friends, religion, nationality, and so on. But due to human beings' long period of immaturity, the relationships formed in the first few years have a special quality. That special quality is the **attachment** between the infant and the mother or primary caregiver. Even a young infant can tell the difference between the mother and other people: the baby's eyes follow her more than anyone else and it smiles more enthusiastically at her. By 8 months, most infants have a strong attachment to their mothers. They smile, coo, and attempt to stay close to her. When frightened, they go to her and cling to her leg or demand to be picked up. As long as she is near, an infant feels free to explore.

Because infants have learned the concept of object permanence and so are able to think about their absent mothers, at about 8 months, they often show extreme distress when the mother leaves (Figure 2-10). This distress is known as **separation anxiety.** When the mother returns, the children will often cling to her desperately. The children cannot be comforted by just anyone; only the mother or primary caregiver brings relief. This bonding and early attachment serves to keep the helpless infant close to the mother where it can be protected. Early in our evolutionary history, infants who wandered too far probably did not survive to reproduce.

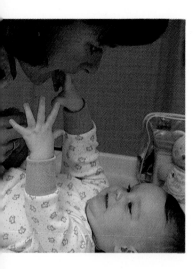

As infants develop separation anxiety, they also become afraid of strangers, a fear called **stranger anxiety.** At 4 or 5 months, infants smile at people almost indiscriminately; they can be comforted by almost anyone, even a stranger. By 8 to 9 months, however, they are likely to scream and cry if a stranger approaches, especially if they are in a strange place or if their mothers are not around (Bretherton & Waters, 1985).

WHY DO INFANTS ATTACH TO THEIR MOTHERS?   The attachment of the baby to the mother is an important event in development and involves many different factors. It is probably an innate bond that develops due to the necessity for mother love, the gratification of needs, the infant's cognitive development, and the communication between mother (or caregiver) and child.

FIGURE 2-10
Separation Anxiety
Beginning about 8 months of age, most infants become so strongly attached to their mothers that they become extremely distressed when left with anyone else, even a grandparent or other person they know, like, and trust.

1. John Bowlby (1982) and Mary Ainsworth (1982) believe that attachment is innate and that strong attachments have a survival function. Because an infant relies for protection on his primary caregiver, it is safer for the infant to spend most of his time clinging to or close by the mother. Babies do not necessarily become attached solely to their primary caregivers; they also develop attachments to people who interact with them socially. The connection to others is stimulated early.

    Bowlby also noted that separation from an affectional attachment, such as the mother-child bond, has three stages: (a) anxiety, disbelief, and searching for the lost one; (b) depression, withdrawal, and despair; and (c) acceptance and recovery. These stages have physiological effects, similar in the first two stages to the physiological arousal of the fight-or-flight response (See Chapter 19). Reite and his colleagues (Reite & Fields, 1985) implanted telemetry equipment in infant monkeys to record their physiology when they were separated from their mothers. On the first day, the monkeys experienced agitation and increased heart rate. A day later the infants settled into depression, marked by decreased heart rate and low body temperature. After four days, the physiological signs returned to normal. Similar attachments occur in adult human beings, who feel the same agitation, the same arousal, and the same feelings of grief. There are also dire health consequences of losing a loved one: breaking attachments can affect the immune system and the heart.

2. Harlow and Harlow (1966) tested the hypothesis that attachment was due to a necessity for love and care. They raised rhesus monkeys with two surrogate ''mothers'' made out of wire mesh. One wire mesh mother had a feeding bottle attached to its chest; the other was covered with terry cloth. The infant monkeys spent most of their time clinging to the terry cloth

FIGURE 2-11
Studies of Attachment

Harlow and Harlow showed that infant monkeys would go to a wire mesh surrogate mother for food, but were more attached to their soft terry cloth surrogate mother, to whom they clung for warmth, security, and a semblance of affection.

MARY AINSWORTH

mothers. They would go to the wire mother when hungry but then return to the cloth mother. When frightened, they would run to the cloth mother rather than to the one that fed them (Figure 2-11). So food is not the primary basis for attachment.

3. Sigmund Freud (1920) believed that the basis for attachment lies in the fact that the mother gratifies the baby's needs, especially for food. Similarly, learning theorists believe that the pleasure infants feel at having their needs gratified becomes associated with the mother and that such emotional needs are important.

4. Piaget (1932) believed that attachment of the child depends on object permanence. A baby must be far enough along in cognitive development to be able to have a permanent conception of the mother before the child can miss her when she is gone. Similarly, the baby has to recognize that something is strange or different before thinking that there may be something to be afraid of.

5. Babies do not necessarily become attached solely to their primary caregivers (Schaffer & Emerson, 1964). Generally, human infants become more attached to *people who interact with them socially*, whether or not they provide any caregiving functions. Many researchers believe that communication is the primary ingredient in the development of attachment (Maccoby, 1980). This argument is supported by observations of father attachment. Infants' whose fathers participate centrally in caregiving show early, strong attachments to their fathers as well as their mothers (Kotelchuck, 1976).

THE STRANGE SITUATION   Ainsworth and colleagues have experimented extensively in home and laboratory settings with attachment, separation anxiety, and stranger anxiety (Ainsworth, Blehar, Waters, & Wall, 1978). She developed an experiment called the **strange situation,** which has become a classic test of the nature of mother-child attachment. In this experiment a stranger enters a room where a baby and mother are playing with toys. The mother then leaves the room, so that the child is alone with the stranger and the toys. The experimenter observes how the child reacts to mother's departure, how much the child plays with the toys, and how the child responds to the stranger and to the mother upon her return (Figure 2-12).

Ainsworth found three basic patterns of attachment:

■ *Anxious/avoidant* (unattached) infants showed little or no interest in either the mother or the stranger and only sometimes cried if she left the room. If they did cry, strangers could comfort them as well as their mothers.

■ *Securely attached* infants appeared to be very happy around their mothers, using her as a security base for exploration. When the mother left the room, they showed varying amounts of distress, but always greeted her happily when she returned.

■ *Anxious/resistant* (insecurely attached) infants explored less and stayed close to their mothers, especially when the stranger was there and showed great distress when the mother left the room. When the mother returned, they remained distressed and both sought out and resisted her efforts to comfort.

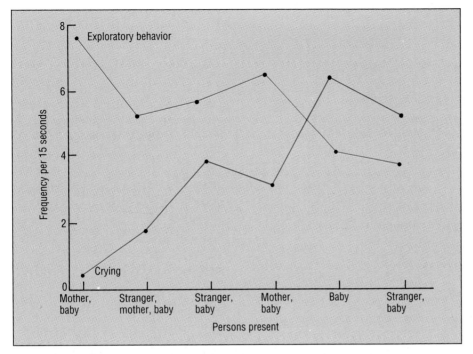

FIGURE 2-12
An Infant's Reaction to the Strange Situation

A 1-year-old child will cry more and explore its environment less when a stranger enters the room. Presence of a stranger combined with absence of the mother increases these negative effects. Such interactions, over a period of about a half an hour, are charted here.
(Ainsworth & Bell, 1970)

ATTACHMENT AND COMPETENCE Being securely attached may be an advantage in early development. At 20 months of age, securely attached children are more advanced in cognitive and social skills. They play more intensely and more enjoyably than babies who were judged either unattached or insecurely attached 10 months earlier (Main, 1973).

Experiments with children at 2 years of age showed that secure children were more adept at problem solving and approached problems with enthusiasm, interest, and pleasure. Unattached and insecure children, however, were easily frustrated and gave up on problems. They seldom asked for help; they simply clung to their mothers (Matas, Arend, & Sroufe, 1978). At 3 1/2 years, children who at 1 1/2 had been judged securely attached played well with others and tended to be leaders, whereas insecurely attached children tended to be more anxious, withdrawn, and less curious (Richards & Light, 1986).

The quality of attachments in the first two years of life leads to competence and social adjustment for a few years afterward. Better adjustment in later life may not be due to attachment in the first year, but to a *continuing* good relationship with parents.

PLAY

For a young child, all the world is a toy. Children play with their bodies and with language, objects, ideas, animals, and other people. *How* they play reflects the degree of their motor, cognitive, and social development. A toddler shrieks with delight at being able to roll a ball back and forth to his mother; a few years

Psychologists agree that mother-infant attachment is the single most important social and emotional task of infancy. Yet in the U.S., half of all mothers of infants under 12 months are employed outside of the home, and the majority of their babies are cared for by nonrelatives. The numbers are rising. We have witnessed more than a 40 percent increase in day-care usage since the mid-1970s (Belsky, 1988). Virtually everyone has an opinion about whether babies should spend time in day care. What does the research say?

Answers to many of the questions about child care are unknown. Most researchers agree that day care has no negative effect on cognitive development; in fact, cognitive *benefits* occur for infants from impoverished home environments. The greatest controversy surrounds social and emotional development. While some psychologists claim that there are no differences in social and emotional development of children reared in day care (Scarr, 1984), others assert that insecure attachment can result from separation from the mother early in life (Belsky & Rovine, 1988; Belsky & Steinberg, 1978).

Jay Belsky and his colleagues claim that children placed in day care before the age of 1 are less responsive and cooperative and more aggressive with adults in subsequent years (Belsky, 1985). He argues that these problems are especially compelling because they are the outcomes attachment theory predicts will occur when children do not form secure attachments with their primary caregivers. Compared to children reared exclusively by their mothers, children in day care are more likely to display behavior patterns consistent with insecure-avoidant attachment (Vaughn, Gove, & Egeland, 1980).

Other experts caution that Belsky's assertions are dangerously premature. Clarke-Stewart (1989) argues that the heart of the problem stems from the exclusive reliance on the Strange Situation paradigm to assess maternal attachment. Recall that the paradigm is designed to create an anxiety-provoking situation so that experimenters can observe the infants' behavior while stressed. Belsky's entire argument rests on the assumption that the SSP creates equivalent conditions for children in or out of day care. Clarke-Stewart claims that this assumption is doubtful, citing cross-cultural evidence that the paradigm creates different situations in different cultures (Grossmann, Grossmann, Spangler, Suess & Unzner, 1985; Takahashi, 1986). Infants who have a great deal of experience in situations with strangers are less anxious during the paradigm and, consequently, behave differently. Their mothers behave differently too. You can see the problem. If observing experimenters assume that the infants are in a stressful situation and don't go to the mother, they worry about the mother-infant relationship. Clarke-Stewart's point is that the situation is so familiar that they are not stressed! Thus, their behavior is quite normal. Clarke-Stewart argues that infants who attend day care participate in a different culture from children reared at home. Therefore, the validity of the measures used to index attachment must be improved if we are to draw definitive answers about it.

Identifying both positive and negative effects of childrearing practices is enormously important. It is also enormously complex. Many factors affect child welfare aside from the use of nonmaternal caregivers. Some argue the focus on maternal employment or non-employment is misguided because it ignores the many moderating factors that provide the context for day care (Scarr, Phillips, & McCartney, 1989). Few doubt that family attitudes and behavior exert far more powerful effects on child well-being than does day care. Researchers who study the effects of day care on infants often find themselves in the middle of political and emotional battlefields outside of the laboratory. Yet, the pursuit of this line of research will one day lead to more predictable outcomes and more accurate knowledge about optimal conditions for our children.

later he may hit the winning home run for his Little League team. Play gives children practice in activities that will be important later in life (Vygotsky, 1978).

As the child ages, play becomes more complex and is combined with other aspects of play. A 9-year-old playing baseball plays with more objects and uses more skilled motions and more cognitive skills than a toddler rolling a ball.

The concrete properties of materials become less important as fantasy and imaginative play become more complex. To a 2-year-old a toy is usually the

TABLE 2-2
Erikson's Eight Stages of Life

Age	Psychological Issue	Positive Product
1. First year	Basic trust vs. mistrust	Optimism
2. Second year	Autonomy vs. shame and doubt	Autonomy
3. Third through fifth years	Initiative vs. guilt	Purpose
4. Sixth year to puberty	Industry vs. inferiority	Competence
5. Adolescence	Identity vs. role confusion	Uniqueness and self
6. Early adulthood	Intimacy vs. isolation	Commitment
7. Middle adulthood	Generativity vs. self-absorbtion	Concern for family and society
8. Old age	Integrity vs. despair	Fulfillment and wisdom

focus of play. The child dials and talks into a toy telephone. An 8-year-old is more likely to use a toy as a prop in a complex situation: the toy telephone may be part of a supermarket he or she has built.

As children gain more experience with the outside world, they incorporate new people, situations, and skills into fantasy play. A common activity of 3-year-olds is to play house: they pretend to cook, iron, or maybe drive to work. The fantasy play of 8-year-olds is more complicated and imaginative; they play Robocop using sticks as guns and chairs as police cars.

ERIKSON'S STAGES

Erik Erikson divides psychosocial development into eight stages. According to his theory, each stage has a characteristic crisis and the way an individual resolves that crisis influences his or her later experience (Table 2-2).

FIRST YEAR   The most important influence in the first year of life is the primary caregiver. The crisis of this year is *basic trust versus mistrust*. Whether the infant has a sense of basic trust or confidence in the outside world depends on his relationship with his mother or other primary caregiver. The positive product is *optimism.*

SECOND YEAR   The important influence at this stage is parental authority. The crisis is *autonomy versus shame and doubt.* A child must learn self-control (toileting, frustration, anger, and so on). If his parents are overly critical, the child may come to doubt his own adequacy (resulting in shame). If they allow him to work through difficult problems himself, he develops a sense of self (*autonomy*).

THIRD TO FIFTH YEARS   The major influence in life at this stage is again parental authority. The crisis is *initiative versus guilt.* How the family reacts to a child's

ERIK ERIKSON

individuality will affect the degree to which the child feels free to express him- or herself. If initiative or innovation is condemned, the child will suffer guilt; if they are encouraged, the child will gain a sense of *purpose*.

SIXTH YEAR TO PUBERTY   The important influences in life at this stage are neighborhood and school. The crisis is *industry versus inferiority*. Children during this stage try to find out how things work. If they succeed, they are likely to become more industrious and will gain a sense of *competence*. If they do not, they may consider themselves inferior.

ADOLESCENCE   Friends are the dominant influences on life in adolescence. The crisis is *identity versus role confusion*. Adolescents are on the brink of adulthood. They have achieved the flexible thinking of the formal operational stage and can imagine many possibilities for their own lives. The choices they make now will determine who they will become. The danger is role confusion: if adolescents do not succeed in making a choice (distinguishing among the many possibilities), they may not be able to establish their own sense of identity. If they do succeed, they will gain a sense of *uniqueness and self*.

EARLY ADULTHOOD   The job of early adulthood is to establish intimate bonds of love and friendship. These bonds typically include marriage and children. The crisis is *intimacy versus isolation*, whether they will develop lasting intimate relationships or remain isolated. The positive product is *commitment*.

MIDDLE ADULTHOOD   At this age, the primary relationships of individuals' lives are the people they live and work with. The crisis in this period is *generativity versus self-absorption*. The choice is between concern for others, family, and a preoccupation with oneself. The danger is of becoming too self-absorbed, concerned primarily with self and not others. A successful resolution will bring an outward focus: *concern and care for family and society*.

THE AGING YEARS   The crisis is *integrity versus despair*. Persons can have a sense of satisfaction and fulfillment looking back over their lives, or they can have a sense of despair at lost opportunities and regrettable actions. At this stage the dominant influence is a sense of "mankind is my kind." How they face the approach of death is largely determined by their assessment of having lived a worthwhile life or having wasted possibilities. A positive assessment of their lives brings *fulfillment, wisdom, and a willingness to face death*.

Erikson's theory is considered by most psychologists to be an idealized narration of development and not an explanation. Few people completely resolve or fail the crises he proposes. However, Erikson's ideas have stimulated research in attachment in infancy, the search for identity in adolescence, and psychology's concerns with adulthood.

THE DEVELOPMENT OF GENDER ROLES

One of the central tasks of childhood is the acquisition of gender. Sometime during the second year of life, children identify their own sex. At that point they begin selectively to adopt behaviors that are consistent with the *social* definitions of male or female. These social roles are termed **gender roles.** Sex identification is straightforward: a person belongs to one category or the other; there is no middle ground. Masculinity versus femininity, however, is another question. They are categories whereby having any one feature is not sufficient to ensure that a person does or does not belong to it. The acquisition of gender identity is much more complicated than the identification of sex.

As you recall from Chapter 1, there are highly diverse theories of gender development. Common to all, however, is consensus about the power of gender in the lives of young children. The most common question asked following the birth of a child is "Is it a boy or a girl?" (Intons-Peterson & Reddel, 1984). And from that moment on newborn boys and girls are treated quite differently. In a hospital nursery, girls are covered in pink blankets, boys in blue. Parents, especially fathers, are more likely to rate their day-old daughters as soft, small, delicate, and weak and their boys as strong, firm, and hardy, whether the infants are or not. When asked to interpret their baby's crying, parents generally interpreted their son's crying as anger and their daughter's as fear (Rubin, Provenzano, & Luria, 1974).

In another study experienced mothers interacted with a 6-month-old male infant (Will, Self, & Datan, 1976). Half of the mothers were told that the baby was a girl; the other half were told that the baby was a boy. The mothers handled the baby differently depending on the perceived sex. Perhaps most interesting was the finding that when mothers were interviewed afterward, they denied differential treatment of children by sex.

At 1 year of age there is no difference between boys and girls in the toys they prefer. Boys and girls are equally happy with a doll or a truck. But parents typically give girls dolls, doll houses, and stuffed animals, whereas boys are given blocks, trucks, and sports equipment. By age 3 children begin to show a clear preference for sex-typed toys.

Parents also play with their infant sons and daughters differently. Mothers touch their little girls more and prefer to keep them close by. By age 2, girls generally prefer to play closer to their mothers than do boys. Little boys also receive more gross motor stimulation than girls; they are more likely to be tossed, swung, and chased (Figure 2-13).

From the age of 2 on, boys show a higher activity level in their play and are more likely to engage in rough-and-tumble play. In most cultures they are also more likely than girls to be aggressive and to get into confrontations (Fausto-Sterling, 1986). Fathers tend to perpetuate sex roles in their children more than do mothers (Block, 1979); the fathers are more likely to reward their daughters for playing with other girls but punish their sons for playing with girls (Langlois & Downs, 1980).

While the parental influence on gender acquisition is undeniable, adult socialization of gender is not the whole story. Shortly after children can identify their own sex, they begin to show strong preferences for same-sex social partners, even if adults encourage mixed-sex play (Maccoby, 1988). This tendency does not vary with the degree of femininity or masculinity of the child. By the age of 4, little girls prefer to play with other girls and little boys with other boys. In fact, children who do have opposite-sex play partners often choose to keep the friendship a secret (Gottman & Parker, in press). Strong sex segregation persists until adolescence when heterosocial contact emerges.

FIGURE 2-13
Gender Roles and Gender-Typed Behavior
Children of both sexes will happily play with toys and engage in behavior traditionally identified with their own or the other gender. The critical factor is whether and how early adults encourage children in their care to engage in gender-typed behavior.

Parents and teachers place different expectations on boys and girls. Teachers pay more attention to boys than girls: they scold boys more and praise them more (LaFrance, 1988). Adults are likely to encourage boys to compete and achieve, to be independent and responsible, and to control their feelings. Fathers, especially, are stricter with their sons than with their daughters and punish their sons more readily. Girls generally get more warmth and physical closeness from their parents; they are more trusted and receive less punishment. They are also encouraged to be nurturant and obedient and are more likely to be closely supervised than boys (Block, 1979).

Girls tend to form small, quiet playgroups of two and three; boys move in larger, more active groups and differ in the way they play team games. Boys engage in rough play, whereas girls tend to negotiate social interactions with verbal persuasiveness (Maccoby, 1988). This pattern has been observed in Swiss and African children also (Omark & Edelman, 1973).

No one escapes the influence of gender, but it is important to keep in mind that differences between males and females are highly variable and typically quite small (Maccoby & Jacklin, 1974). In the gender literature the largest differences are found in the way we *think* about gender and the smallest in actual behavior. Re-read the section above and you will notice that most of the differences we mention are differences in the way we treat males and females, not in the way that they *behave*. Given the major discrepancies in socialization, it is actually quite amazing that males and females are as similar as they are.

ADOLESCENCE

After late childhood a major developmental change occurs. Increases in the level of sex hormones transform the child's appearance into that of an adult. Sex organs and secondary sex characteristics begin to develop at about the same time; the child goes through a growth spurt. Although growth in the first few years of life is also rapid, young children are not aware enough of themselves or the world to be aware of the physical changes. But teenagers are acutely aware of their growth, which is often upsetting to them.

Another source of instability is cognitive: adolescents have just entered the formal operational stage, which involves a more abstract way of thinking and problem solving. These new mental abilities often cause conflicts between themselves and their family and society.

Other factors are personal and social. Adolescents are becoming more independent from home and family. And perhaps most important, for the first time adolescents are aware of and concerned with sexuality, leading to new desires and exploration. Nevertheless, society and family still regard adolescents as children. By considering them children, they receive greater protection (by families and from the law) and also have more restrictions (curfews, drinking age), which are further causes of conflict.

PHYSICAL GROWTH

Adolescence is marked by a sudden increase in physical growth, the growth spurt, which lasts about three years (Figure 2-14). Boys at about age 12 and girls at about age 10 begin to gain weight. Bones grow thicker and wider, and muscle bulk and weight increase (especially around the hips in girls). This "pudginess" is a sign that the changes of puberty are fast approaching.

At the peak of their growth spurt, girls may gain 20 pounds and boys as much as 26 pounds in a year. A sharp increase in height follows the weight gain. The stored fat is then redistributed, particularly in boys. Typically, adolescents gain 2 to 5 inches in height during the growth spurt, fueled by a dramatic increase in caloric intake. Many teenage boys consume as many as 6,000 calories per day (about twice what a normal adult eats).

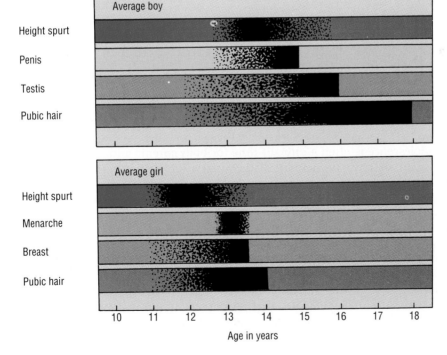

FIGURE 2-14
Physical Development in Puberty

The darkest areas on this chart indicate growth spurts during which adolescent boys and girls grow and change most. Individual patterns of development may vary greatly from these averages.
(Tanner, 1962)

The body during adolescence does not change uniformly and simultaneously. Hands, head, and feet grow more than the central trunk, which causes many adolescents to feel awkward or gangly. More upsetting, sometimes one side of the body develops a bit more quickly than the other (for example, one breast or one ear). Almost 50 percent of all adolescents are dissatisfied with their appearance. Boys wish they were taller; girls wish they were thinner.

PUBERTY

The word **puberty** comes from the Latin "to be covered with hair," and the appearance of darkened hair on the legs, genitals, and underarms for both sexes, and on the face and chest for boys, is one of the first signs of puberty. In males, the larynx lengthens and the voice deepens.

Puberty officially begins for boys when they produce live sperm cells. The scrotum, testes, and penis grow and eventually ejaculation is possible. For girls, puberty officially begins at **menarche,** the onset of menstruation. Their breasts and pubic hair develop simultaneously with the growth of the uterus, vagina, clitoris, and labia.

COGNITIVE DEVELOPMENT

Adolescents undergo a major shift in thinking: the emergence of *formal operations,* the ability to transform information. For many adolescents this new mental ability causes a radical break in their previous schemata. For the first time they realize that the way they have done things and the way their parents, school, or country operates is not necessarily the only way or the "right" way.

QUESTIONING AND IDEALISM

The new level of abstract thought often is characterized by an intense period of questioning, searching, and rebellion. The adolescent begins to see that there are many possible choices in life—choices of careers, of lifestyle, of identity: "Who am I? What do I want to do?" On the threshold of adult life, adolescents imagine it to be ideal; experience inevitably tempers some of this idealism. Because teenagers cannot reconcile the fact that their parents are less than ideal, adolescence is often a difficult time for both parents and children.

Adolescents become idealistic because for the first time they can imagine what an ideal world and an ideal society might be like. This ability can also lead toward ideologies and organizations that claim to offer a utopian life, such as cults led by gurus.

PSYCHOSOCIAL DEVELOPMENT

EGOCENTRISM   Although adolescents tend to be idealistic, they remain emotionally egocentric. They imagine that their new and thrilling experiences, discoveries, and feelings are unique. A girl may reproach her mother, saying "But Mother, you don't know how it feels to be in love." Adolescents are often so preoccupied with their physical appearance that they assume everyone else notices minute details about them.

They are extremely self-conscious; they may even avoid going to a party when they have a pimple. It may be years before such egocentrism abates, before a young person can acknowledge that others feel as deeply as he does (even those who disagree), and before he can no one pays as much attention to him as he pays himself.

IDENTITY AND TURBULENCE As children move into adulthood, they begin to realize that their actions may have long-range consequences on their lives. How well they do in high school determines the colleges they go to, which in turn is important to their careers. Adolescents begin to make their own choices for their lives. Thus, adolescence and young adulthood are often marked by a search for identity: "Who am I? What makes me different from other people? Do I want to be like my parents? What am I going to do with my life?"

Not knowing who you are or what you are going to do can be at once exhilarating and anxiety provoking. College or military service may provide a testing ground for the young person to explore his or her possibilities. Questioning, searching, and conflicts, especially with parents (Figures 2-15, 2-16), are characteristic of the teenager's search for identity. This search is made more urgent by changes in the body and by developments in cognition that occur in adolescence.

Adolescence is characteristically typified as a turbulent time. For many adolescents it is. But others never question their predefined roles and travel through adolescence without anxiety; for these teenagers adolescence is not

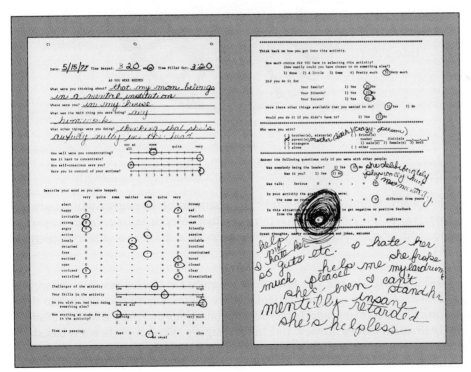

FIGURE 2-15
Adolescent Anger

Teenagers often have angry feelings about their parents, which is well shown on this questionnaire filled out by a wrathful teenager.
(Csikszentmihalyi & Larson, 1984)

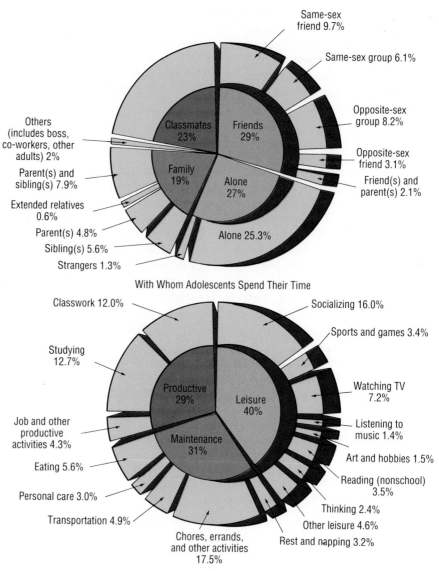

**FIGURE 2-16
How and With Whom
Adolescents Spend
Their Time**
(Csikszentmihalyi & Larson, 1984)

Same-sex
friend 9.7%

Same-sex group 6.1%

Opposite-sex
group 8.2%

Opposite-sex
friend 3.1%

Friend(s) and
parent(s) 2.1%

Others
(includes boss,
co-workers, other
adults) 2%

Parent(s) and
sibling(s) 7.9%

Extended relatives
0.6%

Parent(s) 4.8%

Sibling(s) 5.6%

Strangers 1.3%

Classmates
23%

Friends
29%

Family
19%

Alone
27%

Alone 25.3%

With Whom Adolescents Spend Their Time

Classwork 12.0%

Socializing 16.0%

Sports and games 3.4%

Studying
12.7%

Watching TV
7.2%

Job and other
productive
activities 4.3%

Listening to
music 1.4%

Eating 5.6%

Art and hobbies 1.5%

Personal care 3.0%

Reading (nonschool)
3.5%

Transportation 4.9%

Thinking 2.4%

Other leisure 4.6%

Chores, errands,
and other activities
17.5%

Rest and napping 3.2%

Productive
29%

Leisure
40%

Maintenance
31%

How Adolescents Spend Their Time

dramatically turbulent. In a study of a sample of teenagers who could be characterized, 35 percent had reported rather smooth sailing through adolescence, indicating that not everyone experiences such crises and storms (Berger, 1984).

TEENAGE SEXUALITY   In the last few decades, attitudes toward sex have changed, and all adolescents, girls in particular, have become more sexually active than before. The first major reports on sexual habits of normal people were published in 1948 and 1953 by Kinsey and his colleagues. Their reports were based on interviews with white middle-class people in the 1940s. They found that only 3 percent of women and 40 percent of the men interviewed had had sex by the age of 16 (Kinsey, Pomeroy, Martin, & Gebhard, 1953).

Absolute answers to this question continue to elude psychologists. Sometimes children raised under very stressful, even traumatic, conditions grow up to be surprisingly well-adjusted. Other times, the most idyllic families produce children who grow up to be troubled adults.

Many of our early assumptions about child rearing have not borne out. Children raised in the absence of a father, for example, usually develop quite normally. And it has become apparent that many fathers are quite capable of mothering. Even in cases where parents divorce when children are young, most mature without notable problems. No one concludes from these observations that unfortunate conditions are good for children; rather we can conclude that children are highly resilient and adaptable. The circumstances noted above are better viewed as risk factors than emotional sentences.

But developmental psychologists do not believe that children can weather any storm, just that general indexes, like the presence or absence of natural parents, may not be the most informative ones. There is fairly good consensus about some general principles. First, children need consistency. They flourish under regular schedules and routines. They also need

HOW DO YOU RAISE A WELL-ADJUSTED CHILD?

to experience social and emotional consistency from others. For example, different parents have very distinct parenting styles. It seems to matter less what the style is than how consistently it is practiced. Like adults, children need to predict their worlds. If a parent is typically effusive with praise and one day only mildly pleasant the child may experience the pleasant-ness as rejection. In contrast, the child of a very solemn, stern parent may feel great joy when greeted with a partial smile.

Not unrelated, children appreciate the enforcement of rules. Laissez-faire approaches to child-rearing seem to make everyone nervous—the parent, the child, and anyone else present. The world is a dangerous place and children appreciate it when limits are set. It allows the child to feel safe and comfortable, to explore freely within the designated limits.

Last but not least, children need to feel loved and appreciated. When children receive praise and warmth as well as discipline and structure, the most important ingredients are there. Intact nuclear families are not necessary to produce happy, healthy children. Rather, stable relationships with stable adults—whether parent, sibling, teacher, or friend—provide the best guarantee for happy children to become happy adults.

However, in the mid-1970s a survey of people having the same age and background asked teenagers when they would like to have first sexual intercourse. In response, 23 percent of 15- to 16-year-old boys but only 0.5 percent of the girls said, "On a first or second date." Even with the liberalizing of attitudes in the society, losing virginity seems to be a different experience for boys and girls. For boys it is almost a rite of passage into manhood. Their attitudes about it are overwhelmingly positive (Haas, 1978).

Emotional involvement with the sexual partner is often more important for young women than it is for young men. In one study, almost half of the young men interviewed said they were not emotionally involved with their first sex partner; however, over 80 percent of the women said they were in love with their first partner (Simon, Berger, & Gagnon, 1972). This distinction is also reflected in the patterns of male and female sexual activity. Young men typically have more sexual partners than young women, whereas young women generally have more enduring relationships. (See Chapter 18 for a discussion of sexuality and love.)

THE SEEDS AND THE FRUITS OF DEVELOPMENT

Psychology considers an organism, the human organism, from its biological inheritance, through life in society, to maturity, and to death. But nowhere is the continuity between the different parts more clear than in the development of a child into an adult. The adaption of the infant to his or her small world gradually widens into the social worlds of adulthood.

The same cognitive processes that the child uses to make sense of its small world continue throughout life. Schemata developed in childhood become important for thinking, for relating to others, and for operating intelligently. The processes of mental growth involved in assimilating and accommodating new experiences change as perception and thought become more sophisticated. Slight differences among infants grow into separate and distinct personalities.

Remember, it is the *same person* who grows up and then grows old; the same one who first tries to put things together and who later gets a job in a factory. The person who makes childhood friends is the same one who gets married and has children, letting the cycle begin again.

ADULTHOOD

ISSUES AND PRINCIPLES IN ADULT DEVELOPMENT

Adulthood has traditionally been viewed as the period when people live out psychological lives that were determined during their first six years. The last four decades, however, have witnessed considerable change in this view. Today many theories of development extend into adulthood, and even concepts like attachment, which were originally viewed as a task of infancy, are being studied in adulthood.

Life-span psychology differs from child developmental psychology in two important ways. First, a fundamental assumption in child development is that observed changes are rooted in biological maturation: improvements in vision allow the infant to make finer discriminations than were possible at birth (Banks & Solapatek, 1983). Children enter dramatically changed social worlds once they learn how to crawl and then to walk (Campos & Berenthal, 1989). In adulthood, changes are not based on biological development. In fact, adulthood may provide the first opportunity to study the effects of *experience* independent of maturation (Flavell, 1970).

Second, we typically label as "developmental" changes that are assumed to occur in virtually all people during relatively circumscribed periods of time. Essentially all children learn to walk by the age of 1 and acquire rudimentary language by 2. Making temporal predictions about adulthood is not so easily done. Most people have children, but some begin to do so in their teens; others in their twenties, thirties, or forties; and still others elect not to parent at all. In contrast to child development, adult development is highly diverse. It is commonly referred to as the *process of differentiation*.

EARLY THEORIES OF LIFE-SPAN DEVELOPMENT

JUNG   Carl Jung, who had been a student of Freud's, objected to the idea that development halted in early childhood. In fact, Jung's major interest was in the "psyche," or the self, and he contended that before adolescence people could not have problems with their psyches because they had not yet been formed (Jung, 1933). Only in *puberty* did prohibitions and limitations become internalized and conflict with the self begin (Jung, 1953). According to Jung, *youth* runs from puberty to about age 35. During this time the person confronts problems of sexuality, widening horizons, and establishing oneself in the world. Around age 35 or 40, subtle changes begin.

There may be changes in character; traits and interests long suppressed from childhood may begin to assert themselves. Often, men who have buried themselves in their careers may find themselves becoming more interested in their families. Women who took time off for child rearing may now look forward to starting a career. Conversely, a person may become more rigid in his or her convictions and principles, as if they are becoming endangered and it is now necessary to reinforce them.

Jung characterized a person's values in the first half of life as expanding in an *outward* direction. In the second half of life, he felt the values become more *inward* directed. These include self-knowledge, cultural concerns, and preparation for death.

Jung clearly saw adulthood as the most inspired period of the life-span. Change was evident and growth paramount. According to Jung, adulthood—particularly middle age—is the time when human potential is realized. Spirituality is refined, and commitment to life and loved ones is expressed more fully than possible in earlier years.

BÜHLER   Charlotte Bühler (1968) was the first stage theorist to extend her theory to include the entire life-span. Based on analyses of biographies and autobiographies collected during the 1930s, she formulated five *psychosocial* phases of life that parallel five biological phases. In general, the psychosocial phases that accompanied the biological phases represent psychological expansion, culmination, and, finally, contraction in activities (Kimmel, 1974; Kuhlen, 1964). She theorized that the phases revolve around reproductive capacity. The biological phases they mimic are progressive growth (ages 0–15), the emergence of sexual reproductive capacity (ages 15–25), stability (ages 25–45), loss of sexual reproductive capacity (ages 45–65), and, finally, biological decline (age 65 and older). Note that both biology and psychosocial changes can be conceptualized as growth curves that expand and then contract. Note also the similarity between Bühler and Jung in their thinking about outward and inward focus.

ERIKSON   Erik Erikson's stage model of human development (detailed on pages 65–66) is clearly the most renowned of theories of adult development. Erikson was heavily influenced by Freudian thinking. Like Freud, he believed that we progress through a fixed sequence of stages, and in each stage we face new challenges that must be conquered. If the challenge is mastered successfully, we move on to the next stage as psychologically healthy individuals. If not, all subsequent development is influenced negatively. In spite of the fact that Erikson's stages were psycho*social* whereas Freud's were psycho*sexual*, the first four stages in Erikson's model correspond closely to Freudian stages of child development. Erikson's fifth stage, marked by the onset of puberty, carried stage theory beyond the period where Freud believed development ended. The eighth and final stage is triggered by retirement and ends in death.

THE BIRTH OF LIFE-SPAN PSYCHOLOGY

During the 1970s, life-span developmental psychology emerged as a new subdiscipline of developmental psychology. As the name implies, life-span psychology refers to the study of the entire life-span from birth to old age. It aims to identify systematic, predictable changes that are related to chronological age. It would be ridiculous to think that 20 year olds are identical to 50 year olds in their views of the world and of themselves. During the past two decades, considerable research has nullified many of our preconceptions about the aging process and has provided new grounds for theory building about adult life.

EARLY ADULTHOOD: WORK AND INTIMACY

Adolescence is a time of exploration. Unless individuals are burdened with adult responsibilities and commitments, this pattern of exploration continues into early adulthood. College or military service can provide a hiatus of a sort, in which young persons may be physically separate from their parents while not completely independent. They have time to build a basis for living in the adult world.

While there is no definite biological event that signals the beginning of early adulthood, for most people there are several hallmarks of this period: beginning a career, getting married, and becoming a parent.

WORK AND CAREER

People assume that in their early 20s they must decide on an occupation and settle down. Actually, the process of forming a career is very complicated and may take several years or even decades. Professions are becoming more specialized and require more lengthy training times. Kimmel (1980) identifies six factors that influence occupational choice: background factors, role models, experience, interests, personality, and research.

Early adulthood is usually a time of deciding on a career, getting married, setting up a household, and starting a family.

Background factors include socioeconomic status, ethnic origin, intelligence, race, sex, and education. In practice, psychologists sometimes view these factors as relatively nonpsychological nuisance variables that they must control in their research. But no one doubts their significance. Gender, race, and socioeconomic factors influence occupational choice more than most psychological ones. They set boundaries and limitations on virtually all life choices.

A person may choose an occupation on the basis of identification with a *role model*. A woman may decide to become a dentist like her uncle. Of course, such a person may be more than a role model; he or she may also provide entry opportunities. An important figure in this regard is a *mentor*, someone who eases the youth into adulthood (Levinson, 1978). A mentor ideally aids a person in developing his or her own autonomy, interests, and commitment to an occupation. The mentor may be a teacher, an older colleague, or a family friend.

A person's *experience* is also an important factor. Pre-med students often mention that they want to become a doctor because of the care given to them during a serious illness as a child. Of course, the individual's *personality* and *interests* may be better expressed in or matched to a particular field. Finally, a person may *research* the job market and decide that the best opportunities exist in computer programming or in setting up a mail-order business, for example, and then obtain the specialized training needed in those fields.

INTIMATE RELATIONSHIPS

Intimate relationships have a profound influence on nearly all of our lives. More than 95 percent of all people eventually marry (Bureau of the Census, 1982). Of course, the 5 percent who do not marry are not exempt from intimate relationships. Rather, they include unmarried heterosexual, lesbian, and gay couples. Very few people remain immune to romantic relationships. The modern expectation of intimate relationships is that they will serve as a primary emotional resource. The vast majority of the existing literature has been directed toward marriage.

MARRIAGE   When we ask our undergraduate students how many plan to marry, the vast majority raise their hands. If we ask why they plan to marry, few have even thought about it. If we ask a person why he or she marries a particular person, the automatic answer is, "Because I love so-and-so." If we probe a little deeper, other reasons for marriage become more apparent. The socialization pressures to marry are so pervasive that many people do not question their decisions. Instead they describe a vague feeling that they "should" because it "feels like the right thing to do."

Some researchers class marriages into two subtypes: instrumental and companionship-based. Instrumental marriages, according to Cuber and Haroff (1965), are traditional marriages, based on clear role distinctions influenced heavily by gender roles. Satisfaction in these marriages is predicted by the husband's vocational success and wife's performance as a homemaker and mother. Women in instrumental relationships tend to have close emotional bonds with friends outside of the marital relationship (Lopata, 1971), whereas men tend to have few if any close relationships (Komarovsky, 1976). Companionship-based marriages, which have become common since more and more women have chosen to work outside of the home, are quite different. Here, the emotional closeness between husbands and wives is paramount, forming the basis of the relationship. In companionship-based marriages, roles tend to be shared.

MARITAL SATISFACTION   Throughout marriage, husbands are more satisfied with their relationships than are their wives (Skolnick, 1986). Among married men, general life satisfaction is also higher as compared to single men. But the reverse holds for women: single women report greater life satisfaction than married women (Steil, 1984). Still, for most women, their role as wife and mother comprises the most central aspect of their identity (Hyde, 1985; Luria, 1974).

Both husbands and wives have unfailing complaints about marriage, and the complaints are different. Married women contend that their husbands are emotionally withdrawn (Komarovsky, 1962; Markman & Kraft, 1989; Terman, Buttenweiser, Ferguson, Johnson, & Wilson, 1938), whereas married men complain that their wives are overly expressive and emotional (Markman & Kraft, 1989).

Being married (even a bad marriage) appears better than no relationship at all, however. And an Israeli study of 10,000 marriages found that those who reported a happy marriage had lower death rates than those who said they were unhappy with their relationship (Gerstel & Riesman, 1981).

Several years ago, Robert Levenson and John Gottman began research on marriage that focused on the emotions spouses experience while they interact (Gottman & Levenson, 1986, 1988; Levenson & Gottman, 1983, 1985). They ask both distressed and nondistressed couples to come to the psychophysiology laboratory. When the couples arrive they first sit silently together in one of the experimental rooms, then they discuss the events of the day (something most couples seem to do anyway), and finally discuss a problem area that causes them conflict.

Levenson and Gottman measured each partner's physiological arousal (heart rate, temperature, breathing, and so on) during all three interactions—the silent period, the events of the day, and the conflict discussion. The discussions were videotaped, and later each spouse independently watched the videotape and rated the emotions they had experienced during the interaction.

The higher the negative emotions during the interaction, the more distressed the couple reported themselves as being. There were gender differences in the emotional dialogue. Specifically, when wives expressed negative feelings, husbands tended to be nonresponsive. However, wives answered the negative emotion expressed by the husband with more negative affect, and again men withdrew from marital conflict while women escalated emotionally.

Three years later these same couples were contacted and asked about their current satisfaction with their marriages. As you might expect, some couples had become more dissatisfied, and others had grown more compatible. Interestingly, the level of physiological arousal measured in the original study during the initial silent phase proved to be an excellent predictor of current marital satisfaction. It seems that even though couples were asked not to interact during the baseline (silent) condition, there was a good deal of nonverbal interaction going on. Some couples remained physiologically calm during this condition, they may have looked at each other and smiled, but overall they were not aroused. Other couples were highly aroused during this condition. Interestingly, the lower the arousal was during the baseline condition, the happier the couple was three years later. So much for passion. Levenson and Gottman believe that couples that stay together are, first and foremost, good friends.

"HIS AND HER" MARRIAGES   Marriage is clearly beneficial for men. But for women the benefits are not so clear. Compared to men who are divorced, widowed, or never married, married men live much longer, have fewer mental and physical illnesses, and appear happier. After being laid off work, men with supportive wives show fewer negative effects of stress (Cobb & Kasl, 1977). Divorced and widowed men also remarry very quickly. In contrast, married women have higher rates of mental illness than married men, while single women have lower rates of mental illness than single men (Radloff, 1975).

BECOMING A PARENT

Having a baby can be one of the most significant and wonderful events in life. Women and men alike describe the moment their child was born as one of sheer exhilaration, filled with joy and a sense of unmatched pride and fulfillment. In becoming parents couples form a bond that will last a lifetime. As exciting as it is, parenthood also involves tremendous responsibilities. It is not as much a crisis as a developmental stage; it is most certainly disruptive, with some possibility of harm, but it also affords the possibility of considerable growth (Grossman, Eichler, & Winickhoff, 1980).

The transition to parenthood changes women's lives more than men's in both positive and negative ways (Feldman & Nash, 1984). For women changes are dramatic and occur overnight. Yet they quickly incorporate the role of mother into their self-identity. For men changes occur more gradually and often focus on becoming a provider rather than a caretaker. It may be a year before a man feels comfortable in his new role as father (Cowan et al., 1985). Day-to-day life changes less for men. New fathers soon return to work and resume previous activities.

Several years ago, Philip Cowan and Carolyn Pape Cowan, experts on parenthood at the University of California at Berkeley, launched a prospective study of parenthood, named the "Becoming a Family Project." They recruited 72 couples who were expecting their first child and assessed the couples' marital satisfaction, personal well-being, and expectations about parenting. They also observed the couples with each other and later with the child. They followed the sample over the years, reassessing periodically the variables of interest. At the time of this writing, the children of these couples are 3 to 5 years old and are entering school.

This research is shedding much light on the transition to parenthood. For years, researchers have known that happy, well-adjusted parents tend to have happy, well-adjusted children. But more specific aspects of the transition to parenthood, such as differences in parenting style and their effects on the children, were unknown. Why are parents less satisfied with their marriages after they become parents? Do infants wear their mothers out to the point where they are dissatisfied with their marriages and themselves? Or are other factors more central to adjustment? What happens to a child when parents are distressed?

Because the "Becoming a Family Project" began to follow couples before they had children, the picture has become much clearer. The answers are not simple. Many factors influence the child's development, such as the characteristics of each individual in the family, the parent's marital relationship, the relationship of each parent with the child (even intergenerational relationships involving grandparents), and the relationship of the nuclear family to the friends and community.

Cowan and Cowan (1988) feel strongly that the baby is not at the root of the distress. Rather, distressed couples have distressed children. Parents who are dissatisfied with themselves, their marriages and their jobs late in pregnancy have the most difficult transitions to parenthood. And this distress signals trouble for the child. In fact, the quality of the parent's marriage and each spouse's individual well-being *before the baby is born* predict the child's intellectual and social competence in kindergarten (Cowan, Cowan, Heming, & Miller, 1990)! It seems that previous problems in the marriage at the individual level *worsen* after becoming a parent. On the positive side, if problems did not exist before the baby, new ones are unlikely to be debilitating. One thing is certain, however, having a baby to improve a bad marriage is highly inadvisable.

Because women generally assume more child care responsibilities, their experience of parenthood is quite different. Sometimes women begin to identify themselves more as mothers than as other aspects of their identity (architect, gymnast, gourmet cook, lover, and so on). New mothers often become more sympathetic to their own mothers (Cowan et al., 1978). Today, most mothers do return to work. Interestingly, self-reports of mothers who are also wage earners suggest that their lives are not more stressful than the lives of unemployed mothers (Crosby, 1987). While outside employment may introduce some new stressors, it may also provide a temporary reprieve from the stresses of child care.

Increased gender differentiation following the birth of a child seems to be common (Cowan et al., 1985). Even if a couple shares all household and financial responsibilities before the child is born, this pre-existing division of labor rarely lasts after the baby. A few months after the birth of a child, women report greater marital distress (Miller & Sollie, 1980) and a decrease in autonomy (Belsky et al., 1983). Physical exhaustion may account, in part, for low morale. Having a very young infant is time-consuming and tiring. In addition, a woman who shifts from full-time employment to full-time motherhood may find this disruptive (Cowan et al., 1978). And loss of her income may produce financial strain at a time when expenses increase.

The transition to fatherhood also brings change, but it is qualitatively and quantitatively different from changes associated with motherhood. Men report gradual changes in their self-concept as they integrate the role of father with previous roles. Some men also report increasing closeness to their own fathers (although some vow to do a better job). Many men say that they want to be more involved with their children than their fathers were with them. In addition, some new fathers express a new perspective on life and an ability to see the bigger picture.

Some argue that marital distress stems directly from the different experiences of parenthood men and women have (Cowan, 1988). Becoming a parent introduces disruption in daily life for both mother and father. But the timing and the types of change are often quite different for each parent. Disparities in the experience of parenthood can lead to an increase in conflicts, which leads to increased emotional distance and subsequent distress. We do know that marital satisfaction (for both men and women) declines after the birth of a child and improves after the children leave home.

The focus of psychological research on parenting has been on the problems parents experience; much less attention has been paid to positive developmental growth (Cowan, 1988). No parent will deny that along with the trials and tribulations, there is immense satisfaction in watching their children grow from helpless infants to independent adults. As one father said, "It opens up a whole new world, just to see her looking out the window at the rain making puddles on the sidewalk" (Cowan, 1988, p. 14).

DIVORCE

The rate of divorce has gradually declined from an all-time high at the end of the 1970s. Of those currently married, one-third can expect their marriage to end in divorce. One-half of new marriages end in divorce. Fifteen percent will occur within 18 months after the birth of the first child. Since 80 percent of men and 75 percent of women eventually remarry, a substantial number of children (25 percent) live in stepfamilies before they reach adulthood, and some children encounter more than one stepfamily due to their parents' multiple divorces and remarriages (Hetherington, 1989).

No one would doubt that divorce can seriously affect an individual's mental health; it also can affect physical health. Separated and divorced individuals have high rates of illness and disability (White & Bloom, 1981). One study (Table 2-3) showed that the effect of divorce on the death rate was about the same as smoking a pack of cigarettes a day (Morcowitz, 1975).

Some people are more likely to divorce than others. People who were married when they were teenagers and have little education and low incomes are most likely to divorce (Glick & Norton, 1977). A low income puts a great strain on a marriage. People who marry very young are less likely to have the maturity necessary to cope with the various problems of a marital relationship, household economics, and child rearing.

Obviously, such a widespread phenomenon has attracted a great deal of attention. There is legitimate concern for what effect divorce has on individuals and on society. How stressful is divorce? Is it harder on men or on women? What are the problems divorced men and women are likely to face? Which is

TABLE 2-3
Divorce and Death Rate

	Nonsmokers	Smokers
Married	796	1,560
Divorced	1,420	2,675

Divorce may merit a warning from the Surgeon General: divorce may be hazardous to your health

worse: living with a bad marriage or divorcing? What are the best strategies for coping with divorce? And perhaps most important of all, what does it do to the children?

EFFECTS OF DIVORCE ON ADULTS For men the increased illness following divorce relates mainly to the loss of a confidant, the loneliness, and the loss of the social networks that the marriage provided. For women the increases in symptoms and mental health problems after divorce correlate most significantly to the increased financial strain coupled with child-care responsibilities. Divorced women also suffer from loneliness, but women confide in a variety of friends. So adverse affects of divorce are buffered somewhat.

There are four periods of the divorce process: marital distress, the decision to divorce, separation, and post divorce. There is no doubt that the whole process is very painful: people who are separating are often lonely, anxious, angry, depressed, feel rejected, and have low self-esteem.

The separation period is more stressful than either the preceding marital distress or the post-divorce period. The process of separation is painful whether one is leaving a relatively good marriage or a relatively bad one (Bloom & White, 1981). However, in post-divorce, both men and women are likely to state that their situation is better than it was before the divorce (Albrecht, 1980). Nevertheless, it still takes approximately two years after a divorce for adults to regain their sense of equilibrium.

Indeed, women are more likely than men to report divorce as being traumatic and stressful (Albrecht, 1980). However, assessments of emotional distress and psychosomatic symptoms show that divorce is as painful for men, if not more so. Women are distressed at the beginning of the divorce process, whereas men's distress appears later (Argyle & Henderson, 1985).

The establishment of a new satisfying sexual relationship, for both men and women, helps the most in recovering from divorce (Berman & Turk, 1981). This underscores the importance of interpersonal relationships in our lives.

COPING WITH DIVORCE Getting divorced, especially when there are children, may bring about a host of problems. They involve contacts with the former spouse, problems with interpersonal relationships, loneliness, practical problems, financial concerns, and problems with parent-child interaction (Berman & Turk,

1981). Income generally drops precipitously, although this may be more true for women than for men (White & Bloom, 1981). Only about one-third of ex-husbands contribute to the financial support of their children and former wives (Brandwein, Brown, & Fox, 1974). Thirty-four percent of all households headed by single women are below the poverty level (Shortridge, 1984).

There are practical problems of taking over the tasks previously done by the ex-spouse, such as cooking, household and car maintenance, and child care and discipline. Men with primary custody of children are especially likely to feel disorganized and have problems coping with practical demands. Social adjustment is also difficult. A person may discover that some friends were actually closer to the other spouse, and social networks become disrupted. Women with children may have an especially hard time establishing new romantic relationships, whereas men usually enter into a flurry of social activity (Hetherington et al., 1977). Contacts with former spouses are often distressing.

Problems with parent-child combinations may increase, especially when mothers must discipline male children (Argyle & Henderson, 1985). Although, at first glance, joint custody might be expected to soften the problems children suffer in divorce, we are just beginning to understand its effects. In some ways it may extend exposure to distress. Marital discord, whether it ends in divorce or not, appears to be the primary cause of harm to the child (Hetherington, Cox, & Cox, 1983; Wallerstein & Kelley, 1980).

SETTLING DOWN

I once heard a friend (turning 30) say that the 30s must be the best decade in life. He commented that during your 20s you are trying to figure out who you are and taking the necessary steps to become who you want to be. During the 30s you can begin to reap the benefits. For people who have followed the traditional family and career patterns, the beginning of middle adulthood in the 30s is often a time of settling down (Levinson, 1978). If a marriage has survived the tumultuous beginnings, the husband and wife have largely learned how to accommodate each other. For persons on less traditional tracks, the 30s may bring comfort as well. Gays and lesbians may gain acceptance from themselves and their families and establish themselves in accepting communities.

With children a little older, parenthood is a little easier. Jobs have become more stable, and financial security is better. A person has often developed some skills and acquires some seniority at work. He or she is less likely to be fired or laid off. He or she may have had some rewarding promotions and may feel on the way to becoming established in the field.

For others, the 30s are a time for crucial decisions. A woman who has intentionally foregone having children for the sake of a career must now make the decision whether or not to become a mother. Her biological clock is running out. Past the age of 35, a woman faces increasing risk of difficulty in pregnancy. After she is 40, her child has an increased risk of birth defects, especially Down's syndrome.

Those who have not yet settled into a career may feel time pressure to find one that better suits his or her needs or interests. Women who have been full-time homemakers may start going back to school or working.

MIDDLE AGE

Middle age is more of a social stage of life than a specific biological event. Most researchers set its boundaries from about age 40 to about 65, although today age 60 is still part of the prime of life. However, since it is socially influenced, the boundaries of middle age differ in different groups. In the upper-middle class, the 40s are considered the prime of life, in which case middle age starts at about age 50. In the lower income groups, the 30s are the prime of life, so middle age starts at age 40. Marriage and parenthood begin earlier in lower economic groups, thus children leave the home when the parents are younger. The earnings and prestige of blue-collar jobs peak in the 30s, whereas for the upper-middle class, the peak is usually in the 40s and sometimes 50s (Kimmel, 1980).

MIDLIFE CRISIS

In midlife, whether it's in their 40s or 50s, people review and assess their early adulthood. They may try to change those facets of their lives with which they are dissatisfied. They may attempt to resolve the psychological issues introduced by entering the final half of life (Levinson, 1978). Most people, however, do not have midlife crises (Cavanaugh, 1990; McCrae & Costa, 1984). Long held as normative, we now know that, for most, middle age is a time of heightened self-confidence and insight (Haan, 1985). Still, some people do have problems.

A **midlife crisis** occurs when a person discovers that he or she is not happy with life, and that goals either have not been attained or do not bring the expected satisfactions. The awareness of mortality—that a whole lifetime no longer lies ahead—may also prompt radical changes (Golan, 1986).

Two personality types are prone to depression in midlife (Block, 1971). Early maturing, socially gregarious men may have a hard time with the passing of their youth. They are often athletically oriented and nonintellectual. Lonely, independent women may also become depressed as their chances to have a family fade. They have often primarily invested in their intellect to the exclusion of social relationships. Conversely, the woman who remains strongly involved with her children may have difficulty in the "empty nest" stage (see the next section) (Argyle & Henderson, 1985).

Midlife is a time of transition for many, and transitions are often stressful (Lowenthal, Fiske, Thurner, & Chiriboga, 1974). However, most of these transitions are eagerly anticipated and provide opportunities for growth as well as crisis. Middle age may be a spicier time of life than youth realize.

MENOPAUSE AND THE "EMPTY NEST"

Not all of the important events in middle age cause a crisis. **Menopause** and the "empty nest" are good examples of this. Menopause, the cessation of a woman's menstrual cycle, generally occurs between the ages of 48 and 51

(Talbert, 1977). It may be signaled by hot flashes, irritability, crying spells, and depression. However, in a study of over 700 Japanese and American women, 75 percent reported none of the symptoms usually associated with menopause (Goodman, Stewart, & Gilbert, 1977).

It is primarily younger women who feel that menopause is a disagreeable event. Older women (aged 45–55) were more likely to feel that menopause creates no major changes (Neugarten, Wood, Kraines, & Loomis, 1963). Loss of fertility may have a profound effect on some women's self-esteem, but most women feel that not having to worry about menstruation or getting pregnant is positive.

Similarly, the **empty nest period,** when children leave home and become independent, is often thought to be a time of crisis for the family. A woman who is no longer a mother and who has no other interests may become depressed (Bart, 1971). However, most women do not become despondent. The best predictor of adjustment during menopause is the number of children in the home: the *fewer* the children, the *better* the woman adjusts. In an analysis of ethnic differences, Bart (1971) found that Jewish mothers had the highest rate of depression, WASPs an intermediate rate, and Blacks the lowest. This may reflect differences in family patterns in these groups.

Other responsibilities may also keep a woman at home at this stage of her life. With increasing age, the middle-aged person's own parents are likely to become more dependent and may need extensive assistance. This responsibility usually falls to the woman (Robinson & Thurner, 1979). Daughters care for mothers, and when there are only sons, a daughter-in-law becomes the caretaker of the elderly parent. Caring for the ailing parent may entail great sacrifices of time and money. Having an active, healthy parent may be a source of comfort and reassurance in middle age, but having to care for parents who show increasing signs of mental deterioration may be a source of great stress.

For many women, however, the empty nest period is a time of great satisfaction. Once the adolescent rebellion is over, families may have improved relationships with their children. Parents report being closest to their children and most satisfied with their relationships with them after the children have left home (and they see them the least) (Carstensen, 1989). Parents usually take great pride in the accomplishments of their offspring and may delight in becoming grandparents (Neugarten & Weinstein, 1964). Also, for a woman, the empty nest period may be a time of decreased responsibility, and a time when she can finally pursue her own interests (Deutscher, 1964). Couples may find that they have time again not only for themselves but also for each other. Marital satisfaction begins to improve, and the increased privacy and leisure time may improve their sexual relationship. Many look forward to various leisure activities such as traveling.

While the early theories that spawned life-span psychology provide a useful framework for thinking about adulthood, research has unveiled problems as well. Many of the predictions posited by theories of adulthood have not been supported by empirical evidence. For example, longitudinal studies of personality over the life course suggest that personality profiles remain highly consistent throughout life (Costa & McRae, 1984; Costa et al., 1986). And turbulence during early stages in life does not necessarily lead to difficulty later in life. In some cases persons who suffered horrendous childhoods adjust very well in adulthood; likewise, some people who seemed to be ideal adolescents have miserable adulthoods (MacFarlane, 1968).

Moreover, existing theories are biased toward Western culture. Underlying assumptions are that people pursue education during puberty and very early adulthood, subsequently marry, raise families, and pursue meaningful work. Yet the timing and the tasks are very different in other cultures. Assumptions are also made about the meaning of life events. Consider retirement, seen as a universal crisis. What about the man who has worked all his life on an assembly line and *begins* his life at retirement? What about the middle-aged woman who pursues her college education *after* her children are raised? What about the lesbian couple who opts not to have children? All of these situations represent common occurrences that present challenges to existing theory. In Chapter 21, we will pick up from where we leave you now as we focus on the final stage of life, old age.

SUMMARY

1. *Maturation* is the emergence of individual characteristics through normal growth processes. *Physical maturation* is controlled by the information in the genes and is relatively unaffected by learning or experience. *Psychological maturation* is the development of mental abilities that result from the normal growth of the brain and nervous system and from experience.

2. When babies are born, they have many innate *reflexes.* Only two hours after birth, they can track a slowly moving light, and if a nipple or finger is put into their mouths, they will begin to suck automatically. Newborns also have many visual preferences. They prefer to look at faces, and prefer small amounts of change and variation. Babies open their eyes when awake and alert. They look away from darkness and toward light. They look along edges.

3. *Motor development* and *cognitive development* are intimately tied. Growth affects all sensory systems. Locomotion is particularly central to cognitive development. As the child begins to crawl and walk, new cognitive challenges are encountered which facilitate understanding.

4. The *acquisition of language* is a central task of early development. The *environment* plays an important role in language development, but there is general agreement that an *innate organization* for language is present at birth. Children pass through predictable stages of language development, they produce sentences that they have never heard before, and they make highly consistent grammatical errors. Children communicate not only through words but also through facial and vocal expressions.

5. The most influential theory of cognitive development was proposed by *Piaget.* Piaget assumes (a) knowledge guides action, (b) knowledge develops through experience and action, and (c) the complexity of mental structures is determined largely by chronological age.

6. *Schemata* are the knowledge of how things are organized and how they relate to one another. Other important concepts of Piaget's are *assimilation* and *accommodation.* When children encounter a new event, they may attempt to assimilate it into their

existing knowledge structure. As long as there is an acceptable fit between the existing schemata, information can be assimilated. If it cannot be assimilated, they *accommodate* this new knowledge by changing their knowledge structure. As they learn about the world, schemata join to form repeated mental routines that Piaget calls *operations*—rules for transforming and manipulating information in the world. world.

7. Piaget's theory involves several stages of cognitive development. In the *sensorimotor stage* (birth to 2 years), children learn through motor and sensory play. The *preoperational stage* (2 to 7 years) finds children less bound by their senses and able to represent objects in drawings and words. Schemata that were just being organized are now able to be used intentionally. *Concrete operations* (7 to 12 years) is when thinking abstractly is possible. Children can carry a task through to completion and can understand some of the basic characteristics of things in the world, such as number, weight, and order. *Formal operations* (12 years to adult) concerns higher-level thinking: thinking abstractly, thinking through situations logically and systematically, and being able to imagine worlds that do not exist.

8. Important indicators of cognitive development are *egocentrism* and *decentration*. At each stage of development, children become increasingly aware of the world around them and less focused on only their thoughts and points of view.

9. Piaget's theory has been criticized by many, although it is generally accepted as very useful. Some of the criticisms are that (a) Piaget underestimates the reasoning abilities of children and overestimates verbal abilities, (b) stages of cognitive development are not exactly fixed, and (c) Piaget's focus on cognitive aspects of development lead the field to pay insufficient attention to social and emotional factors in development.

10. *Morality* is the knowledge of what is right and wrong. Like other aspects of cognition, a child's morals also undergo development. *Kohlberg's* theory suggests that there are three stages of moral reasoning, each with different levels. The first stage is *premoral*, in which rules are obeyed to avoid punishment; the second is *conventional morality*, in which rules are obeyed for the good of all; the third is *postconventional morality*, in which rules are obeyed because of respect for individual rights.

11. One criticism of *Kohlberg's* stages is that they seem to describe only male development. In fact, many theories of development, child and adult, are based on a masculine model. Some scholars argue that females value relationships between people more than abstract rights, which are more characteristic of the male world. Gilligan points out that the highest stages of moral development reflect traditionally masculine values, such as individuality, rationality, and detachment. Other values such as caring and responsibility for others (traditionally feminine) are given lower moral value by Kohlberg.

12. *Erikson's* theory divides *psychosocial development* into eight stages, each associated with a characteristic crisis. In the first year of life, the crisis is *trust versus mistrust*; in the second year, *autonomy versus shame and doubt*; in the third to fifth years, *initiative versus guilt*; in the sixth year to puberty, *industry versus inferiority*; in adolescence, *identity versus role confusion*; in early adulthood, *intimacy versus isolation*; in middle adulthood, *generativity versus self-absorption*; and in the aging years, *integrity versus despair*.

13. An important part of child development is emotional *attachment*—the quality of the relationship between the infant and the mother or other caregivers. Attachment is probably an innate bond that develops due to the necessity for maternal love, the gratification of needs, the infant's cognitive development, and communication between the primary caregiver and the child. Studies of attachment rely heavily on the *strange situation* paradigm. A stranger enters a room where a baby and mother are playing with toys; the mother leaves and the child is alone with the stranger and toys. Babies' reactions to separating and reuniting with the mother reveal differences in attachment. Three basic patterns of attachment are observed: (a) *unattached infants*, (b) *securely attached infants*, and (c) *insecurely attached infants*.

14. Children's *play* reflects four developmental trends: (a) biological maturation permits increasing skill; (b) play becomes more complex; (c) play becomes more abstract; and (d) children incorporate new people, situations, and skills into their fantasies.

15. Gender roles are acquired in early development. *Gender identity* means that a child knows and identifies with his or her sex. A *gender role* is society's expectations of how a male or female should behave. Society encourages gender-typed behavior in both males and females. *Self-socialization* also occurs once children acquire *gender constancy*, the knowledge that gender is permanent.

16. At the beginning of adolescence (puberty), there is a characteristic growth spurt and a major shift in thinking—the emergence of formal operations. The first exercise of this new level of abstract thought is questioning, searching, and rebeling, commonly called the *identity crisis*. It is occasioned by the emergence of the ability to imagine a world as the adolescent thinks it *ought to be* rather than the world as it is.

17. Ideas that development continues throughout adulthood date back to Jung, but more formal theories of life-span development did not appear until the 1960s and 1970s. Erikson's stage theory of development is the most widely influential model of development in late life.

18. Obtaining an intimate relationship with another adult is a central task of *early adulthood*. Most people find this relationship in marriage, although this is clearly determined by social convention, and other types of relationships serve the same function. Males and females experience marriage differently. Husbands are generally happier with marriage than wives.

19. Becoming a parent is considered by most to be a powerful growth experience in adulthood, carrying with it both tremendous responsibilities and rewards. There is a marked increase in gender differentiation during the transition to parenthood. For females, the change is more dramatic than for males. Marital distress is greatest during the childrearing years.

20. *Middle age* is often a time of stability. Even though some people do experience *midlife crisis*, there are exaggerations about the severity of these problems. For example, the *empty-nest syndrome* is far less frequent than previously assumed. Most women experience few problems with *menopause*.

21. Stage theories of adult development have been based primarily on Western, male, middle-class models. Predictability across diverse samples is quite limited.

accommodation
adaptation
assimilation
attachment
concrete operational stage
conservation
conventional morality
critical periods
decentration
egocentrism
embryonic period
empty nest period
fetal period
formal operational stage
gender role
germinal period
in utero
maturation
menarche
menopause

morality
motherese
object permanence
operations
physical maturation
postconventional morality
premoral morality
preoperational stage
psychological maturation
psychosocial development
puberty
reflexes
representational (symbolic) thought
schema
schemata
sensorimotor stage
separation anxiety
social referencing
strange situation
stranger anxiety

Bretherton, I., & Waters, E. (1985). *Growing points of attachment theory and research.* SRCD monographs.
A collection of up-to-date papers on research on attachment.

Chess, S., & Thomas, A. (1987). *Know your child.* New York: Basic Books.
An important contribution to child rearing in that it presents the modern evidence on the inheritance of temperament and its importance in childhood.

Colby, A., & Kohlberg, L. (1987). *The measurement of moral judgment.* New York: Cambridge University Press.
An enormous compendium of the testing procedure for classifying behaviors as moral or not.

Gelman, R., & Galistel, C. R. (1986). *The child's understanding of number.* Cambridge, MA: Harvard University Press.
An update of the classic study of how children understand.

Kagan, J. (1984). *The nature of the child.* New York: Basic Books.
A controversial analysis of the ability of the child to recover from early experiences.

Newman, B. N., & Newman, P. R. (1987). *Development through life.* Chicago: Dorsey.

Richards, M., & Light, P. (1986). *Children of social worlds.* Cambridge, MA: Harvard University Press.
Two up-to-date accounts of the psychosocial perspective on development throughout the life cycle.

Roazen, P. (1986). *Erik H. Erikson: The power & limits of a vision.* New York: Free Press.
A perceptive introduction to Erikson.

Scarr, S. (1984). *Mothercare-Othercare.* New York: Basic Books.
An analysis of how different styles of upbringing affect the child.

Skolnick, A. (1986). *The psychology of human development.* San Diego: Harcourt Brace Jovanovich.
Perhaps the best balanced of the current texts on development.

"HYBRIDS"

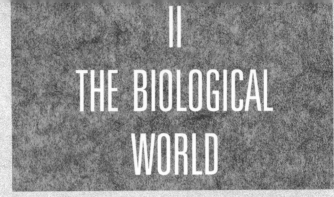

The cell that develops into the adult does so in a precise form, governed by millennia of our genetic inheritance. How much we inherit and how much we can go beyond out inheritance are questions that psychologists 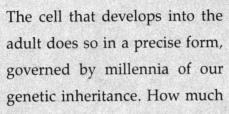 have been grappling with since the beginning of the science. Are we locked into our selves by our cells?

The brain, once an undifferentiated part of that single cell, becomes an organ so complex that no computer, no matter how large, could mimic its function. The number of possible interconnections in our brains is greater than the number of atomic particles in the universe. The cell also contains the specifications for the design and construction of the nervous system and the senses, sensors (and censors) so intricate that they capture only one trillionth of the information reaching them. Then the neural network analyzes these outside signals, processing them further as they ascend to the higher functions of the brain.

This is all part of our genetic endowment, and in this part we consider many of the questions of our evolution, where we came from, and what we may become. How much does the genetic code specify? What were our ancestors like?

The story of human beginnings and physiology is amazing, one filled with spectacular feats of knowledge and of a development unlike any other animal on Earth.

3
THE BRAIN AND THE NERVOUS SYSTEM

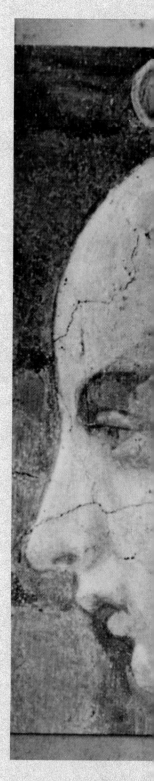

Throughout our lives, brain processes underlie our experiences. The adult brain is a little larger than a grapefruit, and it weighs about three and one-half pounds. It is the one organ we cannot transplant and still be ourselves. It regulates all body functions, controls our most primitive behavior, and is the source of all our most sophisticated creations of civilization, including music, art, science, and language. Hopes, thoughts, emotions, and personality all nest—somewhere—in the brain. Even though thousands of scientists have studied it for centuries, it still remains, in some ways, an awesome mystery. In a single human brain the number of *potential* interconnections between cells is greater than the number of atoms in the known universe.

Although psychologists may never unravel all the mysteries of the brain, much is known about its history, how brain cells communicate with one another, and how injuries to certain areas of the brain affect behavior. Individuals' brains are distinct from one another; they are even different between the sexes. Changes in diet and in the air we breathe affect brain chemistry, which in turn influences mood. The brain is a pharmacy; it produces more chemical substances than any other organ of the body. Some of these chemicals stop pain and aid in healing. The brain can recover from damage, grow in response to new experiences, and grow and develop in old age.

There is a kind of architecture to the brain because the brain evolved partly by "design," partly by accident over hundreds of millions of years. So think of it like an old ramshackle house, one originally built long ago for a small family, then added on to over generations of growth and change. Like such a house, the brain's original structure remains basically intact. Some of the original functions moved elsewhere, as when one builds a modern kitchen and converts the old one into a pantry.

The brain is not like a well-designed modern house, each foot well planned and organized. We just were not built that way. The brain has an irregular design, embodying some structures adapted to the needs of animals and situations long gone.

This chapter reveals some of the complex architecture of the brain. Comparing it to an old house, it begins with the overall shape of the house, then the design of the rooms, and finally the components, the bricks. *It is in this structure that our experience resides.*

THE ARCHITECTURE OF THE BRAIN

Here is a way to help you visualize the rooms of the brain. Place your fingers on both sides of your head beneath the earlobes. In the center of the space between your fingertips is the oldest part of the brain, called the *brain stem*. Now imagine an area in the very center of your head. That is the *limbic system*, which governs emotions and regulates the internal workings of the body.

To visualize the whole brain, make two fists and join them at the heels of the hands. This is about the size and shape of the entire brain, which is divided into

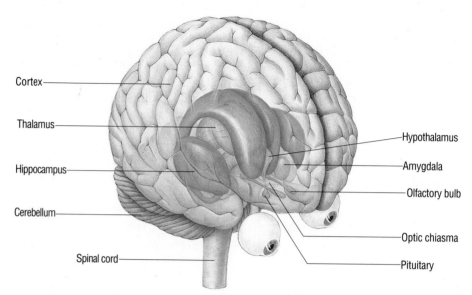

Cortex

Thalamus

Hippocampus

Cerebellum

Spinal cord

Hypothalamus

Amygdala

Olfactory bulb

Optic chiasma

Pituitary

two hemispheres, each about the size of one fist. The front of the brain is where your little fingers are; the back, your thumbs. The middle fingers represent the area where the brain controls movement, and the index fingers where the brain receives sensory information. Now imagine your hands covered with thick gray gloves. These gloves represent the *cortex*, which is Latin for "bark" (Figure 3-1). The cortex was the last part of the brain to evolve and produces the most distinctive human activities, such as language and art.

THE ARCHAEOLOGY OF THE BRAIN

In addition to an architecture, the brain has what we could call an archaeology. Like an archaeological dig, there are layers to the brain—four different levels of functions that developed as the brain evolved. The structures seem to be laid on top of each other, and many of these separate parts of the brain have, loosely speaking, minds of their own. There are minds for alertness, for emotions, for danger, for comparing sensory information, for avoiding scarcity, and for many other functions.

The human brain is in part archaic. Many scientists think that it evolved from the neural mechanisms of primates, earlier mammals and, before that, more primitive vertebrates. The structure of the codfish's brain, for instance, contains many of the same basic elements as the human brain. The codfish even has a cerebral cortex (although it is small), a pituitary gland for controlling hormone production, a cerebellum, and most of the other parts of the brain that we possess. In turn, vertebrates like the codfish obtained many of their neural circuits and routines from earlier and simpler multicelled creatures.

Many of our commonplace preferences stem from the antiquated nature of the nervous system. We maintain concentrations of trace minerals in internal fluids that are appropriate in a fish living deep in the Mediterranean Sea, and we prefer the temperatures found on the East African plains where our first true ancestors came from—that is, 60 to 85 degrees Fahrenheit. We experience a work slump in the late afternoon because of the ancient body rhythms of our savanna-dwelling precursors; they took their "siesta" at that time. Even in Norway in November, this same slump occurs. Our hackles raise during a business meeting because, when threatened, our ancestors fluffed their hair to appear larger and menacing. We raise up goose flesh to provide an insulating layer of air in fur that disappeared millions of years ago.

KEEPING ALIVE: THE BRAIN STEM

What may be the oldest part of the brain evolved over 500 million years ago, before the evolution of mammals (MacLean, 1989). The **brain stem** is primarily concerned with basic life support. It governs the control of breathing and heart rate. In the center of the brain stem and traveling its full length is a core of neural tissue known as the **reticular activating system (RAS)** (Figure 3-2). Like a bell, the RAS alerts the cortex to arriving information, such as "visual stimulus on its way." When a sleeping dog is stimulated by electrodes in the RAS, it awakens immediately and searches the environment. The RAS also controls the general level of arousal—wakefulness, sleep, attention, excitement, and so on (Thompson, 1986).

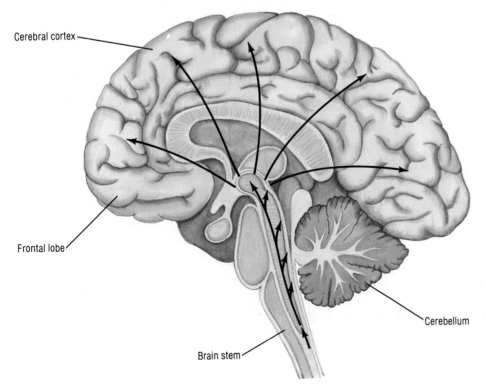

FIGURE 3-2
The Reticular Activating System (RAS)

The RAS, buried in the brain stem, communicates with wide areas of the cortex, informing it of incoming stimuli and controlling its general level of arousal.
(Thompson, 1967)

95

Most sensory information from the outside world enters the lower brain stem. The **thalamus** then relays the information to the appropriate part of the cortex (Figure 3-1). The thalamus classifies external, sensory information ("Is it visual or auditory?") and then relays it to the cortex.

On the side of the brain stem is the **cerebellum,** which originally developed to improve control of balance, body position, and movement in space. Its job has changed throughout the course of evolution, however. Now, memory for simple learned responses is stored there. The cerebellum's change in function is typical of how the brain evolved: original structures took over new functions as evolution proceeded.

KEEPING ALIVE: THE LIMBIC SYSTEM

A person in a coma cannot respond to or interact with the outside world. He or she continues to live, however, because the area of the brain that regulates vital body functions continues to operate. This area of the brain is the **limbic system** (Figure 3-3), which is a group of structures in the center of the brain immediately atop the brain stem. The limbic system probably evolved to its present form during the period from 300 to 200 million years ago, during the transition from sea-dwelling to land animals.

The limbic system helps to maintain **homeostasis,** a constant environment in the body; it regulates body temperature, blood pressure, heart rate, and blood sugar level. Without a limbic system, we would be cold-blooded, like reptiles, unable to adjust our internal state to maintain its constant climate.

The limbic system also directs emotional reactions such as self-protection through fighting or escaping. One way to remember limbic functions is through

**FIGURE 3-3
The Limbic System in Relation to the Cerebral Cortex**

Centrally located between the cerebral hemispheres—which are connected by the corpus callosum—and in touch with the frontal lobes and the brain stem, the limbic system is ideally placed for coordinating many of the brain's operations.

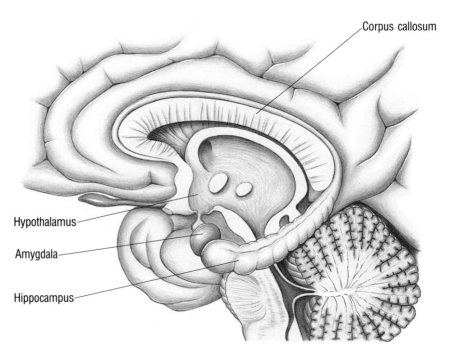

Corpus callosum

Hypothalamus

Amygdala

Hippocampus

the four *f*'s of survival: feeding, fighting, fleeing, and sexual reproduction. It includes many of the most important structures of the brain: the hypothalamus, the pituitary gland, the hippocampus, the amygdala, and part of the frontal lobes of the cortex, which we will discuss later.

THE HYPOTHALAMUS AND THE PITUITARY

The **hypothalamus** is the most intricate and amazing structure of the brain. It is small and weighs about 4 grams. It regulates eating, drinking, sleeping, waking, body temperature, chemical balances, heart rate, hormones, sex, and emotions. It operates through negative feedback. Body temperature is registered in the hypothalamus via blood temperature. If the blood becomes too cool, the hypothalamus stimulates heat production and conservation of energy. An animal with an injured hypothalamus may not eat or drink, no matter how long it has been deprived of food or water. Conversely, stimulation or destruction of points of the hypothalamus provokes incessant eating, which can be fatal.

Through a combination of electrical and chemical messages, the hypothalamus directs the **pituitary,** the master gland of the brain. This gland regulates the body through **hormones,** which are chemicals manufactured and secreted by special neurons in the brain. Hormones flow through the blood to target cells in the body (Figure 3-4).

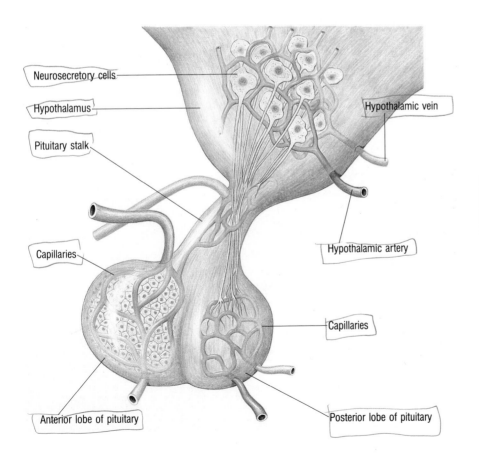

Neurosecretory cells

Hypothalamus

Pituitary stalk

Capillaries

Hypothalamic vein

Hypothalamic artery

Capillaries

Anterior lobe of pituitary

Posterior lobe of pituitary

**FIGURE 3-4
The Vital
Hypothalamus–Pituitary
Link**

The hypothalamus is able to integrate functions of the neuroendocrine and nervous systems because it is structurally connected to the cerebral cortex and to the pituitary gland, with which it communicates both by nerve impulses and by chemical messages sent directly or through the general bloodstream.
(Vannini & Pogliani, 1980)

97

THE HIPPOCAMPUS AND AMYGDALA

The word **hippocampus** is Greek for "sea horse," which is what it looks like (Figure 3-3). Information from the senses passes through the hippocampus, which determines whether it is new or whether it matches stored information. The hippocampus influences learning, the recognition of novelty, and the storage of recent events into memory. The **amygdala** is a small structure between the hypothalamus and the hippocampus. Its functions are not completely understood, but it is basically a large relay, like the thalamus. Surgery on the amygdala results in emotional deficiencies in humans. (See the discussion of the brain's chemical system, page 122.)

CREATING ANEW: THE CEREBRAL CORTEX

The top level of the brain, the **cerebral cortex,** developed in vertebrates about 50 million years ago. It performs the functions that have increased our human adaptability and that make us uniquely human. In the cortex, decisions are conceived, the world is organized, individual experiences are stored in memory, speech is produced and understood, paintings are seen, and music is heard.

The cortex is only about one-eighth of an inch thick and is convoluted and enfolded (Figure 3-5). If it were unfolded and spread out, it would be about the

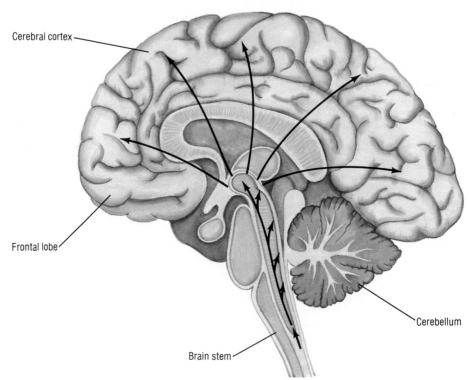

FIGURE 3-5
The Cerebral Cortex

The visible part of the brain is the surface of the cortex, which is thin and enfolded compactly to fit inside the skull. Fifty percent of the cortex is enfolded. The cortex is shown here in relation to the brain stem and cerebellum and to the limbic system, to which it is linked and which it surrounds.
(Thompson, 1967)

Cerebral cortex

Frontal lobe

Cerebellum

Brain stem

size of a newspaper page. Of all mammals, human beings have the most enfolded cortex, perhaps because such a large cortex had to fit into a head small enough to survive birth.

The cortex is the "executive branch" of the brain, responsible for making decisions and judgments on all the information coming into it from the body and the outside world. It performs three distinct functions. First, it receives information from the outside world. Second, it analyzes and compares it with stored information from prior experiences and knowledge and then makes a decision. Third, it sends its own messages and instructions out to the appropriate muscles and glands.

The cortex is layered with specialized cells arranged in columns. The columns each have specific functions, such as the visual detection of corners and edges. They act as *data processing centers* in the cortex and serve as modules for the basic interpretation of information. So, the "rooms" of the brain have "columns"!

These columns of cells are thought to do the basic analysis work of the mind. They interpret a pattern of sounds and translate it into language. They analyze millions of bits of visual information to determine an object's size, shape, and position. They decode a set of squiggles such as 2 + 2 = 4 into meaningful mathematical symbols. They track the position of the limbs to allow the body to turn and avoid an oncoming car. They interpret the sounds in music, and much, much more. There are probably modules for specific reactions and patterns of activity, too (Gazzaniga, 1987; Thompson, 1986).

Side by side inside the cortex lie separate centers of what I call "talents." This may be an unusual word to use but I think it describes this level of brain operation. Most people probably have more of one "talent" than another. These abilities, such as the ability to move gracefully or to speak fluently, seem to exist as coherent mental and behavioral units as well as specific anatomical units (Galin & Ornstein, 1972; Ornstein, 1986).

The cortex divides into different and well-defined areas. Each has a rich concentration of certain abilities. If you imagine each of these areas as a patch, the cortex would look much like a folded patchwork quilt.

The cortex is divided into two hemispheres, each of which has four lobes: the frontal, parietal, temporal, and occipital. We discuss these lobes first and then take a detailed look at the two hemispheres and their significance.

THE FRONTAL LOBES

The **frontal lobes** lie just behind the forehead. They are the largest of the four lobes and oversee much of the rest of the brain's activity. Information about the worlds inside and outside of the body as well as plans and controls are all assembled by a uniquely human talent—a system concerned with the maintenance of the individual self. While it is not possible to find a location for the self in the brain, the functions related to the self seem to depend on decisions carried out in the frontal lobes.

The frontal lobes are a crossroads. They lie at the intersection of the neural pathways that convey information from the parietal areas of the brain about

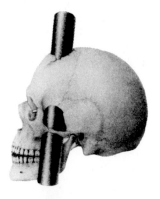

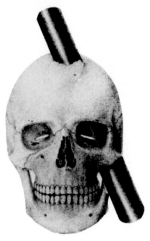

FIGURE 3-6
Frontal Lobe Damage

Phineas Gage, a railroad worker, suffered severe damage to the left frontal lobe of his brain when a device to set tamping irons accidently exploded and lodged the spike in his skull. He survived, but his personality was drastically altered.

people and events in the world as well as information from the limbic system about the body's own state. The frontal lobes also contribute to the control of basic systems such as heart rate. They are so intimately connected to the limbic functions that many psychobiologists classify the frontal lobes as part of the limbic system. There are also different forms of emotions represented within each of the frontal lobes, as well as some control of the expression of emotions. In tragic cases, damage to the frontal areas results in the inability to carry out plans and to know on a long-term basis who one is.

The most famous case of such frontal lobe damage was to a railroad worker named Phineas Gage, who in 1868 accidentally had a piece of a rail line permanently embedded in his skull (Figure 3-6). He survived, but his personality and sense of self disappeared. Here is a record of his condition from one of his doctors:

> His physical health is good, and I am inclined to say that he has recovered. . . . The equilibrium or balance, so to speak, between his intellectual faculty and animal propensities, seems to have been destroyed. He is fitful, irreverent, indulging at times in the grossest profanity (which was not previously his custom), manifesting but little deference for his fellows, impatient of restraint or advice when it conflicts with his desires, at times pertinaciously obstinate, yet capricious and vacillating, devising many plans of future operation, which are not sooner arranged than they are abandoned in turn for others appearing more feasible. A child in his intellectual capacity and manifestations, he has the animal passions of a strong man. Previous to his injury, though untrained in the schools, he possessed a well-balanced mind, and was looked upon by those who knew him as a shrewd, smart business man, very energetic and persistent in executing all his plans of operation. In this regard, his mind was radically changed, so decidedly that his friends and acquaintances said he was "no longer Gage." (Heilman & Satz, 1984)

The self-system in the frontal lobes influences many life processes to seek out different information, to remember differently, and to think and evaluate differently. Problems in the frontal lobes also cause health problems, among them cancer and sudden heart attacks, which we will discuss later.

The frontal lobes participate in planning, decision making, and purposeful behavior. If they are destroyed or removed, the individual becomes incapable of planning, carrying out, or comprehending a complex action or idea and is unable to adapt to new situations, as we can see in the Phineas Gage example. Such people are unable to focus attention and become distracted by irrelevant stimuli (Luria, 1973). Their language and consciousness are fine. However, the loss of the ability to adapt and plan ahead makes those abilities useless.

In a wonderfully titled book, *The Man Who Mistook His Wife for a Hat*, neurologist Oliver Sacks describes a woman with frontal lobe damage.

> Mrs. B., a former research chemist, had presented with a rapid personality change, becoming "funny" (facetious, given to wisecracks and puns), impulsive —and "superficial" ("You feel she doesn't care about you," one of her friends said. "She no longer seems to care about anything at all.") At first it was thought that she might be hypomanic, but she turned out to have a cerebral tumor. At craniotomy there was found, not a meningioma as had been hoped, but a huge carcinoma involving the orbitofrontal aspects of both frontal lobes.
>
> When I saw her, she seemed high-spirited, volatile—"a riot" (the nurses called her)—full of quips and cracks, often clever and funny.

"Yes, Father," she said to me on one occasion.

"Yes, Sister," on another.

"Yes, Doctor," on a third.

She seemed to use the terms interchangeably.

"What *am* I?" I asked, stung, after a while.

"I see your face, your beard," she said, "I think of an Archimandrite Priest. I see your white uniform—I think of the Sisters. I see your stethoscope—I think of a doctor."

"You don't look at *all* of me?"

"No, I don't look at all of you."

"You realise the difference between a father, a sister, a doctor?"

"I *know* the difference, but it means nothing to me. Father, sister, doctor—what's the big deal?"

Thereafter, teasingly, she would say: "Yes, father-sister. Yes, sister-doctor", and other combinations.

Testing left-right discrimination was oddly difficult, because she said left or right indifferently (though there was not, in reaction, any confusion of the two, as when there is a lateralising defect of perception or attention). When I drew her attention to this, she said: "Left/right. Right/left. Why the fuss? What's the difference?"

"*Is* there a difference?" I asked.

"Of course," she said, with a chemist's precision. "You could call them *enantiomorphs* of each other. But they mean nothing to *me*. They're no different from *me*. Hands . . . Doctors . . . Sisters . . ." she added, seeing my puzzlement. "Don't you understand? They mean nothing—nothing to me. *Nothing means anything* . . . at least to me."

"And . . . this meaning nothing . . ." I hesitated, afraid to go on. "This meaninglessness . . . does *this* bother you? Does *this* mean anything to you?"

"Nothing at all," she said promptly, with a bright smile, in the tone of one who makes a joke, wins an argument, wins at poker.

Was this denial? Was this a brave show? Was this the "cover" of some unbearable emotion? Her face bore no deeper expression whatever. Her world had been voided of feeling and meaning. Nothing any longer felt "real" (or "unreal"). Everything was now "equivalent" or "equal"—the whole world reduced to a facetious insignificance.

I found this somewhat shocking—her friends and family did too—but she herself, though not without insight, was uncaring, indifferent, even with a sort of funny-dreadful nonchalance or levity.

Mrs. B., though acute and intelligent, was somehow not present—"desouled"—as a person. (Sacks, 1985)

People seem to lose their selves in a most terrifying and disheartening way when something in the frontal lobes is destroyed. But also important—and keep this in mind—is that this self is separate from other mental faculties, which are governed by another component of the brain.

THE SENSORY AND MOTOR AREAS

The **sensory** and **motor areas** are at the juncture of the frontal and parietal lobes (Figure 3-7). They are proportionately smaller in human beings than in other animals (Figure 3-8). The sensory areas receive information about body position, muscles, touch, and pressure from all over the body. The motor areas control the movements of the different parts of the body.

Figure 3-9 shows the body as it is represented proportionally in the brain. In the *homunculus*, various parts of the body are distorted out of proportion to their

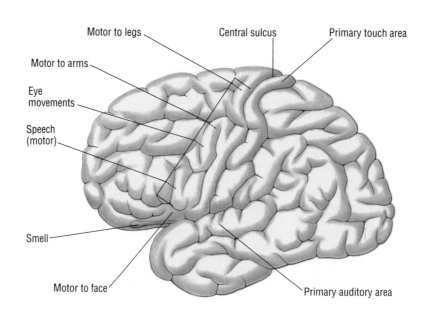

**FIGURE 3-7
Sensory and Motor
Areas of the Brain**

Control of the senses and body movements is located in an area of the brain between the frontal and parietal lobes.

Motor to legs · Central sulcus · Primary touch area · Motor to arms · Eye movements · Speech (motor) · Smell · Motor to face · Primary auditory area

**FIGURE 3-8
The Range of
Complexity of Animal
Brains**

Although not drawn to scale, the differences between human and subhuman brains are obvious, particularly the proportionally smaller human sensory and motor areas and the vastly larger human cortex.

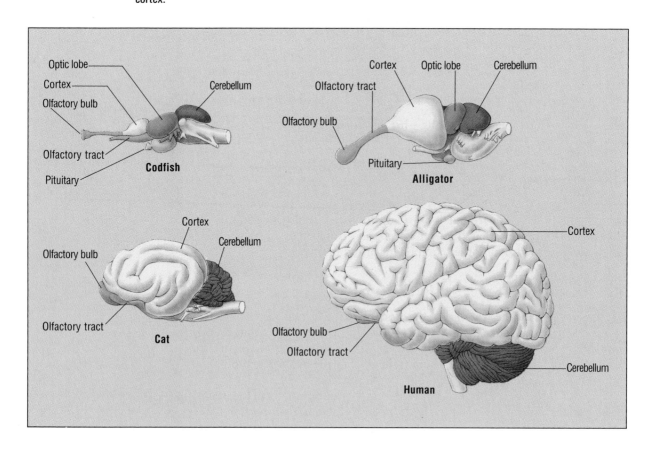

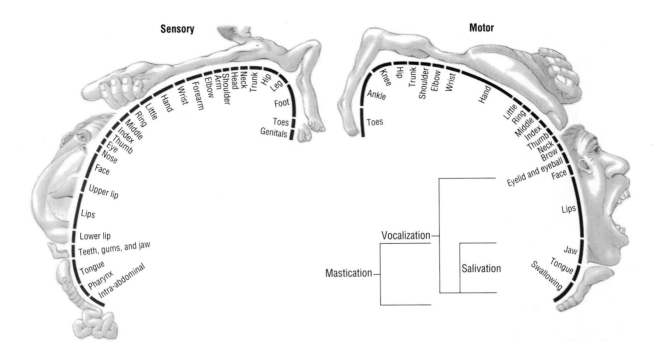

Sensory

Little · Ring · Middle · Index · Thumb · Eye · Nose · Face · Upper lip · Lips · Lower lip · Teeth, gums, and jaw · Tongue · Pharynx · Intra-abdominal · Hand · Wrist · Forearm · Elbow · Arm · Shoulder · Head · Neck · Trunk · Hip · Leg · Foot · Toes · Genitals

Motor

Knee · Hip · Trunk · Shoulder · Elbow · Wrist · Hand · Little · Ring · Middle · Index · Thumb · Neck · Brow · Eyelid and eyeball · Face · Lips · Jaw · Tongue · Swallowing · Ankle · Toes

Mastication — Vocalization — Salivation

FIGURE 3-9
A Homunculus of the Sensory and Motor Areas

A cross-section of the cortex shows the relative space devoted to different functions. Parts of the body that engage in important activities involving great sensitivity— such as speech, touch, and dexterity—are shown much larger proportionally than their actual relative size in the body.
(Penfield & Rasmussen, 1950)

physical size. *The more complex the function, the more space the brain devotes to it.* Although the back is much larger than the tongue, it makes fewer intricate movements and is less sensitive, thus it seems smaller to the brain. Our hands are terribly important to us. They process information about touch and pressure and are also capable of extremely complex movements. But this is different for other species: in the homunculus of a cat's brain, paws have little space, but the more sensitive whiskers have a very large area (Thompson, 1986). Whiskers are also important to a mouse, and the corresponding area of the animal's cortex reflects this (Figure 3-10).

THE PARIETAL LOBES

The **parietal lobes** *analyze* sensory input. It is probably here where letters come together as words and where words are put together into thoughts.

Damage to the parietal lobes can result in a form of *agnosia* (which means "not knowing"). Mountcastle (1976) studied a person with parietal lobe damage who was unaware of a whole side of his body. This is a condition called *amorphosynthesis.* Because he had right parietal lobe damage, he ignored or did not know the left side of his body or the left side of anything. Drawings by Mountcastle's patient are shown in Figure 3-11. Notice how the numbers of the clock squeeze into the right half. Most everything on the left side of his world is ignored. A person who has damage to half the parietal lobe may dress and groom only one side of his or her body (Figure 3-12). Some individuals lose the ability to follow audio or visual cues and cannot recognize familiar objects by touch.

TEMPORAL LOBES

The **temporal lobes** (Figure 3-13) have several important functions. The auditory cortex, a small area in each lobe, interprets the information that the ears sense. Other temporal lobe functions involve perception, memory, and dreaming.

Most of our knowledge of temporal lobe functions comes from people who have suffered some sort of damage to this region. Sometimes these persons experience dramatic hallucinations, while in other cases, they lose memories of events that occur after the damage.

APHASIA AND OTHER TEMPORAL LOBE DEFICITS

Severe damage to certain areas of the left temporal lobe may result in **aphasia,** which is language impairment. Here is an example of how a person with temporal lobe damage may speak. Howard Gardner describes an interview with a Coast Guard operator.

> "Were you in the Coast Guard?"
> "No, er, yes, yes . . . ship . . . Massachu . . . chusetts Coastguard . . . years." He raised his hands twice, indicating the number nineteen.
> "Oh, you were in the Coast Guard for nineteen years."
> "Oh . . . boy . . . right . . . right." (Gardner, 1975)

This was a man who had normal speech before his left hemisphere injury. He clearly wants to communicate but cannot find the words to do it.

That there are clearly separate verbal abilities is shown by another type of brain injury to a different portion of the left temporal lobe. The tragic result is called *Wernicke's aphasia.* Gardner gives an example:

> "What brings you to the hospital?" I asked the 72-year-old retired butcher four weeks after his admission to the hospital.
> "Boy, I'm sweating, I'm awful nervous, you know, once in a while I get caught up, I can't mention the tarripoi, a month ago, quite a while. I've done a lot well, I impose a lot, while, on the other hand, you know what I mean, I have to run around, look it over, trebbin and all that sort of stuff."
> I attempted several times to break in, but was unable to do so against this relentlessly steady and rapid outflow. . . .
> "Thank you, Mr. Gorgan, I want to ask you a few—"
> "Oh sure, go ahead, any old think you want. If I could I would. Oh, I'm taking the word the wrong way to say, all of the barbers here whenever they stop you it's going around and around, if you know what I mean, that is tying and tying for repucer, repuceration, well, we were trying the best that we could while another time it was with the beds over there the same thing. . . ." (Gardner, 1975)

In the first example, the patient is trying to convey meaning but cannot speak the words. In the second example, the patient speaks the words but conveys no meaning, just sounds roughly coherent, unconfined by any direction. Producing the words and producing the meaning seem to be two separate verbal talents.

After temporal lobe stimulation, some people report the feeling of being in two places at once. The memory of an event and the present *coexist* in the

FIGURE 3-10
Brain Function and Structure

Whiskers are so important to a mouse that its brain has a section whose structure almost exactly reflects the external layout of the mouse's snout. For each row of whiskers in the bottom photograph, there is a row of patches of cells, each corresponding to a whisker, in the mouse's cortex (top photograph and insert).
(Woolsey & van der Loos, 1970)

FIGURE 3-11
A One-sided View of the World

A patient with right parietal damage is unaware of the left side of things. The drawings of the watch— the top one made two days after the injury and the bottom one seven days later—in which all the numbers are crowded into the right half of the watch face, show that the patient ignores left-hand external reality. (The house drawings on the far left are the physician's, which the patient tried to duplicate.)
(Mountcastle, 1962)

FIGURE 3-12
A Shattered Mind

Lovis Corinth, an important turn-of-the-century German artist, did the portrait of his wife on the left in 1910. The portrait on the right was done in 1912 after he had suffered a right-hemisphere stroke that, among other deficits, impaired his ability to render the left side of his subject.

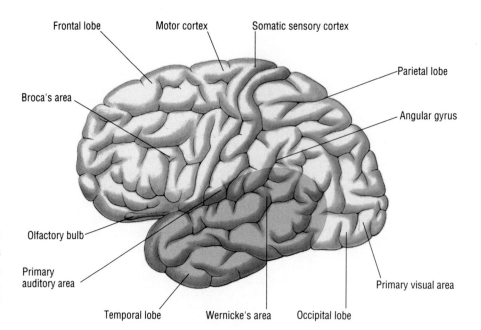

Frontal lobe   Motor cortex   Somatic sensory cortex

Parietal lobe

Broca's area

Angular gyrus

FIGURE 3-13
The Temporal Lobes

The left temporal lobe is
shown here as a darker patch
in relation to the rest of the
left hemisphere.

Olfactory bulb

Primary
auditory area

Primary visual area

Temporal lobe   Wernicke's area   Occipital lobe

person's consciousness. While fully conscious and aware of the activity of the moment, a person might suddenly feel elsewhere. He may be in a kitchen, 30 years ago, and the sounds and smells seem real. Recall Penfield's dramatic finding of memory in the brain during electrical stimulation of his patient's temporal lobe. (See Figure 1-9, page 20.) A person undergoing such stimulation seems to *relive* specific past experiences.

THE OCCIPITAL LOBES: THE VISUAL CORTEX

At the rear of the brain are the **occipital lobes.** Because this area analyzes vision, it is often called the *visual cortex.* Information from the eyes enters the visual cortex for analysis of orientation, position, and movement. Damage to the occipital lobes can result in blindness even if the rest of the visual system is unaffected.

THE TWO HEMISPHERES

The cerebral cortex is divided into two hemispheres connected by a large structure of 300 million neurons called the **corpus callosum.** Only in human beings do these hemispheres specialize for different functions. This lateral specialization is the most recent development in human evolution; it is less than 4 million years old and perhaps "only" 1 million years old.

The left hemisphere controls the right side of the body. It also controls language and logical activities—that is, things that happen in a specific order. The right hemisphere controls the left side of the body. It directs spatial and simultaneous actions as well as artistic activities. These differences in function between the hemispheres probably appeared at the time human beings began to make and use symbols (both language and art).

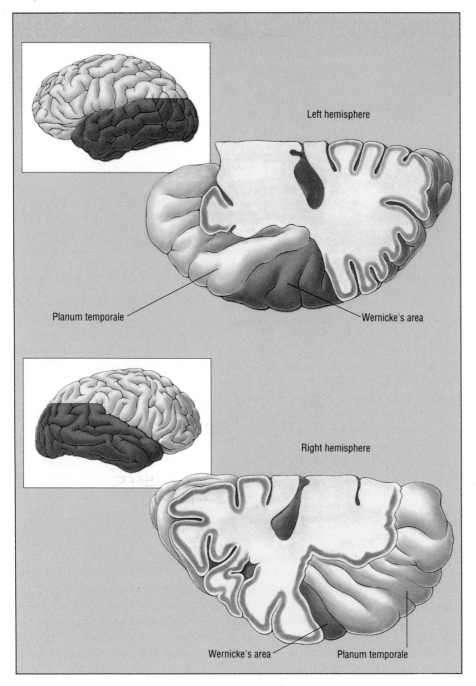

Left hemisphere

Planum temporale

Wernicke's area

Right hemisphere

Wernicke's area

Planum temporale

**FIGURE 3-14
Asymmetry of the Cortex**

In most people the left hemisphere of the cortex is larger than the right, which is thought to be due to the left hemisphere's linguistic dominance. The shaded areas in the boxed drawings show the temporal lobes in the left (top) and right (bottom) hemispheres. Cross-sections of the two lobes show differences in the sizes of Wernicke's area and the planum temporale, which contribute to the brain's asymmetry.

The two hemispheres look about the same, but they have significant anatomical differences. In 95 percent of fetuses, the left hemisphere is larger than the right (Geschwind & Levitsky, 1976). The enlarged area is the *planum temporale* in the temporal lobe, and it governs speech and written language (Figure 3-14). As we have seen, damage to the temporal lobe of the left hemisphere causes aphasia, the loss of the ability to speak language. Damage to the right hemisphere results in impaired performance of spatial tasks, such as the ability to draw or to recognize faces.

Although each hemisphere specializes in different tasks, the division between them is not absolute. Rather, they are in constant communication with each other. Rarely is one hemisphere completely idle and the other frantic with activity.

The two hemispheres are not *separate* systems or two brains. An activity as complex as language, although predominantly controlled by the left hemisphere, involves the interaction of both hemispheres. If either hemisphere is damaged, the remaining intact hemisphere can take over, but this becomes less easy as we age. If the left hemisphere is damaged at birth, the right will take over language. However, the person may be less adept at language than he or she would have otherwise been (Sternglass, 1988).

THE SPLIT BRAIN

The two cerebral hemispheres communicate through the corpus callosum, which joins the two sides anatomically (Figure 3-15). To control severe epilepsy in some patients, Roger Sperry and Joseph Bogen initiated radical treatment by cutting the callosum, producing a so-called **split brain** (Sperry, 1982). After the surgery, if patients held an object, such as a pencil, hidden from sight in the right hand, they could describe it verbally. However, if the object was in the left hand, they could not describe it at all. Recall that the left hand informs the right hemisphere, which has a limited capability for speech. With the corpus callosum severed, the verbal (left) hemisphere is no longer connected to the right hemisphere, which communicates largely with the left hand. Here the *verbal apparatus literally does not know what is in the left hand.*

Sometimes, however, the patients were offered a set of objects out of sight, such as keys, books, pencils, and so on. They were asked to select the previously given object with the left hand. The patients chose correctly, although they still could not say verbally just what object they were taking. It was as if they were

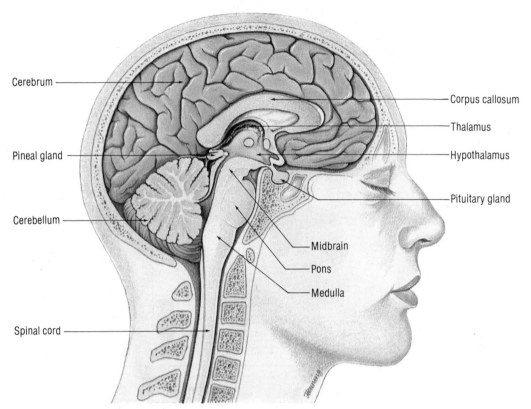

Cerebrum

Corpus callosum

Thalamus

Pineal gland

Hypothalamus

Pituitary gland

Cerebellum

Midbrain

Pons

Medulla

Spinal cord

FIGURE 3-15
Splitting the Brain

In split-brain operations, called commissures, the connective nerve tissue of the corpus callosum, through which the two hemispheres communicate, is severed. This procedure has caused radical changes in patients' perception and behavior.
(Gaudin & Jones, 1989)

asked to perform an action and someone else was discussing it (Gazzaniga et al., 1989).

The right half of each eye sends its messages to the left hemisphere; the left half to the right hemisphere. In an experiment using divided visual input, the word "heart" flashed before the patients. The "he" was to the left of the eye's fixation point, and the "art" to the right. A normal person would report seeing the word "heart." The split-brain patients responded differently, depending on which hemisphere was controlling the response. When asked to point with the left hand to the word seen, the patients pointed to "he," but with the right hand they pointed to "art." The experience of each hemisphere was independent of each other in these patients. The verbal hemisphere gave one answer; the nonverbal hemisphere another (Figure 3-16).

Most right-handed people write and draw with the right hand only. However many can also write and draw to some extent with their left. After surgery, Bogen (1969) tested the ability of the split-brain patients to draw with either hand. The right hand retained the ability to write, but it could no longer draw very well (Figure 3-17). The left hand was able to convey the relationship of the parts, even though the line quality was poor. Note the right hand's performance: the cross contains the correct elements, yet the ability to link the disconnected elements is lacking. Normally, a square would never be considered as a set of disconnected corners!

THE TWO HEMISPHERES

FIGURE 3-16
Hemisphere Specialization and Visual Input

A composite photograph of two different faces is flashed before a split-brain subject (A). When shown a group of photographs and asked to pick out the person he saw in the composite, he will *say* it is the face from the *right* half of the composite (B). But if asked to *point out* which one he originally saw, he will indicate the picture from the *left* side of the composite (C). Such experiments suggest the two hemispheres are independent to some degree, each performing different functions in different ways.

(Levy, Trevarthen, & Sperry, 1972)

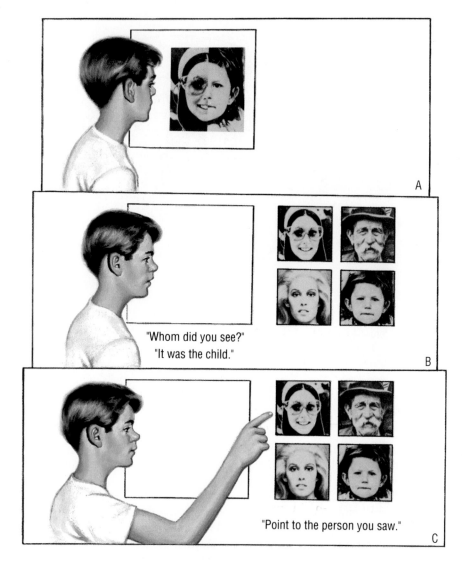

"Whom did you see?"
"It was the child." B

"Point to the person you saw." C

Tests of hemisphere functioning confirm that the right hemisphere is superior at part-to-whole relations. Robert Nebes (1972) asked split-brain patients to match arcs of circles to completed circles, a task that requires the ability to generalize from a segment to the whole. The right hemisphere was superior in doing this.

In a recent study, Gazzaniga, Kutas, Van Petten, and Fendrich (1989) asked a partial commissurotomy (split-brain) patient to judge whether pairs of words rhymed. They presented one word in each pair to her left visual field and the other to her right visual field. The two words in each pair either sounded and looked alike, sounded alike but looked different, sounded different but looked alike, or both sounded and looked different. She was able to perform the rhyming judgment significantly better than chance when the words both looked and sounded alike, but not in the other three conditions. Thus, there are differences in specificity of the information carried by groups of callosal fibers.

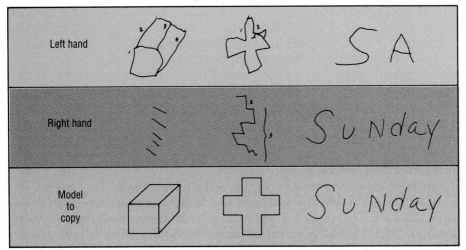

FIGURE 3-17
The Role of the Hemispheres in Controlling Writing and Drawing

After split-brain surgery, the right hand, which is controlled by the left hemisphere of the cortex, cannot integrate the elements of a drawing as well as the left hand, which is controlled by the right hemisphere, the one that specializes in dealing with spatial relationships and other visual information.
(Bogen, 1969)

Kutas, Hillyard, and Gazzaniga (1988) studied the ability of five commissurotomized patients to appreciate semantic anomalies presented to their right and left hemispheres. In all cases, the patients heard sentence fragments that ended either with congruous or incongruous words briefly flashed to the left visual field, to the right visual field, or to both fields simultaneously. All five could indicate by pointing with greater-than-chance accuracy whether the terminal word of a sentence made sense—that is, appropriate for the context—or was nonsensical. This was true regardless of the hemisphere.

WORKINGS OF THE NORMAL BRAIN

As startling as the split-brain studies are, an important question remains. How do the hemispheres operate in *normal* people doing *normal* things? One way to find out what an intact brain is doing is to measure electrical activity in the brain through an electroencephalograph, or an EEG. Brain activity produces various kinds of electrical waves on the scalp: alpha wave activity indicates an awake brain on ''idle,'' and beta waves indicate an awake brain actively processing information.

In one study (Galin & Ornstein, 1972) the right hemisphere showed more alpha activity than the left while the subject was writing a letter, and the left hemisphere showed more beta activity. While arranging blocks, the left hemisphere showed more alpha than the right and the right hemisphere showed beta waves. When people write, they turn off the right side of the brain. While arranging blocks in space they turn off the left hemisphere (Davidson, 1989).

The primary component of hemispheric specialization is *not* the *type* of information processed (words and pictures versus sounds and shapes); rather, it is *how* the brain processes the information. One study compared subjects' brain activity while reading technical passages and folk tales. There was no change in the level of activity in the left hemisphere between the technical material and the folk tales. However, the right hemisphere activated while the subjects read

111

the folk stories, but it did not while they read the technical material (Ornstein, Herron, Johnstone, & Swencionis, 1979). Technical material is almost exclusively logical. Stories, on the other hand, are simultaneous; many things happen at once. The sense of a story emerges through style, plot, images, and feelings. Thus, it appears that language *in the form of stories* can stimulate activity of the right hemisphere.

Another experiment recorded brain activity while subjects mentally rotated objects in space. This normally involves the right hemisphere. When asked to do the task analytically, by counting the boxes, subjects by and large switched over to their left hemisphere (Ornstein & Swencionis, 1985). Thus, people can use their hemispheres at will.

So there are two systems at the top of the human brain. They govern our abilities to create, in language and in art, and to discover new connections in the world. These two hemispheres appeared in our ancestors as *specialized systems* sometime during the long period of human evolution. There is evidence for them at least 100,000 years ago and probably earlier. They are the most distinctively human part of the brain (Ornstein, Thompson, & Macaulay, 1984).

HOW THE BRAIN "MINDS" THE BODY

The most recently developed areas of the brain contain the rational abilities that we human beings prize and develop. But the brain as a whole is *not* primarily designed for thinking. Those attributes we consider most human—language, perception, and intelligence—represent only a *small fraction* of the brain's functions. What the brain does is to regulate or "mind" the body. It controls temperature, blood flow, and digestion. It monitors every sensation, each breath and heartbeat, every movement, every blink and swallow. It directs movement: walk this way, take the hand off the stove, lift the arm to catch the ball, smile.

RUNNING THE BODY

The brain translates several worlds: the internal molecules, the organs, the individual, other people, and more. The brain has separate and independent modular systems, which maintain cellular, organ, and individual health. If you think about the brain this way, its evolution and functions become clearer. Its

FIGURE 3-18
The Brain's Response to the Unexpected

The left hemisphere of the brain responds to an inappropriate word inserted at the end of an otherwise ordinary sentence by registering a marked change in its pattern of electrical activity.
(Kulas & Hillyard, 1980)

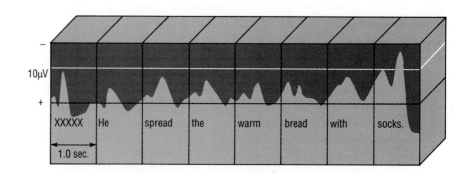

10μV

XXXXX He spread the warm bread with socks.

1.0 sec.

CHAPTER 3 / THE BRAIN AND THE NERVOUS SYSTEM

basic job is health and running the body. The brain directs all voluntary and involuntary movements. It communicates with the body via the glands of the *endocrine system* and three interconnected systems of nerves. They are the *central nervous system (CNS)*, the *peripheral nervous system (PNS)*, and the *autonomic nervous system (ANS)*, which is a portion of the PNS. The brain and spinal cord comprise the CNS.

The brain is the control center of all the neural networks. The spinal cord is the central trunk through which all neural communications pass on the way to the brain. The somatic PNS is a two-way communication system between the brain and muscles for controlling *voluntary* movements. *Involuntary* movements, such as heart rate, digestion, blood flow, and heat regulation, are regulated by the autonomic PNS and the glands of the endocrine system.

The brain responds to changes in the external and internal worlds. Through the senses the brain receives information about occurrences in the outside world. The **endocrine system** controls the internal state of the body, the blood sugar level, and pain.

Changes in stimuli are what the brain perceives. The change may be as subtle as a slight variation in air pressure or as jarring as a strange and unexpected statement. Read the sentence, "He spread the warm bread with jam." A record of the electrical activity of the brain as someone reads this sentence shows little disruption. Now read the sentence, "He spread the warm bread with socks." Brain activity changes significantly at the last word (Figure 3-18), which is an indication of surprise (Kutas & Hillyard, 1980).

As a health system, the brain is the major organ of adaptation. It tells the body what to do based on its information of the changing state of the world. The ability to respond quickly to change and to be flexible in responding is the primary ingredient of adaptability. Consider what happens when a frog is confronted by a fallen tree. The frog has a very specialized sensory system and brain. It probably will not even notice the tree unless it runs into it. A human, however, will see the fallen tree for all the possibilities it provides: he or she can cut it, play seesaw on it, make tables out of it, even make paper for this book. This greater flexibility of action is in part due to a larger brain.

THE LANGUAGE OF THE BRAIN

Whether an activity is simple or complex, voluntary or involuntary, the brain has only *one* way of communicating: by electrical and chemical codes. This language of the brain is the action of very simple signals sent at varying rates among billions of neurons. It is the *pattern of firing* of the neurons in the brain that encodes all experience—if we can learn to read the encryptions.

NEURONS

Neurons, the nerve cells that are the major constituent of the brain, are the most remarkable of all biological cells (Figure 3-19). They are the building blocks that make up the rooms of the brain. The nucleus of the neuron is the **cell body.** It contains the biochemical apparatus for powering the electrical charge and for

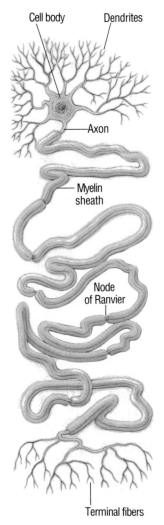

FIGURE 3-19
The Parts of Neuron

113

FIGURE 3-20
The Dendrites of a
Single Neuron

This highly magnified
photograph shows the axons
and branching dendrites
through which the neuron can
receive information from many
other neurons.

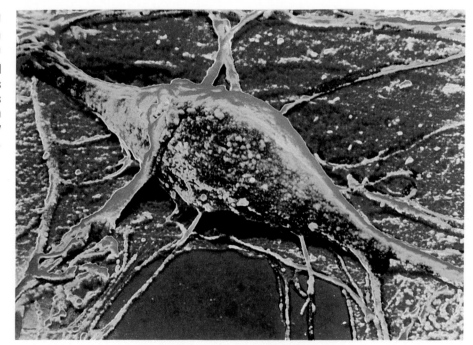

maintaining the life of the cell. The **axon** extends outward from the cell body (Figure 3-19). The axon is the transmitter end of the neuron; signals sent from the neuron exit through the axon. The **dendrites,** which look like the branches of a tree (Figure 3-20), are the receiving end of the neuron. They receive information from the axons of other neurons. Because of the extensive branching of the dendrites, one neuron is able to communicate with thousands of other neurons.

THE NEURAL IMPULSE: ACTION POTENTIAL

If we could see the brain working, we would see millions of miniature explosions going on and off each instant. Neurons fire, then stop, and then fire their electrical charges again and again. In the pattern and composition of those explosions lie our thought and individuality. An enormous amount of research over the past few years has begun to uncover the secrets of this neural code.

Minute quantities of chemical transmitter molecules are the ultimate unit of action of the nervous system. Different concentrations of these various *neurotransmitters* in the brain may well determine activity level, temperament, and mood. They also seem to influence the healing systems of the brain.

Earlier neuroscientists thought there were only a very few such chemicals, perhaps three or four. It now appears there may be hundreds of different chemical messenger molecules. These neurotransmitters are the "words" with which the brain uses to communicate. These transmitters, including acetylcholine, norepinephrine, serotonin, dopamine, and endorphins, govern excitability, sleep and dreams, hallucinations, pain regulation, mood, and thought. In short, these chemicals underlie all the different brain functions.

If we were to look inside a neuron itself, we would see scores of chemicals being released, going from cell to cell and back again. The brain communicates with and controls the body through this continuous flow of chemical messages. *Neurotransmitter* molecules convey messages between cells, and *neurohormones* produced and secreted by the brain carry messages through the bloodstream to distant target organs. In this sense each nerve cell and the brain itself is like an internal pharmacy. It dispenses a stream of powerful drugs to influence and control moods, thoughts, and bodily functions (Thompson, 1986).

Communication between neurons occurs by **neurotransmission,** which is accomplished through the release of chemical molecules, called **neurotransmitters.** Like a battery, a neuron at rest has an electrical charge called the *resting potential.* When the neuron is adequately stimulated by another neuron, it fires. The firing of the neuron releases its stored energy.

The neural impulse of a firing neuron is the **action potential.** The action potential sweeps down the axon. Once it fires, the neuron is temporarily depleted of energy and does not immediately fire again. In the period of time between firings, called the *absolute refractory period,* firing is possible only if the neuron receives greater than normal stimulus. These refractory periods are not long; they are measured in thousandths of a second.

MYELIN SHEATH   The axons of many neurons are coated with a fatty substance called the **myelin sheath.** This sheath begins to develop in infancy and contributes to the weight added to the brain after birth. It *insulates* the neuron and prevents loss of electrical potential; it *isolates* the neuron, preventing it from communicating randomly with other neurons; and it *accelerates neurotransmission.*

NEUROTRANSMISSION   The action potential inside a neuron is *electrical,* but the transmission of the neural impulse from one neuron to the next is *chemical.* Between the axon of one neuron and the dendrite of the next is a tiny space called the **synapse** (Greek for "connection"). The neuron sending the information is the *presynaptic* neuron. The neuron receiving the chemical message is the *postsynaptic* neuron (Figure 3-21). A neuron transmits its signal to the next

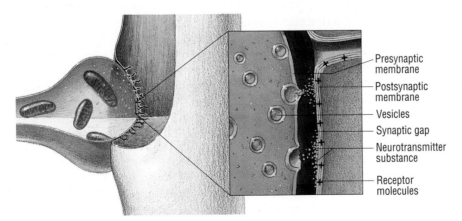

Presynaptic membrane
Postsynaptic membrane
Vesicles
Synaptic gap
Neurotransmitter substance
Receptor molecules

FIGURE 3-21
Neurotransmission

The presynaptic neuron meet at a tiny gap called the synapse across which the transmitter chemicals "jump" to transmit their signals.
(Gaudin & Jones, 1989)

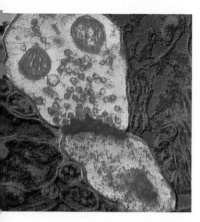

A micrograph of a synapse in the cerebral cortex.

neuron at the synapse between the two. The transmitter chemicals are stored in pouches, called *synaptic vesicles,* at the terminal of the axon. When the action potential arrives at the synapse, it triggers the release of some of the neurotransmitters into the synaptic opening, called the *synaptic cleft.* The transmitters cross the cleft and either *stimulate* or *inhibit* the firing of the postsynaptic neuron. After the transmission the whole process is deactivated (the refractory period). Some transmitters may break down, and others return to the axon of the presynaptic neuron; the latter process is called *re-uptake.*

NEUROTRANSMITTERS

The brain probably has hundreds of different neurotransmitters—researchers discover new ones almost monthly. The chemical compound **acetylcholine (ACh)** is one of the major transmitters in the nervous system. It relates to the arousal of the organism and is most concentrated in the brain during sleep. ACh conveys information from the brain to the muscles. The Amazon Indians knew the results, though not the mechanism, of interfering with neurotransmission when they dipped their arrows in the poison curare. Curare is fatal because it blocks ACh transmission, thereby paralyzing the victim. Such a victim will die quickly without some assistance in breathing.

Individual neurotransmitters cluster into different chemical pathways. These networks connect parts of the brain in complex mosaics unimagined even a few years ago. The following pathways are especially noteworthy:

NOREPINEPHRINE **Norepinephrine** (formerly called adrenaline) is important in the coding of memory and in the reward system of the brain. This is a group of structures that are activated in pleasurable moments. The pathway connects the outer brain stem to the cortex. Norepinephrine exists outside the brain in the autonomic nervous system.

DOPAMINE The **dopamine** pathway connects the limbic system to the cortex. It also participates in the brain's reward system and in the control of motor activity. Parkinson's disease, in which the sufferer exhibits severe motor tremors, is caused by a lack of dopamine and can be aided by administration of the drug L-dopa, transformed by the brain into dopamine (Figure 3-22).

SEROTONIN The **serotonin** pathways are widespread in the brain. They connect the brain stem and the reticular activating system to the cortex and to the limbic system at the hypothalamus and hippocampus. Serotonin controls sleep and many activities associated with sleep. Loss of serotonin causes insomnia.

The drug LSD seems to affect the serotonin system by blocking the firing of serotonin neurons. Because hallucinations are common in LSD "trips," serotonin may be involved in hallucinations and even in psychosis. Since serotonin inhibits neural firing, blocking its transmission speeds up sensory transmission. The great increase in neuronal activity from the LSD thereby distorts the normal mode of perception.

MOOD AND NEUROTRANSMITTERS

People have long believed that internal substances affect mood, disposition, and even personality. The ancient Greeks mistakenly believed that there were

CHAPTER 3 / THE BRAIN AND THE NERVOUS SYSTEM

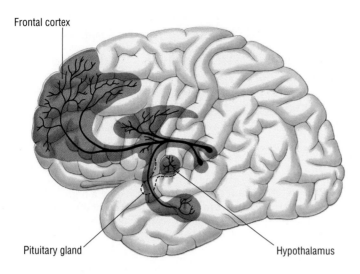

Frontal cortex

Pituitary gland

Hypothalamus

FIGURE 3-22
**Dopamine Pathways in
the Brain**

specific body *humors* that determined mood. A characteristically angry person was thought to have an excess of *bile,* and a calm one too much *phlegm;* hence, the descriptions "bilious" and "phlegmatic." Perhaps different concentrations of various neurotransmitters may affect temperament and mood. Many of the transmitters are involved in excitability, sleep and dreams, and hallucinations.

THE BRAIN'S NEURAL AND CHEMICAL SYSTEMS

The complexities of the neural and chemical organization of the brain and its four different levels of organization all serve one master: the body. The brain activity creates mental and physical action: plans and ideas as well as walking, turning, dancing, or following an object with the eyes. The brain, through its neural and chemical connections, monitors activity in every cell in the body. It communicates with and controls the body via two kinds of systems: the nervous system and the neuroendocrine system (Figure 3-23).

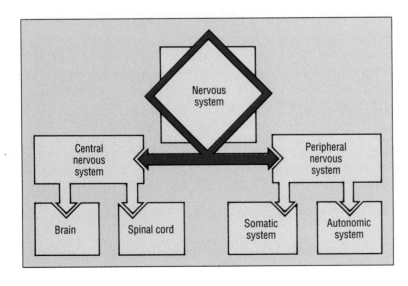

FIGURE 3-23
**Subdivisions of the
Human Nervous System**

The brain is precious tissue and is specially protected from the outside world. The skull provides a strong barrier against blows, but there are also internal barriers to guard the brain. A special network of cells called the *blood-brain barrier* keeps toxins in the blood from reaching the brain. Because of such protections, scientists had thought that the inner workings of the brain were almost completely isolated from the state of the body or the external world.

This view is now challenged. Some recent experiments have found striking short-term changes in brain chemistry associated with

diet. In an early study, eating substances rich in choline increased ACh throughout the brain. This is true particularly in the brain stem and cerebral cortex (Wurtman & Wurtman, 1984). Choline is present in egg yolks (1.7 percent by weight), meat (0.6 percent), and in

lesser amounts in fish, cereal, and legumes.

Whether specific diets can help learning and memory is far from proven, but research may show that this is possible. Other foods also have specific effects on the workings of the brain. A high carbohydrate diet increases serotonin levels (Wurtman & Wurtman, 1984). Tryptophan, a neurotransmitter active in sleep, is also increased by a high carbohydrate intake. The brain seems much more responsive to its internal environment than has been thought, even to the short-term environment of the last meal.

THE NERVOUS SYSTEMS

The nervous systems that link the brain to the body are the central nervous system and the peripheral nervous system.

CENTRAL NERVOUS SYSTEM   The brain and spinal cord together make up the **central nervous system (CNS).** The *spinal cord* extends from the base of the brain to the base of the spine. It is the central trunk of the nervous system, delivering both the brain's commands to the body and the body's messages to the brain.

Reflexes that protect the body from damage are commanded from the spinal cord. A **reflex** is an immediate, inborn response. Place your hand on a hot stove and you will immediately withdraw it, literally without thinking. The spinal cord handles such emergencies without involving the brain. These are the only movements that take place without the brain.

The spinal cord contains all the basic elements of the nervous systems. There are three types of neurons in the spinal cord:

1. **Afferent neurons** bring information to the brain from the sensory system.
2. **Efferent neurons** take messages from the brain and activate muscles and glands.
3. **Interneurons** connect the afferent and efferent neurons.

Encased in the vertebrae, the spinal cord is further protected by the spinal fluid, which acts as a shock absorber. The spinal cord is subject to thousands of shocks during the course of a day. As a result, the average person is a half inch shorter at night than in the morning.

PERIPHERAL NERVOUS SYSTEM   Commands to the muscles move through the **peripheral nervous system (PNS).** Nerves flow from the spinal cord into the muscles and organs of the body. The PNS gathers information about body states, muscle and limb position, and the internal states of organs, and if it determines something is awry, it takes action.

The vast network of nerves in the PNS (Figure 3-24) ultimately reaches every organ and muscle of the body. The PNS is divided into two parts: the somatic and autonomic. The **somatic nervous system (SNS)** controls the voluntary movements of the body, such as reaching for a glass or picking up a pencil. These movements begin in the sensory motor area of the brain. *Afferent* nerves convey information about the skin, sensory organs, muscles, and joints to the brain, and efferent nerves bring instructions from the brain to the muscles.

The **autonomic nervous system (ANS)** is primarily responsible for running the automatic processes of the body (Figure 3-25). The heart beats about 70 times per minute without us consciously instructing it to beat. The kidneys purify the blood without us telling them to. The liver and gastrointestinal tract

FIGURE 3-24
The Network of Nerves in the Peripheral Nervous System

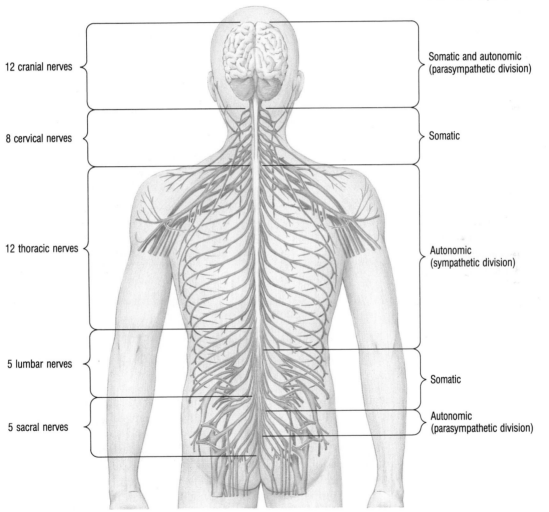

12 cranial nerves

8 cervical nerves

12 thoracic nerves

5 lumbar nerves

5 sacral nerves

Somatic and autonomic (parasympathetic division)

Somatic

Autonomic (sympathetic division)

Somatic

Autonomic (parasympathetic division)

THE BRAIN'S NEURAL AND CHEMICAL SYSTEMS

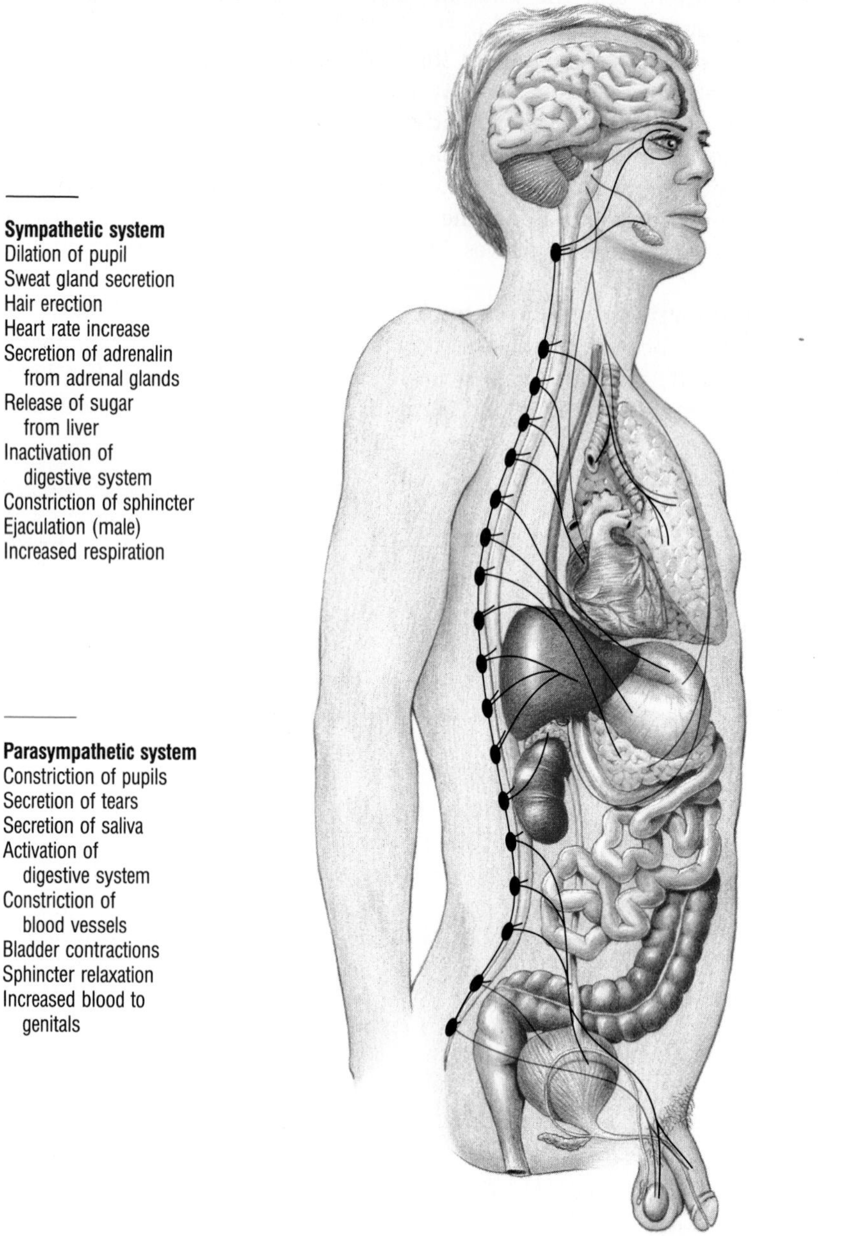

Sympathetic system
Dilation of pupil
Sweat gland secretion
Hair erection
Heart rate increase
Secretion of adrenalin
    from adrenal glands
Release of sugar
    from liver
Inactivation of
    digestive system
Constriction of sphincter
Ejaculation (male)
Increased respiration

Parasympathetic system
Constriction of pupils
Secretion of tears
Secretion of saliva
Activation of
    digestive system
Constriction of
    blood vessels
Bladder contractions
Sphincter relaxation
Increased blood to
    genitals

FIGURE 3-25
Autonomic Nervous
System

This simplified diagram shows
the different functions of the
two systems of the
autonomic nervous system:
the sympathetic system
(black lines) and the
parasympathetic system (red
lines).

also work outside conscious control. The ANS is largely under the control of the limbic system (usually without the involvement of the cortex). It regulates emotional reactions, such as crying, sweating, and stomach pains.

The ANS divides into two systems. The **sympathetic system** prepares the internal organs for emergencies, when there are extra demands on the body. It operates in sympathy with the emotions, like an accelerator, telling the body to go. Signs of sympathetic activation include sweating and other symptoms of

CHAPTER 3 / THE BRAIN AND THE NERVOUS SYSTEM

Heroin produces exultation; LSD, even in minute quantities, can produce hallucinations. How does this happen? We are born with certain locks within our nervous system. Drugs such as heroin are the keys that open these locks; that is why they are so powerful.

Specific neurotransmitters have many different effects on their cells, but the cells can exert these effects only when their messenger molecules (or drugs that mimic the messenger molecules) combine with them. If the chemical molecule fits, the receptor will attach it and be triggered into action. This is the reason why very tiny amounts of many drugs have such powerful effects on the brain and mind. Their shapes resemble the shapes of normal synaptic transmitter chemicals. The similar shapes fool the receptors into believing that they are receiving their normal messenger molecules (Figure 3-26). The nature of this relation-

LOCK AND KEY: ARCHITECTURE OF MOLECULES

ship has been discovered only in the past few decades. It is fundamental to our research into how the brain works. It allows scientists to understand how drugs affect the brain and how psychological disorders can be treated chemically.

On the surfaces of cell membranes are hundreds, perhaps thousands, of different types of molecular structures called *receptors*. Each type of receptor has a characteristic three-dimensional shape and, like a lock, can only be opened or activated by a chemical key. The *shape* of the drug or the neurotransmitter molecule is the key. It fits a receptor whose shape matches it, as a key fits into a lock.

This lock-and-key relationship describes how the chemical messages of the body connect with their target cells. The messenger molecules move through the bloodstream or across synapses until they fit the receptors designed for them. Once the receptor activates, the cell is either stimulated or inhibited. Drugs stimulate body processes because they mimic the shape of naturally existing substances in the body. Every neurotransmitter and hormone molecule has a specific shape that can fit only specific receptors.

Many mental disorders, such as schizophrenia, may be caused by alterations in neurotransmission. Many psychoactive drugs, such as cocaine, work because they affect the process of neurotransmission. Cocaine may prevent reuptake, so that the firing of the neurons involved *does not cease*. This seems to be how cocaine functions as a stimulant.

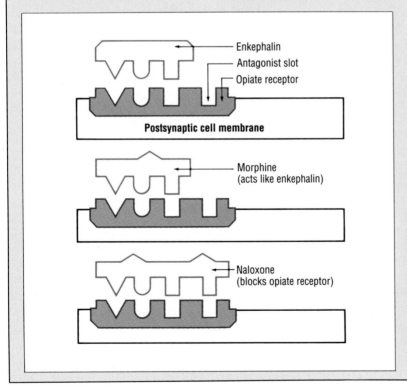

FIGURE 3-26
Opiate Receptors in the Brain

The shapes of special molecules in the brain allow them to act as receptors to natural opiates produced by the brain (enkephalin, top); to opiate drugs made from the poppy plants (morphine, middle); and to a drug antagonistic to morphine but having the same basic shape (naloxone, bottom).
(Ornstein, Thompson, & Macaulay, 1984)

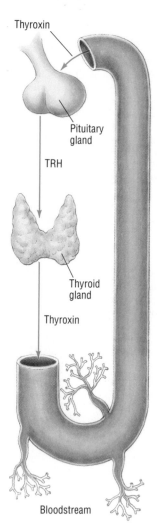

Thyroxin

Pituitary
gland

TRH

Thyroid
gland

Thyroxin

Bloodstream

FIGURE 3-27
Hormone Regulation

This schematic drawing
exemplifies the feedback
process that regulates
hormone production. The level
of thyroxin in the blood may
trigger the pituitary to
produce thyroid-releasing
hormon (TRH); this signals
the thyroid to produce
thyroxin, thereby raising the
level of that hormone in the
blood, which on reaching the
pituitary, informs it that TRH
production can be reduced.

physical arousal. The sympathetic nervous system is commonly activated by unusual circumstances, such as emergencies, ecstasy, or excitement (Williams, 1989).

The **parasympathetic system** is more conservative. It acts like a brake on the sympathetic system and returns the body to normal after an emergency. Typically, when an exciting event has passed, the parasympathetic system actively slows heart rate and deactivates internal organs (Williams, 1989).

The two forms of signals, "go" and "slow down," are carried by different nerve circuits. The messages move via different neurotransmitters. Norepinephrine carries the sympathetic message, ACh the parasympathetic message. The sympathetic neurons are centralized in the brain, acting on their target from a distance. The parasympathetic system is decentralized; each ganglion (collection of neurons) is located near the organ it serves.

THE CHEMICAL SYSTEM

Another way the brain controls the body is via the **neuroendocrine system,** which comprises the ANS and the endocrine glands. Think about the brain this way: each neuron is like a little gland, and the brain acts like an organ of secretion. The understanding of this final level of the brain's operations has come about only since the 1960s. It will provide the key to the ultimate workings of the brain.

HORMONES AND THE PITUITARY   The **pituitary** is the control gland of the endocrine system. It lies below the hypothalamus in the limbic system of the brain (Figure 3-4). Many important behaviors, such as sex, are under its direct control. The pituitary also controls many other glands, such as the adrenal and thyroid glands, and it synthesizes a wide variety of hormones.

A **hormone** is a chemical messenger molecule secreted by specialized cells called *neurosecretory cells.* Hormones are larger molecules than neurotransmitters. Molecules of hormones migrate within the bloodstream to locations where they stimulate production of other hormones. Neuroendocrine communication operates on the lock-and-key principle (see box). A hormone secreted into the bloodstream passes many organs until it fits into its intended receptor. This receptor identifies itself by its shape.

Hormone regulation works through feedback. To stimulate the thyroid gland, the pituitary produces *thyroid-releasing hormone* or TRH. When the thyroid receives TRH, it produces its own hormone, *thyroxin,* which it releases into the bloodstream. Some thyroxin reaches the pituitary, which then measures the amount of the hormone and either increases or decreases production of TRH (Figure 3-27). Similar feedback processes operate for other hormones.

ADRENAL GLANDS   The adrenal glands start up in emergency situations. They have two parts: the outer *adrenal cortex* and the inner *adrenal medulla.* When activated by the ANS, the adrenal medulla secretes epinephrine and norepinephrine. Both of these hormones stimulate the cardiovascular (heart-lung) system. Adrenal gland activity is coordinated with the ANS during emergency situations. If there is injury to the body, adrenal cortisol, an antinflammatory agent, travels to the site of the injury.

THE INDIVIDUAL BRAIN

People's brains are as different as their noses. The brain can respond and grow depending on different experiences. The environment determines the languages that one speaks, and early experience can affect the brain as well. There are even temporary reactions caused by changes in the local environment, such as nutrition and air quality.

BRAIN GROWTH WITH EXPERIENCE

Environmental conditions play a greater role in the brain development of human beings than in any other animal. Psychologists had believed that at birth the neurons begin to make connections, and these connections increase as we age and acquire experience. The opposite is actually the case (Greenough, 1975). There are many *more* connections in the brain of an infant than in an elderly adult. Development seems to be a matter of pruning original connections rather than making new ones. Consider this about infant babbling. In the first months of life, a baby utters almost *every sound of every known language* (Miller, 1951) and later on *loses* the ability to make sounds that are not in the language he or she has learned to speak. There is thus a universe of potential sound patterns available to us at birth, but we *learn* only a few of them. Similarly, the brain may be set up at birth to do a myriad of different things, but we only get around to doing a few of them.

Severe malnutrition may cause inadequate brain development, a smaller brain than normal, and severe mental retardation (Livingston, Callaway, MacGregor, Fischer, & Hastings, 1975). Rats deprived of normal food show distortions in brain structure and even shrinkage of certain brain structures. The illustration at the top of Figure 3-28 shows a brain cell from an undernourished rat.

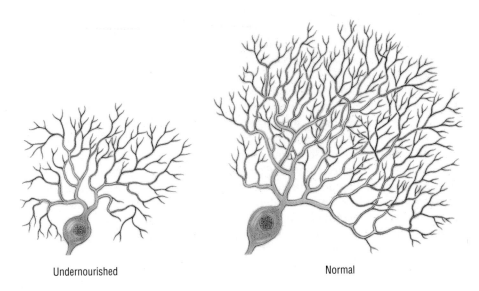

Undernourished

Normal

**FIGURE 3-28
Malnutrition and the Brain**

A brain cell from an undernourished rat is clearly less developed, with fewer and smaller dendrites.
(McConnell & Berry, 1978)

123

The brain, like a muscle, grows in response to certain experiences: the neurons actually become larger. Rats brought up in an enriched environment have a larger cortex than those brought up in a deprived one. This developmental process goes on as long as the organism lives and is active. Brain growth can be increased in *old* rats who are stimulated for as little as one week (Connor & Diamond, 1982). The brain is *modifiable,* and it grows with experience and stimulation.

THE BRAIN OF THE LEFT-HANDER

In most right-handed people, language and other sequential abilities are controlled by the left hemisphere. Spatial abilities and simultaneous thinking reside primarily in the right hemisphere. In left-handed people, however, brain organization is often different (Herron, 1980).

There are three types of hemispheric organization in left-handers: (1) those whose cortical organization is similar to right-handers, (2) those whose organization is reversed, and (3) those who have language and spatial abilities in both hemispheres. EEG studies of left-handers show all three patterns of hemisphere organization in different individuals (Galin, Ornstein, Herron, & Johnstone, 1982).

Left-handers are a distinct minority; about 10 percent of the population is left-handed. They face some difficulty living in a right-handed world. For example, it is sometimes difficult for them to write alphabet languages because these were designed by and for right-handers. Some left-handers write in a hooked position, while others write in the same way as right-handers.

There is controversy about whether being left-handed affects intellectual abilities. A great percentage of left-handers have *mixed dominance*—that is both sides of their brain control language. Some researchers argue that spatial ability is interfered with. However, most investigators who have studied many subjects show equivocal results (Miller, 1971). What is less equivocal is the cultural bias against things of the left. The word *gauche* (meaning "awkward") is the French word for left. The word *sinister* comes from the Latin for left *(sinistra).*

Whether brain differences manifest themselves as personality or intellectual traits is unknown, but the existence of strong brain differences is certain. However, some left-handedness may result from birth trauma, when the brain may be damaged in delivery, upsetting a "natural" right-hander. When this happens there *can* be damage. Segal (1989) studied the relationship of handedness and IQ and found that left-handedness combined with low birth weight can result in lower IQ. And there may be more difficulties for lefties.

Recently Coren (1989) turned up some intriguing evidence about left-handedness, accident-related injury risk, and longevity. He compared self-reported injuries among left-handed and right-handed people in a survey of 1,896 college students in British Columbia, Canada. Left-handers were more likely to report having an injury requiring medical attention during the last two years—especially for left-handed males when driving motor vehicles. And more intriguing is that there are fewer and fewer left-handers as the years go by. Coren has looked at these data and concludes that left-handers have shorter lives (Coren et al., 1989).

Why should this be so? First, there is the problem of being left-handed in a right-handed world. Signs and controls on machinery are designed for righties.

The shift lever on the car falls naturally to the right hand, for instance, not the left. Industrial tools are designed for righties. So lefties might have more accidents. However, being left-handed may also be a result of birth trauma, which may well affect other systems and interfere with longevity.

The research of others shows different brain organizations in left-handers, in control of language, in movement, and in other areas (Galin, et al., 1982). It may well be that this different orientation disorganizes many immune and cardiac functions, perhaps leading to more susceptibility to disease.

THE CHANGING BRAIN

The brain continuously changes in response to a changing environment. Some alterations are in response to temporary, short-term conditions, while some are long-range, permanent conditions.

SHORT-TERM CHANGES

As we have seen, the concentration of neurotransmitters changes rapidly after a meal. A meal of eggs increases the available levels of ACh in the brain, whereas a meal rich in carbohydrates increases the brain's supply of serotonin (Wurtman & Wurtman, 1984). Neurotransmitters also respond to changes in the air. Hot, dry winds (such as the Santa Ana winds in Southern California) often precede outbreaks of violence, including suicide (Krueger, 1978). These "ill winds" contain a preponderance of positive ions. An *ion* is the electrical charge attached to a gaseous molecule. In contrast, air full of negatively charged ions has a refreshing and stimulating effect. Negative ions predominate around waterfalls, in clean mountain air, and at beaches but disappear in polluted urban centers or enclosed spaces. Ionization of the air has a direct effect on the serotonin system of the brain (Krueger, 1978) and the growth of the cortex. Rats raised in a negatively ionized atmosphere have a cortex 9 percent larger than those in a nonionized atmosphere (Diamond, 1980). Further, an increase in negative ionization seems to elevate mood (Krueger, 1978).

LONG-TERM ALTERATIONS

The brain also changes its chemistry and size in response to long-term conditions. It can often rearrange its organization to compensate for accidents. People with left hemisphere damage can learn to produce language using the right hemisphere, although this flexibility decreases with age. The right hemisphere takes over language functions in young children who have suffered severe damage to the left hemisphere (Kohn & Dennis, 1974). In deaf people, areas of the temporal cortex normally used for the processing of speech sounds are used instead for processing visual information (Neville, 1977).

When a person learns a second language, the brain's representation of language changes. In some people, when the second language is learned, the first language *may migrate from the left hemisphere to the right.* In others, the second language may occupy only the right hemisphere or may be represented in both (Albert & Obler, 1978).

The brain is continually changing and developing, responding to influences ranging from the language one hears in infancy to the meal just eaten. The brain has evolved to adapt to conditions in a changing world; our brains still change continuously to aid us in our adaptation to an unpredictable world.

SUMMARY

1. Brain processes underlie experiences. The brain regulates all body functions and controls our behavior. The structure of the brain reflects the evolutionary development of nervous systems from primitive vertebrates to human primates. The parts of the brain include the *brain stem,* the *limbic system,* and the *cerebral cortex.*

2. The oldest part of the brain is the *brain stem.* The *reticular activating system* (RAS) governs breathing and heart rate and alerts the cortex to arriving sensory information. Most sensory information is relayed through the *thalamus,* which classifies it. The *cerebellum,* developed in evolution to regulate movement, functions in humans to store learned responses.

3. In the *limbic system,* the *hypothalamus* and the *pituitary gland* maintain *homeostasis* in the body by regulating vital bodily functions. The *hippocampus* and *amygdala* direct emotional responses (feeding, fighting, fleeing, and sexual reproduction) and store memories of life experiences.

4. The *cerebral cortex* is the most recently developed part of the brain. It receives sensory information, analyzes it, makes decisions, and sends instructions to muscles and glands. The structure of the cortex includes *columns,* which act as data-processing centers, and *talent centers,* which have specialized abilities. The cortex has two hemispheres, each with four lobes. The *frontal lobes* are involved in planning,

decision-making, emotion, and personality. The *sensory and motor control* areas are located at the juncture of the frontal and parietal lobes. The *parietal lobes* analyze sensory input. The *temporal lobes* contribute to sound perception, memory, and language. The *occipital lobes* are called the *visual cortex* because they analyze visual information.

5. The *left and right cerebral hemispheres* are connected by the *corpus callosum*. When this connection is severed, the hemispheres function independently. EEG studies show that in normal people the left brain specializes in logical processes, the right in simultaneous comprehension.

6. The brain responds to changes in the external and internal worlds of an organism. It uses the senses to receive information about the outside world. It directs the responses of the body via the *endocrine glands*, the *central nervous system*, and the *autonomic nervous system*. The brain is the major organ of adaptation.

7. The brain uses *electrical and chemical codes* to send messages to the body. *Neurons* are the basic building blocks of the brain and nervous system. The transmitting end of a neuron is called the *axon*, and the receiving ends are called the *dendrites*. Communication between neurons occurs through *neurotransmission*. When one neuron is stimulated by another neuron, it *fires* and causes action potential. Neurons trigger other neurons to fire by means of chemicals called *neurotransmitters*. Neurotransmitters are stored in synaptic vesicles in the axon and released by action potentials across a gap called the *synapse* to stimulate the dendrites of other neurons.

8. The brain probably contains hundreds of neurotransmitters. *Acetylcholine* is associated with arousal and conveys information from the brain to the muscles. *Norepinephrine* is involved in memory and the reward system of the brain. It is also present in the autonomic nervous system. The *dopamine* pathways connect the limbic system to the cortex, participating in the reward system and motor control. *Serotonin* pathways connect the RAS to the cortex and the limbic system. Serotonin controls sleep and affects the transmission of sensory information.

9. The *central nervous system (CNS)* consists of the brain and the spinal cord. The spinal cord delivers the brain's commands to the body through *efferent neurons* and the body's messages to the brain through *afferent neurons*. The spinal cord is responsible for *reflex* actions. The *peripheral nervous system (PNS)* transmits information from the spinal cord to the organs and muscles. The two parts of the PNS are the *somatic nervous system*, which controls voluntary body movements, and the *autonomic nervous system (ANS)*, which regulates nonvoluntary body processes. The ANS is composed of the *sympathetic* and *parasympathetic systems*, which have complementary actions.

10. The *neuroendocrine system* helps the brain control the body. *Endocrine glands* secrete *hormones* that are designed to affect specific organs by means of their molecular shapes. The *pituitary gland* controls the other endocrine glands. The *adrenal glands* operate in emergencies to stimulate the cardiovascular system.

11. Environmental conditions affect the development of the human brain. The brain grows when exposed to learning experiences, even in mature organisms. Brains are as individual as people. Left-handed people have different brain organizations from right-handers. Some behavioral differences between the sexes originate with differences in brain organization.

12. The operation of the brain is affected by short-term and long-term conditions. In the short term, foods recently eaten and ions in the air affect neurotransmitter levels. In the long term, the organization of brain specialization can change to compensate for injury or even for learning a new language. The brain continuously changes to help us adapt to the changing world.

TERMS AND CONCEPTS

action potential
afferent neurons
amygdala
aphasia
autonomic nervous system (ANS)
axon
brain stem
cell body
central nervous system (CNS)
cerebellum
cerebral cortex
corpus callosum
dendrites
dopamine
efferent neurons
frontal lobes
hippocampus
homeostasis
hormones
interneurons
limbic system

myelin sheath
neuroendocrine system
neuron
neurotransmission
neurotransmitter
norepinephrine
occipital lobes
parasympathetic system
parietal lobes
peripheral nervous system (PNS)
pituitary gland
reflex
reticular activating system (RAS)
serotonin
somatic nervous system (SNS)
split brain
sympathetic system
synapse
temporal lobes
thalamus

SUGGESTIONS FOR FURTHER READING

The Behavioral and Brain Sciences. Quarterly.

It presents important research areas such as cortical function and intelligence and presents commentary from many scientists. Difficult, but gives a good view of the controversies in the field.

Ornstein, R., & Swencionis, C., eds. (1990). *The healing brain: A scientific reader.* New York: Guilford Press.

Papers by noted experts on how the brain operates in its mission to run the body.

Ornstein, R., Thompson, R., & Macaulay, D. (1985). *The amazing brain.* Boston: Houghton Mifflin.

Describes in drawings how the brain evolved and the functional architecture of the cortex. Amplifies material in the text.

Sacks, O. (1987). *The man who mistook his wife for a hat.* New York: Simon & Schuster.

A wonderfully written memoir of different patients' disorders.

Searle, J. (1984). *Minds, brains, and science.* Cambridge, MA: Harvard University Press.

An interesting, brief book which analyzes many of the developments and the follies of mind-brain relations from a philosopher's perspective.

Thompson, R. F. (1986). *The brain: an introduction to neuroscience.* New York: Freeman.

An excellent summary of the brain's inner workings.

4
GENETICS AND EVOLUTION

How do we become the person we are? The answers are quite complex, as you've already seen, but some of the ingredients are from our inheritance, which is the subject of this chapter. Each person is dealt a complex genetic hand at birth, a set of biological instructions for fabricating a human body and brain. There is an overt inheritance: specific physical traits, such as sex and eye color, set at conception and unaffected by environment or experience. And there is a more subtle inheritance: dispositions toward discrete traits, towards tallness, or to different diseases—such as diabetes or schizophrenia (a severe form of mental disturbance)—even certain interests and attitudes (Scarr & Weinberg, 1978).

You are your parents' donation to human evolution. You can probably see much of them in your looks and bearing. But the common human heritage is manifold: all of us develop a large brain, erect posture, color vision. But each human being is also one of a kind—at once like all others and yet like no other person who has ever lived. Human individuality is the subject of genetics, the science of heredity.

THE GENETIC CODE

FIGURE 4-1
Chromosomes during the Phases of Mitosis

The **gene** is the basic component of heredity in all living things. Genes are made of a substance called **DNA** (deoxyribonucleic acid), which is contained in the nucleus of every living cell. The DNA molecule is shaped like a long flexible

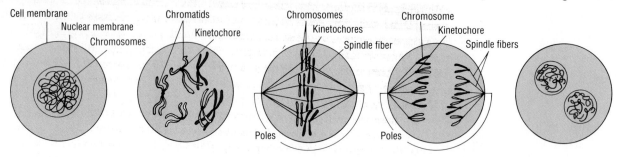

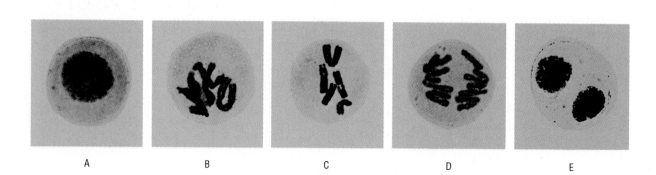

A   B   C   D   E

ladder twisted into a spiral. The rungs of the ladder contain the genetic information. They consist of four chemical substances: adenine, thymine, guanine, and cytosine. These chemicals are called **bases.** Each rung is actually made of two paired bases, going across from one side of the ladder to the other (Figure 4-2). The spiral ladder of DNA is more commonly known as the *double helix.*

Virtually every living thing gets its blueprint for growth and development from these bases. What differs between species and between individual organisms of a species is only the arrangement of the four bases along the double helix of the DNA molecule. The language of DNA is limited to three-letter "words." Starting at one end of a DNA ladder and only going up one side, if we count off the rungs in threes, we find that each three rungs spells one word of building instructions. Each word usually stands for 1 of 20 amino acids, the building blocks of proteins.

The groups of three bases, which we have been calling words, are more properly termed **codons.** The "code" that tells us which amino acid will be used for a given three-base codon is called the **genetic code.** It translates from one kind of chemical (DNA) into another (protein). DNA is the blueprint chemical; protein is the structural and functional chemical that actually makes up the physical body and allows it to perform its many functions, from digestion to reading. The order in which the bases appear along the double helix spells out for the organism exactly what structural and functional proteins to make, when to make them and where to put them. Thus, the fundamental difference between humans and turtles, at the molecular level, is only in the *pattern* of the four chemical substances within the DNA molecule.

Organisms grow by cell division, a process called **mitosis** (Figure 4-1). One cell divides into two, two into four, and so forth. In mitosis, the DNA spirals separate by splitting down the middle, separating the pairs of bases that formed the rungs, yet each new cell has the same genetic code as the original cell. That is because each half of the DNA spiral can replicate the other half.

In 1953 two molecular biologists at Cambridge University in England, Watson and Crick, clarified how this operates. On a DNA double strand, like the spiral ladder we have been describing, guanine and cytosine are always across from each other, forming a rung; and adenine is always connected with thymine (Figure 4-2). Thus the presence of one, such as adenine, is in itself an instruction: "thymine goes across from here." Each *single* strand has all the information needed to reproduce a complementary strand and complete a new double helix.

CHROMOSOMES

Genes are arranged on a chromosome like beads on a string. Human beings have 23 pairs of chromosomes, for a total of 46 chromosomes; one member of each pair of chromosomes comes from each parent. These chromosomes carry an individual's entire genetic program, so each human chromosome contains thousands of genes. Human beings have a total of about a million genes. Because all of the genes exist in the nucleus of every cell of the body, each cell contains the information necessary to produce all the other cells of the body.

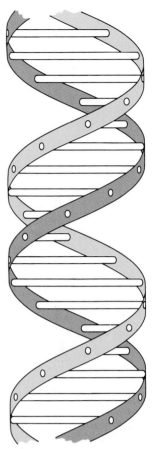

FIGURE 4-2
DNA Molecule

The rungs of the double-helix structure of the DNA molecule are formed by four different amines—adenine (A), guanine (G), thymine (T), and cytosine (C). The order in which these chemicals appear forms the genetic code.

THE GENETIC CODE

DOMINANT AND RECESSIVE GENES

Each parent has a pair of genes for eye color. When the mother's ovum or the father's sperm is formed, the pair of genes is split. Then a new pair can form when egg and sperm join in the conception of a child. The eye-color gene from the mother pairs up with the eye-color gene from the father. Now the child has her own set of eye-color genes. But a mother may donate a gene for brown eyes and a father a gene for blue eyes. Which gene will win out and be expressed in the child's appearance?

All the genes an individual carries are called his **genotype.** But not all genes in an individual are expressed. The portion of the genotype that is expressed is called the **phenotype.**

Gene selection operates on a dominant-recessive basis. When one dominant gene is present, the traits it governs appear in the person's physical makeup. In other words, dominant genes are always expressed. In the case of the eye-color gene, the child's eyes will be brown because genes for brown eyes are dominant over those for blue. However, even though only the gene for brown eyes is expressed, the gene for blue eye color is still part of the child's genetic makeup. Later, when the child grows up and becomes a parent, her own child could have blue eyes if her mate also contributes a blue-eye gene. A recessive trait, such as blue eyes, will normally be expressed only if both parents contribute the recessive gene.

SEX

An important responsibility of chromosomes is sex. The chromosome combination of pair 23 (Figure 4-3) determines an individual's sex. The sex chromosomes have two different shapes: one looks like an X, the other like a Y. A female has two X chromosomes in pair 23, whereas a male has one X and one Y chromosome. Thus, because he can contribute either kind of chromosome, the sex of a child is always determined by the father's sperm: if he contributes the X chromosome, the child will be a girl; if he contributes the Y chromosome, the child will be a boy.

One might assume, therefore, that the chance of conceiving a male or female is 50–50, but it is not so. For every 100 females conceived, 140 males are

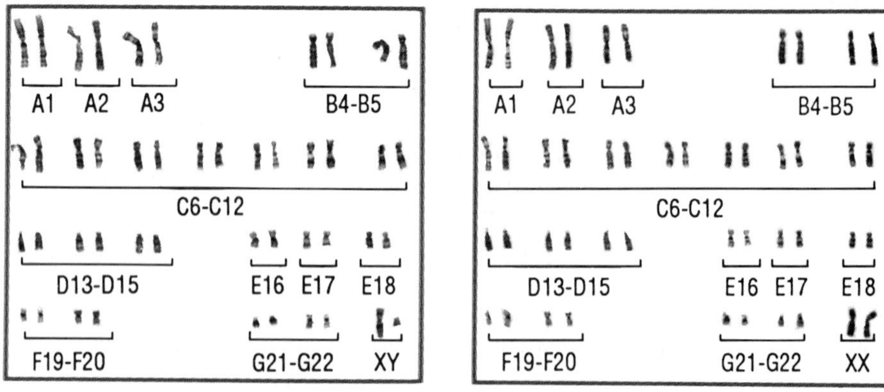

FIGURE 4-3
The 23 Pairs of Human Chromosomes

The 23rd pair, XX (right) shows that individual to be a female, while the one on the left has an XY 23rd pair, indicating those are the chromosomes of a male.

TABLE 4-1
Approximate Sex Ratio for the Human Species

Conception	120 to 150 males for every 100 females
Birth	105 males for every 100 females
Age 15	100 males for every 100 females
Age 50	90 males for every 100 females
Age 60	70 males for every 100 females
Age 70	60 males for every 100 females
Age 80	50 males for every 100 females
Age 100	20 males for every 100 females

SOURCE: Berger, 1980, as adapted from McMillen, 1979; Nagle, 1979.

conceived. Sperm carrying Y chromosomes may be more mobile than those carrying X chromosomes and so may reach the egg first.

Remember that males are more "expendable". They are more fragile too: only 105 boys are born for every 100 girls. The XY (male) unit is more frail than the XX unit in the womb. This fragility continues: more males than females die at every age level in infancy, childhood, and adulthood until there are so few males left that the death rate is higher for females. Thus, women typically live longer than men, and there are more females in the population than males (Singer & Hilgard, 1978). See Table 4-1.

ABNORMAL CHROMOSOMES AND BIRTH DEFECTS

Sometimes a mistake occurs in the process of making the parents' sperm or eggs. A chromosome can be lost, broken, or turned around, or an extra one can be added. If a chromosome is lost at the first cell division—that is, one parent donates only 22, not 23 chromosomes—the fertilized egg almost never develops. If an extra chromosome is donated, the egg generally develops with tragic results. Note in Figure 4-4 that pair 21 contains an extra chromosome. If a child with three chromosomes (a trisome) in pair 21 is born, that individual will have Down's syndrome: he or she will be very short, have a malformed heart, and be severely mentally retarded. Down's syndrome is quite a common birth defect; it occurs in one out of every 600 live births.

In pair 23, the sex chromosomes, another trisome can occur. If a sperm containing both X and Y chromosomes fertilizes the ovum, the result will be a child with two X chromosomes and one Y chromosome: a male child with very feminine characteristics (enlarged breasts, more feminine body contours). In a few recent Olympic contests, the Soviets entered males with this abnormal chromosome composition in women's events. Their performances were unusual for women and so were their genes!

MUTATIONS

Generations can differ in characteristics in two ways: through the sexual recombinations that occur when each parent donates half of his or her

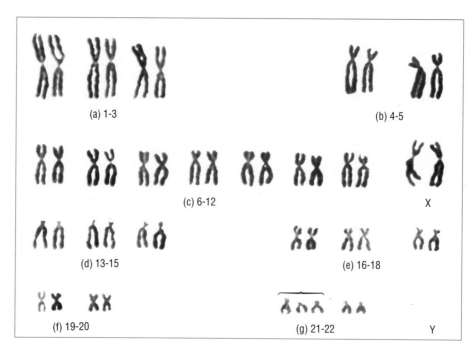

**FIGURE 4-4
Chromosomal
Abnormality in Down's
Syndrome**

The extra chromosome in pair 21, called trisomy 21, is responsible for this relatively common birth defect.

(a) 1-3 (b) 4-5 (c) 6-12 X (d) 13-15 (e) 16-18 (f) 19-20 (g) 21-22 Y

chromosomes and through mutations. A **mutation** is a spontaneous change in the structure of one or more genes. Mutations, then, are accidents in the normal functioning of genetic replication, but they differ from abnormal chromosomes. Mutations can occur in a variety of ways: a mistake when the chromosomes from the mother and the father are combined at conception; mistakes in DNA replication; or physical damage to DNA molecules, which can be caused by environmental events such as radiation.

Mutations can affect the life of an individual in different ways: negatively, positively, or not at all. Some mutations have no effect at all. Most mutations, however, are decidedly negative. They result in serious diseases, physical deformity, or mental retardation. Although dire for the individual, these mutations have little or no effect on the evolution of the species, because the individuals do not often reproduce successfully. Mutations with a positive adaptive value obey the laws of natural selection.

TWINS

The only exception to the rule of genetic uniqueness is identical twins. Identical twins are **monozygotic**—that is, they develop from the same fertilized egg. (Fraternal twins develop when the mother releases two eggs and each is fertilized by different sperms. Fraternal twins are genetically no more alike than any other two siblings.) Because genetic makeup determines much of an individual's behavior and abilities, in addition to physical appearance, genetic similarity is important to psychologists in tracing the role of genetic factors in intelligence, disease, and personality. Because identical twins offer the only possible instance of identical heredity, they are prized as subjects by psycholo-

Events that occur on the microscopic level during fertilization drastically affect the nature of the children who are born. An extra chromosome will produce a child with Down's syndrome (left); a split in the fertilized egg will produce monozygous (identical) twins (right).

gists interested in tackling the nature-nurture issue. The group next most similar in genetic makeup is siblings, who share many of the same genes from their parents.

There is some degree of genetic similarity between all relatives: parents, aunts, uncles, half-brothers, and so on. When we speak of "blood relatives," we are actually speaking about genetic relatives.

GENETICS, BEHAVIOR, AND EXPERIENCE

Some inherited traits may not show up right away, such as myopia (hereditary nearsightedness). Eye color is determined by one gene or at the most a pair of genes, but most human traits are determined by a combination of many. It is possible for a child to have nostrils like the mother's and the bridge of the nose like the father's. Some characteristics are so strong that they come to characterize a family: the Hapsburgs, the ruling family of the Holy Roman Empire for generations, for instance, had a characteristic protruding lip (Figure 4-5). Some are rather inconsequential: whether you have attached or detached earlobes, whether or not you can roll your tongue, or whether your second toe is longer than your big toe.

We are certainly dealt a hand at birth, but how we play the hand is equally important. Most complex human abilities are determined by an interplay between inheritance and the environment; these are the kinds of abilities governed by what is called the **range of reaction.** The range of reaction is contained in a person's *genetic inheritance*. The specific genetic endowment may predispose an individual to an ability or a trait. Whether the predisposition develops into a reality depends largely on experience. There is probably a genetic component in intelligence, but another influence on the development of

FIGURE 4-5
Hereditary Traits

The characteristic Hapsburg lip gives most of these relatives a strong family resemblance.

intelligence is environment. Height, too, may be influenced by environment in the form of nutrition. A genetic predisposition for a particular disease may or may not express itself, depending on specific experiences, such as diet, stress, and culture.

The interaction of the *genotype* (the individual's genetic inheritance) with the environment influences what will be expressed in the *phenotype*. Every organism, even the simplest bacterium, contains more genetic potential than can be expressed. The expression depends on circumstances and opportunity. For example, Caucasians are generally taller than Orientals because the genetic potential for height in the Caucasian gene pool produces taller people. However, a study of Japanese brought up in North America showed that, with better nutrition, these Japanese grew taller than their countrymen in Japan. Therefore, it can be said that Japanese Americans express the upper range of their height potential (Gottesman, 1974). (See Figure 4-6.)

It is easy to analyze the comparative contributions of heredity and environment in a physical trait, such as height. Mental abilities or disabilities are much more difficult to spell out.

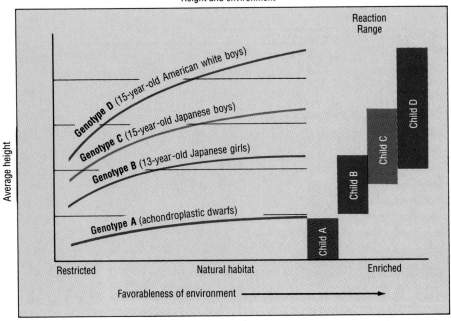

Height and environment

FIGURE 4-6
Range of Reaction to
the Environment

One individual may have a
genetic potential for greater
height than another, but the
height each achieves depends
on the environment in which
each develops.
(Gottesman, 1974)

Schizophrenia is a severe mental disorder, affecting about one percent of the world's population, which has a genetic component as well as social causes. The genetic contribution was discovered by examining the family histories of schizophrenics and correlating them with those of nonschizophrenics. That comparison revealed a higher incidence of schizophrenia within the schizophrenic's families than among the families of nonschizophrenics. Moreover, within schizophrenic families, the greater the genetic similarity, the greater the incidence of schizophrenia (Kessler, 1980). (See Table 4-2.) The identical twin of a schizophrenic is more likely to suffer from the disorder than a fraternal twin. Similarly, a sibling of a schizophrenic has a greater chance of being one than a cousin, and the child of a schizophrenic has 12–13 times the average chance of

TABLE 4-2
Concordance Rates in Recent Twin Studies of Schizophrenia (%)

	Identical Twins	Fraternal Twins
Norway	45	15
Denmark	56	26
United States	43	9
Finland	35	13
United Kingdom	58	12

SOURCE: Data from Gottesman & Shields, 1972.

TABLE 4-3

Estimates of the Risk for Schizophrenia among Relatives of Schizophrenics (%)

	Rosenthal (1970)	Slater & Cowie (1971)
Parents	4.2	4.4
Siblings (neither parent affected)	6.7	8.2
Siblings (one parent affected)	12.5	13.8
All Siblings	7.5	8.5
Children	9.7	12.3
Children (both parents affected)	35.0*	36.6–46.3
Half-Siblings	—	3.2
Aunts and Uncles	1.7	2.0
Nephews and Nieces	2.3	2.3
Grandchildren	2.6	2.8
First Cousins	1.7	2.9

*Excludes Kallmann's (1938) study.
SOURCE: Data from Rosenthal, 1970; Slater & Cowie, 1971.

being a schizophrenic (Kessler, 1980). (See Table 4-3.) This is a predisposition only; in a favorable and healthy environment, the serious disorder of schizophrenia stands less of a chance of being expressed.

THE BEGINNINGS: OUR HERITAGE

There is a footprint in Africa, impressed into the sand more than 3½ million years ago (Figure 4-7). It preserves an occasion when our human ancestors began to diverge from the great apes. The footprint is of a creature standing on two legs. Those pioneering steps made present human beings possible.

The adjustment from walking on all fours to walking on just two encouraged our predecessors' reliance on vision. Also, the weight of the body that had previously been supported by the front limbs shifted to the legs and pelvis, so that the front limbs were freed for other responsibilities, such as toolmaking and tool carrying. The pelvis thickened to haul the weight of the upper body; this refashioned childbirth, begetting immature human beings. This physical evolution also set off an explosion in the mind, as the brain swiftly became larger and ultimately words were spoken.

We are the result of these changes and have certain distinct physical features. Modern human beings stand up on two legs and walk erect. *Homo sapiens* are the most sexual primate. Although other animals typically mate a few times a year when they are in heat, human beings have intercourse repeatedly at any time of the year. We have the largest brain of any animal in relation to body size and have hands capable of fine movements.

FIGURE 4-7

The footprint of one of our prehuman ancestors, left in the sands of Africa more than three and a half million years ago and discovered by Mary Leakey.

These unique physical features are not the only things that make us such an extraordinary animal. The lion has its mane, the penguin its feathers, the deer its antlers. But most animals are able to survive only in their own original habitat. A lion abruptly transported to New York would not survive the winter, a penguin could not survive a New York summer.

However, human beings can and do prevail all over the world, in the bleak heights of the Himalayas, in the deserts of Africa, in the frozen north of Alaska, and in crowded cities. *We are an animal that lives far outside our original habitat* and who makes drastic changes in the environment to suit itself. Think of the differences between your life, with television and air and space travel, and the life of a Stone Age tribesman.

How we did we become such a novel animal? In the long sweep of human history, which spans millions of years, one occasion is noteworthy: that first time the human ancestors stood upright and began to move away from the trees into a new world filled with new circumstances and challenges. In a way, we are still doing that. Sometimes we meet the challenges well, other times not. We respond strongly to new upsets to our lives, such as a terrorist attack, but not to the increasing dangers from chemical pollution because of the way we have evolved. The evolutionary understanding of human thought makes it possible to know where we are matched and where we are mismatched to the world we live in (Barash, 1986; Ornstein & Ehrlich 1989).

PRINCIPLES AND ISSUES IN HUMAN ORIGINS

NATURE-NURTURE

Are human beings naturally violent? Are women more fluent in language than men? Do men want sex more, or differently, than women? Are white people more intelligent than black? These questions reflect one of the oldest controversies in psychology: whether people are *determined* by nature or by nurture—that is, by heredity or by the influence of the environment.

The pure **nature** view holds that human beings are dominated by **innate** characteristics such as instinct. Instincts are inborn, fixed patterns of behavior, such as the salmon's inevitable return to the river of its birth. Love or attachment of a mother for her child is thought by many psychologists to be a human instinct. Because human behavior is more complex than the salmon's, advocates of the nature view presume the existence of hundreds of instincts to account for human behavior.

In contrast, the **nurture** view asserts that people are the result of their environment and that it is life circumstances that make one person into a thief, another into a banker.

Both these views are, of course, extreme. Neither is sufficient to explain the full range of human behavior. Human beings have certain universal patterns of behavior in common, such as their emotions, the use of language, and tool making. At the same time, an individual's specific experience affects the way these universal patterns will be expressed in his or her own life. For example all normal human beings are capable of learning language (nature), but the *particular* language they learn depends on their specific experiences (nurture). Most behavior is the *product of both factors,* as the area of a rectangle is determined by its length *and* width. Some behaviors may be more determined by nature, some by nurture, but all are shaped by differing combinations of both.

But the nature-nurture argument remains in a new form. While most psychologists now accept some biological background to different behaviors, there is great controversy now over *just how much is specified in the genes,* and how far conscious influence pulls us away from our heritage.

THE PRINCIPLE OF ADAPTATION

The first order of business in life is to survive. To endure, an organism must be able to function in its environment. **Adaptation** is an organism's ability to change—adapt—in order to fit better in its environment. A trait such as color vision or speech has **adaptive value** if it assists an organism to function in its environment. Human adaptation is very intricate; it takes many forms because human beings are very complicated animals and are always adjusting to meet new circumstances.

Different forms of human adaptations involve different mechanisms. When you enter a darkened theater, your eyes will gradually adapt to the change in illumination. This form of **sensory adaptation** is called *dark adaptation.* When you put on a new set of glasses, the world seems bent at first, but your perception will adjust. This is a form of **perceptual adaptation.** Many kinds of adaptation will be treated in later chapters in the book: adapting to different temperatures, adapting to the pressures of the contemporary world, as well as the breakdown of adaptation which results in stress.

ORIGINS AND DEVELOPMENT OF HUMAN BEINGS

This is a story about human origins, because we cannot be completely sure of events that occurred millions of years ago. Scientists now have a reasonably good idea of how our human ancestors, over millions of years, underwent successive physical changes to adapt to their new circumstances. Each change, such as standing on two legs, a bigger brain, and the uniquely human style of sex, fed into a positive feedback loop. Modern human beings are the result of this long process of feedback.

The only records of these important changes are a few fragments of tools and some skeletons preserved as fossils. But with new evidence being discovered, the full story of human history is emerging—the line of the species from 4 million years ago to the present day.

A NOTE ON EVOLUTIONARY TIME

Because the human story spans millennia, we must reset our idea of time: in evolutionary time, a few million years, give or take a few thousand, is not very much. Given the time scale of the history of the earth, humanity has developed and bred with unprecedented speed. In only a few million years, human beings have spread from the African plains to inhabit every part of the planet and have grown from a population of a scattered few thousand to well over 5 billion.

If we charted Earth's history as a single year's calendar, making midnight on December 31 represent the present, the first form of life would appear about April 1. Fish appear about November 20. The first recognizable human ancestor would not come forth until the *morning of December 31*. The first human being would emerge at about 11:45 p.m. *All that has happened in recorded history would occur in the final minute of the year* (Figure 4-8). The forces that fashion our lives are much older than we usually think!

PREHUMANS

Between 25 million and 13 million years ago, a succession of events led to the divergence of two primates: human beings and chimpanzees. Prehuman ancestors descended from tree-dwelling animals in East Africa. Sometime before 13 million years ago, the forests of East Africa began to thin out, forcing many of the tree-dwelling primates out of their homes and inviting others to try living in ecological niches on the ground.

Those who were able to remain in their tree homes evolved into chimpanzees. Of those who were forced or attracted out of the trees, some did not adapt and became extinct (Lancaster, 1978), but others did adapt. They learned how to live in the surrounding grasslands, prospered and survived, and evolved into prehuman beings and the first members of the **hominid,** or human, family. The change from prehuman to human involved the development of four important hominid characteristics: a progressively upright stance, increased use of tools, growth of the brain, and the emergence of a cooperative society.

Prehumans had both apelike and humanlike characteristics. The first humanlike ancestor was *Ramapithecus*, who appeared sometime between 9 million and 13 million years ago. The tiny **Australopithecus** (3–4 million years ago) were the first direct ancestors. Of these species, *Homo habilis* (handy men) seems to have prevailed, although this is not certain. The advantages that might have ensured the survival of *Homo habilis* or like species were the capacities to use tools and to hunt. In addition to having these social skills, the hominids were physically more nearly human: their brains were larger and they walked more upright. (See Figure 4-9.)

Tool use probably made *Homo habilis* a more efficient worker. Tools would have made it possible to build shelters and construct primitive settlements. Perhaps more important, *Homo habilis* hunted in groups. Feeding a group on fruits and berries is difficult; most of the day must be spent foraging for food. But a group of hunters can bring home enough food for several families for days. Food-sharing allowed *Homo habilis* to begin to establish a stable home base and a more permanent cooperative society.

Consider what hunting requires: speed and accuracy are obvious, but the ability to plan, communicate, and cooperate are even more important. These abilities foretell superior intelligence: to think and reason, speak a language, and create a culture.

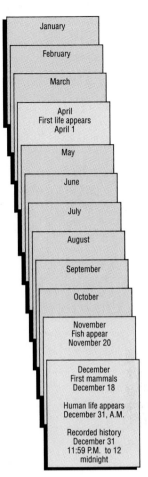

FIGURE 4-8
The History of Life on Earth

Representing the entire history of the earth on a one-year calendar puts human beings' short stay on our planet in a new perspective.

Australopithecus   Homo habilis   Homo erectus

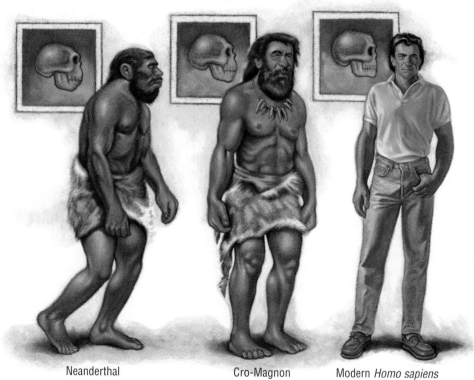

FIGURE 4-9
From Prehuman to
Human

The characteristics and
abilities that distinguish
modern human beings
gradually emerged over
millions of years of
adaptation by our humanlike
ancestors.

Neanderthal   Cro-Magnon   Modern *Homo sapiens*

It took 6–9 million years for the prehuman brain to grow significantly, for some communal living to develop, and for the invention and use of tools (Figure 4-10). But once these things happened, *they affected each other*, and began to work together, and this process spurred further and more rapid change. It has been only about 1½ million years since the emergence of *Homo erectus*. In this time the brain has doubled in size, primitive tools have developed into complex technology, and civilizations have risen and fallen.

Physical differences between prehumans and human beings are obvious (Table 4-4 and Figure 4-9). The skull is greater to contain a larger brain. The brain of *Australopithecus* was 450 cc.; the modern human brain is between 1,000 and 2,000 cc. (Campbell, 1982). Human beings stand more fully erect and walk and run better than prehumans. As human evolution progressed, society became increasingly stable: home bases became permanent and more central to life. Social organization grew in complexity.

HOMO ERECTUS (FROM 1.6 MILLION TO ABOUT 500,000 YEARS AGO) **Homo erectus** ("upright man") stood erect and walked. What most distinguished them from their predecessors was a large brain and the complexity of behavior that it made possible. Their appearance was generally modern: they were probably over five feet tall, and their skeletons were very similar to ours, at least from the neck down. *Homo erectus* migrated and settled in places as far north as present-day Germany and as far east as China.

In 1965 archaeologists uncovered a preserved settlement they called *Terra Amata*, which unlocked many of the mysteries of *Homo erectus* (de Lumley, 1969). Today, in a housing complex built on that same site, people engage in many of the same activities as their ancestors 400,000 years ago. The remains at Terra Amata indicate that the culture of *Homo erectus* was very advanced.

TABLE 4-4
Comparison of Cranial Capacities

	Range of Cranial Capacity (cc)	Average Cranial Capacity (cc)
Lemur	10–70	—
Chimpanzee	282–500	383
Gorilla	340–752	505
Australopithecus africanus	435–530	450
A. robustus	—	500
A. boisei	506–530	515
Homo habilis	600–752	666
H. erectus	775–1,225	950
Modern adult human	1,000–2,000	1,330

SOURCE: Campbell, 1982.

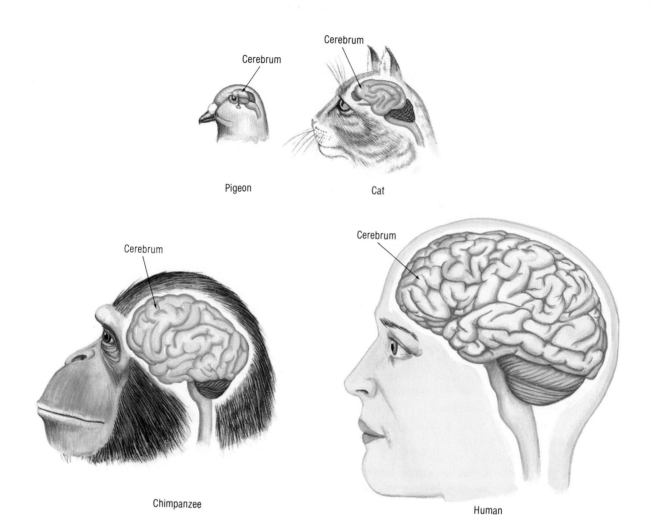

Cerebrum — Pigeon

Cerebrum — Cat

Cerebrum — Chimpanzee

Cerebrum — Human

**FIGURE 4-10
Brain Size**

Progressive increase in the size of the cerebrum in vertebrates is evident in these drawings, which show a representative selection of vertebrate brains, all drawn to the same scale. Note the dramatic increase in size and complexity of the primate brains over lower vertebrates.

Adapted from "The Brain" by David H. Hubel. Copyright © 1979 by Scientific American, Inc. All rights reserved.

Cooking pots, skins, marrow scrapers, and other advanced tools have been unearthed.

Homo erectus built elaborate shelters, invented clothing, and used fire in a controlled manner. The taming of fire is an important landmark in human history. Along with the inventions of clothing and shelter, it made life in cold climates possible. Even today, 75 percent of people use fire as their primary source of heat. Another major benefit of fire was that it cooked food which does not spoil as quickly as raw food and is more versatile.

Fire is also a social landmark. People are drawn to fires not only for warmth but also for socializing. Because brain size had increased considerably by this time, and because of the increased time spent around a fire, it is possible that *Homo erectus* was the first to use speech. (See Figure 4-10.)

NEANDERTHAL (FROM BEFORE 100,000 TO ABOUT 40,000 YEARS AGO)   A cave near what is now Shanidar, Iraq, marks the spot where, on a day 60,000 years ago, a Neanderthal man was buried. But this was not merely a burial, it was a funeral, an organized ceremony. The fossilized remains of several kinds of flowers and grains are distributed in an orderly fashion around the skeleton. The bones of the deceased lie on a woven bed.

Evidence of a deliberate burial this far in the past is impressive. Evidence of an organized ceremony is even more impressive. What is most impressive is that the particular species of flowers located at the burial are still used today in local herbal medicine, which indicates that Neanderthals understood the medicinal properties of plants (Leakey & Lewin, 1977).

Neanderthals first appeared during the Ice Age. The range they inhabited was similar to that of *Homo erectus:* probably from Germany to China, predominantly in northern regions. They had adapted primarily to cold weather, and some archaeologists believe that they became extinct when the Ice Age ended. More likely they merged into the group of modern humanity.

Neanderthals probably refined the inventions of *Homo erectus.* Their shelters were more elaborate than their predecessors'. They clothed themselves in animal skins for warmth and created quite complex tools. Early forms of cooperation had evolved into a genuine society. Thus Neanderthals were not very different from us (their brains were 1,500 cc., larger than our average size).

The Neanderthal culture was advanced. Evidence from archaeological excavations shows a division of labor, increased inventiveness (as seen by the tools and other found artifacts), and even organized warfare. Neanderthals probably were the first to wage wars and the first to conceive of a spiritual life. There is evidence of both worship and ritual: bear skulls and bones are carefully placed in caves.

HOMO SAPIENS (FROM ABOUT 50,000 YEARS AGO TO THE PRESENT)   In 1868, railway workers were cutting through a hillside in the south of France when they came upon four human skeletons. The skeletons looked modern, but what was next to them did not: stone tools, seashells, and animal teeth with holes drilled in them, apparently for stringing as an ornament. These skeletons are verified as the earliest remains (from about 50,000 years ago) of *Homo sapiens* ("intelligent human being").

These people were called **Cro-Magnon,** after the site of their discovery. There are critical distinctions in the shape of the skull of a Cro-Magnon and a Neanderthal (Figure 4-9). Between their eras the entire shape of the face altered and the physiological apparatus for producing a great range of sounds expanded. The brain did not change much but *elevated* in the skull. The palate also (inside the mouth) enlarged, which allowed greater precision in speech.

Speech is the most sophisticated tool human beings have. With the emergence of language, the pace of evolution, quickening since *Homo erectus,* began to accelerate. Because of their language skill, Cro-Magnons had a tremendous advantage over Neanderthals: they could plan, organize, and cooperate much more efficiently. The tools Cro-Magnons used were more elaborate than those of Neanderthals. Shelters and settlements, too, were more complex.

Art and language are both critical milestones in human evolution because they signify a mind capable of abstraction, symbolism, and invention. Making art is an abstraction of a world not present and is often a representation of a world view or a spiritual system. The Cro-Magnon paintings found on the caves of Lascaux in France, done 15,000 years ago, are as beautiful as anything ever

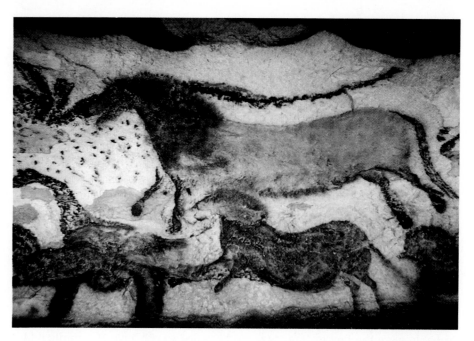

FIGURE 4-11
Cro-Magnon Art

The Cro-Magnon paintings from the caves of Lascaux, France, reveal highly developed artistic ability and sensibility, powers of abstraction, and both an appreciation of the realistic details and the spiritual essence of life and living things.

created (Figure 4-11). Language, too, is abstract, involving the use of arbitrary sounds in arbitrary sequences to represent real objects in the world. Fifteen thousand years ago, our ancestors were fully human (Marshak, 1978).

HUNTING, GATHERING, AND THE AGRICULTURAL REVOLUTION

HUNTER-GATHERERS For most of history, human beings lived in hunting-and-gathering societies; many still do. In this form of society are two main activities: the search for meat and the gathering of available fruits, vegetables, and grains. Such **hunter-gatherers** lead a nomadic existence, moving as grains become scarce or following the seasonal migration of animals. But their lives are not necessarily impoverished; one anthropologist (Johnson, 1978) found that an individual in a contemporary hunter-gatherer tribe, an "original affluent society," spends less time working and has more leisure time than an average French person today (Figure 4-12). Still, the life of hunter-gatherers does not provide a very *stable* society, because it changes as they migrate.

THE AGRICULTURAL REVOLUTION The creation of agriculture unshackled human beings from the vulnerability of the nomadic life of hunter-gatherers. The first crops, planted about 10,000 years ago, were the first extensive effort to prevail over the environment. A hunter-gatherer is at the mercy of nature; a farmer can harness it to some extent.

The cultivation of crops transformed human societies from mobile hunting-and-gathering ones to stable groups. Freed from the recurring search for food, people now literally put down roots. Agriculture made possible the origin of civilization as we know it. In what is now Iran and Iraq, our recent ancestors

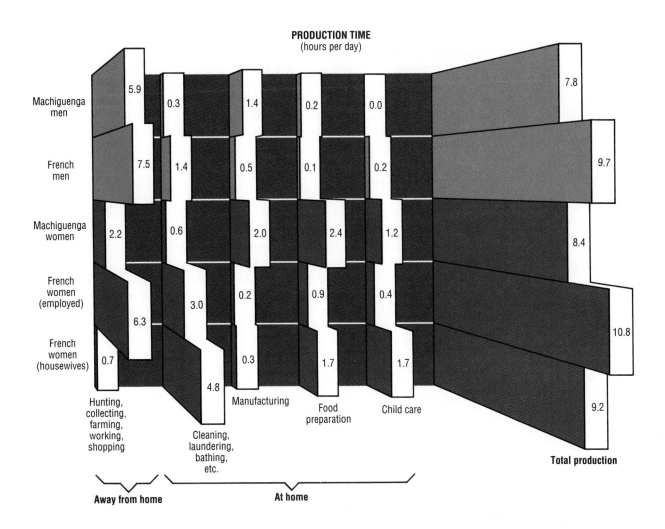

PRODUCTION TIME
(hours per day)

	Machiguenga men	French men	Machiguenga women	French women (employed)	French women (housewives)
Hunting, collecting, farming, working, shopping	5.9	7.5	2.2	6.3	0.7
Cleaning, laundering, bathing, etc.	0.3	1.4	0.6	3.0	4.8
Manufacturing	1.4	0.5	2.0	0.2	0.3
Food preparation	0.2	0.1	2.4	0.9	1.7
Child care	0.0	0.2	1.2	0.4	1.7
Total production	7.8	9.7	8.4	10.8	9.2

Away from home   At home

began to plant grains they collected and to domesticate animals and build permanent settlements. These first, tentative settlements later developed into communities and, still later, into cities.

Then, almost in an instant, the great ancient civilizations emerged in the regions where agriculture was first developed—in the Middle East, China, and India. The pace of change quickened. In a few thousand years, human society had transformed from nomadic to settled, and the foundations of advanced human culture were cemented.

THE PROCESS OF ADAPTATION AND EVOLUTION

Before the origin of modern science, most people believed that all creatures were individually created to suit their special environments. Organisms were thought to be fixed: human beings had been created as humans, monkeys had been created monkeys, and so on. But by the nineteenth century, the scientific view had begun to understand that all animals did change and had developed from

FIGURE 4-12
The Affluence of Hunting and Gathering Societies

Hunter-gatherers, such as the Machiguenga, lack the material wealth of modern French men and women, but—as this chart shows—they spend less time working and caring for their homes and possessions, so they are richer in leisure time than the average member of our modern technological society.
(Johnson, 1978)

CHARLES DARWIN
(1809–1882)

earlier forms of life. Evolution of organisms was accepted, but its mechanism remained a riddle.

The answer appeared when the English naturalist Charles Darwin (1809–1882) proposed his theory of how adaptation occurs. He called the process "descent with modification." In 1859 he published a revolutionary book, *On the Origin of Species*, in which he described the mechanism by which organisms adapt to the environment, termed **natural selection.** Darwin's theory, joined with modern genetics, is the basis of the modern *theory of evolution*.

NATURAL SELECTION

How populations change over time is their *evolution*; natural selection is the crucial factor. A *population* is a group of similar organisms who can produce fertile offspring. For a group of animals to survive as a population, each generation must replace itself through sexual reproduction.

Any group of organisms produces far more offspring than are needed to replace itself. One salmon lays thousands of eggs, a cat can give birth to several litters of 6 to 7 kittens in her lifetime, a woman can have 10 or more children. But populations usually remain at a fairly constant size from one generation to the next. That observation led to two important insights.

1. Some individuals produce more surviving offspring than others. *Therefore, the individuals who do survive must in some way be more fit and better able to live in and adapt to their environment.*

2. Although the offspring are by and large like the parents, they also *differ from them* in many important respects.

Sexual reproduction and the occasional mutation yield offspring that are *combinations* of two different *individuals,* not an exact copy of one or the other parent. Variations that permit the offspring to adapt better and to reproduce would be likely to be passed on to the next generation, and that generation in turn would change or evolve (Darwin, 1859).

Consider, as did Darwin, the selective breeding of animals. To breed a small poodle, we would need the smallest female and the smallest male poodle. The dogs in the resulting litter would probably be smaller on average than the parents. If we repeat this process, each succeeding generation, *on average,* will be smaller than the previous one by this *artificial* selection.

In nature, there is no such calculated manipulation. There is only natural selection, in which successful organisms survive in the environment. Animals more or less choose their own mates and produce offspring that, because they are combinations of their parents' characteristics, diverge slightly from their parents. Adaptive traits are passed on.

ADAPTIVE VALUE AND FITNESS

Darwin's ideas thus became known as the "survival of the fittest," referring to the popular belief that life is a struggle between different *individuals* to survive. But that belief is partly incorrect. The struggle for survival in this theory of evolution is the struggle of a *species,* not an individual.

The advantage of a new trait is not seen in the individual in whom the new trait appears but in *succeeding generations.* Individuals born with characteristics that enable them to adapt better to their environment reproduce more successfully and pass on those characteristics to others. "Fitness" in this context refers to *a match between the traits of a population and its environment.* The greater the fitness, the more surviving offspring.

For example, sunlight stimulates synthesis of vitamin D, which is a necessary nutrient for humans. Human beings can absorb sunlight through the skin. In a tropical environment, however, where there is an abundance of sunlight, human beings run the risk of producing excessive vitamin D, so a mechanism blocking the sun's rays would have *adaptive value.* In contrast, in a northern environment, where there is not much sunlight, individuals who have some mechanism for stimulating production of vitamin D would be more fit for their climate. This is possibly why there are different skin colors in human populations. As human beings settled farther and farther north, those who better survived had lighter skin color, which allows sunlight to be absorbed through the skin at a higher rate. Conversely, the closer humans lived to the equator, the darker the skin.

Darwin's insight enabled later scientists to comprehend evolution: to understand how our ancestors became us, how populations could change over time. To recap, the process by which the environment "selects" the individuals best adapted to it is *natural selection.* The change in the composition of population that follows is its *evolution.*

THE IMPACT OF DARWIN'S THEORY: OUR VIEW OF OURSELVES

Although the principles of evolution are straightforward, they have probably had more impact than any others in the human sciences. The theory of evolution shifted the conception of human nature and our place in the universe. It provides the paradigm for most research in the life sciences and has greatly influenced psychology.

For most of history the prevailing view was that human beings were at the center of the universe: the sun and the planets revolved around the earth and the earth was the center of the universe. Human beings were specially created to dwell at the center of creation. This conception first was attacked in 1543 when the Polish astronomer Nicolaus Copernicus demonstrated that the planets did *not* revolve around the earth; rather, Earth was one of many planets that revolved around the sun. The Catholic Church considered this theory heretical for many years, until the evidence supporting the theory was undeniable and it had to be accepted. Still, Copernicus did not upset the belief that human beings were unique creatures, especially created to rule Earth.

Three hundred years later, Darwin's theory placed human beings under the same rules of life that applied to all creatures. It postulated that all organisms have a common ancestor and, adding insult to injury, that human beings are directly descended from apes. The Victorian world was appalled. There is a vast distinction between thinking of yourself as "created in God's own image" and "descended from the apes." One proper Victorian lady, on learning of Darwin's theory, said "I pray that it is not true, but if it is true, I pray that it does not become widely known" (Leakey & Lewin, 1977).

Darwin was the subject of ridicule, lampooned in cartoons and attacked in sermons, debates, and editorials. His theory has continued to be controversial to this day. In 1925, an American biology teacher was fired for teaching the principles of evolution in a Tennessee school, in violation of a state law. The controversy ended in the famous "Monkey Trial." Today, in the United States, many fundamentalist Christian groups protest the teaching of the theory of evolution in public schools, at least in the absence of any teaching of "creationism", the conception that God created the world as written in the Bible.

Darwin's work, and the later development of evolutionary theory, did more than shock the world. It placed human beings as members of the animal kingdom, subject to the same forces that act on all animals, and, more than any other contribution, it launched the scientific inquiry of human nature. It produces a different view of human beings in the universe. The complexity of the world is not an example of God's work; rather it is an evolved system without general direction. In this view, if there is a controlling force, it is exemplified by the title of a significant book, *The Blind Watchmaker* (Dawkins, 1956)—that is, the controlling force sets a complex system in motion but has no idea what it is doing.

HUMAN ADAPTATION

Human beings have many physical, behavioral, and mental characteristics that set us apart from other animals. One physical characteristic, standing up, was crucial in human evolution because, among other benefits, it led to increased reproduction. Somewhat later (although it is an oversimplification to separate each characteristic) came tool use, an increasingly large brain, and self-awareness. These physical changes resulted in countless behavioral changes, among them the development of a cooperative society. The physical developments in turn prompted vast changes in human society so that cultures and behavior changed rapidly over a very short time.

We present the distinctly human characteristics here in the rough order in which they evolved. But it is better to think of the process of **human adaptation** as the *simultaneous* development of all these characteristics, in a positive feedback loop (Figure 4-13). The effects of the loop have continuously increased the difference between our nearest ancestors and us.

BIPEDALISM: STANDING UP AND WALKING

Human beings are **bipedal**—that is, we walk on two feet instead of on all fours. Chimps and gorillas can stand upright at times, but when they move they typically do so on all fours. A fossil skeleton called Lucy, our first ancestor found whose bones show that she walked on two legs, dates from about 3.75 million years ago, about 1 million years before the use of tools (Johansen & Edey, 1981).

Bipedal walking and running are efficient modes of locomotion. People can cover greater distances over time than any other animal. We are the only animals that can climb a tree, swim a mile across a river, and walk 20 miles in a day

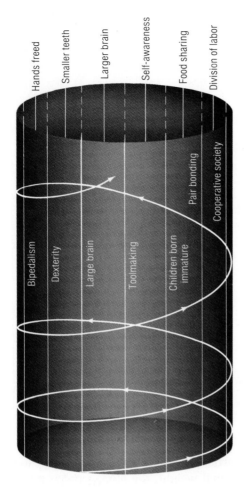

FIGURE 4-13
Human Adaptation and the Power of Positive Feedback

Unique human characteristics include the following: (1) we stand on two legs and walk; (2) children are born immature and need care for a long time; (3) females are biologically sexually receptive all the time and usually pair off with one male; (4) we have forelimbs capable of fine motor control and use tools; (5) our human brain is the largest (relative to body size) and is capable of sophisticated communication; (6) our society is cooperative and organized around food sharing and division of labor; and (7) we have the capacity to change our environment and live anywhere on earth.

(Haldane, 1986). Walking enabled our ancestors to travel into unexplored territory, which in turn led them into new and often dangerous situations. Almost all other animals live their lives in the environment in which they are born.

The view from two feet off the ground is more limited than the view from four to five feet. To four-legged animals smell is important. A standing animal can see farther than it can smell. Since standing animals can spot approaching danger as well as opportunities farther away, a more sophisticated visual system developed along with upright posture.

Hands were freed from weight-bearing responsibilities, making tool use possible. Erect posture also led to profound changes in human sexuality and social systems. Although we cannot be sure, this complex of factors surrounding bipedalism was probably our first adaptive advantage (Johansen & Edey, 1981).

IMMATURITY AND ITS CONSEQUENCES

With the freeing of the front limbs, the hind limbs had to adapt to bearing the entire weight of the body. The human back was not originally "designed" to

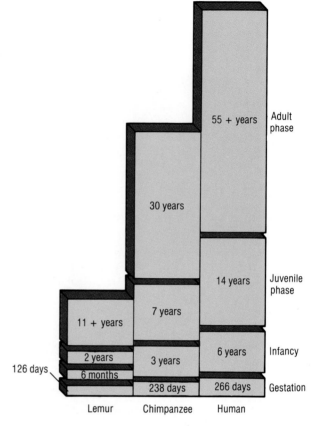

FIGURE 4-14
Long Infancy

With the longest infancy of any animal, human young are wholly dependent upon their parents for twice as long as baby chimpanzees. But the long period of protecting the helpless infants gives human family groups greater cohesion and the infants have the time to learn all that is involved in being human.

Chart data:

	Lemur	Chimpanzee	Human	
Adult phase	11 + years	30 years	55 + years	
Juvenile phase		7 years	14 years	
Infancy	2 years	3 years	6 years	
	6 months			
Gestation	126 days	238 days	266 days	

support upright posture (which partially explains why back pains are a common complaint). To support the additional weight, the human pelvis grew thicker than that of the great apes (Washburn, 1960). As a result, the thickened pelvis made the female's birth canal, the opening through which infants are born, much smaller.

While the birth canal was becoming smaller, however, the fetus's brain and head were growing larger. If there had been no evolutionary correction for this new disadvantage, the human species would have eventually died out because of inefficient childbirth. The evolutionary solution was to have human babies born very early in their development.

At birth a chimp's brain is about 45 percent of its adult weight, while a human baby's brain is 25 percent of its adult weight (Lovejoy, 1974). Human children have the longest infancy in the animal kingdom (Figure 4-14); they are not as competent and independent as baby chimps or baboons. Within a day, baby baboons can hold onto their mothers by themselves (Campbell, 1982). The human child is helpless and will die if not taken care of for years.

The major portion of the brain's development occurs outside the womb, exposed to and influenced by many different environments, events, and people. The environment plays a much greater role in the development of the human brain than in any other animal's brain development. And because the environment is different for each person, the specific abilities each of us develops differs considerably.

A helpless infant requires at least one caretaking parent to survive. In other species, a newborn can fend for itself within a relatively short time, and the mother can almost immediately resume her place in the group, providing her young with food and protection. But taking care of a human infant is a full-time job.

For most of human history, taking care of the infant has been the mother's job. In subsistence societies, like hunter-gatherers, parents working together as a team were better able to get enough food than a nursing mother alone. (Benshoof & Thornhill, 1979). The father can hunt for meat and bring it home to the mother, who stays close to home gathering fruits and vegetables. Human fathers take an active role in feeding their young (Alexander, Hoogland, Howard, Noonan, & Sherman, 1979).

DEXTERITY AND TOOL USE

Once the early humans walked, and the forelimbs were freed from their weight-bearing function, the limbs developed into hands with great **dexterity**, capable of more precise movements such as those needed for fashioning and **using specialized tools.** Human ancestors began to make tools as early as 3 million years ago.

Specialized tools for chopping, digging, killing, cooking, washing, and skinning led to specialized labor by those who used them. Some people gathered wood or nuts, others dug for roots, still others hunted and killed animals (Washburn, 1960). Axes made the hunt more efficient; choppers and scrapers could be used to butcher a large animal at the kill. At home, tools helped scrape the nutritious marrow out of the bones; animal hides could be scraped to make warm clothing.

One mark of improved dexterity is the modification in the tools themselves. Those made by *Homo erectus* about 1 million years ago took 35 blows to make. The knives of Cro-Magnon, made about 20,000 years ago, were more delicately fashioned, requiring at least 250 separate blows (Figure 4-15).

FIGURE 4-15
The Increasing Complexity of Toolmaking

The growing sophistication of human stone implements, and of their manufacture, is illustrated here. Each wedge symbol represents a blow struck in making the tool and the clusters of symbols stand for the different operations during manufacture.
(Campbell, 1979)

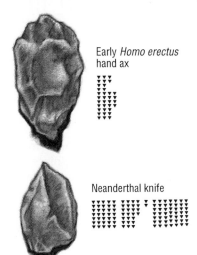

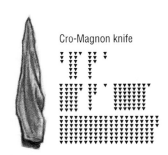

Primitive pebble chopper

Early *Homo erectus* hand ax

Late *Homo erectus* hand ax

Neanderthal knife

Cro-Magnon knife

In about 5000 B.C., human beings began to extract and use metals. This advanced technology and created the need for more specialized labor. Specialization led inevitably to greater interdependence among individuals.

THE BRAIN

Pivotal to human adaptation is our large brain, which has evolved faster than any other human organ. It took hundreds of millions of years to create the 400 cc. brain of *Australopithecus*, yet in only a few million years the brain had grown to 1250–1500 cc. and had developed the capacity for abstract thought: the key to the human adaptation. It has helped us to adapt to every kind of geography and climate. It enables us still today to transcend our biological inheritance.

The brain underlies mental life: to learn, to create, to invent, to think and say things no one has ever thought. The brain increased in size radically from *Ramapithecus* to *Homo sapiens*. It is the largest, relative to body size, of all land mammals, but the size of the brain is not what matters. What is crucial is *where* the brain expanded. Although the anatomy of much of our brain is identical with that of other primates, our cerebral cortex, the uppermost part of the brain, is the largest and most elaborate of all primates. The cortex is the area of the brain devoted to learning, organizing, planning, and other mental activities.

All primates have developed varying degrees of fine motor control. The main mode of locomotion of nonhuman primates is swinging through trees, which requires the ability to grasp tightly onto branches. To do this, an animal must have extremely well-developed motor control in the fine muscles of his limbs. A kind of grammar is necessary to know how to get from one place to another, which hand to use, and where and how tightly to grasp. Those areas of the brain that control fine motor movements, and which became further developed in toolmaking, are the same ones involved in language (Gallup, 1979). The increasing size of the cerebral cortex thus gave our ancestors great advantages—from control of delicate muscle movements to the development of speech and written language.

ETHOLOGY AND BIOLOGICAL FIXED ACTION PATTERNS

If we and other organisms are the result of such an extended evolutionary process, then which responses are its result? Many of the significant studies of such inborn behaviors have been the domain of **ethology:** the study of behavior under natural conditions.

IMPRINTING

When a newly hatched duckling is from 12 to 18 hours old, something quite remarkable happens: if it recognizes something moving, and it follows that movement for 10 minutes, it becomes *imprinted* on the moving object. It continues to follow the object anywhere (Hess, 1973). In nature, of course, the most likely object that a baby duckling sees is its mother, so this prepared reaction is a *stable strategy;* it leads to a greater chance of survival.

However, if a scientist wishing to examine the routine intervenes, and shows the duckling anything at that crucial period, be it a rectangle or a decoy on wheels, it will follow. In the most dramatic demonstration, Konrad Lorenz,

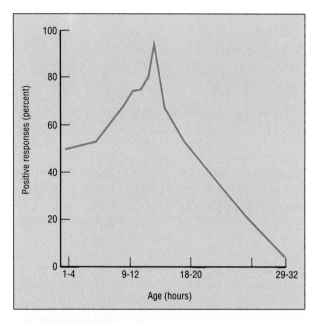

FIGURE 4-17
Imprinting

This is the classic photo of
the famous ethologist Konrad
Lorenz and his imprinted
graylag geese.

one of the most influential ethologists, *himself* appeared in front of goslings at the right time. The tiny goslings followed him as if he were their mother, crying when he was not around. So, a predisposition to bond to the mother is encouraged by this innate reaction (Figures 4-16 and 4-17).

The success of child rearing is the product of evolution and is too important to be left to finicky individual choices. For instance, what if the mother doesn't like the child? Many innate reactions of the child, among them *distress calls* (crying) stimulate an immediate, innate reaction in the mother (feeding, cleaning, or soothing the baby). There is, in addition, a network of *attachments* that persist between mothers (or caregivers) and their offspring. See Chapter 3 for a discussion.

CUTENESS AND ATTRACTION A general way evolution stimulates an attachment is the *cuteness of the baby.* All babies, human or animal (Lorenz, 1943), have much larger foreheads, eyes, and cheeks than the adult (Figure 4-18). This is called the *neotenic face:* the more the face approaches that of the proportions of the baby, the more we goo and gaa, ooh and ahh.

The media have taken advantage of our seemingly built-in tendency to be strongly attracted to these proportions. Mickey Mouse is beloved throughout the world, not only because of his antics, but also because of his brow and eyes. Walt Disney, as well as Konrad Lorenz, are both good observers of innate predilections. And attractive faces on magazine covers show similarly large eyes and forehead.

FIXED ACTION PATTERNS: THE STICKLEBACK ATTACK

The neural program for imprinting is simpler than the behavior: the baby usually attaches to the mother, but all that seems necessary is instructions something like "follow anything that appears within 12–18 hours after you are hatched." By observing animals closely, additional innate patterns have been observed. These **fixed action patterns** are unlearned behaviors, generic to a species, that appear or are released in the presence of certain stimuli.

Tinbergen (1951) identified the simple stimuli which cause the three-spined stickleback to attack. Show the fish a perfect model of a stickleback (Figure 4-19), and it will not attack. But if the belly of the model is painted red, this seems to be the sign to attack. Thus, the models that spark stickleback attack do not have to look at all like the fish; rather, they have to see the critical sign.

Again, there is a principle here: it is probably more economical in the world of the stickleback to instigate attacks against anything with a red belly. But in these ethological analyses we see two points: many reactions may be built in, and they may be quite simple in their composition.

FIGURE 4-18
Cuteness

Cute features of babies of many species—namely, a round head, protruding forehead, and large eyes—trigger a nurturing, caring response in adults.

DO OUR GENES WEAR US?

Genetic mechanisms explain how characteristics of one individual can pass on to succeeding generations. It was only because Darwin's theory of evolution was consistent with the findings of modern genetics in the 1930s and 1940s that evolution became dominant in modern science.

One important question in evolution remains highly controversial: What does natural selection "select"? Darwin's idea was that natural selection is made

CHAPTER 4 / GENETICS AND EVOLUTION

up of countless individuals, struggling for survival, and these individuals pass on their genes to the succeeding generation. Other investigators have hypothesized that natural selection can work on a *group* of related organisms or on the entire *population* of organisms themselves (the species). Thus, anything that helps a *family unit* to survive will be selected, or anything that helps human beings as a whole will also be selected.

Recently, to these three factors—the individual, the group (such as a tribe), and the population—a fourth has been added: the gene itself. The role of the gene in evolution is crucial to a new scientific theory called sociobiology. **Sociobiology** attempts to account for *social* behavior in *biological* terms. There are, however, many different approaches that attempt to understand the biological basis of social behavior. What is different is that sociobiology concentrates on the *gene* as the determinant of our behavior. According to this view, much of our social behavior can be the outcome of genes trying to ensure their *own survival* through their temporary hosts, us—"A hen is an egg's way of making another egg."

INCLUSIVE FITNESS AND THE CONCEPT OF ALTRUISM

The chicken and egg statement turns the normal inquiry around: instead of looking at the individual as the central element in evolution, the focus shifts to the gene, operating through the individual. This viewpoint has given rise to the important concept of inclusive fitness. To understand this we must go back to Darwin. His survival of the fittest theory focuses on the individual ability to produce genetically related (of course) surviving offspring. However, many human behaviors make little or no sense: Why give up one's life for that of another? Why do Eskimos commit suicide when they are no longer viable? Why is infanticide common to many cultures? (Barash, 1986).

The concept of **inclusive fitness** is broader than that of reproductive fitness. It theorizes that an individual will act in such a way to maximize not only his offspring, but the number of copies of his genetic material. This would include actions that benefit his or her family and those who are closely related. This means that motives other than the sexual alone are important in evolution.

An important example of inclusive fitness is the analysis of *altruism*. In some extreme situations, an individual will give up his or her life for that of others. Why, if the individual is the unit of natural selection, would anyone do this? This behavior could eradicate any chance of that individual passing on his or her characteristics to the next generation. From the point of view of the individual, such behavior would make no sense.

FIGURE 4-19
Stickleback Attack

Of the five models used to provoke a fighting response in male sticklebacks, only the four above on the right with red bellies worked, even though the left one is shaped most like a stickleback. It lacked the critical sign stimulus of a red belly.
(Based on Tinbergen, 1951)

157

But it might make sense from the "point of view" of the *gene:* the altruistic act ensures the survival of those genes that the individual has in common with the others. Thus, the more related any individuals are, the more genes they have in common and the higher the probability of altruism. Indeed, homicide rates decline steadily as genetic commonality increases (Daly & Wilson, 1989). In studies of nonhuman beings this seems to be the case: almost all instances of altruism occur between immediate family members (Hamilton, 1964). Haldane (1986) quipped: "I would give up my own life for three of my children, or eight cousins. In each case, the number of one's own genes is increased."

An inclusive fitness analysis reveals that the *closer the relationship* (the more genes in common), the *higher the probability of altruism.* Another example is schizophrenia. It is difficult to see how such a devastating disorder could persist, yet as we shall see later in Chapter 16, relatives of schizophrenics have a high probability of being unusually creative, and thus of value to society. In this concept, the inclusive fitness of the gene which can manifest as schizophrenia is of value to the population (Wenegrat, 1984).

PARENTAL INVESTMENT

The concept of reproductive fitness, although important, does not completely take into account all the actions and decisions that take place after conception. Sometimes a parent must weigh the benefits of supporting one child well versus supporting many less well, or one child against the other. **Parental investment** is any care, food, support, risk, or resource given by a parent that enhances the survival potential of an offspring. The analysis draws from and is similar to economic cost-benefit analyses (Trivers, 1971).

At low levels of parental investment, with little daily care of an infant, the offspring may die. But at very high levels of investment, when parents devote almost all their resources to one infant, the parent's ability to invest in another offspring is limited. Here, such high investment may not be in the parent's genetic interest, for it would be better to have more survivors (Figure 4-20).

It is, of course to the child's benefit to increase investment as much as possible, for the child is acting (in this analysis) to maximize *his or her* genes. So this analysis provides a feasible underpinning for many of the common conflicts between parents and children. As a child, the rule would be to seek the greatest investment, even at the expense of siblings. But as an adult, an individual's *own* children will similarly seek more investment than he or she is willing to give. Individuals will act differently at different stages of the lifespan (Wenegrat, 1984). Males and females, too, because of different parental investments, will also have differing priorities.

SOCIOBIOLOGY, EVOLUTION, AND THE GENE-CENTERED VIEWPOINT

While it is important to note that the gene-centered view of evolution does provide a good explanation of several puzzles, it seems that natural selection in human beings works mainly in the individual, who exercises conscious choices

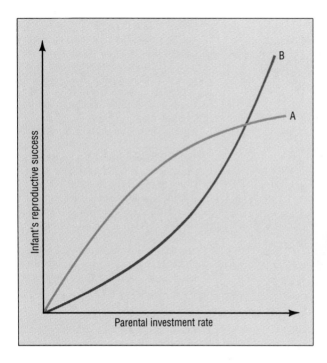

FIGURE 4-20
Parental Investment

Inclusive fitness benefits (curve A) and costs (curve B) as functions of parental investment rate (horizontal axis).
(Wenegrat, 1984)

and passes on a *very large number* of different genes to the offspring (Hamilton, 1964). It is unlikely that *one* individual gene, of the million or so within us, could have a major effect on our behavior.

However, there is more to the evolutionary viewpoint than this specific doctrine, although it is often confused. Psychology is beginning to draw from the vast literature on evolution in many ways. Of course, when major traditions, such as biological and psychological, begin to merge, there are some misconceptions. One is that sociobiology is evolution.

More reasonably, we could distinguish the phylogenetic and the selectionist viewpoints. The *phylogenetic* simply assumes the fact of evolution, that organisms changed to suit the features of the world. This means that some features of perception and cognition are more probable than others. So psychologists like Shepard (1984), Marr (1982), and Chomsky (1980) look to *specialized computational mechanisms* in the nervous system which allow the person to decode, for instance, syntax, the constancies of sensation, and of vision. Others look to universals in the expression of emotions (Ekman, 1984) as another part of the program. Chomsky (1980) thus compares the mind to a collection of different organs, such as exist in the body. Even Skinner (1986) feels that modern life has eroded the original, built-in relationship between an organism's actions and consequences.

The *selectionist* viewpoint is slightly more complex. It assumes that specific selection mechanisms are at work in human judgment and choice. Some psychologists use this approach to analyze biases in moral judgments (Cosmides & Tooby, 1986) as well as other calculations.

THE ARGUMENT FOR AN EVOLUTIONARY BASIS FOR SEXUALITY

Does evolutionary theory have anything to say about gender differences in sexuality? Cross-cultural diversity in sexuality shows clearly that socialization plays an essential role. But are there also universal differences between the sexes? If so, are they rooted in our evolutionary past? Let's consider the arguments.

The evolutionary task for males and females is exactly the same: survive and reproduce, leaving behind as many genes as possible in offspring who will also survive and reproduce. But optimal strategies for accomplishing this goal differ for males and females, particularly for our ancestors. Evolutionary theorists believe that these differences underlie sex differences in behavioral mating strategies (Symons, 1979).

If the ultimate goal is the same for men and women, why would our reproductive strategies differ? The answer lies in the differences in reproductive capacity between

BEING FEMALE

BEING MALE

males and females. Human reproduction is a slow process, and its costs differ for males and females. Males have virtually limitless sperm, so they can father literally hundreds of children with a minimal investment of resources. Of course, in order to maximize

this reproductive potential, males must mate with multiple females.

Still, in evolutionary perspective the male's investment is relatively minor compared to the female's because females play the pivotal role in infant survival. Females can bear only a limited number of offspring in a lifetime, and their investment of resources is enormous: nine months of gestation followed by years of lactation and caregiving. Since the cost is so great, females are highly invested in their offspring. Moreover, females need to be relatively choosy about their mates. The males should be physically fit and control a sufficient number of resources to assist the females in the protection of their progeny.

Can you begin to see the conflict of interest? The scenario above provides the basis for what some scholars feel are the inherent differences between the sexes. Women desire monogamy and men desire promiscuity. Women are attracted to the best providers and men are attracted to the youthful

BEYOND OUR INHERITANCE: THE DISTINCTIVENESS OF THE HUMAN CONDITION

At the end of this swift history, it seems that the unique characteristics of the human animal are the source of our greatest triumphs and obstacles. Human beings are the only animals who have gone beyond their original birthplace to live under almost any conditions on Earth—in the desert, on frozen mountains, on the sea, in small settlements, in large cities—and even beyond the boundaries of the earth to live in space, for a while. We inherit a lot of physical characteristics as do other animals, but our most important characteristic is the *ability to go beyond our inheritance.*

We humans have created our own environment and are constantly adapting to our created world. This is why we have the pervasive physical and mental disorders of civilization—stress, mental disturbances, and so forth. It is as if our feet are rooted in the inheritance we share with other animals, but we are reaching beyond ourselves. In this aspiration we sometimes break in the middle. A new kind of adaptation is now necessary, one which will call on the capacities of mind and adaptations in behavior. So far we've dealt with some of the basic biological underpinnings to psychology, our brain, senses, genes, evolution. For

and fertile. Such characteristics permeate stereotypes of sex differences. Do they reflect a reality?

This is an interesting proposition but is not without its problems. Many feel that it reflects the application of Western ethnocentrism to our evolutionary heritage. Others feel that it is a male interpretation of a much more complicated story.

Let's take another look. Do men really prefer promiscuity and females prefer monogamy? We could argue, in evolutionary terms, that in fact both men and women are deeply ambivalent about monogamy. There is some evidence, for example, that the best way for a female to ensure impregnation is to have multiple partners. This may be why females are more likely than males to have multiple orgasms (Hrdy, 1981).

But females do best when males are around to help the survival of offspring. It is also in the males' best interest to ensure the survival of the offspring. Without it, the probability that the infant will survive to reproductive age is reduced. Many argue that too much has been made of the mother's need for the father to defend, feed, and protect her and her child. During the hunting and gathering period, food was abundant, and females could gather while they carried infants. Moreover, this interpretation presumes the existence of the nuclear family when the extended family was in full force. There were many relatives—that is, persons with shared genes—to assist a lactating female.

For males, however, there is a real advantage to monogamy. It is the *only* way they know that the offspring are theirs! Genetically speaking, the worst thing that can happen to a man is to be duped into providing for an offspring that is not his. So there are very good reasons why males should want loyal mates. In contrast, reproducing with more than one male holds advantages for the female in that her genes are packaged in more than one version. Variability goes a long way in evolutionary fitness.

Finally, do women want good providers as mates, and do men prefer younger females? David Buss (1989) provided compelling support for an affirmative answer to these questions. In a study of 36 different cultures, Buss found that females consistently expressed preferences for powerful mates, whereas males expressed the desire for young, attractive mates.

How should we interpret these findings? Evolutionary psychologists are searching for universals in psychological mechanisms. This is not to be confused with a search for universal human *behavior* (Tooby & Cosmides, 1989). The underlying mechanism may be inherited, but the behavioral expression will depend on environmental input. Thus, great caution must be exercised when using evolutionary approaches to *justify* modern-day behavior as human nature. If a universal human psychology is to be useful we must understand the way that it might operate. Remember, in evolutionary terms, variability is an advantage.

much of the rest of this book we will try to understand how we behave and think, judge and speak, learn and forget, stay healthy and become ill. Then we might know which new steps, succeeding those of our ancestors', we might now take.

1. *Genetic inheritance* plays a significant role in determining our individuality. Some genetic traits are set at conception; others are dispositions, which can be affected by environment or experience. The *gene* is the basic unit of heredity. Genes are made of DNA molecules, which encode heredity with four chemical substances arranged on a double helix.

2. Humans have about a million genes arranged on 23 pairs of chromosomes. One-half of each pair comes from one parent; the other half from the other parent. The *genotype* is the set of all the genes an individual carries. The subset of genes that is expressed in the individual is the *phenotype*. When a *dominant gene* is paired on the chromosomes with a *recessive gene*, the dominant one is expressed. Sex is determined by whether the father contributes an X or a Y chromosome. Abnormal chromosomes result in birth defects.

SUMMARY

3. Children differ genetically from their parents. Most of this variation is due to sexual recombination, but some comes from *mutation*. Most mutations are negative. Identical twins make excellent subjects for the study of the roles of inheritance and environment in development because they are the only examples of genetically identical humans.

4. Most complex human abilities are determined by an interplay between inheritance and environment. The *range of reaction* is a person's genetically determined potential. The experience of the individual affects what part of the genotype is expressed in the phenotype. Schizophrenia is an example of a mental disorder with both a genetic and an environmental component.

5. Humans began to evolve unique characteristics when our ancestors left the trees and began to walk upright. Humans are more *adaptable* than other animals to environments outside their original habitat. However, the evolutionary roots of humanity still affect how we deal with crises and challenges.

6. *Nature versus nurture* refers to the question of which is the greater determinant of behavior, heredity or environment. Neither is sufficient to explain all human behaviors; these two factors work together. To endure, individuals must be able to function and to adapt to the conditions of their environments.

7. The development of the human species spans only a tiny fraction of Earth history. *Prehumans* diverged from chimpanzees 25–13 million years ago. *Homo habilis* was a tool-using, hunting, social *hominid*. *Homo erectus* arose about 1.5 million years ago, with a larger brain and complex social behavior, and developed the ability to use fire. In the last several hundred thousand years, *Neanderthal* men appeared. They had advanced culture and rituals but seem to have disappeared after the Ice Age. *Cro-Magnon* man is the earliest known specimen of *Homo sapiens* (about 50,000 years old). Cro-Magnon was capable of language and art.

8. The invention of *agriculture* transformed human societies from nomadic hunter-gatherer groups to stable settlements. The great civilizations of China, India, and the Near East developed where agriculture was first developed.

9. *Evolution* is the process by which populations change over time. *Natural selection* is the crucial factor behind evolution. Sexual reproduction and mutation result in variations in offspring, some of which survive and reproduce better than others. The term *survival of the fittest* refers to the struggle of *species* to survive and reproduce, not to individuals.

10. Darwin's theory of evolution created controversy because it purported that human beings were not created by God to rule the Earth, but are subject to the same rules of life that apply to all creatures. Nevertheless, humans have many characteristics that set them apart from other animals. Bipedalism, immature birth, environmental influences on brain development, family structure, and tool use are interrelated adaptive advantages that helped make humans enormously successful and different from other animals.

11. Evolution has resulted in organisms having inborn behavior patterns. Ducklings will *imprint* any moving object they see between 12 and 18 hours after hatching and will follow it as if it is their mother. An example of innate behavior in humans is the *cuteness response*.

12. *Sociobiology* attempts to account for social behavior in biological terms, focusing on genes as determinants of behavior. This approach helps explain some human behaviors unexplained by Darwin's theory, such as altruism and infanticide. The concept of *inclusive fitness* states that an individual will act to maximize not only his own offspring, but also the number of copies of his genetic material. There are two theoretical approaches to the role of genetic evolution in psychology: the *phylogenetic* and the *selectionist viewpoints*. Further evolution will require humans to develop their capacities and consciously adapt their behavior to suit the new demands of the world.

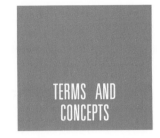

TERMS AND CONCEPTS

adaptation
adaptive value
Australopithecus
bases
bipedal
codons
Cro-Magnon
dexterity
DNA
ethology
fixed action patterns
genetic code
genotype
hominid
Homo erectus
human adaptation

hunter-gatherers
innate
mitosis
monozygotic
mutation
natural selection
nature
nurture
parental investment
perceptual adaptation
phenotype
prehumans
range of reaction
sensory adaptation
sociobiology
using specialized tools

SUGGESTIONS FOR FURTHER READING

Barash, D. (1986). *The tortoise and the hare.* New York: Viking Penguin.

An interesting analysis of human behavior from the sociobiological perspective.

Cosmidies, L., & Tooby, J. (1986). *From evolution to behavior: Evolutionary psychology as the missing link.* In Dupre, J. (Ed.), *The latest on the best: Essays on evolution and optimality.* Cambridge, MA: MIT Press.

An essay in a new collection that tries to carry the evolutionary view further into psychology.

Dawkins, R. (1986). *The blind watchmaker.* New York: Norton.

A brilliantly written work, by the author of The Selfish Gene, *that portrays the human world as an interconnected set of evolved actions, unguided. Very controversial, especially to religious viewpoints, but worth knowing about.*

Haldane, J. B. S. (1986). *On being the right size.* New York: Oxford University Press.

The great evolutionary biologist's essays, edited by Maynard Smith. It allows the reader to begin thinking like a biologist and look at common phenomena in a different way.

Johansen, D., & Shreve, J. (1989). *Lucy's child.* New York: Morrow.

The discovery of our oldest ancestor, written in an engaging style.

Ornstein, R., & Ehrlich, P. (1989). *New world, new mind.* New York: Doubleday.

The mismatches between the world that made us and the world we made. Amplifies much of the discussion in this chapter.

5
SENSORY EXPERIENCE

For years my house had been plagued by squirrels. They nested under the eaves of the roof and held meetings in the recesses of the attic. When they got hungry, they made a nice meal out of the side of my house. For years I harbored destructive thoughts about them. Then one day I saw an advertisement for a rodent eliminator: "Rids you once and for all of all pesty rodents!" I was not only delighted but also filled with ideas of how the rodent eliminator would torture the critters that brought me such grief.

The gadget arrived. It was not a giant flame thrower or an electric jail, but a box with an on–off switch. The instructions advised to set the box near the "rodent infestation" and "watch the rodents disappear forever." When I turned the machine on, nothing happened as far as I could tell. But suddenly there was a great scurrying commotion. The squirrels were running over one another to get out. There were so many that they had to eat a new hole in the house to escape. Even so, I was delighted.

The rodent eliminator projects a very high frequency sound wave, beyond the range of human hearing but within the sensitivity of most rodents. Our worlds are different: I heard nothing, but the squirrels, in the words of the manual, "will feel that a 747 jet has landed inside their heads." No sound heard by me and, now, no squirrels either.

The world appears to us as it does because of the way we are built. Compare yourself with a cat. When you see a chocolate cake, you see its dark color and sense its sweetness; the human body is attuned to color and taste. But when a cat sees the cake, it does not see colors or taste sweetness because its body doesn't need to. However, because the cat family often stalks nighttime prey, the cat can see objects at night that you cannot; it has a reflective layer in its eye that doubles the intensity of light.

REFLECTING AND SELECTING THE WORLD

The outside world is silent and dull in and of itself. There is no color in nature, no sound, no touch, no smell or feel. All these wonders exist inside nerve circuits. Each organism's mental system blinds it to most of the world so it can avoid dangers and exploit opportunities.

The senses are the outposts of the brain and connect the physical and psychological worlds. They "catch" a bit of the outside world and reject the rest. Although there is an astronomical amount of information in the world, human experience is limited to the visual, audible, olfactory, taste, and tactile stimuli. In addition to telling us about the world "out there," senses inform us about the world of our bodies: they help us maintain balance, coordinate and control body movements, and sense internal conditions, like pain and nausea.

Most of our experience of the world is of change: the sun coming up, a sudden loud noise, a change in the weather. Our sensory systems are designed to notice the beginnings and endings of events. When an air conditioner turns on in a room, you notice the hum. Soon you become habituated, or accustomed, to the noise. When it turns off, you again take note, this time because of the sudden absence of the noise. The senses are thus interested in news; loosely speaking their orders are, "Call me when something new happens."

The first need for any animal is to find out what is happening in the world and how to respond to it. The world is full of events, from simple wind shifts, sunrises, and miniscule movement of particles in the air to the sudden alighting of hawks. The earth shifts on its large surface plates, rotates upon its axis, and moves around the sun. On its surface are millions of tiny particles and vast populations of bacteria. Pressure waves (sounds) and radiant electromagnetic energy fill the air.

When you make a telephone call, you don't want to hear all possible human voices. Similarly, the mind needs to limit the information it receives to a small fraction of that actually present in the outside world. It extracts from the cacophony of the entire "big world" a specialized "small world" in which an individual organism can act and live. This radical sensory blindness is effective; sensory systems accurately reflect the regularities of the world (Shepard, 1984).

SIMPLIFICATION AND SELECTIVITY

William James wrote:

> We see that the mind is at every stage a theatre of simultaneous possibilities. Consciousness consists in the comparison of these with each other, the selection of some, and the suppression of others, of the rest by the reinforcing and inhibiting agency of attention. The highest and most celebrated mental products are filtered from the data chosen by the faculty below that, which mass was in turn sifted from a still larger amount of simpler material, and so on. The mind, in short, works on this block of stone. In a sense, the statue stood there from eternity. But there were a thousand different ones beside it. The sculptor alone is to thank for having extracted this one from the rest. . . . Other minds, other worlds, from the same monotonous and inexpressive chaos! My world is but one in a million, alike embedded and alike real to those who may abstract them. How different must be the world in the consciousness of ants, cuttle-fish, or crab! (James, 1890)

Our senses' first selection is the result of the biological nature of the senses themselves. We have only the operations of sight, hearing, taste, smell, and touch available to us. Second, each sense receives only a limited range of stimuli. The eye responds to only a minute portion (one-trillionth) of the entire spectrum of radiant electromagnetic energy. What we see, then, is less than one-trillionth of the energy that actually meets the eye. Like other creatures, we are economical; we sense only what is necessary for our survival.

Consider an animal that simplifies even more than we do. Jerome Lettvin and his associates (1959) at Massachusetts Institute of Technology devised an experiment in which visual stimulation was offered to one eye of an immobilized frog. The frog was placed so that its eye was at the center of a hemisphere seven inches in radius. Small objects were placed in different positions on the inner surface of this hemisphere by means of magnets and could be moved around in the space inside the hemisphere.

The investigators measured "what the frog's eye tells the frog's brain"—that is, the electrical impulses sent to the brain by the eye. However, when an assortment of objects, colors, and patterns were shown to the frog, the investigators noticed a remarkable phenomenon. Despite the great variety of stimuli presented, the eye sent only four kinds of "messages" to the brain.

These four messages contained information relating directly to the two most important aspects of a frog's survival: obtaining food and escaping danger. The first message provided a general outline of the environment. Two of the messages formed a kind of bug-perceiving system: one detected moving edges and the other responded to small, dark objects entering the field of vision. Frogs catch and eat only live insects. A frog surrounded by food that did not move would starve to death because it has no means for detecting unmoving objects.

The fourth message responded to sudden decreases in light, as would happen if a large enemy approached. The frog's brain is "wired" to ignore all but a very few specific types of information. Although higher level animals, ourselves included, are not as restricted in sensory experience as the frog, the sensory systems of all animals simplify their organism's world by the act of selection.

The human brain simplifies our experience by selecting only important stimuli for the brain to respond to. Otherwise, we would not be able to function under conditions of sensory overload, such as shown in this busy scene.

DECONSTRUCTION   To the ordinary observer, the world seems to consist of specific, different objects: cats and chocolate cakes, mountains and water. But think about it: How could a cat, or an image of a cat, get inside our brain? It doesn't enter directly, there are no "cat paths" inside us. And if there were such paths, what about buildings, trees, grass, and the sky? Obviously, we don't have a single brain area for perceiving each and every thing in the world.

How, then, do we perceive all the variety we do? No one knows for sure, but psychologists have figured out that there must first be a process of deconstruction of the physical world so that selected parts of the information available enter the nervous system (Marr, 1982). **Deconstruction** means just what it sounds like, a breakup of a whole object into parts. The technical task for psychologists and other analysts of sensation is to determine which components of the outside world our brain analyzes and how it assembles them later on. Sensation is a complex subject and perception is a complex analysis. It will take the next two chapters just to begin to understand the process, but after reading about it, you may never think the same way about your own experiences again.

SELECTIVITY   The senses are both sensors and censors. Obviously, our senses show us the outside world, but if we were bombarded with all the sensations in the world, our experience would be extremely chaotic. The air in the room you are in is filled with various forms of energy: an entire spectrum of light, sound, and radio waves, and more. Yet you are aware of only a small portion of that energy. The light that we see is actually just a small portion of the band of radiant **electromagnetic energy** (Figure 5-1). **Selection,** then, involves both inclusion and exclusion. The senses select what is important and keep the rest of the world out. And each sense has evolved to extract a very specific kind of information. You see light; you do not hear it. You cannot taste an apricot by squeezing it into your ear!

Each organism's sensory system simplifies the world to see only what it needs. The cat is a nocturnal animal and so needs its reflective eye to see in the dark; insects see infrared radiation, which we feel as warmth; and a frog sees only things that move.

REFLECTING AND SELECTING THE WORLD

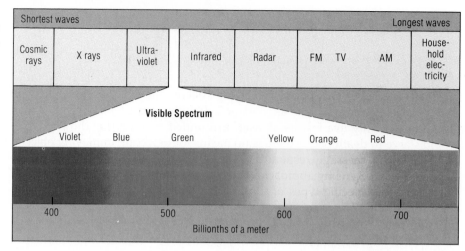

FIGURE 5-1
The Spectrum of Electromagnetic Energy

The visible spectrum—what our unaided senses can detect—is a small fraction of the total range of radiation around us.

HOW THE SENSES SIMPLIFY AND ORGANIZE THE WORLD

SENSORY ADAPTATION

When a stimulus continues for a while, we stop noticing it. The air conditioner in the room, the noise of the street, our breathing—all seem to disappear. This happens because our senses respond vigorously to beginnings and endings of events; they respond less to constant stimulation. This decline in response is called **sensory adaptation.** It reduces the number of irrelevant sensations, allowing us to focus on new events in the environment.

SENSORY COMPARISON

Although each sensory system can discriminate millions of gradients of stimulation, it does not have a specific receptor for, say, each shade of color or each tone of sound. This is an important part of how we are built: since we rarely experience the exact situation twice, it would be uneconomical to have a system that responds in a different way to each new stimulus. Thus, sensory systems operate primarily by **comparison.** Judgments are comparative: the color seen at one moment is brighter or redder than the previous one; a sound is louder or more complex than an earlier one (Figure 5-2).

Here is a demonstration of sensory adaptation, change, and comparison. Fill three bowls with water, one hot, one cold, and one tepid. Put one hand in the hot water and the other in the cold water. Wait a few moments. Now place both hands in the tepid bowl. Notice that the hand that was in the hot water feels cold, while the hand that was in the cold water feels warm. Both hands had adapted to their relative temperatures. Then, when the hands were put in the tepid bowl, they sensed a change. Although both hands were in the same bowl of water, each responded differently to it. The particular message of change that each hand signaled to the brain was based on a comparison of two events.

A sensory change is a difference in a stimulus from one moment to the next. One sensation always follows and precedes another, so one stimulus is louder,

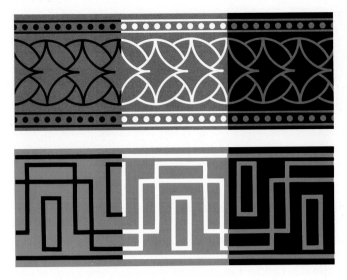

FIGURE 5-2
The Spreading Effect

Because we judge sensory stimuli largely by comparison, even if the red or blue in an illustration is actually all one shade, the so-called spreading effect of the adjacent lines can make us perceive the red or blue as lighter or darker in different parts of the drawing.

softer, brighter, dimmer, warmer, colder, greener, or redder than something else (Figure 5-3). We compare relative differences between stimuli. Try this demonstration: put a three-way bulb (50–100–150 watt) in a lamp in a dark room. Turn on the lamp; the difference between darkness and the 50-watt illumination seems to be significant. But the next two increases in light, from 50 to 100 watts, and from 100 to 150 watts, do not seem to be as great. Although the change in the physical stimulus (a difference of 50 watts) is the same each time, you hardly notice the difference of the two higher wattages.

HOW PHYSICAL AND PSYCHOLOGICAL WORLDS ARE RELATED

The senses connect the external physical world with internal psychological experience. When scientists began to study this relationship in the late nineteenth century, they called it **psychophysics;** their efforts were the beginning of scientific psychology. Using physics as their model, the first psychologists tried to determine precisely how changes in the outside world affected the internal world of human experience. They pursued their investigations in a straightforward manner: they clanged bells and shone lights of varying degrees of brightness at people and then measured how much a stimulus had to change in order for a person to report a change in experience.

THRESHOLDS   There are limits to what we can sense, limits set by the range of physical energy to which the senses respond. A light must attain a certain intensity before we notice it; a sound must be loud enough for us to hear it. The smallest amount of energy necessary for us to notice a stimulus is called the **absolute threshold.** It is defined as the minimum strength for a stimulus to be noticed by an observer 50 percent of the time.

The absolute threshold is not the amount of energy required to activate the sensory system; rather, it is the amount required for us to *experience* the stimulus. The senses can be activated with little energy. The eye will respond to the smallest quantity of light and the ear to movements in the air only slightly

FIGURE 5-3

Stare at the dot at the center of this figure. Those shadowy squares at the intersections of the white lines do not actually exist in the drawing. They are "seen" only because of the way your sensory systems work.
(Verheijen, 1961)

HOW THE SENSES SIMPLIFY AND ORGANIZE THE WORLD

greater than those of the air molecules themselves, but we rarely become aware of this response.

The minimum increase in a physical stimulus necessary for us to notice a difference is called the **difference threshold** or, more commonly, the **just noticeable difference (j.n.d.).** Unlike the absolute threshold, the j.n.d. is not constant. If it takes one additional candle to notice a difference in illumination in a room with 10 candles, then in a room with 100 candles, there would need to be 10 additional candles to notice a difference. There would be no noticeable difference if 101 rather than 100 candles were lit (Coren & Ward, 1989).

THE GENERAL PRINCIPLES OF SENSATION

WEBER'S LAW   A single candle flame emits a fixed amount of physical energy, but we experience it differently depending on the surrounding circumstances. In a darkened room, it provides much illumination; in a bright room, it is hardly noticed. This first principle of sensation was uncovered by Ernst Weber (1834). He noted that equal changes in physical intensity do not produce equal changes in experience. This means that the relationship between the inner world and the external world is not a simple one. Although the psychological world does not have a one-to-one relationship with the physical world, Weber noted that there is a consistent relationship between them. The amount of added energy in a stimulus required to produce a j.n.d. is always the same proportion of the stimulus. If a 64-watt light is required to notice a change in illumination from 60 watts, then 128 watts would be needed to detect a change from 120 watts. This consistent proportional relationship, known as Weber's Law, can be stated mathematically as follows:

$$\frac{\text{change in stimulus}}{\text{stimulus}} = \text{constant}$$

In our example,

$$\frac{4}{60} = \frac{1}{15} \quad \text{and} \quad \frac{8}{120} = \frac{1}{15}.$$

The practical principle is that our sensory systems are sensitive to changes in the intensity of stimuli rather than to the absolute levels of stimuli. One researcher explained how this is adaptive:

CHAPTER 5 / SENSORY EXPERIENCE

Imagine yourself sitting in front of a fire surrounded by forests, without any effective weapons, listening to the growl of a large and hungry animal. The most important information would be the ratio between the loudness of two successive growls. If the present growl is twice as loud as the last one, you know that the animal has covered half the distance toward you in that time. So you know that it will be arriving in just that much time! That information is really much more important than estimating the actual loudness of each growl or the actual difference in loudness of two growls. (Ludel, 1978)

FECHNER'S LAW   Gustave Fechner continued Weber's search for the laws governing how the mind responds to external stimuli. He attempted to discover the relationship between the physical intensity of a stimulus and its perceived intensity. He based his work on Weber's and assumed that the j.n.d. for a particular stimulus would always be produced by the same ratio of intensities regardless of the intensity of the original stimulus.

Fechner postulated that the subjective impression associated with the j.n.d. would also be the same regardless of the actual intensity of the stimuli. Because the j.n.d. is smaller for weak stimuli, the perceptual system would then be more sensitive to changes in the level of stimulation for weak stimuli than for intense stimuli. Fechner's Law states that there is a logarithmic relationship between physical stimulus intensity and perceived stimulus intensity.

Fechner's Law: $S = W \log I$,
where S = the magnitude of sensation produced by the stimulus,
      W = a constant derived from Weber's Law (I/I), and
      I = the physical magnitude of the stimulus.

THE POWER LAW   A third principle, discovered by S. S. Stevens, is that each sense transforms the information it selects differently from the other senses. Using a technique called magnitude estimation to test Fechner's Law, he had people assign numbers to stimuli ranking their perceived intensity. He found that Fechner's Law did not accurately describe the changes in perceived intensity produced by changes in physical intensity because the relationships differed for the different senses. This principle, called the **Power Law,** states that within each sensory system equal ratios of stimulus intensity produce equal ratios of change in experience.

When these relationships are charted on a graph (Stevens, 1956), they reveal much about the function of different sensory systems. The straight line for length in Figure 5-4 indicates that the relationship between the experience of length and the actual physical length is direct. This makes sense because we do not often have to estimate very long distances visually.

However, we encounter a large range of brightness: we can see a single candle flame on a clear night 30 miles away and are able to glance at the sun, which is about 1,000 billion times brighter. Since there is such a variety of brightness to judge daily, our sensory system has to reduce that range. The flattened curve of brightness on the graph indicates that brightness information is indeed compressed.

The upward curve of pain reflects our experience. Because it is important to be aware of potential injury as fast as possible, the experience of pain is amplified, not lessened; a small amount of pain gets our undivided attention

Even a little bit of pain gets an immediate reaction.

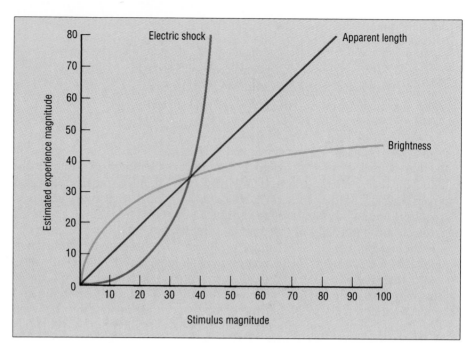

FIGURE 5-4
Power Curves for
Different Stimuli

There is great variation in the
power curves charting the
magnitude of your experience
of such stimuli as pain
(electric shock), apparent
length, and brightness.
(Stevens, 1961)

very quickly. Our amplified response to pain makes it an extremely effective early warning system for possible bodily harm.

Psychophysics has thus revealed four major related principles: (1) there is a consistent relationship between changes in the physical world and changes in experience; (2) these relationships are proportional; (3) each sense system has a different internal representation of the outside world; and (4) the internal representation of these relationships reveals how closely tied our senses are to survival.

HOW PHYSICAL ENERGY IS CHANGED INTO EXPERIENCE: TRANSDUCTION

Although each sense responds to a different form of physical energy, the brain has only one way of receiving and responding to information: neural firing. The senses transform physical energy, such as waves in the air and mechanical pressure (touch), into electrical or chemical action.

The senses routinely perform two miracles. First, each sensory organ transforms a particular kind of physical energy into neural firing. This process is called **transduction.** The eye transduces light, the ear transduces sound waves, the nose transduces gaseous molecules. Second, all of these electrical and chemical reactions in the brain somehow become human experience. What we perceive as trees, birds, light, sound, or thoughts are only electrical and chemical activity in the brain. These two miracles occur every moment of life and are so routine that we are unaware of them. Psychologists are on the way to understanding the first miracle, but science remains mystified by the second.

VISION

Vision is the dominant sense of human beings, responsible for the control of almost all the basic actions necessary for living in the human world. James Gibson (1966) classified the basic functions of vision.

- *Detecting the layout of the surroundings.* This involves the ability to notice large features of the environment and to distinguish objects and other animals.
- *Detecting change or sequence.* We can distinguish between day and night, between fine and gross movements, and between motion and events in the world.
- *Detecting and controlling movement.* We are able to see what we are doing and where we are going. If we did not have visual feedback, movements would be uncontrolled.

Where is the image that we see? We can see what a camera does by looking through its lens, but the eye does not work like a camera. The brain does not "see" the image on the retina; neural impulses, not images, are received by the brain. The visual system of the eye works more like television. Your television set does not receive a "picture"; it receives coded patterns that it translates into colors and shapes.

The eye is the most complex of all the sense organs. In the *retina,* a single layer inside the eye, there are over 120 million receptor cells called *rods* and 6 million receptor cells called *cones.* The *optic nerve,* which connects the eye to the brain, contains more than 1 million nerve cells (Figure 5-5).

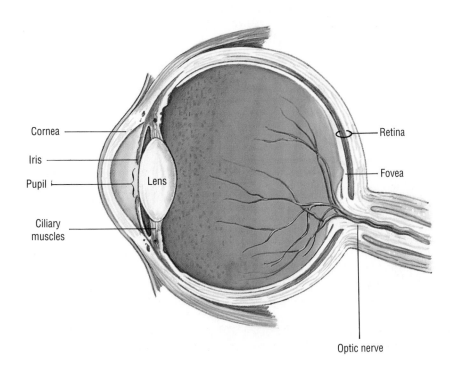

FIGURE 5-5
Major Structures of the Human Eye
(Bloom & Fawcett, 1968)

Light first enters the eye through the **cornea,** a transparent membrane that covers the front of the eye. It travels inside the eye through the *pupil,* which is an opening in the *iris,* the colored part of the eye. The *iris* is composed of two kinds of muscles, circular and radial. The circular muscles make the pupil smaller; the radial muscles open it up to make the pupil larger. Like the aperture of a camera, the size of the opening of the pupil determines the amount of light that is admitted. Light then passes through the *lens,* which focuses the light on the receptor cells of the retina at the back of the eye. The lens is held in place by the interocular ("inside the eye") muscles, which pull the lens and thus change its shape to focus on objects at different distances.

THE RETINA

The **retina** is the key structure of vision. It begins its development as part of the brain but becomes part of the eye in the embryonic stage. It is comprised of neural tissue that is about the thickness of this page. The retina has three main layers of nerve cells (Figure 5-6):

FIGURE 5-6
The Human Retina:
Major Structures and
Their Relative Positions

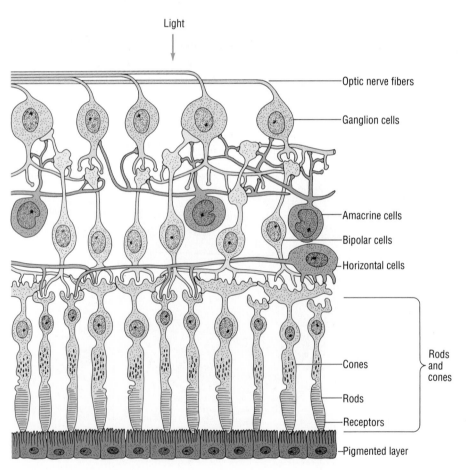

Light

Optic nerve fibers

Ganglion cells

Amacrine cells

Bipolar cells

Horizontal cells

Cones

Rods

Receptors

Rods and cones

Pigmented layer

1. **Photoreceptors** (*photo* comes from the Greek word for "light"). The first layer consists of two types of photoreceptors, the rods and cones, which contain chemicals that respond to light. (See the detailed discussion below.)

2. **Intermediate layer.** Three kinds of cells in the intermediate layer connect the two other layers. The *bipolar cells* take information from the rods and cones to the third layer of cells, called *ganglia* (the singular form is ganglion). The *horizontal cells* transfer information from rods and cones horizontally. The *amacrine cells* transfer information from rods and cones and all cells in the intermediate layer and send it to other intermediate layer cells or to cells in the ganglia.

3. **Ganglion cells.** The third layer is composed of ganglion cells. Each cell has a long axon, the part of a neuron that carries information from the cell to other neurons. All the axons from the eye's ganglion cells leave the eye at the same point, where they are bundled together to form the *optic nerve*. This tiny spot where the ganglion cells exit the eye on the way to the brain is commonly called the *blind spot*. There are no photoreceptor cells here, so this part of the eye cannot respond to light (Figure 5-7). We are not normally aware of the blind spot because normally we do not see it (Figure 5-8).

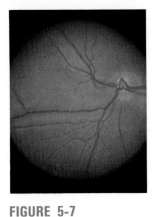

FIGURE 5-7
The Blind Spot

There are no photoreceptors in the area of the retina where the ganglion cells meet to form the optic nerve. It is thus known as the blind spot.

PHOTORECEPTORS: RODS AND CONES

The rods and cones are shaped as their names imply (Figure 5-9). But even though their shapes are different, their internal structures are similar: like stacks of discs. The photochemicals are inside the discs. The major differences between rods and cones are the kind of light they respond to and their distribution in the eye.

FIGURE 5-8
Finding Your Blind Spot

Close your right eye and stare at the circle on the right. Holding the book about one foot from your face, slowly move it back and forth until the square on the left disappears. The square cannot be seen at that point because its image falls on your blind spot.

175

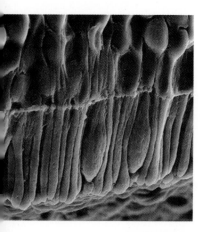

**FIGURE 5-9
Rods and Cones
in the Retina**

This photomicrograph (a photograph taken through a light microscope) shows the thicker cones among the slender rods. Compare this real view with the schematic diagram in Figure 5-6.

Rods respond most to light energy at low levels. They respond best to wavelengths of 480 nanometers (nm) which register in vision as a blue-green color. About 120 million rods are distributed over the retina, with the heaviest concentration at the sides. Light vision is most sensitive slightly to the side of the eye rather than dead center. The rods are like black and white television; they sense all the "colors" in the world as relative shades of blue-green "grays." They allow us to see when the illumination is low.

The retina contains about 6 million **cones,** which are responsible for color vision and are less sensitive than rods. They need bright light to be activated. There are three different kinds of cones, each of which responds to a certain range of wavelengths. For instance, one responds best to 575 nm, which is seen as red-orange; another to 550 nm, seen as green; and yet another to 440 nm, seen as blue-violet (Figure 5-10).

The greatest concentration of cones is in the center of the retina. This area, which has no rods, is called the **fovea.** To examine an object closely, you move your head, body, and eyes until the image of the object falls on your fovea. The fovea is especially well represented in the brain; more brain cells receive input from the fovea than from any other part of the eye. The cones operate like a color television camera and screen, which also have sensors for three colors of light: red-orange, green, and blue-violet. These are the colors from which all other colors can be made.

**FIGURE 5-10
Relative Wavelength
Absorption of Different
Kinds of Cones in the
Human Eye**

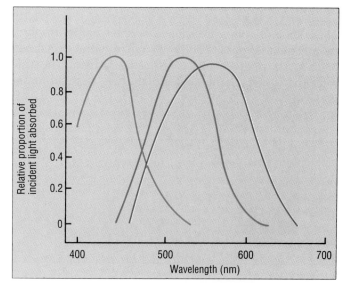

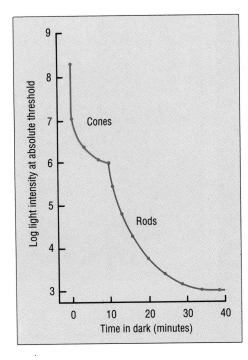

FIGURE 5-11
Testing Dark Adaptation
Subjects whose eyes had become adapted to bright light were then placed in darkness. The curve shows how their retinas adapted to the dark. They became more sensitive to even fainter flashes of light. The abrupt turn at about 10 minutes is called the rod-cone break, indicating where the cones have reached their maximum sensitivity while the rods continue becoming more sensitive over another half hour or so.

The photosensitive rods and cones face away from the light and are located in the innermost layer of the retina. The reason for this surprising arrangement is the need for oxygen. Although all parts of the eye require oxygen (supplied by blood vessels throughout the eye), the photochemicals of the rods and cones need much more.

If the rods and cones were in the outermost layer of the retina, there would have to be many more blood vessels, which would block so much light that it would be impossible to see. So, the layer of cells right behind the retina has an additional network of blood vessels that supply the rods and cones with the necessary amount of oxygen (Figure 5-6).

DARK ADAPTATION

It is difficult to see upon entering a darkened movie theater. Within a couple of minutes, however, the outlines of people and seats become visible. The eyes, through the process of **dark adaptation,** become sensitive to the dark. The cones quickly adapt to the dark, but after 10 minutes they stop adapting. The rods continue becoming increasingly sensitive to light stimulation, reaching their maximum sensitivity in 30 to 40 minutes (Figure 5-11). At first you see objects only in black and white, then in shades of blue-green. After 15 minutes more color becomes visible.

THE BASIS OF COLOR VISION

Human beings can make roughly 8 million distinctions in color! As you might expect, color vision has adaptive value. Seeing in color enables us to make more precise judgments about the outside world. Look at Figure 5-12. One view

177

FIGURE 5-12
The Advantages of
Seeing in Color

As these photographs demonstrate, seeing the world in black and white could impair your ability to recognize and quickly exploit opportunities. Seeing in color makes it easier to evaluate what is desirable or dangerous, inviting or inimical.

shows a scene in black and white, in which the fruit is difficult to distinguish. In the color view of the same scene, however, the ripe fruit immediately stands out.

There is no color in nature. What we see as color is actually variations in the wavelengths of light reflected from different surfaces. These wavelengths activate one of the three kinds of cones, which in turn send their coded information to the brain. The experience of color is a product of our sensory systems.

FIGURE 5-13
How the Retina Codes
Color Information

We see primary colors (red, green, blue, yellow) and their variations, as well as brightness (dark and light, white and black), because of the way our visual system responds to different wavelengths of light. This diagram represents connections in an opponent process that elicits responses from various cone cells. The round and the flat connections may arbitrarily be considered either excitatory or inhibitory, and the numbers indicate the wavelength of the cones' maximum sensitivity.
(Hurvich & Jameson, 1974)

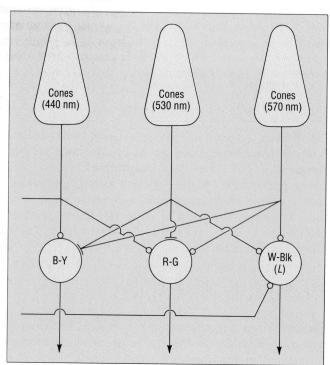

CODING OF COLOR

Figure 5-13 shows a wiring diagram for the retina that has been proposed to explain how the retina codes color information. The nature of this coding process determines much of color experience. Four colors, called *psychological primaries*, are seen as pure. These are red, green, blue, and yellow. Like all other colors, the primaries are associated with specific wavelengths of light. What makes these colors seem pure is not the colors themselves; it is the way the visual system responds to different wavelengths of light.

Three systems of color information are sent from the eye to the brain. Each sends information on two opposite dimensions; therefore, the brain's method for color coding is called an **opponent process**. The first two systems are transmitted only by cone cells and relay information about hue: one transmits the blue-yellow component of color; the other, the red-green. The third system, which is transmitted by both cones and rods, provides information about the color's brightness (dark-light).

AFTERIMAGES Stare at a red square against a white background for a minute. Then take the square away and look at the background. You will see an afterimage of its complementary color, green. Staring at a black square produces white, and blue produces a yellow afterimage. The color of these afterimages results from the brain's opponent process of coding information (Figure 5-14).

COLOR BLINDNESS Color blindness is a genetic defect of one of the color systems and occurs predominantly in males. Seven out of 100 men have some form of color blindness, while only about one woman in 1,000 suffers from this defect (Figure 5-15). The most common form is red-green color blindness; blue-yellow color blindness is rare. But because of opponent processing, there is no such

FIGURE 5-14
Afterimages

Stare at the dot in the center of the colorful left circle for at least 30 seconds. Then shift your gaze to the right circle and concentrate on the dark spot in its center. The afterimage you see in the right circle results from how the brain's opponent process codes information to register complementary colors.

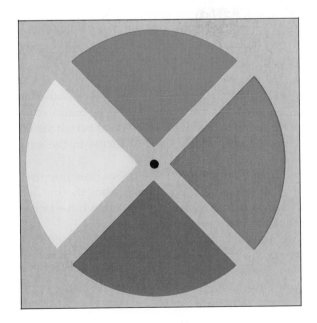

FIGURE 5-15
The World to a
Color-Blind Person

The view at the left is what a person sees who has red-green color blindness, the most common form of defect in the color-sensing system. The right view is what this same scene looks like to a person with normal vision.

thing as red-blue color blindness. Many of the tests for color blindness involve discriminating figures composed of color circles against a background composed of other color circles.

PSYCHOLOGICAL ASPECTS OF COLOR

Like all other perceptual systems, color perception is not a simple, direct process of measuring the wavelength of reflected light. Color perception is intricately connected with other human systems of assessing the environment. The color of a box of detergent on a grocery store shelf can influence a consumer's belief in the effectiveness of the detergent (Kupchella, 1976).

Colors also influence the other senses. It is common, for instance, to hear people refer to blue colors as cool and bright reds and yellows as warm or hot. This is true to such an extent that, as one study found, people turn the heat up higher in a blue room than they do in a yellow room (Boynton, 1971). The obvious association between colors and weather is likely to be responsible for this effect.

WHAT THE EYE TELLS THE BRAIN

As we have seen, sight does not take place in the eyes but with the assistance of the eyes. The first part of visual experience is what the eye tells the brain—that is, the neural impulses that the eye sends to the brain. The second part of visual experience is what the brain tells the eye, which we will discuss in the next section.

In each eye there are about 126 million photoreceptor cells whose impulses are channeled into about 1 million ganglion cells. Stimuli from the outside world are increasingly simplified and abstracted as the information travels from the outside to the visual cortex of the brain (Figure 5-16).

Information from the left eye travels via the left optic nerve, and information from the right eye goes through the right optic nerve. But notice in Figure 5-17 that a change takes place at an intersection called the *optic chiasma:* some of the axons cross over. Those from the left sides of both eyes go off to the right,

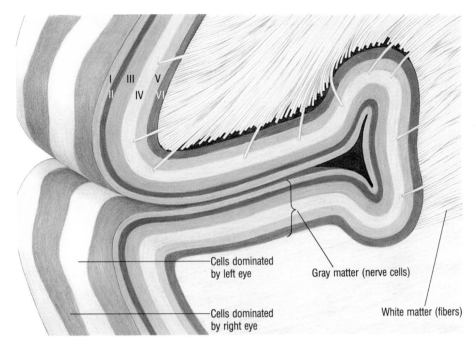

FIGURE 5-16
Detail of the Visual
Cortex

A cross-section of the visual cortex shows its six-layered construction, I–VI, in which each layer contains cells of certain shapes and complexity that specialize in responding to different kinds of information. The black and white stripes on the surface represent the tendency of each eye to dominate alternating areas of cells—those dominated by the right eye are shown by white stripes and those by the left eye, black stripes.

Cells dominated by left eye

Gray matter (nerve cells)

Cells dominated by right eye

White matter (fibers)

and vice versa. Only the arrangement, not the structure, of the axons changes. After the crossover, the optic nerve is called the optic tract.

THE MANY PATHS OF VISUAL PROCESSING

The million nerve fibers in each of the two optic tracts split into two pathways. The larger of the two pathways travels to the **lateral geniculate nucleus (LGN)** in the thalamus (*lateral* means "sideways"; a *geniculate* is a bend or joint). Because of the similarity between LGN cells and ganglion cells, it appears that the LGN is a kind of switching station, relaying messages to the visual cortex. The LGN also analyzes color signals. The neural fibers that leave the LGN fan out to inform the primary **visual cortex.**

The second pathway from the optic tract passes to a region of the brain stem called the **tectum.** This is a much older structure than the visual cortex in an evolutionary sense. From there the pathway goes on to the *pulvinar* and *lateral posterior nuclei* in the thalamus and then to the **secondary visual cortex** at the back of the brain.

The two visual pathways seem to serve specialized functions. The *tectopulvinar system*, which passes through the tectum, may be responsible for the localization of objects in space, guiding eye movements and the crude perception of patterns. The *geniculostriate system*, which passes through the LGN, is probably responsible for detailed perception of patterns and colors and the identification of objects (Essen, 1984; Ungerleider & Mishkin, 1982).

Recent research indicates that two types of cell within the LGN serve specialized purposes (Livingston, 1988). They are called the *magnocellular* (large cell) and *parvocellular* (small cell) divisions. They project to different parts of the

181

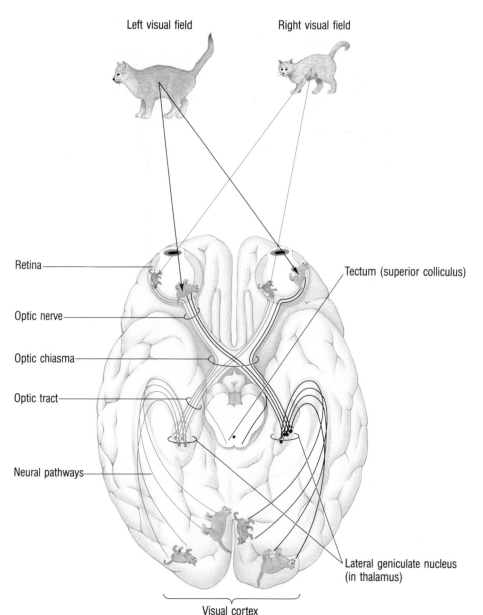

Left visual field

Right visual field

Retina

Optic nerve

Optic chiasma

Optic tract

Neural pathways

Tectum (superior colliculus)

Lateral geniculate nucleus
(in thalamus)

Visual cortex

**FIGURE 5-17
Visual Pathways in the
Brain**

The right half of each retina
picks up light rays from the
left visual field, and those
from the right visual field fall
on the left half of each
retina. The optic nerves meet
at the optic chiasma, where
information from the right
sides of both retinas is
channeled to the visual cortex
of the right cerebral
hemisphere and that from the
left sides of both retinas
goes to the left hemisphere.

primary visual cortex in a way that results in three complementary visual
pathways. The magno cells are faster and less acute to fine patterns than the
parvo cells. The parvo cells pass on color information, and the magno cells,
which are color blind, transmit information about brightness contrast.

In the visual cortex, the information from the two areas is combined to
produce the perception of color and shading. They are also processed separately, in the case of the parvo system, to acquire high-resolution information about
borders, and by the magno system to perceive movement and stereoscopic
depth. All three pathways merge to produce a unified perception of an object.

The color pathway is much less discriminating than the·others. Because of this, our perception of color patterns is less precise than our ability to see borders and movement. You can see this in an impressionist painting where the tiny strokes or dots of color seem to blend together because our color perception system cannot distinguish them in such a fine pattern. If you look closer at the painting, you will see individual strokes. Similarly, in watercolors, the coloration does not need to conform to the outlines of the figures for us to see the colors as part of the figures (Figure 5-18).

LATERAL INHIBITION

Every sensory experience depends on the previous sensory experience. A lump of coal in bright sunlight reflects more light than this page in the shade. But we always experience or perceive the coal as dark and the page as light because the coal is darker than its surroundings and the page is lighter. In Figure 5-19, all the central squares are exactly the same shade of gray, but the darker the surrounding figure is, the brighter each square appears. An edge or corner or sharp change in color is a clear demarcation between two objects or planes. Things appear brighter at edges and corners than in the middle.

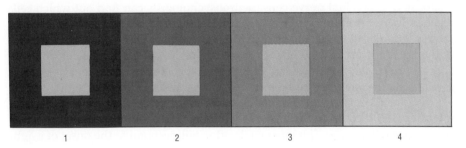

FIGURE 5-18
Pattern Perception

Impressionist and watercolor paintings exploit our visual system's ability to perceive patterns from coloration. (Left, Claude Monet, *Rouen Cathedral, Façade*, 1894; right, Winslow Homer, *Hurricane, Bahamas.*)

FIGURE 5-19
How Simultaneous Brightness Contrast Fools Your Eye

All the central squares are the same shade of gray. But how each contrasts with its lighter or darker background triggers the lateral inhibition mechanism of retinal cells and alters your perception so the central squares seem to be of different shades.

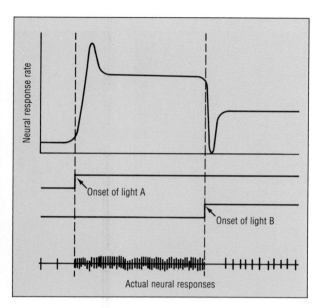

The physiological mechanism by which certain cells inhibit or stimulate one another is called **lateral inhibition.** Most of the evidence on lateral inhibition comes from studies on the horseshoe crab *Limulus,* whose visual system is both simple and large. Retinal cells respond to light by firing: the brighter the light, the more they fire. Whenever a cell fires, it inhibits the cells next to it (laterally) from firing. In Figure 5-20, you can see that the brighter the stimulus, the greater the inhibition. Thus, the basic mechanism of lateral inhibition is that the more a retinal cell fires, the more it inhibits neighboring cells from firing. The firing of cell A inhibits the firing of cell B.

Lateral inhibition helps us see sharp changes, like corners, in the environment (Figure 5-21). It may enhance discrimination between two slightly different figures. Because it exaggerates changes in the environment, we can be fooled. Look at the two illustrations in Figure 5-22. If you stare at the center of the left illustration, the fuzzy-edged circle disappears. This does not happen if you stare at the center of the well-defined circle on the right.

RECEPTIVE FIELDS IN THE RETINA AND VISUAL CORTEX

The rate of firing in a single axon can be measured and recorded by a hairlike electrical probe. By flashing a light at an animal's eye and recording the response to individual nerve cells, neuropsychologists can find out which cells respond to the stimulus. The area of stimulation that a cell responds to is called the **receptive field** (Figure 5-23). The function of the cells in the visual cortex is different from that of cells in the optic tract: the cortical cells respond best to specific features in the environment and are called **feature analyzers.** (However, the cells may actually serve other functions unknown to us.)

The ganglion cells in the retina also have receptive fields. A typical retinal receptive field is composed of input cells arranged in a circle. In the center of the circle is a smaller circle. The inner circle often will respond to the onset of a light

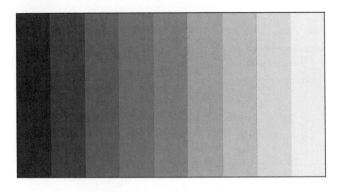

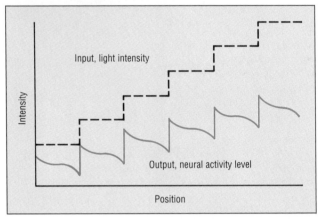

FIGURE 5-21
Lateral Inhibition Accentuates Change

There is a uniform progression of changes between successive steps in this photograph. But you do not perceive the changes as uniform. Lateral inhibition makes nerve cells in the retina respond so that changes are accentuated—the relationship between the input (light intensity) and the output (neural activity level) is not uniform.
(Cornsweet, 1970)

stimulus, while the outer part will respond when the light turns off. The cells in the outer part of the circle and the inner part will also laterally inhibit each other if they are stimulated at the same time. Complex feature selectors are constructed by combining the information from many of these receptive fields further along in visual processing.

There are over 100 million neurons in the human visual cortex, and it is currently hard to know the extent of their specialization. Isolating and identifying receptive fields is one way that investigators can determine what features

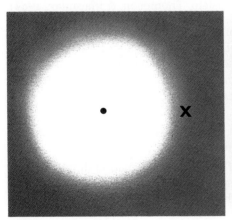

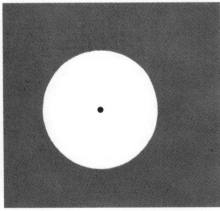

FIGURE 5-22
Sensitivity to the Changes Presented by Stabilized Images

Your visual system is especially sensitive to the sharp-edged circle on the right, so if you stare at it, the photoreceptors continue firing and it remains sharp. In contrast, the fuzzy circle on the right disappears as you stare at the dot. But it will come back into view if your gaze shifts to the X.

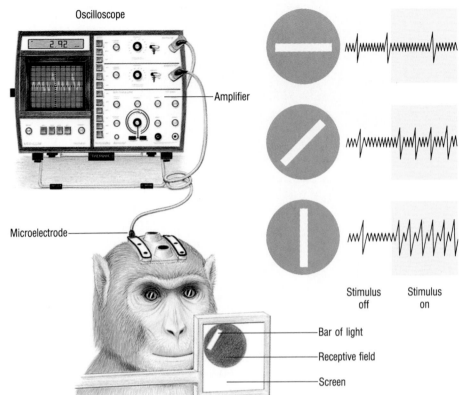

**FIGURE 5-23
Feature Analyzers'
Responses to Different
Receptive Fields**

The response of single
cortical cells to various
stimuli can be measured by
an oscilloscope. When bars of
light (left) are flashed in the
subject's eye, the most
vigorous neural response is to
the vertical bar. This
suggests that this particular
cell is a feature analyzer
intended to detect and react
to visual stimuli that have a
vertical orientation.
(Hubel & Weisel, 1962)

specific cells are designed to notice. It appears that each species of animal possesses a special set of feature analyzers that pick out the objects and events that are important for its survival. Recall that the frog responds to only four small aspects of the environment. The visual system of the cat, which so far is the most thoroughly studied (Hubel, 1979; Hubel & Weisel, 1962), selects for edges, angles, and objects moving in different directions.

Three kinds of cells that detect specific kinds of patterns have been identified in the visual cortex of cats (Ornstein, Thompson, & Macaulay, 1984).

1. *Simple cells* respond to a bar, line, or edge. Figure 5-24 shows the different kinds of receptive fields of simple cells and the stimulus that can cause them to fire at maximum strength. Because simple cells respond most strongly to particular angles, they are called *orientation detectors.* They are arranged in columns in the visual cortex; each column contains cells that respond to a particular orientation.

2. *Complex cells* respond to orientation and to movement, such as a diagonal line moving from left to right (Figure 5-25).

3. *Hypercomplex cells* respond to bars of light in any orientation. It may well be that other cells will be found that respond to even more specialized features of the environment (such as the hand-responding cell of the monkey, discussed below).

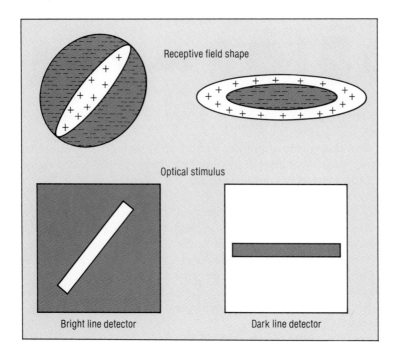

In monkeys, some cells seem to respond to other specific features of the environment. For example, Gross, Rocha-Miranda, and Bender (1972) probed a single cell in the cortex of a rhesus monkey to find out what would make that particular cell respond. They placed food in front of the monkey, showed it cards, moving objects, and so on. They tried everything they could think of and found no response. Finally one of the experimenters began waving his hand "good-bye" to the monkey; there was an immediate response from the cortical cell. They then began showing lots of new stimuli to the monkey. The more

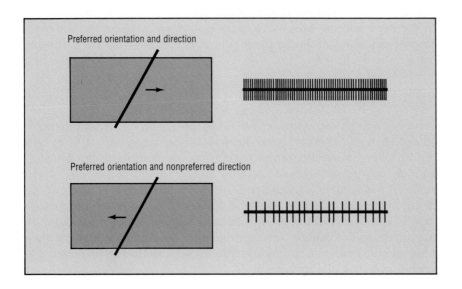

Preferred orientation and direction

Preferred orientation and nonpreferred direction

FIGURE 5-26
The Monkey Paw
Detector

These shapes are arranged in
order of their ability to make
a single cell in a monkey's
brain respond. Some shapes
(1) produced no response;
some made a neuron react a
little (2 and 3). Those
shapes somewhat like a
monkey's paw (4 and 5)
produced a greater response,
and the maximum neural
response was to the shape
most closely resembling a
monkey's paw (6). Clearly,
there are brain cells intended
to detect and react to very
complex, highly specific
features.
(Gross, 1972)

similar a stimulus was to a monkey's hand, the greater the response was in the cell (Figure 5-26). So, at least in the monkey, there is a single cell that responds strongly to an extremely specific feature.

MODULES OF SENSORY ANALYSIS   The discovery of the functions of these cells in the visual cortex has had a great effect on neuropsychology and psychology. The cells are arranged in columns, each column corresponding to one kind of analysis, such as edges and corners. As electrophysiology becomes more and more precise, many researchers believe that more and more complex modules will be discovered. The word *module* means a fixed plan or program, as when a house is described as modular, signifying that the components from which it is built are standard.

Many psychologists (Fodor, 1983; Gazzaniga, 1985; Ornstein, 1986a) now think that there are many different kinds of sensory modules in the brain and that they are encapsulated—that is, they do not communicate with other modules. The sensory modules may also be domain specific; the analysis routine for smell, for instance, may be very different from the analysis for shape or for language. Just how complex and hard-wired these modules are is the subject of much current research (Coren, Porac, Aks, & Morikawa, 1988).

WHAT THE BRAIN TELLS THE EYE

So far, this analysis has considered visual experience as if it occurred to a stationary observer looking straight ahead. But an observer is rarely stationary; both the head and the eyes move to look at an object. The eye is never still. When we look at a painting or photo, our eyes seem to trace the outline of the figure (Figure 5-27).

EYE MOVEMENTS AND THE BRAIN

For an organism to see, it must relate body movements and visual experience. Held and Hein (1963) investigated this relationship using kittens. They raised a group of kittens in total darkness except for one hour each day. During this hour, one group was allowed to move freely around a patterned cylinder; another sat passively in a gondola pulled by a cat from the active group. Later, both groups were exposed to the same visual stimulation. The kittens with an "active" experience moving around in light learned to see normally, but the vision of the other kittens was permanently impaired. Visual information coming into the brain must in some way be correlated, through experience, with an organism's muscular movements.

188

Sensory experience is determined in part by movement. Look straight ahead, then move your eyes sharply to the left. Your view of the scene has changed dramatically, but the "world" remains stable. The brain keeps a record of current movements to account for the changes in the *movement-produced stimulation.* Now, gently tap your right eye on the right side with your right index finger so that your eye jumps slightly to the left. When it does, the world seems to jump. The difference between this and the previous movement is that we rarely, if ever, move our eye with our hand, so there is no record of eye-movement signals to the brain to account for the change in stimulation.

Eye movements stimulate change in the information reaching retinal receptors. Normally, eyes move in fast, sharp movements called **saccades.** We hardly ever stare at any one point very long. Even if you try to fix your vision at one point on an object, very small involuntary movements occur. Portions of the retina are constantly stimulated as a result of both types of eye movements, although at any given moment only some receptor cells are stimulated.

Close your eyes, then open them. What you just saw is a result of all the processes discussed here. Light enters, passes through the retina, and is transduced to the brain. Orientation analyzers and color analyzers do their jobs. A neuropsychologist can follow the sequence from light impinging on the eye to the firing of cells on the visual cortex and understand some of the workings of the cells. But how all this becomes visual experience somewhere in the brain is still a great mystery.

HEARING

Hearing is our second most important sense. The external part of the ear (called the *pinna*) has little to do with hearing itself. Its function is to direct sound waves into the auditory channel. The process of hearing begins in the middle and inner ear. The stimuli for hearing are sound waves—vibrations of air. Sound waves are invisible, but you can see their effects on the surface of a drum as it is beaten.

The ear, like other sensory organs, is both highly sensitive and highly selective. The loudest sounds are millions of times louder than the softest. The sensory cells of the ear transmit to the brain only a fraction of the energy reaching them, but they are precise in what they do transmit. A mosquito buzzing around your ear can keep you up all night, yet the energy in that buzz would have to be 100 quadrillion times greater to light a small lamp.

THE EAR AND HOW IT WORKS

The ear picks up vibrations in the air. The auditory system performs the two miracles mentioned earlier: it transduces the mechanical energy of sound waves from the outside world into chemical or electrical activity in nerve cells, which in turn becomes the raw material for the experience of sound.

Hearing allows us to locate events and discriminate between quite disparate sounds—a bird's song, a car approaching from the left or right, a musical note. When an exciting event occurs, we try to focus on it visually by moving the image onto the fovea. The ear helps guide the eye to that positioning by sensing differences in loudness. A sound to one side will cause us to turn our heads until

FIGURE 5-27
Your Roving Eye

The pattern of lines trace the eye movements of a subject who looked at this picture of the little girl for 3 minutes. The lines not only outline the picture, they indicate points of fixation where the subject's eye paused over areas of visual interest.
(Yarbus, 1967)

the sound is equal in both ears; at that point we will be looking straight at the object.

Hearing gives us feedback on the sounds we make and is especially important for speech. If the auditory feedback from speech is interrupted, distorted, or delayed by even one second, it may completely disrupt the ability to speak coherently.

SOUND WAVES

Sound waves have two major characteristics: amplitude and frequency. *Amplitude* refers to the height of the wave; *frequency* refers to the number of cycles the wave makes each second. Amplitude governs the experience of loudness so that the higher the amplitude, the louder the sound. Frequency governs the pitch; we hear a high-frequency sound wave as a high-pitched tone. Sound waves must travel through a medium such as air, water, or a solid material; there is no sound in a vacuum. Sound waves travel through the ear under pressure; sound that is too intense can therefore be painful because of the increased pressure on sensitive tissue in the ear.

THE STRUCTURE OF THE EAR

The ear is a marvelous system of great complexity (Figure 5-28). It contains a wide-range sound wave analyzer, an amplification system, a two-way commu-

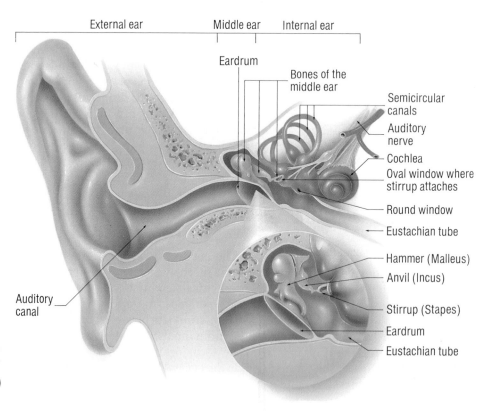

**FIGURE 5-28
The Structure of the
Human Ear**

(Gaudin & Jones, 1989)

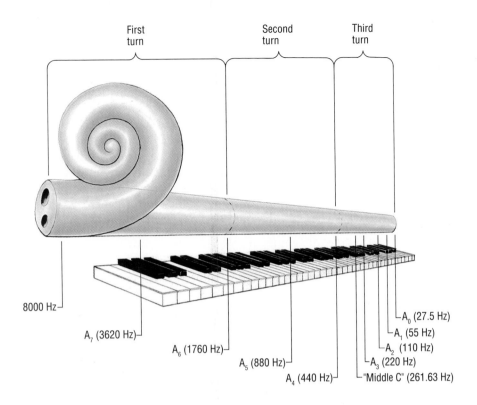

First turn   Second turn   Third turn

8000 Hz

A_7 (3620 Hz)

A_6 (1760 Hz)

A_5 (880 Hz)

A_4 (440 Hz)

A_0 (27.5 Hz)
A_1 (55 Hz)
A_2 (110 Hz)
A_3 (220 Hz)
"Middle C" (261.63 Hz)

FIGURE 5-29
The Auditory Response Range of the Cochlea Compared to That of a Piano

Hz = hertz.

nication system, a relay unit, a multichannel transducer that converts mechanical energy into electrical energy, and a hydraulic balance system. All this is compressed into two cubic centimeters (Stevens & Warshofsky, 1965).

Pressure moves sound waves down the auditory canal to the eardrum, causing it to vibrate. The vibration of the eardrum causes the three bones of the middle ear *(ossicles)* to vibrate. These bones, named after their shapes, are the *hammer* (malleus), the *anvil* (incus), and the *stirrup* (stapes). Their vibrations match the original signal in frequency but are of greater amplitude (25 times greater). The pressure of that amplification forces the waves into the inner ear, where it is transduced into electrical energy in the nerve cells.

THE COCHLEA   Hearing really begins in the **cochlea** (named for its shape, *cochlea* is the Latin word for snail). The liquid that fills the cochlea is an ideal medium for transmitting sound waves. The cochlea has an impressive auditory response range that can be compared to that of a piano (Figure 5-29).

At the base of the cochlea is the **basilar membrane.** When the stirrup beats on the cochlea at the *oval window*, the basilar membrane moves just like a whip being cracked. This whipping movement creates a traveling wave of the fluid through the cochlea (Von Bekesy, 1949). A short wave produces a high frequency; its bulge is closer to the oval window. On top of the basilar membrane is the *organ of Corti*. The membrane's movements bend the outer hair cells of the organ of Corti and its cells fire. Here the pressure waves are transduced into neural firing, sent up the auditory nerve, and then to the brain. The pressure is finally released through the *round window*.

Although the auditory nerve contains far fewer neurons than the optic nerve (28,000 versus 1 million), the number of sound discriminations that the ear is able to make is about equal to the number of visual discriminations that the eye can make. A typical auditory receptor has a *tuning curve* (Figure 5-30), which represents its ability to respond to tones of different frequencies. The nerve cells in the ear are as sensitive and specific in the kinds of stimuli they respond to as those in the eye. Some cells respond only to complex sounds, others to pure tones, and so on. Each auditory neuron is generally thought to collect information from a specific place in the basilar membrane. As the amplitude of the sound wave increases, the rate of firing of the neurons increases. As the frequency of the wave changes, different neurons begin to fire.

SUBJECTIVE DIMENSIONS OF SOUND

Psychophysicists once thought that the auditory system could detect only the actual physical properties of a sound wave—its amplitude (loudness) and frequency (pitch). However, we can detect many more dimensions than these two. For example, we can judge the origin of a sound in space, how long it lasts, its timbre (the harmonics produced by the instrument that makes the sound), its volume (how much it seems to fill space), and its harmonic relationship to other sounds.

Hearing, like vision, is affected by context. Even the perception of the physical dimensions of the sound wave is affected by other perceptions. The judgment of the loudness of a tone is influenced by its pitch. Of two sounds with the same intensity, one that falls within the range of frequencies between 600 and 6,000 Hertz (the normal range of the speaking voice) will be perceived as louder than one that falls outside this range. This is why stereo systems are often equipped with a loudness control to boost the high and low frequency

FIGURE 5-30
The Tuning Curve of a Typical Auditory Receptor

When an auditory neuron is presented tones of various frequencies, the pattern of its responses traces a tuning curve such as this one. The point of the receptor's peak response is called the *critical frequency*—in this example, about 400 Hz—which departs most from the neuron's spontaneous background rate.
(Lindsay & Norman, 1977)

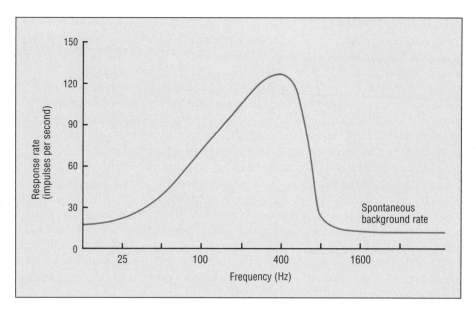

output from the speakers. Otherwise, these high and lows would tend to be overwhelmed by our more sensitive perception of the middle ranges.

Pitch is also influenced by loudness. When a trained singer is asked to match the tone from a tuning fork, she can do so quite accurately unless the tuning fork is only a few inches from her ear, in which case she sings a lower tone. For higher frequency tones (above about 2,000 Hz), pitch rises as loudness increases, but for lower frequency tones it tends to drop with loudness (Stevens, 1935).

AUDITORY CORTEX

The first stop after a signal has left the ear on its way to the brain is the *cochlear nucleus*. Its axons carry the information to the *superior olive* on the opposite side of the brain, where they enter the auditory cortex through the *medial geniculate*. These nerve fibers respond similarly to the tuned neurons in the ear.

Selection and analysis take place in the **auditory cortex;** 60 percent of the cortical cells, which behave in much the same way as those in the visual cortex, respond to specific tones. There are three types of cortical cells: *on* cells respond when a tone starts, *off* cells respond when the tone stops, and *on-off* cells respond when there is any change. The other 40 percent are more specialized. They respond to bursts of specific waves, sharp sounds, or clicks. For example, frequency sweep detectors respond to the small changes in frequency produced in normal speech. Some auditory cells with even more specific functions have been found in other animals. Whitfield (1976) even found cells in the auditory system of the squirrel monkey that respond most strongly to the sounds of other squirrel monkeys.

Like the visual system, the auditory system is one of great selectivity and sensitivity. In both systems, physical stimulation of the body by the outside world—the radiation of light or the movement of sound waves—is translated in the respective cortexes until it somehow becomes the inner world of experience: sight and sound, luminance and tone.

CHEMICAL, SKIN, AND INTERNAL SENSES

Smell, taste, touch, and the internal senses are much simpler than sight and hearing, but they are a substantial part of our sensory experience. Without smell and taste we could not judge if food were fresh or spoiled. People born without a sense of touch feel no pain and must be specially protected from injuring themselves.

We are least aware of the internal senses, which keep us standing up, help us maintain balance while moving, inform us of internal feelings, and let us know where each part of the body is. Without information on body position or movements, we could not do something as simple as walking.

SMELL

Our sense of smell helps discriminate tastes and also is useful in judging distance, location, and danger. For example, people usually smell something burning before they see the fire. The nose is the sensory organ for smell, and the

Because of their superior sense of smell, dogs are used to sniff out illegal drugs brought into the country by drug traffickers.

FIGURE 5-31
**The Structure of the
Olfactory Epithelium**

Smells reaching the surface
of the olfactory epithelium
stimulate the olfactory cilia,
which are embedded in
mucus secreted by glands
situated only in that part of
the nasal passage. The cilia
protrude from the olfactory
knobs, expanded portions of
the olfactory rods that extend
from the receptors' cell
bodies, which are attached by
their axons to the brain.

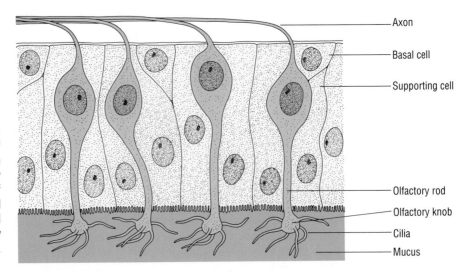

stimulus it responds to is gaseous molecules carried on currents of air. The
receptors for smell, the **olfactory cilia,** are located at the end of the nasal cavity
in the outer surface of the *olfactory epithelium* (which means "smell skin")
(Figure 5-31). These receptors also analyze food. It is difficult to taste the
difference between an apple, an onion, and a potato if the nose is
blocked.

Smell is the most direct sense. The neural information about smell is sent
directly to the brain without any intermediate nerves. Since it has a straight line
into the brain, smell information is less complex than other sensory information
reaching the brain. The direct connection of the nose to the brain may explain
why once one smells something, it is rarely forgotten.

TASTE

A professional wine taster can often tell the vintage, type of grape, and vineyard
of a wine from a single sip. Similarly, coffee, tea, and liquor manufacturers
employ professional tasters to make sure their products are appealing. The
human ability to discriminate and remember tastes is remarkably precise. What
is especially interesting about human taste is that complex taste sensations are
detected by an extremely simple receptor system.

Look at your tongue in the mirror. Its surface is covered with small bumps
called *papillae*. Each has 200 taste buds in and around it (Figure 5-32). Taste buds
are a collection of taste cells. They do not live very long and are replaced every
few days. When you burn your tongue on hot food, you cannot taste anything in
that spot for a few days. This is because the taste buds have been killed and new
ones have not yet replaced them.

There are four basic taste elements in our palate: sour, bitter, sweet, and
salty. Like the other senses, taste stimuli are coded and transmitted to the brain
as one of these four basic categories. Each cell has a different threshold for each

**FIGURE 5-32
Human Taste Buds**

Taste buds, here greatly
magnified, are collections of
taste cells concentrated in
various places on the surface
of the tongue to respond to
the four basic elements of
taste: sour, sweet, bitter, and
salty.

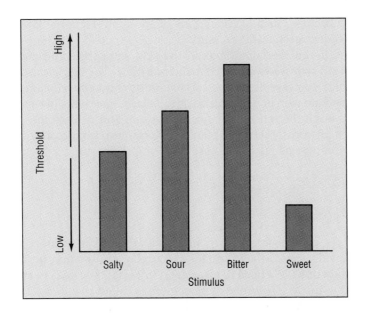

FIGURE 5-33
Taste Buds' Response Thresholds

The single taste bud, whose responses are charted here, is highly responsive to sweet tastes and fairly sensitive to salt tastes. Relatively low thresholds characterize individual taste buds because taste receptors often have no reaction to certain tastes and therefore have infinitely high thresholdls for such stimulation.
(Ludel, 1978)

taste (Figure 5-33). Different parts of the tongue are more sensitive to one taste than another. The tip of the tongue is most sensitive to sweet and salty, while the sides are most sensitive to sour, and the back to bitter (Coren et al., 1984). The taste buds also respond to temperature: hot, warm, and cold (Figure 5-34).

All other senses develop more complexity and sensitivity with age, but the opposite occurs in taste. An adult has fewer taste cells than a child. This difference means that children are more sensitive to taste, which helps explain why children are picky eaters and why adults add seasoning to food.

TOUCHING AND FEELING

Touching informs and communicates. The skin is the primary sensory organ for touch, and it responds to three dimensions of stimuli: pressure, pain, and temperature. The skin is the largest sense organ of the body, and one of its most important functions is to define the boundary between ourselves and the outside world. We also obtain information about the surface textures of the outside world through the skin. Touch gives us feedback on motor movements: whether we are holding a pencil correctly, walking, throwing or catching a ball, bumping into a wall, or cutting our finger with a paring knife. Touch also communicates. In our culture a good indicator of the closeness of two people is how much they touch each other. Sexual intimacy is largely an experience of touching, as is the bond between mother and infant.

Different parts of the body are more sensitive to touch than others. The most sensitive regions of the body are the fingers, cheek, nose, lips, genitals, and soles of the feet. Least sensitive are the arms, back, thighs, and calves.

The skin has many types of receptors, each of which responds to a different kind of stimulation. One is the *pacinian corpuscle* (Lowenstein, 1960), which has

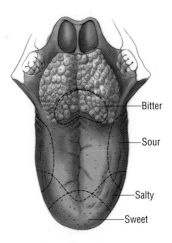

FIGURE 5-34
Areas of the Human Tongue and Their Relative Sensitivity to the Four Basic Tastes
(Ludel, 1978)

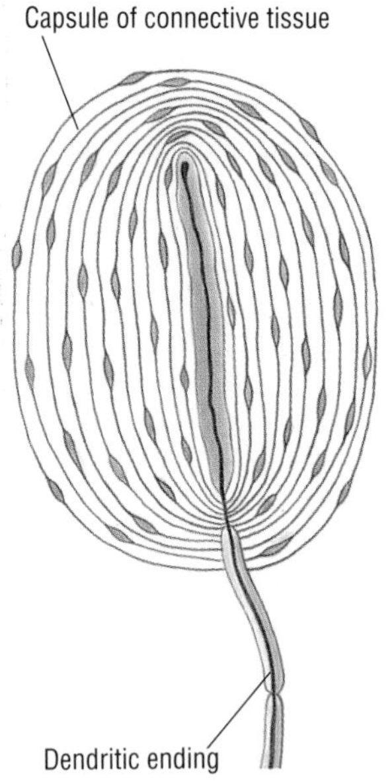

Capsule of connective tissue

Dendritic ending

FIGURE 5-35
The Pacinian Corpuscle

Sensitive to touch, such receptors respond to direct mechanical pressure, adapt to it, and then are ready to respond again soon after the pressure is removed.

(Ludel, 1978)

an internal structure much like the layers of an onion (Figure 5-35). It seems to respond to direct mechanical pressure.

All the different nerve endings in the skin send their information to the brain via one of two systems, one fast and one slow. The fast *lemniscal system,* is comprised of large nerve fibers that conduct information directly into the cortex, like the immediate pain of a blow. The *spinothalamic system* is slow and diffuse, is regulated through the reticular activating system, and reaches the brain at the limbic system. It conveys chronic pain from long-term injuries and ailments, as well as internal pains such as those resulting from surgery or a toothache (Figure 5-36).

INTERNAL SENSES

While the eyes, ears, nose, and skin inform us primarily of events coming to us from the outside world, the internal senses relay information on movements and bodily functions. We need to be aware of internal processes to maintain our balance and to move. The sense of movement is called *kinesthesis.* The sense of balance is one of the *vestibular senses.* The **somesthetic system** conveys to the brain information concerning sensations in the internal environment, such as deep pain or nausea. We also need to know where each part of the body is in relation to all other parts. The sense that performs that function is called **proprioception.**

KINESTHESIS Close your eyes and concentrate on each movement you make while walking across the room. The legs must flex, then extend a certain distance, while movements of the arms and back must be coordinated. At every instant you are aware of the position of your body. The sense that makes this possible is **kinesthesis** (from the Greek *kine,* meaning "movement"). Even when we are not moving—when we are sitting, lying down, or relaxed—we have kinesthetic feedback. At every moment of life we respond to the unseen force of gravity. Without looking at them, you know where your limbs are, what their angles are, and what they are doing. Special nerve cells in the muscles, called *joint position receptors,* relay information on movements of the muscles, and nerve endings in the skin and muscles respond to these signals.

Like the other senses, habituation occurs in the neurons that signal the location of limbs: if the hand is held in one place, the neurons stop firing. We receive no information if we do not move.

VESTIBULAR SENSES   The **vestibular system** consists of organs sensitive to motion, position, and balance. Our organs of balance are in the inner ear next to the cochlea. They are called the *otolith organs* (meaning "ear stone," from their shape), and they are the exception to the rule that sensory systems respond only to changes in stimuli. The otolith organs contain three *semicircular canals* that lie in different planes so that movement of the head in any direction registers in the canals. The enlarged area at the end of the canals is called the *ampulla,* inside of which are hair cells like those in the organ of Corti. When we tilt our heads, the fluid in the canals stimulates certain hair cells to fire. The firing of the cells signals specific directions of movement.

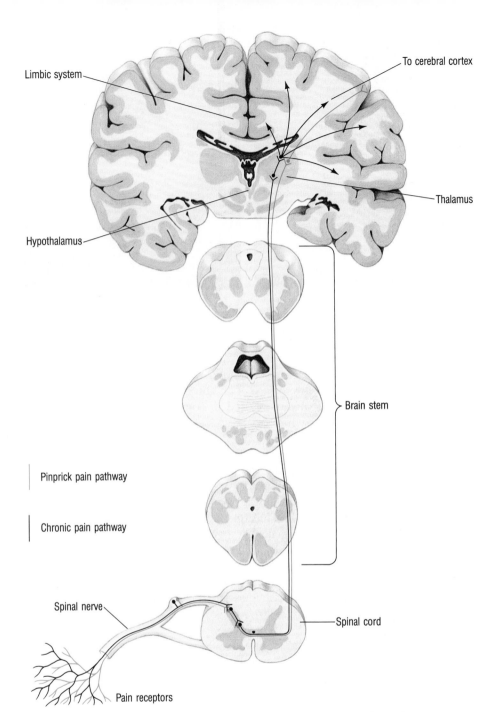

Limbic system

To cerebral cortex

Thalamus

Hypothalamus

Brain stem

Pinprick pain pathway

Chronic pain pathway

Spinal nerve

Spinal cord

Pain receptors

FIGURE 5-36
Pain Pathways

The fast pathway (lemniscal system) carries information on such sudden pain as that from a blow or a pinprick, conducting it directly to the cerebral cortex. Information on chronic pain travels the slow pathway (the spinothalamic system), being routed through the limbic system before coming to the attention of the cortex.
(Snyder, 1977)

The semicircular canals signal the actual position of the head. These organs respond constantly so that the head and body are always oriented in relation to the only constant force in the world of sensation, gravity. They do not adapt because their stimulus, the force of gravity, never changes throughout an organism's lifetime.

FIGURE 5-37
The Relativity of
Sensory Experience

Both these pictures are of the same car. But the left photograph was taken at noon, with white sunlight overhead accentuating the whiteness of the car. The right photograph was shot as the sunset bathed the car with its red rays, making it look as red as some red cars would look at noon. And yet we still perceive it as a white car because it remains relatively whiter than its uniformly redder surroundings. Sensory experience is a highly relative matter, depending on contrast, change, and adaptation.

THE RELATIVITY OF SENSORY EXPERIENCE

Sensory experiences do not occur separately. We may see red but do not see only pure red; it may be on the surface of an automobile, in bright or dim light, or next to a green car. We always see red in comparison to other colors and objects. A photograph of a white car at sunset may be much redder than a tomato at noon (Figure 5-37).

Animals are always adapting. We reset the level of adaptation according to the situation. In winter we experience 50 degrees Fahrenheit as warm, while the same temperature in summer feels cold. I visited Hawaii one winter when the temperature was 68 degrees. On the beach were tourists from Minnesota in bathing suits; the weather they had left was -20 degrees. At the end of the beach were Hawaiian workers wearing heavy sheepskin coats. The native workers were experiencing the low end of their temperature range, the tourists the high end (in winter). That we constantly maintain and interpret experience by comparison to a standard is a principle to keep well in mind, not only for sensory judgments, but for all kinds of judgments, of wealth, people, or politics.

ADAPTATION LEVEL

In trying to adjust to the changes in the external world, an organism sets an **adaptation level,** which is determined by three factors (Helson, 1964).

1. *Focal stimuli.* These stimuli are at the center of our attention; they constitute immediate experience.
2. *Background stimuli.* These are the contextual stimuli in which the focal stimuli are embedded, such as contrasts in brightness and the constant sounds in a room.
3. *Residual stimuli.* These are stimuli that the observer has experienced in the past.

198

If you look at a television sportscaster of normal height interviewing a jockey, you are likely to judge the sportscaster as tall. If you see him interviewing a basketball star, he seems short. The height of the sportscaster is the focal stimulus. The heights of the jockey and the basketball player are the background stimuli. The residual stimulus is the range of experienced human heights. They all combine to create the adaptation level in this situation. You can see an example of this in Figure 5-38.

The adaptation level approach allows us to quantify comparative sensory experience. One important finding is the **anchoring effect,** which is the effect of the preceding stimuli on the judgment of subsequent stimuli. In one experiment, people were given either heavy (400 to 600 grams) or light (100 to 300 grams) weights to judge. Then half of each group switched. Those going from the heavy to the light weights experienced the light weights as lighter than those who had lifted light weights all along.

Adaptation levels affect stimuli in many senses at once. The sense of sight is not entirely independent from hearing or touch. For example, a small object that weighs the same as a larger one is likely to be perceived as weighing more (Helson, 1964). This is because we have set an adaptation level based on the "smallness" of the object, which we compare its weight to.

Adaptation levels also influence our ability to discriminate the difference between stimuli. Stimuli that fall on one side or the other of an adaptation level are harder to tell apart than those which lie on either side.

Research has shown that our perception of the world is far from direct. We do not photographically reproduce the patterns of sound or light in our environment. Instead we perceive everything in relation to its context in both present and past experience. Our senses select, adapt, and compare information in a way that is most effective for helping us survive. They are biased toward

FIGURE 5-38
Adaptation Level

Look at the left-hand photograph. You will quickly form the impression that one woman is "tall," that she is probably above average height. Now look at the right-hand photograph. The "tall" woman from the other picture is obviously the shorter of the two here. From the initial sensory experience you set an adaptive level, a conviction about what "average" and "tall" are. But the second picture forced you to modify it. We judge people and things against such internal standards, which can be altered by new experience that shows them to be in error.

THE RELATIVITY OF SENSORY EXPERIENCE

Every animal senses the world for sources of pleasure. Human beings evolved to find pleasure in sensing the sweetness of a peach, the satisfactions of sex, the flow of a river, the view from a mountaintop to the horizon.

However, many sensual pleasures that we are primed to receive are blunted in the modern world. City dwellers miss the glory of the sunrise and sunset as they hustle in their commutes. Synthetic foods bear little resemblance to the tasty real foods we were built to eat. Our ancestors heard the pleasant sounds of wind rustling in the trees but for us it's the din of traffic.

Not surprisingly, sensual pleasures are vital to physical and mental health. Smell and taste encourage us to eat a variety of foods with a full range of essential nutrients. Pleasurable touch and sex sensations make procreation more likely. Sensory stimulation activates brain pleasure centers, evoking a sense of well-being and a positive mood. We'll concentrate on touch here.

You're sitting in a coffee shop watching the young couple across from you. He leans forward and gently touches her arm. She smiles. He then brushes a wisp of hair back off her forehead. They speak quietly and sip their coffee. As she excuses herself and gets up from the table, her hand rests for a second on his shoulder. He hugs her. She holds his hand tightly, then walks away. In the past hour this couple has touched each other no less than 150 times.

Where are you: England, the United States, France, or Puerto Rico? In the 1960s psychologist Sidney Jourard (1969; Ornstein & Sobel, 1989) roamed cafés record-

ON THE PLEASURES OF THE SENSES

ing how many times people touched each other. In Puerto Rico he tallied 180 contacts per hour. In Paris, the pairs touched 110 times per hour. In Florida, twosomes touched twice an hour. In England, they *never* touched.

OUT OF TOUCH

The scientific investigation of the health benefits of touching and handling began by accident. In the 1920s, anatomist Frederick Hammett removed rats' thyroid and parathyroid glands. To his surprise, some of the rats survived the operation. Most of the survivors came from a colony in which the animals were customarily petted and gentled by their keepers. These rats were much less timid, apprehensive, and high strung than the less handled rats. The gentled rats were also six times more likely to survive the operation.

THE UNTOUCHABLES

Being touched and cuddled is essential for healthy human development. During the late nineteenth century, if a child was lost or separated from its parents it was sent to a "foundling" institution, which was, in effect, a death sentence. A study of 10 such institutions in 1915 revealed that, in all but 1, every single baby under the age of 2 died. The reasons for this tragedy were unknown. Nutrition appeared sufficient. Sanitation was adequate, if not overzealous; the fear of germs and transmission of infectious disease led to "no touch" policies. The infants were seldom touched or handled.

In the 1920s, the respected psychologist James B. Watson promoted his theory that maternal touch spoiled the child.

There is a sensible way of treating children. . . . Never hug and kiss them, never let them sit

seeing, hearing, touching, tasting, and smelling only what is required for avoiding danger and satisfying needs. The senses are the bridge between the outer, physical world and the inner world of perception, consciousness, thought, and intelligence. It is to these subjects that we now return.

SUMMARY

1. The *senses connect* the physical and psychological worlds. The sensory systems are designed to notice *change*. They detect and select only a small portion of the energy in the world. *Deconstruction* is the process by which the brain breaks down and analyzes sensations.

2. The senses *simplify* our perception of the world through *adaptation* and *comparison*. There are limits to what we can sense. The *absolute threshold* is the smallest amount of energy necessary for one to notice stimulus. The *just noticeable difference (j.n.d.)* is the minimum change in the energy of a stimulus detectable by the senses.

in your lap. If you must, kiss them once on the forehead when they say good night. Shake hands with them in the morning. Give them a pat on the head if they have made an extraordinary good job of a difficult task. Try it out. In a week's time you will find how easy it is to be perfectly objective with your child and at the same time kindly. You will be utterly ashamed of the mawkish, sentimental way you have been handling it. (Watson, 1929)

In the 1940s, physician Fritz Talbot visited the Children's Clinic in Dusseldorf. The wards were neat and tidy, but something caught his attention. He noticed an old, fat woman stroking and carrying around a sickly baby on her hip. He asked, "Who's that?" The medical director responded, "Oh, that is Old Anna. When we have done everything we can medically for a baby, and it is still not doing well, we turn it over to Old Anna, and she is always successful."

This observation, and others, led to a dramatic change in treatment of children in foundling institutions. Bellevue Hospital in New York instituted a new policy: every baby was to be picked up, held, touched, gentled, and mothered several times a day. The death rate

for infants plummeted to less than 10 percent. A vital nutrient in the human diet had been discovered: touch.

Until recently, such findings have had little influence on the care of premature infants in the hospital. The standard policy in nurseries and intensive care units was the minimal touch rule: hands off. This minimized exposure to germs. It also avoided arousing the infant and was thought to reduce the strain on its tiny, underdeveloped lungs and heart.

However, premature infants,

like other infants, require touch. Touch can comfort the infant and cause it to increase weight, thereby decreasing medical costs. In one study (Field et al., 1986), premature, underweight babies received special stimulation. For 10 days, the infants were given three 15-minute massages. Warm hands lightly stroked the baby from head to toe and then gently exercised the arms and legs. The massaged babies thrived compared to other premies left in their incubators. Even though they had the same number of feedings and consumed the same number of calories as their untouched counterparts, the massaged babies gained nearly 50 percent more weight per day, a critical factor in the survival of a preemie. Touching seems to improve the efficiency of the baby's metabolism, and the stimulated infants were more active and more responsive to such things as a face or a rattle.

Further, the massaged infants were sent home from the hospital six days earlier, a savings of nearly $3,000 per infant. This early tactile stimulation also produces lasting benefits. Eight to 12 months later, the stroked babies maintained their growth advantage and had better mental and physical abilities—all for a few minutes of gentle touch for 10 days. We'll have more to say about different senses later on.

3. *Weber's law,* the first discovered principle of sensation, states that the amount of added energy to produce a j.n.d. is always the same proportion of a stimulus. *Fechner's law* claims that there is a logarithmic relationship between physical stimulus intensity and perceived stimulus intensity, meaning that we are more sensitive to changes in weak stimuli. Stevens discovered that different senses transform the information they select differently. *Stevens' power law* states that for each sensory system, equal ratios of stimulus intensity produce equal ratios of change in experience.

4. The senses *transform* physical energy into patterns of neural firing through the process of *transduction.* The brain analyzes these patterns in order to create human experience.

5. The visual system works more like a television than a camera. Light enters the eye through the *cornea,* the *pupil,* and the *lens,* and is focused on the *retina.* In the retina

are three layers of cells: *photoreceptors,* the *intermediate layer* (bipolar, horizontal and amacrine cells), and the *ganglion cells. Rods* are photoreceptors that respond best to dim light. *Cones* are responsible for color vision, and are concentrated in the *fovea.*

6. The four *psychological primary colors* are red, green, blue, and yellow. There are three systems of color information: the hue component, the blue-yellow component, and the red-green component. The discrimination of color works by an *opponent process.*

7. Information leaves the eye via the *optic nerve.* The fibers from the two eyes meet and some cross over at the *optic chiasma.* Then the optic tracts split into two pathways, the geniculostriate and the tectopulvinar, which serve specialized functions. There are two types of cells in the *lateral geniculate nucleus (LGN)* which work together to create three paths of visual processing. These produce perception of color and shading, borders, and movement and depth. The color system has relatively poor resolution.

8. In the visual system, *lateral inhibition* acts to help us see sharp changes in the environment and discriminate objects. Cells in the retina work together as receptive fields. Information from *receptive fields* is combined and conveyed to *feature analyzer cells,* which are sensitive to specific features in the environment. Three kinds of feature analyzers are: simple cells, complex cells, and hypercomplex cells. These cells are arranged in columns in the cortex; each "module" column specializes in one kind of analysis.

9. Organisms learn through experience to correlate visual information with muscular movements. Our vision of the world remains stable and stationary, although our eyes are constantly moving.

10. The *ear* picks up vibrations in the air: *sound waves.* The experience of *loudness* is based on the amplitude of the wave, and *pitch* is governed by frequency. Sound waves cause the *eardrum* to vibrate. This vibration is amplified by the *ossicles,* which set up a traveling wave in the *basilar membrane* of the *cochlea.* The cells of *organ of Corti* are stimulated to fire by the movement of the *basilar membrane* and transmit information through the *auditory nerve* to the brain.

11. As in the visual system, sound stimuli are perceived in relation to their context. Our brains extract more information from sound waves than what is conveyed by amplitude and frequency. Perception of sound is not direct: loudness is influenced by pitch and vice versa. The auditory system operates much like the visual system, with on-off receptive field and feature analyzers.

12. *Smell* helps discriminate tastes and judge distance, location, and danger. The *olfactory cilia* respond to gaseous molecules in the air. Neural information about smell is sent directly to the brain without any intermediate nerves.

13. The elements of *taste* are *sour, bitter, sweet,* and *salty.* Different parts of the tongue specialize in different tastes. Taste sensitivity and discrimination decrease with age.

14. The skin is the primary sense organ of *touch.* It responds to three types of stimuli: *pressure, pain,* and *temperature.* Touch helps define the boundary between ourselves and the world and gives feedback on motor movements. Touch also communicates. There are two neural systems for touch: the fast *lemniscal* and *spinothalamic.*

15. The internal senses, *kinesthesis* and the *vestibular senses,* relay information on movements and bodily functions. Kinesthesis is the sense of movement. Joint

position receptors in the muscles inform us about the position of our limbs. The vestibular system is sensitive to motion, position, and balance. The vestibular sensors (*otolith organs*) are in the inner ear. The *semicircular canals* do not adapt; they constantly transmit information about the position of the head.

16. All sensory experiences are relative. Our experience is constantly being compared to a standard: the *adaptation level*. The adaptation level is determined by focal stimuli, background stimuli, and residual stimuli. The effect of preceding stimuli on the judgment of subsequent stimuli is called the *anchoring effect*.

TERMS AND CONCEPTS

absolute threshold
adaption level
auditory cortex
basilar membrane
comparison
cones
dark adaptation
deconstruction
difference threshold
electromagnetic energy
feature analyzers
fovea
ganglion cells
intermediate layer
just noticeable difference (j.n.d.)
kinesthesis
lateral geniculate nucleus (LGN)
lateral inhibition
olfactory cilia

opponent process
photoreceptors
Power Law
proprioception
psychophysics
receptive field
retina
rods
saccades
secondary visual cortex
selection
sensory adaptation
somesthetic system
sound waves
tectum
transduction
vestibular system
visual cortex

SUGGESTIONS FOR FURTHER READING

Coren, S., & Ward, L. M. (1989). *Sensation and perception* (3rd ed.). San Diego: Harcourt Brace Jovanovich.

The best textbook on the senses.

Kosslyn, S. (1986). *Image and mind.* Cambridge, MA: Harvard University Press.

A chance to read a leading psychologist's analysis of mental processing.

Pinker, S. (Ed.). (1985). *Visual cognition.* Cambridge, MA: MIT Press/Bradford.

An excellent current collection about the analysis of the computations of vision.

"VOID"

III
THE MENTAL WORLD

The mind is hard to grasp. Biology is at least tangible: fossils, neurons, sense organs. The mind, however, cannot be uncovered so easily. It can be analyzed using concepts like those of chemistry before atomic particles were discovered. The "atoms" of the mind are the basic associations: a red light means stop. The "elements" are the schemata, linked associations that simplify actions: walking, talking, dancing. The "compounds" are prototypes and categories that instantly decode the arriving information.

The mind is not a single entity; it is made up of a multitude of components, which combine and recombine differently in different people. The nature of those components is becoming clear, just as particles, once only theories, became understood as science progressed.

6
PERCEIVING THE WORLD

How do we perceive the real world? Our sensory neural networks merely gather and transform various forms of energy. Here is a simplified and abbreviated example of sensory information as it is transmitted to the brain: "increasing 700 nanometer waves to the right, accompanied by increasing pressure of sound waves of 60–80 Hertz at 40° to the left." Information in this form does not mean much to us. However, the message "a bear is coming, and fast, from the left" certainly does.

Perception is *the organization of sensory information into simple, meaningful patterns.* It is an active process. It begins with the *reception* of information by the senses and then involves *selection* as well as *computation* and *creation*. This chapter considers the diverse mechanisms through which mental processes harvest meaning and examines the primary achievement of perception: how it provides us with a stable, "constant," experience of the world, even though the physical information we receive from nature is constantly changing.

THE PROCESS OF PERCEPTION

If you don't stop to analyze the process, nothing seems simpler than perceiving the environment. At this moment I see grass and the sky beyond. I hear kids playing in the street, and I smell the musty odor of old books in my study. Let us consider another simple, typical scene. I walk into a room and see my friend Dennis. I might speak to him, perhaps ask him about a project he is working on. This is a simple, ordinary experience, not worthy of much analysis—or so it would seem.

It takes a lot of work to keep perception simple: no modern-day computer can accomplish this simple feat. I know hundreds of people, and I know what to talk about with each one. This ordinary ability is the result of many difficult and complex operations. We may be aware of what we perceive, but we are not normally aware of the mental processes that make perception possible.

Let's go back to Dennis in the room. Only a few of the millions of stimuli reaching my sense receptors tell me anything about Dennis. This raw sensory information is first picked up and organized. That expanse of red I see is the couch and the gray is his shirt; the voice identifies Dennis, not Fred. But my perception of Dennis also goes beyond what meets my eyes and ears. Once I have assembled Dennis, I go beyond that immediate information and make assumptions—that he is the same person he was before, with the same memories, interests, and experiences.

To be useful, perceptions must accurately reflect the world around us. We must see people approaching if we are to avoid bumping into them. We have to be able to identify food before we can eat it. The senses select information about color, taste, and sound relevant for survival. What an organism perceives depends on what elements exist in the environment—what the environment *affords*. The characteristics of environments that we perceive have been studied by specialists called ecological psychologists. Two such characteristics are affordance and invariance.

FIGURE 6-1
The Invariance of Perception

Although some are close and others farther away, some are seen from the front and others from the side, and some are blocked from view by those in front, all the objects in this drawing are clearly perceived as grave markers because they present us unchanging, or invariant, information from all perspectives.

AFFORDANCE   Each object in the environment offers, or affords, a rich source of information (Doner & Lappin, 1980). A wooden post affords information about its right angles; a tomato, about its roundness, color, and taste; a tree, about its greenness, the color of its fruit, and its height.

INVARIANCE   The external environment contains many different objects. Each offers to the perceiver certain *invariant* features, which are constant patterns of stimulation (Michaels & Carello, 1981). Even a common object such as a post presents unchanging, or invariant, information about itself as we walk around it (Figure 6-1). From every angle, we see that the post has right angles, is perpendicular to the earth, and is white. There are invariant patterns that are common to all objects: all objects get smaller as their distance from the perceiver increases, lines converge at the horizon, and when one object is nearer it blocks out another.

THE RULES OF ORGANIZATION

Sensory information is often so complex that to be useful our minds must simplify and organize it. The perceptual system is so specialized for organizing sensory information that it attempts to organize disconnected things into a pattern even when there is none. We look up at a cloud and see shapes in it—a whale, perhaps, or a bird.

Op art, popular in the 1960s, played with the mind's predisposition to organize. Op art is at once intriguing and unsettling because we try continually to organize certain figures that are designed by the artist to have no organization (Figure 6-2). To interpret meaning from raw sensory information, the mental system asks What is the simplest meaningful thing into which the sensory stimuli can be organized? We do not experience a "semirectangular expanse of a certain wavelength," but rather a "red book"; when we hear sounds getting louder, we experience an object approaching; when an object looks smaller and smaller, this means it is moving away from us. Two important components of perceptual analysis are organization and interpretation.

PERCEPTUAL ORGANIZATION

The mind's fusion and coordination of separate stimuli into something meaningful is **perceptual organization.** The disorganized sensations that I feel on awakening are organized into one experience: "I'm at home in bed on a cloudy morning." This organization made sense of all the different sensory information reaching me.

Once stimuli are organized into a *percept*, it becomes difficult to see them once again as separate and disorganized. Look at Figure 6-3 for a few moments. At first it seems to be only a collection of dots strewn at random. At some moment, however, your mind will organize them into a scene of a Dalmatian dog near a tree. Once so organized, it is almost impossible to see the picture as a random collection of dots again.

INTERPRETATION

The second step in constructing meaning is **interpretation.** Consider the approaching bear: first the information from the senses is organized into the perception "bear." But what is the meaning of a bear in your presence? What action do you take? Suppose the bear suddenly says "trick or treat!" Now you remember that it is Halloween, and the significance of "bear" becomes quite different than if you had been camping in the woods and heard a growl!

FIGURE 6-2
Resistance to Stable Organization

Op art such as this can present many different and changing meaningful patterns of organization. This runs counter to our perceptual preference for stable, invariant patterns of organization.
(Carraher & Thurston, 1968)

FIGURE 6-3
Organizing Sensory Stimuli

It takes your perception to make a meaningful pattern emerge from what at first seems to be a random collection of spots and dots. And once you have made sense of it, it is hard to recapture your impression of the picture as random or meaningless.
(Carraher & Thurston, 1968)

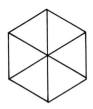

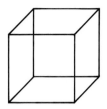

SIMPLICITY

When something is organized, it is **simplified.** The experience of many different dots on a page is quite complex, but a Dalmatian near a tree is organized and simple. Because of the vast amount of information in the world, it is important that we simplify it so we can act quickly.

Our experience of the world is far simpler than the external world itself. In any situation we tend to experience the simplest meaningful organization of the stimuli registered. Look at the two drawings in Figure 6-4: both are of a cube, but from different angles. The simplest interpretation of the one on the left is to see it as a two dimensional hexagon rather than a cube viewed from one of its corners. We see the drawing on the right as a cube in three dimensions because this is simpler than seeing it as a group of rectangles.

FIGURE 6-4
Three Dimensionality and Organizational Simplicity

The continuous lines in each drawing make it easier to perceive one as a two-dimensional pattern (top) and the other as a three-dimensional cube (bottom), although both are views of a cube.
(Hochberg & McAlister, 1953; Kopfermann, 1930)

GESTALT: PRINCIPLES OF ORGANIZATION

The rules of perceptual organization are the basis of the gestalt approach to psychology. **Gestalt** is a German word with no direct English equivalent, but it roughly means to create a form. A gestalt is the immediate organization of the form of an object. In gestalt psychology, an object is more than the sum of its parts. In Figure 6-5, you instantly perceive the lines as a square; you don't start by seeing four individual lines, and then later notice that they are all at right angles to one another, then judge that they are of equal length, and then count them and say, "Aha, that's a square." The figure is immediately perceived as a whole, not as the sum of its parts. Gestalt psychologists identified four rules governing the organizing principles of perception: figure-ground, proximity, similarity, and good continuation (Rock, 1985).

FIGURE 6-5
Perception of the Whole

We tend to organize our perceptions immediately into wholes, rather than seeing them as their constituent parts—which is why you first see this figure as one square, not four individual lines.

FIGURE 6-6
Seeing Figure and Ground

Because you can perceive either the light or the dark portions of these illustrations as figures against a background of the opposite shade, the meaning of what you see can vary dramatically even as you gaze at them. (The vase features the profiles of Queen Elizabeth II and Prince Philip.)

FIGURE-GROUND   What you see in Figure 6-6 depends on which color you decide is the background, or *ground*, and which is the foreground, or *figure*. These illustrations are called *ambiguous figures* because it is not clear which is the figure and which is the ground. You may see either a vase or two human profiles and either some stones from an ancient ruin or the word *TIE*.

PROXIMITY   When elements are close together, they tend to be perceived as a unit—that is, they seem to become a form (Figure 6-7).

SIMILARITY   Like elements tend to be grouped together (Figure 6-8).

GOOD CONTINUATION   It is simpler to see continuous patterns and lines. In Figure 6-9, it is much easier to perceive the whole and parts of the continuous figure at the top than to perceive the identical elements in the other two discontinuous figures.

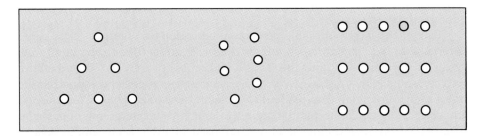

FIGURE 6-7
Organization by Proximity

Separate elements placed close together tend to be perceived as a unit and seem to describe a form rather than being seen as distinct and unrelated.

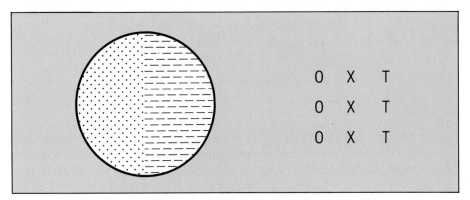

FIGURE 6-8
Organization by Similarity

We tend to perceive similar elements and group them with one another. Thus, we are likely to see the two halves of the spheres as separate and to perceive three groups of the *same* letters rather than groups of the letters *OXT*.

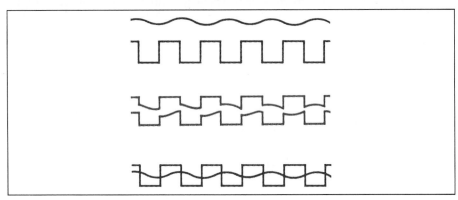

FIGURE 6-9
Organization by Continuity

It is much easier to perceive the whole and the parts of the top figure than to see those identical elements presented in the other two discontinuous drawings.

FIGURE 6-10
Cleaning up Perceptual Information

After looking at these figures for a few seconds, cover them and draw what you saw. What does your drawing indicate about how you interpret what you perceive?

GOING BEYOND THE INFORMATION GIVEN

Although a great richness of information is always available in the environment, what we receive at any one moment from an object or situation is often incomplete. We may catch only a glimpse of Dennis' shirt or hear only a word or two of his voice, yet we recognize him. We go beyond the immediate information to fill in the gaps of missing information (Hochberg, 1978). This is why, for example, it is so easy to miss typographical errors when you are proofreading a paper.

One of the most noticeable perceptual operations is one that "cleans up" information and "straightens it out." Look at Figure 6-10 for a moment; now cover up the figure and draw the shapes. You probably drew the slanted ellipse as a circle, made the "square" with straight sides, completed and connected the sides of the "triangle," and made the "X" with two straight lines. You cleaned up, corrected, and connected the figures to match your interpretation of them. The final diagram in Figure 6-11 is composed of three acute angles spaced equidistantly between three squares, each square with a small piece missing at the corners. What you probably saw, however, was three squares with two overlapping triangles. The topmost white triangle is something you filled in by the process of interpretation. We fit our experiences to the best forms available to us.

FIGURE 6-11
Filling in Perceptual Information

Look at the first three figures in the sequence: you don't see a triangle overlaid. But when you see the figure as a whole (far right), you see two overlying triangles. You are interpreting or subjectively "filling in" the white central one, which does not actually exist.
(Coren, 1972)

UNCONSCIOUS INFERENCES

We are usually unaware of the acts of perception and the rules of organization; we make what psychologists call **unconscious inferences.** We draw conclusions about reality based on the suggestions and clues supplied by the senses. Many demonstrations show the effect of inferences on experience. As you look at the cube in Figure 6-12, its structure may seem to shift before your eyes. Is the shaded portion at the rear or the front of the cube? The figure itself does not

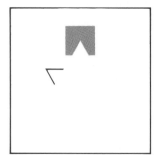
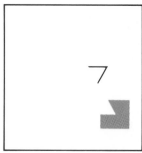
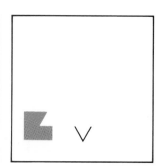
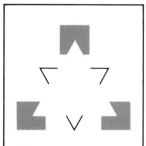

change, of course; what changes is your perception of the cube. The eyes send the brain bits of information about the arrangement of a set of lines. The next step is to organize the information and interpret what it is. Your perception of the cube shifts because the interpretation changes; indeed the shift in experience is actually a shift in interpretation.

ASSUMPTIVE WORLD

If I say that Dennis is in a room, you immediately assume the room has four walls, a floor, a ceiling, and probably furniture. Upon entering a room you do not inspect whether the walls are at right angles, nor do you run back to check if the room is still there after you leave it. If you constantly verified everything in the environment, there would be no time to do anything else. Thus, perceptual experience, such as "Dennis in the room," involves many assumptions.

If much of experience is assumed, then it follows that if assumptions change, perceptions will too. This was the hypothesis of Adelbert Ames and his colleagues at Dartmouth in the late 1940s and early 1950s (Ittleson, 1952). Hastorf (1950) showed that judgment of the distance of an object depends on how big we assume it to be. A ping-pong ball up close might look like a volley ball farther away. How we experience the ball and judge distance from it depends on our assumptions about what it is. (See the section on cultural effects on perception, page 222.)

Another demonstration involves the shapes of rooms. Space is three-dimensional, but representations of space on paper, such as photographs, are only two-dimensional. Thus, sometimes our assumptions are wrong, such as in the left and center photos of Figure 6-13. We assume that a room is rectilinear and so see the boy and dogs as impossible sizes. This trick room fools us and our perception of reality.

NEEDS AND VALUES

Bruner and Goodman (1946) compared the perceptual experiences of children from poor and well-to-do families. When shown a coin, children from poor homes saw it as larger than did the richer children. This finding has been

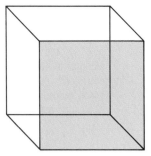

FIGURE 6-12
Inference and Perceptual Ambiguity

The shaded part of this so-called Necker cube seems to shift from the front to the back as you look at it. Your perception changes as your brain organizes and interprets the ambiguous perceptual information it receives.
(Gregory, 1970)

FIGURE 6-13
Perceptual Assumptions

Because we assume rooms are rectilinear, a trick room like this can destroy our perception and fool us into seeing the boy and the dog as impossibly different sizes. The last photo shows how the room actually looks.

FIGURE 6-14
Assimilation

The *I*, the *d*, and the *l* are all identical but are seen differently (and accurately) because of our ability to assimilate.

I do what I please.

repeated in other cultures, such as in Hong Kong (Dawson, 1975). In a similar study, students in one class were asked to draw a picture of their teacher. The honor students drew the teacher as being shorter than themselves, while the poorer students drew themselves as smaller than the teacher. Needs and values determine perception in many ways.

HOW PERCEPTUAL EXPERIENCE CHANGES

**FIGURE 6-15
Context and Ambiguity**

Depending on its context, this ambiguous figure can be perceived as either a duck or a rabbit.

Perceptual experience changes in the same ways that children's schemata change as they get older: by assimilation and accommodation. We constantly update schemata as our search of the external environment relays information that requires new interpretation.

We interpret incoming information to match existing schemata through **assimilation.** Read the message in Figure 6-14. You probably had no trouble deciphering "I do what I please." But notice that the *l* in "please," the *I*, and the *d* in the "do" are identical. We experience the identical element differently, and appropriately, in each case. We do not perceive the individual letters of words, but rather the words they signify. Similarly, Figure 6-15 is seen as a rabbit if shown with rabbits, a bird if among birds.

**FIGURE 6-16
Seeing What You Are
Prepared to See**

See how quickly you can count the number of aces of spades in this illustration; then finish reading this caption. If you are like most people, you may have gotten the wrong total because you have learned spades are black cards, not red. With these anomalous playing cards, Bruner demonstrated how people tend to see what they expect to see, not necessarily what is actually there.

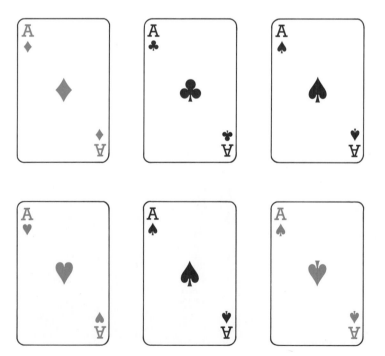

Accommodation is the process by which schemata change to fit new information, if the discrepancy between the outside world and schemata is great enough. Look quickly at the playing cards in Figure 6-16 and then turn away. (Do this before reading any more of this paragraph.) How many aces of spades are there? Now look again, but this time keep in mind that an ace of spades can be red or black. Now how many are there? The difference in the two answers was because of a change in your "playing card schema," which changed what you were prepared to see the second time. A normal "playing card schema" directs us to look for black spades only. When our schemata changed, we saw things more "as they really are."

CONSTANCY: COMPUTING THE STABLE WORLD

We experience little change even though the sensory information reaching us changes radically. A building may appear as a small dot on the horizon or it may completely fill our visual world. Yet we perceive the building to be the same size and shape regardless of our vantage point. The main purpose of the reception, organization, and interpretation by the perceptual processes is to achieve **constancy,** the perception of a stable, constant world.

TYPES OF CONSTANCY

You can easily demonstrate three kinds of perceptual constancies with your hand. Hold it with the palm facing toward you; then turn the palm away; then turn it so that you see the side of the hand. Even though the sensory impression of the hand is very different in each orientation, you perceive the same shape. That is shape constancy.

Now hold your hand close to your face; then hold it at arm's length. Even though the image on the retina is very different in each case, the hand seems to be the same size. That is size constancy. Now hold your hand under a lamp, and turn the lamp out. What color is your hand? You experience the hand as having the same underlying color and brightness, even though the information is different. That is brightness and color constancy.

SHAPE CONSTANCY   We experience the same object presented in very different aspects as the same. In Figure 6-17, a cup is shown from several different angles. Even though the actual image is different, you see the same cup. Changes in the slant of an object cause the retinal image to change, but not your experience of the object.

FIGURE 6-17
Shape Constancy
Like most objects we perceive, this cup, though viewed from various angles, is always recognized as a cup. Such changes of orientation may alter the retinal image, but not what is experienced.

FIGURE 6-18
Size Constancy

In the left photograph the "small" man in the center seems of normal height, about the same as the man leaning against the lamp post. But in the right photo, that *identical* figure is ridiculously smaller than the man on the right. What do your responses to these specially prepared photographs tell you about how size constancy works?

SIZE CONSTANCY   The size of the object can be accurately judged whether it is near or far away. As someone walks toward you from the horizon, that person's image on your retina can increase by more than 100 times (Figure 6-18), but you do not think the person is actually growing larger before your eyes. Our conscious knowledge or assumptions about the distance of an object can affect how large we believe it to be (Pasnak, Tyler & Allen, 1985). Interestingly, if we are not actively attending to the object whose size is being perceived, our size constancy mechanisms may fail (Epstein & Broota, 1986).

BRIGHTNESS AND COLOR CONSTANCY   Although the brightness and color of an object vary in different illuminations, we perceive them to be the same. The whiteness of the pages of this book will look to us to be about the same in sunlight as it does in an unlit room at twilight. In experiments on brightness constancy, people are asked to adjust a light source to match the brightness of a test object.

The subjects are shown a test object (A in Figure 6-19). The outer circle is assigned a brightness level of 200, the inner circle, 100. Then drawing B is presented; here the outer circle has a brightness level of 200. The subjects are

FIGURE 6-19
Brightness Constancy

As explained in the accompanying text, it is the relativity of brightness, not absolute values, that remain constant in perception.

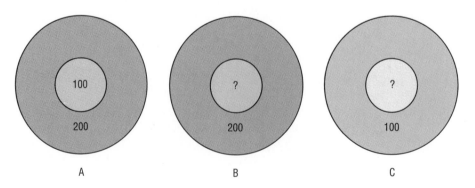

A   B   C

asked to produce the gray that matches the inner circle of the test object (A). The subjects usually choose accurately, producing a gray with 100 units of brightness.

Then they are shown another drawing, C, in which the outer circle has a brightness of 100. Again, they are asked to match the gray of the outer circle to the test object (A). This time they are most likely to produce a gray with brightness level 50. This demonstrates that people do not perceive absolute values of brightness; instead, they judge the relative brightness of objects to achieve a sense of constancy.

We experience color as we do brightness. Recall the photos of the car in Figure 5-37, page 198. The white car at sunset reflects the red color of the setting rays of the sun. But it appears white because we see it as relatively whiter than the surrounding environment.

The color of light also affects our perception of brightness. Yellow light generally appears brighter to us than blue light. Humans are most sensitive to the brightness of colors in the middle of our range of color perception—yellows, oranges, and greens. However, this sensitivity to wavelength of light shifts down about 50 nanometers in conditions of dim illumination, when all colors appear gray. People still see differences in brightness in these conditions, but they see bluish colors better than in brightly lit conditions. This is called the **Purkinje shift.**

The length of time and the size of the area that a light stimulates the retina also affect both how bright it seems and how easily we can see it. Another way to think of human sensitivity to different stimuli is in terms of how well we can detect stimuli. The varying sensitivities of the perceptual system show what factors of our environment have been most necessary to our survival and, thus, what we are most ready to perceive and what we are ill-equipped to perceive.

An illusion that we see frequently is the moon's apparent reduction in size as it rises from the horizon.

ILLUSIONS

Perceptual mechanisms work so quickly and generally so well that we are unaware of the operations involved. Illusions are prized by psychologists not only for their amusing qualities but also because they reveal the normal processes of perception. Many illusions cause us to misapply the rules that govern constancy. Sometimes we may go from the processes of filling in the gaps to jumping to conclusions as a consequence of the speed necessary for making quick judgments, and thus we often make mistakes.

COMPARATIVE SIZE   The central circle on the left of Figure 6-20A looks larger than the central circle on the right, although they are the same size. They are perceived incorrectly because the circle surrounded by larger circles is smaller relative to its context than the other central circle. We perceive in a comparative way rather than according to absolute values (Rock, 1985).

A common illusion partly created by this effect is the moon illusion. When the moon is near the horizon, it appears much larger than when it is overhead. This is not due to a movement of the moon relative to the Earth. When the moon is at the horizon, we see it across many cues to depth and distance (the ground, sea, mountains, and so on). It seems farther away than when we look up at it with no cues to distance. Since we perceive the moon at the zenith as closer to us than the moon at the horizon, we also see it as smaller.

FIGURE 6-20
The Illusion of
Comparative Size

The central circle on the left (A) only looks bigger because it is surrounded by smaller circles than the identical central circle next to it. Likewise, the upper horizontal line in the lower part of the right-hand drawing (B) seems longer no matter how you look at it—even turning the book sideways or upside down does not destroy the illusion. Even knowing that the lines are the same length cannot overcome the power of the rules of perspective and the principle of comparative values.

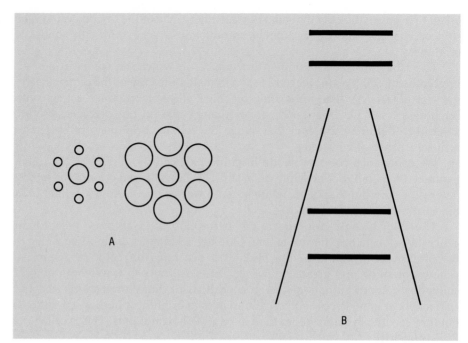

PONZO ILLUSION   Look at the parallel lines at the top of Figure 6-20B. Do you think they are the same length? Now look at the parallel lines at the bottom of the illustration. Putting two converging lines next to these lines makes the top line seem longer. The rules of perspective that normally help us judge size and distance accurately mislead us in this picture.

MÜLLER-LYER ILLUSION   Although both center lines in Figure 6-21 are equal in length, the line with the arrows pointing inward looks longer than the line with the arrows pointing outward. Our brains probably use the arrows as depth cues: the arrows pointing inward cause us to judge the lines as farther away and, thus, longer (Gregory, 1973). The pair of photos in Figure 6-21 is an example of this illusion in the world. The central vertical line of the corner of the left photo looks longer and appears to be farther away than that in the right photo. In this illusion, two schemata, the appearance of things that recede into the background and things that approach and open up toward us, have probably been activated and misapplied.

ADAPTING TO THE ENVIRONMENT

The optical image on the retina is upside down from the way it actually exists and from what we perceive. How is it that we see the world right side up? Where is the image reversed? The answer reveals an important principle of perception: the image is never actually turned right side up. We do not need such an image; all we need to be able to adapt to the external world is consistent information.

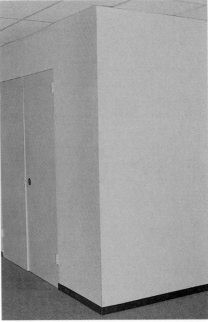

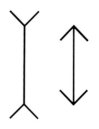

FIGURE 6-21
The Müller–Lyer Illusion

Depth cues can alter our perception of lines of equal length. Because the arrows in the sketch below and the arrowlike intersecting lines at the corners in the photographs make us judge the vertical lines as closer or farther away, we see each line as shorter or longer than the other.

The image on the retina, in fact, is inverted and consistently obscured by blinks, blind spots, and blood vessels, yet we adapt to it all.

ADAPTATION TO DISTORTION

In the late nineteenth century, the psychologist George Stratton reasoned that if perception is a process of adaptation to the environment, then it ought to be possible to learn to adapt to an entirely different arrangement of visual information, as long as it were consistent. To test this hypothesis, Stratton wore a special prism lens over one eye, so that he saw the world inverted and turned 180°: the world was upside down, and left-right were reversed.

Stratton had great difficulty at first in doing even simple things like reaching for or grasping an object. He felt very dizzy when he walked, and he bumped into things. But within days he began to adapt. After only three days of wearing the inverted lens, he wrote, "Walking through the narrow spaces between pieces of furniture required much less art than hitherto. I could watch my hands as they wrote, without hesitating or becoming embarrassed thereby" (Stratton, 1897).

By the fifth day he could move around the house easily. On the seventh day he enjoyed his evening walk as usual. On the eighth day he removed the lenses and wrote, "The reversal of everything from the order to which I had grown accustomed during the last week gave the scene a surprisingly bewildering air which lasted for several hours." Once Stratton had adapted to the new relationship between information and perception, it took some time to unlearn it. As Stratton wrote in his preliminary study,

The different sense-perceptions, whatever may be the ultimate course of their extension, are organized into one harmonious spatial system. *The harmony is found to consist in having outer experiences meet our expectations.* (1896; emphasis added)

More than 60 years later, Ivo Köhler (1962) conducted further experiments on the effects of optical rearrangement. His observers wore various kinds of distorting lenses for weeks. At first they all had great difficulty in seeing the world. But in a few weeks they had adapted. One of Köhler's subjects was even able to ski while wearing the distorting lenses!

People can also adapt to color distortions. In another of Köhler's demonstrations, his subjects wore glasses in which one lens was green and the other was red. Within a few hours they sensed no difference in color between the lenses (Köhler, 1962).

IS PERCEPTION INNATE OR LEARNED?

Suppose a blind person were suddenly able to see after years of blindness. What would he or she experience? Psychologists have studied the question of what is innate and what is learned in perception in many ways, using children, people from various cultures, blind people, and even a person born blind who gained sight as an adult from an operation.

We come into the world with many abilities enabling us to perceive immediately. Children prefer to look at faces and become disturbed when the facial elements are rearranged. They seem to be born with, at the very least, the preference to perceive human beings before other things in the world. (See Figure 2-3 on page 45.) The newborn's ability to imitate others, to discriminate between the mother's odor and that of other women, and to turn toward sounds all point to the likelihood of innate perceptual abilities.

DEVELOPMENT OF PERCEPTION

Our perceptual systems are part of our genetic heritage. However, sensory experience has important effects on the development of perceptual abilities. We can learn from practice to detect smaller or subtler stimuli, such as words flashed for a very brief period of time (Uhlarik & Johnson, 1978). We can also be prevented from learning to perceive types of stimuli by sensory restrictions during a certain period of physical development, called the *critical period* (Mitchell, 1981).

Many studies of the effects of restricting the visual environments of kittens in the first few months of life have shown that experience influences perceptual development. Kittens raised so that they see only horizontal lines can never develop the capacity to detect vertical lines to the same degree as horizontal lines. They can learn to see vertical lines, but not very well (Blasdel, Mitchel, Muir, & Pettigrew, 1977; Hirsch, 1972). A similar effect occurs with binocular vision (the integration of images from both eyes) when kittens are raised in the dark. Without the opportunity to use the eyes together in the developmental critical period, the kittens can never develop the capacity to overlap the visual fields of the two eyes (Sherman, 1973).

The effects of restricted sensory experience on development in kittens have been confirmed with humans, in people born with visual handicaps that were later corrected and in people raised in urban environments. Annis & Frost (1973) compared students from Western cities, which contain many horizontal and vertical outlines, but few oblique ones, to a group of Cree Indians whose homes contained lines in all orientations. The students had less acuity for oblique lines than the Indians.

RECOVERY FROM BLINDNESS

What would the visual experience be like of a person who had been born blind but was suddenly able to see? Richard Gregory had the good fortune to study such a case. At 52 a man called S. B., blind from birth, had a successful corneal transplant. When the bandages were removed, he heard the voice of the surgeon, turned to look at him, and saw nothing but a blur. Within a few days his sight had improved and he could walk around the hospital corridors without touching the walls and could tell time from a wall clock. Even so, he could not see the world as crisply as most people. He was able almost immediately, however, to recognize objects for which he had already developed an internal picture through touch (Gregory, 1973).

S. B. could see and draw objects that he had known previously by touch but had difficulty with objects that he had not had the opportunity to touch while blind. He was surprised by the appearance of the moon. His drawings of a London bus even a year after the operation omitted the front of the bus, which he had never touched. His drawings of windows and wheels, however, were in pretty fair detail right from the beginning (Figure 6-22). When Gregory showed S. B. a lathe, a tool which S. B. was experienced in using, he had no idea what it was. Then he was asked to touch the lathe; he closed his eyes, examined it thoroughly with his hand, and said, "Now that I have felt it, I can see." Although S. B. had been deprived of sight, he had not been deprived of perception.

FIGURE 6-22
Blindness and Perception

Regaining his sight after an operation did not instantly enable the man who drew these pictures to perceive the world as it is. Both the left-hand drawing, done 48 days after the operation, and the other, done a year later, show more detail for parts of the bus the man used—and especially touched—while he was blind. His perceptions from when he was blind still influenced his experience of the world.
(Gregory, 1973)

IS PERCEPTION INNATE OR LEARNED

What do blind people think the world looks like? Are their mental images of people and things very different from those of sighted people? Since the early 1970s John Kennedy has conducted experiments that begin to answer these questions. He asked people, blind since birth, to draw pictures. At first we might think that was a ridiculous request; most of the blind people thought it was. A picture is, after all, a two-dimensional representation of a three-dimensional object, and the blind sense their world primarily through touch, a strictly three-dimensional experience. Kennedy gave each subject a plastic sheet that makes a raised line when a ballpoint pen is moved across it. He first asked them to draw simple objects—a cup, a hand, a table—and later, more complicated scenes.

To his surprise, Kennedy found that the blind realized almost immediately that some aspects of reality must be sacrificed in a drawing. We cannot draw a cup from all sides at once; a point of view must be selected. The blind

SEEING WITHOUT EYES

artists devised ways to convey their meaning. Their solutions were easily understood by sighted people either at a glance or with brief captions, such as, "This is how it would look from the side." What most surprised Kennedy was that his blind artists understood perspective (Kennedy, 1974).

There is more to seeing than meets the eye, and more to visual perception than sight. Although we rarely experience the difference, sensation and perception are not the same. Perception fills in the gaps left by incomplete sensory information. We recognize a cup even though we see only one side; we are not likely to check for a bottom before pouring coffee. The properties of weight, size, texture, form, function, and color all figure into the final perception of what an

object actually is. Through touch, a blind person can gain almost all the same information as a sighted person.

In fact, the sense of touch appears to be part of the visual perceptual system. Carter Collins and his colleagues on the Tactile Sensory Replacement (TSR) project at the Smith-Kettlewell Institute of Visual Sciences in San Francisco have devised a machine that takes advantage of a blind person's fine-tuned sense of touch. The machine impresses televised images onto the skin using electrical stimulation (Figure 6-23). The felt pattern of the image allows individuals to recognize objects in front of them. In fact, blind people have been able to "see" and work with instruments as precise as an oscilloscope using the TSR device.

The reason Collins and his co-workers chose touch instead of another sense is that, of all senses, touch is the closest to vision. Collins explains:

No matter how acute your hearing is, it is a cue for location and

In a study that echoes the tale of "The Elephant in the Dark," Kennedy gave blind children pictures of parts of an elephant (the lines in the pictures were raised, in relief, so they could be felt). In 39 out of 41 cases, the children recognized that together the pieces made up a picture of an elephant. These children lacked *sight* but not perception; the wise men in the story had sight but not perception.

CULTURAL EFFECTS ON PERCEPTION

Although we appear to have some innate perceptual abilities, a completely prewired, built-in perceptual system seems unlikely. Humans live in all types of environments in the world and in many cultures. It is almost certain that much of perceptual experience is learned. Pygmies of the Congo of Africa dwell primarily in dense forest and thus rarely see across large distances. As a result, they do not develop as strong a concept of size constancy as we do. Colin Turnbull, an anthropologist who studied pygmies, once took his pygmy guide on a trip out of the forest. As they were crossing a wide plain, they saw a herd of buffalo in the distance.

distance only—not forms. But . . . vision and touch . . . are both three-dimensional systems. What you see in front of you is essentially a frame on which patterns of light and shadow are played. You see in three dimensions because you move your neck and eyes and you have binocular vision. When a person wears the TSR vest, the camera moves just as the eyes do in sighted people.

Still I could not understand how such representations might actually "look." So I went to the institute and tried it myself. I sat blindfolded in the chair, the cones cold against my back. At first I felt only formless waves of sensation. Collins said he was just waving his hand in front of me so that I could get used to the feelings. Suddenly I felt, or saw, I wasn't sure which, a black triangle in the lower left corner of a square. The sensation was hard to get a fix on. I felt vibrations on my back, but the triangle appeared in a square frame in my head. Although there was no color,

FIGURE 6-23
The Tactile Sensory Replacement Device
This device enables blind people to "see" by television-guided electrical stimulation of their skin.

there were light and dark areas. If you close your eyes and face a strong light or the sun and pass an object in front of your eyes, a difference appears in the darkness. That difference is approximately what I saw. The TSR image was fuzzy at first, but within 10 minutes of sitting in the chair it became clearer. When Collins confirmed that he was indeed holding a triangle, it became clearer still.

For me, believing that there is a difference between sensation and perception has always required an enormous leap of faith. It is hard to believe that I do not see with my eyes or hear with my ears. Although we are taught that there is a difference between sensation and perception, at the TSR lab I experienced the difference for the first time. The sensation was on my back, the perception was in my head. Feeling is believing.

(This report was researched and written by Nancy Hechinger, Institute for the Study of Human Knowledge, especially for this textbook.)

Kenge looked over the plain and down to a herd of buffalo some miles away. He asked me what kind of insects they were, and I told him buffalo, twice as big as the forest buffalo known to him. He laughed loudly and told me not to tell him such stupid stories. . . . We got into the car and drove down to where the animals were grazing. He watched them getting larger and larger, and though he was as courageous as any pygmy, he moved over and sat close to me and muttered that it was witchcraft. . . . When he realized they were real buffalo he was no longer afraid, but what puzzled him was why they had been so small, and whether they had really been small and suddenly grown larger or whether it had been some kind of trickery. (Turnbull, 1961)

People from different cultures may not be fooled by the same optical tricks because they do not share the same schemata. Illusions such as the Müller-Lyer and the Ponzo depend to a certain extent on growing up in a world in which right angles and straight lines predominate. Our Western world is a carpentered world. By contrast, some African tribes, such as the Zulu, live in round huts with round doors (Figure 6-24) and plough their fields in circles; they do not experience the Müller-Lyer illusion as strongly as we do (Segal, Campbell, & Herskovits, 1963).

Look at Figure 6-25. Is the hunter closer to the baboon or the rhinoceros? We say the baboon. However, many Africans, who do not share the Western use

FIGURE 6-24
Culture and Perception
People who live in round houses do not experience the Müller–Lyer illusion as strongly as people who live in square houses.

FIGURE 6-25
Cultural Assumptions and Three Dimensionality

Most of us would say the hunter is closer to the baboon, while many Africans would say the rhinoceros is closer.
(Hudson, 1962)

of perspective in drawing and do not make the same assumptions we make regarding the representation of three dimensions, answer that the rhinoceros is closer. This seems odd to us. However, if you look at the drawing as it is, in two dimensions, the rhinoceros actually is closer to the hunter.

The conventions for representing three dimensions on a two-dimensional surface can lead to some interesting confusions. Look at the ''impossible'' object in Figure 6-26, sometimes called the Devil's tuning fork, and try to draw it from memory. The figure itself is obviously not impossible—after all, it's there on the page. But most Western people cannot reproduce the drawing because we interpret it as an object that could not exist in three dimensions. It is our interpretation, not the figure itself, that is impossible. Schemata for translating two-dimensional drawings into three-dimensional figures prevent us from seeing the figure as it is. Africans who do not share these conventions have little difficulty in reproducing this figure from memory (Deregowski, 1987).

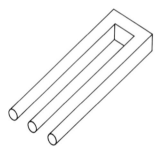

FIGURE 6-26
The Devil's Tuning Fork

CULTURE AND COLOR

Some perceptual abilities are clearly affected by culture, especially when the culture limits the perceptual environment of its members in their developmental years (like the students from Western cities). Some researchers have proposed that people from cultures with limited reference to colors in their language are more limited in their ability to see color variations than people in our Western culture (Whorf, 1956; Robertson, 1967). However, when these people demonstrate their abilities to match, discriminate, or reproduce colors, they are as capable as anyone (Berlin & Kay, 1969; Bornstein, 1973, 1975). Development plays a role in perceptual capacity, but we should be cautious in how we make our inferences about the abilities of others.

PERCEPTION OF SPACE

How do we perceive objects and events in space? How do we know when an object is far away from us? In 1790 Bishop George Berkeley initiated the modern argument over space perception. He stated that information regarding distance must be inferred. "We cannot sense distance in and of itself," he wrote. According to his theory, distance must be constructed from a set of cues, such as the relative size of an object. Although we certainly make inferences, this view is now thought to be incorrect. Recent research has shown that there is a great amount of distance information directly available to the perceiver.

INTERNAL CUES TO DISTANCE

To focus the lens of a camera, we adjust the angle at which incoming light is bent and falls on the film. We do this so the object of interest will be clear and in focus. As a result, things in front of or far behind the object will be less clear.

The eye works in a similar way. When we look at objects at different distances, contractions of the ciliary muscles cause the width of the lens to change. This change is called **ocular accommodation.** To demonstrate this for yourself, hold a pen about 10 inches in front of your face. Choose a distant object to look at. When you focus on the far object, the pen becomes blurred. When you focus on the pen, the background becomes blurred. Changes in the width of the lens are monitored by the brain and coupled with other information to develop distance information. This other information includes the convergence of the eyes (the eyes are turned more sharply inward as they look at closer objects) and the difference between the information reaching the left versus the right eye and ear.

BINOCULAR DISPARITY   Because the eyes are in different locations in the head, each eye receives slightly different information (Figure 6-27). This difference in information, called **binocular disparity,** increases the closer we get to the object we are looking at. The difference in the left and right images is analyzed by the brain to provide information on distance (Coren & Ward, 1989).

BINAURAL DISPARITY   Likewise, the difference in location of the two ears also provides us with distance information. A sound directly in front of us strikes both ears at the same time; one to the left strikes the left ear before the right. Also, since sound is composed of physical pressure waves, the wave can strike the two ears at different points in its cycle, producing **binaural disparity.** This information is also used to judge distance (Kaufman, 1974).

EXTERNAL STATIONARY CUES TO DISTANCE

A great amount of information in the external environment contributes to the perception of distance. These cues include interposition, perspective, size, texture gradient, and relative brightness.

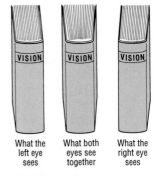

What the left eye sees   What both eyes see together   What the right eye sees

FIGURE 6-27
Binocular Disparity

FIGURE 6-28
Interposition

The largest balloon appears closest because of its size and also because it blocks parts of balloons behind it.

INTERPOSITION Because most objects are not transparent, an object in front of another will block part of the one behind. This is called **interposition.** In most cases interposition is a simple, reliable, and unambiguous cue to depth, so much so that when the cues are unusual and misleading, the rule of interposition governs judgment (Figure 6-28).

PERSPECTIVE When you look at a long stretch of road or railroad tracks, the parallel lines seem to converge on the horizon. This apparent convergence is called **perspective.** Because it is a powerful cue for judging distance, it is crucial in two-dimensional representations of three dimensions. Artists manipulate perspective to create different impressions and evoke different emotions. The exaggerated perspective in Van Gogh's *Hospital Corridor* expresses tension and a

FIGURE 6-29
The Power of Perspective

Perspective is normally used to judge distance, but artists also rely on it to make their paintings more evocative. Van Gogh's *Hospital Corridor* (left) uses perspective to create a constricting view, capturing his feelings about the place. Esher's *Waterfall* (right) shows the artist's habit of using perspective and other depth cues to fashion scenes in which the laws of nature are playfully violated.

closed-in, cramped feeling; M. C. Escher uses perspective and other depth cues to create an impossible world in which water runs uphill (Figure 6-29).

SIZE The size of objects on the retina gets smaller as objects recede into the distance. These size variables are valuable depth cues.

BRIGHTNESS The closer an object is, the brighter it appears. The amount of light from distant objects that hits the eyes is less because particles in the air diffuse the intensity of light. In the absence of other cues, the brighter of the two objects will be judged to be closer (Figure 6-30).

TEXTURE GRADIENT As you look over a uniform surface, like a pebbled beach or grassy field, the density of the texture increases with distance. A change in density, or texture gradient, can also signal a change in the angle of the surface (Figure 6-31). Consequently, information about distance may be directly available to the perceiver.

EXTERNAL MOVEMENT CUES TO DISTANCE

As we move, the stimulus information changes. This changing information gives us additional and important information about distance.

MOTION PARALLAX When you look out the window of a moving car, stationary objects outside the car appear to move. However, objects at varying distances move in different directions at different speeds. Some objects in the far distance seem to move in the same direction; the moon may even appear to be following you. Objects quite close, however, move in the opposite direction. This difference in movement is called **motion parallax.**

FIGURE 6-30
Brightness as a Depth Cue

The brighter, sunlit building here appears closer even though it is further away.

FIGURE 6-31
Texture Gradients as a Depth Cue

Because the density of the texture of a uniform surface increases with distance, such texture gradients can help you judge distance. Changes in the angle, tilt, or level of an otherwise uniform surface (here due to an earthquake) change the density of texture, providing a texture gradient cue to depth.

227

**FIGURE 6-32
Optical Expansion: The
Looming Effect**

The fact that objects you
approach, or that are
approaching you, appear to be
moving faster when closer
than when farther away gives
you cues to speed of
approach, angle of approach,
and relative distance between
objects in the scene affected
by optical expansion.
(Gibson et al., 1969)

OPTICAL EXPANSION   As you approach a scene, close objects appear to be moving
toward you faster than are those far away (Figure 6-32). This apparent
difference, called **optical expansion,** or the "looming effect," provides information on how fast you are approaching, at what angle, and the relative distances
of objects in the scene.

A NOTE ON SPACE

Although many sources of spatial information are available to us, we probably
use only some of them at any given time. It is probably only when the

developmental environment is extremely limited, as in the case of Kenge, the pygmy, that we do not learn all the relevant cues. Berkeley greatly underestimated our ability to pick up the information in the environment that is available to us (Gibson, 1979).

THEORIES OF PERCEPTION

Do we receive, invent, or compute the external world? There are three major theoretical approaches to the process of perception. The *ecological* approach emphasizes the relevance of the external information in perception. Proponents of this theory compare the perceiver to a radio set; they both tune into the environment and pick up information they are built to receive (Gibson, 1979). The *constructivist* approach emphasizes the role of schemata in perception. This view likens the perceiver to a computer, making judgments and decisions about the external world according to past experience or programs. Finally, the *computational* approach analyzes mechanisms of perception. It emphasizes that the mind contains special mechanisms to compute an analysis of what is in the world.

ECOLOGICAL APPROACH

The **ecological approach** emphasizes that perception is direct; it works like a radio receiving specific features of the world (Gibson, 1979; Michaels & Carello, 1981; Shephard, 1984). The information for color vision is directly present at the receptors. It stimulates the receptors, and we experience color. The proponents of this view say that information about distance, relative size, shape, and perspective are all similarly available to the human perceiver. A good example is the invariance of the qualities of the post mentioned earlier.

CONSTRUCTIVIST APPROACH

The **constructivist approach** asserts that perception is not receptive; rather, it is a construction in the mind and involves our making representations or models of the world (as an ordinary globe is fashioned to represent the Earth). Hence, the information from the senses stimulates the creation of an image of what could have caused this sensation. Many of the classic demonstrations, such as the figure-ground illustrations (Figure 6-6, page 210) and the distorted room (Figure 6-13, page 213) support the view that perception involves an act of creation as well as passive reception of information. We process, infer, and analyze information until we arrive at a reliable solution, the percept. Of course, percepts must also be correct when checked out in the real world: they should keep us from bumping into walls or drinking boiling hot fluids.

CRITICISM OF THE ECOLOGICAL AND CONSTRUCTIVIST APPROACHES

These two views emphasize different aspects of the perceptual process. The ecological approach deals with the adaptive nature of perception. Like all other organisms, we have evolved in response to a physical environment. It is thus highly likely that we would possess some built-in systems for the reception of external information important to survival, like color. However, few cells or neural networks have been found that pick up complex features of the world.

Many psychologists feel that the view that all perception is direct cannot account for perception in the complex world (Hayes-Roth, 1980; Ullman, 1980). The ecological view does not account well for the fact that the same stimulus can mean different things to different people; the meaning of a police siren is not the same to a thief as it is to the victim. It also ignores the role of assumptions. The ecological approach, then, does not account for the elements of meaning that depend on interpretation.

The constructivist approach assumes that we must invent a stable world anew, each moment, and that this invention is the product of trial and error. This view, too, is extreme. It ignores evolution, which causes an organism to select important information in the environment. Obviously, most organisms evolved to take advantage of their environment, and human beings are not exceptions.

Perception involves the processes proposed by *both* theories and much more. What is the meaning of the man approaching or of an object disappearing into the distance? We need not restrict ourselves to a one-track view of perception; we are probably a little like a radio and a little like a computer, but neither idea is wholly satisfying to the student looking for an idea of how it might work.

DECONSTRUCTION, COMPUTATION, AND RECONSTRUCTION

The ecological and constructivist approaches have dominated psychology for a long time. The argument continues in large part because neither of them really answers in a satisfactory manner the question of how the mind composes experience.

Many questions remain. What information does the mind use to perform all this composing, constructing, and interpretation? Which elements of the outside world are transformed in the brain? We cannot, for instance, pick up an entire post or leaf or cat somewhere in our heads, nor can we construct a perfect model based upon nothing inside the nervous system.

MARR'S THEORY   David Marr, among others, began to see the limits of these classical approaches. He set out to analyze the mechanisms of the way the mind breaks up the outside world (**decomposition**) into elements that the nervous system can deal with, and how these elements are later assembled, or composed, into perceptions. Some internal system has to compute the way the outside world gets represented inside.

Marr began to develop a **computational approach** to visual perception. His analysis is also lacking in completeness, partly because he died tragically and prematurely before he could fully develop his theory. According to Marr, vision cannot be understood by looking only at the cells of the sensory system (as we did in Chapter 5) or at the environment. It all has to work together: the sensors, the neural networks, the computer models of the networks, the necessity of the

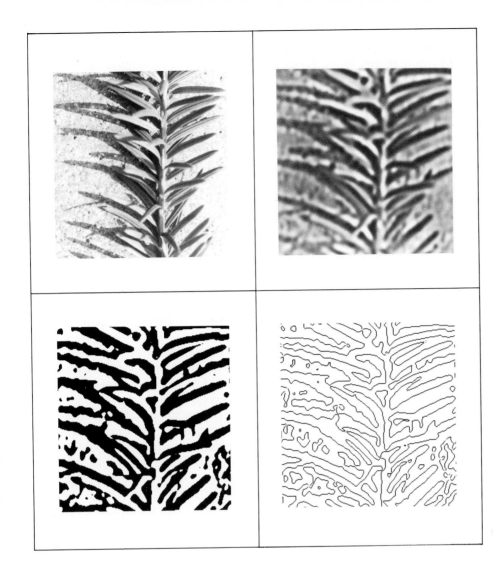

FIGURE 6-33
Decomposition

A visual image such as this branch of a pine tree (A) is *decomposed* (or broken up) by the brain into its most basic elements: first, simple blurs (B) and then blacks and whites (C). The places where zero-crossings occur (where light goes to dark) are shown in the final figure (D).
(Marr, 1982)

organism, and the nature of the world. He wrote in his book, *Vision:*

> It is not enough to be able to predict locally the results of psychophysical experiments. Nor is it enough even to be able to write computer programs that perform in the desired way. One has to do all these things at once and also be very aware of the additional level of explanation that I have called the level of computational theory." (Marr, 1982)

To carry out perception, the nervous system does not produce a picture of the outside world within. Very few cells have been found to be like the "monkey paw" cell to account for perceptions (see Figure 5-26, page 188). So how does it happen? In Marr's view the first operation of the mind is to analyze the light and dark features of an image (what he called the "raw primal sketch"). The major points of change from light to dark, and the reverse, seem to be important, as well as the rough geometry of the image (Figure 6-33). The places on the image where the light changes from positive to negative (that is, light to dark) are called *zero-crossings*. From these, we can produce a two-dimensional sketch which is centered from the viewpoint of the viewer.

The progression of internal analysis follows from (1) the "raw primal sketch" to what Marr calls the "full primal sketch," to (2) the two-dimensional sketch, and finally (3) to a full three-dimensional representation. Details aside, the important fact is that some kind of computational analysis of the visual field by the nervous system is likely.

If this theory is right, then there should be cells or networks of cells in the brain that respond to the relative size of two objects, to the convergence at the horizon, and other features of the natural world, just in the same way that cells in the visual system respond to colors and corners. If such networks are discovered, we would have a more precise understanding of what is built in and what is built up in the perceptual process.

The details of Marr's system have not been worked out, but this kind of analysis might help us understand how experience comes to be composed by the nervous system. Marr's theory is only in its infancy, but it may someday have the power to bring together much of what is known about sensation and perception.

NEURAL SPATIAL FREQUENCY CHANNELS   Recent research into the way the brain analyzes the extremely complex patterns of information detected by the eye have begun to confirm Marr's computational theory of perception. This new line in vision research studies the response of the visual system to spatial frequencies. To understand the concept of spatial frequencies, consider the way in which we measure resolution in a photograph. Coarse resolution, analogous to low spatial frequency, consists of relatively large areas of black and white, like the wide stripes in Figure 6-34. Finer resolution is analogous to higher spatial frequency, represented in the figure by narrow stripes. Many different sizes of alterations in dark and light combine to create the scene before us. Our entire visual field can be reduced to a mathematical expression based on the distribution of different spatial frequencies within it. Thus, all the information presented to our retinas by patterns on light could be processed into one compact equation represented by a pattern of neuronal activity.

How can our visual system detect spatial frequencies? Recall the circular on-off receptive fields of the retinal ganglion cells from Figure 5-24 (page 187). They are perfectly designed to act as tuned spatial frequency detectors. Only the frequency with light and dark bands that exactly fit the "on" and "off" centers and their surroundings will cause the ganglion cells to fire optimally. All other frequencies will pass light and dark over both center and surroundings, and lateral inhibition will prevent the ganglion cell from receiving a message to fire. Only six tuned spatial frequency channels, or collections of cells that respond to a specific frequency of alterations of light and dark, would be required to explain human visual acuity (Bradley & Skottun, 1987; Wilson, 1986).

Evidence has shown that there are cells in the cortex that may intergrate the spatial frequency information collected by the retinal ganglion cells. Certain cells in the visual cortex respond maximally to certain ranges of spatial frequency (Derrington & Fuchs, 1981; DeValois, Albrecht, & Thorell, 1982;

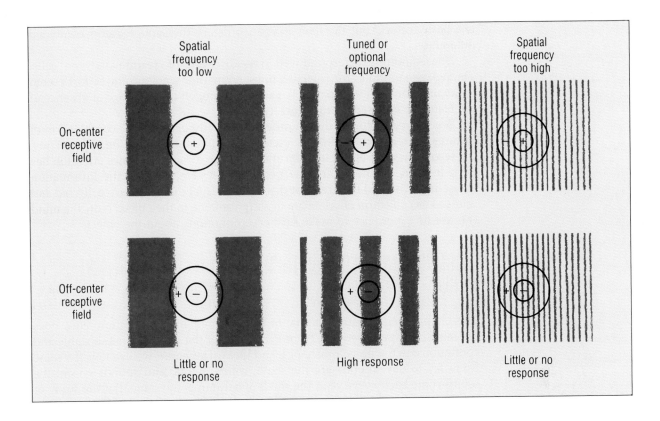

Spatial
frequency
too low

Tuned or
optional
frequency

Spatial
frequency
too high

On-center
receptive
field

Off-center
receptive
field

Little or no
response

High response

Little or no
response

DeValois & DeValois, 1987). Though we are not yet certain that the brain actually analyzes patterns of light according to frequency distributions, this theory explains how humans can resolve details smaller even than the size of a retinal cone (Klein & Levi, 1985; Westheimer, 1979). It also helps explain how the brain can interpret the overwhelming quantity of information present in the patterns of light available to the human eye.

FEATURE AND OBJECT DETECTION   Marr's theory was based on the idea that in visual processing patterns of light must first be encoded into lines, edges, locations, orientations, and colors. Recent research by Anne Treisman (Treisman, 1986) has demonstrated that object perception may proceed in two stages. In the first stage, our visual system detects certain primary features in the patterns of light in our visual field. In the second stage, the visual system identifies the objects composed of the primary features and localizes them in space.

The first stage, which occurs outside of our awareness and independent of the focus of our attention, is to identify a limited number of basic features, which include color, size, contrast, tilt, curvature, and line ends. These are the building blocks of vision. The boundaries between objects are easier to detect if the basic features of the objects are different, and less easy to detect if only the combination of features is different. For example, a red tag on a suitcase is easy to distinguish from a blue tag, but a red tag that says "Amsterdam" is not as easy to distinguish from a red tag that says "New York." The color of the tag

FIGURE 6-34
How Brain Cells Analyze Frequencies of Waves

Cells in the visual cortex analyze wave forms of particular wavelengths and frequencies. If the part of the cell marked in the diagram with a "+" coincides with the size of the wave, as in the two middle figures, it will fire, thus detecting that wave frequency.
(Coren & Ward, 1989)

is a basic feature, but the lines in the words are the same features combined differently.

These findings correspond well to the discovery of "feature analyzer" cells. The separate modules for detecting lines, orientations, colors, and so forth seem to act simultaneously (in parallel), each reporting on the presence or absence of the feature it is designed to detect.

Treisman also found that in order to correctly perceive the combination of features in an object, a person's attention must be focused on the object. Thus, the second stage of object identification requires awareness. Once attention has been focused on the object, the perceptual system accesses the information about the individual features that the various visual modules have collected and refers to its collection of schemata to assign a name to the object. Now the mind can use its experience to make further assumptions about the object.

DECOMPOSITION, COMPOSITION, AND THE MODEL OF THE WORLD

This chapter began with what might have seemed an odd question: How does the mind *compose* experience? Our experience of the world seems so stable and continuous, rich with color, shapes, and ideas. The house we live in is the same from day to day; friends are the same; colors, lights, and sounds go on; the robins come back every year; the smell of autumn is the same. But the study of brain processes, perception, and sensation has shown that the human experience of a stable outside world is a consistent illusion created by the brain. The illusion begins at the first neuron. Our senses grab only a little of reality: the eye

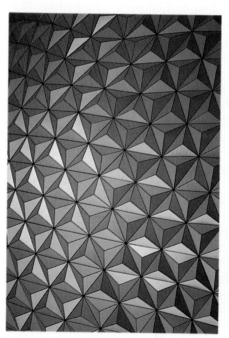
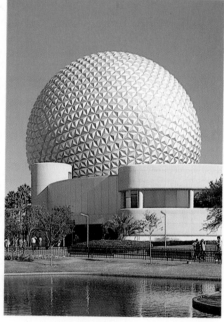

takes in one-trillionth of the energy that reaches it; the ear, similarly. So, we experience the world as stable only because of the way the brain organizes it, not because of the way the world is.

As the primitive brain of lower organisms evolved, a strategy gradually emerged. The nervous system evolved to radically reduce and limit the information transmitted to the brain. Otherwise it would have been flooded with information. It would not have "known" which changes in the environment were relevant and which were not—that is, which represented threats to survival or to the organism.

At each step in the path from sensory nerve cell to the brain, the world becomes more organized and more simplified. Our minds develop a network of schemata representing the world so that the external world, so chaotic and changing, becomes stable, simplified, and seemingly coherent. Instead of thousands of reflecting bits of glass, gray stone, scores of doors opening and closing, many high ceilings, and so on, we perceive one building. The parts fit together as a whole.

These percepts correspond closely enough with reality and help us survive. But, as difficult as it is to imagine, they are not really a complete portrait of the outside world, any more than the frog's four programs are.

SUMMARY

1. *Perception* is the process of organizing sensory information into simple, meaningful patterns. It begins with the reception of information by the senses and continues with selection, computation, and creation. Perception provides us with a constant experience of the world.
2. What an organism perceives depends on the elements in the environment. Two characteristics of objects important to perception are *affordance* and *invariance.*
3. The perceptual system is specialized for organizing complex information into simplified patterns. We experience the simplest meaningful interpretation of sensory information. This process involves perceptual organization and interpretation.
4. *Gestalt* psychology is based on the organizing principles of perception, which are figure-ground, proximity, similarity, and good continuation.
5. The information we receive from the environment is often incomplete. We use *unconscious inferences* to draw conclusions about reality from clues supplied by the senses. Assumptions, needs, and values all affect perception; when they change, perception also changes.
6. Perceptual experience changes through *assimilation* and *accommodation.* Incoming information is either assimilated into existing schemata, or schemata are updated to accommodate new information.
7. The main purpose of the perceptual process is to achieve *constancy,* the perception of a stable world. *Shape* constancy assures that we see an object as having the same form from many different aspects. *Size* constancy allows us to judge accurately the size of an object at different distances. The *brightness* and *color* of a thing are seen as constant under different levels of illumination.

8. Illusions illustrate the normal, automatic processes of perception. The illusion of comparative size shows how we judge size relative to context. The *Ponzo* illusion demonstrates how we use perspective to judge size and distance. The *Müller-Lyer* illusion shows how depth cues are used to assess the length of lines.

9. Perception adapts to fit the environment. This principle has been demonstrated by experiments in distorting visual information. We are born with some innate perceptual abilities, but they can be affected by sensory experience, especially during the critical period of development.

10. Much of perceptual experience is learned. Humans in different cultures develop different perceptual abilities because of the environments in which they are raised.

11. Distance is judged both by direct perception and by inference. Internal cues include *ocular accommodation, binocular disparity,* and *binaural disparity.* External cues are *interposition, perspective, size, brightness, texture gradient, movement, motion parallax,* and *optical expansion.*

12. There are three major theoretical approaches to the process of perception. Proponents of the *ecological* approach compare the perceiver to a radio: they both pick up information they are designed to receive directly from the environment. The *constructivist* approach asserts that perception is a construction in the mind of a model of the world, based on past experience and innate "programs." Both theories account for some aspects of perception, but neither fully explains it.

13. David Marr developed a *computational* theory of perception. The mind decomposes information from the outside world and uses it to compute perception. From a "raw primal sketch" of changes in light and dark, the brain computes a full three-dimensional representation.

14. The visual system responds to spatial frequencies, which are analogous to levels of resolution in a photograph. The on-off receptive fields of retinal ganglion cells work as tuned spatial frequency detectors. Some cells in the visual cortex respond maximally to specific spatial frequencies.

15. *Object perception* seems to proceed in two stages. First we identify the basic features of the object (color, size, contrast, tilt, curvature, and line ends); then we combine them into an object and locate it in space. Basic features are processed simultaneously; this may be accomplished by the feature analyzer modules of the cortex.

TERMS AND CONCEPTS

accommodation
assimilation
binaural disparity
binocular disparity
computational approach
constancy
constructivist approach
decomposition
ecological approach
gestalt
interposition

interpretation
motion parallax
occular accommodation
optical expansion
perception
perceptual organization
perspective
Purkinje shift
simplification
unconscious inferences

Freeman, N., & Cox, C. (1986). *Visual order.* New York: Cambridge University Press.

One approach to how pictures get represented in the mind. Not an easy read, but worth considering.

Marr, D. (1982). *Vision.* New York: Freeman.

The beginnings of the computational approach to perception, to be continued by Marr's successors, owing to his early death.

Rock, I. (1985). *Perception.* New York: Scientific American.

Well-illustrated and compelling. A good treatment of perception as traditionally understood.

SUGGESTIONS
FOR FURTHER
READING

7

CONSCIOUSNESS AND THE NATURE OF THE MIND

W hat are you going to do now? You can stop reading. You can continue reading. Maybe you'll hear something that makes you angry or maybe a loud noise will roust you up from the book (Johnson-Laird, 1988). How do you decide? How many different kinds of decisions are there inside you?

The part of the mind where different decisions cross is **consciousness,** which exists on several levels. Most of our *conscious* thoughts and actions are deliberate. We don't, however, attend to everything we're doing. Some of our actions are automatic, such as driving a car, and some are even more basic like the recoil of the hand when it brushes a flame. Some are unconscious, as when we frown when someone appears. Our actions are not simple: we don't always do what we want, nor do we always know what we are doing or why we are doing it. This multiple-level system is, of course, based on the way the brain is built, and has fascinated scientists and writers for centuries. Its analysis was Sigmund Freud's interest, in psychoanalysis, and it underlies our thoughts and motives as well. This system of mind and its different controls is the focus of cognitive science (Johnson-Laird, 1988; Ornstein, 1986). Here we begin our discussion of how the mind is put together and how it changes.

Consciousness is a word with many meanings, including being awake and being aware of ourselves, of what is going on around us, and of what we are doing (Natsoulas, 1978, 1983). Being conscious is being aware of mental activity, and the essential criterion of whether we are conscious of something or not is whether or not we can describe it.

Our normal waking consciousness is a model of the world. It is a construction based on current sensory input, information about expected regularities of experience (memory), and other cognitive processes. If any of these factors are radically altered, an **altered state of consciousness** results. For example, if sensory input is eliminated through either anesthesia or sleep, and our brains are still active enough to construct a world model, we dream.

In the normal course of a day we undergo profound alterations in our consciousness: at minimum, we sleep, we dream, and we wake. Under special circumstances, whether accidental or deliberate, we can experience forms of consciousness that are entirely different from our normal state of awareness, such as out-of-body experiences, mystical experiences, and drug-induced states.

This chapter will survey some of these varieties of consciousness; but first we need to prepare by comparing the characteristics of conscious and unconscious information processing.

CONSCIOUS AND UNCONSCIOUS PROCESSING

We are consciously aware of only a small part of what our minds are taking in at any one time. Reading a sentence, we are consiously aware of meaning, but we're not usually aware of the spelling of the words (hence the difficulty with proof reading—did you notice that "consciously" was misspelled earlier in this sentence?). And we're not conscious of grammar unless it is wrong. But since we automatically notice mistakes in grammar, we unconsciously analyze the syntax of what we read and hear.

The mind contains dozens of independent, *unconscious* processors—or modules—that operate automatically and in parallel (Fodor, 1983; Ornstein, 1986). Each module specializes in doing only one thing, and it does it rapidly, efficiently, and effortlessly. There are probably modules for language, face and object recognition, music, emotion, and for general memory, such as experiences or academic subjects.

Conscious processes, in contrast, occur one at a time, take effort, and are relatively inefficient (Barrs, 1988). They are also much more flexible than unconscious processes. Although unconscious processors can simultaneously

FIGURE 7-1
Automatization

The division of attention to deal simultaneously with a variety of stimuli requires both conscious processing and automatization, or automatic processing.

CHAPTER 7 / CONSCIOUSNESS AND THE NATURE OF THE MIND

produce contradictory interpretations of experience, consciousness provides us with a unique, consistent interpretation. We see only one interpretation of a Necker cube at a time.

ATTENTION

Attention refers to a set of processes that determine what comes into consciousness (Johnston & Dark, 1986). Attention can be either automatic or voluntary. If something unexpected suddenly happens, we automatically *attend* to it. We can also consciously decide to attend to any area of our current experience, whether novel or not, such as our breathing, sounds in our environment, and so on. Generally, we attend to one thing at a time.

AUTOMATIZATION

We **automatize** procedures or processes when we repeat a series of movements or actions, as in writing a set of letters to make a word. Automatization occurs in difficult skills that are practiced or repeated, such as sports and musical activities (Figures 7-1 and 7-2). We accomplish familiar actions without thinking—meaning without much involvement of consciousness—leaving us free to notice new events.

Do you remember how it was when you first learned to drive a car? "Let's see. Press the left foot down on the clutch. Move the stick shift into first gear. Lift the left foot off the clutch. Press on the gas with the right foot." While learning to operate a car, it is very hard to think about anything else, including driving somewhere. But once the movements become automatized, you can carry on a conversation, sing along with the radio, or admire the scenery without being conscious of operating the car. Shifting gears, even the total activity of driving, becomes automatized.

FIGURE 7-2
Automatization of Complex Tasks

Activities such as playing a musical instrument, assembling devices, driving a car, or flying an airplane involve automatization. Because we automatize, we can accomplish demanding routine tasks without really thinking or worrying about how we are performing the many separate actions that go into accomplishing the tasks.

FUNCTIONS OF CONSCIOUSNESS

In addition to simplifying and selecting information, consciousness guides and oversees actions. At any moment the content of consciousness is what we are prepared to act on next. In consciousness the priority system of the brain is administered. This system gives events that affect survival fast access to consciousness. Although hunger will not intrude on consciousness as dramatically as pain, we will strongly feel the need to eat if we do not eat. (See Chapter 13, section on physiological and safety needs.)

When there is a discrepancy between existing knowledge about the world (schemata) and an event, it is more likely to come to consciousness. A woman in a bikini is hardly noticeable on the beach, but if she wore the same outfit on a busy city street she would certainly be noticed (Figure 7-3).

LEVELS OF AWARENESS

When something is in awareness, *we are keeping track of it.* We are aware of much more than we are conscious of. To walk we must be aware of our movements, our feet on the pavement, and whether there is a crack, a curb, or a stone to step over. But we are not conscious of these things as we walk, nor are we conscious of breathing, arm movements, background noises, or traffic. At least four distinct levels of awareness can be distinguished (Kihlstrom, 1987). (See Figure 7-4.)

CONSCIOUS AWARENESS When we *know* we are aware of something, we are *conscious* of it. For example, we are consciously aware of whether or not this sentence ends with a period. We are also consciously aware of seeing the page and the writing in front of us.

SUBCONSCIOUS AWARENESS We may be aware of something without being conscious of it. This state of awareness below consciousness is *subconscious* awareness. During sleep, for example, when our conscious attention to the environment is

FIGURE 7-3
Consciousness and Discrepancies

Because consciousness tends to be stimulated by change, contrast, and the unusual, we are sure to become conscious of a perceptual discrepancy, such as seeing a man wearing a suit on the beach.

242

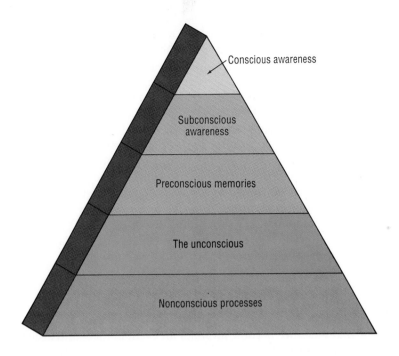

FIGURE 7-4
Levels of Awareness

There are various levels in the structure of our conscious and subconscious.

shut off, we are nevertheless aware of sounds. If the sounds have a particular significance, consciousness can be aroused. Sleepers will awaken to their own names or to a word like "fire," although they will not awaken to random spoken words. A mother sleeps through the noise of sirens in the streets but awakens at the far softer sound of her baby crying. For this to occur, she must be *aware* of the words and sounds of the environment and select only the important ones to enter consciousness.

PRECONSCIOUS   If a schema is activated above a certain level of awareness, it becomes conscious; otherwise it is unconscious. There is evidence suggesting that cognitive processing can interact with partially activated schemas, not themselves conscious. *Blindsight* is an example (see the box on page 245). People who have suffered damage to the visual cortex are completely blind as far as they are consciously aware, but they can accurately guess the direction of flashes of light (Poeppel, Held, & Frost, 1973) and point at objects they cannot see (Weiskrantz, Warrington, Sanders, & Marshall, 1974).

Another example is provided by the phenomenon of *subliminal perception:* sometimes stimuli too weak to be consciously recognized have a measurable impact on the mind. For example, people express a preference for what is familiar. In one experiment geometric shapes were presented for such brief intervals that the subjects could not consciously see them. When later asked to choose between pairs of previously (subliminally) presented figures and new figures, subjects preferred the familiar figures (Kunst-Wilson & Zajonc, 1979).

UNCONSCIOUS   Many mental processes that contribute to perception, thought, and action are not accessible to conscious awareness under any circumstances. For example, speak out loud for 30 seconds on any topic. While doing so, notice that you are conscious of what you say, but not of how you say it. You are conscious of the ideas you want to express, but not of the process that converts ideas into words. A great deal of procedural knowledge is unconscious in this sense.

UNCONSCIOUS MOTIVATION   Freud popularized the idea that we sometimes behave or misbehave as the result of unconscious motivation. There is, in fact, good evidence for "Freudian" slips and the like. Recent studies have shown that *Freudian slips* in the form of spoonerisms—that is, transposed sounds—occur more frequently when subjects are influenced by a conscious or unconscious motivation. When threatened with electric shock, male subjects were more likely to convert "worst cottage" to "cursed wattage"; when in the presence of an attractive female experimenter, they were more likely to convert "past fashion" to "fast passion" and "sappy hex" to "happy sex." Subjects scoring high on a sex-guilt scale showed more sexual spoonerisms (Barrs & Mattson, 1981; Motley, Barrs, & Camden, 1983).

ARE WE DIRECTLY AWARE OF WHAT WE DO?

We assume that when we become aware of an event in the world around us, we perceive it as it happens. Adding to our knowledge of the way consciousness works, Benjamin Libet (1978; Libet et al., 1979) has produced evidence that suggests that we may not actually see things *when* they happen. Libet studied neurological patients who had electrodes implanted in their cortexes for therapeutic purposes. By applying direct electrical stimulation to the somato-sensory cortex, which is responsible for conscious perception of touch, he was able to cause the subject to feel a nearly natural sensation near the wrist. He found that the electrical impulses to the brain had to last about 500 milliseconds (ms) before the subject became aware of the sensation.

He then gave subjects a very short electrical stimulus to their wrists 200 ms *after* initiating a 500-ms-long cortical stimulus. He expected that in each case there would be a 500-ms delay before the patient felt the stimuli, and that since the cortical stimulus came first, it would be felt first. However, the subjects felt the sensation from the skin stimulus *before* the one resulting from cortical stimulation. Since they had reported no awareness of cortical stimuli less than 500 ms long, the skin stimulus must have been processed in another way. Libet then applied the brain stimulus to neuronal pathways before they reached the cortex. This time he found that the subjects perceived the skin stimulus at the same time as the stimulus to the brain.

What difference does it make to the brain if the stimulus begins at the skin, before the cortex, or at the cortex? Both skin stimulation and subcortical stimulation produce what brain scientists call a *primary evoked response*—a spike of neuronal activity in the somatosensory cortex. Stimulation directly at the cortex does not produce this response.

Given the half second required for a stimulus to reach neuronal adequacy, why does it take almost no time to feel an electrical pulse at the wrist? Libet's startling conclusion is that when the skin stimuli were strong enough to be consciously felt, the brain somehow referred the experience back to the time that it actually occurred, using the start of the evoked response as a marker.

Libet's research is just the latest showing that there can be many levels of awareness; we can sometimes be *unconsciously* aware of things. In 1973 and 1974, several researchers discovered that people with damaged visual cortexes, who were blind to parts of the visual field, could actually report on things they could not consciously see (Poppell et al., 1973; Weiskrantz et al., 1974). This phenomenon was labeled **blindsight.**

When people who display blindsight are asked if they can see an image presented in the area of their visual field once served by the damaged part of their visual cortex, they claim to see nothing. However, when asked to guess about the nature or aspects of the object, they generally guess correctly. They can fairly accurately point to where the object is and say whether it is an *X* or an *O* or a line in a specific orientation (Sanders et al., 1974).

One patient had a slightly different kind of deficit in that she could not consciously see the left side of objects: when asked to draw an object, she would draw only the right side of it, without being aware that her drawing was incomplete. (Recall Figure 3-11). Her injury evidently occurred in a brain area involved with more abstract visual processing. Nonetheless, she could make judgments based on the information she could not consciously see. When shown two pictures of a house, identical except that the left side of the house was in flames, she would say they were exactly the same. But if she was asked which one she would prefer to live in, she chose the house that wasn't burning more than 80 percent of the time (Marshall & Halligan, 1988).

Interestingly, patients with this kind of damage can be trained to use the unconscious visual information they receive. They can learn to detect the presence of an object in their blind area and turn to focus on it (Zihl, 1980).

The phenomenon of blindsight indicates that people, at some preconscious level, can perceive and act on information that they do not know they are seeing. If this finding extends to normal human functioning, we may commonly respond to stimuli in our environment without ever knowing they are there or that they are what we are responding to. We may have less conscious control over our actions than we think.

There may be other explanations for these findings (see Libet, 1989), but if true they offer important implications. The delay required between a stimulus and the attainment of neuronal adequacy may provide a time in which perceptions could be modified or excluded from consciousness. This could be a mechanism for repressing unwanted perceptions, something like the 5-second tape loop used by radio and television stations to catch and bleep undesirable speech or actions.

The requirement for neuronal adequacy could serve as a filter to prevent too much information from entering consciousness. And the referral back in time would allow this brain "tape delay" to occur without putting us a half-second out of synchrony with the world. The delay between the occurrence of events and the brain's response may mean that any fast (less than 500 ms) responses to events that are processed in this way must happen before the stimulus reaches conscious levels. Thus, we may react to many things we are not even conscious of.

CONSCIOUSNESS AND PREPARATION TO ACT

And how does the conscious self know what is going on in the head? The answer is that it doesn't. In some of the most important research in years, Libet examined patients who were undergoing open head surgery. This allowed him to record from different areas of the brain, while the patients were awake. (There

is no pain in the brain, so no anesthetic is needed, and it is very useful for the patient to remain conscious so he or she can describe the results of stimulation.) Libet (Libet et al., 1983a, 1983b) asked the patients to tell him when they were going to do something. He compared the readiness potential (particular brain waves) that precedes an act with the patient's report of the subjective experience of wanting to act. For example, if the subject is asked to prepare to move at a certain time, the readiness potential appears; and when he is asked to prepare to move but to veto the move just before the time, the readiness potential also appears.

These findings imply that before an intention to act reaches consciousness, it has already triggered processes in the brain. Thus, much of our behavior may arise unconsciously. However, the ability of the subject to veto the intention to act after the unconscious process had begun indicates that we may have some kind of retroactive control of our behavior—but only if we are aware that an intention to act has been triggered. One function of consciousness may be to veto spontaneous plans, even if those plans are made within our own brain.

SELF-AWARENESS

We are conscious of our existence and our mortality; we know who we are and we have a sense of personal self. Other animals show little evidence of *self-awareness*—although a variation can be elicited in the pigeon (Skinner, 1981). If you put a cat in front of a mirror, it will approach its own reflection as if its reflection were another animal.

A chimpanzee, however, who has a considerably larger brain and a more developed cortex, shows some self-recognition. When Gallup (1979) put chimps in front of a mirror, they acted as though they knew it was a reflection of themselves. In an experiment, Gallup put a red mark on a chimp's forehead, then put him in front of a mirror. The chimp responded to his reflection by touching the mark on himself, not the mirror. This action indicated that he recognized himself and knew that something was unusual. All sighted human beings, from the age of 10 months on, can recognize themselves in a mirror.

Awareness of one's own existence can lead to further questions about the nature of existence (Where do we come from? What will happen when we die?) and to philosophical questions, to a search for universal principles of human life—morality, spirituality, and religions.

EVERYDAY VARIATIONS IN CONSCIOUSNESS

Our normal waking consciousness, rational consciousness as we call it, is but one special type of consciousness, whilst all about it, parted from it by the filmiest of screens there lie potential forms of consciousness entirely different. We may go through life without suspecting their existence; but apply the requisite stimulus, and at a touch they are there in all their completeness, definite types of mentality which probably somewhere have their field of application and adaptation. No account of the universe in its totality can be final which leaves these other forms of consciousness quite disregarded. How to regard them is the question—for they are so discontinuous with ordinary consciousness. . . . At any rate, they forbid a premature closing of our accounts with reality. (James, 1890)

William James made these observations on the nature of consciousness a century ago as a result of his own experiments with nitrous oxide (see page 264), but every day we undergo a series of more or less extreme alterations in our states of consciousness. If we are awake active (walking, talking, reading, etc.), our brain is actively processing external sensory input from the environment, which together with input from our memory systems, provides the raw material from which our normal state of consciousness is constructed—a mental model of ourselves engaged in the activity and interacting with the environment.

If we are awake but inactive, the balance of input moves from the external to the internal: our thinking becomes to a certain extent independent of external stimuli; our mind wanders; we daydream. Our consciousness is now modeling worlds that might be, rather than the current actual environment. Still, we tend to maintain some sort of model of the external world, and our attention can easily be drawn back to it, if some sign of danger appears.

WILLIAM JAMES
(1842-1910)

DAYDREAMING

Everyone daydreams daily. Daydreams usually occur when external events are boring, automatized, or unchanging (such as riding in a car or listening to a dull lecture). At these times, consciousness tunes out the outside world and tunes in the inside world.

We routinely simplify sensory information by tuning out unchanging events to direct attention to novel events. But since consciousness does not turn off when novel events are absent in the environment, we create our own. During daydreams we lose conscious awareness of the external world and our effectiveness is diminished. Even so, daydreaming may have some important functions. During daydreams, thoughts are more free flowing and uncensored, making us more receptive to new courses of action and new ideas, even to reflecting honestly on faults and mistakes. Such thoughts are less likely to enter consciousness in an active state (Singer, 1984).

According to Singer (1976), daydreams fall into four distinct categories:

1. *Self-recriminating.* These daydreams are prompted by the question, "What should I have done (or said)?"

2. *Well-controlled and thoughtful.* These daydreams are a form of planning, such as organizing the day, planning a party, rehearsing a presentation, and so forth.

3. *Autistic.* In these daydreams, material usually associated with nighttime dreams breaks through and disrupts consciousness, such as seeing a horse flying through the lecture hall.

4. *Neurotic or self-conscious.* These daydreams include exaggerated fantasies: "How I can score the winning point and become revered by all the fans?" or "How I can be discovered by a Hollywood director?"

The tendency to daydream waxes and wanes throughout the day, peaking approximately every 90–100 minutes (Kripke & Sonnenschein, 1978). The same conditions of monotonous stimulation that favor daydreaming also frequently lead to a more profound alteration of consciousness—sleep.

SLEEP

When so little sensory input is available that we stop maintaining a conscious model of the external world, we sleep. If the sleeping brain is activated enough to construct a conscious world model, it is the model of a world relatively independent from what is happening in the environment of the sleeper; in other words, it is a dream. The sleeping brain isn't always creating a conscious multidimensional world model. Sometimes, it seems to be merely thinking or perhaps idling. The differences in mental activity during sleep depend largely upon differences in the physiological state of the sleeper.

TWO KINDS OF SLEEP   Sleep is by no means a uniform state of passive withdrawal from the world, as scientists thought until recently. In fact, there are two distinct kinds of sleep, a quiet phase and an active phase, that are differentiated by many biochemical, physiological, psychological, and behavioral factors. Prominent differences in brain waves (from electrical activity measured at the scalp), eye movements, and muscle tone are used to define the two states. The quiet phase mostly fits the common view of sleep as a state of restful inactivity: the brain tends to be running on idle, breathing is slow and deep, metabolic rate is at a minimum, and growth hormones are released facilitating restorative processes. When awakened from this state, sleepers feel disoriented and rarely remember dreaming.

The second, active kind of sleep was discovered in 1952 by a graduate student, Eugene Aserinsky, who was observing the sleep of infants. Aserinsky noticed the periodic occurrence of active eye movements during sleep. During this phase, now called **Rapid Eye Movement** or **REM sleep,** the eyes move rapidly about (under closed lids, of course), much as they would if the sleeper were awake (Aserinsky & Kleitman, 1953). The brain becomes activated, and vivid dreams are reported following 80–90 percent of awakenings from REM sleep (Dement & Kleitman, 1957).

THE NIGHT JOURNEY   By studying the physiology of the body during sleep, researchers have discovered cyclical variations in bodily processes that occur throughout the night and classified these phases of sleep into different stages. In addition to the quiet and active brain states of sleep—non-REM and REM— researchers have classified sleep into four different stages.

The primary instrument used to judge what stage of sleep someone is in is the electroencephalograph (EEG), which monitors brain wave activity. To further distinguish sleep stages, the investigator needs a measure of eye movement activity and of muscle tension. While the sleep subject lies quietly awake in bed before sleep with his eyes closed, his EEG shows predominantly alpha rhythm brain waves. As he drifts off to sleep, the alpha rhythm gradually disappears and is replaced by less regular, low amplitude waves. His eyes roll slowly from side to side. This is called Stage 1 sleep (Figure 7-5). Mental activity at this stage is characterized by brief, bizarre, dreamlike *hypnagogic* (from Greek, meaning leading into sleep) imagery.

Hypnagogic dreams can be as interesting as REM dreams but tend to be much shorter. One sleep subject experienced the following:

> I saw the huge torso of a man rising out of the depths of a profoundly dark-blue sea. I knew, somehow, that he was a god. Between his shoulders, in place of a

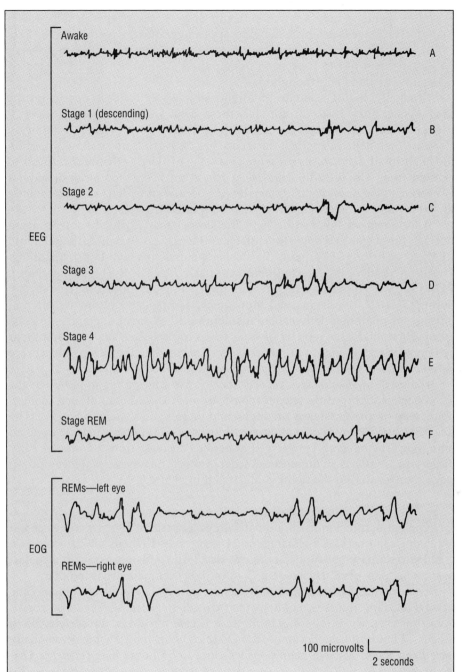

Awake — A

Stage 1 (descending) — B

Stage 2 — C

Stage 3 — D

Stage 4 — E

Stage REM — F

EEG

REMs—left eye

EOG

REMs—right eye

100 microvolts

2 seconds

FIGURE 7-5
Stages of Sleep

These electroencephalograph (EEG) records (A-F) show brain wave activity during the five stages of sleep. The electrooculogram (EOG) records at the bottom record eye movement during the REM stage.

head, he had a large golden disc engraved with ancient designs. It reminded me of the high art of the Incas. . . . The rays of light streaming out from behind him told me the sun was setting. People, clothed in dark garments, were diving into his face—the golden disc. I knew they were dead, and it seemed to me they were being "redeemed" by this action. This image was very significant for me, yet I did not know exactly why. (LaBerge, 1985, p. 48)

After spending only a few minutes in Stage 1, the sleeper usually enters Stage 2. This stage is determined by the appearance of wave patterns in the EEG called *sleep spindles* and *K-complexes.* If awakened from this stage, the sleeper will often claim not to have been asleep at all. Mental activity in Stage 2 is generally mundane and thoughtlike.

Gradually, high-amplitude, rhythmic, slow waves begin to appear on the EEG. When, after 10 to 30 minutes, these delta waves compose at least 20 percent of the EEG, the subject is said to be in *delta sleep.* Stage 3 and Stage 4 sleep are both delta sleep; their difference has been arbitrarily defined based on the quantity of delta waves present. This stage of sleep is the most difficult to awaken from. Children in delta sleep can often be carried around without awakening. Sleep walking and sleep talking occur during delta sleep. Very little dream content or other mental activity is reported from delta sleep.

After about an hour and a half, the sleeper may gradually ascend again through the stages and enter REM sleep, or he may go straight from delta into REM. At or before REM onset, the sleeper's muscle tension drops to nothing. This is the result of the direct inhibition of the muscles by the brainstem during REM sleep, which prevents the dreamer from acting out the dream. Periodically during this state, the sleeper will show quick, darting eye movements, often in bursts, and small muscle twitches. Also during REM, breathing and heart rate become irregular, the genitals of both sexes are aroused, and the vestibular system is activated. Eighty to ninety percent of the time that sleep subjects are awakened from REM sleep, they report vivid, detailed dreams.

The cycle of sleep stages repeats four or five times a night, although the same stage is slightly different at each occurrence. The amount of time spent in delta sleep decreases later in the night, and more time is spent in Stage 2. The first REM period may last 10 minutes, while later REM periods may be up to an hour long. The intervals between REM periods decrease from 90 minutes early in sleep to as little as 30 minutes toward morning. The typical sequence of sleep stage changes during the night is illustrated in Figure 7-6.

FIGURE 7-6
Sequence of Sleep Stages

This graph shows how the brain cycles through REM sleep and the four stages of non-REM (NREM) sleep throughout the night.
(Van de Castle, 1971)

CIRCADIAN RHYTHMS   Organisms as complex as a single cell have daily rhythms in their biological functioning. In human beings, more than 100 physiological and psychological processes fluctuate on a 24-hour cycle (Dement, 1972). This cycle is called **circadian,** meaning "about one day." The cycle of sleep and wakefulness is the most obvious circadian rhythm. Body temperature is another.

Even when isolated from signals such as light and dark that accompany the passage of days, humans maintain their circadian cycles. Under these conditions, however, when the inner body clock is given free run, the cycle is rarely exactly 24 hours; it usually can be from 24 to 28 hours long. People occasionally have been found to have natural cycles close to 50 hours long (Hauri & Orr,

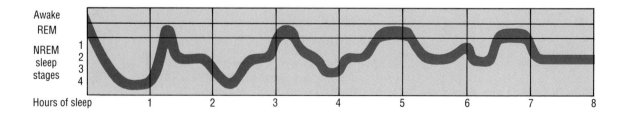

1982). Alterations in light and dark, clocks, meal times, and perhaps other more subtle cues all keep us entrained to the natural rhythm of the planetary day.

Disruptions in our normal cycles cause difficulty in sleeping and waking, as well as excess sleepiness. Jet lag is a common form of such disruption. The traveler who flies east across three time zones finds it hard to awaken at 7 a.m., because to her body it is 4 a.m. Likewise, she may have difficulty sleeping at midnight, because her body thinks it is 9 p.m. Excess sleepiness develops in this case not because of lack of sleep but because of the lack of coordination of body rhythm with activity cycle. After a few days the traveler's circadian rhythms catch up with her, and her sleep returns to normal (Dement, 1972).

THE FUNCTIONS OF SLEEP

We spend 20 years asleep, a third of our lives. During all that time we are functionally inert as far as the outside world is concerned. Why do we do this? All mammals sleep, so sleep must be an important factor in mammalian biology.

Sleep probably evolved about 180 million years ago, in the first warm-blooded animals (Allison & Cicchetti, 1976). Reptiles, cold-blooded creatures from which mammals evolved, depend upon the sun to maintain a high enough body temperature to eat, breed, and avoid danger. At night, when it is cold, they must find a place safe from predators, since they lack the energy to escape.

Mammals, on the other hand, maintain their own internal body temperatures at a steady level, and thus are not forced to become immobile at night. However, when they first evolved from the sunlight-loving reptiles, they were not equipped to function at night: they could not see predators in the darkness. This is one reason why it was healthier for mammals to enter an inert state at night. Animals sleep during the period of time when it is most dangerous or least productive for them.

Sleep may have begun as a simple state of inertness but, over millions of years, evolved into a state in which many useful biological and psychological functions are accomplished. A sleeper may seem to be wasting time but is actually engaged in maintaining a healthy condition of brain and body.

SLEEP DEPRIVATION

Since we all sleep (most) every night and experience a strong drive to sleep when we have stayed awake for an unusual length of time, it seems natural to assume that some harm must come from not sleeping. Researchers have conducted many studies of *sleep deprivation* (Dement, 1972).

Complete sleep deprivation has its most profound effect on the feeling of sleepiness, as we might guess. However, after one to three sleepless nights, people can usually still function quite well. The main detriments are to mood, vigilance, and performance on highly creative or extremely monotonous tasks (Hauri & Orr, 1982). After 2 or 3 days without sleep, people start to show *microsleeps*—brief moments of sleep in the midst of waking—on their EEG. After 10 days, the microsleeps become so frequent that it is hard to tell whether people are awake or asleep, although they function as if they are awake (Hauri & Orr, 1982).

INSOMNIA

The most common sleep disorder is *insomnia,* the inability to sleep. Insomnia is less likely to be a disease in itself than a symptom of some other problem (Cartwright, 1978). Clinical depression is often accompanied by serious insomnia. Other causes are anxiety, worry over not being able to sleep, and drug side-effects. An interesting sidelight on insomnia is that some people who believe they are not sleeping actually are. These people and those who have shorter sleep requirements than most sometimes complain that they have insomnia because they think they should sleep more, though they are not excessively sleepy during the day (Cartwright, 1978).

AROUSAL DISORDERS

A number of strange sleep behaviors are classified as *arousal disorders* (Cartwright, 1978). These events usually occur during the deepest part of delta sleep. They tend to be most common in children, who have much more delta

sleep than adults (Hauri & Orr, 1982). They are characterized by the intrusion of waking-type behaviors into sleep. The three most common are night terrors, sleep-talking, and sleepwalking. Sleep-talking is harmless (except perhaps to the sleep of a bed partner) but demonstrates that people are quite able to talk without thinking.

One to three percent of children under 12 experience night terrors (Cartwright, 1978). In the typical incident, the child awakens and screams in terror, but cannot recall any reason for the fear (Dement, 1972). The probable cause is sudden change in arousal, or an awakening, which is interpreted by the child as the result of something

frightening. Night terrors can be induced by awakening those prone to them from delta sleep with a buzzer (Cartwright, 1978). Several researchers have suggested night terrors are caused by some emotional conflict emerging into consciousness while the sleeper is most vulnerable (Cartwright, 1978).

Sleepwalking (somnambulism) is another arousal disorder. The EEG of a sleepwalker shows a mixture of delta with waking brainwaves (Houri & Orr, 1982). Sleepwalkers and even some normal children can be induced to exhibit somnambulism by taking them out of bed and putting them on their feet (Cartwright, 1978). Sleepwalking can be hazardous to the sleeper. According to one study, one sufferer "occasionally urinated on the living-room carpet, had severely hurt himself after stumbling over furniture, and twice had been found trying to climb out of a window in the couple's fourth story apartment" (Hauri & Orr, 1982).

Excessively prolonged sleeplessness can lead to paranoia, occasional hallucinations, and short-term personality changes (Dement, 1972). These effects are probably due to the effect of REM sleep deprivation. Deprivation of REM sleep was thought in the early 1960s to lead to psychosis. This was an exaggeration, however. REM sleep deprivation probably increases the excitability of the central nervous system.

DREAMING

Dreams are unquestionably the most fascinating phenomena associated with sleep. Most of us have at times awakened from dreams of incomparable mystery, delight, and terror, and we have all probably wondered why we dream and what dreams mean. Research has begun to cast light on these shadows of the night.

Different people report extremely different kinds of dreams: dreams can be more or less interesting, creative, emotional, vivid, lucid, and so on. What determines the different kinds of dreams? First, the individual's personality traits influence dreams. We are basically the same personalities whether awake or dreaming, so depressed patients have dreams of helplessness, hopelessness, and escape (Kramer et al., 1966); creative people have creative dreams (Sylvia

CHAPTER 7 / CONSCIOUSNESS AND THE NATURE OF THE MIND

et al., 1978); and schizophrenics have extraordinarily bizarre dreams (Carrington, 1972).

Second, society determines many of our basic attitudes about the importance and meaning of dreams (Domhoff, 1985). Cultures that regard dreams as airy nothings do not encourage their members to make use of them.

Third, there is evidence that the physiology of the brain during dreaming sleep plays an important role in creating the sometimes bizarre features of dreams (Hobson & McCarley, 1977).

But why do we dream in the first place?

THEORIES OF DREAMING   Sigmund Freud believed that we dream in order to remain asleep. Freud's influential wish fulfillment model of dreaming (1955) held that dreams were the disguised symbols of primitive, unacceptable needs and desires welling up from the unconscious mind. If these repressed instinctual impulses were allowed free expression, they would cause the sleeper to awaken.

Freud distinguished two levels of dream content: the *manifest content,* which is the obvious surface level, the dream itself; and the *latent content,* which is the hypothetical underlying dream thoughts that give rise to the manifest content. Freud believed that every dream was instigated by an unconscious wish, generally sexual and infantile in nature. And everything in every dream was symbolic—of what the reader can guess from the following list of dream symbols according to Freud:

> All elongated objects, such as sticks, tree-trunks and umbrellas . . . may stand for the male organ—as well as all long sharp weapons, such as knives, daggers and pikes. . . . Boxes, cases, chests, cupboards and ovens represent the uterus, and also hollow objects, ships, and vessels of all kinds.—Rooms in dreams are usually women. (1955, p. 389)

Opposing theories of dreaming have pointedly challenged Freud in every particular. Hobson and McCarley (1977) proposed that dreams are instigated not by wishes but by a biological process—REM sleep. According to their *activation-synthesis model,* neurons in the brain stem are activated during REM, causing random signals to bombard the cortex which tries to synthesize an interpretation. The dream is the result of the brain's attempt to make sense of meaningless physiological noise. Dreams, according to Hobson and McCarley, are no more meaningful than inkblots; there is nothing to disguise and nothing to symbolize.

Freud stands on one side, and Hobson and McCarley stand on the other of a centuries old debate. Are dreams meaningful? Is the proverb correct that asserts that an uninterpreted dream is like an unopened letter? Or are dreams the addled children of an idle brain? The answer may be somewhere in between. LaBerge (1985) argues that a modified activation-synthesis model is capable of accounting for both the sense and nonsense of dreams. The dreaming brain is not randomly activated; rather, previously activated schemas (Freud's day residue) are selectively brought into consciousness by the same constructive processes that function in wakefulness. Dreams are more or less meaningful, not because they are intended as messages, but because they are the dreamer's own creation. A fearful dream is the creation of a fearful dreamer.

Because Freud believed that every dream was the fulfillment of a wish, he concluded that nightmares are the result of masochistic wish fulfillment. A more likely explanation is that dreams reveal what we expect to find in the world: either what we wish for or what we fear. Expectation and motivation strongly influence waking perception and, in the case of sleep, with little sensory input, these processes become predominant (LaBerge, 1985).

DREAM RECALL Dreams are difficult to remember. Though we all dream several times a night, most people remember less than one-tenth of these experiences. LaBerge (1985) has argued that this selective amnesia of dream experience may be the result of biological evolution. All mammals have REM sleep; therefore, it is likely that all mammals dream. However, most mammals do not possess the cognitive ability required to distinguish a dream event from a "real world" event, which makes it maladaptive to recall dreams. Think, for example, of how dangerous it would be for a cat to remember a dream that the vicious dog next door had died and been replaced by a family of mice. The cat, upon awakening, might be hungry and decide to go hunting next door, where the dog waits. Obviously, those animals who tended to remember such dreams as real would be less likely to live to pass on the tendency to their offspring.

Humans may be the only animals who can remember dreams (LaBerge, 1985). This ability may be one of the benefits of language. We remember our dreams by making stories—linear sequences of events—out of them. Dreams that do not conform well to a storylike pattern are more difficult to retain. As children, we have to learn to understand the difference between dreams and reality.

When our parents tell us that there isn't a witch in the closet, that it was only a dream, they help us make this distinction. The process of learning to distinguish between waking and dreaming can go further. People can learn to recognize they are dreaming while still in the dream.

FIGURE 7-7
Sleep Research

Research in sleep labs discovered that some people are aware that they are dreaming and can alter their dreams.

LUCID DREAMING Most people have had the experience at least once in a dream of realizing, "This is a dream!" The idea that this could actually happen during sleep had been discounted for years by scientists. Since we are unconscious of the external world during sleep, dreams had been considered the most involuntary and unconscious of mental processes. A decade ago, however, researchers scientifically validated that we can be fully conscious in our dreams while remaining soundly in REM sleep (LaBerge, Nagel, & Dement, 1981). This state is called **lucid dreaming** (Figure 7-7). While lucid, dreamers can often consciously alter the events of the dream.

The scientific discovery of lucid dreaming has many implications. One is that more processes may be accessible to conscious manipulation than many scientists have thought. Also, lucidity brings with it the ability to interact with dream imagery while fully aware that it is a product of one's mind. Because of this, and because it is learnable, lucid dreaming can be used as a therapeutic tool. Lucid dreamers can use their dreams to try out new behaviors without fear of embarrassment or failure. Those plagued by nightmares can use lucidity to face their frightening dream images, armed with the knowledge that the images can do them no real harm. Lucid dreaming is also becoming an important technique for psychologists to study mind-body relationships during REM sleep (LaBerge, 1985).

The same experiment that confirmed the existence of lucid dreams in REM sleep also confirmed the *scanning hypothesis* of the origin of rapid eye movements. This proposed that the eye movements of REM sleep were the result of the dreamer watching the events in the dream (Dement, 1972). The eye muscles are some of the very few muscle groups that are not paralyzed by the REM process. Researchers instructed sleep subjects who were experienced lucid dreamers to make distinctive movements with their eyes once they knew they were dreaming. These unmistakable eye movement patterns appeared on the record of the subjects' eye movements in REM, proving that they had in fact been lucid while in REM sleep, and that *dreamed* eye movements cause *real* rapid eye movements (LaBerge et al., 1981).

Before the discovery of lucid dreaming, efforts to study the relationship between dream behavior and physiology were quite tedious because the experimenters had to wait for subjects to spontaneously dream the behavior they were interested in studying. In lucid dreams, trained subjects can remember to carry out previously agreed upon experimental tasks. In this way the relationship between subjectively experienced dream events and corresponding objectively measured physiological processes can be studied.

There are striking physiological correlations for a variety of dreamed behaviors, including time estimation, breathing, singing, counting, and sexual activity. The strength of the psychophysiological correlations observed in these studies suggests that, from the brain's perspective, *dreaming* of doing something is more similar to actually doing it than merely *imagining* doing it. Perhaps that is why dreams seem so real while they last (LaBerge, 1985).

DELIBERATE ALTERATIONS OF CONSCIOUSNESS

Practices for altering consciousness exist in every society. These mind alterations may be undertaken simply for amusement, as in recreational drug taking, or as a disciplined way of deepening one's understanding of reality.

Since normal consciousness is geared to action, reducing the requirements for action can offer consciousness a chance to change. In laboratory studies, consciousness can be altered by removing the normal requirements for action and attention, as in sensory deprivation. In meditation and in many religious practices, the practitioner is removed from normal routines.

SENSORY DEPRIVATION AND ISOLATION

As we have seen, low levels of environmental stimulation lead to sleep, and decreasing sensory stimulation has been used to alter consciousness. For centuries, techniques to eliminate awareness of change have been used: mystics remove themselves to a cave or to the desert, or they perform repetitive movements or sounds. The effect of these practices has been duplicated in isolation rooms designed to keep perceived changes to a minimum (Figure 7-8).

In early experiments in sensory deprivation, people reported unusual experiences, temporal disorientation, hallucinations, and extreme psychopathology (Bexton, Heron, & Scott, 1954). Yet such bizarre results depend on the

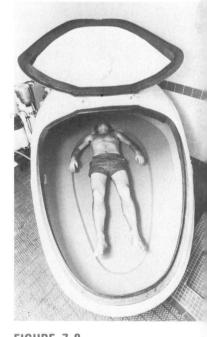

FIGURE 7-8
Sensory Deprivation

This person is in a dark, soundless chamber, floating in water.

The dying *process* may be more or less painful or distressing. However, intriguing clinical reports show that the *experience* of death may be quite different. Ring (1980) studied 102 men and women who had near-death experiences—they had all been very close to death or had actually been clinically dead and then revived. The results were fascinating. These people reported experiencing intense feelings of peace or joy, or felt that they had left their bodies and had traveled through a dark tunnel. In addition, they reported seeing a brilliant light or beautiful colors. A few reported speaking with deceased relatives or friends or a "presence" who convinced the person to return to life. Some felt that they had taken stock of their lives by reviewing all or parts of it; this was sometimes seen in the form of a movie.

This core experience seems to be ordered in five distinct stages: (1) feelings of peace and affective well-being, (2) body separation, (3) entering darkness, (4) seeing a light, and (5) entering the light. People who experienced the first stage reported a cessation of pain and intense feelings of joy, peace, or calm, usually unlike anything they had previously experienced. This has led to some speculation that production of endorphins (neurotransmitters that block pain) in the brain are involved (Thomas, 1982). In the second stage, some people reported a sense of being detached from their bodies. Some even felt they were somehow looking down at their own bodies. Those who did also reported an unusual brightness of the environment.

The third stage seems to be one of transition. People experienced moving through a dark space, sometimes described as a tunnel. At the end of the tunnel was often a brilliant light. Although very bright, it did not hurt the eyes. They described it as very comforting and beautiful. Finally, a few people reported entering the light. This light was somehow a different land—a field or valley, always very bright and beautiful, and indescribable.

There are other elements of the core experience that cut across these stages, such as the life review, meeting with a presence or

---

expectations of the subjects and the experimenter (Suedfield, 1980). The disorienting effects of sensory deprivation and isolation may be potentially beneficial for some purposes. Sensory isolation, for instance, has been useful for relaxation and in clinics for the control of smoking, by removing cues that prompt the subject to smoke.

A recent study looked at the relationship between varying levels of environmental stimulation in wakefulness and sleep and the thematic sequencing of spontaneous thought and imagery. Reinsel, Wollman, & Antrobus (1986) tested the idea that sensory stimulation disrupts the spontaneous stream of consciousness, resulting in more changes of topic per unit of time. They found that REM sleep dreams had the longest periods of uninterrupted, and therefore elaborated imagery, as predicted.

MEDITATION

The aim of **meditation** in spiritual practices is knowledge of oneself and one's place in the world. Instead of coming to an intellectual understanding of different mechanisms of attention, meditation seeks to teach individuals to experience the world differently. Meditation is used by nearly all traditional psychologies of the East—among them Sufism, Zen Buddhism, and Yoga—and in the West by religious orders such as the Franciscans.

CONCENTRATIVE MEDITATION The instructions for **concentrative meditation** are strikingly similar in different traditions. In the book *What the Buddha Taught*, the Buddhist monk Rahula (1969) gives these instructions:

deceased loved ones, and the decision to return to life. In the life review, a person may experience all or part of his or her life in visual, instantaneous images. This experience is usually positive. People report a sense of detachment and sometimes also an ability to edit, to move backward or forward to skip certain parts.

One-fifth of the people in Ring's sample experienced a presence, which was rarely seen. It somehow communicated directly with the person, offering him or her the opportunity to go back. This presence was sometimes interpreted within a religious framework; God or Jesus for Christians and Krishna for Hindus (Osis & Hanalosen, 1977). Alternatively, a person may be greeted by the "spirits" of deceased loved ones, usually relatives, who inform the person that it is not time yet and that he or she must go back to life.

While not everyone in Ring's sample experienced all or any of these phenomena, *not one person had a negative experience*. The experience of nearly dying almost always had a positive effect on the person's life. Everyone who had a brush with death came away a different person. As Ring (1980) stated,

The typical near-death survivor emerges from the experience with a heightened sense of appreciation for life, determined to live life to the fullest. Survivors report a strong sense of purpose in living, even when they cannot articulate just what this purpose is. As one young man said:

"[I had an] awareness that something more was going on in life than just the physical part of it. . . . It was just a total awareness of not just the material and how much we can buy. . . . There's more than just consuming life. There's a point where you have to give to it and that's real important. And there was an awareness at that point that I had to give more of myself out of life. That awareness has come to me."

Some psychologists have argued that these experiences are little more than hallucinations (Siegel, 1980). In response, Ring (1984) has begun to blur the point and become vague about his findings. But hallucinations or not, they indicate that the experience of dying is not as terrible as we once thought and that the similarity described in religious literature between mystical states and death may be intriguing.

Breathe in or out as usual, without any effort or strain. Now, bring your mind to concentrate on your breathing-in and breathing-out. Let your mind watch and observe your breathing in and out. . . . Forget all other things, your surroundings, your environment; do not raise your eyes and look at anything. . . .

At the beginning, you will find it extremely difficult. . . . You will be astonished how your mind runs away. It does not stay. You begin to think of various things. You hear sounds outside. Your mind is disturbed and distracted. You may be dismayed and disappointed. But if you continue to practice this exercise twice a day . . . you will experience just that split second when your mind is fully concentrated on your breathing, when you will not hear even sounds nearby, when no external world exists for you.

Practices of concentrative meditation are similar throughout the world, which suggests that they may stimulate a common experience, regardless of minor variations in technique. The important factor common to all meditations is that the same information is repeatedly cycled through consciousness.

OPENING-UP MEDITATION A second form of meditation is more related to daily activity. The exercises employed do not isolate the practitioner from the world; rather, they attempt to involve everyday events in the training of consciousness. In these exercises—some of which are called "just sitting" in Zen, "mindfulness" in Yoga, and "self-observation" in Sufism—consciousness is opened up to everything that occurs.

Opening-up exercises emphasize the difference between the information that reaches consciousness and the interpretation of that information. Western psychology has also made efforts to study this difference. The early introspectionist psychologists, such as William James, strove to analyze, within their own

An important technique for upsetting routine and opening consciousness is to study a narrative containing paradoxes and unusual events. Such tales are called **teaching stories** (Shah, 1982). One aim of many esoteric traditions is to introduce students to unfamiliar ideas and information. Teaching stories are said to contain certain specially chosen patterns of events that encourage openness to new concepts. Repeated reading of a teaching story strengthens these patterns in the mind of the reader, thus slowly enhancing his capacity to understand formerly foreign ideas (Shah 1986).

Here is a tale about a town in which everyone was blind.

The Elephant in the Dark

One day, an elephant appeared in the town square. No one in town had ever heard of or knew of this strange animal. The King of the Blind sent his three wisest men to find out what manner of creature this elephant was. Each sage approached the elephant from a different side. The one

whose hand had touched the ear reported back that he had discovered the true nature of the elephant. "It is large and flat, rough—like a rug." The second, who had felt only the trunk, said, "That's not it at all—I know the answer. It is like a trumpet, but capable of dramatic movement." The third touched only the legs, and he disagreed vehemently with the other two, "No, no, no. You've got it all wrong. The elephant is mighty and firm like a pillar." Needless to say, none of the single observations could reveal the true nature of the elephant. (Shah, 1970)

Suppose *you* were curious about the discovery of a strange creature, but instead of an ele-

TEACHING STORIES

phant, it was a human being. How would you find out what it is like? You would need to understand where it came from, its past, its family history, its physiology. You would ask, How does its brain work? How does it behave and communicate? What is its sex? What pleases it? How does it act with others? How do culture, groups, and family affect it? How is it like all other individuals of its species? You would have to ask all these questions—and many more. Each answer would lead to more questions. One question that seems quite simple, such as "What is sleep?" might remain unanswered, even after years of inquiry.

Psychologists are in this situation. They approach their study from numerous directions, ask different questions, and use diverse methods. Each aspect of psychology tries to shed some small light on

a previously mysterious part of being human: to illuminate the "person in the dark." Psychology tries to answer many of the questions we have about ourselves, other people, and the nature of human life: Why do I feel lonely? What is "going crazy" like? What makes someone "creative"? What happens when I take drugs? What is a mystical experience? What makes someone help another?

The Man With the Inexplicable Life

There was once a man named Mojud. He lived in a town where he had obtained a post as a small official, and it seemed likely that he would end his days as Inspector of Weights and Measures.

One day when he was walking through the gardens of an ancient building near his home, Khidr, the mysterious Guide of the Sufis, appeared to him, dressed in shimmering green. Khidr said: "Man of bright prospects! Leave your work and meet me at the riverside in three days' time." Then he disappeared.

Mojud went to his superior in trepidation and said that he had to leave. Everyone in the town soon heard of this and they said: "Poor Mojud! He has gone mad." But, as there were many candidates for his job, they soon forgot him. On the appointed day, Mojud met Khidr, who said to him, "Tear your clothes and throw yourself into the stream. Perhaps someone will save you."

Mojud did so, even though he wondered if he were mad.

Since he could swim, he did not drown, but drifted a long way before a fisherman hauled him into his boat, saying, "Foolish man! The current is strong. What are you trying to do?"

Mojud said: "I do not really know."

"You are mad," said the fisherman, "but I will take you into my reed-hut by the river yonder, and we shall see what can be done for you."

When he discovered that Mojud was well-spoken, he learned from him how to write.

After a few months, Khidr again appeared, this time at the foot of Mojud's bed, and said: "Get up now and leave this fisherman. You will be provided for."

Mojud immediately quit the hut, dressed as a fisherman, and wandered about until he came to a highway. As dawn was breaking, he saw a farmer on a donkey on his way to market. "Do you seek work?" asked the farmer. "Because I need a man to help me to bring back some purchases."

Mojud followed him. He worked for the farmer for nearly two years, by which time he had learned a great deal about agriculture but little else.

One afternoon when he was baling wool, Khidr appeared to him and said: "Leave that work, walk to the city of Mosul, and use your savings to become a skin merchant."

Mojud obeyed. In Mosul he became known as a skin merchant, never seeing Khidr while he plied his trade for three years. He had saved quite a large sum of money, and was thinking of buying a house, when Khidr appeared and said: "Give me your money, walk out of this town as far as distant Samarkand, and work for a grocer there." Mojud did so.

Presently he began to show undoubted signs of illumination. He healed the sick, served his fellow men in the shop during his spare time, and his knowledge of the mysteries became deeper and deeper.

Clerics, philosophers and others visited him and asked: "Under whom did you study?"

"It is difficult to say," said Mojud.

His disciples asked: "How did you start your career?"

He said: "As a small official."

"And you gave it up to devote yourself to self-mortification?"

"No, I just gave it up."

They did not understand him.

People approached him to write the story of his life.

"What have you been in your life?" they asked.

"I jumped into a river, became a fisherman, then walked out of his reed-hut in the middle of one night. After that, I became a farmhand. While I was baling wool, I changed and went to Mosul, where I became a skin merchant. I saved some money there, but gave it away. Then I walked to Samarkand where I worked for a grocer. And this is where I am now."

"But this inexplicable behavior throws no light upon your strange gifts and wonderful examples," said the biographers.

"That is so," said Mojud.

So the biographers constructed for Mojud a wonderful and exciting history; because all saints must have their story, and the story must be in accordance with the appetite of the listener, not with the realities of the life.

And nobody is allowed to speak of Khidr directly. That is why this story is not true. It is a representation of a life. This is the real life of one of the greatest Sufis.

The High Cost of Learning
Nasrudin is interested in learning to play the lute. He searches out the lute master and asks, "How much do you charge for

lessons?" The lute master replies, "Ten gold pieces for the first month, one gold piece for the succeeding months." "Excellent," says Nasrudin. "I shall begin with the second month."

See What I Mean?
Nasrudin was walking on the main street of a town, throwing out bread crumbs. His neighbors asked, "What are you doing, Nasrudin?"

"Keeping the tigers away."

"There have not been tigers in these parts for hundreds of years."

"Exactly. Effective, isn't it?"

I Believe You Are Right
During Nasrudin's first case as a magistrate, the plaintiff argues so persuasively that he exclaims, "I believe you are right." The clerk of the court begs him to restrain himself, for the defendant has not yet been heard. Nasrudin is so carried away by the eloquence of the defendant that he cries out as soon as the man has finished his evidence, "I believe you are right." The clerk of the court cannot allow this. "Your honor, they cannot both be right." "I believe you are right," says Nasrudin. (Shah, 1986)

These stories, hundreds of which have been collected by Idries Shah, are important documents of a different type of psychology than the one we are studying in this book. Knowledge of the different divisions of the mind, or the different personalities within an individual, is given full expression in these stories. The interested reader can begin to see the different selves within himself and perhaps understand the nature of his or her mind, composed of diverse and often contradictory forces (Ornstein, 1988).

DELIBERATE ALTERATIONS OF CONSCIOUSNESS

minds, the difference between sensation and perception. Spiritual disciplines use the methods for a different purpose than psychologists do: they seek to disassociate a person's models of the world from the actual outside world. In Zen this process is described as stopping "conceptualizing while remaining fully awake."

Opening-up meditation aims at altering the selective nature of consciousness. One exercise might be to listen to all the sounds inside and outside of the room you are in: the noises of the buildings and traffic, static on the radio, creaks in the walls. These sounds are everpresent but almost never noticed. Because the selectivity of consciousness evolved as an adaptive advantage for survival, this exercise is difficult and could be dangerous if it were done all the time. Opening-up meditation exercises also attempt to de-automatize perception, to undo some of the selectivity and interpretation that take place in normal perception.

EFFECTS OF MEDITATION   Human sensory systems are specialized to attend primarily to changes in the environment; meditation defeats these systems by producing unchanging stimulation. The purpose of heightening consciousness in this way is to restructure schemata and thus de-automatize one's response to the world.

One aim of many forms of conscious development is to awaken a fresh perception. The words *enlightenment* or *illumination* are often used to refer to achievement in these disciplines. The psychological term is **de-automatization,** meaning an undoing of the normal automated structure of consciousness (Deikman, 1966).

The effects of meditation are complex, diverse, and predominantly beneficial (Murphy & Donovan, 1988). Meditation, for example, can lead to decreased blood pressure (Bagga & Gandhi, 1983) and enhanced sensory, perceptual, and cognitive function (e.g., Brown, Forte, & Dysart, 1984).

RELIGIOUS EXPERIENCES

Many meditation and spiritual exercises result in what are called **religious experiences.** In his classic *The Varieties of Religious Experience,* William James (1917) quoted and analyzed the mystical experience of a Canadian psychiatrist, who referred to his experience as "cosmic consciousness":

> I was walking in a state of quiet, almost passive enjoyment. . . . All at once, without warning of any kind, I found myself wrapped in a flame-colored cloud. For an instant I thought of fire, an immense conflagration somewhere close by in that great city; the next, I knew that the fire was within myself. Directly afterward there came upon me a sense of exultation, an immense joyousness accompanied or immediately followed by an intellectual illumination impossible to describe. Among other things, I did not merely come to believe, but I saw that the universe is not composed of dead matter, but is, on the contrary, a living Presence; I became conscious in myself of eternal life. It was not a conviction that I would have eternal life, but a consciousness that I possessed eternal life then; I saw that all men are immortal; that the cosmic order is such that without any peradventure all things work together for the good of each and all; that the foundation principle of the world, of all the worlds, is what we call love, and that the happiness of each and all is in the long run absolutely certain. . . . That view, that conviction, I may say that consciousness, has never, even during periods of the deepest depression, been lost.

James (1890) delineated four characteristics of the mystical or religious experience:

1. *Unity or oneness.* Experience becomes comprehensive rather than fragmented; relationships are seen between things normally separate.

2. *A sense of realness.* The person has the sensation that the relations between things he or she experiences are closer to truth than ordinary experiences.

3. *Ineffability.* The experience is said to be impossible to communicate in ordinary words.

4. *Vividness and richness.* Perceptions take on a glow of freshness and clarity not present in ordinary consciousness. These experiences happen to millions, in all cultures. They may take the form of a "born again" experience or of the religious illumination of a monk.

CONSCIOUSNESS-ALTERING DRUGS

Psychoactive drugs interact with the brain, causing alterations in mood, perception, and behavior. They are interesting to scientists because their effects and the mechanisms of their actions help to show how the brain and mind function. To the millions of people who use them outside of a research setting, psychoactive drugs serve many roles, from pure escapism and pleasure seeking to what William James called "artificial mysticism."

HOW DRUGS WORK   For a substance to affect consciousness, it must interact with the brain. This interaction may occur at a neurotransmitter receptor site, on the structure of the cell membrane, or within the cell by affecting the enzymes controlling neurotransmission. The action of any drug is due to its effect on a normally occurring physiological process. A drug may either mimic, facilitate, or disrupt a natural function.

Part of the psychological effect of any drug results from the expectations of the drug user, called *mental set,* and the situation in which the drug is taken, called *setting.* The different effects of one barbiturate with different sets and settings have been described thus:

> When 200 mg. of secobarbital are taken with the expectation of going to sleep in a suitable sleeping place, most individuals will respond in the predicted way. When the same amount of secobarbital is taken in a stimulating environment with the expectation of "having a good time," many individuals will experience intoxication and excitement. (Wesson & Smith, 1971)

PSYCHEDELICS (HALLUCINOGENS)   The word **psychedelic** in Greek means "mind-manifesting." Psychedelic drugs are also called *hallucinogens* because they tend to induce perceptual distortions, enhancements, and elaborations. The psychedelics also have strong effects on thinking processes and emotionality.

Some of the more common psychedelic drugs are *LSD,* a compound synthesized from a natural chemical occurring in a mold (ergot) that grows on rye; *mescaline,* derived from the peyote cactus native to the Americas; and *psilocybin,* the active ingredient in "magic mushrooms." The effects of these compounds in general are very similar. Different people, however, may have very different types of experiences with them.

FIGURE 7-9
Drawings Made under
the Influence of LSD

The first drawing (A), made 25 minutes after the first dose, shows the drug had not yet taken effect. After a second dose (B), the man had little control of his hand's movements. The man was unhappy with the third drawing (C), and 2 hours and 45 minutes after the first dose the full effect of the LSD was discernible in the highly distorted fourth drawing (D). After 5 hours and 45 minutes the drug's influence was still obvious (E), but the effects were starting to wear off. Eight hours after the first dose the intoxication had worn off, but the quality of the last drawing (F) was not on par with that of the first.

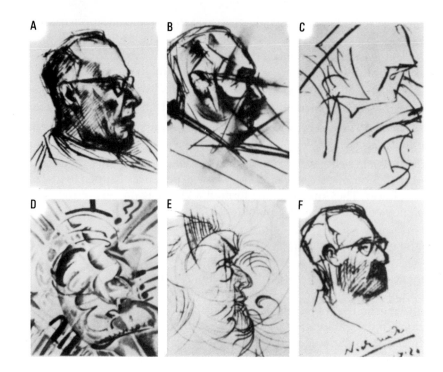

The psychedelics inhibit the modulation of sensory input by an area of the reticular activating system. As a result, the brain becomes much more sensitive and less selective to sensory input, and the normal pattern recognition functions of the brain start to work overtime and perceive patterns and motion in everything. It would seem that this process extends to thought as well, for the person on psychedelics is likely to see connections between seemingly unrelated things and ideas, and his thoughts elaborate in a manner analogous to his perceptions. (See Figure 7-9.)

These drugs also have profound effects on the emotions, probably due to interaction with the limbic system. Euphoria is common, but the experience of extreme dysphoria is also possible. Thus, the psychedelic experience can be either a personal heaven or hell.

For a person on psychedelics, the vividness and intensity of perception increases; objects or one's own body may seem bizarrely distorted; time may seem to slow down or even stop; synesthesias may occur, in which one sees sounds, or feels light; thoughts and ideas take on new significance and meaning; and the boundaries of self dissolve, resulting in a feeling of fusion with objects or a oneness with humanity or the universe.

The aspect of the experience which leads people to become more aware of their own minds is the sudden undeniable evidence, provided by the effects of psychedelics, that perception is a mental process—that the world they have all along thought was "out there" is really "in here," at least in the sense that what we know of the world is far from objective.

Mental set and setting are extremely important to the experience of the psychedelic user. Unpleasant reactions are more likely to occur in people who are afraid of the drug or who don't expect the intensity of its effects and try to fight them. As one writer summarized the LSD experience,

Thirty minutes after the exploding ticket is swallowed, life is dramatically changed. Objects are luminescent, vibrating, "more real." Colors shift and split into the spectrum of charged, electric color and light. Perceptions come as killing insights—true! true! who couldn't have seen it before! There is an oceanic sense of involvement in the mortal drama in a deeply emotional new way. Colors are heard as notes of music, ideas have substance and fire. A crystal vision comes: how full is the cosmos, how sweet the flowers! (Farrell, 1966)

MARIJUANA   For millennia, marijuana has been widely used in the East. In the last three decades its use has become common in the United States. It is usually ingested by smoking the dried leaves or flowering buds of the cannabis plant.

Little is known about how marijuana works to alter consciousness. One expert report said, "The pharmacological action of marijuana has some similarities to properties of the stimulant, sedative, analgesic and [hallucinogenic] classes of drugs." (HEW, 1971)

An excellent description of the psychological effects of marijuana was provided in an anonymous essay:

> A marijuana high usually lasts two or three hours. . . . The usual, most noticeable effect is intensification of sensation and increased clarity of perception. Visually, colors are brighter, scenes have more depth, patterns are more evident, and figure-ground relations both more distinct and more easily reversible. . . . Sounds become more distinct, with the user aware of sounds he otherwise might not have noticed. Music, recorded and live, is heard with increased fidelity and dimension, as though there were less distance between the source and the listener. Taste and smell are also enhanced under marijuana. The spice rack is a treasure of sensation, and food develops a rich variety of tastes. (Anonymous, in Tart, 1971)

Two other common parts of the marijuana experience are increased appetite and deficits to short-term memory. It can also be difficult to remember what happened during a marijuana high after it has ended.

METHOXYLATED AMPHETAMINES   One class of amphetamine derivatives, because of some of its effects, could be grouped with the psychedelics. These drugs, MDA, MMDA, and other variations, are commonly known in the drug world by such names as "Adam," and "Ecstasy." Their primary effect is on the thoughts and emotions of the user. The closeness of the structure of MDA and MMDA to that of amphetamines indicates that their mode of action is also similar.

Naranjo has described the effects of MDA on normal volunteers:

> Not one of the eight subjects reported hallucinations, visual distortions, color enhancement, or mental imagery, while all of them evidenced other pronounced reactions: enhancement of feelings, increased communication, and heightened reflectiveness, which led to a concern with their own problems or those of society or mankind. (1973, pp. 23–24)

ANESTHETICS   Anesthetics are drugs whose primary medical purpose is the induction of a state of decreased consciousness in which the experience of pain is blocked. A number of these substances have effects that could definitely be described as psychedelic.

PCP AND KETAMINE   PCP, or phencyclidine (or "angel dust") was first synthesized in 1957 and tested as an effective, potent, and short-acting anesthetic. The

primary reason for its loss of popularity as an anesthetic in humans was that, as one study describes, it had ''the decided disadvantage of producing in some patients severe excitement on emergence [from anesthesia] and severe hallucinatory disturbances'' (Greifenstein et al., 1958).

PCP has a derivative, ketamine, which sometimes finds its way into the recreational pharmacopoeia. Ketamine acts similarly to PCP but is shorter lasting.

PCP and ketamine, like all anesthetics, block sensation, especially from the body. Unlike some anesthetics, such as barbiturates, these drugs stimulate activity in the central nervous system. Probably the combination of decreased sensory input with brain activation works to create the hallucinatory experience of users of these so-called dissociative anesthetics. The same process that causes disorientation and hallucination in sensory deprivation could be involved.

The most commonly experienced effect of PCP (and ketamine) is the perception of an alteration in body image. The lack of sensory input from the body can cause the user to feel as if the limbs are getting longer, or even that he is outside of the body entirely. The user may also feel as if he is floating, without feet ever touching the ground. The CNS stimulation can cause bizarre dreamlike thoughts, or even the feeling of going on long journeys away from this world.

NITROUS OXIDE AND ETHER   Nitrous oxide, commonly called ''laughing gas,'' is in widespread use today as a general anesthetic in surgery and dentistry. Ether preceded it as the most popular such anesthetic; however, ether's toxicity and flammability makes it dangerous.

Anesthetics may dissolve into the cell membrane neurons and then seem to disrupt the normal energy production and utilization within the neuron. They appear to inhibit synaptic transmission in some parts of the brain. It is likely that these areas are involved in passing on sensory perceptions to consciousness.

William James's experiences with nitrous oxide prompted him to exhort us not to close our accounts prematurely with reality. He described the experience (extendable to ether, as well) in the following terms:

> With me, as with every other person of whom I have heard, the keynote of the experience is the tremendously exciting sense of an intense metaphysical illumination. Truth lies open to the view in depth beneath depth of almost blinding evidence. The mind sees all the logical relations of being with an apparent subtlety and instantaneity to which its normal consciousness offers no parallel; only as sobriety returns, the feeling of insight fades, and one is left staring vacantly at a few disjointed words and phrases, as one stares at a cadaverous-looking snow-peak from which the sunset glow has just fled, or at the black cinder left by an extinguished brand. (James, 1890)

HYPNOSIS

While the word *hypnosis* stems from the name of the Greek god of sleep, Hypnos, the hypnotic state bears only a superficial resemblance to sleep. There are many ideas about what hypnosis is, but behaviorally and physiologically, it is not sleep. Some researchers believe hypnosis is a distinct state of consciousness, whereas others believe it is simply an extreme case of role playing (Sarbin & Coe, 1972). Probably the most essential characteristic of the hypnotic state is hypersuggestibility.

HYPNOTIC SUSCEPTIBILITY   Not everyone is capable of being hypnotized. Those who enter the hypnotic state easily are called *hypnotically susceptible.* Susceptible people share several characteristics; among them is the capacity for imaginative involvement. Everyday forms of this include reading science fiction or drama, adventurousness in physical activities, such as exploration, and adventurousness of a mental nature, such as experimentation with drugs. Hypnotic susceptibility is measured by the degree to which subjects accept suggestions, such as "your arm is heavy" and "you hear a fly buzzing nearby."

TRANCE LOGIC   There is more to hypnosis than mere suggestibility. Hypnotized people act as if they register information on some levels but not on others, thus leading to apparently contradictory behavior. In the hypnotic procedure of age regression, subjects are given suggestions to return to an earlier time in their lives. Subjects may exhibit a curious "trance logic" while age regressed. Orne (1972) reported an experiment with a subject who spoke only German until age 6. When regressed to age 6 and asked whether he understood English, he answered "Nein" ("no").

> When this question was rephrased to him 10 times in English, he indicated each time in German that he was unable to comprehend English, explaining in childlike German such details as that his parents speak English in order that he not understand. While professing his inability to comprehend English, he continued responding appropriately in German to the hypnotist's complex English questions. (Orne, 1972, p. 427)

POSTHYPNOTIC SUGGESTIONS   Numerous experiments have demonstrated that subjects, given suggestions under hypnosis to perform specific actions at a later time in the normal state, will in fact frequently carry out the posthypnotic suggestions. Again, evidence indicates that subjects who were really hypnotized are much more likely to carry out posthypnotic suggestions than simulators (Orne, Sheehan, & Evans, 1968).

Remarkable examples, anecdotal as well as experimental, demonstrate how the body can be affected through hypnosis and suggestion. Controlled studies have shown that warts can sometimes indeed be wished away. Sinclair-Gieben and Chalmers (1959) reported success in hypnotic treatment of 14 patients with intractable generalized warts on both sides of their bodies. The subjects were hypnotized and instructed that the warts on one side of their bodies would disappear, while the other side would serve as the control. Within several weeks the warts in nine of the patients had regressed significantly but only on the "treated" side. The "untreated" side had as many warts as ever, except in one subject, whose warts on the untreated side also showed spontaneous disappearance six weeks after the treated side had been cured.

In a later study at Massachusetts General Hospital, 9 of 17 patients treated with hypnosis demonstrated significant wart regression, while none of an untreated control group showed any improvement (Surman, Gottlieb, Hackett, & Silverberg, 1973).

The implications of the disappearance of warts by suggestion are tremendous to medical science. The virus that causes warts is ubiquitous, and since not everyone develops warts, some type of immune defense must protect the majority of people. The mental wart cures presumably work by either activating the immune system or by altering the blood flow to these growths, or both.

Consider how elegant the mind's approach is: quick, painless, no side effects, and no scars compared to the crude freezing, burning, cutting, and cautery employed in the modern medical treatment of warts. Furthermore, think what is involved in the mental cures. The brain must translate such vague suggestions as "warts go away" into detailed battle plans. Chemical messengers are sent to marshal the cells of the immune system in an assault on the virus-induced tumor. Or perhaps small arterioles are selectively constricted, strangling the wart but sparing neighboring healthy skin. All in all, it seems a remarkable feat.

A popular misconception holds that hypnosis cannot be used to make a person do something contrary to their ethical or moral principles. It is true that a hypnotic subject will not respond to a direct suggestion to do something morally repugnant, but since hypnosis can alter a person's perception of reality, an unscrupulous hypnotist could trick a susceptible person into actions that they might later regret (Echterling & Emmerling, 1987).

THE HIDDEN OBSERVER   In 1960 Kaplan hypnotized a college student and induced "automatic writing," in which the subject's right hand was instructed to "write anything it wanted to, not subject to control or restriction of the 'conscious' personality." Then the hypnotist told the subject he would feel no pain in his left hand. He began pricking the left hand with pins, which ordinarily would have been unbearable. The student showed no pain, but his right hand seemed to know what his left hand was feeling, for it wrote, "Ouch, damn it, you're hurting me!" (Kaplan, 1960, p. 568). This demonstration was one of the first and most important examples of *dissociation* of consciousness. In dissociation, one part of the person is conscious of experiences (and can report them) and another part is not.

In another study, Hilgard hypnotized a man and gave him the suggestion that he would become completely deaf; the subject no longer reacted to sounds. At this point Hilgard said, "Although you are hypnotically deaf, perhaps some part of you is hearing my voice and processing this information. If there is, I should like the index finger of your right hand to rise as a sign that this is the case." When the finger rose, the subject asked to be brought out of hypnosis. He wanted to know why his finger was moving by itself! Hilgard called this phenomenon the **hidden observer** (Hilgard, 1978).

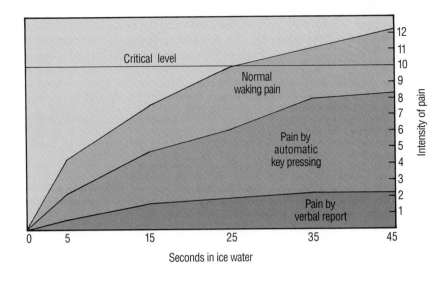

FIGURE 7-10
The Hidden Observer

People hypnotized not to feel pain while their hands are in ice water signal pain during an experiment by automatic key pressing or by reporting it later. This is done through the hidden observer, a level of awareness apparently not affected by hypnosis.
(Hilgard, 1978)

We may be instructed under hypnosis not to feel pain and indeed to report no pain. But because the hidden observer does report pain (Figure 7–10), it may be assumed that the hypnotic state affects only one part of awareness.

HYPNOTIC ANALGESIA In the nineteenth century a British surgeon, James Esdaile, demonstrated hypnosis to an audience of the Royal College of Physicians. The demonstration was dramatic: a man under hypnosis had his gangrenous leg amputated without anesthetic! The patient showed no evidence of pain, and the surgery was successful. Still, Esdaile was ridiculed. In the *Lancet*, a respected British medical journal, it was asserted that "the patient was an imposter who had been trained not to show pain." Another nonplussed observer reported that Esdaile must have hired a "hardened rogue" to undergo the operation for a fee! More recent research has confirmed the value of hypnosis for a variety of clinical applications including surgical anesthesia, the treatment of allergies, insomnia, and pain (Wadden & Anderton, 1982).

Consciousness, then, is the crossroads of the mind, where acts are registered, initiated, or blocked. It exists on several levels, some of which are directly in our focus, as when we are avoiding danger, and some are completely blocked from our attention, such as maintaining respiration. It is the great middle area that is of such interest to psychologists, how we can change our minds, how things get on our minds. Many of the later chapters help flesh out the role of the complete workings of the mind.

1. *Consciousness* is the part of the mind where decisions are made. Being conscious is being aware of some aspect of mental activity. If we are conscious of something, we can describe it. Normal waking consciousness is a model of the world based on sensory input, experience, and other mental processes. Changes in these factors can alter consciousness.

2. Only a small fraction of mental processes are in consciousness at any one time. The mind contains a large number of independent unconscious modules that operate automatically and in parallel. Conscious processes occur one at a time and take effort. Consciousness provides us with consistent interpretations of experience.

SUMMARY

3. *Attention* determines what enters consciousness and can be automatic or voluntary. *Automatization* occurs when an action is repeated so frequently that its components become unconscious. The flexibility of consciousness enables us to adapt to the present situation. It selects the item most relevant to survival at any moment and is geared to the needs of the individual. The contents of consciousness are what we are prepared to act on next. Discrepancies from expectation are likely to enter consciousness.

4. We are aware of more than we are conscious of. There are levels of consciousness. *Conscious awareness* is what you know directly and can spell out. When we are aware of something, but not conscious of it, it is in *subconscious awareness*. Items can affect our minds at a *preconscious* level if they are below the threshold of conscious perception. Mental processes that are never available to consciousness are called *unconscious*. Sometimes we act based on motivations not in consciousness.

5. Libet has provided evidence that many of our actions and decisions may be initiated outside of our consciousness. His experiments show a time delay between stimulation and consciousness. The preparation to initiate an action also begins before a person knows he wants to act. However, voluntary intention can "veto" the action.

6. Humans are conscious of their selves, and this awareness leads to profound questions about the nature of existence. Everyday we experience radical alterations in our states of consciousness. *Daydreaming* occurs when external events provide us with new input for consciousness. There are different kinds of daydreams. The tendency to daydream varies in 90–100 minute cycles.

7. In *sleep*, the brain stops maintaining a conscious model of the external world. Mental activity ranges from nearly nil to vivid dreaming. The two types of sleep are quiet, *non-REM* sleep and active *REM* sleep. Sleep stages are determined from the EEG. Sleep stages run in an approximate 90-minute cycle throughout the night.

8. In *Stage 1* sleep, people experience dreamlike hypnagogic imagery. Mental activity in *Stage 2* is generally mundane and thoughtlike. Little mental activity is reported from *delta* sleep, which is characterized by high amplitude, slow brain waves. Sleepwalking and sleep talking occur in delta sleep. After about 90 minutes, the sleeper enters REM, muscle tone drops and the eyes move rapidly. Most dreams occur in REM sleep.

9. Almost all organisms have daily rhythms of biological function, called *circadian rhythms*. These cycles continue in the absence of cues to the time of day. Jet lag is a disruption of circadian cycles.

10. All mammals sleep. Sleep probably evolved to keep animals inert at night. However, it now serves many biological and psychological functions. *Sleep deprivation* results in profound sleepiness and detriments to mood, vigilance, and performance on some tasks. REM deprivation probably increases the excitability of the nervous system.

11. Freud believed we dream in order to remain asleep, and that dreams are disguised symbols welling up from the unconscious mind. Hobson and McCarley proposed that dreams are the result of the biological process of REM sleep—the brain's attempt to make sense of "physiological noise." Others have argued that dreams are meaningful because they are the unique product of the dreamer's individual mind.

12. Dreams are difficult to recall. This may be the result of biological evolution. Humans may be able to remember dreams because of their capacity for language. Researchers have demonstrated that people can become aware that they are dreaming while dreaming *(lucid dreaming)*.

13. Practices for altering consciousness are found in every society. Alterations in normal routines can cause changes in consciousness. Some means of achieving this are sensory deprivation, meditation, and drug use. One purpose of altering consciousness is to awaken a fresh perspective, called illumination, enlightenment, or de-automatization. Four characteristics of mystical experiences are unity or oneness, a sense of "realness," ineffability, and vividness or richness.

14. Drugs alter consciousness by interacting with the brain. Set and setting influence the psychological effects of drugs. Psychedelics affect the modulation of sensory input and tend to induce perceptual distortions, enhancements, and elaborations. Marijuana and the methoxylated amphetamines share some of the properties of the psychedelics. Anesthetics have been used to induce mystical-type experiences, notably by William James.

15. Not everyone is hypnotically susceptible. Hypnotic subjects can be given post-hypnotic suggestions. Hypnotized people exhibit dissociation—some parts of their minds are aware of an experience, others are not. Hypnosis has been used to induce surgical anesthesia and to treat allergies, insomnia, and pain.

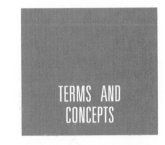

TERMS AND CONCEPTS

altered state of consciousness
attention
automatization
blindsight
circadian rhythm
concentrative meditation
consciousness
de-automatization
hidden observer

lucid dreaming
meditation
opening-up meditation
psychedelic
psychoactive drugs
Rapid Eye Movement (REM) sleep
religious experiences
teaching stories

SUGGESTIONS FOR FURTHER READING

Goleman, D. (1990). *Psychology update.* New York: Harper Collins.

An excellent collection of Goleman's New York Times *articles, that would serve as good supplemental reading to this text.*

LaBerge, S. (1986). *Lucid dreaming.* New York: Ballantine.

A well-written and even lucid account of self-control of dreams.

Ornstein R. (1986). *The psychology of consciousness* (3rd ed.). New York: Penguin Books.

An attempt to bring together much of the diverse literature on consciousness for students who wish to take matters in this chapter further.

Wolman, B. B., & Ullman, M. (Eds.). (1986). *Handbook of states of consciousness.* New York: Van Nostrand Reinhold.

A collection of diverse approaches to the study of consciousness.

8

THE BASICS OF LEARNING

Nothing seems more helpless than a newborn baby. As infants, we are completely dependent on adults. We cannot feed ourselves or move without assistance, and we can express our needs in only the most rudimentary ways, by babbling and crying. Yet, we later become astute business owners, graceful dancers, resourceful engineers, thoughtful writers, and more. The transformation from unskilled babyhood to the competence of adulthood is partly the result of growth and maturation, but in great part is the result of learning.

Learning is, essentially, a process by which we change our thinking or behavior as a result of experience, to adapt to our surroundings and circumstances. After we have learned, we have a different perspective or act differently. Most of our learning is beneficial, as when we learn to read, to play games, to perform useful work. But sometimes our learning is detrimental, as when we acquire severe anxieties or unhealthy habits. Learning is most valuable when it increases our flexibility in adapting to various situations. For instance, it is more useful to learn to swim than it is to learn to fear large bodies of water. Both learned responses are adaptive (they prevent drowning), but one leads to greater flexibility of action than the other.

How do we learn? Actually, we learn different kinds of things in different ways. We learn some things because we readily *associate* some aspects of our experience with other aspects. For instance, when a traffic light switches to red, we step on the brakes because the light has come to "mean" stop. When we smell smoke, we look for fire. These kinds of *stimulus-response* associations, acquired through the process of *conditioning*, form the basis of much of our knowledge of the world. They underlie our ability to predict events, and they shape our actions to help us get what we want and avoid what we don't want.

Another form of conditioning occurs when we learn to associate various behaviors with rewards or punishments. We tend to repeat actions that are satisfying and to avoid actions that bring us discomfort. As the proverb puts it, "Once bitten, twice shy."

Although a great deal of our behavior is conditioned, we do not all form the same associations. Some people learn to fear being in high places while others become enthusiastic sky divers; some people keep pets while others avoid animals. Some of our conditioned responses are the result of our individual experiences. For instance, if we are rewarded with praise for early attempts at drawing, we are likely to draw more often as a result. Many of our conditioned responses are the result of our upbringing in a particular social circle or culture. Food preferences, for example, are heavily influenced by societal customs: a culinary delight of one culture arouses disgust in another. Social behavior, too, is shaped by cultural influences. The manners that we learn in our own culture seem inherently right to us but may be considered strange or objectionable among other peoples.

Other kinds of learning go beyond the formation of simple associations. For instance, we master the intricacies of language; we test hypotheses by performing experiments; we learn to design machines, create beautiful and meaningful works of art, and govern societies. These more complex kinds of learning require us to form concepts, combine information, perceive relationships, and make judgments; this complex, interrelated form of learning is known as *cognitive* learning.

Learning enables us to survive in the world and adapt to changing circumstances. In this chapter, you will learn more about the different processes of learning and also find out how we, as humans, are born prepared to learn certain things.

CLASSICAL OR RESPONDENT CONDITIONING

The process of conditioning has been the subject of more research in psychology than any other topic. In fact, the basis of conditioning, **association,** is one of the oldest principles of psychology. The study of associations began with the Greek philosophers and was revived by the British empiricists in the seventeenth century. Such philosophers as John Locke, David Hume, and John Stuart Mill felt that the association of ideas is the bond that connects all experience.

A student of mine was watching a television program about how bees make honey. At one point in the program, the narrator shook a box of flowers to demonstrate how much pollen there is in them. When the yellow stuff appeared on the screen, my student began to sneeze violently. Of course, she was allergic to the pollen itself, not the sight of it. But a long period of experiencing bouts of sneezing after inhaling pollen made her sneeze when she only *saw* the pollen. Her response (sneezing) had become *conditioned* to the sight of pollen.

We all have similar experiences. We may, for instance, be so engrossed in study or work that we lose track of time. Then we glance at the clock and discover that it is noon. Suddenly we feel hunger. We have come to associate noon on the clock with having lunch, and just seeing the time arouses a sensation of hunger. Or glancing through a magazine we may see a picture of a favorite beverage and become thirsty.

How do these associations develop? What are the rules governing their formation? Once formed, do associations disappear? Some of the earliest scientific experiments designed to answer these questions were performed by Ivan Pavlov, the famous Russian physiologist.

PAVLOV'S EXPERIMENTS

Pavlov's work on digestive processes earned him a Nobel Prize in 1904. Today, he is most remembered for his contribution to the psychology of learning. This work, like many important experiments, began by accident. To study the role of salivation in digestion, Pavlov inserted tubes into the salivary glands of a laboratory dog and connected the tubes to a measuring device (Figure 8-1). When a piece of meat or meat powder was put into the dog's mouth, the amount of resultant salivary flow could be conveniently measured.

The dogs soon began to ruin Pavlov's experiments. After a few trials with the same dog, it began to salivate before the food was put in its mouth. The dogs went so far as to salivate when they heard the rattling of the food trays or even when they saw the person who usually brought the food. Pavlov realized that the dogs were making connections between certain events and the arrival of food and that he could study this process of association with his experimental

IVAN PAVLOV
(1849–1936)

setup. At this time, studying associations was in the realm of philosophy and psychology, both of which Pavlov deemed unscientific. Yet he was able to produce an observable, measurable response (salivation) that could be objectively used as an index of associative strength. So he set out to apply rigorous scientific methods to the study of associations.

Pavlov designed a special, soundproof environment in which he could present all stimuli by remote control. The dog was harnessed and presented with the experimental stimulus. Pavlov watched from behind a one-way mirror. First, Pavlov rang a bell. The dog did not salivate. Then, food was presented, and the dog salivated and ate. Again the bell was rung just before the food was presented. After a number of repetitions, or *trials,* the dog salivated when the bell was rung before the food was presented. Later, the dog salivated when the bell was rung even if food was not presented. This was evidence that the dog had learned to associate the bell with the food.

SOME DEFINITIONS

Over 60 percent of the terms we use today in the study of animal learning were first coined by Pavlov (Bower & Hilgard, 1981). Pavlov set out to discover the conditions under which a dog would form an association between a neutral stimulus and food. Hence, he called the process **conditioning.** How a previously neutral stimulus (NS) comes to influence an organism's behavior is called **classical** or **respondent conditioning.**

The process works as follows (Figure 8-2). When food is in the dog's mouth, salivation always occurs. This salivary reflex is called an **unconditioned response (UCR).** The taste of food is the **unconditioned stimulus (UCS)** that elicits the UCR. The sound of the bell affected the dog's behavior but only under a specific condition: after it had been paired with the taste of food (the UCS). Thus the bell is called the **conditioned stimulus (CS),** and the dog's salivation

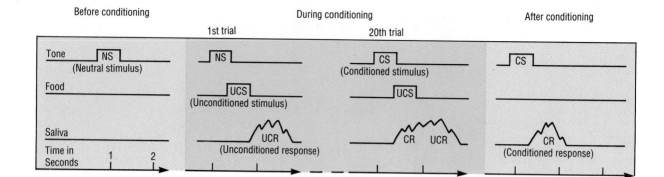

FIGURE 8-2
Relationship of Stimuli to Responses Before, During, and After Classical Conditioning

at the bell is the **conditioned response (CR).** (Pavlov used the adjective "conditional" to mean that the response is conditional upon the presence of the stimulus. We now use the term "conditioned.") The UCR and the CR are often the same response—for example, the dog's salivation. However, the CR is not always identical to the UCR. For instance, if a dog is shocked, it will jump and flinch (UCR). But if a light is paired with the shock, the dog will soon crouch or freeze (CR) when the light is flashed.

WHAT CAN BE CONDITIONED?

The process of conditioning gives animals great flexibility for adapting to novel environments. Humans can learn to associate virtually any two stimuli they are conscious of, and perhaps some they are not conscious of. Many processes once thought automatic have been shown to be subject to conditioning. Ader and Cohen (1981) showed that suppression of immune function (as measured by resistance to infection) could be conditioned to a taste stimulus.

CONDITIONS OF CONDITIONING

STIMULUS SIGNIFICANCE   If you are reading in a library and someone nearby drops a book, certain physiological changes will probably take place within your body. Your senses will sharpen and your muscles will tense. You will stop reading, turn in the direction of the noise, and prepare for possible action. This set of responses is called the **orienting reflex.** It occurs in response to any stimulus that is consciously perceived as novel or unexpected. Pavlov found that only stimuli that initially elicit an orienting reflex can become successfully associated with neutral stimuli. That is, respondent conditioning can occur only with unconditioned stimuli that are *significant* to the organism.

There are two classes of significant stimuli: those the organism seeks to approach, and those it tries to avoid. There are two corresponding kinds of respondent conditioning: appetitive and aversive. Food, water, and sex are unconditioned stimuli that an organism will instinctively approach (when hungry, thirsty, or aroused). These are used in **appetitive conditioning.** Shock, pain, and loud noises are stimuli that an organism will instinctively try to avoid. These are used in **aversive conditioning.**

Whether or not a neutral stimulus becomes a CS depends on when and how often it is paired with a UCS. That is, conditioning is dependent on an effective application of the principles of **recency** and **frequency.**

RECENCY There are five different temporal arrangements of CS and UCS that may be used:

1. *Simultaneous.* The CS and UCS are presented at the same time.
2. *Delay.* The CS is presented and continues until the UCS is presented.
3. *Trace.* The CS is presented but is discontinued before presentation of the UCS.
4. *Backward.* The CS is presented after the UCS.
5. *Temporal.* The CS in this case is time; the UCS is presented at precisely regular intervals.

Delay is the most effective, and *backward* is the least effective. Delay is probably effective because a stimulus presented just before the UCS prepares the organism for the UCS. When the UCS is presented first (backward arrangement), no such preparation is possible. Given that the CS must be presented before the UCS, does it matter how long before? If there is very little time between the CS and the UCS, the organism will not be able to take advantage of the "warning." If there is too much time between the two, the organism may not associate the CS with the UCS. The optimal interval is usually about half a second for muscular reflexes such as an eye blink or a knee jerk and from 5 to 30 seconds for glandular responses such as salivation.

FREQUENCY How *often* must a CS be paired with a UCS before it elicits a CR by itself? That depends on the nature of both the stimulus and the response. Some associations are so easily formed that they require only a trial or two. For example, people readily associate food and sickness. If you become ill after eating a certain food, that single experience will probably be all it takes for you to avoid that food in the future (Garcia, 1989). The more often a CS is paired with a UCS, the faster the CR will be acquired.

EXTINCTION

Conditioned responses are reinforced when the CS and UCS are paired repeatedly. But what happens to a CR if the bell continues to sound but no food is presented? If, after a CR has been acquired, the CS is repeatedly presented without the UCS, the CR gradually decreases (Figure 8-3). This phenomenon is called **extinction.** However, if, after some time has elapsed, the CS is again presented, the CR will often reappear. This phenomenon is known as **spontaneous recovery.** As a result, it is easier to acquire a CR than to get rid of it, as you may have noted in regard to bad habits.

GENERALIZATION AND DISCRIMINATION

Respondent conditioning would have little effect on overall learning if an organism could not generalize from a specific stimulus-response association.

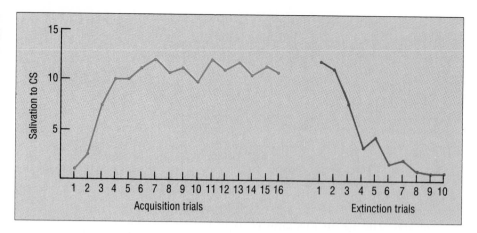

FIGURE 8-3
Acquisition and Extinction

A CR is gradually acquired by repeated pairings of UCS and CS. But when the reinforcement in the form of the UCS is removed and the CS is presented alone, the CR steadily decreases, which is called extinction.

Generalization means that once a specific stimulus has become a CS, similar stimuli will elicit the CR. For example, a child who has been bitten by a poodle is likely also to be afraid of boxers, collies, and German Shepards. The more similar the stimuli, the stronger the generalization.

In a now-classic study, Watson and Raynor (1920) gave 1-year-old Albert a white rat to play with. As Albert crawled to the rat to pet it, Watson stood behind him and banged a steel bar. This procedure was repeated, and soon Albert began to cry (CR) as soon as he saw the rat (CS). Although Albert was conditioned to fear only white rats, this fear generalized to a white dog, a rabbit, a fur coat, and even a Santa Claus mask. (Of course, an experiment like this would not be allowed by today's research ethics.) It is possible that Albert, who would now be in his 70s, may still be afraid of white rats and Santa Claus beards. But it is more likely that his fear underwent extinction as, in later years, he encountered many furry white things that were not paired with alarming sounds.

Gregory Razran (1939) demonstrated the principle of generalization in an experiment on semantic conditioning. Razran flashed the words *style, urn,* and *freeze* on a screen while college students sucked lollipops. Soon, when those words appeared on the screen (CS), the students salivated (CR). New words were then flashed that were either homonyms or synonyms of the original words. There was little salivary response to homonyms *(stile, earn, frieze)*, but the synonyms *(fashion, vase, chill)* did elicit the CR. Thus, the CR was generalized to the meaning of words.

In addition to generalizing, organisms can also learn to discriminate among stimuli. **Discrimination** occurs when an organism learns to respond to some stimuli and not to other, similar stimuli. For instance, if a dog is conditioned to salivate to a tone, it will generalize that response and salivate to another, similar tone. If food does not follow that second tone, the dog will eventually stop responding to it, but it will keep responding to the original tone; it will have discriminated between the two tones (Pavlov, 1927).

If impossible discriminations are demanded, an animal can become "neurotic." Pavlov conditioned a dog to salivate (CR) to the sight of a circle (CS) projected on a screen. Then he projected a picture of an elongated ellipse, without pairing this stimulus with food. The dog soon learned to discriminate between the two stimuli. Then Pavlov began presenting increasingly circular ellipses. The dog was able to make the discriminations, but its behavior underwent a radical change. The quiet dog began to squeal and wriggle about. It tore off part of the apparatus which was attached to its body. It also bit through the tubes connecting its room with the observers' room, a behavior that had never occurred before. On being taken from the experimental room, the dog barked violently, which was also contrary to its usual custom.

APPLICATIONS OF RESPONDENT CONDITIONING

Respondent conditioning can be highly useful to our survival. For example, we can learn to act quickly in emergencies. As children in school, we are conditioned to line up and walk briskly from the room when the fire alarm sounds. Early experience with warning signals generalizes in later life: we act quickly when we hear a smoke alarm and when we hear an ambulance or fire truck siren behind us on the street. When we learn to drive, we become conditioned to stop when the light turns red. Then too, aversive respondent conditioning is sometimes used to eliminate bad or dangerous habits. When alcoholics are given Antabuse, they suffer violent nausea if they drink alcohol. In many cases, they avoid the taste of alcohol because they associated it with the sensation of nausea.

Mary Cover Jones (1924) discovered a method of conditioning that helps people overcome their fears. With this method, **counterconditioning,** an unwanted CR is eliminated by training the subject to form a new association. Jones used counterconditioning on a boy named Peter who was afraid of rabbits. He would become frightened (CR) and scream when he saw a rabbit (CS). First, Peter was put in a high chair and given candy to eat. While he was happily eating the candy, Jones slowly moved a rabbit toward the high chair. When Peter screamed, Jones withdrew the rabbit until Peter was again calm. Each day, she inched the rabbit closer. After six weeks of trials, the rabbit was sitting in the high chair alongside a now-fearless Peter. Once the boy even asked for the rabbit when it wasn't there. Peter had come to associate the rabbit with something pleasant (eating candy); the unwanted CR (screaming) had been eliminated.

INSTRUMENTAL OR OPERANT CONDITIONING

In respondent conditioning, our behavior is shaped by conditioned stimuli that elicit certain unconditioned responses: when the stimulus is presented, we act in a certain way. In **instrumental** or **operant conditioning,** our behavior is shaped by what happens after we act. A major principle of instrumental conditioning will sound very familiar: *we act in such a way as to obtain pleasure and avoid pain.* In psychology, this is called the *law of effect.*

THE LAW OF EFFECT

Edward Thorndike (1874–1949) was an early investigator of how organisms learn new behaviors. He proposed that learning is governed by the **law of effect:** any action that is followed by a "satisfying state of affairs" is likely to be

B. F. SKINNER
(1904–1990)

repeated, and any action that results in an "annoying state of affairs" probably will not. One of Thorndike's experiments involved hungry cats trying to escape a cage to get food. A cat would move around and claw the cage, which was held closed by a latch of string. Eventually, the cat would accidently loosen the string and release the door. Each time it was put in the cage, its behavior became increasingly organized. Instead of clawing randomly, it would head right for the string and unlatch the door. This was evidence that the cat had learned to open the cage. The process of learning was called **instrumental conditioning** because the cat's actions were instrumental in getting what the cat wanted (Hilgard & Marquis, 1940). The law of effect explains the cat's behavior: the cat's moves to unlatch the door were repeated because the food was satisfying to the hungry cat (and also because cats like their freedom as much as any other creatures).

The law of effect is a useful way to predict many behaviors. If you win at the racetrack, you are likely to bet again. If you put your hand into a fire and get burned, you are unlikely to do it again. The result or state of affairs following your actions shapes your future behavior; the association that you form between your action and a succeeding event influences your later actions.

THE BASICS OF OPERANT CONDITIONING

B. F. Skinner, one of the most famous proponents of behaviorist psychology, renamed instrumental conditioning, calling it **operant conditioning** because it is the organism's operations or actions that are conditioned. The basis of operant conditioning is a principle similar to the law of effect: all actions have consequences, and those consequences increase or decrease the likelihood that the action (response) will be repeated. In an important series of studies in the late 1930s, Skinner investigated the process of operant conditioning.

For his experiments, Skinner invented a controlled environment which came to be known as the **Skinner box.** A Skinner box contains a food tray, a lever, and a water spout (Figure 8-4). In a typical experiment, a rat is trained to

FIGURE 8-4
A Skinner Box

This apparatus provides the controlled environment in which a rat (or other animal) can receive operant or instrumental conditioning by emitting responses that are measured, shaped, and reinforced.

press the lever. Before training begins, a record is made of how many times the rat presses the bar by chance. This baseline number is known as the **operant level** of the response. Once the operant level is determined, the lever is hooked up to the food-dispensing device. When the rat again presses the bar, a food pellet is dispensed. Because food is desirable to a hungry rat, bar pressing increases: the rat has been conditioned to press the bar. The experimenter measures the rate at which the rat presses the bar after conditioning. This measurement indicates the strength of the association between bar pressing and food and is thus called the **operant strength** of the response.

In other typical operant conditioning experiments, bar pressing is the conditioned behavior, but the consequences of that behavior vary. For instance, the box may be wired to give the rat a mild electric shock. When the rat presses the bar, the shock stops. In this case, bar pressing increases because not being shocked is a desirable consequence to the rat. If, on the contrary, the box is wired to give the rat a mild shock when it does press the lever, bar pressing decreases because getting shocked is an undesirable consequence. The consequences of behavior, as reinforcement or punishment, are central to the process of operant conditioning.

REINFORCEMENT AND PUNISHMENT: THE CARROT AND THE STICK

Proverbially, there are two ways to motivate a donkey: dangle a carrot in front of it or prod it with a stick from behind. According to the principles of operant conditioning, these are the two basic ways that all behavior can be shaped. The first is to reward the behavior: the carrot. The second is to punish the behavior: the stick. If the consequence of an action increases the frequency of the behavior, the consequence is, by definition, rewarding. If the consequence decreases the frequency of the behavior, the consequence is, by definition, punishing. Let's consider reward and punishment in more detail.

Another word for reward is **reinforcement.** A reinforcement is something that strengthens the possibility that a certain response will occur. Whatever consequence leads to an increase in the desired response can be considered a reinforcer. There are two kinds of reinforcers: positive and negative (Figure 8-5). When something is given to an animal or a person after the desired response, this is positive reinforcement. Press the bar, get food; eat your vegetables, get dessert. When something unpleasant is taken away after a desired response, this

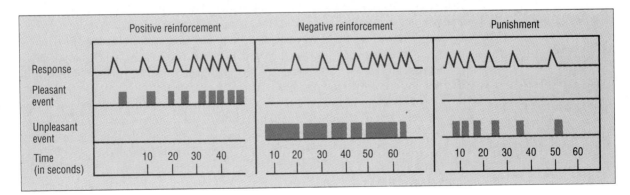

Skinner was a graduate student when he developed the first Skinner box. He had been conducting an experiment in which a rat repeatedly had to run an eight-foot maze. Each time, when the rat finished, Skinner gave it food and recorded its responses.

Skinner redesigned the apparatus so he did not have to do so much repetitive work. He figured out a way to dispense the food automatically. Also, noting that a wheel in the food box turned one notch per trial, Skinner wound a string around the wheel's spindle, attached a pen to the string, and placed the pen on a moving drum of paper. Then he had an accurate record of the rat's behavior that was kept automatically. Skinner could spend a night on the town and collect his data at the same time.

In Skinner's own theoretical terms, certain behaviors within his repertoire (designing mechanisms, attaching string to wheels) increased because they were reinforced by the avoidance of lab drudgery. Thus, from Skinner's point of view, the "invention" of the Skinner box was merely a new combination of existing behaviors, brought into play by the contingencies of the environment. Skinner would say that while he conditioned rats to perform new tasks for food, he himself was being conditioned to perform new tasks to avoid tedious work: a good example of positive reinforcement.

is negative reinforcement. Press the bar, the electric shock stops; take an aspirin, your headache goes away. The terms *positive* and *negative* are not used in the judgmental sense of good or bad but rather in an arithmetic sense. Positive reinforcement is something added; negative reinforcement is something taken away.

Punishment is the opposite of reinforcement. It is a consequence that decreases the likelihood that a behavior will occur. Punishments, like reinforcers, can be positive or negative. *Positive punishment* is something added: press the bar, get a shock; go through a red light, get a ticket. *Negative punishment* is something subtracted: press the bar, get no food; drive recklessly, lose your license.

THE RELATIVE VALUE OF CONSEQUENCES

Reinforcements and punishments are relative. A hungry rat will press a bar for food; a rat that has just eaten will not. One hundred dollars is a lot of money to a poor person but small change to a millionaire. What is reinforcement for one may be punishment for another: "One man's meat is another man's poison."

To change behavior through operant conditioning, an appropriate reinforcement (or punishment) has to be chosen. For example, let's say that a child very much likes jelly beans. The child's behavior can probably be influenced by giving the child a jelly bean each time he or she makes a desired response. The desired behavior is likely to increase because the candy acts as a positive reinforcer. Obviously, the same strategy will not work, however, with a child who is indifferent to jelly beans.

Psychologists have studied the ways that behaviors themselves can act as reinforcers. David Premack (1965) has shown that a more-favored behavior can be used to reinforce a less-favored behavior. He demonstrated this principle, later termed **Premack's principle,** with a group of elementary school children in a room with a pinball machine and chocolate. Observing the children's voluntary actions, he noted that some preferred to play pinball, and these he

In some cases, punishment is quite effective in discouraging undesirable behavior. For instance, once you have burned your hand in a fire, you learn to keep your distance from an open flame; and a spank from a parent can deter a child from again running into the street. However, punishment can affect far more than a specific undesirable behavior. For instance, there is always a danger that the person being punished will perceive the action as a personal attack rather than as a consequence of a specific behavior. When a parent angrily shouts, "Go to your room!" the child may be affected more strongly by the show of anger than by being sent away. The message, from the child's point of view, may be "Go away; I don't love you" rather than "Time out is the penalty for that action." Thus, what is intended as a behavior corrective may actually function as a threat to the child's sense of security or self-esteem.

Punishment seems to be especially detrimental when it is severe and capricious, as when a parent punishes a child harshly on some occasions and ignores or even rewards the same behavior on others. Holmes and Robbins (1987), for example, found that this sort of parental discipline was correlated with alcoholism and depression later in life. Then too, frequent attempts at punishment may just exacerbate the problem. For example, Rutter et al. (1979) found that in schools with a great deal of corporal punishment and other comparable discipline practices, student behavior only became worse. Also, an emphasis on punishment as a means of shaping behavior may lead to fearful or sullen obedience rather than well-considered voluntary actions.

So it seems that punishment, unless it is used selectively and with care, may create more problems than it solves. The chances of changing behavior in the desired direction are probably greater if reinforcement, rather than punishment, is used.

called "manipulators." The ones who preferred chocolate he called "eaters." A few days later, the children went back to the room, but this time their play was restricted. Before the "manipulators" were allowed to play pinball, they had to eat a piece of chocolate. The result was an increase in their consumption of chocolate. Likewise, the "eaters" had to play pinball first, which caused a parallel increase in their pinball playing, thus supporting Premack's principle of one behavior reinforcing another.

Ayllon and Azrin (1968) used Premack's principle on psychotic patients in an Illinois State Hospital. Their goal was to teach the patients social skills so they could live in the community. Ayllon and Azrin observed the patients closely and discovered each person's preferred behaviors. One liked to sit in a certain chair; another hid things under his mattress; some liked to be alone, hidden from others. These behaviors then became the consequences of participating in a new social activity or practicing a new skill. For example, in order to indulge in their favorite pursuits, the patients had to ask questions, follow directions, keep appointments, keep clean, and so on. The project was quite successful and has been applied in a variety of institutional situations.

Operant conditioning will be successful to the extent that a careful analysis is made of what actually influences an organism's behavior. What seems, according to common sense, to be reinforcement or punishment may, in fact, function quite differently. For example, let's say that a parent scolds a child repeatedly for an undesirable behavior, but the behavior does not decrease. It may be that, to the child, a highly desirable consequence is to win the parent's attention. Although the scolding is unpleasant, it is still attention and thus can act as reinforcement. Curwin and Mendler (1988) point out that this holds true for many students who cause trouble in school. When they act in undesirable ways, they are reprimanded or they lose privileges. But what is intended as punishment may actually be reinforcement—attention. This may be especially true for students who are low achievers and are thus seldom rewarded for their academic work. As Curwin and Mendler point out, many of these students seem to be motivated by a face-saving notion: "To be recognized as a troublemaker is better than being seen as stupid."

PRIMARY AND CONDITIONED REINFORCERS

There are two broad categories of reinforcers: primary and conditioned. **Primary reinforcers** include food, water, sex, sleep, comfort, and relief from pain. These are naturally reinforcing. A **secondary** (conditioned) **reinforcer** is something that has come to be associated with a primary reinforcer. For instance, once we learn that money buys food and other primary reinforcers, receiving money is in itself reinforcing, so we work to get money.

Wolfe (1936) demonstrated how secondary reinforcers shape behavior by performing experiments with chimpanzees. Wolfe used operant conditioning to teach the chimps to put poker chips into a machine to get grapes (Figure 8-6). Soon, the chimps performed new behaviors to earn poker chips. Such secondary reinforcers as poker chips are especially useful in maintaining behavior when there is a delay between the behavior and a primary reinforcer. Wolfe's chimps could use the grape machine only at certain times, but they could earn chips any time. When a chimp deposited a chip in the machine and had to wait a long time for a grape, the operant strength of the new behavior decreased. But if the chimp could earn chips during the delay, operant strength was maintained. In a similar way, we continue to work even though we are paid only at relatively infrequent intervals.

PHYSIOLOGICAL REINFORCERS

We have seen that the receipt of tokens that are not in themselves rewarding can be reinforcing if the tokens become associated with primary reinforcers. On the other side of the coin, electrical stimulation to certain locations of the brain can be extremely rewarding, despite the lack of any real connection with primary reinforcers. Olds and Milner (1954) implanted electrodes in the "pleasure zones" of a rat's brain and ran electrical current through them. The rats began to repeat actions that immediately preceded the stimulation. Thus the direct brain stimulation was a reinforcer. Electrode implantation has also been tried in efforts to help people suffering from neurological disorders like epilepsy. In such research, the patient sits in front of an array of buttons; each button sends electrical stimulation to a different part of the brain. Heath (1963) found that certain buttons were pressed more than others. The patients reported sensations ranging from intoxication to specific tastes to the intense feeling of pleasure right before orgasm.

SCHEDULES OF REINFORCEMENT

Another important aspect of operant conditioning is *timing*. Like respondent conditioning, in general the best time for administering reinforcement or

FIGURE 8-6
Conditioned Reinforcers, Chimpanzees, and People

This chimpanzee earned poker chips (conditioned reinforcers) in a learning experiment and is now using one to get food (primary reinforcer). Most people are rewarded in this way, being paid later for work done now, with money that can be converted into primary reinforcers of their choice.

punishment is immediately following the desired response. In this way, the consequence of the behavior is clearly demonstrated. Learning will not occur if there is too much delay between a behavior and its consequence. For example, Grice (1948) had rats run a maze for food. The reinforcement delays for different groups of rats ranged from 0 to 10 seconds. The shorter the delay, the faster the rats learned. The rats who faced a 10-second delay showed no improvement after even hundreds of trials. Likewise, when administering a punishment, it is more effective to do so as soon as the undesirable response is made. Thus, if punishment seems appropriate for a young child who misbehaves, the child should be punished immediately, not made to wait "until Mommy or Daddy comes home."

CONTINUOUS AND PARTIAL REINFORCEMENT   There are two possible patterns of reinforcement: continuous and partial. **Continuous reinforcement** means that each time the animal makes the desired response, it is reinforced. In most situations, this results in very rapid learning. **Partial reinforcement** means that not every response is followed by reinforcement.

Continuous reinforcement is almost essential if an animal is to learn a complex new behavior that is beyond the bounds of its species' normal behavior. For instance, a seal must be reinforced with a fish every time it balances a ball on its nose. Extinction is also quite fast when continuous reinforcement is withdrawn.

Humans do not usually need continuous reinforcements to learn, as you may realize. There is not always someone to throw a fish to us for each job well done. Rather, our behavior is more often shaped by some kind of partial reinforcement schedule, of which there are four kinds.

PARTIAL REINFORCEMENT SCHEDULES

FIXED INTERVAL (FI)   On a **fixed interval schedule,** reinforcement is presented at regular intervals after the desired response. For example, a fixed interval schedule of seven seconds (abbreviated FI-7), means reinforcement every seven seconds. The pigeon pecks and receives food. Every seven seconds thereafter, no matter how many times it pecks, it receives food. As a rule, response on an FI schedule increases just before reinforcement and decreases immediately following it.

Mawhinney, Bostow, Laws, Blumenfeld, and Hopkins (1971) asked their students to use a special room for study and then observed the actual amount of time the students studied. Once the operant level of studying was determined, the experimenters manipulated conditions. First, they gave a test every day. The students studied about the same amount of time each day. Later, the teachers gave a test once every three weeks (FI-3 weeks). Under those conditions, students studied very little immediately after a test but increased their study noticeably later in the three-week interval. The most studying was done in the few days before the test. When the teachers again began giving daily tests, studying was once again regular.

VARIABLE INTERVAL (VI)   On a **variable interval schedule,** the intervals between reinforcement vary randomly about an average. A VI-5 (minute) schedule means that the intervals could vary from a few seconds to several minutes,

Gamblers are rewarded on a variable ratio schedule, because if they win it is after a randomly varying number of bets—but this also allows them to expect to win at *any* time.

while the average of all the intervals would be five minutes. Under these conditions, it is impossible for an organism to adjust its response rate to the schedule. For instance, a cat watching intently at a mouse hole is on a variable interval schedule. "Superstitious" behavior often develops in animals (humans included!) that are on a VI schedule because the relationship between response and reinforcement is uncertain (see the box on superstitions).

FIXED RATIO (FR)   On a **fixed ratio schedule,** reinforcement is given after a certain number of responses. A rat on an FR-5 schedule is reinforced every fifth time it presses the bar. Pieceworkers are paid on an FR schedule. For example, farmers are on an FR-10 schedule if they are paid a fixed amount for 10 bushels of produce. Similarly, garment workers are paid by the number of pants or shirts they make.

VARIABLE RATIO (VR)   On a **variable ratio schedule,** reinforcement occurs after a randomly varying number of responses. A VR-5 schedule means that, on the average, every fifth response will be reinforced, but reinforcement may occur sometimes after 1 or 2 responses and sometimes only after 9 or 10 responses. People gambling on slot machines are on a VR schedule.

An animal's response patterns vary with the kind of schedule it is on. On an FI schedule, the response rate decreases immediately after the reinforcement and then gradually increases: the students' studying dropped off after a thrice-weekly test and then picked up before the next test. On a VI schedule, there is not much change in response rate from reinforcement to reinforcement; "superstitious" behavior, once established, is steady. On both FR and VR schedules, the rate of response is rapid. Garment workers paid on a piecemeal basis will usually work quickly; slot-machine players will insert coins at a very rapid rate.

Superstitions result when a behavior is *accidentally* associated with reinforcement. Skinner created superstitious behavior in pigeons by dispensing food randomly, entirely independently of the birds' responses. The pigeons all made associations between their actions and the dropping pellet. When Skinner returned to the laboratory after a weekend, he found pigeons exhibiting a variety of behaviors. For example, some were turning in circles, some jumping up and down, and some pecking. None of these behaviors was related to the actual consequence. Whatever the pigeons happened to have been doing at the time of the reinforcement, they continued to do.

Baseball players, too, exhibit quite a bit of superstitious behavior. After winning a game or playing well, they often isolate one specific action or series of actions as the cause of their success. Some players have developed an elaborate ritual. For example, on each pitching day for the first three months of a winning season, Dennis Grossini, a pitcher on a Detroit Tiger farm team, arose from bed at exactly 10 a.m. At 1 p.m. he went to the nearest restaurant for two glasses of iced tea and a tuna fish sandwich. Although the afternoon was free, he changed into the sweat shirt and supporter he wore during his last winning game. One hour before the game, he chewed a wad of Beech-Nut chewing tobacco. During the game, he touched his letters (the team name on his uniform) after each pitch. He also strained his cap after each ball. Before the start of each inning, he replaced the pitcher's rosin bag to the spot where it was the inning before. And after every inning in which he gave up a run he would wash his hands (Gmelch, 1978).

Baseball players are renowned for their superstitious behavior. Here are the Mets in their dugout trying to get a rally going.

The four schedules of reinforcement are analogous to the way we are reinforced in life. As a rule, we are not rewarded for every good thing we do. Rather, we are subject to receiving intermittent rewards, and this circumstance keeps us responding. In fact, the most notable effect of partial reinforcement is the increased persistence of the learned response. An animal will respond much longer after reinforcement ceases if it has been trained with partial, rather than continuous, reinforcement. Under continuous reinforcement, the animal learns to expect a reward each time, so the first unrewarded response signals that the contingency has changed, and the animal quickly stops responding. But if the

INSTRUMENTAL OR OPERANT CONDITIONING

animal learns to expect a reward only now and then, an unrewarded response does not clearly signal that the situation has changed. Responses that are conditioned by a variable-ratio schedule are particularly resistant to extinction. This helps to explain why gamblers can lose all their money to one-armed bandits. They expect to win eventually, but they never know how many coins it will take to hit the jackpot. Their coin-insertion behavior is thus remarkably persistent.

OTHER ASPECTS OF OPERANT CONDITIONING

The phenomena of generalization, discrimination, and extinction appear in operant conditioning as they do in respondent conditioning. For instance, generalization and discrimination are evident in infants' language learning (Brown, 1965). Initially, infants are positively reinforced for saying "da-da" and "ma-ma" in the presence of parents. The infants then generalize these words and apply them to all adults, strangers included. Since the infants are not rewarded for the incorrect responses, they learn to discriminate among stimuli (parents and other adults) and to use the words correctly. Also, children's behavior can sometimes be changed through the process of extinction. For instance, a child may have developed the habit of whining because whining has been reinforced with attention. If those around the child ignore the whining, thereby providing no reinforcement, the behavior will probably be extinguished.

APPLICATIONS OF OPERANT CONDITIONING

Skinner applied the principles of operant conditioning to teaching his own daughter, Deborah. For instance, he designed a controlled environment for the girl. This was a box in which all of Deborah's needs were immediately met when she performed desired behaviors. He also invented a toilet-training device: he wired a music box to the toilet so that it began to play when she urinated into the toilet.

Another example of a practical application of operant conditioning is a certain posture-improving device. A specially wired apparatus worn under the clothing sounds a buzzer if the person is not standing up straight. The only way to turn off the buzzer is to straighten up. As you might imagine, the wearer's posture improves greatly as long as he wears these "slump straps."

Operant conditioning has also been effectively used in classrooms. Behavior modification programs use various reinforcers (candy, gold stars, preferred activities, and so forth) to shape children's behavior. Target behaviors may include completing assigned work, keeping quiet during study times, or contributing positively to group activities. Some teaching materials have also been based on operant-conditioning principles. For instance, computers are programmed to reward a child with special displays for solving problems correctly.

The principles of operant conditioning are used in many other situations as well, from settling labor disputes to rearing children to healing physical ailments. In psychotherapy, they are sometimes used to help people overcome fears or learn to interact with others in more positive ways. (See Chapter 16 for further discussion on behavior therapy.)

RESPONDENT AND OPERANT CONDITIONING COMPARED

There are many similarities between respondent and operant conditioning. In both cases, what is learned is an association between relatively contiguous events. In humans, this association is normally conscious. In both cases some sort of reinforcement is required for learning to occur. (The unconditioned stimulus in respondent conditioning is equivalent to the reinforcer in operant conditioning.) The phenomena of discrimination, generalization, and extinction are similar for both. Both respondent and operant conditioning are basic learning processes without which we could not survive.

The essential distinction between the two forms of conditioning is that in instrumental conditioning, *reinforcement is contingent on the occurrence of the correct response;* in respondent conditioning, *reinforcement* (that is, the UCS) *is given independent of what responses are made.* Generally, respondent conditioning involves *involuntary* (reflexive) *responses* that are elicited by stimuli: *the response follows the stimulus.* Operant conditioning involves *voluntary responses* that are followed by reinforcement (or punishment): *the stimulus follows the response.*

But how deep are these distinctions? As you may have realized already, in some situations the differences are not clearly apparent. The learning process called biofeedback, for instance, involves the voluntary or operant conditioning of autonomic responses which would usually be considered unconditioned responses. Through biofeedback training, people can learn to alter their heart rates, their brain wave patterns, or other physiological functions that were once considered beyond voluntary control. The key is providing people with conscious information about processes of which they are normally unconscious. Under these conditions, learning occurs.

A CONCLUDING NOTE

For many years, a large majority of psychologists concentrated on studying respondent and operant conditioning. Because the emphasis was on observable behavior (salivation, bar presses, and so on), this branch of research and its attendant explanations of human actions came to be known as *behaviorism.* From the behaviorist point of view, animals and humans are basically reactive organisms whose actions are shaped in predictable ways by external stimuli and reinforcers. Some scientists have contended that all learning can be explained in behavioristic terms—that learning is simply a matter of developing conditioned responses. The principles of behaviorism do explain a great deal about how we adapt to our surroundings. But there is more to learning than classical and operant conditioning. In the next section, we examine another perspective.

COGNITIVE LEARNING

At the heart of **cognitive learning** is the individual's intention. Unlike the process of forming associations, which can occur without our being fully aware of it, cognitive learning is purposeful. We engage in cognitive learning, for example, because we want to communicate ideas, obtain information, solve problems, or become competent in some field of endeavor.

As toddlers, we discover the rules of language by listening to those around us. Later in life, we engage in formal programs of study to learn the principles of, say, mathematics or psychology. We gain some knowledge and solve some problems by using our intuition and achieving *insight,* and we acquire many skills through *observational* learning—watching and imitating others. We can even learn how to learn. All forms of cognitive learning require motivation, attention, and active involvement.

This approach emphasizes that the learner is an active part of the learning process; what goes on inside the mind of the individual is as significant as the external, observable behavior. Cognitive psychologists maintain that learning depends to a great degree on the ability to perceive similarities and relationships among objects or situations, to recombine information, and to weigh alternative courses of action. This explains why people learn different things from the same situation; they are influenced by their own unique perceptions and expectations. As one psychologist explains,

> When we take in our surroundings, we select from them, not at random, but in accordance with our past experience and our purposes. To a degree, we take out of the scene those elements which will forward our purposes and also those elements which we fear may frustrate our purposes. These are the only parts of the scene which attain functional reality, and they attain it only to the degree that they are taken account of and acted upon by a person. This he can only do in relation to his experience and purpose. (Kelley, 1947, p. 321)

INSIGHT

One kind of learning that is best explained from a cognitive perspective is insight. When the explanation for a situation or the solution to a problem appears all at once, in a flash, we say we have experienced **insight.**

In a classic experiment that demonstrates insight, German psychologist, Wolfgang Köhler (1925) placed a chimp in a cage with a short stick (Figure 8-7).

FIGURE 8-7
Chimpanzee Insight

After apparent contemplation, this chimpanzee used a short stick to pull a longer stick into his cage and then used it to reach some fruit.

CHAPTER 8 / THE BASICS OF LEARNING

A few feet outside the cage was a longer stick, beyond which was some enticing fruit. The chimp immediately tried to reach the fruit, but his arms were too short. Next he tried using the short stick to get the fruit, but it too was not long enough. He stopped all obvious activity for a while. Then, all of a sudden, the solution seemed to pop into his mind. He picked up the short stick, used it to get the long stick, then used the long stick to get the fruit. In a similar experiment, a bunch of bananas was suspended from the ceiling of a room in which there was nothing but a few boxes. The chimp jumped in vain, then stopped, seemed to ponder, and perused the room. He then piled the boxes one upon the other, climbed up, and got the bananas. Köhler points out that what was learned in each case was a *relationship*, not a response: the chimps learned the way in which objects and events in the environment related to one another, not a specific association between a stimulus and a response.

Bruner (1960) points out that insight results from the process of intuitive thinking, which involves an overall or holistic perception of the problem. He goes on to say that the thinker

> rarely can provide an adequate account of how he obtained his answer, and he may be unaware of just what aspects of the problem situation he was responding to. Usually intuitive thinking rests on familiarity with the domain of knowledge involved and with its structure, which makes it possible for the thinker to leap about, skipping steps and employing short cuts. (Bruner, 1960)

Grasping the structure of a field of knowledge or of a situation involves not only noting individual phenomena but also perceiving relationships. "Leaping about" and "skipping steps" involve combining information in various non-methodical ways and, in so doing, being able to see the familiar from different perspectives.

In Köhler's experiments, chimps learned to combine familiar objects and behaviors in new ways to solve problems. The same mental operations of reorganizing and recombining familiar information are the basis of insight in human learning.

COGNITIVE MAPPING

Tolman and Honzik (1930) believed that learning goes far deeper than what behaviorists would expect, and they conducted an experiment to prove his point. Two groups of rats were to run a cross-shaped maze, such as the one in Figure 8-8. The maze was open so that the rats could see any objects in the experimental room. There were two start boxes and two goal boxes with food. Half the time the rats began in start box 1, and half the time in 2. Group A rats always found food in goal box 1 no matter which start box they left from. Sometimes they needed to turn right to get food and sometimes left. Group B rats found food in goal box 1 only when they left start box 1, and they found food in goal box 2 only when leaving start box 2. Group B rats always turned right to get food.

There was a great difference in the rate at which these two groups learned the maze. One group learned in about eight runs, while some rats in the other group never learned. Which group do you suppose performed better? From a strict conditioning point of view, the prediction would be that group B would

FIGURE 8-8
Learning by Developing
Cognitive Maps

The rats who had to run this cross-shaped maze in a natural foraging pattern learned the maze faster than those who always found food by turning one way after leaving their start box. Tolman believed that the more successful foraging group developed wider expectations and a kind of cognitive map of the relationships in their environment.
(Tolman & Honzik, 1930)

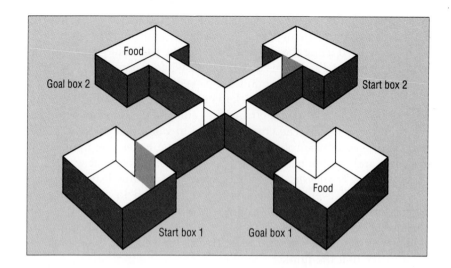

learn faster since their association was simple: "turn right for food." However, group A learned faster, not B. Tolman argued that the way an animal naturally finds food in the environment is through foraging. It comes to know the lay of the land by random exploration and that this learning influences later behavior. Specifically, Tolman noted that animals learn not only by responding to simple stimuli but also by developing a set of expectations about the relationship of elements in the environment, a sort of cognitive map.

We too develop expectations—**cognitive maps**—that enable us to adapt to our surroundings. In visiting a new city, we also learn the lay of the land through exploration. Once we get our bearings, we can reach desired places by different routes; we are not bound by rigid behaviors of "turning right" or "keeping to the left." Similarly, when we go into a new store, we have certain expectations about where to find what we are looking for and how to go about paying for a purchase even though the features of the store are unfamiliar to us. We have a cognitive map that might be called "store" that enables us to adapt our behavior to the specific demands of shopping in the new store.

LATENT LEARNING

Performance is the ultimate test of learning. If an organism shows consistent reductions in errors while performing a task, we say learning is taking place. However, there is evidence that learning can occur without showing immediately in performance improvement. Such **latent learning** amounts to a change in ability not yet demonstrated by performance.

Tolman and Honzik (1930) provided the classic demonstration of latent learning. Three groups of rats ran a complex maze once a day for two to three weeks. Group A always found food in its goal box. Group B never found food. Group C found no food for the first 10 days. On the eleventh day, Group C rats found food in their box, and then food was presented every day thereafter. Figure 8-9 shows the results. The performance of Group C rats was, for the first 10 days, like that of Group B. After the eleventh day, Group C's performance was immediately equal to or better than Group A's. This demonstrated that

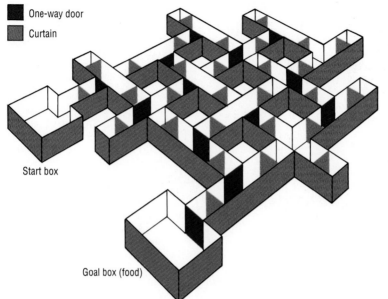

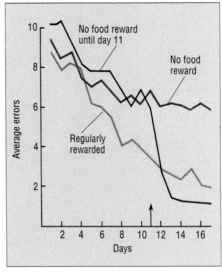

One-way door
Curtain

Start box

Goal box (food)

Group C had learned during the previous 10 days and that its performance had been low only because of the lack of reward.

One example of latent learning in humans can be seen in language acquisition. When learners are acquiring a language (either their native language or a second language), they usually go through a *silent period* during which they listen to but rarely produce the language. In time, they begin speaking, and the learning that occurred during the silent period then becomes evident (Krashen, 1981; Krashen & Terrell, 1983).

LEARNING HOW TO LEARN

Experience with a learning task will often lead to improved performance on later similar tasks. For example, Ward (1927) arranged for subjects to learn 16 word lists of equal length with one new list being learned on each of 16 successive days. The subjects showed a striking decrease in the number of trials required to learn the lists as a function of practice: they needed nearly 40 trials to learn the first list but less than 20 trials to learn the last list. Obviously, they had learned more than associations between stimuli and responses: they learned something about what strategies to use in the task of learning word lists. For this task at least, they had learned how to learn.

Another way of describing this behavior is to say that the subjects were able to *generalize* or transfer their learning to similar situations (learning new lists). That is, once a skill or relationship has been learned, it often becomes part of an organism's behavioral repertoire and can be used in new situations. For instance, if the chimp in Köhler's experiment were to be placed in a similar predicament with wires instead of sticks, he would probably use the wires to get the bananas. Bruner (1960) points out that transfer is evident in many forms of human learning, from the learning of specific skills to the more complex learning of underlying structures of relationships. He cites, as one example, the learning of mathematics. Once basic principles and operations are mastered, the student can use this knowledge to perceive new relationships and to solve a variety of new problems; the student has "learned how to learn" mathematics.

OBSERVATIONAL LEARNING: MULTIPROCESS ANALYSIS

Primates are social animals, and an important function of a group is to teach the young how to act in society. This process is called **socialization.** Implicit in socialization is the ability to learn from the experience of others. One child watches another touch a hot stove and get burned. In the future, they both are less likely to put their hands on the hot stove. The child with the burned finger has learned the lesson by operant conditioning; the other has learned by painless observation.

Albert Bandura, a leading theorist in **observational learning** (also called *social learning*), says that people would not learn much if they had to rely only on the effects of their own actions to inform them what to do. People can learn behavior from observing others, at least in approximate form, before performing any behavior themselves (Bandura, 1986).

Although observational learning has been reported in many species, the capacity is most highly developed in the primates.

292

fantasies. Good stories appeal to students of all ages. In visualizing events and identifying with characters, listeners or readers bring the story to life in their own minds, gaining information and achieving new perspectives.

Simulation games incorporate some fantasy, and this is part of their appeal. Abt (1970), for example, describes how first-grade children enjoyed playing "Transportation," a game that required them to assume the roles of trains, airplanes, and so on, in order to learn basic principles of economical vehicle movement. As he writes, "the flapping of wings, salivating splutter of motors, whine of buses, and hoarse cries of foghorns [were] a little noisy, but the children really identified with those vehicles and got to where they were going as quickly as possible."

CONTROL

The desire to control one's environment is fundamental (Rodin, 1986). Many people find computer games appealing because, as players, they can achieve a powerful sense of control, as when, for example, they save the galaxy from alien invaders.

Learning environments can exploit the desire for control by giving learners choices. Students may be allowed to choose which activities they will complete first or how they will summarize what they have learned. Perhaps the most valuable way of empowering students is to encourage them to set their own purposes for learning. For instance, they can pose their own questions before a unit of study or can choose their own topics for independent research. By exercising some control over

what and how they study, students are more likely to remain interested in the work.

INTERPERSONAL MOTIVATION

Doing well at an activity often results in recognition from others, and the attention is rewarding. When more than one person is included in a learning situation, recognition can come either from competing successfully or cooperating successfully. Although some competition is healthy and motivating, too much emphasis on competition can demoralize the least skilled in the group while causing the most skilled to feel smugly overconfident. On the other hand, if the activity requires cooperation, all have a chance of gaining suitable recognition, and the price of one's success is not the downfall of another.

MODELING

What an organism learns in classical and operant conditioning is clear enough: in the former it is the association between events in the world, and in the latter it is an association between the organism's actions and their effect on the environment. One is the result of frequent pairing, the other the result of reinforcements. In observational learning, what the observing organism acquires is a mental model, or scheme, that directs behavior. These schemata can then direct behavior at appropriate times. They are learned through the process of **modeling:** watching others perform and then, eventually, performing in the same way. Among Peruvian weavers, for example, young girls are taught to weave solely by observing others. For years, the girls simply watch their mothers while they weave the traditional patterns. The girls do not work on a loom until their teens. Everything from the setting up of the loom to weaving itself, even creating the intricate patterns that set each tribe apart, is learned entirely by observation (Franquemont, 1979).

It appears that intense phobic-like fears can also be learned by observation. Monkeys reared in the wild show intense fear of snakes, while those reared in the laboratory do not. In a series of experiments (Mineka, 1990; Mineka & Cook, 1990; Mineka & Tomarken, 1989), lab-reared monkeys observed wild-reared monkeys exhibiting fear of snakes. Three-quarters of the observer monkeys acquired intense and persistent fear of snakes after exposure to the fearful models.

According to the social cognitive perspective (Bandura, 1986), four process-es are involved in observational learning. *Attentional processes* determine the perception and exploration of the modeled behavior; *retention processes* involve the development of mental models or schemata to guide the *production processes,* which organize schemata into action; and *motivational processes* determine whether or not the observationally acquired behaviors will actually be per-formed.

IMITATION

Behavior resulting from observational learning is called **imitation.** The ability to imitate is not as simple as it might seem. To imitate, observers must be able to recognize similarities between the model's behavior and their own and must be able to re-create that behavior. The processes of attention, retention, motivation, and reproduction are involved in even the simplest imitation. Imitation may be the earliest form of human complex learning. A 4-day-old baby can imitate the mother smiling or sticking out her tongue.

Humans also imitate behavior when the model is not present. Rosekrans and Hartup (1967) conducted an experiment that showed this imitation in the form of aggression. Children watched a videotape in which an adult model punched a Bobo doll, shouting, "Wham, bam, I'll knock your head off." Some saw a version in which the model's behavior was punished by another adult's reprimands, while others saw a different version, showing the model being rewarded by the other adult's praise. A control group saw a nonviolent tape.

All the children were later taken to a playroom with lots of normal nursery school toys and a Bobo doll. They were left alone and observed through a one-way mirror. The children's behavior was greatly influenced by their observation of the model. The group that had seen aggression rewarded acted much more aggressively than the group that saw no aggression. Both of these groups were more aggressive than the group that saw aggression punished. (See Figure 1-10, page 21.)

Many psychologists believe that children *learn* to behave aggressively and that many of their lessons in aggression come from television. Their concern is shared by many parents, some of whom have founded Action for Children's Television (ACT). ACT monitors children's television shows and commercials and has been instrumental in banning extremely violent shows.

ABSTRACT MODELING

If we learned only actions that we had observed, our abilities would be much more limited than they are. Children don't just learn how to say the exact sentences modeled by their parents; they learn the grammatical rules and then generalize them to produce unlimited classes of grammatical sentences. In this process of **abstract modeling,** observers generate and test hypotheses about the rules guiding the performance of models. Such modeling plays a crucial role in the highest forms of human behavior. Creativity is an example. You might think that it is contradictory to view innovation as the product of modeling, but the fact is that creative achievements are based on the preceding creations of others. Creative thinking is largely a matter of combining familiar elements in a new way, and creativity can itself be learned through modeling. People who have observed innovative models themselves perform more creatively than people who have observed conventional models (Belcher, 1975; Harris & Evans, 1973).

A CONCLUDING NOTE

The differences between the cognitive and behavioral approaches to learning produced a bitter controversy that lasted more than a generation and centered on one question: Could psychologists study anything other than external, observable responses? The behaviorists maintained that to talk about internal, mental states led to conjectures that could not be substantiated; cognitive psychologists maintained that to focus only on external responses significantly limited the field of inquiry.

With the advent of new technology enabling scientists to observe many internal processes, such as brain waves and blood pressure, the flood gates opened. Psychologists now study observable behavior, internal physiological processes, and the unobservable mind all together (Bandura, 1986).

The new lines of inquiry raise complex and challenging questions. For instance, phenomena such as observational learning cannot easily be described and explained. The most important factors in this form of learning are the hardest to pin down: the characteristics of the model and the learner and the interaction between the two. Thus the exact conditions under which observational learning takes place have not been firmly established. Of course, researchers have gathered much information about this form of learning, but it is far from being understood as well as conditioning. Similarly, such phenomena as insight, latent learning, learning how to learn, and abstract modeling require extensive further exploration.

WHAT WE ARE "PREPARED" TO LEARN

Early empiricists, as we've seen, felt that at birth the mind is a blank slate and that during life an individual's specific experiences are written on this slate. But even with a blank slate, the individual would still have to be born with the innate ability to learn from experience (Cosmides & Tooby, 1986).

In fact, each organism comes into the world with many inborn abilities or potentials: birds learn to fly, human beings do not; we learn to read and write, birds do not. The set of abilities each organism is born with is its behavioral repertoire. This repertoire varies greatly among species. There is, however, a more subtle question that psychologists have recently addressed: Are some things easier to learn than others?

THE ASSUMPTION OF EQUIVALENCE OF ASSOCIABILITY

This question could also be phrased: Are all events equally associable? Most students of conditioning have assumed that any CS and any UCS could be associated equally easily. Pavlov (1928), for instance, wrote, "Any natural phenomenon chosen at will may be converted into a conditional stimulus . . . any visual stimulus, any desired sound, any odor, and the stimulation of any part of the skin."

Similarly, Skinner assumed that any response could be conditioned by any reinforcer. He and other behaviorists believed that the laws of learning governing the association of arbitrary events would apply to all events. The problem, as we shall see, is that these laws may apply only to arbitrary associations in the lab and not to more typical and biologically adaptive learning in nature.

CONTINUUM OF PREPAREDNESS

In an influential paper, Martin Seligman (1970) questioned the assumption of equivalence of associability and suggested that organisms are more predisposed, or prepared, to associate some events than others. He proposed that there is a **continuum of preparedness** ranging from prepared to unprepared to counterprepared.

RESPONSE DIFFERENCE One of the first indications that something was wrong with the classical assumptions about learning came from the experiences of animal trainers Keller and Marion Breland with the "misbehavior of organisms." For example, pigs were rewarded with food for depositing coins in a "piggy bank," a task they learned with some difficulty. But the pigs made poor savers: instead of depositing the coins as they were supposed to do, they would tend to drop the coins and root them about with their snouts, as if they were food. This phenomenon is called **instinctive drift,** in which "Learned behavior drifts toward instinctive behavior" (Breland & Breland, 1961).

Many other studies have shown difficulties with getting organisms to learn certain responses. Cats, in experiments by Thorndike (1954), had great difficulty learning to escape by scratching or licking themselves. Moreover, when they did learn, Thorndike explained, the response degenerated to a "mere vestige of a lick or scratch." Other experiments showed that dogs found it extremely difficult, if not impossible, to learn to yawn for food. Neither rats nor pigeons are prepared to avoid shock by lever pressing. Yet pigeons easily learn to escape shock by flying, as do rats by running. Bolles (1970) observed that the easily learned responses in avoidance situations are closely related to innate species-specific defense reactions. Organisms do not usually have the opportunity to *learn* how to escape from predators. A rat cannot afford to try pressing levers when it sees a cat. In fact, it is counterprepared to do so; it must run if it is to survive. Any avoidance response inconsistent with an organism's specific defenses will be difficult or impossible to condition.

STIMULUS DIFFERENCE We know that some responses are easier to condition than others, but what about stimuli? Again, the assumption of equivalence of associability appears to be mistaken; that is, some stimuli are more easily conditioned than others. For example, dogs are counterprepared to learn to associate different locations of the trainer's voice with responding to commands, yet they easily learn to use voice tone as a discriminative stimulus, as with "go!" or "stay!" (Dobrzecka & Konorowski, 1968).

An important series of experiments showing differences in the associability of different stimuli and reinforcers was performed by Garcia and Koelling (1966). They arranged for rats to drink either saccharin-flavored ("tasty") water or unflavored water that was accompanied by flashing lights and clicking noises ("bright-noisy"). The bright-noisy and tasty water was made aversive in three ways: rats' feet were shocked as they drank, the water was slightly poisoned, or they were given doses of radiation. Afterward, the rats were tested with tasty water and bright-noisy water separately. The rats that had been made ill by poison or radiation avoided the tasty water but not the bright-noisy water. The rats that had been shocked showed exactly the opposite result, avoiding the bright-noisy water but not the tasty water (Figure 8-10).

These results can be understood from an evolutionary perspective. Organisms that survived developed either adaptive fixed action patterns or the ability to master their environment. Garcia and Koelling's (1966) experiment makes this point clear. The rats were "prepared" to associate one external event (shock) with another external event (bright-noisy water) but not with nausea, an

FIGURE 8-10
The "Bright-Noisy" Water Experiment

Whether or not a rat avoided the water depended on the water's characteristics and on the consequences that followed drinking it. Avoidance developed if tasty water and illness were paired (both internal) or if bright-noisy water was paired with shock (both external) —but not if these pairings were reversed.
(Garcia & Koelling, 1966)

		Consequences	
		Illness	Shock
Cues	Taste	Avoid	Not avoid
	Sound-sight	Not avoid	Avoid

internal event. They were also prepared to associate nausea with an internal event (tasty water), but not with a shock, the external event (Garcia & Garcia y Robertson, 1985). Doesn't this make sense? How well would a rat (or a human being, for that matter) survive if it decided it was sick because of something it heard or saw? Or reacted to a sore foot by concluding it must be something it ate?

HUMAN PREPAREDNESS You might be thinking that the notion of preparedness applies only or mainly to animal learning. But the evolutionary history of *Homo sapiens* has selectively prepared human beings for certain kinds of learning as well. Some of the things we find easy to learn are common to other species, while others appear to be uniquely human.

An example of one kind of human prepared learning is taste aversion—the "sauce bearnaise" phenomenon. Seligman (1970) describes how the problem of preparedness first became compelling to him. One evening he had gone to the opera with his wife. For dinner, he had one of his favorite dishes, a filet mignon with bearnaise sauce. In the middle of the night, Seligman became violently ill. As a result, he developed an aversion to the taste of what had been his favorite sauce. This was in spite of knowing that the cause of his sickness was not food, but flu. Moreover, he did not develop an aversion to the opera, his wife, or the friend from whom he caught the flu. Similarly, ocean voyagers may acquire aversions to food eaten prior to seasickness, in spite of knowing that the cause of their sickness is the ship's motion, not the food (Garcia & Koelling, 1966). The tendency to make a connection between nausea and prior food taste is so strongly prepared in us that it defies reason. Even conscious knowledge of why such associations are formed makes little difference.

The tendency for prepared learning is perhaps a root cause of some phobias as well. For example, a little girl saw a snake while playing in the park. Some hours later she accidentally slammed a car door on her hand. The result? A fear of snakes! Evidently humans are more highly prepared to fear snakes than cars, all logic aside (Seligman & Hager, 1972).

As a final, and more positive, example of human preparedness, consider language acquisition. Our species appears to be uniquely prepared to learn language with ease (Lenneberg, 1967). With very informal training, children in all cultures learn the intricacies of their native language. (See the language section in Chapter 10.) The conditions under which normal children fail to learn language must be impoverished indeed, amounting essentially to complete linguistic isolation.

LEARNING THEORY AND THE MODERN WORLD

How do all these principles of learning contribute to our knowledge of what governs behavior in the modern world? Our complex, high-technology society requires specialized and sophisticated behaviors: communicating through computers, working with toxic chemicals, maneuvering on crowded highways, collecting and interpreting enormous amounts of information. Some people seem to adjust easily to the demands of complex, often stressful circumstances. But many people's lives are out of control, and their behavior drifts far from what is desirable in a society whose members are now more and more interdependent.

Where do the principles of reinforcement come into play in the modern world? Skinner (1986) addressed this question in an article entitled "What Is Wrong With Daily Life in the Western World?" (See Chapter 4, page 157.) The problem, as Skinner sees it, is that current society has eroded the normal feedback between actions and consequences. Bureaucratic rules, intended to solve problems, may impose hardships on those who are required to follow them. A well-meaning welfare system results in people being rewarded for not working. Rewards and punishments often occur not because of an individual's action but because of the individual's membership in a group, as when insurance premiums skyrocket for people in certain age brackets. People in the work force often get no feedback from their bosses and co-workers and may begin to feel like unappreciated cogs in the organizational wheel. If you work in a large company, for example, whether or not you have a job next year might have little to do with the effort you invest.

What do the principles of cognitive learning tell us about our present-day behavior? The most prominent people in society are our models, but in observing these models we see conflicting attitudes and actions. The terrorist shares the headlines with the statesman who works for world peace. We hear celebrities say that money isn't everything, but we see that wealth and status are admired, often regardless of how they are acquired. Children who are brought up by gentle parents witness acts of violence daily on television and sometimes on the streets of their neighborhoods. The people and events that shape perceptions, motivations, and expectations vary considerably, leaving many people confused about how they themselves should behave and about what, in fact, they should learn.

Human beings evolved to suit a world long gone, a world of perhaps 20,000 years ago. Some of the problems in today's modern world are due to a mismatch between our adaptations to this ancient world and the nature of the modern world we have made. For instance, the orienting reflex, useful in preparing us to meet danger, is now activated by the impatient honking of drivers caught in a traffic jam or by the sound effects in a Hollywood film. The kind of aggressive behavior that warded off an attacking animal may now be directed at a person who cuts in line. The laws of learning still hold, but what we learn does not always match the demands of our complex society. Chapter 20 presents what many psychologists are now doing to reduce the mismatch in the hopes of making people aware of the problems. This awareness, in turn, may encourage people to seek greater control of their own learning and thus make useful changes in the way they act in society.

A CONCLUDING NOTE

We have learned much about the basic processes of learning. Organisms learn to associate events that occur together in the lab and in life. These simple associations, developed by means of classical and operant conditioning, form the groundwork of our knowledge of what goes on around us and of our behavior in the world. Understanding the processes of conditioning helps us realize why being embarrassed once in class can affect our behavior for years, why we have superstitions, and why we often behave as we do—from playing a slot machine that once hit the jackpot, to avoiding certain foods even though there is no rational reason for our aversion. Although conditioning is an important aspect of our learning, we also make use of such cognitive forms of learning as insight, cognitive mapping, and observational learning. Our perceptions, expectations, and purposes strongly influence how and what we learn. How we organize and remember what we have learned is the topic of the next chapter.

SUMMARY

1. Learning is a process by which we change our thinking or behavior as a result of experience, to adapt to our environment. Learning can be beneficial or detrimental. We learn by making simple associations and by more complex processes.

2. The basis of conditioning, *association*, is one of the oldest principles of psychology. *Classical* or *respondent conditioning* occurs when a previously neutral stimulus comes to influence an organism's behavior. An *unconditioned stimulus (UCS)* evokes an *unconditioned response (UCR)*. When an organism learns to associate a neutral stimulus with a UCS, it becomes a *conditioned stimulus (CS)*, and the behavior it evokes is a *conditioned response (CR)*.

3. The effectiveness of conditioning is dependent on the application of the principles of recency and frequency. The delay arrangement of CS and UCS is the most effective. The more often a CS is paired with an UCS, the faster the CR will be learned. *Extinction* occurs if a CS is repeatedly presented without the UCS. Once a stimulus has become a CS, similar stimuli will elicit the CR; this is called *generalization*. Organisms can also learn to discriminate between stimuli. Respondent conditioning helps us act quickly in emergencies and has been used to overcome irrational fears.

4. Through *instrumental* or *operant conditioning*, our behavior is shaped by what happens after we act. The *law of effect* states that we act in order to avoid pain and obtain pleasure. Behavior can be shaped by reward *(reinforcement)* or punishment, both of which can be negative or positive. Primary reinforcers, such as food and water, are naturally reinforcing. Secondary (conditioned) reinforcers work because they are associated with primary reinforcers. Electrical stimulation to certain parts of the brain can act like primary reinforcers.

5. Timing has a strong effect on operant conditioning. If an animal receives a reward every time it makes the desired response, this is *continuous reinforcement*. There are several kinds of *partial reinforcement* schedules. Reinforcement can be given at regular intervals *(fixed interval)*, at *variable intervals*, after a certain number of responses *(fixed ratio)*, or after a varying number of responses *(variable ratio)*. The variable schedules produce the most frequent responses.

6. *Generalization, discrimination,* and *extinction* appear in operant conditioning as they do in respondent conditioning. Operant conditioning can be used to shape behavior in diverse areas, such as in the classroom or in psychotherapy. The distinction between classical and operant conditioning is not always clear.

7. The *cognitive learning approach* emphasizes that the learner is an active part of the learning process. The ability to perceive relationships, recombine information, and weigh alternatives is essential to learning. Insight occurs when an animal makes a leap of understanding in the relationship of objects and actions. *Insight* is the result of intuitive thinking. The thinker may be unaware of the source of his insight.

8. Animal learning does not always follow the pattern predicted by the *behaviorist* perspective of operant conditioning. Animals develop *cognitive maps* of the environment, not just responses to simple stimuli. *Latent learning* can be shown in animals that learn the layout of a maze without a reward and then demonstrate their knowledge when rewarded for performance. Experience with a learning task leads to improved performance on later, similar tasks. People can "learn how to learn."

9. People learn behaviors by observing others. In *observational learning,* the organism acquires a mental model or schema that directs behavior. *Modeling* can teach complex skills or to transmit phobias. Four processes are involved: *attentional processes,* which determine the perception and exploration of modeled behavior; *retention processes,* or the development of schemata; *production processes,* in which schemata guide actions; and *motivational processes,* which determine when a behavior will be performed.

10. Each organism comes into the world with many inborn potentials. Early students of conditioning believed all stimuli to be equally associable. More recently, researchers have found that animals are prepared to learn some associations more than others. Avoidance responses inconsistent with natural defenses are difficult to condition. Organisms are also predisposed to associate some stimuli with others. Taste aversion, common phobias, and language acquisition are examples of prepared learning in humans.

11. The modern world is a challenge for humans, who evolved to suit a world long gone. The rewards and punishments provided by society do not shape behavior effectively, and our role models give us conflicting and unconstructive input. Unconditioned responses may be evoked in inappropriate situations. Psychologists are working on the problem of how to improve society based on our increasing understanding of learning processes.

abstract modeling
appetitive conditioning
aversive conditioning
classical (respondent) conditioning
cognitive learning
cognitive maps
conditioned response (CR)
conditioned stimulus (CS)
continuous reinforcement
continuum of preparedness
counterconditioning
discrimination
extinction
fixed interval schedule
fixed ratio schedule
frequency
generalization
imitation
insight
instinctive drift
instrumental (operant) conditioning

latent learning
law of effect
learning
modeling
observational learning
operant level
operant strength
orienting reflex
partial reinforcement
Premack's principle
primary reinforcers
punishment
recency
reinforcement
secondary reinforcer
Skinner box
spontaneous recovery
unconditioned response (UCR)
unconditioned stimulus (UCS)
variable interval schedule
variable ratio schedule

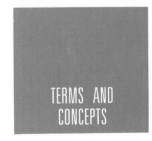

TERMS AND
CONCEPTS

Bandura, A. (1986). *Social foundations of thought and action.* Englewood Cliffs, N.J.: Prentice-Hall.

A masterful and readable account of observational learning.

Chance, P. (1987). *Learning and behavior* (2nd Ed.). San Francisco: Wadsworth.

A very good current introduction to more contemporary viewpoints on learning.

Leahey, T. H., & Harris, R. J. (1985). *Human learning.* Englewood Cliffs, N.J.: Prentice-Hall.

An excellent current introduction to the field.

Norman, D. (1983). *Learning and memory.* San Francisco: W. H. Freeman.

A well-written introduction to the joint analysis of learning and remembering.

Pavlov, I. P. (1927). *Conditioned reflexes.* New York: Oxford University Press.

Skinner, B. F. (1938). *The behavior of organisms.* New York: Appleton-Century-Crofts.

This book and the Pavlov book are the major classics in the discovery of the basic laws of learning. It may be very useful to see how these men wrote and how they related their discoveries to contemporary knowledge.

Snow, R. E., & M. J. Farr (Eds.). (1989). *Aptitude, learning, and instruction: III, Conative and affective process analysis.* Hillsdale, N. J.: Erlbaum.

A modern analysis of learning, in which psychologists try to apply their research to different problems such as making things fun to learn.

9
REMEMBERING AND FORGETTING

One night a friend put on a record that was popular when I was in graduate school. I hadn't listened to the record for 15 years, and as soon as I heard the first note I had a strange experience. I could smell once again the orchard that I had lived in, and I could see the faces of friends whom I hadn't seen (or even thought of) in 15 years. I saw my old blue '56 Chevy convertible; it had a top that never worked, I remembered. I often drove that car to the beach at night. When I heard that song, I could smell the night air once again, see the night sky, and feel the car slipping around the winding curves of the road out to the beach. As I listened to the music, I was transported back in time.

I once worked in a mental hospital. One day I was taking care of Michael S., a patient who suffered from amnesia, due in this case to a blow to the head. He told me a story I will never forget.

> This morning a woman came to see me in my room. I felt attracted to her. She was very pretty, and I liked talking to her. I asked her for her name. "Ellen," she said. I asked why she had come to visit me, as I thought she was a hospital volunteer. She slumped and burst into tears. She said, "Michael, I'm your *wife*. We've been married for 20 years!" I just didn't know what to say. I don't remember her at all.

And consider Clive Waring, a Renaissance music conductor. He contracted encephalitis, which left him with a memory span of only a few seconds. He cannot remember the meal he just ate or the conversation he just had, but he can still conduct a choir (Sacks, 1986).

Memory is a great mystery. How can a song suddenly bring up memories of an orchard, an automobile, a lost era? How can someone forget a spouse of 20 years? How can someone remember a performance long ago, yet not his last spoken sentence? No one really knows, but the answers must lie in the nature of our system of memory. There are *different kinds* of memory, too: Michael lost his memory of Ellen, but not of the English language.

Our memories give meaning to our life, a sense of continuity between the past and present. To live and function, we must be able to remember our friends, our house, how to drive, how to walk, and even who we are. And at the end, what do we have but memories? Thanks to our memory, one poet wrote, "we can have roses in December."

SOME PRINCIPLES OF MEMORY

This chapter discusses the principles and operation of memory—that is, our system of memory, not our specific, personal memories. The analysis here is like that of perception—not an examination of what is on stage, but of the operations behind the scenes. Many of the principles that underlie perception, such as simplicity, organization, and meaning (see Chapter 6), also hold true for memory.

William James (1890) described three important principles of memory:

> The more other facts a fact is associated with in the mind, the better possession of it our memory retains. Each of its associates becomes a hook to which it hangs, a means to fish it up when sunk beneath the surface. Together they form

a network of attachments by which it is woven into the tissue of our thought. The "secret of a good memory" is the secret of forming diverse and multiple associations with every fact we care to retain. . . . Most men have a good memory for facts connected with their own pursuits. . . . The merchant remembers prices, the politician other politicians' speeches and votes. . . . The great memory for facts which a Darwin and a Spencer reveal in their books is not incompatible with the possession on their part of a brain with only a middling degree of physiological retentiveness. . . . Let a man early in life set himself the task of verifying such a theory as that of evolution, and facts will soon cluster and cling to him like grapes to their stem. Their relations to the theory will hold them fast, and the more of these the mind is able to discern, the greater the erudition will become.

1. *Memory involves associations.* The mind is a network of associations formed from past experiences. The more we associate an event with something we already know, the more our memory of it will stick with us—for me, a car, friends, an orchard, and the beach are all associated with a song. When I hear that song now, I am reminded of experiences I had while listening to the song. If you listened to that same song, there is no way you could have the same memories as I do.

2. *Memories are much simpler than actual experience.* Because there is simply too much information available to us, we remember a few of the many things that happen to us. How many of the billions of momentary experiences you had last summer do you remember? Perhaps one glorious day at the beach, some fine times lazing about, but certainly not every bite of food, every right turn, every conversation, every moment of every day.

3. *We remember meaningful events.* We remember events of personal importance or aspects of events that at the time appeared important to us: your lecture notes transcribe the meaning of the talk, not the shape of the room.

Since we remember only the meaningful details, we often overlook familiar details of everyday life. Which of the drawings in Figure 9-1 is an accurate

**FIGURE 9-1
Familiar Details**

Which drawing of the penny is accurate? It may be hard to pick the correct one because the few details that identify it are not sufficiently meaningful that you would remember them.
(Nickerson & Adams, 1979)

SOME PRINCIPLES OF MEMORY

representation of a penny? Most people cannot readily tell, although we see pennies daily. We need to remember little more about a penny than that it is a small copper coin worth one cent with Lincoln on it. Whether Lincoln faces left or right and where the date is placed don't matter to us, and they are normally not remembered, even though we see pennies thousands of times.

THE FUNCTIONS OF MEMORY

Memory records specific episodes in life *(episodic memory)* and the symbols we use to think and communicate *(semantic memory)*. It also contains the general rules for operating in the world, called *procedural memory*. Memory is continuously updated as new events occur, a process that allows us to respond to continuous changes in the world. Memory allows us to organize past experiences and to make them accessible when needed (Baddeley, 1986).

We bring an enormous amount of background knowledge to everyday experience, much more than we may realize. We have a representation of the world in our mind—of general knowledge of the world, common sense, and skills. People who share the same culture have basically a similar representation about the rules of language, inference, and logic and about general facts of the world, such as the effects of gravity, how to ride a bicycle, and who the president is. This memory underlies perception because it allows us to fill in the gaps when we get new information and to assume facts on the basis of partial information. We know that people living in Timbuktu eat and sleep, have children, and work. We know this even though we may never have visited Timbuktu and witnessed these facts firsthand (Wickelgren, 1977). This representation divides into declarative and procedural memory.

DECLARATIVE MEMORY

Declarative memory is our mental record of information that we use to recall events, to think, and to communicate. Tulving (1984) described declarative memory as containing information about which we can verbalize our belief that it is true or false. For example, you could say from your declarative memory that either, yes, you did climb trees as a child or, no, you did not. There are two types of declarative memory, episodic and semantic.

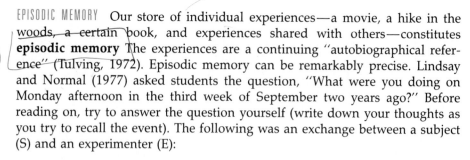

EPISODIC MEMORY   Our store of individual experiences—a movie, a hike in the woods, a certain book, and experiences shared with others—constitutes **episodic memory** The experiences are a continuing "autobiographical reference" (Tulving, 1972). Episodic memory can be remarkably precise. Lindsay and Normal (1977) asked students the question, "What were you doing on Monday afternoon in the third week of September two years ago?" Before reading on, try to answer the question yourself (write down your thoughts as you try to recall the event). The following was an exchange between a subject (S) and an experimenter (E):

S: Come on. How should I know?
E: Just try it anyhow.

Episodic memory records the major events of our lives and is a continuing autobiographical reference for each of us.

S: OK. Let's see: Two years ago . . . I would be in high school in Pittsburgh. . . . That would be my senior year. Third week in September—that's just after summer—that would be the fall term. . . . Let me see. I think I had chemistry lab on Mondays. I don't know. I was probably in chemistry lab. Wait a minute—that would be the second week of school. I remember he started off with the atomic table—a big fancy chart. I thought he was crazy trying to make us memorize that thing. You know, I think I can remember sitting. . . .

Specific episodes can endure in memory a long time, sometimes for decades.

SEMANTIC MEMORY The knowledge of languages, including the shape of letters, the sounds of language (phonemes), and the meaning (semantic content) of words constitutes **semantic memory** (Tulving, 1972). Semantic memory stores our knowledge of the world independent of context in time and space, in contrast to episodic memory, which is primarily concerned with the time and local context of events.

Our quantity of semantic knowledge is vast; the average college student has a vocabulary of about 50,000 words in semantic memory, along with the knowledge of how to combine those words properly, how to write them, and how to speak them. Semantic memory also permits commonsense logical inferences. Suppose you ask your mother where her keys are, and she says, "They are either in the bag or on the mantle." You look in the bag and they are not there; you then know without any further information that they are on the mantle.

Semantic memory also contains the rules for everyday inferences. If someone says, "I hate country music," you know not to invite that person to a Willie Nelson concert. Sometimes semantic memory errs, as in the common

THE FUNCTIONS OF MEMORY

FIGURE 9-2
Errors in
Representational
Memory

Which map is correct? Most
people choose the one on the
left because Reno is
"represented" in our minds
as inland from Los Angeles,
therefore we think it must be
east of Los Angeles. But,
believe it or not, Reno is
actually *west* of Los Angeles.

mistake shown in Figure 9-2. We represent Los Angeles as being on the California coast and Reno, Nevada, as being inland. Therefore, we assume that anything on the coast must be west of anything inland. But, as the map shows, this is not the case.

PROCEDURAL MEMORY

Procedural memory contains the automatized schemata for performing routine actions, whether they are simple, like throwing a ball or getting dressed, or complex, like driving a car or playing baseball. It also guides our movements in space, using our knowledge of perspective and constancy. This kind of memory also underlies much of our ordinary perceptual experience—that we are drinking coffee not tea, that the milk is sour, or that someone is singing off key.

Procedural memory, unlike declarative memory, is not subject to verbalization; it's easier done than said. We cannot really describe how we ride a bicycle; it is a series of muscular responses that we have learned on a nonverbal level. The establishment of procedural memories is somewhat like stimulus-response conditioning. In learning to catch a baseball, we learn which movements are "rewarded" by the ball landing firmly in the glove. We may not be able to describe how it is done, but we can do it over and over again.

MEMORY ORGANIZES AND MAKES PAST EXPERIENCE ACCESSIBLE

ORGANIZATION

Memory is organized around associated events. When you think about your father, you recall things that relate to your knowledge of him. Memories of other people and events unrelated to him do not intrude (Baddeley, 1986).

If memory were a random collection of bits of information, you would have to rifle through millions of memories simply to recognize a face or the voice of

Consider this simple question: What day is it? Answering the question requires a representational knowledge of the days of the week, and it must be updated: today's answer is not the same as yesterday's or tomorrow's.

If our memory system were simple, like a date counter on a digital watch, we would be able to answer the question just as quickly on one day as on any other. However, if people are asked what day it is on Wednesday, it takes twice as long to answer as when they are asked on Sunday (Figure 9-3).

However, our memory is not updated and stored only in simplified schemata. Weekdays take longer to recall than weekends, probably because there are five weekdays and only two weekend days. The closer the weekday is to the weekend, the faster it is recalled (Shannon, 1979). In the real world, the length of every day is equal, but their meaning to us is not. Weekends are perhaps more central to our lives and therefore we may represent our weeks largely with reference to weekends.

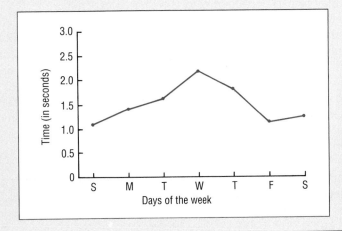

FIGURE 9-3
Memory and Meaning

In timed responses to the question, "What day of the week is it?" people take longer to respond in the middle of the week, perhaps showing that we represent our weeks with reference to the more "meaningful" weekends.
(Shannon, 1979)

someone calling your name. Let's use the analogy of a library. Suppose you wanted the book *The Theory of the Leisure Class* by Thorstein Veblen, and suppose that the library you went to was a random collection of books—that is, no book had an assigned place. The only way you would be able to find Veblen's book would be to look at one book after another, perhaps tens of thousands, until you found it. Even in a small town library with a few thousand books, it might take days to find.

Libraries aren't just buildings; they are *organized systems* for locating books. You could find Veblen's book by looking up the author's name, or if you had forgotten the author's name, you could do a quick search through a subject catalog.

Similarly, memory is richly interrelated and organized. If I ask you to tell me what you know about U.S. presidents, a variety of information may come to mind: names of presidents, what the powers of the president are, and important policies of past presidents.

If memory becomes disorganized, efficiency is impaired. Consider the question, "What are the months of the year?" You would probably answer by reciting the months in chronological order, beginning with January. Try it. This takes about 5 seconds because the months are usually organized in that order in

We can liken our memory to a card catalog. We locate specific bits of information by recalling what events, or drawers, the information is stored with.

your memory. Now, try to name the months of the year in reverse order. This usually takes about 12 to 15 seconds. Finally, name the months of the year in *alphabetical* order. Although you know the months and how to alphabetize, you rarely use these two criteria together and have no organization to speed the response. It takes more than a minute for this task, and most people make several mistakes.

ACCESSIBILITY

Only a limited amount of information in memory is accessible at any one time, and the information constantly changes. This helps us to adapt to different situations: an old song makes certain memories accessible to me or talking to a good friend may bring forth the memory of shared experiences.

The schemata associated with conscious content become accessible as we think about them: during exam week you may have tests in English literature, psychology, and history one right after the other. When you are writing your English exam, the information relevant to literature is easily accessible and recedes when you plunge into your psychology exam.

An analogy is a storehouse: often-ordered items are at the front where they are easy to get to, and items that are rarely called for are tucked away in corners and are less accessible. In one experiment, subjects were asked to name any fruit that begins with the letter *a*; next, they were asked to name fruits that begin with the letter *p*. The second question was answered faster. The first question summoned up the storehouse of information about fruits, making the names of fruits more readily accessible for the second question (Loftus & Loftus, 1975).

THE PROCESSES OF MEMORY

Although distinguishing between the functions of memory is a relatively straightforward matter, how these functions are performed is a question of much debate. This section describes the overall processes of memory in terms of the memory cycle and the memory system. The **memory cycle** describes the process by which we experience something, retain it, and later retrieve it. The **memory system** includes the different divisions of memory from momentary visual impressions to the lifelong retention of important moments in our lives.

THE MEMORY CYCLE

Recall of a specific event depends on three prior processes. First, of course, is *perception:* the event must be sensed, transduced into neural language, and perceived. The second process is *retention:* the new information must be stored and kept. *Retrieval* is the third process, by which the stored information is brought forward into consciousness at the appropriate time.

PERCEPTUAL ENCODING To be remembered, an event must be *perceived.* This occurs when information picked up by the senses stimulates appropriate receptors, which then relay it by neural firing to the brain. Sensory information is then organized by perceptual processes into the simplest meaningful percepts; this process is called **encoding.**

RETENTION The theory of **retention** states that a remembered event is retained as long as needed. The retention time may be a few seconds, a few years, or an entire lifetime. Occasionally we direct retention ("I am going to remember that term"), but usually we select things on the basis of a few rules: an experience or percept is striking or new, related to other memories, important to our career, and so on.

Specialists have not yet pinpointed the locations in the brain of specific memories or even of different kinds of memories. Childhood memories do not seem to be stored in one corner of the brain and memories of songs in another. But the mere fact that we do have memories means that there must be physical changes that occur somewhere in the brain when we remember something.

RETRIEVAL When a past event is brought into consciousness, we regain, or **retrieve,** information previously stored. Two types of retrieval are recognition and recall.

Recognition is the ability to identify an object or event. This identification involves a match between present perception and your memory of the information presented to you. *Recognition,* meaning "to know again," is the most common experience of memory.

Recall is the ability to summon up stored information in the absence of the actual event or object. An exam question, such as "Which of Shakespeare's plays is concerned with the emotion of jealousy?" tests *recall.* The same question presented with a choice of answers would test *recognition:* "Jealousy is the central theme of which Shakespeare play? (a) *Merchant of Venice,* (b) *Macbeth,* (c) *All's Well That Ends Well,* or (d) *Othello.*"

It is easier to recognize something than to recall it because in recognition the stimulus is present and calls up all the relevant associated schemata. This is why multiple-choice tests are easier than tests that require recall. The capacity of recognition memory is enormous. Haber and Standig (1966) showed subjects 2,560 photographs for 10 seconds each. A few days later, subjects' recognition of the pictures was greater than 90 percent.

THE MEMORY SYSTEM

We remember some information, like the name or phone number of someone you have just met, for only a brief time before we forget it altogether. Other information that we use continually, like our own name and address, we do not forget. The difference between these two types of information has led many psychologists to hypothesize that memory has two distinct components: short-term and long-term memory (see Johnson-Laird, 1988).

SHORT-TERM MEMORY Information that is retained temporarily, for only a few seconds, is stored in **short-term memory.** The storage capacity of short-term memory is about seven items, such as a seven-digit number. Short-term memory can be regarded as scratch paper, on which immediate information for

Our short-term memory allows us to remember telephone numbers just long enough to dial them.

Richard Thompson, with whom I wrote a book called *The Amazing Brain* (1984), tries to find brain mechanisms that code and store memories. He writes of his work,

The fundamental problem has been to localize the engrams, or memory traces, in the brain. The cellular basis of memory, how neurons code and store memories, cannot be analyzed until the places and neurons that store memories are found. We were most fortunate recently to discover a tiny region in the brain where certain types of memories may be stored.

We began our search for the engram some years ago, following the lead of ground-breaking scientists such as Ivan Pavlov and Karl Lashley. The strategy we used was to choose a very simple form of learning that is shown equally by humans and animals, particularly mammals, since the basic architecture of the brain is similar from rat and rabbit to human, although much smaller and simpler in the former. We selected eyelid conditioning, a simple situation where a brief sound (a tone) is given, followed by a puff of air to the eye. After a number of such pairings of tone and air puff, the eyelid develops a learned closing response to the tone before the air puff comes. This is a simple adaptive conditioned response learned to try to protect the eye. Rabbits and humans learn the eye-blink response equally well.

ONE SCIENTIST'S SEARCH FOR THE ENGRAM

Indeed, the learned eye-blink response is widely used to study basic properties of simple learning in both animals and humans. Rabbits are docile and cooperative and make good subjects for studies of the brain.

It seemed very likely that the memory for such a simple learned response would not be stored in the highest regions of the brain, regions like the cerebral cortex and hippocampus. Indeed, rabbits with these structures removed can learn the eye-blink response relatively normally. This still leaves a great deal of brain tissue. We were able to rule out some possibilities, such as the motor neurons that control the eye-blink response and the auditory nuclei in the brainstem that relay to the rest of the brain the information that the tone is on.

There was no way to make even a good guess as to where the memory for the learned eye-blink response might be stored. Consequently, we undertook a systematic study to map the activity of nerve cells in all the regions of the brain that might store the memory. To do this we recorded the electrical nerve impulse discharges of nerve cells with a tiny electrode sys-

tem. This system is fixed to the rabbit's skull while the rabbit is deeply anesthetized. After the animal recovers from this minor operation, it is trained in the eye-blink task and tiny electrodes are inserted in the brain to record nerve cell activity. The brain itself has no feeling of pain or touch, and the animals are quite unaware of the inserted electrodes.

These long and laborious brain mapping studies finally paid off. We found a very small region in a part of the cerebellum where the nerve cell discharges increased markedly over the training period. The cerebellum is a large structure of the brain below the forebrain much concerned with movement and had been suggested by some scientists as a possible locus for certain kinds of memory traces having to do with learned movements. The pattern of increased neural activity in this region of the cerebellum actually formed a "model," in time, of the learned eye-blink response to the tone but not of the reflex eye blink to the air puff. Finding this region of neurons that showed learned responses was most encouraging, but it did not establish that this small region was the site of the memory. Some other critical region might simply be relaying neuronal activity about the learned response to this region.

We next made lesions in this region—that is, we destroyed a small amount of brain

a specific purpose is written and continuously erased as new information comes into consciousness. When you look up a phone number, you have to remember the number only long enough to dial it. If you encounter interference—a busy signal or a loud noise next to you —you may have to look the number up again. That act can be thought of as constantly replacing the number in short-term memory or nudging it into the more permanent component of the memory system: long-term memory.

tissue. After the lesion, the animals completely forgot the task and could never learn it again. However, the eye-blink response to the air puff was still normal—the animals had no trouble making the eye-blink response. Instead, they lost the memory for the *learned* eye-blink response and could never relearn it. We have also found that this region of the cerebellum is essential for another kind of learned response that is widely used in the laboratory—learning to lift the leg to avoid a shock to the paw. It appears to be where the memories may be stored for a whole class of simple learned responses.

The critical locus for destroying the memory of the learned eye-blink response is very small. Tiny chemical lesions that destroy no more than one cubic millimeter of nerve cells destroy the memory. Several other lines of evidence in our current work point to this tiny region of the cerebellum as being where the memory is stored, but we have not yet proved that beyond all possible doubt. However, having identified a critical part of a memory circuit, we can now identify the entire memory circuit, from "ear to eyelid," which we are now in the process of doing. This will allow us to establish with certainty the exact location of the memory trace. We will then be in a position to tackle the most important question of all—how it is that neurons code and store memories in the brain.

At the cellular level there are two fundamental types of information coding or memory. One of these is the genetic code. In higher animals literally millions of bits of information are coded in the DNA of the cell, the genetic memory. This information is vast, and it determines not only whether we will be a mouse or a man but the myriad characteristics that make up each individual.

Over the course of evolution a quite different kind of information coding has developed—the cellular encoding of memory in the brain. This memory code is no less remarkable than the genetic code. As we have seen, a well-educated adult has literally millions of bits of acquired information stored in the brain.

The fundamental difference between the genetic code and the memory code is, of course, that each individual human's memory store is acquired through experience and learning. The uniqueness of each human being is due largely to the memory store, the biological residue of memory from a lifetime of experience. We will someday understand the genetic basis of the ability of the brain to store memory, but we can never know the actual memories that are stored from studying the genes, only from studying the brain.

The ability to learn is an emergent property of cellular tissue. The ability, as such, has a clear genetic base; it is dependent on the structural and functional organization, the architecture of the brain, and on cellular storage processes. It would not be entirely surprising if the genetic material itself plays a role in the process of learning. After all, the actions of nerve cells at synapses can engage the interior of neurons and even act on the DNA itself. (Ornstein, Thompson, & Macaulay, 1984, pp. 147–50; see also Thompson, 1989)

Thompson considers classical conditioning the Rosetta stone for brain components of deficits in learning and memory that occur with increased age (1988). He feels that classical conditioning of discrete behavioral responses in rabbits and other mammals is among the most promising animal models of the human condition in which to analyze brain mechanisms of normally occurring age-related deficits in learning and memory. In one study, Knowlton, Lavond, and Thompson (1988) found great effect of lesions of the cerebellar cortex on retention of the classically conditioned eye-blink response. They implanted rabbits with stimulating electrodes in the lateral reticular nucleus (LRN) and gave them classical conditioning training. They then cut the rabbit's cerebellar cortex. Later they again gave the rabbits classical conditioning training. The lesioned rabbits did not retain the CR after the lesion but were able to relearn it.

LONG-TERM MEMORY Information retained for more than a few seconds is stored in what is termed **long-term memory.** You do not have to look up your *own* telephone number when you call home, nor do you have to recite your name over and over to remember it. Both episodic and representational memories are long-term memories. The storage capacity of long-term memory is huge; many psychologists consider it limitless. In a subsequent section we look in more detail at this amazing ability.

ALTERNATIVE INTERPRETATIONS OF MEMORY CYCLE AND SYSTEM

MEMORY CHANGES WITH EXPERIENCE

The concept of a memory cycle is appealing. It describes in a clear manner how a specific experience enters consciousness and is remembered through the stages of encoding, storage, and recall. Many experiments support this hypothesis. Still, it is unlikely that memory operates this way all the time. One important cognitive psychologist, William Estes, describes a different view: "Human memory does not, in a literal sense, store anything; it simply changes as a function of experience" (Estes, 1980).

We have discussed human memory as being similar to that of a computer: acquiring specific information, filing it, and retrieving it. The alternative idea, that memory simply indicates changes within, is similar to the ecological and computational approaches discussed in Chapter 6. According to this view, memory changes are more like changing the dial on a radio set: when the tuning is changed, new stations can be received. The changes that we call "memory" may be more like other changes within us: perhaps they resemble physical changes to the body that occur by reason of experience. With exercise, muscles change shape and change their performance; perhaps "memory" indexes similar changes in the brain. After experiences we are more likely to search the world differently, select words differently, act differently. But our internal alteration doesn't mean we have captured a specific bit of information inside.

Both views are partially accurate and agree that experiences change us and are reflected in memory. They differ on the question of how those changes are reflected in memory. A part of memory is probably a little like a computer, storing words, phrases, and specific events that can later be retrieved. But for much of our life, we don't store exact bits of information simply because we might need them in the future.

Rather, our general concern is *adaptation:* being able to change behavior as a result of experience. We may wish to avoid someone who once caused us pain. Previous experience with that person produced changes in us. We then begin to pick up information about other people who we think may also cause us pain, by noticing similarities between them and the person who has hurt us before. But in these cases we are not retrieving specific information as a computer does. Instead, we become tuned differently; we perceive and act differently. Probably no single machine analogy is sufficient to explain the complexity of the human mind, even a machine as complex as a computer.

MEMORY AS A CONTINUOUS PROCESS

Many psychologists do not believe that *separate* processes for short-term and long-term memory are plausible. Instead, they think of the memory system as a *single* and *continuous* process. In this view, each repetition of an event strengthens the association of that event and increases the probability that it will be remembered later on.

The single process hypothesis seems to be an accurate description of real life (Wickelgren, 1977). There is no sharp distinction between not remembering and fully remembering. You may forget a phone number the first time you dial it, then remember a few of the numbers the next time, and finally the whole thing if you keep using it.

The single-process hypothesis regards short-term and long-term memory not as separate mechanisms but as the extreme ends of a single process. Each exposure to a situation increases the probability of its being remembered. In this view, all memories are generated by the same system. Because the continuous memory approach postulates only a single process for all normal memory experience, it has the advantage of being simpler and more inclusive. The majority of psychologists now seem to be shifting toward this hypothesis.

HOW WE FORGET AND WHAT WE REMEMBER

The modern scientific study of memory began 100 years ago with controlled experiments designed to uncover the fundamental characteristics of human memory by determining the basic rate of forgetting. More recently, the emphasis has been on research outside the laboratory, on determining how and what we remember and forget of real-life events.

FACTORS OF FORGETTING

The first paradigm for controlled research on memory was developed in 1885 by Hermann Ebbinghaus. He devised long lists of **nonsense syllables,** such as "dof," "zam," and "fok." By using such nonsense syllables to test memory, Ebbinghaus hoped to eliminate any effect that subjects' personal experiences might have on their ability to recall information. In this way, he hoped to obtain a precise measure of learning and memory independent of previous experience.

His method was heroic; he used himself as a subject through long hours of investigations. He learned a list of syllables by heart, well enough to recite it two times in a row. He then tested his recall of the list over several days. He designated his measure of forgetting as the time needed to relearn the list until he recalled it perfectly. This method yielded a precise measurement of the rate of forgetting. He discovered that the rate of forgetting follows a predictable curve; most forgetting occurs immediately and tapers off as time goes on (Figure 9-4). Ebbinghaus's curve is a general description of the rate at which material with no previous associations is forgotten.

DECAY OF MEMORY In movies, scenes of the distant past are commonly shot in dulled, faded colors. Although the idea of memory literally fading with time is appealing, this use of imagery is an oversimplification of a very complex process. For instance, a senile person may not be able to recall the day's events but may clearly remember events from youth. The memory of motor skills, such as how to ride a bicycle, does not seem to fade over time, even without practice.

In one important test of the fading belief, Jenkins and Dallenbach (1924) asked two groups to learn lists of nonsense syllables in the same way

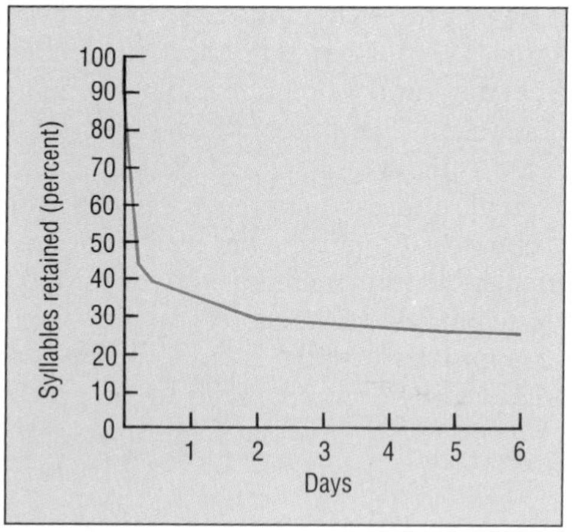

FIGURE 9-4
Curve of Forgetting

Ebbinghaus showed that at first we forget quickly, but then our rate of forgetting evens out and becomes stable.

Ebbinghaus had done. Immediately after the memorization task, one group was allowed to go to sleep, while the second was required to stay awake. The researchers reasoned that if memory fades with time alone, then there should be no difference in recall between the two groups if both groups are tested for recall at the same time. The results showed, however, that those who slept retained far more than those who had stayed awake. The most likely explanation for this result is that the awake group had experiences in the meantime that *interfered* with retention. The decay of memory is not just a matter of time; the particular events that occur during that time are also a factor.

INTERFERENCE   Some kinds of events interfere with memory more than others. Two kinds of interference have been studied in the laboratory. **Proactive interference** occurs when previous knowledge interferes with present memory. The term *proactive* is a combination of "pro," meaning forward, and "active," which together means that the interference *moves forward* from previous to present knowledge. Proactive interference is easily demonstrated in the following test. Two groups learn the same list, B. However, the first group has learned another list, A, before. Both groups are tested for their ability to recall list B.

	Learn	Learn	Test
Group 1	A	B	B
Group 2	—	B	B

On testing, Group 2 can remember more of list B than Group 1 can.

Retroactive interference occurs when new information interferes with previous memories. It can be demonstrated as follows. Two groups learn list C. The first group then learns list D; the other does not. Both groups are tested for their memory of list C.

	Learn	Learn	Test
Group 1	C	D	C
Group 2	C	—	C

On testing, Group 1 will remember less of list C than will Group 2. Similarly, suppose you are making a list of people to invite to a party. You are about to write down John's name, but before you do, someone interrupts with, "Hey, don't forget we have to invite June and Sally." You write their names down but then find that you cannot remember the name of the person you had thought of before.

Two general factors in interference are (1) the *longer* the interval between the first and second event, the *less* interference; (2) the more *similar* the items, the *more* interference. For example, suppose you are trying to remember the phone numbers of two people. If the first number is 524-5318 and the second is 883-2299, you will experience less interference between the two numbers than if the second number were 542-5218.

PRIMACY AND RECENCY   We seem to be structured, even at the most rudimentary physiological level, to notice and retain elements at transition points. Recall that the senses respond most vigorously at the beginnings and endings of stimuli; in between, they habituate, or stop responding. (See the section on sensory adaptation and comparison in Chapter 5.)

Similarly, we *remember* the beginning and ending of an event better than the middle, and the ending better than the beginning. We can recall a word at the beginning of a list 70 percent of the time, words in the middle less than 20 percent, and words at the end almost 100 percent (Loftus & Loftus, 1975). Our enhanced recall of beginnings is an example of the effect of **primacy**. Our enhanced recall of endings is an example of the effect of **recency**. The principles of primacy and recency in memory have been extensively demonstrated experimentally using lists of nonsense syllables. They also hold as general principles in many areas of life, from the basic characteristics of the sensory systems to our involvement in political campaigns, love affairs, and theater performances. In 1980, presidential candidate Ronald Reagan illustrated these principles by saying, "Politics is just like show business. You need a big opening. Then you coast for a while. Then you need a big finish."

MEMORY FOR LIFE EXPERIENCES

Although studies in the laboratory make clear some of the basic operations of the memory system, they shed little light on our real-life memories; lists of syllables and numbers are not important parts of our lives. The most memorable events of our lives would be impossible to duplicate in the lab. When I was 6 years old I almost drowned trying to learn how to swim. I remember as if it just happened, the blue water turning to black as I lost consciousness and the blinding light when my father pulled me out. I will never forget it. If you ask people of your parents' generation where they were when President Kennedy was shot, they will probably remember every detail. But we cannot deliberately create such powerful events and then check on people 20 years later to see what they remember about them.

Psychologists study what kinds of things people recall in the normal course of their lives. Some of the studies discussed here involve considerable amounts of time (sometimes decades) between the event and the recall test, while others involve memory for visual scenes, faces, and odors.

MEMORY FOR RECENT REAL-WORLD EVENTS The forgetting curve of Ebbinghaus (Figure 9-4) shows that the greater part of relatively meaningless information, such as nonsense syllables, is quickly forgotten. But how long do you remember a tennis victory, a good movie, a passionate kiss? Marigold Linton studied her memory of her life events over a period of six years (Neisser, 1982). During this time she recorded 5,500 events and tested some of them for recall every two months. Her record includes such items as "narrowly beat HEO at tennis today," and "received a call from Maureen, Strassberger's secretary, indicating that she will make the travel arrangements to Washington."

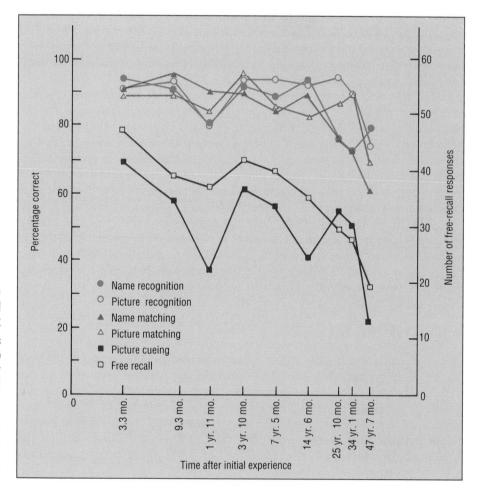

FIGURE 9-5
Remembering Faces and Names from the Past

When high school graduates were tested on their ability to recall the faces of former classmates, even very old subjects showed remarkable memory. The retention in various categories is shown here; the test is discussed in the accompanying text.
(Bahrick, Bahrick, & Wittlinger, 1975)

CHAPTER 9 / REMEMBERING AND FORGETTING

She expected that her rate of forgetting would follow the Ebbinghaus curve. Surprisingly, it was much less rapid. Where Ebbinghaus found that forgetting was rapid at first, Linton's loss of memory for the details of her own life proceeded at a slower, more constant rate. Although there are many differences in the two test situations, the key difference may be that because events in your life have *personal meaning,* they are not quickly forgotten. Many laboratory tests are designed to have no meaning, so there is no reason to remember them when the experiment is over.

MEMORY FOR DISTANT EVENTS To investigate memory for events long past, Bahrick, Bahrick, and Wittlinger (1975) tested the ability of high school graduates to recognize the names and faces of their former classmates. They chose nine groups from a variety of graduating classes (the youngest had graduated 3.3 months before, and the oldest, 47 years before). Each group consisted of about 50 people. All groups were shown photographs and asked to pick out any pictures they recognized. The data were quite surprising (Figure 9-5). Recognition of the faces of old classmates remained at over 90 percent for intervals up to 34 years! However, name recognition was not as durable; it dropped after 15 years (still a considerably long interval). This finding suggests that memory for names might be organized differently from memory for faces.

In another test of what is often called "very long-term" memory, Rubin (1977) tested elementary and college students on their recall of passages most of us learn in school: Hamlet's soliloquy, the Preamble to the Constitution, and the Twenty-third Psalm. There seem to be certain words and phrases that are remembered of each passage, although individuals differ in how many of them they remember. Figure 9-6 shows how many words 50 people remembered of Hamlet's soliloquy "To be or not to be."

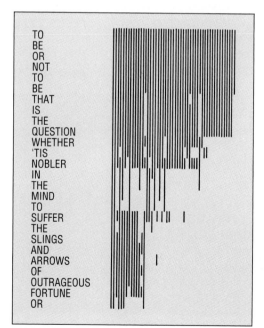

FIGURE 9-6
Very Long-Term Memory

Fifty subjects tested on how much of Hamlet's soliloquy they remembered showed the results charted here: each vertical line represents recall by one subject. How much do you recall of such material learned when you were in high school?
(Rubin, 1977)

Larry Squire (1989) recently tried to determine the time course of forgetting in very long-term memory. He asked about former television programs that had been broadcast for only one season from 1 to 15 years ago. He repeated the questions each year for nine consecutive years and calculated a forgetting curve by superimposing the results from the nine tests. Again, forgetting in very long-term memory was gradual and continuous for many years after learning.

FLASHBULB MEMORIES

When dramatic, life-altering, or life-threatening events happen, people are likely to recall an unusual amount of detail about their circumstances at the time the event occurs. Brown and Kulik (1977) called these vivid memories **flashbulb memories** because it seems as though, at these tense moments, the mind "takes a picture" of the scene. Your parents' generation likely remembers exactly where they were and what they were doing when they heard the news that President Kennedy was assassinated. You probably recall vividly your own circumstances when you saw or heard about the space shuttle *Challenger* explosion (Figure 9-7).

Two explanations have been offered for this phenomenon. The first is that the heightened affect of the person at the time of the event increases the strength of the person's memory. The fact that emotion affects recall has been demonstrated by Craik and Rubin (Craik, 1989), who had subjects listen to lists of words, some of which had emotional associations (breast, corpse, rapist). The subjects showed increased recall both of the emotional words over nonemotional words and of the context of hearing emotional words, in this case, which voice had spoken the word.

FIGURE 9-7
Flashbulb Memories

The image of the *Challenger* explosion is a flashbulb memory for many people.

The other proposed mechanism for flashbulb memories is that these memories are recalled with such detail because we use them as reference points in our lives. In our personal histories, we refer to these exciting events as turning points and rehearse them over and over (Neisser, 1982; Reisberg et al., 1984).

RECOGNITION OF PICTURES AND ODORS

Our ability to remember our high school classmates for so long is impressive. We have an enormous capacity in recognition memory for pictures. In one study, Shepard (1967) selected 612 familiar pictures and allowed subjects to review slides of the pictures at their own pace. Immediately afterward, recognition was 96.7 percent. After 120 days, the subjects still recognized more than 50 percent of the pictures (Figure 9-8).

Are other kinds of information remembered as vividly as pictures? Smell is our most direct sense, so an important component of real-world memories is odor. Marcel Proust, in the famous passage from *Swann's Way,* describes how the smell of madeleine cookies summoned up details of his childhood. You have probably noticed how cities have characteristic odors. The London underground has an unpleasant but distinctive odor; I always feel I am *really* in London when I smell it.

Brown University has a collection of more than 100 different odors, ranging from a skunk's scent to whiskey. In one experiment, subjects sniffed 48 cotton balls, each saturated with a different odor. Afterward, a second group of odors was presented, including many from the first group; 69 percent of the odors were recognized as having been in the first group (Engen & Ross, 1973). While this is very high, it is not as high as picture recognition. However, there seems to be no decline in odor recognition; recognition was 70 percent one week later and 68 percent one month later.

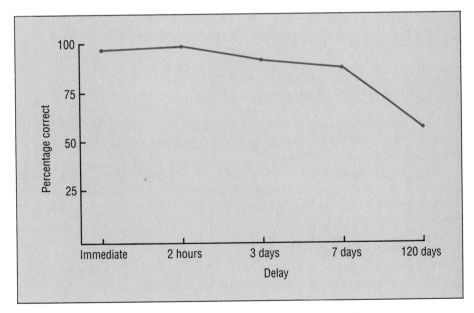

FIGURE 9-8
Recognition of Pictures

People have a great ability to recognize photographs, even long after they are first seen.
(Shepard, 1967)

HOW WE FORGET AND WHAT WE REMEMBER

We all know people who seem to have a good memory for faces but not for numbers. Other people can remember stories well but not directions. "Absent-minded professors" may remember specific details of the Peloponnesian War but cannot remember to pick up their laundry.

Francis Galton (1874) surveyed an eminent group of subjects: British men of science. He found that some relied primarily on vision to remember things, while others relied more on words. In a more recent, though still exploratory, study, Herrmann and Neisser (1978) developed a questionnaire called the Inventory of Memory Experiences (IME), which asks respondents how often they remember and forget different kinds of things. Their analysis reveals eight characteristics that distinguish individual memories (Herrmann & Neisser, 1978):

1. *Rote memory.* Forgetting such things as numbers and addresses and having to recheck them.
2. *Absentmindedness.* Forgetting what one has just done or intended to do.
3. *Names.* The ability or inability to recall people's names.
4. *People.* Recognizing individuals by their appearance.
5. *Conversation.* Remembering jokes, stories, and conversations.
6. *Errands.* Remembering things to do.
7. *Retrieval.* Inability to recall why something seems familiar.
8. *Place.* Where things are.

Although these findings are tentative, they suggest that an individual's memory may be assembled out of these components. One person may have a great memory for jokes and names but forget things to do. Another may easily remember where things are but have difficulty in remembering why someone's face is familiar. Further research may reveal which of these components of memory are associated with one another.

MEMORY AND THE BRAIN

Different forms of damage to the brain can affect the storing and retrieval of memory. This search for how memory is distributed in the brain is one of psychology's most exciting pursuits.

Epileptic seizures often overstimulate and damage parts of the limbic system. When the hippocampus is affected, either by the epilepsy or by subsequent surgery, there are profound affects on memory. Here is an example of an interview with such a patient:

You: Good morning Mr. H. M.

H. M.: Good morning.

You: I wonder whether you could answer a few questions?

H. M.: Fine, go ahead.

You: Who was president of the US during World War II?

H. M.: Franklin Roosevelt, later Truman.

You: What did Truman do when a national rail strike was threatened?

H. M.: He nationalized the railways, or he threatened to.

The questions and answers continue, until you begin to wonder whether there is any deficit in memory. Then the phone rings and you excuse yourself to take an urgent call. You return.

You: Sorry, H.M., to interrupt our session.

H. M.: I beg your pardon, have we met before? I don't seem to remember you. (Ornstein, Thompson, & Macaulay, 1984).

It hits you: H. M. cannot remember what is happening to him *now;* he lives in a kind of perpetual present. Everything he has learned since his surgery is forgotten almost immediately, just as when you jot down a phone number and then quickly forget it. But note that H. M. has retained his previous memories, such as language and what an interview is. Perhaps the damage to the hippocampus has affected his ability to lay down new memories, while leaving alone his ability to retrieve old ones.

AMNESIA

Amnesia, the general name for deficits in learning and memory that occur abruptly, can take many different forms and can involve many different brain mechanisms. This multiplicity of causes suggests that there are a great variety of pathways for memory storage in the brain (Squire, 1987). Amnesia can occur from damage to the frontal lobe, from damage due to electroconvulsive shock, and from lesions to the hippocampus and amygdala. Lesions can occur in one or both hemispheres of the brain.

Thus, all amnesia is not the same, just as all memory is not one system (Squire, Amaral, Zola-Morgan, Kritchevsky, & Press, 1989). People may be deficient in recalling past events or current events, in learning new distinctions or remembering old ones, or in recognizing people or places. All these distinctions, confusing as they may be to the student and the scientist, are nevertheless of great excitement. For the first time, different forms of memory (such as those distinctions proposed by Hermann & Neisser) have been identified by different lesions in the brain (Lynch, McGaugh, & Weinberger, 1984; Squire, 1987).

Janowsky et al. (1989) showed that frontal lobe pathology accounts for some of the cognitive impairment. They gave various cognitive and memory tests to patients with circumscribed frontal lobe lesions, to those with other forms of brain damage, and to control subjects. Patients with frontal lobe lesions showed impairment on the Wisconsin Card Sorting Test and on subscales of the Dementia Rating Scale.

Benzing and Squire (1989) showed that amnesia is specific because amnesic patients acquired at a normal rate the ability to perceive binocular depth using random-dot stereograms. So amnesics benefited from recent experience, despite the fact that they could not remember their prior experience accurately.

So, what kind of information do amnesic patients acquire when they can do well on tests of cued recall and recognition memory? Shimamura and Squire (1988) had amnesic patients and control subjects try to learn sets of sentences. Memory for the last word in each sentence was tested after one hour in the case of the amnesic patients, or after one to two weeks in the case of control subjects. Amnesics and controls performed at similar levels. The amnesics were just as confident of their correct answers as were the control subjects and were not any more disadvantaged than the control subjects when they were given paraphrases of the original sentences. So the representational memory retained by amnesic patients can be as flexible, as accessible to indirect cues, and as available to awareness as normal.

THE BRAIN'S STORAGE OF INFORMATION

Mortimer Mishkin and his colleagues may have uncovered some of the basic memory pathways and mechanisms. They studied the role that various parts of the brain play in the transmission and storage of information in memory by testing what deficits appeared in monkeys' abilities to perform memory tasks when parts of the brains had been surgically destroyed.

Monkey brains are similar to human brains, but the human brain is far more complex, thus we have to be careful about assuming that the human brain works like a monkey's. For example, monkeys do not have language abilities, so human memory circuits might be considerably modified from a monkey's to accommodate language memories.

Mishkin's work suggests that memories are actually stored in the higher level processing areas of sensory systems. One of these areas is the *inferotemporal cortex*, part of the visual system which has cells that respond to complex shapes, rather than the simple line-detection cells common in the primary visual cortex. If memories are stored in the sensory areas, this would explain why people with damaged limbic systems, like H. M., can remember past events but cannot record new ones. The hippocampus and amygdala seem to be involved in processing and transmitting sensory messages so that they are stored in memory. If both hippocampus and amygdala of a monkey are removed, the monkey will no longer be able to learn to recognize new objects.

This deficit is like H. M.'s, and is called *global anterograde amnesia* (global because it encompasses all senses; anterograde because the deficit is to memory following damage). The amygdala appears to be involved in the formation of many types of memory and association, and the hippocampus seems to help with remembering the location of objects. Mishkin hypothesized that sensory impressions are sent from sensory areas of the cortex to the hippocampus and amygdala.

Several integrating processes may occur here: information from different sensory areas is linked in the amygdala. Monkeys with damaged amygdalas could recognize past seen objects when seen again, but they could not recognize an object by sight that they had previously only felt. Normal monkeys can do this task easily.

The amygdala may also connect sensory memories with emotions by sending opiumlike neurotransmitters to the sensory areas as memories are stored. Once the hippocampal and amygdal memory circuits are activated by sensory input, they may in turn activate an area called the *basal forebrain.* The basal forebrain receives input from the hippocampus and amygdala and sends fibers back out to the limbic system and the cortex. It transmits with acetylcholine, a neurotransmitter known to have a strong affect on memory. The messages it sends to the sensory cortex may act to strengthen and thereby store the neural representation of a sensory event. A chemical reaction that may be related to long-term changes in synapses, which may be how memories are laid down, has been found to occur mostly in the final stations of cortical sensory processing.

Mishkin and his co-workers have also found hints about how we can learn habitlike skills, which are more like stimulus-response behaviors. Monkeys that cannot do recognition tasks because they lack a hippocampus and an amygdala can learn to respond to a stimulus that always results in a reward. This type of memory shares features with the idea of procedural memory. In the forebrain is a structure called the *striatum,* which receives input from the cortex (including the sensory cortex) and projects to movement centers of the brain. These connections seem to be ideal for linking sensory perceptions with actions. Disruption of the striatum prevents monkeys from learning new habits.

It is likely that there will soon be a breakthrough in the neural coding of memory (Thompson, 1989). Many theories have been proposed (Lynch et al., 1984; Squire, 1987; Thompson, 1985); but none yet can encompass even one of the different forms of memory considered in this chapter.

MEANINGFULNESS AND ORGANIZATION IN MEMORY

THE IMPORTANCE OF CONTEXT

Quickly read the following story, and then, before reading on, jot down what you remember of it.

> With hocked gems financing him, our hero bravely defied all scornful laughter that tried to prevent his scheme. "Your eyes deceive," he had said. "An egg, not a table, correctly typifies this unexplored planet." Now three sturdy sisters sought proof. Forging along, sometimes through calm vastness, yet more often very turbulent peaks and valleys, days became weeks as many doubters spread fearful rumors about the edge. At last from nowhere welcome winged creatures appeared, signifying momentous success. (Dooling & Lachman, 1971)

You probably remembered next to nothing of this passage. Now read the story again, but this time consider the context: the story is about Columbus's voyage to America. Dooling and Lachman found that people who had been given the *context* remembered much more than those who had not. The main function of **context** is to provide a way of organizing information *beforehand,* therefore making it more memorable. A title usually announces an overall context and makes part of what is read more accessible, as naming fruits aids recall of other fruits.

The context of a story affects what we remember. Because of context, we remember some events better than others. Although it is difficult to study how different people organize information into a meaningful memory, here is a demonstration of how context, when deliberately altered, can affect memory.

Read the following story (Bransford & Johnson, 1974) *once* and do not reread any part of it. Then write down or recite what you remember of it.

Watching a Peace March from the 40th Floor

The view was breathtaking. From the window one could see the crowd below. Everything looked extremely small from such a distance but the colorful costumes could still be seen. Everyone seemed to be moving in one direction in an orderly fashion, and there seemed to be little children as well as adults. The landing was gentle, and luckily the atmosphere was such that no special suits had to be worn. At first there was a great deal of activity. Later, when the speeches started, the crowd quieted down. The man with the television camera took many shots of the setting and the crowds. Everyone was very friendly and seemed glad when the music started.

Did you write down anything about the sentence "The landing was gentle and luckily the atmosphere was such that no special suits had to be worn"? In one experiment, only 18 percent of the subjects recalled something about the sentence. With a different context, however, recollection of this sentence is improved. Now reread the story, but this time under the title "A Space Trip to an Uninhabited Planet." Now the sentence "The landing was gentle . . ." makes sense. Of the subjects who read the story with this title, 53 percent recalled the sentence. You might try this out on a couple of friends, giving both of them the story, but each one a different title. Then compare their recollections.

The word *context* comes from the Latin word meaning "to weave together." When information is presented in a context that is meaningful to an individual, it is remembered more easily. Information is woven into an already meaningful background. All the schemata associated with the new information are activated.

THE EXPERIENCE OF TIME

The same process underlies how we experience time. We may feel these events passing quickly or dragging on. We say we have a sense of time, but there is no actual sensory organ (like the eye) for the experience of time.

TIME THAT HAS PASSED: DURATION   The experience of time passing is based on the same principles of memory we describe. Albert Einstein once explained his theory of relativity this way: "When you sit with a pretty girl for two hours, it seems like two minutes; when you sit on a hot stove for two minutes, it seems like two hours. That's relativity." Enjoyable activity seems to go by quickly.

Memory of duration, however, is also based on the number of things that occur during that time. The fewer the number of events in a given time, the shorter it will seem when you remember it later (Ornstein, 1969). People who have taken mind-stimulating drugs (like LSD) report later that time seems to be expanded under the drug. If you wait an hour with nothing to do, it may seem like an eternity while you are waiting, but that hour will probably disappear from memory and in retrospect seem quite short.

MEMORY STORAGE SPACE AND TIME   The more we remember of a given situation, the longer it seems. We experience a piece of music that contains 40 sounds per

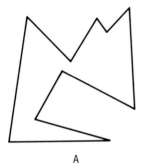

**FIGURE 9-9
Time Worth
Remembering**

The same amount of time spent looking at the simpler pattern (A) will be recalled as shorter than the same period spent contemplating the more interesting figure (B). The effect holds true for experiences of all kinds.
(Ornstein, 1969)

CHAPTER 9 / REMEMBERING AND FORGETTING

minute as shorter than one with 80 per minute (Ornstein, 1969). In one study, people were given 30 seconds to look at Figure 9-9A; then they were given 30 seconds to look at Figure 9-9B. Later they were asked which time period was longer. The subjects estimated that the time spent looking at the more complicated figure (B) was 20 percent longer than the time looking at the simple figure (A).

Ultimately, the sense of time is constructed out of memory of experience. We judge periods of time by how much we remember about them—that is, how much **storage space** they take up. If you are on an interesting vacation, each day is filled with new experiences, people, and places. At the end of a couple of weeks, it is as if you have been on vacation forever. When you return home, at first your memories and descriptions of the experience are quite complex: "We went to Waikiki Beach, ate mahi-mahi in a famous restaurant, listened to Dorman's orchestra, traveled by sailboat to Maui, stayed in the little cottage. . . ." Later, memory may change. It may be simply, "I went to Hawaii for two weeks last year and had a great time." In a study that bears on this, people perceived and remembered an interval containing a successful event as shorter than one with a failure (Harton, 1938). Increased organization and automatization decrease the storage space required and the time needed to recall a memory. Automatic experiences, such as driving a car over familiar terrain, seem shorter than the same amount of time in unfamiliar territory.

I conducted an experiment on the effect of organizing memory on the experience of time. Look at Figure 9-10A. Before reading on or turning the page to look at Figure 9-10B, try to describe Figure 9-10A. Groups of subjects were also asked to look at and describe this figure. One group was given no organizing principle, the second group was told the figure was the word *Man* written on top of its mirror image, and the third group was told that it was an insect. Those who were told it was the word *Man* were able to construct it much faster than the other two groups. The more organized the figure was in memory, the easier and faster it was described, in other words, the experience of duration shortened. Time experience, then, seems to be based on how much we remember and how that memory is organized (Ornstein, 1969).

FIGURE 9-10A
Time and Memory Experiment

Study this figure for a few moments then cover it. Now try to draw it from memory (do this *before* you look at the next page). Difficult, isn't it?
(Ornstein, 1969)

HOW INFORMATION IS ORGANIZED INTO MEANINGFUL UNITS

EFFECT OF SCHEMATA ON MEMORY

In 1932, F. C. Bartlett wrote an important book on remembering, in which he demonstrated the important effects of a person's existing knowledge structure on memory. The method he used in his experiments is similar to the children's games "telephone" and "whisper down the lane." A subject is given an original stimulus, either a drawing or a story, and asked to reproduce it. That person then passes on his or her reproduction to the next person, who reproduces it, and so on. Bartlett called this method *serial reproduction*. The stimuli Bartlett chose were deliberately exotic, unfamiliar to residents of Cambridge, England, where he did his research.

One example of serial reproduction is a series of drawings that begin with an African drawing, *Portrait d'Homme* (Figure 9-11). In these drawings, the

subjects transformed figures to correspond with what was already in their memories. According to Bartlett, unfamiliar features "invariably suffer transformation in the direction of the familiar" (1932)—that is, people have a tendency to transform odd or unfamiliar figures into conventional or familiar ones. In each successive reproduction of the African drawing, the original unconventional characteristics are dropped. The final figure is an ordinary schematic representation of a face. It is interesting, however, that the exotic qualities of the original drawing are retained in the transformation of the name *Portrait d'Homme* (portrait of a man) to *L'Homme Egyptien* (Egyptian man).

Bartlett also presented an unusual story to his students, an Indian tale. Again, each subject was asked to reproduce what he or she remembered from the previous subject's version of the story. The original story is recounted below.

FIGURE 9-10B

This figure contains the same basic elements as Figure 9-10A only moved further apart so that the organizing principle emerges. It now would be much easier and faster to draw from memory.
(Ornstein, 1969)

The War of the Ghosts

One night two young men from Egulac went down to the river to hunt seals, and while they were there it became foggy and calm. Then they heard war-cries, and they thought: "Maybe this is a war-party." They escaped to the shore, and hid behind a log. Now canoes came up, and they heard the noise of the paddle, and saw one canoe coming up to them. There were five men in the canoe, and they said:

"What do you think? We wish to take you along. We are going up the river to make war on the people."

One of the young men said: "I have no arrows."

"Arrows are in the canoe," they said.

"I will not go along. I might be killed. My relatives do not know where I have gone. But you," he said, turning to the other, "may go with them."

So one of the young men went, but the other returned home.

And the warriors went on up the river to a town on the other side of Kalama. The people came down to the water, and they began to fight, and many were killed. But presently the young man heard one of the warriors say: "Quick, let us go home: that Indian has been hit." Now he thought: "Oh, they are ghosts." He did not feel sick, but they said he had been shot.

So the canoes went back to Egulac, and the young man went ashore to his house, and made a fire. And he told everybody and said: "Behold I accompanied the ghosts, and we went to fight. Many of our fellows were killed, and many of those who attacked us were killed. They said I was hit, and I did not feel sick."

He told it all, and then he became quiet. When the sun rose he fell down. Something black came out of his mouth. His face became contorted. The people jumped up and cried.

He was dead.

Now here is an example of one of the final reproductions of the story:

Two Indians from Momapan were fishing for seals when a boat came along containing five warriors. "Come with us," they said to the Indians, "and help us to fight the warriors further on." The first Indian replied: "I have a mother at home, and she would grieve greatly if I were not to return." The other Indian said, "I have no weapons." "We have some in the boat," said the warriors. The Indian stepped into the boat.

In the course of the fight further on, the Indian was mortally wounded, and his spirit fled. "Take me to my home," he said, "at Momapan, for I am going to die." "No, you will not die," said a warrior. In spite of this, however, he died, and before he could be carried back to the boat, his spirit had left this world.

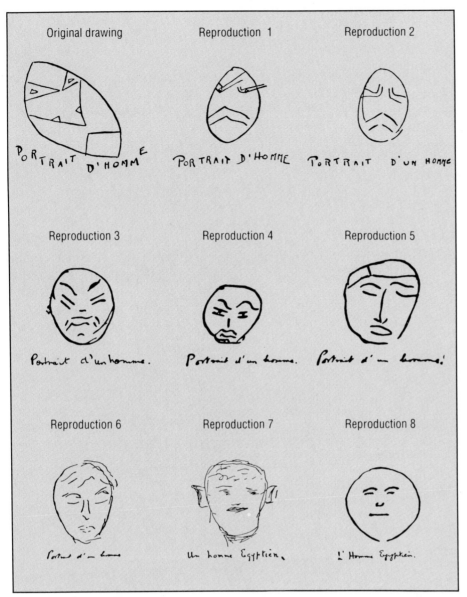

FIGURE 9-11
Portrait d'Homme

These successive drawings
show the transformation of
the unfamiliar in the direction
of the familiar.
(Bartlett, 1932)

The effects of the English student's organization are clear: the story has been transformed into a more conventional one. The original distinctive names are gone, although "Momapan" has been added. Bartlett says, "The story has become more coherent, as well as much shorter. No trace of any odd or supernatural element is left: we have a perfectly straightforward story of a fight and a death." Things that do not match the common schemata of an Englishman are omitted or transformed into the familiar: canoes become boats, and references to ghosts are omitted. What occurred here is similar to what happened in your recollection of "Watching a Peace March from the 40th Floor." We tend to omit elements that do not fit in with what we know already.

A unit of memory is called a *chunk*. In perceiving and remembering bits of information, **chunking** is the process of using a *code* to organize the individual items into units of memory. GEAIMNN is a list of seven bits that you can probably retain only briefly. MEANING is a list of the same seven bits, but you have a code (in this case, the English language) that organizes them into a chunk (in this case, the word *meaning*). The ability to chunk information greatly expands the storage capacity of memory because small chunks can be combined into larger chunks that are then more easily remembered (Figure 9-12).

Knowing a code increases the capacity of memory and the ability to remember. Read the following list of numbers quickly: 41236108324972. Now write down what you remember; most likely you remembered only about seven of the numbers. Now, here is a code to follow: begin with 4, then multiply it by 3; then multiply this product by 3 again; repeat this multiplication three more times. With these instructions, you need not *memorize* any of the numbers; the code tells you where to begin, what to do, and where to stop.

Here is another example. Read the following lists quickly and see if you can devise a code to help you remember them.

IB MF BI TW AJ FK

816 449 362 516 941

If you had to reproduce the two lists above, the simple way would be to notice that the top line includes four well-known acronyms (such as IBM) and that the bottom row includes the squares of all single-digit numbers in descending order from 9. We could easily reproduce the lists as

IBM FBI TWA JFK

81 64 49 36 25 16 9 4 1

FIGURE 9-12
Chunking

It is easier to count the dots on the right (B) because they are arranged in groups, or chunks.

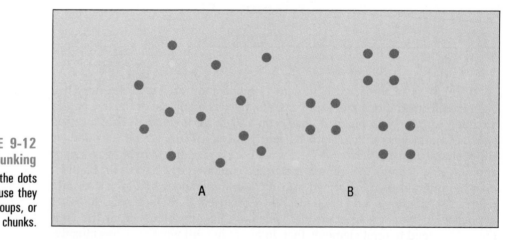

THE RECONSTRUCTIVE NATURE OF REMEMBERING

Various kinds of information can color or change our memory of the past. In one study designed by Elizabeth Loftus, researchers showed subjects a reddish orange disc. One group was told it was a tomato; the other group was told it was an orange. Later the two groups were shown colors and were asked to select the color that most closely matched the color they saw. The group that had been told the disc was an orange selected a color close to orange; the group that had been told the disc was a tomato selected a color closer to red (Loftus, 1978). In another demonstration, two groups of subjects were presented with ambiguous sketches (Figure 9-13). Each drawing was labeled with a word. Although both groups saw the same drawings, they were each given a different set of word labels. For example, the first sketch was presented with the word *eyeglasses* or with the word *dumbbell.*

Immediately after each presentation, the subjects were asked to reproduce the figure they had seen as accurately as possible. The subjects' drawings were influenced by the label they had been given. In the case of the first sketch, some subjects attempted to reproduce eyeglasses or a dumbbell rather than the original ambiguous figure (Carmichael, Hogan, & Walters, 1932).

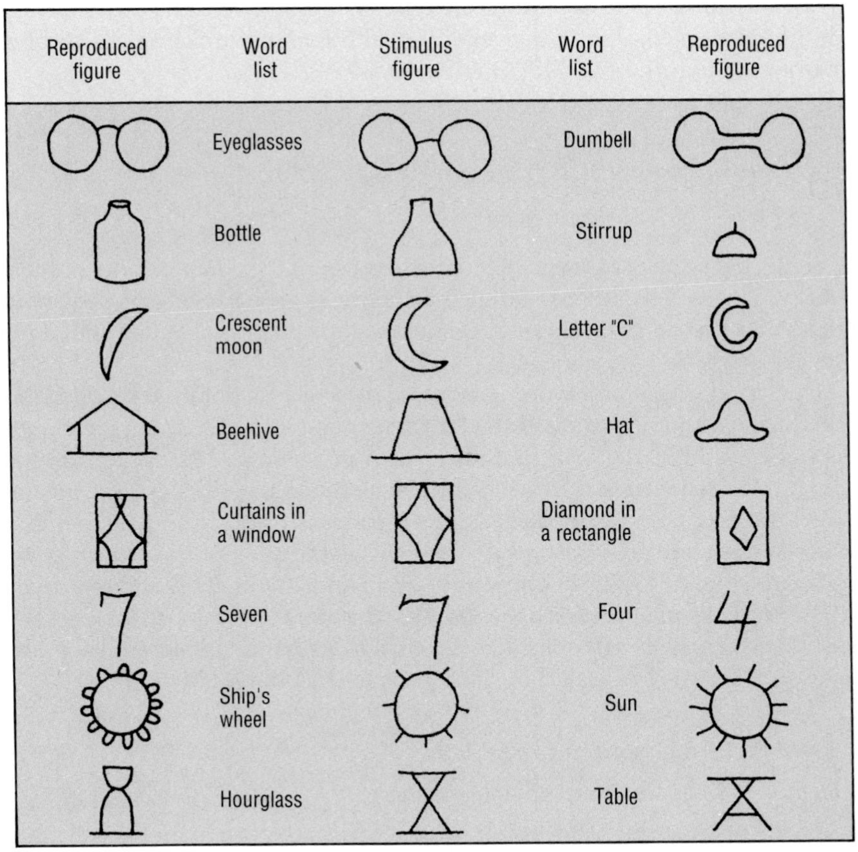

FIGURE 9-13
Labeling and Remembering

The name something is given influences our memory of it, as this chart demonstrates. Subjects in an experiment recalled and reproduced ambiguous doodles as more like the labels given them than did subjects given different labels for the same doodles.
(Carmichael, Hogan, & Walters, 1932)

EYEWITNESS TESTIMONY

The reconstructive nature of memory is sufficient for everyday life. We do not need to know things in complete detail, nor are we capable of recalling literally *every* detail of an experience, even what a penny looks like. But when details are important, perhaps a matter of life and death, the reconstructive nature of memory can become a problem.

No courtroom testimony is more effective than a witness who stands, points a finger at someone, and says, "It's him. I saw him do it with my own eyes." We have such confidence in our memory that the power of an eyewitness's testimony is not easily overcome, even if it is successfully challenged by other testimony. But an understanding of the malleability of memory should make us more wary. Many innocent people have been accused and sentenced to prison on the basis on the testimony of an eyewitness (Loftus et al., 1978).

Memory is influenced not only by previous knowledge but also by events that happen between the time an event is perceived and the time it is recalled. In one experiment, people were shown a film of a traffic accident and later asked questions about what they had seen (Figure 9-14). The key question in the first part of the test was "How fast were the cars going when they *smashed* into each other?" For some groups the word *smashed* was replaced by less aggressive verbs, such as *hit, bumped,* or *collided.* A week later the groups were asked, "Did you see any broken glass?" More of those who had been asked the question with the word *smashed* in it answered yes, although no broken glass had been shown in the film (Loftus, Miller, & Burns, 1978).

LEVELS OF PROCESSING

No single theory has yet been able to tie together all the complex phenomena of memory. One recent attempt at such a theory is called **levels of processing,** which states that all information presented to us is processed at different depths or levels.

The visual image of a word is received as sensory stimuli, transduced into neural signals, and then transformed by perception into something meaningful. This stage would be the first, shallow level of processing. At a deeper level, the word and the sentence it is in are identified and understood. Next, the meaning of the sentence may trigger associations (images, stories, or similar events) on the basis of the subject's past experience; this is the deepest level of processing (Craik & Lockhart, 1972). In one study, Craik and Tulving (1975) hypothesized that the more deeply processed a word was, the more likely it would be recalled. Their method was to ask questions about the "semantic qualities" of a word. These qualities were revealed by such questions as the following:

- *Structural:* Is the word in capital letters?
- *Phonemic:* Does the word rhyme with *weight?*
- *Semantic:* Would the word fit into a sentence, such as "He met a _____ in the street"?

FIGURE 9-14
Eyewitness Testimony

Memory can be influenced by what is experienced between perceiving an event and when it is recalled. Thus, being told two cars collided or bumped into each other will make us recall a milder accident (top) than if we were told the cars "smashed" (bottom).

(Loftus, 1979)

Each type of question was intended to evoke a deeper level of processing, the deepest being the semantic, which concerns the *meaning* of the word.

Craik and Tulving found that it takes longer to process a word deeply, but that recognition and recall of words increase according to the depth at which they are processed. The semantic processing produced a higher amount of recall than the phonemic; the phonemic higher than the structural.

The levels of processing theory helps to explain why we may remember the same item differently depending upon how we process it. Reading a page of text to type it requires only shallow processing; less information is remembered than if it were being read to understand it.

RELATING INFORMATION TO YOURSELF

An important way to deepen processing is to try to relate the information to yourself. To the list of questions in Craik and Tulving's experiment, Rogers and his colleagues (1977) added the question "Describes you?" They found that people best remembered words they could relate to themselves (Figure 9-15). Both asking yourself such questions as "What would have made me do that?" and considering whether or not a given experience happened to you once increases the likelihood of recall. The reason for this increase in remembering may be that the richest set of associations in memory relates to ourselves. When information can be referred to an event in your own life, it is remembered longer (Bower, Gilligan, & Monteiro, 1981).

WHY DO WE REMEMBER MEANINGFUL EVENTS BETTER?

Although the idea of levels of processing offers a useful framework for understanding memory, it has been criticized as circular reasoning: "Deep processing leads to better memory because we remember something that is deeply processed." A possibly simpler, and therefore preferable, explanation is that successfully remembering an event depends primarily on the number of associations that this particular event calls up. One dominant view in psychology, which began with the British empiricists such as Locke and Hume and continued with James and many current researchers, is that the mind is best

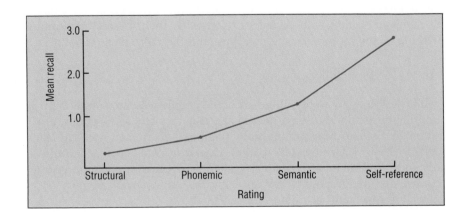

FIGURE 9-15
Memory and Self-Reference

You can deepen the processing of what you perceive and want to recall if you relate that information to yourself or to an event in your life.
(Rogers, Kulper, & Kirker, 1977)

How many times have you heard someone say, "I'll never forget the time I . . ."? Even though we often forget new things we learn, many important events in our lives and facts about the world seem almost impossible to forget. Here is a story that illustrates an extreme form of this phenomenon:

I'll Make You Remember

One day Latif the Thief ambushed the commander of the Royal Guard, captured him and took him to a cave.

"I am going to say something that, no matter how much you try, you will be unable to forget," he told the infuriated officer.

Latif made his prisoner take off all his clothes. Then he tied him, facing backwards, on a donkey.

"You may be able to make a fool of me," screamed the soldier, "but you'll never make me think of something if I want to keep it out of my mind."

"You have not yet heard the phrase which I want you to remember," said Latif. "I am turning you loose now, for the donkey to take back to town. And the phrase is: 'I'll catch and kill Latif the Thief, if it takes me the rest of my life!'" (Shah, 1982).

Why is Latif so sure the commander will remember the phrase? First of all, the phrase is highly

THINGS THAT ARE IMPOSSIBLE TO FORGET

meaningful. Most psychologists would explain this in terms of the number and strength of associations between the new phrase and the other knowledge in the commander's mind. All the words in the phrase are associated in his mind with their meanings and with all sorts of other information —both semantic and episodic memories. The associations to the concept of the commander's "self" are especially rich.

But more importantly, Latif knows that the commander will go on thinking about the phrase, constructing more and stronger associations between it and other knowledge all the time. Every time the commander looks at himself, the donkey, or anything else as he rides back to town, he will be reminded of how he got to be in this humiliating situation. And every time he thinks of that, he is likely to think again about how he will get revenge on Latif. Every image in his mind of another way of catching and killing the thief will add more and stronger associations to the phrase Latif wants him to remember. Thus, the phrase will be processed very deeply indeed and will be associated so strongly with so many other things that it will be almost impossible to forget.

TRYING NOT TO REMEMBER

Can you go for one minute without thinking of the word *elephant*? If

described as a network of associations. When something arises in consciousness, all associated schemata arise with it. Associations may be semantic, visual, or emotional.

Something is meaningful to us because it evokes many associations. Because the most meaningful information has the most associations, it is remembered better. They cluster, as James wrote, "like grapes to a stem." Each time a particular event occurs, the number of associations to it increases, and memory of that event is improved. Thus, relating information to ourselves serves to increase the number of associations to that event because we have the most items associated with ourselves. Generally, then, the more meaningful something is, the more associations it has, and the more memorable it is.

GREAT FEATS OF MEMORY

As with every human ability, there are some people who are simply born with extraordinary memories. Some people can play as many as 60 games of chess blindfolded. Some people can multiply long numbers in their heads as fast as a calculator (789054.78 times 657483.86). One man could look at 70 unrelated words and recall them perfectly a day later, and sometimes even a year later. These feats are made possible by applying the principles of memory and the memory improvement techniques described above.

you have ever tried it, you know it is very difficult. To understand this phenomenon (and much else about memory), you can imagine that each concept in your mind is like a dot (or node) and the associations between concepts are like lines (or links) between the dots. When you think about a concept, you activate that dot and the activation spreads along the lines to other concepts with which it is associated. In this way, you remember the other concepts as well (Collins & Quillian, 1972).

Now, when you are trying not to think about an elephant, you will have remembered your task by creating links between the concept of "what I am trying to do" and the concept of "elephant." Every time you think of what you are trying to do, activation spreads to the concept of elephant, and you are reminded of it whether you want to be or not.

In general, memory seems to depend mostly on the kinds of links you create in your mind and

very little on your direct intentions to remember. If you are trying to remember something, you can process it more deeply and thus establish more associations with it,

but unless you do establish these associations, you probably will not remember it any better than if you had not tried to remember it at all (Nelson, 1976).

IMPLICATIONS FOR TEACHING
This story has a lesson for teachers, too. If you are trying to get a student to learn something (whether the person wants to learn it or not), you should try to construct a situation in which the learner's own interests and inclinations will lead to the thoughts you want to encourage. Students' inclinations to be competitive are harmful in some situations, just as the commander's tendency to be vengeful was sometimes harmful. But, in the same way that Latif harnessed this vengefulness to achieve his goals, good teachers can sometimes harness their students' competitiveness for constructive purposes. For example, spelling bees use this competitive motivation to encourage students to learn spelling.

CHUNKING IN CHESS The chess masters who can play several games at once and blindfolded are not necessarily possessed of supernatural memory but are simply able to combine or chunk larger units of a chess game than ordinary chess players (see the earlier section on chunking and coding). Figure 9-16 shows a fairly common arrangement of chess pieces during an actual game.

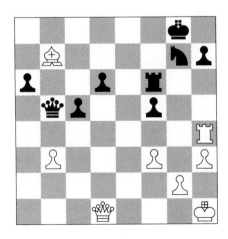

FIGURE 9-16
Chunking in Chess
Look briefly at the positions of the chess pieces and try to reproduce them without looking back at the page.

Several principles in this chapter may help you remember things better.

IMPROVING MEMORY BY CHANGING ENCODING

It is not useful to have learned something by heart if the information cannot be retrieved when needed. Exams test your ability to retrieve information, either by recognition or by recall. Have you ever heard someone say after an exam, "I knew the answer, but not the way the question was asked"? Concerning this problem, one psychologist writes:

The critical thing for most of the material you learn in school is to *understand* it, which means encoding it in a way that makes it distinctive from unrelated material and related to all the things it ought to be related to in order for you to use it. . . . The time you spend thinking about material you are reading and relating it to previously stored material is about the most useful thing you can do in learning any new subject matters. (Wickelgren, 1977)

Instead of simply memorizing by heart, ask "What does this mean?" Talking to a friend about what you have read is a good way to make sure you have grasped the central meaning.

IMPROVING MEMORY BY RELATING INFORMATION TO YOURSELF

As discussed previously, the self is the most efficient context for remembering. Try to relate material to your own past experience and knowledge. Psychology is almost tailor-made for efficient studying, since its subject is you. The demonstrations and examples in this book have been selected to help

IMPROVING MEMORY

you relate concepts to your own experience. So far, every chapter concerns information that bears on your life in some way. As we progress into the more individual aspects of psychology, you may have to associate information to a less familiar concept. Most people do not suffer from severe psychological abnormalities. However, noticing how you *differ* from someone who is seriously disturbed will help you retain the information.

TECHNIQUES FOR IMPROVING MEMORY

It is always easier to remember something according to a rule than by rote. It is simpler to remember the spelling rule "*i* before *e* except after *c*" and the few exceptions than to learn to spell every word containing *ie* or *c*.

Mnemonics

The best way to remember material with no apparent meaning is to *impose a context* that will serve as an aid to memory or will convert the material into something meaningful. Here is one of two methods for improving memory of meaningless events.

Mnemonics (the initial *m* is silent) is a straightforward, and sometimes fun, technique for aiding memory. There is nothing about the names of the months of the year that gives clues to the number of days they have. The rhyme "Thirty days hath September . . ." is a mnemonic to help you retrieve that information when you need it. To remember which way to change your clocks for Daylight Savings Time, a useful mnemonic is "Spring forward, fall back." People often use mnemonics to remember names. To remember someone named Scott McDonald, you might remember that his last name is the same as the fast food restaurant.

Mnemonics is often useful for remembering lists in a certain or-

Look at it briefly and, if you have a board, try to reproduce it quickly without referring back to the book. In one study, chess masters were able very quickly to reproduce most common chess arrangements; beginners could not (Chase & Simon, 1973). The arrangement formed one meaningful chunk of information to the masters. When Chase and Simon placed the chess pieces on a board at random, masters and beginners were equally inept at reproducing the positions.

THE GREAT RUSSIAN MNEMONIST   The most famous case of memorization is "S.," who was studied by the Russian psychologist Luria (1968). To gain a sense of the greatness of his feats, study this arrangement of numbers for three minutes.

563908972   878992111   389763009

der. Try associating each item with a previously learned, organized set of "peg words" such as in this example.

One is a bun   Six is sticks

Two is a shoe   Seven is heaven

Three is a tree   Eight is a gate

Four is a door   Nine is wine

Five is a hive   Ten is a hen

Now let's say you want to buy the following at the grocery store: lettuce, soup, paper towels, tomatoes, and chicken. Try to visualize these items with the above peg words. The more outrageous the association, the more likely you will remember it. Imagine lettuce on a bun, soup spilling out of your shoe, a tree with paper towels for leaves, eggs splattered all over the door, a hive full of tomatoes, and a chicken picking up sticks.

A word to the wise: choose your mnemonic carefully. A friend of mine, Betty Cone, said she knew exactly how the principle of her school tried to remember her name: he always called her Betty Pine.

Method of Loci

Visualizing items is another powerful aid to memory of meaning-less events (Bower, 1973). The **method of loci,** is a memory trick devised by the Greeks to create new and different associations to improve recall. Select a group of places that have some relationship with one another. As an illustration, every day you awaken in your bedroom, wash up in the bathroom, have breakfast in the kitchen or dining room, and walk or drive along a certain route. Associate the items in order with the different places, such as your bed, the sink, the dining room wall, and a tree that you pass. For the shopping list used above, you could imagine that the sheets on your bed are lettuce, that you are eating soup out of the sink, that paper towels are on the dining room table, and so on. The method of loci is effective because human memory is associative, and "putting things in their place" increases the number of associations.

Students can use several techniques to encode information and recall it.

Now try to reproduce it without looking. S. was able to do it in 40 seconds. Even more impressively, he could repeat it several months later! Luria writes: "The only difference in the two performances was that for the later one he needed time to revive the entire situation in which the experiment had been carried out; to 'see' the room in which he had been sitting; to 'hear' my voice; to 'reproduce' an image of himself looking at the board." S. thus encoded information with as *many meaningful associations as possible* to aid retrieval. He was especially adept at associating information with specific visual imagery. When trying to recall a particular list, S. said, "Yes . . . yes, that was a series you gave to me once when you were sitting in your apartment. You were sitting at the table and I was in the rocking chair. . . . You were wearing a gray suit and you looked at me like this" (Luria, 1968).

S. also used the *method of loci* in remembering, and this sometimes led to interesting mistakes. Trying to recall a particular list of words, he imagined a "mental walk" but missed the words *pencil* and *egg*.

> I put the image of the pencil near a fence . . . , the one down the street, you know. But what happened was that the image fused with that of the fence and I walked right on past without noticing it. The same thing happened with the word "egg." I had put it up against a white wall and it blended in with the background. How could I possibly spot a white egg up against a white wall?

S. had an extraordinary ability to visualize, but even so his methods are merely extensions of the principles discussed in this chapter: *making the associations between information meaningful by making those associations rich and complex.* Thus, as James said at the beginning of the chapter, facts will "cluster and cling" in the mind.

SUMMARY

1. *Memories* give us a sense of continuity between past and present. The more *associations* we have to something, the better we remember it. Memories are simpler than actual experiences. Meaningful events are remembered best.

2. Memory stores specific episodes, symbols, and rules for operating in the world. There are two types of declarative memory, which is our mental record of information used to recall events, think, and communicate. *Episodic memory* is our store of individual experiences. The many aspects of language are stored in *semantic memory*. *Procedural memory* contains automatized schemata for performing routine actions and guides movement. Unlike *declarative memory,* it is not subject to verbalization.

3. Memories are organized by related associations. Only a limited amount of information is accessible at a time. Items relevant to the current situation are brought to the fore. Three processes make up the memory cycle. In *perceptual encoding,* sensory information is organized into the simplest meaningful percepts. In most cases, memories are retained as long as needed. Things recalled tend to be striking, new, or important. Past events are brought into consciousness through *retrieval. Recognition* is the correct identification of an object or event. *Recall* is the ability to retrieve stored information in the absence of the relevant object or event.

4. Many psychologists hypothesize that there are two types of memory: short-term and long-term. The storage capacity of *short-term memory* is limited to about seven items, and it retains information for only a few seconds. Both declarative and procedural memories are stored as *long-term memories*. The storage capacity of long-term memory may be limitless. Scientists are using animal models to learn more about the way the brain stores memories.

5. Memory may not actually function like a computer memory storing data. It may be more like other physical changes caused by experience, like changes in muscle tissue resulting from exercise. The process of memory may act by causing us to change our modes of interacting with the world.

6. Instead of memory being divided into short- and long-term components, it may be a single, continuous process. The more an event or action is repeated, the greater the strength of associations to it, and the greater the likelihood that it will be

remembered. Because this theory is simpler and more inclusive than that of short- and long-term memory, many psychologists accept it as being more accurate.

7. The scientific study of memory began with controlled experiments on the rate of forgetting. Ebbinghaus discovered that most forgetting occurs immediately and tapers off with time. Experiences can interfere with remembering, either proactively or retroactively. *Interference* decreases with increased length of time between the first and second event. Similar events are more likely to interfere with each other.

8. Memory for real-life events proceeds at a slow, constant rate, unlike that for meaningless information such as is used in laboratory tests of memory. Memory for faces lasts longer than memory for names. People remember an unusual amount of detail about the circumstances in which dramatic events occur. Proposed mechanisms for these *flashbulb memories* are enhancements of memory by heightened affect. These memories are frequently rehearsed because they represent turning points in people's lives.

9. *Recognition memory* has an enormous capacity for pictures. Our ability to recognize odors is not as good, but there seems to be no decline in memory for odors. There are individual differences in memory, perhaps accountable for by individuals possessing different abilities for performing different types of memory tasks.

10. Studies of people with damaged brains reveal information about how the brain stores memories. The *hippocampus* is important to memory, as demonstrated by the deficiencies of H. M., who could remember events that had occurred prior to his injury but could not remember post-injury events. *Amnesia* is the general name for abruptly induced deficits in learning and memory. Amnesia can result from damage to the frontal lobes, electroconvulsive shock, or from lesions to the hippocampus or amygdala. Amnesics who cannot recall past events may function normally in remembering post-injury information.

11. Tests on monkeys suggest that memories are stored in the higher-level processing areas of sensory systems. The hippocampus and amygdala seem to be involved in processing and transmitting sensory messages so that they are stored in memory. The *amygdala* may integrate information from different sensory areas and connect sensory memories to emotions. Stimulus-response behaviors may be stored in the striatum of the forebrain.

12. *Context* provides a means of organizing information, making it more memorable. The more meaningful the context, the better information will be recalled. Context also affects the experience of time. Memory of duration is based on the number of events that occur during a period of time. The more that is remembered of a scene, the longer it seems. Organized and simple memories are recalled easier and faster than complex or chaotic ones.

13. We use schemata that we already possess to transform our memories of experience into familiar patterns. We tend to omit elements that don't fit with what we already know. Using a code to organize items in memory is called *chunking*. Knowing a code increases the capacity of memory. Memory is *reconstructive*, not photographic. It is influenced by previous knowledge and events between the remembered event and the attempt to recall it.

14. The theory of *levels of processing* states that information is processed to different depths, from neural transduction to semantic processing. It takes more time to process words deeply, but memory for them increases with depth of processing. One way to increase depth of processing is to relate events to oneself. This may work by creating more associations with schemata in our minds. We cannot easily try not to remember something because of the way associations are linked.

15. When teaching, it may be useful to construct situations in which the material being taught is associated with the learner's personal interests. People who perform extraordinary feats of memory use the basic principles of *chunking* to enhance the associations and meaningfulness of memories.

TERMS AND CONCEPTS

amnesia
chunking
context
declarative memory
encoding
episodic memory
flashbulb memory
levels of processing
long-term memory
memory cycle
memory system
method of loci
mnemonics

nonsense syllables
primacy
proactive interference
procedural memory
recall
recency
recognition
retention
retrieval
retroactive interference
semantic memory
short-term memory
storage space

SUGGESTIONS FOR FURTHER READING

Squire, L. (1987). *Memory and the brain.* New York: Oxford.

One of the leading theorists about how memory is stored in the brain presents his theories.

10
THINKING AND LANGUAGE

magine that you are an executive of your town council, and you receive a report saying that a large capital expense is essential to correct hazards on a main road on the outskirts of your town. Repaving is needed and a guard rail should be put up at Goose Curve. But during the town meeting financial consultants caution you that the $100,000 assessment would raise property taxes. You feel it is irresponsible to spend so much at a time when money is tight, so you decide against the improvements for now.

You drive home thinking it's too bad the funds aren't there for the highway safety measures. You know they are important; you think, maybe next year. You decide to go two miles out of your way and look at Goose Curve yourself. It has gotten dark and begun raining; the boring budget battles still pack your mind. Then, suddenly, you see skid marks all over the road. You follow slowly and hope all is well. It is probably old Johnson drunk again, you think, most likely driving too fast under the influence. You hope that he didn't go over the edge of the cliff.

But he did. Wild, slashing tire tracks lead to a spot where the lip of the gully has been broken off very recently. It's pouring and late, but you slam on the brakes and leap out of the car, your mind filled with fear. You begin to climb down the hill, and then you see Johnson, lying in a pool of blood, thrown out of his car, his arm and head bleeding.

You struggle up the hill carrying Johnson on your shoulder, blood pouring over your suit and shoes, but you don't care. Your heart is pounding, and a surge of adrenaline gives you the strength to make it to the top of the hill. You breathe a sigh of relief and gently lay Johnson in the back seat of your car and you race to the hospital. On the way to the hospital you think, if only that guard rail had been there, this could have been prevented. You make a firm resolve that tomorrow you will convene a special session of the town council and push to get the guard rail issue passed immediately.

Follow the trains of thought during both the budget meeting and the emergency. In both, the thought processes seem logical and lead to obvious conclusions. From the perspective of the town council, the matter of the guard rail was of minor concern and did not seem to warrant any increase in expenditures in an already tight budget. Most people would agree that this makes sense.

But our point of view can shift drastically from encounter to encounter. In the emergency, this same issue (of putting in a guard rail) is suddenly magnified to fill our perspective. It becomes impossible not to help someone who is badly injured, and the issue of the guard rail becomes dominant.

The processes we examine in this chapter share a common theme: our minds select a few simplified elements, which can be combined and recombined to create new and diverse thoughts. A similar process underlies language. English has only a few elements—26 letters—but those few elements can be combined to form an almost infinite number of different sentences. The creative process, then, is as basic to us as simplification and selection.

CLASSIFICATION INTO CATEGORIES

Thinking involves simplification: we select a bit of information and base our decisions on it. Helping us to cut our way through the complex world are the simplifying mental structures that underlie thought. Psychologists have defined two different structures of thought: we classify using *categories* and simplify using *heuristics.*

Classification is a major simplifying function in mental life. Without it we would have to identify and decide on *each* shading of color, *each* idea, and *each* feeling every time we encountered it. For example, the human visual system can discriminate 7,500,000 colors; however, we commonly use only 8 color names (Coren & Ward, 1989).

THE FUNCTION OF CATEGORIES

The primary function of categorizing is to *simplify;* to give the most information with the least effort. It is simpler to call a tomato, a sunset, and an apple "red" than to identify them by "orangey red," "luminescent red-orange with streaks of blue and black," and "pure red speckled with green." We *can* do all this, but it is unnecessary and wasteful unless we are engaged in creative writing. For most purposes, the word "red" is enough. A **category,** then, is a grouping of objects or concepts that can be considered equivalent in an important dimension.

Categories are not random and arbitrary; rather, they are part of a mental model that reflects events and occurrences in the world. Most objects in our world are made up of a combination of predictable features. Wings are more likely to have feathers than fur on them; legs are found on animals, not trees. Rooms do not move on their own; people breathe, rocks do not. Certain aspects of the world seem to go together, and categories reflect this: we can consider dogs to be more similar to cats than to airplanes.

NATURAL AND ARTIFICIAL CATEGORIES

Some categories are universal, probably because there are universal truths in the world. These categories of natural phenomena are called **natural categories.** Color is a natural category because it is a universal response to the environment. Recall from Figure 5-13 that the human visual system codes information in two ways: in black-white and in color combinations of red, yellow, green, and blue. In a study of almost 100 languages, Berlin and Kay (1969) determined that color terms always appear in the following sequence:

$$\begin{Bmatrix} \text{white} \\ \text{black} \end{Bmatrix} \rightarrow \text{red} \rightarrow \begin{Bmatrix} \text{green} \\ \text{yellow} \\ \text{blue} \end{Bmatrix} \rightarrow \text{brown} \rightarrow \begin{Bmatrix} \text{purple} \\ \text{pink} \\ \text{orange} \\ \text{gray} \end{Bmatrix}$$

If a language has only two color terms, they will be black and white; if it has three, they will be black, white, and red. If it contains four, that fourth color will be green, yellow, or blue. The fifth and sixth colors will be the remaining two of green, yellow, and blue. Any additional color terms will identify the remaining secondary and tertiary colors. So the categories of our color descriptions follow the structure of the nervous system (Brown, in press).

In addition to these basic natural categories, there are other **artificial categories** that refer to the attributes of *constructed* objects such as chairs or buildings. People have no trouble judging the relative qualities of natural categories but have more disagreement and difficulty in artificial categories; it is easier to judge whether something is "more red" than whether something is "more of a chair" than another.

Categories can also be influenced by culture. An American traveling in Italy would probably have to convert 15,000 lira into dollars to find out if that was a good price for a pair of shoes. In the United States the most commonly used measures are inches, feet, yards, miles, Fahrenheit, and so on. If the weather report predicted that it was going to be 38 degrees Celsius, most of us would have to translate that figure into Fahrenheit to know if it were hot or cold.

CHARACTERISTICS OF CATEGORIES

BASIC LEVEL   Categories can range from extremely broad to quite detailed. A broad category is, say, the concept *furniture*. Furniture is relatively abstract; there are few specific features common to all items of furniture, but furniture may be many different things: chairs, beds, cabinets, tables. Each of these is also a category itself (Figure 10-1). Tables have clear perceptual distinctions: they have legs, a flat top, and other features in common that differentiate them from chairs. Tables even have subdivisions: diningroom tables, coffee tables, wood tables, antique tables. The category *table*, however, seems to represent the level at which we most naturally divide the world. It is called a **basic level category,** which generally comprises the concepts first learned by children, such as table, apple, and dog (Glass et al., 1989).

FIGURE 10-1
Categories

This diagram shows how the category "furniture" might be divided into basic levels and further subdivided into subcategories.

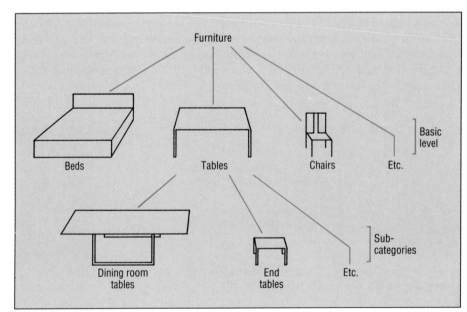

CHAPTER 10 / THINKING AND LANGUAGE

Which is more typical of the prototype *bird*: a chicken or a robin?

TYPICALITY AND PROTOTYPES   A category centers around a **prototype,** which is the example that most typifies the category (Rosch & Mervis, 1975)—as when a strong, agile man is a "typical athlete" or when love of wine is "typically French." Still, a typical example may not always be the one we meet most frequently. Consider this: Which bird do you think is mentioned most often in written English? Most people think it is the robin. A robin flies, has feathers, tugs at worms, makes a nest, sings, announces the arrival of spring; this fits our prototype of a bird. True, but the bird that is most often mentioned is not the robin; it is the chicken. The chicken is very familiar to us, but it does not *typify* our concept of bird. We are more likely to put chicken in the category of food. A robin is more prototypical, "more of a bird" than a chicken is, at least in the human mind.

One way to study how people categorize things is to see how quickly they can make a judgment. One study found that the sentence "A robin is a bird" is recognized *more quickly* than the sentence "A chicken is a bird." In another study, Rosch (1975) asked people to fill in the blanks in the sentence, "_____ is virtually _____ " with the numbers 100 and 103. There was a clear preference for "103 is virtually 100" over the reverse, "100 is virtually 103." It appears that 100 is a more prototypical number than 103. Our preference for round numbers and multiples of 10 is an example of our use of prototypes and categories.

GENERALIZATION AND OVERGENERALIZATION   The ability to **generalize** saves effort. We need not waste time discriminating one car horn from another to get out of the way; different-sounding door bells all mean the same thing. Also, we are conscious of only a few things at once. Thus, what happens is that *whatever enters our consciousness is overemphasized.* It does not matter how the information enters. Whether it is a television program, a newspaper story, a friend mentioning something, or a strong emotional reaction—all get overemphasized. The following excerpt illustrates our tendency to overemphasize:

Let us suppose that you wish to buy a new car and have decided [on] either a Volvo or a Saab. . . . *Consumer Reports* informs you that the consensus of their experts is that the Volvo is mechanically superior, and the consensus of their readership is that the Volvo has the better repair record. Armed with this information, you decide to go and strike a bargain with the Volvo dealer before the week is over. In the interim, however, you go to a cocktail party where you announce this intention to an acquaintance. He reacts with disbelief and alarm: "A Volvo! You've got to be kidding. My brother-in-law had a Volvo. First, that fancy fuel injection computer thing went out. $250. Next he started having trouble with the rear end. Had to replace it. Then the transmission and the clutch. Finally he sold it in three years for junk." (Ross & Nisbett, 1981)

How would you feel about a Volvo now? Most likely you would strongly reconsider buying one. But think about it; the information you received is that *one* person out of thousands does not like the Volvo, but nevertheless, you are strongly influenced by this single case.

Overgeneralization accents the most recent information, even at the cost of ignoring past knowledge. In 1985 there was a toxic leak from a chemical plant in Bhopal, India. Would you have gone into the country at that time? Probably you would have canceled your travel plans there. Our tendency to overgeneralize is adaptive: it helps protect against dangers associated with *changing circumstances*. This mechanism can trip the emergency reaction, and it may have gotten our ancestors out of a lot of trouble.

HEURISTICS IN CATEGORIZATION

Heuristics are simplifying strategies that we use to generalize and solve problems; they could be called the "fast paths" of the mind. There is a trade-off in the use of heuristics: accuracy may be sacrificed for speed. We must usually rely on incomplete information to make judgments, to reason, and to solve problems. Heuristics are the rules of thumb that guide our decisions. Three common forms of heuristics are representativeness, availability, and comparison.

REPRESENTATIVENESS   The judgment that an object is *typical* of its category is called **representativeness.** This heuristic involves matching prototypes: we quickly judge a robin to be a bird; it is *representative* of birds. A chicken is less so. However, using representativeness as a heuristic can lead to mistakes or overgeneralization. *Concrete* or *vivid* events overpower other evidence. When there was a nearly catastrophic accident at the Three Mile Island nuclear reactor in 1979, its influence on people to protest against nuclear power was dramatic. The accident was judged to be representative of nuclear power plants, and this overgeneralization entirely overwhelmed the generally good safety records of these plants. A single case has a striking influence; statistics are readily ignored. Our tendency to use representativeness is so strong that at the beginning of a movie or novel, a disclaimer usually appears that warns against its overuse: "Any resemblance to persons living or dead is purely coincidental."

AVAILABILITY   **Availability** is the ease with which relevant instances come to mind (Tversky 1990). Recall that events that occur more frequently are more easily retrieved from memory since they are more accessible for use. We use the

availability heuristic when we are asked to guess the frequency or the probability of events. In general it is useful; things that occur more frequently are more available.

But availability can lead to error. A man from Indiana may remark, "Haven't you noticed how many famous Hoosiers (people from Indiana) there are?" Because he is a Hoosier himself, he finds more Hoosiers available, causing a bias or error in his judgment. People out of work may overestimate the rate of unemployment (Nisbett & Ross, 1981). One experiment asked, Are there more words in English that start with *K* or in which *K* is the third letter? Two-thirds of the subjects felt that more words begin with *K*; however, they are wrong. Why? Probably because of the way we index and categorize words; it is much easier to remember those that *begin* with *K* than it is to remember those in which *K* is the third letter (Kahneman & Tversky, 1973).

COMPARISON   We judge by **comparison,** and our standard of comparison constantly shifts. We judge an outside air temperature of 50 degrees Fahrenheit as warm in winter but as cold in summer; a salary of $500 a week is enormous to a college student but might insult an executive. We experience a 200-gram weight as heavy when it is in a series of weights ranging from 100 to 200 grams, but in a series of weights from 200 to 500 grams we experience it as light. So *the same processes underlie judgments of sensory, cognitive, and social matters.*

One common effect of comparisons is **anchoring:** once a standard has been used in trying to solve a problem, a person is less likely to change or adjust, even if compelling new data are present or common sense would dictate a change. A person becomes anchored in his or her strategy.

CLASSIFICATION INTO CATEGORIES

Our minds contain a hidden set of priorities and policies. You can feel this system working when you are in the middle of a "hot" conversation while driving. Suddenly the brake lights of the car in front of you go on. Immediately the conversation goes out of your mind, and you attend to the potential threat. Extreme hunger crowds out ideas; pain pre-empts plans. We constantly shift up and down along the set of priorities, governed by conscious and unconscious brain processes.

There is a progression of plans and behaviors (see Figure 13-2). At the bottom and taking priority are physiological needs, then come needs for safety, love, and belonging. Higher up are esteem, cognitive needs, aesthetic needs, self-actualization, and transcendence. So avoiding the car ahead takes precedence, automatically over what you are talking about.

When the most basic and immediate physiological needs, such as hunger and thirst, are met, other higher ones need to be satisfied: safety must be maintained, pain

PRIORITIES AND POLICIES

avoided and pleasure sought; and social needs, like belonging, met. Similarly, we reduce the amount of information that we attend to by following certain "policies." Keep in mind that these are only general, and somewhat whimsical, descriptions of mental tendencies.

1. *What have you done for me lately?* People are extremely sensitive to recent information; emotional upsets like bad feelings last for a while and then are forgiven. Terrible disasters like an airplane crash force attention on airliners for a while, all sorts of reforms are initiated, and then the spotlight fades away.

2. *Don't call me unless anything new and exciting happens.* Most mental operations focus upon "the news", a sudden appearance of something unknown. Unexpected

or extraordinary events seem to have fast access to consciousness, while an unchanging background noise, or a constant weight, or a chronic problem, soon gets shunted into the background. It is easy to raise money for emergencies, like the few victims of a well-publicized disaster, whereas it is much more difficult to raise money for the many victims of continuous malnutrition. We respond quickly to scarcity and danger.

Gradual changes in the world go unnoticed while sharp changes are immediately seized upon by the mind. Gasoline prices increased in the 1970s from about $0.30 per gallon to about $0.95 with little decrease in consumption. When prices went over $1.00, there was an immediate decline in consumption as we had been "awakened" somehow by the change. This happens too on the simple sensory registration of information: a sudden loud noise is commanding, whereas a continual low din as in a factory next door is well, probably too well, tolerated. A sudden scarcity of food is imme-

CHANGING STANDARDS OF COMPARISON We may apply different standards of comparison to different situations at different times. What is enough money at one time is not enough at another. Tversky and Kahneman conceptualize these changing standards as *psychological accounting*—that is, people shift into different "accounts." Suppose you were going to a play and lost $20 on the way. Would you still pay $20 for a ticket? Most people say they would. Now suppose you had already bought your $20 ticket and lost it on the way. Would you pay $20 for another ticket? Most people say they would not. *The loss in both of these situations is exactly the same,* $20, but they are not the same in psychological accounting terms. In the first case, the loss is not applied to our "ticket account"; in the second case, the account has been used up (Tversky, 1990).

Would you drive 20 minutes to save $5? Whether you would or not depends upon comparison. If you were going to buy a toaster, and a store close to you has it for $25 and another store 20 minutes away has it on sale for $20, would you drive? Most people say that they would. Suppose you are going to buy a jacket at a nearby store for $165 and a store 20 minutes away has the same one for $160. Most people say that they would not drive the extra miles. *They are less likely to drive when the savings represent a smaller amount of the total.* The savings are equal, but how they are compared is not (Tversky & Kahneman, 1981).

diately signaled, and we respond.

3. The comedian Henny Youngman was asked: "How do you like your wife?" *"Compared to what?"* he responded. Youngman's answer points out that our judgment of any item depends upon what we are comparing it to at that moment. Suppose your boss hands you $1,000 at the end of the year. You are delighted because you are expecting nothing. But suppose he had told you that he was going to give you $10,000 and changed his mind? The same is true of Youngman's wife, or anybody's spouse. Our standards for other people are very different: actions that are alluring in others might be regarded as unbecoming in a spouse. Comparison processes span everything from judgments of primitive sensations, like heaviness and heat, to social status.

4. *What does this mean to* me? The mental system determines the meaning of any event, and it throws out almost all the information that reaches us. Of the billions of leaves you saw last summer, how many do you remember? A siren is frightening because it *means* that the police want you to stop. Almost automatically, new information is processed in terms of what we have to do next.

All these policies and procedures exist to simplify the amount of information current in the mind. "What have you done for me lately" allows a focus on recent events, "Don't call me . . ." allows many of the real changes in the world to go ignored; only when they are great do they enter the system. Most people do not "mind" the slow increases in the prices they are paying for milk, bread, wine, meat and other items they buy every day. However, the increase in car prices meets with great dismay, even though car prices have increased less than the average of the Consumer Price Index. The reason, as in buying gasoline, is "Policy number 2": we don't notice the slow, monthly price increases in an item like milk, but a car, which we buy only every three or four years contains the accumulated price increase—and we notice it quickly!

The policy "Get to the point!" allows us to operate on and to remember only the meaning or the gist of conversations, meetings, and different situations: "You mean you talked for three hours and you only decided to paint the house blue?"

Our own understanding of ourselves is also processed by these policies and procedures, so we don't always know ourselves directly. We hold a well-organized and simplified version of our environment, of the nature of other people, and *even of our own lives and our own beliefs* in our minds.

We are constantly sifting through evidence, making decisions, inferring from information, deciding what a person is talking about, sorting through different hypotheses, deciding whether the situation is an emergency, whether resources are scarce, whether that noise needs action, whether something is larger or brighter or smaller than another, which decision to make about a purchase, and countless more (Ornstein, 1990).

DECISION MAKING AND JUDGMENT

Which car should you buy? Which job offer should you accept? What should you have for lunch? Life is an endless series of decisions, one after another. Although in a sense every decision is a problem, and every problem requires making a decision, psychologists distinguish between the two. *Problems* require finding a series of steps that allow you to reach a goal. *Decisions* require making a choice among several options. In this section we will consider decision making; in the next, problem solving.

ELEMENTS OF DECISION MAKING

There are four basic elements in every decision:

1. A set of *alternatives* to choose from.
2. A set of possible *outcomes*.
3. The decision maker's *preferences* among the different outcomes.
4. The decision maker's judgments of the *probabilities* that a particular choice will lead to a particular outcome.

Suppose you have to decide whether or not to buy collision insurance for your car at $300 a year. Your *alternatives* are to buy or not to buy the insurance. The *outcomes* are that you do or do not have a collision. Your *preference* is the outcome that will cost the least, but you are not sure which choice will lead to that outcome. This uncertainty can be represented as *probabilities*.

Assume you project that you have a 10 percent chance of having a collision in a year that would cost about $2,000. In this example, you can quantify the various factors since the numbers are specified; you can compute the expected value of each alternative by multiplying the probabilities by the values of the outcomes. According to these numbers, you should not buy the insurance since it costs $300 a year and your expected loss without it would be only $200 a year (10 percent of $2,000). Obviously the decision would not be this simple in reality. There may be other factors involved in your choice than just the amount of money, such as the peace of mind of having insurance. Also, there is no way to know whether or not you will have a car accident.

Even though many decisions are more complex than this, the four basic elements—alternatives, outcomes, preferences, and probabilities—are present in decision making in some form. Often just thinking about decisions in this way can help clarify decision making. Suppose you were having trouble getting along with your roommate; you might make a list of alternative actions you could take and the possible outcomes of each choice. Then you could consider which outcomes seem most likely from each choice and which outcomes you would prefer most. This way of thinking about decisions is called **decision analysis.**

BIASES IN DECISION MAKING

We use heuristics to make decisions. These shortcuts probably result in more efficient decision making overall, but they also lead to systematic **biases,** preventing impartiality in certain kinds of judgments (Einhorn & Hogarth, 1981). Knowing about these common biases may help you avoid them in your judgments and decision making.

AVAILABILITY When people are asked to judge the relative frequency of different causes of death, they overestimate the frequency of well-publicized causes such as homicide, tornadoes, and cancer, and they underestimate the frequency of less remarkable causes such as diabetes, asthma, and emphysema. This is an example of how people's judgments are biased by *how easily they recall specific examples.* This bias was also demonstrated in an experiment by Tversky and Kahneman (1973), in which they read subjects lists of names of well-known people of both sexes. In each list the people of one sex were more famous than those of the other sex. When the subjects were asked to estimate the proportion of men and women on the lists, they overestimated the proportion of the sex having more famous people on the list. If the list contained very famous women (such as Elizabeth Taylor) and only moderately well-known men (such as Alan Ladd), then subjects overestimated the proportion of women on the list. How *available* memories are affects our judgment.

REPRESENTATIVENESS People often overestimate the probability that something belongs in a particular category. Kahneman and Tversky (1973) told subjects to read the following passage, which was written by a psychologist when Tom (the subject of the passage) was in his senior year of high school:

> Tom W. is of high intelligence, although lacking in true creativity. He has a need for order and clarity, and for neat and tidy systems in which every detail finds its appropriate place. His writing is rather dull and mechanical, occasionally enlivened by somewhat corny puns and by flashes of imagination of the sci-fi type. He has a strong drive for competence. He seems to have little feel and little sympathy for other people and does not enjoy interacting with others. Self-centered, he nonetheless has a deep moral sense.

Then they were told to imagine that Tom W. is now a graduate student and to rank the following categories in order of the likelihood that they are Tom's area of graduate specialization:

- business administration
- computer science
- engineering
- humanities and education
- social work
- library science
- medicine
- physical and life sciences
- social science and law

What area of graduate specialization would you expect Tom W. to be in?

If you are like the people Kahneman and Tversky studied, you probably chose computer science or engineering as Tom's most likely area of specialization and thought that humanities, education, social science, and social work were least likely. The character description probably fits your *prototype* of what "typical" computer science or engineering students are like. The *representativeness* heuristic leads you to think these are likely categories for his field of study. But there are many more graduate students in humanities, education, social science, and social work than there are in computer science or engineering. Even people who know these *base rates* of students in different fields and who have very little faith in the predictive value of the character sketch disregard the base rates in making their predictions.

VIVID INFORMATION One particularly important consequence of availability and representativeness is that concrete or **vivid information** is highly influential in judgment. The tendency to disregard statistical information and to overemphasize vivid examples extends even to some of society's most important decision makers. Nisbett and Ross (1981) described an acquaintance of theirs

> who often testifies at congressional committees on behalf of the Environmental Protection Agency. . . . She reported that the bane of her professional existence is the frequency with which she reports test data such as EPA mileage estimates based on samples of ten or more cars, only to be contradicted by a congressman who retorts with information about a single case: "What do you mean, the Blatzmobile gets twenty miles per gallon on the road?" he says. "My neighbor has one, and he only gets fifteen." His fellow legislators then usually respond as if matters were at a stand-off—one EPA estimate versus one colleague's estimate obtained from his neighbor.

General heuristics like *hill climbing* and *means-end analysis* are sometimes called weak methods. Even though they can be used to help solve almost any kind of problem, they are so general that it would still take you a very long time to solve a problem if all you used were these heuristics.

In addition to these general heuristics, people also use a great deal of specialized knowledge in solving problems. For instance, if you need to get to the store, you don't usually consider all possible modes of transportation (such as car, train, bus, walking, bicycle). Instead, you usually try first the things that have worked in the past (such as borrowing your roommate's car). This specialized knowledge about what has worked in the past is usually much more helpful for solving a specific problem than are the general heuristics.

Recent models of human thinking suggest how the two kinds of knowledge can be combined: when we are trying to solve a new kind of problem (or when something unexpected happens in a familiar situation), we can use general heuristics to explore many possible solutions. And whenever we find a solution that works, we remember it and try it first when we come upon a similar situation in the future (Anderson, 1987; Laird, Newell, & Rosenbloom, 1987).

PROBLEM SOLVING

People are continuously **problem solving.** Some of the problems we deal with may be simple and unstructured, such as ''What should I make for dinner?''; some may be chronic, such as ''How can I get along better with my boss?''; and some may be formal, such as an intricate move in chess. Different problems demand different kinds of solutions and approaches. Many everyday problems are fairly simple and may be dealt with by simple trial and error, and some life problems involve hypothesis testing. More formal problems may draw on both of these methods, but also may involve structured analyses and strategies, some of which involve heuristics. Earlier we emphasized how heuristics interfere with judgment; here we will see how they help in solutions. Also examined here is how people go beyond problem solving to the creative invention of new ways to deal with unexpected situations.

SOLVING SIMPLE PROBLEMS

We are faced with problems so frequently that we often do not notice that they are problems until they are solved. Trivial ones, such as how to open a tightly closed jar or how to get the sofa through the door, are usually solved by *trial and error.* Some problems are more substantial (although not formal), such as ''How do I get a checkmate?'' or ''Why isn't my car working?'' We may use *hypothesis testing* for the solution to these problems.

TRIAL AND ERROR   Suppose you arrive in your hotel room in Tibet. There are three faucets in the shower with strange markings on them. How do you turn the hot water on? The only way to find out is to turn the faucets and see what happens. This is **trial and error** (Johnson-Laird, 1989). Trial and error is the most basic problem-solving strategy. When we are stuck in a situation and do not know how to get out of it, we start trying things to get unstuck. Trial and error usually involves a series of different actions aimed at solving a problem to which there seems to be no logical solution. What do you do to stop a car going downhill if the brakes fail?

HYPOTHESIS TESTING Suppose one night you come home and find all the lights out. You check all the switches, turn them on and off and still no light. You call the electric company and find that there has not been a power failure. You check the fuse box and all the fuses are okay. Then you check the main switch to the house; it is off. You switch it on and the lights brighten your house. What you did, even in this simple situation, was to entertain a series of hypotheses about the problem in a systematic and structured way. Using **hypothesis testing,** you eliminated each hypothesis until you found the solution. To do this you must have a *set of possible hypotheses* stored, each of which could account for the situation. In this case it could have been something wrong with the fuse box or the power line. You must also be able to take appropriate *actions* to test and *eliminate* certain hypotheses (in this case, turning on switches in different rooms eliminated the hypothesis that the lights were out in only one room.)

Even animals use hypotheses. David Krechevsky (1932) had rats run a maze with four choice points. At each one the rats could turn left or right. Behind each choice point was a door that could be opened or closed and that either blocked the rats or allowed them to continue. The rats did not treat the situation in a trial-and-error way; rather, they seemed to test hypotheses. They would try a series of all right turns or all left turns until they had arrived at a satisfactory solution.

PROBLEM-SOLVING STRATEGIES

Situations that can be solved by simple trial and error or hypothesis testing are not that common because most human actions and interactions are more complex than mazes or home electrical problems. In chess there are literally millions of possible moves. Players would be stymied unless they used some simplifying strategies and procedures (heuristics).

The variety of problems we face in life are too numerous to allow a neat classification. However, most problems have three basic elements:

1. The *initial state* or starting point of the problem.
2. A set of *operations* or actions that the problem solver can use to change the state of the problem.
3. A *goal* or a description of the states that would be solutions to the problem.

The game of tic-tac-toe, although simple, provides a good example of these three elements. The *initial state* is a set of nine empty squares. The *operations* are marking an X or an O in the squares and all the possible ways the squares can be marked. The *goal* is to be the first player to get three of the same marks in a row. Most puzzles and mathematical problems are similarly well defined, but most problems in life are not. If your problem is to write a paper for an English class, you might say that the initial state of the problem includes a blank sheet of paper and all your knowledge about the subject of the paper. The operations are researching and writing words on the page, and the goal is a completed paper. However, in this example and in most other real-life problems, it is difficult to specify all the possible states, operations, and especially, goals. But even though many real problems are not completely well defined, it still may be useful to distinguish these elements.

SEQUENCE OF PROBLEM SOLVING   The process of problem solving involves four basic steps (Adams, 1989):

1. Understanding the problem.
2. Planning a solution.
3. Carrying out the plan.
4. Checking the results.

You must first *understand* the elements discussed above—the starting point, the operations, and the goal. Then you *plan* a sequence of operations to change the initial state into a goal. Finally, you *carry out* the operations and judge whether the solution is correct by *checking* the results. Of course, you may have to repeat the cycle many times before you reach a solution.

PROBLEM REPRESENTATION   Each step in problem solving contains a number of choices. Two of the most important parts of solving problems are how to *represent* the problem and what *strategy* to use to solve it.

Problem representation, the way you think about or represent a problem, may make the problem harder or easier to solve. Although logical reasoning often helps solve problems, sometimes it makes solution more difficult. Consider the following:

> One morning, exactly at sunrise, a Buddhist monk began to climb a tall mountain. A narrow path, no more than a foot or two wide, spiraled around the mountain to a glittering temple at the summit. The monk ascended at varying rates of speed, stopping many times along the way to rest and eat dried fruit he carried with him. He reached the temple shortly before sunset. After several days of fasting and meditation, he began his journey back along the same path, starting [at] sunrise and again walking at variable speeds with many pauses along the way. His average speed descending was, of course, greater than his average climbing speed. Show that there is a spot along the path that the monk will occupy on both trips at exactly the same time of day (Glass et al., 1989).

Try to think about this problem verbally and mathematically. Most people find the solution difficult: how can we be sure the monk would find himself at the same spot at the same time on two different days, when we do not know how fast he walked? The best way to *represent* this problem is visually. One woman describes her solution: "When you graph the position of the monk on the mountain for the two different days, there must be a point at which they cross, and this is the solution to the problem" (Glass et al., 1989).

However, visual solutions do not always work. Suppose you take a piece of paper 0.01 inch thick and fold it on itself 50 times. How high is it? Most people, visually estimating the solution, say "5 inches" or "2 feet," or perhaps "10 feet." They all greatly underestimate the height. Now attack the problem mathematically: we find that 50 folds increases the height by two multiplied by two 50 times, or 2^{50} times 0.01 inch. When the problem is solved mathematically, the answer is surprising: the thickness of the paper would reach from the earth nearly to Jupiter! Successful problem-solving strategy may require visual, verbal, mathematical, and other kinds of representation.

ALGORITHMS   After you have a representation for a problem, you can use several different strategies. Some strategies guarantee that you will find the solution if you keep working long enough. These strategies are called **algorithms.** If you follow the procedure exactly, you will reach a correct answer to the problem. One algorithm is a strategy for playing tic-tac-toe, in which you consider all the possible moves you could make, then all the possible replies your opponent could make to that move, then all the possible next moves you could make, and so on. Then you select a move that cannot lead to a win for your opponent. This strategy is called *generate-and-test* because at each point you *generate* a set of alternative moves and *test* each one to see if it works. Looking at many alternative actions in this way is called *searching the test* (or *problem*) *space.*

Algorithms are used extensively in solving problems in the structured language of computer programs. (See the section, "The Computer and the Mind" later in this chapter.) For example, computer chess programs are based on the use of algorithms. The computer generates and tests an immense number of possible moves and selects the best one. The number of moves it tests determines the level of difficulty of the chess game. However, computers can do this incredibly fast; it would take us far too long to play chess this way. People have the advantage of using heuristics and insight in solving complex problems such as chess strategies.

HEURISTICS IN PROBLEM SOLVING   People use heuristics as shortcuts in complex situations. Heuristics do not guarantee a solution in all cases but are often very useful in reaching a solution. Some examples of chess-playing heuristics might be "Capture any piece you can" and "Never expose your king." This drastically reduces the amount of information that needs to be considered in solving a problem.

Because computer chess games are based on algorithms, they can be programmed to match any level of ability.

One heuristic that is often useful is called *hill climbing*. For example, if your goal were to reach the top of a hill, a good strategy would be to walk uphill from where you were. Using this heuristic you would always apply operations that would bring the state of the problem more in line with the goal state. As a simplifying strategy in complex problems, the hill-climbing heuristic might help: someone with a poor sense of direction, for instance, would remember that in California you always drive west to reach the ocean. But this strategy can sometimes get you into trouble if used blindly. In checkers the goal is to capture all the opponent's pieces. Using the hill-climbing strategy, you would try to capture any piece you could because this would bring you closer to the goal. But if done indiscriminately, this could lead you into a trap in which more of your own pieces were captured.

Another heuristic that is often useful is to break a larger problem into **subgoals.** Consider the algebraic problem $2x + y = 8$ and $x - y = 1$. To solve this, you might first set the subgoal of finding x and look for a way to reach it. The two equations added give $3x = 9$ or $x = 3$; now y can be easily derived. Breaking a problem into pieces makes it easier to solve (Gazzaniga, 1989).

A particularly useful way of breaking a problem into subgoals is called **means-end analysis.** This heuristic involves working backward from the goal through the things needed to achieve it. If the goal is to cook spaghetti, you need a kitchen to cook in and all the ingredients for spaghetti. Suppose you need to buy the ingredients, but you have no transportation to the store. Your new subgoal is to get to the store. You might ask to borrow your roommate's car. If you get permission to use it, then your next subgoal is to find the keys. If permission is denied, then you may have to consider other means of transportation.

INSIGHT   Not all problems are necessarily solvable using only systematic, step-by-step methods such as those treated thus far. Often a crucial **insight** is needed to solve a problem, a sudden vision of how all the parts fit together or of how to represent the problem differently. Deciding to visually represent the Buddhist monk problem is one example of an insight. "Aha, that's it!" is the feeling of insight when all the different elements of a problem suddenly come together. This experience can come at the end of a directed process of hypothesis testing or seemingly out of the blue. The mathematician Poincaré described his insight into a mathematical formula that he had worked on constantly for 15 days, after which he went on a trip:

> Just at this time I left Caen, where I was living, to go on a geologic excursion under the auspices of the School of Mines. The changes of travel made me forget my mathematical world. Having reached Coutances, we entered an omnibus to go some place or other. At the moment when I put my foot on the step, the idea came to me, without anything in my former thoughts seeming to have paved the way for it. . . . I did not verify the idea, . . . as upon taking my seat in the omnibus I went on with a conversation already commenced, but I felt a perfect certainty. On my return to Caen, for conscience's sake, I verified the result at my leisure. (Poincaré, 1921)

An insight is often visual and seems to consist of a simultaneous vision of the total problem. Some of the earliest experimental work on insight was done by Wolfgang Köhler. Köhler (1925) demonstrated that insight can occur even in

animals. (Recall the discussion of insight in Chapter 8). In an experiment similar to the one in which a chimpanzee had to learn to use different lengths of stick to reach an apple, Köhler hung a bunch of bananas from the ceiling just out of reach of a chimpanzee (Figure 10-2). He also randomly arranged a set of boxes in the cage. After exhausting various trial-and-error approaches, the chimp suddenly stopped, perused the situation, and then appeared to see the solution: he stacked the boxes one on top of another, stood on the boxes, and reached the bananas. This is insight: the sudden arrangement of a set of elements in a new way.

FIGURE 10-2
Problem Solving
This chimpanzee had a flash of insight and was thus able to solve the problem of how to reach the bananas.

STUDYING PROBLEM SOLVING

PROTOCOL ANALYSIS   One way psychologists study problem solving is by asking people to *introspect* (literally "look within") and talk while they are working. If they wait until they are finished, their memory may distort what they actually did to solve the problem. The use of this "thinking aloud" technique is called **protocol analysis.** Newell and Simon (1972) used protocol analysis to study how people solved puzzles in which each letter stood for a digit and the goal was to figure out which digit each letter stood for. Newell and Simon analyzed such protocols by means of a *problem behavior graph* that showed the path the person followed in solving the problem, including all the false starts and backtracking.

PROBLEMS OF "SET" IN PROBLEM SOLVING   One important problem in problem solving (and in thinking in general) is that people tend to repeat actions that have been successful in other circumstances. In other words, they become **set** into a pattern of thought or behavior by activating stored schemata, which sometimes can lead to inefficiency and difficulty in solving new problems. The classical demonstration of the problem of set is in a series of experiments by Luchins (1942). Luchins tested more than 9,000 people on this water jar problem. For example, start with three jars: jar A holds 21 quarts, B holds 127 quarts, and C holds 3 quarts. How can you measure out 100 quarts? Most likely you would fill

FIGURE 10-3
The Luchins Water Jar
Problem

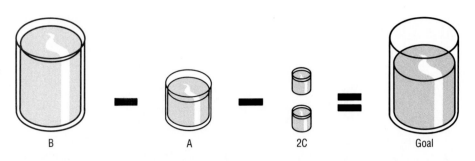

B   A   2C   Goal

TABLE 10-1 Water Jar Problems				
Problem	**Jar A**	**Jar B**	**Jar C**	**Goal**
1.	2	40	4	30
2.	1	27	6	14
3.	2	16	3	8
4.	7	59	12	28
5.	23	49	3	20

Source: Luchins & Luchins, 1959.

the 127-quart jar, then pour 21 quarts into jar A, then 3 quarts into jar C twice (Figure 10-3). The participants were asked to solve the five problems shown in Table 10-1, which begin with different quantities of water in each jar.

All of these problems can be solved using the formula

$$Goal = B - A - 2C.$$

However, look again at the fifth problem in the table. A much simpler solution is $A - C$. People who work through the first four problems tend to use the more complicated formula $(B - A - 2C)$ for the fifth problem because their minds are set on the formula; they usually fail to see the simpler solution at all. Thus, success and efficiency using one approach with certain kinds of problems can cause difficulty or inefficiency in solving other problems.

CREATIVITY

Life is more than solving problems. People go beyond normal problem solving to *inventing* solutions. One characteristic of creativity is that it may involve things as simple as cooking a new dish or as grand as devising a new scientific theory. Humans' need to create is quite basic. We have been inventing ways to deal with unexpected situations for at least a million years.

GENERATION AND EVALUATION

One theory proposes that we generate ideas at random and retain (select) some because they are useful or have adaptive value (Hogarth, 1989). Creativity is thus considered to be a process similar to natural selection, in which there are random variations, some of which prove useful and are "selected" by the environment. Chance plays a great role in both the *generation* and the *evaluation* of ideas. People who have a lot of ideas are more likely to have creative ones, but a *useful* creative idea is rare. As Campbell (1960) emphasizes, the tremendous amount of nonproductive thought

> must not be underestimated. Think of what a small proportion of thought becomes conscious, and of conscious thought what a small proportion gets uttered, what a still smaller fragment gets published, and what a small portion of what is published is used by the next intellectual generation. There is a tremendous wastefulness, slowness and rarity of achievement.

Thousands of small and wrong ideas help prepare the way for an occasional useful one. Thomas Edison is believed to have evaluated his progress on an invention by saying that he now knew a hundred ways that wouldn't work.

Creativity involves hard work and the relentless generation of ideas and thoughts to produce a few that pass evaluation. *Evaluation* is the assessment of the worth of an idea. In an important passage, the psychologist Wickelgren (1979) wrote that "it is perhaps more important to *recognize* a good idea than it is to possess one."

THE PROCESS OF CREATION

There have been many analyses of creativity in problem solving, and most conclude that creativity involves preparation, generation, evaluation, and implementation (Johnson, 1972). *Preparation* entails immersion in the subject and often an especially intense period just before the solution. Recall that the

Individuals are not totally "creative" or "noncreative." However, there are certain human characteristics that may make it easier for some people to express ideas creatively. It seems that people who think unusual thoughts often lead lives differently from the rest of us. Isaac Newton, for example, spent almost 16 hours a day locked up in his rooms at Cambridge working on his theories. We could thus conclude that if we spend too much time being like everybody else, we *decrease* our chances of coming up with something different.

mathematician Poincaré began the description of his insight by saying that the problem had occupied him for 15 days. The next two steps consist of *generating* ideas for solutions to the problem and *evaluating* their worth. *Implementation* involves actually carrying out the idea or ideas that are judged to be more useful. Only a few ideas get implemented because only rarely is anyone willing and able to do the further work needed to carry them out. Thomas Edison remarked that genius is 1 percent inspiration and 99 percent perspiration.

LANGUAGE

The primary way we express our thoughts, share our ideas, and reveal our solutions and decisions is through speech. Language is probably the greatest human achievement. Talking makes it possible for a group to plan and carry out a complex activity together; it makes it possible to teach and to transmit to a new generation what happened in the past. In our society and in most civilized countries, history and culture are passed down in books. But even among illiterate, primitive people, the primary vehicle for the transmission of culture is language. Every human culture has a language; every normal human being has the ability to speak.

Language is creation; every sentence we utter is an on-the-spot invention. Unless you are giving a prepared speech, everything you say is instantly put together in response to a new situation. *All children as they grow up can generate and recognize millions of sentences and exclamations that they have never heard before!*

Education increases our store of knowledge, and most of that knowledge is stored in words. Every profession has its own vocabulary, or jargon, which speeds up communication among colleagues. For instance, words such as *schema, cognitive,* and *neurotransmitter pathways* used in psychology should contain meaning for you now (I hope!).

Even a 3-year-old child, with little complex language ability, can communicate basic needs, ideas, and questions. A single word such as "hungry" will serve as important communication. "Where's Daddy?" communicates a different, more complex thought. Sentences can be extraordinarily complex in structure, but "I wonder where father might possibly have gone today?" is not much more complex than "Where's Daddy?"

ELEMENTS OF LANGUAGE

SPEECH ACTS   The different forms of language are termed **speech acts** (Clark, 1988). Three important speech acts are associated with different kinds of sentences. A *declarative sentence* conveys specific information, such as "Jamaica is a country in the Caribbean." A *question* demands information, as in "Do you have any quarters?" or "Will you give me a kiss?" An *imperative* conveys a command: "Please pass the salad."

PHONEMES   The individual sounds of a language are called **phonemes.** A particular sound is considered a phoneme only if it is used in language. The sound of *d* is used in words and is a phoneme; the grumbling sound we make when we clear our throat is not. A way to isolate a phoneme is to say a word and systematically change one of the sounds until the word changes into a different word. If a change in a single sound transforms one word into another, this identifies a phoneme. There are three phonemes in the word *bat* (b/a/t). A change in the first phoneme can give *pat* or *vat*; a change in the second phoneme can give *bit* or *bet*; a change in the third can give *ban* or *bad*. The phonemes in standard American English are listed in Table 10-2. Note that phonemes within words differ between different dialects; for example, merry, marry, and Mary are pronounced identically in parts of the midwestern United States.

MORPHEMES   Phonemes have meaning only when combined to make units called **morphemes.** A morpheme can be a whole word, such as *car, but,* or *teach* or it can be a word fragment. Prefixes and suffixes are themselves morphemes, such as *pre-, dis-, un-, -ing, -es,* and *-est.*

Words such as "dis-em-body" are composed of three morphemes; the spelling bee favorite, *antidisestablishmentarianism,* is made up of seven morphemes (anti-dis-es-tab-lish-ment-ari-an-ism). English has only 26 letters, but they combine to make more than 90,000 morphemes, which in turn combine to make about 600,000 words, which can be made into an almost infinite number of sentences.

TABLE 10-2
Phonemes in General American English

Vowels		Consonants	
ee as in h*ea*t	*λ* as in t*o*n	*t* as in *t*ee	*s* as in *s*ee
I as in h*i*t	*uh* as in th*e*	*p* as in *p*ea	*sh* as in *sh*ell
ε as in h*ea*d	*εr* as in b*ir*d	*k* as in *k*ey	*h* as in *h*e
ae as in h*a*d	*oi* as in t*oi*l	*b* as in *b*ee	*v* as in *v*iew
ah as in f*a*ther	*au* as in sh*ou*t	*d* as in *d*awn	*th* as in *th*en
aw as in c*a*ll	*ei* as in t*a*ke	*g* as in *g*o	*z* as in *z*oo
U as in p*u*t	*ou* as in t*o*ne	*m* as in *m*e	*zh* as in gara*g*e
oo as in c*oo*l	*ai* as in m*i*ght	*n* as in *n*o	*l* as in *l*aw
		ng as in si*ng*	*r* as in *r*ed
		f as in *f*ee	*y* as in *y*ou
		θ as in *th*in	*w* as in *w*e

Source: Denes & Pinson, 1963.

GRAMMAR AND SYNTAX   A word is the normal unit of meaning. Words form sentences, and spoken sentences form conversations. We speak without being conscious of the elements; children learning to talk often do not actually know they are speaking words (Scarr, 1988). However, written language is by nature more formal and self-conscious. The thought contained in a sentence is meaningful only if it follows the specific rules of language. **Grammar** is the study of those rules of language, and how words are arranged to convey meaning is called **syntax.** Although syntax and grammar are the bane of most students in school, most of us actually speak fairly grammatically all the time.

There are specific rules in language, both written and spoken. For example, "The boy the ball the road hit on" is meaningless; it is not a sentence. But, "The boy hit the ball on the road" conveys a thought. When children begin to speak they utter *essentially* grammatical sentences, and although children's sentences are simple and not in perfect syntax, almost every sentence is original, not an imitation of other sentences they have heard.

DEEP AND SURFACE STRUCTURE

When children begin to speak, they are naturally adept and make relatively few grammatical errors. Thus, many scientists characterize the grammar of language as being *innate.* The leading proponent of this view, which is called **transformational grammar,** is Noam Chomsky (1966). He believes there is an important distinction in syntax between "deep" and "surface" structure. *Deep structure* is the underlying network of thought conveyed in a sentence, and *surface structure* is the actual sentence that carries the deep structure. A *transformation* occurs that changes the deep structure (or meaning) into the surface structure (the expression in words). Because there are many ways to say the same thing, a single deep structure has many possible variations in surface structure. "The large elephant saw the small mouse" and "The small mouse was seen by the large elephant" have the same deep structure, but a different surface structure.

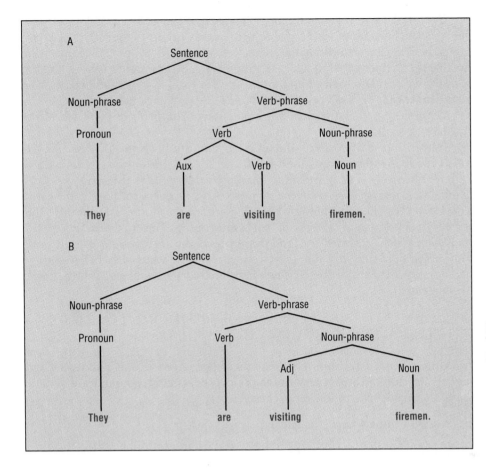

FIGURE 10-4
Transformational Grammar Analysis
Analysis A indicates that some people are paying a visit to firemen, whereas analysis B identifies "they" as firemen who are visiting.
(Chomsky, 1966)

Sometimes the surface structure can be confusing and could derive from two different deep structures. In this case, knowing the deep structure is the only way to understand the sentence. In other words, the listener must have an idea of what the speaker is talking about. The sentence "They are visiting firemen" is ambiguous. Figure 10-4 shows transformational grammar analyses of the sentence that shows the two possible deep structures. A similar analysis of the two sentences above about the large elephant and the small mouse would reveal that they share the same deep structure.

MEANING IN LANGUAGE

Mental activities search for order and meaning and go beyond the information given to fill in the gaps. This tendency is called *active processing.* When we listen and when we read, we attend selectively and fill in an enormous amount of information. The meaning of something causes us to complete the gaps in the elements of language—in the words and letters. As we read text, we are able to make good predictions the words we expect to see. These predictions, for example, were probably good enough to allow you to fill in the missing word "about" in the preceding sentence.

Context determines what we hear. "I went to the new display last night" can get a shocked reaction from someone who heard "I went to the nudist play last night" because the sounds are the same. When I was very young, my father told me that the "Prince of Whales" was coming to the United States. I asked him for weeks if we could go to the aquarium to see this royal marine mammal. We use active processing to analyze specific sounds and language patterns and search for meaning. When the sounds are ambiguous or difficult to hear, we fill in the gaps.

Warren and Warren (1920) did an interesting study on this process. People heard the following: "It was found that the ___ eel was on the _____ ." Different subjects were given four different words to end the sentence: *axle, orange, shoe,* and *table.* They were then asked to repeat what they had heard. Those who had heard "axle" recalled the sentence as "It was found that the *wheel* was on the axle." Those who had heard "orange" inserted *peel;* those who had heard "shoe" inserted *heel;* and those who had heard "table" inserted *meal.* The subjects did not *think* that they were *guessing* the word; they believed they had *actually heard* the sentence. They had filled in the sentence with the most likely element.

CONVERSATIONAL MAXIMS

It is a long leap to go from the elements of language, such as phonemes and surface structure, to an understanding of how we actually communicate in daily speech. Consider the following exchange:

SARAH: I think I have a headache.

JANE: Well, there's a store open around the corner. (Miller, 1981)

What are these people doing? What is the relationship between the first and second statements? The relationship between two speakers follows the **cooperativeness principle:** each speaker tries to understand *why* the other said what he or she did. In this case, the implication is that the store sells something that might relieve the headache. Otherwise the exchange makes no sense.

Following the cooperativeness principle, there are four **conversational maxims** that speakers usually obey when they speak (Grice, 1967; Miller, 1988):

1. *Quantity.* Make your contribution as informative as required, but not more so. If someone asks, "Where do you live?" the answer will depend on where you are. If you live in San Francisco, and you are in your neighborhood, you may say "Green Street." If you are in London, you may say "the United States" or "California." It would be idiotic to tell someone in London that you live on "Green Street." Likewise, if you are in San Francisco, you would never say "I live in the United States." Both of these violate the maxim of quantity.

   However, sometimes this maxim is deliberately violated.

   BILL: How did you like your date last night?

   BOB: Well, she had nice shoes.

Here Bob is not being as informative as is usually required and therefore implies something about his date. Since he says nothing about her personality, it most likely means that he did not like her much.

2. *Quality.* Try to be truthful in conversation. This maxim is often violated in the use of metaphor and in sarcasm. If you say, "I hated the movie," and your friend responds, "Swell, wasn't it," he or she is signaling agreement by violating the principle.

3. *Relation.* Contributions should be relevant to the conversation. Suppose you are a building engineer and your boss says, "It's warm in here." Your response in relation to the situation might be, "Yes, it's time for a maintenance check on the air conditioning." But if your date that night in your apartment says, "It's warm in here," it is doubtful that you would respond the same way!

4. *Manner.* Be clear and orderly. When this maxim is violated, the underlying intention usually is still clear. For example, here is a critique of a would-be singer's audition: "Ms. Mallam managed to produce a number of sounds that seemed to resemble the song 'How're You Gonna Keep 'em Down on the Farm after They've Seen Paree.'" The implication is clear.

The perception of meaning in language, like all perception, is complex and arises from a combination of specific elements, their organization, and the rules that guide our conversation.

LANGUAGE AND THOUGHT

It is nearly impossible for us to separate language and thinking: we formulate our hypotheses through language when we solve a problem; we often actively think it out in words. But language is not the only vehicle for thought; thoughts can be expressed in gestures and movement as well as in music, art, and many other ways. Still, the nature of the relationship of thinking and language has been an important and controversial one in psychology.

Benjamin Lee Whorf proposed that language determines the structure of thinking.

> We dissect nature along lines laid down by our native language. The categories and types that we isolate from the world of phenomena we do not find here because they stare every observer in the face; on the contrary, the world is presented in a kaleidoscopic flux of impressions which has to be organized by our minds—and this means largely by the linguistic systems in our minds. We put nature up, organize it into concepts, and ascribe significances as we do, largely because we are parties to an agreement to organize it this way—an agreement that holds throughout our speech community and is codified in the patterns of our language. The agreement is, of course, an implicit and unstated one, but its terms are absolutely obligatory; we cannot talk at all except by subscribing to the organization and classification of data which the agreement decrees. (Whorf, 1942)

The Arab, for example, has several words for *camel*; the Eskimo has many words for *snow*. Certain languages, like the Hopi, have no words for past and future.

Whorf's hypothesis, in its strongest form—that language reflects the structure of our reality—has excited many psychologists and anthropologists and has created a great controversy. Eleanor Rosch (1973) studied this hypothesis on the Dani, a New Guinean culture, who have only two words for color; one roughly corresponds to *black,* the other to *white.* If Whorf's proposition were right, then the Dani would not be able to discriminate among colors such as *gray, blue,* and *hot pink.* When carefully questioned, however, the Dani *do* show the ability to perceive colors as we see them (Brown, in press). Thus, language does not *entirely* determine thought. Color perception is strongly determined by the innate receptive characteristics of the eye, presumably common to all cultures.

So, a diluted version of Whorf's hypothesis would be that language *influences* thought, not that it determines it. A particular language makes certain ideas more available than others. There are words in all languages that are not translatable into other languages. *Gemütlichkeit* and *gestalt* are German words that have no direct English equivalents. Similarly, there is no word for *consciousness* in French.

It is, however, just as likely that languages are the way they are because our thinking is the way it is. The Eskimo may need hundreds of words for snow because they encounter it daily and need fine distinctions for survival. If it were necessary, we could learn them too. The more specialized we become in a field, the finer the linguistic distinctions we make. For instance, physicians learn a vocabulary that *follows,* not precedes, their thought. As we become more expert in an area, the nature of our category system changes; categories become more intricate and complex, and language develops along with them. An automobile enthusiast may see "a Jaguar XK 120 drophead"; an uninitiated person may notice "an old sports car."

THE COMPUTER AND THE MIND

Consider intelligence, artificial and natural. The goal of making an "artificial person" is one that has tantalized humanity for centuries. In recent years, scientists have made important progress toward one of the most important parts of this goal—building machines that do "intelligent" things. As we will see in Chapter 11, it is very hard to even define precisely what we mean by "intelligence," but most of us have a general idea of what it means for a person to seem intelligent. One useful definition of **artificial intelligence** is the study of ideas that enable computers to do the things that make people seem intelligent (Winston, 1979).

GOALS OF ARTIFICIAL INTELLIGENCE

From its inception in the late 1950s, artificial intelligence inquiry has combined two different goals. The first is to get computers to do intelligent things using whatever techniques succeed. The second goal is to get computers to do intelligent things in the same way that people do them. Both of these approaches have been successful.

The first approach has led to programs that now have commercial applications in such fields as factory automation, geological interpretation, and computer configuration (Winston & Prendergast, 1984). Computer programs are now being used to help geologists interpret the complex readings they receive from various instruments (such as seismographs) and predict the location of petroleum and mineral deposits.

The second approach has contributed to many of the insights discussed throughout this book about how people think, reason, communicate, and solve problems. Consider trying to program computers to understand language. The problem of getting computers to understand "natural languages" (like English and French) instead of "artificial languages" (like computer programming languages) has turned out to be much more difficult than researchers initially expected. One of the most important reasons for this difficulty is that understanding language requires knowing much more than just the rules of grammar and the definitions of words. A great deal of detailed knowledge about the world is also required.

Consider again the exchange we saw above:

SARAH: I think I have a headache.

JANE: Well, there's a store open around the corner. (Miller, 1981)

Understanding this simple dialogue requires knowledge about the relationship between headaches and medications, about the kinds of medications that are sold in stores, and about regular business hours. There is so much knowledge like this that is potentially relevant to understanding language that no one has yet succeeded in representing more than a tiny fraction of it in a computer program.

One current project is attempting to represent in a computer the kind of commonsense knowledge found in an encyclopedia (Lenat & Guha, 1988). Their estimates (which other researchers find optimistic) are that this project will take a staff of dozens of people working for at least 10 years. Also, computers still have very limited language-understanding capabilities. Trying to program computers to understand sentences such as this one has helped us realize how much world knowledge is used every day by people to understand the same sentences.

Artificial intelligence was popularized in movies like *2001: A Space Odyssey*, which featured the independent-thinking computer, HAL.

SIMILARITIES BETWEEN THE COMPUTER AND THE MIND

One of the reasons why research in artificial intelligence is important to psychologists is because comparing how people's minds work with how computers work can help us learn more about both. The degree of similarity between minds and computers, however, is an issue about which many people disagree.

Many researchers believe that human beings and computers can be comprehended as physical systems that process meaningful symbols (Arkes & Hammond, 1986). People and computers do the same kinds of things: they receive information from the world, they process it in some way, and then they perform some actions. The specific ways in which this occurs may be very different in the two cases. Most computers have limited ways of receiving information and performing actions (for example, typewriter keyboards and television screens). Certainly the "hardware" in the two kinds of systems (human and computer) is very different: neurons in one case, silicon in the other. But since the same general kinds of behavior *can* occur in both cases, perhaps much of human thought can be analyzed in terms of how a computer might perform the same function.

A test of a computer as a model of human intelligence is whether a computer can actually produce the same kind of behavior a human being can. In many cases, computer programs today can pass this test. Recall the computer programs that can play chess at the level of a good college chess team member—although the best human players can still beat these programs.

An extreme version of this kind of test is called the *Turing test* (Turing, 1950). A person communicates by typing on a computer console with two other "people." One of the "people" is in fact a computer program, and the other is a real person. The test is to see whether the first person can distinguish the human from the computer program by asking questions and looking at the answers. In part because of the difficulties of understanding natural language, no computer program today is close to being able to pass the most general form of this test.

DIFFERENCES BETWEEN THE COMPUTER AND THE MIND

There are certainly differences in the things people and computers can do and in how the two kinds of systems do the things of which both are capable. Computers can perform well-defined sequential calculations much more rapidly than people. People are much better than computers at understanding the ambiguous, such as seeing analogies or learning new concepts.

Some of these differences are simply because a human brain is many orders of magnitude more complex than even the largest of today's computers. There are also other important ways in which the basic processes of present-day computers may differ from human minds. Two of these involve analog versus digital processing and serial versus parallel processing.

ANALOG VERSUS DIGITAL PROCESSING   Almost all computers used today are *digital* computers. This means that their basic processing occurs in terms of exact categories: a switch is either on or off. Thus, a number may be 4.1397 or 4.1396, but it is always *exactly* something. Human brains, on the other hand, seem to depend at least in part on what are called *analog* properties of the behavior of neurons. This means that there are not always exact categories; instead there may be shades of gray that gradually change from one thing to another without sharp boundaries. This distinction is a complicated one because either kind of system can behave like the other. Given enough time and storage capacity, digital systems can represent gradients, just as they represent decimal digits, with as much precision as necessary. Also, analog systems can be constructed to detect sharp boundaries. For example, the voltage potential on a neuron may change very gradually, but at some point, the neuron fires. Nevertheless, these differences between what is easy and what is hard to accomplish in the two different kinds of systems may have important consequences for their overall behavior (Haugeland, 1985).

SERIAL VERSUS PARALLEL PROCESSING Most computers today use *serial processing*, which means that even when they do things very rapidly, they still do them one step at a time, one after another. Human brains, in contrast, appear to use a great deal of *parallel processing*. Even though we usually cannot pay attention to more than one thing at a time, much processing in our brain is occurring simultaneously; our brain is regulating breathing and heart rate while we are thinking about other things. Even the processes we are conscious of, such as trying to remember someone's name, seem to occur with many different neurons in many different parts of the brain, all at once.

Some researchers feel that, because the basic processes by which humans and computers do things are so different, the resulting behavior must be fundamentally different, too. According to this view, even if computers behaved exactly like people we would still not want to call what computers do "thinking." A somewhat less extreme position holds that, because the basic processes are so different, we will never be able to reproduce much interesting human behavior using computers. Therefore, according to this view, computers will not turn out to be very useful in explaining most human behavior because of practical rather than philosophical reasons.

Interestingly, computers of the future are likely to use much more parallel processing than the computers we have today. In fact, a great deal of current research in computer science is devoted to making "neural network" computers that are much more like human brains than today's computers are (see, for instance, Anderson & Rosenfeld, 1988).

NEURAL NETWORK MODELS OF THINKING AND LEARNING

So far most psychological theories of thinking and learning have focused on processes that occur one step at a time. For instance, a cognitive theory about how we read a sentence might involve the following series of steps, occurring in very rapid succession: first, we convert the visual input from our eyes into letters; then, we recognize the words that those letters spell; next, we use our knowledge of grammar to determine what role each word plays in the sentence; finally, we use our knowledge of word meanings and of the context to figure out the meaning of the sentence.

Recently, psychologists have begun to develop theories that involve all these processes occurring at once, instead of one after the other (see Holyoak, Koh, & Nisbett, 1989; Rumelhart & McClelland, 1986). For instance, these new theories can explain more easily the fact that our knowledge of the context can help us recognize a blurred letter in the middle of a word.

These theories are often called *neural network models* because they are inspired by our knowledge of how neurons in the brain work (see Anderson & Rosenfeld, 1988). In the brain, many neurons operate at the same time, and the intelligence of the brain seems to come not from the fact that the individual neurons are "intelligent" but from the way the neurons are connected to each other.

A SIMPLE NEURAL NETWORK MODEL McClelland and Rumelhart (1981) have developed a neural network model of how we might recognize words (Figure 10-5). The

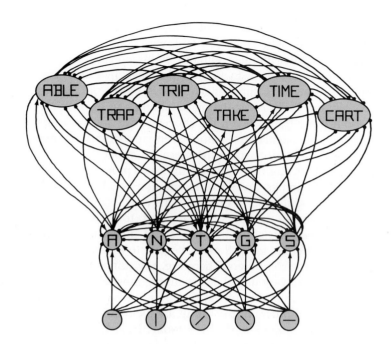

FIGURE 10-5
Neural Network Model

A prominent model of how we recognize words theorizes that neurons first identify the visual features of a letter, then identify the letter, and eventually recognize the word by identifying each of its letters in turn.
(McClelland & Rumelhart, 1981)

basic idea in these models is that "nodes" are connected to each other in a network and are "activated" by stimulation from the other nodes they are connected to. At a very general level, this resembles the way neurons in the brain activate other neurons via their synaptic connections. Also as in the brain, some of the connections increase activation; others decrease it.

In this example, the nodes at the bottom of the figure are assumed to be activated when we see simple visual features such as vertical or horizontal bars. Then activation spreads throughout the network until, eventually, one of the words at the top is more activated than any other, and we "recognize" this word. If no one word is more activated than the others, we would not be able to recognize any word in the pattern we were seeing (for instance, the word might be too blurred, or it might not be a word we know).

Most psychologists who develop neural network models do not take them as literal models of how neurons are actually connected in the brain, but the models are able to explain aspects of human behavior that are hard to explain with other models. For instance, consider how we might recognize the word shown in Figure 10-6 (Rumelhart & McClelland, 1986). Even though the last letter is partly obscured, the node for the word *WORK* might receive a fairly large amount of activation anyway. The activation from this word would then spread back to all the letters it contains, making it more likely that we will recognize the blurred letter as a *K*.

FIGURE 10-6
Model of Word Recognition
(Rumelhart & McClelland, 1986)

LEARNING IN NEURAL NETWORKS One of the most intriguing aspects of neural network models is how they can learn new things from experience. A network can be "trained" to associate particular input patterns with particular outputs by gradually increasing the strength of the connections that lead to right answers and decreasing the others.

If you are like most people, you have a desk. If your desk is neat, you probably have few piles on it, and you have places for everything. On the other hand, if your desk is messy, there may be piles all over it, and you may have little idea of where most things are. But have you ever wondered why piles arise in the first place? In a sense, your desk is a kind of external memory for you: you use it to store information you don't keep in your brain. What are the psychological processes at work when you use this external memory? In trying to design computers that help people keep track of lots of personal information—like that found on a desk—researchers have studied how people organize the information on their desks today (e.g., Malone, 1983).

FINDING AND REMINDING

One of the first insights of this study was that there are two primary functions a desk must serve. It is probably no surprise that you organize the things on your desk, at least in part, so you can find them later, and this *finding* function is clearly important.

A second, equally important function, however, is *reminding*. Much of the information that people keep on top of their desks and tables is there to remind them to do something, not just to be available when they look for it. If you put something away in a file, it may be lost forever ("out of sight, out of mind"). But if you leave it out on top of your desk you will (at least in theory) be reminded of it again without making any conscious effort to look for it. The problem with this often unconscious strategy is, of course, that it is self-defeating: when your desktop becomes overloaded with too many things you need to be reminded of, most of them become buried and you are not reminded of them after all.

PILES AND FILES

A second pattern found in this study was the prevalence of two

primary structures for desk organization: "files" and "piles." These two structures have different characteristics and different relative advantages. For instance, one of the obvious advantages of files is that, even when they contain large volumes of information, you can locate specific items fairly easily by their "key." A disadvantage of files, however, is that you must exert mental (and sometimes physical) effort to assign a key to something before you put it into the file.

One of the advantages of piles, on the other hand, is that they don't require explicit verbal keys. You can create a pile of papers on your desk, grouping them according to some criteria you vaguely sense but have never explicitly articulated, and you can still retrieve items from the pile using its spatial location rather than an explicit key. Another reason for creating piles, therefore, in addition to the reminding function, is to avoid the cognitive effort of explicitly classifying it with a key.

WHAT CAN YOU DO?

If you have a messy desk, but are still able to function reasonably well, you may already be spending about the right amount of effort organizing your desk. On the other hand, if you often find yourself wasting large amounts of time looking for things in your desk, or if important things you are supposed to do often "slip through the cracks," then you probably need to spend more time keeping your desk organized.

Many time management experts say you should try to "touch every piece of paper only once," instead of leaving it around on your desk for later action. A potential problem with this approach, however, is that you may spend an inordinate amount of time dealing with relatively unimportant pieces of paper, while important things go undone.

For instance, Sejnowski and Rosenberg (1987) trained a computer version of a neural network model to pronounce letters correctly by "rewarding" it for right answers and "punishing" it for wrong answers. Interestingly, this computer model resembled the way people learn in two important ways: (1) it made mistakes that were similar to those made by children; and (2) the more words the computer model learned, the better it was able to pronounce correctly new words it had never seen before.

It is not yet clear whether neural network theories are ultimately any better than their precursors at explaining psychological phenomena (see Richman & Simon, 1989). However, they have provided psychologists (and computer scientists) with an intriguing new way of thinking about how we think.

SUMMARY

1. Thought processes and language work by selecting a few simplified elements and combining them to create new possibilities. Psychologists have defined two basic structures of thought: *classification with categories* and *simplification with heuristics.*

2. *Categories* simplify to give the most information with the least effort. They are part of our mental models and reflect the nature of the world. Categories that are a universal part of human experience are called *natural categories.* Color is an example. People may disagree about the qualities of artificial categories. *Basic-level categories* are the ones we most often use to break up the world. For each category, there is a prototype which exemplifies its qualities. The *prototype* is not always the most common example.

3. We tend to *overgeneralize* because we can maintain only limited information in our consciousness. The importance of our current experience is overemphasized. *Heuristics* are strategies we use to generalize and solve problems. They often sacrifice accuracy for speed in decision making. Using representativeness, we *generalize* from the qualities of a single event to an entire category. We use the *availability* of memories of events to judge the probability of events, though our personal experience may not be generally applicable. We compare current events to standards, but our standards are always shifting.

4. *Decision making* requires choosing among several options. The four basic elements of a decision are: a set of alternatives, a set of possible outcomes, one's preferences among the outcomes, and one's judgement of the probabilities of the outcomes. Heuristics help us make decisions, resulting in faster decisions, but also biasing our judgement. People tend to overestimate the importance of events that are easily recalled *(availability).* They will judge that a thing belongs in an improbable category because it shares some of its features *(representativeness),* and will weigh vivid, concrete information more heavily than statistical probabilities.

5. When we first approach a problem, we are likely to use *heuristics* to solve it. Thereafter, we will try solutions that have worked in the past. Simple problems are often solved by *trial and error,* or by *hypothesis testing.* Most problems have three basic elements: the initial state, a set of possible operations by the problem-solver, and a goal that would be a solution to the problem. The four basic steps in problem-solving are: understanding the problem, planning a solution, carrying out the plan, and checking your results.

6. Part of understanding a problem is finding the best way to represent it. Some problems are best represented visually and others mathematically. *Algorithms* are strategies that guarantee that one will find a solution eventually but that take a lot of

processing. People use heuristics and insight as shortcuts in complex situations. Two problem-solving heuristics are *hill climbing,* or constantly moving toward a goal; and *means-end analysis,* working backward from the goal to the means needed to achieve it. Problems are sometimes solved by a sudden *insight*—the sudden understanding of how to arrange a set of elements in a new way.

7. Psychologists study problem solving by *protocol analysis,* which is having people think out loud as they solve problems. People tend to repeat actions that have been successful in the past, although they may not be the most effective means of solving a current problem.

8. *Creativity* allows people to go beyond normal problem solving and invent new solutions. One theory proposes that the creative process is like natural selection: a few random variations out of many ideas are selected as being appropriate. Creativity involves the stages of preparation, generation, evaluation, and implementation.

9. Different forms of language are termed *speech acts.* Three important speech acts are: conveying information, demanding information, and giving a command. The individual sounds of a language are called *phonemes.* Phonemes are meaningless by themselves. *Morphemes* are units of meaning created by combining phonemes. *Grammar* is the study of the formal rules of language. The way words are arranged to convey meaning is called *syntax.*

10. Because children are naturally adept at language, some scientists believe grammar is an innate human ability. The transformational view of grammar distinguishes between the *deep* and *surface structure* of syntax. One deep structure can produce many different surface structures—sentences that carry the same deep meaning.

11. The tendency in language to search for order and meaning and to go beyond the information given is called *active processing. Meaning* and *context* help us fill in information when language is ambiguous and can determine what we hear.

12. In conversation, people generally follow the *cooperativeness principle:* both speakers try to understand the other's meaning. Four conversational maxims are: *quantity,* give an appropriate amount of information; *quality,* be truthful; *relation,* speak relevantly to the current conversation and situation; and *manner,* speak clearly. These maxims can be violated to convey alternative meanings.

13. Language influences thought but does not determine it. As we develop specialization and knowledge about a field, we make finer linguistic distinctions about it, and our categories become more complex.

14. The two goals of *artificial intelligence* research are to program computers to act intelligently and to use intelligence in the same manner as humans. Attempts to get computers to understand "natural language" have revealed the complexity of analysis humans regularly employ in speaking. Computers and minds are similar in that they both can be explained as physical systems that process meaningful symbols. Computers are better than humans at sequential calculations, but people are better at understanding ambiguous concepts.

15. Most computers use *serial processing,* but the human brain processes much information in *parallel.* Current research in computer science is focusing on developing *neural network* computers that function similarly to the brain. Neural network models can learn from experience in a pattern similar to operant conditioning. They have provided psychologists with new ways of analyzing thought processes.

TERMS AND CONCEPTS

algorithms
artificial category
artificial intelligence
availability
basic-level category
biases
category
classification
comparison
conversational maxims
cooperativeness principle
decision analysis
generalize
grammar
heuristics
hypothesis testing
insight

means-end analysis
morphemes
natural categories
overgeneralization
phonemes
problem representation
problem solving
protocol analysis
prototype
representativeness
set
speech acts
subgoals
syntax
transformational grammar
trial and error
vivid information

SUGGESTIONS FOR FURTHER READING

Arkes, H. R., & Hammond, K. R. (1986). *Judgment and decision making.* New York: Cambridge University Press.

An up-to-date summary of research in the field with articles on rationality, expert judgment, decisions in clinical practice, and the like.

Haugeland, J. (Ed.). (1985). *Mind design: Philosophy, psychology, and artificial intelligence.* Cambridge: MIT Press.

An excellent collection of readings by leading computer scientists and philosophers about such questions as whether machines really "think" and whether people are really "information processors."

Johnson-Laird, P. N. (1983). *Mental models.* Cambridge: Harvard University Press.

A recent and interesting account of problems in the nature of the mind, such as "Why do we have to think everything in order, not at once?"

Kahneman, D., Slovic, P., & Tversky, A. (Eds.). (1982). *Judgment under uncertainty.* New York: Cambridge University Press.

A compilation of much of the classic work on how we use heuristics in judgment, how we make mistakes, and the nature of the mental system that underlies these processes. Technical, but interesting and worthwhile.

Miller, G. A. (1981). *Language and speech.* San Francisco: W. H. Freeman.

An elegant, entertaining, and witty introduction to the question and the problem of understanding language.

Penrose, R. (1989). *The emperor's new mind: Concerning computers, minds, and the laws of physics.* New York: Oxford University Press.

The argument that the computer can never model the mind.

11
THE MEASUREMENT OF INTELLIGENCE

P

robably the first bit of psychology you encountered was an intelligence test. Perhaps you were asked to take it in your childhood or perhaps later on. Here, we offer some of the intelligence behind studying intelligence.

The most public and probably the most important endeavor in the history of intelligence testing has been the search for a measurement of intelligence: what it is, who has it, and whether it is inherited. Until quite recently, it has been difficult to come up with anything more useful than the early, simplified approaches.

In 1859, Charles Darwin published *On the Origin of Species,* which marked the beginning of the modern scientific era in biology and related sciences. In psychology, his theory of evolution sparked interest in the variations in human mental abilities. The early psychologists thought that if survival depends on adaptation to the environment, then the superior intelligence of human beings must have been important in human evolution. The most intelligent human beings, because of their superior adaptability, would have been selected. These new ideas ignited a great interest in measuring intelligence.

Darwin's cousin, Francis Galton (1822–1911), was the first modern scientist to try systematically to determine what intelligence was. What is obvious to us now was the result of a great deal of hard work! Galton tried to measure the key elements in intelligence, and some of what he did may seem strange to us now.

Galton examined the concepts of head size and **sensory acuity** as the primary indicators of intelligence. Thus, he began by measuring heads until he found that, in contrast to the popular supposition, a big head does not mean a big mind. He reasoned that "the more perceptive the senses are of differences, the larger is the field upon which our judgment and intelligence can act." Thus, to measure intelligence, Galton devised tests of sensory acuity. He studied reaction times in response to sound, the speed in naming colors, the judgment of points on the skin, and so on. As you might guess, this didn't get too far.

BINET: THE BEGINNINGS OF MODERN INTELLIGENCE TESTING

The next great attempt to measure intelligence took place in France. It eventually led to testing the intelligence of millions of children, which greatly affected the course of their lives. Universal public education became compulsory in the late nineteenth century (up to that point, only the rich could afford to educate their children). Teachers did not know how to teach all these children from different backgrounds who had different degrees of preparation for school. The testing that became necessary was to have a profound effect on our ideas of intelligence.

In 1904 the French government asked Alfred Binet to devise a test to predict which children would be least likely to succeed in school. In the preceding years, Binet and his colleagues had charted an important new approach to intelligence, an approach still in use today. Among the insights of Binet's group were these:

1. Why not directly test actions that teachers and school administrators regard as intelligent? No one had ever done that before. Binet and his associates designed tests of sentence comprehension, visual memory, reasoning, and the ability to detect errors in thinking.

ALFRED BINET
(1857–1911)

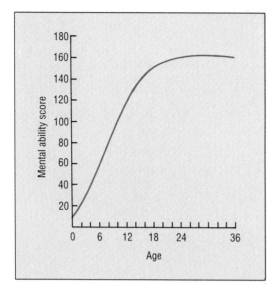

FIGURE 11-1
Increased Mental Abilities in Childhood

There is a rapid increase in intelligence in childhood and a leveling off in early adulthood.
(From W. Bayley, Development of mental abilities, in Mussen, P. (ed.), *Carmichael's manual of child psychology*, Vol. 1, copyright © 1970, John Wiley and Sons.)

2. Intelligence testing would have to be applicable to ranking large numbers of children into "bright," "average," and "below average" groups. To get an idea of how to do this, Binet first tested children who were *already known* to be performing at these levels in schools. Tests developed from these children were used to test other children whose scholastic abilities were unknown.

3. Binet noted that *as children age, their intellectual abilities increase* (Figure 11-1). Thus, he developed tests to measure cognitive development. The measurements were converted into scores to identify which children were exceptionally intelligent, which were normal, and which were retarded. In this testing scheme, a bright child is one whose *mental age* is greater than his or her chronological age, and a slow child is one whose mental age is less than his or her chronological age.

The French education system benefited from Binet's work. The tests were given individually by one examiner to one student and took hours to attain a score. The French schools then used the results of these tests to assign children to classes. Below-average children were either given special training or released from attendance.

MASS TESTING

A few years later, another profound change in society directly affected intelligence testing: World War I broke out. This was a war vastly different from any waged previously. It was the first war in which millions of men from the general population were required to fight. In the United States, the Army needed to know the capabilities of its unknown, untrained, and untried soldiers.

Psychologists were called upon to develop intelligence tests that could be given to large groups and could be scored quickly. The quantified scores took on more importance than they had in Binet's original tests. They were used directly to determine the assignments of soldiers.

Intelligence testing was first used on a mass scale at the beginning of World War I to test untrained recruits.

377

MODERN INTELLIGENCE TESTING

THE WECHSLER TEST

David Wechsler introduced the *deviation IQ*. Individuals are scored according to their relationship to their age group's average score on the test. The current test is standardized at a norm of 100 with a *standard deviation* of 16. (See the appendix, "Statistics: Making Sense of Fallible Data," for an explanation of standard deviation.) An individual who scores one standard deviation above the norm is assigned an IQ of 116; two above the norm, 132; and so on. The test is continually modified to assess people at the low end of the range more adequately.

Wechsler then devised the **Wechsler Adult Intelligence Scale (WAIS-R)** (Table 11-1) and the **Wechsler Intelligence Scale for Children (WISC-R)** (Figure 11-2). Their advantage over the Binet tests is that they measure two major areas of intelligence—*verbal* and *performance*—and yield three scores—

FIGURE 11-2
The Wechsler Intelligence Scale for Children

This scale uses modified versions of the tests in the adult scale, such as the block design test shown being taken by this child.

TABLE 11-1
Tests Used in the Wechsler Adult Intelligence Scale-Revised

Test	Description
VERBAL SCALE	
Information	Questions tap a general range of information; for example, "How many nickels make a dime?"
Comprehension	Tests practical information and ability to evaluate past experience; for example, "What is the advantage of keeping money in a bank?"
Arithmetic	Verbal problems testing arithmetic reasoning.
Similarities	Asks in what way certain objects or concepts (for example, *egg* and *seed*) are similar; measures abstract thinking.
Digit span	A series of digits presented auditorily (for example, 7-5-6-3-8) is repeated in a forward or backward direction; tests attention and rote memory.
Vocabulary	Tests word knowledge.
PERFORMANCE SCALE	
Digit symbol	A timed coding task in which numbers must be associated with marks of various shapes; tests speed of learning and writing.
Picture completion	The missing part of an incompletely drawn picture must be discovered and named; tests visual alertness and visual memory.
Block design	Pictured designs must be copied with blocks (see Figure 11-3); tests ability to perceive and analyze patterns.
Picture arrangement	A series of comic-strip pictures must be arranged in the right sequence to tell a story; tests understanding of social situations.
Object assembly	Puzzle pieces must be assembled to form a complete object; tests ability to deal with part-whole relationships.

Source: Wechsler Adult Intelligence Scale and Wechsler Adult Intelligence Scale-Revised. Copyright © 1955, 1981 by The Psychological Corporation. All rights reserved.

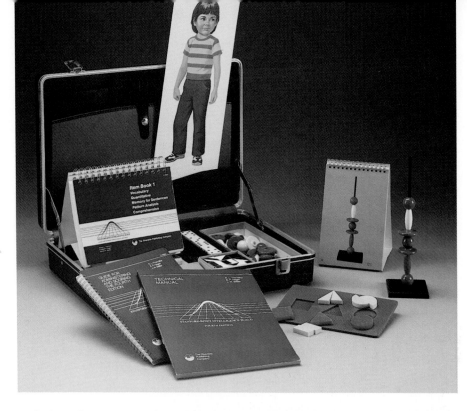

Test materials from the 1986 Stanford-Binet intelligence scale

verbal, performance, and combined. This separation of abilities gives a slightly better portrait of the dimensions of intellectual abilities. Recent developments have gone even further in this regard.

THE STANFORD-BINET TEST

The original Binet test was adapted by Lewis Terman of Stanford University who standardized it for American students in 1916. This **Stanford-Binet test** was restandardized many times. Figure 11-3 shows the distribution used to

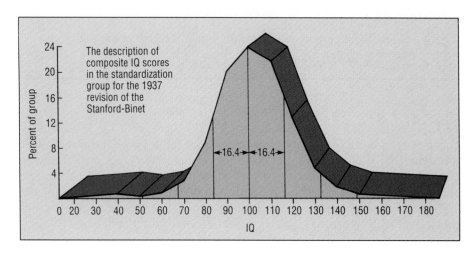

The description of composite IQ scores in the standardization group for the 1937 revision of the Stanford-Binet

FIGURE 11-3
IQ Scores

This graph, from an early form of the Stanford-Binet intelligence Scale (L–M), shows the normal distribution of the standardized IQ scores. (Terman & Merrill, 1973)

TABLE 11-2
Descriptions of Items from the 1986 Stanford-Binet Intelligence Scale

Verbal Reasoning

Vocabulary   Defines words, such as "telephone" and "bus."

Comprehension   Answers questions, such as "Where do people buy clothes?" and "Why do people take baths?"

Absurdities   Identifies the "funny" aspect of a picture, such as a person driving a car from the back seat.

Verbal Relations   Tells how the first three items in a sequence are alike and how they differ from the fourth: slipper, sandal, sneaker, watch.

Quantitative Reasoning

Quantitative   Performs simple arithmetic tasks, such as selecting a die with five spots because the number of spots equals the combination of a two-spot and a three-spot die.

Number Series   Gives the next two numbers in a series, such as

$$10 \quad 8 \quad 6 \quad 4 \quad \_\_ \quad \_\_ .$$

Equation Building   Builds an equation from the following array:

$$2 \quad 4 \quad 6 \quad + \quad = .$$ One of several correct responses would be $2 + 4 = 6$.

Abstract/Visual Reasoning

Pattern Analysis   Copies a simple design with blocks.

Copying   Copies a geometrical drawing demonstrated by the examiner, such as a rectangle interesected by two diagonals.

Short-Term Memory

Bead Memory   Shown a picture of different-shaped beads stacked on a stick. Reproduces the sequence from memory by placing real beads on a stick.

Memory for Sentences   Repeats after the examiner sentences such as "She locked the door and put the key in her pocket."

Memory for Digits   Repeats after the examiner a series of digits, such as 6-8-9-4, forward and backward.

Memory for Objects   Shown pictures of individual objects, such as a lamp and a dog, one at a time. Identifies the objects in the correct order of their appearance in a picture that also includes extraneous objects; for example, a truck, a whale, a *lamp,* a squirrel, a *dog,* and an apple.

Note: These are typical items for 6- to 8-year-olds.

standardize it in 1937. Sample items appear in Table 11-2. The **intelligence quotient (IQ)** was originally a ratio that related a person's mental age to chronological age. It is derived by dividing the mental age (MA) by the chronologial age (CA) and then multiplying by 100. Binet's concept of mental age signified increasing amounts of intelligence. Thus, a child who tests at a mental age of 10 when he or she is 8 years old has an IQ of 125.

STABILITY AND VALIDITY

If IQ reflects a constant and general faculty of a unitary and constant intelligence, then a child's IQ should be the same when he or she is 2, 7, 14, and so on. IQ is not stable, however, for a child's early years. An IQ test given to a 2-year-old child does not predict well what the IQ will be later on in life. For example, the relationship of the IQ at 2 years to the IQ at 14 years is very low. At older ages the relationship is better, though; IQ at 14 years of age is well predicted by the IQ at 7 years. As the young person moves into adulthood, the IQ appears to stabilize (recall Figure 11-1).

Do IQs predict later success in school and in society? This is an important question because it relates to the purpose for which the test was designed. A review of data on IQ scores and school grades found that it does: the higher the IQ, the better the school grades. As expected, IQs in the normal range do predict success in society. On the *average*, accountants have higher IQs than sales clerks, and sales clerks have higher IQs than miners. However, some miners have much higher IQs than the average for accountants and lawyers. The best use of IQ seems to be close to Binet's original purpose: to identify those children who are most likely to profit from different types of schooling. In its original intent it was a great step forward; it could quickly sort children as to what kind of education they might need. Educators are greatly in Binet's debt for this.

TESTING FOR GENERAL VERSUS SPECIFIC INTELLIGENCE

THE SEARCH FOR A GENERAL INTELLIGENCE

Early psychologists expended considerable effort on the search for a single, *general intelligence*. Charles Spearman's (1927) investigations sprang from his belief that general intelligence, which he called *g*, represented an entity related to "cerebral energy." The notion of a single, general intelligence, however, is too limited for an animal as complex as a human being.

Individuals differ in their intelligence as they do in their memories, perceptions, and abilities to learn. People have a great variety of abilities. One person may perform well on verbal tasks; another may be good at fitting objects together; and a third may write well. When children take several different tests of mental ability, some excel on some measures, others on different ones. However, there is a general agreement between ordinary people in our society and experts on who is more or less intelligent (Sternberg, 1985, 1989).

THE SEARCH FOR SPECIFIC INTELLECTUAL ABILITIES

Raymond Cattell (1971) divides intelligence into two major kinds of abilities. **Fluid abilities** involve perception of the world and are thought to be genetically based and independent of culture. **Crystallized abilities** derive from *specific* cultural experiences. They represent the store of gradually accumulated knowledge: vocabulary, mathematics, and social reasoning.

Guilford and his colleagues (1971) conceive of intelligence as being a *large set of independent abilities,* each different and distinct from the other. In Guilford's view the different mental factors can be organized in three categories:

1. *Contents* describe the information in the mind.
2. *Operations* are the working rules of the mind.
3. *Products* are units, systems, relationships, and so on that have to do with how things are related to one another in the mind.

This model may not be accurate in detail, but it is important in its general concept: a person's intelligence is composed of a mosaic of specific intellectual abilities and talents. There are people with good memories for faces, and others who are good with names but not good with faces. There are people who are good at finding their way around in new surroundings but who have trouble thinking abstractly. There are those who have great musical abilities but who have little intelligence in the areas that Howard Gardner (1983) calls the "personal."

THE DISTRIBUTION OF INTELLIGENCE

The distribution of the Binet-type intelligence test has caused more controversy than any other product of psychology. The IQ tests are used to classify children in schools, and those who score low—60 to 70, for example—may be placed in classes of "educable mentally retarded" (EMR). Sometimes this division is warranted and humane. There are some severely retarded or disturbed people who could not function academically in a traditional public school classroom. However, much of the time, the standard tests discriminate against children whose backgrounds differ from the norm, and the norm is usually white, middle class, and male.

The issue of race and intelligence is a controversial topic that must be addressed squarely. We need to clarify the genetic basis of intelligence, understand what we mean by "intelligence" and "race," and analyze the extreme claims of some experts. These issues touch on everyone in society, of all skin colors, ages, and educational levels.

INHERITANCE OF IQ AND INTELLIGENCE

The story of *heritability* is only beginning to be told. Knowing that a condition has a biological basis does not tell us what that basis is. It may be that genetic factors result in brains being more or less sensitive to electrical signals that allow cells to communicate with one another. Physiological reactions to identical substances, like alcohol, may be stronger or weaker depending on a person's genetic make-up. Reactions to experience, too, may differ, leaving one child vulnerable to a difficult situation and another safe (Scarr, 1988).

The problem of assessing the relative roles of genetics and environment are complex (Loehlin, Willerman, & Horn, 1988; Plomin, 1989; Scarr, 1988). Stevenson, Graham, Fredman, and McLoughlin (1989) tested twins to determine genetic influences, using standardized measures of intelligence, reading, and spelling ability. The genetic contribution to reading ability was assessed by examination of correlations in monozygotic (MZ) and same-sex dizygotic (DZ) twins and by analyzing differences between MZ and DZ twins in reading disability rates. Surprisingly, genetic factors play only a moderate role in general reading backwardness or specific reading retardation. However, when spelling ability was investigated, a heritability of 0.53 was obtained, increasing to 0.75 when intelligence was controlled. Strong genetic influences on spelling were also found when concordance rates for spelling disability were compared for MZ and DZ pairs.

Plomin and Loehlin have tried to resolve the puzzle of direct and indirect IQ heritability *estimates* (1989). They note that direct estimates of IQ heritability based on a single-family relationship such as adopted-apart relatives are often 50 percent greater than indirect estimates that rely on correlations such as the classical twin method or nonadoptive-adoptive comparisons. However, selective placement, measurement error, age differences, and genotype-environment correlation and interaction do not obviously explain the difference between direct and indirect IQ heritability estimates. It seems that some aspect of the within-family environment seems a likely candidate, but its exact nature remains to be understood.

In the past several years, many human attributes have been found to have a genetic basis, and even important biological functions such as the electrocardiogram (EKG) vary between individuals on a genetic basis (Brown, 1990). Hanson and others (1989) recorded EKGs on a sample of MZ and DZ twins reared apart since birth or early infancy and found a significant contribution of genetic effects (most heritabilities ranged from 30 to 60 percent). In an important study, Tellegen and others (1988) administered the Multidimensional Personality Questionnaire (MPQ) to 217 MZ and 114 DZ reared-together adult twin pairs and 44 MZ and 27 DZ reared-apart adult twin pairs and analyzed for genetic

The identical genetic makeup of monozygotic (identical) twins makes them uniquely valuable in research on the relative influence of heredity and environment factors on IQ.

383

TABLE 11-3	
IQ and Genetic Relationship	Correlation
Identical twins	
Reared together	0.86
Reared apart	0.72
Fraternal twins	
Reared together	0.60
Siblings	
Reared together	0.47
Reared apart	0.24
Parent/child	0.40
Foster parent/child	0.31
Cousins	0.15
SOURCE: Bouchard & McGue, 1981.	

effects on such factors as interestedness, arousability, and lying. They found heritabilities ranging from 0.39 to 0.58, much higher than anyone would have previously believed. Even responsibility seems to have a genetic component.

Contrary to widely held beliefs, the overall contribution of a common family-environment component was small, and negligible for all but 2 of the 14 personality measures. We'll take up more of this later on in our treatment of personality. For now, the genetic component of our nature seems larger than most people had thought, and one researcher (Plomin, 1989) believes that the only variable that seems *not* to have a strong genetic component is agreeableness, which seems dependent on the early environment.

So there *is* an inherited component to the elusive qualities we call intelligence. It is the nature of that inheritance that is in question. Compare the relationship of IQ to genetic similarity in Table 11-3. If IQ is inherited, then the more similar people's genetic structures are, the more similar their IQs should be, which is, in fact, the case in the table. Note that the more genetically similar individuals are, the more similar are their IQs.

Identical twins have an identical genetic makeup, and they also have the closest IQ resemblance. Next in similarity come fraternal twins and siblings; their similarity is less but is still substantial. Parents and children also show a relationship, but as the genetic similarity decreases, so does the correspondence between their IQs.

Still, the environment has an important effect. The IQs of genetically related children reared together are much more similar than those for genetically related children reared apart. The correlation of IQ of identical twins reared apart is 0.72; together it is 0.86. The correlation between foster parents and children is about 0.30, a good indicator that the environment is important.

PROBLEMS WITH STUDYING HEREDITY AND IQ

Most studies that attempt to relate heredity to IQ do seem to indicate *some* relationship between them, but the precise estimate of heritability of intelligence is still in great dispute. The studies are fraught with problems and have been criticized on several grounds.

Consider the problems of the studies of adopted children and of twins raised apart. Any precise estimate of heritability from these studies is difficult because *adoptions aren't random.* Usually the environments of two separated twins are similar; sometimes they are raised by relatives, often close relatives. Many times twins know each other and know that they are twins.

Adoption agencies go to great lengths to place children in homes that are not only stable and middle class but also compatible with their biological parents. Many times a black family adopts a black child, an Oriental family adopts an Oriental one, and so on (Kamin, 1979). This matching of children and family is laudable from the point of view of the child and the family, but it makes precise measurement of the heritability of IQ very difficult. The adoptive family is often similar to the biological family. Thus, the influence of the similar environment makes the observed correlation between the IQ of the biological parents and that of the child appear greater than it is.

Matters are made even worse by cases of fraudulent studies. Much of the evidence amassed in support of the genetic viewpoint came from Sir Cyril Burt (1963) in England. Burt's work with his two colleagues was, for a time, the basis for many respectable scientists' positions. Burt had apparently documented a strong association between inheritance and IQ. But the work turned out to be a complete fraud. Burt had made up whole studies and had even invented his two famous colleagues! Overall, it is very difficult to estimate precisely the exact relationship between heritability and the IQ. One work (Jensen, 1980) proposes that 81 percent of IQ is inherited, but another important study (Willerman, 1979) estimates the heritability of the biological mother's IQ with the adopted child at only 25 percent. The estimates do vary, and may in fact be different for different groups, but there is clearly some strong inherited component to IQ, as there is to other portions of our personalities. Many if not most reviewers now assume a heritability of 0.6–0.7 is certainly possible, which is a much more direct influence of genes than psychologists had previously estimated.

Indeed, it would be surprising if there were *no* genetic component to IQ. The information encoded in the genes could fill approximately 1,700 full-sized pages. It seems reasonable that some of that information might relate to the reasoning and problem-solving skills that are so important in human evolution.

Researchers still dispute the heritability of intelligence. Adoptive studies evaluate the relationship of the parents' IQs to the adopted child's.

RACIAL DIFFERENCES IN IQ

No issue in psychology is more controversial than the question of inherited differences in intelligence among the different races. The evidence is straightforward, but it has been subject to different interpretations. The average IQ for black Americans is 85 to 90, whereas for whites it is 100.

In 1916, Lewis Terman, the adaptor of the Stanford-Binet test, stated that "high grade moronity [was] very common among Spanish, Indian, and Mexican families . . . and also among Negroes." In a celebrated article in 1969, Arthur Jensen argued that compensatory education programs that attempt to improve the intelligence of black children fail because the difference in IQ is innate. Richard Herrnstein thinks that the United States will eventually develop into a "meritocracy" based on heredity.

As the wealth and complexity of human society grow, there will be precipitated out of the mass of humanity a low capacity [group of people] that . . . cannot compete for success and achievement and are more likely to be born to parents who have similarly failed. . . . The tendency to be unemployed may run in the genes of the family about as certainly as bad teeth do now. (Herrnstein, 1973).

Every ethnic group that has migrated to the United States has been the subject of these arguments (Willerman, 1979). When the descendants of the people of the Italian Renaissance first came to the United States, they too were considered to be of inferior intelligence.

MISCONCEPTIONS ABOUT RACE AND IQ

The claim that certain races are *genetically* inferior in intelligence rests on several erroneous assumptions:

1. *IQ represents a fixed capacity.* Actually, change in the environment strongly affects IQ. A severely impoverished early experience stunts intellectual growth. However, when children in an impoverished environment get more stimulation, their IQs increase. The quality of education, coaching on test taking, and improvements in motivation and in facility with language all increase test scores. Less-educated people score less well on IQ tests. A low score probably means that the individual needs some compensatory education, as Binet had originally intended, not that he or she has a limited intellectual capacity.

2. *Racial differences are important.* The division of the human species into races was first formally classified by Linnaeus (1707–1778). He believed that races differed not only in color but also in personality characteristics. However, his racial classifications were essentially arbitrary. There are many ways to categorize and classify human beings into so-called races. One could differentiate them on the basis of height, hair color, blood type, eye color, hand or head size, and much more.

   The problem is the nature of the mind doing the judging: as in attractiveness and personal perception, surface appearances dominate in prejudice (see Chapter 17). In truth, the major characteristic differences between races are skin deep: they consist of superficial adaptations such as skin color, eye folds, and sweat glands. There is no evidence of differences between races in brain size, shape, organization, or structure.

3. *The difference in intellect between blacks and whites is due entirely to heredity.* There is a profound confusion between the ideas that genes can influence IQ and the inference that the matter is racial. Just because individual mental predispositions can be inherited does not mean that the characteristics of a specific group are inherited. *People get their genes from their parents, not from a group.* There is no way to extrapolate from individual differences to group differences. There are many times more differences among individuals within a racial group than there are among group averages.

INVESTIGATIONS OF RACIAL DIFFERENCES AND IQ

The evidence is scanty regarding any real differences between "black" and "white" genes with respect to IQ. A study of heredity and IQ compared the

GENDER DIFFERENCES IN COGNITIVE ABILITIES

Are females more verbally facile than males? Are males better in quantitative and spatial skills? If so, are these differences based on differences in the brain's ability to process information or do they reflect differential socialization? As you might expect, much controversy surrounds these issues. Argument remains, not only about whether the differences are large enough to be meaningful, but also about their basis.

Let's consider the differences. Although there are no differences between males and females in overall intelligence, hundreds of reports have documented significant differences in subcomponents of intelligence, specifically in verbal and spatial abilities (Maccoby & Jacklin, 1974). Differences favoring girls are found in verbal abilities, such as spelling, language, and perceptual speed and accuracy. Boys outperform girls on tests of mechanical reasoning and spatial relations. Interestingly, studies of young girls and boys show minimal, if any, differences in abilities. The differences emerge in late childhood and early adolescence and become increasingly prominent throughout the teenage years. Even at their peak, the differences are very small. Moreover, there is great variability within the sexes. In other words, even though *on*

BEING FEMALE

BEING MALE

average females are superior to males in language skills, some males will be better than some females. The same logic holds for quantitative skills: a lot of women will outperform the average man.

Why are the differences found so consistently? One interesting biological possibility is that female brains are less lateralized, which improves some brain functions but impedes others, such as spatial skills (Levy, 1972). Others feel differences in early childhood play provide practice in different skills. Boys play with blocks and trucks, while girls talk to their dolls and thus cultivate cognitive abilities.

Still others feel that we are spinning intellectual tales about small differences when all we have to do to explain them is look at the high school course work taken by males and females (Fausto-Sterling, 1985; Sherman, 1982). For example, around the tenth grade, girls begin to opt out of advanced math classes. (In fact, sometimes they are actively encouraged by high school counselors to redirect their attention to more "useful" studies.) It is thus no surprise that they score more poorly on tests requiring trigonometry and calculus!

The latter explanation recently gained considerable support in a study of gender differences in cognitive abilities conducted by Alan Feingold (1988). Feingold analyzed the results of standardized tests, like the SAT, taken by thousands of students over the past 27 years. In 1983, boys had closed the gap on tests of language skill and reduced by 50 percent earlier differences in perceptual speed. Girls had also narrowed the gap considerably in tests of spatial and numerical skill. Only in test scores on the highest levels of mathematics did differences continue to persist, with males scoring better than females. Few doubt the influence of course work on tests of advanced math.

So are there real differences in gender differences in cognitive abilities? Perhaps a better question is, Will there be gender differences in 2040?

ancestry of a group of blacks with their IQ scores. If whites are innately more intelligent than blacks, the study postulated, then blacks having more "white" genes should have higher IQs. This was not the case: more white genes did not increase IQ (Scarr, 1981, 1988).

Consider the results of interracial marriages, in which the genes for intelligence should be approximately equal. Interestingly, one study (Scarr, 1981) found that the IQs of children of mixed races are not equal. Children of a black father and a white mother have higher IQs than children of a white father and a black mother. This only makes sense if we consider the environment: white women on the average seem to talk to their children more than black mothers do. The home environment, especially the mother-child relationship, seems to have an important influence on IQ.

SANDRA SCARR

Many other factors can influence IQ. Educators in Israel noted large IQ differences between Jews of European ancestry and Jews from Arabic countries. European Jews scored higher. These differences were larger than the black versus white differences in the United States. However, when both European and Arabic Jewish children were raised communally on the kibbutzim, where they received the same opportunities and education, the IQ differences disappeared and the children's IQs rose to average above 100 (Smilansky, 1974).

There are many other influences on IQ in the United States. Early experiences and nutrition have long-lasting effects on intelligence; environmental deprivations, if continuous, can be devastating to the child. Blacks on the average live in poorer environments and have more nutritional deficiencies than whites. Also, the larger the size of the family is, the more IQ decreases (Zajonc, 1986); blacks on the whole have larger families than whites. Even when blacks have the same income as whites, they often cannot live where they choose or go to the schools they choose.

There are many reasons to doubt that there are *important* genetic differences in intelligence between racial and ethnic groups. Intelligence is not just a single IQ score, and it is still not adequately defined. Furthermore, although biological differences among races are superficial, environmental differences are profound, at least in the United States.

It is more productive to use the concept of IQ to enrich the environment of children who score lower on intelligence tests. Psychologists are working to develop other measures of intelligence than the IQ alone. Perhaps we should reconsider Binet's earliest notion: use the IQ to aid children whose environment has been deficient, and to identify those with organic deficits. It would certainly help compensate for early loss.

ENHANCING INTELLIGENCE

Many programs and studies attempt to develop various components of intelligence. Experiences in the environment seem to be the important factor that affects the IQ differences between whites and blacks in the United States. Fortunately, the environment can be changed: improved nutrition and more stimulating environments increase IQ test scores. Preschools and Head Start programs in the United States and an ambitious program in Israel are currently attempting to enhance the early years of disadvantaged children.

INFLUENCE OF NUTRITION

Different brain structures underlie different parts of the mind, and their growth and development influence our array of mental abilities. During gestation and in the first year of life, the brain is the fastest-growing organ in the body. It consumes nutrients at twice the rate of the adult brain and is thus heavily dependent upon dietary intake. A severe deficiency in nutrition in the very first months of pregnancy can cause lasting and irremediable damage to the brain. Severe childhood malnutrition can produce many effects lasting seven or eight years (Kagan, 1984), or in extreme cases, a lifetime (NIH, 1989).

Some effects of early deprivation, however, can be overcome by later improvements in nutrition. A specific program of nutritional supplements can increase intellectual ability. In one study, iron and B-complex vitamins were given to one group of pregnant black women, while another group received a placebo. When the children were 4 years old, the mean IQ of those whose mothers had received supplements was 102. Those whose diets were unsupplemented had an average IQ of 94 (Harrell et al., 1956).

In another study, Snowman and Dibble (1979) integrated nutritional supplements in a comprehensive child development program for 68 disadvantaged urban families in an attempt to promote maximum cognitive and psychosocial functioning in their children. Child development trainers made weekly home visits starting in the mother's pregnancy, which combined data gathering, direct nutritional counseling, and early sensory exercises for infants. The greater nutrition raised children's scores by 15% over the controls on the Cattell Scales at 6 months of age.

STIMULATION IN EARLY EXPERIENCE

Most of the brain's growth (75 percent of its weight) occurs outside the womb. Therefore, certain early experiences can have a strong effect on brain growth and, consequently, on intelligence. Rats reared in "enriched" environments develop enlarged brains, as measured by the depth of the cortex. Cortical growth can continue into very old age if the environment remains stimulating. The brain is quite responsive to changes in the outside environment. Thus, changes in early experience can affect the brain and perhaps intelligence.

For instance, some rural Guatemalan children are reared in windowless huts, have no toys, and are rarely spoken to for the first year of life; they show extreme retardation at the end of the year (Kagan & Klein, 1973). When the environment is changed and they are allowed to explore, communicate, and eat better, their development begins to proceed more normally, although it takes many years for them to catch up to children whose first year of life was more stimulating. There is much less difference between them and normal children at 10 years of age than at 1 year of age (Kagan, 1978). The human brain is

The environmental deprivations experienced by children raised in poverty or in institutions can produce extreme retardation. But if the quality of their environment is improved, such children begin to show more normal development and they can eventually catch up to those who have enjoyed the benefits of a stimulating environment and a good diet from the first year of life.

remarkably resilient. Early traumas and deprivations can be overcome if later experience is more benign. Changed diet can overcome the early effects of poor nutrition on intelligence. Intelligence, which suffers in a deprived environment, improves in a normal environment.

ORPHANAGE STUDIES

Even though they provide a sound nutrition, orphanages can have a negative effect on a child's mind. They are often bleak places that offer little human contact and minimal external stimulation. In a Lebanese orphanage, the average IQ of the orphans was 63; in a well-baby clinic, the average was 101 (Dennis & Najarian, 1957). When the orphan infants were simply propped up in their cribs for an hour a day, they could see what was going on and showed dramatic improvement.

Howard Skeels (1966) decided to find out whether stimulation and attention (tender loving care) is important in the development of intelligence. He placed 13 orphanage children with an average IQ of 64 (range 35–85) in an institution for retarded adults. An older woman "adopted" each orphan. All the adoptees became favorites of and were doted on by the patients and staff. A control group of children between 1½ and 6 years of age remained in the same or a similar orphanage. The control group's IQ *dropped* an average of 20 IQ points, while the "adopted" orphans *gained* an average of 28 points.

PROGRAMS TO DEVELOP INTELLIGENCE

GENERAL ENRICHMENT

Skeels's results encouraged development of various enrichment programs aimed at increasing intelligence. For example, many parents now send their children to preschools in the hope that such early training will enhance intellectual development. Children in preschools typically show an initial increase in IQ followed by a decline to the norm at around the second grade. Interestingly, children in the programs that only emphasize academic skills are most likely to show a later decline in IQ. The preschools that emphasize *curiosity* and *self-motivation,* such as the Montessori schools, show the greatest long-term gains. Clearly, there are different parts of the mental structure that develop by different means. For example, students from well-motivated families will test as more intelligent than students from families who prize other abilities, such as serving others.

HEAD START   In 1965 a large-scale experimental program of preschool enrichment, called *Head Start,* began in underprivileged areas. It was one of many **general enrichment programs** that seek to increase general stimulation and interaction for a child. All over the country many preschools began trying to enrich the environment of 4-year-olds, particularly racial minorities. Each Head Start center provided many different curricula (Figure 11-4), which ensured that programs might fit a community's needs more closely, and research could

390

FIGURE 11-4
Head Start Program
Children in the Head Start preschool enrichment program tend on the average to get better grades and score higher on achievement tests. Although there is some controversy over whether their IQs increase, they do show improved health and nutrition and they benefit from their parents' increased involvement in their education.

discover which programs were the most successful. The results followed a pattern similar to the study of more traditional preschools. They demonstrated an initial increase in intellectual functioning followed by a decline almost back down to the level of the norm (Berger, 1980).

A major setback to the Head Start program came in 1969 when the Westinghouse Report claimed that Head Start did not work because children in the program showed no improvement in IQ over non-Head Start children. That report prompted Arthur Jensen to conclude that blacks cannot benefit from an improved environment. Jensen proposed that the reason Head Start did not work is because blacks are inferior intellectually to whites, so the program was a waste of time and money to try to develop compensatory education programs.

The evaluation of the program probably had unrealistic expectations, however. The Westinghouse study evaluated the Head Start program after only a few years of operation while it was still in an experimental phase. When we consider the original goals of Head Start and its results over the long term, we see that the program *has* been effective. Extremes of cultural differences and deprivations can't be completely overcome by a few hours a day of enrichment during one summer. Two major goals of Head Start were improvements in health and nutrition and encouraging parental involvement in their children's education. Also, the programs are different in different areas and are of uneven quality. However, children in Head Start programs on the average get better grades at school and score higher on achievement tests than those from impoverished areas who did not participate in Head Start.

THE TOY DEMONSTRATORS PROGRAM   Successful interventions to improve IQ, at least in the United States, can change the pattern of mother-child interaction. The most successful of these was devised by Phyllis Levenstein (1970). In this program, a "toy demonstrator" visits mother and children at home. Usually she visits twice a week for two years, beginning when the child is between 24 and 28 months old. The visitor brings a toy or a book as a gift (Figure 11-5). She demonstrates to the mother how to play games with the child, especially those involving language.

FIGURE 11-5
Toy Demonstrator's Program

Increasing the meaningful interaction between mothers and children—especially in games involving the development of language skills—seems to contribute to increasing a child's intelligence.

The IQ of the children involved increased during the two years of the program, and the improvement lasted for a long time. Three years after the program ended, the "toy demonstrator" children had IQs 13 points higher than a comparable group not visited. Further, nonprofessionals were equally successful as demonstrators as the original ones who had been professionals. Some of the first mothers who had been visited later joined the project.

The success of this program is probably because many intellectual skills important in schooling depend on language. Language skills develop within the family. The mother spends much more time with her child than do teachers. She is the primary teacher of language—at least in the pretelevision age (Bruner, 1978). *Improving the mother-child interaction thus seems to be an important intervention in increasing intelligence.*

INSTRUMENTAL ENRICHMENT

In addition to the general enrichment programs discussed thus far, many new programs to improve intelligence are in the works. **Instrumental enrichment (I.E.)** is a recent approach. Reuven Feuerstein (1989), the developer of I.E., makes several important distinctions and points out certain concepts that may well aid in the effort to improve intelligence.

1. *There is a difference between* cultural deprivation *and* cultural differences. Individuals who are culturally *deprived* lack something in their own culture. Those who are culturally *different* may belong to a culture that is different from the one they are living in; cultural *differences* can lead to a deficiency or an improvement in the *content* of intelligence. Cultural deprivation in this analysis can lead to a deficiency in the *structure* of the mind. Testers often confuse these differences. A wrong answer on a test by the culturally different person might simply be due to not knowing the language, whereas a culturally deprived person may lack the reasoning and thinking skills necessary to answer. These two varieties of mistakes are very different and indicate very different needs of the person taking the test.

2. *Intelligence has to do with making adaptive responses in new situations.* The Binet-type tests are tests of current *achievement* rather than tests of an

underlying mental structure. A testee should *learn* something during the test rather than simply recall information. I.E. attempts to measure directly the learning ability of the individual.

3. *Cognitive modifiability.* The ability to *change* one's mental structure and contents is **cognitive modifiability.** Learning, for instance, involves a change in contents; thinking involves a change in the structure of information in consciousness. Since the function of all the mental processes is adaptation to the environment, it should also be the focus of testing.

4. *Mediated learning experience.* Interaction with people in their environment gives children **mediated learning experience.** This means that other people, usually parents or siblings, interpret experience and give meaning to events. Consider a child who sees a growling dog and approaches it, but the mother says "Watch out!" The child learns to avoid growling animals through its mother's *mediation.* As Feuerstein (1980) points out, "The mediator selects the stimuli that are most appropriate and then frames, filters, and schedules them; . . . he determines the appearance or disappearance of certain stimuli and ignores others."

How well does I.E. work? The appropriate comparison for instrumental enrichment is a program of general enrichment. With a sample of Israeli children, the I.E. program has shown significant, though not immense, improvement over controls in a general enrichment program, using as assessments the LPAD and other measures such as the Stanford-Binet test. An assessment of I.E. programs by the Israeli military reveals impressive gains. The results show that, after I.E., formerly retarded service-age youths are equal to controls from the general population (Feuerstein & Rand, 1977). (See Figure 11-6).

So, the debates about intelligence are coming to an end as science progresses. We all inherit a complex set of abilities and characteristics from our parents, and some are quite specific, such as responsibility and arousal. Some of these abilities influence what we call intelligence, some influence personality, some predispose us to disorders. We've learned much about how to test people to see how well they will benefit from schooling and how well they will do in life, and we've learned much about the specific components of mind within ourselves that our world can bring out. We shall have more to say on this later on.

ANALYSIS OF THE COMPONENTS OF THE MIND

The work on intelligence has provided us with an insight into the different components of thought and intelligence. This type of analysis derives from the knowledge of brain function, sensation, perception, learning, memory, and cognition. It is perhaps the most promising new trend in the study of intelligence. Several new all-encompassing theories of the mind and intelligence are presented here.

TRIARCHIC THEORY OF INTELLIGENCE

Robert J. Sternberg's **triarchic theory of intelligence,** as its name indicates, consists of three parts. The first is intelligence and the internal world of the

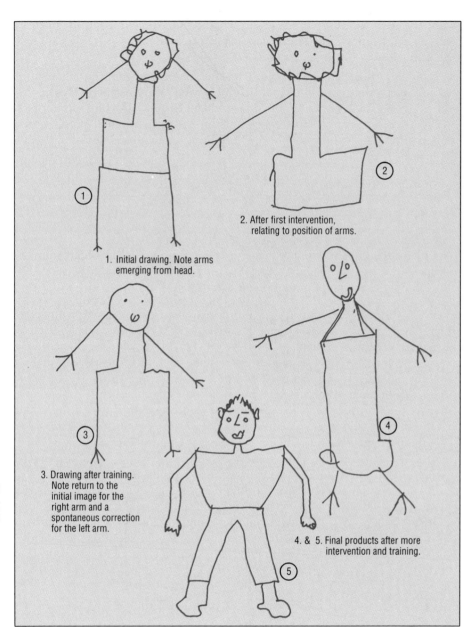

FIGURE 11-6
Instrumental Enrichment Using LPAD

LPAD procedures helped an intellectually retarded, culturally deprived 10-year-old show progressive improvement in drawing a human figure.
(Feuerstein, 1979)

1. Initial drawing. Note arms emerging from head.

2. After first intervention, relating to position of arms.

3. Drawing after training. Note return to the initial image for the right arm and a spontaneous correction for the left arm.

4. & 5. Final products after more intervention and training.

individual, the second is the point of critical involvement of intelligence, and the third is how the external world affects intelligence. Sternberg is attempting to discover which aspects of intelligence are universal and which are specific to individuals and groups.

INFORMATION-PROCESSING COMPONENTS The first part of Sternberg's theory considers information-processing components, which are the mental mechanisms that translate sensory or mental representations (Sternberg, 1988, 1989). He proposes three such components:

1. *Metacomponents.* These are executive or higher order processes, such as planning or evaluating, that are responsible for working out task strategy. They keep in touch with the other components and modify the strategy as the need arises.

   There is a pervasive Western assumption that speed is a measure of intelligence. Known as *speed selection,* it is the ability to judge the appropriate speed at which to think or act depending on the situation. Everyday experience, according to Sternberg, supports this view. We might need to make instant decisions when driving a car, but snap judgments are not necessarily always intelligent judgments. For example, it is smart to alphabetize bookshelves to avoid wasting hours looking for a title on a disorganized shelf. When studying for an exam we might give more time to reading important passages and less time reading passages that are less likely to be asked about.

2. *Performance components.* These are used in performing tasks and carrying out decisions made by the metacomponents. Binet tests measure performance components, but they are not adequately differentiated. Tests do evaluate one type of performance component, inductive reasoning, which includes inferring or applying relationships, but people use many other performance components in carrying out tasks. Linguistic and spatial strategies are two types of performance components that people use in solving problems.

   Developing a method to test the performance components a person uses would be an important diagnostic tool for the assessment and improvement of intelligence. It would show up individual weaknesses and strengths. It would reveal the difficulties experienced by someone who reasoned well but had difficulty reading, or lacked education. Existing tests that result in a total score hide rather than elucidate a person's strengths and weaknesses.

3. *Knowledge-acquisition components.* These help us learn new things. They assess previous experience relevant to the task at hand, rather than the quantity of experience a person has had in the area. An individual may have the knowledge required, but if he fails to employ this experience in a new context, he is less intelligent. If he has the same amount of experience as another person, but has learned more from it, he is more intelligent. More intelligent people are better able to acquire information in context, as shown in vocabulary tests.

COPING AND AUTOMATIZING   The ability to deal with novelty and the ability to cope in extraordinary situations are also measures of intelligence. Sternberg describes this process in terms of three kinds of insights.

1. *Selective encoding.* This form of insight distinguishes between irrelevant and relevant information. A less intelligent scientist than Fleming would merely have thrown away the spoiled culture, bemoaning a failed experiment. Fleming noticed the mold had killed the bacteria and used this knowledge to provide the basis for his discovery of penicillin.

2. *Selective combination.* This form takes the encoded information and processes it in a novel but productive way. Recall the theory of evolution: it was Darwin's ability to combine information available for a long time that produced the theory of natural selection.

3. *Selective comparison.* This is the ability to relate new information to old information. The chemist Kekule dreamed of a snake who bit its tail. When he awoke, he realized that his dreamed image formed the geometric shape for the structure of the benzene ring.

Sternberg proposes that the extent of an individual's ability to *automatize* information processing is a measure of intelligence. A complex task works by automatizating the operations involved. The ability to automatize information may frequently affect the ability to *cope* with novel tasks or situations. The more efficient the person is at the one, the more the resources there are left over for the other. This experiential view reveals difficulties in judging intelligence, particularly across members of different sociocultural groups. A fair comparison between groups must have equivalent degrees of novelty and automatization of test items and comparable processes and strategies.

ADAPTABILITY   The triarchic theory defines intelligence as "mental activity involved in purposive adaptation to shaping of, and selection of, real-world environments relevant to one's life." Accordingly, we can judge intelligence only within a given culture. Again, the shortcomings of our ability to measure intelligence appear with regard to *adaptive* skills. For example, we cannot ignore the ingenuity used by retarded individuals to camouflage their problems. One individual who could not tell time wore a broken watch and would often look at it. He would then say to a passerby, "Excuse me. I see my watch is broken, could you tell me the correct time?"

Adaptability is also culture dependent. Being on time can be maladaptive in cultures where everyone is late. According to U.S. standards, sorting things "intelligently" is done by taxonomic category. Fruit sorts with fruit, animals with animals, cars with cars, and so on. In contrast, the Kpelle tribe in Nigeria prefers a functional sorting but is easily able to sort our way when asked to sort the way "stupid" people would!

There are instances in which it is actually maladaptive to be adaptive. We might prefer to leave a boring job rather than adapt to it. Intelligence also

The ingenuity of some retarded adults to adapt to the real-world environment enables many of them to fit well into the mainstream of society.

enables us to shape our environment in preference to adapting to it. Rather than divorce, a couple might decide to reshape their relationship.

Intelligence is not a single function: it comprises a wide array of cognitive and other skills. We ought to define these skills and learn how best to assess and train them, not combine them into a single but possibly meaningless number. Many educators welcome Sternberg's views as a step toward more of a "real world" intelligence test. Many psychologists think it is not entirely adequate to portray the mind's operations.

FRAMES OF MIND

Another view expands on Sternberg's divisions of intelligence. Howard Gardner postulates six major **frames of mind.** He believes that the many mental activities of human beings are separate and potentially independent abilities. His divisions are summarized here (Gardner, 1983):

1. *Linguistic intelligence.* The fundamental use of language, especially creative language, as in poetry.

2. *Musical intelligence.* One of the most striking early talents. Composing the sounds of music has a logic of its own, quite distinct from that of language.

3. *Logical-mathematical intelligence.* The ability to manipulate quantities, which is separate from the abilities of language and music. Mathematicians often show their talents early in life as well.

4. *Spatial intelligence.* The ability to design and build a table, to assemble a model airplane, to design an office floor plan, or to find your way around town. All of these are independent of the "intellectual" abilities above. This spatial ability is most likely linked to the right hemisphere of the brain.

5. *Bodily-kinesthetic intelligence.* The ability to use one's body in skilled ways for expressive purposes, like a dancer, including the capacity to work skillfully with objects using the fine motor movements of the fingers and hands, like an artist. People with a high degree of "body intelligence" may excel in sports or dance, but this ability does not necessarily preclude intelligence in other areas.

6. *Personal intelligence.* The ability to read another's feelings and intentions. Human beings are bonded to one another from birth, thus, this ability is very important. Is he angry? Will I hurt her if I say that? Is this a good time to ask for a raise? Our survival in the modern world depends on an understanding of other people's intentions and feelings. As we will see in the chapter on psychotherapy, some people are good "empathetic" judges of others and some are not. Gardner considers this ability to be a separate form of intelligence.

Gardner's theory is important for psychologists because it is the first modern cognitive approach that has broadened the concept of IQ. The inclusion of personal and spatial intelligences further extends the view of the mind. However, a focus on high-level abilities such as music and mathematics is not conducive to an analysis of the mind because these are not typical human activities. More fundamental are the ordinary objects of our perception, physiology, and cognition, as discussed throughout this book.

SUMMARY

1. Darwin's theory of evolution provoked interest in human intelligence because it implied that human intelligence evolved through natural selection. Galton tried to correlate head size and sensory acuity with intelligence, to little avail. Binet developed the first useful intelligence test, based on the ideas that tests should test abilities considered intelligent by teachers and be able to rank intelligence, and that intelligence scores should be relevant to a child's age.

2. The Stanford-Binet test was first standardized in 1916. It measures IQ as a ratio of mental age to chronological age. Individuals are scored according to their relationship to their age group's average score. The norm of the present version is 100 with a standard deviation of 16. The Wechsler intelligence scales have advantages over the Binet tests because they separate and measure two major areas of intelligence: verbal and performance skills.

3. A child's scores on IQ tests do not remain constant through development. IQ seems to stabilize as a person reaches adulthood. IQ scores predict school grades and tend to correlate with success in society. The best use of IQ tests seems to be for identifying children who will benefit best from different types of schooling.

4. There does not seem to be any measure of general intelligence. People possess a great variety of abilities; intelligence in one capacity may not generalize to another. Cattel divided intelligence into two major levels of abilities: *fluid abilities*, thought to be genetically based, and *crystallized abilities*, which derive from cultural experiences. Guilford classified intelligence into three categories: *contents* (the information in the mind), *operations* (the working rules of the mind), and *products* (the relation of things in the mind).

5. Much research has been done on whether intelligence is genetically inherited. Inheritance contributes to intelligence, as has been shown with studies of people of differing genetic relationships to each other. Identical twins have the most closely matched IQs. However, environment is an important factor. Exactly how much intelligence is inherited and how much is due to environment is still unknown.

6. People who are not from mainstream, white American culture tend to score lower on the average on IQ tests than whites. The probably mistaken idea that this difference is genetically based is based on several erroneous assumptions: that IQ represents a fixed capacity independent of environment, that there are important differences between races, and that the difference between races is due to heredity. Black people with more white genes do not have higher IQs than others.

7. The IQ of disadvantaged children can be improved by providing nutrition before and after birth. Stimulating environments are also important for normal intellectual development. A baby retarded by a deprived environment can rebound if provided with an enriched one.

8. Recent analyses of intelligence derive from knowledge of brain function. Sternberg's *triarchic theory* proposes three aspects of intelligence: the internal world of the individual, the point of critical involvement of intelligence, and external influences.

9. According to Sternberg's theory there are three information-processing components in intelligence: *metacomponents*, responsible for working out strategies; *performance components*, used in performing tasks; and *knowledge-acquisition components*, which can help us learn new things and apply previous experience in new contexts. Three

kinds of insights contribute to ability to deal with novel and extraordinary situations: selective encoding, selective combination, and selective comparison. Ability to automatize information processing may also be a measure of intelligence.

10. Sternberg's theory defines intelligence as "mental capacity involved in purposive adaptation to shaping of, and selection of, real world environments relevant to one's life." Present tests of intelligence do not adequately measure adaptive skills. Adaptive behaviors vary with culture; what may seem intelligent in one culture seems stupid in another. Intelligence is composed of a wide array of skills which cannot easily be combined into a single measure.

11. Gardner postulates six *frames of mind* that represent separate and potentially independent abilities. They are *linguistic intelligence, musical intelligence, logical-mathematical intelligence, spatial intelligence, bodily-kinesthetic intelligence,* and *personal intelligence.* This list expands the concept of IQ by including personal and spatial ability.

12. Several programs for improving IQ have been tested. Among them are *Head Start,* which sought to enrich the environments of culturally disadvantaged 4-year-olds, the *Toy Demonstrators* program, which taught mothers how to enhance their interactions with their children, and *instrumental enrichment.*

13. The precepts of instrumental enrichment (I.E.) distinguish between cultural deprivation and cultural differences. They are based on the idea that learning ability should be measured directly, along with adaptability. They also assert that interaction with others teaches an individual the meaning of events. I.E. programs seem to work better for improving intelligence than general enrichment programs.

TERMS AND CONCEPTS

cognitive modifiability
crystallized abilities
fluid abilities
frames of mind theory of intelligence
general enrichment programs
information-processing components
instrumental enrichment (I.E.)
intelligence quotient (IQ)

mediated learning experience
Stanford-Binet test
triarchic theory of intelligence
Wechsler Adult Intelligence Scale (WAIS-R)
Wechsler Intelligence Scale for Children (WISC-R)

SUGGESTIONS FOR FURTHER READING

Feuerstein, R. (1980). *Instrumental enrichment.* Baltimore: University Park Press.
   An important early statement about the possibility of improving intelligence.

Gardner, H. (1983). *Frames of mind.* New York: Basic Books.
   A good introduction to the theory of "multiple intelligence."

Ornstein, R. (1986). *Multimind.* Boston: Houghton Mifflin.
   A further description of the complexity and "wheeling and dealing" of the mind. It includes intelligence and multiple personality.

Scarr, S. (1982). *Race, social class, and individual differences in IQ.* Hillsdale, N.J.: Lawrence Erlbaum.

"TRANSMISSION"

IV
THE WORLD OF
THE SELF

We are a puzzle to ourselves and to others. Some people seem like different people at different times. Someone is rude when you thought her nice; another surprises you with his generosity. You may have this same experience with yourself: you are different to your lover than to your boss.

Is someone "emotional," "money motivated," "generous," or "cynical," we may ask. We discuss it with others and try to come up with a single, simple description.

It is the same puzzle as understanding intelligence. People cannot be characterized by a single number or phrase. We are a mosaic of abilities, predispositions, moods, and quirks. We are not the same person at all times.

Each of us is a number of people.

12
EMOTIONS AND HAPPINESS

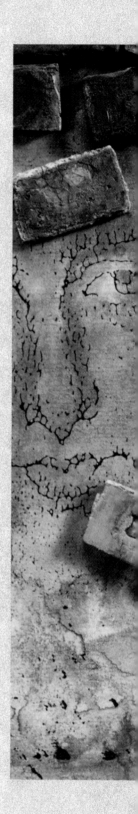

One summer evening I was stuck in traffic while on the way home from the beach. The man ahead of me got out of his car and walked over to the car next to him. A pretty young woman in a bathing suit sat behind the wheel. He swaggered toward the car. She said nothing but frowned, then snarled and almost hissed at him. There was no verbal communication, but the man got the message without any doubt! He returned quickly to his car. The woman smiled in relief.

Emotions are intense experiences, and they immediately communicate our feelings to other people. They can also, in a very real sense, protect us from harm. The woman, as she reacted to the man, quickly tensed to defend herself, although she might not have been aware of this. Emotions have an *automatic* and *involuntary* quality that sets them apart from thinking and reasoning. When frightened, we are almost automatically primed to run or to defend ourselves. You may try to ignore someone who embarrasses you, but your blush may give you away. To borrow from the poet e. e. cummings, "Feelings is first."

Emotions such as fear, anger, joy, and surprise are basic and immediate. We hear a strange noise and feel afraid instantly; we then determine in a logical way if there is something to be afraid of. The basic emotions were around even before human beings were; most of our emotions are common to other animals.

WHAT EMOTIONS ARE AND WHAT THEY DO

We often get angry and embarrassed when we don't want to, and we fall in love almost by accident. Emotions are similar among all peoples of the world and even between human beings and other animals. Emotions embody relatively automatic patterns of responding to different situations. They are *involuntary* and seem to be outside conscious control (Averill, 1978). They simplify an organism's experience by preparing it for action. The range of complex human emotions almost certainly evolved before language and other forms of human knowledge.

THE FUNCTION OF EMOTIONS

The word *emotion* has roots in the Latin word for "movement," originating from the idea that emotions both guide and goad our actions. Basic emotions and expressions coincide in many species of animals. However, human emotional experience is far more complex than that of any other animal. We are the only animal that laughs when happy and almost the only one that cries when sad (the bear is the other).

Why do we have emotions? Emotions *arouse* us, help *organize* experience, *direct* and *sustain* actions, and *communicate* actions (Fridja, 1989).

AROUSAL

Emotions move us to action; they signal that something important is happening. An animal who becomes fearful and excited about an approaching attacker is ready to respond and to defend itself. It would, therefore, be more likely to survive. A human being who experiences sexual love is more likely to reproduce than one who does not. Emotions give action its intensity. Emotions as opposite as elation and anger rouse the emergency system of the body.

ORGANIZATION

Emotions help organize experience. Our emotional state colors perception of ourselves and of others. If your professor is in a grumpy mood, you know it is not the time to ask if you can hand in your paper late. The grumpy mood might follow a family argument the night before or a traffic tie-up on the way to work. The emotions spread and organize the professor's opinion of other events.

Emotions, then, can serve as schemata that aid in organizing consciousness (Bower, 1981). If we are in a good mood, everything seems right with the world: we see it through rose-colored glasses. In a bad mood, everything from foreign policy to friendships seems more negative. Recall from Chapter 9 that when an event enters consciousness, *all associated schemata* actuate as well. So it is with feelings: feeling in consciousness influences perception. When you are angry, you also see others as angry, even if they are not (Bower, 1981).

In one experiment people were hypnotized to feel anger and were later taught something. They remembered what they had learned better in the angry emotional state than in other emotional states (Bower & Gilligan, 1980). However, recent evidence (Bower, personal communication) has thrown some doubt on the evidence about mood effects on memory, so it is wise to remain cautious about these specific studies.

DIRECTING AND SUSTAINING ACTIONS

An enraged animal may attack. A fearful one may flee. A joyous one is willing and eager. Emotions are simplifying guides to behavior, and they have adaptive roles. Consider the pleasure we derive from eating sweet-tasting foods: it encourages us to search for and find sweet things to eat. A sweet tooth has adaptive value because naturally sweet fruits are nutritious and unlikely to be

FIGURE 12-1
Sustaining and Engaging Action

A football coach gets his players "pumped up" emotionally to initiate, direct, and sustain their actions on the field.

poisonous. Psychologist Silvan Tomkins (1979) described this adaptive value colorfully: "If, instead of pain, we had an orgasm to injury, we would . . . bleed to death."

Emotions not only initiate and direct action but also *sustain* and engage action. If you are fearful, you will probably run longer and faster than if you are bored. This reaction is useful in avoiding danger. Coaches recognize this by giving pregame pep talks, making the team emotionally involved (Figure 12-1). Athletes use the expression "pumped up," which is one case when slang is quite accurate.

COMMUNICATION

Most animals have evolved effective display signals, such as odors, postures, facial expressions, and gestures (Figure 12-2), that communicate information about probable behavior to other animals. These signals and gestures are **social releasers.** A dog cannot say "please go away," so it snarls. The message gets across. Emotional signals like facial expression, tone of voice, and body posture convey meaning "between the lines." A person may verbally express interest in what you are saying, but the blank stares, yawns, and passivity signify boredom.

THE BASIC EMOTIONS

We rarely experience a pure emotion, just as we rarely see primary colors. Emotions mix. Some psychologists hypothesize several basic or pure emotions similar to the primary colors. These emotions then combine in different

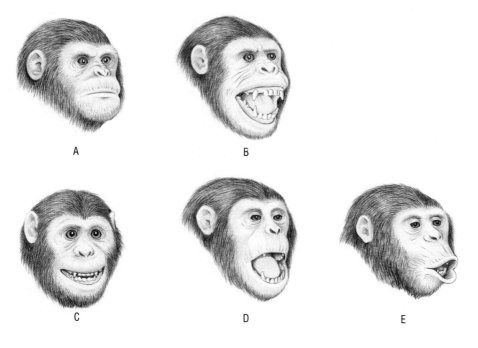

A

B

C

D

E

FIGURE 12-2
Facial Expressions Chimpanzees Use to Communicate Emotions

These diagrammatic drawings, done from photographs and descriptions, illustrate "glare," anger (A); "scream calls," fear-anger (B); infant's "cry face," frustration-sadness (C); "play face," playfulness (D); "hoot face," excitement-affection (E).
(Ekman, 1973)

GENDER DIFFERENCES IN NONVERBAL BEHAVIOR

We communicate a great deal through our nonverbal behavior. Our body posture, facial expressions, gestures, touch, and eye contact often convey our feelings better than our words. We can smile in a way that communicates friendliness, sexual interest, or hostility. Even our use of space communicates our intentions. Standing very close to someone can indicate attraction, or it can signal dominance. Nonverbal behavior is a powerful communication tool. And it is always on—even when we wish we could turn it off—for instance, when we are fearful and we don't want others to know. In fact, we cannot *not* communicate this way because the absence of behavior is as meaningful as its presence. Perhaps most interestingly, when a person's nonverbal behavior and verbal behavior don't match, we tend to consider the nonverbal behavior more valid.

Gender differences exist in several dimensions of nonverbal behavior. We speak of different channels of nonverbal communication. Channels are the paths through which communication flows—the face, voice, and body. Some channels are more leaky than others—that is, they are more difficult to control. In general, people are most skilled at controlling facial expression and less able to control their body language. *Encoding* refers to the way that we display our attitudes and emotions; *decoding* is the ability to interpret these displays in others.

Women are somewhat better than men at decoding nonverbal cues, particularly those expressed by the face (Hall, 1984). In other words, women outperform men at inferring the emotional state of a target person by his or her facial expression. As is true with most gender differences, the differences

BEING FEMALE

BEING MALE

are not large, but they have been found reliably across hundreds of studies and numerous laboratories. Robert Rosenthal, a prominent Harvard psychologist and one of the leading researchers in nonverbal behavior, believes that gender differences are greatest in facial decoding, and that they are smaller in the more leaky channels.

Women are also more facially expressive than men, although they are also more deceptive. In one study, facial expressions of fathers and mothers were compared when talking with their children (Bugenthal, Love, & Gainetto, 1971). The researchers found that fathers' facial expressions were consistent with their verbal statements, but there was no relationship in mothers. Even while mothers verbally reprimanded their children, they smiled. (Interestingly, the children seemed to have figured this out, so they responded to the statement, not the smile).

Overall, women smile a good deal more than men. Two females talking together smile the most, followed by mixed-sex pairs. Male-male pairs smile the least. The smile of a woman, however, is interpreted differently than the smile of a man. Men who smile a lot are described as happy, affiliative, and sociable. Women who smile a lot are described as anxious and uncomfortable. It seems that the smiles of women occur independent of emotional content.

Body language also distinguishes males from females. Males are afforded more interpersonal space; females are approached more closely. Unidirectional touch, such as placing a hand on the shoulder of another, also varies by sex. Men touch women more than women touch men (Henley, 1973).

Several explanations have been offered to explain observed gender differences. One involves dominance. Nancy Henley (1977) believes that gender differences in nonverbal behavior and interpretive skill reflect the subordinate position of women in our society. She maintains that the asymmetry in touch and space reflect dominance on the part of men and deference on the part of women. Women become better decoders because their well-being depends on quickly sizing up the emotional state of a dominant member of society. Others disagree. Rosenthal, for example, believes females are better at decoding because they are more attentive and polite. He goes so far as to say that the reason why gender differences become smaller in the more leaky channels is because reading a leaky channel is comparable to "eavesdropping," and subsequently avoided. Still others argue that hemispheric specialization is at the root of females' superior decoding skills.

Affect refers to the feeling dimension of life. It is part of the general outward emotional expression. Someone with a *flat affect* displays little or no emotion.

Emotions are relatively specific and automatic patterns of short-lived physiological and mental responses. They arouse, communicate, direct, and sustain behavior.

Feelings are the subjective experience of emotions; they can be complex experiences. Jealousy is not, then, an emotion but a feeling comprised of many different emotions, including envy and anger.

Moods are relatively long-lasting states of feeling. A mood sets the emotional backdrop of experience. People who are in a good mood are more likely to help others than someone in a bad mood. Moods color experience. Color words describe moods: blue mood, black mood, rosy or sunny mood.

Temperament is the most permanent and characteristic aspect of emotional life. Temperament is a predisposition to specific emotional reactions in certain situations. One person will become angry at social injustice, another will be sad, a third indifferent. One person has a sunny disposition, and usually sees the bright side of things. Another is a sourpuss and sees misfortune in the same things. (From Ekman, 1984)

mixtures to make complex emotional experiences. Many theories concern the origin of emotional experience and are in general agreement over basic emotions (see Ekman, 1985; Fridja, 1989; Izard et al., 1986; Plutchik, 1984; Scherer et al., 1986; Tomkins, 1984).

Robert Plutchik's (1984) theory of emotions compares them to color experience. Recall from Chapter 5 that the psychological primary colors (red, green, yellow, and blue) exist because of the receptive characteristics of the eyes. All other colors are combinations of these primary colors. Based on evidence from extensive scaling of subjective responses, Plutchik postulates that there are eight **primary emotions.** They include *joy, acceptance, fear, surprise, sadness, disgust, anger,* and *anticipation.* These primary emotions produce new combinations in the way they vary in three dimensions:

1. They may vary in *intensity.* Surprise intensified is amazement; intense anger is rage; intense disgust is loathing. Less intense fear is apprehension; less intense disgust is boredom.

2. They may vary in *similarity.* Disgust is more similar to sadness than it is to joy.

3. Emotions also vary on the dimension of *polarity.* Love is the opposite of hate; sadness is the opposite of joy.

THE EMOTION WHEEL

Plutchik (1984) proposes a general model of emotions called the **emotion wheel** (Figure 12-3). Here the eight primary emotions form a circle of opposites. Simple emotions combine to make complex ones. For example, the mix of the adjacent pair of joy and acceptance yields love. The composite of emotions that are once-removed from one another, such as fear and sadness, results in despair; anger and joy make pride.

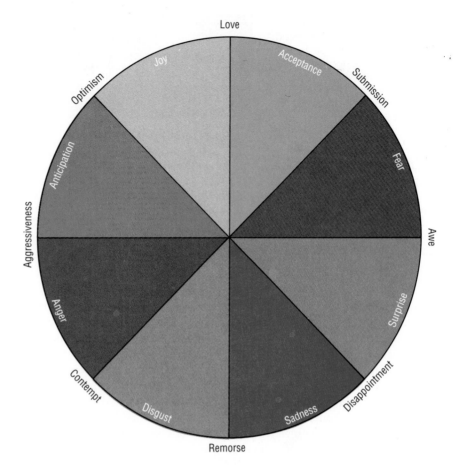

FIGURE 12-3
Plutchik's Emotion Wheel

This model has the eight primary emotions arranged in a circle of opposites. More complex emotions (dyads) resulting from combinations of adjacent primaries are shown just outside the wheel. Additional combinations, of primary emotions once removed on the wheel, produce such emotions as despair (from fear and sadness) and pride (from anger and joy).
(Plutchik, 1980)

Plutchik's view is that emotions are most distinct from one another at the highest levels of intensity, and they are least distinguishable at the lowest levels. Loathing and grief, both being very intense, are very different, while disgust is only slightly different from sadness. Boredom and pensiveness are very similar.

ARE EMOTIONS UNIVERSAL?

Does everyone have the same emotions? Different things make different people happy, obviously, but is the *experience* of happiness the same for everyone? You have probably noticed individual differences in the role one emotion or another plays in different people's lives. One person is easily angered, another apprehensive. Some people give their emotions more weight in actions and in decision making than others; these people are sometimes called "emotional."

The evidence for the *universality* of emotion rests on several different observations. They include the striking similarities of emotional expressions among different species, among different human groups with no contact, and among blind infants, normal infants, and adults (Scherer et al., 1986).

Charles Darwin (1872) observed that all peoples of the world express grief by contracting the facial muscles in the same way. This is true from an Oxford don to an aborigine. It is the same for other emotions as well. In rage, the lips retract and the teeth clench. Similar are the snarl and disgust. All over the world, flirting is signaled by a lowering of the eyelids or the head, followed by direct eye contact. All over the world, embarrassed people turn their heads away or cover their faces. And anger is easily recognizable in all cultures (Figure 12-4).

In human beings, emotions are primarily displayed by the face (Ekman, 1984; Tomkins, 1984). Mammals, especially primates and human beings, have complicated patterns of muscles that allow a variety of facial expressions. The facial muscles of most other animals do not permit much more than the opening and closing of the mouth and eyes.

FIGURE 12-4
Universality of Emotional Expression
People in different cultures all over the world express emotion in very similar ways. This suggests there is an innate component to emotion. You can notice this yourself: you immediately know what these people from New Guinea are feeling.

409

Gorillas, chimpanzees, and human beings have an upright posture. Thus, their faces are much more conspicuous to others than in lower animals. The eyes are in the front of the head, and human beings have stereoscopic vision. Central eyesight leads to a sharper focus on other animals' faces. Facial hair is relatively lacking in human beings and is further accentuated by the framing of head hair. The face is the primary organ of human social communication, followed by bodily gestures (Ekman, 1984).

EMOTIONAL EXPRESSION IN INFANTS

Emotional expression develops naturally in a predictable sequence. Like motor skills, it begins as undifferentiated and disorganized and gradually becomes more refined and precise. Bridges (1932) observed the progressive differentiation of emotions in a study of 62 Canadian babies over a period of several months. At first, infants show general excitement to all stimuli; signs of this include increased muscle tension, quickness of breath, and increased movements. This general arousal gradually becomes differentiated into expressions of distress (at 3 weeks) and anger (3 months). Later are disgust (3–6 months), fear of strangers (7–8 months), and jealousy and envy (15–18 months). The predictable, reliable sequence of these changes indicates an innate maturational component to emotions.

The universality of emotional expression extends to infants (even infants born blind). The forms of emotional expression that babies gradually develop are similar to those seen in adults.

Crying occurs earlier than smiling, perhaps because crying serves immediate survival needs. In addition, *attachment* seems to be an inborn biological and emotional bond between the mother and the child (Ainsworth, 1982). (See Chapter 2, section on Attachment.)

Eibl-Eibesfeld (1970) observed children who were born deaf and blind and found that they displayed basic facial expressions—smiling, laughing, pouting,

crying, surprise, anger—in appropriate situations. Blind children show the same pattern of development of smiling as sighted children. The difference is that around 6 months of age social smiling becomes increasingly responsive to the mother's voice and touch instead of to her face (Fraiberg, 1971).

HOW WE EXPERIENCE EMOTIONS

Emotional reactions involve the autonomic nervous system. Interestingly, the actual bodily response pattern in emotions closely matches the cliché expressions: "My heart leapt when I saw her" or "I've got butterflies in my stomach." Most emotional reactions involve the cardiovascular and gastrointestinal systems and signify emergency arousal in the sympathetic nervous system. Similar patterns are common to all emotions. That we differentiate emotions, and experience one as fear, another as lust, means that we must *interpret* our physical reactions. Just as ambiguous figures and illusions can fool our perceptual processes, emotions can be mislabeled and misunderstood.

For example, a few years ago, I flew to Los Angeles to give a lecture. I enjoy lecturing and was looking forward to the meeting. I was listening to the speaker who preceded me, waiting for my turn, when a most bizarre thing happened. I began to feel shaky, worried, uneasy. When I noticed this, I began to berate myself, silently: "I should have prepared more. I should have written out my speech. Why didn't I fly in last night and get a good night's sleep before the talk?" And there were more worries and ideas about what I should have done.

What was most surprising was that I had never felt like this before in my life. I lecture often on subjects I know well and I was prepared. But was I nervous! Then it began to dawn on me, slowly. I truly felt "shaky." My arms were shaking, so was my hand. Then I looked around. The *table* was shaking, the glasses on it almost spilled their water. The podium was shaking. I turned around, and there it was. The old air conditioner was rumbling and vibrating everything around it, including me. As soon as I saw what was actually happening, I wasn't nervous anymore.

What happened to me was almost a classic experiment in emotion. It is similar to what happened to you when you looked at the cube in the perception chapter (page 213): your hypothesis about the cube became your *experience* of the cube. My hypothesis about why I was shaking (that I was nervous) *became* my experience. The hypothesis "the whole room is shaking" is very unlikely, but when I saw that this was the case, my experience changed. I had appraised myself wrongly. However, most times our appraisals are accurate, and it is only in unusual circumstances such as this one that we can observe them go wrong.

ACTIVATION OF THE EMERGENCY REACTION

The strongest physiological effect of emotion is **activation.** Emotions turn on (activate) the body's **emergency reaction,** allowing us to prepare for immediate action such as the "fight-or-flight" response (see Figure 19-1). Most of the reactions involved in emotions involve the activating mechanisms of the sympathetic nervous system. They underlie most strong feelings such as anger, fear, and joy.

411

The face of emotion is complex. The brain's control of the facial muscles is exquisite. There is more area in the brain devoted to the control of the face than to any other surface of the body. This very detailed control serves a purpose: to express feelings. What a person's feelings are can be directly read as patterns of muscle movements on the face. We continually send emotional messages to others by our facial expression: a raise of the eyebrows here, a downward turn of the mouth there. Our facial expressions are a large part of the impression we communicate to others. Sometimes we are unaware of the messages we are sending to others and of the messages others send to us. However, since many expressions of emotion are universal, it is possible to learn how to identify the emotions in various facial expressions.

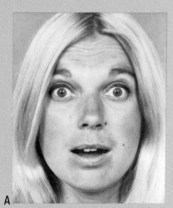

A

B

The face provides three types of signals: *static* (such as skin color), *slow* (wrinkles), and *rapid* (a smile). Emotions communicate by the rapid movements of the facial muscles, which constantly alter the appearance of the face. These changes flash over the face in fractions of a second. It is rare for a facial expression of emotion to last more than 5 to 10 seconds, and some are much faster. The accompanying pictures illustrate several facial expressions of emotion and the specific characteristics of the emotional expression.

HOW TO READ FACES

SURPRISE

Surprise is a sudden experience (Figures A and B):

- The brows raise and are curved.
- Horizontal wrinkles mark the forehead.
- The eyelids open, and the white of the eye is more prominent, particularly above the iris.
- The jaw drops open, but there is no tension in the mouth.

Each one of these clues may express part of the feeling. And since our perception fills in the gaps, the rest of the face may seem to convey the emotion as well. A face may seem to express mild surprise, but only the raised brows give that impression (Figure C).

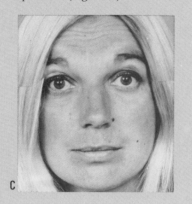

C

FEAR

- The brows raise and draw together.
- The forehead wrinkles in the center, not sides.
- Both the upper and lower eyelids raise.
- The mouth opens and the lips tense slightly (Figures D and E).

Fear may occur with other emotions as well. Fear and surprise blend in when someone looks afraid, but not as afraid as in outright fear.

D

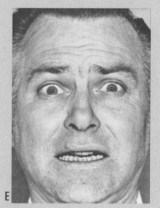

E

DISGUST

Disgust usually involves a response of getting away or getting rid of something offensive. Disgust is shown largely in the lower face and eyelid (Figures F and G):

- The upper lip raises, as does the lower lip.

CHAPTER 12 / EMOTIONS AND HAPPINESS

- The nose wrinkles.
- The cheeks raise.
- The brow lowers.

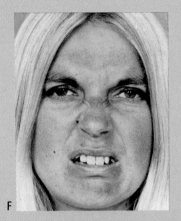

F

G

If we mix disgust and surprise, we get a new expression that seems to be disbelief or skepticism (Figure H).

H

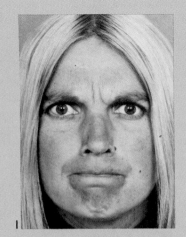

I

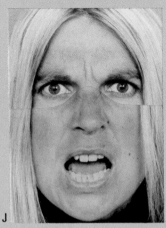

J

ANGER

The expression of anger is strong and direct, and the emotion conveys strong displeasure. It is easy to read. There is much redundancy in the anger message, making it clear to all.

- The brows lower and draw together, causing vertical lines to appear.
- The eyes may have a hard stare and may bulge out.
- The lips may press together or open into a squarish shape as in shouting.

Anger often blends with disgust. Here the wrinkled nose blends with the angry eyes and brows: "How dare you do this to me?" (Figures I and J).

HAPPINESS

Happiness is welcome after all these negative emotions. It shows in the lower face and eyelids.

- The corners of the lips draw back and up.
- The mouth is upturned in a smile, either open or not.
- The cheeks raise, causing a wrinkle from the outer edges of the mouth to the nose.
- Laugh lines or crow's feet wrinkle outward from the outer corners of the eye (Figures K and L).

Anger can blend with happiness into a gleeful "gotcha" expression.

K

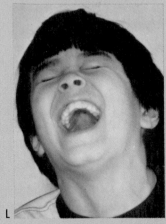

L

This section was adapted in large part from the work of Ekman and Friesen (1983).

413

The process works in several steps. An increase in the secretion of norepinephrine in the bloodstream by the adrenals activates the internal organs. Then heart rate, blood pressure, and blood volume increase. This allows more blood to flow to the muscles and the face—and is the origin of the expression "flushed with excitement." Skin resistance decreases; respiration, sweating, salivation, and gastric motility all increase; pupil size increases. As is becoming apparent, there seems to be nothing in the physical arousal system *alone* that defines what the emotion is.

PATTERNS OF ACTIVATION

It seems that different emotions are similar in their activating capacity, but is the "go–no go" system the only important aspect of emotions? This is too much of an oversimplification. Different emotions, such as grief and elation, anger and joy, *feel* different, so it seems logical that our brains are being activated differently, too. New research shows that changing physiology can produce different emotions.

CONTROLLING FACIAL EXPRESSIONS AND EMOTION

A link between our face and our feelings is deep in our culture. We "put on a happy face" in times of adversity, or say "have a nice day" or say "cheese" to a photo. Recent research shows, surprisingly, that the position of our facial muscles influences our feelings. Try it: pronounce "cheese" and hold that facial expression for a few moments, or purse your lips in a pout and hold the word "few" on your lips. Doing so changes your feelings. Saying "cheese" (a smile-like pose), produces pleasant feelings, while the pout produces feelings of unhappiness (Riccelli, Antila, et al., 1989; Zajonc, 1989).

Thus, we *can* control different emotions using only simple poses of the face, somewhat like method acting. In his pioneering study, Ekman (1984) asked people to assume facial expressions, such as raising the eyebrows and lowering the lips. When they did, they *felt* the emotions they were expressing, such as anger and happiness. Ekman consistently recorded different patterns of autonomic nervous system activity for different emotions, especially anger. This research points to the possibility that people can begin to learn to control their emotions using deliberate techniques. However, no one has yet discovered specific structures in the brain that correspond to specific emotions (McCanne & Anderson, 1987).

Bob Zajonc, however (Adelmann & Zajonc, 1989; Zajonc, Murphy, & Inglehart, 1989), proposes a new theory of emotional expression. He suggests that facial muscles act to tighten facial blood vessels and regulate cerebral blood flow, which in turn influences subjective feeling through a readout in the brain of subjective temperature. The theory, developed by Israel Waynbaum, a French physician, hypothesizes that the subjective experience of emotions *follows* facial expression rather than precedes it.

The internal carotid crosses the cavernous sinus, which, in Zajonc's theory, may respond to facial muscle tightening and relaxing. In this view, raising the temperature of brain blood leads to unpleasant feelings, and lowering it leads to pleasant ones (Adelman & Zajonc, 1989). However, this particular theory has little support from the anatomy, however intriguing it may be.

FIGURE 12-5A
Mona Lisa's Smile

The celebrated ambiguity of the smile of Leonardo da Vinci's *Mona Lisa* might be attributable to the fact that she is smiling only on the left side, the side controlled by the right hemisphere of the brain. To aid you in considering whether or not this could be the source of the enigma, look at the related picture in Figure 12-5B.

FIGURE 12-5B

Look at the smile on this reversed *Mona Lisa*. Is her smile as enigmatic, as ambiguous? Here, because she is smiling only on the right side of her face, the impact is different. Your response may be different because the smile is on the side controlled by the left hemisphere of the brain.

What *has* been found is that each of us shows *characteristic* emotional responses to certain situations. For example, one person flushes with anger as well as joy, another sweats with both, while a third may have stomach reactions (Lacey & Lacey, 1958). In other words, the pattern of activation is different among people experiencing the same emotion. In one study of students' anxiety over an examination, some sweated while others had increased heart rates (Lacey, Bateman, & Van Lehn, 1953). The only specific body pattern that universally relates to all people's emotions is facial expression.

EMOTIONS AND THE BRAIN

Two major divisions of the brain act differently with regard to the emotions. The limbic system is largely responsible for many emotional reactions. Stimulation of the pleasure center in the hypothalamus yields intense awareness of pleasure. Other areas of the limbic system, when stimulated, can produce rage and attack reactions (Delgado, 1969).

Yet many emotional situations are consciously controlled by the cortex. The *emergency reaction* releases hormones into the blood stream. It can often occur involuntarily, as when trembling with fright before a job interview. Some scientists speculate that there is a discord between our "old" emotional brain and the "new" thinking brain. This clash is at the root of many conflicts between rational thought and our gut feelings (Koestler, 1974).

However, most recent analysis about the brain and emotions concerns the two cerebral hemispheres. They seem to be specialized for emotions, as they are for thought. The left hemisphere responds to the verbal content of emotional expression and the right to the tone and gesture (Kolb & Milner, 1980). Since the right hemisphere controls the left side of the body and the left hemisphere the right side, are there differences in the expression of emotions on both sides of the body? Look at Leonardo da Vinci's *Mona Lisa* (Figure 12-5A). She has a smile described as enigmatic, puzzling, ambiguous. Why? Look carefully at each side of her face, then look at the reversed image in Figure 12-5B. Only the left side is

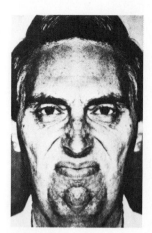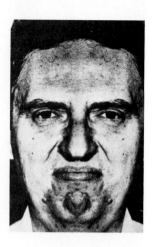

**FIGURE 12-6
Expressing Emotion: The
Two Sides of the Face
and the Brain**

The far left photo shows a man expressing disgust. The middle photo is a composite of two right sides of the man's face, and the one on the right is a composite of two left sides of his face. Do you agree with most people that the photograph on the right—a double image of the side of the face controlled by the right side of the brain—shows disgust most strongly?

smiling, the side controlled by the right hemisphere! Perhaps this is why the expression is so ambiguous.

As another demonstration, look at the three faces in Figure 12-6. Which of the faces seems to express the emotion of disgust most strongly? These three photographs were specially created: the one on the left is a normal photograph of a man expressing disgust. The middle photograph is a double image, a composite of two *right* sides of the man's face. The one on the far right is a double image of the *left* side of his face. Most people feel that the far-right photograph, which expresses the right cerebral hemisphere, shows the emotions strongest. The results are the same with eye movements (Schwartz, Davidson, & Maer, 1975) and with interpreting a facial expression. We seem to express emotion on the left side more than the right (at least in deliberate expressions), and we interpret emotions better on the left than the right (Campbell, 1978).

We should note that in both of these demonstrations, the expressions were *posed*. You may have noticed that a posed smile is not the same as a genuine smile. It is often easy to tell if another's facial expression is not a genuine one. Ekman and colleagues point out that a forced smile is more asymmetrical than a normal one, and this may account for the results shown here.

However, there have also been studies on asymmetry of spontaneous expressions. Moscovitch and Olds (1980) unobtrusively recorded the asymmetry of facial expressions of people seated in restaurants. They found the same result: the right hemisphere controls the left side of the face, the side seen better by the viewer's right hemisphere. In a social situation there may be two kinds of messages sent: one from the left hemisphere to the left through words, and one from the right hemisphere to the right through facial and other expressions.

In an intriguing series of studies, Davidson (1984) showed that the left hemisphere may involve different emotions from the right. The left seems to involve positive emotions, such as happiness, and the right, negative ones such as anger. Fox and Davidson (1986) gave newborns water followed by a sucrose solution and then by a citric acid solution while taping facial expression. They also recorded EEGs from the frontal and parietal scalp regions on the left and right side. They found characteristic brain patterns in response to disgust and pleasure, disclosing that stimulus-elicited affective asymmetries in brain electrical activity are present at birth.

However, not all investigators find this result each time. Mammucari, Caltagirone, Ekman, and Friesen (1988) studied spontaneous facial expression of emotion in right and left brain-damaged patients and in a control group of normal subjects. To elicit emotions the experimenters showed them four short movies, constructed to produce positive, negative, or neutral emotional responses. They found no difference between subjects with right- and left-sided lesions, which is inconsistent with the hypothesis of a specialization of the right hemisphere for facial emotional expressions. An unexpected difference was observed in response to the unpleasant movie. Both normal controls and left brain-damaged patients often averted their gaze from the screen when unpleasant material was displayed, whereas right brain-damaged patients rarely showed gaze aversion. This finding suggests that the degree of emotional involvement or manner of coping with stressful input may be reduced as a result of right brain damage (also see Pizzamiglio, Caltagirone, Mammucari, Ekman, & Friesen, 1987).

In more recent work, Borod et al. (1988) examined emotional facial expression in brain-damaged adults with right- or left-hemisphere lesions. Patients with right-hemisphere pathology showed less facial emotion than patients with left-hemisphere pathology. Ahern and Schwartz (1985) used EEG spectral analysis to investigate lateralization for emotional processes in the human brain and observed, in frontal zones, lateralization for positive and negative emotion.

KNOWING WHAT WE FEEL

A basic emotional reaction such as fear is probably innate, a shortcut to action. In the long course of evolution, emotions probably evolved to match well the needs of most organisms. Fear of snakes probably saved many lives. However, the situation for human beings is now different: the dangers of the modern world are unprecedented in our evolutionary history. The fear of nuclear war is not as palpable as fear of snakes. For a war, there is no identifiable stimulus, no obvious and immediate course of action. The *meaning* of a situation and its *appraisal* are major components in human emotional life.

APPRAISAL AND REAPPRAISAL

Appraisal is the understanding of the meaning of an event. There are three basic dimensions to the appraisal process. The first is *evaluation:* Is the situation good or bad, benign or threatening? The second is *potency:* Is it alive or dead, strong or weak, fast or slow? The third is *activity:* Is the threat active or passive? Osgood and colleagues (1971), who proposed these dimensions of emotions, describe their value:

> What is important to us now, as it was way back in the age of Neanderthal Man, about the sign of a thing is: First, does it refer to something *good* or *bad* for me (is it an antelope or a saber-toothed tiger)? Second, does it refer to something that

417

is *strong* or *weak* with respect to me (saber-toothed tiger, or a mosquito)? And third . . . does it refer to something which is *active* or *passive* (is it a saber-toothed tiger or merely a pool of quicksand, which I can simply walk around)?

Emotions are not a succession of isolated, unrelated feelings and reactions to situations. Perception, consciousness, and memory operate in a cycle; emotions do too. The cycle involves a primary appraisal of the situation, feedback of that information, continuous reappraisals, and feedback from the reappraisals. Feelings change as new information comes in.

One night I awakened to the sound of a strange noise upstairs in my house. I became aroused and fearful. What could the sound be? Did I lock the door? Was the roof falling? With each thought something inside me immediately prepared me to act differently. Then I remembered that a friend of mine had asked to stay over. He must have noticed that I was asleep and then let himself in. Once I realized what had happened, I went back to sleep.

My first reaction was the primary appraisal: "Something's happening." I awoke, aroused. This *primary appraisal* first arouses the organism. *Reappraisal* considers whether an event is *benign* or *threatening* and what actions to take. When I decided that the noise was only my friend's footsteps, all my defensive plans vanished. I no longer felt the need to call the police; the desire to run like mad from the roof caving in went away. The result of my reappraisal was that I went back to sleep.

Almost every situation is complex enough to require continuous appraisal. When a man sees that a cook has prepared his favorite dish, his primary appraisal is benign. When the dish is set in front of him, he sees that the dish is burnt. This new information causes a reappraisal: disappointment. This may lead to an action such as complaining to the cook or going to a different place to eat, which results in a new cycle of feelings (Lazarus & Folkman, 1986).

INTERPRETATION OF EMOTIONS

Because the internal states of many different emotions are similar, our minds need to appraise the situations and make a conscious interpretation of their meaning. Most times these appraisals are accurate and serve us well. Someone may insult us, so we get angry. Another person may snuggle up to us, and we become activated in a blizzard of lustful joy.

The *cognitive appraisal theory of emotion* (Schacter & Singer, 1962) states that the interpretation of the physiological state leads to different emotional experiences. In this view, our interpretation occurs in the same way as most perceptual interpretations: "What is the simplest explanation for my excitement?" But, as with most perception, the interpretation can be difficult when the circumstance is ambiguous.

One factor that may cause confusion in our lives is that arousal is common to quite different emotions. When the situation is ambiguous we may misinterpret our own emotional state. Although this happens infrequently in life, psychologists can design experiments to test it in the lab. My experience shaking before a lecture is an example from real life. I *interpreted* my shaking as nervousness. Once I understood the situation, I was no longer nervous. My interpretation had real consequences: I *felt* worried.

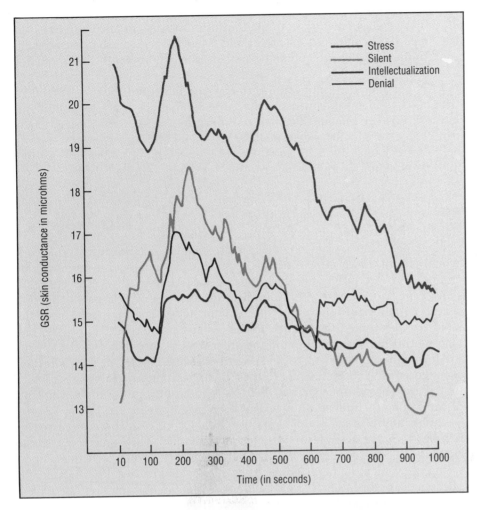

FIGURE 12-7
Cognitive Influences or Emotional Reactions

In the experiment charted in this graph, different groups of people watched a stress-provoking movie. Those who heard a narration that denied or intellectualized the distressing parts of the film, or who saw the film without any narration, had less stressful emotional reactions than people in the group that heard a narration intended to increase stress.
(Speisman, Lazarus, Davidson, & Mordkoff, 1964)

The conscious interpretation can affect the internal state itself. In one study, students saw a very arousing film while psychologists measured autonomic nervous system arousal during the viewing (Speisman, Lazarus, Davidson, & Mordkoff, 1964). The measure of arousal used was a standard measure of skin resistance, called the *galvanic skin response* (GSR). The film was of a ceremony an aboriginal tribe used to mark manhood. The rituals included the subincision of the penis with a knife. Most people find these scenes quite negatively arousing.

One group saw the film silently. A second group heard a narration that emphasized the cruelty of the ritual. Two other groups heard narrations that minimized the cruelty by denying or intellectualizing it. GSR measures of arousal increased in the narration that emphasized the cruelty, whereas the arousal decreased in the narrations that minimized it (Figure 12-7).

To test interpretation of emotion, Schacter and Singer (1962) injected epinephrine into students who were told it was a vitamin. Half of the students were placed in a situation with a euphoric person (a confederate of the experimenters). He tossed paper airplanes and used the wastebasket to shoot baskets with wads of paper. These students later reported feeling euphoric. The other half of the students confronted an insulting and irritated person. They later reported being angry. Schacter and Singer concluded that these results confirm the theory that emotional experiences depend upon the interpretation of arousal.

Abundant studies support Schacter's hypothesis, but there are problems with his experiments. Many people have tried with little success to replicate the result of this experiment (Marshall & Zimbardo, 1979). Since it is no longer permissible to conduct experiments with epinephrine injections, there will be no further replication attempts. However, many other studies indicate that the interpretation of inner states can have profound effects on emotional experience.

One way to test the theory is to offer *false feedback* on the internal state itself. If emotional experience depends on interpretation, then false information should also have an effect on experience. In one study men were shown photographs of nude women while listening to their own heartbeat. What each actually heard, however, was not his own heart beating, but a recording. One group heard a recording in which the heart rate increased when 5 of the 10 slides were shown. A second group heard the heart rate decrease for these 5 slides. Later they rated the attractiveness of the nudes. The group who heard the rapid heartbeat rated the women in the 5 slides as more attractive. The one whose heart rate decreased found the other 5 more appealing (Valins, 1966).

In another experiment, women were shown slides of people who had experienced violent death. Some "heard" their heart rate increase in reaction to the slides. These women rated them as significantly more unpleasant and discomforting than those who had not been misinformed.

The study of sexual attraction on a wobbly bridge that we discussed in Chapter 1 is an example of this misinterpretation. The arousal caused by crossing a dangerous bridge was misinterpreted as sexual excitement upon seeing a woman. Other studies have shown similar results, and similar phenomena occur in life. For example, many people find that exercise with a partner of the opposite sex is very provocative. Why? In one study (Cantor, Zillman, & Bryant, 1974), people were asked to exercise for a period of time. The activation resulting from the exercise diminished with time. Soon after exercise one no longer *feels* activated. However, subtle measures of autonomic activation such as blood pressure are still elevated. If people see erotic stimuli during this phase, they are more easily aroused than when they have fully recovered from the exercise. The interpretation of the unexplained activation is sexual excitement. So activation, especially in contrived or ambiguous situations, is subject to misinterpretation (Mandler, 1980). However, most situations are *not* ambiguous, and our emotions are usually an accurate and immediate guide for us.

CONSEQUENCES OF FRUSTRATION

Frustration is a normal reaction to stress. It results when a desired outcome is thwarted or delayed (Lazarus, 1976). A person may also feel threatened if he or she anticipates harm or frustration.

At one time psychologists thought that *all* frustrations increase the probability of *aggressive* behavior, and that all aggression was due to frustration. This was the "frustration-aggression hypothesis" proposed by Dollard and associates (1939). Aggression *is* a common response to frustration (Bandura, 1965), but frustration may lead to many things besides aggression (Mischel, 1976). A frustrated person may become depressed or may feel guilty, disappointed, apathetic, anxious, or fearful—to mention only a few.

CONFLICTS

There are different types of conflicting emotions that may result in threats or frustration. Needs or motives may be in opposition or may be incompatible, or an internal need or motive may oppose an external demand (Lazarus, 1976). Obviously, if the motivation or demands are weak, little threat or frustration may be felt. However, when they are strong, the conflict may be severe.

An example of *internal conflicting demands* is found in combat stress (Grinker & Spiegel, 1945). A soldier has a very strong need to survive, but he may also have a strong need to be respected by others, which requires that he live up to their expectations—that is, go into combat. Usually, the soldier overcomes or at least puts aside his fear of death and completes his combat tour of duty. Sometimes the conflict is so severe that it results in neurotic symptoms.

A person may also be subject to *external conflicting demands*. This may happen, for example, when one parent insists a child become an athlete and the other demands excellence in music to the exclusion of athletics. The frustration and threat of failure may be so great that the child ends up doing neither.

Finally, most people experience *internal demands* or desires that conflict with *external* ones. A child may want to eat nothing but junk food, but the parents will forbid it and insist he or she also eat vegetables.

FEELING AND THINKING

How do feelings relate to thinking and decision making? Many psychologists consider that mental functions such as perception, consciousness, memory, and thinking come before emotions. We first analyze and appraise information, then evaluate it and experience it emotionally. However, Robert Zajonc has proposed that feelings come first or, to use his phrase, "Preferences need no inferences" (Zajonc, 1980).

Zajonc argues that mental functions often service emotions, not the reverse. We evaluate first and think of the reasons second. He offers many examples of his theory. Consider a woman trying to decide rationally whom to marry: "Let's see, Jack has more money, one point for him. He wants to live where I do, another point in his favor. He's handsomer than Bill. . . . Wait a minute, this isn't coming out right, I want to marry Bill. Let's see. . . ." In a contest between emotion and reason, emotion is more likely to win, according this view.

It may be that the question "Which comes first, emotions or cognitions?" is similar to asking about the chicken and egg. It is perhaps more profitable to view emotions and thoughts as part of the same feedback system. Each influences the other, and appraisals and reappraisals follow each other. Sometimes emotional evaluation may come first: "I like wine," is an evaluation. Sometimes the evaluation may well come after a long analysis: "I don't like this white wine after all, it's too sweet." Emotions probably influence every mental process.

They may cause us to seek out different information, to remember differently, and to think and evaluate differently.

FEAR AND ANXIETY

An important emotion resulting from stress is anxiety, which is apparently at the root of a variety of psychological disorders. Fear and anxiety are closely related, but there are differences.

Fear is an immediate and specific emotional reaction to a specific threatening stimulus. Young birds show fear if the shadow of a hawk—even a wooden one—passes over them. However, as we go up the phylogenetic scale, fear may become abstract.

Anxiety is a more general reaction that occurs in higher animals and human beings that may develop in response to the *anticipation* that something harmful may occur. The harm may not be just physical but also psychological, as in a threat to a person's self-esteem. The stimulus for fear is usually clear and immediate. When a situation is ambiguous and the person is not sure what is going to occur, he or she may feel a vague sense of apprehension and become anxious (Lazarus, 1976).

The stress emotions, while unpleasant, usually alert a person that something is (potentially) wrong and that action is necessary. A student who is anxious about an exam is more likely to study harder than another who is not particularly anxious. Healthy fear may keep someone from walking alone at night in dangerous sections of town. However, when emotional reactions become too great, they disrupt a person's life. The student may be too anxious to study for the test, or a person may become too afraid to leave the house even during the day.

Antianxiety drugs, such as alcohol, barbiturates, and Valium may be useful in helping a person to function. However, these drugs lessen anxiety at a cost. They seem to interfere with complex learning (Gray, 1984), and they inhibit REM sleep, or dreaming (Greenberg & Pearlman, 1974). Antianxiety drugs may reduce the fear of the consequences of action without lessening a person's aggression. In some situations this can be useful, but in others it can be harmful. For example, giving Valium to an anxious parent with a tendency toward child abuse may actually increase the parent's aggression toward the child (Gray, 1978). Thus, such drugs should be used spartanly and with full consideration of the consequences of using them.

HOW FEAR BYPASSES CONSCIOUSNESS

As we said earlier, emotions are often automatic and involuntary. But how can this be since we can consciously control our actions? First, we need to remember that we function on many different levels of awareness at any time. And second, the brain evolved in different layers, and each layer has some precedence. New evidence that the lower center can bypass consciousness has recently appeared.

For example, a psychiatrist once received an emergency telephone call from the San Mateo (California) Police Department: "This is officer Thomas, your patient Alfred R. is standing over the edge of a cliff on Skyline Drive and Aronda road, and he is threatening to jump off. Can you get out here and help?" Alfred's psychiatrist leapt into his car and drove up the hill.

There was Alfred on the ledge, over the canyon. What do you say to someone ready to jump? The doctor tried asking Alfred if he knew what this would do to his mother. How hurt would she be? But Alfred knew. Think how this will affect your kids, it will hurt them for their whole lives! But Alfred knew. What about his robotics company, just about to make a breakthrough? He knew. And didn't Alfred feel he was at last coming to grips with some of his problems, and with a few more weeks he could re-establish his relationship with his wife? Nothing the psychiatrist said seemed to do the trick.

Finally, the psychiatrist walked away, desolate, hoping that one of the police's experts, who would be more trained in these matters than himself, could say something, or do something, or promise something, anything, to avoid the suicide. He didn't have much hope for Alfred, though.

But the expert never arrived and Alfred didn't jump. What happened was that another police officer, on patrol, pulled up his car to the site, unaware of the drama. He took out his power bullhorn and blared very loudly to the bunch of people on the cliff: "Who's the ass who left that Pontiac station wagon double parked out there in the middle of the road, I almost hit it. Move it *now* whoever you are." Alfred R. heard the message and got down at once from his perch, dutifully shuffled out to his car, parked it precisely on the side of the road and then went off, without a word, to the hospital.

These disruptions happen since emotions can be routed specially and separately to the brain. They form the ground plan of the brain, in the limbic system. Alfred R. had a conscious plan but he had not realized, and neither did his psychiatrist, that emotions like fear have a higher priority than personal life crises. So his suicidal resolution was not overcome or worked through; rather, it was *bypassed*, moved out of place by the emotional shifting of his mind, which replaced the suicidal fanatic with a simple reflexive law-abiding citizen.

How do strong emotional reactions like these seemingly bypass consciousness? Most neuroscience assumes that signals go to the thalamus for sorting, then to the cortex. However, in an innovative set of studies, Joseph LeDoux and his collaborators have begun to establish routings, primarily in the amygdala of the limbic system, of these "emotional bypasses." Thus, we can respond emotionally before we can think of what we're doing—a response mechanism that is very useful in emergencies. This may be why we can't control fears of loud noises, heights, or other dangers, even though we "know" they're dangerous.

THE PURSUIT OF HAPPINESS

I've been riding the carousel in Central Park since I was five years old. Back then there were silver and gold rings. You had to get five silver rings or one gold ring to get a free ride. I spent my childhood in Central Park because I went to school on Central Park West. If I'm very depressed or if something's bothering me today, my husband, Larry, and I go back to the park. We get on the carousel horse and we start riding, and I start singing at the top of my lungs. It is pure and absolute joy and happiness.   —EDA LESHAN

While happiness is a feeling most of us wish we had, only recently have psychologists uncovered some of the ways we experience it. People carry with them very different ideas about *what* should make them happy. And, in each of us, these ideas form stories about growing up, marriage, work, morality, pleasure, and life in general. These stories come to reside within us like a political ideology. Sometime while growing up, no one really knows exactly how or when, most people establish their life story—a set of beliefs, assumptions, and expectations about themselves and the world they live in (Beck, 1989).

These schemes are basic to the way the mind works and determine a lot more of our lives than we think, for we make most of our judgments based upon a shifting scale of standards and not on the actual facts. A person may have a comfortable income, but because she is not doing as well as her sister or classmates in business school, she may be unhappy. Another person may have a perfectly wonderful family, but because he doesn't live in exactly the right status home, a residence that his parents might have approved of, he may be miserable. Still others base their happiness on the amount of social injustice in the world, often discounting any improvements made or how much their own life is pleasurable.

Since *happiness* is so central to our lives, it's surprising that the majority of women and men don't target it as a primary goal. Most of us lower our sights and aim for halfway rewards. Many of us believe that well-being depends strongly upon success in the job, so in "work life" we shoot for wealth, status, power, and property. But happiness doesn't seem all that related to money (Argyle, 1988). Here we consider much of the new work on happiness that shows the value of small moments of positive emotion, and the value of concentrating on positive present events (and, surprisingly, negative past events). Of course other factors are important, such as the amount of control we feel (Larson, 1989).

Let's examine how you and most people rate their own happiness. To begin, please mark the place on the scale below which indicates how happy you are at the present time in your life. On this scale, 9 is the most *happy* experience that you believe to be possi-

not at all	1	2	3	4	5	6	7	8	9	very

ble, and 1 is the most *unhappy* you could ever feel.

Where do you think most people in our society would judge themselves? The average self-rated happiness turns out to be approximately 6.5 on the scale we constructed.

Now let's see how some major events, positive and negative, seem to effect people's sense of their own well-being. First, contemplate a couple of the best and the worst experiences that could happen to you: winning first prize in a large lottery or becoming incurably paraplegic.

Suppose you won a lottery and got a tax-free windfall of $10 million? How happy do you think you would be a year after winning this lottery? Again, on a scale of 1 to 9, choose a number that best reflects how happy you would feel.

And suppose the worst happened: you were in a terrible accident that left you alive, barely, and you lost the use of your legs and became paraplegic. A year later, how happy do you think you would be? Pick a number between 1 and 9.

If you are like most people, you would assume that winning the lottery would move you right up the scale toward the top—a 9—and that becoming a paraplegic

would stretch you downward and more or less zero you out. However, the results in reality turn out to be quite different. When actual lottery winners are surveyed immediately after winning they *are* much happier. But one year after winning, their average self-rated happiness remains nearly *unchanged* from where they were before the lottery, increasing only slightly from 6.5 to 6.8. And when paraplegics are surveyed the average drop in self-rated happiness after one year has passed is only about one point lower, from more or less 6.5 to 6. These scores are approximated below, the paraplegics' marked as *P*, average as *A*, and lottery winners as *L*.

You are probably a bit surprised with how little happiness changes even after delightful or devastating life changes. The majority of people guess that they would be devastated forever if they lost the use of their limbs. Getting around town would be a major difficulty; even getting something from the refrigerator would be hard. They may ask, What if I lost my key on the floor? Could I ever enjoy sports? And, of course, what about romance?

The paraplegics' actual happiness doesn't match our expectations. Of course, there is an initial

period of shock and dismay after the trauma. But even after this extreme damage, the sufferers aren't as dismal as most people would imagine.

The same kind of surprisingly small change in happiness comes about to lottery winners a year after they won. Imagine how happy you'd be winning first prize in a lottery. No more worry about work or school. You might buy a big new house with a pool, quit school, and travel around the world. It seems obvious that a person who has the great luck of winning a lottery would be much happier over the long term than those who have not won.

Nonetheless, lottery winners are *almost no happier* one year after winning than before they won (Brickman, 1974; Tversky, in press). Interestingly, the winners found considerably *less* pleasure in daily life activities—their relationships, working around the house, their job if they did not leave it, taking care of the garden—than did those who had not won. Why? The lottery winners may have adapted to their new fortune and their expectations, and what is called their "comparison level" probably shifted upward.

The negative comparisons, of course, depreciate our happiness. Our minds, trying to keep things uniform, adjust our comparison level. In getting rich, our comparison level has changed: it takes more to keep us happy now. It changes, too, in other areas of life —in education, in food, in friendships, in marriages and in health.

So, we don't experience happiness as a result of what happens to us. Instead we gauge happiness by a flexible mental yardstick that we use to compare experiences. This knowledge of our shifting basis of judgement can allow us to increase happiness, in part, by changing our frame of reference. We'll discuss how later on.

not at all	1	2	3	4	5	P6 A	L7	8	9	very

WEALTH AND HAPPINESS

Though many people stake their happiness (and lives) on the accumulation of wealth, great amounts of wealth don't increase happiness much, perhaps as an end result of shifted comparison levels. What, then, happens when an entire society, as ours, increases prosperity year after year? Surveys in the United States find that happiness goes up and down, and up and down again, from era to era, from 39 percent in 1946 saying they are very happy (7–9 on our scale) to 53 percent in the late 1950s, 27 percent in 1971–74, and 35 percent in the late 1970s. However, during this time, the average income in America has increased dramatically, by more than 50 percent (Argyle, 1988).

In our culture, once we are over a minimal standard of wealth—when we have a car (even if it is not the best) and an adequate, if not palatial, place to live; when we can get an education (even in public schools and universities); and can buy adequate, if not gourmet, food—then increases in wealth don't seem to matter as much as we think and certainly not as much as we plan our whole lives around. The bottom line is, if we want money to make us happy, then we'll have to be poor.

HAPPINESS AND SMALL PLEASURES

One of the sources of my happiness is small things. I get great joy from absolute nonsense. I'm very weather reactive. A sunny day can just start things wonderfully. I also love encounters with strangers that bespeak a kind of human warmth. It makes me happy.

I'm a great reader. I get pleasure from reading something that I think is just wonderfully done. I care how the words get together. I can feel on top of the world sitting around with a good newspaper and a cup of coffee and killing three hours.   —MARGO HOWARD

Present happiness is also strongly, and sometimes surprisingly, shaped by our past. You might assume that thinking about an unhappy childhood is a one-way ticket to depression while savoring the memory of a former lover would brighten your day. However, the effects of these mental gymnastics can sometimes be paradoxical.

First, think about an event that was unpleasant concerning your life 10–15 years ago, perhaps something related to school, work, or family that you were unhappy about. Second, think about something that was exceedingly pleasant that happened to you 10–15 years ago. Third, think about the most *negative current* experiences that you have. Finally, think about the most *positive current* experiences that you have. Which condition do you think would make you feel happiest, and which worst?

When subjects were asked to follow these steps, dwelling on present negative events produced the most unhappiness. However, unhappiness also increased after thinking about *past positive* events. Savoring *present positive* happenings improved mood, but the greatest mood boost came from contemplating *past negative* events (Schwartz, 1989; Strack & Schwartz, 1989; Tversky, in press)!

Why does thinking about a negative event in the past produce increased happiness in the present? It is probably a result of changing the level of comparison in the mind (Tversky, in press). An adequate present experience (you've got sufficient money, not enough to travel but enough to go to the movies a few times a week and to get good clothes) may seem pretty good compared with childhood poverty. People who were brought up in poverty during the

INCREASING YOUR CURRENT HAPPINESS

Great Depression are more likely to rate times of relative prosperity as being very positive than people who are brought up prosperous.

So, a remembrance of bad things past has a contrast effect: our present seems brighter. However, a glance back at a well-remembered cheery moment makes the work-a-day world of the present seem very dull if not disagreeable. On the other hand, thinking about one's past poverty, past difficulties, past long hours at work, perhaps a past failed marriage, may make us evaluate more highly a present marriage, a present work life, or a present family life.

Remember, then, to think about what is going on in your life now that makes you happy, be it your team winning, a good meal, a craft project you're doing, or the joys of parenting. It's important to dwell on your present happiness because this concentration can act as a buffer against sad times and can directly influence your current well-being. Keep what is pleasing you higher in your mind. Count your blessings and be thankful.

Also, try to think as much as possible about how you've progressed in life from early days. Focus on those ways in which your life is better off than before. Be aware of the effect on your present mood of savoring past loves, triumphs, and achievements. Dwelling on lost loves or opportunities can hurt your current happiness.

Of course, the benefits of reflecting upon an unhappy past has its limits. If your past is troubled by severe traumatic experiences, these unresolved feelings can overwhelm your present capacities for happiness. Other techniques, which we discuss later, can help you clear your mind and open the way to happier thoughts (Pennebaker, 1990).

Is it necessary to have intense emotional moments, or are little pleasures more important? Is happiness built up over many small occurrences, or is it somehow organized around a few fantastic events, such as one's first love, a long-awaited job promotion, or a once-in-a-lifetime trip to Europe? The answers may surprise you.

Psychologist Ed Diener asked people to carry a beeper and report their mood at random (beeped) moments over six weeks. After that time, he and his colleagues asked the subjects to rate their overall happiness for the period (Diener et al., 1990; Smith, Diener, & Wedell, 1989). Was it *how positive* people felt or *how often* people felt positive that mattered most for happiness? The answer was clear: happiness springs from *how much of the time* a person spends feeling good, not from the momentary peaks of ecstasy. Simple pleasures— hours spent walking on a sunny day, gardening, running with the dog, chopping wood, or working on a new craft—are more allied with happiness than are strong feelings.

It seems that a life filled with *many small moments* of happiness, even simple ones, such as playing hide and seek with a child, strapping on a portable cassette player and blotting out the delay of your plane's departure with your favorite Mozart, playing the harmonica (badly), trying to paint a landscape, or doing meaningful work, seems to deliver happiness.

So don't bet your whole life on the big events—winning the lottery, becoming president of the company, or doubling your income. Instead, make sure you have enough daily small things and attend to the daily pleasures of smells, tastes, and sounds, rewarding relationships, and meaningful work.

SUMMARY

1. *Emotions* are similar among all peoples of the world and between human beings and other animals. They are relatively automatic patterns of response. Emotions cause *arousal,* preparing an animal to respond. They help to organize experience and influence perception. They act as simplifying guides to behavior by directing and sustaining actions. In most animals, emotions are communicated by means of display signals, such as odors, postures, facial expressions, and gestures. In humans, nonverbal behavior often communicates emotional states better than words do.

2. Some psychologists hypothesize that there is a set of basic, pure emotions, analogous to the primary colors. The eight pure emotions postulated by Pluchak are joy, acceptance, fear, surprise, sadness, disgust, anger, and anticipation. They vary on the dimensions of intensity, similarity, and polarity. Combinations of these emotions produce other emotions. Emotions become more distinct from each other at increased intensities.

3. There are striking similarities between emotional expressions among different species, human groups with no contact, and blind and normal infants and adults. Thus, emotional expressions seem to be *universal* to humanity. In humans, emotions are displayed primarily in the face. Babies exhibit a predictable sequence of development of emotional expression, indicating that there is an innate maturational component to emotion.

4. Most emotional reactions involve the cardiovascular and gastrointestinal systems and signify emergency arousal in the *sympathetic nervous system.* Physical reactions are interpreted as various emotional experiences. Because the source of the physical reaction can be ambiguous, emotions can be mislabeled and misunderstood.

5. There is more brain area devoted to the face than to any other part of the body's surface. This detailed control allows us to communicate complex emotions through facial expression. Emotions communicate through rapid movements of facial muscles. They can be identified by the facial expressions with which they are associated.

6. The strongest physiological effect of emotion is *activation.* Most of the reactions involved in emotions involve the activating mechanisms of the *sympathetic nervous system.* The different emotions have similar effects on physiology. Deliberate manipulations of facial expressions can affect the experience of emotion. Autonomic physiological responses vary greatly from person to person, but the relationships between facial expression and emotion remain constant.

7. The *limbic system* is largely responsible for many emotional reactions. Recent research shows that there may be specialization of emotional processing in the cerebral cortex. The left hemisphere responds to the verbal content of emotional expression, and the right to tone and gesture. The right and left sides of the face express emotion to different degrees. Some research indicates that the left hemisphere may be more involved in positive emotions and the right in negative.

8. *Appraisal* is the understanding of the meaning of an event. The three basic dimensions in the appraisal process are evaluation, potency, and activity. The cycle of operations of emotions involves a primary appraisal of the situation, feedback, continuous reappraisal and more feedback.

9. Appraisals of emotionally arousing circumstances must be consciously interpreted because the internal states of emotions are similar. The *cognitive appraisal theory of emotion* states that interpretations of physiological states lead to different emotional experiences. The mind seeks the simplest explanation for the arousal. Conscious interpretations can also influence internal states, as has been demonstrated by studies on the effect of false feedback of internal states on emotional experience. Activation in ambiguous situations is subject to misinterpretation.

10. *Frustration* results when a desired outcome is thwarted or delayed. Although psychologists once believed that all frustration increases the probability of aggressive behavior, research has shown that it can also cause depression, guilt, disappointment, apathy, anxiety, and other emotions. Three types of conflict cause feelings of being threatened or frustrated: when needs and motivations are in opposition, when external demands are incompatible, and when an internal need or motive opposes an external demand.

11. Many psychologists believe emotions follow appraisal by other mental functions. However, Zajonc has argued that mental functions often service emotions, not the reverse. It may be more useful to view emotions and thoughts as part of the same feedback system, each influencing the other.

12. *Anxiety* is an emotion that may lead to a variety of psychological disorders. It is related to fear. *Fear* is an immediate and specific reaction to a specific threatening situation. Anxiety is a more general reaction that occurs in higher animals, including humans. It may develop in response to anticipation of potential harm in the future. This harm may be psychological or physical. Anxiety may occur in ambiguous situations. Stress emotions act to alert a person that something may be wrong and that action should be taken. When emotions are too strong, they can disrupt healthy functioning. Antianxiety drugs can help a stressed person to function, if they are used cautiously.

13. Even though we can exert conscious control over our actions, emotions are often *automatic* and *involuntary*. Processes in lower levels of the brain can bypass consciousness. Neuroscientists have discovered pathways by which the amygdala and hypothalamic structures can directly mediate autonomic aspects of emotional responses while bypassing consciousness.

14. People have different ideas about what should make them happy. Most judgments of *happiness* are based on a shifting scale of standards. Increases in wealth above a minimal standard do not much affect happiness ratings. General happiness is more dependent on how much time a person spends feeling good than on momentary peaks of intense pleasure.

activation	feelings
affect	frustration
anxiety	moods
appraisal	polarity
emergency reaction	potency
emotions	primary (basic) emotions
emotion wheel	social releasers
fear	temperament

SUGGESTIONS
FOR FURTHER
READING

Argyle, M. (1988). *The psychology of happiness.* New York: Penguin.

A compendium of knowledge about happiness.

Ekman, P. (1985). *Telling lies.* New York: Norton.

A psychologist's attempt to explain how to detect deceit in business and in life. The book explains how difficult it is.

Ekman, P., & Friesen, W. (1983). *Unmasking the face.* Palo Alto, CA: Consulting Psychologists Press.

The complete test of facial expression of emotions.

Goleman, D. (1985). *Vital lies, simple truths.* New York: Simon & Schuster.

A popular and well thought out book about how the nervous system, by design, denies feelings.

Izard, C. E., et al. (1986). *Emotions, cognition and behavior.* New York: Cambridge University Press.

A definitive collection of essays on the relationship of emotions to other psychological processes.

Lazarus, R., & Folkman, S. (1986). Coping and adaptation. In W. Gentry (Ed.).*Handbook of behavioral medicine.* New York: Guildford Press.

How emotions, stress, and coping all relate.

Ornstein, R., & Sobel, D. (1989). *Healthy pleasures.* Reading, MA: Addison-Wesley.

Information on how to increase happiness and improve mood to strengthen health.

Scherer, K., Wallbott, H., & Summerfield, A. (1986). *Experiencing emotion: A cross-cultural study.* New York: Cambridge University Press.

How emotion is displayed in different social locales. A different approach to that taken in this text and in psychology.

13
NEEDS AND GOALS

A woman stops going out in the evening; she studies late, works extra hours at a waitress job, and saves all her money. Why? She has decided to go to medical school. At every moment we face an almost infinite number of choices. We can do things enthusiastically, half-heartedly, persistently, or lackadaisically. Well-motivated people do better on intelligence tests than others less motivated. People will give up their lives for their country. They may work all night tending the wounded, or they may eat nothing but bread and cheese to save for something special. People act in very different ways depending on what *motivates* them.

Motives are much more variable and individual than any other process we have considered so far. They can determine the course of your life. A person motivated by love may forgo the possibility of making a scientific contribution. Another motivated by achievement may have little time for a family.

Not only do different people have different motives, but each person has different *levels* of motivation. Motives range from the basic and universal, such as hunger and thirst, to the ethereal, such as the desire for self-actualization. Motives build upon one another in a progression, from the simple to the complex.

As far as we know, we are the only animals aware of our own existence. This awareness, probably coupled with the awareness of death, leads us to wonder about the purpose of life. We create our life in the pursuit of our goals, be they financial, intellectual, family, or others. This chapter considers motives common to all animals, such as basic hunger and thirst, and those common only to human beings, such as creativity and individuality.

AN OVERVIEW OF NEEDS AND GOALS

We share with other animals certain purely biologic needs that are basic to the survival of the individual and the species—namely, thirst, hunger, and temperature regulation. But we do not live by bread and water alone. We also *need* to be safe and warm, to care and be cared for. In addition, we look for *meaning* and strive for specific *goals* in life. To be driven by ambition is to be moved by a goal, be it the construction of a building or the composition of a symphony.

SOME DEFINITIONS

NEEDS There are two different types of motives: needs and goals. **Needs** are specific deficits that any animal must satisfy, such as hunger and thirst. We have needs for food, water, rest, safety, and protection, among many others. Needs give rise to *drives*. The need itself is a deficiency that drives the organism into action to satisfy it.

DRIVES **Drives** are physiologically based prompts to behavior: they literally move us to action. A hungry person feels "driven" to find food. We often experience a drive as a specific feeling, such as thirst, hunger, or sex. At one time psychologists hypothesized that all behavior resulted from the reduction of a drive (Hull, 1943): the hunger drive increases when the organism has not fed.

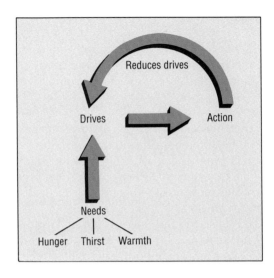

FIGURE 13-1
Drive Reduction

After eating that drive is reduced, and the motivation to seek food is lessened (Figure 13-1). Much of animal and human action is certainly "driven" in this way.

Nevertheless, the concept of *drive reduction* accounts only for behavior associated with very basic needs, such as hunger and thirst. It does not account for much that is characteristically human, such as curiosity and exploration. It hardly explains some behaviors that *increase* drives, such as watching pornographic movies, not to mention jumping out of airplanes for fun.

INSTINCTS   Psychologists once thought that all behaviors, animal and human, could be understood by innate patterns of behavior called **instincts,** which programmed the animal to satisfy needs. An instinct is a behavior typical of every member of a species, and it appears without learning on the first occasion that the appropriate situation occurs.

Motivation theory today places less emphasis on instincts (McClelland, 1985b). Psychologists generally accept that certain *predispositions* are inherited as part of the human genetic program. Some are specific, such as the patterns of mother-infant attachment, while others are general, such as learning a language. General behavior, however, is a mixture of innate and environmental factors. Most humans learn a language, but their culture determines the specific language they learn.

GOALS   What is unique about human motivation is the creation of goals. A **goal** is a desired outcome that has not yet occurred. Human beings do not merely adjust to the demands of their environment, they adapt the environment to suit themselves. If the satisfaction of needs is homeostatic adaptation, then the satisfaction of goals is creative adaptation. *Creative adaptation* changes the environment to meet the goals of the organism (Dubos, 1978). It brings about the construction of cities, human culture and art, science and technology, books, and businesses. What makes human beings unique is our ability to go beyond our inheritance.

We can think of human motives as a pyramid of ascending needs and goals (Frager & Fadiman, 1987). At the bottom are the most basic needs. As we progress to the top, the needs and the goals become more complex (Figure 13-2).

PREPOTENCE What distinguishes the different levels of Maslow's hierarchy is **prepotence:** the *relative strength* of the different needs. In this view, the stronger needs are lower on the hierarchy. Given the lack of both friendship and water, the need for water is stronger—that is, prepotent. The need for water preempts consciousness until it is satisfied. The general rule, then, is *once the lower needs are satisfied, the higher ones can be sought after.*

Keys and colleagues studied 32 conscientious objectors during World War II. The volunteers had their caloric intake reduced from 3,500 to 1,600 per day for six months. During this time they lost an average of 24 percent of their body weight. The thought of food completely preempted their consciousness. They talked, dreamed, and read about food more than anything else. They were extremely disturbed by the slightest waste of available food and even licked their plates clean. Their motivation for anything not associated with food vanished (Keys, Brozek, Henschel, Mickelson, & Taylor, 1950).

Maslow's pyramid of motivation is a general and somewhat idealistic scheme. While thirst is certainly more basic than self-actualization, people may

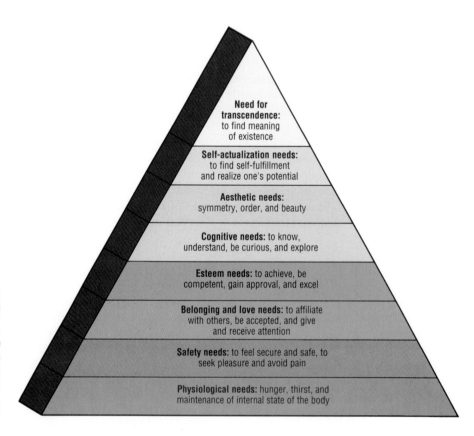

FIGURE 13-2
Maslow's Pyramid of Motivation
Efforts must be made to satisfy needs lower in the hierarchy before needs and goals at higher levels can be expected to motivate action.
(Maslow, 1970)

often satisfy many different needs at one time. The hierarchy does not really work for the higher end. Esteem, knowledge, and the like are much more equivalent to one another than Maslow presumed.

Also, the prepotence of the different levels may vary from individual to individual. The need for transcendence may be so strong that a person may forget friendship and esteem. Sometimes even survival needs are forgotten; religious figures such as Moses, Buddha, and Christ are examples. Still, the hierarchy is a useful way to organize the enormous range of human motives. This chapter begins with basic physiological needs, such as temperature regulation, thirst, and hunger, and it continues with social and intellectual needs, such as belongingness, curiosity, knowledge, and achievement.

PHYSIOLOGICAL AND SAFETY NEEDS

ABRAHAM MASLOW
(1908–1970)

The primary motivation for all organisms is *survival*. Enough oxygen must be breathed, and ample food and liquid must be consumed for animals to stay alive and healthy. All animals, too, try to avoid pain and injury and seek shelter and safety. These needs operate via homeostasis. A deficiency in any of them leads to actions designed to correct the deficiency and a return to the original state.

Because these needs are so important, the complex and precise regulation of these processes has been the subject of much research. Many of our experiences seem quite simple: we are thirsty so we drink; we are hungry so we eat. However, much work and organization goes on within our bodies without our awareness.

KEEPING STABLE

The brain adapts to keep the body stable (but not *static*) in a changing world. Neither the world nor we remain the same. We need more strength as an adult than we did as a child. Blood supply that is adequate for resting does not suffice for running. Metabolic processes that keep the energy supply adequate in winter do not do so in spring.

Countless systems integrate this constant adaptation as the world changes, as the organism changes, as needs change. Think about how much must be organized. We need to control blood flow through heart rate, blood pressure, blood composition, and volume. Metabolism involves breathing, the infusion of oxygen into the bloodstream, and the production, combination, and distribution of thousands of chemicals. Our needs for physical safety involve the integrity of the internal organs, the detection of danger, and mobilizing the emergency system. Internal stability depends, too, on those perceptual processes that generate constancy of perception.

HOMEOSTASIS: THE STABILITY OF THE BODY Mental processes maintain a constancy of the perceived world, and homeostasis maintains a constancy in our internal, physiological world. **Homeostasis** is the tendency to keep the organism in a constant *(stasis)* state. The regulatory systems of the body seek to maintain constant internal processes: constant temperature, water content, and food supply. (See Chapter 3.) Our body must maintain this constancy during extremes of temperature and during long periods without food or drink (Toates, 1986).

Most people like to get hot. We seek out warm and sunny climates, saunas, steam baths, hot tubs, and solariums. Few of us show the same enthusiasm for stripping down for a skinny-dip in a frozen lake or for a mid-winter vacation spent sitting outside freezing in a bikini. We don't like the darkness or the cold.

Most research on heat ignores our love of feeling warm, but one of the few areas in which the potential health benefits of heat have been studied is the sauna. Exposure to high temperatures for brief periods produces profound physiological changes: stress hormones are released, heart rate accelerates, respiration increases, sweating increases, and the skin flushes as the body struggles to maintain a normal body temperature.

People subject themselves to heat stress because they find saunas pleasurable and relaxing and believe that saunas are good for health. The heat of the sauna helps relax tense muscles; electrical discharges in muscles show a more relaxed pattern following a sauna.

An intriguing study in Czechoslovakia demonstrated that sitting in a sauna for 30 minutes doubled beta-endorphin levels in the blood. Recall that *endorphins* are internally produced chemicals that relieve pain and may also produce a sense of well-being and euphoria. So it may not be so far-fetched to speak of a "sauna-bather's high."

The feeling of relaxation following a sauna may also be due to other chemical changes in the brain. The heat may deplete our body stores of stress hormones.

This makes us less likely to respond later to stress—a beneficial type of burnout. Saunas also increase *serotonin*, a powerful hormone associated with relaxation and sleep. Following a sauna, people show more brain waves related to deeper, more restful sleep. So a sauna or a hot bath may be an excellent way to relax before sleep.

Many sauna bathers claim that a sauna helps ward off colds and other infections. They may well be right. Children who regularly take saunas have better resistance to infection. Forty-four kindergarten children in Germany were divided into two groups, with half the children partaking in a weekly sauna.

GETTING HEAT

Over the following 18 months, the number of sick days due to colds, ear infections, and associated maladies for each group was tallied. The children taking the regular sauna bath had only *half* the number of sick days compared to the cooler control group.

The high temperatures produced by the sauna may simply cook and kill the germs. Or the elevated body temperatures may simulate the beneficial effects of a fever. When the body is infected, pyrogens, chemicals that turn up the body's thermostat, flood the bloodstream and bolster the immune system. The invading germs are simultaneously attacked and starved of vital nutrients.

This moderate rise in temperature appears to be healthful: when experimental animals are prevented from raising their body temperature in response to an infection, the death rate increases. A sauna may be a more pleasurable way to produce an artificial fever and may be more functional; wouldn't you rather lie back in the heat once in a while, killing germs, than be forced to lie back for a week or so killing the germs with a fever?

Sauna bathing may even be a pleasant adjunct to physical exercise for burning calories and conditioning the heart. Sweating is an active physiological response to help lower body temperature. It involves the expenditure of a considerable number of calories; a person can burn up 300 to 800 calories during a sauna. Sauna bathing, like physical exercise, also places a stress on the heart and may improve conditioning to some degree.

The healthy pleasures of sauna bathing and hot baths may go well beyond these beneficial physiological measures. A dip in the heat is a great excuse for a protected, quiet rest period in an otherwise harried lifestyle. Again, we need to return to our origins: remember that human beings evolved as a tropical animal, well adapted to the warmer temperatures of the African savannah. For those of us living in the northern hemisphere, separated by thousands of miles and by many degrees from the tropical climes of our ancestors, a sauna or a hot bath may provide a brief respite, a reminder of warm times and warm pleasures.

Homeostasis operates by the process of *feedback*. If the set point of a thermostat is 68° F, higher temperatures cause the cooling systems to come on. Temperatures below 68° F will cause the furnace to produce heat. Any deviation from the desired state is minimized by the thermostatic control of heat and cooling.

Homeostatic principles underlie many bodily processes. We eat when we are hungry; we are hungry when our body needs more fuel. When we are cold, we shiver, which warms us up. Sweat cools us off when we are hot.

TEMPERATURE REGULATION   One of the body's most basic homeostats is the mechanism of temperature regulation. In human beings the set point temperature of 98.6° F (37° C) that is maintained by **thermometer neurons** in the hypothalamus of the brain measure that temperature. If there is a discrepancy of about 1° C from the set point, the thermometer neurons alter their firing rate, which triggers actions either to warm or cool the blood. *Warming* is accomplished by increasing muscle tension, shivering, and constricting the peripheral blood vessels, which decreases heat loss. *Cooling* is attained by sweating and vasodilation in the arms, legs, and head (Toates, 1986).

A fever occurs when the hypothalamic set point itself is raised. There is some evidence that the development of a fever itself may be beneficial. The increased body temperature during fever may kill viruses that cause common febrile diseases such as influenza (Dinarello & Wolfe, 1979).

THIRST

Fluids are essential: every cell of the body is bathed in them. They have the appropriate mineral concentration of sea water, and they constitute 75 percent of our body weight. The maintenance of proper fluid intake and regulation is an extremely important and intricate job, since a small loss of fluid or change in concentration of the electrolytes in the body fluids can kill us.

When our mouths feel dry, we drink; it seems so simple. However, a complicated brain-directed system regulates body fluids. Our mouths become dry because the water content of the blood has dropped, which dries out the salivary glands (Figure 13-3). Usually the glands dry out gradually, but this drying may occur suddenly, as when we exercise on a hot day.

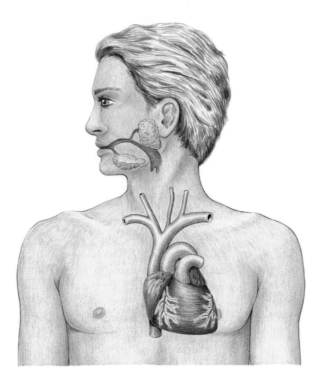

FIGURE 13-3
Thirst

A drop in the water content of your blood, which dries out your salivary glands and makes your mouth dry, is only part of what is involved in thirst. The extremely complex system for regulating body fluids is explained in the accompanying text and Figure 13-4.

PHYSIOLOGICAL AND SAFETY NEEDS

However, **thirst** can be quenched in several ways, only one of which is wetting the salivary glands. Water placed directly into the stomach through a tube reduces thirst. Thus, there is a more central mechanism for fluid control than the glands in the mouth. When the water content outside the cells (primarily in the blood) drops, the concentration of salt (which is usually 0.9 percent) in bodily fluids increases. That increase causes fluid from the cells to be released into the bloodstream, increasing blood volume and hence blood pressure (Figure 13-4). Pressure receptors in blood vessels also detect even the smallest reduction in the water content of the blood (Toates, 1986). This leads, by means of messages transmitted from the vessels by the sympathetic nervous system, to the release of *renin,* an enzyme produced by the kidney. (See Chapter 3, section on the limbic system.) Renin changes blood protein into a new compound, a "thirst substance," which acts on receptors in the hypothalamus and other parts of the limbic system. This activates the sensation of thirst.

How we know when to stop drinking is less clear than why we start, because we stop drinking before the fluid has time to enter the cells of the body. Pressure receptors in the blood vessels detect entering fluid; they then reduce renin production, which diminishes the activity in the area of the hypothalamus concerned with thirst. This cannot be the whole story, though, because much of the liquid is still unabsorbed when we cease drinking. Perhaps increased stomach volume is used as a feedback signal as well.

If there is no fluid intake, as occurs in sleep, and the fluid content within cells is too low, then a hormonal feedback system is activated. The anterior hypothalamus produces *antidiuretic hormone* (ADH), which signals the kidneys to divert some of the water in the urine to the bloodstream. The absence of ADH, which may result from damage to the hypothalamus, as in the disease *diabetes insipidus*, leads to an increase of 10 to 15 times the normal amount of urine and almost constant thirst and drinking (Bellows, 1939).

HUNGER

Thirst regulation is more complex than temperature regulation, and the processes regulating **hunger** are even more complex than those regulating thirst. So, while disorders of temperature regulation and thirst are unusual, hunger disorders such as obesity are common.

HOW DO WE KNOW WE ARE HUNGRY?   When you feel hungry, you eat; as with thirst, it seems so simple. But there is an even more complex system underlying our experience of hunger. *Gastric* and *metabolic* factors are at work telling us when to eat and when to stop.

GASTRIC FACTORS   Walter Cannon, who pioneered much research on the wisdom of the body, emphasized the gastric (stomach) component of hunger. He cajoled his research assistant into swallowing a balloon attached to a graph that recorded the changes in size of the balloon. When the stomach expanded or contracted, so did the balloon. The assistant's reports of hunger pangs coincided with contractions of the balloon (Cannon, 1929). Thus, Cannon proposed that stomach contractions were the primary signal of hunger.

438

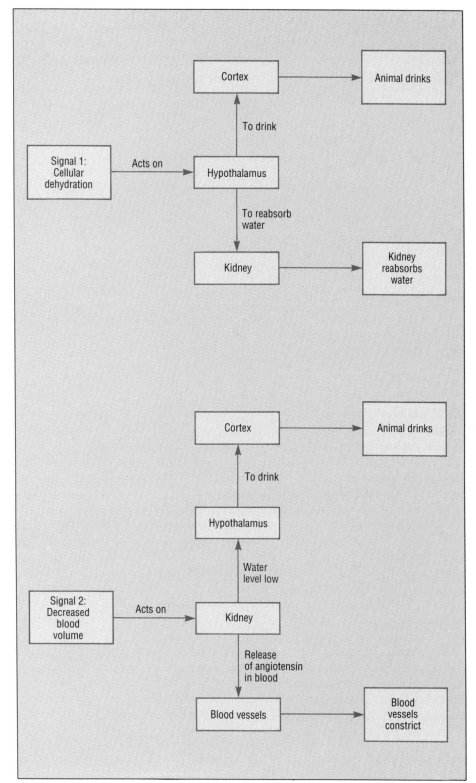

FIGURE 13-4
Regulation of Water Intake

In the upper flow chart cellular dehydration signals the hypothalamus to tell the kidney to reabsorb water and the cerebral cortex to have the animal drink. In the lower flow chart decreased blood volume prompts the kidney to trigger constriction of the blood vessels and to signal the hypothalamus of the need for water intake.

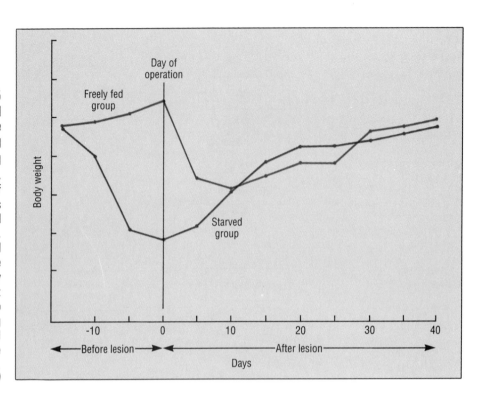

FIGURE 13-5
The Lateral Hypothalamus and the Control of Eating

When their lateral hypothalamus is destroyed, rats will not eat or drink. If tube fed, such animals usually resume eating and drinking on their own in time. But those that were starved before the operation increase their eating, and those freely fed prior to the operation eat less. Eventually, the two groups' weight and eating and drinking patterns will stabilize at about the same relatively normal level.
(Powley & Keesey, 1970.)

FIGURE 13-6
A Case of Overeating

When part of its hypothalamus was destroyed, this rat had no way to tell when it was satiated, so it gorged itself to a weight three to four times normal.

METABOLIC FACTORS   There is more to hunger than stomach contractions, however, and there is more to stomach contractions than simple stomach emptiness. For instance, stomach contractions stop when sugar is injected into the bloodstream, even though the stomach is empty. Metabolic factors relate hunger to the maintenance of energy and body weight. They are registered in the brain in terms of level of blood sugar and the amount of fat deposited in the body. We get hungry when blood sugar (glucose) is low (Mayer, 1953). However, we do not stop eating only because blood sugar is restored to the proper level (Thompson, 1986). Although the control of eating is complex, it involves several brain structures, especially the hypothalamus (Le Magnen, 1986). Consider what happens when the lateral hypothalamus of a rat is destroyed. The rat will stop eating and will actually starve to death without tube feeding (Anand & Brobeck, 1951). If these rats are tube fed, their normal eating and drinking patterns are gradually restored (Figure 13-5). This means that the lateral hypothalamus is not the eating and drinking center.

Destruction of some areas of the hypothalamus leads to very specific deficits. There may be an inability to regulate blood sugar level, but response to food deprivation, is untouched (Blass & Kety, 1974). The hypothalamus is intimately involved in feeding, but in a complex way. Also, disruption of eating and drinking is associated with lesions in a number of other brain areas (Grossman, 1979).

HOW DO WE KNOW WHEN TO STOP EATING?   Destruction of the *ventromedial nuclei* (VMN) of the hypothalamus results in **hyperphagia,** or extreme overeating. This

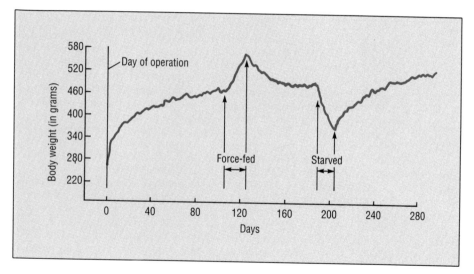

FIGURE 13-7
The Ventromedial
Hypothalamus and
Hyperphagia
Destruction of the
ventromedial area of a rat's
hypothalamus causes
hyperphagia—extreme
overeating. The weight of
such rats eventually stabilizes
at a new, obese level that is
only temporarily influenced by
either force feeding or
starvation.
(Hoebel & Teitelbaum, 1966)

produces some extremely fat rats that are unable to stop eating (Figure 13-6) (Hetherington & Ranson, 1942). Teitelbaum (1957) discovered that these rats are picky eaters. They consume an enormous amount, but are more sensitive to the taste of the food than normal rats. They only eat a lot of what they like.

This is also true of human beings. Obese people with VMN lesions have lost internal mechanisms or cues that control eating, such as stomach contractions or low blood sugar. They seem to eat more because of external cues (Schacter, 1971; Schacter & Rodin, 1974), such as a lunch whistle or the appearance of food.

Rats with VMN lesions do not go on eating until they explode. They simply maintain a new, higher body weight (Figure 13-7) (King & Gaston, 1977). When the VMN is damaged, *growth hormone*, which modulates the effect of insulin, decreases. The level of circulating insulin increases, which decreases the burning of fatty acids. The result is increased deposits of fat. Normally, circulating insulin increases as soon as the organism begins to eat (Struble & Steffens, 1975). When the VMN is damaged, this normal process may be exaggerated (Steffens, Mogenson, & Stevenson, 1972; Toates, 1986).

How does the VMN work when it is working well? It might be a direct sensory process. Food passing through several stages of digestion may be signaled to the VMN, or perhaps the production of insulin is the cue.

OBESITY

The search for the edible and the delicious is constant in modern culture with new cuisines, new restaurants, and new food crazes. Some foods are even sought as aphrodisiacs. Food is strongly associated with feelings: an image of daily love and togetherness might be a family gathered around a holiday table. Some people have thought that "the way to a man's heart is through his stomach." Jewish mothers cure everything with chicken soup. As some researchers have observed,

Maintaining the stability of fluids and nourishment are important motivators, and so is the stability to resist diseases. How are we motivated to repel viruses and bacteria? The immune system defends the body; it has similarities to the nervous system. Both respond to a variety of outside information and regulate the body; both receive and transmit either excitatory or inhibitory signals. But most important and most revolutionary is that both systems learn and remember. The immune system identifies and recognizes what is foreign (not of the body) and what is not.

MECHANISMS OF IMMUNITY

Antigens are foreign cells or large molecules of origin outside the body. Their intrusion into the body stimulates the immune responses to defend the organism. At the same time, the immune system must not attack the cellular and molecular constituents of the body itself. The ability of the immune system to recognize and keep track of millions of different substances is another miracle of our bodies. However, the immune system isn't perfect. If it overreacts to harmless antigens, it causes allergies. It can also fail to recognize the body's own cells attacking itself, as is the case in autoimmune diseases.

Natural immunity involves general inflammatory processes for reacting to tissue damage. When most cells are damaged, they release molecules that increase the permeability of the capillaries. This allows cells and large molecules to enter the tissues and help to neutralize bacteria and viruses. Other molecules, such as *interferon*, inhibit viruses from spreading by replicating themselves.

Acquired immunity works through a type of white blood cell known as *lymphocytes*. Lympho-

cytes patrol the blood stream and are ideally suited for the recognition and destruction of millions of different antigens. Embryonic cells and (later in life) the bone marrow create lymphocytes which then undergo further specialization. Some are carried by the circulation to the thymus where they mature to become *T-cells* (the *T* is from thymus). Other lymphocytes called *B-cells* mature in the fetal liver and later in bone marrow. Other cell types in the immune army include *macrophages* (Greek for "big eaters"), which are large scavenger cells that ingest and destroy antigens, natural killer cells that attack tumors, and virus-infected cells.

The immune system has to patrol constantly and be able to make millions of duplicate cells upon demand. It can work this way because the lymphocytes mutate

RESISTING DISEASE

wildly very early in embryonic life and produce a vast range of cells. Each one, like the transmission of neural impulses, has different shapes of surface receptors. These cells remain available for defense against practically any kind of invader.

It works through the lock-and-key principle (see Chapter 3). The antigen, through its own molecular shape, automatically selects its worst enemy from an army of potential defenders. When the lymphocyte cell pool is exposed to a foreign antigen, a battle follows in rapid succession. Cells matching the pattern reproduce and generate an enormous army of identical lymphocytes. These instant defenders produce specific antibodies

that combine with and inactivate the antigen. At the same time, other sensitized T-cells migrate to the source of the antigen (say a tumor). There they secrete chemicals called *lymphokines*, which are toxic to the foreign tissue.

The state of the immune system motivates the resistance of the organism. This motivation is perhaps more important in the development of diseases than in the exposure to actual diseases (viral or bacterial) or toxins. Some viruses such as herpes simplex are always present but become active only when something goes wrong with the immune system.

THE BRAIN AND THE IMMUNE SYSTEM

Recall the study in Chapter 1, in which the death of a spouse in a train wreck resulted in decreases in immune system functioning. Recent scientific efforts are beginning to track the many influences on the immune system. The influences range from laughter to empathy and from bereavement to anger.

But how do mental factors or even specific brain processes affect the immune system? Answering this question has barely begun, yet there are many important and promising new indications. Psychologists know that extensive connections exist between the nervous system and the immune system. The immune system is the center of the defense against disease. It is also of current interest because AIDS is a disorder of the immune system.

Removal of certain areas in the hypothalamus leads to suppression, while stimulation leads to enhanced immune system response. In an early study in Hungary in the 1950s, two researchers first sensitized guinea pigs to allergic substances. When the hypothalamus was lesioned, those animals did not respond to the allergen. The intact animals responded with standard violent allergic reactions. Later research revealed that damage to certain areas of the hypothalamus resulted in decreased function in the thymus gland. Recall that the thymus is responsible for the maturation of the T-cells that control immune surveillance and antibody production.

Not only does the hypothalamus communicate with the immune system but also the immune system talks back. Besedovsky et al. (1977) recorded the rate of firing of neurons in the hypothalamus when an animal was challenged by foreign and virulent antigens. The neuron firing rate increased greatly. This indicates that information about the immune system is registered, if not organized, in the hypothalamus.

The stronger the immune reaction is, the stronger the brain response is. Since the hypothalamus controls the *pituitary,* the pharmacy of the brain, there were also significant changes in levels of the neurotransmitter *norepinephrine.* All this evidence suggests that the immune system can change brain function and vice versa.

EMOTIONS AND IMMUNITY

As discussed in other chapters, research is beginning to show that mental factors influence resistance to disease. Kasl et al. (1979) studied the development of infectious mononucleosis in West Point cadets. The cadets were given blood tests to screen for antibodies to Epstein-Barr virus, which causes infectious mono. In addition, the investigators reviewed interview data about the cadets, which included information about their expectations and family backgrounds.

Each year about one-fifth of the cadets were infected, but only about one-fourth of them developed mono. What predicted those who were likely to become ill? Cadets who wanted a military career but were doing poorly academically were most likely to develop symptoms. The combination of high expectation and poor performance was reflected in increased susceptibility to infectious disease.

Even mild upsets affect the immune system. Medical students were observed for the number of their "life-change events" in the previous months as well as their loneliness. Both loneliness and the mild amount of life stress these students experienced (they were doing well on exams) preceded decreased natural killer immune cells (Kiecolt-Glaser, 1985).

The immune system responds directly to a break in the mother-infant attachment. Christopher Coe and his colleagues (1985) separated 6-month-old squirrel monkeys from their mothers. Immune function (which appeared as decreased antibody response and levels of complement and immunoglobulins) were suppressed in those suffering maternal loss. However, this separation-induced immune suppression was less when the infant was placed in a familiar home environment or with familiar peers.

Anxiety and depression also affect natural killer cell activity, which is a measure of cellular immune function. Stephen Locke studied a group of 114 Harvard undergraduates. "Good copers"—those who reported few psychiatric symptoms in the face of high levels of stress—had significantly higher cell activity than "poor copers" (Locke, et al., 1984). Poor coping in the face of stressful life changes may adversely affect immunity.

PSYCHOIMMUNOLOGY

Can positive states of mind enhance the functioning of the immune system? This is the subject of a growing amount of research. There is some evidence that an individual can voluntarily improve immune functions. Hall and colleagues studied 20 healthy people to assess the response of the lymphocytes in their immune systems to positive suggestions during hypnosis (Hall et al., 1984; Hall, 1986).

While under hypnosis, the subjects were told to visualize their white blood cells as strong powerful sharks swimming through the bloodstream attacking weak confused germs. They were given a posthypnotic suggestion that these shark-like cells would protect their body against germs. They did self-hypnosis two times each week and told themselves the shark story. Those who were easily hypnotized showed *increased numbers* of lymphocytes after their hypnotic sessions!

There seems to be a benefit from laughing, as well. Ten students viewed a humorous videotape *(Richard Pryor Live)* and a didactic control tape. Their levels of salivary IgA were measured before and after each videotape. (Salivary IgA is a type of antibody that appears to defend against viral infections of the upper respiratory tract.) Viewing Richard Pryor's antics temporarily boosted the average concentrations of this antibody (Dillon et al., 1985–86, 1989).

The immune system may be the central point of a body's motivation to resist disease, and research in this field promises to link mental and physical components of motivation (Ornstein & Sobel, 1987).

Our ideas of obesity and beauty change through time and from culture to culture. People who are fat can be considered healthy and attractive in their own culture. But in our culture today, thinness is equated with health and beauty, while obesity is viewed as unattractive and unhealthy.

Humans will swallow almost anything that does not swallow them first. The animals they relish range in size from termites to whales; the Chinese of Hunan Province eat shrimp that are still wriggling, while North Americans and Europeans eat live oysters. . . . Strong preferences have been shown for the fetuses of rodents, the tongues of larks, the eyes of sheep, the spawn of eels, the stomach contents of whales, and the windpipes of pigs. (Farb & Armelagos, 1980)

Our love of and preoccupation with food has had great adaptive value, until recently. When the food supply was uncertain, people who had gorged themselves when food was plentiful had more chance of survival later. When most work required strenuous manual labor, huge meals were needed as fuel. Until recently, unheated homes made it necessary for people to produce heat from what went into their stomachs, not from a furnace.

TEMPERATURE AND FOOD INTAKE REGULATION   The body operates like a furnace: **metabolism** is a process in which fuel (food) is burned to make heat to keep the body warm and to provide energy. When the body is fed more fuel than can be metabolized, it stores the excess fuel as fat, to be used when needed.

The body's metabolic regulation is dishearteningly accurate. Each of us eats, over a lifetime, more than 45 tons of food, yet our weight varies little. Suppose you ate just 200 calories a day more than you burn (one small chocolate bar), and didn't increase other activities. If there were no adaptation in the body, you would gain about 20 pounds a year!

Modern Western culture has experienced a drastic increase in the availability of food, a decrease in strenuous activities, and the invention of central heating. The result of these advances is often great human stores of fat. In some contemporary Western European countries, such as Germany, more than 75 percent of the population is thought to be overweight.

THE SET POINT   A body gains weight when it takes in more calories than it expends. A *calorie* is a measure of heat production: it is the amount of energy required to increase the temperature of one gram of water by 1° C. Losing and gaining weight is *not* simply a matter of decreasing calorie intake, however, because the homeostatic mechanisms of the body regulate weight around a **set point** (Cabanac, 1971). The hypothalamus can control appetite, absorption of food into the body, and metabolic level to change caloric expenditure (Bennett, 1984; Le Magnen, 1986).

Our metabolisms, not primarily our conscious decisions, keep our weight around a predetermined level. It is almost impossible to consciously regulate food intake to a few hundred calories a day. Even a nutritionist could not estimate caloric intake that precisely (Bennett, 1984). The set point makes it more difficult both to gain and to lose weight than we would predict by merely counting calories.

INNATE FACTORS IN OBESITY   Here are some common excuses for being overweight:
1. "I've lost hundreds of pounds in my life" (the implication being that it is always gained back).
2. "It doesn't matter how much I eat—I am just naturally fat."
3. "I can gain weight by just looking at food."

Recent evidence suggests that these clichés are true. Unfortunately, some persons *are* born to be fat. The set point for weight is simply higher in these people, and it makes losing weight to a desired ideal very difficult, if not impossible.

Fatness is related to the number and size of the body's fat cells, called **adipocytes**. Obese people have three times the numbers of adipocytes as do people of normal weight (Bjorntorp, 1972). Fat cells are established in the first two years of life. Overfeeding in those years results in an increased number of fat cells. No amount of weight loss after that age lessens the number of fat cells. They abide inside the unfortunate person, waiting to be bloated. Critical periods of fat cell production are from the ages 6 to 10 and during adolescence (Nisbett, 1972).

A person with too many fat cells has a high set point for food consumption and will continue to be hungry even when his or her weight is at the supposed "norm." The problem for the constitutionally obese is that their own set point is higher than the cultural norm. They then face two bleak alternatives: either constant hunger or being thought of as overweight. So these people lose and gain weight constantly; their diets do not work. The reason is that they are fighting a powerful biological enemy.

THE LOSING BATTLE   The brain handles incoming food in many sophisticated ways. It is not a matter of simple "calories in and calories out," as was once thought. Not all calories are equally fattening. Fat in food leads to more fat deposit in the body since it deposits directly in the tissue. An equal amount of calories of carbohydrates has to be metabolized first and does not contribute as much to deposited fat.

Calories are handled with great precision. After eating too large a meal the brain lights an internal fire, using brown adipocyte cells. People with a lot of this

PHYSIOLOGICAL AND SAFETY NEEDS

English couple Maurice and Marilyn Bailey were sailing from Panama to the Galapagos Islands on a trans-Pacific voyage when their boat was hit by a sperm whale and capsized. They survived adrift for 118 days (Mar. 4–June 30, 1973), longer than any other human beings lost at sea, in a five-foot rubber life raft. They drifted across an area of the Pacific known as the tropical convergence where there are frequent rains and a variety of marine life.

At first, they limited themselves to a ration of one pint of water each per day. During this time they drifted under an intense heat. During the last two months, however, they were able to catch ample rainwater.

Their diet consisted mostly of trigger fish and turtles (raw). Their revulsion to the former in particular was soon conquered by their hunger. Thus they had a high protein, low fat diet. Because protein digestion requires much water (as opposed to sugar, which is much less demanding in this respect),

HOW DOES MOTIVATION CHANGE IN EXTREME SITUATIONS?

they were fortunate that water was never completely unavailable to them.

Given sufficient fresh water and adequate heat, a person can endure a shortage of food for quite some time before showing signs of starvation. The Baileys declined physically and lost about 40 pounds each. However, the rate at which they lost weight slowed considerably after the first month.

They had a preoccupation with and long discussions about food. They planned menus and holiday meals, remembered favorite childhood foods and talked about restaurants to revisit and food that they'd buy.

The Baileys experienced a de-

gree of mental deterioration from dietary deficiencies compounded by prolonged isolation under adverse environmental conditions. As this story attests, however, these negative effects are not necessarily irreversible. (These were also particularly enduring people.)

They devised ways of coping with the isolation and boredom by playing games with improvised equipment, kept diaries, fantasized about the future, and designed in careful detail the new yacht they planned to have.

They were eventually rescued by a Korean fishing vessel (the eighth ship they had sighted). Marilyn was in better physical condition at the end of the ordeal than Maurice because she, as the average woman typically does, required less energy input and had more resources in the form of fat (than the average man). She also had a higher hemoglobin level, even though men normally have more hemoglobin per unit volume than women. Generally, females do better in the face of starvation.

''brown fat'' sweat out the excess calories overnight and return to a good weight in the morning (Rothwell & Stock, 1979).

The stabilizing mechanisms of the body also serve to discourage weight loss: at the beginning of an attempt to lose weight, when people may be high above their real set points, weight loss is easier; as they approach their set points, however, weight loss is more difficult. This causes many people to go off their diet and return to their original weight. Also, people try to establish a new, lower set point; when this cannot be reached, they abandon all discipline. This reaction is known in technical terms as the ''what the hell'' effect (Polivy & Herman, 1983).

The body has a built-in protection against famine that lowers the set point drastically when the food supply is low. Then weight loss may be extremely difficult. The limits to which the body can conserve were determined by Jewish doctors during the Nazi occupation of Poland. The caloric intake of the residents of the Warsaw ghetto was decreased by the Nazis from about 2,400 per day to about 300. Protein intake was cut to about 10 percent of normal (Winnick, 1979).

The record these doctors made of the human body was of an organism struggling heroically to adapt. Body temperature dropped, blood pressure decreased, and blood circulated at a slower rate. The body burned fuel in the

Sometimes a young person, most often a woman, simply refuses to eat and begins to waste away. Why does this happen? How are they treated? Here is one case and the way it was treated.

Ellen West had great artistic abilities, wrote poetry, and kept a diary, before and after she became sick. . . . After graduation from high school she took up horseback riding and attained great skill, doing it in the same over-intense way with which she approached every task. In her nineteenth year, she noticed the beginning of a *new anxiety*, namely the *fear of becoming fat*. She had developed an enormous appetite and grew so heavy that her friends would tease her. Immediately thereafter she began to castigate herself, denying herself sweets and other fattening foods, dropping supper altogether, and went on long exhausting walks. Though she looked miserable, she was only *worried about getting too fat* and continued her endless walks. Parallel to this fear of becoming fat, her desire for food increased. The persisting conflict between the dread of fatness and the craving for food overshadowed her whole life. After many years of illness she wrote: "It is this external tension between wanting to be thin and not to give up eating that is so exhausting. In all other aspects I am reasonable, but I know on this point I am crazy. I am really ruining myself in this endless struggle against my na-

ANOREXIA NERVOSA AND ITS TREATMENT

ture. Fate wanted me to be heavy and strong, but I want to be thin and delicate." (Ullman & Krasner, 1965)

In the treatment of this case, reconditioning was used, and was often effective. All meals were brought to her by a nurse and were to be taken in her room. The experimenters set up a reinforcement schedule that consisted of verbal rewards for any movements associated with eating. For example, when she lifted her fork to move toward spearing a piece of food, the experimenter would talk to her about something in which the patient was interested. The required response was then shaped by reinforcing successive movements associated with raising or lifting food toward her mouth, chewing and so on.

The same reinforcement procedures were followed to increase the amount of food consumed. At first, any portion of the meal that was eaten would be rewarded by having the nurse come into her room with a radio, TV set, or phonograph. If she did not touch any of the food before her, she received no reinforcement, and she would be left alone until the next meal. As time went on, more and more of her meal had to be eaten, until eventually she had to finish every-

thing on the plate in order to be reinforced. Her meals were slowly increased in caloric value, with the cooperation of the dieticians, and her weight gradually rose to a level of 85 pounds.

After discharge from the hospital, the question became, "How does one generalize the eating response that was acquired under controlled conditions to a situation where such controls are lacking?" This problem was solved by enlisting the help of the patient's family. They were instructed specifically (1) to avoid reinforcing any irrelevant behavior or complaints; (2) not to make any issue of eating; (3) to reinforce maintenance of her weight gain by complimenting with comments about her beginning to fill out her clothes; (4) not to prepare any special diet for her; (5) to refrain from weighing her at home because this was to be recorded only when she made periodic visits to see the medical student; (6) to discuss only pleasant topics at meal times; (7) never to allow her to eat alone; (8) to follow a rigid schedule for meals, with an alarm clock to be present for each meal; (9) to use a purple table cloth initially as a discriminative stimulus for mealtime table behavior associated with eating; and (10) to encourage her to dine out with other people under enjoyable conditions (Ullman & Krasner, 1965).

In anorexia, we see how many "rules" are normally taken care of by the body's stabilizing systems. Specifying all these conditions to make a person eat helps to make us aware of the complexity of the regulation within.

most efficient way possible. Only as a last resort was the stored protein in muscles, including the heart, burned. The human body's ability to slow its metabolism to conserve resources saved lives in the ghetto and the concentration camps. Our ancestors, when confronted with famine, probably experienced the same changes.

In less extreme circumstances, deliberately eating less is one means of adjusting weight. However, to maintain weight loss, *food intake must be continually decreased as the diet continues,* since our caloric needs decrease at lower weights. A diet low enough in calories to decrease weight early in dieting may cause no weight loss or even a weight gain later on. The brain creates a new stabilizing point.

An alternative to reducing caloric intake is to increase exercise, which reduces appetite. Exercise increases the caloric consumption (heat production) during the exercise itself and it also increases heat production *after* a meal. More importantly, the increase in calories burned during exercise *continues during the day.* The set-point regulation mechanism evolved in a setting in which our ancestors habitually engaged in a moderate amount of physical activity during the course of the day. There are substantial weight benefits for those who walk about 25 to 30 miles per week. Exercise about equivalent to this seems to adjust the set point, since this is about the workload that our ancestors adapted to, and it is probably the average stabilizing point of the system.

There is a consolation for those who will never match the ideal figure in the jeans ads. Remember that the average weight gain is a little less than one pound per year for people of average height. A man who weighed 165 at age 30 will usually weigh about 185 at age 60. Millions of people gain weight through their lives. This gain plagues the middle aged; it is the boon for fitness centers, fad diets, and diet aids.

But from the point of view of keeping the body stable, why should this occur? It is for health. Our culture usually assumes that thin people are healthier—for years, actuarial tables have been built around this assumption. But some research, especially by Reuben Andres (Andres et al., 1985), shows that people who are of average weight for their ages or slightly overweight are the healthiest (Figure 13-8).

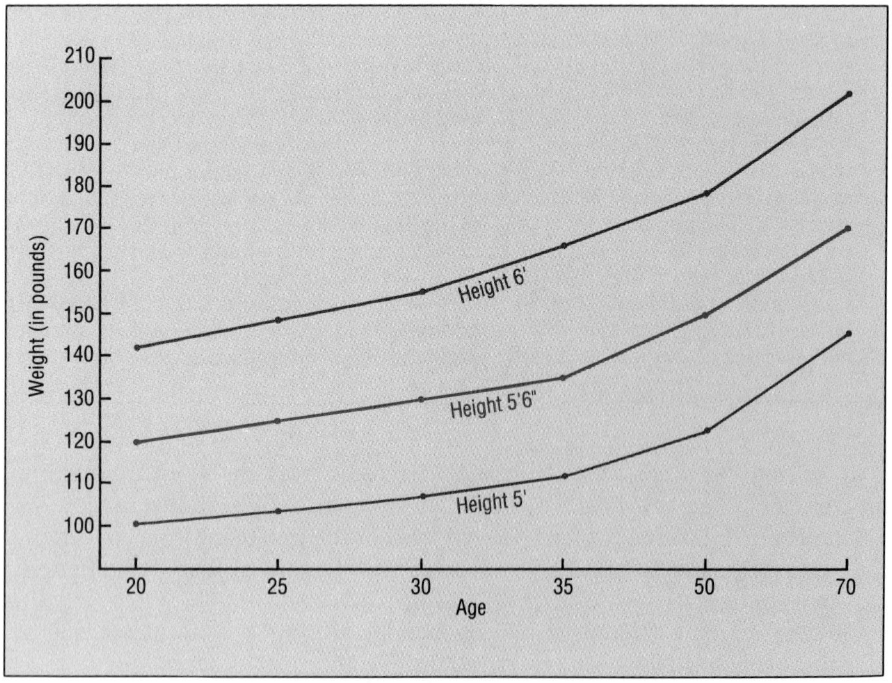

FIGURE 13-8
"Natural Weight"

The most recent research indicates that natural weight depends only on your height and age. This table graphs the natural weight for people of three heights at different ages in their lives. Weight within 15 pounds of each of these points should not interfere with health. For example, a 25-year-old woman who is 5'6" can weigh between 110 and 140 with little effect on her health.
(Andres et al., 1985)

Most of the social advice about weight is more likely advice about appearance (looking thin means looking young) rather than useful health information. Brain processes, having evolved over millions of years to adjust weight for health, are wiser than our current cultural ideal. So being "overweight" for those who are not obese may not be such a losing battle after all.

BELONGING AND SAFETY

When the most basic and immediate physiological needs are met, others then need to be satisfied. Safety must be maintained, pain must be avoided, and pleasures are usually sought. There are human needs to belong to groups and social networks and to give and receive attention.

The underground man, Dostoevsky's narrator in *Notes from the Underground,* is a classic (however complex) social outcast. Self-exiled from human society, he leads an extremely solitary existence.

> It seems that the underground man was driven to an extreme form of the detached solution by a singularly bleak and loveless childhood. He was completely deprived of the warmth, re-enforcement, and protection of family life; and his resulting oddness (defensiveness) made him an object of scorn and derision to his peers.

And Dostoevsky draws him, foresightedly, as having health problems, especially those of the liver. The underground man is keenly aware of why he is how he is:

> "If I had a home from childhood I shouldn't be what I am now. I often think that. However bad it may be at home," he tells another character, Liza, "anyway they are your father and mother, and not enemies, strangers. Once a year, at least, they'll show their love of you. Anyway, you are at home. I grew up without a home; and perhaps that's why I've turned so . . . unfeeling."

PAIN AND PLEASURE

The motives of avoiding pain and seeking pleasure guide the behavior of most animals. In fact, the nervous system contains well-defined pain and pleasure centers. These serve as a feedback system about actions that may be injurious or helpful to the organism's survival or reproductive success. An organism's feelings are a guide to action. It is here that emotions and motives are most closely related (Mook, 1986).

Different networks send pain information to the brain. Sudden pain preempts consciousness. This happens when you put your hand on something hot. The *lemniscal system* quickly transmits sudden pain information. The *spinothalamic system* transmits slow pain information, like that of an old back problem.

A part of the brain's limbic system is probably the final common pathway of the feeling of pleasure. Animals with electrodes inserted in the "pleasure center" of their brain will perform almost any action to keep that center stimulated. They even forgo food and drink under certain conditions (Routenberg, 1976).

People Need to Belong

Taking a class, being a member of a team, joining a social organization, or just getting together with the gang provides a sense of belonging that can improve an individual's health and outlook on life.

BELONGING

At first glance you might be surprised to find **belonging** as a human need. After all, we have defined a need as something that, if not satisfied, results in harm to the organism, such as starvation from lack of food. Why, then, is belonging a need? Recent evidence suggests that when people are deprived of belonging to a group, they may suffer health consequences. Human beings are social animals.

In one Australian aboriginal tribe, a person may become the victim of "bone pointing" when a powerful witch casts a spell condemning the unfortunate person to death. The people in the tribe then treat such individuals as if they were actually dead. They do not speak to them or acknowledge their presence, and they act as if they cannot see the condemned persons. Unless the "spell" is lifted, the condemned often do die.

Cases of people deprived of normal social interaction show significant negative effects on intelligence and on health. Recall that children in a Lebanese orphanage who were neglected showed much lower intelligence (Dennis & Dennis, 1948). When some children in an orphanage were "adopted" by caring people, their intelligence increased (Skeels & Dye, 1939). (See Chapter 11, section on enhancing intelligence.)

So *people need people and need the attention of others.* In an extensive study of the effect of social networks on health, Syme and others found that healthy people have a more extensive network of friends than those less healthy. Syme often begins his lectures by saying, "When I was young and felt bad, my grandmother used to tell me, 'Go out and play with your friends'; now I find there is good evidence for this" (Syme, 1984).

When people who lack friends or a group are encouraged to join one, their health improves. A large project in San Francisco's "Tenderloin" area seeks to improve the health of the impoverished elderly residents by forming neighborhood associations. The results show significant health improvements when people belong to a group (Minkler, 1984). Almost any improvement in "belonging" seems to help, whether there is another person involved or not. Patients in a nursing home who were given a plant to care for showed improvements in health (Rodin & Langer, 1977). To belong and to be needed by a family, group, or club is more of a basic human need than we might expect.

CHAPTER 13 / NEEDS AND GOALS

MATERNAL CARE One of the strongest attachments is the mother-child bond. Maternal care in female rats seems largely under hormonal control. Some experiments have transferred hormones in the blood from a mother rat to another rat. The receptor rat later will begin to exhibit the characteristic maternal behavior pattern of rats. This includes nesting, licking, retrieving, and nursing the young rats. In humans, hormonal regulation probably does not completely determine maternal behavior. However, hormones under the control of the pituitary do play a specific role in lactation and nursing.

Male rats never care for their offspring. Human males may come to take an active role in child care, and some women abandon their children. The hormones associated with lactation may predispose the mother toward loving and caring for the child (Newton & Modahl, 1978). It is more likely that it is the closeness involved in the activity of nursing itself that cements the love bond.

HUMAN GOALS

Many needs are common to all animals: food, drink, avoiding pain, and safety. Belonging needs and needs for attention are common to social animals such as human beings and chimpanzees. What is uniquely human is not our needs but our **goals.** Human beings are not only motivated by biological *deficits* but by the invention of *possibilities* (Dubos, 1978). Homeostatic adaptation is important to all organisms, and it is to us as well. However, our most important inheritance is the ability to go beyond our inheritance.

Goals serve the function of creative adaptation: the ability to create a new world to suit ourselves. These motives are more mental than biological. They are highly individual and are capable of being expressed differently by different people. If we had no goals, we would have no civilization.

What makes us unique also makes us difficult to study. Why someone creates or is driven to form a new company is not as clear as the thirst drive. Thus, some of the most important human experiences are not as well understood as the most basic.

COMPETENCE AND EXCELLENCE: ESTEEM

Competence is how well we can carry out an intended action. It earns us the esteem of others and builds our self-respect. Early in life, competence may involve simple tasks, such as getting food into the mouth or lifting a cup. At around age 2, a child smiles when he or she is able to perform a task successfully. Competence is a part of the emerging human consciousness.

Later on there are other challenges to competence—learning new tasks such as riding a bike, reading, making friends, and being liked. Challenges to one's competence appear throughout life, especially to people of high aspiration. The desired *level* of competence increases with age, from the toddler to the student to the worker to the executive.

ACHIEVEMENT

Competence produces its own reward: **achievement.** The sense of achievement is so reinforcing that it is itself a motivating force. David McClelland, a major investigator of human motivation, defines the drive for achievement as "competition with a standard of excellence" (McClelland, 1985b).

McClelland and his associates have concentrated their study on what they call the need for achievement. **Achievement motivation** is what enables us to carry through and complete the goals we set for ourselves. Many human goals are long-term and not immediately attainable. We can quench thirst right away, but it takes years to become a great pianist. The need to achieve keeps us on the path toward a distant goal.

Achievement motivation is different at different times. The value placed on achievement itself and the kinds of achievements that are valued vary within cultures and across time. High achievers were the heroes in stories in the years prior to and following the American Revolution. In nineteenth-century America, the folklore was dominated by stories of remarkable achievements. The stories described inventions, mastery over the wild environment, and people making huge fortunes. Success stories are not as popular today. This idea of achievement has never been central in such cultures as those of the Egyptians and the American Indians. The rise and fall of a civilization can sometimes be correlated with the achievement level in literature. Striving is a major theme in early Greek literature, but by the peak of the civilization, it had declined (McClelland, 1985a, 1985b). Revolutions also bring forth changes in achievement. The children's books in Russia and China urged a higher level of achievement after their communist revolutions than before.

CHARACTERISTICS OF ACHIEVERS

One successful man described his view of how to get things done:
"First try opening the door by turning the handle," he said. "If that doesn't work, try a key. Failing that, break the door down. If you can't, get in by a window."
"What happens if everything fails?" a young listener interrupted.
The great overachiever responded instantly and with total sincerity, "That is totally unthinkable," he said. (Engel, 1986)

The *need* for achievement is a characteristic component of a person's personality (McClelland, 1985a). There are striking differences between people in whom the need for achievement is high and those in whom the need is low. People with a high level of *n-Ach* (a measure of the strength of the achievement motive) set *moderately high, realizable* goals. High achievers are more likely to succeed. They do not worry as much as others about avoiding failure, and they are willing to take some risks. They are more internally motivated than low achievers. They make decisions and judgments on their own, independently of the opinion of others. They are more likely to associate with others on the basis of their competence than on the basis of friendship. Their fantasies often concern unique accomplishments (McClelland, 1985b). They like concrete feedback and criticism, and they prefer to direct activities with definable goals and clear-cut results.

McClelland suggests that these tendencies may be why high achievers are more attracted to business careers than academic ones. A business usually has a definable outcome: "the bottom line." An academic contribution is often difficult to evaluate.

The need for achievement is often determined by environmental factors. But achievement does seem to breed achievement. The standards parents set for their children and the parents' accomplishments themselves are critical in the development of a high level of n-Ach. Parental training and expectations are the most important factors, specifically encouraging their children from an early age to do things well on their own (McClelland, 1985b).

Upper- and middle-income homes produce twice as many high achievers as lower-income homes. Middle- and upper-class parents are high achievers and set higher standards for their children. Over the past few decades, opportunities for advancement have become more available to lower-income families. Consequently, there has been an increase not only in their income, but also in their level of n-Ach (Banks, McQuarter, & Hubbard, 1977; Rokeach, 1973; Rosen, 1959).

Achievement motivation can be easily and quickly learned, even in adulthood. In one study, businessmen in India took an achievement motivation course and subsequently made more investments, employed more people, and made more money than before they took the course (McClelland, 1985a).

Necessity is also a primary motivator of achievement, just as it is the mother of invention. Recall the amazing surge of creativity *and* implementation that came over the people of England during the Second World War when the entire nation was fighting for its life. Men and women, who in their civilian lives had contentedly pushed paper from pile to pile, suddenly created fantastically efficient administrative systems for rationing food, for civil defense, for the production necessary for the war effort, for national health, and for a myriad of other programs dictated by necessity. Men who had been entirely satisfied to sit back behind little shop counters suddenly, on their own initiative, led desperate attacks across the front lines into the face of the enemy's fire—and won! Men and women who had been content to fish in the waters of the English Channel, as their forebears had, suddenly and spontaneously organized themselves into a civilian armada and rescued the British Army at Dunkirk. Here was innovation and implementation of an incredible order carried out by individuals who in more normal circumstances had been neither creative nor action-oriented.

THE LIVES OF ACHIEVERS A key quality of achievers is *perseverance*. Robert the Bruce (1274–1329), who would become Robert I, King of Scotland, was reminded of this by a spider. Grim battles with the English to win the independence of Scotland had left him discouraged until he observed a spider who, repeatedly falling from the ceiling and working its way back up its thread, finally managed to conquer gravity. Bruce was moved by this to persevere one more time and prevail over England.

Achievement is often the *execution* of an idea. Edwin Land, inventor of the Polaroid camera, was not responsible for the original idea of a camera that developed its own film. A restless, activist type, he acted out of a desire to remedy the small nuisance of having to wait a week to get film developed. Using an idea available to anyone, he achieved by inventing the instant camera, then by manufacturing and selling it.

We might think that a high achiever drives to dominate. But Jane Goodall's research on chimpanzees, as documented in her book *In the Shadow of Man,* would appear to refute this and posit the reverse. The chimps develop

Sally Ride, first U.S. woman astronaut, and Mikhail Gorbachev, whose political and economic restructuring efforts in the U.S.S.R. led to the end of the cold war, are examples of high achievers who have contributed much to society.

dominance by learning that they can achieve. In the case of chimps, hunger motivates achievement; the experience of having achieved leads them to possess feelings of dominance and be viewed as dominant. Similarly, making opportunities available to young businessmen in training is a method that has been employed by business to foster traits common to the achiever or the over-achiever. Many sales companies begin the workday with a series of early-morning chants to stimulate their salesmen who might otherwise be lethargic or not be able to motivate themselves to the same extent.

KNOWLEDGE

A vital human motive is the search for **knowledge** and understanding of the world. Systems of education and philosophical, scientific, and fictional works all are evidence of our efforts to further our understanding. What might not be so evident, however, is that our search for how the world is organized is so basic that our health suffers when our understanding of the world is in disarray (Antonovsky, 1984, 1987).

ORGANIZATION   Recall from Chapter 6 that our nervous system organizes the world. It selects only the meaningful elements from all the stimuli that reach us. Our mind organizes them into the most likely occurrence and remembers only a small sample of what has occurred. At each step the world becomes more organized and more simplified in our mind. A network of schemata develops to represent the world. The external world, so chaotic and changing, becomes stable, simplified, and seemingly coherent in the mind. What we see may be thousands of reflecting bits of glass, gray stone, and scores of doors opening and closing. But we *perceive one building;* the parts fit together as a whole.

We need a sense of organization or of coherence. When this sense of coherence is disrupted, we are more likely to become ill (Antonovsky, 1987). If the world is disorganized, it is not clear what appropriate action to take in any situation.

FIGURE 13-9
Curious Monkeys

Experiments have shown that monkeys and other animals are motivated by curiosity and prefer stimulating, complex environments.

CURIOSITY AND EXPLORATION   The other side of our voracious organizational ability is that we become restless when things get too organized. We get bored, we need to change, we need to create something new. We explore our environment as much to find what it is like as to find something in particular. Other organisms are also curious. Monkeys will work for the reward of the sight of another monkey or a stimulating toy (Figure 13-9). Indeed, even rats are motivated by curiosity: they will choose a more complex environment over a less complex one (Dember, Earl, & Paradise, 1957).

Curiosity increases mental activity by conveying more stimulation from the outside environment (Berlyne, 1960). If you had to eat your favorite meal every day, you would soon wince at the sight of it. A confirmed chocoholic was thrilled about getting a job in a candy store selling chocolates. She could eat all the chocolate she wanted, and for the first few days she was in paradise. After two weeks, however, she never wanted to see chocolate again! We are restless, stimulus-hungry creatures, even at the most basic physiological level of our nervous system.

BOREDOM   In today's world, the number of repetitions of work, travel, and daily life are such that boredom is becoming a great problem; some people become workaholics because they are afraid of becoming bored. Boredom is most prevalent in cultures where achievement, accumulated wealth, and status are highly prized (Rediger, 1986).

Boredom is often described as a hunger for human experience. At first, the longer the hunger is not satisfied, the more it grows. But when all hope of satisfying it falls away, the hunger turns to apathy and the person wastes away. For secondary needs—that is, those not strictly necessary for maintaining life—this indifference (boredom) represents adjustment to the deprivation and a figurative wasting away.

As people grow older they become more selective about what kind of stimulation they need. When patterns of satisfaction (habits) develop, boredom can follow if the patterns aren't periodically changed. Stimulation pushed to unlimited satiation (overeating, playing too many video games, having too many religious "highs") creates boredom by overwhelming the human system.

The brain appears to have another set point, like the one that determines body weight. This one is for the amount of information, stimulation, and change that is optimal for the organism. What is stressful noise to one person may be another's Beethoven; what is delightful peace and quiet to one may drive another up the wall.

We are motivated to regulate the amount of information we receive within our own set range just as we regulate temperature and weight. The brain apparently has a need for a certain amount of stimulation and information to maintain its organization. When there is either too much or too little stimulation, instability results and illness may follow.

As the brain evolved, its ability to handle the world became comprehensive. It developed increasingly sophisticated cortical and subcortical systems for receiving, decoding, analyzing, and reducing the varied and complicated flow of information. And the individual brain follows a similar pattern of development throughout the life span.

Remember at age 5 or so what a delight it was to discover what a letter meant, then to discover that these letters go together to make whole words, and later that words go together to make sentences, that sentences go together to make paragraphs, and that paragraphs go together to make stories? But now that you are older, you can sit reading the newspaper for half an hour and when you are asked "What's in the paper today?" you answer "Nothing, really." The world becomes organized, automatized, and familiar.

The paradox is that, as the human brain matures and develops, it both enormously increases its ability to find out new things and, at the same time, develops an enormous capacity for getting bored. It is easy for us to adapt, to

learn, and to develop, and so we are in the crux of a two-horned dilemma—too much too soon, and too little too late, both at the same time.

We must deal, on the one hand, with the destabilizing challenges of life changes (see Chapter 20) and, on the other, with the destabilization that can result when the brain is understimulated: stop lights all the same, repetitive conversations, stereotyped relationships, and a world that can become too familiar, too routine. Out of this need to stimulate themselves people have produced great works of art, while other attempts such as thrill-seeking, fast cars, and drugs, can be maladaptive. Car-

AVOIDING BOREDOM

toonist Sol Steinberg, discussing his art, said, "Avoiding boredom is one of our most important purposes."

Compared to a less experienced or less developed brain, our more experienced brain does receive less sensory information because we have learned to extract just those bits of information that we need. We need only to catch a glimpse of a spouse's expression to know whether he or she is angry or not. We need only to hear the beginning of someone's tone of voice to know whether we are welcome or not.

At each step we need less and less and we need to attempt less and less. As we age we need stronger and stronger stimuli. Young children are prone to be frightened by unfamiliar stimulation, and any parent of young chil-

dren knows that they seem to enjoy repetition of the familiar more than older children or adults (Ornstein & Sobel, 1987).

The maturing brain develops the capacity to organize the world better, reducing unnecessary information so that critical threats and instabilities can be recognized and responded to. This process of brain organization begins at the earliest moments of life. Even in the first days of life the stabilizing tendencies of motivation—to seek stimulation and to reduce complexity—are apparent.

People try to keep a stable level of stimulation in consciousness. Different people like different levels of stimulation, just as different people prefer their music at different loudness or different amounts of spice in their food. Much research has been done on changing levels of sensory stimulation since, as you might expect, this would change consciousness. Remember from Chapter 7 that when a person is put into a sensory deprivation chamber, he will immediately try to seek stimulation by moving about, brushing his hand against his leg, or making noises. It seems that consciousness, accustomed to a supply of "news," also needs its fix to keep going.

What happens when people are prevented from stimulating themselves? They rapidly become disorganized and they lose their intellectual ability, concentration, and coordination.

People constantly need stimulation to develop, grow, and maintain an organization of the world, and they need to not get bored with it. There is even some speculation among psychologists that lack of proper information flow can result in disease such as cancer (de la Peña, 1984).

We're motivated to look out over the world even when we don't have to, so motivated that it affects health. When given a choice between viewing a natural scene rich in foliage or an urban landscape devoid of vegetation or water, human beings favor the nature scene. This may come as no surprise, but there is now mounting evidence that such choices may be more than simple aesthetic preferences. Flooding our brains with rich natural visual stimulation helps us recover from surgery, tolerate pain, and manage stress, and it bolsters well-being.

Most of us are aware that extreme environmental conditions like heat and cold as well as noise and air pollution can be stressful. But can minor changes in our visual world nurture our response to and recovery from stress?

Look out your window. What do you see? A world of buildings and cement or a scene of natural beauty? When people view photographs of natural scenes, they report much higher levels of positive feelings, such as friendliness and elation, and reduced feelings of sadness and fear than those looking at man-made, urban scenes. Pictures of ponds, streams, trees, and other vegetation produce lower levels of arousal and higher alpha brain waves, a brain state associated with wakeful relaxation, than pictures of treeless urban streets.

What we see also affects our recovery when we are stressed. After watching a 10-minute film on the blood and gore of disabling work accidents, people responded with increased anxiety, muscle tension, blood pressure, and skin conductance—measures of a stress reaction. However, if the stress-provoking film was followed by a 10-minute film of scenes of trees and water, the recovery from stress on all physiological measures was faster than if they watched a film of an urban scene (Ornstein & Sobel, 1989).

A ROOM WITH A VIEW Imagine Sarah and Sally, identical twins, age 45. They both have gallstones and their doctor recommends surgical removal of their gallbladders. They check into the same hospital together. Sarah is escorted to her room. It is a typical aesthetically sterile room. She looks out the window and contemplates the view of a brown brick wall of another wing of the hospital. She thinks, "Oh, that's too bad, but I'll only be here a few days." Meanwhile her sister Sally checks into her typical hospital room but can look out her window onto a park with a small stand of trees. She thinks, "Oh, that's nice."

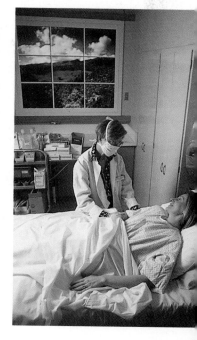

The next day they both have uneventful operations and are returned to their rooms. They receive identical treatment. However, Sally, in her room with a view, *recovers faster, requires less pain medication, is noted to be in better spirits, and is sent home from the hospital one day sooner than her sister in the room with a wall view.*

Could curiosity, looking out at the world, really influence recovery from surgery? Ulrich (1984) reviewed the hospital charts of 46 patients who had undergone gallbladder surgery. Half the patients had hospital rooms with a window looking out onto a small stand of trees, while the others viewed a brown brick wall. The patients with a view of the trees spent less time in the hospital after surgery (by nearly one day), were less upset, and took fewer doses of moderate and strong pain medications. They also had slightly fewer postoperative complications such as persistent headache and nausea. Whether similar salutary effects could be achieved by pictures or murals depicting outdoor scenes is not known but is worth considering.

Human beings seem designed to explore natural scenes, and this is reflected in our moods and physical well-being. We prefer certain types of landscapes, perhaps as a result of a deep-rooted evolutionary experience. People, regardless of cultural background, tend to favor parklike scenes with smooth ground cover, scattered trees, lakes, and a degree of openness and depth. It is a scene not too different from the savannahs of central Africa where our ancestors first stepped down from the trees onto the plains.

Evolution may have given us a deep need to look at life. So, try to include some elements from the natural environment in your home and work environment. Plants, pets, windows with views of natural scenes, paintings or photographs of nature, or even an aquarium can transform a lifeless manmade environment and reconnect you with nature. We're motivated to look out at the world we evolved to see. If we cannot see nature, our nervous system seems to signal to us that we are lacking something.

OPTIMAL LEVEL OF AROUSAL Curiosity keeps us stimulated, but when the arousal level is too low, just before sleep or in a boring situation, the level of performance suffers. Likewise, overarousal—being highly excited at bedtime or restless when we are trying to study—hurts performance. Each of us has an **optimum level of arousal.** Many psychologists (see Hebb, 1972) use an *n*-shaped curve (sometimes called an *inverted-U*) to describe this (Figure 13-10). The optimum level is in the middle of an organism's response range. Here pleasure is greatest, reinforcement is most efficient, and the processing of information is most efficient.

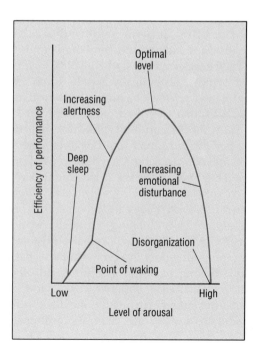

**FIGURE 13-10
Arousal and Performance**

As this *n*-shaped curve shows, arousal helps performance but overarousal can lower efficiency of performance.
(Hebb, 1972)

CHAPTER 13 / NEEDS AND GOALS

Sensation seeking is a common human activity.

Many of our behaviors are motivated by the need to achieve our optimum level. Some people cannot study without loud music on; they need to increase their activation level. Others cannot be in a room with any distractions; they need to decrease their activation level. It is probable that individual differences in optimum level of arousal are relatively stable characteristics in individuals. Many actions during the day—working hard, exercising, resting, having a cup of coffee, playing music—change arousal level. The maintenance of the optimum level is another feedback process in human motivation. It is more complex but similar to the homeostatic mechanisms in the body.

But many people also seek to upset homeostasis and try to move their arousal level up, even if it is unpleasant. They do this presumably for the pleasure that occurs when that stimulation is reduced. People *sensation-seek* by riding roller coasters, driving quickly, eating spicy food, jumping out of airplanes, going to horror movies, and watching erotic films (Zuckerman, 1984).

BEYOND KNOWLEDGE

Human beings do not live for bread alone, or for safety or love or their work. Abraham Maslow (1970) felt that there is a goal to develop oneself, called *self-actualization,* and a goal to go beyond the normal range of knowledge, that is, to *transcendence.*

SELF-ACTUALIZATION

Maslow was concerned that psychologists restrict their study to problems and breakdowns because these issues are more easily studied. It is easier and more

FIGURE 13-11
Self-Actualizers

Eleanor Roosevelt (left), Martin Luther King, Jr. (center), and Mother Teresa (right) are among the rare individuals whom Maslow calls *self-actualizers*, people who have reached the pinnacle of human motivation.

fun to study mistakes in thinking than errorless thinking. It is easier to study a need such as hunger than a goal that makes people strive for years to achieve excellence.

Maslow used the term **self-actualization** to refer to the growth motivation of the healthy individual. He believed this motive to be natural, that every person, unless obstructed, tends toward growth and health. He thought that once the lower motives are fulfilled, people begin to feel the need to expand their inner lives. He studied such great people as Eleanor Roosevelt, Albert Einstein, and Ghandi, to isolate those common characteristics that might be the defining characteristics of the self-actualized individual (Figure 13-11). Maslow identified the following as the distinguishing features of self-actualized individuals:

1. Creativity and inventiveness
2. Problem centering rather than ego centering; capacity for concern about larger problems of society and humankind
3. Strong purpose to life
4. Objectivity and detachment; acceptance of self and others
5. High tolerance of the unknown and of ambiguity
6. Mystical or peak experiences of a special quality that serve to organize and give direction to one's life
7. Freedom from prejudice and cultural conventions; an unconventional morality about what is right and what is wrong (Frager & Fadiman, 1987)

TRANSCENDENCE

We seek meaning, from the meaning of sensory stimulation to the remembrance of actions that mean the most to us. At the highest level, the search for meaning involves the search for the order of the world and the meaning of life. This is generally termed the *spiritual* aspect of life, and it is embodied in organized religions such as Christianity, Judaism, and Islam, and by spiritual groupings such as Sufism (Shah, 1982).

Transcendence, then, means to go beyond the ordinary understanding of life. Some of the questions that lead to this search are "What is the meaning of life?" or "What is God?" There has been little attention given to transcendence in psychology since William James's *The Varieties of Religious Experience* appeared in 1900, but transcendence nevertheless is a major organizing principle in the lives of many throughout the world. More than 2.5 billion people belong to the major religious groups of the world. Religions guide motivation; they determine morality, what one eats, whom one can marry, and many of the "lower" motives we have considered.

Thoreau's inspired experiment at Walden pond, as described in his poetically philosophical book *Walden*, sought to merge the self with nature. Experiencing life in its most essential terms, away from the establishment and artifice, was to experience it most vividly, truthfully, and fully. He wished, he wrote "to live deliberately, to front only the essential facts of life, and see if I could not learn what it had to teach, and not, when I came to die, discover that I had not lived."

Many aspects of religions serve social functions. However, the foremost purpose of religious activity is to attain a direct knowledge of how the world is organized and the purpose of human life. This knowledge may take the form of a born-again experience in contemporary Christianity; a mystical experience, either deliberately stimulated or accidental; or a continuously deepening understanding of the nature of human life. In any case, it is a powerful motivator. For millennia, people have fasted, prayed, meditated, given up their possessions, and even gone to war in the service of religious knowledge.

THE MOTIVES COMBINED

At any moment we are doing many things. Our brain monitors body temperature and food and fluid intake on the most basic level. At the same time, we may be trying to join a club or struggling to understand a new concept. Sometimes we fulfill more than one need in a single action: we may combine the need for food with that of learning and become a chef. Or we may combine achievement with understanding and become a rich inventor.

Some people *may* move up the hierarchy of motives during their lives in the idealized way Maslow describes. They first satisfy basic physiological and safety needs, belonging, and gaining esteem. They then develop competence and understanding and, finally, become self-actualized. However, few people follow this strict sequence. The art collector Hirschorn described his motive for collecting: "After the first million, money doesn't make much difference. I tried eating four meals a day and I got sick. I can't change my suits more than three times a day. So I collect art." Sometimes an individual may become dominated by one particular motive. This occurs, for example, when the lower needs are not satisfied. All thoughts turn to food or drink or to the maintenance of other body processes.

However, some may skip stages on the way up; some may stay at one level. Some people may operate in a way contrary to Maslow's scheme. A person may

The optimistic beliefs and confidence we have are sometimes more important than the reality of our situation. For example, we seem to have a deep-rooted need to feel in control. If we are in a stressful situation and have the illusion that we can control it, *even if we can't,* our stress reaction will be less. Researchers asked people to perform difficult math problems while distracting them with random bursts of loud, nerve-jangling noise. Half the people were told that they could stop the noise by pressing a button (the button actually had no effect on the noise). The other subjects were given no such illusion of control. *Even though no one pressed the button, the people who thought they could control the stressor experienced fewer symptoms of stress and anxiety:* sweaty hands, racing hearts, ringing ears, and headaches.

The sense of control even affects immune function. Some laboratory rats learned to shut off a mild electric shock by turning a wheel in their cages. Other rats got shocked every time the first group did, but nothing they could do could control the shocks. The immune function dropped in the helpless rats, but not in the rats who could end the shocks (Ader, 1981). Uncontrollable stress also appears to promote the growth of cancer in experimental animals (de la Peña, 1984).

Confidence, too, is critical to health. Consider a series of experiments conducted at the Stanford Arthritis Center. The project began innocently enough. An arthritis self-management course was designed to help patients cope better with the pain, disability, fear and depression often associated with arthritis. The program consisted of six weekly two-hour sessions attended by patients and their families and led by instructors, many of whom had arthritis themselves. They learned a lot of detailed basic information about the physiology and treatment of arthritis, strengthening and endurance exercises, relaxation techniques, joint protection, nutrition, and the interrelationship of stress, pain, and depression. Impressively, participants began to demonstrate significantly greater self-management behavior and less pain. But why?

BUILDING CONFIDENCE

The people who improved were not those who knew more about arthritis or who had the therapeutic exercise. Those who improved had a *positive outlook on and felt a sense of control over* their arthritis. Those who failed to improve, even if they exercised, felt that there was nothing they could do about the disease.

The key difference appeared to be the patients' perception of their own capability to control or change their arthritis symptoms. Notice that the critical feature here is the persons' *belief* in their capacity, not what skills or capacities they actually have.

There is a biology of self-confidence. Think about all of your good intentions—the plans for new diets, exercise regimens, stress reduction techniques. If asked, most people can recount a litany of failures. What are the consequences of failing at a health behavior change? So much emphasis has been placed on changing lifestyles, adopting the good life, that what is often missed is that the *feelings of success or failure* may be more important to health than the actual behaviors. Success, even in small things, supports a feeling of self-confidence and competence.

One mistake people make is trying to change everything at once. Part of the problem is most of us can't attain our ultimate, often unrealistic, goal immediately and then don't take the small steps that could move us forward. Recall a previous experience in which you successfully changed. Why did you change? What were the keys to your success?

If feeling confident and successful is perhaps more important than the specific behavior changed, then the focus should be on developing a series of successful experiences in changing something, no matter how small. Set yourself up for success. Choose something that *you* want to change and select a small step that you are confident you can achieve. Make sure that at regular intervals in your life you take up something new—maybe playing a musical instrument, learning to cook a new dish, studying a new language—something you can learn, something that makes you grow, something you

ignore needs such as esteem and belonging in the search for achievement or for transcendence.

FUNCTIONAL AUTONOMY

Some motives seem to persist even after they are satisfied. Students may work hard to obtain the esteem of their peers and may find it so rewarding that they continue to seek esteem for the rest of their lives. In doing so, they may neglect

like and is yours. It may be exercising, losing weight, managing stress more effectively, developing a new hobby—anything you really want to do. It all bolsters hope and optimism.

That sense of confidence may not only make it more likely you will succeed in changing a behavior, from pain control to smoking, but itself fosters health. Successful change in any part of your life, in hobbies or work, can reinforce this vital sense of confidence.

Even the health consequences associated with confidence are striking. For example, a person's confidence in his or her own health turns out to be one of the best predictors of future health—even better than the results of extensive laboratory testing or a physician's examination. People who rate their health as poorly die earlier and have more disease than their counterparts who view themselves as healthy. Even people with objective diseases seem to do better when they believe themselves to be healthy than when they believe themselves to be weak.

LEARNING TO INCREASE MOTIVATION BY BEING OPTIMISTIC

What you expect is what you get. Or so it seems. Try this: write down as many of the wonderful experiences you look forward to in the future as you can think of. Then describe all the difficult and trying things you expect to happen. How many positive experiences did you write down? How many negative?

The way a person responds to this surprisingly simple test seems to predict future health and well-being. In one study (Carver & Scheier, 1987), a group of elderly considered their future just as you have. They listed all the positive things they had to look forward to during the immediate future. Two years later the optimists reported fewer physical symptoms of ill-health and more positive physical and psychological well-being than the pessimists. They felt less tension, and reported fewer colds and days off from work, and had more energy.

Another way to assess motivational optimism is by taking the Life Orientation Test (LOT) developed by psychologists Charles Carver and Michael Scheier (1987). You might want to try filling it out yourself. Mark how much you agree with each of the items, using the following scale: 4, strongly agree; 3, agree; 2, neutral; 1, disagree; and 0, strongly disagree.

1. In uncertain times, I usually expect the best.

2. If something can go wrong for me, it will.*

3. I always look on the bright side of things.

4. I'm always optimistic about my future.

5. I hardly ever expect things to go my way.*

6. Things never work out the way I want them to.*

7. I'm a believer in the idea that every cloud has a silver lining.

8. I rarely count on good things happening to me.*

In scoring the test you'll need to reverse the numbers for the items marked with an asterisk (*). That is, if you strongly agree with the statement "If something can go wrong for me, it will," then give yourself a score of 1 instead of 4. Do this for items 2, 5, 6, and 8. Then total your score.

When college students completed this test four weeks before final exams, the higher-scoring optimists (20 and over) reported many fewer health symptoms. The pessimists complained of more dizziness, fatigue, sore muscles, coughs, and the like in the weeks leading up to exam time.

The effects of a bright outlook on the future are perhaps even more striking for people facing major trauma, like open-heart surgery. The attitudes of patients about to undergo coronary by-pass surgery were assessed just before the operation. Those with a more hopeful, positive outlook showed fewer complications during surgery: their electrocardiograms and blood tests reveal less evidence of heart muscle damage. Those with a sunny disposition also recovered quicker: their lung function returned speedily, they sat up in bed sooner, and they were able to walk around the room earlier than their gloomier counterparts. Six months later, those who expected an improved quality of life, that they would return to work quickly and be active with hobbies and exercise, tended to get just what they expected (Carver & Scheier, 1987).

Pollyanna may have been onto something.

achievement and understanding. Politicians may find that they love to run for office and win, but they give little attention to the process of governing later on, as they continually run for office.

An important determinant of the motives an individual expresses is **functional autonomy,** which is the tendency for any action repeated often enough to become a motive in its own right (Allport, 1961). Functional autonomy may cause an individual to stay at one level of motivation or may lead him or her upward in the hierarchy. The motive to earn money may be prepotent when one is poor. Nevertheless, it may continue for life, even when the person has enough money or is very rich. Habits persist. A child may learn to play a musical instrument simply to gain approval but might later develop a true love for music.

It is in the particular motives that a person expresses that we find the roots of individual personality.

SUMMARY

1. *Motives* can determine the course of your life. They range from basic and universal to ethereal. The two groups of motives are needs and goals. *Needs* are specific deficits that all animals must satisfy. They give rise to *drives,* which move us to act to satisfy needs. *Instincts* are behaviors typical to all members of a species that are exhibited without learning in the first appropriate situation encountered by an organism. Psychologists no longer believe that all behavior can be explained in terms of instincts. *Goals* are desired outcomes that have not yet occurred. The satisfaction of goals can be called "creative adaptation." In satisfying goals, humans adapt the environment to suit themselves.

2. *Maslow* conceived of a *hierarchy of human motivations* in the form of a pyramid. The most basic needs are at the bottom of the pyramid. At each higher level, the needs and goals become progressively more complex. The levels are distinguished by the relative strength of different needs, called *prepotence.* Lower needs preempt higher ones. Maslow's pyramid is useful, but not entirely accurate. Prepotence varies with the individual, and the hierarchy tends to break down at the higher levels.

3. The primary motivation of all organisms is *survival.* Needs related to survival operate via *homeostasis,* the tendency to keep the organism in a constant state. The regulatory systems of the body use *feedback* to maintain constant levels in internal processes, such as temperature, water content, and food. Human body *temperature* is normally maintained around a *set point* of 98.6° F (37° C). Discrepancies of more than 1° are corrected by mechanisms like shivering and sweating. Fever occurs when the hypothalamic set point for temperature is raised.

4. *Fluid regulation* is important because small changes in the fluid content of the body can be fatal. Body fluids are regulated by a complicated brain-directed system. *Thirst* can be quenched by wetting the salivary glands or by putting water directly into the stomach. Pressure receptors in blood vessels detect small changes in the water content of blood and trigger the release of renin which activates brain centers that produce the sensation of thirst. A hormonal feedback system maintains fluid levels by reclaiming water from urine.

5. *Hunger* is more complex than temperature or thirst. As a result, disorders of hunger are common. Feelings of hunger come from gastric and metabolic factors. Stomach contractions are a primary signal of hunger. Hunger is related to the maintenance of energy and body weight, registered in the brain in terms of levels of blood sugar and the amount of fat deposited in the body. The hypothalamus is important in the control of eating.

6. *Metabolism* is the process by which food is burned to make heat to keep the body warm and provide energy. When more food is consumed than is metabolized, the excess is stored as fat to be used when needed. The *set point* is the body weight around which the brain attempts to maintain homeostasis. The set point keeps our

weight around a predetermined level, independent of our conscious decisions to alter it. Obese people often have higher body weight set points than the norm. Their set points are the result of having more *adipocytes* (fat cells) than the average person.

7. The brain and body have complex systems for handling incoming food. Fat from food deposits directly into the tissue, and carbohydrates are metabolized first. Brown adipocyte cells burn off excess calories. The stabilizing mechanisms of the body discourage weight loss. When the food supply is low, the set point can be lowered drastically, making weight loss extremely difficult. *Exercise* helps weight loss by increasing caloric consumption by the body both during and following the activity. The average person gains a little less than one pound a year. The healthiest people are either of average weight for their age or slightly overweight.

8. When basic physiological needs are met, others become important. Most animals act to *avoid pain* and *seek pleasure*. Pain and pleasure centers in the nervous system provide feedback about actions that may be injurious or helpful to survival and reproduction. Human beings are social animals. When they are deprived of *belonging* to a group, they may suffer detriments to health and intelligence. Feelings of belonging can improve health. Maternal care is a drive that is partly controlled by hormones.

9. *Goals* are more mental than biological, and they are highly individual. *Competence* earns us esteem and self-respect. It leads to the sense of achievement, which is in itself a motivating force. Achievements often require long-term goals. The need for *achievement* is a characteristic component of personality. High achievers pursue success, take risks, and are internally motivated and independent. Parental training and expectations are the most important contributing factors to the need for achievement. The role of *necessity* in achievement motivation was demonstrated by the behavior of English people during World War II.

10. The human motivation to search for knowledge and understand the world derives from our need to organize and explore our environments. Disruption of a person's sense of *coherence of the world* can lead to an increased chance of illness. *Curiosity* drives us to explore the environment. It increases mental activity by taking stimulation from the outside world. *Boredom* results from lack of change in stimulation. Humans seem designed to explore natural scenes, and this is reflected in our moods and physical well-being. Surgical patients with views of nature scenes recover faster than those who don't.

11. When arousal levels are too low or too high, levels of performance suffer. The *optimal level of arousal* for an organism lies in the middle of its response range. Many behaviors are motivated by the need to achieve an optimal level of activation. This level varies with the individual and is maintained by a feedback process.

12. Maslow felt that humans are motivated to develop themselves (*self-actualization*) and to go beyond the normal range of knowledge (*transcendence*). He believed that once lower motives are fulfilled, people begin to feel the need to expand their inner lives. The distinguishing features of *self-actualized individuals* are creativity and inventiveness, problem centering rather than ego centering, strong purpose to life, objectivity, detachment, acceptance of self and others, high tolerance of the unknown, mystical or peak experiences, and freedom from prejudice and cultural conventions.

13. At the highest level, the search for meaning involves the search for the meaning of life. This is generally called *spirituality* and is embodied in organized religion and spiritual groupings. *Transcendence* means to go beyond the ordinary understanding of life. The foremost purpose of religious activity is to attain a direct knowledge of how the world is organized and the purpose of human life. The pursuit of religious knowledge is a powerful motivator.

14. Few people strictly follow Maslow's hierarchy. Another important determinant of motivation is *functional autonomy*, the tendency for an action to be repeated often enough that it becomes a motive in its own right. Some people may stay at one level of the hierarchy, while others may skip stages on the way up.

TERMS AND
CONCEPTS

achievement
achievement motivation
adipocytes
boredom
competence
curiosity
drives
functional autonomy
goals
homeostasis
hunger
hyperphagia
instincts

knowledge
metabolism
motives
natural immunity
needs
optimum level of arousal
prepotence
self-actualization
set point
thermometer neurons
thirst
transcendence

SUGGESTIONS
FOR FURTHER
READING

Antonovsky, A. (1987). *Unraveling the mystery of health.* San Francisco: Jossey-Bass.

The most recent discussion of how coherence affects health, and how psychological factors pertain.

Bennett, W. S., & Gurin, J. (1982). *The dieter's dilemma.* New York: Basic Books.

A good read and synopsis of the "set point" approach to weight regulation.

Frager, R., & Fadiman, J. (1987). *Maslow's motivation and personality.* New York: Harper & Row.

One of the few texts which gives a version of Maslow's approach to psychology.

McClelland, D. (1985a). How motives, skills, and values determine what people do. *American Psychologist, 40,* 812–825.

A leading theorist of motivation tries to explain how it operates in the person.

McClelland, D. (1985b). *Human motivation.* Chicago: Scott, Foresman.

Perhaps the best statement of, as McClelland told me, "All I know about motivation."

Mook, D. E. (1986). *Motivation, the organization of action.* New York: Norton.

An important text which helps outline the different components of motivation.

Zuckerman, M. (1984). Sensation-seeking: A comparative approach to a human trait. *Behavioral and Brain Sciences. 73,* 413–433.

An account of the sensation-seeking theory, with responses from other professionals.

14
PERSONALITY

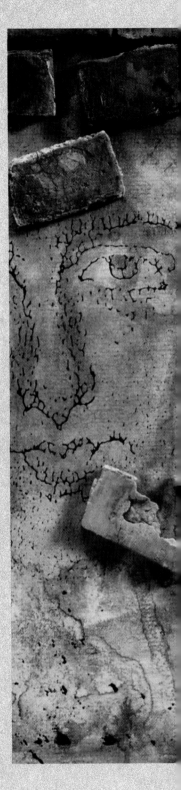

W ho are you? How do you know? Are you sure? How would you find out? To the government you are a social security number. To your mother you are a child, no matter what your age. To your friends you are a source of pleasure. Each of us plays many roles in our lives. In fact, *personality* comes from the Latin *persona*, for actors wearing masks in a play. But even with this array of roles we somehow retain a sense of continuity over our lives. As much as we may change over time and alter our behavior in different situations, we still feel a connection with who we are when we are 5, or 15, or 50. We know that we are somehow still the same person, only different. This illustrates one of the problems that the study of personality poses for psychologists: How do you take a frame from a movie and make sense of it?

What is **personality?** A formal definition might be that it consists of the unique and stable qualities, including thoughts, feelings, and actions, that characterize an individual over time and across situations. But, does it exist? In your head? In your heart? In your actions? In your closet?

Before we can answer those questions, we must first ask some others. For example, what is the nature of human nature? Are humans basically animals that must be controlled by society? Or are they fundamentally good and would behave in a way that creates society? Followers of Sigmund Freud and Carl Rogers would argue over the answer to this question. Freud saw humans as having an animal element that must be controlled by society. Rogers believed that, if left alone in the right environment, humans naturally grow to be warm, caring, and good. These ideas influenced the way these theorists thought about personality. You probably have your own idea about which of these you think is right.

Another question is, Which accounts most for your behavior, the situation you are in or some quality in you? In this argument, followers of Freud and Rogers would be together on the side of inner qualities determining behavior. They would be arguing with B. F. Skinner and Albert Bandura who believe that behavior is determined by the situation. What do you think?

Why do we want to know? Part of it is curiosity about ourselves and about other people. Maybe you have wondered about yourself, who you are, how you got this way. Or, you might have wondered about those things and worried that you might never change. This is the second reason to study personality. You can't change something unless you know what it is made of, how it is put together, and what makes it go. Many of the ideas about personality have come from psychologists and counselors working to understand the people they help. These ideas come out of the clinic and are based on troubled people. Other ideas have come from research settings as a result of psychologists struggling to understand normal personality. All of these ideas have been used to help people understand themselves and each other.

So far we have lined up the elements needed to understand personality: perceiving, thinking, feeling, remembering, learning, needing. Now we must weave them to try to answer some of these questions.

SIGMUND FREUD

Sigmund Freud (1856–1939) is one of the most influential figures in modern psychology, and many consider him to be the most influential in twentieth-century thought. His theory of personality is the most complete and detailed theory in psychology. It is a grand theory of another era, a time when it seemed possible to combine evolutionary, developmental, and social components of human nature. It incorporates what motivates people and the development and structure of personality. The appeal of Freud is his breathtaking ambition and his startling insights. His thinking combined Victorian ideas about science, reason, and morality with residue from the Romantic era. These romantic ideas include an emphasis on the emotional and irrational aspects of the personality, the development of a unique inner self, and conflict between the individual and society (McAdams, 1990). Freud took science into the realm of poets.

Freud studied medicine in nineteenth-century Vienna and began a research career in neurology. In 1885 he traveled to Paris to study with the charismatic neurologist Jean Martin Charcot who influenced him in the direction of psychology (Brenner, 1974). When Freud returned to Vienna he began a practice treating patients with nervous disorders. Common among these disorders was *hysteria*, a disorder in which a physical symptom such as blindness, numbness, or paralysis has no basis in physiology. While in Paris, Freud had observed Charcot take seriously the symptoms of hysteria rather than dismiss them as malingering. He had watched as Charcot used hypnotic suggestion to remove his patients' symptoms (Gay, 1988).

Freud tried Charcot's method with mixed success. He then remembered that his friend Josef Breuer had once told him of a patient he had treated successfully with hypnosis. Freud recalled that Breuer found that symptoms disappeared when the hypnotized patient remembered the emotions and events that had occurred when the symptoms began. This release of emotion is called **catharsis.** Freud tried this method with some success, but he discovered that

SIGMUND FREUD
(1856–1939)

Charcot made hypnosis respectable as a topic for scientific investigation. Here he demonstrates his methods before his colleagues at the Salpêtrière in Paris.

often the symptoms would return. What was needed was not simply catharsis but *insight*. The patient needed to understand the early events, not simply recall them. To do this, Freud abandoned hypnosis and devised other ways to gain access to the buried memories—namely, free association, dreams, and analysis of faulty actions (called *parapraxes*) such as forgetting names, misremembering facts, or breaking objects. Thus, psychoanalysis was born, and Freud sometimes acknowledged Breuer as its father (Freud, 1937).

FUNDAMENTAL IDEAS

Psychoanalysis is based on two fundamental hypotheses (Brenner, 1974). If you have ever forgotten a name or lost the pen your father gave you and then asked yourself, "I wonder why I did that," you are linking these two hypotheses. The first is the principle of **psychic determinism,** which is the idea that no behavior happens by chance. Freud believed that all present thoughts, behavior, and symptoms have meaning and are determined by events in the past, particularly in childhood. The second fundamental hypothesis is the notion that **consciousness** is the exception rather than the rule. That is, we are unaware of most of what determines our behavior. He likened consciousness to an iceberg with only a small part observable and accessible. Not only is a thought or an action meaningful, but the reason for it is to be found in the past which we have, meaningfully, forgotten.

DYNAMICS OF PERSONALITY: THE DRIVES

With the advent of Darwin's theory of evolution, scientists began to assume that animals are dominated by inherited instincts that improve reproduction. Freud believed that a *drive* produces *psychological tension,* which motivates a person to act to reduce that tension. This action is mediated by thought and influenced by the environment. This is what distinguishes it from an instinct. Animals react, people decide. He believed that all human behavior is motivated by the desire to increase pleasure and avoid pain. In the final version of his theory, which he termed the **pleasure principle,** Freud suggested that there are two major drives, sex and aggression.

Freud sometimes referred to the sexual drive as **Eros.** By this he meant not just a drive for sex but for all pleasurable experience. Later in his career, after living through the First World War with its unprecedented carnage, Freud pessimistically balanced the sexual drive with a drive for aggression, sometimes called **Thanatos.** As with sex, aggression is broadly conceived as a drive for destruction. In his book *Beyond the Pleasure Principle* (1920), Freud suggested the highly controversial idea that organisms seek a quiescent state, such as death, a state of greatly reduced tension! "The aim of life," Freud wrote, "is death."

These two drives, Eros and Thanatos, are thought to operate together at all times. Sexual acts are always in some part aggressive, and aggressive acts are always partly sexual. We can both love and hate at the same time. So when Freud wrote of the sexual and aggressive drives, he was describing something much more complex than simply aggression and sex as we normally think of them. These drives are present at birth and guide our development through childhood.

Freud offered the term **libido** for the psychic energy associated with the sexual drive but suggested no corresponding term for the aggressive drive. But since these two drives are thought to operate together, the term *libido* has come to be used for psychic energy in general. Psychic energy becomes invested in the mental representations—that is, thoughts and fantasies—of a person or an object. This psychological investment is called **cathexis.** The more important and desired the object or person, the stronger the cathexis. How a personality develops is largely a matter of the distribution of the psychic energy, or changes in what is cathected.

HUMAN DEVELOPMENT

Human development, according to Freud, proceeds through a series of **psychosexual stages.** Each of the five stages is named for an erogenous zone, which is a part of the body that, when stimulated, produces pleasure. Freud theorized that unsuccessful resolution of major conflicts at a given stage would *fixate* an individual's personality at that stage. The person's libido would remain focused on the pleasures of that stage.

In the **oral stage,** which extends from birth to about 18 months, the infant's pleasure is derived from the mouth. The infant sucks, makes noises, and grimaces—that is, his or her needs and their satisfaction are centered around the tongue, lips, and mouth.

In the **anal stage,** for the next 18 months, pleasure comes from both the retention and expulsion of feces. The toddler attends to elimination and takes great interest and joy in it. With this ability, or lack of it, the child begins to develop control over his or her world.

At about age 3 the child enters the **phallic stage,** in which the genitals are the focus of pleasure. It is during this stage, which lasts until about the age of 6,

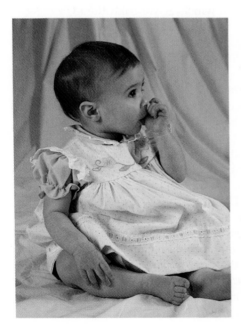

The oral stage (left) and the phallic stage (right) are two of the psychosexual stages a child must successfully pass through, according to Freud.

that the child must resolve the most crucial crisis he or she will ever face (Brenner, 1974). Freud believed that during this stage, as an outgrowth of newly found pleasure in the genitals, the child's love for the opposite-sex parent takes on a sexual element. In boys, this is called the **Oedipus complex,** after the legendary Greek character who unwittingly murdered his father and married his mother. Its counterpart in girls is sometimes known as the **Electra complex,** after the mythical Greek character who persuaded her brother to kill their mother. In each case, the child wants to become the only love object of the opposite-sex parent and eliminate any rivals. Gradually, however, the child comes to realize that these impulses are unacceptable. Repressing them, the child then turns to the same-sex parent as a model. It is through identification with the same-sex parent that the child incorporates the values and standards of society as filtered through the parent. The resolution of this conflict results in development of conscience.

With the struggles of the phallic phase behind, the child enters the **latency stage,** in which, as the name suggests, the child's sensual desires become dormant. This stage lasts from age 6 until puberty.

With the development of mature sexual interests, the **genital stage,** the time of adult sexuality, begins. According to Freud, the personality is fully formed by the end of the phallic stage—that is, by age 6. He had relatively little to say about the last two stages.

THE STRUCTURE OF PERSONALITY

Freud divided personality into the *id*, the *ego*, and the *superego*. The **id** is considered to be the psychic representative of the drives. The id is like a newborn. It wants what it wants and it wants it *now*. When a drive such as hunger creates tension, a newborn doesn't negotiate with the world, it cries. According to Freud, when we are born, we are all id. It is the "reservoir" of psychic energy for the ego and superego, which derive from the id.

The pleasure principle guides the id, but the id cannot act directly on the outside world to avoid pain and obtain pleasure. The id is not logical and doesn't make a distinction between reality and fantasy. It is governed by *primary process thought*, which is irrational. It is visual, metaphoric, and timeless. The id attempts to fulfill wishes, often by creating primary process images or hallucinations; dreams are the best example. Since the id is entirely in the unconscious, to fulfill its wishes it needs an intermediary through which to operate on the outside world.

The **ego** comes into existence to gratify the id's wishes. It does this through exploring the environment and differentiating between reality and images from the id. The ego begins to develop about age 6–8 months, as the baby is able to move around and manipulate objects. The ego is guided by the *reality principle,* which delays the "discharge of tension" or action until an appropriate object is found. The id says, "I want"; the ego responds, "okay, but wait a minute until I figure out how to get it." The ego is the only part of the personality that interacts with the world, and its job is to exploit the environment to gratify the wishes of the id. The ego is characterized by *secondary process thought*. This mode of thought is rational and is responsible for the ego's capacity to delay action until the proper time to satisfy the id's demands.

The **superego** is the last part of the personality to develop. It appears as a resolution of the struggles encountered in the phallic stage of development. It is the internal representation of society's values and morals, the sense of what is right and wrong; it is our conscience. While the ego goes about taking care of the id's demands, the superego sits in judgment of the ego's solutions. The main functions of the superego restrain the aggressive and sexual impulses of the id by pressuring the ego to substitute moralistic goals for realistic ones. It complicates the ego's task by placing conditions on how the ego can satisfy the wishes of the id. Like the id, the superego is unyielding, but its goal is moral perfection rather than pleasure.

CIVILIZATION AND NEUROSES

For Freud, a central problem in human life is the conflict between biological inheritance and the demands of society represented in the personality by the id and the superego. This analysis was much influenced by Darwin's ideas on evolution. Other animals express instincts for sex and aggression. However, for human beings to coexist in civilization, these instincts must be restrained. Personality develops for purposes of restraint: people cannot have sex with anyone at any time, nor can they kill their rivals.

Freud thought that almost all that is noble in our culture—religion, justice, family—exists primarily to control animal instincts. This conflict puts a tremendous strain on the individual, which may result in neuroses. **Neuroses** are unconscious conflicts between the desires of the id and the demands of the superego. They often occur as a result of traumatic experiences in early childhood. The primary symptom of a neurosis is **anxiety.**

The major problem for the ego is how to cope with anxiety, which signals danger for the personality. Freud identified three sources of anxiety, one each for the pressures on the ego: from the id comes **neurotic anxiety,** fears of yielding to passions of the id; from reality comes **realistic anxiety,** real dangers in the environment; and from the superego comes **moral anxiety,** fears of not living up to standards. With realistic anxiety there is the possibility of confronting the source directly or running away. But this solution is impossible when dealing with the superego or the id. With moral or neurotic anxiety, the ego must distort or deny the situation by using **defense mechanisms,** which ward off anxiety by either *separating* the source from consciousness or by *distorting* it.

There are many kinds of defense mechanisms, but they all begin with *repression*. Freud observed that his patients often were unable to recall hurtful childhood events. He hypothesized that the ego deliberately pushes the memory of the event into the unconscious. It is a kind of self-deception. Because the anxiety-producing stimulus is first repressed, the other defenses operate unconsciously. The ego has a number of methods to defend against anxiety, many of which were defined and elaborated on by Freud's daughter Anna (1936). Other defense mechanisms include *projection*, by which the person attributes his or her own undesirable thoughts and behaviors to another person; *reaction formation*, by which the person replaces one emotion or behavior with its opposite; *regression*, in which the person retreats to an earlier behavior that had been controllable or nonthreatening; and *sublimation*, by which the person converts the energy from basic impulses, such as sexual or aggressive energy, to behavior that is socially acceptable.

EVALUATION OF FREUD'S THEORY OF PERSONALITY

Freud was a genius. He brilliantly integrated many turn-of-the-century ideas from biology, medicine, philosophy, and psychology. Some of his radical ideas stemmed from the evolutionary idea of his time, that we share most of our characteristics with other animals. Other ideas were rooted in the Romantic notion of conflict between the individual and society represented within the person by the struggle between the id and the superego. It remains a brilliant synthesis.

Freud focused attention on many of the most fundamental questions about personality and human nature. How much of our personality is inherited and how much is determined by early childhood experiences? Do we know what motivates us? Why and how do personality and civilization develop? How much conscious control can a person have over life? However, Freud's specific concepts are difficult to test experimentally because many of the answers are to be found in the unconscious and must be made conscious in order to be studied. When psychologists have been able to raise a conflict to consciousness, his theories do not seem to hold up well.

There is little evidence that specific disorders, such as impotence, can be traced to difficulties in early childhood experience. Most importantly, it does not seem to be true that our psychological problems are so deeply rooted that removing one symptom (such as fear of snakes) may lead to "symptom substitution," as Freud postulated. If you remove a symptom, it does not always reappear in a new form (Mischel, 1986).

There has, however, been some confirmation of his theories. For example, researchers have found that subliminal suggestions do affect conscious process-es (Silverman, 1983). Some of Freud's ideas are being tested by those interested in the effects of schemata on the mind (Erdelyi, 1986). The conception of an unconscious defense system is generally thought to be a useful description of many mental processes. But, even after almost a century, the theory remains lacking in scientific proof. The ideas that schemata outside consciousness have great influence receives support from cognitive psychology. However, attempts to find genuine confirmation of Freud's theories in the modern analysis of the mind are exaggerated. There is little direct relationship between the two, although the same terms are used in both (Liebert & Spiegler, 1987; Mischel, 1986; however, see Erdelyi, 1986, for a different view). Research on the effectiveness of psychoanalysis as a therapy provides little evidence that the method is successful. But these findings are difficult to interpret because psychoanalysts define success as patient insight—that is, a clear understanding—whereas other therapists define success as relief from psychological distress (Carver & Scheier, 1988).

In some ways our situation is worse than Freud imagined, in some ways better. It is not only internal conflict that controls our lives but also many other forces beyond our control. The food we eat affects thought processes. The structure of our nervous system is a profound barrier to adaptive thought. Even the weather and electrical current in the air affect brain processes. From the

474

perspective of current scientific knowledge, however, it is most clear that Freud greatly underestimated the human ability to develop and change throughout life. Aggressive and sexual "instincts" can be modified more than Freud thought (Bandura, 1986).

However, Freud's work was an astonishing synthesis, and it has set the agenda for psychologists, especially those involved in psychotherapy and personality. Freud's place in Western thought was described by Janet Malcolm (1981):

> By 1909, Freud's unassuming quest for a cure for nervous disorders . . . had improbably flowered into the vast system of thought about human nature—psychoanalysis—which has detonated throughout the intellectual, social, artistic, and ordinary life of our century as no cultural force has (it may not be off the mark to say) since Christianity. (Freud himself preferred to align the psychoanalytic revolution with the revolution of Copernicus and then the revolution of Darwin, saying that the first showed that the earth was not the center of the universe, the second that man was not a unique creation, and the third that man was not even master of his own house.) It was as if a lonely terrorist working in his cellar on a modest explosive device to blow up the local brewery had unaccountably found his way to the hydrogen bomb and blown up half the world. The fallout from this bomb has yet to settle. It isn't even clear whether the original target—the neurotic patient—wasn't overshot; "proof" of the efficacy of psychoanalytic cure has yet to be established and no analyst claims it.

NEO-FREUDIANS

Much behavior does not seem to be linked to unconscious forces of sex and aggression nor to the id-superego conflicts. Infants playing with their hands seem to be motivated more by curiosity and new knowledge than by the release of "tension." Exploration does not serve tension reduction; rather, it serves higher mental needs, such as achievement. Furthermore, Freud neglected some major social influences on behavior. Later psychologists, called **neo-Freudians,** sought to modify Freud's theories about the important determinants of personality. They de-emphasized determinism, emphasized higher mental functions, and included social influence.

EGO PSYCHOLOGY

As Freud's ideas became known, a group of followers gathered. Some of these followers eventually disagreed with him on certain aspects of psychoanalytic theory and broke off on their own. One group of neo-Freudians was called **ego psychologists** because they expanded the role of the ego. In their view, rather than simply trying to keep the peace, the ego is responsible for such behaviors as exploration and mastery. They emphasized the ego's independence from the id and the importance of its role of interacting with the environment. Among this group was Freud's daughter, Anna.

Some neo-Freudians, such as Alfred Adler (1870–1937), Harry Stack Sullivan (1892–1949), Karen Horney (1885–1952), and Erich Fromm (1900–1979), minimized the importance of instincts in favor of social interactions and processes. Adler was an early follower of Freud. He was the first president of the Viennese Psychoanalytic Society and was the first of Freud's followers to break with him. He called his own theory *individual psychology* but emphasized that "the individual becomes an individual only within a social context" (Adler, 1929). Adler made no distinction between individual and social psychology. He believed that people are innately ready to relate to others and that social interest guides development. The outcome of successful development is a strong social feeling and a capacity for cooperation that can be used to solve the three great tasks of life: society, work, and love (Potkay & Allen, 1986).

Harry Stack Sullivan defined personality in terms of interpersonal interactions and also emphasized such social urges as participation and cooperation. He believed that our personality is defined by the way we perceive our selves and are perceived by others (Hall & Lindzey, 1978). Both Horney and Fromm stressed unconscious motives but elaborated in different ways on the importance of social interaction. Horney emphasized the role of anxiety and insecurity in the development of neurosis in childhood. Fromm emphasized the importance of cultural context in shaping personality. In contrast to Freud, these theorists viewed society as something to be embraced rather succumbed to.

ERIK ERIKSON

Erik Erikson (1902–   ) is a psychoanalyst who has considered the formative effect of social interaction on personality. His theory of psychosocial stages demonstrates the shift to ego processes and social influences in psychoanalytic thought. (See the discussion of Erikson's stages in Chapter 2, pages 65 and 66.) Erikson believes that the ego develops independently rather than derives from the id. In addition to defending the personality, the ego is responsible for maintaining a sense of identity. According to Erikson, in modern times identity confusion rather than sexuality is the core problem confronted in psychoanalysis (Erikson, 1968).

Erikson's theory differs from Freud's in two basic ways. First, Erikson suggests that the ultimate goal of people is not to reduce tension, but rather to become integrated human beings. Second, although early childhood experiences are important, Erikson (1986) emphasizes that development continues throughout the life span. Over the course of their lives, people encounter an ever-widening range of human relationships. Thus, Erikson described psycho*social* rather than psycho*sexual* stages. According to Erikson, personality develops through the resolution of the crises associated with each stage.

JUNG'S ANALYTICAL PSYCHOLOGY

While most of the neo-Freudians emphasized the role of the ego and expanded on the importance of the individual's outward interaction with society, one of his followers turned inward. Carl Jung was an early follower of Freud's who was also interested in the role that instincts and the transformation of energy play in the development of personality. However, Jung disagreed with Freud on a number of important points. First, Jung rejected Freud's strong emphasis on sexuality as a primary motivator. Second, Jung also rejected Freud's idea that all behavior is determined by unconscious forces from the past. He emphasized that humans also strive toward goals and are thus motivated by future events.

Jung formed his own school of thought, called **analytical psychology,** and developed a personality theory that is second only to Freud's in its reach and complexity. Analytical psychology is based on the principle of opposites. Jung believed that psychic energy is created by tension between opposites within the personality. These include such polarities as extraversion and introversion, thinking and feeling, and masculinity and femininity. If you meet someone whom you experience as cold and rejecting, Jung would suggest that the opposing warmth exists but is buried in that person's unconscious. According to Jung, unconscious contents can be positive as well as negative. Jung considered extreme one-sidedness to be a psychological symptom, so a developmental task for the personality is to integrate the two poles. Your cold acquaintance needs to get in touch with unconscious warmth. And you might need to acknowledge the dark side of your own sunny nature.

Jung called the process of development **individuation** and believed that it occurs throughout the life span. Recognizing four stages in human development—childhood, youth, middle age, and old age (Hall & Nordby, 1973)—he was particularly interested in the changes of middle age which he saw as a critical transition from concern with the outer world to an inward focus on meaning and values.

CARL JUNG
(1875–1962)

THE EGO

According to Jung, the **ego** is the conscious mind and is composed of thoughts, feelings, perceptions, and memories. It is the gatekeeper to consciousness (Hall & Nordby, 1973) and forms the basis for our sense of identity and continuity. The **persona** is the social mask worn when interacting with others in the roles we play in our lives. The **shadow** is the part of our personality that we reject and repress into our unconscious. It is what we deny about ourselves. Part of the process of individuation is to acknowledge the shadow, dismantle the persona, and reconcile the opposites within the personality.

THE PERSONAL UNCONSCIOUS

Jung believed that the **unconscious** is even more vast and complex than Freud suggested. In his view, the unconscious contains not only impulses but also positive psychic material that, if brought to light, can help the conscious personality to develop. He suggested that the unconscious is comprised of two parts, the personal unconscious and the collective unconscious. The **personal unconscious** consists of memories that have been forgotten, suppressed, or are too weak to enter consciousness in the first place. Within the personal unconscious are **complexes**—organized groups or constellations of emotionally charged memories, thoughts, feelings, and perceptions. For example, experiences with a domineering mother may cause a mother complex. That person's thoughts, feelings, and actions will be guided by his or her conception of the mother. If the complex becomes strong enough, it may even take control of the personality. Conversely, a complex can also be the source of drive needed for achievement. This, again, reflects Jung's thinking about the importance of opposites within the personality.

THE COLLECTIVE UNCONSCIOUS

The **collective unconscious** is the most innovative and significant of Jung's contributions. It is the inherited foundation of personality, the experience common to all peoples, and is not dependent on an individual's experience. It consists of **archetypes,** which are the inherited predispositions to have certain experiences or to react to the world in a certain way. For example, we don't have to learn to fear the dark, snakes, or spiders because they have been dangerous to man throughout the ages. On the other hand, unless we have had a bad experience, few of us develop a fear of light sockets even though they too can be dangerous. Archetypes include such universal images as God, birth, rebirth, the hero, the child, the wise old man, and the earth mother and are found all over the world in legends and in literature. They reflect what is common about human experience and are expressed in common symbols found throughout the world. While the archetypes contribute to the formation of complexes in the personal unconscious, they also provide energy for the personality and a fund of wisdom and creativity that the ego can draw on.

Jung agreed with Freud that dreams are meaningful. However, Jung felt that dreams are not simply wish fulfillment but the way in which both the personal and collective unconscious seek to provide information to the conscious. Jung's viewpoint has been significant as a bridge between the Western psychoanalytic viewpoint and the Eastern esoteric viewpoints on the great range of influences on personality.

EXPLORING PERSONALITY: MAKING THE UNCONSCIOUS CONSCIOUS

PSYCHOANALYSIS

Even though Freud and his followers were clinicians, *psychoanalysis* was at first regarded as a technique for exploring the unconscious (Peterson, 1988). Relief of symptoms was considered to be a by-product in the search for understanding.

According to Freud, the best that can be hoped for within the personality is a kind of armed truce in the war between "I want" (from the id) and "Don't you dare" (from the superego). With luck, the ego maintains a balance between demands of the id, the superego, and reality by using repression and distortion to manage anxiety.

Psychoanalysis analyzes the way the ego defends the personality. In order to do this, the analyst must gain access to the unconscious and its repressed contents. This is achieved through the tools of free association, dream analysis, and the analysis of parapraxes, which Freud discovered or invented when he abandoned hypnosis as a therapeutic tool. The task of **psychoanalysis** is to find a way into the unconscious, into the base of the iceberg, in search of clues from the past that explain the present personality.

Psychoanalysis begins with **free association**. The patient is told to relax and simply say whatever comes to mind. It is more difficult than it sounds to short-circuit the censor that normally governs our speech, to let go of conscious control. Try it. The psychoanalyst listens intently but doesn't speak or interrupt. If the patient stops speaking, the analyst remains silent.

This led to the second method used in psychoanalysis, which is **dream analysis**. Freud found that his patient's free associations often would lead to a dream (Freud, 1914). He believed that, during sleep, the ego relaxes and allows repressed contents to surface. The ego maintains some control, however, so the id must use *symbols* to communicate repressed wishes. The dream is then interpreted by transforming its *manifest content* (the story as constructed by the id) into *latent content* (the meaning) (Brenner, 1974).

The third method of reaching unconscious material is the **psychoanalytic interpretation** of faulty actions or slips. Such actions, such as calling someone by the wrong name, losing objects, or forgetting an appointment, are all subject to interpretation. Since all behavior is meaningful, according to Freud, these slips provide clues to unconscious desires.

Psychoanalytic interpretation is much like interpreting a poem or a work of art. Clues from the unconscious come disguised in their meaning. They are complex enough to be interpreted at many levels, so their interpretation must also be multilevel. Like art, there is not a single correct interpretation; rather many interpretations contribute to understanding (McAdams, 1990). Psychoanalytic interpretation is used as a first step toward *insight*, which is the goal of psychoanalysis.

WORD ASSOCIATION TEST

Carl Jung's view of the unconscious is even more complex than Freud's, so access to its contents is also important in Jungian analysis. Jung used dream interpretation extensively and encouraged such activities as sand play and painting because he thought these provide clues to unconscious material. One widely used method devised by Jung is the **word association test,** in which a person is presented with a standard list of 100 words, one at a time, and is asked to say the first word that comes to mind. Jung wasn't simply interested in the response itself but also in the length of time it takes to come up with the response, as well as other nonverbal clues such as vocal inflection, shifts in posture, and facial expression. These signals of emotion are thought to indicate a complex related to the stimulus word. In fact, the publication of investigations using the word association test established Jung's reputation in the United States (Hall & Nordby, 1973).

PROJECTIVE TECHNIQUES

Projective techniques induce the subject to project inner needs and conflicts onto ambiguous stimuli. The techniques are more standardized than the methods used by Freud and Jung, but they rest on the same assumption—that is, that the unconscious must be approached indirectly.

Two of these techniques are the **Rorschach ink blot test** and the **Thematic Apperception Test** (TAT). (See Figures 14-1 and 14-2.) With the Rorschach, the

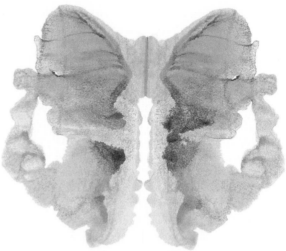

FIGURE 14-1
Rorshach Inkblot

The subject can view the inkblot from any angle to describe what he or she sees in the color, design, or pattern.

subject freely describes a series of 10 ink blots. Half of the cards are black and white; the other half contain color. The analyst then examines the descriptions to see if the subject mentioned the whole blot or part, the presence of humans or animals, and color and movement, among other things.

The TAT comprises a series of 19 pictures portraying people in ambiguous situations. The twentieth card is blank. The subject is asked to tell a story about the situation pictured, including what led up to the situation, what is happening at the moment, and how things turn out. These stories are then analyzed for themes demonstrating inner needs and external pressures. The analysis of the way an individual responds to these standard stimuli is thought to provide a glimpse of unconscious conflicts in much the same way that a dream interpretation or the analysis of a verbal slip might. The projective techniques are widely used in conjunction with objective tests to help evaluate personality in clinical settings.

FIGURE 14-2
Thematic Apperception
Test

The ambiguous pictures in the TAT are intended to uncover a subject's inner conflicts and needs as he or she describes the pictures.

A **case study** is a long-term observation of a single subject (Runyan, 1984). In the clinic, that single subject is a person. A single life, richly explored, can be a source of important insights about human personality in general. Much of psychoanalytic theory was developed from case histories of patients seen in the consulting room, and it is still an important tool used by clinicians. As a research strategy, however, it is controversial because case studies are not objective or verifiable, and there is no way of knowing how generalizable case study findings might be. Overall, case studies are best used for developing theories rather than for testing them (McAdams, 1990).

TEMPERAMENT, TRAITS, AND TYPES

Some personality theorists have attempted to devise ways to describe personality characteristics and individual differences accurately. Instead of grand conceptions about the structure of personality and its underlying dynamics, these psychologists have tried to determine how people differ. They have been interested in the differences for two reasons. First, psychologists believe the differences are consistent and enduring within the individual. Second, by classifying people accordingly, we learn something important about how that person will behave. For example, classifying someone as a narcissist would lead us to expect the person to be self-absorbed and difficult to develop any kind of intimacy with. This is not a person we are likely to call when we are troubled and need someone to listen to us.

CATEGORIZING PEOPLE

Categorizing people is an intuitively appealing idea, and theories of types and temperaments are to be found throughout history. Did you look at your horoscope this morning? Sometimes classification is based on date of birth, as with signs of the zodiac. Often, though, classification has been based on presumed differences in biology. The Greeks classified people according to their predominant "humors" (fluids in the body). Depressed (melancholic type) people were thought to have too much black bile, while too much yellow bile resulted in an excitable (choleric type) person. An excess of blood accounted for emotional expressiveness (sanguine type), and too much phlegm (phlegmatic type) was thought to result in a person who is unflappable.

Body type was the basis for a more recent attempt to classify people. Sheldon (1942) classified people according to "somatotype." According to this classification scheme, if you have a muscular build (mesomorph) you are inclined to be physically active. Thin people (ectomorph) are sensitive and high strung, while round (endomorph) people are thought to be affable and relaxed. (Figure 14-3). Sheldon's work has been criticized on methodological grounds (Humphreys, 1957), but there is evidence (Tanner, 1955) that these stereotypes have some truth. The kind of environments we choose may be influenced by the kind of build we have. These environments may in turn emphasize and develop certain physical characteristics at the expense of others. For example, it is

FIGURE 14-3
Body Type and Personality

How much does a person's physical build reflect or determine his or her personality? According to Sheldon's classification, Mike Tyson would be a mesomorph, Andy Warhol an ectomorph, and Luciano Pavarotti an endomorph.

difficult to imagine Santa Claus playing the saxophone in a bohemian dive or the Incredible Hulk sitting still for hours listening patiently to children's Christmas requests. Or, try to imagine Woody Allen in a red four-by-four with guns hung in the back window and a deer slung across the hood. So a physically active person might come to develop a muscular build, or a naturally muscular person might find physical activity easier and more fun. A naturally sedentary person might not move around as much and as a result burn too few calories. People who are naturally bulky or slight of build might choose very different environments and, as a result, develop different personality qualities. It is also possible that, given a particular build, a person comes to enact the appropriate stereotype because it is expected by others (Peterson, 1988).

TEMPERAMENT

Modern psychologists still classify people according to differences. Some of the categories they use are temperament, trait, and type. **Temperament** is a genetic predisposition to respond to specific events in a specific way (Peterson, 1988). It is one of the terms psychologists use to describe emotional life (Ekman, 1984). Temperament is expressed in the way a person goes about doing things. It is the style of behavior. For example, think of the different ways a person can approach a task such as cleaning a desk. One person suddenly decides that the time has come to clean up and jumps right in, mercilessly discarding old papers, stopping only when the job is finished. Another person sets aside a specific time to clean up and then carefully sorts through all the papers, stopping to read and create new files along the way. The task may be the same, but the style of behavior differs quite a bit. Some psychologists consider temperament to be a foundation upon which the personality is developed rather than part of the personality itself (Peterson, 1988).

Temperament is thought to be biologically based because the differences in activity level and sociability observed in infants seem to remain into adolescence. That is, a placid baby often develops into an easy-going teenager (Kagan & Moss, 1962). Recently, Jerome Kagan (1989) suggested that physiological differences related to the limbic system may account for differences in inhibition found in young children. Further support for the idea of a genetic basis for temperament was reported by psychologists Arnold Buss and Robert Plomin (1984), who measured adult behavior for frequency, intensity, and duration. They reported stable differences on three aspects of personality: emotionality, activity level, and sociability (extraversion–introversion). **Emotionality** is the degree of emotional responsiveness that a person displays. When confronted with a spider, you might shriek and run from the room while your friend might calmly pick it up and place it outside. **Activity level** refers to how energetically a person behaves. For example, your sister may amble along and call it hiking while your brother scampers along the trail, exploring all rocks and trees. Finally, **sociability** is the desire to be around others and respond to them. Some people approach a roomful of strangers with anticipation while others feel dread. These findings were supported by studies using the twin method (Buss, Plomin, & Willerman, 1973; Plomin & Rowe, 1977).

Using factor analysis as a research tool, British psychologist Hans Eysenck (1981) concludes that there are three personality types, or *superfactors,* that he believes are genetically based. These are extraversion–introversion, instability–stability, and psychoticism–superegofunctioning. Eysenck believes that the *extraversion–introversion dimension* is linked to the brain's ascending reticular activating system, which controls arousal level. In his view, introverts are easily aroused, and so they withdraw from stimulation. Extraverts are just the reverse: they seek stimulation in order to maintain an optimal arousal level. He links the *instability–stability dimension* to the limbic system with its control of the "fight or flight" response. Individuals high in instability are emotionally reactive and are thought likely to develop neurotic symptoms in response to severe stress. The third dimension is the *psychoticism–superego* functioning, which Eysenck believes is less important in determining personality than the first two dimensions. A person high in psychoticism is isolated, hostile, and insensitive to others (Eysenck, 1975). He believes this dimension is related to the androgen hormone system. Eysenck notes the similarity of his trait dimensions to those proposed by the Greek theory of humours. He also claims that these factors can be found in animals as well as in humans (Eysenck, 1981).

TRAITS

Traits are the general and enduring qualities that exist within us and underlie our thoughts, feelings, and actions over time and across situations. Some psychologists believe they are the basic units of personality (Allport, 1937). There are nearly 18,000 words (Allport & Odbert, 1936) that we use to describe other people and ourselves. Over 4,500 of these are trait terms. Trait terms are not simply descriptions; they are also predictions of behavior. If someone has been described to you as stingy, you would be surprised if that person picked up the check in a restaurant. The word *stingy* may describe behavior, but it doesn't explain why that behavior occurs.

Allport (1937) identified two kinds of traits: cardinal and secondary. **Cardinal traits** are highly generalized dispositions that organize the whole personality. John McEnroe's cardinal trait could be said to be competitiveness. **Secondary traits** occur in only a few specific situations. A person may be generally calm but may become anxious on airplanes, so anxiety is a secondary trait.

Raymond Cattell (1971), who also analyzed intelligence, gathered personality traits from many different sources. They included lists of adjectives, personality tests, and observations of behavior in real-life situations. Through a series of complex factor analyses, he developed 16 factors that he believes are the basic trait dimensions. Each factor is represented by two expressions, one indicating a high score, the other a low score. For this he developed the **Sixteen Personality Factor** (or **16PF) questionnaire,** a list of 100 yes-or-no questions. By plotting a person's factor scores on a graph, a psychologist can identify that individual's personality profile (Table 14-1).

TYPES

With trait terms, a person can be described as somewhat introverted, very stable, and not at all open. With types, however, an individual is usually described in absolute terms. A person would be described as either introverted or extraverted, either stable or neurotic. A **type** is a cluster of related traits—that is, a superfactor. Like traits, types are descriptions of personality that imply prediction. A **typology** is a summary statement about what a person is like. The Greek classification scheme of the four humors is a typology. So is the American Psychiatric Association's *Diagnostic and Statistical Manual of Mental Disorders,* or *DSM* (see Chapter 15, page 508).

ARE TRAITS AND TYPES USEFUL?

We all have our own implicit theories of personality. We use them not only to type other people ("Joe is an honest person"), but also to predict ("Marie is generous, so I'll ask her if I can borrow a dollar"). Belief in the importance of traits and types rests on the assumption that knowing a person's characteristics will tell us something about how that person will behave. Not only that, we see a person behave and attribute the behavior to a trait. People assume that others are consistent and that their behavior is understandable. But some psychologists question whether people really are consistent enough across situations to make knowledge of traits useful in predicting behavior (Mischel, 1968).

By thinking in terms of traits that influence behavior, most of us believe that other people are more predictable than they really are. We think that someone who is honest does not lie to friends, does not cheat, and doesn't steal. But what would happen if you actually followed a person around for several days and kept a record of whether his or her actions were honest?

Hartshorne and his colleagues (Hartshorne & May, 1929) did just that. They studied 8,000 children and assessed their "moral character" by looking at their behavior in a number of diverse circumstances: cheating in the classroom and on exams, stealing money, lying, and cheating during games. They found surpris-

TABLE 14-1
Cattell's Basic Trait Dimensions

	Low score description	Average	High score description	
A	1 2 3 4 Reserved, cool impersonal	5 6	7 8 9 10 Warm, easygoing, likes people	WARM
B	1 2 3 4 Concrete-thinking	5 6	7 8 9 10 Abstract-thinking	INTELLIGENT
C	1 2 3 4 Easily upset, emotional, impatient	5 6	7 8 9 10 Emotionally stable, mature, patient	EMOTIONALLY STABLE
E	1 2 3 4 Submissive, accommodating	5 6	7 8 9 10 Dominant, assertive, opinionated	DOMINANT
F	1 2 3 4 Serious, sober, prudent, quiet	5 6	7 8 9 10 Cheerful, expressive, enthusiastic	CHEERFUL
G	1 2 3 4 Expedient, disregards rules	5 6	7 8 9 10 Conforming, persevering, rule-bound	CONSCIENTIOUS
H	1 2 3 4 Shy, timid, threat-sensitive	5 6	7 8 9 10 Socially bold, unafraid, can take stress	BOLD
I	1 2 3 4 Tough-minded, insensitive, rough	5 6	7 8 9 10 Sensitive, tender-minded, refined	SENSITIVE
L	1 2 3 4 Trusting, adaptable, accepting	5 6	7 8 9 10 Suspicious, hard-to-fool, skeptical	SUSPICIOUS
M	1 2 3 4 Practical, "down to earth," conventional		Imaginative, absent-minded, impractical	IMAGINATIVE
N	1 2 3 4 Forthright, unpretentious, open	5 6	7 8 9 10 Shrewd, polished, calculating	SHREWD
O	1 2 3 4 Confident, self-satisfied, complacent	5 6	7 8 9 10 Insecure, apprehensive, self-blaming	GUILT PRONE
Q_1	1 2 3 4 Conservative, traditional, resists change	5 6	7 8 9 10 Liberal, innovative, open to change	EXPERIMENTING
Q_2	1 2 3 4 Group-oriented, sociable	5 6	7 8 9 10 Self-sufficient, resourceful, self-directed	SELF-SUFFICIENT
Q_3	1 2 3 4 Undisciplined, uncontrolled, impulsive	5 6	7 8 9 10 Controlled, socially precise, compulsive	SELF-DISCIPLINED
Q_4	1 2 3 4 Relaxed, composed, has lower drive	5 6	7 8 9 10 Tense, restless, has high drive	TENSE

SOURCE: Cattel, 1986.

ingly little consistency of behavior across situations. They concluded that being honest in one situation does not mean that a person will be honest in another. This finding has been demonstrated repeatedly (Bem & Allen, 1974) and calls into question one of the defining characteristics of a trait—that it be consistent across situations.

With the evidence for biologically based differences in personality comes support for the idea of consistency of personality over time. Most people's self-descriptions are remarkably stable across years or even decades (Block & Block, 1980). Lutsky and colleagues (1978) measured consistency in conscientiousness both across time and across situations. People were consistent over time in the same situations, but not in different situations.

Bem and Allen (1974) studied consistent and inconsistent people. Then they measured their behavior across situations in three ways: observing a subject's behavior, subject's filling out a questionnaire, and ratings of subject by parents and friends. All three measures showed the same thing. Individuals who said they were friendly were more friendly in specific situations and were judged friendly by their parents and peers. However, these findings were much weaker for the trait "conscientious." Possibly, "being friendly" means about the same thing to most people, but people have very different conceptions about what "being conscientious" entails.

So consistency itself may be a trait. Some people actually are more consistent than others. Epstein (1979) found that some people are almost completely consistent, with average correlation coefficients higher than 0.9, while others are much less consistent. Furthermore, people are quite accurate in predicting how consistently they (themselves) demonstrate certain traits across situations.

How consistent are people's personalities across situations? Will this woman display the same personality traits at home as at the office?

Mark Snyder (1979, 1983, 1987) has also found that some people are more consistent than others. He believes that some of us are very sensitive to the impression we make on others, and he calls those *high self-monitors*. They continually monitor the impression they are making and adjust their behavior accordingly. High self-monitors are particularly concerned about how they appear to others and how appropriately they behave. They are sensitive to the wishes of others and use others' behavior as a guideline. If a high self-monitor went to a meeting where everyone was serious and staid, he or she would try to act appropriately sedate. He or she is making behavior unpredictable from knowledge of traits alone. In order to predict the behavior of a high self-monitor, we must know something about the situation he or she is in.

CHAPTER 14 / PERSONALITY

One reason we may feel that others act inconsistently is that we're not accurately interpreting what they're doing. This is because different actions can have different meanings to a person. Suppose you are sitting at the computer writing a paper for your biology class and a friend walks in and asks you what you are doing. You might say, "I am writing a biology paper" because that is how you are thinking about it. But that is just one way to answer the question.

Robin Vallacher and Daniel Wegner's (1985, 1987) theory of action identification suggests that how we think about what we do can be located on a hierarchy ranging from a low-level focus on performing the action to a high-level concern with its meaning. Possible responses to your friend's question range from "I am pressing the letter *q* with my little finger" all the way to "I am preparing myself for medical school" or even "I am on my way to winning the Nobel Prize."

Since there are so many ways to think about what we are doing, what determines which one we choose? According to the first principle of action identification theory, the identification we choose will be the one that helps most in

ACTION IDENTIFICATION

maintaining the action. If you concentrate too much on your fingers and worry about typos, you might never get your paper written. But if you focus too much on medical school you might choke and not be able to finish your paper. So by thinking about the task as "writing a paper for my biology class," you are able to maintain the action and complete it.

Sometimes thinking about the *mechanics* of what we are doing is more effective than thinking about what it *means*. But we tend to prefer thinking about the meaning of our actions, particularly if the action is one that is easy for us (Vallacher, Wegner, & Somoza, 1989). Wegner and Vallacher have found that when there is available both a lower and higher level of identification, people tend to be open to the higher-level interpretations of the action (Wegner, Vallacher, Kiersted, & Dizadji, 1986; Wegner, Vallacher, Macomber, Wood, & Arps,

1984). This is the second principle of the theory. So, if the writing of your biology paper is going well, you might find yourself entertaining thoughts of white coats as you type. You may even wonder what Stockholm will be like in December.

But if you do too much of this, or if your roommate turns on his heavy-metal albums, or the paper isn't going well, you might find yourself making mistakes or accidentally erasing your file. In this case, action identification's third principle would come into play, which states that when you can't maintain the action at a high level of identification, then identification must drop back to a lower level. If the action is a difficult one, then it is best to identify it in low-level terms (Vallacher, Wegner, & Somoza, 1989). The mechanics of writing the paper or retrieving your lost file would be how you identify your action to your friend. This loops us back around to the first principle of the theory, which states that we choose the level of identification that helps to maintain the action. So next time you ask someone what they are doing, listen carefully to what they say. They might be telling you more than they realize.

Low self-monitors, on the other hand, express what they truly think and feel no matter what the situation. They are not so concerned about what others think, and they look to their own standards as a guide. They are, as they say, being true to themselves. Low self-monitors are therefore more consistent in their behavior across situations. Their behavior is more predictable from knowledge of traits than is the behavior of the situationally sensitive high self-monitors.

There are a number of reasons for our belief that people are consistent across situations. First, we have a tendency to underestimate the influence of the situation a person is in (Ross, 1977). For example, we are likely to assume that the hostile act we just witnessed expresses a trait of hostility rather than being a reaction to a frustrating situation. Second, our own behavior shapes the behavior of those around us. If we approach someone for help with the expectation that they will be friendly, it is likely that we will elicit friendliness from them. Third, we tend to see people repeatedly in the same situation. You

487

see Helen at work every day and admire her cool competence as she performs her job. You come to think of her in these terms. However, because you don't commute with her, you don't see how unglued she becomes every time something goes wrong with her car. The tow-truck driver would describe her in very different terms. Fourth, most of us have theories about "the type of person who . . ." or about what personality characteristics go together. These *implicit personality theories* (Schneider, 1973) are based, in part, on our schemata about people. Remember that schemata affect the way we perceive the world and how we remember events. They act as filters, shaping our impressions about people as well. These *person schemata* (Fiske & Taylor, 1984) help us categorize people and influence the way we treat them. While people may indeed possess unique and stable qualities that endure over time (Block, 1971, 1977; Costa & McCrae, 1980), some of the consistency we see in others across situations may actually exist only in our minds.

MEASURING PERSONALITY

There are literally hundreds of personality tests, most based on various trait assumptions. That is, they assume that traits are stable over time and across situations. Personality tests are important for research on personality and are also widely used in applied settings. In clinical and counseling situations they are used for diagnosis and to chart client progress. They are also commonly used for personnel selection.

Most of these personality tests are objective, self-report questionnaires. They are called objective because the subjects or clients are asked to respond to standardized questions. Instead of interpreting ink blots or telling stories, the subjects fill in bubbles on a computer-scored answer sheet.

The most widely used personality test is the **Minnesota Multiphasic Personality Inventory (MMPI)**. It is a personality atlas consisting of more than 500 true-false items. Originally devised to distinguish between normal people and those with psychiatric difficulties such as paranoia, anxiety, or depression, it is also used for research in personality. The test can be scored by hand or by computer. Thirteen scale scores are reported on the MMPI: 3 of these are validity scales, which are designed to determine whether the test was being taken seriously; the remaining 10 are clinical scales, named after various clinical diagnoses such as depression and schizophrenia (Figure 14-4). Interpretation of the MMPI is configural—that is, the person interpreting the results looks at the relationship of the scores rather than simply using single scales to diagnose. Scales are usually referred to by number rather than by name, so a patient is referred to as a "2-8" or a "4-6" rather than by some clinical term (Graham, 1977). As a result of extensive research using the MMPI, codebooks for interpretation have been developed which allow psychologists to employ computer interpretation.

Another kind of personality test is the **interest inventory.** The best known is the **Strong-Campbell Interest Inventory.** You have probably taken it at one time or another. It is used to counsel people about what careers might suit them. Like the MMPI, it is a fill-in-the-bubble test. Reported interests are compared with those expressed by people who are satisfied in their occupation. These

SCALE NAME	SCALE ABBREVIATION	INTERPRETATION OF HIGH SCORES
Lie	L	Denial of common frailties
Frequency	F	Invalidity of profile
Correction	K	Defensive, evasive
Hypochondriasis	Hs	Emphasis on physical complaints
Depression	D	Unhappy, depressed
Hysteria	Hy	Reacts to stress by denying problems
Psychopathic deviancy	Pd	Lack of social conformity; often in trouble with the law
Masculinity—feminitity	Mf	Feminine orientation (males); masculine orientation (females)
Paranoia	Pa	Suspicious
Psychasthenia	Pt	Worried, anxious
Schizophrenia	Sc	Withdrawn, bizarre thinking
Hypomania	Ma	Impulsive, excitable
Social introversion—extraversion	Si	Introverted, shy

FIGURE 14-4
An MMPI Profile

The table lists the categories that are scored on the personality profile. The computer printout analyzes the results of a subject's test and interprets them to describe his personality.

ROCHE PSYCHIATRIC SERVICE INSTITUTE

MMPI REPORT

CASE NO: 718365　　　　　　　　　　　　RPSI. NO: 10000
AGE 39 MALE

THE PATIENT'S RESPONSES TO THE TEST SUGGEST THAT HE UNDERSTOOD ITEMS AND FOLLOWED THE INSTRUCTIONS ADEQUATELY. IT APPEARS HOWEVER, THAT HE MAY HAVE BEEN OVERLY SELF-CRITICAL. THE VALIDITY OF THE TEST MAY HAVE BEEN AFFECTED BY HIS TENDENCY TO ADMIT TO SYMPTOMS EVEN WHEN THEY ARE MINIMAL. THIS MAY REPRESENT AN EFFORT TO CALL ATTENTION TO HIS DIFFICULTIES TO ASSURE OBTAINING HELP. IT FURTHER SUGGESTS THAT HE CURRENTLY FEELS VULNERABLE AND DEFENSELESS, WHICH MAY REFLECT A READINESS TO ACCEPT PROFESSIONAL ASSISTANCE.

THIS PATIENT MAY EXHIBIT CONCERN OVER PHYSICAL SYMPTOMS WHICH, ON EXAMINATION, REVEAL NO ORGANIC PATHOLOGY. HE MAY BE IRRITABLE, DEPRESSED, SHY AND SECLUSIVE, WITH A RIGIDITY OF OUTLOOK AND AN INABILITY TO FEEL COMFORTABLE WITH PEOPLE. HE SHOWS LITTLE INSIGHT INTO HIS PERSONAL ADJUSTMENT. PSYCHIATRIC PATIENTS WITH THIS PATTERN ARE LIKELY TO BE DIAGNOSED NEUROTIC, CHIEFLY WITH SOMATIC FEATURES. MEDICAL PATIENTS WITH THIS PATTERN ARE DIFFICULT TO TREAT BECAUSE THEY APPEAR TO HAVE LEARNED TO LIVE WITH AND TO USE THEIR COMPLAINTS. ALTHOUGH THE PATIENT MAY SHOW A GOOD RESPONSE TO SHORT-TERM TREATMENT, THE SYMPTOMS ARE LIKELY TO RETURN.

IN TIMES OF PROLONGED EMOTIONAL STRESS HE MAY DEVELOP PSYCHOPHYSIOLOGICAL SYMPTOMS SUCH AS HEADACHES AND GASTROINTESTINAL DISORDERS. HE APPEARS TO BE A PERSON WHO REPRESSES AND DENIES EMOTIONAL DISTRESS. WHILE HE MAY RESPOND READILY TO ADVICE AND REASSURANCE, HE MAY BE UNWILLING TO ACCEPT A PSYCHOLOGICAL INTERPRETATION OF HIS DIFFICULTIES.

THERE ARE SOME UNUSUAL QUALITIES IN THIS PATIENT'S THINKING WHICH MAY REPRESENT AN ORIGINAL OR INVENTIVE ORIENTATION OR PERHAPS SOME SCHIZOID TENDENCIES. FURTHER INFORMATION WOULD BE REQUIRED TO MAKE THIS DETERMINATION.

THIS PERSON MAY BE HESITANT TO BECOME INVOLVED IN SOCIAL RELATIONSHIPS. HE IS SENSITIVE, RESERVED AND SOMEWHAT UNCOMFORTABLE, ESPECIALLY IN NEW AND UNFAMILIAR SITUATIONS.

THIS PERSON IS LIKELY TO BE AN INDECISIVE INDIVIDUAL WHO LACKS SELF-CONFIDENCE AND POISE AND IS LIKELY TO BE INHIBITED AND SLOW IN RESPONSE. HE HAS DIFFICULTY CONCENTRATING, AND MAY BECOME DISORGANIZED UNDER STRESS. ALTHOUGH SUPERFICIALLY CONFORMING AND COMPLIANT, HE MAY EXHIBIT CONSIDERABLE PASSIVE RESISTANCE.

THIS PATIENT HAS A TEST PATTERN WHICH SUGGESTS THE POSSIBILITY OF SEVERE EMOTIONAL PROBLEMS. PROFESSIONAL CARE IS INDICATED.

THIS PATIENT'S CONDITION APPEARS TO FALL WITHIN THE NEUROTIC RANGE. HE IS USING NEUROTIC DEFENSES IN AN EFFORT TO CONTROL HIS ANXIETY.

NOTE: ALTHOUGH NOT A SUBSTITUTE FOR THE CLINICIAN'S PROFESSIONAL JUDGMENT AND SKILL, THE MMPI CAN BE A USEFUL ADJUNCT IN THE EVALUATION AND MANAGEMENT OF EMOTIONAL DISORDERS. THE REPORT IS FOR PROFESSIONAL USE ONLY AND SHOULD NOT BE SHOWN OR RELEASED TO THE PATIENT.

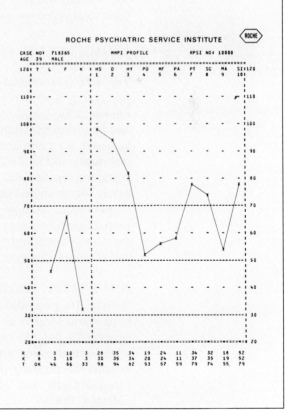

interests are not necessarily related to the occupation itself; they can be such things as a preference for whistling in the shower, gardening, or "fixing things" that aren't broken. The premise of the interest inventory is that having interests similar to those of people in an occupation indicates suitability for that occupation.

These tests are objective in the sense that they are standardized and can be scored by a computer. But think of when you last took one of these tests. Did you try to be honest? Did you care? Would it have made a difference? The answer to this last question is yes. While the tests themselves may be objective, the people who take them have a variety of motives when they fill in those bubbles. Sometimes we don't want to answer truthfully, sometimes we can't, and sometimes we just don't care. This is one of the problems with such tests. The results are only as good as the information that went in. A good clinician will use these tests along with other methods to devise a plan for treatment, to assess progress, or to counsel.

THE SELF

Many centuries ago, Socrates proclaimed "Know thyself," but how do we do this? Is there a real self that we are meant to be? We talk about finding ourselves or actualizing ourselves. This implies that our real self is either lost in the wilderness somewhere or is inside us but undernourished in some way. What is the self and where is it? In the 100 years since William James introduced the topic to psychology, psychologists have attempted to answer these questions.

HUMANISTIC PSYCHOLOGY

The **self** is a central concept in **humanistic psychology.** This branch of psychology is primarily concerned with the experience of the whole person. It is known as the "third force" in psychology, the other two being psychoanalysis and behaviorism. Humanistic psychologists criticize psychoanalysis because it is based on emotionally disordered people. The resulting theory is thus pessimistic and limited in its conception of people. Behaviorists are criticized for being too mechanistic. The proponents of humanistic psychology argue that psychologists should study the healthy, growth-oriented facet of human nature.

Abraham Maslow and Carl Rogers were two of the central figures in humanistic psychology. They each conceived of the self and something within the person that is trying to develop, to actualize. In addition to being clinicians and teachers, these men also conducted research in support of their ideas.

ABRAHAM MASLOW Abraham Maslow (1908–1970) was primarily a motivational theorist. He proposed a hierarchy of needs that consisted of basic needs of hunger and security and the psychosocial needs of belonging and esteem. (See Chapter 13, page 434.) Once these needs have been satisfied, the higher needs of self-actualization and transcendence can be approached. This conception extends the thinking of psychoanalytic and ego psychology to include basic social curiosity and achievement as determinants of personality (Frager & Fadiman, 1987).

ROGERS' SELF THEORY Carl Rogers (1902–1987) exemplified the humanistic view that each person has the possibility for healthy, creative growth. His theory rejects Freud's historical determinism to emphasize the immediacy of a person's experience at the moment. Rogers divided the personality into the *organism*, the *experiential field*, and the *self*. In addition to the self, there is an *ideal self*, which is what the person would like to be. By using our organismic valuing process, we evaluate experience according to whether it helps or hinders our self-actualization. As long as our self-concept is congruent with our experience, we develop smoothly as a fully functioning person.

CARL ROGERS
(1902–1987)

But sometimes in order to receive positive regard from the world we change our behavior in ways not consistent with our self-concept. This implies a discrepancy between the actual self and the ideal self. We become what Rogers called *incongruent*. This comes about as a result of negative appraisals from the world and from conditions of worth. *Conditions of worth* are messages like "We love you when you are good (or clean, or polite, or happy)." Since you are not always good, clean, polite, or happy, the message you get is that some of the time you won't be loved. So, in order to gain the love you need, you take more showers or hide your sadness even though you don't feel like it. This interferes with the actualization process because we sometimes internalize these conditions of worth and apply them to ourselves.

Both the organism and the self have related, but separate, self-actualizing tendencies. If the self is relatively congruent with the total experience of the organism, then the actualizing tendency is unified. But if not, the self and the organism may oppose each other. This results in the person becoming unhappy and dissatisfied. Incongruence results in part from differences between the self as perceived and the self as experienced (organism). Rogerian therapy consists of creating a situation of unconditional positive regard within which the client is accepted without conditions and can therefore learn to be congruent, or whole. Rogers (1959) concluded,

> If an individual should experience only unconditional positive regard, then no conditions of worth would develop, self-regard would be unconditional. The need for positive regard would never be at variance with organismic evaluation. The individual would continue to be psychologically adjusted, and would be fully functioning.

For both Maslow and Rogers, the self is like a seed planted within the individual. Given the right growing conditions, enough food, enough water, enough caring, the self will fulfill its potential and grow into Bill or Sally or you. And each of us is a wonderful human being—not a mean or selfish streak to be found. If the environment interferes and fails to supply these needs, the self-seed develops into "not-quite-Bill" or "not-quite-Sally" or "not-quite-you." All of what we are "meant to be" is in there; the environment only serves to help or hinder development.

THE SELF AS A SET OF IDEAS: THE COGNITIVE PERSPECTIVE

To **cognitive psychology,** the self is a set of ideas we have about ourselves. We gather an array of information by monitoring our thoughts and feelings as well as from interactions with others. This information then influences how we think about ourselves and how we interpret the behavior of others.

SELF-SCHEMATA **Self-schemata** are the beliefs we have about ourselves. They guide the selection and processing of information about the different selves that compose us (Markus & Nurvus, 1986; Markus & Wulf, 1987). We pay closer attention to information that is self-relevant (Nuttin, 1985), process it more quickly and efficiently (Kuiper & Rogers, 1979), and remember it better (Greenwald & Banaji, 1989). For example, researchers have found that individuals who think of themselves as independent responded more quickly to words related to the concept of independence than they did to words linked to the concept of dependence (Markus, 1977). We are particularly sensitive to information that confirms our self-schemata and tend to ignore or misinterpret information that is contrary to it. We resist information that we consider to be at odds with our self-concept (Tesser & Campbell 1983). So, if you think of yourself as friendly and smart, then you would pay attention and remember when these words are mentioned and you would interpret the behavior of others in light of this.

INVESTIGATING THE SELF The individual's subjective experience is important to these cognitive views of regarding the self. Of interest is the way the person experiences the world and the self. Since the self is thought to be comprised of feelings, thoughts, and memories of behaviors, that is what an investigator wants to know about. Rather than ask you to fill in bubbles on a personality test, you might be asked by a cognitive researcher to sort a series of statements according to how well they describe you.

Q-Sort (Stephenson, 1953) is a method of ranking statements according to how relevant they are to you. It can also be used to describe another person. The content of these statements can vary according to the interests of the investigator, but the process remains the same. For example, you might be handed a pile of 100 cards, each containing a statement such as "I am a careful person" or "I am moody." You would then be asked to sort them into nine piles. In pile 1 you would place the statements that most describe you, and in pile 9 you would place the statements that least describe you. So if a statement like "I am a conscientious worker" describes you some of the time but not always, you might place it in pile 3 or 4. You are free to move statements around until you feel satisfied that they are distributed correctly according to how you see yourself.

This is a flexible method that can be used in a variety of ways. In the example above you were describing yourself, but you might be asked to describe another person. A number is assigned to an item according to which pile it is in (1–9). This allows correlations to be computed. For example, a Rogerian therapist might ask you to describe yourself as you are (actual self) and then again as you would like to be (ideal self). These two descriptions could then be correlated to see how similar they are.

With a fill-in-the-bubble personality test like the MMPI, the meaning of an item like "I am friendly" is determined by the person who constructed the test. Endorsing that item would count on one of the scales that make up that test. With the Q-Sort method, the person who sorts the items is the one who assigns meaning (or weight) to an item because value is assigned based on the final resting place of that item relative to other items. Thus, the relationship among items is also determined by the person who sorts the cards. This method isn't designed to compare individuals with each other. Instead, a single individual is described by other people or gives self-descriptions at different times or in different situations.

LIFE NARRATIVES

While questions have been raised about the consistency of behavior actions across situations, there is much evidence for the belief in consistency of personality over time (West & Graziano, 1989). In order to document personality stability over time, researchers must follow individual lives over time. One method is the **longitudinal study,** in which a group of subjects is studied over many years. Typically, a group of subjects of about the same age (a *cohort*) is recruited and given a series of personality tests, rated by others, and interviewed. This procedure is repeated at intervals over a long period. There are longitudinal studies still in existence that were started during the 1920s (Block, 1971, 1977; Eichorn, Clause, Haan, Honzik, & Mussen, 1981), but these are rare and costly.

Another method is simply to ask people about their past, much the way Freud did. Researchers interested in life narratives use biographical methods to learn about lives (Runyan, 1984). With a personal history, or **life narrative,** we create a story about ourselves that integrates our thoughts, feelings, and memories (Bruner, 1986; Gergen & Gergen, 1983). It is a way we have of making sense of our lives and constructing our identity (McAdams, 1987, 1988). According to McAdams,

> Identity is a life story. In late adolescence and young adulthood, the person begins to compose, both consciously and unconsciously, an integrative life story—a narrative configuration that binds together his or her past, present, and anticipated future so as to confer upon that person's life the sense of "inner sameness and continuity" that Erikson sees at the heart of ego identity. Able to entertain hypothetical realities as a formal-operational thinker and motivated to reevaluate personal history and to explore new possibilities for the future, the adolescent or young adult operates as both a historian on the past and a prophet of the future. (1990, p. 402)

As with any memory, part of our story is based on fragments that we amplify and color with detail. In one view, the task of the psychotherapy consists, in part, of the therapist helping a client to construct a coherent life story that contains *narrative truth* (Spence, 1982). This life story then becomes text to be interpreted rather than a string of facts that must be proven. This narrative is malleable and often revised as we grow and change (Ross & Conway, 1986).

THE PERSON AND THE ENVIRONMENT

Rather than the self being within us or a set of ideas, it may be that we construct a self through interacting with the environment. Through self-observation and interaction with others we learn what feelings and behavior are appropriate and how to label them.

SOCIAL LEARNING THEORY

Social learning theory emphasizes that most behavior is learned rather than instinctually determined. Its advocates generally reject the idea of an unconscious in favor of an analysis of immediate, situational influences on behavior. According to Bandura, we learn by watching others be rewarded or punished, not simply by being rewarded or punished ourselves. For example, Bandura (1973) believes we learn to be aggressive by observing others. In this view, aggression is not an unconscious drive but the result of watching too many Road-Runner cartoons or Rambo movies. Wile E. Coyote and Rambo act as models of aggression, and since they are seldom arrested for their behavior, we learn that it is okay to be aggressive.

But it isn't simply a case of the environment—in this case, aggressive surroundings—influencing our behavior. We also choose to watch those cartoons and movies. Our aggressiveness is a combination of our preference for aggressive entertainment and what we learned from that entertainment. It is an interaction.

THE MECHANISM: RECIPROCAL DETERMINISM

The idea that the environment has an impact on our thoughts, feelings, and actions while we, in turn, shape the environment is called **reciprocal determinism** (Bandura, 1978). This is another way of saying that it is neither nature (our genes) nor nurture (the environment) that alone determines our personality. It is both: the result of a back-and-forth process of mutual influence. We choose many situations in our lives—where to live, whom to marry, what career to pursue. These choices shape the experiences we have, which in turn shape our expectations about the new situations we encounter.

We can also create situations through our expectations. The behavior of others is interpreted in light of the expectations we have of them. If you believe someone to be attractive, you are more likely to behave in a flirtatious manner when talking to them on the telephone. Your flirtatiousness in turn elicits warm, friendly behavior from the person at the other end of the phone (Snyder, Tanke, & Berscheid, 1977). According to Caspi and his colleagues (1989), the selection and creation of situations is an important expression of our dispositions. It helps maintain continuity within our personality and validate our self-concept.

CREATING IDENTITY: GOALS AND VALUES

One of the ways that Freud's followers changed and expanded his theory was to emphasize the importance of social interaction. In fact, it has been suggested that the neo-Freudians should really be called neo-Adlerians (Peterson, 1988) because their views reflect the social focus of Adler's thinking.

Erikson's conception of the stages of psychosocial development illustrates the way we negotiate with the environment to forge an identity. (See Chapter 2, page 65.) During each of these stages, you will recall, we must confront and resolve a conflict. As we grow, we must negotiate with the ever-increasing demands of society in order to develop a secure sense of identity. According to

494

McAdams (1990), "the individual's experiences give rise to a unique question at each stage which is typically 'asked' and eventually 'answered' through the individual's behavior." For example, the first stage, trust versus mistrust, asks the question, "How can I be secure?" The next stage, autonomy versus shame and doubt, asks the question, "How can I be independent?"

We ask these questions, behaviorally, of our own particular social and cultural environment. Therefore, each of us receives a different answer. The concept of identity is central to Erikson's theory. According to McAdams (1990), the central question of Erikson's fifth stage, identity versus role confusion, is "Who am I? How do I fit into the adult world?" During this stage we go through a period of exploration that includes questioning the assumptions and beliefs that we have been taught. We begin to realize that there are many ways to view the world and that possibly some other system of values and goals may be preferable to the one we have learned. The important task is to explore these alternatives rather than simply to accept what we have been taught. We construct an identity by trying things out: one month black clothes and orange hair; six months later, dressed for success. These are physical manifestation of a search for the ideas and values that are most comfortable for us. While we may finally incorporate many of our original views into our identity, we are making an informed choice. During this stage we are also centrally concerned with committing to an occupation that defines our role in society. This task is heavily dependent on our interests and abilities as well as on the opportunities that our social world presents. Prodigious talent on the violin is unlikely to be realized in a child born in the ghetto. Thus, the response we receive to questions of values and roles and the identity we create depends not only on our skills and abilities but also on the family we belong to and the culture we live in.

Life has its turns: your spouse unexpectedly decides to leave you; the thesis you've been working on for months is flayed to death by your professors. What does it mean to you? What do you say about it to yourself? Everyone has interviews and presentations that fail, relationships that break up, bad luck at the races or a dress sale, but the way we narrate the reasons why things went wrong has a surprisingly strong influence on mood and health.

Consider the following situation: your mate just walked out on you. How would you describe the major reason for the breakup of the relationship? Now consider how your reason reflects your view of the problem, yourself, and others. Do you explain the event as something *stable* ("I always screw up my personal relationships") or *unstable* ("It's a transient, one-time event")? If your explanation is stable, you are likely to link it with past failures and expect the same dismal results in the future.

Now consider whether your reasons are *global* ("I'm incapable of doing anything right" or "I am completely unlovable") or *specific* ("I'm unlovable because I'm so moody and picky"). The more global an explanation is, the more likely you will expect bad things to happen in all areas of your life.

Finally, do your reasons tend to be *internal* ("It was all my fault. My lover did everything possible to keep the relationship going") or *external* ("My mate had significant problems and was very moody")?

Again, internal explanations reflect and reinforce self-blame and lower self-esteem.

When bad events occur, as they will, pessimists explain the causes in *stable, global, internal* terms ("It's going to last forever, it's going to affect everything I do, and it's all my fault"). At the same time, should something good happen to a pessimist, the event is discounted as unstable, specific, and external ("It won't last. It won't change my life. I was just lucky").

USING PSYCHOLOGY: BECOMING A MORE OPTIMISTIC PERSON

Most people, of course, wouldn't want to be caught dead being pessimistic, and would feel even less inclined to think this way after reading this book. But we may not realize that many of our attitudes are pessimistic or can lead to pessimism. Most men and women, for instance, don't necessarily believe that they look on the bad side of events. Yet when confronted with an uncontrollable bad event, they will offer up a litany of subtle explanations that reflect their enduring, global, and self-centered view of the world.

This tendency for creeping pessimism is to some degree a reflection of the brain's attempt to organize and simplify the world.

Believing that things are stable, constant, and revolve around oneself brings order and stability—but at considerable cost in terms of health and happiness.

In one study (Ornstein & Sobel, 1989), a pessimistic explanatory style predicted those college students who would report more days sick and more visits to the doctor. Another long-term study tracked members of the Harvard classes of 1939 through 1944 who had fought in World War II (Seligman et al., 1988). In 1946, the men responded to questionnaires about their experiences in the war. Their responses held clues about their health some 30 years later.

One soldier described his experience: "Giving orders was sometimes very hard, if not impossible, because I always had this problem of dealing with men under me, even later in the war and when I had the appropriate rank." Recognize the tell-tale signs of pessimistic thought: the global, stable, and internal explanation of the problem? Contrast that with the more optimistic narrative, "During the war I was occasionally bored, because anyone who's ever been aboard ship is bored to tears."

Overall, men who explained bad events with stable, global, and self-centered reasoning at age 25 were less healthy later in life than men who believed their troubles were due to short-lived factors outside themselves. Belief seemed to affect health most strongly at age 45, approximately 20 years after their style of self-talk was assessed.

THE IMPACT OF THE GROUP ON PERSONALITY: SOCIOANALYTIC THEORY

Socioanalytic theory combines many of the ways of looking at personality that we have already discussed. Humans have always lived in groups, and each group is characterized by a status hierarchy. Robert Hogan (1982; Cheek & Hogan, 1983) believes that human nature must be understood in this evolutionary context. Hogan theorizes that we have a "real self" comprised of fixed needs

Does pessimism also put a person at risk for early death? Several researchers poured through the sports pages of the *New York Times* and the *Philadelphia Inquirer*. They analyzed the quotes of all the baseball Hall of Fame players who played from 1900 to 1950. The pessimists who said their baseball success was short-lived and due to luck lived significantly shorter lives than the optimists.

Optimism, as we've implied in Chapter 12, may also favorably affect immune function. Comparing blood samples from optimists and pessimists revealed a better ratio of "helper" to "suppressor" lymphocytes, suggesting that the white blood cells of optimists may be more effective in defending the body against tumors (Seligman et al., 1989).

Of course, optimistic attitudes aren't the only determinants of who stays well and who gets sick. The contribution of optimism and pessimism in physical illness seems to depend on the stage and type of disease. If a truck hits you, it probably doesn't matter much what you think. If the magnitude of your cancer is overwhelming, your psychological outlook may help you cope better but is unlikely to enhance your survival. On the other hand, if your cancer is marginal or if an illness is just beginning, your psychological state may be critical.

Optimism is, for Americans in particular, a major cultural trait: as we rate the future, we overwhelmingly believe that the present is better than the past and project that the future will be better still. Most healthy college students think that there are four times as many probable future positive events ahead for them than negative outcomes.

Americans respond so unremittingly to optimism that a content analysis of presidential candidates' speeches shows that voters are likely to pick the most optimistic-speaking president. The only exception in recent years was in 1968 when Richard Nixon beat Hubert Humphrey, but Humphrey was burdened by a disastrous war and political convention. He then came from 14 points behind in the polls to lose by only one point. Presenting good feelings yields votes as well as health!

Optimism, in psychological terms, is the tendency to seek out, to remember, and to expect pleasurable experiences. It is an active priority of the person, not merely a reflex to look on the positive side. Some people learn optimism after they have experienced difficulties, while others are brought up to emphasize the positive.

All optimists expect good things to happen, but for different reasons. One may attribute it to their talents or skills, another to ongoing good fortune, while still others to the benevolence of God. Whatever the reason, optimists, expecting to be pleased, fill their minds with positive moods and their lives with positive experiences. It is the increase in positive mood that crowds out negativity and seems to improve health.

An optimistic frame of mind reshapes the stories we tell ourselves about our past, present, and future. Optimism involves memory: selectively remembering positive events at the expense of negative events. It involves a person's current situation: actively highlighting the more promising and auspicious aspects of the present. It involves the future: looking to a promising tomorrow with an eye toward what can be done instead of what cannot happen. A person who is positive, therefore, is hopeful about his or her future, not helpless.

An optimistic person faces the future and faces difficulties as a challenge and believes that he or she can control the environment. An optimistic person believes that the world is coherent and that his or her actions can make a significant difference. In general, these men and women are passionately engaged and involved in the world and believe in their own abilities. They have a fair measure of self-worth. They feel that they matter. And they appear to live longer, healthier lives.

In contrast, pessimistic thinking undermines life. Pessimists pay twice: first, it feels bad to be so glum about future prospects; and second, it costs in health. It is not as much reality that causes stress and illness as it is personality, selecting the stories they tell themselves about reality. They *can* learn to turn pessimistic stories into optimistic ones.

(for social status) and flexible cognitive structures (our self-concept). However, this self must play the roles and follow the rituals of the group to which we belong. In so doing, we may deny our motives which, according to Hogan, are social rather than sexual, as Freud believed. These social motives include a drive for status within the group while maintaining social success.

Each of us balances a *need for status and success* with a *need for structure and order* in the social environment. We must both get ahead *and* get along. A

socially skilled person is able to do this. Here, there is a faint echo of the id-superego struggle found in Freud's theory: a drive (for status), which we often deny, is curtailed by rules and roles imposed by society.

According to **socioanalytic theory,** a *role* is the natural unit of social behavior. It is within the framework of the roles we enact that we construct our self-concept. This is done through a reciprocal process of interpreting our self-concept to others and being responded to. Our behavior in any interaction is determined by what we want the other person to believe about us. We want them to "buy" our self-image. And this self-image is shaped, in turn, by how others respond to us, including traits attributed to us by others (Cheek & Hogan, 1983).

Since part of what is going on in any social interaction is the negotiation of self-concept, self-presentation strategies are vitally important. Socially skilled people have a choice about how to behave within a situation. You behave in a way that puts forward your view of yourself as likable and warm while the other person responds by agreeing or contradicting you. Hogan suggests that the behavior of people in laboratory experiments or when filling out personality inventories must be interpreted in light of such self-presentational strategies. That is, the researcher must ask "What is this person trying to tell me about himself or herself?" rather than simply interpreting test scores.

Hogan's response to the person-situation debate is to say that "Personality is stable, but behavior varies; it varies largely because, in order to be consistent, people must change their actions when they deal with different people" (Hogan, 1982). What is consistent, but alterable, is the self-concept, which is altered through social interaction.

One clue to the importance of group membership to personality is found when we consider the nature of trait terms. They are useful not only to describe an individual's personality but also to evaluate a person's potential contribution to the group. By carefully analyzing various trait and type theories, Hogan found that there are two underlying dimensions in all of them: *sociability* and *conformity* (getting along and going along). Each of us has within us a unique mix of sociability and conformity that influences the way we are able to seek status while trying to remain acceptable to the group.

Some of us prefer to work alone, while others prefer to work with others. At the same time, some of us try to maintain the traditions of the group while others of us are bent on innovating. These preferences are reflected in the occupations we choose—the task specializations within the group.

Because of the importance of the group to human life, Hogan sees the task of psychotherapy as one of *training in social skills,* since these skills are crucial for negotiating a self-concept and achieving status within the group.

A CONCLUDING NOTE

These are some of the different ways psychologists have attempted to weave the elements of psychology into a tapestry called personality. But it is a living tapestry that changes according to where it is hung and who is nearby. We might come to understand the origin of its yarns and dyes. We might even come to understand the techniques of weaving and the logic of its design. But add to these the responsive changes brought about by interactions with others, who themselves are complex tapestries, and the task of completely understanding personality becomes impossibly complex. This is what makes it such an elusive subject for formal study.

If there is one lesson to be learned, it is that none of us are simple, but the way we understand the world involves a great deal of simplifying. This simplifying costs us more in the perception of other people than it does in the perception of objects. People are very difficult to categorize simply, but we do it anyway. We label a person with a trait name or a diagnosis and then expect him or her to behave according to the label we have assigned. We interpret their behavior accordingly. The problem is that by doing this we are seeing and reacting to a static tapestry instead of to a living one—one that is reverberating to our own woven design.

1. *Personality* contains the unique and stable qualities, including thoughts, feelings, and actions, that characterize an individual over time and across situations.

2. The most complex and important theory of personality is that of Sigmund Freud. His theory, *psychoanalysis,* is the most complete and detailed explanation of what motivates people, how the personality develops, and how it is structured. It is based on two fundamental hypotheses. First, all behavior is meaningful, including mistakes, dreams, and symptoms. Second, consciousness is the exception rather than the rule.

SUMMARY

3. Freud suggested that there are two major drives: sex and aggression. These are broadly conceived as a drive for pleasure and a drive for destruction. Freud offered the term *libido* for the psychic energy associated with the sexual drive. According to Freud, development proceeds through a series of stages, called *psychosexual stages.* Some of these stages are named for an area of the body from which a developing child derives pleasure: *oral, anal, phallic.* The remaining two stages are the *latency* and the *genital* stages. Freud had relatively little to say about the final two stages, since he believed the personality is fully formed by the end of the phallic stage, that is, by age 6.

4. Freud divided personality into three parts: the id, the ego, and the superego. According to Freud, when we are born, we are all *id*. It is the psychic representation of the drives. The *ego* comes into existence to negotiate with the world to gratify the wishes of the id. The *superego*, the last part of the personality to develop, is the internal representation of society's values and morals. While the ego takes care of the id's demands, the superego sits in judgment of the ego's solutions. The major problem for the ego is how to cope with anxiety which signals danger for the personality. *Defense mechanisms* are unconscious processes used by the ego to distort the image of reality to ward off anxiety.

5. Freud's followers expanded on his theory in different ways. One group of *neo-Freudians*, the *ego psychologists*, emphasized the ego's independence from the id and the importance of its role of interacting with the environment. Adler, Sullivan, Horney, and Fromm stressed the importance of social interactions and processes.

6. Carl Jung, an early follower of Freud, expanded on the importance of the unconscious. Jung formed his own school of thought called *analytical psychology* and developed a theory of personality that is second only to Freud's in its reach and complexity. Jung believed that the unconscious is even more vast and complex than Freud suggested. According to Jung, the unconscious is divided into the *personal unconscious* and the *collective unconscious*. The collective unconscious is the inherited foundation of personality; the human archetypes are the inherited predispositions to have certain experiences. Among them are such universal images as God, birth, and the hero, experiences common to all people. Jung called the process of development *individuation* and believed that it occurs throughout the life span.

7. According to the psychoanalytic perspective, exploring personality consists of using various techniques to bring unconscious contents to consciousness. Among these techniques are *free association, dream analysis,* and the *interpretation* of "faulty actions." Carl Jung contributed the word association test to the methods used to tap unconscious contents. Many clinicians use the Thematic Apperception Test and the Rorschach inkblot test, which are *projective techniques* because the subject is thought to project unconscious needs and conflicts onto ambiguous stimuli.

8. *Temperament* is a person's inborn style of behavior including such biologically based differences as activity level and sociability. *Traits* are thought to be general and enduring qualities that exist within an individual and underlie all thoughts, feelings, and behavior, over time and across situations. *A typology* is an attempt to classify people according to categories. It is assumed that by classifying people in one of these ways, their behavior can be predicted. But this assumption has been questioned.

9. Objective, self-report *personality tests* are important for research in personality and are widely used in applied settings. Among the most widely used tests is the Minnesota Multiphasic Personality Inventory (MMPI), a personality "atlas" originally devised to distinguish between normal people and those with psychiatric difficulties. A second widely used test is the Strong-Campbell Interest Inventory, which is used to counsel people about what careers might suit them.

10. The *self* is a central concept in *humanistic psychology*. Rejecting the pessimistic view of the psychoanalysts and the mechanistic view of the behaviorists, proponents of humanistic psychology argue that psychologists should study the healthy, growth-oriented facet of human nature. For Carl Rogers and Abraham Maslow, the self is

like a seed planted within the individual. Given the right growing conditions, it will fulfill its potential and grow into a fully functioning individual. *Cognitive psychologists,* on the other hand, regard the self as a set of ideas that influences how an individual thinks about himself or herself and how he or she intereprets the behavior of others.

11. Since an individual's subjective experience is important to these views of the self, the methods used to explore personality are subjective rather than objective in nature. For example, a researcher might ask an individual to do a Q-Sort which is a method of ranking statements according to how relevant an individual thinks the item is to describing his or her personality. Other researchers interested in life narratives use biographical methods to learn about lives.

12. *Social learning theory* emphasizes that most behavior is learned rather than instinctually determined. The idea that the environment has an impact on an individual's thoughts, feelings, and actions, while in turn the individual shapes the environment, is called *reciprocal determinism.* Erik Erikson's concept of the stages of *psychosocial development* illustrates the way we negotiate with the environment to forge an identity.

13. Robert Hogan's *socioanalytic theory* suggests that human nature must be understood in an evolutionary context. According to this theory, individuals construct a self-concept through a reciprocal process of interpreting the self-concept to others and having it responded to. Each individual is composed of a unique mix of sociability and conformity that influences the way he or she seeks status while trying to remain acceptable to the group. This mix is expressed in the occupations chosen by the individual. This is important because these are the task specializations within the group.

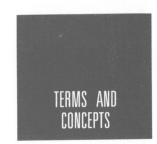

TERMS AND CONCEPTS

activity level
anal stage
analytical psychology
anxiety
archetypes
cardinal traits
case study
catharsis
cathexis
cognitive psychologists
collective unconscious
complexes
consciousness
defense mechanisms
dream analysis
ego
ego psychologists
Electra complex
emotionality
Eros
free association
genital stage

humanistic psychology
id
individuation
interest inventory
latency stage
libido
life narrative
longitudinal study
Minnesota Multiphasic Personality
    Inventory (MMPI)
moral anxiety
neo-Freudians
neuroses
neurotic anxiety
Oedipus complex
oral stage
persona
personality
personal unconscious
phallic stage
pleasure principle
projective techniques

501

psychic determinism
psychoanalysis
psychoanalytic interpretation
psychosexual stages
Q-Sort
realistic anxiety
reciprocal determinism
Rorschach ink blot test
secondary traits
self
self-schemata
shadow
Sixteen Personality Factor (16PF)
    Questionnaire

sociability
social learning theory
socioanalytic theory
Strong-Campbell Interest Inventory
superego
temperament
Thanatos
Thematic Apperception Test (TAT)
traits
types
typology
unconscious
word association test

SUGGESTIONS
FOR FURTHER
READING

Baumeister, R. F. (1986). *Identity: Cultural change and the struggle for self.* New York: Oxford University Press.

A thoughtful and well-written account of the concept of identity and the relationships between the self and society.

Dilman, I. (1986). *Freud and human nature.* New York: Basil Blackwell.

A modern assessment of Freud's important viewpoint, more easily read than most.

Freud, S. (1962). *New introductory lectures on psychoanalysis.* London: Hogarth Press.

Perhaps the best statement of Freud's ideas. However, Freud changed his theory throughout his career, and there is no single definitive work.

Gay, P. (1988). *Freud: A life for our time.* New York: Norton.

A recent biography of Freud by a cultural historian.

Jung, C. G. (1964). *Man and his symbols.* Garden City, NY: Doubleday.

Jung's theory as it relates to the importance of symbolism in everyday life. An excellent introduction to Jungian thought.

Mischel, W. (1984). Convergences and challenges in the search for consistency. *American Psychologist, 39,* 351-364.

A good summary of the emerging research on consistency.

Rogers, C. R. (1980). *A way of being.* Boston: Houghton Mifflin.

A more personal but still definitive statement of Rogers' view of human nature.

Snyder, M. (1987). *Public appearances, private realities.* New York: Freeman.

A recent description of self-monitoring research.

15
PSYCHOLOGICAL DISORDERS

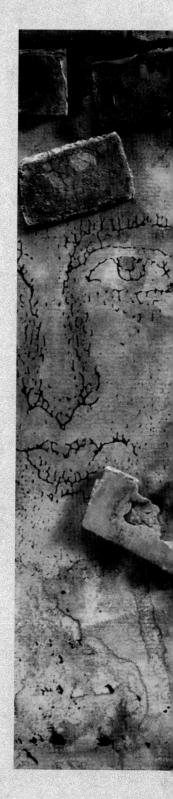

The crisis of mental illness appeared as a nuclear explosion in my life. All that I had known and enjoyed previously was suddenly transformed, like some strange reverse process of nature, from a butterfly's beauty into a pupa's cocoon. There was a binding, confining quality to my life, in part chosen, in part imposed. Repeated rejections, the awkwardness of others around me, and my own discomfort and self-consciousness propelled me into solitary confinement.

My recovery from mental illness and its aftermath involved a struggle—against my own body, which seemed to be without energy and stamina, and against a society that seemed reluctant to embrace me. It seemed that my greatest needs—to be wanted, needed, valued—were the very needs which others could not fulfill. At times, it felt as though I were trying to swim against a tidal wave. (Houghton, 1980)

Sometimes, problems in life become too great and people's ability to adapt can fail. When this happens, all or almost all efforts focus on problems, fears, and distorted thoughts. Little in life remains undisturbed. Psychologists refer to the manifestations of these problems as **psychological disorders.** Many are simply *exaggerations* or *extremes* of normal patterns of thought, action, emotions, personality, and coping.

The distinction between a normal reaction to adversity and a disturbed reaction is not, in truth, clear. In some ways, it is like the difference between a brief bout with the flu and a chronic illness. At one time or another, we all experience anger, sadness and fear, probably as *intensely* as the person who suffers from a clinical disorder. But for some people the reaction gets out of control. It is one thing to cry when a love affair ends or to feel extreme sadness when a parent dies, and it is quite another to be so disturbed that three years later you still cannot experience joy. It is one thing to be anxious about going to a party, and it is quite another to be so afraid of meeting people that you cannot go outside your house at all.

Some types of distress are so common that we do not classify them as disorders at all. Most people feel anxious when speaking to a large audience for the first time, dislike the idea of a bug or a snake crawling across their foot, and are easily spooked while walking through a dark, empty house. Even if these feelings are irrational, they are part and parcel of being human. Psychological disorders, in contrast, are defined by their unusual occurrence or *deviance* from the norm. Most people do not cry themselves to sleep every night; most people do not refuse to leave their homes; most people do not hear voices.

Being different, in and of itself, is not sufficient reason be characterized as disordered. Einstein was a very odd child, but he was not mentally ill. On the contrary, his differences were unquestionably advantageous to us all. Only when unusual thoughts or behavior patterns *detract* substantially from our psychological well-being do we consider it a psychological disorder. The thoughts or behavior must be both **deviant** and **maladaptive.**

Some disorders are relatively mild. They may interfere with our efficiency at work, but we can still hold the job. We may be anxious about meeting people, but we manage to structure our lives so we have little contact with strangers and somehow get through the unavoidable contacts. These disorders do cause discomfort, but they are not so disruptive that we cannot function. Other disorders are so severe that they interfere with virtually every life activity, including the ability to know what is real and what is not.

People may see faces looming over their heads, keeping them from sleep, or hear voices broadcasted from inside their heads. Conditions that alter the experience of what is real are referred to as **psychoses.** In lay terms, *psychosis* means out of touch with reality. When this occurs, people become terribly incapacitated. They usually find it impossible to hold a job or function effectively in their relationships. In extreme cases they may even present a danger to other people or, much more likely, to themselves.

The despair of disorder takes an enormous toll on society. Scores of millions are so depressed that they cannot function adequately. Hundreds of thousands are paralyzed because of their fear of crowds or elevators. Ten million alcoholics in the United States cannot live without a drink, and hundreds of thousands are addicted to street drugs. More than a million are schizophrenic, the condition closest to the common concept of "crazy."

Here are descriptions of the most common psychological disorders and information about possible causes. In addition, we include a number of case histories about persons who have had first-hand experience with these altered states of mind, to give you a sense of the experience itself. As you read you may recall times when you have felt similarly, but don't think you're disturbed. These extracts should convey that most disorders result in *exaggerations* of normal processes that we all experience at one time or another. Hopefully, acquiring information about the psychological disorders—and, indeed, seeing a bit of yourself in some of them—will not result in alarm, but rather in increased understanding and compassion.

AN OVERVIEW OF PSYCHOLOGICAL DISORDERS

There are a few characteristics common to most psychological disorders (Goldstein, Baker, & Jamison, 1986).

LOSS OF CONTROL

Combatting painful feelings and thoughts feels impossible. Life seems meaningless; the afflicted person's actions do not matter. Helplessness and lack of control are both aspects of this. In earlier times, the idea that people were possessed by the devil or a spirit was popular. When the individual was possessed, he or she had no control.

UNHAPPINESS OR DISTRESS

There is a romantic notion that mad people are happy to be different from others or that they have made a breakthrough. However, the experience is more of a **breakdown.** They are almost always unhappy about it. Even mania, characterized by exaggerated excitement, is typically followed by severe depression. People who are considered to be disordered make other people unhappy as well. They may be so unable to function that the lives of their family, friends, and colleagues suffer too.

ISOLATION FROM OTHERS

Individuals suffering from psychological disorders often find themselves alone. This may be due to their own efforts to physically separate themselves from other people, and they may feel withdrawn even while in the presence of others. It may also be due to others' avoiding them. It is often unpleasant to be around people who are suffering psychologically (Coyne, 1976); it is particularly painful when that person is a parent or someone who has previously cared for you.

CAUSES OF PSYCHOLOGICAL DISORDERS

There is no single cause of psychological disorders; they may arise from biological, psychological, or social factors. Some disorders have a strong genetic component because they run in families. But none of the psychological disorders are determined exclusively by genetic make-up. As psychologists advance their understanding of the brain and behavior, the basis for disorders is becoming increasingly clear. But it will be many years before we fully comprehend the wide array of factors that lead to mental illness.

BIOLOGICAL CAUSES

GENETICS Genetic inheritance has been strongly implicated in a number of psychological disorders including schizophrenia, depression, and alcoholism (Gottesman, 1962, 1968; Gottesman & Shields, 1972; Neale & Oltmanns, 1980; Pardes et al., 1989). Recent research suggests that a number of other disorders— long thought to be learned—might be inherited as well, such as violent and antisocial disorders.

One noninvasive way to investigate the genetic basis of psychological disorders is to find out if the disorder is more common among relatives of a person with a disorder than it is in the general population. The person who is known to have the disorder is called a **proband.** A **concordance rate** indicates the degree to which other people have the same disorder as the proband.

You have half of your genes in common with each of your biological parents. Brothers and sisters share one-quarter of their genes—unless the sibling is an identical (monozygotic) twin. Identical twins are both from the same egg and so have identical genetic makeup. Fraternal twins are the product of two eggs; they are no more alike genetically than any brother or sister. So genetic overlap is perfect for identical twins, greatest next for parents, then siblings. It gets weaker and weaker as you move farther away from the proband on the family tree.

Researchers have discovered a great deal about the role of genetic inheritance in the development of psychopathology from studies of **population genetics**—that is, investigations that test the predictions about concordance rates. When we find that a disorder is no more likely among parents and siblings of probands than in the general population, we have every reason to think that it is *not* genetically based. But if there is a greater likelihood of finding the disorder among very close relatives than among more distant relatives, and a greater incidence among distant relatives than nonrelatives, then the picture begins to conform to one of inheritance.

Yet just because something runs in families doesn't mean that it is genetic. After all, the ability to speak French runs in families, too. Because families share common *environments*, much of what is similar may be learned from each other or contracted from exposure to some common element. Although we can use family studies to rule out a genetic basis, positive findings *do not prove* that the basis is genetic.

The best evidence for the genetic basis of psychopathology comes from studies of twins who are adopted away from their natural parents at birth (Gottesman & Shields, 1972). These cases have provided compelling evidence for the heritability of many conditions. An identical twin of a schizophrenic who was adopted into an entirely different family and never even met the other twin is still twice as likely to be schizophrenic as a person identified randomly from the general population. (See a discussion of this on pages 535–36.)

One of the more interesting questions facing behavioral geneticists today is: Why do two people who have identical genes sometimes fail to show concordance for psychological disorders? Even when the disorder is known to have a strong genetic component? Heritability is not complete (i.e., insured) for any of the psychological disorders. At this time, most researchers feel that genetic inheritance leads to some form of biological vulnerability, but that life experiences determine whether the disorder develops or not.

SENSORY IMPAIRMENT   Genetics are not the only biological influences on psychopathology. Physical problems, such as inadequate sensory input, can also set the stage for psychological disorders. Paranoia is more common among people who are deaf or blind (Post, 1980).

PSYCHOLOGICAL CAUSES

Unique experiences influence each person's life. A person may grow up under extremely stressful conditions: being beaten by a father or abandoned by a mother, or even being doted on by both parents but witnessing violent arguments between them. A person may have a strange series of accidents that create an unusual view of the world. He or she might then come to behave in ways that elicit more unusual experiences and so eventually establish a cycle that continually reaffirms distorted beliefs.

SOCIAL-SITUATIONAL CAUSES

There are conditions and times that make a person more vulnerable and less able to cope with the problems of living. Poverty places psychological strains on individuals that are unimaginable to those of us who have not experienced severe deprivation. Mental hospitals admit more people during economic hardship and recessions. Violence and riots occur more often during heat waves. Some people seem to flourish during hard times whereas others succumb. Although we can identify factors that may increase the level of stress, we cannot predict with assurance an *individual's* disorder from the social conditions he or she has experienced.

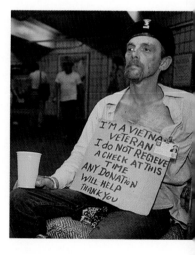

507

Psychological disorders are difficult to isolate, for they are complex and more subject to interpretation than are medical disorders. Sometimes as our culture changes, our views of normal and abnormal change. Homosexuality, for example, was once considered a psychological disorder, but during the early 1970s that interpretation was discredited. Today the practice of witchcraft could land a person in a mental hospital whereas in some cultures it is viewed as a legitimate service to the community.

In the United States, the most widely used classification system is the American Psychiatric Association's *Diagnostic and Statistical Manual of Mental Disorders (DSM)*. The *DSM* was first published in 1952 and has undergone three major revisions. The *DSM* classification system provides a common language for discussing psychological disorders, ranging from the mild to the severe. It has been criticized for being too medical, too atheoretical, and too stringent (depending on the critic), yet the system represents the consensus of committees of experts from a variety of theoretical orientations. To its credit, it is in a constant state of revision, incorporating new empirical evidence and changing existing criteria when they do not hold up to empirical test. We will refer to categories of psychological disorders as classified in its present edition, *DSM-III-R* (Table 15-1).

TABLE 15-1
DSM-III-R Diagnostic Categories

Disorders usually first evident in infancy, childhood, or adolescence
Organic mental disorders
Psychoactive substance use disorders
Schizophrenia
Delusional (paranoid) disorders
Psychotic disorders not elsewhere classified
Mood disorders
Anxiety disorders
Somatoform disorders
Dissociative disorders (hysterical neuroses, dissociative type)
Sexual disorders
Sleep Disorders
Factitious disorders
Impulse control disorders not elsewhere classified
Adjustment disorders
Psychological factors affecting physical condition
Personality disorders

Source: American Psychiatric Association, 1987.

ANXIETY DISORDERS

Fear is arguably the most adaptive emotion. Fear prepares us biologically either to defend ourselves or to flee. With a moderate amount of fear we are faster, more accurate, and more motivated. Fear is also the underlying emotion in a less adaptive state, anxiety. **Anxiety** refers to the enduring experience of fear in the absence of a fear-eliciting stimulus (Marks, 1969). If you were lying in your bed at night and suddenly saw the face of a stranger, you would experience fear. If you were lying in your bed at night *thinking* that if you looked at the window you *might* see the face of a stranger, you would be experiencing anxiety. Invariably, humans experience anxiety, but for some it is uncommon; to others it is a constant companion.

Anxious people recognize and are disturbed by the symptoms they experience. There is little disturbance of thought processes, and behavior is not way out of line with normal social conventions. But anxiety disorders can be extremely limiting and, if left untreated, can persist for a lifetime.

Before the 1980 revision of the *DSM-III*, such disorders were classified as "neurotic disorders." Although people use the word *neurotic* in everyday speech, psychologists have no useful definition of it. The anxiety disorders include a number of specific types of anxiety conditions: the primary ones are generalized anxiety disorder, panic disorder, agoraphobia, simple phobias, and post-traumatic stress disorder.

CAUSES OF ANXIETY DISORDERS

The causes of anxiety disorders are unclear. In some cases they may be entirely psychosocial. Generalized anxiety may result from an extreme reaction to an early trauma. And we know that simple phobias can be conditioned—that is, learned. Recall little Albert, who became afraid of white furry things because they were associated with a frightening, loud noise (see Chapter 8). Moreover, there are real gains from fears. The fears may relieve individuals of responsibilities or gain the attention of others. A child who has *school phobia* (see page 511) may actually fear separation from his or her mother. By refusing to go to school, the child gets to stay home with her.

We also know, however, that anxiety disorders run in families: children of agoraphobics (see page 511) stand a 15 percent greater risk of school phobia than nonrelatives (Berg, 1976). When the global category of "anxiety disorder" is studied in twin populations, the evidence for a biological basis is relatively weak. However, subtypes of anxiety disorders, particularly panic disorders, show strong inheritance patterns (Torgersen, 1983). Familial relationships are strongest in females (Crowe et al., 1983). In general, current thinking about the cause of anxiety disorders is that *vulnerability* is inherited, but environmental stress accounts for the larger piece of the puzzle (Barlow, 1988).

GENERALIZED ANXIETY DISORDER

People suffering from **generalized anxiety** experience persistent tension and worry. They seem uneasy when they are around people and are unusually

sensitive to comments and criticisms. Often they are so terrified of making a mistake that they cannot concentrate or make decisions. Their posture is often strained and rigid, resulting in sore muscles (especially in the neck and shoulders). They may have chronic insomnia and gastrointestinal problems (such as diarrhea), perspire heavily, and experience high blood pressure, heart palpitations, and breathlessness. Irrespective of how well they are actually doing, they are worried that something will go wrong. Here is one case:

> A 27-year-old married electrician complains of dizziness, sweating palms, heart palpitations, and a ringing of the ears of more than eighteen months' duration. He has also experienced dry throat, periods of uncontrollable shaking, and a constant "edgy" and watchful feeling that often interfered with his ability to concentrate. These feelings have been present most of the time over the previous two years; they have not been limited to discrete periods. . . .
>
> For the past two years he has had few social contacts because of his nervous symptoms. Although he has sometimes had to leave work when the symptoms became intolerable, he continues to work for the same company for which he has worked since his apprenticeship following high-school graduation. He tends to hide his symptoms from his wife and children, to whom he wants to appear "perfect," and reports few problems with them as a result of his nervousness. (Spitzer et al., 1981)

PANIC DISORDER

> A 25-year-old married salesman arrives at the emergency room for the fourth time in a month. He insists that he is having a heart attack and is admitted to the hospital by his internist. The cardiologist's workup is completely negative.
>
> The patient states that his "heart problem" started six months ago when he had a sudden episode of terror, chest pain, palpitations, sweating, and shortness of breath while driving across a bridge on his way to visit a prospective client. His father and uncle had both had heart problems, and the patient was sure he was developing a similar illness. Not wanting to alarm his wife and family, he initially said nothing; but when the attacks began to recur several times a month, he consulted his internist. The internist found nothing wrong, and told him he should try to relax, take more time off from work, and develop some leisure interests. In spite of his attempts to follow this advice the attacks recurred with increasing intensity and frequency.
>
> The patient claims that he believes the doctors who say there is nothing wrong with his heart, but during an attack he still becomes concerned that he is having a heart attack and will die. (Spitzer et al., 1981)

Panic disorder is a condition that can exist alone or accompany any of the other anxiety disorders. A common pairing is agoraphobia with panic, where the person is housebound and experiences attacks of panic if he or she thinks about venturing out. The cardinal feature of panic disorder is its sudden onset. Within 10 minutes, the individual goes from feeling completely normal to experiencing an intense set of physiological symptoms accompanied by feelings of "going crazy" or impending doom. Physiological symptoms may include shortness of breath, trembling, choking, accelerated heart rate, chest pain, sweating, lightheadedness, and numbness or tingling sensations.

PHOBIC DISORDERS: THE FEARS

Phobia is Greek for "fear." In psychology, the term refers to an extreme or unfounded fear of a specific object or place. Many objects of phobias do, in fact, represent real danger, such as extreme heights, snakes, or blood. But if you cannot rescue your child who got stuck in a tree because you are too frightened to climb the ladder, or your fear of snakes is so intense that you cannot leave your apartment on the 34th floor in New York City, or you cannot allow a nurse to draw blood even when your life is in jeopardy, then it is a disordered fear, or phobia.

The most common phobias are *zoophobia* (fear of animals), *claustrophobia* (fear of closed spaces), and *acrophobia* (fear of heights). Phobics experience anxiety whenever they try to confront their fear. *DSM-III-R* classifies *agoraphobia* separately. Agoraphobia is the fear of being alone in public places that might be difficult to escape. Agoraphobics may stay in their homes for years at a time, frozen by the thought of journeying out.

Age is important in phobias. Most children are naturally phobic: afraid of the dark or of a certain kind of animal. Many parents of preschoolers have to check their children's closets to get rid of all the gorillas and monsters. These fears are not considered pathological in early childhood. However, *school phobia* develops relatively early and may require help. School phobia is an acquired fear of school in which the child either actively refuses to go to school or avoids it by reporting physical complaints, like stomach aches, whenever he or she is supposed to go to school. Most pathological phobias develop in the late teens or early adulthood.

Also, women are more likely to suffer from phobias than men. We do not know why these gender differences exist in phobias. We could argue that the display of fear is more socially acceptable in females than in males. Also, as you will read in Chapter 16, the best treatment for phobias is exposure to the feared stimulus. Perhaps females are exposed to the feared situation less, which allow the phobias to develop further.

OBSESSIVE-COMPULSIVE DISORDERS

Scientists or artists may be "obsessed" with their work and allow few intrusions. You may check more than once during the day to see that you have brought the tickets for this evening's concert, but this behavior is normal—it actually may enhance daily life. **Obsessive-compulsive disorders,** however, are clear-cut exaggerations of feelings. In an *obsession*, the mind is flooded with a specific thought. In a *compulsive* disorder, the person feels compelled to repeat a certain action over and over. But this behavior does not enhance the obsessive-compulsive's life; it interferes with it. Davison and Neale (1986) describe a client who washed her hands more than 500 times a day to prevent contamination from germs. Below is an excerpt from *The Boy Who Couldn't Stop Washing,* a book about obsessive-compulsive disorders:

> I'm driving down the highway doing 55 MPH. I'm on my way to take a final exam. My seat belt is buckled and I'm vigilantly following all the rules of the road. No one is on the highway—not a living soul. Out of nowhere an Obsessive-Compulsive Disorder (OCD) attack strikes. It's almost magical the way it distorts my perception of reality. While in reality no one is on the road, I'm intruded with the heinous thought that I might have hit someone . . . a human being! God knows where such a fantasy comes from.

511

War continues to destroy lives long after the guns stop firing. Although most veterans resume normal lives after they return home, some are haunted by memories. This is particularly true of persons who served in active combat, and it is particularly true of Vietnam veterans.

The psychology of war is tremendously complex. War violates all the rules of humankind. Killing during peacetime is murder. Killing during war is heroic. During peacetime, helping a small child who is lost is a natural response for most of us. During war, approaching that child may cost you your life. Making the psychological transition to becoming a warrior is no simple task. Characteristics specific to the Vietnam war created even more difficulty for the men and women who served their country in the armed forces during the Vietnam era. Unlike war efforts in World War I and World War II, when we identified a clear enemy and the entire population banded together to fight for the cause, tremendous ambivalence surrounded the Vietnam war. Citizens protested and the government vacillated endlessly. In fact, the U.S. never really declared war on Vietnam.

But there was no ambivalence among the North Vietnamese fighting American soldiers. From the North Vietnamese perspective, the enemy was clear. Their country was being invaded, their families killed. They were defending their homeland. Civilians fought this war. Children carried grenades into army camps. Attacks by young women and old men were as likely as attacks by the military.

Young Americans (the typical age was 18) arrived in Vietnam, fresh out of basic training, ready to fight hard in the name of their country. But they found themselves fighting a war that was not confined to battlefields, a war where land was not conquered but disputed time and again, a war where they came face to face with the enemy, and the enemy was sometimes 9 years old. Day after day they witnessed friends killed. And the news from home was that their peers despised everything about the war, including them.

Veterans of World War I and World War II returned home to parades, celebrations, and the open arms of welcoming citizens. Their tales of adventure were listened to with great admiration. Vietnam veterans returned home to protest marches. Sometimes demonstrations were held at the camps where soldiers were returning. Crowds chanted antiwar slogans and yelled "baby killers" to returning soldiers, some of whom felt that they had become just that. No one wanted to talk about what it was like. Within this context, it comes as no surprise that the psychological trauma was enormous.

Post-traumatic stress disorder (PTSD) is a delayed stress reaction that recurs repeatedly, long after the traumatic event has passed. In PTSD, the precipitating event is something that would cause severe distress in virtually anyone at the time it happens. It can follow any number of traumatic events including war, natural disasters, rape, torture, and even motor vehicle accidents. PTSD is characterized by a persistent re-experiencing of the event through intrusive thoughts and nightmares. Sometimes, flashbacks occur that can be so vivid the person loses touch with reality and believes that he or she is actually in the original situation again.

Other symptoms of PTSD include difficulty concentrating,

I think about this for a second and then say to myself, "That's ridiculous. I didn't hit anybody." Nonetheless, a gnawing anxiety is born. An anxiety I will ultimately not be able to put away until an enormous price has been paid. . . .

The pain is a terrible guilt that I have committed an unthinkable, negligent act. At one level, I know this is ridiculous, but there's a terrible pain in my stomach telling me something quite different. . . . I start ruminating, "Maybe I did hit someone and didn't realize it. . . . Oh my God! I might have killed somebody! I have to go back and check. . . ." I've driven five miles farther down the road since the attack's onset. I turn the car around and head back to the scene of the mythical mishap. (Rapoport, 1989, pp. 21–22)

This case illustrates well the sense of uncontrollability of obsessive-compulsive disorders that persists in spite of the tortuous realization that the thoughts and behaviors are irrational. Recent advances in treatment for OCD are discussed in Chapter 16.

hypervigilance (i.e., being hyper-attentive, jumpy), sleeplessness, flashes of anger alternating with emotional numbness, and feelings of detachment from friends and loved ones. Victims of PTSD try to avoid situations that remind them of the original event. The sound of gunfire or even Fourth of July celebrations may be very difficult for a Vietnam veteran with PTSD. A common concomitant to PTSD is drug or alcohol abuse, to dull or escape from the horrifying memories.

Why does PTSD develop, especially long after the person has returned to safety? The clinical symptoms of PTSD are described as a conditioned response to an originally life-threatening event (Keane, Zimering, & Caddell, 1985). Mower's two-factor learning theory (1947, 1960) can be used to explain the etiology of the disorder. According to two-factor theory, psychopathology is a function of both respondent and operant conditioning.

Recall Pavlov's dogs from Chapter 8. Dogs salivate (the unconditioned response) in the presence of food (the unconditioned stimulus). If the presentation of food is repeatedly paired with a new stimulus (the conditioned stimulus; in Pavlov's case, a bell) the dog will come to salivate in the presence of the new stimulus as well (the conditioned response; i.e., the response that would not have occurred prior to conditioning). This is called *classical conditioning*. It is the first factor in Mower's two-factor theory. The second factor is *operant conditioning*. Recall that operant behaviors are behaviors that increase or decrease in frequency depending on their consequences. In psychopathology, escape behavior is often reinforced by the consequence of removing oneself from the feared stimulus. If the organism escapes once, escape behavior is more likely the next time and the next, and so on.

Conditioning can be weak or strong depending on the circumstances surrounding it. If just prior to receiving a powerful unconditioned shock, an organism is exposed to a constellation of potent stimuli, the conditioning is stronger and persists for a longer period of time (Stampfl & Levis, 1967). And, after one stimulus is strongly conditioned, *it* can be paired with other stimuli, making them conditioned stimuli also. Eventually, through the process of *higher order conditioning*, a complex network of conditioned stimuli develops. Keane et al. argue that the traumatic events experienced by Vietnam veterans were conditioned to multiple stimuli, sights, sounds, smells, even the time of day. The affected individual may go for a long period of time and not flash back to the event, but if a complex assortment of conditioned stimuli are presented together, the individual can experience a severe episode of anxiety remarkably similar to the way he or she felt when the event originally occurred.

In one extreme account, a Vietnam veteran attacked his own 9-year-old son. In Vietnam, he had witnessed a young boy throw a grenade into a truck carrying three of his best friends. The truck exploded, killing all inside. At the time, his own son was only a baby. One hot muggy afternoon, nine years later, he was playing baseball with his son. His son wound up his arm to throw the ball to his father and suddenly the boy appeared to him as the young Vietnamese boy throwing a grenade. The conditions were all there—the heat and humidity, the age of the boy, the time of day, and even the position of the arm.

Based on this behavioral analysis, Keane and his colleagues have developed a very effective treatment based on imaginal flooding (Keane, Fairbank, Caddell, Zimering, & Bender, 1985). You will read more about flooding in Chapter 16.

SOMATOFORM DISORDERS

Somatoform disorders are those in which the individual complains of a physical ailment or pain for which there is no organic or physiological explanation. *DSM-III-R* classifies several kinds of somatoform disorders: somatization disorder, hypochondriasis, conversion disorder, and somatoform pain disorder. **Somatization disorder** is diagnosed when an individual presents with multiple physical complaints over a period of many years but appears to have no physical basis for the complaints. **Hypochondriasis** is similar to somatization disorder but differs in that the person believes he or she suffers from, or may contract, a particular disease. Hypochondriacs interpret heartbeat, perspiration, minor coughing, or even irregular bowel movements as symptoms of serious disease. The belief persists even in the face of medical evidence to the contrary. The "illness" may cause serious restrictions in social, work, and home activities. An important distinction between somatization disorders and feigning or malingering is intentionality. Persons with somatization disorders truly believe in their physical symptoms.

Persons suffering from hypochondriasis or somatization disorder are famous for "doctor shopping." They go to doctor after doctor with their list of symptoms and medical knowledge picked up from popular journals and previous physicians. They search for the doctor who can find the serious disease they know they have.

Conversion disorders are very rare and have become more so over the years. They refer to the loss of some physical function, again without medical basis. Commonly, conversion disorders involve paralysis of a limb, seizures, or blindness. In contrast to somatization disorder and hypochondriasis, a central feature of conversion disorder is a lack of concern about the impairment, referred to as *la belle indifférence*. **Somatoform pain disorder** refers to the experience of pain that is inconsistent with physical findings.

CAUSES OF SOMATOFORM DISORDERS

There is virtually no evidence that somatoform pain disorder or conversion disorder are genetically based. Rather, it is generally thought that these disorders allow the patient to avoid facing psychological problems by "converting" them into physical disorders. In many cultures, including our own, physical distress is more socially acceptable than psychological distress. Thus, by transforming psychological distress into physical symptoms, the individual avoids the internal (emotional) and external (social) consequences of mental distress. Somatization disorders can stem from early childhood learning. Overanxious parents, who pamper their children unduly when they are sick, may be unwittingly teaching their young that sickness is an effective way to gain love and attention. People who become hypochondriacs later in life (usually men in their 30s and women in their 40s) may do so in reaction to a sense that they have not made much of their lives. They may feel that they have not achieved what they wanted professionally or that they are dissatisfied with their marriage. Hypochondriasis is the maladaptive behavior they subconsciously "choose" over what they perceive to be a life full of wrong choices. Again, there is a gain: hypochondriacs gain attention from families, friends, and doctors. They are reinforced and sometimes encouraged to persist in their behavior. These individuals will not have to worry about disappointing people because they are too "sick" to live up to the expectations of others.

PERSONALITY DISORDERS

People with personality disorders perceive, relate to, and think about themselves and their environment in maladaptive ways. The symptoms are acted out in the world rather than simply in the mind of the person. The entire personality seems to be imbued with the disorder. People with personality disorders do not usually want treatment; they do not think anything is wrong, and often it is the people who live with them who do.

Here is one case:

> Charles Clay, aged 45, owned what had been a successful 24-hour-a-day grocery store. . . . Until 5 years ago he had been a cheerful, friendly merchant. Then his wife died, and his personality seemed to undergo a change. Increasingly he worried that people were trying to shoplift his merchandise. . . . As time went on, he began to confront customers with his suspicions and even to demand that some of them submit to a search.
>
> Mr. Clay's business began to decline. When this happened, he got very angry and even more suspicious. The culminating event was an attempt he made to search a woman who entered the store, walked around for a few minutes, and then bought a newspaper. When he tried to search her (at the same time yelling, "Don't tell me you were just looking around!"), she ran from the store and summoned the police. The police investigation led Mr. Clay to seek advice from his lawyer, who had been a friend since high school. Although Mr. Clay insisted that "there is nothing the matter with me," his anger and suspiciousness bothered the lawyer. With deft touches of tact and persuasion, the lawyer got Mr. Clay to agree to visit a psychiatrist. Unfortunately, the visit did not work out well. Mr. Clay was reluctant to talk about his concerns and was angered by what he thought of as the psychiatrist's inquisitiveness. . . . Several months later Mr. Clay was arrested and convicted of physically attacking another customer. (Sarason & Sarason, 1984)

TYPES OF PERSONALITY DISORDERS

Below is a list of major personality disorders and brief definitions from *DSM-III-R*. We will then focus on one of the most interesting disorders, the antisocial personality.

- *Paranoid.* Pervasive and unwarranted suspiciousness and mistrust of people, hypersensitivity.

- *Schizoid.* A defect in the capacity to form social relationships, evidenced by the absence of warm, tender feelings for others, indifference to praise, criticism, and the feelings of others.

- *Histrionic.* Overly dramatic, reactive, and intensely expressed behavior and characteristic disturbances in interpersonal relationships.

- *Narcissistic.* A grandiose sense of self-importance or uniqueness.

- *Borderline.* Instability in a variety of areas, including interpersonal behavior, mood, and self-image; no single feature is invariably present.

- *Avoidant.* Hypersensitivity to potential rejection, humiliation, or shame; an unwillingness to enter into relationships unless given unusually strong guarantees of uncritical acceptance.

- *Dependent.* The individual passively allows others to assume responsibility for major areas of his or her life because of a lack of self-confidence and an inability to function independently.

- *Compulsive.* Restricted ability to express warm and tender emotions; excessive devotion to work and productivity to the exclusion of pleasure; and indecisiveness (goodbye, I think).

515

- *Passive-Aggressive.* Resistance to demands for adequate performance in work and social functioning; the resistance is expressed indirectly rather than directly, and the result is pervasive and persistent social or occupational ineffectiveness.

- *Antisocial.* A history of continuous and chronic antisocial behavior in which the rights of others are violated.

CAUSES OF PERSONALITY DISORDERS

There is little information about why people develop personality disorders or why they develop the specific ones that they do. Because individuals with such disorders have little desire to change, treatment is rarely successful.

ANTISOCIAL BEHAVIOR: SOCIOPATHIC PERSONALITY

Suppose you saw this advertisement:

> Are you adventurous? Psychologists studying adventurous carefree people who've led exciting, impulsive lives. If you're the kind of person who'd do almost anything for a dare and want to participate in a paid experiment, send name, address, phone number and short biography proving how interesting you are.

This ad appeared in several newspapers in Boston. It attracted people who psychological tests later revealed fit the clinical picture of an **antisocial personality (ASP),** also called **psychopath** or **sociopath** (Widom, 1977). Most persons whose antisocial personalities have been studied by psychologists are institutionalized, usually in prisons or reformatories. Widom wanted to see if ASPs within society were similar to those institutionalized. They are. (One respondent determined the true purpose of the ad; he wrote: "Are you looking for hookers or are you trying to make a listing of all the sociopaths in Boston?")

The pattern of antisocial behavior usually begins before age 15. The individual is unable to feel either positive emotions or guilt. Such people also have superficial charm and average or above-average intelligence. They have little sense of responsibility about anything, big or small. They tell lies and have no guilt or regret about any antisocial actions.

A CASE OF AN ANTISOCIAL PERSONALITY Psychologist Elton McNeil described an antisocial personality (Dan F.) whom he knew not as a patient but as a friend.

> One night, a colleague of Dan's committed suicide. My phone started ringing early the next morning with the inevitable question, "Why?" The executives at the station called but Dan F. never did. When I did talk to him, he did not mention the suicide. Later, when I brought it to his attention, all he could say was that it was "the way the ball bounces." At the station, however, he was the one who collected money for the deceased and presented it personally to the new widow. As Dan observed, she was really built and had possibilities. . . .
>
> He was currently involved sexually with girls ranging from the station manager's secretary (calculated) to the weather girl (incidental, based on a shared interest in Chinese food). The females of the "show biz" species seemed

to dote on the high-handed treatment he accorded them. They regularly refused to believe he was "as bad as he pretended to be," and he was always surrounded by intense and glamorous women who needed to own him to feel complete as human beings.

Dan F. had charm plus. He always seemed to know when to say the right thing with exactly the proper degree of concern, seriousness, and understanding for the benighted victim of a harsh world. *But, he was dead inside* [italics added]. People amused him and he watched them with the kind of interest most of us show when examining a tank of guppies. Once, on a whim, he called each of the burlesque theaters in town and left word with the burlesque queens that he was holding a party beginning at midnight with each of them as an honored guest. He indeed held the party, charging it to the station as a talent search, and spent the evening pouring liquor into the girls. By about 3 a.m. the hotel suite was a shambles, but he thought it was hilarious. He had invited the camera and floor crew from the television station and had carefully constructed a fictional identity for each: one was an independent film producer, another a casting director, a third an influential writer, and still another, a talent agent. This giant hoax was easy to get away with since Dan had read correctly and with painful accuracy the not so secret dreams, ambitions, drives, and personal needs of these entertainers. What was staggering was the elaborateness of the cruel joke. He worked incessantly, adding a touch here and a touch there to make it perfect. (McNeil, 1967)

PSYCHOSOCIAL FACTORS   Three percent of American men and less than 1 percent of American women have ASP disorder. The psychosocial factors thought to be important are extreme poverty and poor education, and poor family background; if the father suffers from the disorder the child is often removed from the home and may get little discipline.

BIOLOGICAL FACTORS   Dan F., the antisocial personality just discussed, describes his own situation:

> I can remember the first time in my life when I began to suspect I was a little different from most people. When I was in high school my best friend got leukemia and died and I went to his funeral. Everybody else was crying and feeling sorry for themselves and as they were praying to get him into heaven I suddenly realized that I wasn't feeling anything at all. He was a nice guy but what the hell. That night I thought about it more and found out that I wouldn't miss my mother and father if they died and that I wasn't too nuts about my brothers and sisters, for that matter. I figured there wasn't anybody I really cared for but, then, I didn't need any of them anyway so I rolled over and went to sleep. (McNeil, 1967)

The antisocial personality has *decreased emotional response*, especially to unpleasant stimuli. In studies measuring autonomic system reactions, ASPs have less activation to shock (Wilson & Herrnstein, 1985). When a child is punished or slapped for doing the wrong thing, it activates a feeling of hurt and guilt and makes it less likely that the child will repeat the action. People with "flat" emotions would not feel the hurt and would be less likely to learn law-abiding behavior. Thus, one characteristic of these people is extreme calm, perhaps due to the underarousal. These people constantly search for excitement. They attack others verbally or set up wild scenes, such as Dan F.'s burlesque queen party. This may be due to a characteristic underarousal and the need for extreme stimulation.

GENETIC FACTORS   There is evidence for genetic factors contributing to the antisocial personality. Children of criminal fathers have less reactive autonomic nervous system response than do children of noncriminals. In a very large study, Wadsworth noted the pulse rate of 11-year-old boys just before a mild stress. He compared these to later pulse rates and records of delinquency. Those with low increases in pulse rate were much more likely to become delinquent (Mednick, 1977). Biological relatives of adopted criminals show a higher rate of criminality and antisocial behavior than does the general population (Wilson & Herrnstein, 1985). In studies of the antisocial personality, the same relationship holds: the transmission is significant from the biological father (Schulsinger, 1972). What might be inherited, then, is an autonomic nervous system that is less responsive to stimulation. In the appropriate situation this could lead to some deficiencies in learning law-abiding behavior, to less responsiveness to others' feelings, and to the need to create excitement. These are all characteristic of the antisocial personality.

SUBSTANCE USE DISORDERS

Many people believe that humans have an innate desire to experience altered states of consciousness. The use of mood- or consciousness-altering drugs is common to every culture. Alcohol is the most common recreational drug in our society. The use of illegal drugs such as marijuana and heroin have been widespread in certain subcultures of American society for many years. Cocaine began to rise in popularity among the middle and upper classes in the early 1970s; crack, a cheaper form of cocaine, now heads the list of illegal drugs used by the poor.

Substance use disorder means that there is a consistent pattern of excessive use resulting in impairment of social or occupational functioning. Disordered individuals are dependent on the drug (substance), and they may not be able to get through the day without it, nor can they stop or restrict their use even if they know that they should. Sometimes addictions can develop without the user's awareness; a good example is caffeine intoxication:

> A 35-year-old secretary sought consultation for "anxiety attacks." A thorough history revealed that the attacks occurred in the mid-to-late afternoon, when she became restless, nervous, and easily excited and sometimes was noted to be flushed, sweating, and, according to co-workers, "talking a mile a minute." In response to careful questioning, she acknowledged drinking five or six cups of coffee each day before the usual time the attacks occurred. (Spitzer et al., 1981)

The patient must experience a disturbance in behavior for at least one month before the *DSM-III* will classify him or her as having a drug disorder. There are two forms of substance use disorders: dependence and abuse. **Dependence** is more severe: the drug-dependent person begins to show increased tolerance. He or she thus requires greater amounts of the drug over time and experiences specific physiological symptoms if the drug is withdrawn. **Abuse** refers to drug use that interferes with the person's ability to function but does not involve physical addiction.

There are five categories of substances that may invite abuse or dependence: **alcohol**; barbiturates or other **sedatives**; **analgesics**, such as painkillers or narcotics, which include heroin; **stimulants**, such as amphetamines; and **psychoactive drugs** such as marijuana and LSD.

INCIDENCE OF SUBSTANCE USE DISORDERS

About 16 percent of Americans report alcohol-related problems. More men than women have a substance use disorder with alcohol. Abuse and dependence do not usually appear until adulthood. Alcoholic disorder usually appears between the ages of 20 and 50, whereas problems with marijuana, cocaine, heroin, and other narcotics start earlier, in late teens and early 20s. Substance abuse and dependence may lead to physical problems such as malnutrition or hepatitis.

Although addictions to illegal drugs receive the most media attention, the legal drugs—alcohol, tobacco, and caffeine—affect more people's lives. One in every 10 people who try alcohol becomes addicted to it. Half of all highway deaths in America involve either a driver or pedestrian who was drinking. About one-fourth of all suicides and more than one-half of all murderers *and* their victims were drunk at the time of the death. Cigarettes are highly addicting. Nine out of every 10 people who try cigarettes become addicted; in many, this addiction will lead ultimately to death. Contrasted with cigarettes, the health consequences of caffeine are less dire. However, habitual use of caffeine is our most common addiction (Davison & Neale, 1986).

CAUSES OF SUBSTANCE USE DISORDER

The use of a drug may begin for recreational purposes or to alleviate fear and anxiety in social settings. Lessening anxiety is the reinforcer that maintains the abuse. The factors that contribute to the abuse of different drugs vary. Alcoholism often runs in families, and there is some evidence for a genetic predisposition to the disorder.

Alcoholism provides a useful example of the interplay between biology and environmental factors in the development of psychopathology. If your parents were alcoholics, the substance very likely dampens your physiological reactions to stress more than a person whose parents were not alcoholic—that is, alcohol works *better* as a stress reducer to those who are physiologically more sensitive to it (Levenson, Oyama, & Meek, 1988). This predisposition may play a critical role in the development of alcohol dependence, but *no one* becomes alcoholic without drinking. In other words, however important genetics are in the development of addictions, they do not, in and of themselves, *cause* them. The important factors seem to be psychosocial and involve stress and tension reduction.

In narcotic addiction there is some evidence of neurological causes. Recall that the brain produces its own painkillers and mood modulators called **endorphins.** Specific endorphins fit, as a key does into a lock, specific receptors in the brain, especially in the limbic system. Morphine (of which heroin is a derivative) fits these locks as well. Some researchers hypothesize that morphine addiction may occur in people whose brains produce too few natural endorphins (Coleman et al., 1980).

Sociocultural factors seem to be important in narcotic addiction. In the United States, heroin addiction is more common in lower socioeconomic groups. Fortunately, heroin addiction is often short-lived; this is not true of alcohol or the other narcotics. But the death rate among heroin users is high, due in large part to impurities and continual injections without proper hygiene. If a person survives, dependence rarely lasts more than nine years.

Cocaine has a different neurological action. A chemical found in the brain called **dopamine** plays a central role in the experience of extreme pleasure, euphoria. It is normally released when triggered by an external stimulus; gradually, it is reabsorbed by the same neuron. Cocaine blocks the reabsorption of dopamine. Subsequently, the experience of euphoria becomes more intense and lasts until the brain's supply of dopamine is exhausted (about 30 minutes). Once depleted of dopamine, the euphoria quickly spirals down into a deep depression, described as the "crash" of cocaine. Crack, the common form of cocaine, is highly addicting: one out of every six people who try the drug becomes addicted (see box on facing page).

NARCOTICS (OPIATES)

Opium is harvested from a poppy plant native to the Near East and has been a frequently used drug in those regions for at least 5,000 years. Opium and its derivatives are used medically as painkillers and recreationally to induce euphoria and dreamlike reveries. The two active agents in opium are morphine and codeine. Heroin was first synthesized in 1874 and marketed by Bayer Laboratories in 1898 as a nonaddicting substitute for codeine. Heroin is in fact three times as potent as morphine and just as addictive.

In the 1970s, scientists discovered opiate receptors in the central nervous system. This led to the conclusion that the body itself must produce its own opiatelike substances to interact with these receptors. Two separate systems have since been identified: the endorphin and enkephalin systems. Both of these are involved in the perception of pain. The pleasure-inducing effects of opiates are probably due to opiate receptors in the limbic system of the brain, which is responsible for much of our experience of mood and pleasure.

Opium use became quite popular in nineteenth-century England and is reflected in the literature of the time. In "Confessions of an English Opium Eater," Thomas DeQuincy (1821) described his first opium experience (taken for a toothache):

> I took it: and in an hour, O heavens! . . . what a resurrection, from its lowest depths of the human spirit! what an apocalypse of the world within me! That my pains had vanished was now a trifle in my eyes; this negative effect was swallowed up in the immensity of those positive effects which had opened up before me, in the abyss of divine enjoyment thus suddenly revealed. Here was a panacea . . . for all human woes; here was the secret of happiness, about which philosophers had disputed for so many ages, at once discovered; happiness might now be bought for a penny, and carried in the waistcoat-pocket; portable ecstasies might be had corked up in a pint-bottle, and peace of mind could be sent down by mail.

Due to set and setting, the typical heroin user of today has quite a different experience from the English writers of the nineteenth century. The experience

Crack—a relatively cheap, smokable form of cocaine—has become a major problem among youth in the United States. More addicting than alcohol, crack produces an instant state of euphoria. The immediate high lasts for only a short period of time, however, and is followed by serious depression. The depth of the depression coupled with the memory of the high encourages the user to search out the drug once again. Addiction to crack results in a craving for the drug to the exclusion of everything else that was once important, even food and sleep.

A new crystallized form of cocaine called "ice" is making it's way east from Asia via the West Coast and Hawaii. Ice may be even more dangerous than its predecessors because the euphoric state it

CRACK

produces lasts for as long as 12 hours.

How does a doctor cure addiction to a drug that stimulates the pleasure centers of the brain and from which withdrawal causes severe depression? Researchers are rising to the ominous challenge. New hope has come from experimental findings with a new drug called Flupenthixol, which acts as a cocaine blocker and helps to subdue addicts' cravings for crack. Antidepressants may also be use-

ful in easing the addict off the drug.

Still, unless and until the social environments of addicts change, we can expect the relapse rate to be high. We know from the treatment of other addictions, like heroin, that when an individual's life is filled with reminders (conditioned stimuli) of the drug, maintenance of drug abstinence is far less likely. An article in the *New York Times* described a young man who had been recently released from prison for dealing crack. While in prison he quit using the drug (even though it was available), but when he returned to his West Harlem home he quickly resumed dealing and using. He told the reporter that all of his friends were crack addicts and it was the best way he knew to make money (Kolata, 1989).

sought by the heroin user is the initial rush following injection—a sensation of overflowing warmth and pleasure—followed by several hours of warm, carefree, well-being. As tolerance to the drug develops, however, the user must obtain larger and larger doses to duplicate the intensity of his first rush. Eventually, an addict will find that he or she needs heroin just to feel alright and will no longer derive pleasure from it.

Withdrawal from narcotics is an unpleasant experience, but not deadly. It begins with anxiety and a craving for a fix of the drug. Soon the addict will get goose bumps, twitch, feel hot and cold flashes, generally ache and lose appetite. Still later the person will experience insomnia, fever, restlessness, vomiting, and diarrhea. The process takes four or five days. This, of course, is the "cold turkey" (so-called because of the goose-bumps) method. The more humane way to bring an addict off of heroin is to decrease dosage over time.

DEPRESSANTS

Depressants lower activity in the brain, thereby reducing physical and cognitive activity. Different doses of the same drug can be used in different ways: low doses as *tranquilizers*, which decrease excitability and anxiety; medium doses as *hypnotics*, to induce sleep; and high doses as *anesthetics*, rendering the user unconscious.

All depressants are physiologically addicting and have severe withdrawal symptoms that can lead to death. When combined, depressants can have a *synergistic* effect, meaning that the effect of two drugs together is greater than double that of one alone. Depressants can be quite dangerous because, by slowing down mental processes, they not only impair ability to make reasonable judgements but also impair motor coordination and reflexes. A person sedated by barbiturates or alcohol may lose his ability to judge whether or not he should drive.

ALCOHOL The most commonly used depressant in our culture is the drinkable intoxicant on most Americans' shelves called ethanol. It is produced by the action of certain yeasts on the sugars of a wide variety of grains and fruits (fermentation). The popularity of alcohol is well demonstrated by the innumerable types of alcoholic beverage available in the world today.

Alcohol is the biggest drug problem in the Western world today. Though we hear much in the media about the dangers of cocaine, the few hundred deaths that will result from cocaine use this year can hardly compare to the over 200,000 alcohol-related deaths that will also occur. Alcohol is this nation's third largest health problem.

Alcohol affects neuronal membranes, disrupting the ability of the neuron to fire and transmit normally. The lowest effective dose of alcohol disrupts the functioning of the reticular activating system, causing diminished cortical functioning. The result can be disinhibited behavior and the feeling of being excited or stimulated. The early intoxication, characterized by loss of normal behavioral inhibitions, is the reason why alcohol is enjoyed at parties. The loss of social inhibitions makes people more convivial and carefree (and, for some, more aggressive or amorous).

Higher doses directly affect the cortex, slowing down all of the drinker's brain processes. The greater doses increasingly impair the drinker's reaction time, motor coordination, thinking, and judgment. Eventually, the drinker becomes unresponsive to the world, then unconscious. Finally, at a dose only slightly higher than that causing unconsciousness, alcohol poisoning can result in death, usually caused by respiratory failure.

Alcohol affects memory. An intoxicated person has difficulty processing and retaining new information—thus the experience of not remembering the night before. In the long term, heavy drinking can lead to intellectual impairment.

Withdrawal from alcohol is dangerous. Untreated advanced alcoholics run a one-in-seven risk of dying from alcohol withdrawal (called *delirium tremens* by doctors and "the DTs" on the street) if they stop drinking all at once (Ray, 1983). The experience of delirium tremens includes muscular tremors, rapid heartbeat, sweating, loss of appetite, insomnia, hallucinations, delirium, and seizures (Alcohol and Health Notes, 1973).

BARBITURATES **Barbiturates** were first synthesized around the beginning of the twentieth century. Clinically, they are used to treat anxiety and insomnia and as anesthetics. Recently, safer forms of tranquilizers are replacing barbiturates as prescriptions for anxiety and sleep difficulties. The danger of barbiturates lies in the small difference between an effective and a lethal dose. Also, tolerance develops rapidly to barbiturates, decreasing the difference between the dose that helps and the dose that kills.

The psychological effects of barbiturates are similar to those of alcohol. An expert on drug abuse described the apparent advantages of using barbiturates to get high as follows:

For the youngster barbiturates are a more reliable "high" and less detectable than "pot." They are less strenuous than LSD, less "freaky" than amphetamines, and less expensive than heroin. A school boy can "drop a red" and spend the day in a dreamy floating state of awayness untroubled by reality. It is drunkenness without the odor of alcohol. It is escape for the price of one's lunch money. (Cohen, 1971)

STIMULANTS

CAFFEINE   Caffeine use dates back to the time when tea drinking first began in China. **Caffeine** is the stimulant found in tea, coffee, and chocolate. Coffee tends to contain more caffeine than tea, and chocolate only contains a little. Caffeine is also frequently added to soft drinks.

Caffeine stimulates the brain by blocking the functioning of a natural inhibitor, *adenosine*, which normally acts to inhibit the release of neurotransmitters. Some research also indicates that caffeine causes the release of *norepinephrine*, which causes arousal and activation (Ray, 1983). Tolerance can develop to caffeine, but it is minimal. Withdrawal from caffeine can lead to headaches.

Most people drink coffee when they are tired or sleepy, and caffeine does seem to counter the detrimental effects of fatigue on performance. It also increases the capacity to focus and persist with boring tasks (Ray, 1983). If we did not consider coffee such a mundane drink, perhaps we would experience its effects more as it is described by the French writer, Balzac:

[It] causes an admirable fever. It enters the brain like a bacchante. Upon its attack, imagination runs wild, bares itself, twists like a pytoness, and in this paroxysm a poet enjoys the supreme possession of his faculties, but this is a drunkenness of thought as wine brings about a drunkenness of the body. (quoted in Mickel, 1969)

NICOTINE   **Nicotine** is a highly toxic, extremely addicting substance. The active ingredient of tobacco, a plant native to the Americas, nicotine was used by the American Indians to induce mystical, trancelike states in special ceremonies. The health risks of tobacco use are well-known. If it weren't for the great difficulty in breaking the nicotine habit, and the indefatigability of the advertising campaigns of the tobacco companies, surely very few people would persist in smoking in the face of the findings of modern medicine.

Nicotine mimics the *acetylcholine* molecule and has a very strong affinity for acetylcholine receptors. Initially, nicotine molecules, by attaching to these receptors, stimulate the neurons to fire. After doing so, however, they continue to occupy the receptors and prevent any other molecules from again stimulating the neurons. Thus, nicotine first excites and then depresses functions dependent on acetylcholine activity.

Studies with monkeys show that they will work very hard to earn a dose of nicotine (Goldberg et al., 1981), so the effects must be rewarding. In addition, people are highly motivated to continue to smoke to avoid the unpleasantness of nicotine withdrawal. Some common symptoms of withdrawal are depression, irritability, anxiety, tension, restlessness, drowsiness, and an inability to concentrate.

AMPHETAMINES **Amphetamines** are synthetic central nervous system stimulants. They are medically prescribed for narcolepsy, weight loss, and to keep soldiers on their feet. There are three commonly used members of the amphetamine family: benzedrine, dexedrine, and methedrine. *Methedrine* is the street drug referred to as "meth" or "crystal." The term *speed* is used to refer to any amphetamine.

Amphetamines increase the activity of the reticular activating system by increasing brain level of *norepinephrine* and sometimes *dopamine*. The reticular activating system in turn increases the activity of the cerebral cortex. Amphetamines, especially methedrine, also strongly stimulate the reward centers of the brain, causing the euphoria (Ray, 1983).

People use amphetamines to become more alert, to feel less sleepy, and to feel good. Speed users may be excessively talkative or extraordinarily active. Large doses of amphetamine, ingested by snorting or injection, cause a euphoric rush, which has been described as a "full body orgasm" (followed later by a depressed mood).

Amphetamine taking became a craze amongst the youngsters in England in the early 1960s who called themselves "Mods." One described the following incident:

> This friend of mine was very blocked up, talking away like crazy. We were in a flat on the second floor and he was sitting out on the balcony railings facing in, talking to us. He was so involved in conversation that he forgot where he was, leaned over backwards and fell off the balcony. We all rushed downstairs and when we got to him he was still talking away like mad. He didn't realize he'd fallen off the balcony. (Barnes, 1979)

Heavy amphetamine use can lead to a psychotic state much like paranoid schizophrenia, characterized by auditory and visual hallucinations and often by the feeling of being pursued or persecuted by some agency, such as the CIA. Even short-term use of speed can cause odd, compulsive behavior, such as repeatedly cleaning your room, or counting cornflakes.

MOOD DISORDERS

Mood disorders afflict 5–8 percent of all people at some time in their lives. Of these people, 6 percent of the women and 3 percent of the men have an episode serious enough to require hospitalization.

DEPRESSION

Depression has been referred to as the "common cold of psychological disorders" (Rosenhan & Seligman, 1985). We often use the word *depressed* to mean sad, upset, or in a bad mood. "I'm depressed—the store is out of chocolate chip cookies, and I was thinking about them all day." The clinical syndrome of **depression** is much more than a down mood. It is a severe mental disorder that results in an overwhelming sadness that immobilizes and arrests the entire course of a person's. Here is a case of a college student suffering from severe depression:

Nancy entered the university with a superb high-school record. She had been president and salutatorian of her class, and a popular and pretty cheerleader. Everything she wanted had always fallen into her lap; good grades came easily and boys fell over themselves competing for her attentions. She was an only child, and her parents doted on her, rushing to fulfill her every whim; her successes were their triumphs, her failures their agony. Her friends nicknamed her Golden Girl.

When I met her in her sophomore year, she was no longer a Golden Girl. She said that she felt empty, that nothing touched her any more; her classes were boring and the whole academic system seemed an oppressive conspiracy to stifle her creativity. The previous semester she had received two F's. She had "made it" with a succession of young men, and was currently living with a dropout. She felt exploited and worthless after each sexual adventure; her current relationship was on the rocks, and she felt little but contempt for him and for herself. She had used soft drugs extensively and had once enjoyed being carried away on them. But now even drugs had lost their appeal.

She was majoring in philosophy, and had a marked emotional attraction to Existentialism: like the existentialists, she believed that life is absurd and that people must create their own meaning. This belief filled her with despair. Her despair increased when she perceived her own attempts to create meaning— participation in the movements for women's liberation and against the war in Vietnam—as fruitless. When I reminded her that she had been a talented student and was still an attractive and valuable human being, she burst into tears: "I fooled you, too." (Seligman, 1975)

Depression is classified in *DSM-III-R* as a **mood disorder.** There are two categories of severe depressive disorders. In **unipolar depression** an individual suffers only from depression, whereas in **bipolar depression** a person suffers from depression as well as the opposite emotion of **mania,** which is excessive elation. An individual in a manic episode is in a frenzy of overexcitability and activity; the happiness is as out of control as the sadness (see page 527). A severely depressed or manic person may need to be hospitalized. All of the

GENDER DIFFERENCES IN DEPRESSION

Unipolar affective disorder, more commonly referred to as depression, is much more common in women than in men. A conservative estimate of the sex ratio is 2:1. This is true whether we compare the numbers of men and women treated for clinical depression (Pederson, Barry, & Babigian, 1972) or the frequency of self-reported depressive symptoms in community dwelling populations (Meyers et al, 1984). Most researchers agree that differences in rates of depression reflect true differences, not artifacts related to reporting biases or other extraneous factors (Weissman & Klerman, 1977). Why would a disorder (which is characterized by sadness, loss of pleasure, poor self-esteem, and somatic complaints such as sleep difficulty and fatigue) show differential prevalence rates for the sexes?

Some researchers argue that biological differences between the sexes account for differences in prevalence rates of depression. Although some contend that susceptibility to depression is transmitted genetically via sex-linked chromosomes, the argument that hormonal fluctuations associated with the menstrual cycle make women vulnerable to depression is more popular. Proponents of this hormonal explanation argue that depressed mood is more common during premenstrual, postpartum, and menopausal periods.

However research on women during each of these periods provides only limited support for the widespread beliefs that women are depressed during times of hormonal fluctuation. Although women are more likely to be depressed after the birth of a child, most of the women who are depressed were also depressed before the

BEING FEMALE

BEING MALE

child was born (Atkinson & Rickel, 1984). Research on menopause suggests that, if anything, depressive symptoms become lesser during the climacteric (Frieze, Parsons, Johnson, Ruble, & Zellman, 1978).

Learning theorists often view gender roles as the underlying reason for higher rates of depression in women. Women, for example, may be reinforced for dependent, passive behavior more than men and therefore display these behaviors more frequently than men. In our society, it is also customary for women to defer to men regarding decisions about careers, where the family lives, and even minor day-to-day choices (Hyde, 1985). Thus, gender roles may inherently predispose women to hold beliefs that they have little control over the world around them and may, therefore, become helpless. *Learned helplessness* is a powerful predictor of clinical depression (Seligman, 1975).

Women's traditional role in society does not place them at risk

for all psychological disorders, however. On the contrary, men suffer disproportionately higher rates than women of alcohol and drug abuse, hyperactivity, and antisocial personality disorder. Thus, we would be hard-pressed to make the case that women suffer more than men, but it does appear that women respond differently to despair.

Susan Nolen-Hoeksema(1987) believes that differences in the way that males and females each respond to their own depressed states are at the core of differential rates of depression. She argues that most of us experience transient depressive symptoms some of the time, however, the way that we *respond* to these feelings is actually the cause of the depression. Nolen-Hoeksema contends that males typically cope with initial depressive experiences by engaging in activities that distract them from their mood. Women, in contrast, focus on the mood itself and, in doing so, often amplify it.

In the case of psychopathology, understanding gender differences may lead to better understanding and treatment for males and females. Nolen-Hoeksema's model is appealing because unlike other models that are largely unchangeable, hers points directly to strategies for intervention. If males and females do indeed respond differently to distress—and as a result show different rates of various disorders—both sexes have something to learn from the other. Distraction may help to insulate a person from depression, but used excessively may place him or her at risk for other psychopathology. Similarly, focusing on feelings may be very useful at times but in excess may lead to clinical depression.

mood disorders involve either mania or depression or both. Here we will describe the essential characteristics of both, and in the following subsections begin to examine the causes of the disorder. Before a clinician would diagnose a person as depressed, at least four of the following symptoms have to be present *every day* for *two weeks:*

1. *Loss of interest and pleasure.* This is almost universal. The individual is indifferent to the activities that usually provide interest and pleasure. This loss of interest extends to friends and family. The depressed person often withdraws from people and activities.

2. *Appetite disturbance.* The most common appetite disturbance is loss, although some people experience an increase in appetite, causing a significant change in the person's normal weight. A fairly accurate description of a depressed person is that he or she is "wasting away." One sign that a person is pulling out of a depressive episode is weight gain.

3. *Sleep disturbance.* The most common sleep disturbance is insomnia, although sometimes there is the opposite, hypersomnia.

4. *Psychomotor disturbance.* Those afflicted may be agitated and cannot sit still; they pull their hair, pace up and down the floor, and wring their hands. They may be retarded, with slower and monotonous speech. They move slowly as if carrying a heavy weight.

5. *Decrease in energy level.* A virtually universal trait. People feel tired consistently, although they have slept or done nothing physically taxing. The prospect of having to do even the smallest task is overwhelming.

6. *Sense of worthlessness.* The degree of worthlessness varies from general feelings of inadequacy and negative self-evaluations to feelings of delusional proportion.

7. *Difficulty in concentrating.* Thinking is slower. The depressed person has trouble making decisions and often complains of memory disturbances. They are easily distracted.

8. *Thoughts about death.* A depressed person often seems preoccupied with death. They may be afraid of it, wish for it, or plan or attempt suicide.

9. *Miscellaneous associated symptoms.* Other features that depressed persons may experience are anxiety, phobias, overconcern with health, tearfulness, and irritability.

MANIC EPISODES

The attributes of **mania** are the mirror image of depression. *DSM-III-R* characterizes the mood as predominantly elevated, expansive, or irritable. Patients often experience elevated moods as pure euphoria, and those who know manics will recognize that the euphoria is a bit excessive. Their friends are "not themselves." The happiness has no specific cause and is not under the person's control.

The manic person has unbounded enthusiasm for everyone and everything. The two qualities of euphoria and expansiveness, if not too extreme, are

Almost everyone experiences mood change in the presence or absence of sunlight. On bright, sunny days we feel better, perhaps more energetic and "sunny." On dull, gray days, we may feel moody, blue, and out of sorts. For some light-sensitive people, changes in light exposure can generate mood swings.

Mr. P., a sixty-three year old scientist started experiencing unexplained depressive episodes at thirty-five. After many years, he began to notice a pattern: toward the end of June he would begin to become depressed. He would feel anxious, reluctant to go to work, and fearful of interacting with others. He had difficulty developing new ideas, and his sexual energy declined. He slept fitfully and became reluctant to get out of bed.

Mr. P. remained depressed until about the end of January when he would switch dramatically into a hypomanic state. His energy level surged and he required less sleep, sometimes as little as two to three hours per night. He had taken without success a variety of antidepressant medications.

Mr. P. suffers from seasonal affective disorder (SAD). This newly identified disorder is common. Symptoms begin in the teens and twenties. The symptoms appear directly related to the amount of sunlight which reaches the brain. For people in the Northern Hemisphere the depressive symptoms usually start between September and October and last into March. One patient living in Chile experienced her depressive episodes between June and September, which are the winter months in the Southern Hemisphere. (Rosenthal, 1984)

Norman Rosenthal and his colleagues at the National Institutes of Health have developed a novel approach to treating such patients. Reasoning that the symptoms were due to an extreme reaction of the brain to light deprivation, they prescribed "light therapy." Patients sit directly in front of a bright, full-spectrum fluorescent light source for three hours before dawn and three hours after dusk. A control group sat an equal amount of time in front of a dim yellow light. The high-intensity light treatment dramatically lessened depression, as does diet (Rosenthal et al., 1984; Rosenthal, 1986).

infectious. They enable some manics to be very effective manipulators, as in the following example:

> You look like a couple of bright, alert, hard working, clean-cut, energetic, go-getters and I could use you in my organization! I need guys that are loyal and enthusiastic about the great opportunities life offers on this planet! It's yours for the taking! Too many people pass opportunity by without hearing it knock because they don't know how to grasp the moment and strike while the iron is hot! You've got to grab it when it comes up for air, pick up the ball and run! You've got to be decisive! decisive! decisive! No shilly-shallying! Sweat! Yeah, sweat with a goal! Push, push, push, and you can push over a mountain! Two mountains, maybe. It's not luck! Hell, if it wasn't for bad luck I wouldn't have any luck at all! Be there firstest with the mostest! My guts and your blood! That's the system! I know, you know, he, she, or it knows it's the only way to travel! Get'em off balance, baby, and the rest is leverage! Use your head and save your heels! What's this deal? Who are these guys? Have you got a telephone and a secretary I could have instanter if not sooner? What I need is office space and the old LDO [long-distance operator]. (McNeil, 1967)

INCIDENCE OF MOOD DISORDERS

Bipolar disorder (depression with both depressive and manic periods) is experienced by 0.4 to 1.2 percent of the population. Women are more likely than men to suffer from *unipolar disorder* (depression only). However, there is no sex difference in the bipolar form. A major depression can occur at any age. A person with the bipolar form of the disorder often experiences his or her manic episode before the age of 30. The average age of onset for bipolar is 28 and for unipolar, 36.

CAUSES OF MOOD DISORDERS

The causal factors of both unipolar and bipolar disorder can be divided into two global categories, endogenous and exogenous. **Endogenous** (or within) factors include genetic predisposition and biochemical components; whereas **exogenous** (or without) factors include undue stress, a precipitating event, and psychosocial factors such as helplessness, personality predispositions, and sociocultural factors. In some ways, differentiating exogenous and endogenous factors is misleading because in reality (with the exception of genes) both factors interact with one another to cause depression. That is, an external event such as the death of a loved one can elicit biochemical changes in the brain, and, alternatively, a biochemical change in the brain can color one's perception of the world.

ENDOGENOUS FACTORS   Twin studies provide strong evidence that both unipolar and bipolar forms of the disorder have a genetic component. There is an extremely high concordance rate in identical twins. In bipolar disorder the concordance rate for identical twins is 72 percent, but for fraternal twins, 14 percent; in unipolar disorder, the rate is 40 percent for identical twins but only 11 percent for fraternal twins (Kessler, 1980). This finding is particularly interesting because the bipolar form of the disorder is rarer than the unipolar.

There is probably more of a predisposing genetic factor in bipolar than unipolar depression. Studies of families of bipolar depressives reveal that 11 percent of close relatives also had experienced bipolar depression, whereas only 0.5 percent had the unipolar form. Of close relatives of people with unipolar depression, 7 percent also had experienced a major depression, but only 0.4 percent had experienced the bipolar form (Winokur, Clayton, & Reich, 1969). Other severe psychological disorders and suicide are more prevalent in families of people with bipolar disorder.

Winokur was able to locate and interview the close relatives of 61 bipolar patients. He found that there was a risk of an affective disorder in 56 percent of the mothers and 13 percent of the fathers. He found a much lower incidence in a similar study of unipolar patients. The evidence so far points to a probable genetic component in bipolar disorder, but it is not so clear in unipolar disorder.

Some studies (Cadoret, Winokur, & Clayton, 1971) suggest that a predisposition to bipolar depression might be transmitted as a dominant gene on the X chromosome. Geneticists have traced specific X chromosome traits, such as red-green color blindness, through several generations of families. They have also traced bipolar depression. However, this finding has not always been reproduced and is controversial. Even if they can prove it conclusively, it would indicate only inherited vulnerability to, not a certainty of, depression.

EXOGENOUS CAUSES   Stress and other precipitating causes are important factors in the onset of depression. Depressed patients report two to three times as many

Financial difficulties and marital stress are common exogenous causes of depression.

disruptive events as normal in the period just before a depression. The kinds of events reported are threatening—for example, marital separation or loss of a job. Marital separation increases the probability of depression by five to six times (Deykin, Klerman, & Armor, 1966). Still, fewer than 10 percent of people who separate from their spouse become clinically depressed.

There also seem to be personality characteristics that predispose persons to depression. The individuals are often successful, hard working, and conscientious to the point of obsessiveness. The typical family background of bipolar depressed individuals includes parents who used their children to gain social acceptance for themselves. The children were told that they had to behave better and do better than other kids. Consequently, the children felt they had to earn their parents' love by superior effort. As adults, these people are inclined to be dependent on others and work hard to make other people like them. They still believe that they cannot be loved without extra effort.

AN INTERESTING FINDING ABOUT REALISM

Most people—psychologists among them—believe that a depressed person has a negative perception of how others feel about him or her. However, one study shows that depressed people are *more* realistic in their self-perception than nondepressed people. Normal people overestimate how much others like them, while depressives are fairly accurate in this regard. One sign that depression is abating is that the *realism decreases* and depressives begin to think people view them more favorably than they do (Lewinshohn, Mischel, & Barton, 1980).

SUICIDE

The most serious and tragic outcome of depression is suicide. Although it is important to recognize that not all suicides stem from depression, three-quarters of all suicides are committed by people who are depressed at the time of death (Leonard, 1971). Suicide is among the 10 leading causes of death in

Western countries. Over 200,000 people attempt suicide each year in the United States alone. This means that 5 million living Americans have tried to kill themselves. Each year about 15 percent of those who attempt it succeed. Three times as many women as men attempt to kill themselves, but three times as many men as women are successful. This fact may have something to do with the way they choose to commit suicide. Women are more likely to try to overdose on drugs, especially barbiturates; men are likely to use firearms.

The most likely candidates for suicide are old, alcoholic males. For men, the frequency of suicide increases across the life span, but for women, the frequency rates are highest in middle age. However, in recent years there has been an enormous increase in the number of young adults, 15 to 24 years of age, who have attempted suicide. Each year, an estimated 80,000 young adults will attempt suicide and about 4,000 will succeed. One characteristic of this group of suicides is that they often come from privileged backgrounds. The rate is higher at larger, more prestigious colleges and universities (Peck & Schrut, 1971).

MULTIPLE PERSONALITY

Recall the case of Billy Milligan in Chapter 1 (page 25). While unusual, the breakup of the mind reveals its normally separate components. The number of multiple personality cases is small, so we can't be sure about the cause. But it seems to occur in people whose parents were violent and sadistic to them as children and who were extremely inconsistent—lenient one day, harsh the next; sweet one day, horrible the next. Often the parents inflict almost unspeakable sexual assaults on the child, followed by aloofness. The child simply cannot understand what is happening and does not know how to think, how to act, or what to do.

For some who cannot bear the pain, the solution is to give full and independent voices to those different minds. Then distinct personalities emerge, which are unaware of one another; this may help in avoiding consciousness of the pain and horror of their life. Sometimes two personalities coexist, and later a third may emerge, one who has all the memories of the independent first two. Normally, the mental system maintains coherence and order under most conditions, but under the daily violence that these children are exposed to, it seems to break down, revealing the splits.

In addition to brutality and sexual degradation of the disordered families, multiple personalities can also result from violence experienced later in life. Here is the case of Charles Poultney, in which a third personality of a former soldier comes forward after severe wartime trauma. This case is described by the psychologist Ernest Hilgard in his book *Divided Consciousness*, which also describes the therapy.

> It was found that he had first been picked up in Los Angeles in 1919 in a dazed condition, wandering the streets. Although he had identification papers made out to Charles Poulting of Florida and had British and French war medals with him, he did not know who he was. He spoke with an Irish accent, thought he might be a Canadian, and Michigan seemed to have some importance to him. He was tattooed with Buffalo Bill and an American flag. He had traveled widely since World War I, trying to find himself, for he had lost all memories prior to February 1915. . . .

The police again found him wandering in a dazed condition in March 1930, now having regained the memories and identity of Charles Poultney from birth to 1915, but having lost all recent memories. He now thought he was back to 1914 and looked on newspapers with the 1930 dates as some strange "futuristic" sheets because they gave no war news. He missed his uniform and, when seeking to return things to a pocket, automatically fumbled for the breast pocket of his uniform, where there was no pocket in his civilian clothes.

In this second state, as Charles Poulting, it was possible to "introduce him" to the memories of the first state, as Charles Poultney, by way of the biography that he had written while in that state. This did not help him much, until with a map of Africa before him, two personal memories were integrated in a flood of emotion. The place name of Voi proved to be the trigger. [He was able to recall two events.] About one he felt no guilt, but the other burdened his conscience. Out in the forest with another soldier in leopard country, his companion refused to climb a tree and tie himself there to spend the night. During the night he was attacked and eaten by leopards. This did not bother Poultney; he had seen many battle deaths, and this was the companion's fault for not taking the precaution that he had recommended and himself taken. However, the other event was different. He had a monkey with him when nightfall occurred in the same territory. He tied the monkey to the base of the tree, while he found his own secure place up in the tree. During the night the monkey was attacked and eaten; had Poultney not tied him at the bottom of the tree he could have escaped. By contrast with the death of the human companion, the death of the monkey—his fault—was an intolerable burden and he became amnesic for the event and the other events surrounding it. (Hilgard, 1977)

Once the monkey episode came to light, all the subsequent memories of Poulting and Poultney became fused, and the man felt essentially cured, even though he still had some memory gaps.

SCHIZOPHRENIA

Schizophrenia is considered to be a disease of the central nervous system that affects virtually all cognitive processes and behavior. More precisely, it is referred to as "the schizophrenias" since the category includes many different subtypes. Schizophrenia is diagnosed when *severe deterioration of mental abilities* is observed in a previously normal person and no biological cause is determined. It is considered to be the most serious of all the disorders, interfering with virtually all aspects of life and lasting a lifetime. Here is one case:

Mary Waverly was in her late 20s. A university graduate, she had run a successful boutique in a large western city before her marriage and until shortly before the birth of her daughter, who is now 2. During the year before Mary's daughter was born, Mary's mother had been treated for cancer. She died when Alice, her granddaughter, was 14 months old. During the baby's first year and a half, Mary was also under pressure because her daughter had surgery several times to correct a birth defect.

Recently, Mary's husband attempted to have her committed to a psychiatric hospital. He said he was concerned about their daughter's welfare. Mary had become a religious fanatic. Although she came from a very religious family, her behavior had not seemed unusual until recently, when she joined a cult group. Since joining the group she refused to have sexual relations with her husband because he was not a "believer." Although she seemed to take good care of her child, she made all decisions only after listening to the "voice of the Lord." (Sarason & Sarason, 1984)

Schizophrenia results in a fundamental cognitive disorganization that causes problems in social functioning, feelings, thinking, and behavior. The characteristics of these disturbances are listed here, although no single feature is *always* present.

1. *Content of thought delusions.* These are the most common disturbances of thought. Common delusions are the belief that someone is spying on the individual or spreading rumors. Often schizophrenics give inappropriate, unusual, or impossible significance to events. One man was convinced that Ronald Reagan was instructing him on one of his television broadcasts. Other common delusions that they experience include *thought broadcast*, the belief that others hear their thoughts; *thought insertion*, that others are inserting thoughts into their minds; *thought withdrawal*, the sensation that their thoughts are being stolen from their minds; and *delusions of being controlled*, the belief that their actions and thoughts are being controlled.

2. *Form of thought.* This disturbance involves unusual patterns of formal thought. Typically, associations loosen and ideas shift from one topic to another with no apparent connections. The speaker typically is unaware of the bizarreness of this thought process. Often the associations are so loose as to make speech incoherent and incomprehensible. Also, although the person speaks a lot, there is little content.

3. *Perception hallucinations.* These are the most characteristic perceptual disturbance. Auditory hallucinations ("voices") are the most common, although visual and olfactory ones do occur. Many investigators believe that a breakdown in perceptual filtering is also characteristic of people with schizophrenia.

4. *Affect.* There are three kinds of affect: blunt, flat, or inappropriate. A *blunt affect* means there is little intensity in feeling. A *flat affect* means there are virtually no signs of emotions. An *inappropriate affect* is an expressed emotion that does not fit the situation (giggling at a funeral).

5. *Sense of self.* There is severe disturbance in the sense of self. The persons have the delusion of being controlled or of their most private thoughts being public. Laing (1959) writes that the schizophrenic "may say that he is made of glass, of such transparency and fragility that a look directed at him splinters him to bits and penetrates straight through him."

6. *Volition.* There is often an impairment in goal-directed activity. The reasons for this are either lack of interest, inability to complete something, or lack of initiative.

7. *Relationship to the external world.* The tendency of individuals with schizophrenia is to withdraw from the world. Often their strange behavior may cause other people to withdraw from them. In the withdrawn state they become totally immersed in their own fantasies, delusions, and illogical conclusions.

8. *Psychomotor behavior.* There are several different patterns of psychomotor disturbance. In extreme cases, a person may maintain a rigid posture for hours. In others he or she may assume bizarre postures or make strange gestures. Often there is a "waxy flexibility" to body and muscle movements.

Here is an account by Carol North, a woman who was schizophrenic and recovered to become a psychiatrist.

After supper, I sat quietly in the day room trying to watch TV. The medication was slowing me down considerably, and even the simplest movement seemed to take forever.

The voices gathered behind me, keeping up a running commentary on everything that was happening.

A nurse breezed through the day room on her way down another hallway. "There goes the nurse," said a voice.

A flash of light zoomed across the day room, burning out and disappearing into thin air. Had I really seen that?

"There goes another comet," said a voice.

Okay, I did see it. This could mean only one thing: further leakage of the Other Worlds into this world. The comet had been a sign.

"It's all right," Hal reassured me with his sugary voice. "We're here with you."

Interference Patterns began to materialize in the air. I stared at their colorful swirls, watching new patterns emerge in response to every sound in the room. When the voices spoke, the patterns shifted, just as they did with other sounds. It was like the vampire test: vampires don't have reflections in mirrors; nonexistent voices shouldn't af-fect the patterns the way other sounds did. That was scientific proof that the voices were just as real as everything else in the world; actually they seemed even more real.

Frightening. I didn't know whether existence in the Other World would be divinely magnificent, beyond human description, like heaven, or whether it would be like the worst imaginable hell. I was ambivalent about whether I wanted it to happen. On one hand, I didn't want to stop the emergence of goodness, yet if it threatened to be hellish, I would have to try to prevent it. I froze, not wanting to produce further patterns from the stimulation of my bodily movement. I didn't want to be responsible for encouraging such change in the world. Live your life as a prayer, I reminded myself. I heard a news announcer on TV parrot my words: "Live your life as a prayer."

Yes, that was good advice for the world to know. The newscaster had broadcast my own thought. The communication systems brought in from the Other Worlds were incredi-bly sophisticated, more than I could understand. The whole world was now praying with me. A nurse sat down next to me on the couch and put her hand on my arm. "Carol, what's going on with you? You're just sitting there doing nothing. Are you bored?"

The sound of her voice created new waves of Interference Patterns, sent hurtling through the air in front of us.

Hush! Don't you understand what you're doing? For God's sake, don't help the Other Side.

She shook my arm gently. "Why Carol, I believe you look scared. Am I right?"

Oh, no, now you've done it, you've inadvertently hurled us into that bottomless pit. With the force of your movement you've made us start to fall again.

The nurse got up and went for help. She returned with two male aides, who picked me up off the couch, carried me to my bed, and left me lying there alone in the dark. The whole time, the patterns swirled through the air, crashing over my head like a tidal wave. Would any of us survive this ordeal?

On my bed, undisturbed, unmoving, I applied the powers of my concentration, gradually settling the turbulent waters of the Other Side. The Interference Patterns began to fade back into the air. If I could only lie still indefinitely, I might have a chance. (North, 1987)

9. *Associated features.* Almost any other symptom of any psychological disorder may be present in the schizophrenic. An individual may display anxiety, anger, or a mixture of emotions. Sometimes victims appear disheveled or eccentrically groomed, or they display odd motor activities such as pacing or rocking. (Adapted from DSM-III-R, 1987)

Psychologists estimate that about 1 percent of all populations suffer from a form of schizophrenic disorder. It is far more likely in urban than rural areas. As mentioned earlier, Farris and Dunham (1965) and others have found a greater instance of people hospitalized for schizophrenia from the lower socioeconomic sections of a city. This may be due to the tendency for schizophrenic families to "drift" to the lower classes because of their difficulty managing life. There is no sex difference in the incidence of schizophrenia.

TYPES OF SCHIZOPHRENIC DISORDERS

Bleuler (1923) first classified schizophrenia as a distinct disorder. He chose the term to indicate that "the splitting of the different psychic functions" was the most important characteristic. (*Schiz* means splitting; *phren* refers to the mind.) There are a number of different subtypes. Most psychologists divide them into the following categories:

A stuporous catatonic schizophrenic may hold the same position for days.

HEBEPHRENIC   This is the most severely disorganized form of schizophrenia, characterized by extreme disturbance of affect. Most often the **hebephrenic** appears confused and distractible. There is more disintegration of personality in hebephrenia than any other form of schizophrenia. It also has the worst prognosis for recovery. It often begins in childhood.

PARANOID   This type is dominated by delusions of being persecuted. The **paranoid** person is extremely suspicious. Speech is generally coherent. Sirhan Sirhan, who assassinated Bobby Kennedy, was diagnosed as a paranoid schizophrenic.

CATATONIC   The **catatonic** type is characterized by unusual motor activity: either excitement or stupor. In catatonia with stupor, a person might maintain a single posture for days, usually one that a normal person would find difficult to maintain for more than a few minutes. One woman explained that the reason why she held her arm outstretched in front of her, palm outstretched, was that the forces of good and evil were warring on the palm of her hand and she did not want to upset the balance in favor of evil.

UNDIFFERENTIATED   This type is a rapidly changing mix of all or most of the primary symptoms of schizophrenia. Many people exhibit signs of the **undifferentiated** type in the beginning stages of the disorder.

CAUSES OF SCHIZOPHRENIA

GENETIC FACTORS   As mentioned earlier in the chapter, genetic factors play an essential role in the development of schizophrenic disorder, but the role is not a simple one. Experts now believe that schizophrenia depends on complex interactions among specific parts of a variety of genes, some of which are more important than others, and some of which are expressed only under certain environmental conditions (Eaves et al. 1988). Studies of concordance rates are consistent with this claim. Kringlen (1967) in a study in Norway found a 38 percent concordance rate in identical twins and only 10 percent in fraternal twins. U.S. studies have also shown high concordance rates. Gottesman and

Shields (1972) found 42 percent concordance for identical twins, but only 9 percent for fraternal twins (recall Tables 4-2 and 4-3, pages 137–38). Thus, although the concordance rate is high, it is not perfect. It indicates a predisposition, not a certainty.

Heston (1966) found that 16.6 percent of children reared apart from their schizophrenic parents developed schizophrenic disorder. Schizophrenics often have retarded, neurotic, or psychopathic children (Heston, 1966). They have unusual peer relations, are suspicious, and exhibit strange mental activity and group behavior.

The risk of developing schizophrenia is 5 to 15 times higher in siblings of schizophrenics than in the general population. The risk for developing schizophrenia is less than 1 percent in the general population. It is less than 5 percent in parents of schizophrenics, and it averages 10 percent in siblings and 11 percent in the children. If both parents are schizophrenic, a child has a 35 to 45 percent or more chance of developing the disorder.

In studies of twins reared apart, identical twins showed a concordance rate of 50 to 60 percent, while fraternal twins showed 10 to 15 percent (Rosenthal et al., 1970). Although the evidence for genetic factors is impressive, the biochemist Solomon Snyder offers a caution: "Schizophrenia runs in families, but so does attendance at Harvard."

BIOCHEMICAL AND NEUROPHYSIOLOGICAL FACTORS Certain chemical agents, such as LSD and mescaline, present in the bloodstream can evoke schizophrenic symptoms. Researchers established this in the 1950s. They were excited by the possibility of discovering a substance produced in the body that might be the dominant causal factor. They have made no breakthroughs, but they have one promising theory called the **dopamine hypothesis,** which states that schizophrenia is caused by a surplus of *dopamine*, a neurotransmitter of the catecholamine group, at important synapses. Alternatively, there may be a surplus of dopamine receptor sites. The very effective antipsychotic drugs given to patients to control their schizophrenic symptoms work by blocking dopamine at synapse receptor sites (Snyder, 1979). This supports the dopamine hypothesis. (See Chapter 3, section on neurotransmitters.)

Other neurophysiological abnormalities might be causal factors. One hypothesis is that the disturbance might be due to imbalances in the exciting and inhibiting processes, leading to inappropriate arousal. Disturbances of these processes would interfere with the normal attentional process (Wynne, Cromwell, & Mattysse, 1978). A woman who had suffered a schizophrenic episode later became a psychiatric nurse. She writes: "I had very little ability to sort the relevant from the irrelevant. The filter had broken down. Completely unrelated events became intricately connected in my mind." These attentional deficiencies often occur before the onset of the episode.

Another predisposing factor is the adequacy of sensory information. Schizophrenia affects virtually every aspect of information processing. It interferes with the ways in which people receive, process, and act on information. Deficits such as selective attention, distractibility, and illogical or incoherent speech are key symptoms in schizophrenia influencing the ability to understand all kinds of information, including the social and emotional intentions of others (Holzman et al., 1988).

AGE-RELATED PSYCHOLOGICAL DISORDERS

Several psychological disorders are characterized by their appearance at a particular time in life. Mental retardation and autism never begin in adulthood; rather, they are apparent very early in life. Conversely, Alzheimer's disease is characterized by its onset in the senescence. Other disorders, such as eating disorders, appear throughout life but are much more common at a particular age range. Below we review four of the most common age-related disorders: childhood autism, mental retardation, eating disorders, and organic brain disorders.

CHILDHOOD AUTISM

The essential feature of **childhood autism** is the failure to develop social relationships. The child does not form an attachment to parents or to other children, appearing disinterested and detached. Both verbal and nonverbal communication are impaired. Language may be totally absent or have bizarre features like echolalia (repeating words, sentences, and phrases that others state) and pronoun reversal (using "you" when referring to him- or herself). Serious impairment in intellectual development is typical, although sometimes autistic children show remarkable ability in an isolated area, like math or art (recall Figure 1-1, page 5). Some researchers feel that memory works differently in autistic children; they tend not to remember the context of material but rather focus exclusively on direct memorization of a string of numbers or characters. Autism is much more common among males than females and usually appears before the age of 3.

Autistic disorder is generally linked to a problem in the mother's pregnancy or to birth complications. Most researchers assume that the brain is damaged in some way during gestation or just after birth, but the exact nature of the damage is unknown. For years, autism was considered a disorder that resulted from interaction with a cold and detached mother. Mothers of autistic children were observed to interact less with these disturbed children and seemed to be less involved with them. They were referred to as "refrigerator mothers." Only when controlled research showed that these same mothers were not cold with their other children was the idea abandoned and a search for biochemical bases investigated.

MENTAL RETARDATION

Mental retardation refers to impairment in intellectual functioning and adaptive behavior. Unlike autism, mental retardation involves no impairment in the ability to form close emotional bonds with other people. It is a chronic problem for which there are many causes but no cure. Nevertheless, during the past two decades, training and educational programs based on behavioral techniques have allowed mentally retarded people to function at higher levels than was previously believed possible. As a result, the prognosis for mental retardation has improved remarkably. No longer is institutionalization a likely outcome for mentally retarded children or adults.

A therapist works to stimulate an autistic child.

Mental retardation differs from many other diagnostic categories in that it is purely descriptive of symptoms. It does not represent a specific syndrome. On the contrary, the causes of mental retardation are numerous and include chromosomal abnormalities, exposure to toxins, and social-cultural deprivation. Mental retardation is slightly more common in males than in females.

EATING DISORDERS

The **eating disorders** include pica, anorexia, and bulimia. Obesity is no longer considered an eating disorder, according to *DSM-III-R,* because it may or may not involve psychological or behavioral problems.) **Pica** is a disorder most commonly seen in infants between the ages of 1 and 2. It refers to the persistent eating of non-food substances, such as plants or dirt. On rare occasions, pica is also observed in adults. Anorexia and bulimia are much more common and are described below.

ANOREXIA   The hallmark of **anorexia** is the refusal to eat food, resulting in severe weight loss. The incidence of anorexia has skyrocketed over the past two decades; once a relatively rare disorder, it is now viewed by some as an epidemic among middle- and upper-middle-class women. Although it does occur in males, 95 percent of reported cases are in females. It is most common during late adolescence and early adulthood.

The term *anorexia* literally means "without appetite," but this is misleading. Persons suffering from anorexia do experience hunger pangs, but they ignore them due to an intense fear of gaining weight. Anorexics have a distorted body image. They view themselves as fat even when dangerously underweight. Often menstrual periods stop (amenorrhea), and other physical problems develop.

Typically, these individuals deny the severity of the problem and refuse to seek therapy until friends or relatives force them to face the problem. It's severity must not be minimized. It is estimated that 3–21 percent of anorexics die from starvation or from causes related to the anorexic condition, such as heart failure (Leon & Dinklage, 1989).

BULEMIA   **Bulemia** is a condition marked by recurrent episodes of binge eating and purging. Usually vomiting is induced or laxatives are taken to prevent weight gain. Like anorexia, bulimics report overconcern with their appearance. They are often depressed. Most people with bulimia are normal weight, although some can be too thin whereas others can be overweight. The physical danger associated with bulimia is electrolyte imbalance and dehydration, which can lead to many serious complications, including death.

CAUSES OF ANOREXIA AND BULEMIA   There is no evidence for inheritance of anorexia or bulimia. Most researchers assume that strong cultural influences are responsible for distorted beliefs about perfection and femininity; and that the increased incidence of eating disorders reflects societal pressures to conform to popular stereotypes of beauty and femininity. Pressure also comes from families who desire "model children." In bulimia, the parents are often overweight, so children may be attempting to avoid a similar fate.

ORGANIC MENTAL DISORDERS

Organic mental disorders involve a clear disturbance of brain function from physiological causes. Disorders may be due to physical disease, injury, or substance abuse. We will focus on the brain disorders that arise in old age, referred to globally as the **dementias.**

Old age does not cause dementia. The vast majority of older people live out their lives without serious mental impairment. But the prevalence of dementia is greater in the over-65 age group, and higher still in the over-80 age group. Five percent of people over 65 and 20 percent of people over 80 suffer from *senile dementia* (i.e., brain deterioration occurring in old age). There are hundreds of different dementias with different causes and symptoms, but the most common dementia of old age is Alzheimer's disease.

A daughter observes as her mother struggles with everyday tasks.

ALZHEIMER'S DISEASE   The symptoms of **Alzheimer's disease** include marked defects in memory and other cognitive processes, including language and perceptual abilities. In some people the onset is slow and gradual, but in others it can be quite rapid. The first and most obvious symptom is loss of the ability to remember recent experience and to learn new things. Eventually the person does not remember highly significant people, even loved ones. Confusion, irritability, suspiciousness, and wandering are also common symptoms. Ultimately, Alzheimer's disease leads to death.

The cause seems to be linked to abnormalities in the hippocampus and certain regions of the cerebral cortex, the brain systems most dedicated to complex cognitive processes and memory functions. Although there is no known cure, a number of promising research projects are underway that may lead to improved understanding and treatment.

THE IMPORTANCE OF BEING NORMAL

Does classifying someone as "disordered" do justice to the person? As McNeil (1967) explains,

> Each of us is neurotic in one sense or another. Each of us carries through life a set of unsolved problems, prejudices, and biases in response to our fellow human beings. Since neurosis so often disguises itself as normality and so often is indistinguishable from it, a major problem of adjustment is focused on the correct or incorrect diagnosis each of us makes of the other. The disorder of a single life usually has repercussions in the lives of others, and that is the issue. Normality, then, becomes a very relative term, and its limits are more elastic than most of us suspect. We are all, simultaneously, normal and abnormal.

Often the labels that society places on certain behavior can have serious consequences in a person's life. Individuals who have been diagnosed as schizophrenic are considered to be *in remission* for five years before a diagnosis of "no mental disorder" is made. Aside from the debilitating effect this may have on these people psychologically, it may also interfere with their ability to find work and with their personal relationships. Friends and family may treat them as "disturbed." Often this is a self-fulfilling judgment.

Have you ever turned inward and wondered about the stability of your own mental condition? Most people question, at times, whether other people could possibly have such irrational thoughts and worries. It is human nature to wonder about our own sanity. Most of us sometimes feel so anxious about an upcoming event that we question if we can get through it at all. To make matters worse, you may know someone (who seemed normal enough) who was hospitalized for a nervous breakdown. Perhaps psychopathology has hit even closer to home, a parent may have an alcohol problem or an uncle may have been diagnosed "schizophrenic." There is always an unsettling quality about hearing that a human mind has gone awry. You feel badly for the person, of course, but you also can't help but wonder if the same thing could happen to you. Reading a psychology textbook detailing all sorts of symptoms that you may have experienced at one time or another doesn't help. How do you know if you are normal or not?

First, be assured that wondering whether you are "normal" is very normal. Lots of people experience thoughts like "if only people knew what I was thinking...." There is an important message in this uncomfortable feeling, but it is not that you are "crazy." Rather the message is that psychological disorders are *exaggerations* of normal thought processes. We all feel very sad at times, and we all experience times where we are nervous

WHAT IS "NORMAL"?

past the point where we can hide it. Having experienced occasional symptoms of alienation, anxiety, or sadness does not mean that you are abnormal, or even predisposed toward abnormality. The rule of thumb goes something like this: only when the symptoms begin to disrupt your daily life do you have reason for concern. For example, if you get very nervous before a test, but generally pull through just

fine, you are normal. If you get nervous before tests so regularly that you don't take them, and so put your education in serious jeopardy, you have a problem and you should seek help.

The second important tip to remember is this: "insanity" is not a condition that suddenly happens to you. Rarely does a person go through life just fine and one day —boom!—depression hits. Rather, signs and symptoms are usually present long before serious problems develop.

The bottom line is that psychological discomfort is part of being human. It has great survival value and often guides us to make better decisions about life. Most of us will not experience serious psychopathology. If you feel that a particular discomfort is affecting your daily life or your ability to obtain your life goals, then you should seek help. Sometimes just talking to a friend can help immensely. If not, psychotherapy is another option many people choose and is the topic we address next.

SUMMARY

1. Defining *psychopathology* is difficult because our definitions reflect cultural judgments about the acceptability of behavior. Unusual conditions must be both *deviant* and *maladaptive* to be considered psychopathological.

2. All psychological disorders share several characteristics: (a) loss of control, (b) unhappiness or distress, and (c) isolation from others. The most widely used classification system for mild and severe disorders is in the *Diagnostic and Statistical Manual of Mental Disorders (DSM)*, published by the American Psychiatric Association. The *DSM* is continuously revised to incorporate advances in our understanding of the disorders. The most recent is the *DSM-III-R*, 1987 edition.

3. Psychological disorders are caused by both biological and social-situational factors. There are very few disorders that appear entirely independent of one or the other.

4. Psychological disorders are exaggerations of normal emotions. In *anxiety disorders,* the underlying emotion is fear. *Generalized anxiety disorder* refers to the persistent experience of tension or worry. *Phobias* are extreme, unfounded fears about objects or places. There are many varieties of phobias, including *zoophobia* (fear of animals), *claustrophobia* (fear of closed spaces) and *acrophobia* (fear of heights). *Panic disorder* is characterized by acute onset of panic, during which the person experiences intense physiological and psychological symptoms of terror. *Obsessive-compulsive disorders* refer to disorder of uncontrollable repetition of thoughts (obsessions) or behaviors (compulsions). *Post-traumatic stress disorders* (PTSD) are precipitated by a traumatic event that would occasion extreme fear in any normal person, but the fear reaction continues to appear long after the event.

5. *Somatoform disorders* involve physical ailments or pains for which there are no organic or physiological explanations. There are several types of somatoform disorders: somatization, conversion, psychogenic pain, hypochondriasis, and atypical. *Hypochondriasis* is characterized by an individual's belief that he or she has a disease. Symptoms of somatoform disorders are very real to the individual.

6. *Personality disorders* are enduring sets of maladaptive symptoms that influence the way individuals think about, perceive, and behave in the world. Some of the most common personality disorders are *paranoid,* pervasive and unwarranted suspiciousness and mistrust of people; *schizoid,* a defect in the capacity to form social relationships; *avoidant,* hypersensitivity to potential rejection; *compulsive,* restricted ability to express warm and tender feelings coupled with extreme productivity; and *antisocial,* a history of chronic and continuous antisocial behavior that violates the rights of others.

7. *Substance use disorders* are disturbances in behavior and emotion that result from abuse or dependence on drugs. Six categories of these substances are *alcohol, barbiturates* or other sedatives, *analgesics, painkillers* or narcotics, *stimulants* such as amphetamines, and *psychoactive drugs* such as marijuana and LSD. It is more common for men than women to have a substance use disorder, but this is changing in recent years.

8. A severe mental disorder is *depression,* which is an overwhelming sadness that immobilizes and arrests the entire course of a person's life. There are two types: *unipolar,* in which the person experiences only depression; and *bipolar,* in which the person experiences wide mood swings from extreme sadness to extreme elation *(mania).* Unipolar depression is far more common than bipolar.

9. Symptoms of clinical depression include loss of interest and pleasure; appetite, sleep, and psychomotor disturbances; decrease in energy level; sense of worthlessness; difficulty concentrating; and thoughts of death. There are endogenous (from within) causes of depression, which are the result of biological/genetic factors; and exogenous (from without) causes of depression, the onset of which appears to be related to environmental stress or tragic events. Depressives are usually conventional, well behaved, and often successful, conscientious people.

10. *Schizophrenia* is a uniquely human disorder. It is the name for a group of disorders that involve severe deterioration of mental abilities. This fundamental thought

disorganization causes disturbances in every area of life: social functioning, feeling, thought delusions, form of thought, perception hallucinations, affect, sense of self, volition, relationship to the external world, and psychomotor behavior. Categories of schizophrenic disorders include *hebephrenic,* the most severely disorganized form of schizophrenia, characterized by extreme disturbances of affect; *paranoid,* dominated by delusions of being persecuted, *catatonic,* unusual motor activity, either excitement or stupor; and *undifferentiated,* a rapidly changing mix of all or most of the primary symptoms of schizophrenia.

11. Several psychological disorders are characterized by their appearance at a particular time in life. Mental retardation and autism are disorders of childhood. Alzheimer's disease is a dementia only evidenced in old age. Other forms, like eating disorders, are found at all ages, but are far more common during particular life stages.

12. About being normal: it is possible to classify someone as disordered, but does this do justice to the person? The dividing line between normal and abnormal is not often easy to determine and the cost of being labeled disordered can be extremely high.

TERMS AND CONCEPTS

abnormal
abuse
alcohol
Alzheimer's disease
amphetamines
analgesics
anorexia
antisocial personality (ASP)
anxiety
barbiturates
bipolar depression
breakdown
bulimia
catatonic
childhood autism
concordance rate
conversion disorders
crack
dementia
dependence
depressants
depression
deviant
dopamine
dopamine hypothesis
eating disorders
endogenous
endorphins
exogenous
generalized anxiety disorder

hebephrenic
hypochondriasis
maladaptive
mania
mental retardation
nicotine
norms
obsessive-compulsive disorders
organic mental disorders
panic disorder
paranoia
phobia
pica
population genetics
post-traumatic stress disorder (PTSD)
proband
psychoactive drugs
psychological disorders
psychopath
psychoses
schizophrenia
sedatives
sociopath
somatization disorder
somatoform disorders
somatoform pain disorder
stimulants
substance use disorder
undifferentiated
unipolar depression

CHAPTER 15 / PSYCHOLOGICAL DISORDERS

Barlow, D. (1988). *Anxiety and its disorders: The nature and treatment of anxiety and panic.* New York: Guilford Press.

A thorough review of the literature on treatment of anxiety, including both pharmacological and psychological approaches.

Gottesman, I. I. (1990). *Schizophrenia genesis: The origins of madness.* New York: Freeman.

The genetic and social story of schizophrenia written by the country's foremost authority on behavioral genetics.

Nolen-Hoeksema, S. (1990). *Sex differences in depression.* Stanford: Stanford University Press.

A critical review and theoretical analysis of the literature, which destroys myths and makes sense of sex differences in the prevalence of depression.

Rosenhan, D., & Seligman, M. (1989). *Abnormal psychology* (2nd ed.). New York: Norton.

An important text, especially because it is written by two of the top investigators.

SUGGESTIONS FOR FURTHER READING

16
PSYCHOTHERAPIES

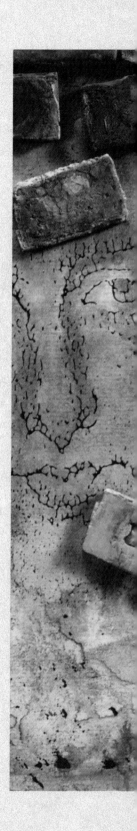

I am nine years old now. When I was six years old I started picking things up with my elbows because I thought I would get my hands dirty if I picked things up with my hands. By the time I was seven I was washing my hands 35 times a day. For the next two years, my fear of getting my hands dirty grew worse. . . . It wrecked my life. It took away all my time. I couldn't do anything. . . . I had to take some toilet paper and rip them up a lot of times into teeny pieces that had to be the right size. . . . From the beginning, I knew something was very wrong. I kind of thought, "It's going to go away tomorrow. It's going to go away the next day or the next day or sometime." But it never went away and I kind of gave up hope. . . . (Rapoport, 1989, pp. 43–45)

As long as people suffer, others undertake to relieve that suffering and to restore adaptive functioning. Throughout history there have been many forms of psychotherapy, reflecting differing beliefs about mental disorder. If society believes that psychological disorder is caused by demons that invade a person, the treatment may include getting the demons out. If the culture thinks that psychological disorder originates in early childhood experiences, the treatment may attempt to root out these experiences. If it is thought that disorders result from learning inappropriate responses, the treatment may involve teaching a new, more adaptive set of responses. If society contends that the problem is essentially biological, then drugs may be administered or surgery performed. If the problem is perceived as a difficulty in cognitive patterns, the person may be helped to restructure his or her ways of thinking. If a psychological problem is thought to be the result of blockage in the normal development of self, treatment would seek to find out where the block is and how it can be removed. Although all psychotherapies have as their goal the restoration of normal functioning, they vary in method, approach, and assumptions. There are many controversies about therapy, about which ones work best and whether any of them work at all.

THE DEBATES ABOUT PSYCHOTHERAPY

Debates about the merit of applying psychological principles to human problems have divided psychology since it declared itself a science. During World War I, the United States government turned to psychologists to ask if they could help in the war effort. A meeting was called at Cornell University, and sparks flew. Robert Yerkes said yes, of course, psychologists could help their country by applying what they knew. Edwin Boring was emphatically opposed and accused John B. Watson of trading a science for a technology. He felt that his colleagues were about to sell out and that a science could remain pure only as long as it remained without power (O'Donnell, 1979).

Whether psychotherapy can (or even should) be a scientific endeavor, whether the search for truth about human behavior is corrupted when the treatment of disorders is the focus, and indeed, whether we know anywhere near enough about human behavior to offer cures are debates that rage on today. Many psychologists view psychotherapy as far too premature in light of our knowledge about psychological problems.

But more psychologists are practitioners than researchers or teachers. And practitioners contend that basic research has generated too little information too slowly and that, in the meantime, people suffer. After all, isn't the ultimate aim of psychology to improve the state of humankind? Perhaps, argue the researchers, but is practice before understanding the answer? Scientist-practitioners answer that the optimal course is one where therapy is practiced and carefully evaluated. There is little consensus within the field of psychology. We will return to these questions and discuss the empirical evidence for the effectiveness of psychotherapy.

MODERN PSYCHOTHERAPISTS

Psychotherapists are not necessarily psychologists. **Psychiatrists** are trained as medical doctors with specialization in the treatment of psychological problems. As physicians, their background is in medicine, and they are licensed to dispense drugs as part of the treatment. A **psychoanalyst** is a psychotherapist trained in the psychoanalytic tradition first formulated by Sigmund Freud. Almost all psychoanalysts are also psychiatrists.

A **clinical psychologist** holds a Ph.D. in psychology. He or she may specialize in a specific psychotherapy, such as behavior modification, cognitive therapy, or even psychodynamic therapy (a more global category than psychoanalysis, encompassing but not limited to Freudian theory). All clinical psychologists have training in research, but the depth of that training varies tremendously depending on the school where the psychologist was trained. Whereas some universities train clinical psychologists to be, first and foremost, researchers of psychopathology—many of whom never practice—other universities place heavy emphasis on clinical skills in training.

After they complete their training, clinical psychologists may work as researchers, teachers, or therapists. Some clinical psychologists are also involved in testing and evaluation, others concentrate their efforts on therapy, and

Before reformers such as Pinel (shown below, left, unchaining the inmates of a Paris asylum) and Dix began having an impact, people with mental disorders continued to be "treated" with such devices as the "circulating swing" (below, right), which seemed to involve as much torture as treatment.

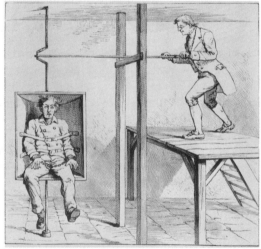

still others consult to industry. In recent years, a new approach has emerged: schools of **professional psychology.** They award a Ph.D. or a Psy.D., but, unlike university programs, their emphasis is on the practice rather than the science of psychology.

A **psychiatric social worker** holds an advanced degree (M.S. or Ph.D.) and usually concentrates on social or community-based problems. **Counselors** are trained to treat problems as well. In general, clinical psychologists trained at professional schools, psychiatric social workers, and counselors are unlikely to be researchers.

Psychotherapists have diverse trainings, scientific and not, and the literature on psychotherapy reflects this diversity. Some of what you read will be familiar, stemming directly from psychological theories that you have read about in previous chapters. Other information will sound remarkably foreign. Such is the nature of psychotherapy.

A BRIEF HISTORY OF PSYCHOTHERAPY

EARLY APPROACHES

One widespread belief during Medieval times was that mental disorder was caused by demons that entered and possessed the victim. One treatment for such demonic possession was **trephining** (Figure 16-1), in which holes were drilled into a person's head to let the demons out. Other treatments included floggings, burnings, and other forms of torture. These treatments were not *intended* to be cruel to the victim, but rather to the devil.

FIGURE 16-1
Trephining

In this medieval treatment, holes were cut into a mentally disturbed person's head in the hope that the demons would pass out through them.

During the eighteenth century, mental disorders were believed to be a moral problem: a result of idleness or bad character. Mad people were lumped together with criminals and vagrants, chained, and thrown into dungeons. The "insane" were considered dangerous nuisances to society and were also used as warnings. They were often put on view so that young people would see the consequences of deviant behavior. In this period, the disturbed were confined, not treated.

Then Philippe Pinel (1745–1826) began a series of reforms in France during the French Revolution. Dorothea Dix (1802–1887) and others started them later in America. Finally, research and advances in biology, medicine, and neurology encouraged a conception of insanity as a disease. This paradigm shifted the blame from the victim. A doctor treated the disease, usually with a certain amount of compassion, although bleeding with leeches and early forms of electroconvulsive shock therapy were not without pain.

A great advance in the late nineteenth century was the discovery that the widespread disease syphilis causes **general paresis,** a slow, degenerative disease that eventually erodes mental faculties. Understanding the cause led to an effective treatment: the administration of the drug *salvarsan*. At a practical level, the elimination of paresis was one of the few decisive victories in the war against mental disorder. At a more theoretical level, the breakthrough showed definitively that the mind could be affected by physical disease. That victory spurred important research: mental disorders began to receive more attention from scientific researchers.

CLASSIFICATION OF DISORDERS

As the body of research grew on the malfunctioning of the mind, diagnostic accuracy became more precise, and intricate classification systems were developed. Today most practitioners refer to the *Diagnostic and Statistical Manual (DSM)* when diagnosing patients. Diagnosis of disorders can assist the therapist in a developing a treatment plan based on research with other similarly disordered individuals and can provide the patient (and relatives) with a sense of relief in knowing what is wrong. Similarly, it can help predict the future course of the disorder. Diagnosis can also cause harm. The therapist may stop looking for new evidence once a diagnosis is made or may rely too heavily on the recommendations in the literature rather than on individual circumstances. Or a diagnosis may be devastating to an individual.

Emphasis on diagnosis varies depending on the theoretical orientation of the therapist. Some therapists see diagnosis as one of the central goals of treatment; others feel that, while interesting, diagnosis contributes relatively little to the formulation of a treatment plan because each case is so different (Longabaugh et al., 1983).

PSYCHOANALYSIS

As we saw in Chapter 14, **psychoanalysis** is a theory of and method of treatment for the conflict between the biological and social (or civilized) selves. Freud believed that "instincts" underlie the state of the mind and that psychological distress arises from basic conflicts of the id and the ego. Unconscious wishes and desires cause anxiety and fear, so they are repressed and forced out of consciousness. Freud believed that the roots of disorder lie in early childhood.

One of Freud's most famous cases concerned "Little Hans," a boy who was so afraid of horses that he would not leave his house. (Freud based his analysis, by the way, on letters from Hans's father; he met the boy only once.) Before Hans became so afraid of horses, he was a perfectly normal boy. But he did show an "uncommon" interest in his penis.

Once his mother caught him masturbating. She told him she would cut off his penis if she ever caught him "at it" again. At age 4, Hans was described as harboring strong sexual desires for his mother. For Freud, sexual desire for one's mother at 4 years of age was quite normal, but this particular young boy seemed to delight (more than most) in his mother's attention to his penis while she groomed or bathed him. At about age 4½, he was out walking with his nurse when a horse and carriage rolled over in front of them. He began crying and said that he wanted to go home to hug his mother.

From that day on, he was terrified of horses and would not leave the house. Freud's analysis was that Hans's real fear was that he so desired his mother that he subconsciously wanted his father out of the way. Since he really feared his impulses, he transferred his fear to horses to relieve himself of guilt. Freud hypothesized that, even though his mother had actually threatened to castrate him, it was his father who represented that threat. By avoiding horses, he thus avoided his fear of castration, and by staying home, he got to stay close to his mother.

THE PSYCHOANALYTIC METHOD

From the "Little Hans" example, you can see that Freud believed that therapy should bring unconscious desires into consciousness where they can be analyzed. However, the unconscious does not give up its secret desires easily or without struggle. The ego "edits" and represses those desires. Thus, Freud at first used hypnosis in his therapy to bring the unconscious to the surface.

Later he developed the technique of **free association,** in which the psychiatrist asks the patient to say anything that comes into his or her mind. There is no criticism or editing of the patient's thoughts—no matter how obscene, unimportant, or silly the thought Free association is difficult, because people characteristically exercise control and are modest about personal subjects.

Because the patients themselves are unconscious of the problems, the task of the therapist is to interpret *symbolic* gestures, displays, or words that the patient uses. For example, a patient may mistakenly call the therapist by the name of her first husband; another patient may appear angry at the therapist after a discussion of his dependency. The therapist would not take either of these behaviors at face value; rather, he or she would delve into the underlying meaning (that even the patient was unaware of).

To aid in the process of uncovering deeply repressed information, the patient lies on a couch facing away from the analyst. Removing normal eye-to-eye contact usually removes some reticence. The analyst usually listens

The therapy couch in Sigmund Freud's office

passively, but occasionally may interrupt the patient's free flow of ideas. He or she may highlight or suggest connections among things that the patient has said. A psychoanalyst often asks the patient to recall dreams and uses the content of dreams as a starting point for free association. Thus, the **interpretation of dreams** is a cornerstone of Freudian analysis.

Patients who seek psychoanalysis commit themselves to a very long process of self-evaluation, criticism, and examination. Psychoanalysis usually requires four to five 50-minute sessions a week for one to several years. These conditions exclude a great number of people from treatment, including most psychotics, people with personality disorders who are not highly motivated to change, nonverbal people, or poor or elderly people.

RESISTANCE   The *opening* phase of treatment usually lasts from three to six months. In this time, the analyst begins to learn the patient's history and the general nature of his or her unconscious conflicts. One of the greatest signals of an unconscious conflict in the opening phase is **resistance,** which is the characteristic way that the patient resists or works against revealing feelings or thoughts. For example, every time some patients start to talk about their mothers, they may change the subject; they might tell a joke or say that the thought is too silly. Another sign of resistance to therapy is when the patient forgets an appointment or is late. Resistance serves to reduce the anxiety of the patient by not allowing anxiety-producing thoughts to surface.

TRANSFERENCE   An important concept in psychoanalytic therapy is how the patient perceives the analyst. At a certain point in treatment, **transference** takes place: the patient transfers onto the analyst attitudes toward people about whom he or she has conflicting feelings. For example, a male patient who has difficulty getting along with people in authority may have had a domineering father who demanded perfection from his son and strict obedience to all his rules. At a certain point in therapy, the patient may begin to show anger at the analyst for requiring him or her to follow the rules of analysis. The analyst comes to play a role in the patient's life whose significance is all out of proportion with reality. Freud believed that transference is extremely important. It is the patient's way of re-creating and re-enacting forgotten or repressed memories from earliest childhood. Instead of recalling events, the patient repeats them.

The therapist then proceeds to an **analysis of the transference.** This is a critical stage. The patients begin to see the nature of their misconceptions, maladaptive responses, and misinterpretations. They have transferred them to the analyst, and thus they can see them in a concrete way. Patients can then begin to evaluate their situation more realistically.

The analysis of the transference should offer patients some insight into the nature of their unconscious conflicts. Usually during this phase the patients recall some extremely important event, desire, or fantasy of their youth. The recollection and their ability to express it produces in them a **catharsis,** which is the release of stored-up or held-back feelings. It is an intensely emotional experience. The immediate result of a catharsis is pleasurable relief.

Resolution of the transference is the last phase of the treatment, in which the patient and therapist agree that they have accomplished their goals. This means that the patient ought to be behaving in different ways. He or she should no longer experience anxiety in situations that previously had been anxiety provoking.

PSYCHODYNAMIC THERAPY

There have been many revisions of classical psychoanalysis since Freud's day. Recall from Chapter 14 that people who accept some of Freud's ideas but practice therapy slightly differently are called **neo-Freudians.** Among psychologists, there are more neo-Freudians than psychoanalysts (who, as we mentioned earlier, are usually psychiatrists). The basic concepts of transference, resistance, free-association, and the unconscious are similar across psychodynamic paradigms. **Psychodynamic therapy** refers to a broad category of therapies including Harry Stack Sullivan's interpersonal psychotherapy and the work of ego-analysts such as Anna Freud, Karen Horney, and Erik Erikson.

SUMMARY COMMENT

The roots of modern psychoanalysis are in Freudian theory, not in psychological empiricism. As a result of this fundamental difference, proponents of psychoanalysis seem to speak a different language from research psychologists. Nevertheless, psychoanalytic theory has had a pervasive influence on the practice of clinical psychology. Like scientists, psychoanalysts seek to discover the truth. But they disagree about suitable instruments and methods to acquire evidence. Practitioners of psychoanalysis have traditionally relied on the case study method and impressions of patient gains to verify hypotheses. Moreover, many actively downplay the role of research in evaluation, placing greater emphasis on "clinical wisdom" (Luborsky & Spence, 1978). In contrast, research psychologists, trained in the scientific method and attuned to problems of uncontrolled research (such as experimenter bias) remain dubious of the method and its effects.

In recent years a number of psychodynamic psychologists have dedicated themselves to establishing a data base that conforms to modern scientific standards. Using larger samples and observations of patient sessions, they seek to document both process and outcomes of the psychoanalytic method (Horowitz et al., 1989; Jones & Zoppell, 1982; Luborsky & Spence, 1978). In addition to gathering evidence, this type of research may—for the first time—open communication lines between psychoanalysis and scientific psychology. The results of this communication may signify the beginning (or the end) of cross-theoretical interchange involving psychoanalysis and empirical psychology.

BEHAVIOR THERAPY

In striking contrast to psychoanalysis, which developed outside of psychology altogether, **behavior therapy** stems directly from learning theory. The behavioristic viewpoint of psychological disorders is that they are the result of faulty learning. Psychotherapy, then, is a process of *relearning*. A behaviorist would view Freud's analysis of little Hans as far-fetched: Hans's fear could be better explained by respondent conditioning. Recall from Chapter 8 the story of "Little Albert": a loud noise presented at the same time as a white rat caused Albert to be afraid of anything white and furry. In Hans's case, it is conceivable that the commotion associated with the accident frightened him. Because his parents reinforced the fear by letting him stay home, the fear was maintained.

Two varieties of therapy are related to two primary modes of learning: **behavior therapy** is based on **respondent conditioning**, and **behavior modification** is based on the theory of **operant conditioning**. The two therapies reflect the historical roots of the approaches. Behavior therapy and behavior modification refer to treatments that reflect different modes of learning, not different types of therapists. In other words, individual therapists are not *either* behavior therapists or behavior modifiers. Rather, behavior therapists (which is the term used to refer to both these days) are persons who base their treatment on a behavioral analysis of the problem.

Behavior therapists believe that *anxiety* is the underlying cause of "neurotic" behavior. Therapy techniques based on *respondent* conditioning aim to recondition anxiety-producing autonomic responses (Wolpe, 1958). Techniques based on *operant* conditioning change the behavior by changing the consequences that follow it. This may involve reinforcement or extinction to alter maladaptive responses.

Behavior therapy proceeds from the assumption that the *behavior* that is causing the person distress is the problem, whereas psychoanalysis assumes that it is only the symptom of an underlying neurosis. As a prominent behavior therapist, Hans Eysenck, wrote, "There is no neurosis underlying the symptom, but merely the symptom itself. Get rid of the symptom . . . and you have eliminated the neurosis." Most behaviorists agree there are many "thinking" components of fears and anxiety. But they assert that the key to unlocking the thoughts is a change in behavior.

Behavior therapy has a wide range of applications and methods. Therapy may be for an individual, a group, a family, or even a community. Therapy may last for a single session or for several months. Only in cases of severe chronic disorders, as in the case of autism or schizophrenia, does treatment last for years. Behavior therapists work with a much wider range of disorders than do psychoanalysts or humanistic psychotherapists, from the most severely disturbed (e.g., chronic schizophrenics) to basically normal persons who encounter situational problems (e.g., test anxiety or sexual dysfunction). They also treat phobias, addictions, depression, and interpersonal difficulties.

METHODS OF BEHAVIOR THERAPY

A first step in a successful therapeutic program is beginning a good relationship between the therapist and the client—the term therapists prefer to use, instead of "patient." Unlike psychoanalysis, the therapist does not *do* therapy *on* a client; rather, the therapist and client work *together* to accomplish agreed-upon outcomes. In the first phase of treatment, the therapist asks the client to give an account of the history of the problem.

The behavior therapist's purpose in knowing the client's history is fundamentally different from that of the psychoanalyst. Behaviorists do not believe that solving the problems of early childhood will solve the problems of adult life. Instead, the aim is to *discover where and how the inappropriate conditioning was acquired.* The therapist also tries to find out how the problem now arises.

To get an accurate account, the therapist may not rely only on the client's own verbal report. The client may be asked to keep diaries of events and feelings during the week. The therapist may interview members of the client's family or engage the client in role playing. In **role playing** the therapist creates a hypothetical situation; the chosen situation is likely to cause the client anxiety, and they act it out together.

RECONDITIONING TECHNIQUES

Once the client achieves an understanding of the problem, **reconditioning** proceeds. There are several behavior therapy techniques to do this. Here we will mention the three most common techniques.

SYSTEMATIC DESENSITIZATION   The technique of **systematic desensitization** is based on the phenomenon of **counterconditioning.** The idea is to *eliminate* an unwanted conditioned response by conditioning the client to another stimulus. The stimulus elicits a response (usually relaxation) that is incompatible with the original response.

Systematic desensitization is very effective in helping people overcome phobias. The therapist asks the client to imagine or role play an anxiety-provoking situation. When the client begins to feel anxious, the therapist instructs him or her in relaxation techniques. When the client is able to relax, the therapist presents a situation *more* likely than the initial situation to produce anxiety. The client again learns to relax. The therapist arranges the situations in a progression from least to most anxiety provoking, and the client reduces fear step by step. The therapist may first ask a person who is afraid of elevators to imagine an elevator, then to imagine being alone in the elevator. Later he or she

Therapists help their clients overcome acrophobia, a fear of heights.

may physically go and stand beside the elevator, then may stand inside it. Finally, the client will ride it alone.

FLOODING   In the technique of **flooding,** the therapist literally floods the client's mind. He or she incessantly presents situations that evoke fear and anxiety. As the client begins to experience anxiety, the therapist elaborates on the story to make the client more and more anxious. Flooding is based on the principle that prolonged exposure to feared stimuli, *while in a safe environment,* will recondition the stimuli to evoke a neutral (or at least less noxious) response.

Take the case of a woman with agoraphobia who is afraid to leave the house. The therapist might begin by asking her to close her eyes and to imagine going out of the house. Then she imagines meeting someone in the street, imagines a group of children running down the sidewalk bumping into her, and imagines getting on a public bus at rush hour. Eventually, the client will notice that her anxiety diminishes even if she does not run away. Then the therapist may ask the client to try to imagine going places on her own. Finally, she actually imagines going to specific places on her own. Flooding is extremely intense. There is no let-up until the client begins to feel the fear and anxiety dissipate. It is a highly effective therapy for phobias.

ASSERTIVENESS TRAINING   **Assertiveness training** is often used for people who have difficulty in interpersonal relationships. Such persons are not viewed as suffering from an intrapsychic disturbance; rather, they are seen as lacking specific skills. The task of the therapist is to teach those skills. Therapists may use role playing. They may also assign clients tasks to force them to confront and overcome their inability to assert themselves.

COGNITIVE-BEHAVIOR THERAPY

Cognitive or **cognitive-behavior therapies** combine many of the techniques of behaviorism with cognitive psychology. The main difference between strict behavior therapy and cognitive-behavior therapy is the latter's emphasis on the *effects of thought on behavior*. We will review two forms of cognitive therapy: cognitive restructuring and stress inoculation. These therapies differ in method and emphasis, but they share two major assumptions: (1) that cognitive processes influence behavior, and (2) that restructuring of the individual's cognitive system can change behavior, by the individual becoming conscious of thought processes and analyzing them. The method of cognitive therapy is hypothesis testing. As in the behavior therapies, the client and therapist work together, and the therapist takes an active role.

COGNITIVE RESTRUCTURING THERAPY

Cognitive restructuring therapy was developed by Beck (1976), who assumes that disorders result from individuals' negative beliefs about events in the world and about themselves. Because people tend to set unrealistic goals for themselves, their efforts are usually self-defeating, and thus their negative beliefs are reinforced. Beck proposed four major areas where a person's thought processes make the beliefs self-fulfilling.

1. Absolute thinking; everything is black or white, all or nothing.
2. Generalizing a few negative events to every aspect of life.
3. Magnifying the importance of negative events.
4. Being overselective in perception, noticing only those events that confirm the negative beliefs.

The therapist in **cognitive restructuring therapy** does not dispute clients' beliefs directly. Rather, he or she encourages clients to engage in *experiments* that will help them to confirm or disconfirm their beliefs. The client and therapist may develop a hypothesis, and then the client has the assignment of gathering information to support or demolish it. For example, a depressed man may decide to wallpaper his living room. His wife papers one side, and he does the other. He predicts that he will not be as good as his wife at the job. When he finishes the papering, he may point out all the places on his side where the pattern does not exactly match or the seams are slightly off kilter. He may point to the excellent job on his wife's side of the room. His therapist may point out that not being good at wallpapering has little effect on his life and may then point out skills in which the client excels. Eventually, this type of feedback may make it possible for the man to change his perception of himself.

An important part of cognitive restructuring therapy, especially in the treatment of depression, is the assignment or scheduling of tasks that interfere with the conduct of the disorder. For example, a depressed person might find no

With all the types of therapies available today (over 250 of them), no wonder people are confused. This extract is presented as a unique opportunity for you to compare how four common therapies work. Perry Turner (1986) asked four therapists to treat a fictional patient named George, and each in turn offered a solution to George's problem. Here is the scenario they were given:

George is 31 years old, works in small business development, and has been married for five years. . . . His wife, who is 30, is four months pregnant with their first child.

George came in complaining of insomnia, "testiness," and anxiety caused by fantasies about another woman and by fears that he would prove inadequate as a father, husband, and musician. George reports no history of significant acute or chronic physical illness. He takes no prescribed or over-the-counter medications. His last physical was seven months ago; all findings were normal.

His childhood was "as happy as anyone's," he says, and his parents were loving and fair. There is no mental illness in the family. . . . His mother, a housewife, was a quiet, passive woman whose principle disciplinary tactic was a doleful look used mostly when George neglected to practice his bassoon and when his sister dated unsuitable boys.

. . . About seven months ago, a new typist named Laura started working in George's office. Laura, a poor typist and a very pretty young woman, behaved quite seductively around George. He found this amusing at first and planned to tell Ann about it—they had always prided themselves on sharing more of their lives than other couples. The night he planned to tell her they had a fight—George

ONE PROBLEM, FOUR TREATMENTS

thinks it has to do with who would be using the car that evening, but he can't remember with certainty. He ended up not telling Ann about Laura, and he remembers feeling a moment of satisfaction in keeping this part of his life to himself. He and Ann made up shortly, but he "never got around to telling her" about Laura, who had made it progressively clearer to George that she wanted to sleep with him.

About two months after she had started working in his office, George played a noon-time concert in a nearby park with a quintet made up of several coworkers. Laura and Ann showed up, though separately. When he saw them, he felt suddenly humiliated by his "artistic pretensions." . . . One night, having awakened at 4:00 a.m., he resolved to get his life in order: the next day he began suggesting to Ann that they start a family, and he asked a coworker to complain about Laura's performance to the office manager and see about getting her transferred. Within three weeks, Laura had been reassigned to an office on another floor, and Ann had conceived.

But George didn't feel any happier, and he began to grow frustrated. He started waking up regularly in the middle of the night and could not fall asleep. He feared Laura would discover he had engineered her transfer and considered taking her out to lunch to "set the record straight," but he soon abandoned this idea, as it made him

too nervous. He grew irritated at his wife's "sickliness"—she was by this time frequently nauseous—and he began taking different elevators to avoid running into Laura at the office. He threw himself into his music and decided if he was going to make anything of himself as a musician, he would need a new bassoon. But there was no extra money now that a baby was on the way, which aggravated his "testiness" with Ann.

He did run into Laura several times at work and was disconcerted because she continued to behave seductively around him, though now he wondered if she was mocking him. One night while making love to Ann he fantasized he was with Laura, and subsequently he has been unable to stop doing this whenever he and Ann make love.

George sought help three weeks after the fantasies commenced. He spoke of finding "self-discipline" to be a good husband, father, and musician. He does not want to resent his child as an intrusion in his life, but fears that he might. And he wants to sleep through the night.

BEHAVIORAL THERAPY

"What I would first try to do," says behavior therapist Marcia Chambers, "is 'operationalize' George's complaints—get him to define them as specifically as possible. What does 'selfdiscipline' mean? Does 'testiness' mean he can't sit in a chair for more than three minutes, does he lose his temper more quickly? Once we had defined behaviors he would like to change, I would have him monitor what he's doing that's a problem. In behavioral therapy, everything is measurable and you can see change. It's important for the person to see the change visually, so clients chart their progress on lots of different kinds of graphs and three-by-five cards.

"In George's case, probably the easiest behavior to monitor would be sleep—what time he wakes up, and either how many times he wakes up in the middle of the night or how long those times were. Sometimes just monitoring a behavior makes it drop out—it just stops happening. For instance, one of the best ways to lose weight is to write down everything you eat. . . .

. . . "I would spend maybe four sessions teaching George relaxation. A very deep relaxation takes 30 to 35 minutes. Once he'd learned that, we could really use it for many different things. For instance, what I could do is once he's very relaxed, have him think about being in bed and having sex with Ann. And then see if he could do it again at home. You first have to train him to have positive thoughts about being with Ann; it gives him a good feeling, and you want to get as much 'positive' in him as possible. So if he starts thinking about Laura, he could signal to me—by closing his eyes tighter, or moving his elbow—and I'd say, 'Stop—think about Ann.' If he can't get into an 'Ann scene' or gets anxious in it, I could get him back to the neutral relaxing scene I taught him earlier, and then ease him back into thinking about Ann."

With practice, George will come to relax when he made love to Ann, and the deeper his relaxation, the higher his resistance to distress—to thoughts of Laura, specifically. As Chambers points out, "It's physiologically impossible to feel relaxed and anxious at the same time." . . . And she would encourage him to devise his own rewards, especially ones that he could work into his day-to-day routines, such as taking Ann to dinner after a week of faithfully practicing his bassoon. "My goal," she explains, "is to put myself out of business."

COGNITIVE THERAPY

Each session, as George recounted the bad moments of the week before, cognitive therapist Dean Schuyler would mark off three columns on a lap-sized blackboard and jot down the critical events and the accompanying thoughts and feelings. He might, for example, record the noontime concert episode this way: *Laura and Ann at concert/"I'm a lousy musician and just fooling myself"/Humiliation.* He would also get George to track his responses in a journal between sessions, either at the time of, or as soon as possible after, an emotional upset.

Schuyler claims that careful monitoring would soon reveal how George's thoughts—thoughts he might not have even been aware of—were setting off feelings of distress. "The therapy," says Schuyler, "would then consist of disputing these thoughts," a process dramatized in the following exchange between Schuyler and George (who appeared via the writer).

S: What is so bad about thinking of someone else while making love to your wife?

G: Your marriage is a hoax—this person [Ann] isn't who you wanted.

S: So what if your marriage is a hoax?

G: Well—then you're destroying someone's chances for happiness because—you bound her into this arrangement under false pretenses.

S: So what if you did that?

G: It's hard enough for each person in the world to be happy—why drag someone else down with your lies?

S: Okay, so all of this miserable stuff that you're doing has resulted from your having thought about someone else while making love to your wife?

G: No, no, but—

S: (smiling a little): Certainly that seems to be what you've been saying.

[This therapy is] "not for everyone. The people who do best in cognitive therapy are the kind who do best with psychoanalytic therapy: psychologically minded, generally bright, verbal individuals who are comfortable dealing with concepts and looking at themselves. For George to get relief from the symptoms presented, six months of once-a-week therapy is not an unreasonable expectation."

FAMILY THERAPY

"What I would do in the first session," says family therapist Joseph Lorio, "is talk to George a little bit about the presenting symptoms, maybe for as little as 10 or 15 minutes. Then I would get a history of the relationship between him and his wife, going back to when they first met, and how the relationship developed, what the big events in it were, and how they each reacted to those events. I would be looking for any changes in the relationship's tone that could have been significant as a trigger for stirring up the anxieties he has."

Lorio would also try to involve Ann in therapy as soon as possible. "I may see George alone the first two times and then try to get his wife in by the third session. I might then spend one session just with her, or see the two of them together, then see her individually, then go back to seeing them together—just depends on what the problem is and how they're dealing with it. You can let them know that when families are in this kind of situation, her distancing from him is pretty typical. And when he understands what's going on between him and his wife, he can understand that what he's reacting to is her distancing, and that what he

(Box continued on next page)

needs to do is be more available to her emotionally.

"The key thing is to change from being an emotional reactor to a better observer. The better you can observe and learn about the interplay between self and relationships, the less you react emotionally to it and the faster you make progress. Oftentimes people with just six sessions feel less anxious, calmer, better in control of their lives. But he could be in therapy a year or two, or even longer, if I could get him to bridge his current situations to his extended family. . . .

PSYCHODYNAMIC THEORY

[Psychoanalyst Robert Winer responded]: I'm struck by the kind of work George does, to begin with—he manages other people's development, but he's having some problem managing his own. It's sort of like that cliché, 'Those who can, do; those who can't, teach.' Then there's his complaint of 'testiness'—the more I thought about that word, the more it struck me that that's not a word that somebody would use about himself. People call *other* people testy, but since he's saying it about himself, I'd think he was reporting someone else's complaint about himself. . . . And his childhood was 'as happy as anyone's'—that struck me as an odd statement; it implies some oversensitivity to other people's opinions, something in his early family life about keeping up with the Joneses.

"He says his parents were 'loving and fair.' Well, 'fair' isn't a word a person normally used to describe his parents, unless fairness was some kind of an issue. . . .

"This is getting me to think about the baby representing some further injury to his sense of masculinity. That's unusual—becoming a father usually helps men feel more phallically potent, more full of themselves. In George's case, it's more as if Ann's growing and he's shrinking. . . . You wonder if he feels some threat to his security with his wife.

"And the whole business of getting Laura transferred represents an overriding concern with his own security and a lack of a reasonable effort to be concerned with someone else's. Laura is nothing to get nervous about. She's being flirtatious, that's all. She's entitled to that in life. He can always say . . . , 'Look I'm a married man; we're not going to have anything happen.' I did think getting her transferred is a strikingly aggressive act for him—though again, it's passively done; . . . he gets someone else to do it.

"And now he becomes obsessed with Laura. Usually obsessions are a way of controlling aggression. You wonder how much anger toward his wife about the pregnancy is tied up in that. And men can experience intercourse with a pregnant wife as an attack on the baby, if they're already feeling aggression toward it, so maybe the obsessive thoughts about Laura are some way of blocking out that aggression.

"He does say that he doesn't want to resent the child as an intrusion so he has some capacity for self-awareness. And he takes the initiative to seek help, which leads me to think that he also has the capacity to make more active decisions. It may be that just seeing him through the end of the pregnancy will be enough to help him make some kind of adjustment around the baby. But if his goal is to realize himself more fully as a man, given that he's been ducking that all his life," concludes Winer, "you're talking about analysis: four or five sessions a week, probably for several years." (Turner, 1986, pp. 38–44).

pleasure in doing things that once gave him pleasure. The therapist may ask him or her to list those things: going to a movie, listening to records, going for walks, cooking meals. The assignment may be to engage in a certain number of these activities before the next session. The client will feel he or she has accomplished something by completing such assignments and may even begin to rediscover the pleasure once felt in participating in these activities. As part of the therapy, the client is called upon to monitor his or her thoughts and to question constantly whether they are realistic.

STRESS INOCULATION THERAPY

Stress inoculation therapy is based on Meichenbaum's (1974) theory of stress inoculation. Meichenbaum proposes that by altering the way people talk to themselves, the way they approach stressful problems will be changed. The training takes place in three phases. First, the therapist and client *examine the situations* causing stress and try to uncover the beliefs and attitudes being carried into these situations. The therapist focuses attention on how and what the clients say to themselves in these situations affect their behavior. For example, a graduate student experiences great stress every time she has to give a lecture. Often the effects of the stress are so overpowering that she begins to stutter; her mind has gone blank on occasion. Before she enters the classroom she says to herself, "I know I am going to do a lousy job. I am not well enough prepared. What if a student asks a question I cannot answer?" When the client realizes how damaging her self-statements are, she and the therapist can work up a new set of statements that will be more constructive.

The second phase is called **acquisition** and **rehearsal.** The client rehearses and learns a new set of statements. The therapist suggests certain self-statements that are helpful for a person who feels overwhelmed by the task he or she must do. Some examples of these include "When the fear comes, just pause," or "It will be over shortly," or "Just think about something else."

Application and *practice* are the third phase of the training. The client begins to use the new set of statements in real situations. Usually he or she begins with the situations that are only slightly stressful and gradually works up to increasingly stressing situations. Stress inoculation training is most helpful in cases in which the situations that cause distress are clearly defined—for example, fear of speaking in front of crowds. Some believe that stress inoculation training may prove to be an effective preventive treatment. Maladaptive behaviors may be prevented from developing if a person has the stress inoculation coping strategy in his or her behavioral repertoire (Mahoney & Arnkoff, 1978).

SUMMARY COMMENT

The chasm that exists between psychoanalysis and empirical psychology does not exist with behavior therapy or cognitive therapy. Both are firmly grounded in psychological principles and based on empirical research. By and large, proponents of these approaches also see evaluation as an integral part of treatment, even if treatment is not part of a formal research project. Therapy is approached as hypothesis testing, with the therapist and client working together identifying goals, developing guesses about what maintains the problem, and then manipulating the environment or improving the skills of the individual. If evidence for one hypothesis is not found, the therapist and client use this information to formulate a new strategy and test another hypothesis. Thus, behavior therapy is a joint venture between therapist and client. The therapist essentially plays a consultant role. That is why cognitive and behavior therapists refer to consumers of services as "clients" rather than "patients." They are not viewed as "sick" but as requiring improved skills of some kind.

HUMANISTIC PSYCHOTHERAPIES

Humanistic therapies are based on the positive assumption that human beings, if unobstructed, tend toward growth, health, and realization of their maximum potentials.

RATIONAL-EMOTIVE THERAPY (RET)

Rational-Emotive Therapy (RET) holds a generally humanistic view of human nature. It is founded on belief in the worth and value of human beings and their potential for growth, self-understanding, and self-acceptance. Developed by Albert Ellis (1970), RET is based on the assumption that a person's perceptual interpretation becomes his or her "world." In this view, a well-adapted person is one in whom there is a good match between behaviors, self-perception, and reality. Maladaptive behavior can result from unrealistic beliefs or expectations. A person might believe that he or she must be loved by everyone, must always show perfect control, or must be good at everything. Because these are unrealistic goals, they are self-defeating. A person may feel a failure and thus no good. This feeling is a consequence of the *interpretation*, not of any external event.

In rational-emotive therapy, the therapist determines what the underlying belief system of the individual is. In contrast to psychoanalysis and behavior therapy, the therapist confronts the client with the faulty belief system and *directly* forces him or her to examine it against reality. For example, a woman's lover breaks a date with her. She interprets this to mean that he does not love her and is trying to avoid her. A RET therapist might point out that she also has broken dates in the past. Did that mean that she did not love her mate? What if her car broke down one day and her lover, suspecting that she was disenchanted with him, left her? Would that be fair? In RET the awareness of the client is *constantly directed* to the *inconsistencies* between his or her beliefs and external reality. There has been some criticism of RET about the therapist's active disputing of the client's beliefs. A person might hold very strict religious beliefs, which may be at the core of the problem. If the religion says that sex is bad, the client may feel sinful every time he or she has sex. The therapist, therefore, may be attacking the person's belief system.

PERSON-CENTERED PSYCHOTHERAPY

In Carl Rogers's view (1959, 1980), psychological disorders arise from a blocking of a person's natural inclination toward **self-actualization**—the tendency of an individual to develop maximum human potential. These blocks arise because of unrealistic demands people make on themselves. Individuals might believe that it is wrong to feel anger or hostility toward others. Rather than admit to feeling these "wrong" emotions, they deny and suppress them. In denying these feelings, people may actually numb themselves emotionally or lose touch with these feelings. When individuals lose touch with their real experience, the self is necessarily more fragmented and less integrated. This

CARL ROGERS
(1902–1987)

Person-centered therapy is often conducted in groups.

state makes relationships and a whole variety of behaviors difficult and maladjusted.

The purpose of **person-centered therapy** (formerly called client-centered therapy), according to Rogers (1959), is to release "an already existing capacity in a potentially competent individual." Under the proper conditions, clients can learn to unblock themselves and allow their self-actualizing capacity to emerge. Perhaps the most important element in person-centered therapy is the relationship between the therapist and client. The client's perception of the therapist is particularly important. The client has to perceive in the therapist three qualities: genuineness, empathy, and unconditional positive regard.

Person-centered therapy is **nondirective.** The therapists gain the trust of clients by showing that they base concern for the clients on their ability to accept the clients nonjudgmentally. The therapist respects the client's feelings, privacy, and reluctance. A psychoanalyst directs, interferes, and (to some extent) shapes the patient's revelations and the connections they make. A person-centered therapist does not probe. Unless it is necessary, he or she does not express either approval or disapproval and does not interpret what clients say. More often, he or she repeats and paraphrases what clients have said. These restatements should help clients further clarify their feelings. They demonstrate that the therapist understands the clients because he or she is experiencing what they are experiencing.

Rogers found that therapy usually progresses in three stages. In the first stage the clients express predominantly *negative feelings* toward themselves, the world, and the future. In the second stage they begin to feel and express a few glimmers of *hope*. They show a few tenuous signs that they are beginning to accept themselves. Finally, *positive feelings* emerge which allow them to care about others. They develop more self-confidence and start to make plans for the future. The therapist then concludes the treatment because the person has allowed his or her natural self-actualizing capacity to emerge.

SUMMARY COMMENT

The influence of humanistic psychology has extended to psychotherapy, religion, education, social work, and other professions (Meador & Rogers, 1984). Virtually all therapists regularly attempt to build the client's self-worth, and confrontation of a clients' belief system is prototypical in many therapies. Many psychotherapists train at the institutes established by Rogers and Ellis. Yet, relative to psychodynamic or behavior therapists, few clinical psychologists identify themselves exclusively as humanistic therapists. Rather, these are approaches that have influenced the practice of therapy in a general way.

Rogers himself made early attempts to establish an empirical data base on humanistic therapy, but his followers have been remiss to continue it. Many researchers from other orientations have studied person-centered therapy, however. Because humanistic techniques are common to most therapies, they are frequently used as a comparison treatment when an investigator wishes to study the effects of a more specific change technique.

BIOLOGICAL THERAPY

The evidence on possible biological factors in disorders comes from two sources. First, patients initially feel and experience many disorders as *somatic* complaints—that is, complaints related to the body. Modern psychotherapy began with Freud's discovery of the power that the mind has over the body. His first patients were primarily "hysterics," people who complained of a *physical* problem that had no underlying physical cause. For example, they would suffer from paralysis or loss of some other sensory modality.

Second, as discussed in Chapters 12 and 15, mood and thought can greatly influence body state and vice versa. Stress can cause physical disease, but it is also possible for *physical disease* to cause psychological distress. Of 100 patients who were about to be committed to a state mental hospital, 46 percent had undiagnosed medical illnesses. These were specifically related to their psychiatric symptoms or exacerbated them significantly. When treated for their medical ailments, 61 percent had reduced psychiatric symptoms. The most common illnesses were Addison's disease, Wilson's disease, low levels of arsenic poisoning, and dietary deficiencies (Hall, Gardner, Stickney, LeCann, & Popkin, 1980).

Certain diseases and medical treatments can have mood-altering side effects. Depression is a side effect of the degenerative blood disease lupus and of the strong chemotherapy used in the treatment of cancer. In this section, we will examine the two main kinds of **biological therapy:** electroconvulsive shock and drugs.

ELECTROCONVULSIVE THERAPY

Shock treatments began as a result of an observation that later proved to be wrong: that epileptics do not suffer schizophrenia. Psychiatrists thought that the brain's intense electrical activity that causes epileptic convulsions was incompatible with schizophrenia. In 1938, two Italian psychiatrists, Cerletti and Bini, developed a method whereby an electrical current of about 160 volts was

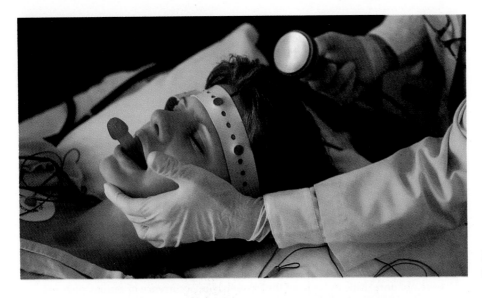

Patient undergoing electroconvulsive therapy

passed through the patient's head from one hemisphere to the other. The patient first loses consciousness and then undergoes convulsive seizures. When the patient wakes up, he or she has amnesia for the period immediately preceding the administration of the shocks. He or she may be disoriented and experience loss of memory for a period lasting up to a few months.

A patient undergoing **electroconvulsive therapy (ECT)** may receive a series of several (usually fewer than 12) shocks. At the completion of the treatment, all or some of the disordered symptoms have often ceased. In the early days of ECT, the convulsions were often so severe that bones were fractured. However, people are now premedicated with a muscle relaxant, which has removed that side effect. A new method of ECT, called **unilateral ECT,** passes the electrical current through only one side of the brain (usually the right hemisphere). This results in fewer of the disorienting verbal side effects of bilateral ECT (Lynch et al., 1984).

Sometimes the cure seems miraculous. Other times the effects are short-lived. Since the development of antipsychotic drugs, the use of ECT has declined. It is an extremely drastic intervention, and the overadministration of ECT may cause significant brain damage.

Furthermore, no one really knows why shock therapy works. The mechanism may simply be the increased amount of electrical firing it induces in the brain, which may in turn facilitate and stimulate the release of greater amounts of neurotransmitters. The inhibition of certain neurotransmitters might underlie severe disorders such as depression and schizophrenia. Today, only in the most severe cases of depression or schizophrenia is ECT used. But it is still the *most effective treatment* (Snyder, 1980).

PHARMACOTHERAPY: ADMINISTERING OF DRUGS

A major change in the treatment of mental disorders came in the 1950s. This was the development of drugs that relieve the major symptoms of several different psychological disorders. **Pharmacotherapy** involves administering drugs from four main categories: antipsychotics, antidepressants, antianxiety drugs, and lithium compounds. Lithium is used exclusively to resolve manic episodes and to control mood swings in bipolar depressive disorder.

ANTIPSYCHOTIC DRUGS Psychiatrists use **antipsychotic drugs** in the treatment of severe disorders such as schizophrenia. They serve to calm the patient (they are often called the major tranquilizers), and they reduce the experience of some of the major symptoms of the disorder, namely, the hallucinations and delusions. It is important to realize what a tremendous impact the use of these drugs has had in mental hospitals. Here is the experience of one psychologist regarding the change that drugs make:

> [I] worked several months in the maximum security ward of (a mental) hospital immediately prior to the introduction of this type of medication in 1955. The ward patients fulfilled the oft-heard stereotypes of individuals "gone mad." Bizarreness, nudity, wild screaming, and the ever present threat of violence pervaded the atmosphere. Fearfulness and a near-total preoccupation with the maintenance of control characterized the attitudes of staff. Such staff attitudes were not unrealistic in terms of the frequency of occurrence of serious physical assaults by patients, but they were hardly conducive to the development or maintenance of an effective therapeutic program.
>
> Then, quite suddenly—within a period of perhaps a month—all of this dramatically changed. The patients were receiving anti-psychotic medication. The ward became a place in which one could seriously get to know one's patients on a personal level and perhaps even initiate programs of "milieu therapy," and the like, promising reports of which had begun to appear in the professional literature. A new era in hospital treatment had arrived aided enormously and in many instances actually made possible by the development of these extraordinary drugs. (Coleman, Butcher, & Carson, 1980)

In recent years, antipsychotic drugs and other advances have allowed many former mental patients to live in halfway houses and become involved with society. Here, a counselor uses art as a form of therapy in the halfway house.

The first antipsychotic drug used in the United States was *reserpine*. It had a calming effect on patients and helped to reduce manic and schizophrenic symptoms. However, it has severe side effects, such as producing low blood pressure and sometimes depression; it may also be carcinogenic. Reserpine is no longer in widespread use because of the introduction of new antipsychotic drugs.

One of the newer drugs is *chlorpromazine* (trade name, Thorazine). Because it has fewer side effects than reserpine, it has become the most widely prescribed drug in the treatment of schizophrenia. Different drug companies manufacture several other compounds of the phenothiazine group, which are all basically variants of chlorpromazine. Chlorpromazine and the other antipsychotics have side effects such as jaundice, stiffness in the muscles, and dryness of the mouth. The most serious side effects are those that affect the motor control areas of the brain. The facial muscles may become so rigid as to make eating difficult, and tremors resembling Parkinson's disease may result. With extended use, these drugs may also cause infertility and cessation of menstruation.

An important result of the use of antipsychotic drugs has been a drastic reduction in the number of people in mental hospitals. Many people who might have remained in institutions for the rest of their lives are able now to live fairly normally. After the development of antipsychotic drugs, the number of people in state and county mental hospitals decreased each year. In 1955 there were almost 560,000; in 1980 there were only 132,000 (Coleman et al., 1980). However, an unfortunate consequence of reducing the number of people hospitalized has been a dramatic increase in the number of released mental patients without homes. They have no jobs and live as street people in our major cities.

The antipsychotic drugs treat schizophrenia but do not cure it. A schizophrenic taking an antipsychotic drug no longer shows overt signs of abnormal behavior, but the evidence suggests that the symptoms are merely suppressed or masked by the drug. The way they work may be analogous to the way insulin controls diabetes. As long as diabetics receive doses of insulin, their disease is under control. But if they stop taking insulin, it will reappear. The analogy is not perfect, because it is not yet clear exactly how the antipsychotics work. We do not know if they work on the basic mechanism of schizophrenia. They may perhaps supplement a short supply of some chemical agent in the brain, or they may only reduce the intensity of the internal experience or inhibit the overt symptoms.

The *dopamine hypothesis* described in Chapter 15 presumes that the drugs work by inhibiting the production of dopamine at the synapse receptor sites (see also Figures 3-26, page 121). In one study, half of a group of schizophrenics were given a placebo, and the other half were maintained on their antipsychotic drug. At the end of six months, the placebo group showed a relapse rate of 60 percent compared to 30 percent of the group on the drugs (Hogarty & Goldberg, 1973). It is still too early to know what the long-term side effects of prolonged treatment with these drugs might be.

ANTIDEPRESSANTS Biochemical abnormalities play an important role in depression. Evidence for this is the effectiveness of drugs used to treat depressive

Obsessions and compulsions are common to us all. We say that we "obsess" when we review a matter again and again in our minds. We laugh about compulsivity in ourselves and in our friends. Have you ever checked the oven more than once to make sure you turned it off? Even when you *knew* that it was off? Most of us know at least one person whose home is so neat we wonder if he or she catches dust before it falls, or who plans his or her wardrobe one week at a time, right down to the underwear, with a kind of precision that *always* ensures a proper match.

For most people this type of behavior is completely harmless. For others it gets out of control. Attempts to control the repetitions only make it worse. **Obsessive-compulsive disorder (OCD)** strikes young and old alike. The handwashing compulsion referred to at the beginning of this chapter is quite common. For others, the compulsion takes the form of repeated measurements of street signs or counting the patterns on the ceiling. In still others, it manifests as a "pack-rat" behavior. I recently heard about a successful lawyer who became homeless after he filled his apartment with so many collectibles that there was no room for him to sleep.

In OCD, the compulsions get worse and worse until eventually they control the victims' lives. They cannot go to school or hold a job because they cannot concentrate on other things. Typically, persons suffering from OCD know that something is terribly wrong, but they can do nothing to stop it.

Attempts to treat OCD with antidepressants or behavior modification have met with only modest success. Research led by Dr. Judith Rapoport, chief of the child psychiatry branch at the National Institute of Mental Health, is beginning to offer a glimmer of hope. She and her colleagues have been conducting drug trials with a new antidepressant called *Anafranil*. The drug has been shown to work in both mild and severe cases of OCD. Treatment appears to be most effective when used in combination with behavior modification techniques that involve repeated exposure to the situations most likely to bring out the compulsion (Rapoport, 1989).

symptoms and the action of these drugs on the neurotransmitters (Snyder, 1980). *Serotonin* and *norepinephrine* are two important transmitters that operate, among other places, along limbic system pathways. Recall that the limbic system of the brain governs emotions, thus depressive symptoms may relate to levels of serotonin and norepinephrine.

To see how researchers arrived at this conclusion, let's look at how two types of **antidepressant** drugs work. One class of drugs are **monoamine oxidase (MAO) inhibitors.** They work by blocking the work of an enzyme, monoamine oxidase, which destroys both neurotransmitters. Thus, MAO inhibitors allow serotonin and norepinephrine concentrations to build up. **Tricyclics** are another class that work by *preventing the inactivation* of serotonin and norepinephrine in the synapse. Recall that neurotransmitters are normally inactivated during the absolute refractory period following transmission across the synapse. During this time, the re-uptake mechanism brings the chemicals back into the presynaptic neuron. *Tricyclics block the re-uptake mechanism,* allowing the released serotonin and norepinephrine to work. Tricyclics have side effects, however; they are sedatives and cause dryness in the mouth, blurry vision, and difficulty in urinating.

ANTIANXIETY DRUGS People suffering from any one of the mild disorders have in common the experience of anxiety. Although there are a variety of ways to relieve anxiety, the most common method of treatment is with drugs. The oldest and most widely used antianxiety drug is *alcohol*, and it is usually self-prescribed.

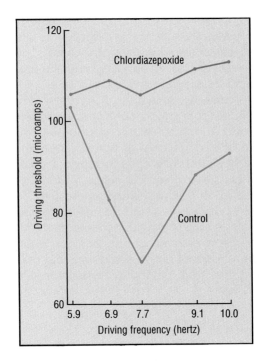

FIGURE 16-2
Antianxiety Drugs and Electrical Activity in the Brain

Antianxiety drugs such as Librium (chlordiazepoxide) alter the rhythm of theta brain waves, and this rhythm can be artifically "driven" to test how such drugs work. The graph here shows that the drug raises the minimum threshold needed to drive the theta rhythm.
(Gray, 1978)

Before the 1950s, the tranquilizers most often prescribed by doctors were sedatives. Today two drugs of the *benzodiazepine* group are the most popular: *Librium* and *Valium*. These drugs work very effectively to reduce the experience of anxiety. People are able to return to work, to sleep, and to confront situations that used to give rise to anxiety reactions.

Antianxiety drugs (minor tranquilizers) are the most prescribed drugs in America (Coleman et al., 1980). There is a growing concern over the overuse of these drugs, first because they are addicting, and second because their indiscriminate use may prevent people from developing coping strategies from within to handle their fears (Gray, 1984). In addition, many people who take antianxiety drugs also drink alcohol. The interactions of antianxiety agents with alcohol can be fatal. In fact, the most common cause of accidental suicide is the mixing of minor tranquilizers and alcohol.

How the antianxiety drugs work is not fully known. One promising approach is Jeffrey Gray's (1984), which proposes that the brain represents anxiety by increased electrical activity (Figure 16-2). The activity is in the parts of the brain that contain the neurotransmitters norepinephrine and serotonin. This increased activity may stimulate increased firing of the neurons and hence the flow of the transmitters. Antianxiety drugs may block synthesis of norepinephrine and serotonin at the receptor sites.

THE EFFECTIVENESS OF PSYCHOTHERAPY

About one out of every seven people in the United States (30 million) will consult a professional for a psychological problem during their lifetime. What will be the outcome? Do therapies work? Does one work better than another? If they work, do we know why? What does "work" mean in this context? The question of the effectiveness of psychotherapy is very difficult to answer. Circumstantial evidence would say that it does work. Why else would 30 million people spend time and money seeking it out? But there are hundreds of therapies available: which ones work best, and for whom?

Empirical evidence is hard to come by. It is difficult to assess why the disordered become "ordered" again. There are many variables to consider, such as the cause and nature of the disorder, the particular experience and personality of the individual seeking help, the competence of the therapist, and the nature of the interaction. Suppose that individuals enter therapy when they are troubled and that therapy is finished when they feel better. Would we then judge that the therapy was effective, that it worked? Suppose they sought additional therapy six months later? What if they went to another psychotherapist? What about the person who comes to therapy with a specific goal and does not obtain that goal, but in the process of therapy becomes happier? Is therapy effective for that person? How can we account for the social pressures that lead patients to tell their therapist (and themselves) that they have changed? Have they changed—really?

EARLY OUTCOME STUDIES

There were virtually no objective data on the effectiveness of psychotherapy until the mid-1940s. Freud and most followers of the psychoanalytic school maintained that the outcome of psychoanalysis was too complex to be studied. Carl Rogers was the first pioneer in the gathering of psychotherapy outcome data. With the development of behavioral therapies, data collection became customary.

In 1952 Hans Eysenck initiated research on the question of psychotherapy's effectiveness. He separated people seeking psychotherapy into two groups. The members of one group were put on a waiting list; the others received psychotherapy. At the end of the study, he concluded, "roughly two-thirds of a group of neurotic patients will recover or improve to a marked extent within about two years of the onset of their illness" (Eysenck, 1952).

This improvement took place whether the person had received therapy or not. He called this two-thirds figure the rate of **spontaneous remission,** meaning that the patient perceived that the neurosis vanished without psychiatry. This figure then would be a baseline to compare the effectiveness of any therapy. At the time he wrote his report, Eysenck claimed that there was no evidence of the usefulness of psychotherapies. However, about 80 percent of the studies since then have shown positive results (Smith, Glass, & Miller, 1980). Thus, the questions that remain are which forms of therapy work better, for whom, and why.

PSYCHOANALYSIS AND PSYCHODYNAMIC PSYCHOTHERAPY

Psychoanalysis is the most difficult of all therapies to evaluate. First, few psychoanalysts undertake research on outcomes. Second, psychoanalysis is available to a very few individuals and suitable for only a few disorders. Freud felt that psychoanalysis was effective in the treatment of mild or "neurotic" disorders only. So more serious disorders, like schizophrenia, are not usually treated with psychoanalysis. Because of the time and expense, psychoanalysis is a route open to a very few. A study conducted by the Menninger Foundation found, however, that psychoanalysis is effective for individuals who score high on scales of ego strength at the beginning of therapy (Smith et al., 1980). In some ways, psychoanalysis is thought of as a therapy for the elite, both psychologically and socially. Research efforts are underway to identify specific characteristics of patients that predict outcomes in psychodynamic therapies (Luborsky et al., 1989).

BEHAVIOR AND COGNITIVE-BEHAVIOR THERAPY

The advent of behavior therapy had several important advantages for the study of outcomes. Primarily, the methods are precise and thus easily measured. Second, the desired outcome is explicit at the beginning—the modification of a certain behavior. How close a client is to that predetermined goal at the end is a good measure of success. Many outcome studies show that behavior therapy is useful when a person has a specific behavior to change, such as a phobia or a habit like smoking or overeating, an addiction, or a sexual dysfunction. Behavioral treatment for phobias has been so successful that, regardless of theoretical orientation, it has been accepted as the treatment of choice. Because behavior therapists use many different techniques, some of which work better than others and with some problems better than others, only a rough statement can be made about the effects of behavior therapy in general (Wilson, 1983). All in all, the cognitive-behavior therapies enjoy a large literature documenting effects. In part, this reflects the dedication to evaluation.

DRUG THERAPY

Results of studies comparing drug treatment to psychotherapy are mixed. Some studies, especially of short-term effects, conclude that drugs are superior to psychotherapy. With certain disorders, there is widespread agreement that this is true. Drugs are the treatment of choice in schizophrenia and in bipolar affective disorder (Hogarty & Goldberg, 1973) but not with major affective disorder (unipolar depression). In major depression, drugs and therapy both work alone, but they work better still if used in conjunction with one another. And without psychotherapy, recovery from depression through drug therapy may be short-lived (Kovacs et al., 1981).

While the benefits of drug treatment are often striking, the side-effects can be similarly potent and, unfortunately, harmful. Long-term use of major tranquilizers can lead to serious disorders such as tardive dyskinesia—impairment of the motor system. Extended use of minor tranquilizers can lead to tolerance, requiring larger and larger doses of the drug. (Today, drugs are used for sleep problems only when they occur during a crisis because these drugs lose their effectiveness in as short a time as four days.) Even when drug therapy is the treatment of choice, there can be problems. Schizophrenics and persons with bipolar disorder are notorious for ceasing to take the drugs once they begin to feel better. Later, they relapse. And even though traditional psychotherapy is ineffective with schizophrenia, for example, research has shown that interventions with *families* of schizophrenics result in improved patient compliance in taking the drugs (Faloon et al., 1982).

"META-ANALYSIS" OF THE OUTCOME OF PSYCHOTHERAPY

The controversy over whether or not psychotherapy works has stimulated some comprehensive studies. Smith and colleagues (1980) analyzed the results of many different studies of effectiveness of psychotherapy. This **meta-analysis** (so-called because it is the analysis of many analyses) finds the following effects (Smith, Glass, & Miller, 1980):

1. The *average* effect of psychotherapy is *positive* in almost all kinds of therapies.
2. The amount of effect is fairly large, enough to move a person who is at the mean (50th percentile) of a population up to the 80th percentile rank.
3. Cognitive therapies seem to be the most effective of all therapies, but all are effective.
4. There is a significant positive effect of "attention-placebo," but it is not as strong as psychotherapy.
5. Drug therapy is as effective as psychotherapy, and the effects of drug therapies and psychotherapy add to one another. Thus, drug plus psychotherapy is the most effective treatment on the average.

Thus, although certain therapies seem to be more beneficial than others, three decades of research and almost a century of treatment show that most therapies are largely effective. Some of the success may be due simply to attention given to the client's problem, some to the specific technique, and some to drugs. The main point is that psychotherapy, on average, can help people.

Some practitioners liken the verdict of the meta-analysis research to the Dodo bird in Lewis Carroll's *Alice in Wonderland* that exclaimed, "Everybody has won and all must have prizes" (Stiles, Shapiro, & Elliott, 1986). Is this really the case for all the therapies? Decidedly no. Many unanswered questions remain. Berman, Miller, and Massmann (1984) found that the theoretical allegiance of the investigators who report the findings predicts which therapy is judged better, even in the meta-analysis studies! A more fundamental problem is that there is no real matching of problem to therapy. The chance to compare alternative therapies, as in the case of George (in the box "One Problem, Four Treatments") is rare. Luborsky (1989), a psychodynamic psychotherapist himself, points out that the extensive criteria for being considered a "good" candidate for psychodynamic therapy result in the approach serving people who are already functioning at a relatively high level. Such a selection bias would be expected to inflate the results of outcome studies.

COMMON MECHANISMS OF CHANGE

Since some psychotherapists from all orientations have been able to produce positive effects, we need to address the common features that they share. Is there something that virtually all therapists do that might account for treatment gains? Some research attention has been paid to these questions. Many studies (Frank, 1983) suggest that the most important factor in therapeutic success is the *therapist-client relationship*. If there is a successful outcome, it may not be because one technique or another was the "right" one. What may matter is that each therapy recognizes the importance of the therapist establishing a good, trusting relationship with the client (or patient) at the start of therapy.

THERAPIST VARIABLES   When I was a behavior therapist in training, I was supervised briefly by an extraordinarily gifted neo-Freudian therapist, Dr. James Capage. I was seeing a young woman who told me that her eating was out of control. I worked week after week carefully recording her eating habits, caloric intake, and assessing the conditions under which she overate. She made no gains (except in pounds). I asked Dr. Capage to sit in one day. As I spoke to her, he sat forward in his chair, listening intently to her talk. After a long pause, he leaned back, inhaled deeply from his pipe and quietly said to her, "Tell me what the real problem is." She burst into tears and began to describe the years that she had been sexually abused as a child.

In thinking back on this case, I am convinced that it was not a question of theoretical orientation (he only asked one question!), but rather the interviewing skill of the therapist. Knowing when to probe more deeply and when to be silent are essential ingredients of effective therapy. Research shows that experienced therapists (regardless of orientation) are more similar to one another than they are to novices of the same theoretical orientation (Fiedler, 1950). A more recent supervision experience convinced me more than ever. For a year (after I had many years of experience as a therapist behind me) I supervised a group of psychology interns along with a Sullivanian therapist and a Freudian therapist. We all listened to the same problems from students and commented on them.

There were days when I felt as if we all came from different planets, and there were days when I left feeling that our differences were actually quite small. In retrospect I realize that when we talked about what we actually *did* I felt that we were similar. Psychoanalysts, although supposedly nondirective, do steer their patients toward more appropriate behaviors. Behavior therapists, while they focus most of their efforts on specific change techniques and do not *write* extensively about establishing a trusting relationship, do work to establish a relationship before requesting patients to change. The days that I felt like a Martian were the days the conversation drifted to *why* we did what we did. In this area there was little agreement.

Does it even matter if a person is trained as a therapist at all? In many studies researchers compared experienced therapists with undergraduates, housewives, graduate students, and inexperienced but trained therapists. In general, inexperienced or nonprofessional people are far more directive and less interpretive; they act the way most nonprofessionals would imagine a therapist to act. But a panel of experts can pick out experienced from inexperienced therapists. However, are professional therapists always more effective than amateurs? In a comparison of 12 outcome studies using inexperienced versus experienced therapists, only 5 showed that patients of experienced therapists achieved better outcomes (Smith et al., 1980). A closer examination of these statistics suggests that the severity of the problem does matter, but it also seems that on a personal level something happens to people involved in therapy, something beyond just the formal training. Are there some general processes that occur during therapy that span all theoretical approaches?

ATTENTION The need to belong is quite basic to us. It follows, then, that some people are helped by the attention they receive from the therapist. In one study, Paul (1965) divided a sample of college students seeking therapy for "performance anxiety" into two groups. One group became involved with an insight-oriented therapy (e.g., psychoanalysis and person-centered). The other group received "attention-placebo" treatment, which means that a person was merely convinced that a therapist was interested in him or her but received no actual treatment. At the end of two years, both groups showed the same rate of improvement.

Many other analyses have shown that the therapeutic situation, regardless of methodology, has many elements in common. People enter therapy feeling as if they have no control over their lives, and they leave with some hope (Frank, 1982).

THE BENEFITS OF CONFESSION Another general mechanism that may operate, regardless of theoretical orientation, is confession. Patients confide in therapists. Frequently they speak of traumas that occurred years earlier and about which they never spoke before. Can talking about a trauma, in and of itself, help reduce the effects? James Pennebaker argues that it can. In a series of studies, he has shown that writing or talking about traumatic events improves physical and psychological health (Pennebaker, 1985; 1988; 1989; Pennebaker & Beall, 1986).

He believes that when most of us worry silently, it is without much mental organization; flashes of emotion and bits and pieces of memories circulate in and out of our consciousness. When we speak or write we are forced to translate the worry into language. Language serves as a catalyst that organizes the emotional turmoil and gives new meaning to it.

PLACEBOS: ARE THEY FOR REAL?

Frank (1983) states that "the placebo *is* psychotherapy." This may seem like an exaggeration, but it points out the power of the placebo and the great importance of mental phenomena. Researchers often compare all kinds of therapies to placebos. However, the placebo itself is an important aspect of therapy. For example, consider Lourdes, in France, the most famous Western religious healing shrine where each year over 2 million pilgrims come to be healed by the springs. Thousands of the pilgrims are chronically ill and, having failed medical treatment, turn to the shrine as a last resort. Even before arriving at the shrine, the ailing pilgrim's hopes are raised by the elaborate preparation. And once there, the ill people are overcome with religious faith and hope. These strong, positive emotions may well act as powerful placebos to cure many of the pilgrims' illnesses.

The word *placebo* itself comes from the Latin, meaning "I shall please," and the implications are intriguing. Does this refer to the doctor or the healer? A **placebo** is a substance that a doctor may give to please or placate a patient, even though it has no specific pharmacological activity for the ailment. Does it refer to the patient's own decision to get better, possibly to please the doctor? In either case, researchers have historically viewed the placebo as a nuisance, something to be shunted aside and "controlled *for*" rather than something to be understood in its own right (White, Tursky, & Schwartz, 1985).

Placebos have been shown to be effective against postoperative wound pain, seasickness, headaches, coughs, anxiety, and other disorders of nervousness. Subsequent studies have also shown improvements from placebos in high blood pressure, angina, depression, acne, asthma, hay fever, colds, insomnia, arthritis, ulcers, gastric acidity, migraine, constipation, obesity, blood counts, and lipoprotein levels (Buckalew & Ross, 1981; Frank, 1982). But not all the results of placebos are positive and therapeutic. Placebos can produce an entire range of symptoms including palpitations, drowsiness, headaches, diarrhea, and nausea (Agras, Horne, & Taylor, 1982).

Some researchers postulate that placebos release natural brain opiates (endorphins) that reduce pain. But since placebos result in many effects other than pain relief, it is unlikely that endorphins mediate the whole range of responses to placebos. Still, findings such as these have led many researchers to wonder whether psychological factors and the doctor-patient relationship are as important as drugs are in medicine and form part of the basis of therapy itself. Remember that physical symptoms sometimes display as psychological ones. The reverse may be true, and it may well be possible to interrupt problems in a variety of ways.

In summary, there are any number of reasons why therapy may work aside from the reasons therapists typically articulate. Speaking to a kind and perceptive person, the simple act of confiding, receiving attention, and the placebo effect are only four. There are many others, including such things as changes in the person's belief system. When people believe that they can accomplish a goal, they are more likely to accomplish it than if they doubt their ability (Bandura, 1982). Other reasons why therapy may work are less affirming to therapists, but not less real. Social cognitive processes like *dissonance reduction*—"I paid all this money, I must be better"—may also play a role.

The effects of these social-psychological phenomena on therapy outcome do not denounce the influence of specific treatment techniques. On the contrary, research controlling for all of these factors shows that many specific techniques do contribute substantially to improvement, above and beyond these more subtle factors. Yet they do point out the need to assess a wide range of factors that might contribute to the overall effectiveness of therapy.

It is not enough to know that most therapies have a positive effect. Perhaps some therapies *only* provide improvement based on demand characteristics. If the improvement persists, we would not want to discount it! But we would want to do better. A scientific approach to psychotherapy is one in which all pieces of the puzzle are studied, their relative contributions to outcome are assessed, and possible areas of improvement are identified. This approach has the potential to lead us to impressive interventions tailor-made to specific problems of specific individuals.

THE SCIENTIFIC FUTURE OF PSYCHOTHERAPY

What will be the status of psychotherapy 100 years from now? The answer depends largely on the steps we take to demystify and evaluate it. One of the greatest barriers to the evaluation of psychotherapy is that different orientations vary in the extent to which they are willing to state clearly what "recovery" means. Therapy goals are quite different depending on the theoretical approach. Some approaches evaluate their effects based on diffuse or easily obtainable goals, such as the patient's statement to the therapist that he or she has improved or even the therapist's *opinion* that the patient has improved (regardless of what the patient thinks!). Other approaches employ specific, observable goals. So the comparison of outcome studies across diverse paradigms provides only limited information. As it stands now, those therapists most committed to the scientific development of their work use the toughest evaluation criteria.

Beware of psychotherapists who go so far as to say that therapy is an "art," not a science and, like religion, is not amenable to scientific evaluation. Imagine a physician saying that a medicine cannot be evaluated because it works for some people and not for others and compliance depends on the way the instructions are given. You would want to know why the drug works for some people and not others, and you would want to know—verbatim—what the dosage instructions were! "Therapy as art form" positions do little more than put up a smoke screen that forbids any evaluation and abdicates all responsibility to provide accountable services to the public.

Psychotherapists who are seriously committed to understanding the therapeutic process recognize that psychotherapy and science are not incompatible. There is much reason, indeed much evidence, to think that psychotherapy has positive effects. But it is far from a perfect science. If we are ever to answer questions such as which treatments work best and for whom, we will have to compare treatments across paradigms in objective, verifiable ways. No doubt, we will find that, in many cases, psychotherapy provides great benefits; and no doubt, in others we will see that "the emperor is not wearing any clothes."

We currently have good ideas about many of the basic elements of effective change techniques. But as with research on intelligence, personality, and the nature of the mind, the need for a complex analysis of multiple components is clear. The analysis of multiple components of successful therapy is an initial step toward scientific psychology becoming more capable of resolving complex human problems.

SUMMARY

1. From psychology's beginnings, there have been debates about the merits of applying psychological principles to human problems. Today most psychologists are practitioners, but there remains much debate within the scientific community about the utility of application. Some feel that treatment is premature given our limited knowledge; others feel that we must act with whatever tools that we have.

2. Mental health workers come from many disciplines. A *psychiatrist* is a physician who specializes in psychiatric disorders. A *psychoanalyst* is a practitioner trained in the Freudian tradition and usually is a physician. A *clinical psychologist* holds a Ph.D. in psychology and may specialize in a particular form of psychotherapy. In recent years, *professional schools* began to award the Ph.D. in clinical psychology as well;

these schools focus primarily on the practice of psychology with little emphasis on the science of psychology. *Psychiatric social workers* and *counselors* are trained in the disciplines of social work and counseling, respectively.

3. In the late eighteenth century, a series of humane reforms allowed disordered people to be treated as victims of disease instead of as "possessed" by them. A great advance in the late nineteenth century was the discovery of the cause of one type of disorder, general paresis, which is a slow degenerative disease that eventually erodes mental faculties. It was discovered to be caused by syphilis. The elimination of paresis by medical means is one of the few decisive victories in the war against mental disorder. That victory led to the hope that researchers would find a specific biological cause for every pathology.

4. Accuracy in diagnosis is a continuing aim of psychopathologists. The benefits of diagnosis include predicting the course of the disorder, help in planning an appropriate treatment, and the conduct of additional research. Diagnosis can be harmful if the therapist overlooks important information pertaining to individual circumstances or if it leads to self-defeating beliefs on the part of the client.

5. The *psychoanalytic* method of treatment is based on *Freudian* theory. Freud believed that disorders are caused by conflicts between conscious and unconscious desires. In this system, therapy brings these desires into consciousness where the patient can acknowledge and analyze them. Freud developed the technique of *free association* in which the psychotherapist asks the patient to say anything that comes to mind, without criticism or editing. The idea is that the thoughts, images, and connections in therapy must come from within the patient. Psychoanalysis is usually very expensive and lasts from one to several years.

6. There are several phases of treatment in psychoanalysis. In the opening phase, *resistance* in the patient emerges, which is the way that patient unconsciously works against revealing feelings or thoughts. At a certain point in treatment, patients *transfer* their feelings toward people in their lives onto the analyst (an important process called *transference),* and these feelings thus come to the surface. The therapist then proceeds to an *analysis of the transference.* Patients begin to see, in a concrete way, the nature of their misconceptions, having transferred them to the analyst. The transference is then *resolved* in the last phase of the treatment, in which patients and the therapist agree that they have achieved their goals.

7. *Behavior therapy* stems directly from *learning theory.* The approach is to work directly on the problems. Treatment is the process of *relearning.* Two forms of behavior therapy are related to two primary modes of learning, respondent and operant conditioning. Treatment based on *respondent conditioning* aims to reduce the discomfort that a person experiences in response to certain key external stimuli. Behavior therapy aims to decondition anxiety-producing autonomic responses. Treatment based on *operant conditioning* attempts to change behavior by changing the conditions that follow it. This form of therapy has been useful in treating test anxiety, sexual dysfunction, phobias, addictions, and interpersonal problems.

8. Important reconditioning techniques in behavior therapy include the following: (a) *systematic desensitization* eliminates unwanted conditioned responses and conditions the client to another stimulus that elicits a response (usually relaxation) incompatible with the original one; (b) *flooding* exposes the client to a noxious stimulus for a prolonged period to produce a more neutral response; (c) *assertiveness training*

teaches people to behave in ways that reduce difficulties and anxieties surrounding interpersonal relationships.

9. *Cognitive-behavior therapy* emphasizes the effects of thought on behavior, holding that restructuring individuals' cognitive systems can change their behavior. Two common treatment approaches are cognitive restructuring and stress inoculation. *Cognitive restructuring* aims to change people's unrealistic goals and self-defeating views of themselves. *Stress inoculation* therapy focuses specifically on the ways that people talk to themselves that lead to anxiety and behavioral dysfunction.

10. *Humanistic therapies* are based on the assumption that human beings will reach their maximum potentials if unobstructed. Thus, the purpose of therapy is to release an already existing capacity in a potentially competent individual. *Rational-emotive therapy (RET)* involves confronting clients with their irrational beliefs about the way that they "should be" in an effort to reduce unrealistic expectations and thereby reduce anxiety. *Person-centered psychotherapy*, also referred to as Rogerian therapy, aims to destroy obstacles that prevent *self-actualization* (maximum potential). This therapy is nondirective. It usually progresses in three stages: (a) the client expresses predominantly negative feelings both inwardly and toward the world and the future, (b) the client begins to feel hope, and (c) impromptu feelings emerge that allow the client to have more self-confidence and to plan for the future.

11. A different approach to therapy is *biological*. Recent research has shown that the areas of the "mental" and "physical" are not as unrelated as previously thought. Brain states affect mental states, and body states affect brain states. This is why placebos work so well. Therefore, the relationship between the biology of the body and therapy is potentially quite important.

12. One important form of therapy is *electroconvulsive therapy (ECT)* in which a patient receives a series of shock treatments. When completed, there is often a complete cessation of disordered symptoms, especially those of depression. Since the invention of antipsychotic drugs, the use of ECT has been in decline because it is a drastic intervention. Today, only in the most severe cases of depression or schizophrenia is ECT used. It is the most effective treatment of such severely disordered cases, in spite of the fact that we do not understand why it works.

13. *Pharmacotherapy* has perhaps been the most revolutionary change in the treatment of mental disorder. Three types of drugs have been developed that relieve the major symptoms of several different psychological disorders. *Antipsychotic drugs* treat severe disorders, such as schizophrenia. They serve to calm the patient and reduce the experience of delusions and hallucinations. Examples of antipsychotic drugs are reserpines and chlorpromazine. *Antidepressants* are an effective class of drugs used to treat depressive symptoms. These drugs seem to act on the neurotransmitters, especially serotonin and norepinephrine. *Antianxiety drugs* are widely used in our culture. Among the most popular are Librium and Valium. These drugs work effectively to reduce the experience of anxiety. There is growing concern because they are addicting, and their indiscriminate use may prevent people from developing coping strategies from within to handle their fears.

14. It is controversial how effective psychotherapy is. Early outcome studies showed that patients improved as much without therapy as with it. Among therapies, psychoanalysis is the most difficult to evaluate; there is little emphasis on successful outcomes because they are so loosely defined. Behavior therapy is much easier to

evaluate because its procedures and the criteria for successful outcome are quite specific. Behavior therapy is more effective than other approaches with specific phobias and habits. Cognitive-behavioral therapies are also highly effective with well-defined problems. On the average, people in therapy are statistically better off than people in matched situations who do not enter therapy. Not everyone is helped by every form of psychotherapy to the maximum extent. Psychotherapy is still in its infancy and much research needs to be done.

15. The fact that most therapies, even those based on contradictory theoretical approaches, result in positive gains leads to questions about common mechanisms of change. The client-therapist relationship, other therapist variables, attention, placebo, and confession are several features of therapy that may contribute a great deal to treatment success.

TERMS AND CONCEPTS

acquisition and rehearsal
analysis of the transference
antidepressant
antipsychotic drugs
assertiveness training
behavior modification
behavior therapy
biological therapy
catharsis
clinical psychologist
cognitive therapy
cognitive-behavior therapy
cognitive restructuring therapy
counselors
counterconditioning
electroconvulsive therapy (ECT)
flooding
free association
general paresis
humanistic therapies
interpretation of dreams
meta-analysis
monoamine oxidase (MAO) inhibitors
neo-Freudians
nondirective

obssesive-compulsive disorder (OCD)
operant conditioning
person-centered therapy
pharmacotherapy
placebo
professional psychology
psychiatrist
psychiatric social worker
psychoanalysis
psychoanalyst
psychodynamic therapy
rational-emotive therapy (RET)
reconditioning
resistance
resolution of the transference
respondent conditioning
role playing
self-actualization
spontaneous remission
stress inoculation therapy
systematic desensitization
transference
trephining
tricyclics
unilateral ECT

SUGGESTIONS FOR FURTHER READING

Beck, A. T. (1989). *Love is never enough.* New York: Harper & Row.

Written by one of the foremost experts in cognitive psychotherapy, this book describes how couples can overcome conflicts and solve relationship problems.

London, P. (1986). *The modes and morals of psychotherapy.* New York: Harper & Row.

The most influential study of therapy of the past period, now revised after 22 years. Recommended.

Rapoport, J. (1989). *The boy who couldn't stop washing: The experience and treatment of obsessive compulsive disorder.* New York: Dutton.

A fascinating account of obsessive-compulsive disorder, including descriptions of clinical cases and the latest research findings on treatment.

Smith, M. L., Glass, G. V., & Miller, T. I. (1980). *The benefits of psychotherapy.* Baltimore: Johns Hopkins University Press.

A technical account of how the different methods of therapy are evaluated and analyzed. Useful.

VandenBos, G. A. (1986). Psychotherapy research [Special issue]. *American Psychologist, 41* (2).

A special issue of the journal, concerning many of the current problems of therapy research. They include its evaluation and the help computers may bring. Also included are some of the difficulties.

Yalom, I. D. (1989). *Love's executioner and other tales of psychotherapy.* New York: Basic Books.

A prominent existential psychotherapist presents 10 case studies of his patients and the treatment of their problems, providing the reader with insights into the therapist-patient relationship rarely made available to the public. The book is thoughtful, interesting, and remarkably well written.

"CASUAL
INFLUENCE"

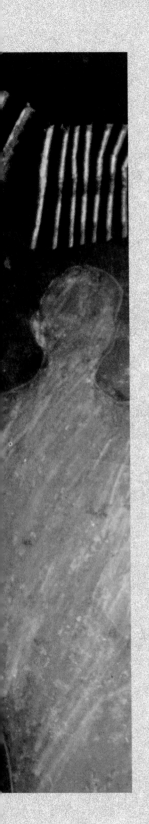

V
THE SOCIAL WORLD OF THE ADULT

If our early development is primarily biological and cognitive, our later development is social. Other people often determine how and where we work, what we like to eat, and how we think. We conform, obey, accept. We may make extreme decisions, such as whether or not to kill, while in a group.

The experiences of adulthood —work, marriage, becoming a grandparent—make many people aware that they are part of something larger than their individual selves. We are workers, citizens, members of a social group. Some people become "citizens of the world," concerned with life on the planet as a whole.

So, we expand away from our biology during our adulthood—until the end, when our biology reclaims us once again.

17

SOCIAL PSYCHOLOGY

Human beings are social animals. Try to imagine anything you might think, feel, or do that is completely without connection to others. Even when we are isolated, thoughts of others keep us company and influence our feelings and actions. The mere presence of other people intensifies and directs our behavior. This intensification phenomenon has been known since the early days of psychology as the **coaction effect.** Bicyclists ride faster against other people than alone against the clock; children reel in their fishing lines faster in groups than alone (Triplett, 1897). Other people influence not only our behavior but also who we are and how we think about ourselves.

This influence can exist only in our thoughts. Our daydreams, memories, explanations, and expectations guide our interpretation of situations and our behavior. Influence can be subtle. An attractive person being particularly friendly to us can cause us to respond in a friendly way. In an unfamiliar situation, we look to others for cues about how to behave. And influence can be overt. The daughter of a friend asks us to buy Girl Scout cookies and we comply. A man in a white coat asks us to administer shock to a stranger and we obey.

Social psychology is the study of how thoughts, feelings and actions are influenced by the actual, imagined, or implied presence of others (Allport, 1985).

OBSERVING OTHERS: SOCIAL PERCEPTION

Perceiving others is fascinating and complex because, unlike objects, other people cause events that affect us. In general, we perceive others the same way we perceive everything else. We pick up sensory information, we have selective schemata, we interpret actions and events, and we reconstruct memories. This process is even more true of our experience of people: we may interpret someone's behavior as "overbearing" and, from then on, select and notice only those actions consistent with our interpretation. Not only that, if we expect that person to be overbearing, we might be a bit timid and actually cause him to behave in an overbearing way.

BEHAVIORAL CONFIRMATION

Our perception of others has a powerful influence on the way we behave toward them. And our beliefs about others create their own reality (Snyder, 1984). Suppose you have been led to believe that the person you are about to meet is a hostile person. How would you behave? What if you were asked to play a competitive game with this person? How would you play? Competitively? As part of a program of research on **behavioral confirmation,** Mark Snyder and William Swann (1978) designed an experiment to test this scenario. They found that the subjects did indeed play competitively. They also found that competitive play by subjects who had been *led* to believe that their partners were hostile elicited hostile behavior from the partners, confirming the subjects' initial expectation of hostility.

Snyder, Tanke, and Berscheid (1977) convinced half of their male subjects that they were talking to an attractive woman on the telephone. The other half believed they were talking to an unattractive woman. Each of the 10-minute conversations was recorded. Next, research assistants who knew nothing about the purpose of the study listened to recordings of the telephone conversation, hearing only the women's half of the conversation.

The assistants then filled out an "impression formation questionnaire." The women who were designated by the research assistants as the most sociable, warm, and interesting were those women whom the male subjects thought to be attractive. In other words, the behavior of the men who thought they were talking to attractive women elicited from the women "attractive" behavior. Reviewing this research, Snyder writes:

> Acting on beliefs about objects and physical events does not influence the reality of those objects and events in the same way that acting on beliefs about people and social events does influence the reality of those people and their behavior. For example, a sedan does not become a sportscar because I think of it as one and try to handle it as one, but a person may become friendly and sociable because I believe him to be, and treat him as if he were, that type of person. (Snyder, 1984)

SOCIAL THINKING: ATTRIBUTION

All of us wonder, either casually or intimately, about what other people's thoughts are; we try to predict what they might do, and we puzzle over why they did what they did. The study of these explanation processes has been guided by **attribution theory** (Heider, 1946 1958; Jones & Davis, 1965; Kelley, 1967). We attempt to attribute people's behavior to a cause. In turn, our own behavior is influenced by the explanations we come up with. We might see Jim snap at Barbara and think, "Jim was rude, he must have had a tough day." Or we might think, "Jim was rude, what a boor." Each of the explanations we gave for Jim's behavior attributed the cause to a different source.

The first cause, a bad day, is an external source of Jim's rudeness. It is a **situational attribution.** Because it is situational, we wouldn't expect Jim to behave the same way in a different situation. Presumably when we see him next, and his day has run smoothly, we will not be surprised to find him charming. On the other hand, the second explanation, he's a boor, is a **dispositional attribution.** It places the cause of his rudeness inside Jim, like a trait. Because of our dispositional attribution, we might expect him to behave like a boor in a different situation—talking to us, for example. So the next time we see him we take care to avoid him. The way we explain other people's behavior influences our expectations of them in the future. And as we now know, these expectations not only influence our own behavior but the behavior of others as well.

MISTAKES AND BIASES IN INFERENCE

Early researchers in attribution assumed that we function much like amateur scientists (Kelley, 1967, 1972). They reasoned that we observe behavior and rationally assign the cause of the action to either of the people involved (the actor or the object) or to the situation. After seeing Jim be rude to Barbara, according to Harold Kelley, we would systematically consider a variety of possible causes for his behavior. We would take into consideration our knowledge of Jim's behavior in the past, our knowledge of the behavior of people on tough days, and our knowledge of Jim's behavior with people other than Barbara. We would then assign a cause to either Jim, Barbara, or the situation.

Researchers soon found, however, that not all of this information carried the same weight (Fiske & Taylor, 1984; Nisbett & Ross, 1980). They found that there are some biases in the attribution process.

THE FUNDAMENTAL ATTRIBUTION ERROR

We tend to assign the cause of events to the person rather than to the situation. This is called the **fundamental attribution error** (Ross, 1977). When observing others, we assume that their behavior is freely chosen and is guided by underlying traits or attitudes (Jones & Davis, 1965). To test this idea, Jones and Harris (1976) asked students to evaluate essays that either supported or opposed Fidel Castro. The subjects were told either that the essays had been assigned or that the writer had chosen the topic. Even when the subjects knew the topic had been assigned—that is, the behavior was caused by the situation rather than the individual—they believed the writers of the pro-Castro essays to be supporters of Castro.

Ross, Amabile, and Steinmetz (1977) randomly assigned the role of questioner in a college bowl quiz to one subject and assigned another subject the role of answerer. The questioner was to compose a set of challenging questions from his or her store of knowledge and to pose these questions to the answerer. Observers, who knew that the assignments had been made randomly, were asked to rate the general knowledge of both the questioner and answerer.

Before looking at the results of this experiment, note that the questioner had an advantage in this situation. Each of us has our own idiosyncratic store of trivia as a result of our interests and experience. You may be able to name the vice presidents of the United States in order while your best friend knows the entire life history of every Marvel Comics super-hero.

In this experiment, subjects assigned to the role of questioner were able to display their own wealth of knowledge by composing difficult questions to which they knew the answers. The role also guaranteed that the questioners could conceal their lack of knowledge in many other areas. The answerers, on the other hand, were prevented any such display. Think how you could dazzle someone with your knowledge of baseball statistics in a situation like that.

But what if you were assigned the role of the answerer? How much do you know about Beethoven symphonies? Did observers in this experiment make allowance for this "role-based situational cause" of behavior? No. Both observers and subjects overlooked it and inferred instead that the questioner was smarter than the answerer, thereby making a dispositional rather than a situational attribution.

There are a number of reasons for this error. First, when we are observing people we may be unaware of the norms and power relationships in the situation. The guy across the room who just spilled guacamole on the dress of the redhead he was talking to isn't necessarily clumsy. It may be that he just saw his boss walk into the room and he is supposed to be at the office or that the redhead is the boss's wife.

A second reason for the fundamental attribution error may be our society-wide belief in personal responsibility (Jellison & Green, 1981). People are held accountable for their actions. Also, we may assign cause to the individual because that is what we are paying attention to. People and what they do stand out against the background of a situation. Finally, it is simply easier to assign cause to a person than to a situation because there are more than 18,000 ways of describing people (Allport & Odbert, 1936) and far fewer for describing situations.

SELF-SERVING BIAS

When observing others, we attribute the cause of events to the person rather than to the situation. But when things go wrong and we are asked to account for our own behavior, we blame the situation. And when things go right, we take credit for it. This is the **self-serving bias** (Miller & Ross, 1975).

Think about the last time you did poorly on an exam or your team lost. Why did that happen? Chances are the reason you give is situational (Lau & Russell, 1980)—the room was too hot or the field was muddy. But if you did well or your team won, you probably took credit for superior ability or effort. Perhaps we do this to protect our egos (Snyder & Swann, 1978; Zuckerman, 1979).

Attributing an event positively is also adaptive. How hard you study or how fiercely your team plays in the future depends on the explanation given for the performance last time. If you were to attribute that exam failure to lack of ability, how hard would you study for the next one? On the other hand, if you attributed that failure to the hot day and broken air conditioner, then you would go ahead and give it your best shot.

MAINTAINING OUR SENSE OF CONTROL

One reason for biases in our social thinking is that they help us maintain our **sense of control.** We like to assume that our behavior is under our own control, and we believe that other people are the same way. If Jim's rude behavior is under his control and freely chosen, then we attribute his behavior to his disposition: he's a boor. We discount the situation in part because it simplifies matters. If we attribute his behavior to a dispositional cause, then Jim's future behavior is easier for us to predict.

Taking credit for our successes and blaming failure on the situation also allows us to feel in control. Our successes should be repeated and our failures are anomalies. In fact, one way that the thoughts of depressed people differ from those of nondepressed people is that they lack this self-serving bias. Unlike the rest of us, depressed people tend to give situational explanations for their success and blame failure on themselves (Sweeny, Anderson, & Bailey, 1986).

Some researchers have suggested that maintaining a sense of personal control is so important that it approaches being a psychological need (Fiske & Taylor, 1984). Researchers have found that people work harder when given

When things go wrong and we feel anguish, we still tend to blame the situation. This tendency is the self-serving bias.

more control over their jobs (Tjosvold, 1986), and retirement home patients improved both psychologically and physically when given some control over their activities (Langer & Rodin, 1976).

ILLUSORY CORRELATIONS

Sometimes we expect things to be connected, and so we perceive a connection between two events that are really random. Many of us come to believe that washing cars causes rain. Others believe that rain is caused by picnics. Have you ever had a "lucky shirt" or a "lucky penny"? This misattribution is called an **illusory correlation.** Once we believe a correlation exists, we tend to notice it whenever it is confirmed. We simply fail to notice all the times the belief is disconfirmed (Ward & Jenkins, 1965; Troiler & Hamilton, 1986). We create illusory correlations to try to make our lives more predictable, to maintain our feeling of control.

One researcher found how much people were willing to pay for control. Ellen Langer (1975) sold lottery tickets for a 50-dollar prize. Each ticket cost 1 dollar. Subjects were either handed a ticket or allowed to choose their own. Later, ticket holders were asked how much they would sell their ticket for. Those who had been handed a ticket asked for an average of $1.96, while those who had control over choosing their own wanted an average of $8.67!

REACTANCE AND HELPLESSNESS

How important is our sense of control to us? Consider what happens when we lose it. We either fight or we fold; it depends on the situation. Usually we expect to have control, that we are free to choose our behavior, and that our efforts will be successful. When this expectation is thwarted we experience psychological reactance.

Reactance is an angry or hostile reaction to a loss of freedom (Brehm & Brehm, 1981). Someone pushing you too hard to see their point of view, to buy their product, or to vote for their candidate may encounter reactance on your part. Their "you have no other choice" approach is likely to result in a reaction of "oh yeah, watch me." Maybe you really wanted to vote for Senator Slick, but now any other candidate will get your vote. In this situation, reclaiming your freedom of action has become more important than the action itself.

But what causes us to fold rather than to fight? Any time we feel that we have no control over the outcome of events, we experience a sense of helplessness. Assume you didn't have time to study for the first exam in your chemistry class and so you got a C. Since that wasn't good enough, you studied very hard for the second exam. And you got another C. For the final exam, you not only studied very hard but also wore your lucky shirt. And you still got a C.

Wouldn't you begin to feel helpless? You might even stop studying altogether. Even rats don't run without rewards. Psychologists believe that we learn to be helpless through repeated experiences of such lack of control (Seligman, 1975). After a while we don't expect to have control, so we give up. Feelings of lack of control may not cause depression in people, but a perception that they lack control over life characterizes the thoughts of depressed people (Weary, Jordan, & Hill, 1985).

ATTITUDES

An **attitude** is a lasting evaluation of an issue, thing, or person (Zanna & Remple, 1988). Attitudes consist of several components, the ABCs of attitude: **affect, behavior,** and **cognition.** An attitude about another person (say, a negative one) has an *affective* component (dislike), a *behavioral* tendency component (avoid that person), and a *cognitive* component (belief that the person is conceited and domineering).

DEVELOPING ATTITUDES

We learn many of our attitudes through basic socialization processes, such as observing others or direct reward and punishment. Approval and disapproval from parents and friends help to shape many of our important beliefs. As a child, observing your father frown and mutter under his breath while the president is speaking helps to shape your political outlook.

Daryl Bem (1972) hypothesized that we infer our own attitudes in the same way we infer the attitudes of others. According to his self-perception theory, we put ourselves into the role of an outside observer who witnesses his or her own behavior. That is, we come to know our attitudes by observing what we do. "I didn't realize I liked X so much until I defended him to my friends," or "I must like chemistry because I got an A on the exam." This is true if the attitude is one that we have not thought much about and is therefore not particularly strong. Of course, we are more likely to think about strong attitudes, and they will be prominent in our memory (Fazio, 1986).

THE LINK BETWEEN ATTITUDES AND BEHAVIOR

We want to know about people's attitudes so we can predict what they might do. If you like one political candidate more than another, you are more likely to say positive things about that candidate, and you will most likely vote for him or her in the election. You say you prefer Hondas to Toyotas, so when it comes time to buy a car you will head for the Honda dealer. Perhaps.

Politicians and businessmen spend vast amounts of money on public opinion polls and market surveys. They assume that by knowing your attitude about what they have to offer, they can predict who you will vote for and what you will buy. The problem is that an expressed attitude doesn't always translate into behavior. That is, thinking and feeling don't automatically lead to acting. You may think jogging is good for you, and you are planning to start any day now. You may prefer Hondas to Toyotas, but the Toyota dealer in your town has a terrific service department and is closer to where you work. So you decide to buy a Toyota. Someone asking you what you prefer couldn't have predicted your behavior.

WHEN ATTITUDES INFLUENCE BEHAVIOR

The relationship between attitudes and behavior has been controversial in social psychology. But this controversy has centered on the definitions and measurements of attitudes and behaviors. The ordinary view that attitudes can and do cause actions is supported when researchers have carefully and specifically measured both. But researchers found that, before they can predict behavior from an attitude, they must also take into account such situational factors as perceived control ("I can act") and the social norms operating ("It's OK to act") (Ajzen & Fishbein, 1980). Something else that influences whether an attitude gets expressed as action is how well it is remembered (Fazio, 1986). And important attitudes are those that are remembered best (Krosnick, 1988).

WHEN BEHAVIOR INFLUENCES ATTITUDES: COGNITIVE DISSONANCE

Not only do attitudes affect behavior, but the opposite is also true: behavior influences attitudes. In fact, one of the most effective methods of persuasion is self-persuasion through justifying our behavior. One perspective on this involves **cognitive dissonance,** which assumes the need for cognitive consistency (Festinger, 1957). An individual experiences cognitive dissonance whenever he or she holds two cognitions—that is, beliefs, attitudes, or knowledge of behaviors—that are psychologically inconsistent with each other. *Dissonance* (literally, disharmony) is a discrepancy between an attitude we hold and our knowledge of something we have done or intend to do. We try constantly to resolve discrepancies because, as in any state of disequilibrium, dissonance is uncomfortable and motivates us to reduce it (Croyle & Cooper, 1983).

Dissonance can be reduced by changing one of the cognitions so that it is no longer inconsistent with the other cognition, or by attempting to reduce the importance of one of the dissonant cognitions. For example, suppose you insulted one of your friends in public. This behavior is *dissonant* with your

A rational person who smokes may have a hard time justifying his or her habit in the face of the strong arguments against smoking, and especially in front of a child.

589

ATTITUDES

perception of yourself as a kind friend. There are several ways you could reduce the dissonance in this situation. Since you can't take back the behavior, you could change how you think about your friend. You might decide that you really don't like her very much, that she really isn't a friend. Or you could change how you think about the behavior.

For example, you could decide that it wasn't really a very great insult. Or you could recall that your friend is quite sensitive, in fact she is really a little too thin-skinned, and you were really doing her a favor by giving her practice dealing with "tough guys." In each of these cases, the result of justifying your behavior is a change in attitude. In one case you changed your attitude about your friend, and in the others you changed your attitude about your behavior.

Another time we might experience dissonance is when we make a difficult decision. Once you buy that new Hyundai instead of the little Ford you were looking at, anyone asking you about your new car would find you extolling its virtues at the expense of small American cars. Finally, expending great effort to achieve something can sometimes create dissonance. After standing in line for hours and paying a small fortune for tickets to that new show about phantom roller skating cats, it would be difficult to admit that the show was boring. Attitudes changed in this way are often particularly strong and resistant to change (Aronson, 1988).

Consider these two statements: (1) *I know cigarette smoking causes cancer;* and (2) *I smoke.* A rational person would be uncomfortable trying to live with these two contradictory facts. So the discrepancy could be solved in several ways. She could give up smoking, or consider cancer not a bad thing. She could assume that researchers will find a cure by the time she gets the disease. In the extreme, she could ignore the data. (Or, as Festinger jokingly suggested, she could give up reading!)

The following experiment, known as the "$1/$20 study," was the most eminent demonstration that justification of behavior can change attitudes (Festinger & Carlsmith, 1959). Sixty undergraduates were randomly assigned to one of three experimental conditions. Experimenters explained that they were interested in "measures of performance" and asked each subject to perform two repetitive tasks. These tasks had been designed to be as dull as possible. First, subjects were to place 12 spools in a tray, empty the tray, place the spools in the tray, empty it, and repeat this for a half hour.

They were then confronted with 48 square pegs embedded in a board and asked to turn each peg clockwise a quarter of a turn. When they had completed this, they were to return to the first peg and again turn each peg clockwise a quarter of a turn. They were to do this also for a half hour. Meanwhile, to make the cover story convincing, an experimenter sat using a stop watch and pretended to take notes. But the real experiment hadn't begun yet.

One-third of the subjects were paid $1. They were asked to help out the experimenter and tell a waiting subject (who was a confederate of the experimenters) about the experiment, including the fact that the task was enjoyable and interesting. Another third of the subjects were paid $20 to say the same thing. The final third simply performed the repetitive task and were not asked to tell anyone how they liked the job.

Later, the subjects were told that the psychology department was evaluating some of the experiments being conducted and wanted to interview them about

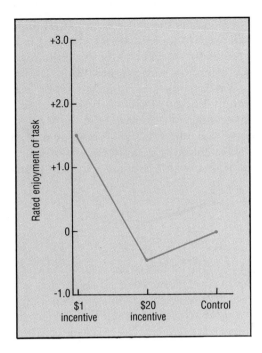

FIGURE 17-1
Behavior, Incentive, and Attitude Change

Paid to perform what they knew would be a boring task, those paid only $1 had more reason to change their attitude about the work to make it consistent with their behavior than did those paid $20, an amount that gave them sufficient reason to perpetuate the inconsistency.
(Festinger & Carlsmith, 1959)

their experience. As part of the interview, they were asked how interesting they thought the task really was. In reality, all subjects initially thought that the task was extremely dull.

Festinger and Carlsmith predicted that subjects in the $1 condition would experience dissonance and would change their attitude about the task. They also predicted that subjects in the $20 condition would not experience dissonance and would not change their attitude. They felt that the $20 subjects would think, "Heck, for $20 it's no skin off my back to lie about such an insignificant thing." The $20 would justify their behavior. On the other hand, the $1 subjects would be left with insufficient justification. Their reasoning would be "I wouldn't lie about such a silly thing for $1, so I must have really enjoyed it."

The results confirmed this prediction. During the final interview, the $1 subjects evaluated the task as significantly more enjoyable than did both the $20 subjects and the control subjects (Figure 17-1). In this case, the behavior produced a change in attitude. The inconsistency between the behavior (saying the task was interesting) and the initial attitude (thinking the task was boring) produced a dissonance. Since the behavior couldn't be changed, the subjects changed their attitude so it was consistent with their behavior. The $1/$20 study was the first of literally hundreds of studies that documented this process of self-persuasion.

Dissonance is aroused whenever we have behaved in a way that is not consistent with our self-concept. We must have freely chosen the behavior ("No one paid us $20 to do it"), so the responsibility is ours. Also, the action must have negative consequences for others ("They will be seriously bored for an hour"), otherwise there is nothing to justify. Finally, we must experience physiological arousal that is attributed to the action (Croyle & Cooper, 1983).

The more responsible we feel and the greater the consequences for others, the greater will be the dissonance aroused (Cooper & Fazio, 1984). Similarly, the greater the dissonance, the more likely we will change our attitude.

Attitudes changed in this way are often particularly strong. Think how difficult it would be to leave an organization after you had spent years of convincing others to join the group. You are likely to have justified your activities by becoming even more convinced of your belief in the value of the organization. With each new convert, your attitude would strengthen. It would be very difficult for anyone to persuade you that the group is, in fact, quite peculiar because you have developed a strong attitude through your own behavior.

PREJUDICE

Prejudice derives from mechanisms similar to those that we use to experience the world and develop our other ideas and attitudes. We are able to judge many different objects and people because of our efficient simplification processes. We sort the infinite variety of things we come across into simpler categories, and we assume that all members of a category are similar. The problem comes when we overextend our simplifying strategies.

Prototypes are central to categories. They are examples that are "best instances," as a robin may be the best instance of a bird. However, when we overextend a prototype, it becomes a stereotype. A **stereotype** is a generalized assumption that attributes identical characteristics to all members of a group: Americans are materialistic, blonds are dumb, the elderly are confused, and the Irish are drunks. But not all stereotypes are negative: Americans are generous, blonds are attractive, the elderly are wise, and the Irish are poets. Because our expectations of others influences their behavior, we are mainly concerned with negative stereotypes.

The content of stereotypes may differ, but the process remains the same. Stereotypes guide our expectations and therefore influence what we notice, what we encode, and what we remember. They are *heuristics* that guide our thinking, and so once they are formed, we resist changing them. Gordon Allport, in *The Nature of Prejudice* (1954), gives this example:

Mr. X: The problem with Jews is that they only care for their own group.

Mr. Y: But the record of the Community Chest campaign shows that they give more generously, in proportion to their numbers, to the general charities of their community than do non-Jews.

Mr. X: That shows they are always trying to buy favor and intrude into Christian affairs. They think of nothing but money. That is why there are so many Jewish bankers.

Mr. Y: But a recent study shows that the percentage of Jews in the banking business is negligible, far smaller than the percentage of non-Jews.

Mr. X: That's just it: they don't go in for respectable businesses. They are only in the movie business or run nightclubs.

DISCRIMINATION Prejudice is an attitude; **discrimination** is the behavior it predicts. Discriminatory behavior ranges from simple avoidance to blatant rejection, such as excluding members of a given group from neighborhoods or jobs. Discrimination can be outlawed, but that doesn't necessarily eliminate prejudice.

COUNTERING PREJUDICE: CHANGING ATTITUDES WITH ACTIONS Some prejudices are learned. One way to fit in is to adopt and conform to many of the existing attitudes of the group, and we sometimes do these without questioning or examining the attitudes. Unfortunately, many of a group's attitudes may be prejudices. Our strongest attitudes, however, are those formed through direct experience (Fazio & Zanna, 1981). One way to counter prejudice is to reverse these processes. Conformity of attitude can also work to reduce prejudice. Prejudiced people, when they join less prejudiced groups, adopt more tolerant attitudes (Aronson, 1988). Another way to reduce prejudice is to increase contact with the prejudged group; direct experience dispels the reasons or basis for the prejudiced attitude.

But simple contact isn't enough to eliminate prejudice. Cooperation is also needed. One interesting study shows both how prejudice can develop and how we might change it (Sherif, Harvey, White, Hood, & Sherif, 1961). Twenty-two boys in summer camp were divided into two groups. For a week the boys lived in these groups, which they named the "eagles" and the "rattlers." The first phase of the experiment was to create strong group affiliation and cohesion of a random groups of individuals. Once each group had become a cohesive unit, they were pitted against one another in competitive sports events. The winning team would receive desirable prizes. Initially, the boys showed good sportsmanship, but gradually resentment, hostility, and discrimination arose between the teams.

In the final phase of the experiment, the goal was to decrease the ill will between the groups. Simply eliminating competition did not work. The groups remained hostile toward each other. The experimenters then arranged for the

Prejudice seems to be reduced through increased cooperative contact with members of the prejudged group.

camp water supply to fail. Since water was vital to all campers, the group had to cooperate to repair the damage. Later the experimenters caused a truck to break down. It required the cooperation of all the campers to tow the truck up the hill with a rope. When both groups worked together toward these common goals, hostility decreased and cooperation and fellowship increased. The cooperative effort to achieve a superordinate goal reduced the feelings of differences between the groups and allowed the two groups to share a sense of accomplishment and to discover similarities.

One systematic attempt to reduce prejudice uses cooperation as the key. Asked by a school district to help reduce racial tension in desegregated classrooms, Elliot Aronson (Aronson, Stephan, Sikes, Blaney, & Snapp, 1978) developed the "jigsaw classroom technique." Noting that classrooms often stress individual competition, Aronson and his colleagues set about developing a technique that creates interdependence.

In this method students are divided into groups, and each group is assigned a project. Each member of the group is given specific information about one part of the assignment—that is, one puzzle piece. Members of the group are to teach their part of the puzzle to the others. The only way to do well on the exam is if each member shares his or her information with the group.

This process makes each person an important and invaluable resource. If a group member is shy or has difficulty speaking English, the other members of the group are forced to pay careful attention and help draw the student out. One by-product of a jigsaw classroom is an increase in empathy exhibited by students (Bridgeman, 1981).

Thus, two major psychological principles can work to reduce prejudice:

1. Stereotypes can be overcome by increasing the availability of information about the groups, especially by increasing direct knowledge of a variety of individuals within the group.

2. Association and cooperation with members of a discriminated group demonstrates and actively proves that group's worth.

PERSUASION: CHANGING ATTITUDES WITH WORDS

Whenever you turn on television, open a magazine, or walk down the street, you are exposed to the efforts of people who are trying to change your attitudes. These **persuasive** messages aim to change your attitude about automobiles, toothpaste, hairspray, dog food, political candidates, or issues. They are trying to change your attitude because they want to influence your behavior—to buy their product or support their view.

We are exposed to so much information that we simply screen out most of it. Persuasive messages have a chance of working only if we can be induced to think about them, carefully. We tend to think about a message if it is relevant to us, if we are exposed to it many times, and if it is in written form (Chaiken & Stangor, 1987). That is, to be persuaded, we must not only pay attention to the message but also understand and remember it. Sometimes, however, we shortcut the process and allow the expertise or attractiveness of the persuader or simply our exposure to the product to change our attitude.

WHO SAYS WHAT TO WHOM? There are many factors that affect whether a persuasive message works or not: the source of the message, the message itself, and the audience to whom it is addressed. Or, who says what to whom. Is the source of the message attractive, or expert, or trustworthy, or similar to us in some way? If so, we are more likely to be convinced (Petty & Cacioppo, 1981).

What kind of message is most effective? It depends. If the message is complex, we will be more convinced if it is in writing and we can read it at our own pace (Chaiken & Eagly, 1976). Otherwise, a verbal or visual presentation is more effective—the more vivid the better.

One kind of presentation, which by its nature is vivid, is one that arouses *fear*, thus trying to persuade people to quit smoking by showing them a photograph of a diseased lung or an antismoking message recorded by a well-known person who had died of lung cancer. Fear appeals work only if they are believed and accompanied by recommendations for specific actions that are believed to be effective (Rogers, 1975). Another kind of presentation is the one-sided message, which works only if the audience is friendly to the position being presented, if it is unlikely to hear the other side, and if temporary opinion change is all that is desired. Otherwise, it is best to present both sides of an argument (Karlins & Abelson, 1970).

But which side should be presented first? If the attitude won't be measured right away—that is, the buying or voting opportunity is a few days away—then you would want to present your side *first*, so the information you present will influence how the audience understands and processes the other argument. This first impression is an example of the **primacy effect.** But if the buying or voting is to happen immediately, then you would want to present your side *last* to take advantage of the **recency effect.** Your argument will be best remembered, for a short time (Petty & Cacioppo, 1981).

Are there some people who are easy to persuade? Again, it depends. Intelligent, educated people are more persuaded by complex messages, while less intelligent people are more persuaded by simple messages. But an intelligent person may counterargue a complex message rather than yield to it (McGuire, 1968). Contrary to folk wisdom, women are no more persuadable than men (Eagly & Carli, 1981).

Overall, as we saw in the case of countering prejudice, the most effective methods of attitude change are those that motivate action. By arousing and directing action, persuasive communications can lead to self-persuasion through behavior.

Who a speaker is, what he is saying, and whom he is speaking to are all factors that affect how persuasive a message is. President John F. Kennedy was a particularly persuasive speaker.

SUBTLE INFLUENCES ON OUR THOUGHTS FEELINGS AND ACTIONS

Our thoughts and feelings are not the only things that influence our behavior. We constantly interact with other people, and they influence our behavior in both subtle and overt ways. The mere presence of others influences how we perform and whether we help or hurt someone. Other people provide cues about norms and values and act as guides to appropriate action. If they belong to a group that is important to us, their influence on us is even stronger.

SOCIAL FACILITATION

Have you ever been practicing your backhand or playing a video game and suddenly become aware that someone was watching you? How did it affect your performance? If you were a beginner, your performance probably deteriorated. But if you were already very good, having an audience probably improved your performance. This is known as the **social facilitation** of dominant responses (Zajonc, 1965).

Having others around is arousing and interferes with difficult tasks. But if the task is easy, having others around is exciting and may cause you to outdo yourself. This is true of animals as well as humans. (Recall the discussion of the optimal level of arousal in Chapter 13, page 458.) But with humans, the effects of an audience on performance also depend on how close, how big, and how important the audience is (Latane, 1981).

SOCIAL COMPARISON

New situations don't usually come with a procedures manual. When you start a new school or a new job, much of the stress of adjusting comes from learning the correct way of doing simple things, such as eating (on a tray or off, out of a bag), getting around (car, subway, bus, feet), and dressing (suits, button-down shirts, tee shirts, sweats). You also want to know whether your attitudes fit in. How do you find these things out? Sometimes you ask, but mostly you simply watch. But who do you look to?

The theory of **social comparison** (Festinger, 1954) states that, when in doubt, we compare ourselves to those we admire or believe are like us. We compare our behavior and attitudes for correctness or our abilities to see where we rank. The group we choose to compare ourselves with is our **reference group.** When there are differences between our attitudes and those of the group, we don't fit in and we often pay a price. The members of the group may dislike us. There may be pressure to change attitudes and to conform. If we refuse to conform, they may reject us (Schachter, 1951).

A classic study demonstrating the effects of group membership on political views was begun in 1935 at Bennington College, then a small expensive college for women in Vermont. The college had just graduated its first senior class, and it had not yet gained a wide reputation. The older students and professors were liberal, but the bulk of the new students came from very conservative families. Thus, there was a wide difference between the attitudes of the new students and those of their new reference group. Theodore Newcomb and his colleagues (1943) charted for over a quarter of a century the effects of exposure to the different attitudes.

The college itself was isolated, and the students were self-sufficient and formed a close-knit group. Over the four years in college, the once-conservative students increasingly adopted the liberal attitude of the older students who had been influenced by the views of their professors. Liberals held many of the leadership positions. The longer the students attended Bennington, the more liberal their views became: 62 percent of the freshman class, 43 percent of the sophomore class, but only 15 percent of the junior and senior classes were Republicans.

Even after 25 years, most of the students were still politically liberal. The change that had been initiated by the college reference group persisted (Newcomb, Koenig, Flacks, & Warwick, 1967). Newcomb explained this persistence by noting that, after college, the students actively sought out other liberals. They joined liberal groups, which then became their reference groups and provided a continuing source of liberal information and identification. Many of the reference group changes that many of us make in college become important for life. But in this extreme case, in only eight months some of the most conservative young people in America had become the most liberal—a substantial and lasting change in attitude—without dramatic brainwashing and with nothing but a change in reference group.

CONFORMITY

To **conform** is to obey the customs or standards of the group. The more desirable and important we find the group, the more difficult it is to resist its pressure. Sometimes, in ambiguous circumstances, we go along with those around us, even if we don't know them. We try to fit in.

Solomon Asch (1956) conducted what has become a classic study of social influence on conformity. Volunteers were recruited for a psychology experiment on visual perception. One real subject and six confederates of the experimenter were seated along a table and shown a card with a vertical line on it. The experimenter then showed a second card that had three vertical lines, one the same length as the line on the first card and two obviously different in length.

Subjects identified which line on the second card was the same length as the one on the first. The subjects answered in turn; the real subject responded last. During many of the trials all of the confederates picked the same obviously incorrect line. While common sense tells you it would be very easy to resist this pressure, overall 37 percent of the responses given by the subjects were incorrect. Some subjects never gave a wrong answer, but 76 percent went along with the group and gave a wrong answer at least once (Figure 17-2).

In this experiment, Asch placed subjects in the dilemma of being right or being liked. By conforming, the subject avoided singling himself out and being

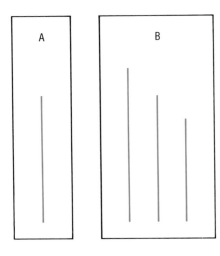

FIGURE 17-2
Social Influence

In the Asch study, subjects viewed display A and then were asked to choose the line in display B that matched it.
(Asch, 1956)

The man third from the right (top) is the subject in this series of Asch photos. The rest of the men are confederates, who were asked to give uniformly incorrect answers. The subject believes he is in a visual judgment experiment and finds himself a lone dissenter when he gives the correct answer. This subject persisted in his opinion, saying that he "has to call them as [he] sees them."

rejected by the group. This is the same dilemma we face when violating the norms of groups that are important to us. When we conform, we are changing our behavior but not our minds. Asch repeated his study but allowed responses to be written rather than stated aloud, and conformity dropped (Asch, 1957).

Several factors determine the degree of conformity. One is group unanimity. People are most likely to conform when faced with unanimous group opinion. In the Asch experiment, the overall conformity was about 36 percent. If, however, there was even one person who did not go along, conformity dropped drastically, to about 8 percent. It does not even matter if the other dissenter's answer is wrong (Wilder & Allen, 1973).

A second factor is group size. If you are sitting with someone in a lecture who says that it is boring, you may or may not agree. But if 10 other people say it is boring, you may begin to agree. In the Asch experiment, only 2.8 percent conformed when there was only one other person in the room, while 12.8 percent conformed with two other people, and about 30 percent with four people. Conformity does not increase with groups over four (Asch, 1951).

A third factor is the person's relationship to the others in the room. If the others were perceived as experts in line length estimation, conformity would have been higher (Campbell, Tesser, & Fairey, 1986). If the others were unlike the subject in age, social group, or status, conformity would have been lower. And what if the others in the room had all been the subject's fraternity brothers or other members of the football team? If the subject felt secure about his position within these groups, conformity would not have been influenced; but if he were insecure, conformity would have been higher (Aronson, 1988).

GROUP INFLUENCE

A **group** is not simply a collection of individuals; it is two or more people who are gathered together or who have a trait, a belief, or an experience in common. Groups influence our behavior through norms, roles, and cohesiveness (Forsyth, 1983).

Norms are the rules of behavior established by the group. Often they are unspoken but understood by all the members. The norms exert pressure to conform: wear a tie, be on time, no eating at your desk. Violation of these rules will result in pressure from the group. A **role** is an assigned task within the group. Suppose you were the designated leader of a group but refused to preside at a meeting or make any decisions. This would violate the group's expectation, and you would be pressured to assume your duties. These norms and roles influence our behavior only if we want to remain in the group. The more cohesive the group, the stronger its influence on the behavior of its members (Baron & Byrne, 1987). If a group is not cohesive, then these subtle social forces operating to keep members in the group won't be effective.

THINKING AND ACTING IN GROUPS

Most of us do much of our work in groups. We might assume that by distributing tasks according to our abilities and coordinating our actions, better products or decisions will result. Not always. Fifty people scrubbing oil off rocks in Alaska should get 10 times as many rocks clean as five people. Right? Probably not. According to Bibb Latane, when our efforts are hidden in a group, we sometimes slack off. He calls this **social loafing** (Latane, Williams, & Harkins, 1979). Testing this idea as part of his social impact theory (Latane, 1981), he found that people clap harder alone than when in a group and leave bigger tips when paying a separate bill than when contributing to a group tab. Social loafing is likely to occur if individual contributions are not identifiable and if the task is not difficult or particularly involving (Jackson & Williams, 1985).

Social life is characterized by many interactions involving both cooperation and competition among members of groups large and small.

Workers clean oil off rocks from the *Exxon Valdez* spill. Did they work as hard in a group as they would have individually?

Social impact theory (Latane, 1981) predicts that, as the number of others around you increases, the total impact on you also increases. But as the group grows, *each added person* has less of an individual impact on you. That is, adding one more person to a 10-person group has less of an impact than adding a fourth person to a 3-person group. The influence of others is also greater if they are physically close rather than far away. Also, if these people are important to you, then their influence is even more pronounced.

GROUP POLARIZATION

As we have seen, groups exert a subtle influence on our behavior—even groups of people we have never seen before, as in the Asch experiment. But, what about the more formal groups in our lives, such as those we work or play with. If, as Latane suggests, the influence of a group increases with closeness and importance to us, what happens when we try to work with people to solve problems and make decisions?

You might think that by pooling expertise, decisions made by a group are better than those made by individuals. Because diverse viewpoints are represented in a group, it seems reasonable that any decision will be more carefully considered and moderate than one made by an individual. Instead, researchers have found that groups make more extreme decisions than individuals. The dominant view of the group as a whole seems to be made stronger through discussion (Myers & Bishop, 1970). When groups discuss a problem, those who are for the decision become stronger in their support, and those who are against it oppose it even more. This results in a polarized decision—decisions tend to end up at one extreme or the other: risky or conservative.

Group polarization is a result of social comparison and persuasion. Group members compare themselves to others in the group and move to greater agreement with those who share their views. They also become even more convinced through developing and giving arguments in support of their position.

GROUPTHINK

Occasionally groups make disastrous decisions. Irving Janis (1982) analyzed a number of such unfortunate decisions made by the U.S. government. Among these were the Bay of Pigs invasion, involvement of the United States in both Korea and Vietnam, United States's unpreparedness for the attack on Pearl Harbor, and the Watergate coverup. Common features of the decision process were a highly cohesive group; a strong, directive leader; and reaching premature agreement in a crisis situation. He termed this phenomenon "groupthink." In each of these situations, conforming to group norms became important, and the group lost touch with the reality of the problem at hand.

Groupthink is characterized by a collective feeling of invulnerability and a belief that all past decisions made by the group were correct and moral ("We are the good guys"). In fact, the feeling of group invulnerability is the group analog of the positive illusions held by individuals (Goleman, 1989). Also, the group is highly cohesive, and opponents are thought of in a stereotyped way ("They are the bad guys").

There is group pressure against dissent, which leads to self-censorship on the part of some members in some situations ("I don't think this will work, but I don't want to lose my job") or to conversion ("Gee, maybe it will work") in others (McCauley, 1989).

This results in an illusion of unanimity, which is sometimes held in place by a "mindguard." A **mindguard** is a member of the group who acts to shield the group from information that might alter the decision ("There aren't enough ships to get the troops there all at once." Or, "The product causes one out of three people to break out in hives"). Criticism is discouraged, so the group process results in an inadequate search for information, thereby limiting the range of proposed solutions.

Avoiding groupthink involves building contentiousness into the group process. Janis suggests that this can be done by assigning a member of the group to be devil's advocate, allowing nongroup members to respond to the group's solutions, forming subgroups to come up with separate solutions, and allowing members a chance to reconsider. These solutions disrupt the pressures to conform and expose the group to a wider array of information and possible solutions.

THE SUNNY SIDE OF SOCIAL INFLUENCE: HELPING OTHERS

WHEN DO PEOPLE HELP?

It might surprise you that having other people around will influence whether or not you will help someone in need. *When* people help and *why* has puzzled psychologists. We are all familiar with stories of apathetic bystanders and people who don't want to get involved. Yet, we are also familiar with stories of great heroism. Why the difference?

Puzzled by a widely publicized incident in which a young woman was attacked and murdered while 38 witnesses did nothing (recall the discussion of

Kitty Genovese in Chapter 1, page 23), Bibb Latane and John Darley (1970) designed a series of experiments to find out when people will help others. They found that, if others are present, individuals are less likely to stop and help someone who appears to need it. Why is this? There are a number of reasons. In an ambiguous situation, such as when someone we can't see yells for help or we see a figure lying in a doorway, what do we do? First, we try to decide if it is really an emergency. As in any other ambiguous situation, we look to others. We compare. If there are others around us, we look to see if they noticed and how they interpret the situation. If others seem to be continuing on unconcerned, we might decide that the call for help was part of a children's game or that the figure in the doorway is a sleeping drunk.

But, if we decide that it really is an emergency, having others around will also affect whether we decide to help. One of several reasons that we are much more likely to help if we are alone is that we would be the only one who *could* help; when others are present, the responsibility diffuses among the bystanders. Whose responsibility is it?

The next question we ask ourselves is Can we help? Can they? If we have some special expertise, such as being trained in first aid, we might decide to help. Otherwise, we will probably look to others. Finally, if others are around and we decide to act, we are likely to worry about what they think. What if it isn't really an emergency? What if others think we are responsible? In all of these ways, the presence of other people will inhibit our helping.

THE GOOD SAMARITAN

Are some people more likely to help than others? Helping someone in need is just one example of **prosocial behavior,** which is behavior that benefits others. Being a Red Cross volunteer, raising money for the Heart Fund, or leading a Boy Scout troop are prosocial actions.

Although whether or not a person will help in a specific situation can't be predicted from a personality test (Gergen, Gergen, & Meter, 1972), there are a few personal characteristics that are associated with prosocial behavior. Among these are where we live, how our parents behaved, how self-interested we are, and how competent we feel. If we live in a rural environment rather than in a city (Amato, 1983) and have parents who had high moral standards and who lived by them (Fogelman & Winer, 1985), then we are likely to be empathetic (Eisenberg & Miller, 1987), oriented to the needs of others (Eisenberg-Berg, 1979), and feel capable of helping (Midlarsky, 1984).

Whether or not we help someone may also depend on who needs help. In both emergency and nonemergency situations, we are more likely to help if the person is someone we know (Pearce, 1980), similar to us in some important way (Krebs, 1975), attractive (Benson, Karabenick, & Lerner, 1976), or appears to be dependent and deserving of help (Berkowitz, 1972).

WHY DO PEOPLE HELP?

Altruism is a prosocial behavior that is personally costly and engaged in without the expectation of reward. Altruism puzzles psychologists: how can unrewarded behavior be explained? How can the behavior of a man diving into

Who will stop to help this person, and why?

A volunteer helps two women learn to read.

a freezing river to rescue victims of a plane crash or someone who gives up a place in a lifeboat be explained? It may depend on how we define reward. Perhaps these people would feel guilty if they didn't act, or they anticipated the praise of others. Or perhaps they simply misjudged their actions. Daniel Batson (1987) has conducted a series of studies testing these various explanations for altruistic behavior. He found that *empathy*—the capacity to experience the emotions of another—is enough to motivate some people to act for the benefit of another in the absence of any personal reward.

THE DARK SIDE OF SOCIAL INFLUENCE: AGGRESSION

Aggression is the forceful intent to do harm. The harm can be psychological as well as physical (Bandura, 1986). Although of a different kind, a malevolent comment can cause as much harm as a well-aimed shoe.

There are two basic types of aggression. *Hostile* aggression is motivated by anger or hatred and is intended only to make the victim suffer. *Instrumental* aggression is motivated by an incentive, usually economic. The victim may be injured incidentally, as when a purse snatcher causes an old woman to fall, breaking her hip. Hostile and instrumental aggression are often combined in the same act.

Aggression is an attribution as well as an act. Whether or not you judge an act to be aggressive depends on the attribution you make about whether the act was intended. Throwing an object with the intent to harm is an aggressive act, even if the object misses its target. On the other hand, if you were seriously injured by a wild pitch or a pop fly, you would not be the victim of aggression.

As with many attributions we make, there is a bias when attributing aggression. The prejudices we hold influence attributions we make. Just as we are likely to excuse friends and loved ones when they have harmed us, the harm caused by favored members of society is usually attributed to accident or circumstance. But when harm is caused by disfavored members, it is attributed instead to personal intent (Bandura, 1986).

WHEN DO PEOPLE HURT ONE ANOTHER?

Many factors affect the aggressive response.

1. *Physiological arousal* increases the probability of aggression, but only when aggression has become a dominant response (Zillman, Johnson, & Day, 1974). A high level of *sexual arousal* increases aggression, and a low level inhibits it, presumably by simply distracting attention from the provocation (Bandura, 1986).

2. *Crowding* intensifies feelings, pleasant or unpleasant. If a person is in an aggressive mood, crowding is likely to make him or her feel more aggressive (Freedman, 1975).

3. *Noise* increases the chance of aggressive behavior when aggression is dominant in the response hierarchy—that is, a likely response (Bandura, 1986).

4. *High temperatures* also facilitate violence. A long, hot summer or heat waves have often contributed to urban riots. Riots occur relatively more frequently in very hot weather (Carlsmith & Anderson, 1979). Aggressive crimes also increase as the weather gets hotter (Anderson & Anderson, 1984).

5. *Alcohol* in small amounts tends to reduce aggression, while in larger amounts it makes aggression more likely (Taylor, Gammon, & Capasso, 1976).

6. *Marijuana* in large amounts inhibits aggression (Taylor, Vardis, Rawitch, Gammon, Cranston, & Lubetkin, 1976).

7. *Tranquilizers,* surprisingly, do not lessen aggressive behavior. In fact, they may even increase it. Tranquilizing drugs seem to interfere with the transmission of the neurotransmitter *norepinephrine,* associated with general arousal. They provide evidence that aggression is not a function of mere arousal; cognitive interpretation of physiological state is crucial (Bandura, 1986).

Some of these elements influence arousal level, and some reduce inhibitions. When these are operating together, aggression will result if there is provocation. Crowding may increase arousal level, and being in the crowd may disinhibit aggression because individual acts are hidden (Zimbardo, 1970). So, if it is a hot night and many persons in a crowd has had too much to drink, it probably won't take much to provoke a riot.

WHY ARE PEOPLE AGGRESSIVE?

FREUD'S THEORY OF AGGRESSION   Freud held that aggression is one of two fundamental human drives. Calling it *Thanatos*, he identified it as a destructive energy that accumulates until it is discharged either inwardly or outwardly, as in self-destructive behavior or in the destruction of others. Our innate aggression was probably more useful in the days before settled society. At that time, killing enemies was important for survival. Civilization puts curbs on aggression and makes it necessary for us to redirect these instinctual urges (Ibisiter, 1986).

ETHOLOGY'S THEORY OF AGGRESSION   Like Freud, ethologists contend that aggression is *instinctive*. Lorenz (1966) and others proposed a complex theory of aggression. Basically, aggression in animals is most often directed at other species. Animals have evolved innate inhibitions against fatal aggression toward members of their own species. These *inhibitions* involve either behavior patterns or physical characteristics. Coloration "turns off" an aggressor before he can do serious damage. *The strength of the inhibition corresponds to the strength of a species' offensive weapons.* Thus, wolves, as predators, are well equipped for violence and also have strong inhibitions against killing other wolves.

However, the human inheritance has provided us with very weak "natural" instruments of physical aggression. We are weak for our size, and we do not have the strength of a tiger or the jaws of a shark. Since we inherit weak weapons, we also *inherit weak inhibitions* on personal aggression. However, human beings can go beyond their inheritance. We have invented weapons that are vastly more destructive than any inherited ones. But we have not evolved corresponding inhibitions.

Our lack of inhibition against violence toward members of our own species explains why we have become so dangerous to ourselves. A whole city can be destroyed by the push of a button by someone in an underground fortification.

SOCIAL LEARNING THEORY OF AGGRESSION   According to social learning theory, there is no simple aggressive instinct (Bandura, 1986). The biological basis of aggression is the same as that of all learning. Organisms, especially human beings, have the ability to learn vicariously. Humans, in particular, learn by observing the behavior of models, especially people who are perceived as important controllers of reward and punishment (Bandura, 1986). According to social learning theory, aggressive behavior is elicited not merely by learning how to do it, but also by rewards and punishments, both experienced and anticipated.

Threatened punishment works to subdue aggression, but only if certain conditions are satisfied (Bower & Hilgard, 1981):

1. The punishment is imminent.
2. The threatened punishment is severe.
3. The potential aggressor understands that punishment is highly likely.

One reason the threat of punishment doesn't act as a deterrent to violent crime is that it seldom meets these criteria. Other ways need to be found to counter human aggression. Social learning theory has provided one possible aide: nonaggressive models are useful in reducing aggression in others (Baron & Kepner, 1970) and appear to be more effective than threats of retaliation.

OVERT INFLUENCES ON OUR THOUGHTS, FEELINGS, AND ACTIONS

COMPLIANCE: DELIBERATE CONFORMITY

Conformity is the changing of behavior to go along with the norms of the group. You enter an elevator in a strange building and find everyone facing the back wall. Do you also face the back wall? Probably. To your surprise, the door to the upper floors opens from the wall everyone is facing. **Compliance,** on the other hand, is going along because someone asks you to. If that person is in a position either to reward you (with friendship perhaps) or punish you (by withholding your paycheck), you are likely to comply. A direct request is a common form of social influence.

OBEDIENCE

When the person asking you to comply with a request is a legitimate authority, going along is called **obedience.** While obedience to authority is a fundamental requirement of organized society, in certain situations ordinary people will follow the commands of an authority figure, even when the commands are extreme and uncalled for and when there is no threat of punishment.

Making reference to the atrocities committed in Nazi Germany, Stanley Milgram (1974) conducted a series of experiments (1960–1963) designed to test the conditions under which people will obey authority. Subjects responded to a newspaper advertisement for "participants in a psychology experiment." The ad said the experiment would take about one hour and they would be paid $4.50. When each subject arrived for the experiment, he was introduced to the experimenter and another "subject" (actually a confederate of the experimenter). The real subjects were told that the experiment was "a study of memory and learning."

The subject and confederate drew lots to see who would be the "teacher" and who would be the "learner." The drawing was rigged, however, so that the confederate was always the learner and the subject was always the teacher. The teacher's job was to administer an electric shock every time the learner made a mistake.

The experimenter took the teacher and learner to an adjoining room and strapped the learner into a chair and attached electrodes to his wrist. The learner (the confederate) then expressed concern about receiving shocks, stating that he had a heart condition (which was not true). The experimenter assured him and the teacher that there were no physical risks in the experiment. The teacher and the experimenter then returned to the original room.

The experimenter asked the teacher first to read a series of word pairs to the learner and then to read the first word of each pair along with four word choices. For each pair, the learner was to recall which word had been the second in the original pair. When the learner answered correctly, the teacher was to press a switch that lit a light in the learner's room. When the learner was wrong, the teacher was supposed to read the correct answer aloud. He was also to punish the learner by pressing a switch that delivered an electric shock to the learner.

There were 30 switches ranging from 15 volts (labeled "Slight Shock") to 420 volts (labeled "Danger: Severe Shock"). The two final switches, for 435 and 450 volts, were simply labeled "XXX." Each time the learner made a mistake, the teacher was to administer an increasingly higher shock (15 more volts than the previous shock).

Unknown to the subject (teacher), the experimenter instructed the learner to make mistakes. He never actually received any shocks. Following a prearranged script, the learner complained about the shocks. He expressed concern over his heart condition and begged for release. After the teacher administered 300 volts, the learner began to pound the wall. Then, ominously, he no longer responded. Whenever the teacher showed hesitation about giving a shock, the experimenter simply instructed him to follow the directions. The experimenter did not threaten or display force (Figure 17-3).

FIGURE 17-3
Milgram Experiment

These photos show some of the actual events in the Milgram experiment on obedience to authority in which subjects (designated as "teachers") gave electric shocks to "learners" (see text).

OVERT INFLUENCES ON OUR THOUGHTS, FEELINGS, AND ACTIONS

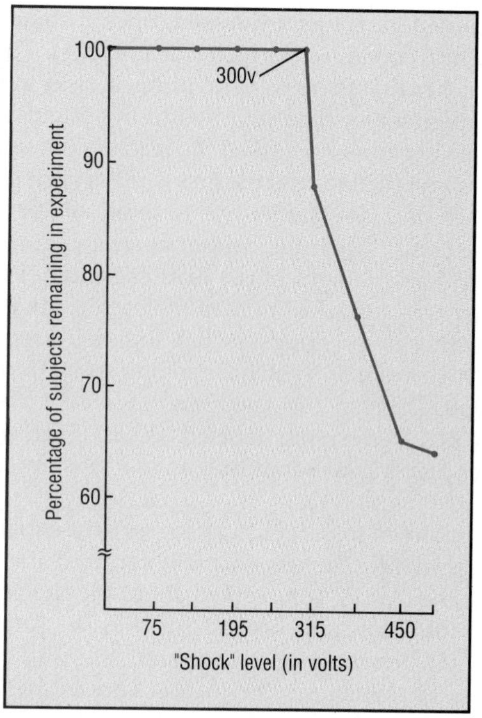

FIGURE 17-4
Obedience to Authority

In the Milgram experiment, all subjects followed instructions and administered what they thought were painful shocks of up to 300 volts. Only above 300 volts did some subjects refuse to go on administering shocks to the protesting "learner."
(Milgram, 1963)

Now, consider this question honestly: How much shock would you have given? Almost no one says he or she would have given the maximum shock.

Before performing this experiment, Milgram described the situation to psychiatrists at a nearby medical center. He asked them how many subjects out of 100 would administer the full 450 volts. The psychiatrists predicted that about one-tenth of 1 percent of the subjects might go all the way (Milgram, 1974). In fact, nearly two-thirds of the subjects in this experiment obeyed the experimenter and gave the maximum shock of 450 volts. Even more startling, only 22.5 percent gave less than 300 volts. In one variation of the experiment, no one gave less than 300 volts (Figure 17-4).

This experiment, extreme though it is, shows how strongly human beings can be influenced by a social situation. The subjects gave the maximum shock because they were in a situation where pressure to comply with an authority figure outweighed their own desire not to cause harm to the "learner."

There were many social forces operating in the situation. Milgram pointed out some of them: subjects had agreed to be in an experiment, they accepted money for their participation, and they felt an obligation to the experimenter. They might have reasoned that the "learner" also volunteered for the experiment, and it was simply bad luck that he was the one being shocked. The pace of the experiment gave subjects little time to stop and consider their actions (Milgram, 1963). All the while, the experimenter assured the subjects that there was no danger to the learner and, if necessary, the experimenter assured subjects that the responsibility was not theirs.

The subjects in the Milgram experiments were placed in a position of great conflict—between obeying authority and not hurting another person. This conflict expressed itself in real suffering on the part of many of the subjects. To call the obedient subjects sadistic is to fall victim to making the fundamental attribution error. These experiments illustrate that it is very difficult to disobey when there are strong social forces urging us to go along.

THE SITUATION TAKES OVER: A MOCK PRISON

Philip Zimbardo sought to investigate the degree to which brutal behavior can be determined by the situation. In one of psychology's most controversial studies, he simulated a prison in the basement of the psychology building at Stanford University (Haney, Banks, & Zimbardo, 1973; Zimbardo, 1972). There is no clearer demonstration of the power of situations to influence human behavior.

He randomly assigned male student volunteers to the roles of "prisoner" and "guard." The local police even cooperated by picking up the prisoners in squad cars, complete with siren. A cameraman from a local television station recorded the arrests. Prisoners were treated realistically. They were fingerprint-ed, stripped, "skin searched," and given demeaning uniforms. The uniforms were dresses, with no underclothing, intended to restrict their movement and to emasculate the male prisoners. The prisoners also wore a chain locked around one ankle. Guards were uniformed and were given handcuffs, cell and gate keys, and billy clubs. They were deindividuated by their uniforms and by wearing reflecting sunglasses that masked the expression in their eyes. Guards were told that physical violence was prohibited; they were simply to maintain law and order (Figure 17-5).

Soon the experiment took an unsettling turn. Some of the guards identified with their roles and began to enjoy their power over the prisoners. They quickly grew to enjoy their power roles. Their apparently complete power over the

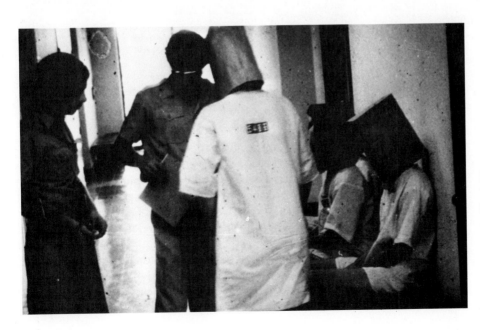

FIGURE 17-5
The Stanford "Prison" Study

Students playing their roles as prisoners and guards in the mock prison in the basement of the psychology building at Stanford University

609

Since we can't possibly process all the information that comes our way, we select and edit what we pay attention to and think about. We place much of our routine behavior on "automatic pilot" while our minds are busy with other things. Think about the last time you were driving on the freeway and the traffic was running smoothly. Chances are there were times when you looked up and suddenly realized you had traveled 10 or 15 miles without being aware of the distance. While you were driving your mind had been focused on those two wild guys explaining car repairs on the radio, or you had been planning your weekend. Because we are not consciously thinking about everything we are doing, we act automatically in an emergency: an object suddenly appears on the highway ahead and we hit the brakes, locking them. If we had been concentrating on driving, it might have been possible to avoid the object or to remember to pump the brakes instead of automatically stomping down.

We need to be able to do many things automatically in order to function in a complex world. It is this gap between thought and action that makes us vulnerable to people using social psychological principles to influence us. Robert Cialdini (1988) likens this automatic responding to the fixed-action patterns of animals (see Chapter 4) and suggests that there are certain "trigger features" that elicit automatic compliance.

One of these social trigger features is the norm of *reciprocation*. Have you ever opened the mail and found an unordered set of return-address labels with your name and address on them? Sometimes the envelope will contain a set of unsolicited greeting cards. Each of these "gifts" was probably accompanied by a description of the charitable organization that sent them and a request for a donation. What do you do in a situation like that? What do you do when a young

USING PSYCHOLOGY: COUNTERING SOCIAL INFLUENCE

person walks up to you on the sidewalk or in an airport and hands you a flower. It is very difficult to turn down the subsequent request for a donation. This is because the **reciprocity norm** requires that we repay our obligations. According to Cialdini, the best way out of this trap is to accept the gifts in good faith. Then, if necessary, redefine the gifts as tricks to get you to comply with a request for donation. That way, you don't have to feel guilty about not reciprocating.

Another element of automatic behavior that can be brought into play when someone wants us to comply is our need to be *consistent*. Inconsistent people are unpredictable, and unpredictability makes others uncomfortable. Consistency also helps us to function automatically. We don't have to make a new decision every time, we just do what we did before. If we can be induced to make a commitment to a position, a product, or a candidate, our need for consistency will likely influence our future actions. Commitments that are public, difficult for us, and uncoerced are the most effective in guaranteeing follow-through. The theory of cognitive dissonance is relevant here. Enduring "hell week" in order to join a fraternity or standing up in front of a group and detailing the importance of the group in our lives are examples of such public commitments. Having made a difficult public commitment, we then justify our behavior and persuade ourselves of the rightness of our action. Cialdini suggests that the way to avoid pressures for consistency is to ask yourself "Knowing what I know, if I could go back in time, would I make the same commitment? Sometimes the answer to this question is simply a feeling—relief perhaps.

Social comparison is another cue we use that can open us to influence. When in ambiguous situations, we look to others for cues about how to behave. We look to those who are similar to us. Televi-

prisoners resulted in arrogant, aggressive, and cruel behavior toward their charges.

The prisoners rebelled at first. After the rebellion was put down, the guards became more aggressive and the prisoners became more passive. Five prisoners were released early because of their severe anxiety and rage reactions. Outside the situation, all the released subjects were normal, nondestructive people, as measured by standard psychological tests.

The subjects weren't the only ones who slipped too deeply into their roles. The experimenters themselves lost some of their objectivity and fell victim to groupthink. Reality finally broke through after a former prison chaplain visited with the prisoners and urged them to hire a lawyer to see about bail or to appeal

sion laugh tracks and "man on the street" testimonials are two examples of using social comparison to influence us. In these cases, the "social evidence" is contrived. One solution is to be alert for impression management.

Avoiding influence is particularly difficult if the person trying to influence us is someone we have come to like. All other things being equal, we naturally want to give our business to our friends. Salespeople are hired and rewarded by their employers for their ability to develop rapport with their clients. Our weapon against this is to be aware of how the power of *liking* influences our behavior and to make decisions based on the issue rather than on the person.

Deference to authority is another automatic behavior that can be used to influence us. Milgram's obedience study demonstrated the difficulty of disobeying authority. Not only do we obey authority, but sometimes we also react automatically to symbols of authority such as a title, a uniform, or expensive possessions. According to Cialdini, the defense against this type of influence is tricky. True authorities often really do know what they are talking about and we should listen to them. He suggests that just to be safe, however, we ask ourselves "Is this authority truly an expert?" Actors who play doctors on television shouldn't influence our choice of aspirin. Second, we should ask, "Is this authority trustworthy?" We shouldn't listen too carefully to wine experts who also own wineries.

A final form of manipulation to gain our compliance is information that something we want is in short supply. Two things happen when we are told that something is *scarce*. First, that item's value increases or we assume it will. Second, we experience the loss of freedom to acquire the scarce commodity. We experience reactance and act to restore our freedom. Both of these principles work to increase our desire for whatever is scarce. This is particularly true if the scarcity is new, and others are competing with us. So the next time you are bidding in an auction or your neighborhood rug gallery goes out of business, be aware that the situation is emotionally arousing. The only real solution is to be aware of the arousal that accompanies such situations and try to define the situation rationally.

One of the most important elements of any situation is the other people who are present. As we have seen, we are all influenced by the groups in which we live and the people we encounter. Sometimes this influence is subtle, and sometimes it is very noticeable. By understanding how the presence of others can influence our own behavior and how we, in turn, influence theirs, we maintain the freedom to choose our actions rather than having them chosen for us.

the charges. When the lawyer arrived to discuss bail, the experimenters realized they had to call off the experiment.

The experiment was originally scheduled to last for two weeks. It had to be terminated after only six days. The experimenters concluded,

> We were no longer dealing with an intellectual exercise in which a hypothesis was being evaluated in the dispassionate manner dictated by the canons of the scientific method. We were caught up in the passion of the present, the suffering, the need to control people not variables, the escalation of power and all of the unexpected things which were erupting around and within us. So our planned two-week simulation was aborted after only six (was it only six?) days and nights. (Zimbardo, Haney, Banks, & Jaffe, 1973)

1. *Social psychology* attempts to understand and explain how our thoughts, feelings, and actions are influenced by the actual, imagined, or implied presence of others.

2. Our perception of others influences expectations we have about them and our behavior toward them. This may influence their behavior in such a way that our initial expectations are confirmed. In this way, beliefs about others may create their own reality.

3. *Attribution theory* guides the study of causal explanations we use to explain our own behavior and the behavior of others. Early researchers in attribution assumed that we observe and rationally assign cause for a behavior to one of the people involved or to the situation.

4. There are, however, some biases in the attribution process. When observing others there is a tendency to attribute the cause of events to the *person* rather than to the situation. This is called the *fundamental attribution error*. On the other hand, when things go wrong and we are asked to account for our *own* behavior, we blame the *situation*. When things go right, we take credit. This is the *self-serving bias*.

5. These biases in our social thinking help us maintain our sense of control. The perception of loss of control may lead to reactance, which results in a fight to reclaim freedom of action. If this fails, however, feelings of helplessness may result and the fight may be abandoned.

6. An *attitude* is a lasting evaluation of an objective or thought. We want to know about a person's attitudes so we can predict what he or she might do. But attitudes don't always lead to behavior. Sometimes behavior affects attitudes. The theory of *cognitive dissonance* predicts that when there is a discrepancy between an attitude and our knowledge of something we have done or intend to do, tension is created and we try to resolve it by changing the attitude. The more responsible we feel for the behavior and the greater the consequence for others, the greater the dissonance aroused. The greater the dissonance, the more likely there will be a change in attitude.

7. *Prejudice* derives from a process basic to our thoughts about many different objects and people. We simplify by sorting into categories. When a category is overextended it becomes a *stereotype*, which is a generalized assumption attributing identical characteristics to all members of a group. *Prejudice* is an attitude; *discrimination* is the behavior it predicts. One way to counter prejudice is to increase contact between the holder of a stereotype and members of the stereotyped groups. Ideally, this contact would include cooperative activity to achieve a superordinate goal.

8. There are many factors that affect whether a persuasive message works or not. Among these are characteristics of the source of the message, the message itself, and the audience to whom it is addressed. Overall, the most effective methods of attitude change are those that motivate action. By arousing and directing action, persuasive communications can lead to self-persuasion through behavior.

9. Although the mere presence of others influences our arousal level and can have an impact on performance, social influence is usually mediated by thoughts. The theory of *social comparison* states that, when in doubt, we compare with others. We compare our behavior and attitudes for correctness or our abilities to see where we rank. The group we choose to compare ourselves to is called our *reference group*. An important reference group can cause a change in attitudes or behavior because deviates are often rejected from a group.

10. *Conformity* is the act of obeying the customs or standards of the group. The more desirable and important the group is, the more difficult it is to resist pressure to conform. Three factors affect conformity: group unanimity, group size, and the individual's relationship to the group. A person is most likely to conform when faced with the unanimous opinion of a group of at least four members. Conformity would be even higher if the person felt insecure and the group was important to him or her.

11. A group is not simply a collection of individuals; it is a collection of *interdependent* individuals. The more cohesive the group is, the stronger its influence is on the behavior of its members. When individual efforts are hidden in a group, individuals sometimes slack off. This is known as *social loafing* and is likely to occur if the task is not difficult or particularly involving. *Social impact theory* predicts that as the number of others increases, their impact on an individual increases. But each added person has less of an individual impact. Influence also increases if others are physically close and are important to the individual.

12. *Group polarization* is the notion that groups make more extreme decisions than individuals do. Through a process of social comparison and persuasion, the dominant view of the group as a whole at the beginning of a discussion is made stronger through discussion. *Groupthink* is a decision process in which a highly cohesive group with a strong, directive leader reaches premature agreement in a crisis situation. It has been blamed for a number of disastrous decisions made by government leaders. Conforming to group norms overtakes information seeking and rational problem solving. Solutions to groupthink involve building contentiousness into the group process.

13. Having other people around influences whether an individual will help someone in need. The presence of others helps to decode the situation as one that requires intervention, but if there are many others, the responsibility for helping may diffuse among them. An individual will help if he or she feels competent to help but may hesitate because of what others might think. Psychologists have been unable to find a personality trait or disposition for helping. Empathy has been found to motivate prosocial behavior.

14. *Aggression* is intentionally harming another. *Hostile aggression* is motivated by anger and intended to make the victim suffer. *Instrumental aggression* is motivated by incentive, and the victim may be injured incidentally. The aggressive response can be affected by arousal, crowding, noise, temperature, and drugs. These factors can interact to ensure aggression if there is provocation.

15. Freud considered aggression an instinct, calling it *Thanatos* or the death instinct. Ethologists also see aggression as instinctive. Animals have evolved innate inhibitions against fatal aggression toward members of their own species. However, the human inheritance has provided us with weak natural instruments of physical aggression. We have therefore developed weapons that are vastly more destructive than any inherited ones, but we have not evolved corresponding inhibitions. *Social learning theory* holds that there is no simple aggressive instinct. Rather, the biological basis of aggression is the same as that of all learning. We learn aggression by observing the behavior of models.

16. *Compliance* is going along because someone asks you to. When the person asking is a legitimate authority, going along is called *obedience.* In an important experiment on obedience to authority performed by Milgram, 60 percent of the subjects in the experiment obeyed an experimenter's request and gave up to 450 volts of shock to a

confederate of the experimenter. These subjects gave the maximum shock because they were in a situation where strong social forces urged them to comply with an authority figure and outweighed their own desire to not cause harm to the confederate.

17. In one of psychology's most controversial studies, Zimbardo simulated a prison to investigate the degree to which brutal behavior can be situationally determined. Student subjects were randomly assigned to roles as prisoner or guard. The experiment caused so much distress, with the prisoners becoming weak and submissive and the guards behaving aggressively, that the experiment had to be called off after only six days.

18. The gap between thought and action makes us vulnerable to people trying to influence us using social psychological principles. Cialdini points out certain trigger features that elicit automatic compliance on our part. These include the *norm of reciprocation,* the need to be *consistent,* social *proof, liking,* symbols of *authority,* and *information* that something we want is in *short supply.*

TERMS AND CONCEPTS

affect	obedience
aggression	persuasion
altruism	prejudice
attitude	primacy effect
attribution theory	prosocial behavior
behavior	prototype
behavioral confirmation	reactance
coaction effect	recency effect
cognition	reciprocity norm
cognitive dissonance	reference group
compliance	role
conform	self-serving bias
conformity	sense of control
discrimination	situational attribution
dispositional attribution	social comparison
fundamental attribution error	social facilitation
group	social impact theory
groupthink	social loafing
illusory correlation	social psychology
mindguard	stereotype
norms	

SUGGESTIONS FOR FURTHER READING

Argyle, M., & Henderson, M. (1985). *The anatomy of relationships.* New York: Penguin.

Information about attraction, marriage, friendship, and life as it unfolds. The conclusions are not always compelling, but the evidence is intriguing.

Aronson, E. (1988). *The social animal.* New York: Freeman.

An engaging introduction to the field of social psychology.

Cialdini, R. (1988). *Influence: Science and practice,* 2nd ed. Chicago: Scott Foresman.

An excellent and useful book about how to avoid being exploited by "influence professionals."

Fiske, S. T., & Taylor, S. E. (1990). *Social cognition,* 2nd ed. Reading, MA: Addison-Wesley.

An overview of the research on social thinking.

Hatfield, E., & Sprecher, S. (1985). *Mirror, mirror: The importance of looks in everyday life.* New York: SUNY Press.

An excellent summary of research on attractiveness, second only in value to Cialdini's book.

Janis, I. L. (1989). *Crucial decisions: Leadership in policy making and crisis management.* New York: Free Press.

A current look at decision-making by the author of Groupthink.

Milgram, S. (1975). *Obedience to authority: An experimental view.* New York: Harper & Row.

The famous study, well presented by its author.

18

HUMAN INTIMACY

ATTRACTIVENESS, LOVE, AND SEXUALITY

L
ove is special to human beings. Friendships that last for many years, attachments between parents and children, and emotional bonds between lovers are familiar to us all. Emotional bonds have great survival value. When parents are bonded together by love, the probability that both will care for the child increases. Human fathers are the only males among primates who play a significant role in the care of their own offspring.

Like thought and behavior, human emotions probably reflect our evolutionary past. One outcome of upright posture and bipedalism is that the female's birth canal is small, leading to human infants being born immature and helpless. In order to survive, the mother must be heavily invested in her offspring. Paternal investment improves the odds even more. Infants' attachment to parents keeps the children close by and wary of strangers. Recall from Chapter 2 that stranger anxiety reaches its height just as the infant learns to crawl or walk independently and is at risk for straying into unsafe territory. Interpersonal bonds—that is, love—attach us to one another. And together, we are more likely to survive.

Any analysis of the nature of love, far from being trivial, is of the utmost importance to our understanding of ourselves. The analysis of love and its evolutionary history is new (Mellen, 1981), and the current studies of love and loving are also in their infancy.

THE HUMAN SEXUAL REVOLUTION

Humans engage in sex more often than other mammals, another likely side effect of our biology. All female mammals except humans are sexually excitable only when "in heat," when *ovulating.* **Ovulation** occurs when the female's

ovaries release the developed egg; it is the time when the female is fertile. The period of ovulation is called **estrus.** Female mammals, other than humans, have an *estrus cycle,* which means that they ovulate only a few times a year. In addition, males are generally excited by a female in estrus, and a female will physically receive the male only when she is ovulating.

A female in estrus communicates her sexual excitability (or receptivity) by emitting certain odors from the vagina. Without estrus, males cannot tell by smell when females are ovulating. However, in a menstrual cycle with ovulation every month, a woman is always sexually receptive, or—to put it a less offensive way—sex is possible at almost any point. Human beings thus have intercourse frequently throughout the year.

HUMAN SEXUALITY

The degree to which sexuality and gender differences in sexuality are determined by biology is highly controversial. Some scholars claim that men and women differ inherently and profoundly in their sexuality (Symons, 1980), while others view gender differences in sexuality as socially constructed (D'Emilio & Freedman, 1988). For example, Symons believes that the shift to upright posture led males to transfer emphasis from odor to visual signs of sexuality. Even males' interest in pornography has been cast as the exploitation of a "natural" tendency for men to look at women sexually. Such views must be considered carefully. It is easy to construct a story to justify sexual practices as we believe them to be today, attributing them to biology, forgetting that different historical periods have viewed sexuality and intimacy very differently (D'Emilio & Freedman, 1988). Nevertheless, examining our evolutionary history and the ways that we differ from other mammals may help us understand our sexual selves.

PAIR BONDING

The frequency of sex, combined with the eye contact during sex and the continual presence of visual sex signals, may be the basis for attachments based on sexual pleasure. There is a sound evolutionary basis for the pleasure derived from sex; it encourages sexual relations and increases the chance of conception. Human beings customarily like to have sex much more than the demands of conception require.

The human style of sex allows a foundation for a stable society built on family units (Sahlins, 1972). The place sex occupies in human life is unique: we do not have sex merely to replace ourselves in the next generation; we "fall in love" and "make love." The sexual bond, or **pair bonding,** is the basis of the family: fathers stay with, care for, and care about their families. The mother can care for several small children if the father assists with the provision of food (Benshoof & Thornhill, 1979).

Consider the female chimpanzee. She lives from 18 to 40 years, but because she bears all the responsibility for her children—nursing, feeding, and protection—it takes her about 16 years to produce and raise two offspring (Gallup, 1977). A human female, if she has a mate or other form of support, theoretically could produce and raise one child each year from the onset of menstruation to menopause. One important part of the adaptive value of bipedalism may lie in

SEX DIFFERENCES AND DIVISION OF LABOR

In all of the 800 primitive societies studied, men hunt and women gather (Friedl, 1978). It is impossible to be an effective hunter while pregnant or while nursing or carrying a child (Washburn, 1960). Also, males are physically bigger and stronger than females and are usually faster runners.

Males do the fighting in every society. This is not only because of their greater physical strength but also because it follows the most basic requirement of a species: survival of the next generation. In a population of 10 males and 10 females, if 9 females die in battle, only 2 or 3 children could possibly be born to the group the next year, and survival of the population would be in peril. But if 9 men died in battle, the 10 surviving females could each produce a child in the next year. Thus, *males are the more expendable* (Leutenegger, 1977).

Even so, in virtually every society, men have held and continue to hold the most powerful and respected positions. Why has this

BEING FEMALE

BEING MALE

male dominance occurred? This question brings up the issue of nature versus nurture. Are males "naturally" dominant? Many theorists (males) contended that males are not only physically stronger but also intellectually superior. But studies in recent years, by both men and women, have not supported this contention.

One theory suggests that control of a society's most valued resources determines who dominates (Friedl, 1978). We need protein to live, and meat is a much more concentrated source of protein than fruits and vegetables. A large gazelle, caught and brought home by a hunting party, can feed several families for several days. Thus, many can eat well for a long period of time from the labor of a few.

An alternative theory is that women's reproductive potential is the most valuable resource of all, and it is the control of this potential that leads to male domination of women. Identification of one's genetic offspring is essential to investing appropriately in them (Wilson, 1989). For females, this presents no problem; they always know who their offspring are. But males cannot be confident about their offspring unless they control sexual access to a particular female. Subsequently, in order to secure rights to children, men must first secure rights to women. Physical domination and the control of other valuable resources is one way to gain access to children.

the human style of sexuality, which creates the family unit and cooperation (Lovejoy, 1981), although this view has been challenged on the grounds that male and female sexual strategies may be different (Symons, 1989).

DIFFERENCES IN SEXUALITY

The description in the text so far has emphasized the harmonious and cooperative nature of the human sexual bond, the monogamous couple-family unit. However, anyone who has had even a small interest in matters sexual cannot fail to see that all is not smooth and harmonious, nor exclusively heterosexual. One of the reasons why males and females do not always get along comes from *evolutionary biology*. It emphasizes that males and females, because of their different roles in reproduction, will have different ways of behaving sexually in order to gain the greatest advantage, but the advantage for the male is not the same as for the female (Symons, 1989).

Dorothy Parker wrote, in her "General Review of the Sex Situation":

> *Woman wants monogamy;*
> *Man delights in novelty.*

Love is woman's moon and sun;
Man has other forms of fun.
Woman lives but in her lord;
Count to ten and man is bored.
With this gist and sum of it;
What earthly good can come of it?

While this poem written in 1926 may be a bit outmoded, especially about woman living for "her lord," it may contain some truth about sex differences in sexual expression and desire.

In Figure 18-1 on the frequency of orgasms of men and women, note that at all ages men have more sex per week than females. One consistent difference in sexuality is this: in all cultures studied, men say that they desire more sex and more variety in sex than women do. In his monumental survey of human sexual activity, Kinsey and his colleagues concluded that "Among all peoples, everywhere in the world, it is understood that the male is more likely than the female to desire sexual relations with a variety of partners" (Kinsey, Pomeroy, Martin, & Gebhard, 1953). However, be aware that these statistics are based on self-report. Even controlling for homosexual sex, men report having intercourse much more often than females. If both reports are true, who are these promiscuous males having sex with?

Still, men seek visual sexual arousal more than women do. Although the recent preference for free sexual expression has narrowed this difference somewhat, men still seek vicarious, visual, and other sexual stimulation far more than women do. The industry in X-rated films and sex-oriented books and magazines, which in the United States alone does over $1 billion business a year, is almost entirely geared to male interests. Prostitution has almost exclusively male clients.

The pattern of sex differences holds in homosexuality as well. Male homosexuality is thought to be a "hypermale" sexuality, uninhibited by females (Symons, 1989). Male homosexuality is characterized, as a rule, by many sexual

FIGURE 18-1
Frequency of Orgasm

At all ages men are more active sexually than women of the same age. But men's highest level of sexual activity is achieved in their teens and twenties, whereas women just begin reaching their highest level of activity in their thirties.
(Kinsey, Pomeroy, Martin, & Gebhard, 1953)

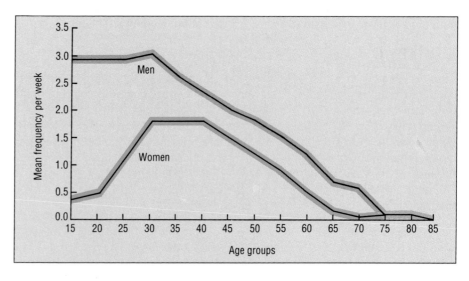

Men are far more likely than women to seek sexual arousal, so the X-rated adult entertainment industry is almost exclusively oriented toward men.

encounters; female homosexuality, by long, stable relationships. Male homosexual prostitution is quite common in large cities; female homosexual prostitution is almost unknown (Symons, 1990).

While experience (environment, cultural conditions) undoubtedly sharpens, develops, and exaggerates the differences in male and female sexuality, some feel there are *fundamental biological differences* in the sexual natures of the sexes. In every known human society, and in primate societies, too, there is a very basic divergence of sexual interest. This may be due to the differences between the reproductive strategies of the male and female. The male can father large numbers of children in a year, whereas the female can carry usually only one. It is "cheap" in biological terms for males to father offspring, while much more expensive for females, which leads to very different strategies, it being more advantageous for a male to mate with a greater number of partners.

With changes in society, such as the acceptability of female sexual expression, the increasing ability of single parents to care for their children, and contraceptives that allow a woman to have sex without worrying about pregnancy, these differences will probably continue to decrease in the coming years, but it is unlikely they will disappear entirely (Symons, 1989).

COOPERATION AND HUMAN SOCIETY

In a mating system governed by estrus, the female is available only at specific times and is available to many males at those times. Mating in most other animal societies is preceded by aggressive competition among males for the females in heat. With the replacement in humans of an estrus cycle by a menstrual cycle and the emergence of pair bonding, this continual sexual competition among males was lessened. Marriage, for example, is a ubiquitous feature of human societies that function to restrict sexual access and form reproductive alliances (Wilson, 1989). Increased cooperation took place, not only within the pair bond but also among members of a society (Johansen & Edey, 1981; Lovejoy, 1981). One characteristic of all human societies studied so far is their cooperation, as defined at least by food sharing and division of labor. The complex and interdependent human society has a biological basis in cooperation.

Every individual begins life dependent on the mother. As humans mature, they recognize increasingly complex networks of interdependence: from family to group to nation to the entire world. Even organized aggression depends on cooperation. Hunting, which is a primary human adaptation, requires planning, division of labor, signals of a complex order, cooperative carrying home of the kill, and a sharing of the prize with those at home (Lancaster, 1978).

HUMAN SEXUALITY: INTIMATE FEELINGS

Human **sexuality** is very difficult to study because the feelings involved with it are the most intimate of all human experiences. Until the last few decades, cultural and personal taboos have made it impossible to study this important aspect of life. For example, many questions about women's orgasms were not settled until the mid-1960s when social mores had relaxed enough to permit laboratory investigation.

As we have seen, people are, simply, very sexual animals. Our love of sex is one of the reasons for the success of our species. In evolutionary terms, the survival of the fittest—those who have the most surviving offspring—determines how a population grows, changes, and develops. Survival is related more to sex than to aggression. Because we make love often, we have been successful.

Sex is different for human beings than for other animals in that the signals for sex are mental as well as biological. The role of emotions and our mental interpretation of love experiences are closely related to sexual feelings. Because how we feel depends on our interpretation of physical arousal, sexual attraction has mental components that include both love and attachment.

PHEROMONES

Smell may have a more direct effect on behavior than was previously thought. Most animals communicate their sexual receptivity through odors. During estrus, the female of a species produces an odor that arouses the male. Such chemical substances that convey information are called **pheromones.** They have been found in insects and in many mammals. Female mice, for instance, secrete a substance, *copulin,* which arouses the male.

The evidence in humans is beginning to become clear. A difference between the smells of women and men can also be discriminated. People have described the male smell as "musky" and the female as "sweet." Some recent evidence indicates that smell plays a role in human sexual behavior and that people can distinguish their own body odor from others (Ornstein & Sobel, 1989). Scent glands in the armpits seem to be part of a human pheromone system.

Females unconsciously respond to the odor of other females. One study showed that the menstrual cycles of women living together became synchronized. One woman can even influence the cycles of other women by smell, even if she is absent (McClintock, 1971). If women sniff the scent of the absent woman, their cycles will become synchronized (Preti et al., 1989).

Unlike other animals, the human male is more odorous than the female. A new and potentially revolutionary set of studies has confirmed the effects of human male pheromones on women (Preti et al., 1989). Women who have intimate contact (usually sexual intercourse) with men at least once a week have longer menstrual cycles, fewer infertility problems, and a less difficult menopause. As in the previous study, the effect can be produced by sniffing male "essence" from pads worn underarm by male volunteers. Women whose menstrual cycles were longer than 33 days or shorter than 26 days synchronized to the normal 29.5 days after the "treatment." The studies also found that the pheromones of males and females act differently: the female scent can diffuse through a room and be effective, while the male scent requires close contact.

Obviously, human sexuality is not completely determined by chemical messages. But the portrayal of scent in sexual experience will have to be expanded. People who say they feel "the right chemistry" with someone of the opposite sex may be right!

THE SEXUAL RESPONSE CYCLE

There are regular physiological changes involved in sexual intercourse and sexual activity (Masters, Johnson, & Kolodney, 1986). The four major phases of the **sexual response cycle** (Figure 18-2) are excitement, plateau, orgasm, and resolution.

1. In the *excitement phase*, there is a general arousal reaction combined with an increase of blood flow *(vasocongestion)* to the genitals. There is increasing muscular tension in the genital area. The penis becomes erect, and the vagina lubricates through vaginal sweat glands.

2. In the *plateau phase,* vasocongestion and muscle tension level off, but sexual and general excitement remain high. This is the phase when intercourse occurs. The plateau may be long or short depending on many factors, including the nature of the sexual act itself, the stimuli, and the training and control of the individual. One person may reach orgasm quickly, while another may wish (and be able) to delay orgasm.

FIGURE 18-2
Human Sexual Response Cycles

These graphs show how males and females differ in their patterns of physiological response during sexual activity.
(Masters & Johnson, 1966)

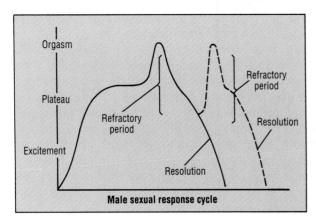

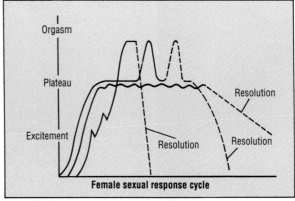

HUMAN SEXUALITY: INTIMATE FEELINGS

3. The third phase is *orgasm*, which is the briefest and most intense phase. Arousal, muscle tension, heart rate, and respiration increase rapidly to a peak. Then there is a sudden reduction of tension accompanied by orgasm. While sexual excitement can begin by purely mental means, such as fantasies, orgasm usually results from the stimulation of the genitals. Almost every male has orgasm. During orgasm men ejaculate semen, which contains sperm. From 10 to 30 percent of women never have orgasms, but about 14 percent report that they always have one or more climaxes during intercourse. The pattern of orgasm differs between the sexes. Men have orgasms more often overall, but women can have multiple orgasms during one sexual act.

4. In the *resolution phase*, the participant rests; arousal has subsided. There is mental and physical relaxation and a feeling of well-being. During resolution a man cannot have an erection. After resolution, the cycle can begin again. There is, however, a physical limit to the number of times a day a man can have sexual intercourse. This number decreases as he ages. Theoretically, there is no limit to the number of times a woman could have sex.

HOMOSEXUALITY

What about attraction to members of one's own sex—that is, homosexuality? Does it signify that something is wrong with one's psychological make-up and adjustment? Today, the consensus in psychology and psychiatry is a decided *no*, but this opinion has not always been the case.

Many investigators have conducted studies aimed at discovering the cause of homosexuality. Hypothetical causes range from hormonal, genetic, psychological, and social, but no one model has gathered persuasive evidence. Viewed as a psychiatric disorder, early investigations aimed to identify the underlying pathology. Initially, studies of lesbians and gay men were based on clinical populations, so not surprisingly, there appeared to be problems. However, beginning with the Kinsey report (Kinsey, Pomeroy & Martin, 1948; Kinsey, Pomeroy, Martin, & Gebhard, 1953), followed by other documentation of the widespread occurrence of homosexuality (Humphreys, 1970), studies shifted to nonclinical populations. After many years, it became clear that lesbians and gays were at no greater risk for psychopathology than heterosexuals (Mannion, 1981). "Therapeutic" efforts to change sexual preference subsided. In 1973, the American Psychiatric Association dropped from its classification manual the category denoting homosexuality as a psychiatric disorder.

Why does homosexuality exist, especially when it is so fundamentally maladaptive for reproductive fitness? Some sociobiologists believe that there may be real benefits; for example, homosexuals may invest more in their nieces and nephews than heterosexuals and ensure the preservation of their genes in the gene pool in this way. The interpretation, however, lacks empirical evidence. Perhaps more important is that even though an evolutionary model of behavior is very helpful in generating hypotheses and explanations about human behavior, it does not explain all behavior, especially complex human behavior, and is not expected to. There are probably many reasons for homosexuality, just as there are many reasons why some people are attracted to people with blue eyes and others to people with brown eyes.

Yet, despite the fact that psychologists have found no differences between heterosexuals and homosexuals in psychological adjustment, homosexuality is clearly bothersome to many. Discrimination and derision toward homosexuals are widespread. And, historically, terrible travesties against women and men have been committed due to their sexual preference (Gartrell, 1987). Rather than pursuing the causes of homosexuality, our time may be better spent trying to understand why so many people seem to fear it.

LOVE AND ATTRACTION

LOVE

Of all our relationships with others, those involving **love** have probably inspired the most comment. It is easy to see why: being in love is among the best and most treasured experiences of life. Being without love is often dismal. The experience of love is complex and involves intense feelings of ecstasy, despair, and uncertainty. We do not know when love will strike or why it goes away. Love is a complicated, private experience, involving intense and intimate feelings. Therefore, it is devilishly hard to study and difficult to analyze scientifically. Many people do not want any of the secrets of love subjected to the "cold eye" of science. In 1975, Senator William Proxmire of Wisconsin denounced the federal government for funding research on love:

> I believe that 200 million other Americans want to leave some things in life a mystery, and right at the top of things we don't want to know is why a man falls in love with a woman, and vice versa. . . . So National Science Foundation— get out of the love racket. Leave that to Elizabeth Barrett Browning and Irving Berlin. Here, if anywhere, Alexander Pope was right when he observed, "If ignorance is bliss, 'tis folly to be wise."

However, the senator is wrong, on many accounts. Love relationships are central in people's lives, and disruption of them is a major cause of personal distress. The most common precipitating factor in severe depression and suicides is disruption of a love relationship. People are hungry for information. Why do we fall in love with a certain person? Why does love turn to hate? Do opposites attract? Love stories are best-selling books; songs exalt or lament over love. Newspaper columnists and advisors to the lovelorn prosper by the thousands. A scientific analysis, flawed as it might be, would begin to expose some of the essential components of love.

In addition, we might want to study love out of sheer curiosity about the hows and whys of a most prized human emotion. It is no less interesting or important than how and why memory works. In a world troubled by wars and discord in national and private affairs, learning how love works seems an important task.

CHARACTERISTICS OF PEOPLE IN LOVE

Something dramatic happens to us when we fall in love (Argyle & Henderson, 1985). When you love someone, that person is suddenly unique, the central person in your world. You may act differently around your lover than around anyone else. The language we use to describe love uses images of movement and distance. We "fall" in love, lovers are "inclined" toward one another, lovers are "close," "as one." The physical and verbal expressions of closeness are related. It is quite easy to tell who are the lovers and who are not. There are three characteristics that researchers have observed as indicators of interest: inclination, closeness, and eye contact.

"INCLINATION" TOWARD ANOTHER   Francis Galton in 1884 first proposed that the ordinary metaphors of speech are useful for the scientific student of love. He wrote: "When two persons have an "inclination" to one another they visibly incline or slope together when sitting side by side."

CLOSENESS   When we are in love, we feel close to the other person. Couples walking with distance between them seem less in love than those entwined arm in arm. In one study, men and women students were introduced and sent off for a cola on a 30-minute "blind date." When they returned they were asked to rate their date's attractiveness. Unknown to the students, the psychologists also rated how closely the couples stood when they returned. There was a high relationship between liking and physical proximity. The more the couple reported liking one another, the closer they stood to each other (Hatfield & Sprecher, 1986).

GAZE   When two people are close to one another, each looks more often into the other's eyes. People who like one another more look more in each other's eyes than those who do not (Argyle & Henderson, 1985)

EXCITEMENT OF SEXUAL LOVE

Love is a grand stirring up of feeling and probably depends on physiological activation more than most other experiences. Walster and her colleagues (1966) sent a group of men on blind dates. They then asked them to come to the lab to fill out a questionnaire. While they were waiting, half were given fairly boring reading material and half were given sexually suggestive magazines. The experimenters thought that the magazines would be more arousing and would lead to a higher rating of attractiveness of the "blind date." The hypothesis was confirmed (Hatfield & Sprecher, 1986).

Many studies confirm the importance of arousal in sexual attraction. The men on the wobbly bridge in the Dutton and Aron experiment discussed in Chapter 1 (pages 10–11) interpreted their arousal (from the danger) as attraction. In other experiments, those given false feedback on their heart rates and those aroused by exercise also showed increased attraction.

The arousal component of love can help make sense of a common problem that occurs when love ends. Many people report that they strongly hate someone they once loved. At first glance that seems odd, but perhaps it is due to the arousal component of sexual love. When the affair ends, the strong positive feelings are replaced by equally strong negative feelings that have been *amplified* by the arousal. Obstacles to love, such as short separations and the exciting effects of dangerous exploits, heighten intensity.

In long-term, loving relationships, passionate love gradually cools to companionate love.

PASSIONATE AND COMPANIONATE LOVE

The strong form of being in love is **passionate love.** It is a state of intense absorption, arousal, and longing for another. (Infatuation is a very brief and limited version of passionate love.) This experience seems to have some similar aspects among most people. It is involuntary, and there are times when many people wish they were not in love. The French writer Stendahl once commented that if he were murdered while he was in the throes of an unrequited passion, he would thank the murderer before he died. The experience often includes these "symptoms":

1. Thinking of the object of desire almost all the time. The person involved intrudes into thinking; attention is narrowed to him or her. One so involved wrote: "Love is a human religion in which another person is believed in."

2. Longing for reciprocation.

3. Dependency of mood on the other's reactions.

4. Inability to react in the same way to more than one person at a time.

5. Fear of rejection.

6. Intensification through adversity.

7. Emphasis and focus on positive qualities of the person, ignoring all negative ones (Tennov, 1979).

In time, however, most passionate relationships fade. Arousal is dependent on novelty, so it is virtually impossible to maintain such intense feeling for long. When the initial passion fades, there are two possibilities. Either the relationship is burned out and over, or it develops into the more sober kind of everyday love, **companionate love** (Walster & Walster, 1980). This second form of love involves less arousal and excitement, but more friendly affection and deep attachment. Companionate love, to be sure, has its moments of passion, but these do not usurp all other concerns.

FALLING IN LOVE

What causes us to fall in love, and what are the characteristics of this "fall"? Each love experience is different, yet there are some similarities of all love experiences.

It is commonly thought that women are the romantics; their lives are said to be organized more around love, while men are thought to be more concerned with work, money, and other activities. But the data contradict that common assumption. Hobart (1958) asked hundreds of men and women questions about romance. He found that men are much more likely to be romantics than women are. Men fall in love faster and have a more romantic view of love relationships than women do. In another study, 20 percent of men fell in love before their fourth date, while 15 percent of women did. Also, it is usually the woman who ends the affair and the men who report greater distress (Walster, Walster, & Traupmann, 1978).

THE "INGREDIENTS" OF LOVE

Robert Sternberg describes loving as having three components: Intimacy, passion, and commitment. **Intimate feelings** include a desire to promote the welfare of the other, holding the loved one in high esteem, and sharing and mutual understanding. **Passion** is the state of intense longing for the other. **Commitment** is both short- and long-term and is the ability to give up others

---

TABLE 18-1
Taxonomy of Kinds of Love

Kind of Love	Intimacy	Passion	Decision/ Commitment
Non-love	—	—	—
Liking	+	—	—
Infatuated love	—	+	—
Empty love	—	—	—
Romantic love	+	+	—
Companionate love	+	—	+
Fatuous love	—	+	+
Consummate love	+	+	+

Note: + = component present; — = component absent. These kinds of love represent idealized cases based on the triangular theory. Most loving relationships will fit between categories, because the components of love occur in varying degrees, rather than being simply present or absent.
Source: Sternberg, 1988.

either for the moment or to stay with the loved one over the ups and downs of the course of life. (See Figure 18-3.)

As Table 18-1 shows, this analysis allows us to understand why loves, lovers, and loving situations are so different from each other. Some have one component, some two, and a few three. Intimacy alone, for example, yields liking, not loving. Couples who have high intimacy share a lot, and have high regard, but do not have intense relationships. Passion alone is infatuation, longing, and lust, but not necessarily regard or commitment. Commitment alone yields a feeling of emptiness; when the passion and intimacy fade, little is left.

Romantic love is intimacy and passion; companionate is intimacy and commitment; while passion and commitment yield "fatuous" love, one of lust and permanency but little else. In Sternberg's ideal scheme, perfect love is all three. This is a suitable way to survey your relationships, and there is increasing research support for it (Sternberg, 1989; Sternberg & Barnes 1987).

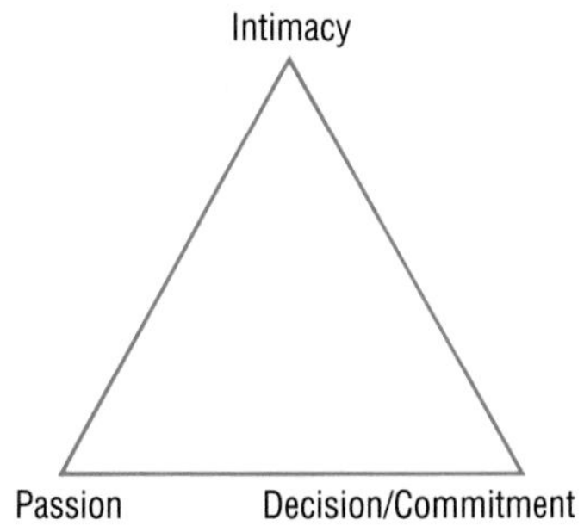

FIGURE 18-3
Triangle of Love
(Sternberg, 1988)

THE RELATIONSHIP BETWEEN ATTRACTIVENESS AND LOVING

We want someone to love us for ourselves, not for external qualities such as a pretty face. However, physical **attractiveness** is very important in the initial tumble into love, particularly in men's eyes. In one study (Walster, Aronson, Abrahams, & Rottmann, 1966), a panel of college students rated the physical attractiveness of 752 college freshmen. Afterward, other information regarding their intelligence, personality, and attitudes was also assembled.

Then the experimenters staged a dance at which the freshmen were randomly assigned a date. The freshmen were later asked how satisfied they were with their date. They were asked how eager they were for another date, and whether they would ask the person out. *The only determinant of interest was physical attractiveness.* Another study found that physical attractiveness was more related to a woman's popularity than to a man's. There was a strong correlation between a woman's physical attractiveness and the number of dates she had, but the relationship was slight for men (Hatfield & Sprecher, 1986).

Physical attractiveness may be most important at the beginning of a love relationship; with time, other "more real" factors come into play. However, the evidence so far disagrees with those who believe that "love" does not depend upon "mere physical" attributes.

ON THE NATURE OF ATTRACTIVENESS: SEXUAL AND GENERAL

Sensitivity to scarcity makes anyone who is difficult to meet seem more valuable. In one study of a singles bar, researchers in Virginia randomly selected customers. They asked them to rate the attractiveness of individuals of the opposite sex who were present three hours, two hours, and then one-half hour before closing. The results were surprising. Those remaining one-half hour before closing were judged the best looking. This is when the chances to meet and strike up a conversation were becoming less and less, scarcer and scarcer (Pennebaker et al., 1979).

629

A person's attractiveness and physical appearance affect other aspects of his or her life as well. One of the quickest ways to judge people is by their appearance. Clothes, manner of speech, skin color, and sex often overwhelm other considerations. So many long-held stereotypes may be influenced by the overwhelming amount of exterior information (appearance) we receive about people.

It is easy to misconstrue the applicability of the immediate impressions from the physical features of others, such as height. One survey of college graduates showed that males six feet two inches tall and over had a starting salary of $125 per week higher than those shorter than six feet. Tall people seem to be judged more trustworthy and generous as well (Deck, 1968).

Unfortunately, this bias affects more than just trivial matters. The same processes are at work in judging job worth and political capabilities. Consider this: in all presidential elections from 1900 to 1968, the taller candidate won. So impressed was the Carter campaign by this fact that when Jimmy Carter had to meet Gerald Ford in debate, he insisted that their lecterns be placed far apart. Even the ritual handshake was analyzed. Carter stood far away and extended his hand as far as possible, then walked away, minimizing the time they were on the screen together (Keyes, 1980).

Surface attractiveness is important to us in selecting a mate and planning a family, especially to males (Argyle & Henderson, 1985). Speaking again in evolutionary terms, beauty is slightly more than skin deep. It indicates good health and thus good reproductive potential. A clean skin may signify freedom from disease.

ATTRACTIVENESS AND CRIMINALS

While most of us believe that attractiveness is important for sex and loving, we do not think that attractiveness should play a role in the courtroom. But there is clear evidence that most people are unable to put their instincts and biases aside and to act on their logical convictions. Criminologists have collected evidence showing that if defendants are good-looking people, they are less likely to get caught at illicit activities. If caught, they are less likely to be reported. And even if the case comes to court, judges and jurors are more likely to be lenient with them.

In one study (Mace, 1972), 440 young men and women were asked to shoplift merchandise from 10 markets in a large city (of course, the markets were told of the study). Clerks were less likely to accuse shoplifters who were well-groomed and neatly dressed than those who were sloppily groomed. Customers were also more likely to report shoplifters of undesirable appearance. In two grocery stores and a discount department store, an accomplice blatantly shoplifted in the presence of customers. The shoplifter looked like a typical professional out on a shopping break. Very few people reported the thefts. In contrast, a "hippie" shoplifter (this study took place in the mid-1970s) was described in great detail in the following way: "He wore soiled patched blue jeans, blue workman's shirt, and blue denim jacket; well-worn, scuffed shoes with no socks. He had long and unruly hair with a ribbon tied around his forehead. He was unshaven and had a small beard" (Stefensmeyer & Terry,

Unattractive people are more likely than attractive people to be both accused and convicted of crimes.

1973). Thus, hippie shoplifters were not only more likely to be reported, but they were reported with more enthusiasm. "That [expletive] hippie over there stuffed a banana down his coat." Apparently, appropriate looks pay off, even when commiting a crime. We are less suspicious of attractive people.

What other effects does a person's attractiveness have on others? In another study people were asked to watch a well-dressed or a slovenly woman shoplifting. The "detectives" were asked how upset the woman would probably be if she were caught, tried, and convicted of shoplifting. Observers felt that the well-dressed woman would suffer most if she were convicted of shoplifting. They thought she would be emotionally upset and concerned about what her family and friends would think of her than the scruffy woman would be (Deseran & Chung, 1979).

Whenever juries decide, they are presumed to use all the information they receive to come to the right decision. Because of the tendency of the mind to ignore the familiar, then unusual or incongruous information may have great influence. Solomon and Schopler (1978) hypothesized that we might judge unusually attractive defendants most leniently. We assume that "what is beautiful is good." Homely defendants may also be judged compassionately out of pity. An average-looking defendant, however, does not get the benefit of the doubt for either reason. Thus, he or she may get the harshest sentence.

Students at the University of North Carolina evaluated a fake case of a young woman accused of hustling $10,000. The woman was presented to the "jury" as attractive, average-looking, or unattractive. The attractive woman got the most magnanimous sentence of 12 months. The unattractive women had an average prison sentence of 18½ months. The average-looking woman, however, received the most restrictive sentence of all: the jury wanted to lock her up for 19 and a half months (Solomon & Schopler, 1978)!

The sentencing of a rapist may depend not only on his crime, but also on his looks. Test yourself on this. Suppose you heard a description such as the following (Jacobsen, 1981, adapted from Jones & Aronson, 1973).

What effect did John De Lorean's attractiveness and wealth have on his acquittal of drug charges?

> It was ten o'clock at night and Judy W. was getting out of an evening class at a large Midwestern university. She walked across the campus toward her car, which was parked two blocks off campus. A man was walking across the campus in the same direction as Judy W. and began to follow her.
>
> Less than a block from Judy W.'s car, the man accosted her. In the ensuing struggle, he stripped her and raped her. A passerby heard her screams and called the police. They arrived at the scene within minutes.
>
> Judy W. told the police that she had never seen her attacker before that night. Based on her description, the police arrested Charles E., a student whom they found in the vicinity of the attack. Judy W. positively identified Charles E. as the man who raped her. Charles E. swears that he is innocent. He testified that he was just taking a break from studying by going out for a walk and that it was just a coincidence that he was in the vicinity and that it was a coincidence that he matched Judy W.'s description of her attacker.

Again, in a psychology experiment, Charles E. was depicted as either good looking or ugly. When he was described as a handsome man, both men and women "judges" (subjects in the experiment) were likely to think he was just out for a walk and that his resemblance to the rapist was coincidental. Not so if Charles E. was described as ugly, then they saw him as guilty.

Some of us seem to be able to do without sex just fine. In others, nature has implanted a powerful need or drive that appears to be as necessary to total health as food, air, sleep, exercise, love, and laughter. Remember that sex combines many needs—i.e., being touched, caressed, feeling close to others. At times when sex is not available, substitute other forms of closeness. Get a massage. Give one. Talk to people in trouble and try to help them. These and other recourses can never completely substitute for sex, but they will help you more than you think as well as helping others. It will put you in a better mood, make you feel better about yourself, less lonely. And, maybe, you'll meet someone compatible.

Unfortunately, many erroneous beliefs can interfere with sexual pleasures—upbringing, cultural traditions, media images —and work, and other interests or demands compete for our time and energy. Sex may be the first thing to go during times of physical and mental stress, illnesses, pregnancy, parenting, and aging. You may take it for granted that you can return to it later on. Don't do so.

USING PSYCHOLOGY: ON SEX

When you decide to enter into a sexual relationship, take time for sex, touching, and loving. Don't let other events interfere. Think about the qualities that make a sexual experience satisfying for you: Is it the setting? What you did before and afterward? The degree of emotional commitment? Make sure you can arrange the scene so it works.

Make sure if your sex life isn't working that you pay attention to it as you would problems in other areas of life. Communicate, even if it's difficult, your likes and dislikes to your partner. Where do you like to be touched, and how? Your partner is not a mind reader, and neither are you. Many lawyers now say that sexual incompatibility is the primary but often hidden issue in divorce. It isn't mentioned in the complaints, which focus on cruelty, lack of commitment, or broken promises, but it can often be sex, whether it's satisfactory to both, whether both have sexual release as frequently as they need. People have very different sexual appetites. If your sexual relationship is a problem for you, even a small one, heed it and give it the attention it needs to make it work.

The subjects were also asked how long a prison sentence they would recommend for Charles E. if he were found guilty. The good-looking Charles E. was given a 10-year sentence, but the homely version was given almost 14 years in prison! Ugliness may be dangerous to your freedom.

The looks of the victim were also important. Judges were more likely to assume Charles E. was guilty when Judy W. was alluring. They were less sympathetic to a rapist of an attractive woman than to a rapist of an unattractive woman (Jacobsen, 1981; Hatfield & Sprecher, 1986). The snap judgments of prejudice and attractiveness are difficult to overcome.

SUMMARY

1. The love bond between men and women plays a key biological role. Human fathers are the only male primates to contribute significantly to the care of their own offspring. Human females are the only female mammals that are sexually receptive at all times of the year.

2. Human sexual signals are more visual than those of other animals. This, combined with frequent sex and eye contact during sex may help establish pair bonds based on sexual pleasure. The pair bond makes possible a stable society based on family units.

3. In all primitive societies, the division of labor is the same: men hunt, women gather. Males do the fighting in every society, partly because of their size and strength, but also because they are more expendable. Male dominance may have originally resulted from men possessing control over a valuable resource: protein. An alternative view is that women's reproductive ability is the most valuable resource.

4. The replacement in humans of the estrus cycle with the menstrual cycle decreased male competition for females. As a result, humans were able to develop cooperative societies.

5. People are very sexual animals. The signals for sex among human beings are psychological as well as biological. Emotions like love and attachment are important in sexual attraction.

6. *Pheromones* are chemicals that convey information about sexual receptivity through odor. They have been found in insects and many mammals. Humans respond unconsciously to the odors of others. The menstrual cycles of women can be synchronized by exposing the women to the scent of each other. Contact with male pheromones affects the reproductive cycle of women.

7. There are four phases of physiological activity in the *sexual response cycle*. During the *excitement* phase, blood flow and muscle tension increases in the genitals. The penis becomes erect and the vagina lubricates. Intercourse occurs during the *plateau phase,* when vasocongestion and muscle tension levels off, but excitement remains high. During *orgasm*, arousal, muscle tension, and heart rate peak. The male ejaculates. Tension is suddenly released following orgasm, in the *resolution* phase; the participant feels relaxed and the male cannot get an erection. Orgasms generally result from genital stimulation. More men than women commonly experience orgasm during intercourse. Some women are capable of multiple orgasms in one sex act.

8. About 10 percent of men and 6 percent of women are *homosexual.* Until 1973, homosexuality was considered a disorder. But studies failed to show any relationship between sexual preferences and psychological distress. Now psychologists are striving to understand the causes of homosexuality.

9. Love relationships are central in people's lives, and disruption of them is a major cause of personal distress. Researchers have identified three characteristics of people in love. They incline, or literally lean, toward one another, they maintain physical closeness, and they look often into each other's eyes.

10. Love is highly dependent on *activation*. Increases of arousal, even if artificially induced, lead to higher ratings of the attractiveness of a partner. Strong positive feelings may turn to strong negative feelings when a love affair ends. Obstacles to love heighten its intensity.

11. *Passionate love* is the strong form of ''being in love.'' Seven characteristics of the state of passion are constant thought about the beloved, longing for reciprocation, dependency of mood on the other's reactions, direction at only one person, fear of rejection, intensification of the feeling through adversity, and focus on only the good qualities of the beloved. Passion generally fades with time. *Companionate love* is the strong, long-term bond of attachment and friendship that evolves when the passionate love fades.

12. According to Sternberg, love has three components. *Intimacy* includes caring for another, respecting another, and mutual understanding. *Passion* is the state of intense longing for another. *Commitment* is the decision to stay together. In Sternberg's ideal, perfect love includes all three components.

13. Physical *attractiveness* plays a primary role in the development of romantic interest. The attractiveness of a woman is more important than that of a man. When potential

partners are more scarce, they seem more attractive. Physical features have a very strong influence on us. Tall people tend to get higher salaries and are judged to be more trustworthy and generous. Good looking people are less likely to be caught, reported, and sentenced for crimes.

TERMS AND CONCEPTS

attractiveness
commitment
companionate love
estrus
homosexuality
intimacy
love

ovulation
pair bonding
passion
passionate love
pheromones
sexual response cycle
sexuality

SUGGESTIONS FOR FURTHER READING

Hatfield, E., & Sprecher, S. (1986). *Mirror, mirror: The importance of looks in everyday life.* New York: SUNY Press.

A wonderful compilation of social psychology on the importance of attractiveness.

Symons, D. (1980). Precis of the evolution of human sexuality. *Behavioral and Brain Sciences, 3,* 171–214.

Mentioned here and elsewhere in the text, an important statement of the evolutionary approach to sexuality and sex differences.

Tennov, D. (1979). *Love and limerence.* New York: Stein & Day.

Mellen, S. L. W. (1981). *The evolution of love.* San Francisco: W. H. Freeman.

Walster, E., & Walster, G. W. (1978). *A new look at love.* Reading, MA: Addison-Wesley.

Three books, from very different perspectives, on the components of loving.

634

19

HEALTH PSYCHOLOGY

L ife did not start out well for Mary. During her childhood her parents had financial difficulties. Between Mary's fifth and tenth birthdays, her mother had several major illnesses and had to undergo surgery many times. Her mother also was hospitalized twice for "unbearable tension," nervousness, annoyance with her children, and fears that she might harm them.

At 18 Mary described herself: "If I say how I am it sounds like bragging—I have a good personality and people like me. I don't like it when people think they can run my own life—I like to be my own judge. I know right from wrong, but I feel I have a lot more to learn and go through. Generally, I hope I can make it—I hope." She planned to enroll in college and was keeping her career goals open. She had high self-esteem and was outgoing, persistent, and concerned for others.

Mary was one of 72 children growing up in Hawaii who was tracked from birth into her early 20s (Werner & Smith, 1982). They came of age from 1955 to 1979—a time of unprecedented social change. They had to confront war in Southeast Asia and the civil rights and antiwar conflicts in their own neighborhoods. They witnessed the assassination of one president and the resignation of another. They were the first generation encountering television, contraceptive pills, and mind-altering drugs. By all standards, these children were at high risk, born and raised in poverty and reared by mothers with little education and with learning and behavioral problems.

Yet some endured and thrived, challenging the stresses. They developed into competent, autonomous adults who worked well, played well, loved well, and expected well. How were these people able to adapt and thrive?

ABOUT HEALTH PSYCHOLOGY

Health psychology helps people improve and maintain their well-being. Traditionally, psychology has been more concerned with mental health than with physical health. It did not encompass physical health until the 1970s. Originally a subdiscipline of psychiatry, not psychology, **psychosomatic medicine** has been based on the premise that particular personality traits were components of the cause of particular illnesses (Dunbar, 1943; Alexander, 1950). Some illnesses considered at least partly psychosomatic are bronchial asthma, essential hypertension, gastric ulcers, and colitis.

As psychosomatic medicine developed, it broadened its concern from the psychogenic in the direction of complex biopsychosocial models. The biopsychosocial model developed by George Engel and the psychobiological model developed by Herbert Weiner assume that psychological factors may influence physical disease at any stage, from predisposition through precipitation to maintenance (Weiner, 1978), and can influence the progress of any disease, not just a few psychosomatic diseases.

Behavioral medicine, an interdisciplinary field, attempts to intervene in health maintenance with behavioral changes. However, the use of behavioral techniques is not limited to psychologists. Social workers, nutritionists, nurses, physicians, health educators, and others are active in behavioral medicine.

STRESS: ADAPTING TO CHANGES IN THE WORLD

THE EMERGENCY REACTION

Imagine that you work in the evening. To get home you must walk a few blocks to your car through a dangerous area. It's dark, and only a few people are around. You begin to hear footsteps behind you, but when you turn around, there's no one there. You start walking faster, but the footsteps keep pace. You remember that a co-worker was mugged last week not too far from here, and you begin to feel afraid. Your heart starts to pound, your mouth gets dry, and your hands get clammy. The footsteps get closer, and you can't decide if you should run for it or turn and face the "mugger."

Suddenly you whirl around and you see a person in the shadows who seems huge and menacing. A man steps into the light and then you realize that it's just the security guard, who offers to escort you to your car. Although you feel relieved, you worry about the next night and wonder if you shouldn't switch to the day shift.

This is an illustration of our most basic and immediate reaction to stress, called the **emergency reaction.** It includes both the fight-or-flight response and the general adaptation syndrome.

THE FIGHT-OR-FLIGHT RESPONSE   If our prehistoric ancestors were confronted by a charging animal, it would be adaptive if they were instantly aroused. (See the section on activation of the emergency reaction in Chapter 12, page 411.) They would be ready for action—to fight or to flee (Cannon, 1929). This **fight-or-flight** emergency response (Figure 19-1) is mediated by the sympathetic nervous system and includes the following changes:

1. The rate and strength of the heartbeat increase, allowing oxygen to be pumped more rapidly.
2. The spleen contracts, releasing stored red blood cells to carry the extra oxygen.
3. The liver releases stored sugar to provide energy to the muscles.
4. The blood supply is redistributed from the skin and viscera to the muscles and brain.
5. Respiration deepens.
6. The pupils dilate.
7. The blood's ability to seal wounds is increased (Gray, 1984).

A variety of physiological systems respond directly to immediate stress.

GENERAL ADAPTATION SYNDROME   As a medical student in the 1920s, Hans Selye, the main proponent of the stress concept, noticed something that eluded his professors. No matter what type of illness a patient had, one thing was common to all: they all *looked* sick. Key to Selye's understanding of stress was that he saw

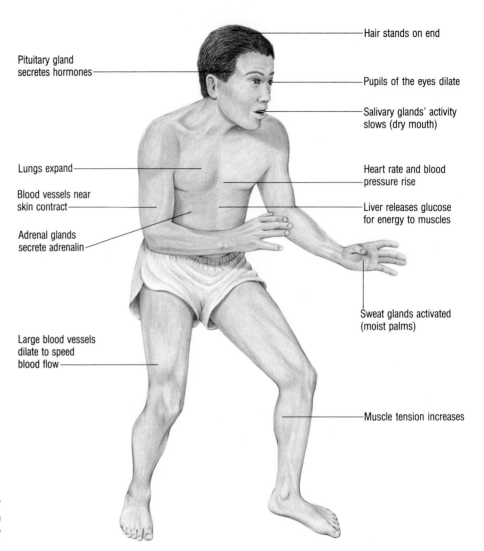

FIGURE 19-1
Fight-or-Flight Reaction

Many physical reactions occur in the body in response to activation of the emergency reaction.

Pituitary gland secretes hormones

Lungs expand

Blood vessels near skin contract

Adrenal glands secrete adrenalin

Large blood vessels dilate to speed blood flow

Hair stands on end

Pupils of the eyes dilate

Salivary glands' activity slows (dry mouth)

Heart rate and blood pressure rise

Liver releases glucose for energy to muscles

Sweat glands activated (moist palms)

Muscle tension increases

it as a *response,* not as the environmental stimulus or as a situation where the demand exceeds the individual's abilities to cope.

Selye (1956) called this response the **general adaptation syndrome** and identified three stages. First is the *alarm reaction,* which prepares the organism for immediate flight or fight. This is the same as the fight-or-flight emergency reaction. Then comes the *resistance* stage, in which many of the physiological changes associated with the alarm reaction are reversed. The organism has increased resistance to the stressor. Selye subjected rats to prolonged cold for five weeks. These animals, having developed resistance, withstood colder temperatures than rats that had been kept at room temperature. The third stage, *exhaustion,* occurs when the body's ability to adapt uses up all of its resources. After several months of cold, the rats lost their resistance and became less tolerant of the cold than ordinary rats and became prone to sickness and death.

To explain this, we need to look at how the emergency reaction is mediated by the sympathetic nervous system (SNS). Its synapses directly stimulate the heart to beat faster and direct the peripheral blood vessels to clamp down. Chemical neurotransmitters at these synapses are *epinephrine* and *norepinephrine*. The SNS stimulates the adrenal medulla to secrete more epinephrine and less norepinephrine.

If the emergency reaction is strong, it brings on the general adaptation syndrome. Then the hypothalamus stimulates the pituitary gland to release an important hormone called *ACTH* into the blood, which stimulates the adrenal cortex to release other hormones. These hormones stimulate the immune system to attack any invading antigens and stimulate the liver to fight the stressor. If glucocorticoids are produced, the body has made the decision to coexist peacefully with the stressor.

STRESS AS A FAILURE TO ADAPT

People today face challenges equipped with a brain and biology suited to a different world than that of today. The fight-or-flight response, which evolved to cope with physical threats, is now evoked by money problems, an unsympathetic boss, traffic jams, or unemployment. Increased adrenaline (epinephrine), rapid heart rate, increased respiration, moist palms, and tense muscles are all inappropriate to today's challenges. Do you need to run, literally, from a low bank balance?

The current popular view of stress is that people are passive, helpless victims. Stressors, from loss of a loved one to loss of car keys, attack us. The answer would seem to be to avoid all stress, change, and challenge. Yet stress does not result simply from exposure to events in the environment. The way we perceive and appraise the event has more to do with the outcome than the event itself.

Stress is the failure to adapt. It occurs when the environment or internal demands exceed an individual's resources to adapt (Lazarus & Launier, 1978). Stressful situations are of several types: *catastrophes,* such as earthquakes, wars, and fires; *major life changes,* such as unemployment or the death of a spouse; *chronic life strains,* such as poor working conditions; and *hassles,* such as having a check bounce.

CATASTROPHES Human adaptation can be overwhelmed by too much change, such as the catastrophic effects of war. The study of stressful situations began with men in combat who suffer extreme psychological distress. This was called "shell shock" in World War I, "combat fatigue" in World War II, and "acute combat reaction" in the Vietnam War.

Under combat conditions, a soldier may have to make extreme demands on his body, going without sleep, food, or shelter for many days. He may be called upon to commit extreme acts such as killing. And he may see his buddies become injured, disfigured, or die, and may fear for his own life. World War II veterans who had combat stress for prolonged periods still have major psychological problems five decades later.

The way we react to stressors, from catastrophes (such as the San Francisco earthquake pictured here) to daily hassles, directly affects our health.

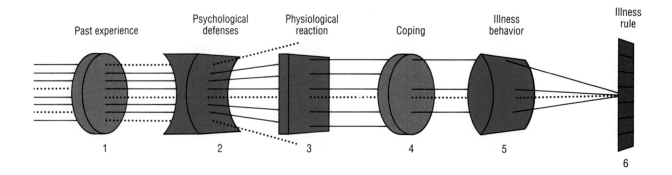

Past experience   Psychological   Physiological   Coping   Illness   Illness
                   defenses   reaction   behavior   rule

1   2   3   4   5   6

FIGURE 19-2
Dealing with Stressful Life Events

Illness is not the inevitable reaction to life changes and stress. Each of us has various ways of deflecting, defusing, or interpreting stressful events to permit coping and possibly to prevent physiological reactions and illness. How such physiological defenses can filter upsets and upheavals is shown diagrammatically above.

From R. H. Rahe, The pathway between subjects' recent life changes and their near-future illness reports, in Dohenwend, B. S., and Dohenwend, B. P. (eds.), *Stressful life events*, copyright © 1974, John Wiley and Sons.

MAJOR LIFE CHANGES   Major alterations in a person's world cause major upsets within because the mental system detects instability and change. A strong connection exists between the unpredictability of life and illness: people are more likely to become ill after extensive life changes (Figure 19-2). **Major life changes** (Holmes & Rahe, 1967) include positive events (such as marriage, vacations, and outstanding personal achievements) and negative events (such as marital separation, death of a family member, and jail terms). Increases in life changes increase the risk of such problems as traffic accidents (Rahe & Arthur, 1978). People who have experienced many major life changes—particularly negative ones—are more likely to develop diabetes, leukemia, cardiovascular disease, schizophrenia, depression, and difficulties in pregnancy (Schwartz & Griffen, 1986).

It is difficult to rate how stressful life events are, so Holmes and Rahe (1967) asked people how much adjustment certain events would require. They set marriage at a value of 50 *life change units* (LCUs). Mild stress occurs at an LCU score of 150–199, moderate stress at 200–299, and high stress at 300 or more. These early findings were startling. However, some researchers began questioning some of the assumptions of the scale and the way it was used.

However, the situation is more complex than Holmes and Rahe assumed. Negative life events relate directly to illness, but positive events relate weakly. Few who experience major life changes get sick. The *nonoccurrence* of a desired

Chronic life strains, at home and at work, wear down our ability to resist stress.

TABLE 19-1
Ratings of Stressful Life Events

LIFE EVENT	Life Change Units[1]		
	AMERICAN	EUROPEAN	JAPANESE
Death of spouse	100 (1)	66 (1)	108 (1)
Divorce	73 (2)	54 (3)	63 (3)
Marital separation	65 (3)	49 (5)	46 (7)
Jail term	63 (4)	57 (2)	72 (2)
Death of close family member	63 (5)	31 (18)	57 (4)
Personal injury or illness	53 (6)	39 (8)	54 (5)
Marriage	50 (7)	50 (4)	50 (6)
Being fired from job	47 (8)	37 (9)	37 (8)
Marital reconciliation	45 (9)	40 (7)	27 (15)
Retirement	45 (10)	31 (17)	29 (11)
Change in health of family member	44 (11)	30 (20)	33 (9)
Pregnancy	40 (12)	43 (6)	27 (13)
Sexual difficulties	39 (13)	32 (15)	31 (10)
Addition of new family member	39 (14)	34 (13)	18 (23)
Major business readjustment	39 (15)	34 (11)	28 (12)

[1]Ranking is shown in parentheses.
SOURCE: Ornstein & Sobel, 1987.

event may also be stressful, as when a person would like to marry someone but does not. Life events are not necessarily *discrete* episodes that occur at once. They are often events that take place over a span of time, with far-reaching consequences for many areas of a person's life. The effects of a bad job or an unhappy marriage endure.

However, not everyone finds that marriage relates in the same way to other events as the original sample did. The loss of a spouse is very different for men versus women. There are also cultural differences: for Americans, the death of close family member is fifth on the scale; for Europeans, eighteenth (Table 19-1).

CHRONIC LIFE STRAINS   Chronic conditions such as an unhappy marriage or poor working conditions are not really events, per se, but may be very stressful (Pearlin, 1980). **Chronic life strains** come under four different roles in life: marriage, parenthood, household economics, and work. The work environment in particular contains stresses that seem to outstrip our capacity to adapt to them. Certain aspects of work add stress, such as the type of work, the workload, and relationships with co-workers and bosses.

However, being out of work may be even more stressful than having work that you don't like. When unemployment increases, the use of physical and mental health services increases dramatically (Cobb & Kasl, 1977). Mental hospital admissions and deaths also increase (Brenner, 1976). Each time the unemployment rate increases by 1 percentage point, 4 percent more people

TABLE 19-2
Ten Most Common Hassles

College Sample (n = 34)	% of Times Checked	Middle-aged Sample (n = 100)	% of Times Checked
1. Troubling thoughts about future	76.6	1. Concerns about weight	52.4
2. Not getting enough sleep	72.5	2. Health of a family member	48.1
3. Wasting time	71.1	3. Rising prices of common goods	43.7
4. Inconsiderate smokers	70.7	4. Home maintenance	42.8
5. Physical appearance	69.9	5. Too many things to do	38.6
6. Too many things to do	69.2	6. Misplacing or losing things	38.1
7. Misplacing or losing things	67.0	7. Yard work or outside home maintenance	38.1
8. Not enough time to do the things you need to do	66.3	8. Property, investment, or taxes	37.6
9. Concerns about meeting high standards	64.0	9. Crime	37.1
10. Being lonely	60.8	10. Physical appearance	35.9

SOURCE: Kanner, Coyne, Schaefer, & Lazarus, 1981.

commit suicide, 5.7 percent more commit murder, and nearly 2 percent more die of cirrhosis of the liver or cardiovascular disease (Gore, 1978).

HASSLES AND UPLIFTS Stressful life events are relatively uncommon compared to daily **hassles.** What about all the frustrating, irritating, and annoying common events? There are traffic jams, waiting in lines, foul-ups at work, arguments, misplacing things, concerns about weight and rising prices, and other daily hassles (see Table 19-2). Even major life events are accompanied by hassles. Getting a divorce unbalances people, partly because of the added extra hassles: having to do all of the chores that had been shared, arranging child care, added expenses, and so on. Hassles better predict psychosomatic and physical symptoms than major life events (Lazarus, 1984).

The experience of stress, of course, does not predict illness; we might expect positive events, **uplifts,** to balance out negative ones. A person with a very active life may have hassles because of it but may also be doing something that gives great pleasure. Consider someone preparing for the Olympics: juggling school and workouts, watching weight, scrounging up money to go to competitions may be a hassle, but the joy of mastery and winning matches more than compensates.

Kanner and his colleagues (1981) devised some scales to assess positive and negative experiences. Not unexpectedly, people of different ages and occupations have different patterns of hassles and uplifts (Tables 19-2 and 19-3). College students were found to be "struggling with the academic and social

TABLE 19-3
Ten Most Common Uplifts

College Sample (n = 34)	% of Times Checked	Middle-aged Sample (n = 100)	% of Times Checked
1. Completing a task	83.7	1. Relating well with your spouse or lover	76.3
2. Relating well with friends	81.6	2. Relating well with friends	74.4
3. Giving a present	81.3	3. Completing a task	73.3
4. Having fun	81.3	4. Feeling healthy	72.7
5. Getting love	81.3	5. Getting enough sleep	69.7
6. Giving love	80.0	6. Eating out	68.4
7. Being visited, phoned, or sent a letter	79.0	7. Meeting your responsibilities	68.1
8. Laughing	79.0	8. Visiting, phoning, or writing someone	67.7
9. Entertainment	78.4	9. Spending time with family	66.7
10. Music	78.0	10. Home (inside) pleasing to you	65.5

SOURCE: Kanner, Coyne, Schaefer, & Lazarus, 1981.

problems typically associated with attending college (wasting time, concerns about meeting high standards, being lonely)." Middle-aged subjects found pleasure and satisfaction primarily in their family and in good health. However, the students preferred hedonic ("fun") activities such as laughing, entertainment, music, and the like. Little solid evidence has yet developed to link uplifts with improved health. However, this approach is probably on the right track.

MEDIATION OF STRESS

Stresses of modern life in part result from living in a modern world that is different from the world we originally adapted to. Thus, psychologists are currently applying their knowledge to aid in a fresh adaptation: to learn to be healthy in our new circumstances. Some of these new studies are examining those who are "better selected" to withstand the difficulties of the modern world. Identifying what makes them "hardy" may make it easier for others. Other studies are developing new treatments and new ways to understand relationships between the mind, the brain, the body, and society, some of which have already been presented, such as the new field of psychoimmunology. Still others consider the surprising changes in the environment that aid health. For example, simply providing a view out of a window may help to heal patients. All these studies hold great promise.

HARDINESS IN THE FACE OF STRESS: COPING MECHANISMS

In *Vulnerable, But Invincible,* Emmy Werner and Ruth Smith (1982) recount their study of 72 resilient children, such as Mary who was described in the beginning of this chapter. The children's mothers reported that they were active and "socially responsive" even when they were infants. Other observers reported that they had positive social orientations as young children. They seemed to have a strong concept of themselves and could follow their interests where they led. These children had

> a more positive self-concept, and a more nurturant, responsible, and achievement-oriented attitude toward life than peers who developed serious coping problems. At the threshold of adulthood, the resilient men and women had developed a sense of coherence in their lives and were able to draw on a number of informal sources of support. They also expressed a desire to "improve themselves," i.e., toward continued psychological growth. (Werner & Smith, 1982)

This study, and others of children with schizophrenic parents and of children surviving war, abuse, and adversity, give testimony to the enormous adaptability of people. These investigations are beginning to reshape our thinking about stress and resistance to disease.

Many experts accept that stress makes us more vulnerable to all disorders from cancer to heart attacks, infections to depression. However, this simple equation—that stress (whether it be psychological trauma or microbes) equals disease—doesn't really work. Most people exposed to stressors don't become ill. Different people confronting the same stressor react differently: some break down while others thrive.

The pessimistic view is that stress kills; yet this impression of people as passive victims of stress doesn't make sense. If we avoided all stressors, no one would ever marry, have children, take a job, write a book, or invent anything. And how would the modern world have come about?

These children in Northern Ireland and others like them who have suffered from life's adversity show a resilience that gives testimony to the amazing ability of human beings to adapt.

CHAPTER 19 / HEALTH PSYCHOLOGY

Most people need change and challenge. They seek out novelty and stimulation. Many come through stressful experiences not with illness but with better strength and health. For many people, disease is not inevitable in the face of difficulty.

Although the relationship between life change events and disease is important, the correlations are modest and hide more than they reveal. If we try to predict who will become ill based on a tally of major life events, we are likely to be correct only about 15 percent of the time. This means that there is a large group of people who are not exposed to high stress but still become ill.

COMMITMENT, CHALLENGE, CONTROL, AND CHANGE More interesting are those who survive changes and challenges in their lives. When confronted with a stressor, some people seem to be able to cope with it without becoming anxious and aroused in a harmful way. Some people appraise the potential stressor in such a way as to avoid stress. The charging lion may elicit a very different reaction in you than in an experienced animal trainer. Some people are able to take action in the face of a stressor that minimizes or eliminates the threat.

Suzanne Kobasa and colleagues (1982) identified the components of psychological hardiness. She studied middle- and upper-level business executives at Illinois Bell Telephone Company when the company was undergoing reorganization, a time of great stress and uncertainty for its employees. Of the 250 business managers surveyed, 200 were selected from those who experienced high stress levels. About half of them had frequent or severe illnesses, whereas the other half remained healthy. The executives were similar in income, job status, educational level, age, ethnic background, and religious practice, but they were opposite in their attitudes about themselves, their jobs, and the people around them.

Low-illness executives showed a strong **commitment** to self, work, and family. They had a sense of **control** over their life, and they saw change as a **challenge** rather than a threat. They agreed with such statements as "I would sacrifice financial stability in my work if something really challenging came along."

In contrast, high-illness executives felt threatened by change and suffered in the face of uncertainty. They agreed with such statements as "It bothers me when I have to deviate from the routine or schedule I have set for myself."

Here is a profile of one of Kobasa's high-illness executives:

> "I'm thinking of making a major change. I'm thinking of leaving the phone company and going to this little electronics company that's a much more risky operation. I figure if what you're going to do is free, I'll come and get the advice. Maybe it'll be helpful."
>
> This man's protocol showed high stress and high illness. He was only in his thirties, but he had hypertension, peptic ulcer, and migraine headaches: many symptoms as well as diseases. He arrives forty-five minutes late, trenchcoat flying behind him, papers under his arm. Then he makes a beeline for my secretary's desk and begins calling people. He's got to call many people to let them know where he's going to be in the next forty-five minutes. All the time I'm in my office waiting, hearing all these phone calls. He comes in and I've prepared what's going to be a fairly difficult conversation with him about his alienation from other people. However it's difficult to do that because the phone

keeps ringing and every time it does he jumps up because he's convinced it's for him. He can't talk in my office so he has to run out to the secretary's office. This happens three times and we're not getting anywhere.

He says to me, "Look, I really need to take all these calls, they're very crucial. But you may have something here. So why don't you talk into my tape recorder?" So he pulls out a tape recorder, puts it on my desk and says, "I'll listen to it at night when I have a chance." (Kobasa, 1987)

In contrast, here is a description of one of the low-illness executives:

Although he has a clear sense of the importance of broader social issues concerning his work, and certainly feels that his role requires innovative planning, it is the moment-to-moment activities of the day that intrigue him the most. He claims to learn fairly continuously, even when the task appears at first to be routine.

When asked his views about the company reorganization, he expresses a clear sense of the magnitude of the changes in the offing. But he shows no signs of the panic we saw in other subjects. He is not more certain than they are about what the changes will mean for him specifically. But he is so involved and interested in the evolutionary process going on that he almost welcomes it. Whatever his new role turns out to be, he is sure he will find a way to make it meaningful and worthwhile. He recognizes the hard work and possible frustrations involved in the company's reorganization, but he treats it as all in a day's work. He looks forward to rolling up his sleeves, working hard, and learning new things—he is involved with the company and wants to help with its reorganization. (Kobasa, 1987)

The business managers were surveyed three times over a two-year period. The characteristics of challenge, commitment, and control predicted which of the stressed executives would become ill and which would remain well. The hardy executives were only half as likely to get sick as the less hardy people confronting the stressors (Kobasa, Maddi, & Kahn, 1982).

HARDINESS INDUCTION Can a person learn to become more hardy? Kobasa and Maddi identified childhood experiences that foster hardiness. *Commitment* seems to emerge from strong parental encouragement and acceptance. *Control* is cultivated in children successfully encountering a variety of tasks that are neither too simple nor too difficult. A *challenge* orientation develops when the child perceives the confusing environment as rich and full rather than chaotic. These features also appear to foster hardiness in adults. A work environment that encourages self-mastery and includes encouragement from superiors assists in the breeding of hardiness (Kobasa, Maddi, & Kahn, 1982).

Maddi and Kobasa (1984) developed "hardiness induction groups," which are small group sessions to encourage commitment, control, and challenge. Group members are taught how to focus on their bodies and mental sensations in response to stressful situations. They are encouraged to ask themselves such questions as "What's keeping me from feeling terrific today?" This focusing increases the person's sense of control over stress.

People are also encouraged to think about a recent stressful episode and to imagine three ways it might have been worse and three ways it could have gone better. In addition, group members plan action when they face a stressor they cannot avoid or control, such as the death of a spouse or a serious illness. They are encouraged to refocus on another area of their lives in which they can master a new challenge and restore their sense of control and competence. They might learn a new skill like swimming or offer their services in tutoring.

The preliminary result of this hardiness training is encouraging. A group of eight high-stress, hypertensive executives attended eight weekly group sessions. At the end, not only were their hardiness scores higher, but they reported fewer symptoms of psychological distress, and their blood pressures were lower in comparison to an untreated control group.

CONTROL   Control mediates stress. One of the first studies on this was the "executive monkey" study by Brady (1958). Brady first found that electric shocks administered over a period of weeks or months were associated with more frequent gastric ulcers in monkeys. Brady wondered whether human executives, who have control and responsibility for serious decisions, might not develop their ulcers in a similar way. He devised an "executive" situation for the monkeys. Monkeys were paired, with one member of each pair designated the "executive." The executive could avoid the shock for both. The other monkey was yoked to the first and received exactly the same shock but could do nothing to avoid it. The executives were quite successful at avoiding the shock, but within two months, all executives were either dead or very sick from gastric ulcers. The paired monkeys who had no control developed few ulcers. Brady interpreted this study as meaning that control and responsibility increased stress.

However, Weiss (1968, 1971) found that Brady's results were due to selection bias rather than control or responsibility. In assigning roles to each member of the pair, the animal assigned to the executive role was always the one that responded quickest. More emotional monkeys seem to learn avoidance responding faster and also to be more susceptible to the effects of stress in general and to ulcers. Weiss also found that the relation of control and the development of ulcers was complicated by the degree of demand. When the task the animals had to perform to avoid the shock was very difficult, the added stress of control made them develop ulcers faster. However, when the task was easy or of moderate difficulty, control was protective against ulcers.

Even the illusion of control may reduce stress. Glass, Singer, and Friedman (1969) exposed people to unpredictable noise. Half of the subjects believed they could shut the noise off with a switch if they wished. They were told not to end the noise unless absolutely necessary. This *belief* that they had control over the noise allowed them to persist longer in working on unsolvable puzzles and proofread with greater accuracy than those who did not believe they could turn the noise off.

LEARNED HELPLESSNESS   The extreme of having no control is **learned helplessness.** When individuals repeatedly are unable to control their environment, they learn to be helpless. Seligman (1975) has demonstrated the results of this with people and with animals. Cohen, Evans, Krantz, and Stokols (1980) found that uncontrollable noise of aircraft flying overhead is associated with feelings of helplessness and health problems in children. When old people are moved to unfamiliar surroundings, negative health results often occur. If the surroundings are similar to the old ones, however, the environments are more predictable and controllable (Schulz & Brenner, 1977).

"MIND-MADE" HEALTH

How would you rate your health overall (poor, fair, good, excellent)? Surprisingly, this simple question better predicts a person's health status than objective assessments made by his or her doctor. People who tend to rate their health poorly die earlier and have more disease than their counterparts who view themselves as healthy. Even people with actual physical illnesses seem to do better when they believe themselves to be healthy than when they believe themselves weak.

In Manitoba, Canada, more than 3,500 senior citizens were interviewed at the outset of a seven-year study. They were asked, "For your age would you say, in general, your health is excellent, good, fair, poor, or bad?" In addition, their objective health status was determined by reports from their physicians on medical problems and how often they required hospitalization or surgery (Mossey & Shapiro, 1982). Those people who rated their health as poor were almost three times more likely to die during the seven years of the study than those who perceived their health as excellent. Was this because those who rated themselves as unhealthy were, in fact, so? The evidence is against it. Surprisingly, subjective self-reported health was more accurate in predicting who would die than the objective health measures from physicians. Those who were in objectively poor health according to physician reports survived at a higher rate as long as they *believed* their own health to be good.

Nearly 15 percent who rated their health as fair or poor had good or excellent health according to the objective health measures. These "health pessimists" had a slightly greater risk of dying than the "health optimists" who viewed themselves as healthy in spite of negative reports from their doctors. The predictive power of self-rated health was the same for male or female, older or younger, objectively sick or well. Only greater age appears to have a more powerful influence on death rates than self-rated health.

Another study of 7,000 adults in Alameda County, California, confirmed the importance of the way a person views his health. Men with poor self-rated health were 2.3 times more likely to die than those who saw their health as excellent. For women, the difference was 5 times greater. The importance of self-reported health remained even when such variables as smoking, drinking, exercising, marriage, social contacts, happiness, and depression were controlled for in the study (Kaplan & Camacho, 1983).

Optimistic attitudes, therefore, bolster an individual's ability to resist disease: those with better self-reported health are less likely to die from any cause. Whatever the mechanism, the message is clear that how people view their own health significantly influences health outcomes. Quickly assessing a person's overall perception of his or her health may help us identify people at greater risk. By encouraging more positive self-perceptions, we may eventually be able to affect physiological processes and improve health outcomes.

DENIAL OF OUR FEELINGS

Sometimes active coping through direct problem solving is not possible even for the hardiest. Some events cannot be avoided and flood us with anxious thoughts. Fortunately, psychological mechanisms clear the deck and make

Mental attitudes have a direct effect on a person's physical well-being.

CHAPTER 19 / HEALTH PSYCHOLOGY

possible other thoughts and actions. **Denial** is the mental operation by which thoughts, feelings, acts, threats, or demands are minimized. Denial is often considered to lead to pathology. It is thought that people must face reality, identify their feelings, and be honest about them. Yet sometimes we need our illusions (Taylor, 1989).

The brain has developed certain adaptive mechanisms, such as denial, to help block perception of certain threatening information when attending to it will only arouse unnecessary anxiety and contribute little to changing the situation. Therefore, whether denial is healthy or not depends on the circumstances and the outcome.

Denial in some circumstances can interfere with necessary actions and thereby undermine health. The diabetic who needs to carefully regulate insulin dosages, the patient with kidney disease who needs to undergo dialysis, or the woman who discovers a breast lump all need to pay attention to information about their health to preserve it. Denying a breast lump can delay treatment for breast cancer.

But denial in other circumstances can be helpful. Frances Cohen and Richard Lazarus (1984) studied 61 patients about to undergo elective surgery for conditions like hernia and gall bladder disease. They asked each patient about how much he or she knew or wanted to know about the disease, the operation, and so on. Two basic coping strategies, *avoidance* and *vigilance,* emerged.

The avoiders denied the emotional or threatening aspects of the surgery and were not interested in thinking about or listening to anything that was related to their illness or surgery. They would say such things as "All I know is that I have a hernia. I just took it for granted. It doesn't disturb me one bit. I have not thought at all about it."

In contrast, the vigilant were alert to the emotional and threatening aspects of their upcoming medical event. They attempted to cope by trying to control every detail of the situation and were aroused to every danger. One vigilant patient commented after a detailed description of the operation: "I have all the facts, my will is prepared. It is major surgery. It's a body opening. You're put out, you could be put out too deep, your heart could quit, you can have a shock. I go not in lightly."

The avoiders had better postsurgical recovery than the vigilant, left the hospital sooner, had fewer headaches, fevers, and infections, required less pain medication, and showed less distress. Of course, some of these differences may be due to the different way the vigilant are treated by the doctor. Since they were more likely to notice and report symptoms after the operation, the doctors were perhaps more likely to conclude that the patient was not ready to go home.

There are other situations in which denial may be healthy. Following a miscarriage or a severe burn, the victim can "buy" some time by denying the implications of the trauma. A temporary disavowal of reality helps the person get through the devastating early period of loss and threat when there is, in truth, little he or she can do. Later the person can face the facts at a gradual, more manageable pace and mobilize other means of coping.

Fear and vigilance alert the brain to settle the threat. But when there is nothing that can be done to aid survival, then denying or ignoring the threat protects the stability and health of the person. And it leaves room for hope.

In Aaron Antonovsky's (1984) view, control may be an example of a **sense of coherence.** He identified a group of women who had been in Nazi concentration camps during World War II. Not surprisingly, he found that the concentration camp survivors, as a group, were in poorer emotional and physical health than other comparable women who had not been in the camps.

Antonovsky was intrigued that some women survived the concentration camps and were healthy by all measures of physical, psychological, and social functioning. As he remarked, "Despite having lived through the most inconceivably inhuman experience, some women were reasonably healthy and happy, had raised families, worked, had friends, and were involved in community activities." How was this possible?

Antonovsky proposed that resources that promote health—whether money, friends, education, or coping strategies—reinforce a certain way of looking at the world, a way of perceiving the stimuli and demands that bombard the person.

> A sense of coherence is a global orientation that expresses the extent to which one has a pervasive, enduring though dynamic feeling of confidence that one's internal and external environments are predictable and that there is a high probability that things will work out as well as can reasonably be expected. (Antonovsky, 1984)

Antonovsky (1987) refined the sense of coherence to include comprehensibility, manageability, and meaningfulness. *Comprehensibility* means that the demands made on the person seem ordered, consistent, structured, clear, and hence predictable, as opposed to random, chaotic, disordered, and unpredictable. *Manageability* is how much people feel that they have resources adequate to meet the demands made upon them. *Meaningfulness* refers to the feeling that the demands posed by living are viewed as worth investing in and worthy of commitment and engagement. The demands are meaningful in the sense that they are viewed as worthwhile challenges, not threats or unwelcome burdens.

A strong sense of coherence can function in many ways to strengthen health. The beliefs that life is meaningful, that resources are available and manageable, and that life is ordered and predictable may allow a person to engage in activities that are more health promoting and avoid those that endanger health. This way of appraising the world may permit a person to see unavoidable stressors as challenges rather than as threats and thereby to short-circuit a stress reaction. Further, people with a stronger sense of coherence may be more likely to mobilize and effectively utilize resistance resources such as friends, material resources, and coping skills to deal with potentially stressful situations.

Coherence is basic to perception and cognition. At each step the world becomes more organized and simplified in the mind. Schemata represent the chaotic and changing external world, so that it becomes stable, simplified, and seemingly coherent. Instead of thousands of reflecting bits of glass, gray stone, scores of doors opening and closing, and several high ceilings, we perceive *one* building. The parts fit together; it makes sense.

This simple, stable organization (coherence) is basic to us in our connections to others. When a person's sense of coherence is disrupted, he or she is more likely to become ill. If the world is disorganized, it is not clear what appropriate action to take in any situation, nor is it clear that the individual can control his or her life to any extent.

SOCIAL SUPPORT

Social support is another important mediator of stress. It means being cared about and valued by other people and belonging to a social network. The number of people we see on a regular basis, the number of people we consider as friends, the people we know who could help with problems in our life—all have positive effects on reducing stress (Berkman & Syme, 1979; Minkler, 1989).

Esteem support is the effect other people have on increasing our feelings of self-esteem. *Informational support* is the kind of social support involved in getting necessary information from social interaction. *Social companionship* is the support received from social activities. *Instrumental support* is the practical help we can get from friends, such as helping fix our car (Wills, 1985). Exactly how social support works to reduce the effects of stress is unclear. The two most popular theories are the **main effect** or **direct hypothesis,** and the **stress-buffering hypothesis.** The main effect hypothesis proposes that social support directly benefits health, regardless of stress. The stress-buffering hypothesis proposes that support reduces the effects of stress (Minkler, 1989).

EXERCISE

Exercise is another stress mediator. Brown and Lawton (1986) studied adolescent women and found that their life-event changes were related to illness and that illness was related to depression. However, exercise was negatively related to depression, so that those women who had high-stress life events showed more illness if they did not exercise regularly.

THE EFFECTS OF STRESS: THE DIATHESIS-STRESS THEORY

Levi (1974) and Sternbach (1966) believe that people react to stress with different physiological patterns. The **diathesis-stress** model has two parts. First, the individual responds to demanding situations with a stereotyped response. That is, the person has a constitutional predisposition to respond physiologically in the same way every time, with some pattern of organs or organ systems. Second, homeostatic restraints, which would keep this response from being exaggerated in other people, are inadequate, because of previous damage or genetic composition. When the individual is repeatedly exposed to stressful situations, the diathesis response is activated. This model helps us understand why stress has such varied effects from person to person.

651

TREATING STRESS AND STRESS-RELATED DISORDERS

COGNITIVE-BEHAVIOR THERAPY

Combinations of behavior therapy with cognitive therapies (see Chapter 16, page 555) have been very useful in treating stress-related problems. These have included rational emotive therapy (RET), cognitive restructuring therapy, and a specialized adaptation of the latter, called stress inoculation therapy. Because most behavior therapists use a combination of treatments to help solve clients' problems, Lazarus (1971) labeled the general nature of their work *broad-spectrum behavior therapy*.

BIOFEEDBACK

Biofeedback is a method of training people to become aware of and control their internal processes. By recording the client's physiological processes, amplifying the signals, and displaying them back to the person, biofeedback has been found useful in understanding and controlling the physiological part of stress responses and such specific stress-related problems as essential hypertension, postural hypotension, cardiac arrhythmias, Raynaud's disease, migraine and tension headaches, asthma, incontinence, epilepsy, motor neuron dysfunctions, dyskinesias, muscle pain, and some anxiety problems (Gatchel & Price, 1979).

RELAXATION

Relaxation exercises may be as effective as biofeedback for controlling the bodily part of the stress response. A wide variety of exercises exist, although the most commonly used in the United States is Jacobsen's Progressive Muscle

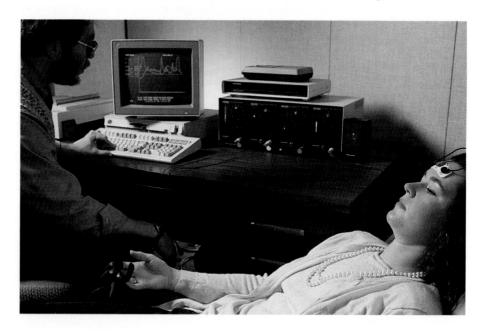

Relaxation. This consists of alternately tensing and relaxing different muscle groups and trying to move them more and more into the direction of relaxation.

CONDITIONED IMMUNE RESPONSES

Perhaps the most powerful demonstration that psychological factors affect immune responses is the research on conditioning immune responses. This conditioning is based on taste aversion; for apparently evolutionary reasons, it is a particularly effective form of conditioning. Ader (1981) found that if he paired the presentation of saccharin-flavored water with an immunosuppressive drug, thereby producing an aversion, then later presentation of the saccharin-flavored water alone would bring about immunosuppressive effects.

HOW PEOPLE BEHAVE AS MEDICAL PATIENTS

COPING WITH CHRONIC ILLNESS

Having a chronic illness, such as diabetes, heart disease, cancer, or hypertension, requires patients to make major changes in their daily lives. They may have to change the foods they eat, change how and how often they exercise and work, and take drugs or even radiation therapy with possible powerful side effects. How people cope with these demands depends on how they see the illness. Three models of how such patients perceive chronic illness are the health belief model, the control and predictability model, and the coping and defense mechanism approaches.

The **health belief model** (Rosenman & Friedman, 1980) proposes three levels: the patient's readiness to act, the costs and benefits of compliance, and the existence of a cue to action. Readiness to act can be influenced by perceived severity of the illness and the susceptibility to the disease. With hypertension, some people are more willing than others to accept that blood pressure, a thing they cannot see or feel, can cause a heart attack or stroke. Some may believe their blood pressure is elevated only when they experience certain, perhaps actually unrelated, symptoms, such as headaches. They may take their antihypertensive medications only at such times.

The **control and predictability model** proposes that chronic diseases pose a stressful and potentially uncontrollable crisis for patients, particularly cardiac patients (Krantz & Deckel, 1983). This brings on helplessness. People who feel more competent, less depressed, and less threatened (or less helpless) will do better emotionally, behaviorally, and physiologically later. Procedures that enhance the patient's sense of control should improve outcome.

Studies of coping—how people deal with stress—and defense mechanisms show complex relationships. As Lazarus (1979) observed, denial may be useful. Hackett and Cassem (1973) described the recovery of cardiac patients from the point of view of psychodynamic defense mechanisms. Immediately after heart attack, the patients usually feel anxiety. However, within about two days, denial predominates, protecting the patient from excessive fear and stress. After about another day, denial is replaced by depression, which keeps the patient from moving about too much. Over a period of three to ten days, depression gradually wanes.

Adherence to medical regimens is the degree to which people carry out their doctor's recommendations. If a physician's diagnosis is correct and the treatment prescribed is effective, a patient who does not follow the regimen may cause the physician either to reconsider the diagnosis and incorrectly diagnose something else or to change the treatment to something with more negative side effects than the first treatment.

Research into *compliance* may make treatments much more effective than they are now. It is estimated that compliance ranges from 18 percent to 89 percent (Epstein & Cluss, 1982). One factor that appears very important in compliance is the patient's satisfaction with the physician. Korsch and Negrete (1972) found that if doctors are seen as warm and caring, patient satisfaction is higher than if doctors are seen as cool and businesslike.

Another factor is *comprehension*. Ley and Spelman (1967) found that often the material presented by doctors is too difficult for patients to understand, that patients often do not understand basic anatomy or physiology or have misconceptions about how the body works so they do not understand what the doctor says. Patients may have different theories about health and illness than the prevailing medical model. People who have such different models and who find themselves being treated in the medical model are likely to take recommendations with a grain of salt (Meyer, Leventhal, & Gutmann, 1985).

PREVENTIVE HEALTH BEHAVIORS

We all know that we should not smoke but many of us do. We also know that we should wear seat belts, eat a balanced diet, and exercise, but many of us do not. Our attitudes toward preventive health behaviors are more a function of our families and peers' attitudes than a reasoned system (Evans et al., 1981). The presence or absence of symptoms of illness is also an important factor (Leventhal et al., 1985). Finally, some people perform risky health behaviors when they are experiencing negative emotions (Marlatt & Gordon, 1985).

Changing preventive health behaviors may involve changing these factors, and also opposing the **gradient of reinforcement** (Miller, 1983). This concept from learning theory states that the closer a reward is to a behavior, the stronger will be the impact of the reward; conversely, the farther a reward is from a behavior, the weaker will be the impact. Thus, a cigarette delivers 20 or more "hits" of pleasure, which are perceived by the brain within about 3 seconds, and costs about 7 cents. It is one of the best buys on the marketplace. The fact that it could cause lung or other cancers, heart disease, or emphysema in 10 or 50 years does not seem much reason to forgo the immediate pleasure of the drug.

The level of fear stimulated by information about the destructive behaviors has an effect. Generally, higher levels of fear lead to more attitude change and somewhat more behavioral change in use of seat belts, dental care, smoking, and inoculations (Leventhal & Hirschman, 1982). The effects of high-fear communications last only about a week, and if they are followed in that time with instructions on how to take action, often lead to change. Leventhal (1970) considers the ways people cope with fear communications as falling into two categories: fear control and danger control. Together these compose a **parallel process model** of fear and attitude change. *Danger control* involves manipulating the threat by reducing or eliminating the source of fear. *Fear control* consists of coping to make one feel better despite the threat.

Helping people change their behavior to follow up perceptions of fear involves understanding their conceptions of illness (Meyer, 1981); the application of behavioral principles to help them learn new behaviors (Stunkard, 1979); and cognitive-behavioral approaches, which combine social learning, health education, and behavior modification (Foreyt et al., 1979).

PAIN

THE PERCEPTION OF PAIN

Melzack and Wall (1965) proposed the **gate-control theory of pain,** which still dominates the way we believe pain is perceived. This theory suggests that neurophysiological mechanisms in the dorsal horns of the spinal cord function as a gate, increasing or decreasing the flow of nerve impulses from peripheral nerve fibers to the central nervous system (CNS). Sensory input is then modulated by the gate before pain is perceived. The theory accounts for the influence of different types of pain receptors and the possibility that different patterns of stimulation and transmission may affect how pain is perceived. It also allows for the influence of descending pathways from the CNS on pain perception, so that anxiety, depression, the meaning of events, and past experience can modify the experience. The theory also led to the procedure of artificially stimulating the nervous system, in hopes of "closing the gate" to reduce chronic pain. (See Chapter 3.)

The psychological aspect of pain perception cannot be underestimated. Beecher (1956) found that 25 percent of soldiers wounded at Anzio asked for pain medication, compared with 80 percent of civilians with similar wounds. Beecher interpreted this as due to the benefits of the wound for the soldier; because of the wound, he would be sent home and removed from further danger. Pavlov (1927) demonstrated that when pain in the form of an electric shock is presented regularly before feeding dogs, they cease responding to it with negative emotional displays and instead salivate and approach it—that is, they become conditioned to regard it as a stimulus rather than as a painful experience. Tursky and Sternbach (1967) showed that cultural background also affected pain reporting. Protestants of British descent had a matter-of-fact orientation toward pain; patients of Irish background inhibited expression of pain; and Italian and Jewish Americans exaggerated expression of their pain.

This is not to say that pain is learned, only that it is an extremely complex combination of stimulation, processing, learning, and behavior. Any approach to treating chronic pain must then take all these features into account.

PSYCHOLOGICAL TREATMENT METHODS FOR CHRONIC PAIN

HYPNOSIS   James Esdaile, a Scottish surgeon in India, performed more than 200 operations between 1845 and 1853 using hypnosis as the anesthetic. The advent of anesthetic drugs caused a decline in the use of *hypnosis* for anesthesia, but it has been used successfully in obstetrics, surgery, dentistry, and treatment for cancer pain (Hilgard & Hilgard, 1975). Hypnosis may become a useful adjunct to drug anesthetic and analgesic agents, especially when the patient is particularly anxious or in cases in which drugs would be dangerous.

ACUPUNCTURE *Acupuncture* is part of ancient Chinese medicine and has been understood as a way to regulate the flow of *chi'i*, or life energy, through a system of meridians under the skin. Although the Chinese no longer necessarily believe this metaphysical explanation, acupuncture is effective in blocking many types of pain. It seems to operate under different mechanisms from hypnosis. Mayer et al. (1976) found that naloxone (an antidote for narcotics) reversed the effectiveness of acupuncture, but not of hypnosis. However, acupuncture has been more effective for short-term pain than for chronic pain (Bakal, 1979; Levine, Gormley, & Fields, 1976).

COGNITIVE STRATEGIES *Cognitive therapies* have been used with acute and chronic pain. Barber and his colleagues (Barber & Cooper; 1972; Chaves & Barber, 1974) trained people to use distracting imagery—imagining pleasant events or attending to other stimuli in their environment or to other sensations, such as imagining that the area of pain was injected with novocaine. Meichenbaum and Turk (1976) trained people in a form of *stress inoculation*, which included a variety of pain-control methods, like those used by Barber, as well as a plan to use when the pain becomes intense, and how to use the plan at these times.

The most comprehensive approach to cognitive pain treatment is the *pain clinic*, begun by Fordyce et al. (1968). In this approach, environmental consequences, such as attention of family and the clinic staff, are made contingent on the decreased frequency of "pain behavior," such as grimacing, complaining, moving slowly, and requesting pain medication. Attention, rest, and medication are made contingent on the performance of adaptive behaviors, teaching patients to reinterpret the sensations of pain and tolerate them, while learning to function better with others.

Another approach to treatment of chronic pain is *functional restoration*. An outgrowth of sports medicine, this approach considers a data base of how other people with similar injuries have been restored to function, permitting the development of treatment programs of graded intensity and duration. Goals include more traditional ones of attempting to alter pain complaints, reduce medications, and improve quality of life. However, goals are enlarged to include more societal problems associated with chronic pain, such as return to work and decreasing use of the medical system. The approach emphasizes "no pain, no gain," and the return of function (Mayer et al., 1987).

ADDICTIVE BEHAVIOR: SMOKING

Cigarette smoking is responsible for more deaths in the United States than crack addiction, but it receives far less attention. It is directly associated with increased incidence of lung cancer and almost every other kind of cancer, coronary artery disease, emphysema, chronic obstructive pulmonary disease, and peptic ulcer. It increases allergies, decreases immune function, causes birth defects, and negatively affects child development (Wynder, Hertzberg, & Parker, 1981). Tobacco is extremely addictive (Russell, 1976). Attempts to quit often result in depression, difficulty concentrating, and irritability.

The habit often begins in imitation of peers, family members, or media role models, or as an expression of adolescent rebellion (Pomerleau, 1979). The *psychoanalytic* understanding of the phenomenon stresses arrested development in the oral stage. Erikson's theory of *psychosocial* development suggests the development of smoking is affected by the struggle to overcome inferiority (ages 6 to 11) and the struggle to establish an identity (ages 12 to 18). Bandura's *social learning* theory stresses the immediate reinforcement of peer approval and imitation of media figures, compared to delayed aversive consequences such as later poor health.

Evans (1981) used these theories to develop *behavioral inoculation* programs for children. He showed them desirable role models declining invitations to smoke in a "cool" manner, so they maintained their social desirability.

The smoking habit is a complex combination of social factors, individual habits, and drug effects. Any attempt to help smokers quit should take all these into account. Thus, the most effective quitting programs have combined many techniques (Schwartz, 1987). Particular therapies often used include *aversive techniques*, such as rapid smoking (Lichtenstein, 1982), which involves smoking at a very rapid rate until the person feels ill, or smoking to satiation, which means smoking two to three times a person's normal amount just before quitting; *stimulus control*, or various methods of making cigarettes hard to obtain; *reinforcement of nonsmoking*, such as giving oneself rewards such as going to the movies; *substitute behaviors*, or doing things such as taking a walk instead of smoking; and *chewing nicotine gum*, which replaces the nicotine normally received from the cigarettes with that in the gum, so the physical addiction does not cause resumption of smoking.

Relapse is a problem in all areas of addictive behaviors. It both causes the frustrations of working with addictions and has provided the most useful advances taken in the area in recent years. Based on self-control principles, the model of *relapse prevention* (Marlatt & Gordon, 1985) puts responsibility on the individual without blame. It is the position advocated by Jesse Jackson, that a person is *not* responsible for being down, but he or she *is* responsible for getting up.

Quitting is only the first stage of change. The *maintenance* stage is much more difficult and lasts a longer time. People are expected to experience *slips*, or small episodes of the old habit; *lapses*, or more serious episodes; and perhaps *relapse*, full-blown recurrences. The key difference between relapse prevention and other approaches is that it views these problems not as failures but as learning experiences. The problems are analyzed to see how the person could cope differently in the future. It asks such questions as the following: What happened to the person's sense of control? Why did he or she enter a high-risk situation? Did a negative emotional state precede the problem? What was out of balance in the person's life-style that could have precipitated the problem? Answers to these questions can help the person plan to avoid the next relapse.

657

ADDICTIVE BEHAVIOR: SMOKING

MAJOR CAUSES OF DEATH

CORONARY HEART DISEASE

Coronary heart disease is caused by deposits on the walls of the coronary arteries, which bring blood to nourish the heart muscle, so that the heart does not get enough blood to supply its need for oxygen, nutrition, and removal of waste. The disease develops over decades and precipitates events such as *angina*, the experience of heart pain when the heart does not get enough oxygen; *myocardial infarction*, or heart attack, when blood is completely cut off to part of the heart and the tissue dies; *arrhythmia*, in which the electrical conduction system that makes the heart beat becomes damaged and the heart beats irregularly; and *sudden death*, when arrhythmia causes the heart to stop pumping blood.

In addition to drug and surgical treatments, the same treatment is recommended for both primary and secondary prevention: the reduction of risk factors associated with the development of arterial deposits. Major risk factors for coronary heart disease include hypertension, high blood cholesterol levels, cigarette smoking, and Type A behavior pattern. Minor risk factors are diabetes, obesity, and a sedentary life-style. Nonmodifiable risk factors are age, sex, and family history of heart disease.

TYPE A AND B BEHAVIORS AND THE HEART   Rosenman and Friedman (1959) reported that people who are coronary prone seem to have certain personality characteristics. They are time urgent, excessively devoted to work and competitive, and they have excessive hostility and deny fatigue. Analyzing only men, the researchers concluded that these "coronary-prone" men were twice as likely to get coronary artery disease as men who do not behave this way.

These Type A's have been characterized as the overbusy type of person, always trying to do everything simultaneously.

> Type A's may be found attempting to view television, read a newspaper or trade journal, and eat lunch or dinner all at the same time. "When the commercials come on, I turn down the volume and read my newspaper," is a statement we hear repeatedly. It is not unusual for a Type A to view two football games on two different television sets as he irons a shirt or treads an exercise bicycle. (Friedman & Ulmer, 1984)

Type A behavior is "an action-emotion complex that can be observed in any person involved in an incessant struggle to achieve more and more in less and less time" (Friedman & Ulmer, 1984). Type A was originally thought to be a very general characteristic of the person. This type reacts to challenge with aggressiveness, impatience, and time urgency.

In contrast, Type B's are placid and speak slowly. They do not try to do several things at once, and are just as successful as Type A's.

What are the two types like? The Type A behavior pattern is discriminated from Type B by the "structured interview" (Friedman & Ulmer, 1984). Since the Type A's respond to challenge with time urgency, the best test would be to challenge them. Rosenman and Friedman designed the interview to be irritat-

The following are from interviews by Professor Charles Swencionis of the Albert Einstein College of Medicine: a Type A.

Q: Do you ever feel rushed or under pressure?

Mr. A: At all times.

Q: How would your wife describe you, as ambitious and hard-driving, or relaxed and easy-going?

Mr. A: Ambitious and hard-driving.

Q: When your children were young, say around six or eight, did you ever play competitive games with them: cards, checkers, Monopoly?

Mr. A: Yes.

Q: Did you ever let them win on purpose?

Mr. A: No, I would beat the hell out of them. [embarrassed]

Q: You mean you would beat a six-year-old child?

Mr. A: I would play with you and try to beat you. I'm always competitive. I'm sorry, it's just the way I am.

Q: Are you competitive off the job?

Mr. A: Yes, everywhere. [Sigh, horizontal smile, tight lips and jaw]

Q: When you have an appointment to be somewhere at, say 2:00, are you on time?

Mr. A: Definitely. I would always be there 15 to 20 minutes ahead.

Q: What's so important about being on time?

Mr. A: I can't answer that. It's just important.

Q: Do you resent it if someone else is late?

Mr. A: Do I. I hate it. [emotional]

INTERVIEWS WITH TYPE A AND TYPE B MEN

Q: Would you say anything to them?

Mr. A: Yes.

Q: What would you say?

Mr. A: All according to the way I felt at the time. I'd say, "What the hell's the matter with you? Can't you keep your appointments? Do you have to keep me waiting?" [loudly]

Q: You would let them know?

Mr. A: Yes, definitely. [angry tone]

Q: Do you remember a time when that happened?

Mr. A: Yes. Just before my heart attack. I had to wait for my sister-in-law. I had called her up about an hour and two hours before and I told her, I said, "_____, be ready." I had to come (about an hour's drive) and I had to wait about 20 minutes or so, almost a half hour. When she finally got to the car, I was muttering a few things. I was trying not to be too abusive, because my father-in-law was there; he's an older man. But boy, I let her know. [angry]

Q: What did you say?

Mr. A: I said, "_____, I had to come here, I had to wait for you, can't you make it on time? What's the matter with you? [angry] I said a lot of things I shouldn't have really said."

An interview with Mr. B, a New York City cabdriver, may show a few of the differences. If ever there were an occupation designed to bring out the Type A in anyone, a cabbie in a big city is it. Mr. B talks slowly, without word emphasis, in a monotone. He rambles and there are long pauses between the questions and his responses.

Q: Do you enjoy the competition for fares?

Mr. B: No, that's an ugly aspect of it. The people who are in it . . . that's not . . . that's not what the business is about. Actually, you're not going to make your quota on the one fare that someone else gets. You're not always up against it. You'll get the next one. The keynote, the whole success of operating a cab is just not to have accidents, so that your car is always available and rolling. If you put the time in, then it . . . a certain average per hour that's just what it's about.

Q: What about the competition in New York to always get to the next space?

Mr. B: Well that gets to you, but only in a delayed way. After you've been driving for 8 or 10 hours, you feel kind of spent, shot. That's how it gets to you. I can get around traffic. You have to be very aggressive to be a New York City cab-driver. Otherwise you couldn't make it as a cabdriver.

Q: Do you enjoy it?

Mr. B: Yes, I do. [flatly, no emotion, no anger] You get to feel as though you could go through a keyhole after a while. (Swencionis, 1987)

ing. They had people take time off from work to come to their hospital. The interviewer kept them waiting without explanation and then asked them questions about being hostile and pressed for time. How did they respond to waiting in bank lines and supermarket lines? How did they like driving behind someone who was going too slowly and whom they couldn't pass? The interviewer interrupted, challenged, irritated, and threw in non sequiturs.

As important as the interview's questions, however, is the challenging manner in which interviewers ask the questions. A challenge such as an implied criticism evokes vigorous and explosive speech in coronary-prone individuals. The interview is scored more on the way that the person answers the questions rather than on the answer itself.

The voice of the extreme A in this situation is very strong. There is a lot of word emphasis and explosive, bombastic, staccato, and loud talk. The A tries to control the interview, and jumps in abruptly when the interviewer stops talking. He raises his volume to talk over the interviewer and can't be interrupted.

The Type A has clipped, telegraphic speech and sighs frequently. The Type A sits in a tense manner, smiles a tight-lipped horizontal smile, and has a nervous laugh. The hallmark of the Type A is that he can describe hostile incidents with such emotional intensity that he seems to be reliving them.

Conversely, the Type B speaks in a monotone, rambles, seems subdued and lethargic, speaks slowly and softly and is easily interrupted. He doesn't raise his voice and sits in a relaxed manner. The Type B smiles with a round mouth and laughs a deep, belly laugh.

HOSTILITY   Flanders Dunbar and Karen Matthews (1983) noticed that people who have coronary artery disease are *hostile* frequently. Easily provoked hostility is a more important indicator of heart disease than the Type A pattern. Anything can cause this irritable eruption. Horn-honking in traffic is a favorite pastime for hostile persons. But they do not like it much when it is done to them. Dr. W. Gifford-Jones was driving with a hostile Type A surgeon who was slow to step on the gas pedal of his car after the signal at the intersection had turned green.

> The result was a sudden and loud horn honk from the car behind us. Immediately the Irish temper flared. My friend jumped up, walked to the car behind us, opened the door, grabbed the keys out of the ignition, and with a mighty toss threw them into a snowbank. (Freedman & Ulmer, 1984).

Hostility is currently the most popular candidate in the search for the destructive Type A component. It links with blood pressure reactivity, severity of coronary artery disease, and death from all causes including coronary heart disease. But what are the reasons for hostility?

SELF-INVOLVEMENT AND PERSONALITY   Persons who are very *self-involved* often think of themselves as better than others and are vulnerable to anyone who appears better than them. Hostility may be a strategy for coping with such challenges by saying, "Who do you think you are to challenge me like this!" To the self-involved, many events are the cause for a threat: the success of a friend, the turn of the stock market, the prospects for their company, the insurance crisis.

Those who were hostile during the Type A interview used more self references (use of "me," "my," "mine," "I") (Dembrowski et al., 1983). In one study, students recalled an incident that made them angry and described it (Leventhal, Berton, & Scherwitz, 1985). The most important predictor of heart activation was the *number of times the students referred to themselves.* Self-involved individuals had the strongest emotional and physical reactions to challenge. They expressed anger more intensely and had much higher blood pressure, again at levels that would qualify for hypertension.

Maybe people became more self-involved after developing heart disease. But this was not the case. Self-involvement and the severity of coronary artery disease were most correlated with those who did not have a heart attack or felt discomfort (Scherwitz et al., 1985). And in an earlier study, Lynda Powell found that people with great self-involvement were more likely to have a second heart attack.

Scherwitz and colleagues (1985) speculate that it is not the activity of people that is dangerous to the heart, nor is it the hurry or the speed; rather, it is the selfishness that underlies the behaviors. "If individuals are ambitious, competitive, or time urgent for purely selfish reasons, they may be at greater risk than if they are ambitious or competitive to serve others or higher ideals," the researchers concluded.

TREATMENT AND PREVENTION   Most of the research into treatment and prevention of coronary heart disease has focused on community intervention and intervention with large groups. The North Karelia Project (Puska, 1984) treated an entire county in Finland, which has one of the highest rates of heart disease in the world. North Karelia was compared to a neighboring county that did not receive the intervention. The intervention used television and other media as well as community demonstrations, posters, and existing community organizations to encourage people to quit smoking, reduce the fat in their diets, and get their blood pressures measured and hypertension treated. Risk factors and the incidence of heart attack and stroke declined in the treated community compared to the untreated.

The *Stanford Heart Disease Prevention Project* (Farquhar et al., 1977, 1984) is really two projects. The first compared three communities which received three different interventions to reduce cardiovascular risk factors: one received mass media interventions only; one received mass media plus group face-to-face behavioral treatment; and the third received no intervention. Results from the first study showed that the mass media plus face-to-face behavioral treatment was more effective than mass media alone, and both were more effective than no treatment. The study was later expanded to address five communities and to treat obesity as well as smoking, hypertension, and blood cholesterol levels.

The *Multiple Risk Factor Intervention Trial (MRFIT)* (MRFIT Group, 1982) followed over 12,000 high-risk men over time to determine whether they could lower their smoking, hypertension, and serum cholesterol. Men were assigned either to an intervention program or to the care of their usual physicians. The men in the intervention group successfully lowered their risk factors, but there was no difference in mortality between the groups because over the years of the study the men in the usual-care group also lowered their risk factors, and because one of the medications used in the intervention group may have been dangerous.

THE CAUSES OF HYPERTENSION **Hypertension** is high blood pressure. Blood pressure is essential to provide blood flow of oxygen and food and removal of waste products to and from tissues. It must be kept within certain levels in order for blood flow to proceed—especially to the brain and heart—despite the body's change of positions, change in exertion, and other changes. Over 20 hormonal and physiological factors are involved in the control of blood pressure (Weiner, 1977). Disruption in any one of these factors, however, can cause blood pressure to become chronically raised. It is difficult to diagnose exactly what the cause is, except for some factors, such as kidney disease. When the obvious physiological causes are excluded, the diagnosis is made of essential, or cause unknown, hypertension.

Lowering blood pressure can be accomplished by changing any one of the factors that affect it, such as obesity, high sodium levels, and chronic psychological stress. Treating *obesity* can be quite effective in reducing blood pressure (Weiner, 1977). A weight loss of as little as 10 pounds can reduce mild hypertension and decrease the amount of medication required for more serious hypertension. Exercise, which is also effective in weight loss, may have independent effects on reducing blood pressure.

Sodium restriction has very limited use. About 33 percent of the population has hypertension, and of these, only a minority are sodium responders—that is, their blood pressure decreases as their sodium decreases. It is also difficult to decrease sodium to the level required to lower blood pressure. Most of the sodium in our diets comes from bread, not from salt shakers. Sodium must be reduced severely to have an effect on blood pressure.

Chronic psychological stress has been treated by biofeedback and other relaxation techniques, with some success (Shapiro & Goldstein, 1982). However, like medications, biofeedback or relaxation must be practiced every day to keep hypertension under control.

BLOOD PRESSURE, HYPERTENSION, AND HEART DISEASE **Blood pressure** is the force (the "pressure") with which blood pushes against the walls of the blood vessels. When the heart beats, it pumps about three ounces of blood into the aorta, the major artery leaving the heart. The aorta divides into smaller arteries that lead into a system of tiny vessels, *arterioles*, which open and shut. The peak pressure when the heart is contracting is the *systolic* pressure, the low point when the heart relaxes and refills is the *diastolic* (Figure 19-3).

Arteries squeeze blood into the arterioles the way water goes through a hose. When water is turned on, it enters the hose. If a valve at the other end of the hose is closed, the pressure in the hose will rise, but no water will go through. As you open the closed end of the hose, water flows out and the pressure will then fall. In the bloodstream, the tiny arterioles are like millions of valves. When they *constrict*, the pressure behind them (in the arteries) increases. Blood pressure is determined by the amount of blood pumped from the heart ("cardiac output") and by the resistance the blood meets in its passage throughout the peripheral circulation (Figure 19-4).

Blood pressure normally changes from heartbeat to heartbeat. People whose pressure is consistently high have *hypertension,* and hypertension, or

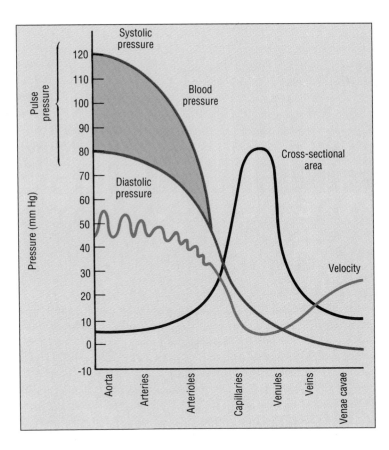

FIGURE 19-3
Blood Pressure

This graph shows the relationship between blood pressure (both systolic and diastolic), velocity of blood flow, and cross-sectional area in the blood vessels. Note that when the vessels are less constricted (high cross-sectional area), the blood pressure is lower.
(Tortora & Anagnostakos, 1987)

sustained elevated blood pressure, contributes to stroke and heart attacks. Hypertensives are two to three times more likely to develop coronary artery disease than are those with normal blood pressure, and four times more likely to suffer from a stroke.

Sixty million Americans are hypertensive, and about half remain untreated, a potentially dangerous condition because high blood pressure injures the

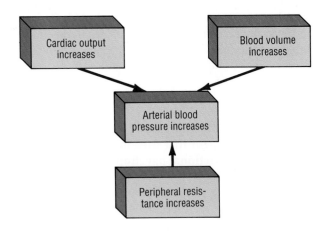

FIGURE 19-4
Factors that Affect
Arterial Blood Pressure

663

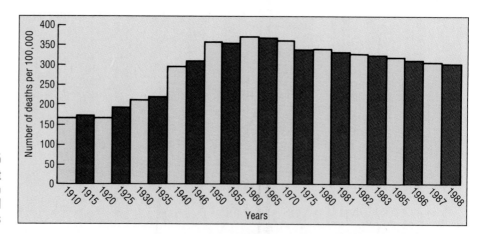

FIGURE 19-5
Deaths Due to Heart Disease from 1910 to 1988 in the United States

blood vessels, which can later damage the brain, heart, kidneys, and eyes. Hypertension usually is not noticeable to those who have it until they suffer a stroke, eye failure, or heart attack.

Cardiovascular diseases cause 45 percent of deaths in the United States, but the rate is decreasing (Figure 19-5). Almost 70 million Americans suffer from diseases of the heart and blood vessels. The economic costs of cardiovascular disorders, including loss of productivity and health expenditures, exceed $80 billion annually in the United States alone.

High blood pressure also forces the heart to work harder. The increased pressure in the arteries can cause enlargement of the heart muscle, especially of the left ventricle, which pumps blood into the body. In addition, the high pressure and turbulent flow of blood can damage the walls of arteries, contributing to the establishment of fatty deposits, which can block the blood flow further.

Such changes place the person under ever-increasing risk of a heart attack. In the brain, the constant strain of high pressure within the blood vessels can cause them to tear or to explode suddenly, leading to a stroke. Brain hemorrhages and other forms of blood vessel blockages are four times more common in people with hypertension.

Except for the few cases of hypertension that are due to kidney abnormalities, the vast majority of hypertension is called "essential hypertension," which means we do not know the essential cause. The search for causes has been restricted to the physician's normal categories of "somatic etiologies," such as too much sodium, too little calcium, too much of this hormone, too little of that. Hypertension is viewed as a matter of the hydraulics of the system; the person has been by and large ignored.

TRANSACTIONAL PSYCHOPHYSIOLOGY: A COMPUTER-BASED TREATMENT   Can a change in communication effect a change in blood pressure? James Lynch and his colleagues (1981) have developed a treatment that tries to link the social world with the internal world. It is called **transactional psychophysiology,** measuring how the heart responds to other people.

A patient is hooked up to a standard blood pressure cuff and a computer. "Sit quietly for a few minutes," the therapist says. Then he shows the patient's blood pressure to her as a graph on the computer's screen. "Now, talk about anything," he says. She speaks about the weather, and he again pushes a key on the computer. Her blood pressure is much higher now, in the hypertensive range.

"Be quiet again," he requests. She sits quietly again for three minutes, and amazingly, when he pushes the key again, her blood pressure is back in the normal range. In successive sessions, for six months, once every week or two, she will watch her blood pressure response on the graph, compared to that of minutes, weeks, and months before. She will learn how it goes up when she speaks rapidly and breathes shallowly, and how it goes down when she speaks slowly, pauses for breath, and breathes deeply. She will learn subtle physical signals, too small to be considered symptoms, such as her forehead feeling tense or perspiration on her upper lip, that warn her when her pressure is rising. This is a complex form of biofeedback.

Most difficult, she will learn to connect these subtle signals to her social interactions. (See Chapter 7, section on self-regulation.) She will learn to change her interactions with people and situations that consistently make her blood pressure go up. In a sense, she will learn how to have a healthy dialogue with herself and others and how she is a part of society.

CANCER

CAUSES, BEHAVIORS, AND EDUCATION
Cancer is the second highest cause of death in the United States. *Smoking* is the single largest reducible cause of cancer. In addition to its relation to lung cancer, smoking is associated with higher rates of almost every other kind of cancer as well (Wynder, Hertzberg, & Parker, 1981).

Nutritional factors in cancer are active areas of research. Many studies have shown relationships between fat intake and cancers of the breast, large intestine, prostate, and possible other sites (Roberts, 1984). Increased intake of dietary fiber in the form of vegetables and whole grains may be protective against colon and rectal cancer, and intake of vegetables rich in beta carotene may protect against cancer at several sites (Roberts, 1984).

DENIAL AND DETECTION
However useful denial may be as a psychological defense mechanism, it poses a strong obstacle in the detection and treatment of cancer. Since treatment of many cancers is effective when done early in the progress of the disease, but difficult or impossible later, early detection and treatment is important. Denial and delay of diagnosis and treatment is more common in poor people, but it is unclear if this is related to psychological factors or to availability of medical services (Bransfield, Hankey, & Wesley, 1989).

AIDS

Acquired Immune Deficiency Syndrome (AIDS) is now probably the most feared and the most deadly epidemic in the world. It affects the immune system and is caused by the *human immunodeficiency virus (HIV)*, which attacks lymphocytes directly. This compromises the immune function of those who contract it,

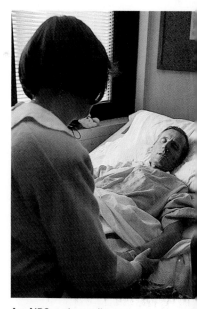

An AIDS patient talks to a social worker about burial plans.

You are probably quite familiar with the claim that confession is good for the soul. But confession is more than a moral issue, it can sometimes be good for the body. This may sound somewhat surprising since we've so far made a very strong case for *not* facing up to reality, emphasizing the positive and ignoring the negative. But shoveling emotional experiences aside and not confronting them has its limits.

The principle is this: if the trauma is minor, then it is a healthy pleasure to minimize, ignore, or deny the problem. However, if the trauma is major, it is probably healthier in the long run to face up to it. Confessing may be unpleasant at the moment but getting it off your chest can clear your mind to enjoy a more pleasurable life and, apparently, a healthier one.

We can live our whole lives holding a secret close to the chest. We may be afraid of hurting others, so we hold our feelings in. Or we may keep traumatic secrets to avoid shame, embarrassment, or pain. But when the cost of holding in our feelings exceeds the benefit of ignoring the displeasing events, we need to shift gears and learn how to remove the negative experiences.

In many lives there are extraordinary traumas, events that can scar for life. We don't mean

USING PSYCHOLOGY: GETTING IT OFF YOUR CHEST

ordinary business disappointments, financial setbacks, or the usual marital upsets. The health-damaging secrets are the major traumas like being raped in childhood, seeing a loved one die in an accident, witnessing a murder, or committing a violent crime.

But can holding in such strong feelings, feelings never discussed with anyone, be demonstrably bad for health? Shouldn't we just ig-nore them? The evidence is that long-buried events can undermine health. One survey showed that individuals who experienced traumatic experiences in childhood *and* who had not confided them to others were more likely to develop cancer, hypertension, ulcers, and even suffer major bouts with influenza than were people either who had not had traumas or who had confided them.

People who had suffered the death of their spouse due to an automobile accident or suicide found that confiding is good for health. Those men and women who spoke with others about their spouses' deaths were healthier in the year following the death than those who had not talked with others (Pennebaker, 1990).

Encouraging people to disclose long-held traumas can measurably improve health. Pennebaker (1990) instructed students as follows:

I want you to write continuously about the most upsetting or

making them susceptible to infections that they could easily have fought off otherwise. The HIV virus also directly affects the central nervous system, with neurological consequences.

TRANSMISSION Not everyone exposed to HIV contracts AIDS. HIV is spread by exchange of bodily fluids. This can occur during sex, sharing of needles or related drug paraphernalia, or blood transfusion or across the placenta during gestation. The disease first appeared in the United States in the homosexual community, and then in the intravenous drug community, making them both high risk groups. Bisexual men and hemophiliacs are also considered high risk groups. It normally requires more than one sexual encounter to become infected, but direct exposure through breaks in the skin are exceptions to this. Intravenous exposure can lead to infection after one episode. Not all babies contract AIDS from their HIV-positive mothers.

There are, as of this writing, no cures for AIDS. There are promising treatments that can slow the virus growth in many people, but prevention is the main tool we have to fight the epidemic. Since prevention involves avoiding high-risk behaviors, psychological techniques are being used in a variety of situations. Anyone can contract AIDS, and it is slowly spreading into the heterosexual community.

traumatic experience of your entire life. . . . Discuss your deepest thoughts and feelings about the experience. You can write about anything you want, but whatever you choose, it should be something that has affected you very deeply. Ideally, it should be about something you have not talked with others about in detail. It is critical, however, that you let yourself go and touch those deepest emotions and thoughts that you have.

Meanwhile, other students simply wrote about trivial daily activities or events.

The students kept these diaries over four days. One man disclosed that while in high school he was beaten by his stepfather. After attempting suicide using the stepfather's gun, the stepfather further mortified him by laughing at his attempt. Another woman in a fit of rage accused her father of marital infidelity in front of her mother.

This disclosure precipitated the divorce of the parents and triggered the daughter's continuing guilt. Another man wrote about his feelings concerning the divorce of his parents. His father told him at age 9 that he was divorcing the boy's mother because their home life had been disrupted ever since the boy had been born.

Disclosing feelings about such traumas was obviously difficult and emotionally distressing. But getting these secrets off their chest paid off in the long run: they had fewer health complaints, fewer visits to their doctor, and fewer drugs prescribed for the next six months of the study and showed improved immune functioning six weeks later. Was it better for their health to disclose the most private aspects of their experiences? Expressing *both* the facts of the trauma and the emotions seems to be critical for health improvement.

Written, even anonymous, disclosures of thoughts and feelings about traumatic experiences, un-

pleasant at the moment, can improve health. And the majority of people seem to appreciate the opportunity to confess. Many students remarked, "It made me think things out and really realize what my problem is," "It helped me look at myself from the outside," or "It was a chance to sort out my thoughts."

So, confessing may be very good for the body. In the mind, a covered-over negative event is never finished. People tend to mull over the trauma again and again in their minds, rehearsing what they should have said, what they might have done. Writing about something or confiding in someone may force you to organize your thoughts and feelings about events, revealing hidden biases and unresolved issues. Once it is out in the open, you can often distance yourself from the traumatic experience. By getting it off your chest, you may be able to break the endless recycling of negative thoughts and feelings.

EDUCATION AND PREVENTION   Education and prevention focus on safer sex, using condoms to avoid exchange of fluids, reducing numbers of sexual partners, not sharing needles or related drug paraphernalia, and making condoms, needles, and syringes readily available. Prevention programs target homosexual and bisexual men, intravenous drug users, and adolescents. Adolescents and college students are at risk even if they are not homosexual or do not use drugs: they have frequent sexual contacts and have a sense of invulnerability because they have not been ill yet much in their lives. Many drug users know of the risks they incur, but they continue their risky behaviors (Coates et al., 1987).

LIVING WITH AIDS   People who test positive for HIV do not necessarily contract AIDS immediately. There may be a period of up to nine years during which the disease develops. The function of the immune system may be important in determining how long the incubation period takes. Stress may be important as well. People who are HIV-positive may benefit from counseling, education in the relations between HIV and the immune system, stress management, safer sex behaviors, knowledge of the effects of alcohol and drug abuse on immune function, medical aspects of HIV, and legal considerations. Support groups focus on managing grief, depression, helplessness and hopelessness, anger, and fear of dying (Morokoff, Holmes-Johnson, & Weisse, 1987).

1. *Health psychology* helps people improve their well-being. Psychosomatic medicine developed as a subdiscipline of psychiatry, not psychology. Behavioral medicine is an interdisciplinary field, focusing on intervention with behavioral techniques in physical health problems.

2. The *fight-or-flight* emergency reaction is mediated by the sympathetic nervous system. It is the first stage of the *general adaptation syndrome*. Then comes the *resistance stage*, in which many of the physiological changes associated with the alarm reaction are reversed. The third stage, *exhaustion*, occurs when the body's ability to adapt runs out.

3. *Stress* can be a failure to adapt. People now face challenges equipped with a brain and biology suited to the world of our distant ancestors. Stress occurs when the environment or internal demands exceed resources to adapt. These situations are of several types: *catastrophes, major life changes, chronic life strains,* and *minor hassles.*

4. Low illness executives have a strong *commitment* to self, work, and family. They have a sense of *control* over their life, and they see change as a *challenge* rather than a threat.

5. Psychological processes and behaviors that mediate stress include *control,* or even the *illusion of control; optimistic attitudes; denial; visual stimulation; sense of coherence; social support;* and *exercise.*

6. The extreme of having no control is *learned helplessness.* When an individual has repeated experiences that whatever he or she does to attempt to control the environment will not succeed, the person learns to be helpless.

7. The *stress-diathesis* model posits that the individual responds internally to demanding situations with a specific response. Homeostatic restraints, which would keep this response from being exaggerated in other people, are inadequate in the individual because of previous damage or genetic composition. The stress part of the model is that the individual is repeatedly exposed to stressful situations which cause activation of this response.

8. Approaches to treating stress-related disorders include *cognitive-behavior therapy, rational emotive therapy, cognitive restructuring therapy, stress inoculation therapy, biofeedback,* and *relaxation exercises.* The term *broad-spectrum behavior therapy* denotes that most behavior therapists use a combination of treatments to help solve clients' problems.

9. Mental factors can influence resistance to disease. Even mild upsets have effects on the immune system, and poor coping may adversely affect immunity. Positive states of mind, including laughing, may enhance the functioning of the immune system. Perhaps the most powerful demonstration that psychological factors affect immune responses is the demonstration that immune responses can be conditioned.

10. The *health belief model* includes the patient's readiness to act, the costs and benefits of compliance, and the existence of a cue to action. The *control and predictability model* proposes that chronic diseases pose a stressful and potentially uncontrollable crisis for patients, particularly cardiac patients. This brings on feelings of helplessness.

11. Helping people change their behavior to follow up perceptions of fear involves understanding their conceptions of illness; the application of behavioral principles to

help them learn new behaviors; and cognitive-behavioral approaches which combine social-learning, health education, and behavior modification.

12. Higher levels of fear lead to more attitude change and somewhat more behavioral change in use of seat belts, care of teeth, smoking, and inoculations. Together these comprise a *parallel process model* of fear and attitude change.

13. The *gate-control theory of pain* suggests that there are neurophysiological mechanisms in the dorsal horns of the spinal cord that function as a gate, increasing or decreasing the flow of nerve impulses from peripheral nerve fibers to the central nervous system. Sensory input is then modulated by the gate before pain is perceived. The theory also led to the procedure of artificially stimulating the nervous system, in the hopes of closing the gate to reduce chronic pain.

14. Treatments for pain include hypnosis, acupuncture, *cognitive strategies,* the *pain clinic,* and *functional restoration.*

15. Addictions such as smoking, alcohol, and drugs, share problems of relapse. Based on self-control principles, the model of relapse prevention puts responsibility on the individual without blame. *Quitting* is only the first stage of change. The *maintenance* stage is much more difficult and lasts a longer time. People are expected to experience *slips,* or small episodes of the old habit; *lapses,* or more serious episodes; and perhaps *relapse,* full-blown recurrences. The key difference between relapse prevention and other approaches is that it views these problems not as failures, but as learning experiences.

16. Major risk factors for coronary heart disease include hypertension, blood cholesterol levels, cigarette smoking, and a Type A behavior pattern. Minor risk factors are diabetes, obesity, and a sedentary lifestyle. Nonmodifiable risk factors are age, sex, and family history of heart disease. People who have coronary artery disease are hostile frequently. Hostility is currently the most popular candidate in the search for the destructive Type A component. It links with blood pressure reactivity, severity of coronary artery disease, and death from all causes including coronary heart disease.

17. Treatment and prevention of coronary heart disease has focused on intervention with large groups, using television and other media as well as community demonstrations, posters, and existing community organizations to encourage people to quit smoking, reduce the fat in their diets, and get their blood pressures measured and hypertension treated. Mass media plus face-to-face behavioral treatment have been more effective than mass media alone, and both have been more effective than no treatment.

18. Lowering blood pressure can be accomplished by changing any one of the factors which control it. Some of the factors involved in raising blood pressure include obesity, excess sodium intake, and chronic psychological stress.

19. Smoking is the single largest reducible cause of cancer. Increased intake of fiber may protect against colon and rectal cancer, and eating vegetables rich in beta-carotene may protect against cancer at several sites. Denial is a problem in the detection and treatment of cancer, since early detection and treatment is important.

20. *Acquired Immune Deficiency Syndrome (AIDS)* is probably the most feared and the most deadly epidemic in the world. Prevention is the main tool we have to fight the epidemic. Since prevention involves avoiding high risk behaviors, psychological techniques are being used in a variety of situations.

TERMS AND CONCEPTS

Acquired Immune Deficiency Syndrome
   (AIDS)
biofeedback
blood pressure
cancer
challenge
chronic life strains
cognitive behavior therapy
commitment
control
control and predictability model
denial
diathesis-stress model
emergency reaction
exercise
fight-or-flight reaction
gate-control theory of pain
general adaptation syndrome

gradient of reinforcement
hassles
health belief model
health psychology
hypertension
learned helplessness
main effect or direct hypothesis
major life changes
parallel process model
psychosomatic medicine
relaxation
sense of coherence
social support
stress
stress-buffering hypothesis
transactional psychophysiology
uplifts

SUGGESTIONS FOR FURTHER READING

Friedman, H. S., & DiMatteo, M. R. (1989). *Health psychology.* Englewood Cliffs, NJ: Prentice Hall.

Gatchel, R. J., Baum, A., & Krantz, D. S. (1989). *An introduction to health psychology.* New York: Random House.

Taylor, S. E. (1990). *Health psychology.* New York: Random House.

Three texts on health psychology.

Ornstein, R., & Swencionis, C. (1990). *The healing brain: A scientific reader.* New York: Guilford.

Recent papers on how the principal role of the brain is to mind the health of the body.

Stone, G. C., et al. (1987). *Health psychology: A discipline and a profession.* Chicago: University of Chicago Press.

Considerations of how the new field of health psychology might grow.

Taylor, S. E. (1989). *Positive illusions.* New York: Basic Books.

Williams, R. (1989) *The trusting heart: Great news about Type A behavior.* New York: Times Books.

A fascinating description of how hostility and cynicism seem to be the culprits in Type A behavior and how trust, forgiveness, and love may be protective against heart disease.

20
ADAPTING TO THE MODERN WORLD

For most of human history, people were delivered by their parents into a world, were taught about it and lived inside that same environment for their entire lives. Now the world is changing for us at an extraordinary rate, and the world of our parents isn't our world; the world of our youth, even, isn't the world we grow old within.

Anyone who is now over 50 was born into a world in which a majority of the present countries did not even exist, and less than half the number of people lived on earth then than are alive today. At the time of the birth of those who are now over 75, there had never been a world war, electricity and pasteurization were rare, and one out of every three people died in childhood.

All of us alive today live in an unprecedented world. We live with the constant threat of 2 billion people dying within one-half hour from a nuclear war. For more than 99 percent of its history, humanity never faced a problem of this magnitude. We have not evolved enough yet to comprehend and solve the problems of the colossal number of people (5 billion human beings) who are alive today. We face problems of a scale and speed for which history and biology have left us poorly prepared. Senses, perception, memory, thought, and social judgment evolved in a stable, small, simple, and slow world, now long gone. We can't sense radiation, or low levels of acid rain, or electromagnetic fields. The problems pose unprecedented, even incalculable dangers. Yet we are only a few hundred generations away from the agricultural revolution and about 2,000 generations from Neanderthal.

Because these changes are so new, they are also new to the study of psychology. But understanding them is important. Thus, this chapter looks at the world around us. Time seems to be passing faster and faster, so it is vital that we learn to comprehend how different our world is from the world that made us. This mismatch in the worlds, *the world that made us* and *the world we made,* is in part responsible for many of our misjudgments about current events. It creates stress and poses the problems of forging a new world. Psychologists are attempting to help in the adaptation by analyzing the mental mismatches in this "new world" of computers, the physical environment we live in, and the ease with which we can travel the world.

HOW AND WHY OUR WORLD IS SO DIFFERENT

Human beings long ago migrated from their original home in subtropical East Africa and now live all over the Earth. We can even live for brief periods away from the Earth itself. From the moment our ancestors stood upright, they began to explore unexpected places and to create new conditions. As a result, we have to adapt to unprecedented challenges.

Until recently, these changes in the relatively stable environments we had adapted to were gradual. This is no longer true. The world we are creating is constantly and rapidly changing. The ability to change the environment also enhanced human evolution. Clothing, fire, dwellings, and agriculture all enabled human beings to live where none had gone before, in wintry climates as well as tropical ones. However, this inventiveness also created problems. Once an invention becomes widespread, such as electricity or jet planes,

CHAPTER 20 / ADAPTING TO THE MODERN WORLD

everyone must adapt to the new conditions that the invention creates. *Our ability to judge lags behind our ability to create.*

Travel that was unimaginable, such as visiting the moon, is now possible. Nuclear power and nuclear weapons, unimagined by our predecessors, now threaten our existence. Much of what is newly invented or created now is done by a lone genius or a small group, isolated from the rest of us. Therefore, our technology can leap way ahead of the ability of the remaining billions of us to adapt.

Think of it this way. Twenty-five thousand years ago the human population was at most a few million, surviving mainly by hunting and gathering. The invention of agriculture 10,000 years ago revolutionized the human experience. Settlements grew up along the fertile flood plains of the Nile, in the Fertile Crescent of the Middle East, and around the Ganges Delta and Huang Ho (Yellow River) in Asia.

The statistics on the rise of the human population, the measure of our reproductive success, are astonishing. At the time of the agricultural revolution, the total human population was less than 10 million. Today, almost that many people are born *each month.* It took from the beginnings of humanity, perhaps a million years ago, to produce the first billion people, and it took less than two decades to produce the most recent billion! In 10,000 years, the population has exploded from 10 million to over 5 billion (Figure 20-1) (Ehrlich, Holdren, & Ehrlich, 1977).

Since surviving offspring are one measure of a species' success, human beings are a notably successful species. Its basis is adaptability. Natural selection favors those who adapt to changing conditions. Physical changes, bipedalism, a larger brain, dexterity, visual acuity—combined with the propensity to cooperate and invent—enabled human beings to transform their world.

When people began to settle down and till the soil, they started on the road to cities, to overpopulation, to smog, and to nuclear weapons. The trip down that road was slow at first. Even in the 10,000 years from the agricultural revolution to the Middle Ages, there was no *great* change in the nature of human lives.

FIGURE 20-1
The Human Population Explosion of Modern Times

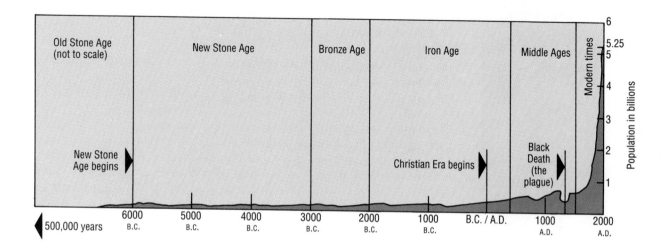

HOW AND WHY OUR WORLD IS SO DIFFERENT

In the Industrial Revolution, from the late eighteenth to the mid-nineteenth centuries, the number of inventions greatly increased: printing presses, factories, steam engines, mass production, railroads, electric power, telegraphs, and more. In this new era, development piled on development and the pace of change picked up. Human society moved faster and faster until it took off into a new and unknown world. Where there were once only prairies and deserts, now farms and factories thrive. Where there were swamps and forests, now high-tech laboratories and launching pads are built.

Many of society's current difficulties are rooted in our evolution. There were no radical changes in the brain in the course of vertebrate, primate, and human evolution. We carry the remains of our long history inside our own heads. And then suddenly, we changed things completely. Our cultural evolution has proceeded enormously faster than our genetic evolution.

Clothing, fire, dwellings, and agriculture all enabled people to live where none could before. The world of prehistoric human beings was a world bounded by a few miles rather than by continents. It contained small groups perhaps of 50 to 500 individuals isolated from other small groups. The tribal network originally designed to accommodate 200 people now tries to deal with a population of more than 5 billion. Early human beings led a nomadic life, moving through familiar terrain but subject to many short-term threats and opportunities.

MENTAL ADAPTATIONS TO A WORLD LONG GONE

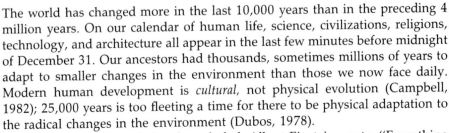

The world has changed more in the last 10,000 years than in the preceding 4 million years. On our calendar of human life, science, civilizations, religions, technology, and architecture all appear in the last few minutes before midnight of December 31. Our ancestors had thousands, sometimes millions of years to adapt to smaller changes in the environment than those we now face daily. Modern human development is *cultural*, not physical evolution (Campbell, 1982); 25,000 years is too fleeting a time for there to be physical adaptation to the radical changes in the environment (Dubos, 1978).

When the first atomic bomb exploded, Albert Einstein wrote, "Everything has now changed except for our way of thinking." More destructive power can now be carried by a single submarine than has been used in all the wars in human history.

Next month the population will increase by more than the number of human beings who lived on the planet 100,000 years ago. In the next two years, more people will be *added* to the earth's population than lived at the time of Christ.

Our mental system may have been helpful in coping with our early environment, but in the complex world of today, people are often upset by new situations and changes in their lives (Holmes & Rahe, 1967). The conflict between our evolutionary capabilities and the demands placed on us today leads to stress-related ailments such as ulcers (Selye, 1978). We are forced *always to adapt* to our own creations—the airplane, television, nuclear power.

The human brain evolved to aid the *survival of individuals*, individuals who had to live in circumstances very different from our own. They lived in small groups, in a stable situation, with only short-term threats to safety and security. The environment, both natural and cultural, remained relatively constant for very long periods, for hundreds of thousands of years. At the time of the agricultural revolution, about 10,000 years ago, this stability gradually began to disappear. The great civilizations arose out of the agricultural revolution. Human societies and cultures began to evolve rapidly.

Many of today's serious problems have their roots in our ability to make a new world that is beyond our ability to live within it. Improvements in agriculture and health make it possible for almost all children to survive infancy, grow to adulthood, and reproduce. There has been no balancing reduction in birth rates. As a result, the world is now badly overpopulated, resources are depleted, and life support systems are damaged.

Families in Bhopal identify the victims of the chemical spill.

MISTAKES AND MISMATCHES IN JUDGMENT

Individuals were more afraid of the first few small atomic bombs than they are of the tens of thousands of much more powerful nuclear weapons that are now in the U.S. and Soviet arsenals. When First Lady Betty Ford was reported to have breast cancer, all over the country women went to their physicians to get examined. Both actions are misapplications to immediate and local phenomena.

This mental emphasis on new and exciting changes in the world makes individuals and society as a whole vulnerable to anyone who can exploit this component of the mind. It leads to the effectiveness of terrorism, to violence spreading as a result of watching brutality on television and in movies, and to ignoring the dangers resulting from acid rain.

Consider these events of the mid-1980s and the responses to them. A chemical spill in a Union Carbide plant in Bhopal, India, exposed hundreds of thousands of people to toxic fumes. It caused severe damage to the health of at least 20,000 people. Soon after the spill, stories appeared in the press describing the dangerous storage procedures in similar chemical plants in the United States. This event stimulated an investigation of such chemicals in the air in the United States and Western Europe that would have been done sooner were it not for the way human beings evolved to receive information. The slow release of toxins stays out of mind because the changes are slight. Then a disaster occurs, and all attention is fixed on it and similar problems.

Movie star Rock Hudson revealed that he had AIDS. Funds for research were increased dramatically only a few days later. As an announcer on ABC News commented, "AIDS has received more attention in the few weeks after Rock Hudson's announcement than in the previous four years." AIDS, growing slowly and continuously, was suddenly noticed as a problem when a single famous person contracted it.

MISPLACED COMPARISONS

Recall from Chapters 5, 10, and 17 that we constantly judge things by comparison, and our judgment shifts constantly. An automobile ad may say "BMW prices range from $70,000 to $24,950." This ad makes your comparison shift, and you begin telling yourself that the $24,950 model is actually quite

The misjudgments people make by using comparison helped to bring down a U.S. president. In 1972, a break-in occurred at the head of the opposition party's headquarters, and the resulting scandal came to be known as "Watergate" —an elaborate, extensive plan to spy on and harass the opposition. How could an experienced group of politicians have approved such a ridiculous operation?

The Watergate break-in was proposed by G. Gordon Liddy, following the strategy of the billiard table salesman—start very high and then lower your demands until something that at first would seem outlandish now appears reasonable. Liddy went to planning sessions of the Committee to Re-Elect the President. He first proposed an outlandish program of compromising the Democrats by spying on them, using walkie-talkies. He also proposed selective kidnappings, break-ins at Democratic headquarters to scrounge information about prominent Democrats' personal lives, and other "dirty tricks" on

THE TALE OF WATERGATE

the Democrats during the entire year, culminating with the live confessions at the Democratic convention in Miami. This plan, which he proposed would cost $1 million, was rejected by the Attorney General.

Liddy later halved the plan, eliminating the most offensive elements—no kidnapping, only a few whores. His cutdown plan costing $500,000 was also rejected. Finally, for "only" $250,000, Mr. Liddy proposed a simple and comparatively mild break-in at the Democratic headquarters in the Watergate office building.

Jeb Magruder, one of the members of the committee, wrote,

After starting at the grandiose sum of $1 million, we thought that probably $250,000 would be an acceptable figure. . . . We . . . signed off on it in the sense of saying "Okay, let's give him a quarter of a million dollars and let's see what he can come up with." A quarter of a million looked small after the initial proposals, as did the simple break-in compared to the wild scheme. It brought down the government.

With a view less clouded by the comparative pressures of the moment, Magruder later wrote,

If he had come to us at the outset and said "I have a plan to burglarize and wiretap Larry O'Brien's office," we might have rejected the idea out of hand. Instead he came to us with his elaborate kidnapping/ mugging/sabotage/wiretapping scheme. He had asked for the whole loaf when he was quite content to settle for half or even a quarter.

cheap for a BMW. The sales and marketing industries readily take advantage of our comparative judgments of reality. Here is an example from one sales strategy:

If you were a billiard-table dealer, which would you advertise—the $329 model or the $3,000 model? The chances are you would promote the low-priced item and hope to trade the customer up when he comes to buy. But G. Warren Kelley, new business promotion manager at Brunswick, says you would be wrong. . . . To prove his point, Kelley has actual sales figures from a representative store. . . . During the first week, customers were shown the low end of the line . . . and then encouraged to consider more expensive models—the traditional trading-up approach. . . . The average table sale that week was $550. However, during the second week, customers . . . were led instantly to a $3,000 table, regardless of what they wanted to see. [They were] then allowed to shop the rest of the line, in declining order of price and quality. The result of selling down was an average sale of over $1,000. (Cialdini, 1985)

Our use of comparison helps us judge the brightness of light, the temperature of water, which items to buy, and whether to harm or help someone. The same neural procedures that originally developed to judge brightness now preside over the life and death of us all. We retain primitive processes of judgment, appropriate to an era long gone. In the modern world, important decisions about the lives and death of millions and political campaigns also funnel through the ancient system, and it sometimes has incalculable consequences.

MISJUDGMENTS OF THE MODERN WORLD

Among our mind's simplifying heuristics is the tendency to analyze everything as an immediate, personal phenomenon: "What does this mean to me?" A personal insult dominates attention, yet in time the insult is forgotten. Whatever gets close to us, in space, time, and thought, is immediately overemphasized. Viewers of violent movies believe there is more violence in the world than those who do not see such films.

Thus, whether it is an emotional slight, a change in the weather, or a matter of government policy, our minds automatically give current information higher weight in making decisions. During the 1985 Geneva summit between Reagan and Gorbachev, the U.S. Secretary of Defense wrote a letter to the president opposing summit accords. It was front-page news in international media, and many commentators felt that it threatened the talks. The letter, however, contained no real change in policy or new information—that is, no "news" of any kind—it simply restated already known positions. Yet it was *perceived* as potentially damaging because it was leaked and it was close to the time of the talks. Thus, the letter was perceived wrongly as "current" information. Had the letter been made public two weeks earlier, it probably would have had no effect.

This incident (and thousands of others like it) are misapplications of a mental system that is basically designed, like a frog's, to respond to immediate and local phenomena. Newly released warnings about hazardous food additives get full attention and full scrutiny, while the enormous, constant dangers of cigarettes are well known and ignored.

INSENSITIVITY TO OLD PROBLEMS

Consider an ordeal of the sort that happens 20 times per day in the United States, yet has little effect on decisions. Sarah Wilson will be forever brain-injured as the result of hitting the windshield of her parent's car when it careened into a dump truck. Three-year-old Sarah became an orphan in the collision, which claimed both her mother and father. The tires on the family car were not able to grip the road and properly stop when the truck abruptly pulled onto the road in front of them.

In 1986 about 500 people were severely injured or killed each month in the United States because of underinflated tires and other results of poor car maintenance. This is a far greater, ongoing, and more important tragedy than a single terrorist murder, yet tire inflation is scarcely as attention-grabbing as General Manuel Noriega or the bombing of the Pan Am flight over Lockerbie, Scotland.

Crack is a great problem and the airwaves and newspapers are surfeited with information on its dangers. We know crack is addictive and a killer. However, if we told you of another drug that is *six times* as addictive as crack and will kill 3–5 million people in this decade, you would certainly be concerned. But this drug is cigarettes, and since it is a continuing killer, and part of our environment, it gets little attention (Kolata, 1989).

So, little is done about the chronic dangers of highway safety or the 300 murders per week or the 100 billion cigarettes smoked each year—because they are familiar problems. A single new event, such as a terrorist strike, is immediately on the front page of newspapers all over the world. We conscript jet fighters to apprehend terrorists who have killed a single man, but little is done to save thousands of lives like the Wilsons' or to improve the lives of many, such as Sarah, who are permanently injured and lost to society. It seems senseless, absurd, and bizarre, but the mental system ignores large daily dangers, even dangers that threaten death.

SENSITIVITY TO SCARCITY

A sensitivity to an immediate scarcity of resources, especially a sudden change leading to scarcity, is a default program in all animals. It is part of how all organisms evolved. Before the agricultural revolution, food supplies were not under human control. A sudden decrease in the number of game animals or a drought that resulted in a decline in the fruit and grain supply needed immediate attention and action. Because such short-term changes are recorded quickly by the nervous system, our human ancestors probably avoided famine by responding to shortage immediately, by changing their diet or foraging in a new area.

This human tendency to respond readily to scarcity is sometimes exploited in interesting ways in modern-day society. Columnist Jon Carrol of The *San Francisco Chronicle* took over as headwaiter for one day in an Oakland restaurant. He learned about scarcity quickly. The title of his article (November 13, 1986) was "Only a Few Clams Left."

> About halfway through my one-night tenure as the substitute maitre d' (or host) at the Bay Wolf, an Oakland restaurant of sole and heart, I checked in with the kitchen.
>
> "The clams aren't moving," said Stephen, chef in charge of first courses. "Tell them about the clams."
>
> Why not? The clams were swell; they just weren't selling. East Bay diners had developed an unaccountable craving for spinach salad. So the next five times I did my small tap dance at the beginning of the meal—"Let me direct your attention to a few special items on the menu"—I described the clams in loving detail. Still nothing.
>
> With the next party, I tried a different approach. "The clams are very popular tonight," I said, "so if you want to start with them, I suggest you tell me now."
>
> Marketing heaven. The clams began walking out the door like little soldiers. Rebecca, one of the waitresses told me: "Gold star on your chart. My whole table ordered clams."
>
> I walked into the kitchen again. "I've got a great way to sell anything," I told Lee, the head chef, "just say it's going fast."
>
> Lee considered carefully. Finally, she said: "Gee, do you think I could sell myself that way?"

(She probably could because "hard to get" people are usually thought to be quite attractive.)

The mental system automatically amplifies short-term scarcity. It makes us vulnerable in the modern world to manipulations of scarcity. The best daily evidence comes from advertising, where the weak points of the mind get illuminated. About 20 years ago, I decided to get my car painted. I noticed a trifling price in an ad for Earl Scheib Auto Painting. The ad listed a "special low price" for paint jobs and then said "last three days" for this price. I went right out and had the job done.

Recently, I was looking for a new paint job on another car and happened to notice the current ad for Earl Scheib Auto Painting. The price was still low (in the context of 20 years of inflation), but what had not changed was the sales pitch: it still said "last three days" for the low price. This must be the longest three days in history! The pitch works because of our propensity to rush to a sudden scarce situation, the scarcity here being *time*.

Another example is the "special, limited time" offers that attract us. One portrait company urges parents to buy as many poses as possible because "stocking limitations force us to burn the unsold pictures of your children within 24 hours." Of course, stocking limitations do not really exist, but this ploy has evolved because it works on the limitations of the purchaser's mind. When something is available for a limited period, people are more likely to value it. A limited performance of a stage play often attracts a larger audience than an extended run.

In a simple "consumer preference" study (Worchel, 1984), individuals were given a chocolate chip cookie taken from a jar. They were then asked to rate its quality, its probable price, and how tasty they thought it was. In the first study, half the people got cookies drawn from a jar containing 10 cookies, half from a jar containing 2 cookies. The subjects judged the cookie in short supply to be of higher quality and more costly than the abundant cookie.

This is bad enough, but we can go a step further. What about *sudden* scarcity of a previously abundant cookie? Worchel then ran the experiment again. One group of people first were given their cookie from the jar of 2 and the second group were given a cookie from the jar containing 10. But then the jar containing 10 was immediately removed and replaced with a jar of 2. Which was valued more? The subjects valued the newly *scarce* cookies more highly than the *previously* scarce cookies, estimating that the newly scarce cookies would be 20 percent more expensive than the old scarce cookies. This experiment demonstrates some fundamental characteristics of the way the mental system evolved: notice the short-term and maximize gain. The same kinds of actions influence all sorts of decisions, in business as well as in cookie evaluation.

In 1973, ABC decided to pay the unheard-of sum of $3.3 million for a showing of a movie, *The Poseidon Adventure*. It was an amount that ABC and other networks admitted, at the time, could not be justified. ABC stood to lose $1 million on the deal. Why did they do it?

The selling of this movie was different from previous sales of films to television. It was the subject of an open bid auction, the first of its kind. In an auction, the commodity, in this case a single showing of a film, automatically becomes scarce. Like the cookies, something scarce gets an automatically higher value within the mind. One competing bidder, CBS president Robert Wood, noted, "Logic goes right out the window." He described the feeling:

> We were very rational at the start. We priced the movie out, in terms of what it could bring in for us, we allowed a certain value on top of that for exploitation.
> But then the bidding started. ABC opened with $2 million. I came back with $2.4. ABC went to $2.8. And the fever of the thing caught us. Like a guy who had lost his mind, I kept bidding. . . . There came a moment when I said to myself, "Good grief, if I get it, what the heck am I going to do with it?"

The "winner's" reaction was expressed later: "ABC has decided regarding its policy for the future that it would never again enter into an auction situation." The manipulation of this short-term spotlight on something rare is a way of life, from the crush of shoppers at opening hour specials ("prices good for the first hour") to the continuance of auction houses. It costs us daily, this vestige of the past. And it also determines how we judge other people.

HOW WE ARE MANIPULATED BY COMPARISONS AND CATEGORIES

Categories can affect comparisons. We seem to possess cutoff points for categories. Retailers are aware of this when they price goods at $99.99 rather than $100.00. They know people may be looking for something "under $100." The shifting nature of our comparisons is shown in the effect the rise in the cost of gasoline had on American drivers. There was little decline in gasoline consumption as gas rose from 38 cents to 60 cents to 90 cents and even 95 cents per gallon; but once gasoline was more than $1.00 a gallon, there was a marked decrease in usage. Later, as prices continued to remain above $1.00 per gallon, consumption rose again.

Knowledge of our decision-making and attention processes makes some of the ways we respond to events more comprehensible. Simply because of the normal processes of the nervous system—the transmission to the brain of sharp changes in the world—human beings are not easily able to register threatening changes that are not immediate emergencies. Such changes are not perceived in the same way as are other threats, and they are often incorporated wrongly into our culture. The typical response is to attend closely to the first occurrence of an event, then tune out; we habituate. (See Chapter 5.) This happens in responding to a noise, to a sudden appearance of the sun from behind a cloud, and to extreme danger.

Consider the responses to atomic threats. Recall that people were more afraid of the first few atomic bombs than they are of the thousands of much more powerful nuclear weapons now in U.S. and Soviet arsenals. The first atomic bombs were kept secret and then were unveiled *suddenly*. The mushroom cloud over Hiroshima and the unparalleled destruction signaled a sharp change in the world; it was easily noticed and properly feared. In contrast, nuclear bombs have accumulated *gradually* until they now number in the tens of thousands, each one much more powerful than the first ones. These arsenals have hardly been given the notice of the first weapons. Yet the growth of these arsenals, as well as countless other alterations in the environment of the contemporary world, are dangers of a dimension that humanity has never known.

The same general processes that evolution developed to judge sensory information are used today to judge more complex information. This is one reason why understanding basic neural processes is important. This kind of perception (and we can find thousands of examples) is a misapplication of a system designed, like a frog's, to respond only to immediate and local phenomena.

ADAPTING TO DENSITY

CROWDING

People and things around us become part of our *selves*. The self extends beyond the body. Anything that we control we consider to be part of us (Miller, 1980). For instance, when someone hits our car, we say "he hit *my* rear end" not "the car's rear end."

The space we live in is also a medium of communication. How close we approach another person may indicate what culture we come from, how much we like the other person, and whether our meeting is casual or for business. Too many people in the same space produces crowding and loss of privacy, but both individuals and cultures differ on what is "too many people."

PERSONAL SPACE   Edward T. Hall wrote that "We treat space somewhat as we treat sex. It is there but we don't talk about it." Hall developed a method of analysis called **proxemics,** which makes our spatial habits explicit. This analysis begins with the concept of **personal space,** which Hall defines as a "small, protective sphere or bubble that an organism maintains between itself and others." **Individual distance,** in contrast, is the basic minimum distance members of a species keep between themselves. The maintenance of a fixed individual distance seems innate in most animals, but the distance varies in different human cultures. Such distance is classified into four basic types (Hall, 1966):

- *Intimate:* from actually touching to 18 inches
- *Personal:* up to 4 feet
- *Social:* 4 to 12 feet
- *Public:* more than 12 feet

Distances that may be considered "invasions" depend on the individual's culture, and this can easily lead to misunderstandings. People from the Middle East and southern Europe interact with each other at close range, touching frequently and gazing intently into each other's eyes (Figure 20-2). North Americans and the English tend to find this very disconcerting. One person interacting with another whose cultural distance is less than his or her own can be driven across a room trying to avoid this "rude pursuer."

However, the English and Americans differ between themselves in their concept of "proper" space. The English are accustomed to less exclusive space than Americans, so they learn ways to enhance mutual privacy when they are with others. The technique of "reserve" serves this function. English people

FIGURE 20-2
Personal Space

Westerners would not feel comfortable being as close to one another as these Middle Easterners are; personal territorial demands are larger in the West.

681

The Kowloon walled city,
Hong Kong

often speak quietly and diplomatically and interact less with the people in their immediate environment than do Americans (Hall, 1969).

Members of different cultures appear to need widely varying amounts of space. In Hong Kong, the world's most densely populated city, low-cost housing provides only 35 square feet of living space per person. One architect reports,

> When the construction supervisor of one Hong Kong project was asked what the effects of doubling the amount of floor area would be upon the living patterns, he replied, "With 60 square feet per person, the tenants would sublet!" (*American Institute of Planners Newsletter*, 1967)

PRIVACY **Privacy** is the need to be alone when desired. We can enhance privacy by different means: behavior, words, and body language (the English "reserve"); space (a large house on spacious grounds); and security measures (locks and alarms). Privacy is sought in different ways throughout the world. Americans create physical barriers, while the English specialize more in psychological barriers. The Japanese developed the movable wall to make space multifunctional while preserving situational privacy (Hall, 1969).

THE EXPERIENCE OF CROWDING **Crowding** is having more people around than one desires. It might seem that the experience of crowding would simply be a function of the number of people in a given amount of space, the population density—a physical measure of the number of people in a given area (Aiello & Thompson, 1980; Freedman, 1975; Stokols, 1972). Yet this is not always the case. The *experience* of crowding depends on many factors: population density as well as the individual and social *interpretation* of that density.

The experience of crowding can be triggered in a number of ways, only some of which are related to density. The effect of density in social pathology has been studied in rats and mice (Calhoun, 1973). In an experimental situation, populations of mice were allowed to increase without external restraint by predators, disease, or lack of food and water. These colonies grew rapidly at first, then leveled off, and finally declined. The mouse population eventually died out completely. (Marsden, 1972). In the process, several curious patterns developed. Dominant males staked out the favorable areas, and the females in their territories produced more offspring than others. As the population grew, territorial defenses broke down, females became more aggressive to protect their litters, but maternal behavior and live births declined. A large population of nonreproducing females developed along with nonviolent and asexual males, which Calhoun called the "beautiful ones." They only ate, drank, slept, and groomed. When mice from this environment were transferred to one of low density, most could not establish a society or reproduce.

Yet density is not the principal cause of deterioration of this mouse society nor of any human society. Rather, as Calhoun notes,

> *Rate and quality of social interaction are paramount issues* [italics added]. The same factors are important in human life. Despite the thousandfold increase in human numbers since the beginning of culture, some forty to fifty thousand years ago, there has been no change in effective density. (Calhoun, 1973)

RESPONSES TO POPULATION DENSITY When an animal population in the wild becomes too large, it may suddenly decline or "crash." For instance, the victims of a

Crowding amplifies our emotions, so that the excitement of the crowd at a football game enhances our own feelings of excitement.

population crash among Sika deer were not sick or undernourished in general, but they did have enlarged adrenal glands, indicating an extreme stress reaction (Christian, Flyger, & Davis, 1960). This is consistent with the evidence from other animal studies: the adrenal glands of *lone* mice in very small enclosures do not enlarge (Freedman, 1975).

The human response to density is much more flexible. Males and females may differ in response to density. In a mock jury deliberation, women became less aggressive and gave lighter sentences in small rooms than in large ones, but men tended to do just the reverse. Similar effects have been found for competition in all-girl and all-boy groups (Freedman, Levy, Buchanon, & Price, 1972). Although this type of relationship has not always been found, it has occurred often enough to suggest that men and women may respond differently to high-density situations.

In general, crowding *amplifies* what is occurring (as do other parts of our social life), whether this is positive or negative (Freedman, 1975). Parties and football games are crowded environments that most of us seek out for pleasure—the excitement of the crowd increases ours. Going to a crowded bar after an irritating day at the office may result in a sudden lifting of a bad mood. Situations that *violate* our distance preferences, however, make us feel stress; we react physiologically and become less creative than under preferred conditions (Aiello & Thompson, 1980).

THE BUILT ENVIRONMENT

"We shape our buildings, and thereafter our buildings shape us." When he said this, Winston Churchill was referring to the reconstruction of the sixteenth-century House of Commons. The Commons was destroyed by bombing in

683

FIGURE 20-3
The Pruitt-Igoe Housing
Project

World War II, and many in England wanted to reconstruct the building along more modern lines. Churchill, however, felt that the design of the building had, in some part, determined the course of British politics. The oblong shape of the Commons room encouraged the existence of two opposed parties that had a number of leaders rather than just one. It encouraged confrontation rather than cooperation. The building was rebuilt as it had been, brick by brick.

Although Churchill was speaking of a political institution, his observation "our buildings shape us" is universally applicable. Our built environment has a profound effect on how well we live and work. Failure to recognize this can lead good intentions into disaster.

The Pruitt-Igoe housing project in St. Louis was built in the 1950s as a radical, new approach to improving life. The hope was to replace the slums of the black ghetto (Jacobs, 1959). It was assumed that new housing would automatically be better. So a large high-rise project was built that effectively and instantly "replaced" the slum. However, it did not include any of the *benefits* of the ghetto. Twenty years later, part of it was torn down because people would not live in it any longer (Figure 20-3). Why?

Many housing projects contain design flaws that a knowledge of human needs and of the relationship of spatial arrangements to behavior could have prevented. High rises, such as the Pruitt-Igoe project, are usually set off in an open space (Figure 20-4). This seems like a good, humane idea at first glance, but on closer inspection, it is clearly the opposite. In poor neighborhoods, there is frequently a network of affiliation that makes the area a true community, even

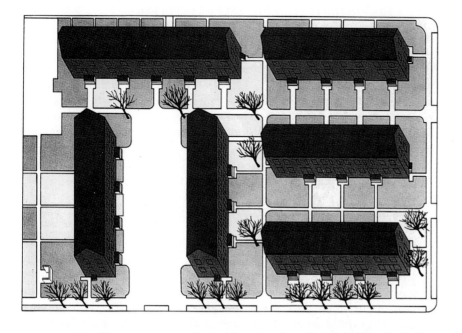

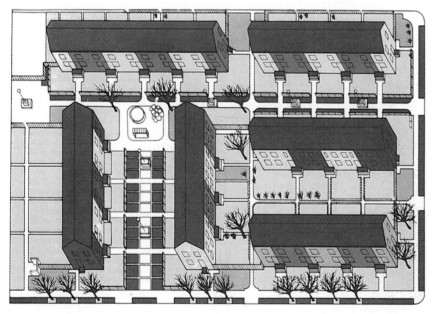

FIGURE 20-4
Modifying the Built
Environment

Before the Clason Point
housing project in New York
City was modified (top), the
crime rate was rising and the
buildings were deteriorating.
The modification (bottom)
assigned parts of the grounds
to the residents to treat as
their own front and rear
yards. This ended the totally
open access from all
directions and, along with
other modifications and
increased community interest
that developed, contributed to
lowering the crime rate and
improving the residents'
attitudes about both their
built environment and their
social environment.
(Newman, 1979)

if it is rundown. The streets are safe because so many people are on them, and
other people keep an eye on the street from their windows. In high rises with
spacious grounds, full surveillance by occupants is not possible, and from about
the fourth floor up, keeping an eye out for trouble is not very effective anyway.
The open spaces therefore become a "no man's land" in which people are
justifiably afraid to walk (Jacobs, 1959).

ADAPTING TO COMPUTERS AND MECHANIZATION

Nothing has increased the pace of change more than computers. A small personal computer on an executive's desk or in his or her lap now has more power than was available to all of the Allied forces of World War II. Fifty years ago, computers did not exist. Twenty-five years ago, people who had seen a computer were rare. Today, it is hard to live in society without coming into daily contact with computers. We use computers when we withdraw money from our bank accounts using automated teller machines, when we play video games, and every time we make a long distance telephone call. We use word-processing programs to write everything from business letters to term papers to this textbook. In the future, computers may be used as often as telephones to send "electronic mail," to access "expert" knowledge in making decisions, and in many other ways that we cannot predict.

The widespread application of computers is the most recent in a series of technological changes that have affected our lives in complex ways. For example, the personal automobile not only enables us to travel long distances more quickly and easily, it also has led to the development of suburbia, smog, and the decay of our inner cities. When the telephone was first invented, many people thought it would be used primarily to broadcast entertainment into people's homes (Pool, 1977). Instead, it has given us new opportunities for convenient (and sometimes inconvenient) social and business communications.

Unlike some areas of psychology where there are "right answers" that most people agree on, no one really knows what the effects of computers will be. Most of the evidence so far is inconclusive and contradictory (Attewell & Rule, 1984). In spite of this uncertainty, some people think that computers will have some inevitable impacts on people and that it is up to us to adapt to these changes (or to resist the use of computers altogether). In fact, the adaptation works both ways. There are many choices that we, as a society, can make about the ways we use computers. Understanding the possibilities for how computers can affect people will help us make these choices wisely.

QUALITY OF WORK LIFE: DESKILLING VERSUS UPGRADING

Most people in our society spend most of their waking hours for most of their adult lives at work, and computers may have profound effects on the experiences that people have during this time. The views are at two extremes: deskilling and upgrading (Attewell & Rule, 1984). Some observers claim that computers will lead to *deskilling* of many jobs. If this occurs, jobs will decrease in status, and much of their satisfying content will be lost (Braverman, 1974; Glenn & Feldberg, 1977). The conceptual and judgmental content of these jobs will be transferred to computer programs or to a smaller number of high-level specialists assisted by computers. Only the routine, uninteresting, and subservient parts will be left. If banks use computer programs to tell their credit officers which loan applications to accept, the role of the loan officer will become more clerical and less decision making.

Computers might eliminate jobs altogether and cause large-scale unemployment. There have been waves of fear since at least the 1950s that automation would put many people out of work. These fears have not materialized for previous technologies, however, and there is no evidence yet that they will be realized for computers either (Attewell & Rule, 1984).

In contrast, other observers believe that the primary effect of computers will be to *upgrade* jobs. They argue that computers are used most often to do the repetitive and uninteresting parts of jobs, leaving people more time to concentrate on conceptual and decision-making tasks (Giuliano, 1982). A secretary who uses a word-processing program no longer has to spend hours retyping entire documents to make changes. The result of this time saving will be that secretarial positions will be upgraded to involve less clerical work and more administrative responsibility.

We do not know for sure which of these two possibilities, deskilling or upgrading, will be the most common effect of computers. There are situations in which each has occurred, and opinion surveys show that people generally feel that their jobs have been improved somewhat by computers. However, no large-scale studies of actual job changes in the economy as a whole have been made (Attewell & Rule, 1984). Zuboff (1988) points out that managers can choose to use computers in either of these ways. If they use computers to substitute for human skill (what she calls "automating"), jobs may be deskilled. On the other hand, if they use the knowledge captured by automated systems as a resource, to inform people throughout an organization (what she calls "informating"), jobs may be upgraded, intellectual skills may become more important, and the whole organization may become more adaptive.

In many ways, the technology is changing faster than researchers can study it. Most studies of the effects of computers on work life were done when large mainframe computers were used. People now use personal computers in many new ways, and the effects of this newer version of technology may be very different from the old.

DESIGNING MACHINES FOR PEOPLE TO USE

Have you ever wondered why almost everyone can dial long distance telephone calls, but almost no one seems to know how to use the complicated features (like call forwarding and conference calling) on modern office telephones? Why is it that when an airplane crashes, or a nuclear power plant melts down, or an oil tanker runs aground, the disaster is so often blamed on "human error"? Why do some microwave ovens and VCRs seem so easy to use while others seem devilishly complicated?

In a high-tech world, our environment is increasingly made up of machines. When these machines are simple and easy to use, our lives can become happier and more productive. But when the machines are needlessly complicated or confusing, our lives become filled with hassles and frustrations. Designing machines that are easy for people to use often requires a great deal of knowledge about people—how they think, react, and learn—and a growing number of psychologists are concerned with designing usable machines. This branch of psychology is sometimes called **human factors psychology** or ergonomics.

A SIMPLE EXAMPLE: DESIGNING EASY-TO-USE DOORS   To see the subtleties involved in designing even simple machines that are easy to use, consider the doors shown in Figure 20-5 (see Norman, 1988). The top two doors are excellently designed to subtly signify how they work. The lever on the left makes you hold your hand vertically, indicating a slide. The lever on the right is horizontal, with an overhang and indentation that make you insert your hand, indicating a pull.

FIGURE 20-5
The Design of Door Handles

CHAPTER 20 / ADAPTING TO THE MODERN WORLD

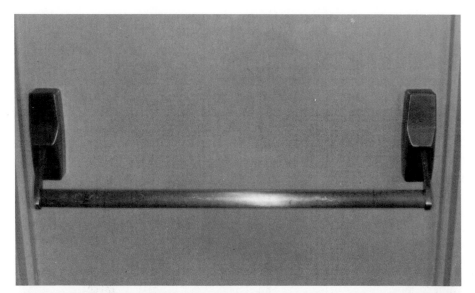

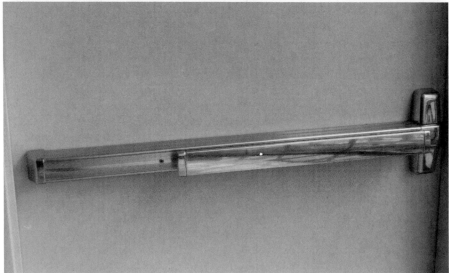

FIGURE 20-6
Push-Bar Levers on
Doors

Even though these two different types of doors are next to each other, there is no confusion about how they each work. The lower door, on the other hand, is very poorly designed for its purpose. This form of handle signifies something you should grasp, twist, or pull—but this door is supposed to slide. Figure 20-6 shows two more doors. In both cases, you push on a bar to open the door. But the top door gives you no clue about which side you should push, while the bottom door gives you a simple, easy-to-interpret signal. How many times have you been fooled by a door like the one at the top?

VISIBILITY AND FEEDBACK   Two characteristics that help make machines easy to use are visibility and feedback (Norman, 1988). **Visibility** means that users should be able to tell what their alternatives for action are and what condition the

A Macintosh II in use

machine is in. **Feedback** means that users' actions have immediate and obvious results.

When you dial a telephone, the alternative number keys you can press are visible in an arrangement that resulted from careful laboratory experimentation, and you receive constant auditory feedback as you pick up the receiver, press different keys, hear a busy signal or ringing, and eventually reach the person you are calling.

With modern office phone systems (and many programmable VCRs), however, the situation is much different. Often the only cues you have about your action options are hidden away in an instruction booklet somewhere. And as you press keys to select options, enter numbers, and so forth, you have very little feedback to help you keep track of where you are in a lengthy series of steps.

Part of the problem is that the designers of these systems have tried to cram too many functions onto too few controls and displays. The problem isn't as bad in VCRs that have on-screen programming, for which commands that appear on the TV screen help you enter the time, date, and channel of the programs you want to tape.

DESIGNING EASY-TO-USE COMPUTERS   Because of their vast flexibility, computers provide some of the most fertile opportunities for designing easy-to-use machines. Designers of computer systems have almost unlimited choices in how they signify action options and give users feedback about what is happening in a program.

Apple's Macintosh computers have been very successful, in part because people find them so easy to use. Macintosh computers (and many other modern computers) use a style of interaction with users that is similar to the way video games work. This style is often called *direct manipulation* because people don't have to remember and type commands to the computer. Instead, they just point to and manipulate documents and other objects that are visible on the screen (Hutchins, Hollan, & Norman, 1986; Shneiderman, 1988).

In an attempt to help computer system designers, some psychologists have also begun developing elaborate models of the cognitive processing that goes on as people use a program (e.g., Card, Moran, & Newell, 1983). For example, these theories try to estimate the amount of time and effort it will take people to accomplish a specific task (such as deleting a sentence in a word processor) using different kinds of word processors.

AN EXPERT SYSTEM

Artificial intelligence programs that are used to help make decisions that ordinarily are made by human experts are often called **expert systems.** One of the first and best-known expert systems was the MYCIN program developed at Stanford University in the early 1970s (Davis, 1984). It helps physicians diagnose and treat certain kinds of infectious diseases. First, it asks the physician dozens of questions about the patient's age, sex, and symptoms and about the results of previous laboratory tests. Then, using its data base of diseases and treatments, the program names which diseases it concludes are present and suggests drugs to treat them. Most of MYCIN's knowledge about diseases and treatments is stored in the form of approximately 500 rules such as this one:

Rule 27:
  IF (1) the gram stain of the organism is gram negative, and
  (2) the morphology of the organism is rod, and
  (3) the aerobicity of the organism is anaerobic,
  THEN there is suggestive evidence (0.7) that the identity of the organism is bacteriodes.

If physicians want to know how the program arrived at its suggestions, they can ask for explanations like this one:

Q: How did you decide that ORGANISM-1 was *E. coli?*

A: I used rule 084 to conclude that the identity of ORGANISM-1 is *E. coli.* This gave a cumulative certainty factor of 0.41. I used rule 003 to conclude that the identity of ORGANISM-1 is *E. coli.* This gave a cumulative certainty factor of 0.43.

Because of MYCIN's extensive knowledge about this small part of medicine, its suggestions are often as good as those of human experts. The range of its knowledge, however, is quite limited. It knows nothing about broken legs or psychiatric conditions.

ORGANIZATIONAL STRUCTURES AND DECISION MAKING

Since computers can process and distribute information in new ways, many people have predicted that computers will affect how organizations are structured and decisions are made. Leavitt and Whisler (1958) predicted that whole levels of middle management would be eliminated as improved information technology led to centralized decision making at higher levels of the corporate hierarchy. Others have argued that computers may lead to greater decentralization of decision making because lower level managers have more access to information or because their decisions can be monitored more easily from above (Pfeffer, 1978). Still other theorists have argued that the increasing use of computers and communication technologies may ultimately lead to an even greater form of decentralization: more small companies and more companies buying components from other companies instead of making them internally (Malone, Yates, & Benjamin, 1990).

Here, too, case studies show both kinds of changes, but we do not know what overall effect, if any, computers will have on the distribution of authority and control in organizations. In many cases, either organizational structures do not change when computers are used, or the existing structure is reinforced (Robey, 1981). Where changes do occur, centralization may be more common than decentralization, but computerized information systems are used in many different kinds of power relationships (Attewell & Rule, 1984).

Much of the research in this area has studied the use of large mainframe computers for such tasks as accounting. Personal computers and new uses of computers for communication tasks, including electronic mail and computer conferencing, may have very different effects (Greif, 1988; Hiltz & Turoff, 1978).

Professors are especially long-lived. Al G., an old friend, was professor emeritus when I entered graduate school; he was 70 years old at the time. For years we continued to talk over ideas and work, hardly noticing that he was getting on in years. He died when he was 94. And his advanced age wasn't unusual among academics. Harvard professors are in the top 1 percent of oldsters. In the modern world, we need to rethink how advantageous it is for society to invest in education. The costs of education are little compared with the benefits to the person in health as well as productivity.

Paralleling the great improvement in health and longevity is the increased education of most individuals. While popular attention focuses on the problems and inadequacies of our schools and the lowering of IQ and achievement scores, we overlook the great rise in both literacy and education that has happened in the last 50 years. More men and women today are educated about the world and know more about what is going on than ever before.

The amount of education seems to correlate with improved health and disease resistance, and even more powerfully than some of the highly publicized risk factors like high cholesterol, smoking, high blood pressure, or obesity. For example, a 1984 study appearing

USING PSYCHOLOGY: GET AHEAD

in the *Irish Medical Journal* compared the different risk factors for heart disease and concluded that

The results confirm a strong association between education and cardiovascular disease which is not entirely explained by differences in age, cigarette smoking, diastolic blood pressure, weight or plasma cholesterol. *Indeed, on the basis of the logistics analysis, the independent effect of education on cardiovascular disease is as strong as the effects of smoking, blood pressure, weight and cholesterol combined.* [emphasis added]

The more the education, then, the *less* the disease. Workers with the least education in this study had four times the rate of heart disease than those with doctorates. So, reading, learning history, mathematics, and above all, literacy seem to relate to better health. It isn't that those who are better educated make more money, either. In a U.S. study comparing men and women with *equal incomes,* those with post-graduate degrees are 2½ times more likely to have good health than those with no education. They are twice as likely to be in good health than those with 1–8 years of education. And they not only report good health but live longer.

It isn't those high-stress, highly publicized sedentary Type A ex-

Groups that communicate via computers to make decisions participate more equally in the decision-making process but take longer to come to a consensus than face-to-face groups. They also engage in more "uninhibited verbal behavior," such as swearing and expressing strong opinions (Kiesler, Siegel, & McGuire, 1984).

COMPUTERS IN EDUCATION

The primary "work" of many people is learning, and computers may have important effects on this process (Taylor, 1980). By giving students highly individualized instruction and immediate feedback, computers can sometimes significantly increase learning speeds (Suppes & Morningstar, 1969). Computers can also be used to create highly motivating instructional environments. When some of the motivational characteristics of computer games are used in designing instructional programs, they may lead students to give more time and higher quality attention to their educational tasks (Malone, 1981). For instance, most people find writing, rewriting, and revising much easier on a word processor.

Depending on how these motivational characteristics are used, however, they might distract students from their educational tasks or lead students to be

ecutives who drop dead in great numbers from cardiovascular diseases; rather, it is the hard-working uneducated physical laborers. And it isn't only heart disease, as in the Irish study, that is affected. Blood pressure also drops with more education. Many more uneducated blacks are hypertensive than educated ones. And with increasing levels of education, rates of kidney disease drop, accidents decline, and all cancers drop dramatically —except for breast cancer, perhaps because of less breast feeding among highly educated women (Ornstein & Sobel, 1989).

To make it a personal example: Consider Maria and Lydia, each 25 years old. Maria has two years of college, while Lydia dropped out of school in the sixth grade. Their incomes and family histories are comparable, but Maria can expect to live fully **10** years longer than Lydia. By comparison, eliminating *all cancer deaths* would add less than two years to life expectancy.

What happens when people become educated? Of course they can read safety warnings and the instructions on their prescription labels. They can read the best health advice and learn of impending health risks and opportunities to improve health. But this is hardly the whole story, although it is certainly a part. There is probably a direct effect of knowing what is going on in the world, understanding how economic and social forces operate to affect one's life, and, in general, understanding how things work.

Education offers a sense of the world, much as when the stories and myths in ancient cultures helped make the world seem more coherent and less threatening. If you know that lightning is followed by thunder, you won't get upset the next time you experience a thunderstorm. If you know that downturns in the economy affect your business, you can diversify your company to avoid weak markets. If you know that you get a runny

nose during the flowering of acacia, you can either avoid exposure to the plant or, at least, not panic. If you know that there is a flu going around, you can care for yourself and if you get it, avoid worrying about otherwise unexplained feelings. If you know that most other people, even famous and accomplished people, have had great difficulty setting up their careers and most usually fail at new projects, you will be less pessimistic or discouraged. Your comparisons are healthier and allow you, in the face of adversity, to keep heart and expect better things.

Persons also feel a sense of mastery and competence from having the benefit of an education. Education helps events in the world cohere, form a pattern, so that some surprises and panics are avoided. And the healthy pleasures of literacy and knowledge can boost self-esteem, optimism, and, as we've seen, they seem to pay off in terms of better health and longevity. So keep on with it!

ADAPTING TO COMPUTERS AND MECHANIZATION

less interested in academic material when it is later presented in a less motivating fashion (Lepper, 1985).

One of the most common uses of computers in education is to teach students how to program computers. This is certainly a skill that will be useful in its own right in our increasingly computerized society. Many people also believe that students can be taught to program in a way that helps them learn more general thinking and problem-solving skills (Papert, 1980). The results of research on this topic are still inconclusive, but some early work indicates that transferring problem-solving skills from programming tasks to other domains is not as simple as proponents would argue (Pea & Kurland, 1989).

SUMMARY

1. Humans did not evolve to comprehend the problems of the over 5 billion people who are alive today. The mismatch between the world that made us and the world we made is partly responsible for misjudgments in current human affairs. Psychologists are attempting to help humanity adapt to the new world.

2. In the modern world, change outpaces the adaptive ability of the majority of people. In 10,000 years, the population has exploded from 10 million to more than 5 billion. The Industrial Revolution sped up the pace of change. However, there have been no similarly radical changes in the brain in the course of vertebrate evolution. Cultural evolution has proceeded enormously faster than our genetic evolution.

3. The human brain evolved to aid the survival of individuals living in small groups in a stable situation. It is not built to cope with long-term changes. This results in misjudgments in the modern world. The mind places emphasis on new and exciting changes, making society vulnerable to sudden threats such as terrorism and to risks from ignoring long-term, slow changes, like acid rain. Our mental mechanism of judging by comparison is easily exploited by salespersons and politicians.

4. Several simplifying heuristics confound our judgments in the modern world. We tend to analyze everything in terms of its personal relevance, and we give current news greater weight in making decisions than old and often more relevant information. We tend to be insensitive to old problems and give attention and energy mostly to new, exciting, but often less dangerous issues.

5. The mental system automatically amplifies short-term scarcity, which makes us vulnerable to deliberate manipulations of scarcity. We consider scarce commodities more valuable than abundant ones. Our judgment in making comparisons is also affected by categories.

6. The normal processes of the brain are designed to transmit sharp changes in the world. Thus, humans are not easily able to register threatening changes that are not immediate threats. People were more afraid of the first atomic bombs than they are of the enormously more destructive present nuclear arsenal because the first bombs were revealed suddenly.

7. Hall developed a method of analysis called *proxemics,* which describes our habits of maintaining personal space. Different levels of proximity are considered appropriate in different social relationships. These standards vary among different cultures. The experience of crowding depends on factors such as population density and

individual and social interpretations of that density. Animals who are too crowded develop various social pathologies, and eventually their populations decline. In general, crowding amplifies whatever behavior is occurring, positive or negative.

8. Our built environment, our homes and offices, has a profound effect on how well we live and work. It is important for us to recognize this whether trying to improve poor housing conditions or constructing important government buildings.

9. Computers have increased the pace of change more than anything else. Today we come into constant contact with computers. Understanding how computers can affect people can help us choose wisely how we want to use them. Some observers claim that computers will lead to deskilling of jobs, but others believe their primary impact will be to upgrade jobs. Managers can choose to use computers either way. Which effect will be most common is unknown, but opinion surveys show that people generally feel their jobs have been improved by computers.

10. Designing machines that are easy for people to use requires knowledge about how people think, react, and learn. Two characteristics that help make machines easy to use are visibility and feedback. Some psychologists have begun to develop models of the cognitive processing people use when working with computers.

11. Artificial intelligence programs that are used to help make decisions ordinarily made by human experts are called *expert systems.* Such systems use sets of rules to make informed decisions bases on probabilities. An example of their use is in medical diagnosis. Computers might have several effects on organizations and businesses, such as the decentralization of decision making, or the establishment of more small companies. Computers can also be used to create highly motivating instructional environments.

crowding   personal space
expert systems   privacy
feedback   proxemics
human factors psychology   visibility
individual distance

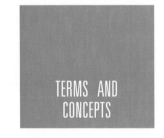

TERMS AND CONCEPTS

Ehrlich, P., & Ehrlich, A. (1990). *The population explosion.* New York: Simon & Schuster.

Ornstein, R., & Ehrlich, P. (1989). *New world new mind.* New York: Doubleday

Zuboff, S. (1989). *In the age of the smart machine: The future of work and power.* New York: Basic Books.

Three books about how our life has changed drastically in the modern world.

SUGGESTIONS FOR FURTHER READING

695

21

OLD AGE

O ne of the benefits of living in modern times is increased longevity. Ironically, however, this country places an extraordinarily high value on youth. We view aging as a dreadful, even if unavoidable, process that robs us of our vitality and eventually of life itself. When younger people describe their images of old people, they include positive terms like *kind* and *gentle* but also negative terms like *rigid, sick, frail,* and *demented.*

Does the term *old* bother you? Would you prefer that we use *senior citizen, seniors,* or *elderly?* Many people feel that *old* is a pejorative term. But think for a minute what that means. I once heard Maggie Kuhn, the founder of the Gray Panthers, speak at a conference of the national meeting of the Gerontological Society. The Gray Panthers aim at uniting young and old people to fight against injustices based on age. They are a very active group.

Her introducer stood at the podium of a large auditorium and said, "I would like to introduce to you a very impressive young lady, Maggie Kuhn." Kuhn rose to the podium, turned to him and said, "I am not young and I am no lady. I am an old woman" and with that she embarked on a powerful speech about age discrimination, beginning by asking the audience to think about why people did not even want to say the word *old.* Only in a culture that devalues old people is the word *old* considered an insult instead of a compliment.

What is old age really like? The new study of life-span development challenges many of the common stereotypes about aging. In this chapter we pick up the threads of our discussion on adult development that we began in Chapter 2.

SPECIAL ISSUES AND TERMS

What do we mean by **old, elderly,** and **aged?** How old is old? As in the transition from adolescence to early adulthood, the transition from middle age to old age is slow but sure. When 19-year-olds say "I am an adult, not a child," they often feel a bit like impostors. But by the age of 30, they no longer feel like children; the impostor feeling is gone. Similarly, there is no magic age when individuals suddenly become old.

In **gerontology,** the scientific discipline that studies aging, there is general agreement that old age begins at 65. But 65 is an arbitrary number. It gained its threshold status in 1935, when the U.S. government established the Social Security Act and had to decide when people could begin receiving their social security pensions. Sixty-five sounded like a reasonable number, and so it came to demarcate entrance into the last stage of life.

Today, 65 is a significant number primarily because of its implications. Persons who reach 65 experience subtle and sometimes dramatic life changes, not necessarily caused by age. In this country, people can retire and receive full Social Security benefits at 65. They also qualify for senior housing programs and Medicare insurance, so some people change their housing and their health care. More subtle changes occur because of *expectations* about old age, because people believe that 65 means something. People might become concerned about forgetting the name of a recent acquaintance, even if they have been bad with names all of their lives. But more on this later.

A final import of the magic number 65 is that most of the research on aging has focused on people who are 65 years and older. So in this chapter, unless specified otherwise, we consider those people who are 65 or older.

Is there really development in old age? Recall from Chapter 2 that only recently has developmental psychology come to include the study of adulthood. Some psychologists feel that extending notions of development to old age is conceptually wrong. These psychologists concede that change occurs, but they view the change as *regressive*, not *progressive*, and therefore the opposite of development. Old age *is* accompanied by loss in a number of ways; health problems and a modest degree of memory impairment occur frequently among older people. But before we conclude that the *central* feature of old age is decline, we must recognize the powerful influence of our beliefs and culture on science.

Scientists are not immune from preconceptions about old age, so they generally approach the study of old age as the study of decline. Psychologists often ask the question, "What goes wrong?" instead of "What goes right?" As a result, the vast majority of the research on aging documents only the *problems* of old age, not the *benefits* that accrue from a lifetime of living.

Age is not the only reason why old people are different from young people. Generations are different from one another. People who are 95 years old today were born in the 1800s, whereas people who are 20 years old today were born in the 1970s. Imagine what a difference that makes! Health care, education, work opportunities, and childrearing practices are strikingly different depending on when you are born.

Consider the Great Depression, the devastating, worldwide economic collapse from 1929 through most of the 1930s. The current elderly population lived through the Great Depression, which affected people differently depending on their age when the depression hit. It was a very different experience for children, young adults, and middle-aged adults. The oldest people were hit the hardest because they had a limited ability to recover their financial losses. Parents of young children had the burden of providing for both their immediate and their extended families. Children were affected in a mixed way. Even though they realized they were poor, they enjoyed the availability of their parents (who were home because they were unemployed) and the fact that neighbors bonded together and helped each other out. As a result of the depression, each of the three generations was changed—and each in a distinct way.

Differences that reflect what people have lived through as opposed to how many years they have lived are called **cohort effects.** They reflect being part of an era, a generation. Studies of aging, whether of physical or psychological change, are always susceptible to criticisms that they are not studies of age per se, but instead are studies of cohorts.

WHY DO WE AGE?

Why we age remains a puzzle to scientists. No doubt, genetics plays a role, but currently there are more than 20 different theories about aging, none of which is definitive. Aging results from a variety of processes.

Some studies focus on changes in the immune and neuroendocrine systems as the basic mechanisms of aging in human beings. As we age, our immune systems become less competent, less able to fight off foreign invaders or *antigens,* such as infections and cancers. We literally lose the ability to recognize ourselves. We then develop **autoantibodies,** which can attack our own organs and joints. One study showed that elderly people with impaired immune functioning die much earlier than elders who maintain more normal immune system functioning. However, immune system changes may either cause or result from other aging processes (Hausman & Weksler, 1985).

Research on the *neuroendocrine* system holds great promise for understanding the effects of aging. The neuroendocrine system, controlled by the hypothalamus and the pituitary, is responsible (among other things) for starting and stopping menstruation in women and may modify other aging processes as well. Overproduction of or artificially increasing the levels of certain neuroendocrines can lead to accelerated aging in fish and rats. Much more research is needed to find out if there are similar mechanisms in humans (Finch & Landfield, 1985).

Leonard Hayflick (1985, 1987), the proponent of the **programmed senescence theory of aging,** believes that aging and death occur due to built-in clocks in our genetic structure. With Paul Moorhead, Hayflick showed that human cells have a limited ability to divide (1961). Prior to their work, it was believed that, outside of the human body, cells would continue to divide indefinitely. Their extraordinary research showed that human cells divide only 50 times. Hayflick is careful to state that physiological change precedes the replicability of the cell (Hayflick, 1980), but his demonstration of the limited life span of the human cell dramatically changed our views of aging.

HOW LONG CAN WE LIVE?

Life-expectancy refers to the average number of years we can expect to live. Since the turn of the century, the life expectancy in the United States has increased dramatically. In 1900, the average life expectancy was 47. Today, among Caucasian Americans, life expectancy is 72 for men and 79 for women. No doubt due to poorer living conditions and limited access to health care, life expectancy is lower for nonwhites. Among Black Americans, the life expectancy is 75 for women and 67 for men. Among American Indians it is about two years lower. Note that the difference in life expectancy between the sexes is maintained regardless of race—no one knows why.

It is commonly believed that people are living much longer today because of improvements in medical care for heart disease and other problems of later life. This is not quite true. While there have been advances in medical care, the increase in life expectancy is due more to reduced infant mortality than to the extension of the adult life span. Life expectancy is an *average* based on the length of time that a specified group of people, born in the same year, will live.

Around the turn of the century, infant mortality was very high. About half of all babies born died before the age of 5. So even though people who reached adulthood stood about as good a chance of living into old age as people do today, their ages at death are averaged with the ages of very young children who died. For example, if we estimated life expectancy for four people, two of whom

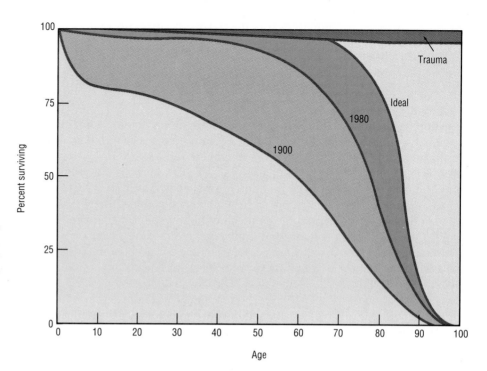

FIGURE 21-1
Survival Curve
If premature death from disease were eliminated in the United States, the population would attain the ideal survival curve. By 1980, more than 80 percent of the discrepancy between the 1900 curve and the ideal curve had been eliminated.
(From Fries & Crapo, 1981)

died before the age of 3 and two died at 80, we would assess that, on average, people live to the age of 42. This misleading figure shows the problem with averages.

Moreover, improvements in sanitation and public health, not medical treatments for disease, account for most of the reduction in infant mortality (Sagan, 1988). Life expectancy at 65—that is, how much longer we can expect to live if we are already 65 years old—has increased only by about four years since 1900, from 77 to 81 years (U.S. Senate Special Committee on Aging, 1985).

The reason why the population of older people is growing at an unprecedented rate is because the *ratio* of older to younger people is changing. In 1900, 3 percent of the population in the United States was over 65. In contrast, in 1990, 12.7 percent of the population was over 65. By 2080, we can expect the over-65 segment of the population to comprise 24 percent of the population. There are two reasons for this shift. First, women are having fewer babies. The average woman today has 1.7 children, as opposed to 4.2 children years ago. (Again, these numbers illustrate the problem with averages. Have you ever met a woman who gave birth to 1.7 babies?) Second, infant mortality has been reduced. A baby born today has an excellent chance of becoming an old person—not so less than a century ago. Interestingly, the fastest growing segment of the population is the over-80 group (Figure 21-1).

Maximal life span, or how long a person *can* live, is a matter of debate. Some villagers in the Caucasus mountains in Russia and Turkey claim to be 120, 130, and even 150 years old (Figure 21-2) (Medvedev, 1974). Many of these elderly people indeed do live a long time and are exceptionally healthy.

However, there is very little evidence, such as birth certificates, to back up these claims. Most scientists agree that the maximal human life span is 115 to 120 years. Kyucharyants (1974) asked one elderly woman in the Caucasus who claimed to be 138 years old whether a fountain of youth existed in her village. She replied, "Of course, it exists, young man. It is inside each of us. Only not everyone knows how to use it."

People who live long lives often had parents and grandparents who also lived long, which indicates that genes may direct the aging process. But life choices also play an important role. Smoking and heavy alcohol consumption shorten lives, as does eating too many fatty foods and refined sugars. Rats kept on a calorie-restricted diet age much slower than rats who gain a lot of weight.

It is not yet clear that the same is true for human beings. We have known for a long time that exercise is very important in staying healthy and living longer. People who exercise retain muscle and bone mass, have faster reflexes, and show better neurological and cognitive functioning in later life; thus, they live longer (Buskirk, 1985; Paffenbarger, 1986). In fact, many of the groups of extremely long-lived persons reside in mountainous terrain, and some scholars attribute their longevity to their rugged life-styles.

FIGURE 21-2
Maximal Life Span

The Caucasus villager in this photo claims to be 113 years old.

BIOLOGICAL AGING

Much research in the past two decades has been directed at biological changes associated with aging. The hallmark of biological aging is *slowing*. Virtually all organ systems slow with age. The heart pumps more slowly. It takes the body a longer time to digest food. Even regulatory systems slow, resulting in a host of functional changes; older bodies take more time to adjust to changes in outside temperature and to settle down following strenuous exercise.

Age-related changes in bodily functioning are different from abnormal or disease-related changes. Birren and his associates (1963) studied 47 men aged 67 to 91 who appeared healthy. They were given lengthy and comprehensive examinations of physiological, psychological, and social functioning. They were divided into two groups according to the results: those in Group A were optimally healthy on every measure; but those in Group B, who appeared healthy, actually had subclinical diseases, such as the beginnings of diabetes, heart disease, and the like. Many of the decrements associated with being old were absent in the healthy men (Group A) but were present in the men in Group B. This is an indication that impairments are often more a function of *disease* than of *age*.

Yet health problems are so common in old age that it is nearly impossible to study aging free from disease. The terms *normal aging* and *abnormal aging*—also termed *primary* and *secondary* (or disease-related) *aging*—are used to differentiate age-related changes that occur independent of disease from those that reflect common but abnormal processes.

Normal aging reflects changes that are age related, gradual, and irreversible. **Abnormal aging** refers to age-related diseases that, at least in theory, are reversible. In many cases, it is almost impossible to differentiate one from the other.

Sometimes scientific breakthroughs force us to reconsider whether a change is normal or abnormal. Twenty years ago, the scientific community believed that *dementia* reflected normal aging. Although the age at onset varied across individuals, it was generally accepted that if people lived long enough, they would suffer serious cognitive impairment. Today, we have recognized dementia as a disease. Some mild cognitive changes do occur as part of normal aging. But the vast majority of us will grow old and die without suffering from senile dementia.

NORMAL CHANGES

What are the normal physical changes we can expect? Most obvious are the changes in physical appearance. Wrinkles occur from a loss of fatty tissue underneath the outer layer of skin, causing the skin to sag. Skin also loses its natural oils and becomes more sensitive with age. Sores and bruises are more likely to develop. Hair also changes. Most notably, the hair grays due to a slowing of the production of pigment. It also becomes thinner and more brittle.

You may have noticed that the vast majority of older people wear glasses. **Presbyopia,** a form of farsightedness, is considered a normal part of aging. Almost all older people need glasses to read. In addition, visual adaptation to changes in light is slowed. If you turn off the lights in a room without windows, at first you will have difficulty seeing. If you are 20 years old, your eyes will adapt within seconds. Older eyes require more time to make this adjustment, and overall, they need more light to see clearly. Discrimination of some colors at the blue-green end of the color spectrum is also impaired in advanced age.

Hearing loss goes hand-in-hand with aging. We refer to this age-related syndrome as **presbycusis,** which is really the sum of losses that occur to the auditory system during life. Hearing difficulty results from the loss of ganglion cells in the cochlea, a spiral tube in the inner ear (see Chapter 5). At birth, we have about 20,000 ganglion cells. They die off throughout life and thereby impair hearing.

Most diminished is the ability to hear high-frequency sounds. We rely on high-frequency sounds to discriminate speech sounds. Loss of high-frequency sensitivity begins in adolescence, but it is typically not sufficient to interfere with everyday hearing until much later in life. Speech understanding in old age is particularly difficult in the presence of background noise. Having a one-on-one conversation in a quiet room may not present a problem. However, having the same conversation in a noisy room, especially where other conversations are ongoing, could present great difficulty.

Musculoskeletal changes also occur. **Kyphosis** is a minor bending of the spine and the settling of the vertebrae on the spinal column. This shift results in a change in stature. Most people are about two inches shorter in their later years compared to their maximum height. Bones also become lighter because less calcium is absorbed. Joints lose flexibility with age. This is because of changes in the connective tissues that provide support to the joints; tendons, ligaments, and muscles break down.

The gastrointestinal system slows because the body produces fewer digestive enzymes. As a result, it takes longer for food to be fully digested. Because the entire digestive process is slowed, older people are prone to constipation and hemorrhoids.

Changes appear in the cardiovascular system as well, but studies of the aging heart have shown that, in the absence of disease, the heart performs exceedingly well into the 80s. Changes that do occur appear to help maintain normal functioning. The larger blood vessels and the left ventricle of the heart thicken, which allows the heart to get more oxygen to the tissues. Because the heart beats more slowly, it pumps more blood per heartbeat during exercise.

Loss of lung function in adulthood occurs at the rate of approximately 1 percent per year and is the result of a gradual decrease in surface area for gas exchange. Because we start with more than we need, this loss does not present a problem for most people. Function is also lost due to a reduction in the elasticity in the joints of the rib cage and a weakening of the muscles that surround the lungs. Additionally, because we lose nose hairs with age (just as we lose the hair on our heads), we expose the lungs to more noxious material.

There is *less* change in the aging brain than in the rest of the body. Nevertheless, functioning in the central nervous system is altered in a number of ways. Neurotransmitters such as serotonin and catecholamines are in shorter supply in old brains. Recall that neurotransmitters communicate electrochemical signals in the spinal cord and brain. We also see *neuronal atrophy*, the loss of brain cells. However, like the lung cells, we came into the world with more brain cells than we need. One result of development is the "pruning" of brain cells (Greenough, 1982), possibly for more efficient functioning. Studies of rats under controlled conditions show that most brain cells are actually lost in the first years of life, and that relatively fewer brain cells are lost in later life (Diamond, 1980).

So both the overall number of brain cells and the communication system in the central nervous system are altered. Some brain structures do not function as well in old age; the hypothalamus, which serves as a thermostat or regulator in the body, is less efficient. Very likely, physical changes in the brain contribute to changes in cognition we discuss later in the chapter.

But the relationship between cognitive functioning and brain atrophy is not a simple one. Autopsy, the surgical dissection of the body after death, has made this very clear. There are documented cases of brilliant individuals whose brains, on autopsy, were visibly degenerated. The opposite is also true, where the brain of a seriously impaired person appears quite normal. We have much to learn about the brain. No doubt, the integrity of the brain influences our thinking and behavior. But effects of age-related changes remain elusive.

Physical changes in the reproductive system result in the **climacteric,** the loss of reproductive capacity. In women this occasion is clearly marked by menopause during middle age. **Menopause** is the cessation of menstruation and ovulation. In men, the climacteric is more gradual and never complete. Like most of the changes we refer to as age-related, the process begins much earlier in life but does not have a functional impact until many years later. Males produce fewer sperm with age and therefore gradually become less able to father children. Although we periodically hear of an 80-year-old man fathering a child, this is highly unusual. Not because 80-year-olds do not have sex! Only fertility is lessened. The loss of reproductive ability has nothing to do with the ability to have sex or the enjoyment of it. Barring disease, there are no physical barriers to sex in old age.

Normal aging results in changes in virtually every organ system in the body. Yet, in and of itself, age presents few obstacles to general functioning. In advanced age we might not be quite as limber, quick, and energetic, but growing old will not limit us substantially. Given the alternative, it's clearly our best bet.

ABNORMAL CHANGES

Abnormal aging, also termed *secondary* or *disease-related aging*, is another story. With age, the risk of chronic health problems and disease increases considerably. Approximately 86 percent of people over 65 require medical care for some kind of health problem (Butler & Lewis, 1973). Chronic conditions like diabetes, arthritis, and hypertension are much more common among the old as compared to the young. Life-threatening problems like heart disease and cancer are far more frequent. This is because normal age-related changes leave us less able to ward off disease.

The heart provides a good illustration of the interface between aging and disease. Normal changes in the heart are quite benign. In fact, as we have seen, the age-related thickening of the larger blood vessels is thought to help the heart adapt to aging. Why, then, does heart disease, specifically coronary artery disease, account for 50 percent of deaths among older people? The thickening of the vessels, coupled with a loss of elasticity, leaves them more susceptible to blockage by substances in the blood. Cholesterol, a fatty substance carried in the blood, accumulates on the walls of the vessels, further narrowing the vessel. If blood flow to the heart is blocked, *myocardial infarction*—better known as heart attack—occurs. Hypertension, another common problem in old age, presents yet another risk factor. And because the body's structural muscles are somewhat weaker, they are less able to defend against insults that do occur.

As we saw, the normal changes in breathing and the lungs are quite modest. Fewer nose hairs is no big deal, right? The catch is that because of hair loss, we are more likely to expose our lungs to toxins. And since our immune systems produce fewer *macrophages* (cells that attack foreign substances), we are less able to defend against infection.

That's the bad news. The good news is that over the past decade it has become clear that our health in old age is influenced by our behavior and the environments we were exposed to in younger days. In fact, some of what we consider normal aging may in fact reflect disuse (Bortz, 1982). Other health-behavior relationships are exceedingly clear. Smoking leads to emphysema and lung cancer. Excessive alcohol consumption leads to liver damage and an increased likelihood of cancer. Diets high in cholesterol impair cardiovascular functioning. (By the way, cholesterol begins to build up on blood vessel walls when we are teenagers.) Exposure to toxins like nicotine lead to cancer.

We cannot assume that all of our new knowledge about health and behavior means that the future population of old people will fare better than the current population of old people. Younger generations are being exposed to new toxins. Even life-style changes aimed at improving health sometimes create new

IS OLD AGE THE SAME FOR MEN AND WOMEN?

Some have said that age is the great equalizer: men and women, rich and poor, black and white—we all grow old. Does gender make a difference? If we look at actuarial data, the answer is decidedly yes, and the implications for psychological well-being are profound.

On average, women live seven years longer than men. No one knows why women outlive men, but given the fact that the seven-year difference is found cross-culturally, most scientists believe that it has a genetic basis. So women can expect a much longer old age than men. Are they lucky? Again, actuarially speaking, yes and no. Most of us don't view death as lucky, but living longer places women at risk for some of the worst problems associated with aging.

Consider Sally and Dick, a prototypical older couple. Sally is 72 and Dick is 77. They have been married 45 years and have two sons with families of their own. Dick retired from a small company at the age of 65. He was division manager when he retired and had accrued a reasonable pension. Sally was never employed because she and Dick had felt that she should stay home with the children, but she has been an active volunteer in her community for 30 years and continues to work about 20 hours a week. One day Dick suffers a serious stroke and his right side is paralyzed. After two weeks in the hospital he is discharged, but since he is bedridden (and Sally cannot

BEING FEMALE

BEING MALE

lift him) he cannot go home. Dick is admitted to a local nursing home. The cost is $2500 a month, but Sally wants only the best for her husband. She visits him every day, feeding and grooming him. Even though he cannot speak, Sally knows that he would not want a stranger to do these things. She quits her volunteer work, losing contact with life-long friends, so that she can be at the nursing home each day. Friends notice that she is physically and emotionally exhausted and urge her to cut back, but she loves her husband dearly and knows that their time together is preciously limited.

Two years later, Dick dies. The nursing home expenses exhausted the couple's life-savings; in fact, Sally took out a second mortgage on their home so she could pay Dick's medical expenses. Two weeks after the funeral she receives a letter from Dick's company informing her that Dick's pension does not include survivor benefits. Her income is cut in half. Since she was never employed, she has no social security benefits of her own. Her sons send her what they can, but they have their own expenses. She cannot pay the mortgage, so she moves into government-subsidized housing, placing her 15 miles away from her old neighborhood and preventing casual contact with previous neighbors and friends. Ten years later, Sally is isolated and poor. The apartment manager notices that newspapers are piling up outside her door. A social worker comes by and finds her confused from malnourishment and infirm. She is placed in a nursing home, paid for by state aid, where she lives out her life, dying at the age of 86.

Gender does make a difference in old age. Wives are more likely to outlive their husbands. They are also likely to be caregivers for very frail spouses. They are less likely to have adequate retirement incomes. Many women in the current cohort of older people have never been employed outside the home; and recall that even full-time female workers, on average, earn less than three-quarters of what males earn in comparable jobs. Women are more likely to live alone in old age and are at much greater risk for nursing home placement. Women do live longer than men, but they often live out those years under very harsh circumstances.

problems. Jogging may help you retain cardiovascular fitness, but your joints may suffer. And if you wear headphones and listen to loud music while you jog, you may lose your hearing as well. Experts predict that the hearing of the future old will be worse than what we observe today because of the widespread appeal of loud music among the youth (Working Group on Speech Understanding and Aging, 1988).

But try not to worry, because excessive worry about our health probably leads to all sorts of health problems! Recognition of the influence our behavior has on our health has led to massive changes in our culture. Exercise regimens and diet programs have become an integral part of American life. Ironically, many of us tend to be excessive even in our attempts to be healthy. In a funny way, we are still looking for a fountain of youth.

The National Institute on Aging has advised the public to be skeptical of claims of life extension through the use of vitamin products and dramatic life-change programs. The reality is that we have come to know that our health is influenced by the way we live our lives. But this observation does not lead to simple answers. Much of the popular thinking about health-behavior relationships is seriously flawed in logic. The bottom line is that it pays to be sensible. A reasonably healthy diet, moderate exercise, and, last but not least, doing things we *enjoy* will probably do more for our health than anything else (Ornstein & Sobel, 1989).

HEALTH AND DAILY FUNCTIONING

If we define health based on the presence or absence of disease, we could conclude that the over-65 age group is sick. If instead we define health in terms of level of functioning, a very different picture emerges.

Where do most old people live? How much assistance do they require? These questions often bring to mind pictures of old people in nursing homes, sitting in wheelchairs or lying in bed. If images like these entered your mind, read on. You are in for a big surprise.

Most old people live out their lives in the community with little or no assistance from others. Only one-fifth of the over-65 age group are sufficiently disabled that they cannot engage in their routine activities (Palmore, 1981). Five percent of people over 65 (and 20 percent of those over 80) live in nursing homes. The character of nursing homes is changing rapidly. Ten years ago, if you lived alone and functioned well but required help with a few things like grocery shopping, you very likely could have ended up in a nursing home. Today, home health care, residential facilities that provide mid-level care, and social service programs provide a continuum of services that enable most people to remain outside of institutions. Simultaneously, nursing homes have become more and more hospital-like, housing only the most frail elderly.

We hear a great deal these days about caregiving for the elderly. Close your eyes and picture a "caregiver." If the person you envisioned was not old, the person was not representative. Most of the caregivers for the elderly are elderly themselves. Wives almost always provide care for their husbands. And adult daughters, themselves often in their 60s and 70s, provide assistance to their mothers.

Among the working poor, grandmothers often function as the heads of households, providing childcare and household assistance. Grandmothers are also the most likely caregivers of many high-risk infants. And among the middle and upper classes, grandparents frequently provide financial assistance to adult children throughout life (Johnson, 1989).

A middle-aged daughter fixes the hair of her invalid mother.

OBSTACLES TO DAILY FUNCTIONING

The high level of functioning of most older people should not be taken as an indicator that problems do not exist. On the contrary, it is a testament to the tenacity, persistence, and love for autonomy that is so prevalent among the old.

When we are young, we cannot imagine not being able to bend over easily or trot across the street. As we grow older, we first experience subtle changes in our bodies and then may face increasing physical limitations. Getting on a bus may become impossible due to arthritis. Fears of slipping on the ice in the winter keep some elderly people housebound. Some gerontologists teach classes in which students put on glasses that impair vision, braces that impede mobility, and ear plugs that limit hearing. Then they go out for the day. The students invariably come to the realization that we live in a environment designed for the young and physically fit. Relatively simple modifications in public transportation, access, and lighting adequate for older people's vision could have profound effects on the quality of life for older people.

AGE AS A PREDICTOR OF CHANGE

In childhood, age is an excellent predictor of physical ability, intellectual functioning, and even social behavior. Age begins to lose its power as a predictor in adulthood, however, and by old age, it is quite poor. Suppose you are told that you will observe two individuals. One is 6 months old and the other is 80 years old. You could make some fairly good guesses about what the 6-month-old infant will be like—even about preferences and dislikes. But you will be hard-pressed to make similarly good guesses about an 80-year-old. No two individuals are ever identical. Aging is the **process of differentiation** (Figure 21-3).

Health status is far superior to age as a predictor of functioning. A longitudinal study conducted at Duke University found that the best predictors of successful aging were physical functioning and happiness. Sex, education, intelligence, and even age were uncorrelated (Palmore, 1979). Studies have also shown that symptoms of old age are mimicked in younger people who are

FIGURE 21-3
The Process of Differentiation

Although we could make generally accurate guesses about the physical, intellectual, and social abilities of 6-month-olds, we could not do so about 80-year-olds. Aging varies so much from one person to the next that only the broadest descriptive terms would apply to all 80-year-olds.

HEALTH AND DAILY FUNCTIONING

Some young-old skiers at a seniors' race (the 70+ class)

Creativity seems to increase in the final years of life. Grandma Moses began painting at age 70 and continued until her death at age 101.

confined to bed rest, suggesting that part of the aging phenomenon reflects disuse (Bortz, 1982).

Many speak of "old people" as if it were a meaningful category, as if people over 65 were a homogenous group. Keep in mind that the period of old age spans 30–40 years. People who are 65 are very different from people who are 85. Neugarten (1974) suggested that the elderly be divided into two groups: the "young-old" and the "old-old." The *young-old*, aged 55 to 75, have good health, relative economic security, and leisure time resulting from a decrease in traditional work and family responsibilities. The *old-old* are more likely to be frail and in ill health. More recently, researchers have suggested further delineation of the old into three groups: young-old, aged 60–74; old-old, aged 75–84; and *very-old*, aged 85 and older (Field & Minkler, 1988). The subclassifications of the elderly population reflect increasing awareness among researchers that classifying the last 30 years of life as one stage is grossly inadequate.

We generally think of age as the number of years since birth. Another way of thinking about age is time until death. In some ways, this reverse index of age is more revealing than chronological age. In the 1960s and 1970s, several researchers observed that a rapid decline in physical and intellectual performance occurs about five years before death (Jarvik & Falek, 1963; Kleemeier, 1962; Reigel & Reigel, 1972).

This phenomenon, called **terminal drop,** suggests that if a person is 80 years old and near death, he or she will perform more poorly on tasks than a person who is 80 but is going to live to be 90. There is some controversy about the timing and size of the decline. Botwinick, West, and Storandt (1978) found that slower response, slower learning and memory, depression, lessened sense of control, and lower self-rated health strongly indicate people who are going to die. It is an intriguing notion that one day we may be able to predict death from a change in intellectual and emotional functioning.

Not all abilities diminish before death. There is some evidence that creativity increases during the final years of life. Traditionally, the literature has suggested that, like intelligence, creativity increases until middle age (when our best work supposedly occurs) and then gradually declines until death. Dean Simonton, however, has found a fascinating connection between age and creative achievement in what he terms the *swan-song effect* (1986, 1989). Simonton had experts rate the works of great composers along several dimensions. He found evidence for declines in areas like productivity and melodic originality, but he found that the truly great masterpieces were likely to have been created near the end of the composer's life. The compositions he termed masterpieces were enormously popular and characterized by their esthetic significance. Simonton commented: "Composers in their final years seem to concentrate on producing masterworks that will permanently establish their reputation, doing so by creating works of a concise directness, as revealed by the brevity and melodic simplicity of their concluding pieces" (1989, p. 45). Simonton's work is an excellent example of the consequences of asking "What goes right?" in old age as opposed to "What goes wrong?"

RACE AND GENDER

Aging does not occur evenly across a population. As we have seen, men die earlier than women and are more susceptible to illness. Women live longer than men but they are much more likely to be poor and alone in old age. Some say being old and female presents a "double jeopardy" and for minority women a "triple jeopardy." If we add poverty to the list (minority groups are twice as likely to be poor in old age), we can safely bet that the golden years will not resemble the popular television show.

We have very limited information on minority elderly in this country. In fact, the diversity among ethnic groups limits the usefulness of the term *minority* (Fujii, 1980). In the United States, minorities include African-Americans, Pacific Asians, Hispanic/Latinos, native Americans, and Vietnamese, among many other groups. Their life-styles, health practices, and support systems are strikingly different from Caucasians and from one another. Thinking in terms of white and non-white is far too simplistic.

Jackson (1989) makes the excellent point that we need to know more about aging in minority cultures not only for practical reasons, but for scientific reasons as well. If we are ever to understand the true effects of aging, we must know what it looks like under all possible living conditions.

SOCIAL CHANGES

It is misleading to view the elderly as isolated and forlorn. They are not. Most old people live near their children and have regular contact with them (Shanas, 1979). But no one survives old age without loss. Deaths of friends and loved ones, loss of mobility through health impairment, and loss of many previously held roles occur for virtually every old person. By and large, the elderly show remarkable resilience through these losses. They seem to accept and cope well, even with losses that present considerable difficulty to younger people.

Retirement from work at the end of life, with its implications of leisure time, is a recent phenomenon. Previously, most people worked until they died or were too ill to continue. Now, with better health and more economic security, the retirement years represent an important phase of life. Some people look forward to them, whereas others dread their retirement years.

The people who most look forward to retirement have an adequate income and are not overinvolved with their work. Retirement is perceived as a chance to have fun and perhaps to practice a skill or hobby that work left little time for. People who dread retirement are those who have erratic work histories and so will not have enough funds for an adequate income after retirement. Incomes are generally halved upon retirement.

Professional people, or those who have a great deal invested in their work and derive much satisfaction from it, often keep working longer. Even after retirement they may continue to work part-time or consult. Most people's lives are structured by the demands of their jobs. Work provides an income and a satisfaction from a sense of having done something well, from practicing a skill, or from helping others. It also provides opportunities for social interaction and friendships. In retirement, people are removed from many of their previous social patterns and sources of satisfaction. Retired spouses tend to see a lot more of each other (which may or may not be a good thing).

For a long time, gerontologists believed that retirement presented a major crisis for older adults. Now it is clear that other factors like health and adequate income are at the root of problems. When both are satisfactory, retirement has almost no effect on well-being. Of course, this is *on average*. Some elderly may feel useless and regret the lack of responsibility of work. Others may have parents in their 80s and 90s who require a good deal of care and so they assume the role of caregiver. Still others assume major responsibility for raising their grandchildren, especially if their adult children are single parents. Among the working poor, grandmothers regularly assume the role of primary caregiver for their grandchildren. For others, retirement may mark the beginning of a new career.

SUPPORT FOR THE ELDERLY

Old age increases the risk of social isolation. Social isolation and disconnection increase susceptibility to disease in general. The death rates for people who are not socially stable are higher for all types of disease, including heart disease and cancer, and for infections and accidents. Perhaps changing the social world can improve health.

Berkman and Syme (1979) studied 7,000 residents of Alameda County in California over nine years to distinguish why some people get ill and die younger than others. Although most of the questions addressed smoking, physical exercise, eating habits, and history of disease, several questions asked how well the people were connected with others. They were asked about their marital status, how many close friends and relatives they had, how much contact they had with these people, and if they were members of community organizations.

Those who were single, widowed, or divorced; those with few close friends or relatives; and those who tended not to join or participate in community organizations died at a rate two to five times greater than those with more extensive social ties. This was true for men and women, old and young, rich and poor. The more social connectedness, the lower the death rate. Similar findings have since been reported by other investigators as well (Blazer, 1980).

FORMS OF SOCIAL SUPPORT

Social support appears to offer a stability that protects people in times of transition and stress. Losing a job, particularly when it is unanticipated, is understandably stressful and is associated with the development of subsequent illness. But not everyone gets ill when there is a recession or when a company folds.

Social support comes in many forms: intimate relationships with friends and family, casual contacts in the community, memberships in religious and other community organizations, and work relationships with bosses, employees, and co-workers (Figure 21-4). These relationships help the elderly in different ways. They can obtain emotional support, such as reassurance, empathy, and someone to rely on and to confide in, as well as the feeling that they are loved and cared about. They can be encouraged by others to adopt healthier behaviors: to stop smoking, eat regularly, exercise, take prescribed medications, or seek medical care. Friends can provide an invaluable source of information on how to do things, find a job, or locate services. Social support can be a source of money, goods, or services.

In a study of the degree of atherosclerosis of the coronary arteries, Seeman (1985) found that people who felt they had someone they could turn to for help, money, or support were the ones with less coronary artery disease. It is becoming clear that the expectation that someone will be there for us is important for our health and well-being across the life span (Antonucci, 1989; Antonucci & Jackson, 1987).

FIGURE 21-4
Social Support

Being part of a group, having a friend, or engaging in social interaction can provide a sense of belonging that can improve an elderly person's health and outlook on life.

711

Consider for a moment the strong and enduring relationships people cultivate with pets. Medical dogma paints a sad picture for pet owners. You can be bitten, scratched, or clawed; you can get rabies, ringworm, cat-scratch fever, or even a rare lung disease from parrots. Nevertheless, people persist in owning pets. Over one-half of American homes have one or more pets.

But now there is good news on the health front for pet owners. A study of victims of a heart attack one year later revealed that pet owners had one-fifth the death rate when compared with the petless. It didn't seem to matter what kind of pet the person owned. Since most people don't walk their fish, increased exercise doesn't account for the difference. It may have something to do with the sense of control and the sense of being needed experienced by pet owners. They may have an added incentive to survive in order to continue to care for their animal companions, who depend upon them (Fitzgerald, 1986; Friedman et al., 1980).

It is important to recognize that social contact is not necessarily supportive. Turbulent relationships can have very negative effects on well-being among the aged (Rook, 1984). Older people seem to prefer familiar longstanding relationships over novel, less predictable ones (Carstensen, 1987; Fredrickson & Carstensen, 1990).

Families provide a tremendous amount of support for older adults. Although we hear much more about attachment to parents during childhood, attachment to siblings also occurs. It appears that these close relationships, begun during our first years of life, assume great importance in the later years (Cicirelli, 1982; Troll, 1971). Having a close relationship with your sister in later life, whether you are male or female, is a good predictor of well-being (Cicirelli, 1989).

A COMPARISON WITH OTHER SOCIETIES

We know that males have a less-structured support system than females and that they suffer for it. What about different societies? If we compare people living in Japan with those in the United States, we find that both countries are highly industrialized, urbanized, polluted, and exhibit a fast pace of life. Yet Japan has the highest life expectancy in the world and one of the lowest rates of heart disease, only one-fifth the rate in the United States. Yet this low rate of heart disease seems to hold only for the Japanese who live in Japan. Those who migrate to Hawaii or California have much higher heart disease rates than those remaining in Japan. How can we explain these different death rates? Is it diet?

Apparently not. Marmot and colleagues (1975) studied Japanese immigrants in California who had low rates of heart disease similar to those who remained in Japan. They found that Japanese immigrants who maintained strong links to the traditional community had less heart disease. In spite of eating Western foods, having high serum cholesterol, smoking cigarettes, and having high blood pressures, those with close ties to the traditional Japanese community had rates of heart disease only one-fifth as high as those who adopted a Western pattern of social relationships.

Those with very low heart disease rates lived a traditional Japanese life. As children, they had lived in Japanese neighborhoods and had attended Japanese language schools. As adults, their friends were Japanese, and they identified with the Japanese community, visited Japanese doctors, and most often attended Japanese cultural events as well as Japanese political and social gatherings.

WIDOWHOOD

In the past, people of all ages had frequent contact with death. The death of infants was more common than not, and longer-lived people could expect to bury two or three spouses. However, in modern society we have much less experience with death. The death of a loved one at any age is a great loss for us. This is especially true for very young children whose parent dies or for parents who lose a child. But in this day and age, such tragedies are unusual. Not so for widowhood. The death of a spouse is something that husband or wife will almost certainly face.

Loss of a spouse after 50 or 60 years of marriage affects virtually every aspect of life. Identity may be so entwined with that of their spouse that they feel as if they have lost a part of themselves. "I feel as if half of myself is missing," said one widow, and another spoke of "a great emptiness" (Parkes, 1972). Many widowed men and women sense the presence of their spouse. They may actually feel that they have seen, heard, or spoken to their spouse. Nearly 50 percent of people in both a British sample (Morris, 1958) and a Welsh one (Rees, 1971) had such experiences. Yamamoto and his colleagues (1969) found this in 90 percent of their sample of 20 Japanese widows. Such experiences are most likely to occur to people who had happy marriages. Most found the experience helpful, although some were disturbed by "seeing" their spouse (Morris, 1974).

Widowhood is much more likely for women. Most women live longer than men and marry men older than themselves. If a woman marries a man 10 years older than herself, she stands an 80 percent chance of being widowed by age 55. Only 35 percent of women over 65 are married. Women are also much less likely than men to remarry in old age. Although some women say they would like to remarry, the majority say that they do not even consider it (Gentry & Shulman, 1988).

The stressful effect of losing a spouse is reflected in health and mortality statistics. The bereaved person's health generally deteriorates, along with loss of weight and sleeplessness, depression, and general irritability. The bereaved increase their use of tranquilizers, alcohol, and cigarettes, and they visit their physicians more often.

Some evidence shows that bereavement is harder on men than on women (Longino & Lipman, 1981). In a large-scale longitudinal study, widowed men had a lower survival rate than still-married men at every follow-up conducted over a 10-year period. There was no effect for women (Helsing et al., 1981). It appears that resistance to disease is impaired in men during bereavement. At Mt. Sinai Hospital, Steven Schleifer, Marvin Stein, and their colleagues conducted a fascinating prospective study of healthy men whose wives had terminal cancer (Schleifer et al., 1983). They measured immune system function in the husbands when their wives were still living and repeated their measurements up to 14 months after their wives had died. As predicted, immune system function significantly worsened during bereavement. It was the worst immediately after the wife died and over the course of a year returned to baseline levels.

In Chapter 2 you read that there are men's and women's marriages. There may be men's and women's widowhoods too. In older traditional marriages, women tend to prepare meals and often are the ones who encourage proper diet and health care. In addition, wives typically maintain the couple's social support network. A wife is more likely than a husband to plan the couple's social events. And women have more friends than men throughout adulthood. When a man loses his wife, he sometimes loses his entire social support network.

For women other factors make widowhood difficult. A widow's income often drops dramatically. As in divorce, the widow may be faced with learning new roles and skills formerly handled by her husband. She may, for the first time, have to face taking care of the car and managing the budget. The woman's social life changes less so than a man's, but—in a couple-oriented society—a widow may feel like the odd person out if she socializes with married friends. As a consequence, she may gradually lose contact with them. Many cultures place severe restrictions on widows (Lopata, 1979).

Most older people do adjust to the death of a spouse. In fact, one year following the death of a spouse many women report a newfound sense of competence and autonomy. Widowers, in contrast, are likely to remarry (George, 1981).

THE GRIEF OF WIDOWHOOD

Regardless of how well a person recovers, the period of grief is terribly difficult. Many aspects of the grief reaction are similar the world over (Glick et al., 1974). The initial reaction is one of shock and disbelief, especially if the death was unexpected. For many, the shock is so great that they feel numb. This prevents them from being overwhelmed by grief and allows them to carry on, at least briefly. But the numbness lasts only a few hours or days and gives way eventually to grief and despair. Lindemann (1944) describes the pangs of grief this way:

> The picture showed by persons in acute grief is remarkably uniform. Common to all is the following syndrome: sensations of somatic distress occurring in waves lasting from twenty minutes to an hour at a time. There is a feeling of tightness in the throat, choking with a shortness of breath, need for sighing, an empty feeling in the abdomen, lack of muscular power, and an intense subjective distress described as tension or mental pain.

While such intense mourning generally lasts only a few weeks, the effects of bereavement last much longer, including exhaustion, loss of appetite, and inability to initiate activity. Feelings of emptiness, guilt, apathy, hostility, and that life has no meaning are common. The person may feel unable to surrender the past. He or she may brood over memories or refuse to let go of possessions. The bereaved may have feelings of unreality. These characteristics are not pathological; they are *normal* reactions to bereavement, which can continue for months.

PSYCHOLOGICAL CHANGES

SOCIAL COGNITION AND OLD AGE

Older people fare remarkably well psychologically. A recent poll conducted by the *Los Angeles Times* (May 4, 1989) found that more than two-thirds of respondents over the age of 65 were very satisfied with the way things were going in their lives, whereas only half of the people between 18 and 49 reported being very satisfied. Compared to middle-aged adults, older people are also less lonely (Revenson, 1984) and less depressed (Bolla-Wilson & Bleecker, 1989). But if we ask young people what older people's lives seem to be like, they will usually paint a dismal picture.

Why do we believe old age is worse than it is? One reason has to do with the *availability heuristic* (Tversky & Kahneman, 1973). Recall from Chapters 10 and 19, that our minds are more likely influenced by the exceptional case than the prototypical. We forget that we passed 30 older people walking in the park, but we remember vividly the one old woman sitting in a wheelchair with her nurse. Later when we think about old age, we envision it as a time of extreme fragility.

Some scholars feel that we distance ourselves from the aged because they present powerful reminders of our own mortality and death. Others feel the age segregation is the cause of faulty stereotypes of the elderly. Retirement eliminates most old people from the workplace. And very few young people count among their friends many 80-year-olds. When younger people do have contact with older age groups, it is often in a helper role serving the very frail elderly. Outside of these circumstances, many young people have contact only with their grandparents or older relatives. Whether low contact is the cause or the result most of us seem to hold distorted images of the old and of old age.

EXPECTATIONS AND ATTITUDES ABOUT OLD AGE

I once watched a friend direct a film that had a part in it for a woman 65 years old. The actress engaged for the part was about 65. The director told her to act like a 65-year-old woman in the scene. Since she was one, she acted like she normally did. She smiled, almost leaped around the room, and walked with a spring in her step. This did not satisfy my friend. The woman was acting too young for him. Finally, because expensive time on the set was adding up, he got an idea. He told her, "Act like you are 110 years old." Then he got the effect he wanted.

Attitudes toward the old are best characterized as ambivalent (Lutsky, 1980). In some ways we observe the old adage "Respect your elders." Yet, at the same time we are paying our respects, we often experience a wave of pity, assuming that the old are feeble in mind and body. College students view older people as less satisfied, less decisive, more dependent, and poorly adjusted (Weinberger & Millham, 1975).

Younger people feel greater interpersonal distance from older people than from younger people (Kidwell & Booth, 1977), and a national survey found that younger people think of the elderly as bored and inactive (Harris, 1975). Some researchers find that older people themselves hold negative attitudes toward the elderly (Ward, 1977). This is very likely due to the fact that we form our attitudes about old age long before we grow old. Negative attitudes toward old people are seen in children as young as 5 (Weinberger, 1979). Then we become old ourselves. Prejudice against the old may have a uniquely harmful effect on self-concept; it is the only minority group that all of us eventually join.

Do these views affect us when we are old? It is reasonable to think that they do. When we hold beliefs about what people are like, we behave in ways that tend to confirm our beliefs (Snyder & Swann, 1978). If you believe that old people are frail and incompetent, you behave differently from someone who views older people as strong and wise. You will not go to an older person for advice, ask directions when you are lost, or ask for help in solving a problem. Since you don't ask, you never get the chance to hear or see the answer. And in the absence of evidence to the contrary, you continue to believe that older people are not very competent. A person who holds the opposite view will behave differently and thereby confirm his or her own view.

DEPENDENCE

By looking at the social context of older nursing home residents, Margret Baltes completely changed the common view of nursing home residents as being dependent "by nature." Rather, she found that the residents became *conditioned* to be **dependent.** Observing the behavior of nursing home residents and staff during the mornings when residents were getting up, dressing, and eating breakfast, her assistants recorded what each resident did and what the staff member did, in turn. They noted that the only time residents got attention from the staff (smiles, conversation, encouragement) was when they needed assistance. Thus, the more independent residents were, the less social contact they received. She and her colleagues have replicated the results in many nursing homes in both Germany and the United States (Baltes, Kindermann, Reisenzein, & Schmid, 1987; Baltes & Werner-Wahl, 1987; Barton, Baltes, & Orzech, 1980).

MINDFULNESS

Ellen Langer (1989) maintains that young and old alike hold grossly oversimplified mindsets about aging. Essentially, we believe that senility and incompetence, if not already present in an elderly person, are just around the corner. Mindsets, according to Langer, lead to mindlessness—that is, unquestioning actions and thoughts that limit all sorts of possibilities. Young people who hold these mindsets treat old people as if they were feeble, even if they are not. Perhaps even more dangerous is that older people may come to treat themselves as if they were frail and feeble.

SELF-EFFICACY AND COGNITIVE AGING

Our beliefs about our abilities to solve problems have a clear effect on our ability to solve them—at any age (Bandura, 1977; Bandura & Wood, 1989; Wood & Bandura, 1989). If you cannot think of a word you are searching for (something that happens to people of all ages) and you are old, you may get frustrated and stop trying, irritated that the aging process had gotten the best of you. Were you 20 years younger (and believed firmly that the word would come to you), you would continue to search until you thought of it. You can see how this can lead to a vicious cycle. Our best cognitive efforts occur when we are maximally motivated. Beliefs that aging undermines our competence can do just that; it is not aging per se that undermines competence, it is the *belief* that aging undermines competence.

THE IMPORTANCE OF CONTROL

Rodin (1986) notes that the connection between health and sense of control is strong in the elderly. She gives three reasons why this should be so. First, **control** is important to older people because they seek to organize their lives more than do the young. Second, the physiological changes of the aging process, such as alterations of the immune system, make psychological effects more potent. Third, since the elderly pay more conscious attention to health, the influence of directed behaviors (such as seeing the physician) is much greater.

Rodin cites much of the evidence covered in this and the previous chapters that enhancements of social support, self-efficacy, hardiness, and the attainment of a sense of coherence can have striking effects on health. In one of her own studies, Rodin and Langer (1977) simply gave plants to the elderly in nursing homes. Some were asked to take care of their own plants, whereas others were told that the staff would be responsible for the plant care. She found that the residents who were directly responsible for their plants were significantly happier, more alert, and spent more time interacting with others.

A follow-up study showed that in a given period the responsibility-induced group was healthier than the comparison group and that less than half as many of the responsibility-induced group died. Rodin feels that psychological interventions (if the need for self-determination is taken into account) can greatly enhance the lives of the elderly (Rodin, 1986).

Research on the study of social support, control, aging, and health is a good example of how psychology is beginning to integrate the work of its subgroups. Here, research on the mind, health psychology, and adult development come together.

CHANGES IN COGNITION

INTELLIGENCE

If we were to take a cross-section of people aged 20, 40, 60, and 80, we would find that IQ scores are lower in the older groups. From this information, we might be tempted to conclude that people lose cognitive function after age 20. However, this conclusion would not take into account that, in this century, each successive generation has been better educated.

Education is a major factor in IQ scores. Recall our discussion of cohort effect at the beginning of the chapter. The apparent decline in intelligence among the age groups is due to *historical* rather than *aging* factors. On average, young people have more formal education than old people, and subsequently perform better on IQ tests. Sometimes historical factors work in favor of older adults. A recent report of age differences in mathematical ability suggests that 60-year-olds now outperform 20-year-olds (Schaie, 1989). Again it is doubtful that this finding means that our mathematical skills continue to improve into the sixth decade. Rather, it more likely reflects an overreliance of the young on computers to the point where they perform poorly on problems requiring mental calculations.

Longitudinal studies attempt to control for this problem. A group or panel is selected and studied over a number of years or decades. In contrast to the earlier conclusion about IQs, data from longitudinal studies show *increases* in IQ scores with age—that we *gain* cognitive function after age 20. However, longitudinal studies also have a problem: the **survivor effect.** People who are more intelligent and better educated tend to live longer and to continue as participants in longitudinal studies. So the survivors in longitudinal studies make it appear as if intelligence increases.

What actually does happen to our intellectual capacity as we age? There appears to be very little actual change, at least not until very late in life. Verbal abilities, or **crystallized intelligence,** seem to remain relatively constant or to increase slightly with age. **Fluid intelligence,** or measures of performance, decline. However, these declines are often not found before age 50 or 60, and even then they are relatively small (Botwinick, 1977). Schaie recently reported findings based on a longitudinal study that 60 percent of the participants experienced no decline in cognitive functioning even when assessed at age 80 (Schaie, 1989).

Encouraging results from brain physiology show that the cortex of the brain in older rats can *increase* in size if they are put in an enriched environment that has a lot of sensory stimulation and activities that the rats can engage in. So the brain continues to adapt and develop throughout life depending on the environment. Thus, the elderly in bland institutional settings seem disoriented or confused, whereas the elderly justices of the Supreme Court—most of whom are in their 70s and 80s—may be at the height of their mental abilities. As Diamond (1984) reminds us, "Use it or lose it."

Recent research has demonstrated a diminishing of cognitive abilities, long thought to be normal, can be reversed with practice (Baltes & Lindenberger, 1988; Schaie & Willis, 1986). Improvement has been shown in spatial abilities (Baltes, Sowarka, & Kliegl, 1989; Willis & Schaie, 1986) and inductive reasoning (Willis & Schaie, 1986). This line of research forces us to question whether the psychological changes observed over the years are due to the *aging process* or to *disuse.*

MEMORY

We may, however, become more forgetful as we age. Older people tend to take longer to learn new things. They seem to learn them in a less organized fashion, which makes retrieval difficult (Poon, 1985). Again, this finding may in part be a function of educational or the cohort effect rather than age differences. Elders with good verbal skills often do not show many decrements in secondary memory with age (Bowles & Poon, 1982). Still, older adults report more memory problems than younger ones, especially when doing things out of their normal daily routine or when they need to remember information not used recently (Cavanaugh, Grady, & Perlmutter, 1983).

Many different theories exist of why memory declines with age. The loss of neurons (Kinsbourne, 1980), or damage to the frontal cortex (Albert & Kaplan, 1980) could account for memory decline. Botwinick et al. (1980) assert the reason may be that neurological processes slow with age. Because memory is often time dependent, this general slowing may account for many of the cognitive deficits found in the elderly. Memory declines can also be reversed by teaching elders *mnemonics,* or memory aids (Poon et al., 1980; Yeasavage, Rose, & Spiegel, 1982).

PERSONALITY

Traditionally, personality theorists have believed that personality alters in old age. Jung believed that in late life people compensate for those aspects of their personality that were neglected in the first half. Men begin to express the more feminine, or nurturant and receptive, tendencies, and women begin to express the more masculine, or aggressive and dominant, aspects. Guttmann (1987) has reported that males across very different cultures become less active and more cognitive (or magical) in their coping responses. Neugarten (1977) described old age as a period of decreasing extraversion. Stage theorists also view later life as organized around discrete crises that arise and subsequently change the individual (Gould, 1978; Levinson et al., 1978.) For many, the crisis is approaching and adjusting to retirement. Lowenthal, Thurnher, and Chiriboga (1975) noted:

> The preretired men are mellow—and significantly less dissatisfied and unhappy—compared to men at earlier stages. . . . They see themselves as less hostile and more reasonable. They feel less ambitious but also less restless than any of the younger men. Unlike the middle-aged, they do not seem to feel the need to control others or to drive themselves. Rather, they manifest a concern for warm interpersonal relations. . . . In sum, the preretired men seem the group most comfortable, not only with others, but with themselves as well.

Most of the work inspired by stage theories has focused on men's lives. Women may age differently. Rather than becoming more passive and accepting, women sometimes shift toward more assertive and independent styles. Again, borrowing from Lowenthal et al. (1975):

> It is in the preretirement stage that women seem finally to hit their stride. The problems with competence, independence and interpersonal relations . . . appear resolved. The preretired women see themselves as less dependent and helpless and as more assertive: "I don't have the fears and tragedies that I had when I was younger. I can say what I feel, I am not embarrassed by many things any more, and my personality is better."

Instead of retiring, many women are just returning to the workforce in middle age and continue to work during old age. Precipitants may include children leaving home, reduced income following their husband's retirement, or

widowhood. Recall that for women, late life frequently involves widowhood. Many women return to the workforce out of financial need.

Certainly lives change in old age. But do these changes result in change in personality? The evidence here is mixed. Based on large cross-sectional and longitudinal studies that use personality inventories to assess change, Costa and McCrae (1984; Costa et al., 1986) contend that *stability* in personality is so striking that the interesting question is not how it changes, but how people live through so many life changes and maintain a consistent personality. Others argue that personality inventories are not sufficiently sensitive to tap the changes that occur with aging. Studies that rely on interviews provide some evidence for change (Haan, Millsap, & Hartka, 1986).

DEATH AND DYING

There are some inescapable facts of life that everyone faces in late adulthood. Bereavement and grief are a part of this phase of life. Just before death, we decline, although we might cling to life for a while. We may want to reach another birthday or to live to see an important date, such as a fiftieth wedding anniversary. Everyone dies and yet, until recently, research on death has been as taboo as research on sex. The early evidence indicates that people go through a series of stages of dying, and it is not all that unpleasant.

The death of others close to us remind us of our own mortality. Everyone goes through specific life stages, from the egg, embryo, and fetus, to the infant, the child, the adolescent, and finally, the adult. These periods are marked by specific maturational changes. Adulthood is less dominated by biology, as conscious choices determine how our adulthood develops. But we are never free of our physical constraints. As the end of life approaches, the last state is biological and is common to us all.

You have probably been told many times what you need to do to be a successful adult. How-to books abound that provide tips about raising children, making your marriage work, and succeeding in your chosen career. Precious few tell us how to succeed at growing old.

Until recently, planning for very old age was not a problem. Most people did not grow old—they died. Death was a common part of life at every age. Accidents, disease, and epidemics claimed lives at every point in the life span. In 1900, mothers expected half of their children to die before the age of 5.

Babies born in this country today can expect to live into old age. Many young people say that they don't want to get old. Why would they want to live to be 90? they ask. Whatever the answer, know that their opinion might be different at 89. The tremendous variability in the way people age tells us with no uncertainty that our behavior and environment when we are young will have consequences when we are old.

Physical health is undeniably the best predictor of happiness in old age. And don't think for a minute that luck and genetics will determine yours. If you are a heavy drinker, and you love to meet new people, you're in luck because you probably won't remember much from one day to the next. If you smoke, stop.

If you never exercise, you may feel like an old person already. The effects of physical disuse mimic normal aging. But don't go overboard either. If you jog 20 miles a day, you may want to rethink your exercise plan. Joints last only so long; take care of them.

Contrary to folk wisdom, if you've got your health, you don't have everything. One of the most precious things in old age are old friends. So take care of your friendships. Someday being able to talk to a friend from the days when the Berlin Wall was being torn down will bring immense pleasure. Women should know that they are at greater risk for being alone in old age than men. The prototypical heterosexual woman will outlive her husband by 15 years. Be prepared. Maybe you could form a household with three old friends in a house on the coast of Maine, . . . or maybe you can think of a even better plan.

But do think about old age. Many people find it the best time in life. The worst thing you can do is to deny that you will grow old. There's only one alternative.

THE YEARS BEFORE DEATH

Most people believe, somehow, that death is something that happens to others, not to them. But in late age, unavoidable events remind us of our own mortality. Parents and friends may die, our health may deteriorate, and so on. We may begin to think in terms of how many years we have left to live rather than how many years we have already lived (Neugarten, 1964).

The effect of psychological and personal processes on health and mortality in the elderly should not be underestimated. Kastenbaum and his colleagues have done a series of studies on raising the morale on geriatric wards in hospitals (Kastenbaum, 1965). Even beer and wine parties for patients and staff have a remarkable effect. They improve both the morale of the staff and the physiological and psychological well-being in the elderly. They even affect the severely impaired. On one "hopeless" ward, elderly who had gross impairment showed marked gains, such as reduced incontinence.

There is also some clinical and anecdotal evidence that psychological factors can affect the timing of a person's death. The person can die prematurely—apparently losing the will to live" (Pattison, 1977)—or postpone death until a special occasion. Statistically, there are fewer deaths before birthdays, before presidential elections, and before important holidays (Phillips & Feldman, 1973). They concluded that this **anniversary effect** results from a person postponing death.

An important study defined five stages that a dying person goes through. We should not think of these as necessarily sequential, rather that they reflect common characteristics of the terminally ill (Kübler-Ross, 1969, 1975).

The first stage is **denial and isolation.** This may function positively to keep the person from being overwhelmed with grief and to maintain hope. The second stage, **anger,** is a natural reaction to disrupted plans and loss of personal control. It is also an individual's way of asserting that he or she is still alive. In the third stage, the person may **bargain with fate**—that is, he or she may offer to devote the remaining life to God in exchange for a little more time. **Depression,** the fourth stage, is an understandable reaction to increasing debilitation. It may include the tremendous financial burden of hospitalization and fear of losing loved ones. A dying person may sometimes be unable to communicate with his or her family or may feel rejected by them. In the final stage, the person **accepts** impending death. This is sometimes aided by religious faith or by the understanding that he or she has lived a full and meaningful life. Kübler-Ross believes that if an individual has accepted his or her death, it is easier to die in peace and dignity.

While acknowledging the importance of Kübler-Ross's work, some researchers caution against a too-literal interpretation (Kastenbaum, 1977). They point out that these stages are not sequential. A person may go from anger to denial to hope to fear, and so on. There are many questions not addressed. For example, what factors affect the way a person handles death? Are age, type of illness, and setting important? Are there personality, sex, or ethnic differences? We know that people do not all die in the same manner. Hinton (1967) found that about half of his sample of patients openly acknowledged and accepted their deaths, but only one-quarter showed a high degree of acceptance and composure. Another one-quarter expressed distress, and the remainder said very little about it.

So, at the end, our biology reclaims us once again, quietly and pleasantly. It completes the story begun before we were born.

SUMMARY

1. The demarcation of entrance to old age at 65 is arbitrary. In fact, the differences between old and young people become evident only over time. Chronological age is not a good predictor of well-being in old age. With age, the heterogeneity of the population increases.

2. *Cohort effects* refer to the effects of growing up in a particular historical era. *Age effects* are assumed to reflect the aging over time.

3. Although more than 20 theories of aging have been proposed, we do not know why we age. The *programmed senescence* theory of aging is the most widely accepted today. According to this theory, human cells are programmed to replicate only 50 times.

4. *Life expectancy* refers to the average number of years we can expect to live from birth under average conditions. *Maximal life span* refers to the number of years we can live

under optimal conditions. The gain in life expectancy since the turn of the century is due primarily to reductions in infant mortality, not to an extension of life in old age.

5. *Normal aging* refers to changes that occur to most people and are assumed to be inevitably linked to the aging process. *Abnormal aging* refers to changes caused by disease processes that are more common in old age. Normal age-related changes are quite small, but most people experience some type of chronic disease process in their later years, so it is difficult to differentiate the two.

6. Our social and physical environments early in life influence how we age. Personal habits (like exercise and drug use) and structural factors (like socioeconomic status, gender, and race) lead to very different outcomes in old age.

7. As people age, their friends tend to age, and older people begin to have more contact with death and dying. Most women live longer than men and marry men older than themselves; thus they have a much higher chance of being widowed than men do. Widowhood is quite different for women than for men. Women face financial hardships and sometimes must learn new roles that their mates once filled. For men, the loss of a wife often leads to abrupt changes in emotional and social support. Widowhood results in marked increases in mortality in men but not in women.

8. *Social support* is an excellent predictor of psychological well-being, morbidity, and mortality in old age. Social support can come in the form of relationships with friends, family, community, church, work, or even pets. Comparative studies show that Japanese migrants who have maintained close ties with the traditional Japanese community have less heart disease than those who have adopted Western ways.

9. Young people tend to view older people as more impaired than they really are. Recent studies show that older people are independent and in remarkably good mental health. They are less lonely and depressed than younger people. Erroneous myths and beliefs about aging can affect the behavior of young and old alike.

10. Changes in intellectual functioning, though small, do occur in many people. Most prominent are changes in *fluid intelligence,* the processing of new information; least prominent are changes in *crystallized intelligence,* acquired knowledge and facts. There is tremendous variability in the onset and the amount of these changes. Many people show no changes in intelligence even into their eighth decade. Changes are most pronounced shortly before death. This period is known as *terminal drop.*

11. Debate surrounds changes in personality with age. Some gerontologists feel that late life crises, like retirement or widowhood, bring about personality change. Longitudinal studies based on the repeated administration of personality inventories show little, if any, change in the personality structure.

12. Kübler-Ross's theory describes five stages that a dying person goes through: *denial and isolation,* which may function positively to keep the person from being overwhelmed with grief; *anger,* a natural reaction to disrupted plans and loss of personal control; trying to *bargain with fate; depression;* and finally, for some people, *acceptance* of impending death. These stages are not sequential, but they do reflect common characteristics of the terminally ill. There are also tentative reports that while the dying process may be painful or distressing, the experience of death may actually be quite pleasant.

TERMS AND CONCEPTS

abnormal aging
acceptance
anger
anniversary effect
autoantibodies
bargain with fate
climacteric
cohort effects
control
crystallized intelligence
denial and isolation
dependence
depression
fluid intelligence
gerontology
kyphosis

life-expectancy
life-span development
longitudinal studies
maximal life-span
menopause
mindfulness
normal aging
presbycusis
presbyopia
process of differentiation
programmed senescence theory of
  aging
retirement
social support
survivor effect
terminal drop

SUGGESTIONS FOR FURTHER READING

Blythe, R. (1979). *The view in winter: Reflections on old age.* New York: Harcourt Brace Jovanovich.

How people see themselves as they age, in their own words. Wonderful reading.

Erikson, E., Erikson, J., & Kivnick, H. (1986). *Vital involvement in old age.* New York: Norton.

The most recent book by this eminent psychologist about enhancing older age.

Langer, E. (1989). *Mindfulness.* Reading, MA: Addison-Wesley.

A fascinating look at the problems of nonthinking behavior and the insights and advantages of questioning our worlds.

Rowe, J. W., & Kahn, R. L. (1987). Human aging: Usual and successful. *Science, 237,* 143–149.

An excellent critique of the research on normal aging, pointing out that much of what is typical is not inevitable.

Skinner, B. F., & Vaughn, M. E. (1983). *Enjoy old age: A program of self-management.* New York: Norton.

A practical guide to designing our life and environment to limit the impact of age declines, written by the distinguished behaviorist himself.

STATISTICS: MAKING SENSE OF FALLIBLE DATA

GEOFFREY IVERSON

INTRODUCTION

Take a long hard look at the world. Try to describe what you see—all of it, as precisely, as completely as you can.

You will soon give up in frustration. There is just too much going on, too much detail, too much change, too much that appears arbitrary. No two peas, no two people, no two pearls are exactly alike. Sometimes dogs chase cats, sometimes they do not.

Fortunately, we spend little time bogged down in this mire of detail. The world, as it actually is, as it really occurs, is something we hardly notice. Individual detail is sacrificed for lucidity; attention is confined to trends, tendencies, and regularities.

Suppose you want to describe (in a precise way) the direction that the wind is blowing. You know the importance of this if you have ever gone sailing. For gauging wind direction, a small flag or wind sock is usually used. Despite the fact that the flag never stays put and is never in exactly the same position twice, it serves well as a directional indicator. We see constancy in its motion that is unaffected by irregular, moment-to-moment fluctuations. Such regularity emerges in our eyes almost automatically, a useful end-product of visual processing and short-term memory. No conscious calculations are involved and none are needed.

We have inherited an amazingly powerful and flexible visual system that, as long as our eyes are open, provides us with the information needed to navigate our way successfully through a world seething with inconsequential detail. How do we extract stability from the irregular, unpredictable motion of a flag? This question is for the psychophysicists and physiologists. But here we are asking a different, less specific question—one that does not require a knowledge of vision: How can we describe things so as to reveal, on a piece of paper, the hidden regularity in "fallible" (that is, variable) data?

Suppose we can measure the direction of the tip of the flag at any designated time. We might take a movie of the flag—a sequence of still shots, each of which yields an instantaneous measurement. Let us record these measurements as compass direction, that is, in degrees with respect to the fixed direction north (Figure 1).

We have recorded 20 such measurements as they occur in our movie, frame by frame. These are given in Table 1. But there is no simple, unitary direction of wind peering up at us from Table 1, just a bunch of different numbers. Perhaps a graph would help to visualize the data better. In Figure 2 the measurements of Table 1 are plotted as flag positions for each movie frame number. This graph is a history of the flag position over time, exactly as it was recorded in the sequence of movie frames.

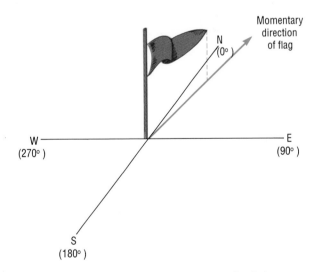

FIGURE 1 Direction of flag (degrees of compass direction)

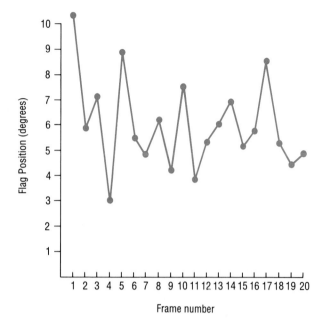

FIGURE 2 Motion of a flag depicted graphically (based on data from Table 1)

Does Figure 2 remind you of anything? If you have any interest in the stock market, it might occur to you that the graph of Figure 2 looks like the Dow-Jones industrial average. To make this analogy clearer, in Figure 3 we have plotted typical Dow-Jones averages for a typical week. Although the units in Figures 2 and 3 are

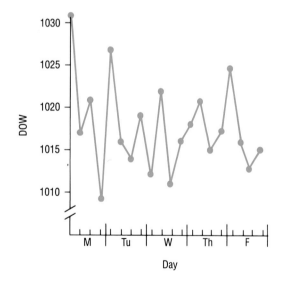

FIGURE 3 Hypothetical weekly record of Dow-Jones industrial average (based on data from Figure 2)

FIGURE 4 A visual representation of data from Table 1
Figure 4 (Source: Table 1)

different (Figure 2 plots position, while Figure 3 plots the Dow-Jones index), the appearance of each figure is essentially the same. If one graph is clear, can we understand the other in the same way? Note that in Figure 3 each day's trading has been divided into four separate values, taken in succession: an opening figure, a morning figure, an afternoon figure, and a closing figure.

Here is a description of Figure 3 in terms of events on Wall Street. In a run that showed only a minor correction after lunch, the Dow dropped 22 points on Monday. A rally early on Tuesday was not sustained, though by Tuesday's close there was a hint of recovery. This promise persisted, somewhat nervously, through Wednesday and Thursday, but on Friday the market began to slide again. By the week's end, the Dow had dropped 16 points altogether.

Can we profit from this blow-by-blow description of the stock market in gauging wind direction? I suggest not. There ought to be a better way of visualizing the data of Table 1 than that conveyed by Figure 2. So let's try another way of representing the data. Figure 4 shows each of the 20 measurements given in Table 1 by a cross (x) on a line.

The picture is easy to interpret. While the x's are scattered, this scatter is limited to about a 7° range (3° to about 10°). Moreover, there is a marked concentration of crosses between 4° and 6°. So we can generalize the data in the following way: the wind direction is approximately 5° east of north.

However, Figure 4 is not visually pleasing. Perhaps we can achieve a more pleasing representation of the data by sacrificing unnecessary precision. We therefore round the measurements of Table 1 to the nearest whole degree. Thus, the first measurement, 10.2°, becomes

Movie frame	1	2	3	4	5	6	7	8	9	10
Direction of flag (degrees)	10.2	5.8	7.1	3.0	8.9	5.4	4.8	6.2	4.1	7.4
Movie frame	11	12	13	14	15	16	17	18	19	20
Direction of flag (degrees)	3.8	5.3	6.0	6.9	5.1	5.7	8.3	5.2	4.3	4.9

TABLE 1 Twenty instantaneous measurements of flag direction

Frame number	1	2	3	4	5	6	7	8	9	10
Direction	10	6	7	3	9	5	5	6	4	7
Frame number	11	12	13	14	15	16	17	18	19	20
Direction	4	5	6	7	5	6	8	5	4	5

TABLE 2 Data of Table 1 rounded to nearest whole number

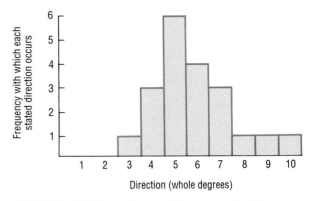

FIGURE 5 A histogram showing the frequency with which each direction occurs in Table 2

10°; the next, 5.8°, becomes 6°; and so on. In this way we obtain the list of rounded measurements shown in Table 2.

Many of the measurements are now identical. This suggests the following strategy: count the number of times each of the rounded measurements occurs in Table 2 and record these counts in a new table (like taking an inventory), as has been done in Table 3. This inventory allows a simple, elegant picture to emerge in the alternative visual form of a bar graph, or *histogram* (Figure 5). The first 20 measurements of wind direction combine into a visual form that displays their regularity. Like vision and our other senses, this regularity was achieved by excluding detail. *Thus, statistics is similar in principle to the kind of simplication processes the mind performs.*

The process we just went through is a rudimentary example of a *statistical analysis*. This is a process of organizing evidence, typically numerical, so as to reveal tendencies, trends, regularities, and so on that are often present in collections of measurements but that are quite difficult, even impossible, to detect in any individual measurement.

A major benefit of a statistical description of data is the simple, clear picture that often emerges. The forest is emphasized at the expense of the individual trees. Should we always analyze information this way? We rejected the "Wall Street" description of the motion of a flag in favor of the simplicity manifested in a histogram. Should we then use a histogram to describe the Dow-Jones fluctuations?

A full answer is complicated, and we content ourselves with a simple "no." To appreciate the difference between the stock market and a piece of cloth flapping in a steady breeze, we need to free ourselves from the shackles of mechanical habit, of blindly following a

recipe. The recipe, "construct a histogram," applied to the data of Figure 2, leads to the highly interpretable representation of Figure 5. If applied to the similar data of Figure 3, it would lead to a similar picture, but one that most stock market analysts would label as worthless.

There seems to be a paradox here. To resolve it, let us examine in more detail what one preserves in a histogram, and more important, what one throws away.

It is useful to go back to the source of our data, namely, a movie, a sequence of individual photographs, each of which gives rise to an individual measurement. Suppose we ran our movie backward. Would the average wind direction change? Of course not. Even more drastically, suppose we arbitrarily shuffled the order of the frames that make up our movie, thereby creating a new one. Would the average wind direction change? Again, the answer is no. While the momentary fluctuations of the flag are different for each of the (roughly) 2.4 billion movies that could be created by shuffling the order of 20 individual frames, the histogram and estimate of average wind direction accompanying each such movie would remain exactly the same.

But this is not so for the stock market descriptions. Taking into account the *sequence* of events in the stock market is of indisputable importance for deciding when to buy and when to sell. Similar considerations of order are irrelevant when one is out sailing. Thus, to follow the recipe, "construct a histogram," is to assume that *the order of measurements is irrelevant* to the object or system under study. We do not usually care if a big cloud follows a little one, or vice versa; only that it might rain. But we behave and feel very differently if the prime lending rate is on the increase rather than on the decline.

In psychology, as in any science, we place a premium on "stable," replicable measurements. Is there any

Direction	1	2	3	4	5	6	7	8	9	10
Frequency	0	0	1	3	6	4	3	1	1	1

TABLE 3 Frequency with which each direction occurs in Table 2

reason to distinguish between the abilities of two students who in a course receive respective homework grades of A, B, B, C, A, B, B, B, C and C, B, B, A, B, B, A, C, B? Each student's performance would be characterized by the same histogram, and each averages to a solid B.

This is not to say that people do not learn, do not change their behavior, do not adopt new habits—of course they do. But to understand learning or to measure a behavior change requires us to calibrate "before and after" learning or change. Those "before and after" measurements are critical, because it is through comparison (just as with the senses) that we detect change or recognize that learning has taken place. Statistics is used for the *description* of stable, practical measurement, but just as important is its related role in *detecting change.*

The question "Has the wind changed?" requires *statistical inference.* However, at least in some circumstances, the issue may not be settled with the mere detection of change. If the wind changes direction by 1°, do we (usually) care? What we do with the outcome of a statistical analysis, what actions we take, is an issue for *decision theory.* Decision theory is still in its infancy, and we will not say much about it here.

In summary, statistics divides into three major areas: *descriptive statistics, statistical inference,* and *decision theory.* These form a hierarchy in which issues that are unresolved at one level become the dominant focus at the next.

DESCRIPTIVE STATISTICS

The purpose of descriptive statistics is to *accurately* represent a set of observations of the world in as condensed a form as seems appropriate. Weather reports, the Dow-Jones average, baseball "stats," grade point averages, IQs, and Nielsen ratings are all examples of the use of descriptive statistics.

Condensing a large set of measurements of facts without destroying their collective integrity is termed *data reduction.* It is characterized by a number of useful procedures, called *algorithms,* of wide applicability. We have already seen one of the most widely used algorithms—"form a histogram." However, blind application of this algorithm may lead nowhere, or worse, to potential misrepresentation. Yet a sensitive, informed descriptive analysis can be of great power and beauty. A good description often allows data to "speak for themselves."

A common form of data reduction is supplied by a *table.* Baseball statistics are usefully represented in this form. Tables are very desirable devices for collecting information related to some specific issue. The visual format of a sensibly organized table allows the eye to quickly pick out clusters of related information that might otherwise go unnoticed. Indeed, important questions and hypotheses often emerge from a scrutiny of tabulated information.

Tables are most commonly used to list categories of some focus of interest; for example, diseases and other causes of death are listed in a historically interesting table from the year 1632 (Table 4). Typically, numerical information accompanies each category; for instance, we see from Table 4 that 62 Londoners died "suddenly" (perhaps by a heart attack?), while 46 were "kil'd by several accidents."

The algorithms "form a table" and "form a bar graph" are sometimes equivalent. For example, there is no more (nor less) information in Table 3 than in the histogram of Figure 5. However, it would not be natural nor helpful to represent a grocery list (with prices) as a bar graph. (If you are not sure why, try it.)

In many applications, categories are artificially formed by grouping measurements (of a single entity) that fall into a narrow range, *bin,* or *interval* of values. Rounding measurements creates categories in this manner (recall the transition from Table 1 to Table 3). When

The Diseases, and Casualties this year being 1632.

Abortive, and Stillborn	445	Grief	11
Affrighted	1	Jaundies	43
Aged	628	Jawfaln	8
Ague	43	Impostume	74
Apoplex, and Meagrom	17	Kil'd by several accidents	46
Bit with a mad dog	1	King's Evil	38
Bleeding	3	Lethargic	2
Bloody flux, scowring, and flux	348	Livergrown	87
Brused, Issues, sores, and ulcers	28	Lunatique	5
Burnt, and Scalded	5	Made away themselves	15
Burst, and Rupture	9	Measles	80
Cancer, and Wolf	10	Murthered	7
Canker	1	Over-laid, and starved at nurse	7
Childbed	171	Palsio	25
Chrisomes, and Infants	2268	Piles	1
Cold, and Cough	55	Plague	8
Colick, Stone, and Strangury	56	Planet	13
Consumption	1797	Pleurisie, and Spleen	36
Convulsion	241	Purples, and spotted Feaver	38
Cut of the Stone	5	Quinsie	7
Dead in the street, and starved	6	Rising of the Lights	98
Dropsie, and Swelling	267	Sciatica	1
Drowned	34	Scurvey, and Itch	9
Executed, and prest to death	18	Suddenly	62
Falling Sickness	7	Surfet	86
Fever	1108	Swine Pox	6
Fistula	13	Teeth	470
Flocks, and small Pox	531	Thrush, and Sore mouth	40
French Pox	12	Tympany	13
Gangrene	5	Tissick	34
Gout	4	Vomiting	1
		Worms	27

	Males	4994			Males	4932	Whereof,
Christened	Females	4590	Buried		Females	4603	of the
	In all	9584			In all	9535	Plague.8

Increased in the Burials in the 122 Parishes, and at the Pesthouse this year 993
Decreased of the Plague in the 122 Parishes, and at the Pesthouse this year 266

TABLE 4 A mortality table for the year 1632 in London. (Source: John Graunt, "Natural and Political Observations made upon the Bills of Mortality," 1662)

STATISTICS: MAKING SENSE OF FALLIBLE DATA

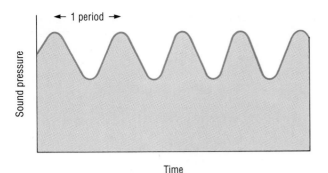

FIGURE 6   According to physics, a representation of a pure tone

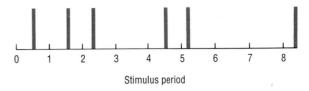

Stimulus period

FIGURE 7   Neural responses to a pure tone

categories of a single quantity, such as wind direction, reaction time, height, or weight, are involved, a histogram is often preferred to a table (compare Table 3 with the visual clarity of Figure 5). Our next example, which requires some preamble, is a beautiful illustration of the power of a well-constructed histogram.

As you know, the nervous system is composed of billions of neurons grouped into bundles according to function. Information is transmitted by these neurons both electrically and chemically. The easiest, most direct way to measure the activity of neurons is to do it electrically. Not surprisingly, recordings of neural events (action potentials, or "spikes") from a single cell are of great importance in neurophysiology. It is possible to record the activity induced in a primary auditory neuron by an externally applied tone of fixed frequency and intensity.

Our ability to hear, particularly, to distinguish one sound from another, strongly suggests that the nervous activity induced by physical sound is a sort of "code," a running record of those aspects of a physical stimulus that are crucial for its recognition and eventual meaning. Physiologists spend a good deal of effort attempting to decode neural activity, especially the activity produced in response to simple stimuli such as pure tones. To a physicist, however, a tone is an undulating pressure wave, as depicted in Figure 6. An obvious feature of a tone is its *period*, the time between two consecutive peaks of physical pressure.

The question naturally arises: is periodicity present in the activity of a single auditory neuron? The answer is "yes," but this is not obvious at first glance. A spike train recorded in response to a tone looks something like that depicted in Figure 7. Disappointingly, no semblance of periodic behavior is apparent, even though it is present. The way to see it is to form an *interval histogram*, that is, an inventory of intervals between successive spikes. (Presenting a tone over and over again allows the

inventory to grow arbitrarily large.) Such a histogram is displayed in Figure 8. The intervals between neural spikes are clustered at precise multiples of the stimulus period. In other words, each cluster is separated by exactly one stimulus period. The activity of a single auditory neuron is locked in synchrony with the stimulus (at least at moderate to low frequencies), thus preserving (or "coding") the periodicity of the stimulus.

It is not uncommon to reduce the information in a histogram or table even further. We did this in our discussion of how to use a flag to measure the direction of a steady breeze. Recall that we reduced 20 individual measurements first to a histogram and then to a single summary statement: "The wind direction is approximately 5° east of north." There are two key issues here; one having to do with the term "approximately," the other being the numerical value "5 degrees." Let's look at the latter first.

Frequently it is useful to condense a set of data or histogram into a single number, which is a measure of *location* or *central tendency*. When we look at the histogram of Figure 5, it is apparent that the data are fairly evenly distributed at a value of about 5°. We can be even more systematic than this.

There are a number of useful indices of location employed in practice, and of these, three are usually

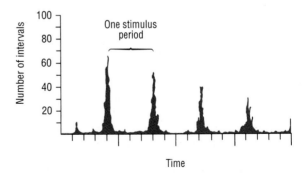

FIGURE 8   Interval histogram of a single auditory neuron driven by a pure tone with a period of 4,060 microseconds—roughly middle C.   (Rose et al., 1967)

singled out at having the widest application. They are the *mode*, the *mean*, and the *median*. The mode is easy to define: it is the most frequently occurring category (the tallest bar in a histogram). In Figure 5, the category "5°" occurs more often than any other, so the mode of that histogram is 5°.

The median of a set of measurements is the value that divides the set in two: half the measurements fall below the median, half above. The median of the set of directions recorded in Table 1 is between 5.3° and 5.7°, and it suffices to record the median as 5.5°.

Finally, the mean of a set of measurements is simply their arithmetic average. If we compute the arithmetic average of the 20 values listed in Table 1, we find that it is 5.9°. These three numerical values, 5°, 5.5°, and 5.9° are different but sufficiently close in magnitude that no one would (usually) care which was selected. The close agreement of these three values will occur whenever a histogram is approximately "heaped symmetrically" about its mode.

However, there are many examples of data that do not distribute themselves in this ideal way. Income provides a notorious example. The average income of people who work in a factory is dramatically influenced by a few large managerial salaries together with many much smaller salaries paid to workers on the production line. The average of one $100,000 salary and ten $10,000 salaries is $18,182, which is not representative of anyone's income. However, both the modal and median salaries in this case are $10,000, which are more reasonable reflections of reality.

A histogram can be a combination of two or more histograms. It is not uncommon for such histograms to have two or more distinct modes. Notice in Figure 9, the bimodal nature of a "living histogram" of men and women arranged according to height. This could be broken down into two histograms, one for each sex, each being characterized by a single mode.

This example should not be taken as indicating that more than one mode necessarily indicates the presence of more than one underlying structure. It can certainly occur that a single system is naturally characterized by several modes. An example is provided by gambling. Have you ever noticed that when playing poker you are either "hot" or "cold"? In fact, in a simple game between two players involving the tossing of a fair (unbiased) coin, it is common for one player to be ahead for the entire duration of the game! Despite this, over many such games of the same length, the average winnings will eventually even out. An appropriately constructed histogram for tossing a coin would be diagrammatically U-shaped, showing two pronounced modes (always ahead and always behind), with a mean of zero in

FIGURE 9   A living bimodal histogram of college students arranged by height

between. Both the modes and the mean are reflections of a single underlying mechanism: pure chance.

An additional comment is in order before we proceed. The calculation of a mean requires the arithmetic operations of addition and multiplication. These operations may be inappropriate, indeed meaningless, if applied without thought. We could facetiously classify the major interests of teenagers into three categories: sex, drugs, and rock 'n' roll. What is the average category of interest? The answer cannot be found in averaging. There simply is no answer, for the question as posed is meaningless. Likewise, to compute a median requires that a meaningful *order* be established for the category values or labels. Only the mode remains unaffected by such considerations of meaningfulness (or *scale type* in statistical jargon). One can always sensibly ask, What is the most frequent category? Unfortunately, the answer may be none, many, or worse, irrelevant.

A histogram is often not well represented by a mere measure of location because such measures are essentially blind to the "width" or dispersion of the histogram. It is one thing to know that the modal direction of a breeze is 5° east of north, but quite another to know that it varies over a 7° range. To state the mean direction of the Mississippi River is to ignore its incredible meandering.

To compensate for the deficiencies of measures in location, measures of *variability* (scatter, spread, and dispersion) are introduced. The *range* of a set of measurements is one such measure. This is simply the difference between the largest and smallest of a set of measurements. The range of the data listed in Table 1 is 7.2° (10.2° − 3.0°).

STATISTICS: MAKING SENSE OF FALLIBLE DATA

Just as there are several useful indices of location, there are also a number of measures of variability in use. The most commonly used of these are *variance* and the closely related *standard deviation*. Like the mean, variance is an arithmetic average, not a set of raw measurements, but of squared *deviations*. A deviation is computed for each raw measurement by subtracting from it the value of the common mean. These deviations are squared so as to eliminate the distinction between positive and negative values, and they are subsequently averaged to produce the variance. In Table 5 these arithmetic operations are illustrated for the data of Table 1.

The variance of the data of Table 1 is given by the average of the squared deviations listed in the right-hand column of Table 5. We see that

$$\text{variance} = \frac{60.644}{20} = 3.032$$

Note that the average of the middle column, that is, the average of the (unsquared) deviations is zero. This is no accident—it is a simple algebraic consequence of the definition of a deviation and provides a useful check on intermediate calculations.

Standard deviation arises from variance by extracting a square root; thus, for the above data,

$$\text{standard deviation} = \sqrt{3.032} = 1.74$$

Why bother with standard deviation when variance will do? The answer is convenience; a standard deviation possesses the same units as the original data and may be pictured as a "distance" from the mean value. Standard deviation provides a gauge of how discrepant individual values are from the mean, and hence how discrepant they are from each other. A rule of thumb for histograms is this: nearly all measurements fall within ± 2 standard deviations from the mean. In other words, one can expect the range of a typical set of data to be a total of about four standard deviations. For example, for the data of Table 1, we noted above that the range was 7.2°. This is close to 6.96, which is 4×1.74 (one standard deviation), in accord with the rule of thumb.

So far we have exclusively considered univariate data, that is, measurements pertaining to a single numerical quantity such as time, direction, salary, and so on, or to a single qualitative variable such as sex, occupation, or marital status. Inventories of such measurements lend themselves to organization in tables, bar graphs, and histograms, which allows for further reduction to a measure of location and one of variability. Sometimes this is enough, especially if all that is required is an assertion of simple fact: "The life expectancy of a Saudi Arabian is presently 42 years"; or "The percentage of 15- to 18-year-olds enrolled in education in the United States was 84% in 1976"; or "The infant mortality rate is 15 per 1000 births in the United States."

However, there are many classes of statements that are more complex: "From 1973 to 1980, average verbal scores on the Scholastic Aptitude Test dropped over 50 points, and average mathematics scores dropped nearly 40 points"; or "Warning: The Surgeon General has determined that cigarette smoking is dangerous to your health"; or "Psychologists have shown a connection between viewing violence on TV and aggressive behavior." When dissected, such statements are seen to involve two or more variables or two or more sets of measurements. The Surgeon General's warning means that there is a difference between the incidence of various diseases (for example, lung cancer, emphysema, and heart ailments) for those who smoke cigarettes and those who do not and, moreover, that such differences cannot reasonably be attributed to other possible sources (for example, alcohol, place of domicile, or anxiety).

Original measurement (Flag directions)	Deviations (Measurement- Mean)	Squared deviations
10.2	4.28	18.318
5.8	−0.12	0.014
7.1	1.18	1.392
3.0	−2.92	8.526
8.9	2.98	8.880
5.4	−0.52	0.270
4.8	−1.12	1.254
6.2	0.28	0.078
4.1	−1.82	3.312
7.4	1.48	2.190
3.8	−2.12	4.494
5.3	−0.62	0.384
6.0	0.08	0.006
6.9	0.98	0.960
5.1	−0.82	0.672
5.7	−0.22	0.048
8.3	2.38	5.664
15.2	−0.72	0.518
4.3	−1.62	2.624
4.9	−1.02	1.040
Average $= \dfrac{118.4}{20}$ $= 5.92$ $= $ Mean	Average $= 0$	Average $= \dfrac{60.644}{20}$ $= 3.032$ $= $ Variance

TABLE 5   Calculating a variance (based on data in Table 1)

The ability to detect change, to recognize differences, and to notice that one variable (say, height) is linked to another (say, weight) are all crucial for what is perhaps the major ambition of science: to provide a simple yet highly precise description of the world. No encyclopedia of bare facts is adequate to this task.

The question "Does juvenile delinquency increase with population density?" is one that typifies many research efforts in the social sciences. It is often dealt with by using *correlational algorithms,* two of which we deal with below. They are distinguished by the type of variables involved (whether the variables are quantitative or qualitative), but their purpose remains the same: to decide if two or more variables *covary* (vary together).

Suppose 40 high school seniors, 20 male and 20 female, are submitted to a battery of tests designed to assess "ability in mathematics." The results of these 40 individual ability scores are compiled and the median is computed. Why the median? This allows individuals of both sexes to be classified as "above the median" or "below the median." In short, we record the number of students falling into each of the four categories "male-above," "male-below," "female-above," and "female-below." It is convenient to record these counts in a "2 × 2" table (Table 6).

Those who score above the median are typically male, while those who score below are typically female. In other words, the variables "gender" and "mathematics ability" are positively *associated.* We can go further and compute an index of *strength* and *direction* of association, designated by the Greek letter ϕ (phi). The index ϕ varies between two extreme values: -1 (complete negative association) and $+1$ (complete positive association). Speed and accuracy are usually negatively associated (quickness begets sloppiness), whereas motivation and effort are often positively correlated. Values of ϕ near zero indicate little or no association.

The algorithm for computing ϕ for any 2 × 2 table is given in Table 7. Applying the algorithm to the data of Table 6, we compute $\phi = 0.3$, confirming what our eye

		B_1	B_2	Totals
A	A_1	a	b	a + b
	A_2	c	d	c + d
	Totals	a + c	b + d	

TABLE 7 Computation of coefficient of association ϕ for an arbitrary 2 × 2 frequency table

$$\phi = \frac{ad - bc}{\sqrt{(a + b)(c + d)(a + c)(b + d)}}$$

told us already, that there is a modest positive association between gender and mathematics ability.

Now, women, do you accept this conclusion without protest? Surely not. There is good reason to believe that the observed association may be a by-product of complex social circumstances that conspire to the detriment of women. (To what extent this more complex and subtle explanation is true is an area of current investigation.) As this example suggests, it is a mistake to confuse association with the notion of cause. Although no one doubts anymore that cigarette smoking is a causal agent for a number of horrible diseases, it took about ten years of research to replace the phrase "may be" with the definitive "is" in the warning that appears on the side of every pack of cigarettes on sale in the United States. Why? Because taking into account other relevant factors can change an observed association between two variables quite dramatically, turning a large value of ϕ into a small one, or even reversing its sign.

	Male	Female	Totals
Above	13	7	20
Below	7	13	20
Totals	20	20	

TABLE 6 A 2 × 2 cross classification of 20 male and 20 female students according to mathematics ability

County	Index of exposure	Cancer mortality per 100,000 person-years
Clatsop	8.34	210.3
Columbia	6.41	177.9
Gilliam	3.41	129.9
Hood River	3.83	162.3
Morrow	2.57	130.1
Portland	11.64	207.5
Sherman	1.25	113.5
Umatilla	2.49	147.1
Wasco	1.62	137.5

TABLE 8 Radioactive contamination and cancer mortality (Fadeley, 1965, cited in Anderson & Sclove, 1986)

STATISTICS: MAKING SENSE OF FALLIBLE DATA

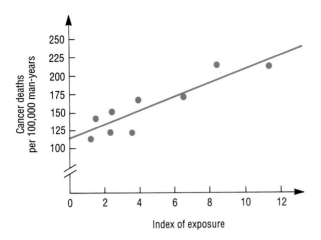

FIGURE 10 Scatter plot of data of Table 8 (Fadeley, 1965, cited in Anderson & Sclove, 1986)

When covariation is suspected between a pair of quantitative variables, a simple *scatter plot* is useful. The data recorded in Table 8 are *pairs* of measurements taken in a few counties in Oregon following leakage of radioactive contaminated waste into the Columbia River. One measurement is an index of exposure; large values indicate more serious exposure than small values. The other is the mortality rate due to various forms of cancer. These pairs of measurements have been plotted on a graph to form a scatter plot (Figure 10), in which the two measurements are used as the horizontal and vertical axes.

The relationship between death from cancer and radioactive exposure is obvious from this plot. An index called *coefficient of correlation*, denoted r, is often employed for the same purpose as the measure ϕ. The coefficient r, like ϕ, also ranges between -1 and $+1$ and has roughly the same interpretation. More precisely, r is a measure of how well the relationship between two quantitative variables conforms to a simple straight line (see Figure 10). The value of r for the present data turns out to be about 0.93, a value which again bolsters what we see by eye in the scatter plot.

Correlations can be very misleading if accepted uncritically. For example, the scatter plot of Figure 11 shows a definite linear relationship between human population size and stork population size in the German city of Oldenburg. The value of r for these data is 0.95. But does this mean that storks bring babies? The answer is surely "no"—in fact, it is closer to the truth to say that babies bring storks. As the Oldenberg population increases, more housing is built, a by-product of which are

chimneys, ideal nesting sites for storks. The large correlation between the populations of inhabitants and storks would drop to zero if the number of chimneys was kept constant and not allowed to increase with new housing.

Problems with the interpretation of indices such as r and ϕ make the task of the social scientist quite difficult. It is not a problem so much for statistics as it is for scientific explanation. There *is* a large positive correlation between the number of storks and the number of babies; that is all that a statistical index is required to report. But the scientific explanation of covariation is not to be found in accepting such indices at face value. Other nonmeasured or hidden variables (e.g., chimneys) may be responsible for superficial appearances.

Problems of interpreting data are usually traced to lack of *control*. It is often difficult to control natural events, so science has invented the laboratory, a place where the individual scientist can, in theory, have the last word as to what will vary and what will remain fixed. A good deal of technology, common sense, intuition, and creative effort goes into a well-controlled scientific experiment. Each scientist brings to bear one or more techniques from a bag of tricks called *scientific method* so as to achieve as much control as he or she can. When successful, scientific explanation and statistical interpretation practically coincide. But in psychology, as in other social sciences, control may not always be possible without disturbing important features of the system being studied. And even in the context of a

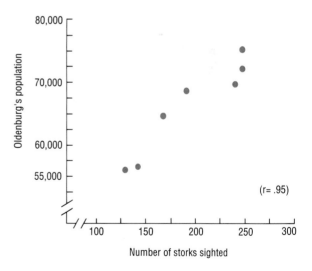

FIGURE 11 The population of Oldenburg, Germany, and the corresponding stork population for the years 1930–1936 (Glass & Hopkins, 1984)

laboratory, control is often only partially achieved. While scientific method is a branch of metaphysics, statistics is a branch of applied mathematics. They should never be confused.

STATISTICAL INFERENCE

Descriptive techniques are helpful in the preliminary search for regularity in variable data. But there are a number of vexing questions that remain unanswered, indeed unanswerable, without further consideration. Suppose we ask the simple question: Has the wind changed? We might mean a number of things by this: Has the breeze shifted its mean direction from 5.9° east of north to a new value? Has the breeze become more variable than before? Or we may be asking both of these questions.

The issue can be stated more clearly and scientifically this way: if the data represented in the histogram of Figure 5 were collected at 10 A.M., for example, and we take another set of measurements on the same flag at 2 P.M., and construct a new histogram from those measurements, can we tell the difference between the two histograms? Large differences will show up quite clearly; one needs no elaborate statistical apparatus to distinguish two clearly different sets of measurements. But what about the two histograms shown in Figure 12? While they are actually different, would you be willing to attribute this difference to a genuine trend?

The problem of detecting change, especially small differences that are difficult to discern, is common in scientific research. Its resolution calls for a new language, supplied by the theory of probability. We do not have the space here to enter into this mathematical theory in any serious way, so we shall content ourselves with the briefest indication of the role it plays.

Probability theory is used by statisticians as a framework for modeling *inherently* variable measurements. Regardless of researcher's attempts to control matters, variability of measurement, especially in the behavioral sciences, cannot be eliminated. Sometimes this may be attributed to "individual differences" among people, but such inherent variation is also present in the behavior of each one of us. For instance, do you chew your food or blink your eyes at precisely regular intervals? The sun rises each morning at the correct time and in the right place, but can you say the same about your own behavior or that of anyone else? Even for people who pride themselves on being punctual, the best we can say is something like "There is a 90% chance that Mr. Discipline will be in the shower between 7:00 and 7:05 A.M. on any given day."

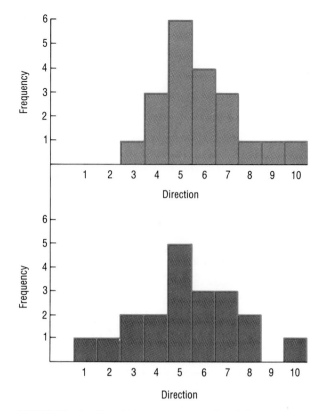

FIGURE 12 Are these histograms representative of the same breeze, or has the breeze changed its direction?

To be sure, not all variability is due to chance, and it is the responsibility of each scientist to attempt the difficult job of partitioning it into two components, one that is controllable and one that is uncontrollable (chance events). A characteristic signature of chance is that its effects disappear in *large* batches of independently repeated measurements; this is called the "law of averages." It is no empirical law or phenomenon, but a mathematical theorem, an inevitable consequence of averaging out the annoying obfuscations of chance. It is testimony to the appropriateness of probability theory for application to data that batches of empirical observations do behave in the manner dictated by that theory.

Not to be outdone by nature, science has exploited the theory of probability to good end in the process of *sampling*. The Nielsen ratings, which greatly influence the television advertising industry, are based on measurements taken in 1,000 households. This is a tiny proportion of the approximately 100 million dwellings in the United States. Political polls, famous for a few outstanding blunders, also deserve to be credited with an otherwise flawless track record. (In fact, they may be

STATISTICS: MAKING SENSE OF FALLIBLE DATA

"too" good. These days it is not uncommon for the results of an election to be announced before the voting has ended.)

While there are various forms of sampling, that is, of selecting a few from a larger *population* of possible measurements, the most useful forms are those called *probability sampling*, in which chance is injected *deliberately* by the scientist or pollster. This is done so that the result of a scientific endeavor, survey, or poll may be subject to the description afforded by probability theory and so that it may gain from the precision offered by that theory.

The simplest form of probability sampling is known as *random sampling*. Here, all samples of a given size (that is, all samples containing a specified number of measurements) are conceptually laid out on a table, and just one of these is chosen "at random" without bias or emotion. It is usually the failure to carry out this conceptual random selection that causes problems in practice. For example, a convenient practical way to research people for survey purposes is to call them on the phone. But this excludes people who do not own telephones, who have limited access to them, and who have unlisted numbers. Such departures from the strict requirements of random sampling can and do lead to unwarranted conclusions in research or to incorrect predictions in a close political contest. For related reasons, psychology has sometimes been dubbed (not entirely without justification) as the "science of college sophomores."

Let us pick some simple notion to examine, such as the average height of 10-year-old American males. This measure is not entirely frivolous. For example, the federal Department of Health and Human Services might be interested in determining whether providing free milk in schools has a measurable effect on mean height. The cost of locating, measuring, and recording *all* 10-year-old males would be about $1 million, so a random sample of 1,000 is selected. The average value of these 1,000 measurements is computed. Now the question arises: to what extent is this sample average indicative of the true, but unknown, population mean? The answer turns out to depend on the *variance of the population*, an unknown quantity, and on the size of the sample. In fact, the "error" of our sample mean falls within

$$\pm 2 \times \frac{\text{unknown population standard deviation}}{\sqrt{\text{sample size}}}$$

We can take a rough guess at the value one would expect of the unmeasured population standard deviation. Remember the rule of thumb mentioned earlier:

almost all the measurements of a single numerical quantity fall between ± 2 standard deviations of the mean. Common experience tells us that the range of heights of typical 10-year-old boys is surely no more than 2 feet, so a reasonable guess at the unknown population standard deviation should be no more than 6 inches. Using the above formula, the "error" incurred by quoting our sample mean as if it were the true population mean is

$$\frac{2 \times 6 \text{ inches}}{\sqrt{1000}} \times 0.38 \text{ inches}$$

Our sample mean (whatever its value) is seen to be an excellent *estimate* of the true population value. We could improve our accuracy further by increasing sample size to, say, 10,000; the error now drops to 0.12 inches. If we were not interested in such precision, a sample size of 100, incurring an error of 1.2 inches, might be tolerable and would certainly be cheaper to obtain.

The use of sample means as estimates of population means is widespread in scientific and commercial enterprises. Similar sample quantities are available for estimating other *parameters* of populations; for instance, it is intuitively reasonable, and theory confirms, that a sample variance provides a good estimate of population variance, at least for large samples.

Now that we know how to estimate the mean height of 10–year–old American males with an accuracy that improves with sample size, we are close to being able to address more serious matters. First, let's look at the question that prompted the measurement of height: Does the school milk program have the effect of increasing height? To address this question requires two samples—one taken just before the program is instituted and one taken, say, five years later. Entirely different 10-year-olds characterize each sample, and each sample typifies different populations, one who received milk and one who did not.

The question can be put this way: Do these populations differ in their means? This question is handled by *statistical inference*, the major application of which involves *hypothesis* testing. Briefly, this means that a skeptical attitude is adopted and the hypothesis of "no effect" (that is, "no difference in height") is made. The hypothesis allows the observed difference in the (undoubtedly different) sample averages to be evaluated under the assumption that all one really has are two samples from the *same* population.

Imagine that the heights from each sample are listed side-by-side in long columns of 1,000 entries each. Suppose the initial sample is listed in the left-hand column and the final sample on the right. Proceeding line by line, imagine subtracting the left-hand number from the right, recording the 1,000 differences in yet a third column. What do you expect the average of those 1,000 differences would be? According to the skeptical hypothesis of no difference, each sample average provides a good estimate of the same population mean; so their difference should be close to zero. Simple algebra tells us that an average of differences is the same as a difference of averages. Thus, we have answered our question: the average of the 1,000 differences should be close to zero, if indeed the sample means are estimating a common population value.

However, what if the hypothesis is wrong; what if milk does in fact have an effect on height? We should then expect many more of our 1,000 differences to be positive and consequently the average difference to be positive. The only question that remains unanswered is this: How discrepant from zero is a *significant* positive difference? This question can be put another way: How likely is it to observe a positive difference of any stated amount?

Such questions are answered by probability theory. We can now use the rule of thumb about the scatter of any distribution of numerical data. Differences are numerical data, so we can apply our rule to them. We expect almost all differences to fall within ±2 standard deviation of their mean (which we are temporarily assuming is zero). We have to somehow come to terms with the standard deviation of differences, and once again it is probability theory that provides the answer: the "error" of our sample differences is $\sqrt{2}$ times the error incurred by either sample mean alone. For samples of size 1,000, we saw above that this latter error was at most 0.38 inches. Multiplying by 2 we find that almost all average differences in height would lie in the interval −0.54 to +0.54 inches, provided that milk has no effect. Thus, if we observe an average difference of 0.25 inches, for example, we attribute it to chance and give up on the milk program (at least insofar as it affects height). However, if we observe a mean difference of 1 inch, we stay with the program and maybe hire some more high school basketball coaches.

While this example is fictitious, it does illustrate a common design strategy. Another more realistic example along similar lines is provided by the 1954 Salk vaccine trials, which constituted possibly the largest public health experiment ever conducted in the world.

The Salk vaccine greatly reduced the incidence of poliomyelitis, a crippling disease to which young children were especially prone. Two very large random samples of young children were chosen, roughly equal

	Placebo	Vaccine	Totals
Children contracting polio	110	33	143
Children not contracting polio	201,119	200,712	401,831
Totals	201,229	200,745	

TABLE 9 Incidence of poliomyelitis (Francis et al., 1957, cited in Anderson & Sclove, 1986)

in number. One group, the "control" group, received a placebo—each child received injections of a harmless substance. Each child in the "treatment" group received injections of the new vaccine. No child, parent, or administering medical staff had any knowledge of the true nature of the substance being injected into any individual; that is, the study was a *double-blind* experiment. This very useful device helps to offset any bias that might otherwise contaminate the interpretation of results.

Partial data from this experiment are given in Table 9. Notice the large sample size, about 200,000 for each group. Why so large? The answer is partially contained in the "placebo" column: the rate of the naturally occurring disease is estimated as 110 per 201,229, or about one case per 2,000 children. A sample of 1,000 children would not be expected to reveal a single case of polio. To obtain an accurate estimate of the incidence of any rare event, such as contracting polio, calls for large sample sizes.

There is another reason for the large number of children studied. While it is important to be conservative in evaluating differences between treatment and control groups, so that small differences are not inappropriately interpreted as an effect of treatment, it is also important to pick up genuine effects of treatment when they do in fact exist. The ability of a statistical test to satisfy the latter requirement involves the notion of *power*. To achieve a high likelihood of detecting genuine effects of vaccine in the polio trials calls for high power, which in the present context, is also achieved by employing very large sample sizes.

We have a tool for evaluating the effect of the vaccine, namely, the coefficient of association ϕ introduced in Table 7. Calculation reveals that $\phi = 0.01$, a shocking result that, taken at face value, would seem to implicate the vaccine as worthless. But this conclusion is unwarranted. Tiny as it is, the 0.01 value of ϕ is wildly significant; that is, it could not have been produced by chance (except in about 1 in every 200 experiments). This example points to the often dramatic difference between a purely descriptive use of statistical indices and a more refined statistical analysis of the same data. A value of ϕ close to zero may be highly significant, but in contrast, it may be routine in smaller scale experiments to observe nonsignificant values of ϕ equal to about 0.5.

There are extensions of the above simple design. One common extension involves two or more *levels* of some treatment. For example, the vaccine may be available in two or more concentrations; all concentrations may be effective, but is one more effective than another?

A more important extension involves the simultaneous experimental manipulation of two or more *independent* variables, so as to study their *joint* effect on a single *dependent* variable. For example, age could have been incorporated into the vaccine trials so that the effectiveness of the of the vaccine on adults as well as children could have been assessed simultaneously.

When two or more variables influence a third, their joint effect is not predictable in any simple way from the effect of each of them taken alone. Consider the influence of fear and rage on the aggressiveness of an animal. We probably expect a frightened animal to be passive, while on the contrary, we would expect an enraged animal to be relatively dangerous. What then can we expect of a frightened, enraged animal? It is possible that the situation depicted in Figure 13 may occur. Notice that a dog in a state of moderate fear and moderate rage (center) appears more vicious than one in a state of no fear and moderate rage. This is contrary to what would have been anticipated from our earlier conjecture about the effect of increasing fear alone. In the jargon of *analysis of variance*—statistical machinery developed for analyzing the effects of two or more variables on a single dependent measure—we say that fear and rage *interact* in their influence on aggressiveness.

CONCLUDING REMARKS

Contrary to popular impression, statisticians do not normally spend much of their time scratching out arithmetic calculations on a piece of paper. Computers compute, but statisticians occupy themselves with "good" methods for organizing data, "good" methods for estimating population quantities, and "good" inferential procedures. The emphasis is always on the term *good* and what it means in a given context.

The advantages of an informed data analysis are obvious and many. Such an analysis is tailored to the requirements of some set of specific data and keeps in prominent view questions that arise naturally from the empirical context generating those data. All too frequently the conservative ("no effect") *null hypothesis* of the working scientist is confirmed. Usually this occurs not because an effect is absent, but as a by-product of an insensitive analysis chosen naively for reasons of convenience or tradition. A competent statistician can often turn an apparently uninteresting set of data into a highly revealing, thought-provoking one. If for no other reason, I leave you with the following advice: support your local statistician.

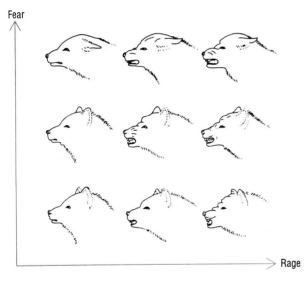

FIGURE 13 The joint effects of fear and rage on aggressiveness. (Zeeman, 1976)

GLOSSARY

A

abnormal An atypical, maladaptive state that leads to the inability to function adequately.

abnormal aging Decrements from disease that are commonly associated with age. Abnormal aging in theory is reversible, unlike normal aging.

absolute threshold The least amount of physical energy necessary for a stimulus to be perceived. The working definition is the minimum strength for a stimulus to be noticed by an observer 50 percent of the time. See also **difference threshold.**

abstract modeling A process in which observers generate and test hypotheses about the rules guiding the performance of others. This helps an observer learn how to produce complex human behaviors.

abuse The use of a drug or drugs in such a way that it interferes with a person's ability to function, but does not involve physical addiction.

acceptance The final stage in the dying process. In reaching this stage, people are sometimes aided by religious faith or by understanding that they have led a full and meaningful life. Acceptance leads to peaceful, dignified dying.

accommodation In vision, the focusing process in which the shape of the lens of the eye adjusts, depending on the distance between the eye and the object being viewed, to consistently project a clear image on the retina. In the theory of Jean Piaget, the process of adjusting existing knowledge so that new information can fit more readily.

acetylcholine (ACH) A common neurotransmitter in both the central and peripheral nervous systems. In the CNS it plays an important role in sleep and wakefulness and in memory. In the PNS it is involved in the first stage of transmission in both sympathetic and parasympathetic systems and in the second stage as well of the parasympathetic system.

achievement, achievement motivation The form of motivation, postulated by McClelland, that enables us to carry through and complete the goals we set for ourselves. Achievement motivation varies in different cultures and in different subgroups within a culture. Many experiments have found that achievement motivation can be developed. See also **goals.**

Acquired Immune Deficiency Syndrome (AIDS) A deadly disease that disables the immune system. The human immunodeficiency virus (HIV) directly attacks lymphocytes, compromising cell-mediated immune function, and it damages the central nervous system.

acquisition and rehearsal The second phase of **stress inoculation therapy,** in which the client learns and practices a new set of constructive self-statements to use in stressful situations.

action potential The electrical impulse that occurs when a **neuron** fires. **Neurotransmitters** released by adjacent neurons trigger the neuron to fire an action potential that sweeps down the axon and causes the release of neurotransmitters into the **synapse.**

activation The major physiological effect of emotion. See also **emergency reaction.**

activity level An aspect of personality that remains stable throughout development. It refers to how energetically a person behaves.

adaptation The process wherein an organism changes in order to fit better in its environment. Varieties of adaptation include sensory adaptation, perceptual adaptation, and biological adaptation through the long processes of evolution.

adaptation level The adjustment an organism makes to respond to differences in its external environment. It is determined by three factors: focal stimuli, background stimuli, and residual stimuli. The general finding in adaptation level research is that we adjust perceptions to match the average of external surroundings. If we are watching a group of tall people, such as basketball players, those "only" 6'5' seem small.

adaptive value Any trait has adaptive value if it enables an organism to function better in its environment. See also **adaptation.**

adipocytes Fat cells in the body, the number and size of which are genetically determined. Fat cells are established in the first 2 years of life.

affect A term used by psychologists to refer to the feeling dimension of life. Someone with a flat affect displays little or no emotion.

affective disorder A psychological disorder in which a disturbance of mood is the distinguishing feature; such disorders include **depression,** manic depression, **mania.**

afferent neurons Nerve cells in the spinal cord that convey information to the brain from the sensory system. See also **efferent neurons, interneurons.**

aggression The intentional harming of another. According to Freud, it is an instinct. According to social learning theory, it is learned behavior. In social psychology, the situation is analyzed to determine how people can be coerced to become aggressive.

alcohol A common term for beverages containing ethanol, a liquid intoxicant. Alcohol acts on neuronal membranes, disrupting the ability of neurons to transmit normally. At low doses alcohol disinhibits behavior, but at higher doses it impairs functioning and leads to unconsciousness.

algorithm A thought strategy for guaranteeing a solution if a person keeps working at the problem long enough.

altered state of consciousness A radical change of the content of awareness from the normal waking state. Altered states can result from sleep, changes of sensory input, meditation, drug use, or **hypnosis.**

altruism Behavior characterized by kindness and concern for others, which in extreme situations may extend to sacrificing one's life for others. The question for evolutionary biologists, since natural selection is presumed to operate on individuals, is why would an individual give up his or her life for another. See also **sociobiology.**

Alzheimer's disease A disease associated with aging that causes the decline of CNS function, resulting in a decrease in memory and other cognitive processes. The first symptom is loss of memory for recent experiences. It later produces confusion, irritability, suspiciousness, and wandering and it eventually leads to death.

amnesia A loss of memory caused by damage or trauma to the brain.

amphetamines Synthetic central nervous system stimulants.

amygdala A small structure between the hypothalamus and the hippocampus. Its functions are not completely understood, but it seems to affect the maintenance and gratification of internal bodily needs and the storage of some memory processes.

anal stage The second **psychosexual stage** of development postulated by Freud that begins at about 18 months and continues until the child is 3 years old. During this period, the infant attains pleasure and derives a sense of control from the retention and expulsion of feces.

analgesics Drugs that reduce the experience of pain. They include aspirin, acetaminophen, ibuprofen, and narcotics such as codeine, morphine, and heroin.

analysis of the transference A process in psychotherapy in which patients learn about their own misconceptions, maladaptive responses and misinterpretations by seeing how they transfer them to their analysts.

analytical psychology An offshoot of psychoanalysis, developed by Jung, that studies individuation, the development of the person through the process by which the unconscious and the conscious unite.

anger A negative emotion, usually prompted by the perception of a threat, that causes the organism to feel aggressive.

anniversary effect The apparent postponing of death until after a special occasion—such as a birthday, election, or special holiday—by persons very near death who might otherwise not be expected to live that long.

anorexia A disorder in which a person develops a distorted body image, seeing him or herself as fat even when dangerously underweight. Anorexics refuse to eat but are frequently obsessed with food. Most anorexics are women.

antidepressant Drugs used in the treatment of chronic endogenous depression. They work by affecting the balance of neurotransmitters in the brain. Two common varieties are MAO inhibitors and tricyclics. See also **monoamine oxidase (MAO) inhibitors** and **tricyclics.**

antipsychotic drugs A substance, often called a major tranquilizer, used in the treatment of severe mental disorders. See also **pharmacotherapy.**

antisocial personali.y (ASP) A personality disorder that is characterized by an extremely calm mood, no sense of responsibility or shame, and a lack of genuine concern or caring for other people. Also called psychopathic or sociopathic.

anxiety A general emotional reaction that develops in response to the anticipation that something may occur in the future. This could be something physical or psychological, such as a threatened insult or a threatened embarrassment.

aphasia Partial or complete loss of the ability to use language, resulting from brain damage.

appetitive conditioning Respondent conditioning involving an **unconditioned stimulus (UCS)** that an organism will instinctively approach.

appraisal The understanding of the meaning of an event. Among the many dimensions along which people appraise events is whether there is harm or loss and whether the situation is a threat, a challenge, or benign.

archetype A predisposition to have certain experiences or reactions to the world, postulated by Jung to be common to all humanity. Archetypes are the elements that make up the **collective unconscious.**

artificial category A system of classification that refer to attributes of constructed objects, like chairs or buildings.

artificial intelligence (A.I.) The study of abilities that enable computers to simulate human intelligence. The two major goals of A.I. research are to get computers to do intelligent things, and in the same way as humans do.

assertiveness training A form of behavior therapy used when the problem entails difficulties in interpersonal relationships. Generally, assertiveness training teaches people that they have a right to their own feelings and opinions, which matter as much as anyone else's.

assimilation The incorporation of a new event into existing knowledge. See also **accommodation.**

association The postulated bond that forms in the mind when two events occur often enough together: the dinner bell and the taste of dinner, for instance.

attachment The special bond between the infant and the mother or other caregiver. It probably is an innate bond that develops due to the necessity for love, the gratification of needs, the infant's cognitive development, and the communication between the caregiver and the child.

attention A set of processes that determine what enters consciousness. Attention can be automatic or involuntary, as when we choose to focus on some aspect of an experience or are automatically drawn to look in the direction of an unexpected loud noise.

attitude A learned tendency to respond in a consistent way to certain groups, ideas, or situations. Attitudes can be positive or negative and are resistant to change.

attractiveness The degree to which a person is considered desirable to associate with, and the degree to which a person's physical features are considered aesthetically pleasing.

attribution theory A theory explaining the processes by which we explain the causes of our own or others' actions or behavior. We try to determine whether people's actions are attributed to a specific situation or whether their behavior reflects something enduring about their personal disposition.

auditory cortex The part of the cortex of the brain responsible for processing input from the ear. The auditory cortex contains specific modules that process certain tones, the beginnings and endings

of sounds, and certain specific types of sounds.

Australopithecus A **hominid,** dating from 3 to 4 million years ago, that might be considered the earliest direct ancestor of humans.

autoantibodies Antibodies that attack one's own organs and joints. Their appearance is associated with aging and lowered competence of the immune system.

automatization When a series of movements or actions are repeated many times, as in writing or walking, the behavior is accomplished automatically—without thinking. Automatization is an important aspect of cognitive functioning; without it we would have to "pay attention" to every action we make during the day.

autonomic nervous system (ANS) A division of the **peripheral nervous system** primarily responsible for running the internal organs, such as the heart, kidneys, liver, and gastrointestinal tract. Its processes are autonomic—that is, without conscious control. See also **somatic nervous system.**

availability A thought judgment that refers to the ease with which relevant instances come to mind. We use availability to judge the frequency or the probability of events. See also **heuristics.**

aversive conditioning Respondent conditioning involving an **unconditioned stimulus** that the organism instinctively avoids.

axon A part of the **neuron** that extends outward from the cell body. The axon is the transmitter end of the neuron. See also **dendrites, neurotransmission.**

B

barbiturates Depressant drugs used clinically to treat anxiety and insomnia. They are illegally used recreationally to produce an effect similar to that of alcohol.

bargain with fate The third of five stages a dying person commonly experiences. The individual offers to behave in a given way, perhaps devoting the rest of his or her life

to God, in exchange for a little more time.

bases The four chemical substances that are the building blocks of **DNA:** adenine, thymine, guanine, and cytosine. A group of three bases makes up a **codon.**

basic level category The part of a categorization system that children learn first—such as table, apple, house—and that is the level at which we most naturally divide the world.

basilar membrane A structure in the ear at the base of the cochlea. It moves like a whip being cracked and creates a traveling wave that is transduced into sound.

behavior For psychologists, observable, verifiable activity; more generally, the final decision about what action to take.

behavior modification A form of therapy based on **operant conditioning,** which attempts to change behaviors by changing the stimuli and conditions. Behavior modification may employ reinforcement or extinction to teach new learned responses and to alter problem situations.

behavior therapy A form of psychotherapy, based primarily on classical conditioning. It attempts to decondition anxiety-producing responses.

behavioral confirmation How our beliefs about others have a powerful influence on the way we behave toward them and create their own reality.

behaviorism Growing out of a desire, in the late nineteenth century, to make psychology objective, it is an approach that studies external, observable behavior of organisms and attempts to infer what caused that behavior.

bias Factor in the decision-making process that prevents impartiality in certain kinds of judgments. Biases include availability, representativeness, and vivid information.

binaural disparity The difference in sound information received by each ear, which provides us with cues to distance, since the sound slightly to the left will strike the left ear before the right and vice versa.

binocular disparity The difference in information received by the left and right eyes, which are in slightly different locations on the head. This difference is analyzed by the brain to provide cues to distance.

biofeedback A method of training people to control internal processes not normally controlled by consciousness, such as glandular and muscular activity, brain waves, blood pressure, and heart rate.

biological therapy The treatment of mental illness with physical means, such as **electroconvulsive therapy (ECT)** and **pharmacotherapy.**

bipedalism Walking on two legs instead of four. Humans are the only organisms that typically walk on the hind limbs. This enables them to carry, to share, to use their delicate forelimbs to manipulate objects, and to accomplish many other tasks that contribute to human uniqueness.

bipolar depression Depression that involves both depressive and manic periods. See also **depression** and **mania.**

blindsight When people with partial blindness can exhibit knowledge about objects in the portions of their visual fields that they cannot consciously see.

blood pressure The force with which blood pushes against the walls of the blood vessels. High blood pressure (**hypertension**) increases one's chances of suffering strokes and heart attacks.

boredom A drive for increased stimulation. The brain appears to require a certain amount of information, stimulation, and change. If this requirement is not met, boredom results.

brain stem The oldest and deepest area of the brain, which evolved over 500 million years ago. It sets the general level of alertness and warns the organism of important incoming information.

breakdown The descent into a mental illness. The experience is disruptive to the sufferer's life and to those with whom he or she has social contact.

bulemia A condition in which people repeatedly eat large amounts (binge) and then vomit or consume laxatives (purge). Most bulemics are of normal weight but overconcerned with their appearance. Bulemia can cause electrolyte imbalance, which can be fatal.

C

cancer An unnatural, malignant growth of body tissues. Cancerous growths (tumors) destroy the tissues around them, disrupt bodily functions, and can spread to other tissues.

capture error A mental error in which an intended action is replaced by the normal, habitual operation of the mind. An example is driving straight home from work instead of remembering to stop at the store as originally planned.

cardinal traits One of two kinds of traits identified by Allport; highly generalized dispositions that organize an individual's whole personality. See also **secondary traits.**

case history A psychologist's report of unique experiences for which little or no other evidence is available.

case study A research method that involves detailed analysis of the experiences of a particular individual, usually over a period of time, in which the effects of some experimental procedure or independent variable are studied.

catatonic A type of **schizophrenia** characterized by unusual motor activity, either excitement or stupor. In catatonia with stupor, a person may maintain a single awkward posture for days.

category A grouping of objects or concepts that can be considered equivalent in at least one important dimension.

catharsis An ancient idea, first proposed by the Greeks, that strong emotional experience will cleanse the mind and release stored energy. In more technical terms, catharsis is the reduction of emotional stress by releasing emotion in controlled circumstances.

cathexis According to Freud, the investment of energy in an object, action, individual, image, or idea that will gratify an instinct.

cell body The central part of a **neuron.** The cell body contains the biochemical apparatus for powering the **action potentials** and maintaining the life of the cell.

central nervous system (CNS) The system of neurons that control the actions of the body. It includes the brain and spinal cord. See also **peripheral nervous system (PNS).**

cerebellum An area of the brain adjacent to the brain stem; originally developed in primates to assist in the control of fine motor movements. In humans it stores simple learned responses.

cerebral cortex The top level of the brain, present in all vertebrates. The cortex is responsible for making decisions and judgments based on information it receives from the body and senses. Its three main functions are to receive information, to analyze information and make decisions, and to transmit instructions to the muscles and glands.

challenge A difficult task that requires one to work at the limits of one's capacity, and which can lead to increased strength and ability. Psychologically hardy people tend to see change as a challenge rather than a threat.

childhood autism A mental disorder characterized by the failure of a child to develop social relationships. The autistic child appears disinterested and detached from all people and has impaired language abilities.

chromosome A tiny, complex structure in every cell and on which the genes are arranged. It carries the organism's entire genetic program and is the basic mechanism of heredity.

chronic life strain Certain condition that persists in a life, such as an unhappy marriage or poor working conditions, and that may be very stressful; can also be produced by the way a society is organized.

chunking A memory process that reorganizes individual bits of items into chunks by using a code. IBM and FBI are not mere sequences of letters; they are chunked into their code.

classical conditioning See **respondent conditioning.**

classification The categorization of objects and ideas that makes it unnecessary for us to identify anew each object or idea we encounter.

climacteric The loss of reproductive capacity. In women the loss is marked by menopause. In men the loss is gradual and never complete.

clinical psychologist A person with a PhD in psychology whose primary focus is on researching, instructing about, or treating psychopathology.

coaction effect A phenomenon in which the presence of other people intensifies and directs an individual's behavior.

codons A group of three **bases** on the **DNA** molecule that spells one ''word'' of building instructions by dictating the identity of one of the twenty amino acids that are used in constructing proteins.

cognition The mental processes we use to combine information and make decisions; thinking.

cognitive-behavior therapy A type of psychotherapy that combines techniques from **behaviorism** with ideas from **cognitive psychology;** emphasizes the effect of thought on behavior.

cognitive dissonance A social cognition theory by Festinger that states that whenever an individual holds two cognitions (beliefs, attitudes, or consciousness of behaviors) that are inconsistent with one another, a disharmony results. There is then a desire to reduce such disharmony either by changing cognitions or by changing behaviors. This has been a most influential theory in social psychology and has led to many imaginative experiments.

cognitive learning An acquisition of new behaviors that requires the motivation, attention, and active involvement of the learner; unlike conditioning, it depends on the intention of the learner. Cognitive learning theory emphasizes that the processes within the individual's mind are as important as the behavior exhibited.

cognitive maps Expectations concerning the relationship of elements in the environment that enable us to adapt readily to our surroundings.

cognitive modifiability The ability to change mental structure and content. For example, learning involves a change in the mental content, and thinking involves rearranging the structure of information in consciousness.

cognitive psychology The study of the mind, which, unlike the brain, is not an observable entity; involves many hidden activities, such as thinking, memory, language, and consciousness.

cognitive restructuring therapy A form of therapy developed by Beck. It assumes that disorders result from individuals' negative beliefs about events in the world and about themselves. Cognitive restructuring therapy encourages clients to engage in experiments that will help them confirm or disconfirm their beliefs and obtain a more realistic picture of themselves in their situation.

cognitive therapy See **cognitive-behavior therapy.**

cohort effect In a sample of people of different age groups, a group that is born in the same period of time. People are grouped into cohorts to avoid the distorting effects of different environmental experiences. For example, people born in the 1960s are, on the average, taller than people born in the 1920s.

collective unconscious Perhaps the most important of Jung's contributions to psychology, it is considered to be the inherited foundation of personality and contains the common reservoir of experience available to all human beings. It consists largely of **archetypes.**

commitment One of the three components of a love relationship in Sternberg's theory. Commitment is the decision to maintain a love relationship over time. In psychological hardiness, commitment to self, work, or family is a contributing factor that helps people cope with stressful situations.

companionate love After **passionate love** fades, it is often replaced (especially in successful relationships) with this more sober, everyday kind of love, in which there is less arousal and excitement but more friendly affection and deep attachment.

comparison A process that underlies judgments in sensory, cognitive, and social experience. All percepts, ideas, or people are assessed in relation to our current standards of comparison, which vary according to context, memory, recent experience, and expectations.

competence How well an individual carries out an intended action; a human goal that helps a person reach another goal: esteem.

complex In the usage developed by Jung, an organized group of constellations of memories, thoughts, feelings, and perceptions that can influence or even control personality.

compliance A type of social influence in which a person alters his or her behavior in response to the requests of others.

concentrative meditation A form of meditation that focuses the mind totally on one aspect of experience, shutting out all other thoughts and sensory input.

concordance rate The degree to which other people have the same disorder as a certain individual (the **proband**). The genetic basis of psychological disorders is measured by comparing the concordance rate between the proband's relatives and the general population.

concrete operational stage The stage of cognitive development, according to Piaget, that lasts from ages 7 to 12. Thinking is no longer dominated by sensory information; children begin to reason abstractly. They become more organized and more able to focus and direct attention for longer periods.

conditioned response (CR) A response that comes to be associated with a **conditioned stimulus,** such as salivating at the dinner bell. See also **respondent conditioning.**

conditioned stimulus (CS) Something that has no inherent meaning, such as a light, a sound, a puff of air, but comes to acquire meaning through a specific learning situation. A puff of air may always signal a loud noise; thus, the puff of air will become a conditioned stimulus to the noise. See also **respondent conditioning.**

conditioning The study of the *conditions* under which simple associations are formed. Extensive experiments in conditioning have been conducted by Ivan Pavlov and B. F. Skinner, among others. See also **operant conditioning, respondent conditioning.**

cone The form of **photoreceptor** in the retina that is responsible for color vision and is less sensitive than **rods;** needs bright light to be activated. Three kinds of cones exist, each of which responds primarily to a different range of wavelengths. One responds best to red/orange, one to green, and one to blue/violet.

conformity The adoption of the behaviors and attitudes of a social group to which one wishes to belong.

consciousness The contents of our awareness. When we are conscious of something, we can describe it. Decisions about conflicts are made in consciousness.

conservation The understanding that an object remains the same, even if it looks different. A ball of clay is the same whether it is spread out into a disc or made into a cylinder. Piaget felt that children under age 3 do not understand this principle.

consistency The degree to which a person's behavior is the same from one situation to the next.

constancy A goal of the perceptual process is to achieve a stable, constant world. So we *experience* surprisingly little change, even though the sensory information changes radically. A building may first appear like small dot, then larger than anything on the horizon, but we see the building as the same, constant building. There are three varieties of constancy: shape, size, and brightness.

constructivist approach Sensory information reaching the brain is chaotic and disorganized. Thus, in this view, perception must be a process of constructing a representation or model of the world, as a globe is fashioned to represent the earth. The information from the senses merely "sparks off" the creation of what could have caused a sensation.

context Prior knowledge that helps us to organize incoming information. We remember information more easily when it is provided in context than when it is not.

continuous reinforcement (CRF) A form of reinforcement in which each time the organism makes the correct response, it is reinforced. See also **operant conditioning, partial reinforcement.**

continuum of preparedness The concept proposed by Seligman that organisms are predisposed to learn to associate some events more than others. The continuum ranges from prepared to unprepared to counterprepared.

control The influence that we have over our environment and the events of our lives.

control and predictability model A model of how people perceive chronic illness. It proposes that chronic diseases can be seen as uncontrollable crises by the patient who then develops an attitude of helplessness. Those who feel some control over their condition should have improved outcomes.

control group That part of the **sample** similar in every way to the experimental group except that it is observed in the absence of the independent variable. See also **experimental group, variable.**

conventional morality In Kohlberg's theory of moral development, the level of moral reasoning that goes beyond individual considerations and takes the view of society as whole. See **postconventional morality, premoral level.**

conversational maxim According to Grice, speakers usually obey four maxims when they speak: quantity, quality, relation, and manner. The existence of these maxims makes it possible to understand the general rules people follow when they have a conversation. See also **cooperativeness principle.**

conversion disorder Rare **somatoform disorder,** characterized by the loss of some physical function without any organic basis. Unlike in somatization disorder, the individual shows no concern about the impairment.

cooperativeness principle The principle that describes the relationships between two speakers: each speaker tries to understand why the other said what he or she did.

corpus callosum A structure of 300 million neurons that connects the two separate cerebral hemispheres. Fibers in the corpus callosum run from one area in the left hemisphere to corresponding areas in the right, serving as an enormous network of communications.

correlation A statistic that measures the relationship between two sets of numbers. Usually used in psychology to measure the relationship between two factors, such as years of drinking and decline in intelligence.

counselors People trained to treat psychological problems.

counterconditioning A method of therapy using **extinction** and **generalization,** often used to help people overcome their fears. In this method, an unwanted **conditioned response** is eliminated by conditioning the subject to another stimulus (a **conditioned stimulus**) that elicits a new, less disruptive conditioned response.

crack Cocaine processed and crystallized to be smokable; produces an intense rapid effect. Crack has only been available on the street for a few years, but it has become a major drug of abuse. While cocaine in a powdered form was used primarily by the middle and upper classes, crack has become a drug of choice for poverty-stricken Americans.

critical period A period during the development of an organism in which the environment influences the development of perceptual capacities. Deprivation of certain stimuli during this period can prevent the organism from acquiring the ability to perceive those stimuli.

Cro-Magnon The first modern humans, members of our species, **homo sapiens.**

crowding The experience of having more people around than we would like; dependent not only on population density but also on the interpretation of that density. Crowding can cause alterations in the rate and quality of social interactions.

crystallized abilities Mental abilities hypothesized by Cattell to derive from specific cultural experiences. See also **fluid abilities.**

crystallized intelligence Abilities such as verbal, that remain relatively constant or improve slightly with age. See also **fluid intelligence.**

curiosity A drive to explore the environment. Curiosity increases mental activity by conveying more stimulation to the mind from outside.

D

dark adaptation The process by which the eye adjusts to see in dim illumination. **Cones** adapt in about 10 minutes, and **rods** reach maximal sensitivity after 30 to 40 minutes. See also **Purkinje shift.**

de-automatization The Western psychological term for enlightenment or illumination, meaning the undoing of normal automated structures of consciousness.

decentration According to Piaget, at each stage of development children and adults become increasingly aware of the world outside of themselves and less focused on themselves. They become progressively less egocentric.

decision analysis Thinking about decisions in terms of alternatives, outcomes, preferences, and probabilities.

declarative memory The mental record of information that we use to recall events, to think, and to communicate. The two types of declarative memory are episodic and semantic. See also **episodic memory, procedural memory,** and **semantic memory.**

decomposition According to Marr, the way the mind breaks up its perceptions of the outside world into elements it can analyze and assemble into simple, whole percepts.

deconstruction See **decomposition.**

defense mechanism An unconscious way of distorting reality to avoid unpleasant facts that might produce **anxiety.** Some defense mechanisms are **denial,** repression, rationalization, displacement, projection, and reaction formation.

dementia A class of brain disorders that arises in old age. The most common dementia is **Alzheimer's disease.**

demonstration Giving people direct experience of the effects of principles discovered by scientific means. For example, we might demonstrate a rule of perception by showing an illusion that results from that rule.

dendrite Part of the **neurons** named after the Greek word for *tree,* indicating the branches of one neuron connecting with another. They receive information from the **axons** of other neurons. See also **neurotransmission.**

denial The mental operation by which thoughts, feelings, acts, threats, or demands are minimized. If denial interferes with necessary actions, it can undermine health. However, denial can help people cope with serious illness, surgery, or trauma by decreasing debilitating anxiety and negative emotions.

denial and isolation The first of the five stages of dying, according to Kübler-Ross. It may help people to maintain hope and to avoid being overwhelmed by grief.

dependence An individual's reliance upon requiring others to assume responsibility for major areas of his or her life, because of either a lack of self-confidence or an inability to function independently.

dependent variable See **variable.**

depressant A drug that lowers activity in the brain, reducing physical and cognitive activity. Depressants can be used as tranquilizers, hypnotics, or anesthetics.

depression A severe mental disorder consisting of an overwhelming sadness that immobilizes and arrests the entire course of a person's life. See also **affective disorder mania.**

deviant A behavior or experience that is significantly different from the norm.

dexterity The ability in humans to use the forelimbs (hands) in a deliberate, manipulative manner. Human dexterity, allowed by bipedalism, encouraged toolmaking and other factors important to human evolutionary development.

diathesis-stress model A theory that some individuals react to stress with stereotyped physiological patterns, have inadequate homeostatic restraints on these physiological processes, and are repeatedly exposed to stress, all of which lead to physical illness.

difference threshold Commonly known as the **just noticeable difference (j.n.d.).** The minimum increase in a physical stimulus necessary for us to notice a difference. The j.n.d. is not constant; the experience of a stimulus is always relative to its surroundings. See also **absolute threshold.**

differentiation The development of individuality. As people age, they become more different from each other.

discrimination In **respondent** and **operant conditioning,** the process of learning to respond to some stimuli and not to other, similar stimuli.

dispositional attribution The act of accounting for another person's behavior by assuming it to be the result of his or her personality rather than the situation.

DNA Deoxyribonucleic acid; each molecule is made of two chains twisted into a spiral. The chains consist of four chemical building blocks: adenine, thymine, guanine, and cytosine. Virtually every living thing is made up of these elements.

dopamine An important **neurotransmitter** whose pathway connects the **limbic system** to the **cerebral cortex;** it also participates in the brain's reward system and in the control of motor activity. The lack of dopamine causes Parkinson's disease.

dopamine hypothesis The theory that **schizophrenia** is caused either by a surplus of dopamine or by a surplus of dopamine receptor sites.

double-blind procedure An experimental procedure in which the experimenter as well as the subject is unaware, ''blind,'' of which is the experimental group and which is the control group, and is thus unable to influence the results.

dream analysis A method in **psychoanalysis** for reaching the contents of the unconscious mind.

Freud believed that repressed thoughts arise in dreams and that these thoughts could be discovered by interpreting the content of dreams.

drive A physiologically based goad to behavior that moves an organism to action; often experienced as a specific need, such as thirst, hunger, or sex.

E

eating disorder A group of mental disorders that are characterized by pathological eating patterns. They include **pica, anorexia,** and **bulimia.** The latter two disorders may have their roots in societal values of attractiveness.

ecological approach A theory of perception that emphasizes the richness of the information available to the perceiver. In this view, perception is a direct function of stimulation.

efferent neuron The nerve cells in the spinal cord that take messages from the brain and activate muscles and glands. See also **afferent neurons, interneurons.**

ego An important part of the personality as described by Freud. It mediates between the demands of the **id** and the reality of the external world. See also **superego.**

ego psychologist Followers of Freud who formed their own school of psychology in which they accorded an expanded role to the ego.

egocentrism An important principle in psychology emphasizing that individuals' experiences tend to be centered upon themselves. With normal development a human being becomes progressively less egocentric from childhood to adulthood. See also **decentration.**

Electra complex In Freud's theory of psychosexual development, the female counterpart to the **Oedipus complex.** During the **phallic stage** of development, the girl wishes to have a sexual relationship with her father and eliminate her mother. See also **psychosexual stages.**

electroconvulsive therapy (ECT) A form of therapy for severe cases of **schizophrenia** and **depression.** It involves the passing of an electric shock through a hemisphere of the brain. In many cases, it is extremely effective. In other cases, it is of marginal use.

electroencephalogram (EEG) The EEG is a record of the brain's electrical activity and is usually recorded on the scalp. Changes in the EEG often relate to changes in arousal and alertness.

electromagnetic energy Radiant energy that spans many frequencies including electric currents, radio waves, microwaves, infrared light, visible light, ultraviolet light, and X-rays. It surrounds us at all times, but we are capable of perceiving only a tiny fraction of it.

embryonic period The first period of pregnancy, lasting in humans until about the ninth week. It is the critical stage of development for the baby's **central nervous system.**

emergency reaction The activation reaction of the body, preparing us to respond to sudden, unexpected events. Most of the emergency reaction involves stimulating the mechanisms of the **sympathetic nervous system:** increases in norepinephrine, heart rate, blood pressure, and blood volume. Skin resistance decreases; respiration, sweating, salivation, and gastric motility all increase; pupil size increases.

emotion wheel A theoretical approach to how emotions are organized. In this framework, proposed by Plutchik, the eight primary emotions are arranged in a circle of opposites. See also **primary emotions.**

emotionality An aspect of personality that remains stable through development. It refers to how readily an individual expresses emotions.

emotions Relatively specific involuntary and autonomic patterns of short-lived physiological and mental responses.

empty nest period The period for a woman in which the children leave home and become increasingly independent.

encoding The process by which perceptual processes organize sensory information into the simplest meaningful percepts.

endogenous Internal to an individual. Some cases of depression result from endogenous factors; these factors can be genetic or biochemical. See also **exogenous.**

endorphins A class of neurochemicals (peptides) that serve as modulators of nervous system activity and seem to be involved in pain and healing and in relief from unpleasant stimulation. The word derives from Greek for "the morphine within."

episodic memory A record of individual and personal experiences; memories that are unique to ourselves, such as a movie, a relationship, or experiences in learning.

Eros According to Freud, the sexual instinct, the primary source of the **libido.**

estrus The period in most female animals' lives when she is sexually receptive. During estrus, she communicates her sexual receptivity to others. See also **ovulation.**

ethology The study of behavior under natural conditions.

evolution The long series of physical changes through which species develop specific characteristics that allow them to adapt to their environment. See also **adaptation.**

exercise Healthy (not unduly stressful) physical exertion; helps to maintain both physical and mental health. It reduces the negative health effects of stress.

exogenous External to an individual. Exogenous factors such as stress, traumatic events, helplessness-inducing situations, and sociocultural circumstances can trigger the occurrence of depression. See also **endogenous.**

experiment A procedure in which a researcher creates a controlled situation in order to test the effect of one factor (the independent variable) on another (the dependent variable). See also **variable.**

experimental group That part of the **sample** with whom the researcher intervenes by manipulating the independent variable and observing this group's reactions. See also **control group, variable.**

experimental method The process of scientific investigation that involves planning and carrying out controlled experiments. See also **experiment, variable.**

expert system Artificial **intelligence** programs that are used to make decisions ordinarily made by human experts. For instance, an expert system has been devised to assist in the diagnosis of infectious diseases.

extinction The process whereby a **conditioned response (CR)** gradually decreases as a result of no longer being reinforced, because of the **conditioned stimulus (CS)** being presented without the **unconditioned stimulus (UCS).** See also **reinforcement.**

F

fear An immediate and specific emotional reaction to a threatening stimulus. Young birds show fear if the shadow of a hawk passes over them.

feature analyzers Cells in the visual area of the **cerebral cortex** that respond best to certain features in the environment. See also **receptive field.**

feedback Information about the operation of a system, used within the system to attain its goal.

feelings The subjective experience of **emotions.** Feelings can be more complex than simple emotions; jealousy is a feeling comprised of several emotions, including envy and anger.

fetal period The period of human development from about 9 weeks after conception until birth.

fight-or-flight reaction See **emergency reaction.**

fixed action pattern An ethological concept of preset behavior stimulated by predictable occurrences in the environment.

fixed interval (FI) schedule One of the four kinds of partial reinforcement schedules, in which reinforcement is presented at regular intervals after the correct response. See also **variable interval (VI), fixed ratio (FR), variable ratio (VR).**

fixed ratio (FR) schedule In this schedule of reinforcement, the reward is given after a specific number of responses.

flashbulb memory An extremely vivid memory associated with a dramatic life-altering or life-threatening event.

flooding A form of **behavior therapy** similar to **systematic desensitization.** In flooding, the therapist fills, literally "floods," the client's mind with a continuing narrative of situations that evoke fear and anxiety.

fluid abilities Mental abilities hypothesized by Cattell to be involved in the perception and registration of the world; thought to be genetically based. See also **crystallized abilities.**

fluid intelligence Measures of performance that tend to decline with advanced age (after age 50 or 60).

formal operational stage The stage from age 12 to adulthood, in Piaget's framework for cognitive development. In this higher-order stage, abstract thinking begins, complex scientific experiments can be followed, and hypotheses can be formulated and tested.

fovea At the center of the **retina,** it contains the greatest concentration of **cones** and no **rods.**

frames of mind theory of intelligence A theory proposed by Gardner that the many mental activities of a human being can be divided into six separate and potentially independent abilities, or frames of mind. These include linguistic intelligence, musical intelligence, logical-mathematical intelligence, spatial intelligence, bodily-kinesthetic intelligence, and personal intelligence.

free association A technique developed by Freud, it is a fundamental feature of psychoanalytic therapy. The patient is asked to say anything that comes into his or her mind, without criticism or editing. Free association is designed to allow normally forbidden thoughts to arise to the surface of consciousness.

frequency In perception, the property of a sound wave that is associated with the perception of pitch. In conditioning, the number of times a stimulus is associated with a reward or punishment; the rapidity with which the organism learns the association is dependent on the frequency of trials.

frontal lobes A part of the cortex intimately connected to the limbic system, so much so that many psychologists regard the frontal lobes as part of the limbic system. They are also involved in planning and seem to contain different emotions: the left side seems to be involved in positive or happy emotions; the right, negative or sad emotions.

frustration An emotion that results when a desired outcome is thwarted or delayed. It is a normal reaction to stress and to the hassles of everyday life.

functional autonomy The tendency for any action repeated often enough to become a motive in its own right. A person who initially strives to make money may continue to try to make money even after becoming very rich.

fundamental attribution error A mistake that people often make in judgment: what little information is available is overused. In judging other people, we tend to overgeneralize from a small sample we have and to underestimate situational forces and overestimate dispositional forces. So if we see someone acting brusquely, we may conclude that person is rude.

G

ganglion cells The third layer of nerve cells in the **retina.** Each ganglion has a long axon, and all these axons exit the eye at the same point, where they are bundled together and form the optic nerve that carries visual information to the brain.

gate-control theory of pain Proposes neurophysiological mechanisms in the dorsal horns of the spinal cord that increase or decrease the flow of pain impulses from peripheral nerve fibers to the central nervous system.

gender Differential behaviors and thought patterns for males and females associated with, but not caused by, biological sex.

gender identity A person's identification with what sex he or she is.

gender role The socially prescribed role within any given culture assigned on the basis of sex.

gene The basic unit of heredity in all living things. Genes are made of deoxyribonucleic acid (**DNA**). See also **chromosome.**

general adaptation syndrome The physiological reaction to extreme change, which occurs in three stages: alarm reaction, resistance, and exhaustion. It was first identified by Selye, who set out to study the syndrome of just being sick—those phenomena that occur in all illnesses. See also **emergency reaction.**

general enrichment program An early childhood education program that seeks to increase general stimulation and interaction for the child. The goal is to increase children's intelligence.

general paresis A slow degenerative disease that eventually erodes mental faculties. A scourge in the late nineteenth century, it was discovered to be caused by syphilis. This understanding of the biological roots of a supposedly mental disorder gave psychiatrists the hope that other biological causes would be found for many mental disorders.

generalization The association of related stimuli; once a specific stimulus has become a **conditioned stimulus,** similar stimuli can elicit the **conditioned response.** Someone who has an aversion to eating a hamburger may also avoid eating steak. See also **discrimination.**

generalized anxiety disorder People suffering from generalized anxiety live in constant tension and worry. They are uneasy around people and are sensitive to comments and criticism. They are often so terrified of making a mistake that they cannot concentrate or make decisions. Generalized anxiety is a very common anxiety disorder.

genetic code The sequence of instructions contained in the four chemical building blocks of the **genes** that guides the construction of any particular organism. The essential differences between human beings and turtles, at the molecular level, is only the arrangement of the chemical substances along the **DNA** molecule.

genetic potential The specific genetic endowment that may predispose an individual to an ability or a trait. See also **range of reaction.**

genetics The study of how specific characteristics are passed physically from one generation to the next.

genital stage According to Freud's stages of **psychosexual development,** the time in a person's life when adult sexuality begins.

genotype The entire complement of an individual's genetic inheritance. See also **phenotype.**

germinal period The 8- to 10-day period immediately following human conception prior to implantation of the embryo in the uterine wall.

gerontology The scientific discipline that studies the aging process and old age.

Gestalt Gestalt means to "create a form." In psychology, it is an immediate organizing of the form of an object. One of the principles of Gestalt psychology is that the whole is greater than the sum of its parts.

goals Desired outcomes that have not yet occurred. See also **achievement motivation, needs.**

gradient of reinforcement A concept from learning theory that states that the sooner a reward is given following a behavior, the stronger will be the impact of the reward.

grammar The study of the rules for formation of a specific language. See also **syntax.**

group A set of individuals, either real or imagined, who are related in some way to an individual, and whom that individual compares him or herself to.

groupthink The tendency of a group to override an individual's judgment and to make decisions that no one member would make on his or her own.

H

hassle A common, daily annoyance—like traffic jams, waiting in long lines, and foul-ups with the computer—that add measurably to emotional conflict and to stress.

Head Start A large-scale preschool enrichment program in underprivileged areas of the United States, begun in 1965.

health belief model This model of recovery from illness includes the patient's readiness to act, the costs and benefits of compliance, and the existence of a cue to action.

health psychology The application of psychological knowledge to teach people to learn to be healthy. Some research involves those who are hardy and can resist disease and those whose behavior makes them susceptible to disease.

hebephrenic A subtype of **schizophrenia** marked by regressive behavior and changeable moods; also referred to as disorganized schizophrenia.

heuristic A simplifying strategy to make judgments and solve problems—our usual mental rules of thumb.

hidden observer An important demonstration of the hypothesis that many experiences below consciousness may enter consciousness through hypnosis. In this demonstration, a person was instructed that he would feel no pain during hypnosis. While his conscious report indicated that he felt no pain, through automatic writing, his hidden observer, operating below consciousness, could still report the experience of pain, indicating that this experience was simply dissociated from consciousness.

hippocampus A structure in the **limbic system** that seems to be involved in three related functions: learning, the recognition of novelty, and the storage of memory.

homeostasis Literally, a return to the same state; the general principle whereby the body maintains a constant environment. Changes in one direction are neutralized, and body functions remain at a constant. For instance, changes in blood flow, heart rate, blood temperature, and breathing rate are all regulated to maintain constant internal processes. The best-known of these is the normal body temperature of 98.6 degrees F. See also **negative feedback.**

hominids Humans and their humanlike ancestors.

Homo erectus Probably one of the first true humans, this so-called upright man stood fully erect, walked much as we do, and had a relatively large brain and a complex culture and technology that included mastery of fire.

Homo habilis Literally "handyman," this hominid was a maker and user of tools and an efficient worker and hunter who was probably a direct ancestor of later humans.

Homo sapiens Literally "intelli-

gent man," our species. See also **Cro-Magnon.**

homosexuality Desiring sexual relations exclusively or primarily with members of one's own sex. Homosexuality was once classified as a disorder by the American Psychiatric Association, but that classification was removed in 1973.

hormones Chemicals manufactured and secreted by special glands, such as the endocrine glands; they are carried through the blood to specific target cells in the body.

human adaptation The simultaneous development, in a positive feedback loop, of all those characteristics that set humans apart from other animals. See also **adaptation.**

human factors psychology The branch of psychology involved in designing and arranging technology that is easy for people to use, also known as **ergonomics** or **human engineering.**

humanistic approach An attempt to analyze human experience by understanding important, positive aspects of life, such as growth and development.

humanistic psychology A field of psychology that studies primarily the healthy, growth-oriented side of human nature.

hunger The drive to eat. A complex system underlies the feeling of hunger, involving gastric and metabolic factors.

hunter-gatherers The typical human group through most of evolutionary history. In this kind of society there are two main activities: the search for meat and the gathering of available fruits, vegetables, and grains.

hyperphagia Extreme overeating.

hypnosis A form of dissociation in which individuals relinquish the normal control of their consciousness to another person. People under hypnosis have been able to recall events otherwise inaccessible to their waking consciousness.

They can also withstand pain and follow quite detailed suggestions.

hypochondriasis An individual's misinterpretation of bodily functions, leading usually to fear of disease or belief that he or she is already suffering from a disease.

hypothalamus A pea-sized organ located in the limbic system that regulates many activities relating to survival: eating, drinking, sleeping, waking, body temperature, balance, heart rate, hormones, sex, and emotions.

hypothesis A specific statement about what will happen if certain events take place: "if A, then B." To be scientific, a hypothesis should be able to be confirmed or disconfirmed.

hypothesis testing The systematic consideration of a series of hypotheses until all are eliminated except the one that solves the given problem.

I

id According to Freud, it is the initial, infant personality and is composed of the primary instincts (those largely concerned with survival) and other inherited psychological characteristics. See also **ego superego.**

illusory correlation Sometimes we expect things to be connected and so we perceive a connection between two events that are really random, such as washing cars makes it rain.

imprinting The process of a newly born or newly hatched animal seeing an object, usually its mother, and following it; a prepared reaction that leads to a greater chance of survival.

in utero Literally, within the uterus; the prenatal period.

independent variable See **variable.**

individual distance The basic minimum distance members of a species keep between themselves.

individuation The term Jung used to refer to the process of development. He believed individuation

to occur across the life-span and to include four stages: childhood, youth, middle age, and old age.

information processing components These comprise one part of Sternberg's triarchic theory of intelligence. They are the mental mechanisms that translate sensory or mental representations and include metacomponents such as planning, performance components, and knowledge-acquisition components.

innate Inborn, unlearned, fixed at birth; usually applied to such characteristics as **instincts.**

insight A vision of how all the parts of a problem fit together or of how to represent the problem differently. The experience of insight can come either at the end of a process of hypothesis testing or seemingly all at once.

instinct An innate, fixed pattern of behavior typical of every member of a given species; thought to be programmed to satisfy needs and to appear without learning as soon as it is needed. The salmon's inevitable return to the river of its birth is instinctual.

instinctive drift A phenomenon identified by Breland and Breland that indicates that various organisms have difficulty learning arbitrary responses because learned behavior drifts toward instinctive behavior.

instrumental enrichment (I.E.) A program devised by Feuerstein in Israel, which attempts to develop a special set of techniques to increase intelligence and to assess increases in intelligence.

instrumental conditioning See **operant conditioning.**

intelligence quotient (IQ) A measure first devised by Binet for testing individuals for their suitability for either normal or remedial school. The IQ test is probably psychology's most visible contribution to society, and its most controversial. Many psychologists feel that it is a useful predictor of how well a person will do in society, while many more feel that

it is only a measure of a kind of achievement and reflects more an individual's background than his or her potential.

interest inventory A kind of personality test used to counsel people about what careers might suit them.

intermediate layer One of the three main layers of nerve cells in the **retina,** comprising bipolar cells, horizontal cells, and amacrine cells. See also **ganglion cells, photoreceptors.**

interneuron Nerve cells in the spinal cord that connect **afferent** and **efferent** neurons.

interposition A cue to depth, provided when one object is in front of another and blocks part or all of the other object.

interpretation After organization, interpretation is the second step in discovering meaning. A question we answer when we interpret phenomena is "What is the simplest meaningful stimulus that gives rise to my experience?"

interpretation of dreams An analytic technique used by psychotherapists to understand patients' subconscious fears and anxieties.

intimacy According to Sternberg's theory of love, one of three components of love, along with passion and commitment. Intimate feelings include the desire to promote the welfare of the loved one, holding the loved one in high esteem, and sharing and mutual understanding.

introspection The primary research method used by late-nineteenth-century psychologists; it involved studying their own minds and examining the contents of their own experience.

J

just noticeable difference (j.n.d.) See **difference threshold.**

K

kinesthesis The feedback from the joints of the body, which allows us to know and coordinate the movement of different parts of the body (where limbs are, what their angle is, and what they are doing).

knowledge Information that helps us understand the world. The search for knowledge is a vital human motive; our health suffers when our understanding of the world is in disarray.

kyphosis A minor bending of the spine that occurs with age.

L

latency stage In Freud's theory of **psychosexual** development, the latency stage follows the **phallic stage.** During this period, the child's sensual desires become dormant from about age 6 until puberty.

latent learning Learning that can occur without being manifested in an observable performance improvement.

lateral geniculate nucleus (LGN) Lateral means "sideways"; a geniculate is a bend or joint. The LGN, a structure in the **thalamus** alerts the primary visual cortex to visual input.

lateral inhibition Retinal cells fire and affect one another. The stronger the sensation, the more they fire. Whenever a cell fires, it inhibits the firing of a cell next to it (laterally). This mechanism sharpens perception of sharp changes, like corners and edges. It sometimes makes edges appear when there are none.

law of effect The principle that we act in such a way as to obtain pleasure and avoid pain. As Thorndike described it, we are likely to repeat actions that are followed by a "satisfying state of affairs."

learned helplessness The belief that one has no control over events and that actions do not lead to goals. This can decrease motivation, decrease the ability to learn new responses, and increase emotional disturbance.

learning In its strictest sense, a change in behavior due to experience.

levels of processing A theory of memory stating that all information presented to us is processed at different depths or levels. According to this theory, the greater the depth of processing, the more likely something is to be remembered. The deepest processing relates information to oneself.

libido In Freud's theory, the animal instincts provide the fuel for actions and for the human mind. In human beings, this biological fuel is transformed into psychic energy, called libido.

life narrative A story we compose about our personal histories that integrate our thoughts, feelings, and memories. This is one way we make sense of our lives and construct our identities.

life expectancy The average number of years a person can expect to live; unless otherwise specified, it refers to life expectancy at birth.

life-span development Changes in humans across the life course.

limbic system A group of cellular structures between the brain stem and the cortex that evolved about 150 million years ago. It is the area of the brain that helps maintain constant environment in the body: regulating the maintenance of body temperature, blood pressure, heart rate, and levels of sugar in the blood. See also **homeostasis.**

lock-and-key principle The principle that each neuron transmitter has a specific shape that fits a specific receptor, as a key fits into a lock. This relationship describes how chemical messages can connect with their target cells.

long-term memory A kind of memory thought to store permanent records of experiences, including both **episodic** and **representational memory.**

longitudinal study Research in which a group of people are studied over a number of years or even decades. See also **cohort effect.**

love Although this is a complex experience, one important theory describes love as having three components: intimacy, passion, and arousal.

lucid dreaming Being aware that one is dreaming while remaining in the dream state.

M

main effect The primary result of an experimental manipulation.

major life changes People are more likely to become ill after extensive life changes, which include positive events—such as marriage, vacations, and outstanding personal achievements —and negative events—such as marital separation, death of a close friend, and jail terms.

maladaptive Not serving the individual's well-being.

mania Excessive elation. An individual in a manic episode may be caught up in a frenzy of overexcitability and activity. Grandiose and impossible plans may be made during such manic episodes. Mania is a serious condition, but it is treatable, often by chemical means.

maturation The emergence of individual characteristics through normal growth processes. It is controlled by the information contained in the genes, relatively unaffected by learning or experience, and follows a universal pattern.

maximal life span Under optimal living conditions, the longest possible time a human can live.

mean The arithmetic average of a set of numbers.

means-end analysis A method of problem solving by which we work backward from the goal through the thing needed to achieve it. If the goal is to cook spaghetti, we need a kitchen to cook it in and all the ingredients for spaghetti.

median From the Latin word for *middle*. It is the middle figure in a distribution of numbers.

mediated learning experience The information about the world, events, and experiences interpreted by others, usually a parent or sibling. Thus the meaning of events is given to us by other people. In Feuerstein's theory of **instrumental enrichment,** the roots of intelligence will be found in the adequacy of the mediated learning experience.

meditation A system of mental training that often involves relaxation and an attempt at knowledge of oneself and one's place in the world. It is a different form of knowledge than the intellectual and academic knowledge taught in the schools.

memory cycle The three linked processes that allow an event to be recalled: perception, retention, and retrieval.

memory system The two components to memory: short-term and long-term. See also **short-term memory** and **long-term memory.**

menarche The onset of first menstruation.

menopause Cessation of a woman's ovulation and menstruation, normally occurring in the late 40s or early 50s, which marks the end of reproductive ability.

mental age Based on the concept that intellectual abilities increase with age, it attributes various levels of attainment (ages) to different **IQ** scores.

mental retardation A syndrome, resulting from multiple causes, characterized by subnormal intellectual functioning.

meta-analysis An examination of the effectiveness of several methods of analysis.

metabolism Bodily processes that maintain a constant energy supply to the brain and body.

method of loci A memory method developed by the Greeks. With it, a person tries to create a new and different association to improve recall by visualizing the items to be recalled.

method of observation Observations are made in three ways: case histories, measurements and tests, and questionnaires in which feelings and opinions may be reported.

mid-life crisis A hypothesized stage in middle adulthood when people review and assess their early adulthood. They may try to change the facets of life that they are dissatisfied with. It may be triggered by awareness of their own mortality and may lead to radical changes, such as job or family disruptions.

mindfulness The awareness of behavior and thoughts, in contrast to automatic behavior and thoughts.

mindguard A member of a group who acts to shield the group from information that might alter the decision and discourages criticism, which results in an inadequate search for information.

Minnesota Multiphasic Personality Inventory (MMPI) The most widely used personality test, used for psychiatric diagnosis and research on personality.

mitosis The process of cell division that underlies normal organism growth.

mnemonic A technique for aiding memory. It involves making up a context in which certain meaningless items can be remembered, such as "Spring ahead, fall back" to remember which way to change clocks for Daylight Savings Time.

modeling How, by observation, we create a mental model or schema that directs behavior. Four processes are involved: attention, retention, production, and motivational processes.

monoamine oxidase (MAO) inhibitors A class of antidepressant drugs that prevents the enzyme monoamine oxidase from deactivating **neurotransmitters,** resulting in an increase in norepinephrine and serotonin, and a subsequent elevation of mood.

monozygotic Developed from the same fertilized egg, as in monozygotic (identical) twins.

mood Long-lasting states of feeling. See also **affective disorders.**

moral anxiety According to Freud, a fear, arising from the **superego,** that one will not live up to standards.

morality The knowledge of what is right and what is wrong. According to Kohlberg, morality develops in several stages, from the **premoral stage** through the **conventional moral stage** to the **postconventional stage** of morality. These stages, in most part, parallel developments in cognition and are based on them.

morpheme The smallest unit of meaning in language. A morpheme can be a word, such as *car,* *but,* or *teach.* It can also be fragments, such as common prefixes and suffixes of words.

motion parallax The difference in apparent speed and direction of movement by objects at varying distances from a moving observer.

motives Processes that guide and drive our behavior. They range from basic and universal, such as hunger or thirst, to ethereal, such as the desire for self-actualization. Maslow described a pyramid of motives, with basic needs at the bottom and complex goals at the top.

mutation A spontaneous change in the structure of one or more genes.

myelin sheath A fatty substance coating the axons of many neurons. It serves to insulate, to accelerate neuronal transmission, and to isolate neurons from one another.

N

natural categories Systems of classification that reflect the structure of the physical world. An example would be categories of color.

natural immunity The general inflammatory processes that respond when tissue is damaged. These processes permit natural agents to enter the damaged tissues and neutralize bacteria and viruses.

natural selection Described by Darwin in 1859, this theory elucidates how populations can change over time. It involves two insights: those individuals who do survive must in some way be more fit, better able to live in and adapt to their environment; and the offspring differ in important respects from the parents. Therefore, differences that are passed on to the offspring usually enable them to fit better in their environment. The ''natural'' selection is made by the environment. See also **adaptation.**

nature Innate characteristics derived from heredity in the argument over whether human behavior is determined by nature or nurture.

nature-nurture The controversy in psychology over whether our behavior is determined more by innate characteristics or by experiences in the environment. Most behavior is the product of both factors.

Neanderthal The cave man of popular folklore but with mental abilities and a culture far more advanced than was once suspected. Very like modern humans in many ways.

needs In psychological terms, the specific deficits that any animal must satisfy, such as hunger and thirst. See also **goals.**

neo-Freudians Psychodynamically oriented therapists who use in their practices a modified version of classical Freudian psychoanalysis.

neuroendocrine system The system comprising the **autonomic nervous system (ANS)** and the endocrine glands, which is one of the means through which the brain controls the body.

neuron Nerve cells that are the building blocks of the brain and the nervous system. The nucleus of the neuron is called the **cell body.** There are approximately ten billion neurons in the human brain, each neuron having as many as thousands of different interconnections.

neurosis In the definition of Freud, an unconscious conflict between the desires of the **id** and the demands of the **superego.** He felt a neurosis often occurrs as a result of traumatic experiences in early childhood.

neurotic anxiety According to Freud, fears of yielding to the passions of the **id,** arising from pressures on the **ego** from the id.

neurotransmission, neurotransmitter The process by which nerve cells in the brain and other parts of the body communicate with one another. This process is largely chemical. When a **neuron** fires, it releases chemicals (neurotransmitters) at its **axon,** which then migrate across the synaptic cleft to a second cell.

nicotine The active ingredient of tobacco. It is highly toxic and extremely addicting.

nondirective In psychotherapy, an approach in which the patient is supported and accepted as he or she is without suggesting change.

nonsense syllables Hermann Ebbinghaus devised lists of syllables such as ''dof,'' ''zam,'' and ''fok'' to eliminate any effect subjects' personal experience might have on their ability to recall information and to obtain a precise measure of learning and memory independent of previous experience.

norepinephrine Formerly called noradrenaline, this **neurotransmitter** is important in coding of memory and in the reward system of the brain. As a **hormone,** it prepares the body to respond to external events.

normal aging Age-related, gradual, and irreversible changes in mental and bodily functions that are not related to disease. See also **abnormal aging.**

norms Standards of permissible thought and behavior shared by members of a group.

nurture Usually thought as opposed to nature; the effect of heredity, nurture refers to the effects on the developing person of experiences in the environment.

O

obedience Unquestioning acquiescence to a request or command.

object permanence An important demonstration first pointed out by Piaget, that children, at about 8 months, begin to be able to form a representation of an object not present. They will follow an object that they have previously seen and attempt to find it. Younger children will not look for such a vanished object.

observational learning Also referred to as **social learning,** it involves learning through watching others and modeling or imitating their behavior.

obsessive-compulsive disorder (OCD) In an obsession the mind is flooded with a specific thought. In a compulsive disorder the person feels compelled to repeat a certain action over and over again.

occipital lobes The area at the back of the brain that is devoted entirely to vision.

ocular accommodation To focus on close objects, the lens of a camera must bend the light so it falls on the film. The eye works in a similar way. When we look at objects at different distances, the width of the lens needs to change to focus light on the retina. This change is called ocular accommodation.

Oedipus complex According to Freud, the conflict that a boy feels in the **phallic stage** of **psychosexual** development. The boy's love for his mother takes on a sexual component and he wishes to eliminate his father as a rival. See also **Electra complex.**

opening-up meditation A type of meditation in which the exercises employed involve everyday activities in the training of consciousness. Consciousness is opened up to everything that occurs, rather than limited to a narrow focus. See also **meditation, concentrative meditation.**

operant conditioning Also called **instrumental conditioning,** it was developed by B. F. Skinner beginning in the 1930s. In this form of conditioning, it is the organism's operations or actions that are conditioned. Operant conditioning is very useful for teaching organisms new responses and the contingencies of different situations. See also **conditioning, reinforcement, respondent conditioning.**

operant strength In **operant conditioning,** the measure of the rate of response after conditioning, of the strength of association between a behavior and its reinforcement.

operations In Piaget's theory of cognitive development, the rules for transforming and manipulating information in the world. A simple arithmetic operation is "If you have two and add two, you will have four."

opponent process Color information sent from the eye to the brain contains opposite dimensions; blue-yellow, red-green, and dark-light.

optical expansion In the analysis of perception, the way items seem to move apart, or expand, as we approach them; used as a cue to judge distance and movement.

optimum level of arousal The ideal condition of stimulation. The optimal level is usually in the middle of an organism's response range. Here pleasure is greatest, and reinforcement and the processing of information is most efficient.

oral stage The first of Freud's stages of **psychosexual development.** The oral stage begins at birth and continues for about 18 months, during which time the infant derives its pleasure from its mouth.

organic mental disorders A class of mental disorders that stems directly from biological dysfunction of the brain.

orgasm The brief and most intense phase of the sexual response cycle, during which arousal, muscle tension, heart rate, and respiration increase rapidly to a peak, which for males also involves ejaculation.

orienting reflex (OR) The physiological changes that prepare the organism for action: muscles tense, neurotransmitters increase, sensory acuity sharpens. See also **emergency reaction.**

ovulation The time when the female's developed egg is released from the ovary, and thus can be fertilized. In human females this takes place every month, rather than only during **estrus,** a more limited period of ovulation during which other female mammals are fertile and sexually receptive to males.

P

pair bonding The sexual bond that is the basis of the family, that encourages fathers to stay with, care for, and care about their mates and their offspring, permitting families to expand faster through the sharing of food and childrearing responsibilities.

panic disorder A form of **anxiety** disorder in which acute episodes of extreme physiological and psychological fear are experienced seemingly independent of threatening external stimuli.

parallel process model A model of mental processing in which several simultaneous processors are assumed to operate on the same information.

paranoia Extreme distrust and suspiciousness of others; in some cases specific individuals are identified and in others a general feeling of persecution is experienced.

parasympathetic nervous system A division of the **autonomic nervous system,** it acts to return the body to normal after emergencies. See also **sympathetic nervous system.**

parental investment The contribution of resources by a parents to offspring that enhances the survival potential of the offspring.

parietal lobes The area between the **frontal lobes** and the **occipital lobes** that is involved in the integration and analysis of sensory input, although its functions are not all that clearly understood.

partial reinforcement (PR) In this form of reinforcement, each time the animal makes a correct response, the reinforcement does not always occur. See also **continuous reinforcement, operant conditioning.**

passion One of the components of Sternberg's theory of love. Passion is a state of intense longing for the other. See also **passionate love.**

passionate love This is the strong physical form of being in love; a state of intense absorption in another person. It includes arousal, longing, and activation of many different emotions.

perception The complex process by which an organism extracts the important meaningful features of its environment.

perceptual adaptation How each organism adjusts perceptions to suit conditions; as in darkness, in which otherwise dim lights are well perceived. See **adaptation.**

perceptual organization The fusion and coordination of separate stimuli into something meaningful.

peripheral nervous system (PNS) Nerves from the spinal cord that conduct impulses to the muscles and organs of the body, gather information about body states, muscle position, limb position, and internal states of organs. See also **central nervous system.**

person-centered therapy An influential form of psychotherapy developed by Rogers. In this **humanistic** therapy, the most important element is the relationship between the therapist and client. Clients are encouraged by means of nondirective statements to explore and reveal their feelings about themselves and their life situations. Once these situations can come to consciousness, a clarification of beliefs and action follow.

persona The term used by Jung to refer to the social mask worn when interacting with others in the various roles we play in our lives.

personal space Defined by Edward Hall as "a small protective space or bubble that an organism maintains between itself and others." See also **individual distance.**

personal unconscious One part of the structure of the unconscious mind postulated by Jung. It consists of forgotten, suppressed, or weak memories and includes complexes. See also **complex.**

personality The unique and stable qualities of an individual. The thoughts, feelings, and actions that characterize an individual over time and across situations.

perspective A cue for judging distance, such as parallel lines converging on the horizon, important in two-dimensional representations of three dimensions.

persuasion The act of convincing someone to do something.

phallic stage According to Freud, the stage of **psychosexual** development the child enters at about age 3, in which the genitals are the focus of pleasure. During this stage, which lasts roughly three years, the child must resolve the conflicts engendered by the **Oedipus** or **Electra complex.**

pharmacotherapy An attempt to treat psychological problems by administering drugs in four major categories: antipsychotics, antidepressants, anti-anxiety drugs, and lithium compounds.

phenotype The portion of the **genotype** (genetic inheritance) that is expressed in the organism.

pheromone Chemical substances used by members of various animal species to communicate with others of their kind.

phobia From the Greek word for *fear.* In psychology the term refers to an extreme or unfounded fear of an object or place.

phoneme The specific sound element of language. A particular sound is considered a phoneme only if it is used in language.

photoreceptor A **rod** or **cone,** nerve cells containing photochemicals that respond to light;

constitute the main layer of the **retina.**

physical maturation Genetically determined biological change that occurs from conception throughout life.

pica An eating disorder marked by the persistent ingestion of non-food substances.

pituitary The control gland of the **neuroendocrine system,** it lies below the **hypothalamus** in the **limbic system.**

placebo From Latin "I shall please." A substance or treatment that has no specific therapeutic value. However, placebos can produce a wide range of physical and psychological effects, some helpful and some detrimental.

pleasure principle In Freud's theory of personality, the principle that organisms seek to reduce tension created by the build-up of **libido.**

polarity In Plutchik's theory of emotions, the opposition of emotions, such as love and hate, sadness and joy. See also **emotion wheel.**

population genetics The study of inheritance patterns of mental and physical disorders based on prevalence in genetically related individuals.

post-traumatic stress disorder (PTSD) An **anxiety** disorder that follows a genuinely traumatic event in which the individual continues to re-experience physiological and psychological symptoms that first occurred during the trauma.

postconventional morality In Kohlberg's theory of moral development, moral reasoning based on individual principles of conscience, which respect both the moral rights of individuals and the welfare of the community. See also **conventional morality, premoral level.**

potency A component of emotional appraisal proposed by Osgood: a person judging an emotional experience asks, "Is it alive or dead, strong or weak, fast or slow?"

Power law A principle of sensation described by Stephens that shows that the different senses transform the information they select differently. Within each sensory system, equal ratios of stimulus intensity produce equal ratios of change in experience. See also **Weber's law.**

preconscious A level of awareness that includes memories that enable us to operate in the world.

prehuman beings Creatures having both apelike and humanlike characteristics. See also **hominids.**

prejudice A negative judgmental attitude toward an identifiable group of people, usually based on a simplistic overgeneralization.

Premack's principle The process by which a more favored behavior can be used to reinforce a less favored behavior.

premoral level In Kohlberg's theory of moral development, the first level of moral reasoning in which individuals consider only their own interest. See also **conventional morality, postconventional morality.**

preoperational stage In Piaget's view of cognitive development, the stage (from 2 to 7 years) at which a child is able to represent objects in drawings or words and in which **schemata** become more integrated and coordinated.

preparedness An influential concept developed by Seligman, which hypothesizes that certain animals are more predisposed (prepared) to learn certain given responses better than other animals.

prepotence In Maslow's hierarchy of motivation, prepotence denotes the relative strength of different needs. In this view, the stronger needs are lower on the hierarchy. The need for water is a stronger need than the need for friendship.

presbycusis Hearing loss that results from the loss of ganglion cells in the inner ear.

presbyopia The form of farsightedness that occurs in normal aging.

primacy Enhanced recall of beginnings in learning: the first words in a list are easier to learn than the latter ones; the first lessons of a course are easier to learn and remember than the latter ones. See also **recency.**

primary (basic) emotions Many psychologists now hypothesize that there are several primary emotions, as there are primary colors. Plutchik names eight primary emotions: joy, acceptance, fear, surprise, sadness, disgust, anger, and anticipation.

primary reinforcer A reinforcement whose effect is direct, such as food, water, sex, sleep, comfort, and relief from pain.

privacy The need to be alone. Privacy is sought in different ways in different cultures.

proactive interference The interference of previous knowledge with present memory. See also **retroactive interference.**

proband In population genetics, the person who serves as the starting point for tracing inheritance patterns of disorders in families.

problem representation The way a person thinks about or presents a problem may make it harder or easier to solve. Some problems need to be represented visually, some purely mathematically. The wrong representation to a problem may dramatically change how it works.

problem solving Making a decision or finding a solution to a conflict. Different kinds of problems require different problem-solving strategies.

procedural memory The kind of memory that contains automated schemata for performing routine actions and underlies perceptual experience. Its contents are not subject to verbalization.

professional psychology The branch of psychology that trains and practices application of psychology rather than research.

programmed senescence A cellular theory of aging, developed by Hayflick, that is based on the limited replicability of human cells.

projective techniques Methods, originally proposed by Jung, of attaining access to the content of an individual's unconscious mind. They induce the subject to project inner needs and conflicts onto ambiguous stimuli. See also **Rorschach ink blot test** and **Thematic Apperception Test (TAT).**

proprioception The sense that allows us to know where each part of the body is in relation to all other parts.

prosocial behavior Behaving in such a way as to enhance social integration and the actions of others.

protocol analysis A method of analysis of thought, used by Newell and Simon to study how people solve puzzles. This method involves recording verbatim statements made by a person while he or she is solving a problem and analyzing the protocol by means of a problem behavior graph.

prototype The sample that most typifies a category. A concept of *house* evokes the prototype of four walls, ceiling, paintings on the wall.

proxemics An analysis of personal space developed by Hall. Personal distance is classified in four different ways: intimate, personal, social, and public.

psychedelic Literally from Greek for "mind manifesting." Commonly used to refer to hallucinogenic drugs because of their effects on thinking and emotional processes.

psychiatric social worker The holder of an advanced degree, such as an MS or PhD. Usually concentrates on social and community-based problems.

psychiatrist A medical doctor whose specialty is the treatment of psychological problems.

psychic determinism A fundamental hypotheses of psychoanalysis. It is the idea that no behavior happens by chance; all thoughts, behaviors, and symptoms have meaning and are determined by past events.

psychoactive drugs Substances—such as marijuana, mescaline, and LSD—that change the overall structure of consciousness.

psychoanalysis The most famous and one of the most influential theories in psychology. Proposed by Freud and developed from the late nineteenth century until 1940, it is a complete theory of personality and a method of treatment. It specifies what motivates people, how personality develops, and how it is built. Its primary aim is to show that the relationship between conscious and unconscious processes is often the root of much of behavior, especially behavior that causes us difficulties.

psychoanalyst A psychotherapist trained in the psychoanalytic techniques formulated by Freud; almost all psychoanalysts are physicians.

psychoanalytic interpretation A method used to reach unconscious material in psychoanalysis. It involves analyzing faulty actions or slips. Freud postulated that these behaviors provide clues to unconscious desires.

psychodynamic therapy Psychotherapeutic approaches in which treatment is based on the resolution of intrapsychic conflict.

psychological disorders Patterns of behaving and thinking that are both deviant and maladaptive.

psychological maturation Change rooted in the development of cognitive and emotional domains; in contrast to physical maturation, which is based on biological change.

psychopath See **antisocial personality.**

psychophysics The beginnings of psychology, in the relationship of the mental world ("psycho") with the external world ("physics"). This study, begun by Weber and Fechner, showed that these two worlds were not at all identical.

psychoses Disorders marked by severe emotional and cognitive impairment in which the person is clearly out of touch with reality.

psychosexual stages The series of five phases of human development proposed by Freud. Each stage is named for an erogenous zone. If an individual were to fail to resolve a major conflict in any given stage, his or her personality would fixate on that stage.

psychosomatic medicine A theory that particular personality traits are components of the cause of particular illnesses such as bronchial asthma, essential hypertension, gastric ulcers, and colitis.

puberty The point in physical maturation when the individual becomes capable of reproduction.

punishment A negative consequence to a behavior that decreases the likelihood that the behavior will occur.

Purkinje shift The change in human sensitivity to wavelengths of light that occurs in conditions of dim illumination. The peak of sensitivity shifts down about 50 nanometers so that bluish colors are seen better than in brightly lit conditions.

Q

Q-sort A test used by cognitive psychologists to assess an individual's concept of his or herself. The person ranks statements according to how personally relevant they are.

questionnaire A formal method for asking specific questions that will provide researchers dependable answers on which to base their judgments.

R

range of reaction The portion of an individual's **genetic potential** that predisposes him or her to a certain ability or trait. Whether the predisposition develops into a reality depends on experience and environmental factors.

Rapid Eye Movement (REM) sleep A stage of sleep that appears in approximately 90-minute cycles throughout the night. It is characterized by an active brain, occasional rapid eye movements, and low muscle tone. This is the stage of sleep during which most dreaming occurs.

rational-emotive therapy (RET) A form of therapy, developed by Ellis, in which the therapist determines what the underlying belief system of the individual is, confronts the client with that belief system and directly forces him or her to examine it against reality.

reactance An angry or hostile reaction to a loss of freedom.

realistic anxiety In Freud's theories, fears that arise from real dangers in the environment to threaten the ego.

recall The ability to summon up stored information in the absence of the actual object or event.

recency Enhanced recall of the end of a string of stimuli; what is last is highly remembered. See also **primacy**.

receptive field The area of stimulation that a retinal cell responds best to. Different cells have been found to have different shaped receptive fields.

reciprocal determinism The idea that the environment has an impact on our thoughts, feelings, and actions, which in turn shape the environment.

reciprocity norm The social contract that requires that we repay our obligations, and which can be employed to create an obligation.

recognition The ability to correctly identify an object or an event.

reconditioning The conditioning of a new, more adaptive set of responses to replace maladaptive responses.

reference group In social comparisons, we learn to compare ourselves to other people on a number of dimensions, such as the speed with which we run, writing ability, and the like. The group we choose to compare ourselves to is the reference group, often a group of peers or appropriate individuals.

reflex Inborn, unlearned responses of newborns, many of which involve sophisticated motor skills. Reflexes include sucking and head turning in response to noise.

reinforcement Any event that strengthens the possibility that a certain response will recur. When something is given to an animal after a desired response, this is called *positive reinforcement*. When something unpleasant is taken away from the animal after a desired response, this is called *negative reinforcement*.

relaxation Decreasing tension in the body. Relaxation exercises can be effective for the bodily aspect of the stress response.

religious experience The aim and occasional result of meditation and spiritual exercises. William James described them as having the characteristics of feelings of unity of all things, the sense that the perceptions of the experience are more real than ordinary reality, ineffability, and extraordinary vividness.

replicability, replication Psychological experiments need to be repeated (replicated) by others. If the findings of a second experiment confirm those of the first, then the findings of the first experiment are more likely to be accepted.

representational memory General knowledge about the world and how to function in it, such as how to speak, how to ride a bicycle, and where Chicago and Scotland are. It is information common to all members of a culture.

representational (symbolic) thought At about 18 months, children begin to develop the capacity to represent objects in their minds. One important kind of symbol is language.

representativeness The judgment that an object is typical of its category. Because we tend to judge vivid examples of a category as representative, a single case, considered representative, can have a disproportionate influence on us.

resistance In psychoanalysis, a characteristic way that the patient unconsciously works against revealing his or her feelings or thoughts. For instance, every time a patient might start to talk about his or her father, he or she might change the subject, tell a joke, or say the thought is too silly.

resolution of the transference In psychodynamic therapy, the working through of problems by projecting onto a therapist neurotic conflicts and resolving them in new, more adaptive ways.

respondent conditioning The process whereby a previously neutral stimulus (NS) comes to have a significant effect on an organism's behavior. Also known as classical conditioning. See also **conditioned response, conditioned stimulus, conditioning, operant conditioning, unconditioned response, unconditioned stimulus.**

retention A process in memory in which new information must be stored and kept. This is a hypothetical stage in the cycle of memory, used by many psychologists. See also **retrieval.**

reticular activating system (RAS) The RAS arouses the cortex to important incoming stimulation. It seems to serve a general alarm function: it tells the cortex that something visual, auditory, or olfactory is on its way. The RAS controls the existence and the intensity of consciousness.

retina The rear part of the eye onto which light is focused. The center of the process of vision, comprised of neural tissues and about the thickness of this page.

retirement The cessation of wage-earning work.

retrieval A process hypothesized by many psychologists in which stored information is brought forward into consciousness at the appropriate time. See also **retention.**

retroactive interference The interference of new information with the memory of old information. See also **proactive interference.**

rods One of the two kinds of photoreceptors in the eye. Rods respond most to light energy at low levels, particularly those of a wave length of 480 nm. There are about 120 million rods distributed over the **retina;** the heaviest concentration is at the sides. See also **cone, photoreceptor.**

role In social psychology, the set of expectations and behaviors associated with a particular personification, such as "the boss" or "the bad child."

role playing In behavior therapy, the simulation of social situations which provides an opportunity to train new ways of handling interpersonal problems.

Rorschach ink blot test A **projective technique** in which people identify the forms they see in the ambiguous figures of inkblots. Psychologists use the clients' responses to make inferences about their personal needs and conflicts.

S

saccades The fast, sharp movements the eyes normally make when looking. They ensure that the **retina** constantly receives fresh information.

sample The group of subjects, representative of an entire population, in an experiment or study.

schema, schemata (pl.) A mental concept; the internal, mental organization of how actions relate to one another, how different internal stimuli relate to one another, and how outside stimuli relate to specific actions. Schemata are the cognitive generalizations about oneself that guide the processing of information and interpretation about oneself.

schizophrenia The group of psychological disorders that involve severe deterioration of mental abilities; fundamental disorganization that causes disturbances in every area of life: social functioning, feeling, behavior.

seasonal affective disorder (SAD) A mood disorder evoked by

changes in light exposure. People with SAD often become severely depressed in the dark winter months and sometimes manic in the light months of the spring and summer.

secondary reinforcer Something associated with a primary reinforcer. Once we learn that money (a secondary reinforcer) buys food and other primary reinforcers, then receiving money is, in itself, reinforcing, and so we work to get money.

secondary traits In Allport's theory of personality, these are traits that only occur in a few specific situations. A person may be generally calm but may become anxious on airplanes. See also cardinal traits.

sedative A type of drug, such as a **barbiturate,** that induces relaxation and sleep.

selection A major principle of sensory and conscious experiences. Since there is so much more information available in the world than can be perceived, we need to limit (select) the information that reaches us. The first selection is the result of the biological nature of the senses themselves.

self A central concept in **humanistic psychology.** The self is the entire experience of an individual, including temperament, traits, memories, thoughts, feelings, and actions.

self-actualization Maslow theorized that we all have within us certain potentials and that we strive to fulfill those potentials (make them actual). Thus, self-actualization is the drive within individuals to actualize their potential.

self-awareness The consciousness of our own existence and mortality; the knowledge of who we are and the sense of personal self.

self-schemata Cognitive generalizations that guide the processing of information and interpretation about the self.

self-serving bias When things go wrong and we are asked to account for our own behavior, we blame the situation; when things go right, we take credit.

semantic memory The knowledge of a specific language, of what words mean, and how they are used within a specific culture. The average college student has a vocabulary of about 50,000 words in semantic memory.

sense of coherence A strong conviction that our environment and life are predictable and that things will work out well. The idea was proposed by Antonevsky as a trait that promotes physical and psychological health and social functioning.

sense of control The assumption that our behavior is under our own control. Some researchers have suggested that maintaining a sense of personal control is so important that it approaches the category of a psychological need.

sensorimotor stage In Piaget's view of cognitive development, the stage (up to 2 years of age) during which a child learns primarily through motor and sensory play, begins to develop a sense of self, and starts to be capable of representational or symbolic thought. See also **object permanence.**

sensory adaptation See **adaptation.**

separation anxiety The extreme distress shown by infants usually around 8 months of age when their mothers leave them in the care of someone else. See also **attachment.**

serotonin A neurotransmitter that connects the brain stem and reticular activating system to the cortex and to the limbic system. It is thought to be very much involved in sleep and sleep regulation.

set A pattern of thought or behavior that becomes habitual because it has worked for solving past problems. Sets can lead to inefficiencies and difficulties in solving new problems.

set point The body tends to maintain a set point for weight, as it does body temperature. The **hypothalamus** can control eating, drinking, and metabolic level to raise or lower caloric expenditure. The implications of this set point are that weight is much more difficult either to gain or to lose than we would like and that people's normal weight is more likely to be higher than the current social norm. See also **homeostasis.**

sex A characteristic determined by the biological structure of reproductive organs. Sex is determined by genetics. See **gender.**

sexual response cycle The regular physiological changes involved in sexual activity and sexual intercourse, described by Masters and Johnson as comprising four phases: excitement, plateau, orgasm, and resolution.

sex roles See **gender roles.**

sexuality The sexual character of a person.

shadow The part of our personality that we reject and repress into our unconscious mind.

short-term memory The process by which information is thought to be stored for temporary retention of only a few seconds. Its capacity is about seven items, such as a seven-digit number.

simplification The process whereby detailed or complex sensations are reduced to a small number of well-organized categories. Simplification is essential to perception.

situational attribution A judgment that the cause of the behavior is due to the particular circumstances, and not to an enduring disposition of the person.

Sixteen Personality Factor (16PF) A questionnaire developed by Cattell based on 16 basic trait dimensions. It is used by psychologists to identify an individual's personality profile.

Skinner box A controlled environment developed by Skinner, the behaviorist psychologist. It contains a food tray, a lever, and a water spout. An animal in the box is trained to press the lever to attain a reward (often food) or to avoid a punishment (often electric shock).

sociability An aspect of personality that tends to remain consistent throughout development. It is the level of desire to be around others and respond to them.

social comparison An important theory in social psychology by Festinger. If there is no objective measure of comparison, we tend to seek out other people whom we admire or believe are like us, and compare our attitudes and behavior to theirs. There is no generally accepted yardstick for determining such questions as How smart am I? Am I well behaved? The only way to achieve such comparisons is to compare oneself to others.

social environmental perspective The study of how other people and environment affect us.

social facilitation The effect of others on our performance. Having others around interferes with difficult tasks. But if the task is easy, having others around improves performance.

social impact theory As the number of others around us increases the total impact on us also increases. But as the group grows, each added person has less of an individual impact.

social learning theory An outgrowth of the learning theory analyses of conditioning in the 1930s. It emphasizes that most behavior is learned rather than instinctually determined. It generally rejects the idea of an unconscious and favors an analysis of the situational and immediate determinants of behavior.

social loafing A phenomenon that occurs when a sizable group is working together on a project, whereby some people do not work to their capacity because they assume others will pick up the burden.

social psychology The attempt to understand and explain how thoughts, feelings, and actions are influenced by the actual, imagined, or implied presence of others.

social referencing The process whereby preverbal infants look to their mothers' expressions for information about uncertain situations.

social releasers Animals' physical signals—such as odors, postures, facial expression, and gestures—that communicate information about probable behavior to other animals.

social support The company and attention of others. Many studies have shown that the more social support a person has, the less likely he or she is to become ill when under stress.

socioanalytic theory A theory developed by Hogan that our motives are primarily social, and that we construct our self-concept within the context of the roles we play in society.

sociobiology A field of study that attempts to account for much social behavior in biological terms. Important questions dealt with by sociobiologists are altruism, male/female sex differences, and territoriality.

sociopath See **antisocial personality.**

somatic nervous system (SNS) A division of the **peripheral nervous system** that controls voluntary movements of the body.

somatization disorder A **somatoform disorder** in which an individual complains of multiple physical complaints over a period of many years but manifests no physical basis for the complaints.

somatoform disorder Disorder in which the individual complains of a physical ailment for which there is no organic or physiological explanation.

somesthetic system Part of the vestibular senses, it conveys to the brain information concerning sensations in the internal environment (body), such as deep pain or nausea.

sound wave A rhythmic variation in the pressure of air molecules.

species-specific behavior See **instinct.**

speech acts The different forms of language associated with different kinds of sentences—for instance, questions and imperatives.

split brain In this surgical operation devised by Sperry and his colleagues, the corpus callosum is severed, producing a person or animal whose hemispheres can no longer communicate with one another. Many studies have been performed on split-brain people and have revealed the dramatic differences between the two hemispheres. Occasionally performed as treatment for severe cases of epilepsy.

spontaneous recovery If, after **extinction** of a **conditioned response (CR),** the **conditioned stimulus** is again presented, the CR will often reappear.

spontaneous remission The process by which people spontaneously recover from psychological disorders without the intervention of psychotherapy. Such spontaneous remission is now used as a control in studies evaluating the outcome of specific therapies.

SQ3R The method of remembering, which stands for "Survey, Question, Read, Recite, and Review." It involves (1) surveying a chapter before you read it, (2) questioning the material before you read it, (3) reading the material only after a framework for remembering is in place, (4) reciting what you have learned, and (5) reviewing the material after retaining the important information.

Stanford-Binet test An adaptation of the original Binet intelligence test first standardized by Terman in 1916. This test has been restandardized several times and is still used to assess **intelligence quotient (IQ).**

statistics The formal, mathematical set of rules for the evaluation of evidence, which enables scientific judgments to be more precise

and quantitative than ordinary judgments.

stereotype A generalized assumption attributing identical characteristics to all members of a group: blondes are dumb, Americans are materialistic, and the like.

stimulant A type of drug, such as amphetamines or cocaine, that elevates mood and increases alertness.

storage space The amount of memory capacity taken up by given experiences, which helps us construct sense of time, because we judge periods of time by how much we remember about them, and thus by how much storage space they take up.

strange situation An experiment developed by Ainsworth and devised to observe an infant's degree of **attachment** and **separation anxiety.** A stranger enters the room where an 8- to 9-month-old baby and mother are playing with toys. The mother leaves the room so that the child is alone with the stranger. The experimenter observes how the baby reacts to the mother's departure.

stranger anxiety Infants' fear of strangers, which often develops around the last quarter of the first year and may cause them to scream and cry if a stranger approaches. See also **attachment.**

stress The failure of adaptability that occurs when environmental or internal demands exceed the adaptive resources of an organism. Also defined, by Selye, as the general reaction of the body to change. See also **emergency reaction, general adaptation syndrome.**

stress-buffering hypothesis A theory explaining how social support contributes to health by reducing the effects of stress.

stress inoculation therapy A therapy proposing that altering the way people talk to themselves will change the way they approach stressful problems. The training takes place in three phases: (1) the therapist and client examine a stressful situation, (2) the client rehearses and learns a new set of statements to help avoid stress, and (3) the client applies and practices these new statements.

Strong—Campbell interest inventory See **interest inventory.**

subgoals A method of thinking that is useful in problem solving. It involves breaking a large problem into shorter problems and setting intermediate or subgoals.

subject A person or animal whose behavior of physiology is observed as part of an **experiment.** See also **control group, experimental group, sample.**

substance abuse disorder A type of psychological disorder marked by a consistent pattern of excessive substance use resulting in impairment of social or occupational functioning and that may involve physical dependence on the substance.

superego According to Freud's theory, this is the last part of the personality to develop. It is the internal representation of society's values and morals. The superego restrains aggression and sexual impulses of the **id,** pressures the **ego** to act in a more moralistic than realistic way, and encourages the individual to strive for perfection.

survivor effect In longitudinal research, the illusive appearance of improvement over time caused by the loss of weaker individuals from the sample due to morbidity and mortality.

sympathetic nervous system A division of the **autonomic nervous system,** it prepares internal organs for emergencies. It operates "in sympathy" with the emotions, telling the body to react. See also **parasympathetic nervous system.**

synapse The point at which two **neurons** meet, usually between the **axon** of one and the **dendrite** of the other, where the chemicals involved in **neurotransmission** pass from the transmitting neuron to the receiving one.

syntax The specific structure or arrangement of words in a specific

language to convey meaning. See also **grammar.**

systematic desensitization A form of behavior therapy based on **counterconditioning.** In this therapy, the aim is to eliminate an unwanted **conditioned response** by conditioning the client to another stimulus that elicits a response (usually relaxation) that is incompatible with the original, undesired response.

T

teaching story A story form predominant in the Sufi tradition, that entices the mind into operating in an unfamiliar manner. Examples of such tales include "The Elephant in the Dark" and "The Man with the Inexplicable Life" by Idries Shah.

tectum A region of the brainstem that receives nerve fibers from the optic tract. See also **lateral geniculate nucleus.**

temperament The enduring emotional characteristics of a person's life.

temporal lobes The area on each side of the brain devoted to hearing, perception, memory, and dreaming. Damage to the temporal lobes may result in a condition known as **aphasia,** the disruption of the ability to use language.

terminal drop A marked decline in intelligence and other measures of cognitive and biological functioning, a few months to a year before death.

texture gradient As we look over a uniform surface, the density of the texture increases with distance. We then analyze this texture gradient for information about distance and the angle of the surface.

thalamus The brain stem structure that relays information to the appropriate areas of the cortex. Certain areas of the thalamus seem to be specialized for specific kinds of sensory information—auditory, visual, and the like.

Thanotos In Freud's theory, the death instinct: organisms seek a quiescent state, and death is, of

course, the ultimate of this. "The aim of life," Freud wrote in a famous passage, "is death."

Thematic Apperception Test (TAT) A projective test consisting of 19 pictures of people in ambiguous situations and 1 blank card. The subject is asked to tell a story about the situation pictured. The stories are analyzed for themes demonstrating inner needs and external pressures.

thermometer neurons Nerve cells that measure blood temperature and can alter their firing rate to trigger actions either to warm or cool the blood. See also **homeostasis.**

thirst The drive to drink water, usually signaled by dryness in the mouth.

trait A general and enduring quality within an individual's psychological makeup that underlies his or her thoughts, feelings, and actions over time and across situations. Some psychologists believe traits are the basic units of personality.

transactional psychophysiology Lynch's method of therapy measuring how the heart responds to other people, most specifically blood pressure changes when speaking about or considering emotional events.

transcendence The form of **motivation** that drives people to go beyond the ordinary understanding of life. Many people try to search for knowledge at the highest level and ask questions such as "What is the meaning of life?" or "What is God?"

transduction A sensory process that transforms each particular kind of physical energy (light, sound, etc.) into neural firing. The eye transduces light, the ear transduces sound waves, the nose transduces gaseous molecules.

transference An important concept of psychoanalytic theory. During therapy, the patient tends to transfer his or her general feelings about life onto the therapist: a person who has difficulty getting along with people in authority may suddenly start to have that problem with the therapist; a person who is suspicious of other people may be suspicious of what the therapist is doing. The clarification of the transference is held to reveal fundamental ways in which the patient acts in the world. Psychoanalysis then proceeds to work through that transference.

transformational grammar An influential theory that a distinction exists in syntax between "surface" and "deep" structure. This theory presupposes that the human brain is designed to produce language and that the structure of language is in some way innate.

trephining A medieval method of treatment of mental disorder. In what must have been heroic treatment, holes were drilled into a person's head to let out the demons who were thought to be causing the disorder.

trial and error A problem-solving strategy that is useful for simple problems. It involves a series of different actions aimed at solving a problem to which there is no obvious logical solution.

triarchic theory of intelligence A theory proposed by Sternberg that divides intelligence into three parts: intelligence in the internal world of the individual, the point of critical involvement of intelligence, and how the external world affects intelligence.

tricyclic A class of antidepressant medications that interfere with the reuptake of **norepinephrine** and serotonin, leaving more of these **neurotransmitters** at the **synapse** and leading to a subsequent elation of mood.

type A cluster of related traits. Types describe people in absolute terms and imply predictions about people's behavior.

Type A, Type B behavior The behavior of individuals who have specific reactions to the stresses of life. Type A people tend to be aggressive, hostile, competitive,

fast-paced, and irritable. They are deeply involved in their work and often deny failure, fatigue, and illness. They try to get more done in less time and are twice as likely to develop heart disease as Type B people, who may be as successful but tend to be calm.

typology A summary statement about what a person is like based on an analysis of **traits** and characteristics. See also **type**.

unconditioned response (UCR) A response that is made without any specific sort of learning, such as salivation to food.

unconditioned stimulus (UCS) A stimulus, such as food or a loud noise, that elicits an **unconditioned response,** such as salivation or being startled.

unconscious Aspects of the mind that are not available to consciousness.

unconscious inferences The nineteenth-century scientist Helmholz described a perceiver as one who must make inferences, fill in gaps in the information reaching him or her. These inferences transform a set of disconnected lines into the living world of objects: cube, train, car.

undifferentiated A type of **schizophrenia** in which all or most of the primary symptoms of schizophrenia are presented in a rapidly changing mix.

unilateral ECT The application of electroconvulsive shock to only one of the cerebral hemispheres; this approach leads to less confusion and memory impairment than bilateral ECT. See **electroconvulsive therapy (ECT).**

unipolar depression Affective disorders of mood in which only depression is experienced; in contrast to bipolar disorder characterized by alternating extremes of elation and depression.

uplifts Positive life events that give a great deal of pleasure and

may, in some instances and to varying degrees, balance the impact of negative events.

using specialized tools A human capacity that in evolution accompanied the development of hands with great **dexterity.**

validity A required characteristic of tests, such as intelligence tests, ensuring that they measure what they are intended to measure. See also **reliability.**

variable interval (VI) schedule In this **reinforcement** schedule, the intervals between reinforcement vary randomly around an average.

variable ratio (VR) schedule In this **reinforcement** schedule, the reward occurs after a randomly varying number of responses.

variable In experiments, only a few things are allowed to change; these are called **variables.** *Independent variables* are those the experimenter may attempt to manipulate, such as how many hours an animal is deprived of food. *Dependent variables* are those that the experimenter measures and those that change after the experimenter's manipulations, such as how much the animal might eat.

vestibular system The sensory organs in the ear that detect motion, position, and balance.

visibility A characteristic of making machines easy to use. Users should be able to tell what their alternatives for action are and what condition the machine is in.

visual cortex The rear area of the brain that receives information from the 126 million **photoreceptor cells.** The cortex is divided into layers, in which different levels of processing occur.

vivid information Concrete examples that strongly influence judgment. People tend to disregard statistical information and overemphasize vivid information.

Weber's law The first major principle of sensation, discovered by

Weber (1834), noted the consistent proportional relationship between a physical stimulus and psychological response to it.

Wechsler Adult Intelligence Scale (WAIS-R) An intelligence test measuring two major areas of intelligence, verbal and performance, yielding three scores: verbal, performance, and combined.

Wechsler Intelligence Scale for Children (WISC-R) The intelligence test for children, based on the **Wechsler Adult Intelligence Scale (WAIS-R).**

word association test A widely used method devised by Jung for gaining access to unconscious material. A person is presented with a standard list of 100 words, one at a time, and is asked to say the first word that comes to mind. The length of time it takes to respond, the vocal inflection, and other nonverbal cues are analyzed as well as the response word.

BIBLIOGRAPHY

ABT, C. C. (1970). *Serious games.* New York: Viking.

ADAM, K., & OSWALD, I. (1977). Sleep is for tissue restoration. *Journal of the Royal College of Physicians, 11,* 376–388.

ADAMOWITZ, S. I. (1969). Locus of control and self-reported depression among college students. *Psychological Reports, 25,* 149–150.

ADER, R. (1981). Behavioral influences on immune responses. In S. M. Weiss, J. A. Herd & B. D. Fox (Eds.), *Perspectives on behavioral medicine.* New York: Academic Press.

ADER, R. (Ed.). (1984). *Psychoneuroimmunology.* New York: Academic Press.

ADER, R., & COHEN, N. (1981). CNS-immune system interactions: Conditioning phenomena. *Behavioral and Brain Sciences, 8,* 379–426.

ADLER, A. (1929). *The practice and theory of individual psychology.* New York: Harcourt.

ADORNO, T. W., FRENKEL-BRUNSWICK, E., LEVINSON, D. S., & SANFORD, R. N. (1950). *The authoritarian personality.* New York: Harper & Row.

AGRAS, W. S., HORNE, M., & TAYLOR, C. B. (1982). Expectation and the blood-pressure-lowering effect of relaxation. *Psychosomatic Medicine, 44,* 389–395.

AHERN, G. L., & SCHWARTZ, G. E. (1985). Differential lateralization for positive and negative emotion in the human brain: EEG spectral analysis. *Neuropsychologia, 23*(6), 744–755.

AIELLO, J. R., & THOMPSON, D. E. (1980). When compensation fails: Mediating effects of sex and locus of control at extended interaction distances. *Basic and Applied Social Psychology, 1,* 65–82.

AIELLO, J. R., DE RISI, D. T., EPSTEIN, Y. M., YAKOV, M., & KARLIN, R. A. (1977). Crowding and the role of interpersonal distance preference. *Sociometry, 40,* 271–282.

AINSWORTH, M. D. S. (1982). Attachment: Retrospect and prospect. In C.M. Parkes & J. Stevenson-Hinde (Eds.), *The place of attachment in human behavior.* New York: Basic Books.

AINSWORTH, M. D. S., & BELL, S. M. (1970). Attachment, exploration and separation: Illustrated by the behavior of one-year-olds in a strange situation. *Child Development, 41.*

AINSWORTH, M. D. S., BLEHAR, M., WATERS, E., & WALL, S. (1978). *Patterns of attachment: A psychological study of the strange situation.* Hillsdale, NJ: Erlbaum.

AINSWORTH, M. D. S., & WHITTIG, B. A. (1965). Attachment and exploratory behavior of one year olds in a strange situation. In B. M. Foxx (Ed.), *Determinants of infant behaviour, 4.* London: Methuen.

AJZEN, I., & FISHBEIN, M. (1980). *Understanding attitudes and predicting social behavior.* Englewood Cliffs: Prentice-Hall.

ALBERT, M. A., & OBLER, L. K. (1978). *The bilingual brain.* New York: Academic Press.

ALBERT, M. S., & KAPLAN, E. (1980). Organic implications in neuropsychological deficits in the elderly. In L. Poor (Ed.), *New directions in memory and aging.* Hillsdale, NJ: Erlbaum.

ALBRECHT, S. (1980). Reactions and adjustments to divorce: Differences in the experiences of males and females. *Family Relations, 29,* 59–68.

ALDWIN, C. M., & LEVENSON, T. A. (1987). Does coping help? A reexamination of the relation between coping and mental health. *Journal of Personality and Social Psychology, 53*(2), 337–348.

ALEXANDER, F. (1950) *Psychosomatic medicine: Its principles and applications.* New York: Norton.

ALEXANDER, R. D., HOOGLAND, J. L., HOWARD, R. D., NOONAN, K. M., & SHERMAN, P. W. (1979). In N. A. Chagnons & W. G. Irons (Eds.), *Evolutionary biology and human social behavior: An anthropological perspective.* North Scituate, MA: Duxbury.

ALLEN, I. M. (1951). Cerebral injury with shock treatment. *New Zealand Medical Journal, 50,* 356–364.

ALLISON, R. (1980). *Minds in many pieces.* New York: Rawson-Wade.

ALLISON, T., & CICCHETTI, D. (1976). Sleep in mammals: Ecological and constitutional correlates. *Science, 194,* 732–734.

ALLPORT, G. W. (1937). *Personality: A psychological interpretation.* New York: Holt.

ALLPORT, G. W. (1954). *The nature of prejudice.* Cambridge, MA: Addison-Wesley.

ALLPORT, G. W. (1955). *Becoming.* New Haven: Yale University Press.

ALLPORT, G. W. (1961). *Pattern and growth in personality.* New York: Holt, Rinehart & Winston.

ALLPORT, G. W. (1985). The historical background of social psychology. In G. Lindzey & E. Aronson (Eds.), *Handbook of Social Psychology* (Vol. 1). New York: Random House.

ALLPORT, G. W., & ODVERT, H. S. (1936). Trait-names: A psycholexical study. *Psychological Monographs, 47,* 1–171.

ALLPORT, G. W., & ROSS, J. M. (1967). Personal religious orientation and prejudice. *Journal of Personality and Social Psychology, 5,* 432–443.

ALPER, T. G. (1974). Achievement motivation in college women: A now-you-see-it-now-you-don't phenomenon. *American Psychologist, 29,* 194–203.

ALPERS, B. J., & HUGHES, J. (1942). Changes in the brain after electrically induced convulsions in cats. *Archives of Neurology and Psychiatry, 47,* 385–398.

ALTROCCHI, J. (1980). *Abnormal behavior.* New York: Harcourt Brace Jovanovich.

AMATO, P. R. (1983). Helping behavior in urban and rural environments: Field studies based on a taxonomic organization of helping episodes. *Journal of Personality and Social Psychology, 45,* 571–586.

AMERICAN INSTITUTE OF PLANNERS NEWS-LETTER. (1967). Baltimore.

AMERICAN PSYCHIATRIC ASSOCIATION. (1980). *Diagnostic and statistical manual of mental disorders* (3rd ed.). Washington, DC: American Psychiatric Association.

ANAND, B. K., & BROBECK, J. R. (1951). Hypothalamic control of food intake in rats and cats. *Yale Journal of Biology and Medicine, 24,* 123–140.

ANDERSON, C. A., & ANDERSON, D. C. (1984). Ambient temperature and violent crime: Tests of the linear and curvilinear hypothesis. *Journal of Personality and Social Psychology, 46,* 91–97.

ANDERSON, J. A., & ROSENFELD, E. (1988) *Neurocomputing: Foundations of research.* Cambridge: MIT Press.

ANDERSON, J. R. (1987). Skill acquisition: Compilation of weak-method problem solutions. *Psychological Review, 94,* 192–210.

ANDRES, R., ELAHI, D., TOBIN, J. D., MULLER, D. C., & BRANT, L. (1985). Impact of age on weight goals. *Annals of Internal Medicine, 103*(6), 1030–1033.

ANNIS, R. C., & FROST, B. (1973). Human visual ecology and orientation anistropies in acuity. *Science, 182,* 729–731.

ANTONOVSKY, A. (1984). The sense of coherence as a determinant of health. In J. D. Matarazzo, S. M. Weiss, J. A. Herd, & N. E. Miller (Eds.), *Behavioral Health.* New York: Wiley.

ANTONOVSKY, A. (1987). *Unraveling the mystery of health.* San Francisco: Jossey-Bass.

ANTONUCCI, T. C. (1989). Social support luences on the disease process. In L. L. Carstensen & J. M. Neale (Eds.), *Mechanisms of psychological influence on physical health.* New York: Plenum.

ANTONUCCI, T. C., & JACKSON, J. (1987). Social support, interpersonal efficacy and health. In L. L. Carstensen & B. A. Edelstein (Eds.), *Handbook of clinical gerontology*. New York: Pergamon Press.

ARCHER, D., ARONSON, E., & PETTIGREW, T. (1983). *An evaluation of the energy conservation research of California's major energy utility companies, 1977–1980* [Report to the Cal. PUC]. Santa Cruz: University of California.

ARCHER, D., PETTIGREW, T., COSTANZO, M., IRITANI, B., WALKER, L., & WHITE, L. (Manuscript in preparation). *Energy conservation and public policy: The mediation of individual behavior.*

ARGYLE, M. (1978). *The psychology of interpersonal behavior*. New York: Penguin Books.

ARGYLE, M., & CROSSLAND, J. (1987). The dimensions of positive emotions. *British Journal of Social Psychology, 26*(2), 127–137.

ARGYLE, M., & HENDERSON, M. (1985). *The anatomy of relationships*. New York: Penguin Books.

ARIES, P. (1962). *Centuries of childhood*. London: Jonathan Cape.

ARKES, H. R., & HAMMOND, K. R. (1986). *Judgment and decision making*. New York: Cambridge University Press.

ARON, A. (1977). Maslow's other child. *Journal of Humanistic Psychology, 17*(2), 9–24.

ARONSON, E. (1958). The need for achievement as measured by graphic expression. In J. W. Atkinson (Ed.), *Motives in fantasy, action and society* (pp. 249–265). Princeton: Van Nostrand Reinhold.

ARONSON, E. (1988). *The social animal*. New York: W. H. Freeman.

ARONSON, E., BLANEY, N., STEPHAN, C., SIKES, J., & SNAPP, M. (1978). *The jigsaw classroom*. Beverly Hills: Sage.

ARONSON, E., & O'LEARY, M. (1983). The relative effects of models and prompts on energy conservation. *Journal of Environmental Systems, 12*, 219–224.

ARONSON, E., & OSHEROW, N. (1980). Co-operation, prosocial behavior, & academic performance: Experiments in the desegregated classroom. In L. Bickman (Ed.), *Applied social psychology annual* (Vol. 1). Beverly Hills: Sage.

ASCH, S. E. (1946). Forming impressions of personality. *Journal of Abnormal and Social Psychology, 41*, 258–290.

ASCH, S. E. (1951). Effects of group pressure upon the modification and distortion of judgments. In H. Guetzkow (Ed.), *Groups, leadership, & men* (pp. 177–190). Pittsburgh: Carnegie Press.

ASCH, S. E. (1956). Studies of independence and conformity: A minority of one against a unanimous majority. *Psychological Monographs, 70*(9, Whole No. 416).

ASCH, S. E. (1957, April). An experimental investigation of group influence. In *Symposium on preventive and social psychiatry* (pp. 15–17). Walter Reed Army Institute of Research, Washington, DC: U.S. Government Printing Office.

ASCHOFF, J. (1965). *Circadian clocks*. Amsterdam: North-Holland.

ASCHOFF, J. (1967). Human circadian rhythms in activity, body temperature, and other functions. In A. H. Brown & F. G. Favoite (Eds.), *Life sciences and space research* (Vol. 5, pp. 159–173). Amsterdam: North-Holland.

ASERINSKY, E., & KLEITMAN, N. (1953). Regularly occurring periods of eye motility and concomitant phenomena during sleep. *Science, 118*, 273–274.

ATKINSON, A. K., & RICKEL, A. O. (1984). Postpartum depression in primiparous patients. *Journal of Abnormal Psychology, 93*, 115–119.

AUSTIN, J. L. (1962). *How to do things with words*. Oxford: Oxford University Press.

AVERILL, J. R. (1978). A constructivist view of emotions. In R. Plutchik, (Ed.), *Theories of emotion*. New York: Academic Press.

AYLLON, T., & AZRIN, N. (1968). *The token economy: A motivational system for therapy and rehabilitation*. New York: Appleton-Century-Crofts.

AZJEN, I., & FISHBEIN, M. (1977). Attitude-behavior relations: A theoretical analysis and review of empirical research. *Psychological Bulletin, 84*, 888–918.

BAARS, B. J. (1988). *A cognitive theory of consciousness*. Cambridge: Cambridge University Press.

BAARS, B. J., & MATTSON, M. E. (1981). Consciousness and intention: A framework and some evidence. *Cognition and Brain Theory, 4*, 247–263.

BAASTRUP, P. C. (1980). Lithium in the treatment of recurrent affective disorders. In F. N. Johnson (Ed.), *Handbook of lithium therapy*. Baltimore: University Park Press.

BADDELEY, A. (1986). *Working memory*. New York: Oxford University Press.

BAGCHI, B. K., & WENGER, M. A. (1957). Electrophysiological correlates of some yogi exercises. *Electroencephalography and Clinical Neurophysiology, 7*, 132–149.

BAGGA, O. P., & GANDHI, A. (1983). A comparative study of the effect of Transcendental Meditation and Shavasana practice on the cardiovascular system. *Indian Heart Journal, 35*, 39–45.

BAHNSON, C. B., & BAHNSON, M. B. (1964). Cancer as an alternative to psychosis: A theoretical model of somatic and psychological regression. In D. M. Kissen & L. L. Leshan (Eds.), *Psychosomatic aspects of neoplastic disease*. London: Pitman.

BAHNSON, M. B., & BAHNSON, C. B., (1969). Ego defenses in cancer patients. *Annals, New York Academy of Science, 164*, 546–559.

BAHRICK, H. P., BAHRICK, P. O., & WHITTLINGER, R. P. (1975). Fifty years of memory for names and faces: A cross-sectional approach. *Journal of Experimental Psychology: General, 104*, 54–75.

BAKAL, D. A. (1979) *Psychology and Medicine: Psychobiological dimenstions of health and illness*. New York: Springer.

BAKAN, P. (1977). Left-handedness and birth order revisited. *Neuropsychology, 15*.

BALTES, M. M., KINDERMAN, REISENZEIN, R., & SCHMID, U. (1987). Further observations of the behavioral and social world of institutions for the aged. *Psychology and Aging, 2*, 390–403.

BALTES, M. M., & WERNER-WAHL, K. (1987). Dependence in old age. In L. L. Carstensen & B. A. Edelstein (Eds.), *Handbook of clinical gerontology*. New York: Pergamon Press.

BALTES, P. B., SOWARKA, D., & KLIEGL, R. (1989). Cognitive training research on fluid intelligence in old age: What can older adults achieve by themselves? *Psychology and aging, 4*, 217–222.

BANDURA, A. (1965). Vicarious processes: A case of no-trial learning. In L. Berkowitz (Ed.), *Advances in experimental social psychology* (Vol. 2). New York: Academic Press.

BANDURA, A. (1977a). Regulation of cognitive processes through perceived self-efficacy. *Developmental Psychology, 25*, 5.

BANDURA, A. (1977b). *Social learning theory*. Englewood Cliffs, NJ: Prentice-Hall.

BANDURA, A. (1978a). Social learning theory of aggression. *Journal of Communication, 28*, 12–29.

BANDURA, A. (1978b). The self system in reciprocal determinism. *American Psychologist, 37*, 122–147.

BANDURA, A. (1979). *Aggression: A social learning analysis* (2nd ed.). Englewood Cliffs, NJ: Prentice-Hall.

BANDURA, A. (1982). Self-efficacy mechanism in human agency. *American Psychologist, 37*, 122–147.

BANDURA, A. (1986). *Social foundations of thought and action: A social cognitive theory*. Englewood Cliffs, NJ: Prentice-Hall.

BANDURA, A. (1990). Regulation of cognitive processes through perceived self-efficacy. *Developmental Psychology, 25*.

BANDURA, A., & ADAMS, N. E. (1977). Analysis of self-efficacy theory of behavioral change. *Cognitive Therapy and Research, 1*(4), 287–310.

BANDURA, A., CIOFFI, D., TAYLOR, C. B., & BROUILLARD, M. E. (1988). Perceived self-efficacy in coping with cognitive stressors and opioid activation. *Journal of Personality and Social Psychology, 55*(3), 479–488.

BANDURA, A., & McDONALD, F. D. (1963). The influence of social reinforcement and the behavior of models in shaping children's moral judgements. *Journal of Abnormal and Social Psychology, 67*, 274–281.

BANDURA, A., ROSS, O., & ROSS, S. A. (1961). Transmission of aggression through imitation of aggressive models. *Journal of Abnnormal and Social Psychology, 63,* 575–582.

BANDURA, A., TAYLOR, C. B., WILLIAMS, S. L., MEFFORD, I. N., & BARCHAS, J. D. (1985). Catecholamine secretion as a function of perceived self-efficacy. *Journal of Consulting and Clinical Psychology, 53,* 406–414.

BANDURA, A., & WOOD, R. E. (1989). Effect of perceived controllability and performance stanfdards on self-regulation of complex decision-making. *Journal of Personality and Social Psychology, 56,* 805–814.

BANE, M. S. (1976). *Here to stay: American families in the twentieth century.* New York. Basic Books.

BANKS, M. S., & SALAPATEK, P. (1983). Infant visual perception. In P. H. Mussen (Ed.), *Handbook of child psychology: Vol 2. Infancy and developmental psychobiology.* New York: Wiley.

BANKS, W. C., McQUARTER, G. V., & HUBBARD, J. L. (1977). Task-liking and intrinsic-extrinsic achievement orientations in black adolescents. *Journal of Black Psychology, 3*(2), 61–71.

BARASH, D. (1986). *The tortoise and the hare.* New York: Viking Penguin.

BARBER, T. X., & COOPER, B. J. (1972). The effects on pain of experimentally induced and spontaneous distraction. *Psychological Reports, 31,* 647–651.

BARKER, R. G., & WRIGHT, H. F. (1951). *One boy's day: A specimen record of behavior.* New York: Harper.

BARLOW, D. (1988). *Anxiety and its disorders: The nature and treatment of anxiety and panic.* New York: Guilford Press.

BARNES, R. (1979). *Mods.* London: Eel Pie.

BARON, R. A. (1977). *Human aggression.* New York: Plenum.

BARON, R. A., & BYRNE, D. (1987). *Social psychology understanding human interaction* (5th ed.). Boston: Allyn & Bacon.

BARON, R. A., & KEPNER, C. R. (1970). Model's behavior and attraction toward the model as determinants of adult aggressive behavior. *Journal of Personality and Social Psychology, 14,* 335–344.

BARR, J., LANGS, R., HOLT, T., GOLDBERGER, L., & KLEIN, G. (1972). *LSD: Personality and experience.* New York: Wiley.

BARSLEY, M. (1979). *Left handed people.* North Hollywood: Wilshire.

BART, P. (1971). Depression in middle-aged women. In V. Goinich & B. K. Moran (Eds.), *Women in sexist society.* New York: Basic Books.

BARTHROP, R. W., LAZARUS, L., LUCKHURST, E., KILOH, L.G., & PENNY, R. (1978). Depressed lymphocyte function after bereavement. *Lancet, 1,* 834–839.

BARTLETT, F. C. (1932). *Remembering: A study in experimental and social psychology.* Cambridge: Cambridge University Press.

BARTON, E., BALTES, M. M., & ORZECH, M. J. (1980). On the etiology of dependence in older nursing home residents during morning care. *Journal of Personality and Social Psychology, 38,* 423–431.

BATESON, G. (1959). *The double bind.* Palo Alto: Science and Behavior Books.

BATESON, G. (1979). *Mind and nature: A necessary unity.* New York: Dutton.

BATESON, G., JACKSON, D. D., HALEY, J., & WEAKLAND, J. H. (1972). Toward a theory of schizophrenia. *Behavioral Science, 1*(4).

BATSON, C. D. (1987). Prosocial motivation: Is it ever truly altruistic? In L. Berkowitz (Ed.), *Advances in experimental social psychology* (Vol. 20). Orlando, FL: Academic Press.

BATSON, C. D., NAIFEL, S. V., & PATE, S. (1978). Social desirability, religious orientation and racial prejudice. *Journal for the Scientific Study of Religion, 17,* 31-41.

BAYNES, K., & GAZZANIGA, M. S. (1988). Right hemisphere language: Insights into normal language mechanisms? Burke Rehabilitation Center, Cornell University Medical College, New York. *Res Publ Assoc Res Nerv Ment Dis, 66,* 117–126.

BECK, A. (1976). *Cognitive therapy and the emotional disorders.* New York: International Universities Press.

BECK, A., & KATCHER, A. (1983). *Between pets and people: The importance of animal companionship.* New York: Putnam.

BECK, A., RUSH, A. J., SHAW, B., & EMERY, G. (1979). *Cognitive therapy of depression: A treatment manual.* New York: Guilford Press.

BEE, H. (1978). *The developing child* (2nd ed.). New York: Harper & Row.

BEECHER, H. W. (1956) *Evolution and religion.* New York: Harper & Row.

BEER, R. R., JR. (1979). *Mechanisms of pain and analgesic compounds.* New York: Raven Press.

BELCHER, T. L. (1975). Effect of different testing situations on creativity scores. *Psychological Reports, 36*(2), 511–514.

BELL, A. P., WEINBERG, M. S., & HAMMERSMITH, S. K. (1981). *Sexual preference: Its development in men and women.* Bloomington: Indiana University Press.

BELLAH, R. N. (1973). Evil and the American ethos. In N. Sanford & C. Comstock (Eds.), *Sanctions for evil* (pp. 187–188). San Francisco: Jossey-Bass.

BELLER, S., & PALMORE, E. (1974). Longevity in Turkey. *The Gerontologist, 14*(5), 373–376.

BELLOWS, R. T. (1939). Time factors in water drinking in dogs. *American Journal of Physiology, 125,* 87–97.

BELOFF, J. (1978). Why parapsychology is still on trial. *Human Nature, 1*(12), 68–76.

BELSKY, J. (1984). The determinants of parenting: A process model. *Child Development, 55,* 83–96.

BELSKY, J. (1988). The 'effects' of infant day care reconsidered. *Early Childhood Research Quarterly, 3*(3), 235–272.

BELSKY, J., GILSRAB, B., & ROVINE, M. (1984). The Pennsylvania Infant and Family Development Project: Pt. 1. Stability and change in mother-infant and father-infant interaction in a family setting at one, three and nine months. *Child Development, 55*(3), 692–705.

BELSKY, J., & ROVINE. (1988). Nonmaternal care in the first year of life and the security of infant-parent attachment. *Child Development, 59,* 157–176.

BELSKY, J., & STEINBERG, L. D. (1978). The effects of day care: A critical review. *Child Development, 49,* 929–949.

BEM, D. J. (1967). Self-perception: An alternative interpretation of cognitive dissonance phenomena. *Psychological Review, 74,* 183–200.

BEM, D. J. (1970). *Beliefs, attitudes and human affairs.* Belmont: Brooks/Cole.

BEM, D. J. (1972). Self-perception theory. In L. Berkowitz (Ed.), *Advances in experimental social psychology* (Vol. 6). New York: Academic Press.

BEM, D. J., & ALLEN, A. (1974). On predicting some of the people some of the time: The search for cross-situational consistencies in behavior. *Psychological Review, 81,* 506–520.

BEM, S. L. (1981). Gender schema theory: A cognitive account of sex-typing. *Psychological Review, 88*(4), 354–364.

BENNETT, W. (Speaker). (1984). *Set point regulation of body weight* (Cassette recording). ISHK.

BENNETT, W. S., & GURIN, J. (1982). *The dieter's dilemma.* New York: Basic Books.

BENSHOOF, L., & THORNHILL, R. (1979). The evolution of monogamy and concealed ovulation in humans. *Journal of Social and Biological Structures, 2*(2), 95–105.

BENSON, P. L., KARABENICK, S. A., & LERNER, R. M. (1976). Pretty pleases: The effects of physical attractiveness, race, & sex on receiving help. *Journal of Experimental Social Psychology, 12,* 409–415.

BENZING, W. C., & SQUIRE, L. R. (1989). Preserved learning and memory in amnesia: Intact adaptation-level effects and learning of stereoscopic depth. *Behavioral Neuroscience, 103*(3), 538–547.

BERDYSHEV, G. D. (1966). *Ecologic and genetic factors of aging and longevity.* Moscow: Nauka.

BERG, I. (1976). School phobia in the children of agoraphobic women. *British Journal of Psychiatry, 128,* 86–89.

BERGER, H. (1984). *The developing person.* New York: Worth.

BERKMAN, L., & SYME, S. L. (1979). Social networks, host resistance, and mortality: A nine-year follow-up study of Alameda County residents. *American Journal of Epidemiology, 109,* 186–204.

BERKMAN, L. F. (1984). Assessing the physical health effects of social networks and social support. *Annual Review of Public Health, 5,* 413–432.

BERKOWITZ, L. (1970). Aggressive humor as a stimulus to aggressive responses. *Journal of Personality and Social Psychology, 16,* 710–717.

BERKOWITZ, L. (1972). Social norms, feelings, and other factors affecting helping and altruism. In L. Berkowitz (Ed.), *Advances in experimental social psychology* (Vol. 6). New York: Academic Press.

BERLIN, B., & KAY, P. (1969). *Basic color terms: Their universality and evolution.* Berkeley and Los Angeles: University of California Press.

BERLYNE, D. E. (1960). *Conflict, arousal, & curiosity.* New York: McGraw Hill.

BERLYNE, D. E. (1966). Curiosity and exploration. *Science, 153,* 25–33.

BERLYNE, D. E. (1967). Arousal and reinforcement. *Nebraska symposium of motivation* (pp. l-ll0). Lincoln: University of Nebraska Press.

BERLYNE, D. E. (1972). Humor and its kin. In J. H. Goldstein & P. E. McGhee (Eds.), *The psychology of humor* (pp. 43–60). London: Academic Press.

BERMAN, J. S., MILLER, R. C., & MASSMAN, P. J. (1984). Cognitive therapy versus systematic desensitization: Is one treatment superior? In J. S. Berman (Chair), *Meta-analytic reviews of psychotherapy outcome research.* Toronto:

BERMAN, W., & TURK, D. (1981, February). Adaptation to divorce: Problems and coping strategies. *Journal of Marriage and the Family,* pp. 179–189.

BERNARD, J. (1972). *The future of marriage.* New York: Bantam Books.

BERTENTHAL, B. I., & CAMPOS, J. J. (1989). A systems approach to the organizing effects of self-produced locomotion during infancy. In C. Rover-Collier (Ed.), *Advances in infant development.* Hillsdale, NJ: Erlbaum.

BERTENHAL, B. I., CAMPOS, J. J., & BARRETT, K. (1984). Self-produced locomotion. In R. Emde & R. Harmon (Eds.), *Continuities and discontinuities in development* (pp. 175–210). New York: Plenum.

BESEDOVSKY, H. O., DEL RAY, A., SORKIN, E., DAPRADA, M., & KELLER, H. H. (1979). Immunoregulation mediated by the sympathetic nervous system. *Cellular Immunology, 48,* 346–355.

BESEDOVSKY, H. O., DEL RAY, A., & SORKIN, E. (1983). What do the immune system and the brain know about each other? *Immunology Today, 4,* 342–346.

BESEDOVSKY, H. O., SORKIN, R., FELIX, D., & HAAS, H. (1977). Hypothalamic changes during the immune response. *European Journal of Immunology, 7,* 325–328.

BETCHER, R. (1981). Intimate play and marital adaption. *Psychiatry, 44,* 13–33.

BETTELHEIM, B. (1960). *The informed heart: Autonomy in a message.* Glencoe, IL: Free Press.

BEXTON, W. H., HERON, W., & SCOTT, T. H. (1954). Effects of decreased variation in the sensory environment. *Canadian Journal of Psychology, 8,* 70–76.

BIBRING, G. (1959). Some consideration of the psychological processes in pregnancy. *Psychoanalytic Study of the Child, 14,* 113–121.

BINFORD, S. R., & BINFORD, L. R. (1969, April). Stone tools and human behavior. *Scientific American, 96.*

BIRREN, J. E., BUTLER, R. N., GREENHOSE, S. W., SOKOLOFF, L., & HARROW, M. R. (Eds.). (1963). *Human aging: A biological and behavioral study.* (Publication No. HSM 71–9051). Washington, DC: U.S. Government Printing Office.

BIRREN, J. E., et al. (1981). *Developmental psychology: A life-span approach.* Boston: Houghton Mifflin.

BJORK, R. A., & LANDAUER, T. K. (1979). On keeping track of the present status of people and things. In M. M. Gruneberg, P. E. Morris, & R. N. Sykes (Eds.), *Practical aspects of memory.* New York: Academic Press.

BJORNTORP, P. (1972). Disturbances in the regulation of food intake. *Advances in Psychosomatic Medicine, 7,* 116–147.

BLACK, S., HUMPHREY, J. H., & NIVEN, J. S. F. (1963). Inhibition of Mantoux reaction by direct suggestion under hypnosis. *British Medical Journal, 1,* 1649–1652.

BLANCHARD, F. A., ADELMAN, L., & COOK, S. W. (1975). Effect of group success and failure upon interpersonal attraction in cooperating interracial groups. *Journal of Personality and Social Psychology, 31,* 1020–1030.

BLANCHARD, F. A., WEIGEL, R. H., & COOK, S. W. (1975). The effect of relative competence of group members upon interpersonal attraction in cooperating interracial groups. *Journal of Personality and Social Psychology, 32*(3), 519–530.

BLASDEL, G. G., MITCHELL, D. E., MUIR, D. W., & PETTIGREW, J. D. (1977). A combined physiological and behavioral study of the effect of early visual experience with contours of a single orientation. *Journal of Physiology, 265,* 615–636.

BLASI, A. (1980). Bridging moral cognition and moral action: A critical review of the literature. *Psychological Bulletin, 88,* l-45.

BLASS, E. M., & KETY, F. S. (1974). Medial forebrain bundle lesions: Specific loss of feeding to decreased glucose utilization in rats. *Journal of Comparative and Physiological Psychology, 86,* 679–692.

BLAZER, D. G. (1982). Social support and mortality in an elderly community population. *American Journal of Epidemiology, 115,* 684–694.

BLEULER, E. (1923). *Lehrbuch der Psychiatre* (4th ed.). Berlin: Springer.

BLOCK, J. (1971). *Lives through time.* Berkeley: Bancroft Books.

BLOCK, J. (1977). Advancing the psychology of personality: Paradigmatic shift of improving the quality of research. In D. Magnussen & N. S. Endler (Eds.), *Personality at the crossroads.* Hillsdale, NJ: Erlbaum.

BLOCK, J. (1978). Another look at sex differences in the socialization of mothers and fathers. In J. Sherman and F. Denmark (Eds.), *The psychology of women: Future directions in research.* New York: Psychological Dimensions.

BLOCK, J. (1979). Socialization influences on personality development in males and females. In M. M. Parkes (Ed.), *APA master lecture series on issues of sex and gender in psychology.* Washington, DC: American Psychological Association.

BLOCK, J. (1981). Some enduring and consequential structures of personality. In A. I. Rabin, J. Aronoff, A. M. Barclay, & R. A. Zucker (Eds.), *Further explorations in personality.* New York: Wiley-Interscience.

BLOCK, J. H., & BLOCK, J. (1980). The role of ego-control and ego resiliency in the organization of behavior. In W. A. Collins (Ed.), *Minnesota Symposium on Child Psychology* (Vol 13). Hillsdale, NJ: Erlbaum.

BLOOM, B. L., ASHER, S. J., & WHITE, S. W. (1978). Marital disruption as a stressor: A review and analysis. *Psychological Bulletin, 85,* 867–894.

BLOOM, B. L., & WHITE, S. W. (1981). Factors related to the adjustment of divorcing men. *Family Relations, 30,* 349–360.

BLUMENTHAL, H., & BURNS, A. (1964). Autoimmunity in aging. In B. Strehler (Ed.), *Advances in gerontological research* (Vol. 1). New York: Academic Press.

BLYTH, R. (1979). *The view in winter: Reflections on old age.* New York: Harcourt Brace Jovanovich.

BOLLA-WILSON, K., & BLEECKER, M. L. (1989). Absence of depression in elderly adults. *Journal of Gerontology, 44,* 53–55.

BOLLES, R. C. (1970). Species-specific defense reactions in avoidance learning. *Psychological Review, 71,* 32–48.

BOLLES, R. N. (annual). *What color is your parachute? A practical manual for job-hunters and career-changers.* Berkeley: Ten Speed Press.

BOLLES, T. C. (1974). Cognition and motivation: Some historical trends. In B. Weiner (Ed.), *Cognitive views on human motivation* (pp. l-32). New York: Academic Press.

BONVILLIAN, J. D., ORLANSKY, M. D., & NOVACK, L. L. (1983). Developmental milestones: Sign language and motor development. *Child Development, 54,* 1435–1445.

BORGES, J. L. (1966). Funes the memorius. In D. A. Yates & J. E. Irbt (Eds.), *Labyrinths.* New York: New Directions.

BORNSTEIN, M. H. (1973). Color vision and color naming: A psychophysiological hypothesis of cultural difference. *Psychological Bulletin, 80,* 257–285.

BOROD, C., KOFF, E., LORCH, M. P., NICHOLAS, M., & WELKOWITZ, J. (1988). Emotional and non-emotional facial behavior in patients with unilateral brain damage. *Journal of Neurological and Neurosurgical Psychiatry, 5*(16), 826–832.

768

BORQUIST, A. (1906). Crying. *American Journal of Psychology, 17,* 149–205.

BORTZ, W. M. (1982). Disuse and aging. *Journal of the American Medical Association, 248,* 1203–1208.

BORTZ, W. M. (in press). Redefining human aging. *Journal of the American Medical Association.*

BORYSENKO, J. Z. (1985). Healing motives: An interview with David McClelland. *Advances, 2,* 29–41.

BOTWINICK, D. E., WOODS, A. M., & WILLIAMS, M. V. (1980). Behavioral slowing of age: Causes, organization, and consequences. In Poon, L. W. (Ed.), *Aging in the 1980s: Psychological issues.* Washington, DC: American Psychological Association.

BOTWINICK, J. (1977). Intellectual abilities. In J. E. Birren & K. W. Schaie (Eds.), *Handbook of the psychology of aging.* New York: Van Nostrand Reinhold.

BOTWINICK, J., WEST, R., & STARANDT, M. (1978). Predicting death from behavioral test performance. *Journal of Gerontology, 33,* 755–762.

BOUCHARD, T., & McGUE, R. (1981). Familial studies of intelligence: A review. *Science, 212,* 1055–1059.

BOWERMAN, M. (1988). Inducing the latent structure of language. In F. S. Kessel (Ed.), *The development of language and language researchers: Essays in honor of Roger Brown.* Hillsdale, NJ: Erlbaum.

BOWER, G. H. (1972, July). How to . . . uh . . . remember! *Psychology Today,* 62–67.

BOWER, G. H. (1978). Improving memory. *Human Nature, 7,* 62–67.

BOWER, G. H. (1981). Mood and memory. *American Psychologist, 36,* 129–148.

BOWER, G. H., & GILLIGAN, S. G. (1980). Remembering information related to one's self. *Journal of Research in Personality, 13,* 420–432.

BOWER, G. H., GILLIGAN, S. G., & MONTEIRO, K. P. (1981). Selectivity of learning caused by affective states. *Journal of Experimental Psychology: General, 110*(4), 451–473.

BOWER, G. H., & HILGARD, E. R. (1981). *Theories of learning* (5th ed.). Englewood Cliffs, NJ: Prentice-Hall.

BOWER, T. G. R. (1974). *Development in infancy.* San Francisco: W. H. Freeman.

BOWLBY, J. (1982). *Attachment: Vol. 1. Attachment and loss.* New York: Basic Books.

BOWLES, N., & POON, L. (1982). An analysis of the effect of aging on memory. *Journal of Gerontology, 37,* 212–219.

BOYNTON, R. M. (1971). Color vision. In J. W. King & L. A. Riggs (Eds.), *Woodwater and Schlossberg's experimental psychology* (3rd ed., pp. 315–368). New York: Holt, Rinehart & Winston.

BRADBURN, W., & CAPLOVITZ, D. (1965). *Reports on happiness,* Chicago: Aldine.

BRADLEY, A., & SKOTTUN, B. C. (1987). Effects of contrast and spatial frequency on vernier activity. *Vision Research, 27,* 1817–1824.

BRADY, J. V. (1958). Ulcers in 'executive' monkeys. *Scientific American, 199,* 95–100.

BRAINERD, C. (1978). *Piaget's theory of intelligence.* Englewood Cliffs, NJ: Prentice-Hall.

BRAINERD, C. J., KINGMAN, J., & HOWE, M. L. (1985). On the development of forgetting. *Child Development, 56,* 1103–1119.

BRANCH, A. Y., FINE, G. A., & JONES, J. M. (1973). Laughter, smiling, & rating scales: An analysis of responses to tape recorded humor. *Proceedings of the 81st Annual Convention of the American Psychological Association.*

BRAND, R. J., ROSENMAN, R. H., SHOLTZ, R. I., & FRIEDMAN, M. (1976). Multivariate prediction of coronary heart disease in the Western Collaborative Group Study compared to the findings of the Framingham Study. *Circulation, 43*(2), 348–355.

BRANDWEIN, R. A., BROWN, A., & FOX, S. M. (1974). Women and children last: The social situation of divorced mothers and their families. *Journal of Marriage and the Family, 36,* 495–514.

BRANSFIELD, D. D., HANKEY, B. F., & WESLEY, M. N. (1989, March). Sociodemographic variables associated with delay among black and white breast cancer patients. *13th Annual Meeting of the American Society of Preventive Oncology,* Bethesda, MD.

BRANSFORD, J. D., & JOHNSON, M. K. (1974). Contextual prerequisites for understanding. Some investigations of comprehension and recall. *Journal of Verbal Learning and Verbal Behavior, 11,* 717–726.

BRANTHWAITE, A., & COOPER, P. (1981). Analgesic effect of branding in treatment of headaches. *British Medical Journal, 282,* 1576–1578.

BRAVERMAN, H. (1974). Labor and monopoly capital: The degradation of work in the Twentieth Century. *Monthly Review.*

BRAY, G. A. (1974). Endocrine factors in the control of food intake. *Federal Proceedings, 33,* 1140–1145.

BRECHER, E. M., & CONSUMER REPORTS (Eds.). (1974). *Licit and illicit drugs.* Boston: Little, Brown.

BREHM, S. S., & BREHM, J. W. (1981). *Psychological reactance: A theory of freedom and control.* New York: Academic Press.

BRELAND, H. (1977). Family configuration and intellectual development. *Journal of Individual Psychology, 31,* 86–96.

BRELAND, K., & BRELAND, M. (1961). The misbehavior of organisms. *American Psychologist, 16,* 661–664.

BRENNER, C. (1974). *An elementary textbook of psychoanalysis* (rev. ed.). New York: Anchor Books. (Reprinted from New York: International Universities Press, 1973)

BRENNER, M. H. (1973). *Mental illness and the economy.* Cambridge: Harvard University Press.

BRENNER, M. H. (1976). *Estimating the social costs of economic policy.* (Paper No. 5, report to the Congressional Research Service of the Library of Congress). Washington, DC: U.S. Government Printing Office.

BRENNER, M. H. (1980). Importance of the economy to the nation's health. In L. Eisenberg & A. Kleinman (Eds.), *The relevance of social science for medicine.* Dordrecht: Reidel.

BRESNITZ, S. (Ed.). (1983). *The Denial of Stress.* New York: International Universities Press.

BRETHERTON, J., & WATERS, L. (1985). *Growing points of attachment theory and research.* SRCD monographs.

BREUER, J., & FREUD, S. (1955). Studies in hysteria. In J. Strachey (Ed.), *The standard edition of the complete psychological works of Sigmund Freud.* London: Hogarth Press. (Original work published 1895)

BREWER, V., & HARTMANN, E. (1973). Variable sleepers: When is more or less sleep required? *Sleep Research, 2,* 128.

BRICKMAN, P. (1974). Adaptation level determinants of satisfaction with equal and unequal outcome distributions in skill and chance situations. *Journal of Personality and Social Psychology, 32,* 191–198.

BRIDGEMAN, D. (1981). Enhanced role taking through cooperative interdependence: A field study. *Child Development, 52,* 1231–1238.

BRIDGES, D. (1927). Occupational interests of three-year-old children. *Journal of Genetic Psychology, 34,* 415–423.

BRIDGES, K. M. B. (1932). Emotional development in early infancy. *Child Development, 3,* 324–341.

BRIM, O. G., JR. (1976). Theories of the male mid-life crisis. *Counseling Psychologist, 6*(1), 2–9.

BRIM, O. G., JR. (1978–1979). In P. Baltes (Ed.), *Life-span development and behavior* (Vols. 1–2). New York: Academic Press.

BROADBENT, D. E. (1961). *Behavior.* New York: Basic Books.

BROADHEAD, W. E., et al. (1983). Epidemiological evidence for a relationship between social support and health. *American Journal of Epidemiology, 117,* 521–537.

BROADHURST, P. L. (1957). Emotionality and the Yerkes-Dodson law. *Journal of Experimental Psychology, 84,* 345–352.

BROBECK, J. R. (1946). Mechanics of the development of obesity in animals with hypothalamic lesions. *Physiological Review, 26,* 541–559.

BROOKS, C. M., & LAMBERT, E. F. (1946). A study of the effect of limitation of food intake and the method of feeding on the rate of weight gain during hypothalamic obesity in the albino rat. *American Journal of Physiology, 147,* 695–707.

BROOKS, G. W., & MUELLER, E. (1966). Serum urate concentrations among university professors: Relation to drive, achievement, & leadership. *Journal of the American Medical Association, 195*(6), 415–418.

BROWN, A. M. (1990). *Human universals.* Unpublished manuscript, University of California, Santa Barbara.

BROWN, D., FORTE, M., & DYSART, M. (1984). Visual sensitivity and mindfulness meditation. *Perceptual & Motor Skills, 58,* 775–784.

BROWN, G. W., & HARRIS, T. (1978). *Social origins of depression.* New York: Free Press.

BROWN, J. (1977). *Mind, brain and consciousness.* New York: Academic Press.

BROWN, J. B., & STERNBERG, J. (1986). *Teaching thinking skills.* New York: W. H. Freeman.

BROWN, J. D., & LAWTON, M. (1986). Stress and well-being in adolescence: The moderating role of physical exercise. *Journal of Human Stress, 12,* 125–131.

BROWN, L. B. (1964). Classifications of religious orientation. *Journal for the Scientific Study of Religion, 4,* 91–99.

BROWN, R. (1965). *Social psychology.* New York: Free Press.

BROWN, R., & HERRNSTEIN, R. J. (1975). *Psychology.* Boston: Little, Brown.

BROWN, R., & KULIK, J. (1977). Flashbulb memories. *Cognition,* pp. 73–99.

BROWN, R. W., & LENNEBERG, E. H. (1954). A study in language and cognition. *Journal of Verbal Learning and Verbal Behavior, 49,* 454–462.

BRUN, J. (1984). Therapeutic value of hope. *Southern Medical Journal, 77,* 215–219.

BRUNER, J. S. (1960). *The process of education.* New York: Random House.

BRUNER, J. S. (1978). Learning the mother tongue. *Human Nature, 1,* 52–59.

BRUNER, J. S. (1986). *Actual minds, possible worlds.* Cambridge: Harvard University Press.

BRUNER, J. S., & GOODMAN, C. C. (1946). Value and need as organizing factors in perception. *Journal of Abnormal and Social Psychology, 42,* 33–44.

BRUNER, J. S., & TAGIURI, R. (1954). Person perception. In G. Lindzey (Ed.), *Handbook of social psychology* (Vol. 2). Reading, MA: Addison-Wesley.

BRYAN, J. H., & TEST, M. (1967). Models and helping: Naturalistic studies in aiding behavior. *Journal of Personality and Social Psychology, 6,* 400–407.

BRYDEN, M. P. (1973). Auditory-visual and sequential-spatial matching in relation to reading ability. *Child Development, 43*(3), 824–832.

BUCKALEW, L. W., & ROSS, S. (1981). Relationships of perceptual characteristics to efficacy of placebos. *Psychological Reports, 49,* 955–961.

BUDZYNSKI, T. (1977). Biofeedback and the twilight states of awareness. In G. Schwartz & D. Shapiro (Eds.), *Consciousness and self-regulation.* New York: Plenum.

BUFFREY, A., & GRAY, J. (1972). Sex differences in the development of spatial and linguistic skills. In C. Ounsted &

D. Taylor (Eds.), *Gender differences: Their ontogeny and significance.* New York: Churchill Livingstone.

BUGENTHAL, D. E., LOVE, L. R., & GIANETTO, R. M. (1971). Perfidious feminine faces. *Journal of Personality and Social Psychology, 17,* 314–318.

BURNES, K., BROWN, W. A., & KEATING, G. W. (1971). Dimensions on control: Correlations between MMPI and I-E scores. *Journal of Consulting and Clinical Psychology, 36,* 301.

BURNS, M.O., & SELIGMAN, M.E. (1989). Explanatory style across the life span: Evidence for stability over 52 years. *Journal of Personality and Social Psychology, 56*(3), 471–477.

BUSKIRK, E. R. (1985). Health maintenance and longevity: Exercises. In C. E. Finch & E. L. Schneider (Eds.), *Handbook of the biology of aging.* New York: Van Nostrand Reinhold.

BUSS, A. H., & PLOMIN, R. (1984). *Temperament: Early developing personality traits.* Hillsdale, NJ: Erlbaum.

BUSS, A. H., PLOMIN, R. & WILLERMAN, L. (1973). The inheritance of temperaments. *Journal of Personality, 41,* 513–524.

BUSS, D. (1989). Sex differences in human mate preferences. *Brain and Behavioral Sciences, 12*(1), 1-3.

BUTLER, R. N. (1963). The life review: An interpretation of reminiscence in the aged. *Psychiatry, 26,* 65–76.

BUTLER, R. N, & LEWIS, M. I. (1983). *Mental health and aging.* St. Louis: Mosby.

BÜHLER, C. (1968). Fulfillment and failure in life. In C. Bühler & F. Massarik (Eds.), *The course of human life.* New York: Springer.

CABANAC, M. (1971). Physiological role of pleasure. *Science, 173,* 1103–1107.

CADORET, R. J., WINOKUR, G., & CLAYTON, P. J. (1971). Family history studies: Pt. 6. Depressive disease types. *Comprehensive Psychiatry, 12,* 148–155.

CALHOUN, J. B. (1973). Population density and social pathology. *Scientific American, 206,* 139–148.

CAMPBELL, B. G. (1982). *Humankind emerging* (3rd ed.). Boston: Little, Brown.

CAMPBELL, D. T. (1960). Blind variation and selective retention in creating thought as in other knowledge processes. *Psychological Review, 67,* 380–400.

CAMPBELL, D. T. (1963). Social attitudes and other acquired behavioral dispositions. In S. Koch (Ed.), *Psychology: A study of a science* (Vol. 6). New York: McGraw-Hill.

CAMPBELL, J. D., TESSER, A., & FAIREY, P. J. (1986). Conformity and attention to the stimulus: Some temporal and contextual dynamics. *Journal of Personality and Social Psychology, 51,* 315–324.

CAMPBELL, R. (1978). Asymmetries in interpreting and expressing a posed facial expression. *Cortex, 14,* 327–342.

CAMPOS, J. J., & BERTENTHAL, B. I. (1989). Locomotion and psychological devel-

opment in infancy. In F. Morrison, K. Lord, & D. Keating (Eds.), *Applied developmental psychology.* New York: Academic Press.

CAMPOS, J. J., & STENBERG, C. R. (1981). Perception, appraisal and emotion: The onset of social referencing. In M. E. Lamb & L. R. Sherrod (Eds.), *Infants social cognition: Empirical and social considerations.* Hillsdale, NJ: Erlbaum.

CANGEMI, J. J. (1976). Characteristics of self-actualizing individuals. *Revista de Psicologia General Aplicada, 31,* 88–90.

CANNON, W. (1929). *Bodily changes in pain, hunger, fear and rage: An account of recent researches into the function of emotional excitement* (2nd ed.). New York: Appleton-Century-Crofts.

CANNON, W. (1977). "Voodoo" death. In A. Monat & R. S. Lazarus (Eds.), *Stress and coping.* New York: Columbia University Press.

CANTOR, J., ZILLMAN, D., & BRYANT, J. (1974). Enhancement of humor appreciation by transferred excitation. *Journal of Personality and Social Psychology, 30,* 812–821.

CANTOR, N., & MISCHEL, W. (1977). Traits and prototypes: Effects on recognition memory. *Journal of Personality and Social Psychology, 35,* 38–48.

CANTOR, N., & NIEDENTHAL, P. (in press). Affective responses as guides to category based inferences. *Motivation and Emotion.*

CARD, S., MORAN, T., & NEWELL, A. (1983). *The psychology of human-computer interaction.* Hillsdale, NJ: Erlbaum Associates.

CARLSMITH, J. M., & ANDERSON, C. A. (1979). Ambient temperature and the occurrence of collective violence: A new analysis. *Journal of Personality and Social Psychology, 37,* 337–344.

CARMICHAEL, L., HOGAN, H. P., & WALTERS, A. (1932). An experimental study of the effects of language on the reproduction of visually perceived form. *Journal of Experimental Psychology, 16,* 73–86.

CARRINGTON, P. (1972). Dreams and schizophrenia. *Archives of General Psychiatry, 26,* 343–350.

CARROLL, W. R., & BANDURA, A. (1985). Role of timing of visual monitoring and motor rehearsal in observational learning of action patterns. *Journal of Motor Behavior, 17,* 269–281.

CARSTENSEN, L. L. (in press). A longitudinal analysis of social and emotional behavior across adulthood.

CARTWRIGHT, R. D. (1978). *A primer on sleep and dreaming.* Reading, MA: Addison-Wesley.

CARVER, C., & GLASS, D. (1977). *The coronary prone behavior pattern and interpersonal aggression.* Unpublished manuscript, University of Texas.

CARVER, C. S., & SCHEIER, M. F. (1988). *Perspectives on personality.* Boston: Allyn & Bacon.

CASPI, A. (in press). *Moving against the*

world: Life course patterns for explosive people.

CASPI, A., BEM, D. J., & ELDER, G. H. (1989). Continuities and consequences of interactional styles across the life course. *Journal of Personality, 57,* 375–406.

CASPI, A., & ELDER, G. H., JR. (in press). Childhood precursors of the life course. In E. M. Hetherington, R. M. Lerner, & M. Perlmutter (Eds.), *Child development in life-span perspective.*

CASSEL, J. C. (1976). The contribution of the social environment to host resistance. *American Journal of Epidemiology, 104,* 107–123.

CASSILETH, B. R., et al. (1988). Patient and physician delay in melanoma diagnosis. *Journal of the American Academy of Dermatology, 18*(3), 591–598.

CASSILETH, B. R., LUSK, E. J., MILLER, D. S., BROWN, L. L., & MILLER, C. (1985). Psychosocial correlates of survival in advanced malignant disease? *New England Journal of Medicine.*

CATTELL, R. B. (1971). *Abilities: Their structure, growth, and action.* Boston: Houghton Mifflin.

CAVANAUGH, J. C. (1990). *Adult development and aging.* Belmont, CA: Wadsworth.

CAVANAUGH, J. C., GRADY, J. G., & PERLINETT, M. P. (1983). Forgetting and using memory aids in 20- to 70-year-olds' everyday life. *International Journal of Aging and Human Development, 14,* 238–246.

CHAIKEN, S., & EAGLY, A. H. (1976). Communication modality as a determinant of message persuasiveness and message comprehensibility. *Journal of Personality and Social Psychology, 34,* 605–614.

CHAIKEN, S., & STANGOR, C. (1987). Attitudes and attitude change. In M. R. Rosenzweig & L. W. Porter (Eds.), *Annual review of psychology* (Vol. 38). Palo Alto, CA: Annual Reviews.

CHANCE, P. (1987). *Learning and behavior* (2nd ed.). San Francisco: Wadsworth.

CHAPMAN, A. J. (1976). Social aspects of humorous laughter. In A. J. Chapman & H. C. Foot (Eds.), *Humour and laughter: Theory, research and applications.* London: Wiley.

CHASE, W. G., & SIMON, N. A. (1973). The mind's eye in chess. In W. G. Chase (Ed.), *Visual information processing.* New York: Academic Press.

CHAVES, J. F., & BARBER, T. X. (1974). Cognitive strategies, experimenter modeling, & expectation in the attenuation of pain. *Journal of Abnormal Psychology, 83,* 356–363.

CHEEK, J. M., & HOGAN, R. (1983). Self-concepts, self-presentations, & moral judgments. In J. Suls & A. G. Greenwald (Eds.), *Psychological perspectives on the self* (Vol. 2). Hillsdale, NJ: Erlbaum.

CHESNEY, M., & ROSEMEAN, R. H. (Eds.). (1985). *Anger and Hostility in Cardiovascular and Behavioral Disorders.* Washington, DC: Hemisphere.

CHESS, S., & THOMAS, A. (1987). *Know your child.* New York: Basic Books.

CHIRIBOGA, D. (1977). Life event weighting systems: A comparative analysis. *Journal of Psychosomatic Research, 21,* 415–422.

CHIRIBOGA, D. (1981). The developmental psychology of middle age. In J. Howells (Ed.), *Modern perspectives in the psychiatry of middle age.* New York: Brunner/Mazel.

CHIRIBOGA, D., & CUTLER, L. (1977). Stress responses among divorcing men and women. *Journal of Divorce, 1*(2), 95–106.

CHIRIBOGA, D., ROBERTS, J., & STEIN, O. (1978). Psychological well-being during marital separation. *Journal of Divorce, 2*(1), 21-35.

CHODOROW, N. (1978). *The reproduction of mothering: Psychoanalysis and the sociology of gender.* Berkeley: University of California Press.

CHOMSKY, N. (1966). *Aspects of the theory of syntax.* Cambridge: MIT Press.

CHOMSKY, N. (1975). *Reflections on language.* New York: Pantheon.

CHOMSKY, N. (1980). *Rules and representations.* Cambridge: MIT Press.

CHRISTIAN, J. J., FLYGER, V., & DAVIS, D. C. (1960). Factors in the mass mortality of a herd of Sika Deer, Cervus Nippon. *Chesapeake Science, 1,* 79–95.

CHUKOVSKY, K. (1963). *From two to five.* Berkeley: University of California Press.

CIALDINI, R. B. (1988). *Influence: Science and practice.* Glenview, IL.: Scott Foresman/Little, Brown.

CICIRELLI, V. G. (1982). Sibling influence throughout the lifespan. In M. E. Lamb & B. Sutton-Smith (Eds.), *Sibling relationships: Their nature and significance across the lifespan* (pp. 267–284). Hillsdale, NJ: Erlbaum.

CICIRELLI, V. G. (1989). Feelings of attachment to siblings and well-being in later life. *Psychology and Aging, 4,* 211–216.

CLARK, E. V. (1987). The principle of contrast: A constraint on language acquisition. In B. MacWhinney (Ed.), *The 20th annual Carnegie symposium on Cognition.* Hillsdale, NJ: Erlbaum.

CLARK, H. H. (1985). Language use and language users. In G. Lindzey & E. Aronson (Eds.), *Handbook of social psychology* (3rd ed., pp. 179–231). New York: Harper & Row.

CLARK, H. H., & CLARK, E. V. (1977). *Psychology and language: An introduction to psycholinguistics.* New York: Harcourt Brace Jovanovich.

CLARK, K., & CLARK, M. (1947). Racial identification and preference in Negro children. In T. M. Newcomb & E. L. Hartley (Eds.), *Readings in social psychology.* New York: Holt, Rinehart & Winston.

CLARK, M. S., & FISKE, S. T. (Eds.). (1982). *Affect and cognition.* Hillsdale, NJ: Erlbaum.

CLARKE-STEWART, A. (1989). Infant day care: Malignant or maligned? *American Psychologist, 44,* 266–273.

CLECKLEY, H. (1954). *The mark of sanity.* St. Louis: Mosby.

COATES, T. A., SOSKOLINE, C. L., et al. (1987). *Canadian Journal of Public Health, 77*(5), 343–348.

COBB, S., & KASL, S. V. (1977, June). *Termination: The consequences of job loss.* (Report No. 76–1261). Cincinnati: National Institute for Occupational Safety and Health, Behavioral and Motivational Factors Research.

COBB, S., & ROSE, R. M. (1973). Hypertension, peptic ulcer, & diabetes in air traffic controllers. *Journal of the American Medical Association, 224,* 489–492.

COE, C. L., ROSENBERG, L. T., & LEVINE, S. (1985). Effect of maternal separation on humoral immunity in infant primates. In Spector, N. H. (Ed.), *Proceedings of the First International Workshop on Neuroimmunomodulation.* Bethesda, MD.

COFER, C. N., & APPLEY, M. H. (1964). *Motivation: Theory and research.* New York: Wiley.

COGEN, M., BAKER, G., COHEN, R. A., FROMM-REICHMANN, F., & WEIGERT, E. V. (1954). An intensive study of twelve cases of manic-depressive psychosis. *Psychiatry, 17,* 103–137.

COHEN, F., & LAZARUS, R. (1973). Active coping processed, coping dispositions, & recovery from surgery. *Psychosomatic Medicine, 35,* 375–389.

COHEN, S., EVANS, G., KRANTZ, D. S., & STOKOLS, D. (1980). Physiological, motivational, & cognitive effects of aircraft noise on children: Moving from the laboratory to the field. *American Psychologist, 35,* 231–243.

COHEN, S., GLASS, D. C., & SINGER, J. E. (1973). Apartment noise, auditory discrimination, & reading ability in children. *Journal of Experimental Social Psychology, 9,* 407–422.

COHEN, S., & SYME, S. L. (Eds.). (1985). *Social Support and Health.* New York: Academic Press.

COHEN, W. (1971, December 15). Statement before the Subcommittee to Investigate Juvenile Delinquency of the U.S. Senate Committee on the Judiciary of Drug Abuse.

COLBY, A., & KOHLBERG, L. (1986). *The measurement of moral behavior.* New York: Cambridge University Press.

COLEMAN, J. C., BUTCHER, J. N., & CARSON, R. C. (1980). *Abnormal psychology and modern life.* Glenview, IL: Scott, Foresman.

COLEMAN, P. O. (1974). Measuring reminiscence: Characteristics from conversation as an adaptive feature of old age. *International Journal of Aging and Human Development, 5,* 281–294.

COLLINS, A. M., & QUILLIAN, M. R. (1972). Experiments on semantic memory and language comprehension. In L. W. Gregg (Ed.), *Cognition and learning.* New York: Wiley.

COMFORT, A. (1974). *The joy of sex*. New York: Simon & Shuster.

CONDRY, J., & CONDRY, S. (1976). Sex differences: A study in the eye of the beholder. *Child Development, 47,* 812–819.

CONDRY, J., & DYER, S. (1976). Fear of success: Attribution of cause to the victim. *Journal of Social Issues, 32*(3), 63–83.

CONNOR, J. R., & DIAMOND, M. C. (1982). A comparison of dendritic spine number and type on pyramidal neuron of the visual cortex of old adult rats from social and isolated environments. *Journal of Comparative Neurology, 210,* 99–106.

COOPER, C., & MARSHALL, J. (1976). Occupational sources of stress: A review of the literature relating to coronary heart disease and mental ill health. *Occupational Psychology, 94,* 11–28.

COOPER, J. E., KENDELL, R. E., GURLAND, B. J., SHARPE, L., COPELAND, J. R. M., & SIMON, R. (1972). *Psychiatric diagnosis in New York and London.* London: Oxford University Press.

CORAH, N., & BOTTA, J. (1970). Perceived control, self-observation, & response to aversion stimulation. *Journal of Personality and Social Psychology, 16*(1), 1-4.

COREN, S. (1989). Left-handedness and accident-related injury risk. *American Journal of Public Health, 79*(8), 1040–1041.

COREN, S., & PORAC, C. (1987). Individual differences in visual-geometric illusions: Predictions from measures of spatial cognitive abilities. *Perception and Psychophysics, 41*(3), 211–219.

COREN, S., PORAC, C., AKS, D. J., & MORIKAWA, K. A. (1988). Method to assess the relative contribution of lateral inhibition to the magnitude of visual-geometric illusions. *Perception and Psychophysics, 43*(6), 551–558.

COREN, S., & WARD, L. M. (1989). *Sensation and Perception* (3rd ed.). San Diego: Harcourt Brace Jovanovich.

CORSINI, R. J. (Ed.). (1984). *Current psychotherapies.* Itasca, IL: Peacock.

CORSO, J. (1977). Auditory perception and communication. In J. Birren & K. Schaie (Eds.), *Handbook of the psychology of aging.* New York: Van Nostrand Reinhold.

COSMIDES, L., & TOOBY, J. (1986). From evolution to behavior: Evolutionary psychology as the missing link. In J. Dupre (Ed.), *The latest on the best: Essays on evolution and optimality.* Cambridge: MIT Press.

COSTA, P. T., & McCRAE, R. R. (1980). Still stable after all these years: Personality as a key to some issues in adulthood and old age. In P. Baltes & O. Brim (Eds.), *Life span development and behavior* (Vol. 3). New York: Academic Press.

COSTA, P., & McCRAE, R. (1984). *Emerging lives, Enduring dispositions.* New York: Guilford Press.

COSTA, P., & McCRAE, R. (1990). *Personality in adulthood: Emerging lives, adult dispositions.* New York: Guilford Press.

COSTA, P. T., McCRAE, R., & ARENBERG, D. (1980). Enduring dispositions in adult males. *Journal of Personality and Social Psychology, 38,* 793–800.

COSTA, P., McCRAE, R., et al. (1986). Cross-sectional studies of personality in a National Sample: Pt. 2. Stability in neuroticism, extraversion, & openness. *Psychology and Aging, 1,* 144–149.

COSTANZO, M., ARCHER, D., ARONSON, E., & PETTIGREW, T. (1986). Energy conservation behavior: The difficult path from information to action. *American Psychologist, 41,* 521–528.

COTMAN, C., & McGAUGH, J. (1980). *Behavioral neuroscience.* New York: Academic Press.

COWAN, C., COWAN, P., COIE, L., & COIE, J. (1978). Becoming a family: The impact of a first child's birth on the couple's relationship. In W. Miller & L. Newman (Eds.), *The first child and family formation.* Chapel Hill: Carolina Population.

COWAN, C. P., et al. (1985). Transitions to parenthood: His, hers and theirs. *Journal of Family Issues, 6,* 451–481.

COWAN, P. (1988). Becoming a father: A time of change, An opportunity for development. In P. Bronstein & Cowan, P. A. (Eds.) *Fatherhood today: Men's changing role in the family.* New York: Wiley.

COWAN, P. & COWAN, P. A. (1988). Changes in marriage during the transition to parenthood. In G. Y. Michaels, & W. A. Goldberg, (Eds.), *The transition to parenthood: Current theory and research.* Cambridge: Cambridge University Press.

COYLE, J., PRICE, D., & DELONG, M. (1983). Alzheimer's disease: A disorder of cortical cholinergic innervation. *Science, 219,* 1184–1190.

COYNE, J., ALDWIN, C., & LAZARUS, R. S. (1981). Depression and coping in stressful episodes. *Journal of Abnormal Psychology, 90,* 439–447.

COYNE, J. C. (1976). Depression and the response to others. *Journal of Abnormal Psychology, 85,* 186–193.

CRAIK, F. (1977). Age differences in human memory. In J. Birren & K. Schaie (Eds.), *Handbook of the psychology of aging.* New York: Van Nostrand Reinhold.

CRAIK, F. I. M., & TULVING, E. (1975). Depth of processing and the retention of words in episodic memory. *Journal of Experimental Psychology: General, 104,* 268–294.

CRAIK, H. L. & LOCKHART, R. R. (1972). Levels of processing: A framework for memory research. *Journal of Verbal Learning and Verbal Behavior, 12,* 599–607.

CROSBY, F. J. (Ed.). (1987). *Spouse, parent, worker: On gender and multiple roles.* New Haven: Yale University Press.

CROWE, R. R., NOYES, R., PAULS, D. L., & SLYMEN, D. J. (1983). A family study of panic disorder. *Archives of General Psychiatry, 40,* 1065–1069.

CROYLE, R. T., & COOPER, J. (1983). Dissonance arousal: Physiological evidence. *Journal of Personality and Social Psychology, 45,* 782–791.

CSIKSZENTMIHALYI, M. (1975). *Beyond freedom and anxiety.* San Francisco: Jossey-Bass.

CUBER, J. F., & HAROFF, P. B. (1965). *Sex and the significant Americans.* Baltimore: Penguin.

CUMMING, E., & HENRY, W. (1961) *Growing old: The process of disengagement.* New York: Basic Books.

CUMMINGS, S. (1977). Family socialization and fatalism among black adolescents. *Journal of Negro Education, 46*(1), 62–75.

CURTIS, H. J. (1966). *Biological mechanisms of aging.* Springfield, IL: Thomas.

CURWIN, R., & MENDLER, A. (1988). *Discipline with dignity.* Washington, DC: Association for Supervision and Curriculum Development.

CUSTANCE, J. (1951). *Wisdom, madness, & folly: The philosophy of a lunatic.* New York: Pellegrini Cudahy.

CZEISLER, C., WEITZMAN, E. D., MOORE-EDE, M. C., ZIMMERMAN, J. C., & KNAUER, R. S. (1980). Human sleep: Its duration and organization depend on its circadian phase. *Science, 210,* 1264–1267.

DANIELS, E. F., et al. (1988). Patterns of thought disorder associated with right cortical damage, schizophrenia and mania. *American Journal of Psychiatry, 145*(8), 944–949.

DARBY, W. J. (1978). The benefits of drink. *Human Nature, 1,* 30–37.

DARLEY, J. M., & BATSON, C. C. (1973). From Jerusalem to Jericho: A study of situational and dispositional variables in helping behavior. *Journal of Personality and Social Psychology, 27,* 100–108.

DARLEY, J. M., & LATANE, B. (1968). Bystander intervention in emergencies. *Journal of Personal and Social Psychology, 8,* 377–383.

DARWIN, C. (1968). *On the origin of species.* New York: Penguin Books. (Original work published 1859).

DARWIN, C. (1872). *The expression of the emotions in man and animals.* London: Longmans.

DAVIDSON, R. (1984). Hemispheric asymmetry and emotion. In K. Scherer & P. Ekman (Eds.), *Approaches to emotion.* Hillsdale, NJ: Erlbaum.

DAVIS, R. (1984). Expert systems: Where are we and where do we go from here? In P. Winston & K. Prendergast (Eds.), *The AI business.* Reading, MA: Addison-Wesley.

DAVISON, G. (1976). Homosexuality: The ethical challenge. *Journal of Consulting and Clinical Psychology, 44,* 156–162.

DAVISON, G., & NEALE, J. (1982). *Abnormal psychology* (3rd ed.). New York: Wiley.

DAWKINS, R. (1986). *The blind watchmaker.* New York: Norton.

DAWSON, J. (1975). Socio-economic differences in size judgments of discs and coins by Chinese primary VI children in Hong Kong. *Perceptual and Motor Skills, 41,* 107–110.

DE LA PEÑA, A. (1984). *The psychobiology of cancer.* New York: Praeger.

DE LUMLEY, H. (1969). A Paleolithic camp at Nice. *Scientific American, 220*(5), 47–59.

DECHARMS, R. (1968). *Personal causation.* New York: Academic Press.

DECI, E. L. (1975). *Intrinsic motivation.* New York: Plenum.

DECK, L. (1968). Report in *Journal of College and University Personnel Association, 19,* 99–37.

DEIKMAN, A. (1966). Deautomatization and the mystic experience. *Psychiatry, 29,* 329–343.

DELGADO, J. M. R. (1969). *Physical control of the mind.* New York: Harper & Row.

DELONGIS, A., COYNE, J. C., DAKOF, G., FOLKMAN, S., & LAZARUS, R. S. (1982). Relationship of daily hassles, uplifts and major life events to health status. *Health Psychology, 1,* 119–136.

DEMBER, W. N. (1974). Motivation and the cognitive revolution. *American Psychologist, 29,* 161–168.

DEMBER, W. N., EARL, R. W., & PARADISE, N. (1957). Response by rats to differential stimulus complexity. *Journal of Comparative and Physiological Psychology, 50,* 514–518.

DEMBROWSKI, T. M., MACDOUGALL, J. M., et al. (1983). Perspectives on coronary prone behavior. In D. S. Krantz, A. Baum, & J. E. Singer (Eds.), *Handbook of psychology and health* (Vol. 3). Hillsdale, NJ: Erlbaum.

DEMBROWSKI, T. M., MACDOUGALL, J. M., ELIOT, R. S., BUELL, J. C. (1984). Moving beyond Type A. *Advances, 1,* 16–26.

DEMENT, W. C., & KLEITMAN, N. (1957). Cyclic variations in EEG and their relation to eye movements, body motility and dreaming. *Electroencephalography and clinical neurophysiology, 9,* 673–690.

DEMENT, W. C. (1972). *Some must watch while some must sleep.* San Francisco: W. H. Freeman.

DEMENT, W. C., & WOLPERT, E. (1958). The relation of eye movements, bodily motility and external stimuli to dream content. *Journal of Experimental Psychology, 55,* 543–553.

D'EMILIO, J., & FREEDMAN, E. (1988). *Intimate matters: A history of sexuality in America.* New York: Harper & Row.

DENES, P. B., & PINSON, E. N. (1963). *The speech chain.* Murray Hill, NJ: Bell Laboratories.

DENGERINK, H. A., O'LEARY, M. R., & KASNER, K. H. (1975). Individual differences in aggressive responses to attack: Internal-external locus of control and field dependence-independence. *Journal of Research in Personality 9*(3), 191–199.

DENNIS, W. (1960). Causes of retardation among institutional children: Iran. *Journal of Genetic Psychology, 96,* 47–59.

DENNIS, W., & DENNIS, S. G. (1948). Development under controlled environmental conditions. In W. Dennis (Ed.),

Readings in child psychology. New York: Prentice-Hall.

DENNIS, W., & NAJARIAN, P. (1957). Infant development under environmental handicap. *Psychological Monographs, 71*(7).

DENTON, D. A. (1967). Salt appetite. In C. F. Code (Ed.), *Handbook of physiology: Alimentary canal* (Vol. 1, pp. 433–459). Washington, DC: American Physiological Society.

DEQUINCY, T. (1822). *Confessions of an English opium eater.*

DEREGOWSKI, J. B. (1973). Illusion and culture. In R. L. Gregory & G. H. Gombrich (Eds.), *Illusion in nature and art* (pp. 161–192). New York: Scribner's.

DEREGOWSKI, J. B. (1987). Unpublished manuscript.

DEROGATIS, L., ABELOFF, M., & MELISARATOS, N. (1979). Psychological coping mechanisms and survival time in metastatic breast cancer. *Journal of the American Medical Association, 112,* 45–56.

DERRINGTON, A. M., & FUCHS, A. F. (1981). The development of spatial frequency selectivity in kitten striate cortex. *Journal of Physiology, 316,* 1–10.

DESERAN, F. A., & CHUNG, C. S. (1979). Appearance, role-taking, & reactions to deviance. *Social Psychology Quarterly, 42,* 426–430.

DEUTSCHER, I. (1964). The quality of postparental life. *Journal of Marriage and the Family, 26*(1), 263–268.

DEVALOIS, R. L., ALBRECHT, D. G., & THORELL, L. G. (1982). Spatial frequency selectivity of cells in the macaque visual cortex. *Vision Research, 22,* 545–559.

DEVALOIS, R. L., & DEVALOIS, K. K. (1987). *Spatial vision.* New York: Oxford University Press.

DEYKIN, E. Y., KLERMAN, G. L., & ARMOR, D. J. (1966). The relatives of schizophrenic patients: Clinical judgment of potential emotional resourcefulness. *American Journal of Orthopsychiatry, 36*(3), 518–528.

DIAMOND, A., ZOLA-MORGAN, S., & SQUIRE, L. R. (1989). Successful performance by monkeys with lesions of the hippocampal formation on AB and object retrieval; Two tasks that mark developmental changes in human infants. *Behavioral Neuroscience, 103*(3), 526–537.

DIAMOND, M. (1978, January/February). The aging brain: Some enlightening-optimistic results. *American Scientist.*

DIAMOND, M. C. (1980, June). Environment, air ions and brain chemistry. *Psychology Today.*

DIAMOND, M. C., & CONNORS, J. R. (1981). A search for the potential of the aging cortex. In M. Diamond (Ed.), *Brain neurotransmitters and receptors in aging and age related disorders.* New York: Raven Press.

DILLON, K., MINCHOFF, G., & BAKER, K. H. (1985–1986). Positive emotional states and enhancement of the immune system. *International Journal of Psychiatry in Medicine, 15,* 13–17.

DILMAN, I. (1986). *Freud and human nature.* New York: Basil Blackwell.

DINARELLO, C., & WOLFE, S. (1979). Fever. *Human Nature, 2*(2), 66–74.

DOBRZECKA, C., & KONOROWSKI, J. (1968). Qualitative versus directional cues in differential conditioning. *Acta Biologiae Experimentale, 28,* 61–69.

DOBZHANSKY, T. (1962). *Mankind evolving.* New Haven: Yale University Press.

DODSON, J. D. (1917). Relative values of reward and punishment in habit formation. *Psychobiology, 1,* 231–276.

DOHRENWEND, B. S., & DOHRENWEND, B. P. (1974). *Stressful life events: Their nature and effects.* New York: Wiley.

DOLLARD, J., DOOB, L. W., MILLER, N. E., MOWRER, O. H., & SEARS, R. R. (1939). *Frustration and aggression.* New Haven: Yale University Press.

DOMHOFF, G. W. (1985). *The mystique of dreams.* Berkeley: University of California Press.

DONALDSON, M. (1978). *Children's minds.* London: Croom Helm.

DONER, J. F., & LAPPIN, J. S. (1980). Commentary in S. Ullman, Against direct perception. *Behavioral and Brain Sciences, 3*(3).

DOOLING, D. J., & LACHMAN, R. (1971). Effects of comprehension on retention of prose. *Journal of Experimental Psychology, 88,* 216–222.

DORE, J. (1985). Holophrases revisited: Their "logical" development from dialogue. In M. D. Barrett (Ed.), *Children's single word speech.* (pp. 23–58). New York: Wiley.

DOUVAN, E. (1956). Social status and success striving. *Journal of Abnormal and Social Psychology, 52,* 219–223.

DOYLE, G., & GENTRY, W. (Ed.). (1984). *Handbook of Behavioral Medicine.* New York: Guilford Press.

DRAKE, R. A., & SELIGMAN, M. E. (1989). Self-serving biases in causal attributions as a function of altered activation asymmetry. *International Journal of Neuroscience, 45*(3-4), 199–204.

DROMI, E. (1987). *Early lexical development.* New York: Cambridge University Press.

DUA, P. S. (1970). Comparison of the effects of behaviorally oriented action and psychotherapy reeducation on introversion-extroversion, emotionality, and internal-external control. *Journal of Counseling Psychology, 17,* 567–572.

DUBOS, R. (1968). *So human an animal.* New York: Scribner.

DUBOS, R. (1979). The price of adapting to work. *Human Nature, 2*(4), 29–35.

DUBOS, R. (1978). Health and creative adaptation. *Human Nature, 1*(1), 14–21.

DUNBAR, F. (1943) *Psychosomatic Diagnosis.* New York: Harper & Row, 1943.

DUNKEL-SCHETTER, C., FOLKMAN, S., & LAZARUS, R. S. (1987). Correlates of social support receipt. *Journal of Personality and Social Psychology, 53*(1), 71–80.

DUNN, J. P., BROOKS, G. W., MAUSNER, J., RODMAN, G. P., & COBB, S. (1963). Social class gradient of serum uric acid levels in males. *Journal of the American Medical Association, 185*(6).

DURKEIM, E. (1951). *Suicide.* New York: Free Press.

DUTTON, D., & ARON, A. (1974). Some evidence for heightened sexual attraction under conditions of high anxiety. *Journal of Personality and Social Psychology 30,* 510–517.

DWORKIN, E. S., & EFRAN, J. S. (1967). The angered: Their susceptibility to varieties of humor. *Journal of Personality and Social Psychology, 6,* 233–236.

DYER, W. G. (1962). Analyzing marital adjustment using role theory. *Marriage and Family Living, 24*(4), 371–375.

EAGLY, A. H., & CARLI, L. L. (1981). Sex of researcher and sex-typed communications as determinants of sex differences in influenceability: A meta-analysis of social influence studies. *Psychological Bulletin, 90,* 1-20.

EAGLY, A. H., & STEFFEN, V. J. (1986). Gender and aggressive behavior: A meta-analytic review of the social psychological literature. *Psychological Bulletin, 100,* 309–330.

EBBINGHAUS, H. (1885). *Ber das gedchtnis (Memory).* Leipzig: Duncher Humbolt. (Translated by H. A. Ruger and E. Bussenius, 1913, and reissued by Dover Publications, 1969)

ECHTERLING, L., & EMMERLING, D. (1987). Impact of stage hypnosis. *American Journal of Clinical Hypnosis, 29,* 149–154.

ECKERMAN, J., WHATLEY, J., & KUTZ, S. (1975). The growth of social play with peers during the second year of life. *Developmental Psychology, 11,* 42–49.

ECKHOLM, E. (1978). Vanishing firewood. *Human Nature, 1*(5), 58–67.

EGBERT, L. D. (1985). Postscript. *Advances, 2,* 56–59.

EHRHARDT, S. A., & MEYER-BAHLBURG, H. (1981). Effects of prenatal sex hormones on gender-related behavior. *Science, 211,* 1312–1318.

EHRLICH, P., & FELDMAN, S. (1977). *The race bomb.* New York: Quadrangle.

EHRLICH, P., HOLDREN, J., & EHRLICH, A. (1977). *Ecoscience.* San Francisco: W. H. Freeman.

EHRLICH, P., & ORNSTEIN, R. (in press). *New world, new mind.* New York: Doubleday.

EIBL-EIBESFELDT, I. (1970). *Ethology: The biology of behavior.* New York: Holt, Rinehart & Winston.

EIBL-EIBESFELDT, I. (1971). *Love and hate: The natural history of behavior patterns* (G. Strachan, Trans.). New York: Holt, Rinehart & Winston.

EIBL-EIBESFELDT, I. (1972). Similarities and differences between cultures in expressive movements. In R. A. Hinde (Ed.), *Non-verbal communication.* Cambridge: Cambridge University Press.

EIBL-EIBESFELDT, I. (1980). Strategies of social interaction. In R. Plutchik & H.

Kelerman (Eds.), *Emotion: Theory, research, and experience.* New York: Academic Press.

EICHORN, D., CLAUSEN, J., HAAN, N., HONZIK, M., & MUSSEN, P. (Eds.). (1981). *Present and past in middle life.* New York: Academic Press.

EILERS, R. E., GAVIN, W. J., & OILER, D. K. (1987). Cross-linguistic perception in infancy: Early effects of linguistic experience. *Journal of Child Language, 9*(2), 289–302.

EINHORN, H. J., & HOGARTH, R. M. (1981). Behavioral decision theory: Processes of judgment and choice. *Annual Review of Psychology, 32,* 53–88.

EINSTEIN, A. (1956). My life as a scientist. In J. Bronowski (Ed.), *The structure of science.* New York: Doubleday.

EISENBERG, N., & MILLER, P. A. (1987). The relation of empathy to prosocial and related behaviors. *Psychological Bulletin, 101,* 91–119.

EKMAN, P. (1984). Expression and the nature of emotion. In K. Scherer & P. Ekman (Eds.), *Approaches to emotion.* Hillsdale, NJ: Erlbaum.

EKMAN, P. (1985). *Telling lies.* New York: Norton.

EKMAN, P. (Ed.). (1982). *Emotion in the human face* (2nd ed.). Cambridge: Cambridge University Press.

EKMAN, P., & FRIESEN, W. (1983). *Unmasking the face.* Palo Alto: Consulting Psychologists Press.

EKMAN, P., FRIESEN, W. V., et al. (1987, October). Universals and cultural differences in the judgments of facial expressions of emotion. *Journal of Personality and Social Psychology, 53*(4), 712–717.

ELIOT, R., & BREO, D. (1984). *Is it worth dying for?* New York: Bantam Books.

ELKIND, D. (1974). *Children and adolescents: Interpretive essays on Jean Piaget* (2nd ed.). New York: Oxford University Press.

ELKIND, D. (1978). *A sympathetic understanding of the child: Birth to sixteen* (2nd ed.). Boston: Allyn & Bacon.

ELLIOTT, J. (1977). The power and pathology of prejudice. In P. G. Zimbardo & F. L. Ruch (Eds.), *Psychology and life* (9th ed.). Glenview: Scott, Foresman.

ELLIS, A. (1970). *Reason and emotion in psychotherapy.* New York: Lyle Stuart.

ENGEL, G. (1971). Sudden and rapid death during psychological stress: Folklore or folk wisdom. *Annals of Internal Medicine, 74,* 771–82.

ENGEN, T. (1977). Taste and smell. In J. E. Birren & J. W. Schaie (Eds.), *Handbook of the psychology of aging.* New York: Van Nostrand Reinhold.

ENGEN, T., & ROSS, B. M. (1973). Long-term memory of odors with and without verbal descriptions. *Journal of Experimental Psychology, 100,* 221-227.

EPSTEIN, J. W., & BROOTA, K. D. (1986). Automatic and attentional components in perception of size-at-a-distance. *Perception & Psychodynamics, 40,* 256–262.

EPSTEIN, L. H., & CLUSS, P. A. (1982). A behavioral medicine perspective on adherence to long-term medical regimens. *Journal of Consulting and Clinical Psychology, 50*(6), 950–971.

EPSTEIN, S., & SMITH, R. (1956). Repression and insight as related to reaction to cartoons. *Journal of Consulting Psychology, 20,* 391–395.

EPSTEIN, S. M. (1967). Toward a unified theory of anxiety. In B. A. Maher (Ed.), *Progress in experimental personality research* (Vol. 4). New York: Academic Press.

EPSTEIN, S. M. (1979). The stability of behavior: Pt. 1. On predicting most of the people much of the time. *Journal of Personality and Social Psychology, 37,* 1097–1126.

ERDELYI, M. H. (1986). *Psychoanalysis: Freud's cognitive psychology.* New York: W. H. Freeman.

ERICSSON, K. A., & SIMON, H. A. (1980). Verbal reports as data. *Psychological Review, 87,* 215–251.

ERIKSON, E. (1968a). *Childhood and society.* New York: Norton.

ERIKSON, E. (1968b). *Identity: Youth and crisis.* New York: Norton.

ERIKSON, E. (1986). *Vital involvement in old age.* New York: Norton.

ESSEN, D. C. VAN. (1984). Functional organization of primate visual cortex. In A. Peters & E. G. Jones (Eds.) *Cerebral cortex* (Vol. 3, p. 250–329). New York: Plenum.

ESTES, W. K. (1980). Is human memory obsolete? *American Scientist, 68,* 62–69.

EVANS, R. I., ROZELLE, R. M., (1981). Social modeling films to deter smoking in adolescents: Results of a three-year field investigation. *Journal of Applied Social Psychology, 66,* 399–414.

EYSENCK, H. J. (1952). The effects of psychotherapy: An evaluation. *Journal of Consulting Psychology, 16,* 319–324.

EYSENCK, H. J. (1975). *The inequality of man.* San Diego: Edits.

EYSENCK, H. J. (Ed.). (1981). *A model for personality.* Berlin: Springer-Verlag.

FALOON, I., BOYD, J., MCGILL, C. RAZANI, J., MOSS, H., & GILDERMAN, A. (1982). Family management in the prevention of and exacerbation of schizophrenia: A controlled study. *New England Journal of Medicine, 306,* 1437–1440.

FANTZ, R. L. (1961). The origin of form perception. *Scientific American, 204,* 66–72.

FARB, P., & ARMELAGOS, G. (1980). *Consuming passions: The anthropology of eating.* Boston: Houghton Mifflin.

FARQUAHAR, J. W., BROWN, B. W., JR., SOLOMON, D. S., & HULLEY, S. B. (1985). The Stanford 5-City project: Design and methods. *American Journal of Epidemiology, 122*(2), 323–334.

FARR, L. E. (1967). Medical consequences of environmental noises. *Journal of the American Medical Association, 202,* 171–174.

FARREL, B. (1966). Scientists, theologians,

mystics swept up in a psychic revolution. *Life, 60,* 31.

FARRIS, R. E. L., & DUNHAM, H. W. (1965). *Mental disorders in urban areas.* Chicago: University of Chicago Press. (Original work published 1939)

FAUSTO-STERLING, A. (1986). *Myths of gender: Biological theories about women and men.* New York: Basic Books.

FAZIO, R. H. (1986). How do attitudes guide behavior? In R. M. Sorrentino & E. T. Higgins (Eds.), *The handbook of motivation and cognition: Foundations of social behavior.* New York: Guilford Press.

FAZIO, R. H., & ZANNA, M. P. (1981). Direct experience and attitude-behavior consistency. In L. Berkowitz (Ed.), *Advances in experimental social psychology* (Vol 14). New York: Academic Press.

FEIN, R. A. (1978). Consideration of men's experiences and the birth of a first child. In W. Miller & L. Newman (Eds.), *The first child and family formation.* Chapel Hill: Carolina Population Center.

FEINGOLD, A. (1988). Are cognitive gender differences dissapearing? *American Psychologist, 43,* 95–103.

FELDMAN, S., & NASH, S. C. (1984). The transition from expectancy to parenthood: Impact of the firstborn child on men and women. *Sex Roles, 11,* 61–78.

FELDMAN-SUMMERS, S., & KIESLER, S. B. (1974). Those who are number two try harder: The effect of sex on attributions of causality. *Journal of Personality and Social Psychology, 30,* 846–855.

FENDRICH, R., & GAZZANIGA, M. S. (1989). Evidence of foveal splitting in a commissurotomy patient. *Neuropsychologia 27(3),* 273–281.

FERENCZI, S. (1954). *Thalassa: A theory of genitality.* New York: W. W. Norton.

FERNALD, A. (1984). The perceptual and affective salience of mothers' speech to infants. In L. Feagans, C. Garvey, & R. Golinkoff (Eds.), *The origins and growth of communication* (pp. 5–29). Norwood, NJ: Ablex.

FERNALD, A., & SIMON, T. (1984). Expanded intonation contours in mothers' speech to newborns. *Developmental Psychology, 20,* 104–113.

FESTINGER, L. (1954). A theory of social comparison processes. *Human Relations, 7,* 117–140.

FESTINGER, L. (1957). *A theory of cognitive dissonance.* Stanford: Stanford University Press.

FESTINGER, L., & CARLSMITH, J. M. (1959). Cognitive consequences of forced compliance. *Journal of Abnormal and Social Psychology, 58,* 203–211.

FESTINGER, L., SCHACHTER, S., & BACK, K. (1950). *Social pressures in informal groups: A study of human factors in housing.* New York: Harper & Row.

FEUERSTEIN, R. (1979). *The dynamic assessment of retarded performers.* Baltimore: University Park Press.

FEUERSTEIN, R. (1980). *Instrumental en-richment.* Baltimore: University Park Press.

FEUERSTEIN, R., & RAND, Y. (1977). *Studies in cognitive modifiability. Instrumental enrichment: Redevelopment of cognitive functions of retarded early adolescents.* Jerusalem: Hadassah-Wizo-Canada Research Institute.

FIEDLER, F. E. (1950). A comparison of therapeutic relationships in psychoanalytic, nondirective, and Adlerian therapy. *Journal of Consulting and Clinical Psychology, 14,* 436–445.

FIELD, D., & MINKLER, M. (1988). Continuity and change in social support between young-old, old-old, and very-old adults. *Journal of Gerontology, 43,* 100–106.

FIELD, T. M., et al. (1986). Tactile-kinesthetic stimulation effects on preterm neurates. *Pediatrics, 77(5),* 654–658.

FIELDS, H. L., & LEVINE, J. D. (1981). Biology of placebo analgesia. *American Journal of Medicine, 70,* 745–46.

FINCH, C. E., & LANDFIELD, P. W. (1985). Neuroendocrine and autonomic functions in aging mammals. In C. E. Finch & E. L. Schneider (Eds.), *Handbook of the biology of aging.* New York: Van Nostrand Reinhold.

FISCHER, C. S. (1976). *The urban experience.* New York: Harcourt Brace Jovanovich.

FISKE, S. T., & TAYLOR, S. E. (1984). *Social Cognition.* Reading, MA: Addison-Wesley.

FITZGERALD, F. T. (1986). The therapeutic value of pets. *Western Journal of Medicine, 144,* 103–105.

FLAVELL, J. (1970). Cognitive changes in adulthood. In L. R. Goulet & P. B. Baltes (Eds.), *Life-span developmental psychology: Research and theory.* New York: Academic Press.

FLAVELL, J. (1981). On cognitive development. *Child Development, 53,* 1–10.

FLAVELL, J. (1985). *Cognitive development* (2nd ed.). Englewood Cliffs, NJ: Prentice-Hall.

FLINN, M. W. (1966). *The origins of the industrial revolution.* London: Longmans, Green.

FODOR, J. (1983). *The modularity of mind.* Cambridge: MIT Press.

FOGELMAN, E., & WIENER, V. L. (1985). The few, the brave, the noble. *Psychology Today, 19(8),* 61–65.

FOLKMAN, S., & LAZARUS, R. (1980). An analysis of coping in a middle-aged population. *Journal of Health and Social Behavior, 21,* 219–239.

FORDYCE, W. E., FOWLER, R. S., LEHMANN, J. F., & DELATEUR (1968). Some implications of learning in problems of chronic pain. *Journal of Chronic Diseases, 21,* 179–190.

FOREYT, J. P., SCOTT, L. W., MITCHELL, R. W., & GOTTO, A. M. (1979). Plasma lipid changes in the normal population following behavioral treatment. *Journal of Consulting and Clinical Psychology, 47,* 440–452.

FORSYTH, D. (1983). *An introduction to group dynamics.* Monterey: Brooks/Cole.

FORT, J. (1970). *The pleasure seekers: The drug crisis, youth and society.* New York: Grove Press.

FOUCAULT, M. (1978). *The history of sexuality: Vol. 1. An introduction.* (Robert Hurley, Trans.). New York: Random House.

FOX, N. A., & DAVIDSON, R. (1986). Taste elicited changes in facial signs of emotion and the asymmetry of brain electrical activity in human newborns. *Neuropsychologia, 24(3),* 417–422.

FOZARD, J., WOLF, E., BELL, B., FARLAND, R., & PODOLSKY, S. (1977). Visual perception and communication. In J. Birren & K. Schaie (Eds.), *Handbook of the psychology of aging.* New York: Van Nostrand Reinhold.

FRAGER, R., & FADIMAN, J. (1987). *Maslow's motivation and personality.* New York: Harper & Row.

FRAIBERG, S. (1971). Blind infants and their mothers: An examination of the sign system. In M. Lewis & L. A. Rosenblum (Eds.), *The effect of the infant on its care-giver* (pp. 215–232). New York: Wiley.

FRANK, J. D. (1982). Therapeutic components shared by all psychotherapies. In J. H. Harvey & M. M. Parks (Eds.), *Psychotherapy research and behavior change.* Washington, DC: American Psychological Association.

FRANK, J. D. (1983). The placebo is psychotherapy. *Behavioral and Brain Sciences, 6,* 291–292.

FRANQUEMONT, C. (1979). Watching, watching, counting, counting. *Human Nature, 2,* 82–84.

FREDRICKSON, B. L., & CARSTENSEN, L. L. (1990). Choosing social partners. *Psychology and Aging.*

FREEDMAN, D. (1979). Ethnic differences in babies. *Human Nature, 2,* 36.

FREEDMAN, J. L. (1975). *Crowding and behavior.* New York: Viking Press.

FREEDMAN, J. L. (1986). Television violence and aggression: A rejoinder. *Psychological Bulletin, 100,* 372–378.

FREEDMAN, J. L., LEVY, A. S., BUCHANAN, R. W., & PRICE, J. (1972). Crowding and human aggressiveness. *Journal of Experimental Social Psychology, 8,* 528–548.

FREEDMAN, J. L., SEARS, D. O., & CARLSMITH, J. M. (1984). *Social psychology.* Englewood Cliffs, NJ: Prentice-Hall.

FREEMAN, N., & COX, C. (1986). *Visual order.* New York: Cambridge University Press.

FREIZE, I. H., PARSONS, J. E., JOHNSON, P. B., RUBLE, E. N., & ZELLERMAN, G. L. (1978). *Women and sex roles: A social psychological perspective.* New York: Norton.

FRENCH, E., & LESSER, G. S. (1964). Some characteristics of the achievement motive in women. *Journal of Abnormal and Social Psychology, 68,* 119–128.

FRENCH, J., & CAPLAN, R. (1970). Psychosocial factors in coronary heart disease. *Industrial Medicine, 39,* 383–397.

FREUD, A. (1966). *The ego and the mechanisms of defense*. New York: International Universities Press. (Original work published 1936)

FREUD, S. (1896). Further remarks on the neuro-psychoses of defence. In *Standard edition* (Vol. 3, p. 159). London: Hogarth Press.

FREUD, S. (1914). On narcissism: an introduction. In *Standard edition* (Vol. 14). London: Hogarth Press.

FREUD, S. (1920). Beyond the pleasure principle. In *Standard edition* (Vol. 18). London: Hogarth Press.

FREUD, S. (1937). Analysis terminable and interminable. In *Standard edition* (Vol. 23). London: Hogarth Press.

FREUD, S. (1953-1966). *The standard edition of the complete psychological works of Sigmund Freud*. (J. Strachey, Ed. and Trans.). London: Hogarth Press.

FREUD, S. (1955). *The interpretation of dreams*. London: Hogarth Press. (Original work published 1900)

FREUD, S. (1962). *New introductory lectures on psychoanalysis*. London: Hogarth Press.

FREY, A. (1982). Personal communication.

FREY, W. H., II, DeSOTA-JOHNSON, D., HOFFMAN, C., & McCALL, J. T. (1981). Effect of stimulus on the chemical composition of human tears. *American Journal of Opthalmology, 92*,(4), 559–567.

FRIEDL, E. (1978). Society and sex roles. *Human Nature, 1*(4), 68–75.

FRIEDMAN, M., & ROSENMAN, R. (1974). *Type A behavior and your heart*. New York: Knopf.

FRIEDMAN, M., & ULMER, D. (1984). *Treating Type A behavior and your heart*. New York: Knopf.

FRIEDMAN, M. I., THORESON, C. E., & GILL, J. J. (1982). Feasibility of altering Type A behavior pattern after myocardial infarction. *Circulation, 66*, 83–92.

FRIEDMANN, E., KATCHER, A., LYNCH, J. J., & THOMAS, S. A. (1980). Animal companions and one-year survival of patients after discharge from a coronary care unit. *Public Health Reports, 95*, 307–312.

FRIEZE, I. H., PARSONS, J. E., JOHNSON, P. B., RUBLE, D. N., & ZELLMAN, G. L. (1978). *Women and sex roles: A social psychological perspective*. New York: Norton.

FROHMAN, L. A., & BERNARDI, L. L. (1968). Growth hormone and insulin levels in weanling rats with ventromedial hypothalmic lesions. *Endocrinology, 82*, 1125–1132.

FROMME, E. (1941). *Escape from freedom*. New York: Holt, Rinehart & Winston.

FUJII, S. M. (1980). Minority group elderly: Demographic characteristics and implications for public policy. In C. Eisdorfer (Ed.), *Annual review of gerontology and geriatrics* (pp. 261–284). New York: Springer.

GALANTER, E. (1962). Contemporary psychophysics. In R. Brown, E. Garlanter, E. Hess, & G. Mandler (Eds.), *New directions in psychology* (pp. 85–157). New York: Holt, Rinehart & Winston.

GALIN, D., & ORNSTEIN, R. (1972). Lateral specialization of cognitive mode: An EEG study. *Psychophysiology, 9*, 412–418.

GALIN, D., ORNSTEIN, R. E., & ADAMS, J. (1977). Midbrain stimulation of the amygdala. *Journal of States of Consciousness, 2*, 34–41.

GALIN, D., ORNSTEIN, R. E., HERRON, J., & JOHNSTONE, J. (1982). Sex and handedness differences in EEG measures of hemispheric specialization. *Brain and Language, 16*(1), 19–55.

GALLUP, G. G. (1977). Self-recognition in primates: A comparative approach to the bi-directional properties of consciousness. *American Psychologist, 32*, 329–338.

GALLUP, G. G. (1979). Self-awareness in primates. *American Scientist, 67*, 417–421.

GALTON, F. (1979). *Hereditary genius*. New York: St. Martin's Press.

GARCIA, J. (1989). Food for Tolman: Cognition and cathexis in concert. In T. Archer & L. Nilsson (Eds.), *Aversion, avoidance, and anxiety* (pp. 45–85). Hillsdale, NJ: Erlbaum.

GARCIA, J., GARCIA, Y., & ROBERTSON, R. (1985). Evolution of learning mechanisms. In B. L. Hammonds (Ed.), *Psychology and learning* (Vol. 4, pp. 191–243). Washington, DC: American Psychological Association.

GARCIA, J., & KOELLING, R. (1966). Relation of cue to consequence in avoidance learning. *Psychonomic Science, 4*, 123–124.

GARDNER, H. (1975). *The shattered mind*. New York: Knopf.

GARDNER, H. (1983). *Frames of mind*. New York: Basic Books.

GARDNER, H. (1985). *The mind's new science*. New York: Basic Books.

GARNER, W. R. (1974). *The processing of information and structure*. Potomac: Erlbaum.

GARRISON, W. (1971, March). Tears and laughter. *Today's Health*, 29–32.

GARVEY, C. (1977). *Play*. Cambridge: Harvard University Press.

GATCHEL, R. J., & PRICE, K. P. (Eds.). (1979). *Clinical applications of biofeedback: Appraisal and status*. Elmsford, NY: Pergamon.

GATRELL, N. (1987). The lesbian as a "single woman." In M. Walsh (Ed.), *The psychology of women: Ongoing debates*. New Haven: Yale University Press.

GAY, P. (1988). *Freud: A life for our time*. New York: Norton.

GAZZANIGA, M. (1985). *The social brain*. New York: Basic Books.

GAZZANIGA, M. S. (1987). Perceptual and attentional processes following callosal section in humans. *Neuropsychologia, 25*(1A), 119–133.

GAZZANIGA, M. S., HOLTZMAN, J. D., & SMYLIE, C. S. (1987). Speech without conscious awareness. *Neurology, 37*(4), 682–685.

GAY, P. (1989). *Freud: Life and work*. New York: Doubleday.

GELMAN, R., & BAILLARGEON, R. (1983). A review of some Piagetian concepts. In J. H. Flavell & E. Markman (Eds.), *Handbook of child psychology* (Vol. 3, pp. 167–230). *Cognitive Development*. New York: Wiley.

GELMAN, R., & GALISTEL, C. R. (1986). *The child's understanding of number*. Cambridge: Harvard University Press.

GENDLIN, E. T. (1986). What comes after traditional psychotherapy research? *American Psychologist, 41*, 131–137.

GENTRY, M., & SCHULMAN, A. D. (1988). Remarriage as a coping response for widowhood. *Psychology and Aging, 3*, 191–196.

GEORGE, L. (1981). *Role transitions in later life*. Monterey: Wadsworth.

GERBNER, G., & GROSS, L. (1976). The scary world of TV's heavy viewer. *Psychology Today, 89*, 41–45.

GERGEN, K. J., & GERGEN, M. M. (1986). Narrative form and the construction of psychological science. In T. R. Sarbin (Ed.), *Narrative psychology: The storied nature of human conduct* (pp. 22–44). New York: Praeger.

GERGEN, K. J., GERGEN, M. M., & METER, K. (1972). Individual orientations to prosocial behavior. *Journal of Social Issues, 8*, 105–130.

GERSTEL, N., & RIESMAN, C. (1981). *Social networks in a vulnerable population: The separated and divorced*. Paper presented at the American Public Health Association Meetings, Los Angeles.

GESCHWIND, N. (1972). Language and the brain. *Scientific American, 226*(4), 76–83.

GESCHWIND, N., & GALABURDA, A. (Eds.). (1984). *Biological foundations of cerebral dominance*. Cambridge: Harvard University Press.

GESCHWIND, N., & LEVITSKY, W. (1976). Left-right asymmetries in temporal speech region. *Science, 161*, 186–187.

GIBSON, E., & WALK, R. (1960). The visual cliff. *Scientific American, 202*, 64–71.

GIBSON, J. J. (1960). *The perception of the visual world*. Boston: Houghton Mifflin.

GIBSON, J. J. (1966). *The senses considered as perceptual systems*. Boston: Houghton Mifflin.

GIBSON, J. J. (1970). On theories for visual space perception: A reply to Johansson. *Scandinavian Journal of Psychology, 11*, 73–79.

GIBSON, J. J. (1979). *The ecological approach to visual perception*. Boston: Houghton Mifflin.

GIBSON, J. J., OLUM, P., & ROSENBLATT, F. (1955). Parallax and perspective during aircraft landings. *American Journal of Psychology, 68*, 372–385.

GIEDION, S. (1948). *Mechanization takes command*. New York: W. W. Norton.

GILLIGAN, C. (1982). *In a different voice: Psychological theory and women's development*. Cambridge: Harvard University Press.

GIULIANO, V. (1982). The mechanization of office work. *Scientific American, 247*, 148–165.

GLADUE, B. A., GREEN, R., & HELLMAN, R. E. (1984). Neuroendocrine response to estrogen and sexual orientation. *Science, 225*, 1496–1499.

GLASER, R., & BOND, L. (Eds.). (1981). Testing: Concepts, policy, practice, and research [special issue]. *American Psychologist, 36*(10).

GLASS, A. L., HOLYOAK, K. J., & SANTA, J. L. (1984). *Cognition.* Reading, MA: Addison-Wesley.

GLASS, D. C., & SINGER, J. E. (1984). *Urban stress: Experiments on noise and social stressors.* New York: Academic Press.

GLASS, D. C., SINGER, J. E., & FRIEDMAN, L. N. (1969). Psychic cost of adaptation to an environmental stressor. *Journal of Personality and Social Psychology, 12*, 200–210.

GLASS, G. V., & HOPKINS, K. D. (1984). *Statistical Methods in Education and Psychology.* Englewood Cliffs, NJ: Prentice-Hall.

GLEESON, P. A., BROWN, J. S., WARING, J. J., & STOCK, M. J. (1979). Thermogenic effects of diet and exercise. *Proceedings of the Nutrition Society, 38*, 82.

GLENN, E., & FELDBERG, R. (1977). Degraded and deskilled: The proletarianization of clerical work. *Social Problems, 25*, 52–64.

GLICK, F. O., WEISS, R. S., & PARKES, C. M. (1974). *The first year of bereavement.* New York: Wiley.

GLICK, P. C., & NORTON, A. J. (1977). Marrying, divorcing and living together in the U.S. today. *Population Bulletin.*

GMELCH, G. (1978). Baseball magic. *Human Nature, 1*, 32–40.

GOLAN, N. (1986). *The perilous bridge: Helping clients through mid-life transitions.* New York: Free Press.

GOLDBERG, P. (1968, April). Are women prejudiced against women? *Trans-Action,* 28–30.

GOLDBERG, S., & LEWIS, M. (1969). Play behavior in the year-old infant: Early sex differences, *Child Development, 40*, 21–31.

GOLDBERG, S. R., et al. (1981). Persistent behavior at high rates maintained by intravenous self-administration of nicotine. *Science, 214*, 573–575.

GOLDSMITH, H. H., BUSS, A. H., PLOMIN, R., & ROTHBART, M. K. (1987). Roundtable: What is temperament? Four approaches. *Child Development, 58*(2), 505–529.

GOLDSTEIN, A. (1980). Thrills in response to music and other stimuli. *Physiological Psychology, 8*, 126–129.

GOLDSTEIN, J. H., DAVIS, R. W., & HERMAN, D. (1975). Escalation of aggression: Experimental studies. *Journal of Personality and Social Psychology, 31*(1), 162–170.

GOLDSTEIN, K. (1974). *Human nature in the light of psychopathology.* Cambridge: Harvard University Press.

GOLDSTEIN, M. J. (1959). The relationship between coping and avoiding behavior and response to fear-arousing propaganda. *Journal of Abnormal and Social Psychology, 58*, 247–252.

GOLDSTEIN, M. J., BAKER, B. L., & JAMISON, K. R. (1986). *Abnormal psychology: Ex-*

periences, origins, and interventions (2nd ed.). Boston: Little, Brown.

GOLEMAN, D. (1984a, December). Denial and hope. *American Health, 3*, 54–60.

GOLEMAN, D. (1984b, December). To dream the impossible dream. *American Health, 3*, 60–61.

GOLEMAN, D. (1985). *Vital lies, simple truths: The psychology of self-deception.* New York: Simon & Schuster.

GOLEMAN, D. (1989). What is negative about positive illusions? When benefits for the individual harm the collective. *Journal of Social and Clinical Psychology, 8*, 190–197.

GOMBRICH, E. H. (1961). *Art and Illusion* (2nd ed.). Princeton: Princeton University Press.

GOODCHILDS, J. D. (1972). On being witty: Causes, correlates and consequences. In J. H. Goldstein & P. E. McGhee (Eds.), *The psychology of humor.* London: Academic Press.

GOODE, E., & HABER, L. (1977). Sexual correlates of homosexual experience: An exploratory study of college women. *Journal of Sex Research, 13*, 12–21.

GOODE, W. (1956). *Women in divorce.* New York: Free Press.

GOODMAN, M. J., STEWART, G. J., & GILBERT, F., JR. (1977). A study of certain medical and pysiological variables among Caucasian and Japanese women living in Hawaii. *Journal of Gerontology, 32*(3), 291–298.

GOODY, J. (1976). *Production and reproduction.* Cambridge: Cambridge University Press.

GORDON, B. (1979). *I'm dancing as fast as I can.* New York: Harper & Row.

GORE, S. (1978). The effect of social support in moderating the health consequences of unemployment. *Journal of Health and Social Behavior, 19*, 157–65.

GORE, S. (1978) *The influence of social support and related variables in ameliorating the consequences of job loss.* Doctoral dissertation, University of Pennsylvania.

GOSS, A., & MOROSKO, I. E. (1970). Relations between a dimension of internal-external control and the MMPI with an alcoholic population. *Journal of Consulting and Clinical Psychology, 34*, 189–192.

GOTTESMAN, I. (1962). Differential inheritance of the psychoneuroses. *Eugenics Quarterly, 9*, 223–227.

GOTTESMAN, I. (1968). Severity/concordance and diagnostic refinement in the Mandsely-Bethlem schizophrenic twin study. In D. Rosenthal & S. S. Kety (Eds.), *The transmission of schizophrenia.* New York: Pergamon Press.

GOTTESMAN, I. (1974). Developmental genetics and ontogenetic psychology. *Minnesota Symposia on Child Psychology, 8.* Minneapolis: University of Minnesota Press.

GOTTESMAN, I., & SHIELDS, J. (1972). *Schizophrenia and genetics: A twin study vantage point.* New York: Academic Press.

GOTTMAN, J. M. (1979). *Marital interaction:*

Experimental investigations. New York: Academic Press.

GOTTMAN, J. M. (in press). *Marital communication.*

GOTTMAN, J. M. & LEVENSON, R. W. (1986). Assessing the role of emotion in marriage. *Behavioral Assessment, 8*, 31–48.

GOTTMAN, J. M., & LEVENSON, R. W. (1988). The social psychophysiology of marriage. In P. Noller & M. A. Fitzpatrick (Eds.) *Perspectives on marital interaction,* Clevedon, Eng,: Multilingual Matters.

GOTTMAN, J. M., & PARKER, J. G. (in press). *Conversations of friends: Speculations in affective development.* New York: Cambridge University Press.

GOULD, R. L. (1978). *Transformations: Growth and change in adult life.* New York: Simon & Schuster.

GOULD, S. J. (1979). *Ever since Darwin.* New York: W. W. Norton.

GOVE, W. R. (1972). Sex roles, marital roles, mental illness. *Social Forces, 51*, 34–44.

GRABOYS, T. B. (1981). Celtic fever: Playoff-induced ventricular arrythmia. *New England Journal of Medicine, 305*, 467–468.

GRAFF, H., & STELLAR, E. (1962). Hyperphagia obesity and finickiness. *Journal of Comparative and Physiological Psychology, 55*, 418–424.

GRAHAM, J. R. (1977). *The MMPI: A practical guide.* New York: Oxford University Press.

GRANICH, S., & PATTERSON, R. (Eds.). (1971). *Human aging II: An eleven year follow-up biomedical and behavioral study* (Publication No. HSM 71-9037). Washington, DC: U.S. Government Printing Office.

GRASTYAN, E., KARMOS, G., VORECZKEY, L., MARTIN, J., & KELLENYI, L. (1965). Hypothalamic motivational processes as reflected by their hippocampal electrical correlates. *Science, 149*, 91–93.

GRAUNT, J. (1986). Natural and political observations made upon the bills of mortality. In J. R. Newman (Ed.), *The world of mathematics* (Vol. 3). New York: Simon & Schuster.

GRAVELLE, K. (1985). Can a feeling of capability reduce arthritis pain? *Advances, 2*, 8-13.

GRAVES, C. W. (1966). Deterioration of work standards. *Harvard Business Review, 44*, 117–128.

GRAY, J. A. (1984). *The neuropsychology of anxiety.* New York: Oxford University Press.

GRAY, R., & SMITH, T. (1960). Effect of employment on sex differences in attitudes toward the parental family. *Marriage and Family Living, 22*, 36–38.

GREELY, A., & SHEATSLEY, P. (1971). The acceptance of desegregation continues to advance. *Scientific American, 225*(6), 13–19.

GREENBERG, R., & PEARLMAN, C. A. (1974). Cutting the REM nerve: An approach to the adaptive role of REM sleep. *Perspectives in Biology and Medicine, 19*, 513–521.

GREENO, C. G., & MACCOBY, E. (1986). How different is the "different" voice? *Signs, 11*(2), 310–316.

GREENOUGH, S. (1975). Experimental modification of the developing brain. *American Scientist, 63,* 37–46.

GREENOUGH, W. T. (1982). Lecture to the Developmental Psychology Research Group, Estes Park, CO.

GREENWALD, A. G., & BANAJI, M. R. (1989). The self as a memory system: Powerful, but ordinary. *Journal of Personality and Social Psychology, 57,* 41–54.

GREER, H. S., MORRIS, T., & PETTINGALE, K. W. (1979). Psychological response to breast cancer: Effect on outcome. *Lancet 11,* 785–87.

GREER, S. (1981, August). *Psychological response to breast cancer and eight-year outcome.* Paper presented at the Annual Meeting of the American Psychological Association, Los Angeles.

GREER, S., & MORRIS, T. (1975) Psychological attributes of women who develop breast cancer. *Psychosomatic Research, 19,* 147–53.

GREGORY, R. L. (1973, 1977). *Eye and brain* (2nd & 3rd eds.). New York: McGraw-Hill.

GREIF, I. (Ed.). (1988). *Computer-Supported Cooperative Work.* Los Altos, CA: Morgan Kaufmann.

GREIFENSTEIN, F. E., et al. (1958). A study of a 1-dryl cycle hexylamine for anesthesia. *Anesthesia and Analgesia, 37*(5), 283–294.

GRICE, G. R. (1948). The relation of secondary reinforcement to delayed reward in visual discrimination learning. *Journal of Experimental Psychology, 38,* 1–16.

GRICE, H. P. (1967). Utterer's meaning, sentence-meaning and word-meaning. *Foundations of Language, 4,* 225–242.

GRIFFITH, R. M., MIYAGI, O., & TAGO, A. (1958). The universality of typical dreams: Japanese vs. American. *American Anthropologist, 60,* 1173–1179.

GRINKER, R. R. (1953). *Emotions and emotional disorders.* New York: Hoeber.

GRINKER, R. R., & SPEIGEL, J. P. (1945). *Men under stress.* Philadelphia: Blackiston.

GRINSPOON, L., & BAKALAR, J. B. (1979). *Psychedelic drugs reconsidered.* New York: Basic Books.

GRIVES, P. M., & THOMPSON, R. F. (1973). A dual process theory of habituation: Neural mechanisms. In H. M. S. Pecks & M. J. Herz (Eds.), *Habituation, physiological substrates II.* New York: Academic Press.

GROSS, C. G., ROCHA-MIRANDA, C. E., & BENDER, D. B. (1972). Visual properties of neurons in inferotemporal cortex of the macaque. *Journal of Neurophysiology, 35,* 96–111.

GROSSMAN, F. K., EICHLER, L., & WINICK-HOFF, S. A. (1980). *Pregnancy, birth, and parenthood.* San Francisco: Jossey-Bass.

GROSSMAN, K., GROSSMAN, K. E., SPANGLER, G., SUESS, G., & UNZNER, L. (1985). Maternal sensitivity and newborns' orientation responses related to quality of attachment in Northern Germany. In I. Bretherton & E. Waters (Eds.), *Growing points of attachment theory and research: Monographs of the Society for Research in Child Development, 50,* (1-2, Serial No. 209).

GROSSMAN, S. (1979). The biology of motivation. *Annual Review of Psychology, 30,* 209–242.

GUILFORD, J. P. (1967). *The nature of human intelligence.* New York: McGraw-Hill.

GUILFORD, J. P., & HOEPFNER, R. (1971). *The analysis of intelligence.* New York: McGraw-Hill.

GUTMANN, D. (1968). Aging among the Himalaya Maya: A comparative study. *Journal of Personality and Social Psychology 7,* 28–35.

GUTMANN, D. (1987). *Reclaimed powers: Toward a new psychology of men and women in later life.* New York: Basic Books.

HAAN, N. (1977). *Coping and defending.* New York: Academic Press.

HAAN, N. (1985). Common personality dimensions or common organization across the life-span? In J. M. Munnichs, P. Mussen, E. Olbrich, & P. G. Coleman (Eds.), *Life-span and change in gerontological perspective* (pp. 17–44). San Diego: Academic Press.

HAAS, J. (1978). *Teenage sexuality.* New York: Simon & Schuster.

HABER, R., & STANDIG, L. G. (1966). Direct measures of short-term visual storage. *Quarterly Journal of Experimental Psychology, 21,* 43–54.

HACKETT, T. P., & CASSEM, N. H. (1973). Psychological adaptation to convalescence in myocardial infarction patients. In J. P. Naughton, H. K. Hellerstein, & I. C. Mohler (Eds.), *Exercise testing and exercise training in coronary heart disease.* New York: Academic Press.

HAITH, M. M. (1980). *Rules that babies look by: The organization of newborn visual activity.* Hillsdale, NJ: Erlbaum.

HALDANE, J. B. S. (1932). *The causes of evolution.* London: Longmans, Green.

HALDANE, J. B. S. (1986). *On being the right size.* New York: Oxford University Press.

HALER, R. N. (1958). Discrepancy from adaptation level as a source of affect. *Journal of Experimental Psychology, 56,* 360–375.

HALL, C. S., & LINDZEY, G. (1978). *Theories of personality* (3rd ed.). New York: Wiley.

HALL, C. S., & NORDBY, V. J. (1973). *A primer of Jungian psychology.* New York: Mentor.

HALL, E. (1978). *Why we do what we do: A look at psychology.* Boston: Houghton Mifflin.

HALL, E. T. (1969). *The hidden dimension.* New York: Anchor Press.

HALL, H. (1983). Hypnosis and the immune system: A review with implications for cancer and the psychology of healing. *American Journal of Clinical Hypnosis, 25,* 92–103.

HALL, H. (1986). Hypnosis, suggestion, and the psychology of healing: A historical perspective. *Advances, 3,* 29–37.

HALL, H., LONGO, S., & DIXON, R. (1981). *Hypnosis and the immune system: The effect of hypnosis on T and B cell function.* Paper presented to the Society for Clinical and Experimental Hypnosis, 33rd Annual Workshops and Scientific Meeting.

HALL, J. A. (1984). *Nonverbal sex differences: Communication accuracy and expressive style.* Baltimore: John Hopkins University Press.

HALL, R. C., GARDNER, E. R., STICKNEY, S. K., LeCANN, A. F., & POPKIN, M. K. (1980). Physical illness manifesting as psychiatric disease: Pt. 2. Analysis of a state hospital inpatient population. *Archives of Central Psychiatry, 37*(9), 989–995.

HALPERN, D. F., & COREN, S. (1988, May 19). Do right-handers live longer? (letter). *Nature, 333*(6170), 213.

HAMILTON, C. L. (1963). Interactions of food intake and temperature regulation in the rat. *Journal of Comparative and Physiological Psychology, 56,* 476–488.

HAMILTON, W. D. (1964). The genetical evolution of social behavior. *Journal of Theoretical Biology, 7,* 1-52.

HAMMOND, B. L., & SCHEIRER, C. J. (1986). *Psychology and Health* (Vols. 1-4). Washington, DC: American Psychological Association.

HANCOCK, K. (1986). *Homophobia: Lesbian and gay issues in psychology.* Washington DC: American Psychological Association.

HANDAL, P. S. (1965). Immediate acceptance of sodium salts by sodium deficient rats. *Psychorem. Sci., 3,* 315–316.

HANEY, C., BANKS, C., & ZIMBARDO, P. G. (1973). Interpersonal dynamics in a simulated prison. *International Journal of Criminology and Penology, 1,* 69–97.

HANSON, B., et al. (1989, March 1). Genetic factors in the electrocardiogram and heart rate of twins reared apart and together. *American Journal of Cardiology, 63*(9), 606–609.

HARE, R. D., & CRAIGEN, D. (1974). Psychopathy and physiological activity in a mixed-motive game situation. *Psychophysiology, 11,* 197–206.

HARLOW, H., & HARLOW, M. H. (1966). Learning to love. *American Scientist, 54,* 244–272.

HARLOW, H. F. (1950). Learning and satiation of response in intrinsically motivated complex puzzle performance by monkeys. *Journal of Comparative and Physiological Psychology, 43,* 289–294.

HARRELL, R. F., WOODYARD, E. R., GATES, E. R., & GATES, I. A. (1956). The influence of vitamin supplementation in the diets of pregnant and lactating women on the intelligence of their offspring. *Metabolism, 5,* 555–562.

HARRINGTON, D. M., BLOCK, J. H., & BLOCK, B. (1978). Intolerance of ambiguity in preschool children: Psychometric considerations, behavioral manifestations and parental correlates. *Developmental Psychology, 14,* 242–256.

HARRIS, L., et al. (1975). *The myth and reality of aging in America.* Washington, DC: The National Council on Aging.

HARRIS, MARVIN. (1971). *Culture, people, nature.* New York: Crowell.

HARRIS, M. B., & EVANS, R. F. (1973). Models and creativity. *Psychological Reports, 33*(3), 763–769.

HARTLINE, H. K., & RATLIFF, F. (1957). Inhibitory interaction of receptor units in the eye of Limulus. *Journal of General Physiology, 40,* 357–376.

HARTMANN, E. (1973). *The functions of sleep.* New Haven: Yale University Press.

HARTON, J. J. (1938). An investigation of the influence of success and failure on the estimation of time. *Journal of General Psychology, 21,* 51–62.

HARTSHORNE, H., & MAY, M. A. (1928). *Studies in the nature of character: Studies in deceit.* New York: Macmillan.

HARTSHORNE, H., & MAY, M. A. (1929). *Studies in the nature of character: Studies in self-control.* New York: Macmillan.

HASKELL, W. (1979). Physical activity in health maintenance. In D. Sobel (Ed.), *Ways of health.* New York: Harcourt Brace Jovanovich.

HASTORF, A. H. (1950). The influence of suggestion of the relationship between stimulus, size and perceived distance. *Journal of Psychology, 19,* 195–217.

HASTORF, A. H., & CANTRIL, H. (1954). They saw a game: A case study. *Journal of Abnormal and Social Psychology, 49,* 129–134.

HATFIELD, E., & SPRECHER, S. (1986). *Mirror, mirror: The importance of looks in everyday life.* New York: SUNY Press.

HAUGELAND, J. (Ed.). (1985). *Mind design: Philosophy, psychology, and artificial intelligence.* Cambridge: MIT Press.

HAURI, P., & ORR, W. C. (1982). *The sleep disorders.* Kalamazoo, MI: Upjohn.

HAUSMAN, P. B., & WEKSLER, M. C. (1985). Changes in the immune response with age. In C. E. Finch & E. L. Schneider (Eds.), *Handbook of the biology of aging.* New York: Van Nostrand Reinhold.

HAVIGHURST, R. J., & GLASER, R. (1972). An exploratory study of reminiscence. *Journal of Gerontology, 27,* 245–253.

HAVIGHURST, R. J., NEUGARTEN, B. L., & TOBIN, S. S. (1968). Disengagement and patterns of aging. In B. L. Neugarten (Ed.), *Middle age and aging.* Chicago: University of Chicago Press.

HAYES-ROTH, F. (1980). Comment regarding "Against direct perception." *Behavioral and Brain Sciences 3*(3), 367–368.

HAYFLICK, L. (1980a). Cell aging. In C.

Eisdorfer (Ed.), *Annual review of gerontology and geriatrics.* New York: Springer.

HAYFLICK, L. (1980b). The cell biology of human aging. *Scientific American, 242*(1), 58–65.

HAYFLICK, L. (1985). Theories of biological aging. *Experimental Gerontology, 20,* 145–159.

HAYFLICK, L. (1987). The cell biology and theoretical basis of human aging. In L. Carstensen & B. Edelstein (Eds.), *Handbook of clinical gerontology.* New York: Pergamon.

HAYFLICK, L., & MOORHEAD, P. S. (1961). The serial cultivation of human diploid cell strains. *Experimental Cell Resources, 25,* 585–621.

HEATH, R. G. (1963). Electrical self-stimulation of the brain in man. *American Journal of Psychiatry, 120,* 571–577.

HEATH, R. G., & MICKLE, W. A. (1960). Evaluation of seven years' experience with depth electrode studies in human patients. In E. R. Ramey & D. S. O'Doherty (Eds.), *Electrical studies of the unanesthetized brain.* New York: Holber.

HEBB, D. O. (1949). *The organization of behavior.* New York: Wiley.

HECKHAUSEN, H. (1967). *The anatomy of achievement motivation.* New York: Academic Press.

HEIDER, F. (1944). Social perception and phenomenal causality. *Psychological Review, 51,* 358–374.

HEIDER, F. (1946). Attitudes and cognitive organization. *Journal of Psychology, 21,* 107–112.

HEIDER, F. (1958). *The psychology of interpersonal relations.* New York: Wiley.

HEILMAN, K. M., & SATZ, P. (Eds.). (1984). *Neuropsychology of human emotion.* New York: Guilford Press.

HELD, R., & HEIN, A. (1963). Movement produced stimulation in the development of visually guided behavior. *Journal of Comparative and Physiological Psychology, 56,* 872–876.

HELSING, K. J., et al. (1981). Factors associated with mortality after widowhood. *American Journal of Public Health, 71,* 802–809.

HELSON, H. (1964). *Adaptation level theory: An experimental and systematic approach to behavior.* New York: Harper & Row.

HENLEY, N. (1973). Status and sex: Some touching observations. *Bulletin of the Psychonomic Society, 2*(2), 91–93.

HENRY, J. P., & STEPHENS, P. M. (1977). *Stress, health and social environment: A sociobiological approach to medicine.* New York: Springer-Verlag.

HENRY, W. (1956). *The analysis of fantasy.* New York: Wiley.

HERBERT, M. J., & HARSH, C. M. (1944). Observational learning by cats. *Journal of Comparative and Physiological Psychology, 37,* 81–95.

HERRMANN, D. J., & NEISSER, U. (1978). An inventory of everyday memory experiences. In M. M. Gruneberg, P. E.

Morris, & R. N. Sykes (Eds.), *Practical aspects of memory.* New York: Academic Press.

HERRNSTEIN, R. J. (1973). *IQ in the meritocracy.* Boston: Little, Brown.

HERRON, J. (1980). *Neuropsychology of left-handers.* New York: Academic Press.

HERZBERG, F. (1966). *Work and the nature of man.* Cleveland: World.

HESS, E. H. (1973). *Imprinting.* New York: Van Nostrand Reinhold.

HESS, E. H. (1975). *The tell-tale eye: How your eyes reveal hidden thoughts and emotions.* New York: Van Nostrand Reinhold.

HESTON, L. (1966). Psychiatric disorders in foster home reared children of schizophrenic mothers. *British Journal of Psychiatry, 112,* 819–825.

HETHERINGTON, A. W., & RANSON, S. W. (1942). The spontaneous activity and food intake of rats with hypothalamic lesions. *American Journal of Physiology, 136,* 609–617.

HETHERINGTON, E., COX, M., & COX, D. (1977). Divorced fathers. *Family Coordination, 25,* 417–428.

HETHERINGTON, M. E. (1989). Coping with family transitions: Winners, losers and survivors. *Child Development, 60,* 1–14.

HETHERINGTON, M. E., COX, M., & COX, R. (1983). Family interaction and the social, emotional, and cognitive development of children following divorce. In V. Vaughan & B. Brazelton (Eds.), *The family: Setting priorities.* New York: Science and Behavior Books.

HILGARD, E. R. (1966). *The experience of hypnosis.* New York: Harcourt Brace Jovanovich.

HILGARD, E. R. (1977). *Divided consciousness: Multiple controls in human thought and action.* New York: Wiley-Interscience.

HILGARD, E. R. (1978). Hypnosis and consciousness. *Human Nature, 1,* 42–51.

HILGARD, E. R. (1986). *Psychology in America: A historical survey.* San Diego: Harcourt Brace Jovanovich.

HILGARD, E. R., & HILGARD, J. R. (1975). *Hypnosis in the relief of pain.* Los Altos, CA: Kaufmann.

HILGARD, E. R., & MARQUIS, D. G. (1940). *Conditioning and learning.* New York: Appleton-Century.

HILLYARD, S. A., & KUTAS, M. (1980). Reading senseless sentences: Brain potentials reflect semantic incongruity. *Science, 207,* 203–207.

HILTZ, S. R., & TUROFF, M. (1978). *The network nation.* Reading, MA: Addison-Wesley.

HINES, M. (1982). Prenatal gonadal hormones and sex differences in human behavior. *Psychological Bulletin, 92,* 56–80.

HINES, T., & FOZARD, J. (1980). Memory and aging: Relevance of recent developments for research and application. In *Annual Review of Gerontology and Geriatrics* (Vol. 1). New York: Springer.

HINTON, J. (1967). *Dying*. Baltimore: Penguin Books.

HIRSCH, H. V. (1972). Visual perception in cats after surgery. *Experimental Brain Research, 15*, 409–423.

HIRST, W., NEISSER, U., & SPELKE, E. (1978). Divided attention. *Human Nature, 1*, 54–61.

HOBART, C. W. (1958). The incidence of romanticism during courtship. *Social Forces, 36*, 362–367.

HOBSON, J. A., & McCARLEY, R. W. (1977). The brain as a dream state generator: An activation-synthesis hypothesis of the dream process. *The American Journal of Psychiatry, 134(12)*, 1335–1348.

HOCHBERG, J. E. (1978). *Perception* (2nd ed.). Englewood Cliffs, NJ: Prentice-Hall.

HOCKETT, C. F., & ASHER, R. (1964). Human revolution. *Current Anthropology, 135*, 142.

HOEBEL, B., & TEITELBAUM, P. (1962). Hypothalamic control of feeding and self-stimulation. *Science, 135*, 375–376.

HOFFMAN, A. (1968). Psychotomimetic agents. In A. Burger (Ed.), *Drugs affecting the central nervous system* (Vol. 2). New York: Marcel Dekker.

HOFFMAN, L. W. (1974). Fear of success in males and females: 1965 and 1972. *Journal of Consulting and Clinical Psychology, 42*, 353–358.

HOFSTADTER, R. (1959). *Social Darwinism in American thought*. New York: George Braziller.

HOGAN, R. (1982). A socioanalytic theory of personality. In M. Page (Ed.), *Nebraska symposium on motivation* (Vol. 30, p. 55–89). Lincoln: University of Nebraska Press.

HOGARTY, G. E., & GOLDBERG, S. C. (1973). Drug and sociotherapy in the aftercare of schizophrenic patients. *Archives of General Psychiatry, 28*, 54–63.

HOLLAND, J. L. (1973). *Making vocational choices: A theory of careers*. Englewood Cliffs, NJ: Prentice-Hall.

HOLMES, L. (1978). How fathers can cause the Down's syndrome. *Human Nature, 1(10)*, 70–73.

HOLMES, S. J., & ROBBINS, L. N. (1987). The influence of childhood disciplinary experience on the development of alcoholism and depression. *Journal of Child Psychology and Psychiatry and Allied Disciplines, 28*, 399–415.

HOLMES, T. H., & RAHE, R. H. (1967). The social readjustment rating scale. *Journal of Psychosomatic Research, 11*, 213–218.

HOLYOAK, K. J., KOH, K., & NISBETT, R. E. (1989). A theory of conditioning: Inductive learning within rule-based default hierarchies. *Psychological Review, 96*, 315–340.

HORN, J. L., & KNAPP, J. R. (1973). On the subjective character of the empirical base of Guilford's structure of intellect model. *Psychological Bulletin, 80*, 33–43.

HORN, J. M., LOEHLIN, J. C., & WILLERMAN, L.

(1982). Personality resemblances between unwed mothers and their adopted-away offspring. *Journal of Personality and Social Psychology, 42(6)*, 1089–1099.

HORN, M. (1989). *Before it's too late: The child guidance movement in the United States, 1922–1945*. Philadelphia: Temple University Press.

HORNER, M. S. (1968). *Sex differences in achievement motivation and performance in competitive and non-competitive situations*. Doctoral dissertation, University of Michigan. (University Microfilms No. 69–12, 135)

HORNEY, K. (1950). *Neurosis and human growth*. New York: W. W. Norton.

HOROWITZ, M. J., MARMAR, C., WEISS, D. S., SEWITT, K. N., & ROSENBAUM, R. (1984). Brief psychotherapy of bereavement reactions: The relationship of process to outcome. *Archives of General Psychiatry, 41*, 438–448.

HOUGHTON, J. F. (1980). One personal experience: Before and after mental illness. In J. G. Rabkin, L. Gelb, & J. B. Lazar (Eds.), *Attitudes toward the mentally ill: Research perspectives*. Rockville, MD: National Institute of Mental Health.

HOUGHTON, J. F. (1982). First person account: Maintaining mental health in a turbulent world. *Schizophrenia Bulletin, 8*, 548–549.

HOUSE, J. S., ROBBINS, C., & METZNER, H. L. (1982). The association of social relationships and activities with mortality. *American Journal of Epidemiology, 116*, 123–140.

HRDY, S. (1981). *The woman that never evolved*. Cambridge: Harvard University Press.

HUBEL, D. H. (1979). The brain. *Scientific American, 241*, 44–35.

HUBEL, D. H., & WIESEL, T. N. (1962). Receptive fields, binocular interactions and functional architecture in the cat's visual cortex. *Journal of Physiology, 160*, 106–154.

HUBEL, D. H., & WIESEL, T. N. (1979). Brain mechanisms of vision. *Scientific American, 241*, 150–162.

HUCK, S. W., & SANDLER, H. M. (1979). *Rival hypotheses: Alternative interpretations of data-based conclusions*. New York: Harper & Row

HUDSON, W. (1960). Pictorial depth perception in sub-cultural groups in Africa. *Journal of Social Psychology, 52*, 183–208.

HULICKA, I. M., & GROSSMAN, J. L. (1967). Age group comparisons for the use of mediators in paired associate learning. *Journal of Gerontology, 22*, 46–51.

HULL, C. L. (1943). *Principles of behavior*. New York: Appleton-Century-Crofts.

HUMPHREY, N. K. (1978). The origins of human intelligence. *Human Nature, 1 (12)*, 42–49.

HUMPHREYS, L. (1970). *Tearoom trade: Impersonal sex in public places*. Chicago: Aldine.

HUMPHREYS, L. G. (1957). Characteristics of type concepts with special reference

to Sheldon's typology. *Psychological Bulletin, 54*, 218–228.

HUNT, J. McV. (1965). Intrinsic motivation and its role in psychological development. *Nebraska Symposium on Motivation 1965*, (pp. 189–282). Lincoln: University of Nebraska Press.

HUNT, M. (1974). *Sexual behavior in the 1970s*. New York: Dell.

HURVICH, L. M., & JAMESON, D. (1957). An opponent-process theory of color. *Psychological Reviews, 64*, 384–404.

HURVICH, L. M., & JAMESON, D. (1974). Opponent processes as a model of neural organization. *American Psychologist, 29*, 88–102.

HUTCHINGS, B., & MEDNICK, S. A. (1974). Registered criminality in the adoptive and biological parents of registered male adoptees. In S. A. Mednick, F. Schulsinger, J. Higgins, & B. Bell (Eds.), *Genetics, environment and psychopathology*. New York: Elsevier.

HUTCHINS, E., HOLLAN, J. D., & NORMAN, D. A. (1986). Direct manipulation interfaces. In D. A. Norman & S. W. Draper (Eds.), *User centered system design: New perspectives on human-computer interactions*. Hillsdale, NJ: Erlbaum.

HUXLEY, A. (1971). Fifth philosopher's song. In D. Watt (Ed.), *The collected poetry of Aldous Huxley*. New York: Harper & Row.

HYDE, J. S. (1985). *Half the human experience: The psychology of women*. Lexington, MA: Heath.

ICKES, W., REIDHEAD, S., PATTERSON, M., (1986). Machiavellianism and self-monitoring: As different as me and you. *Socal Cognition, 400(1)*, 58–74.

INTONS-PETERSON, M. J., & REDDEL, M. (1984). What do people ask about a neonate? *Developmental Psychology, 20*, 358–359.

ISBISTER, J. N. (1986). *Freud*. New York: Polity/Blackwell.

ISEN, A. M. (1984). Affect, cognition, and social behavior. In R. S. Wyer & T. K. Srull (Eds.), *Handbook of social cognition* (Vol. 3, pp. 179–236). Hillsdale, NJ: Erlbaum.

ISEN, A. M., DAUBMAN, K. A., & NOWICKI, G. P. (1987). Positive affect facilitates creative problem solving. *Journal of Personality and Social Psychology, 52(6)*, 1122–1131.

ISEN, A. M., JOHNSON, M. M., MERTZ, E., & ROBINSON, G. F. (1985). The influence of positive affect on the unusualness of word associations. *Journal of Personality and Social Psychology, 48(6)*, 1413–1426.

ISEN, A. M., & LEVIN, P. F. (1972). Effect of feeling good on helping: Cookies and kindness. *Journal of Personality and Social Psychology, 21(3)*, 384–388.

ISEN, A. M., NYGREN, T. E., & ASHBY, F. G. (1988). Influence of positive affect on the subjective utility of gains and losses: It is just not worth the risk. *Journal of Personality and Social Psychology, 55(5)*, 710–717.

ISEN, A. M., SHALKER, T. E., CLARK, M., & KARP, L. (1978). Affect, accessibility of material in memory, and behavior: A cognitive loop? *Journal of Personality and Social Psychology, 36*(1), 1-12.

ITTLESON, H. (1952). The constancies in perceptual theory. In F. R. Kilpatrick (Ed.), *Human behavior from the transactional point of view*. Hanover, NH: Institute for Associated Research.

IWATA, J., & LEDOUX, J. E. (1988). Dissociation of associative and nonassociative concomitants of classical fear conditioning in the freely behaving rat. *Behavioral Neuroscience, 102*(1), 66-76.

IWATA, J., LEDOUX, J. E., MEELEY, M. P., ARNERIC, S., & REIS, D. J. (1986). Intrinsic neurons in the amygdaloid field projected to by the medial geniculate body mediate emotional responses conditioned to acoustic stimuli. *Brain Research, 383*(1-2), 195-214.

IZARD, C. E., KAGAN, J., & ZAJONC, R. B. (Eds.). (1986). *Emotions, cognition and behavior*. New York: Cambridge University Press.

JACKSON, J. (1989). Race, ethnicity and psychological theory and research. *Journal of Gerontology, 44*, P1-2.

JACKSON, J., & WILLIAMS, K. D. (1985). Social loafing on difficult tasks: Working collectively can improve performance. *Journal of Personality and Social Psychology, 49*, 937-942.

JACOBS, B., & MOSS, H. (1976). Birth order and sex of sibling as determinants of mother-infant interaction. *Child Development, 47*, 315-322.

JACOBS, J. (1959). *Death and life of great American cities*. New York: Vintage Books.

JACOBS, J. (1971). *Adolescent suicide*. New York: Wiley.

JACOBSON, J. (1977). *The development of peer play and cautiousness toward peers in infancy*. Doctoral dissertation, Harvard University.

JACOBSON, M. B. (1981). Effects of victims' and defendants' physical attractiveness on subjects' judgements in a rape case. *Sex Roles 4*: 169-174.

JACQUES, E. (1951). *The changing culture of a factory*. London: Tavistock.

JACQUES, E. (1965). Death and the midlife crisis. *International Journal of Psychoanalysis, 46*, 502-514.

JAHODA, M., & WEST, P. (1951). Race relations in public housing. *Journal of Social Issues, 7*, 132-139.

JAMES, S., & KLEINBAUM, D. G. (1976). Socioecologic stress and hypertension: Related mortality rates in North Carolina. *American Journal of Public Health, 66*, 354-58.

JAMES, W. (1970). *The principles of psychology* (Vol. 1.) New York: Dover. (Original work published 1890)

JAMES, W. (1980). *The varieties of religious experience*. New York: Longmans Green. (Original work published 1917)

JANIS, I. L. (1982). *Groupthink* (2nd ed.). Boston: Houghton Mifflin.

JANIS, I. L. , & MANN, L. (1977). *Decision-making*. New York: Free Press.

JANOWSKY, J. S., SHIMAMURA, A. P., KRITCH-EVSKY, M., & SQUIRE, L. R. (1989). Cognitive impairment following frontal lobe damage and its relevance to human amnesia. *Behavioral Neuroscience, 103*(3), 548-560.

JARVICK, L. F., & DECKARD, B. S. (1977). The Odyssean personality: A survival advantage for carriers of genes predisposing to schizophrenia. *Neuropsychobiology, 3*(2-3), 179-191.

JARVIK, L. F., & FALEK, A. (1963). Intellectual stability and survival in the aged. *Journal of Gerontology, 18*, 173-176.

JELLISON, J. M., & GREEN, J. (1981). A self-presentation approach to the fundamental attribution error: The norm of internality. *Journal of Personality and Social Psychology, 40*, 643-649.

JEMMOTT, J. B., et al. (1983). Academic stress, power motivation, and decrease in secretion rate of salivary secretory immunoglobulin A. *Lancet*, 1400-1402.

JEMMOTT, J. B., & LOCKE, S. E. (1984). Psychosocial factors, immunologic mediation and human susceptibility to infection: How much do we know? *Psychological Bulletin, 95*, 78-108.

JENKINS, J. G., & DALLENBACH, K. M. (1924). Oblivescence during sleep and waking. *American Journal of Psychology, 35*, 605-612.

JENKINS, R. L. (1966). Psychiatric syndromes in children and their relation to family background. *American Journal of Orthopsychiatry, 36*, 450-457.

JENKINS, R. L. (1969). Classification of behavior problems of children. *American Journal of Psychiatry, 125*(8), 1032-1039.

JENSEN, A. R. (1969). How much can we boost IQ and scholastic achievement? *Harvard Educational Review, 39*, 1-123.

JENSEN, A. R. (1980). *Bias in mental testing*. New York: Free Press.

JESSOR, R., & JESSOR, S. L. (1977). *Problem behavior and psychosocial development: A longitudinal study of youth*. New York: Academic Press.

JESSOR, S. L., & JESSOR, R. (1975). Transition from virginity to nonvirginity among youth: A social-psychological study over time. *Developmental Psychology, 11*, 473-484.

JOHANSEN, D., & EDEY, M. (1981). *Lucy: The beginnings of human kind*. New York: Simon & Schuster.

JOHNSON, A. (1978). In search of the affluent society. *Human Nature, 1*(9), 50-60.

JOHNSON, D. M. (1972). *Systematic introduction to the psychology of thinking*. New York: Harper & Row.

JOHNSON-LAIRD, T. N. (1983). *Mental models*. Cambridge: Harvard University Press.

JOHNSON-LAIRD, T. N. (1988). *The computer and the mind*. Cambridge: Harvard University Press.

JOHNSON-LAIRD, T. N., & WASON, P. C. (Eds.). (1977). *Thinking: Readings in cognitive science*. New York: Cambridge University Press.

JOHNSTON, T. (1981). Contrasting approaches to a theory of learning. *Behavioral and Brain Sciences, 4*, 125-139.

JOHNSTON, W., & DARK, V. (1986). Selective attention. *Annual Review of Psychology, 37*, 43-75.

JOINER, B. L. (1975). Living histograms. *International Statistical Review, 43*, 339-340.

JONES, C., & ARONSON, E. (1973). Attribution of fault to a rape victim as a function of responsibility of the victim. *Journal of Personality and Social Psychology, 26*; 415-491.

JONES, E., & ZOPPEL, C. L. (1982). Impact of client and therapist gender on psychotherapy process and outcome. *Journal of Consulting and Clinical Psychology, 50*, 259-272.

JONES, E. E., & DAVIS, K. E. (1965). From acts to dispositions: The attribution process in person perception. In L. Berkowitz (Ed.), *Advances in experimental social psychology* (Vol. 2). New York: Academic Press.

JONES, E. E., & HARRIS, V. A. (1967). The attribution of attitudes. *Journal of Experimental Social Psychology, 3*, 1-24.

JONES, E. E., & NISBETT, R. E. (1971). *The actor and the observer: Divergent perception of the causes of behavior*. Morristown, NJ: General Learning Press.

JONES, M. C. (1924). A laboratory study of fear: The case of Peter. *Journal of Genetic Psychology, 31*, 308-315.

JOSEPH, S. A., & KNIGGEE, J. M. (1968). Effects of VMH lesions in adult and newborn guinea pigs. *Neuroendocrinology, 3*, 309-331.

JOURARD, S. M. (1966). An exploratory study of body accessibility. *British Journal of Social and Clinical Psychology, 5*, 221-231.

JULIEN, R. M. (1978). *A primer of drug action*. San Francisco: W. H. Freeman.

JUNG, C. (1921). Psychological types. In *Collected works* (Vol. 6). Princeton: Princeton University Press.

JUNG, C. (1953). *Collected works*. (H. Read, M. Fordham & G. Adler, Eds.). New York: Bollingen Series/Pantheon Books.

KAGAN, J. (1978). *The growth of the child: Reflections on human development*. New York: W. W. Norton.

KAGAN, J. (1981). *The second year: The emergence of self-awareness*. Cambridge: Harvard University Press.

KAGAN, J. (1984). *The nature of the child*. New York: Basic Books.

KAGAN, J. (1989). Temperamental contributions to social behavior. *American Psychologist, 44*, 668-683.

KAGAN, J., & KLEIN, R. E. (1973). Cross cultural perspectives on early development. *American Psychologist, 28*, 947-961.

KAGAN, J., & MOSS, H. A. (1983). *Birth to maturity*. New Haven: Yale University Press. (Original work published 1962)

KAGAN, J., RESNICK, J. S., & GIBBON, J. (1989). Inhibited and unihibited types of children. *Child Development, 60*(40), 838-845.

781

KAGAN, J., RESNICK, J. S., SNIDMAN, N., GIBBONS, J., & JOHNSON, M. C. (1988). Childhood derivatives of inhibition and lack of inhibition to the unfamiliar. *Child Development, 59*(6), 1580–1589.

KAHN, M. (1970). Non-verbal communication and marital satisfaction. *Family Process, 9,* 449–456.

KAHN, R. L., HEIN, K., HOUSE, J., McLEAN, A., & KASL, S. (1980, July). *Stress in organizational settings.* Paper prepared for the National Academy of Sciences, Institute of Medicine, Committee on Stress in Health and Disease.

KAHNEMAN, D. (1973). *Attention and effort.* Englewood Cliffs: Prentice-Hall.

KAHNEMAN, D., & TVERSKY, A. (1973). On the psychology of prediction. *Psychological Review, 80,* 237–251.

KAHNEMAN, D., SLOVIC, P., & TVERSKY, A. (Eds.). (1982). *Judgment under uncertainty.* New York: Cambridge University Press.

KALISH, R. A. (1976). Death and dying in a social context. In R. H. Binstock & E. Shanas (Eds.), *Handbook of aging and the social sciences.* New York: Van Nostrand Reinhold.

KAMIN, L. (1979, April). *Psychology as social science: The Jensen affair, ten years after.* Presidential address to Eastern Psychological Assn., Philadelphia.

KAMIN, L. (with EYSENCK, H. J.). (1981). *The intelligence controversy.* New York: Wiley.

KANNER, J. D., COYNE, J. C., SCHAEFER, C., & LAZARUS, R. S. (1981). Comparison of two modes of stress management: Daily hassles and uplifts versus major life events. *Journal of Behavioral Medicine, 4*(1), 1–39.

KAPLAN, E. A. (1960). Hypnosis and pain. *AMA Archives of General Psychiatry, 2,* 567–568.

KAPLAN, G. A., & CAMACHO, T. (1983). Perceived health and mortality: A nine-year follow-up of the Human Population Laboratory cohort. *American Journal of Epidemiology, 117,* 292–304.

KAPLEAU, P. (1980). *The three pillars of Zen.* New York: Anchor Press.

KARLINS, M., & ABELSON, J. I. (1970). *How opinions and attitudes are changed* (2nd ed.). New York: Springer.

KARLSSON, J. L. (1986). Genetics of myopia and associated mental traits. *Hereditas, 105*(2), 205–208.

KARMILOFF-SMITH, A. (1979). Language development after five. In P. Fletcher & M. Garmon (Eds.), *Language acquisition* (pp. 307–323). Cambridge: Cambridge University Press.

KASAMATSU, A., & HIRAI, T. (1963). An electroencephalographic study on the Zen meditation (Zazen). *Folia Psychiatria et Neurologia, 20,* 315–336.

KASL, S. V., EVANS, A. S., & NEIDERMAN, J. C. (1979). Psychosocial risk factors in the development of infectious mononucleosis. *Psychosomatic Medicine, 41,* 445–66.

KASTENBAUM, R. (1965). Wine and fellowship in aging: An exploratory action program. *Journal of Human Relations, 13* 266–275.

KASTENBAUM, R. (1977). Is death a crisis? In Daton, N., & Ginsberg, L. H. (Eds.). *Life-span developmental psychology.* New York: Academic Press.

KASTENBAUM, R., & AISENBERG, R. (1977). *Psychology of death.* New York: Springer.

KATCHER, A., & BECK, A. (Eds.). (1983). *New Perspectives on our lives with companion animals.* Philadelphia: University of Pennsylvania Press.

KATZ, M. L. (1973). *Female motive to avoid success: A psychological barrier or a response to deviancy?* Princeton: Educational Testing Service.

KAUFMAN, L. (1974). *Sight and mind: An introduction to visual perception.* New York: Oxford University Press.

KEANE, T. M., FAIRBANK, J. A., CADDELL, J. M., ZIMERING, R. T., & BENDER, M. E. (1985). A behavioral approach to assessing and treating post-traumatic stress disorder in Vietnam Veterans. In C. R. Figley (Eds.), *Trauma and its wake.* New York: Bruner/Mazel.

KEANE, T. M., ZIMERING, R. T., & CADDELL, J. M. (1985). A behavioral formulation of posttraumatic stress disorder in Vietnam Veterans. *Behavior Therapist, 8,* 9–12.

KEESEY, R., & POWLEY, T. (1975, September-October). Hypothalamic regulation of body weight. *American Scientist, 63,* 558–565.

KELLEY, E. (1947). Education for what is real. New York: Harper & Brothers.

KELLEY, H. H. (1967). Attribution theory in social psychology. In D. Levine (Ed.), *Nebraska Symposium on Motivation, 15,* 192–238. Lincoln: University of Nebraska Press.

KELLEY, H. H. (1972). Causal schemata and the attribution process. In E. E. Jones, et al. (Eds.), *Attribution: Perceiving the causes of behavior.* Morristown, NJ: General Learning.

KENNEDY, J. M. (1974). *A psychology of picture perception.* San Francisco: Jossey-Bass.

KERMOIAN, R., & CAMPOS, J. J. (1988). Locomotor experience: A facilitator of spatial cognitive development. *Child Development, 59,* 908–917.

KESSEN, W., HAITH, M., & SALAPATEK, P. H. (1970). Infancy. In P. H. Mussen (Ed.), *Charmichael's manual of child psychology* (3rd ed.). New York: Wiley.

KESSLER, S. (1980). *Schizophrenic families.* New York: Raven Press.

KEYES, D. (1982). *The minds of Billy Milligan.* New York: Bantam Books.

KEYES, R. (1980). *The height of your life.* New York: Warner Books.

KEYS, A., BROZEK, J., HENSCHEL, A., MICKELSON, O., & TAYLOR, H. (1950). *The biology of human starvation* (Vols. 1-2). Minneapolis: University of Minnesota Press.

KIDSON, M. A., & JONES, I. H. (1952). Psychiatric disorders among aborigines of the Australian western desert. *Archives of General Psychiatry.*

KIDWELL, I. J., & BOOTH, A. (1977). Social distance and intergenerational relations. *The Gerontologist, 17,* 412–420.

KIECOLT-GLASER, J. K., GLASER, R., et al. (1985). Psychosocial enhancement of immunocompetence in a geriatric population. *Health Psychology, 4,* 25–41.

KIESLER, S., SIEGEL, J., & McGUIRE, T. W. (1984). Social psychological aspects of computer-mediated communication. *American Psychologist, 39,* 1123–1134.

KIHLSTROM, J. F. (1987). The cognitive unconscious. *Science, 237,* 1445–1452.

KIMBLE, G. A. (1961). *Hilgard and Marquis's Conditioning and learning* (2nd ed.). New York: Appleton-Century-Crofts.

KIMMEL, D. C. (1980). *Adulthood and aging: An interdisciplinary developmental view* (2nd ed.). New York: Wiley.

KIMURA, D. (1963). Right temporal lobe damage. *Archives of Neurology, 8,* 264–271.

KING, B. M., & GASTON, M. G. (1977). Reappearance of dynamic hyperphagia during the static phase in medial hypothalamic lesioned rats. *Physiology and Behavior, 18,* 463–473.

KINSBOURNE, M. (1980). Attentional dysfunctions in the elderly: Theoretical models and research proceedings. In L. Poon et al. (Eds.), *New directions in memory and aging.* Hillsdale, NJ: Erlbaum.

KINSEY, A., POMEROY, W., & MARTIN, C. (1948). *Sexual behavior in the human male.* Philadelphia: Saunders.

KINSEY, A., POMEROY, W., & MARTIN, C. (1953). *Sexual behavior in the human female.* Philadelphia: Saunders.

KINSEY, A., POMEROY, W., MARTIN, C., & GEBHARD, P. H. (1953). *Sexual behavior in the human female.* Philadelphia: Saunders.

KISSEN, D. M. (1966). The significance of personality in lung cancer in men. *Annals of the New York Academy of Science, 125,* 820–826.

KLEEMEIER, R. W. (1962). Intellectual change in the senium. *Proceedings of the Social Statistics Section of the American Statistical Association, 1,* 290–295.

KLEIN, S. A., & LEVI, D. M. (1985). Hyperacuity threshold of 1.0 second: Theoretical predictions and empirical validation. *Journal of the Optical Society of America, A2,* 1170–1190.

KLEINKE, C. (1978). *Self-perception: The psychology of personal awareness.* San Francisco: W. H. Freeman.

KNOWLTON, B. J., LAVOND, D. S., & THOMPSON, R. F. (1988). The effect of lesions of cerebellar cortex on the retention of the classically conditioned eye-blink response when stimulation of the lateral reticular nucleus is used as the conditioned stimulus. *Behavioral Neural Biology, 49*(5), 293–301.

KOBASA, S. (1990). The stress resistant personality. In R. Ornstein & C. Swencionis (Eds.), *The healing brain: A scientific reader.* New York: Guilford Press.

KOBASA, S. C. (1984, September). How much stress can you survive? *American Health, 3,* 64–77.

KOBASA, S. C., MADDI, S., & KAHN, S. (1982). Hardiness and health: A prospective study. *Journal of Personality and Social Psychology, 42,* 168–177.

KOBASA, S. C., MADDI, S. R., & PUCCETTI, M. C. (1982). Personality and exercise as buffers in the stress-illness relationship. *Journal of Behavioral Medicine, 4,* 391–404.

KOBASA, S. C., & PUCCETTI, M. C. (1983). Personality and social resources in stress-resistance. *Journal of Personality and Social Psychology, 45,* 839–50.

KOESTLER, A. (1974). *The heel of Achilles: Essays, 1968–1973.* London: Hutchinson.

KOGAN, N., & WALLACH, M. A. (1967). Risk taking as a function of the situation, the person, and the group. In G. Mandler (Ed.), *New directions in psychology* (Vol. 3). New York: Holt, Rinehart & Winston.

KOHLBERG, L. (1969). Stage and sequence: The cognitive developmental approach to socialization. In D. A. Goslin (Ed.), *Handbook of socialization theory and research.* Chicago: Rand McNally.

KOHLER, I. (1962). Experiments with goggles. *Scientific American, 206,* 62–86.

KOHLER, W. (1925). *The mentality of apes.* New York: Harcourt Brace Jovanovich.

KOHN, B., & DENNIS, M. (1974). Selective impairments of visual-spatial abilities in infantile hemiplegics after right hemidecortication. *Neuropsychologia, 12,* 505–512.

KOLB, B., & MILNER, B. (1980). Observations on spontaneous facial expression in patients. In B. Kolb & I. Q. Whishaw (Eds.), *Fundamentals of human neuropsychology* (2nd ed.). San Francisco: W. H. Freeman.

KOLB, B., & WHISHAW, I. Q. (1984). *Fundamentals of human neuropsychology.* (2nd ed.). San Francisco: W. H. Freeman.

KOMAROVSKY, M. (1967). *Blue collar marriage.* New York: Random House, Vintage Books.

KOMMER, D., SCHWARZ, N., STRACK, F., & BECHTEL, G. (1986). [Mood and social information processing in depressive disorders] Z *Klinikisch, Psychologisch, Psychopathisch, Psychotherapie, 34*(2), 127–139.

KORSCH, B. M., & NEGRETE, V. F. (1972). Doctor-patient communication. *Scientific American, 227,* 66–74.

KOSSLYN, S. (1986). *Image and mind.* Cambridge: Harvard University Press.

KOSSLYN, S. M., HOLTZMAN, J. D., FARAH, M. J., & GAZZANIGA, M. S. (1985). A computational analysis of mental image generation: Evidence from functional dissociations in split-brain patients. *Journal of Experimental Psychology, 114*(3), 311–341.

KOTELCHUCK, M. (1976). The infant's relationship to the father: Experimental evidence. In M. E. Lamb (Ed.), *The role of the father in child development,* New York: Wiley.

KOVACS, M., RUSH, A. J., BECK, A. T., & HOLLON, S. D. (1981). Depressed outpatients treated with cognitive therapy or pharmacotherapy: A one-year follow-up. *Archives of General Psychology, 38,* 33–39.

KRAMER, M., et al. (1966). Dreaming in the depressed. *Canadian Psychiatric Association Journal, 11* (suppl), S178-S192.

KRANTZ, D. S., & DECKEL, W. (1983). Coping with coronary heart disease and stroke. In T. G. Burish & L. A. Bradley (Eds.), *Coping with chronic disease: Research and applications.* New York: Academic Press.

KRASHEN, S. (1981). Second language acquisition and second language learning. Oxford: Pergamon Press.

KRASHEN, S., & TERRELL, T. (1983). The natural approach: Language acquisition in the classroom. San Francisco: Alemany Press.

KREBS, D. (1975). Empathy and altruism. *Journal of Personality and Social Psychology, 32,* 1134–1146.

KRECH, D., ROSENZWEIG, M., & BENNETT, E. L. (1962). Relations between brain chemistry and problem-solving among rats raised in enriched and impoverished environments. *Journal of Comparative and Physiological Psychology, 55,* 801–807.

KRECHEVSKY, D. (1932). "Hypotheses" in rats. *Psychological Review, 39,* 516–532.

KRINGLEN, E. (1967). *Heredity and environment in the functional psychosis: An epidemiological-clinical twin study.* Oslo: Universitsforlaget.

KRIPKE, D. F., & SONNENSCHEIN, D. (1978). *A 90 minute daydream cycle.* Paper presented at the meeting of the Association for the Psychophysiological Study of Sleep, San Diego.

KRITCHEVSKY, M., & SQUIRE, L. R. (1989). Transient global amnesia: Evidence for extensive, temporally graded retrograde amnesia. *Neurology, 39*(2 Pt. 1), 213–218.

KROSNICK, J. A. (1988). The role of attitude importance in social evaluation: A study of policy preference, presidential candidate evaluations, and voting behavior. *Journal of Personality and Social Psychology, 55,* 196–210.

KRUEGER, A. (1978). Ions in the air. *Human Nature, 1*(7), 46–53.

KUHLEN, R. (1964). Developmental changes in motivation during the adult years. In J. E. Birren (Ed.), *Relations of development and again.* Springfield, IL: Thomas.

KUHN, T. S. (1962). *The structure of scientific revolutions.* Chicago: University of Chicago Press.

KUIPER, N. A., & ROGERS, T. B. (1979). Encoding of personal information: Self-other differences. *Journal of Personality and Social Psychology, 37,* 499–514.

KUNST-WILSON, W. R., & ZAJONC, R. B. (1979). Affective discrimination of stimuli that cannot be recognized. *Science, 207,* 557–558.

KUPCHELLA, C. (1976). *Sights and sounds.* Indianapolis: Bobbs-Merrill.

KURLAND, D. M., PEA, R. D., CLEMENT, C., & MAWBY, R. (in press). A study of the development of programming ability and thinking skills in high school students. *Journal of Educational Computing Research.*

KURTINES, W., & GRIEF, E. B. (1974). The development of moral thought: Review and evaluation of Kohlberg's approach. *Psychological Bulletin, 81,* 453–470.

KUTAS, M., & HILLYARD, S. A. (1980). Reading senseless sentences: Brain potentials reflect semantic incongruity. *Science, 207,* 203–204.

KUTAS, M., HILLYARD, S. A., & GAZZANIGA, M. S. (1988, June). Processing of semantic anomaly by right and left hemispheres of commissurotomy patients: Evidence from event-related brain potentials. *Brain, 111; 553–576.*

KÜBLER-ROSS, E. (1975). *Death: The final stage of growth.* Englewood Cliffs, NJ: Prentice-Hall.

KÜBLER-ROSS, E. (1969). *On death and dying.* New York: Macmillan.

KYUCHARYANTS, V. (1974). Will the human life-span reach one hundred? *The Gerontologist, 14*(5).

LACEY, J. I. (1950). Individual differences in somatic response patterns. *Journal of Comparative and Physiological Psychology, 43,* 338–50.

LACEY, J. I., BATEMAN, D. E., & VAN LEHN, R. (1953). Automatic response specificity and Rorschach color responses. *Psychosomatic Medicine, 14,* 256–260.

LACEY, J. I., & LACEY, B. C. (1958). Verification and extension of the principle of autonomic response stereotypy. *American Journal of Psychology, 71,* 50–73.

LAFRANCE, M. (November, 1987). *The school of hard-knocks: Challenging subtle sexism in the classroom.* Paper presented at the Association for Moral Education, Harvard University.

LAING, R. D. (1959). *The divided self.* London: Tavistock.

LAIRD, J. E., NEWELL, A., & ROSENBLOOM, P. (1987) Soar: An architecture for general intelligence. *Artificial Intelligence.*

LAMARK, J. B. (1951). Evolution through environmentally produced modifications. In *A source book in animal biology.* (Trans. of original statement of hypothesis by LaMark.)

LANCASTER, J. L. (1978). Carrying and sharing in human evolution. *Human Nature, 1*(2), 82–89.

LANGER, E. (1989). *Mindfulness.* Reading, MA: Addison-Wesley.

LANGER, E. (1975). The illusion of control. *Journal of Personality and Social Psychology, 32,* 311–328.

LANGER, E. J., & ABELSON, R. P. (1974). A patient by any other name. *Journal of Consulting and Clinical Psychology, 42,* 4-9.

LANGER, E. J., & RODIN, J. (1976). The effects of choice and enhanced personal responsibilty for the aged: A field experiment in an institutional setting. *Journal of Personality and Social Psychology, 34*, 191–198.

LANGFORD, H. G., et al. (1985). Dietary therapy slows the return of hypertension after stopping medication. *Journal of the American Medical Association, 253*, 657–664. (DISH ref.)

LANGLOIS, J. H., & DOWNS, A. C. (1980). Mothers, fathers and peers as socialization agents of sex-typed behaviors. *Child Development, 51*, 1237–1247.

LARSEN, R. J., DIENER, E., & CROPANZO, R. S. (1987). Cognitive operations associated with individual differences in affect intensity. *Journal of Personality and Social Psychology, 53* (4), 767–774.

LATANE, B. (1981). The psychology of social impact. *American Psychologist, 36*, 343–356.

LATANE, B., & DARLEY, J. M. (1970). *The unresponsive bystander: Why doesn't he help?* New York: Appleton-Century-Crofts.

LATANE, B., & RODIN, J. (1969). A lady in distress: Inhibiting effects of friends and strangers on bystander intervention. *Journal of Experimental Social Psychology, 5*, 189–202.

LATANE, B., WILLIAMS, K., & HAWKINS, S. (1979). Many hands make light work: The causes and consequences of social loafing. *Journal of Personality and Social Psychology, 37*, 822–832.

LAU, R. R., & RUSSELL, D. (1980). Attributions in the sports pages. *Journal of Personality and Social Psychology, 39*, 29–38.

LAZARUS, A. A. (1971). *Behavior therapy and beyond.* New York: McGraw-Hill.

LAZARUS, R. S. (1976). *Patterns of adjustment* (3rd ed.). New York: McGraw-Hill.

LAZARUS, R. S. (1979, November). Positive denial: The case for not facing reality. *Psychology Today*, 44–60.

LAZARUS, R. S. (1984). Puzzles in the study of daily hassles. *Journal of Behavioral Medicine, 7*, 375–389.

LAZARUS, R., & FOLKMAN, S. (1986). Coping and adaptation. In W. Gentry, *Handbook of behavioral medicine.* New York: Guilford Press.

LAZARUS, R. S., & LAUNIER, R. (1978). Stress-related transactions between the person and the environment. In L. A. Pervin & M. Lewis (Eds.), *Internal and external determinants of behavior.* New York: Plenum.

LABERGE, S. (1985). Lucid dreaming. New York: Ballantine.

LABERGE, S., NAGEL, L.E., DEMENT, W. C., & ZARCONE, V. P. (1981). Lucid dreaming verified by volitional communication during REM sleep. *Perceptual and Motor Skills, 52*, 727–732.

LABUDA, M. C., DeFRIES, J. C., PLOMIN, R., & FULKER, D. W. (1986). Longitudinal stability of cognitive ability from infancy to early childhood: Genetic and environmental etiologies. *Child Development, 57*(5), 1142–1150.

LEAHEY, T. H., & HARRIS, R. J. (1985). *Human learning.* Englewood Cliffs, NJ: Prentice-Hall.

LEAKEY, R., & LEWIN, R. (1977). *Origins.* New York: Dutton.

LEAVITT, H., & WHISLER, T. (1958). Management in the 1980s. *Harvard Business Review, 36*, 41–48.

LEDOUX, J., CHIDA, K., & LEDOUX, J. E. (1987). Cardiovascular responses elicited by stimulation of neurons in the central amygdaloid nucleus in awake but not anesthetized rats resemble conditioned emotional responses. *Brain Research, 418*(1), 183–188.

LEDOUX, J. E., IWATA, J., CICCHETTI, P., & REIS, D. J. (1988). Different projections of the central amygdaloid nucleus mediate autonomic and behavioral correlates of conditioned fear. *Journal of Neuroscience, 8*(7), 2517–2529.

LEDOUX, J. E., RUGGIERO, D. A., FOREST, R., STORNETTA, R., & REIS, D. J. (1987). Topographic organization of convergent projections to the thalamus from the inferior colliculus and spinal cord in the rat. *Journal of Comparative Neurology, 264*(1), 123–146.

LEFCOURT, H. (1976). *Locus of control.* New York: Wiley.

LEHMAN, H. C. (1953). *Age and achievement.* Princeton: Princeton University Press.

LEHMAN, H. C. (1966). The psychologist's most creative years. *American Psychologist, 21*(4), 363–369.

LEMAGNEN, J. (1986). *Hunger.* New York: Cambridge University Press.

LENAT, D., & GUHA, R. V. (1988, September). *The world according to CYC.* Microelectronics and Computer Technology Corporation Technical Report, Austin, TX.

LENNEBERG, E. H. (1967). *The biological foundations of language.* New York: Wiley.

LEON, G., & DINKLAGE, D. (1989). Obesity and anorexia nervosa. In T. H. Ollendick & M. Hersen (Eds.), *Handbook of child psychopathology* (pp. 247–264). New York: Plenum Press.

LEONARD, C. B. (1971). Depression and suicidality. *Journal of Consulting and Clinical Psychology, 42*, 98–104.

LEPPER, M. (1985). Microcomputers in education: Motivational and social issues. *American Psychologist 40*, 1–18.

LETTVIN, J. Y., MATURANA, H. R., MCCULLOCH, S. W., & PITTS, W. H. (1959). What the frog's eye tells the frog's brain. *Proceedings of the Institute of Radio Engineers, 47*, 140–151.

LEUTENEGGER, W. (1977). Scaling of sexual dimorphism in body size and breeding system in primates. *Nature, 272*, 610–611.

LEVENSON, R. W., & GOTTMAN, J. M. (1983). Marital interaction: Physiological linkage and affective exchange. *Journal of Personality and Social Psychology, 45*, 587–597.

LEVENSON, R. W., & GOTTMAN, J. M. (1985). Physiological and affective predictors of change in relationship satisfaction. *Journal of Personality and Social Psychology, 49*, 85–94.

LEVENSON, R. W., OYAMA, O., & MEEK, P. (1988). Alcohol. *Journal of Abnormal Psychology.*

LEVENSTEIN, P. (1970). Cognitive growth in pre-schooler through verbal interaction with mothers. *American Journal of Orthopsychology. 40*, 426–432.

LEVENTHAL., H. (1970). Findings and theory in the study of fear communications. In L. Berkowitz (Ed.), *Advances in experimental social psychology* (Vol. 5). New York: Academic Press.

LEVENTHAL, H., PROHASKA, T. R., & HIRSHMAN, R. S. (1985). Preventive health behavior across the life span. In J. C. Rosen & L. J. Solomon (Eds.), *Prevention in health psychology.* Hanover, NH: University Press of New England.

LEVENTHAL, H., & HIRSCHMAN, R. S. (1982). Social psychology and prevention. In G. E. Sanders & J. Suls (Eds.), *Social psychology of health and illness.* Hillsdale, NJ: Erlbaum.

LEVINE, J. D., & GORDON, N. C. (1984). Influence of the method of drug administration on analgesic response. *Nature, 312*, 755–756.

LEVINE, J. D., GORDON, N. C., BORNSTEIN, J. C., & FIELDS, H. L. (1979). Role of pain in placebo analgesia. *Proceedings of the National Academy of Sciences, 76*, 3528–3531.

LEVINE, J. D., GORMLEY, J., & FIELDS, H. L. (1976). Observations on the analgesic effects of needle puncture (acupuncture). *Pain, 2*, 149–159.

LEVINE, S., & URSIN, H. (1980). *Coping and health.* New York: Plenum.

LEVINSON, D. J. (1977). The mid-life transition: A period in adult psychosocial development. *Psychiatry, 40*, 208–226.

LEVINSON, D. J. (1978). *The seasons of a man's life.* New York: Knopf.

LEVINSON, D. J., DARROW, C. N., KLEIN, E. B., LEVINSON, M. L., & MCKEE, B. (1978). *The seasons of a man's life.* New York: Knopf.

LEVI, L. (1974). Psychosocial stress and disease: A conceptual model. In E. K. Gunderson & R. H. Rahe (Eds.), *Life stress and illness.* Springfield, IL: Thomas.

LEVY, J. (1972). Lateral specialization of the human brain: Behavioral manifestation and possible evolutionary basis. In J. A. Kiger Corvalis (Ed.), *The biology of behavior.* Eugene: University of Oregon Press.

LEVY, S. M. (1984). Emotions and the progression of cancer: A review. *Advances, 1*, 10–15.

LEWINSHOHN, P. M., MISCHEL, W., & BARTON, R. (1980). Social competence and depression: The role of illusory self-perceptions. *Journal of Abnormal Psychology, 89*(2), 203–212.

LEWIS, C. N. (1971). Reminiscing and self-concept in old age. *Journal of Gerontology*, 26, 240–243.

LEWIS, M., & FREEDLE, R. (1973). Mother-infant dyad: The cradle of meaning. In P. Pliner, L. Kramer, & T. Alloway (Eds.), *Communication and affect: Language and thought*. New York: Academic Press.

LEY, P., & SPELMAN, M. S. (1967). *Communicating with the patient*. London: Staples Press.

LIBET, B. (1978). Neuronal vs. subjective timing for a conscious experience. In D. Buser & A. Rouseul-Buser (Eds.), *Cerebral correlates of conscious experience*. Amsterdam: Elsevier.

LIBET, B. (1985). Subjective antedating of a sensory experience and mind-brain theories: Reply to Honderich. *Journal of Theoretical Biology*, 114(4), 563–570.

LIBET, B. (1989). The timing of a subjective experience: Reply to Salter. *Behavioral and Brain Sciences*, 12(1), 183–185.

LIBET, B., GLEASON, C. A., WRIGHT, E. W., & PEARL, D. K. (1983). Time of conscious intention to act in relation to onset of cerebral activity (readiness-potential): Pt. 3. The unconscious initiation of a freely voluntary act. *Brain*, 106, 623–642.

LIBET, B., & MOCHIDA, S. (1988). Long-term enhancement (LTE) of postsynaptic potentials following neural conditioning, in mammalian sympathetic ganglia. *Brain Research*, 473(2), 271–282.

LIBET, B., WRIGHT, E. W., & GLEASON, C. A. (1982). Readiness-potentials preceding unrestricted "spontaneous" vs. pre-planned voluntary acts. *Electroencephalography and Clinical Neurophysiology*, 54(3), 322–335.

LIBET, B., WRIGHT, E. W., JR., GLEASON, C. A. (1983). Preparation or intention-to-act in relation to pre-event potentials recorded at the vertex. *Electroencephalography and Clinical Neurophysiology*, 56(4), 367–372.

LICHTENSTEIN, E. (1982). The smoking problem: A behavioral perspective. *Journal of Consulting and Clinical Psychology*, 50(6), 804–819.

LIEBERMAN, M. A., & FALK, J. (1971). The remembered past as a source of data for research on the life cycle. *Human Development*, 14, 132–141.

LIEBERT, R. M., & BARON, R. A. (1972). Some immediate effects of televised violence on children's behavior. *Developmental Psychology*, 6, 469–478.

LIEBERT, R. M., & SPIEGLER, M. D. (1987). *Personality: Strategies and issues* (5th ed.). Chicago: Dorsey Press.

LIFTON, R. J. (1963). *Thought reform and the psychology of totalism: A study of 'brainwashing' in China*. New York: W. W. Norton.

LINDEMANN, E. (1944). The symptomatology and management of acute grief. *American Journal of Psychiatry*, 101, 141.

LINDSAY, P. H., & NORMAN, D. A. (1977). *Human information processing* (2nd ed.). New York: Academic Press.

LIVINGSTON, M. (1988). Art, illusion and the visual system. *Scientific American*, 258, 78–85.

LIVINGSTON, R. B, CALLAWAY, D. F., MACGREGOR, J. S., FISCHER, G. J., & HASTINGS, A. B. (1975). U.S. poverty impact on brain development. In M. A. B. Brazier (Ed.), *Growth and development of the brain: Nutritional, genetic, and environmental*. New York: Raven Press.

LOCKE, H. J. (1951). *Predicting adjustment in marriage: A comparison of a divorced and a happily married group*. New York: Henry Holt.

LOCKE, J. (1670). *An essay concerning human understanding*. New York: Meridian.

LOCKE, S., & COLLIGAN, D. (1986). *The healer within*. New York: Dutton.

LOCKE, S. E., KRAUS, L., LESERMAN, J., HURST, M. W., HEISEL, J. S., & WILLIAMS, R. M. (1984). Life change stress, psychiatric symptoms, and natural killer cell activity. *Psychosomatic Medicine*, 46(5), 441–453.

LOEHLIN, J. C., WILLERMAN, L., & HORN, J. M. (1988). Human behavior genetics. *Annual Review of Psychology*, 39, 101–133.

LOFTUS, E. F. (1978). Shifting human color memory. *Memory and Cognition*, 5, 696–699.

LOFTUS, E. F., MILLER, D. G., & BURNS, H. J. (1978). Semantic integration of verbal information into a visual memory. *Journal of Experimental Psychology*, 4, 19–31.

LOFTUS, E. F., & PALMER, J. C. (1974). Reconstruction of automobile destruction: An example of the interation between language and memory. *Journal of Verbal Learning and Verbal Behavior*, 13, 585–589.

LOFTUS, G. R., & LOFTUS, E. F. (1974). The influence of one memory retrieval on a subsequent memory retrieval. *Memory and Cognition*, 3, 467–471.

LOFTUS, G. R., & LOFTUS, E. F. (1975). *Human memory: The processing of information*. New York: Halsted Press.

LONDON, P. (1986). *The modes and morals of psychotherapy*. New York: Harper & Row.

LONGABAUGH, R., et al. (1983). Validation of a problem-focused nomenclature. *Archives of General Psychiatry*, 40, 453–461.

LONGINO, C. F., & LIPMAN, A. (1981). Married and spouseless men and women in planned retirement communities: Support network differentials. *Journal of Marriage and the Family*, 43, 169–177.

LOPATA, H. Z. (1971). Living arrangements of urban widows and their married children. *Sociological Focus*, 5, 41–61.

LOPATA, H. Z. (1973). *Widowhood in an American city*. Cambridge, MA: Schenkman.

LOPATA, H. Z. (1979). *Women as widows: Support systems*. New York: Elsevier.

LORENZ, K. (1966). *On aggression* (M. K.

Wilson, Trans.). New York: Harcourt Brace Jovanovich.

LORENZ, K. Z. (1943). Die angeborenen Formen moeglicher Erfahrung. *Zeitschrift Fur Tierpsychologie*, 5, 276.

LORIG, K., LAURIN, J., & HOLMAN, H. (1984). Arthritis self-management: A study of the effectiveness of patient education for the elderly. *The Gerontologist*, 24, 455–457.

LORIG, K., LAURIN, J., HOLMAN, H., BRAINERD, C., KINGMAN, J., & HOWE, M. L. (1985). On the development of forgetting. *Child development*, 56, 1103–1119.

LOVEJOY, C. O. (1974). The gait of Australopithecines. *Yearbook of Physical Anthropology*, 17, 147–161.

LOVEJOY, C. O. (1981). The origin of man. *Science*, 211, 128–130.

LOWENSTEIN, W. R. (1960). Biological transducers. *Scientific American*, 203, 98–108.

LOWENTHAL, M. F. (1964). *Lives in distress*. New York: Basic Books.

LOWENTHAL, M. F. (1975). *The four stages of life*. San Francisco: Jossey-Bass.

LOWN, B., DESILVA, R. A., REICH, P., & MURAWSKI, B. J. (1980). Psychophysiologic factors in sudden cardiac death. *American Journal of Psychiatry*, 137, 1325–1335.

LUBORSKY, L., CRITS-CHRISTOPH, P., MINTZ, J., & AUBERBACK, A. (1989). *Who will benefit from psychotherapy? Predicting therapeutic outcomes*. New York: Basic Books.

LUBORSKY, L., SINGER, B., & LUBORSKY, L. (1975). Comparative studies of psychotherapies. *Archives of General Psychiatry*, 32, 995–1008.

LUBORSKY, L., & SPENCE, D. P. (1978). Quantitative research on psychoanalytic therapy. In S. L. Garfield & A. E. Bergin (Eds.), *Handbook of psychotherapy and behavior change: An empirical analysis*. New York: Wiley.

LUCE, G. (1970). *Biological rhythms in psychiatry and medicine*. U.S. Public Health Service Publication No. 2088.

LUCERO, M. (1970). Lengthening of REM sleep duration consecutive to learning in the rat. *Brain Research*, 20, 319–322.

LUCHINS, A. (1942). Mechanization in problem solving. *Psychological Monographs*, 54(248).

LUDEL, J. (1978). *Introduction to sensory processes*. San Francisco: W. Freeman.

LURIA, A. R. (1968). *The mind of a mnemonist*. New York: Basic Books.

LURIA, A. R. (1973). *The working brain*. New York: Penguin Books.

LURIA, Z. (1974). Recent women college graduates: A study of rising expectations. *American Journal of Orthopsychiatry*, 44, 312–326.

LUTSKY, N. (1980). Attitudes toward old age and elderly persons. In C. Eisdorfer (Ed.) *Annual Review of Gerontology and Geriatrics* (Vol. 1). New York: Springer.

LUTSKY, N., PEAKE, P. K., & WRAY, L. (1978). *Inconsistencies in the search for cross-*

situational consistencies in behavior: A critique of the Bem and Allen study. Paper presented to the Midwestern Psychological Association, Chicago.

LYNCH, G., et al. (Eds.). (1984). *Neurobiology of learning and memory.* New York: Guilford Press.

LYNCH, G., McGAUGH, J., & WEINBERGER, N. (1984). *Neurobiology of learning and memory* New York: Guilford Press.

LYNCH, J. J. (1977). *The broken heart: The medical consequences of loneliness.* New York: Basic Books.

LYNCH, J. J. (1985). *The language of the heart.* New York: Basic Books.

LYNCH, J. J., et al. (1974). The effects of human contact on the heart activity of curarized patients in a shock-trauma unit. *American Heart Journal, 88,* 160–69.

LYNCH, J. J., et al. (1977). Psychological aspects of cardiac arrhythmia. *American Heart Journal, 93,* 645–57.

LYNCH, J. J., et al. (1982). Blood pressure changes while talking. *Israeli Journal of Medical Science, 18*(5), 575–579.

LYNN, M., & OLDENQUIST, A. (1986, May). Egoistic and nonegoistic motives in social dilemmas. *American Psychologist,* 456–463.

MACCOBY, E. (1980). *Social development: Psychological growth and the parent-child relationship.* New York: Harcourt Brace Jovanovich.

MACCOBY, E. (1988). Gender as a social category. *Developmental Psychology, 24,* 755–765.

MACCOBY, E., & JACKLIN, C. N. (1974). *The psychology of sex differences.* Stanford: Stanford University Press.

MACE, K. C. (1972). The "overt-bluff" shoplifter: Who gets caught? *Journal of Forensic Psychology 4,* 26–30.

MACFARLANE, A. (1978). What a baby knows. *Human Nature, 1,* 74–81.

MACFARLANE, A. (1977). *The psychology of childbirth.* Cambridge: Harvard University Press.

MACLEAN, P. (1978). The triune brain. *American Scientist, 66,* 101–113.

MADDI, S. R., & KOBASA, S. C. (1984). *The hardy executive: Health under stress.* Homewood, IL: Dow Jones-Irwin.

MAHONEY, M., & ARNKOFF, D. (1978). Cognitive and self-control therapies. In S. Garfield & A. Bergin (Eds.), *Handbook of psychotherapy and behavior change: An empirical analysis.* New York: Wiley.

MAIER, S. F., & LAUDENSLAGER, M. (1985, August). Stress and health: Exploring the links. *Psychology Today,* 44–49.

MAIN, M. (1973). *Exploration, play and level of cognitive functioning as related to child-mother attachment.* Unpublished doctoral dissertation, Johns Hopkins University.

MAKINODAN, T. (1977). Immunity and aging. In C. Finch & L. Hayflick (Eds.), *Handbook of the biology of aging.* New York: Van Nostrand Reinhold.

MALCOLM, J. (1981). *Psychoanalysis: The impossible profession.* New York: Knopf.

MALINOWSKI, B. (1928). *Sex and repression in savage society.* New York: Meridian.

MALONE, T. W. (1981). Toward a theory of intrinsically motivating instruction. *Cognitive Science 4,* 333–369.

MALONE, T. W. (1983). How do people organize their desks? Implications for designing office automation systems. *ACM Transactions on Office Information Systems, 1,* 99–112.

MALONE, T. W., & LEPPER, M. R. (1987). Making learning fun. In R. E. Snow & M. J. Farr, *Aptitude, learning and instruction: Vol. 3. Cognitive and affective process analysis.* Hillsdale, NJ: Erlbaum.

MALONE, T. W., YATES, R. M., & BENJAMIN, T. (1990). Electronic markets and electronic hierarchies. *Communications of the ACM, 30,* 390–402.

MAMMUCARI, A., et al. (1988). Spontaneous facial expression of emotions in brain-damaged patients. *Cortex, 24*(4), 521–533.

MANDLER, G. (1980). *Mind and emotion.* New York: Wiley.

MANION, K. (1981). Psychology and the lesbian: A critical view of the research. In S. Cox (Ed.), *Female psychology: The emerging self* (2nd ed., pp. 256–274). New York: St. Martin's Press.

MARKMAN, E. M. (1989). *Categorization and naming in children: Problems of induction.* Cambridge: MIT Press, Bradford Books.

MARKMAN, H. J., & KRAFT, S. A. (1989). Men and women in marriage: Dealing with gender differences in marital therapy. *Behavior Therapist, 12,* 51–56.

MARKS, I. (1969). *Fears and phobias.* New York: Academic Press.

MARKUS, H. (1977). Self-schemata and processing information about the self. *Journal of Personality and Social Psychology, 35,* 63–78.

MARKUS, H., & NURVUS, P. (1986). Possible selves. *American Psychologist, 41*(9), 954–969.

MARKUS, H., & WULT, E. (1987). The dynamic self-concept: A social psychological perspective. *Annual Review of Psychology, 38,* 299–337.

MARKUS, S., SMITH, J., & HALL, C. (1985). Role of self-conception in the perception of others. *Journal of Personality and Social Psychology, 49,* 1494–1512.

MARLATT, G. A., & GORDON, J. R. (Eds.). (1985). *Relapse Prevention.* New York: Guilford Press.

MARMOT, M. G., et al. (1975). Epidemiological studies of cornonary heart disease and stroke in Japanese men living in Japan, Hawaii, and California. *American Journal of Epidemiology,102,* 514–525.

MARMOT, M. G., & SYME, S. L. (1976). Acculturation and cornonary heart disease in Japanese-Americans. *American Journal of Epidemiology, 104,* 225–247.

MARR, D. (1982). *Vision.* New York: W.H. Freeman.

MARSDEN, H. M. (1972). Crowding and animal behavior. In J. F. Wohlwill & D. H. Carson (Eds.), *Environment and the social sciences: Perspectives and applications.* Washington, DC: American Psychological Association.

MARSHAK, A. (1978). The art and symbols of Ice Age man. *Human Nature, 1*(9), 32–41.

MARSHALL, G. D., & ZIMBARDO, P. G. (1979). Affective consequences of inadequately explained physiological arousal. *Journal of Personality and Social Psychology, 37*(6), 970–988.

MARSHALL, J. C., & HALLIGAN, P. W. (1988). Blindsight and insight in visuo-spatial neglect. *Nature, 336,* 766–767.

MASLOW, A. H. (1970). *Motivation and personality* (2nd ed.). New York: Harper & Row.

MASLOW, A. H. (1971). *The farther reaches of human nature* (2nd ed.). New York: Viking Press.

MASON, M. A. (1988). *The equality trap.* New York: Simon & Schuster.

MASTERS, W. H., & JOHNSON, V. E. (1966). *Human sexual response.* Boston: Little, Brown.

MASTERS, W. H., JOHNSON, V. E., & KOLODNY, R. C. (1986). *Human sexuality* (2nd ed.). Boston: Little, Brown.

MATARAZZO, J., WEISS, S. M., HERD, J. A., & MILLER, N. E. (Eds.). (1984). *Behavioral Health.* New York: Wiley.

MATAS, L., AREND, R., & SROUFE, L. A. (1978). Continuity of adaptation in the second year: The relationship between quality of attachment and later competence. *Child Development, 49,* 547–556.

MAWHINNEY, V. T., BOSTON, D. E., LAWS, D. R., BLUMENFELD, G. J., & HOPKINS, B. L. (1971). A comparison of students studying: Behavior produced by daily, weekly, and three-week testing schedules. *Journal of Applied Behavior Analysis, 4,* 257–264.

MAYER, A. D., & ROSENBLATT, J. S. (1979). Hormonal influences during the ontogeny of maternal behavior in female rats. *Journal of Comparative and Physiological Psychology, 93,* 879–898.

MAYER, D. J., PRICE, D. D., et al. (1976). Acupuncture analgesia. In J. J. Bonica & D. Albe-Fessard (Eds.), *Advances in pain research and therapy* (Vol. 1). New York: Raven.

MAYER, J. (1953a). Genetic, traumatic and environment factors in the etiology of obesity. *Physiological Review, 33,* 472–508.

MAYER, J. (1953b). Glucostatic mechanism of regulation of food intake. *New England Journal of Medicine, 249,* 13–16.

MAYER, T. G., GATCHEL, R. J., et al. (1987). A prospective two-year study of functional restoration in industrial low back injury utilizing objective assessment. *Journal of the American Medical Association, 258,* 1763–1767.

MAYNARD SMITH, J. (1978). The evolution of behavior. In Scientific American staff, (Eds.). *Evolution.* San Francisco: W. H. Freeman.

McGUIRE, W. J. (1968). Personality and

susceptibility to social influence. In E. F. Borgatta & W. W. Lambert (Eds.), *Handbook of personality theory and research.* Chicago: Rand McNally.

MCADAMS, D. P. (1987). A life-story model of identity. In R. Hogan & W. H. Jones (Eds.), *Perspectives in personality* (Vol. 2), pp. 15–20). Greenwich, CT: JAI Press.

MCADAMS, D. P. (1988). Self and story. In A. J. Stewart, J. M. Healy, & D. J. Özer (Eds.), *Perspectives in personality: Approaches to understanding lives.* Greenwich, CT: JAI Press.

MCADAMS, D. P. (1990). *The person: An introduction to personality psychology.* San Diego: Harcourt Brace Jovanovich.

MCCAULEY, C. (1989). The nature of social influence in Groupthink: Compliance and internalization. *Journal of Personality and Social Psychology, 57,* 250–260.

MCCLELLAND, D. C. (1971). *Motivational trends in society.* Morristown, NJ: General Learning Press.

MCCLELLAND, D. C. (1975). *Power: The inner experience.* New York: Irvington.

MCCLELLAND, D. C. (1984). *Achievement motivation.* New York: Free Press.

MCCLELLAND, D. C. (1985a). How motives, skills, and values determine what people do. *American Psychologist, 40(7),* 812–825.

MCCLELLAND, D. C. (1985b). *Human Motivation.* Chicago: Scott, Foresman.

MCCLELLAND, D. C., ATKINSON, J. W., CLARK, R. A., & LOWELL, E. L. (1953). *The achievement motive.* New York: Appleton-Century-Crofts.

MCCLELLAND, D. C., FLOOR, E., DAVIDSON, R.J., & SARON, C. (1980). Stressed power motivation, sympathetic activation, immune function, and illness. *Journal of Human Stress, 6,* 11–19.

MCCLELLAND, D. C., & JEMMOTT, J. B. (1980). Power motivation, stress and physical illness. *Journal of Human Stress, 6,* 6-15.

MCCLELLAND, D. C., ROSS, G., & PATEL, V. (1985). The effect of an academic examination on salivary norepinephrine and immunoglobulin levels. *Journal of Human Stress, 11,* 52–59.

MCCLELLAND, D. C., & WINTER, D. G. (1971). *Motivating economic achievement: Accelerating economic development through psychological training.* New York: Free Press.

MCCLELLAND, J. L., & RUMELHART, D. E. (1981). An interactive activation model of context effects in letter perception: Pt. 1. An account of basic findings. *Psychological Review, 88,* 287–330.

MCCLINTOCK, M. K. (1971). Menstrual synchrony and suppression. *Nature, 229,* 244–245.

MCCONNELL, P., & BERRY, M. (1978). The effects of undernutrition on Purkinje cell dendritic growth in the rat. *Journal of Comparative Neurology, 177,* 159–171.

MCCRAE, R. & COSTA, P. (1984). *Emerging lives, enduring dispositions.* Boston: Little, Brown

MCGLONE, J. (1980). Sex differences in human brain asymmetry: A critical survey. *Behavioral and Brain Sciences, 3(2),* 215–263.

MCGRATH, J. E. (1984). *Groups: Interaction and performance.* Englewood Cliffs, NJ: Prentice-Hall.

MCLEAN, A. (1979). *Work stress.* Reading, MA: Addison-Wesley.

MCNEIL, E. B. (1967). *The quiet furies: Man and disorder.* Englewood Cliffs, NJ: Prentice-Hall.

MEADOR, B. D., & ROGERS, C. R. (1984). Person-centered therapy. In Corsini, R. J. (Ed.) *Current psychotherapies* (pp. 142–195). Itasca, IL: Peacock.

MEDNICK, S. A. (1977). A bio-social theory of the learning of law-abiding behavior. In S. A. Mednick & K. O. Christiansen (Eds.), *Biosocial bases of criminal behavior.* New York: Gardner Press.

MEDVEDEV, Z. A. (1974). Caucasus and Altay longevity: A biological or social problem. *Gerontologist, 14(5),* 31–37.

MEDVEDEV, Z. A. (1975). Aging and longevity: New approaches and new perspectives. *Gerontologist 15(3),* 196–201.

MEICHENBAUM, D. (1974). *Cognitive behavior modification.* Boston: General Learning Press.

MEICHENBAUM, D., & TURK, D. (1976) The cognitive-behavioral management of anxiety, anger, and pain. In P. O. Davidson (Ed.), *The behavioral management of anxiety, depression, and pain.* New York: Brunner/Mazel.

MELLEN, S. L. W. (1981). *The evolution of love.* San Francisco: W. H. Freeman.

MELNECHUK, T. (1985). Why has psychoneuroimmunology been controversial? *Advances, 2,* 22–38.

MELZACK, R., & WALL, P. D. (1965) Pain mechanisms: A new theory. *Science, 150,* 971–979.

MENNINGER, K. A. (1945). *The human mind* (3rd ed.). New York: Knopf.

MEYER, A. J., MACCOBY, N., et al., (1977). Community education for cardiovascular health. *Lancet, 1,* 1192–1195.

MEYER, D., LEVENTHAL, H., & GUTTMANN, M. (1985). Common-sense models of illness: The example of hypertension. *Health Psychology, 4(2),* 115–135.

MEYER, D. L. (1981). *The effects of patients' representations of high blood pressure on behavior in treatment.* Ph.D. dissertation, University of Wisconsin.

MEYEROWITZ, B. E. (Ed.), *Cancer, nutrition, and eating behavior: A biobehavioral perspective.* Hillsdale, NJ: Erlbaum.

MICHAELS, C. F., & CARELLO, C. (1981). *Direct perception.* Englewood Cliffs, NJ: Prentice-Hall.

MICKEL, E. J. (1969). *The artificial paradises in French literature.* Chapel Hill, NC: University of North Carolina Press. (Free translation from French)

MIDLARSKY, E. (1984). Competence and helping: Notes toward a model. In E. Staub, D. Bar-Tal, J. Karylowski, & J. Reykowski (Eds.), *The development and maintenance of prosocial behavior: International perspectives.* New York: Plenum.

MILGRAM, S. (1963). Behavioral study of obedience. *Journal of Abnormal and Social Psychology, 67,* 371–378.

MILGRAM, S. (1970). The experience of living in cities. *Science, 13,* 1461–1468.

MILGRAM, S. (1974). *Obedience to authority.* New York: Harper & Row.

MILLER, B. C., & SOLLIE, D. L. (1980). Normal stresses during the transition to parenthood. *Family Relations, 29,* 459–465.

MILLER, D. T., & ROSS, M. (1975). Self-serving biases in attribution of causality: Fact or fiction? *Psychological Bulletin, 82,* 213–225.

MILLER, E. (1971). Handedness and the pattern of human ability. *British Journal of Psychology, 62,* 111–112.

MILLER, G. A. (1951). *Language and communication.* New York: McGraw-Hill.

MILLER, G. A. (1981). *Language and speech.* San Francisco: W. H. Freeman.

MILLER, G. A., & BUCKHOUT, R. (1973). *Psychology: The science of mental life* (2nd ed.). New York: Harper & Row.

MILLER, G. A., GALANTER, E., & PRIBRAM, K. H. (1960). *Plans and the structure of behavior.* New York: Holt, Rinehart & Winston.

MILLER, J. (1978). *General systems theory.* New York: McGraw-Hill.

MILLER, J. (1980). *The body in question.* New York: Holt, Rinehart & Winston.

MILLER, N. (1978). Biofeedback and visceral learning. *Annual Review of Psychology, 29,* 421–452.

MILLER, N. (1980). Lecture at 'The Healing Brain,' Albert Einstein College of Medicine.

MILLER, N. (1983) Behavioral medicine: Symbiosis between laboratory and clinic. *Annual Review of Psychology, 34,* 1-31.

MINEKA, S. (1990). A primate model of phobic fears. In H. Eysenck & I. Martin (Eds.), *Theoretical foundations of behavior therapy.* New York: Plenum.

MINEKA, S., & COOK, M. (1990). Social learning and the acquisition of snake fear in monkeys. In T. Zentall & J. Galef (Eds.), *Comparative social learning.* Hillsdale, NJ: Erlbaum.

MINEKA, S., & SUOMI, S. J. (1978). Social separation in monkeys. *Psychological Bulletin, 85,* 1376–1400.

MINEKA, S., & TOMARKEN, A. (1989). The role of cognitive biases in the origins and maintenance of fear and anxiety disorders. In T. Archer & L. Nilsson (Eds.), *Aversion, avoidance, and anxiety* (pp. 195–221). Hillsdale, NJ: Erlbaum.

MINKLER, M. (1984). *Social networks and health: People need people.* Los Altos, CA: Institute for the Study of Human Knowledge.

MINKLER, M. (1989). Health education, health promotion and the open society: An historical perspective. *Health Education Quarterly, 16(1),* 17–30.

MINKLER, M. (1990). People need people: Social support and health. In R. Ornstein & C. Swencionis (Eds.), *The Healing Brain: A Scientific Reader*. New York: Guilford Press.

MISCHEL, W. (1968, 1981). *Personality and assessment* (1st and 3rd eds.). New York: Wiley.

MISCHEL, W. (1984). Convergences and challenges in the search for consistency. *American Psychologist 39*, 351–364.

MISCHEL, W. (1986). *Introduction to personality* (4th ed.). New York: Holt, Rinehart & Winston.

MISCHEL, W., & PEAKE, P. K. (1982). Beyond déjà vu in the search for cross-situational consistency. *Psychological Review, 89*, 730–755.

MISHKIN, M., & APPENZELLER, T. (1987, June). The anatomy of memory. *Scientific American*, 80–89.

MITCHELL, D. (1981). Sensitive periods in visual development. In R. Aslin, J. Alberts, & M. Peterson (Eds.), *Development of Perception* (pp. 1-43). New York: Academic Press.

MONAGAN, D. (1986). Sudden death. *Discover, 7*(1), 64–71. (Also see Lown, B., Verrier, R. L., & Rabinowitz, S. H. (1977). Neural and psychologic mechanisms and the problem of sudden cardiac death. *American Journal of Cardiology, 39*, 890–902.)

MONTE, C. F. (1987). *Beneath the mask: An introduction to the theories of personality* (3rd ed.). New York: Holt, Rinehart & Winston.

MOOK, D. E. (1986). *Motivation: The organization of action*. New York: Norton.

MORISKY, D. E., DEMUTH, N. M., FIELD-FASS, M., GREEN, L. W., & LEVINE, D. M. (1985). Evaluation of family health education to build social support for long-term control of high blood pressure. *Health Education Quarterly, 12*, 35–50.

MORISKY, D. E., LEVINE, D. M., GREEN, L. W., SHAPIRO, S., RUSSELL, R. P., & SMITH, C. R. (1983). Five-year blood pressure control and mortality following health education for hypertensive patients. *American Journal of Public Health, 73*, 153–62.

MOROKOFF, P. J., HOLMES-JOHNSON, E., & WEISSE, C. S. (1987). A psychosocial program for HIV-seropositive persons. *Patient Education and Counseling, 10*, 287–300.

MORRIS, P. (1958). *Widows and their families*. London: Routledge.

MORRIS, P. (1974). *Loss and change*. New York: Pantheon Books.

MOSCOVITCH, M., & OLDS, J. (1980). *Asymmetries in spontaneous facial expressions and their possible relation to hemispheric specialization*. Paper presented at the meeting of the International Neuropsychology Society, Holland.

MOSCOWITZ, H. (1975, August). Hiding in the Hammond report. *Hospital Practice*, 35–39.

MOSSEY, J. M., & SHAPIRO, E. (1982). Self-rated health: A predictor of mortality among the elderly. *American Journal of Public Health, 72*, 800–807.

MOTLEY, M. T., BARRS, B. J., & CAMDEN, C. T. (1983). Syntactic criteria in pre-articulatory editing: Evidence from laboratory-induced slips of the tongue. *Journal of Psycholinguistic Research, 10*, 503–522.

MOUNTCASTLE, V. B. (1976). The world around us: Neural command functions for selective attention. *Neurosciences Research Program Bulletin, 14* (Suppl.), 1-47.

MOWER, O. H. (1947). On the dual nature of learning: A reinterpretation of "conditioning" and "problem solving." *Harvard Educational Review, 17*, 102–148.

MOWER, O. H. (1950). *Learning theory and personality*. New York: Ronald Press.

MRFIT Research Group. (1982). Multiple risk factor intervention trial: Risk factor changes and mortality results. *Journal of the American Medical Association, 248*, 1465–1477.

MUMFORD, L. (1970). *The pentagon of power*. New York: Harcourt Brace Jovanovich.

MURPHY, M., & DONOVAN, S. (1988). *The physiological and psychological effects of meditation*. San Rafael, CA: Esalen Institute.

MYERS, D. G., & BISHOP, G. D. (1970). Discussion effects on racial attitudes. *Science, 169*, 778–789.

MYERS, D. G., & LAMM, H. (1976). The group polarization phenomenon. *Psychological Bulletin, 83*, 602–627.

MYERS, J. K., et al. (1984). Six-month prevalence of psychiatric disorders in three communities. *Archives of General Psychiatry, 41*, 959–967.

MYERS, R. D. (1971). Hypothalamic mechanisms of pyrogen action in the cat and monkey. In G. E. V. Wolstenholme & J. Birch (Eds.), *CIBA Foundation symposium on pyrogens and fever* (pp. 131–153). London: Churchill.

NAGLE, J. J. (1979). *Heredity and human affairs* (2nd ed.). St. Louis: Mosby.

NARANJO, C. (1973). *The healing journey*. New York: Pantheon Books.

NATSOULAS, T. (1978). Consciousness. *American Psychologist, 33*, 906–914.

NATSOULAS, T. (1983). Addendum to "Consciousness." *American Psychologist, 38*, 121–122.

NAUTA, W. J. H. (1971). The problem of the frontal lobe: A reinterpretation. *Journal of Psychiatric Research, 8*, 167–187.

NAUTA, W. J. H. (1973). Connections of the frontal lobe with the limbic system. In L. V. Laitinen & R. E. Livingston (Eds.), *Surgical approaches in psychiatry*. Baltimore: University Park Press.

NAVRAN, L. (1967). Communication and adjustment in marriage. *Family Process, 6*, 173–184.

NEALE, J. M., & OHMANNS, T. F. (1980). *Schizophrenia*. New York: Wiley.

NEBES, R. (1972). Dominance of the minor hemisphere in commissurotomized man in a test of figural unification. *Brain, 95*, 633–638.

NEISSER, U. C. (1967). Snapshots or benchmarks? In U. Neisser, T. M.

Newcomb, K. E. Koenig, R. Flacks, & D. P. Warwick (Eds.), *Persistence and change: Bennington College and its students after twenty-five years*. New York: Wiley.

NEISSER, U. C. (1976). *Cognition and reality*. San Francisco: W. H. Freeman.

NEISSER, U. C. (1979). *Cognitive psychology*. New York: Appleton-Century-Crofts.

NEISSER, U. C. (1982). *Memory observed: Remembering in natural context*. San Francisco: W. H. Freeman.

NELSON, T. O. (1976). Reinforcement and human memory. In W. K. Estes (Ed.), *Handbook of learning and cognitive processes* (Vol. 3). Hillsdale, NJ: Erlbaum.

NER, U. (1970). *Two worlds of childhood*. New York: Russell Sage, 1970.

NESER, W. B., TYROLER, H. A., & CASSEL, J. C. (1971). Social disorganization and stroke mortality in the Black population of North Carolina. *American Journal of Epidemiology, 93*, 166–75.

NEUGARTEN, B. L. (1964). Summary and implications. In B. Neugarten et al., *Personality in middle and late life*. New York: Atherton.

NEUGARTEN, B. L. (1974). Age groups in American society and the rise of the young-old. *The Annual of the American Academy of Political and Social Science*, 187–198.

NEUGARTEN, B. L. (1977). Personality and aging. In J. E. Birren & K. W. Schaie (Eds.), *Handbook of the psychology of aging*. New York: Van Nostrand Reinhold.

NEUGARTEN, B. L., & HAGESTAD, G. O. (1976). Age and the life course. In R. H. Binstock & E. Shanas (Eds.), *Handbook of aging and the social sciences*. New York: Van Nostrand Reinhold.

NEUGARTEN, B. L., HAVIGHURST, D. J., & TOBIN, S. S. (1968). Personality and patterns of aging. In B. L. Neugarten (Ed.), *Middle age and aging*. Chicago: University of Chicago Press.

NEUGARTEN, B. L., MOORE, J. W., & LOWE, J. C. (1965). Age norms, age constraints, and adult socialization. *American Journal of Sociology, 70*(6), 710–717.

NEUGARTEN, B. L., & PETERSON, W. (1957). A study of the American age-grade system. *Fourth Congress of the International Association of Gerontology* (Vol. 3). Firenzi, It.: Tito Mattiolo.

NEUGARTEN, B. L., & WEINSTEIN, K. (1964). The changing American grandparent. *Journal of Marriage and Family, 24*(2), 199–204.

NEUGARTEN, B. L., WOOD, V., KRAINES, R. J., & LOOMIS, B. (1963). Women's attitudes toward the menopause. *Vita Humana, 6*(3), 140–151.

NEVILLE, H. (1977). EEG testing of cerebral specialization in normal and congenitally deaf children: A preliminary report. In S. J. Segalowitz & F. A. Gruber (Eds.), *Language development and neurological theory*. New York: Academic Press.

NEWCOMB, T. M. (1943). *Personality and*

social change. New York: Dryden Press.

NEWCOMB, T. M., KOENIG, K. E., FLACKS, R., & WARWICK, D. P. (1967). *Persistence and change: Bennington College and its students after twenty-five years.* New York: Wiley.

NEWELL, A., & SIMON, H. A. (1972). *Human problem solving.* Englewood Cliffs, NJ: Prentice-Hall.

NEWELL, A., & SIMON, H. A. (1976). Computer science as empirical enquiry: Symbols and search. *Communications of the ACM, 19,* 113–126.

NEWMAN, B. N., & NEWMAN, P. R. (1987). *Development through life.* Chicago: Dorsey.

NEWMAN, J., & MCCAULEY, C. (1977). Eye contact with strangers in city, suburb, and small town. *Environment and Behavior, 9*(4), 547–558.

NEWMAN, O. (1979). Community of interest. *Human Nature, 2*(1).

NEWTON, N., & MODAHL, C. (1978). Pregnancy: The closest human relationship. *Human Nature, 1*(3), 40–50.

NISAN, M., & KOHLBERG, L. (1982). Universality and variation in moral judgment: A longitudinal and cross-sectional study in Turkey. *Child Development, 53,* 865–876.

NISBETT, R. E. (1968). Taste, deprivation, and weight determinants of eating behavior. *Journal of Personality and Social Psychology, 10,* 107–116.

NISBETT, R. E. (1972). Hunger, obesity, and the ventromedial hypothalamus. *Psychological Review, 79*(6), 433–453.

NISBETT, R. E., & ROSS, L. (1980). *Human inference: Strategies and shortcomings of social judgment.* Englewood Cliffs, NJ: Prentice-Hall.

NISBETT, R. E., CAPUTO, C., LEGANT, P., & MARACEK, J. (1973). Behavior as seen by the actor and as seen by the observer. *Journal of Personality and Social Psychology, 27,* 154–164.

NOLEN-HOEKSEMA, S. (1987). Sex differences in unipolar depression: Evidence and theory. *Psychological Bulletin, 101,* 259–282.

NORMAN, D. (1983). *Learning and memory* San Francisco: Freeman.

NORMAN, D. (1988). *The psychology of everyday things.* New York: Basic Books.

NORTH, C. (1987). *Welcome, silence.* New York: Simon & Schuster.

NUCKOLLS, K. B., CASSEL, J., & KAPLAN, B. H. (1972). Psychosocial assets, life crisis, and the prognosis of pregnancy. *American Journal of Epidemiology, 95,* 431–441.

NUTTIN, J. M. (1985). Narcissism beyond Gestalt and awareness: The name-letter effect. *European Journal of Social Psychology, 15,* 353–61.

O'DONNELL, J. M. (1979). The crisis of experimentalism in the 1920s. *American Psychologist, 34,* 289–295.

OLDS, J. (1958). Self-stimulation of the brain. *Science, 127,* 315–323.

OLDS, J., & MILNER, P. (1954). Positive reinforcement produced by electrical stimulation of septal area and other regions of rat brain. *Journal of Comparative Physiological Psychology, 47,* 419–427.

O'LEARY A. (1985). Self-efficacy and health. *Behavioral Research and Therapy, 23,* 437–51.

OMARK, D. R., & EDELMAN, M. (1973). *Peer group social interactions from an evolutionary perspective.* Paper presented at the meetings of the Society for Research in Child Development, Philadelphia.

OPPENHEIM, J. S., LEE B. C., NASS R., & GAZZANIGA, M. S. (1987). No sex-related differences in human corpus callosum based on magnetic resonance imagery. *Annals of Neurology, 21*(6), 604–606.

ORNE, M. T. (1972). On the simulating subject as a quasi-control group in hypnosis research: What, why, and how? In E. Fromm & R. Shor (Eds.), *Hypnosis, research developments, and perspectives.* Chicago: Aldine.

ORNE, M. T., SHEEHAN, P. W., & EVANS, F. J. (1968). Occurence of posthypnotic behavior outside of the experimental setting. *Journal of Personality and Social Psychology, 9,* 189–196.

ORNSTEIN, R. (1969). *On the experience of time.* London: Penguin Books.

ORNSTEIN, R. (1976). *The mind field.* London: Octagon Press.

ORNSTEIN, R. (1986a). *Multimind.* Boston: Houghton Mifflin Company.

ORNSTEIN, R. (1986b). *The psychology of consciousness* (3rd ed.). New York: Penguin.

ORNSTEIN, R. (1991). *Mindworks.* New York: Prentice-Hall.

ORNSTEIN, R. (Ed.). (1973). *The nature of human consciousness.* San Francisco: W. H. Freeman.

ORNSTEIN, R., & EHRLICH, P. E. (1989). *New world new mind.* New York: Doubleday.

ORNSTEIN, R., HERRON, J., JOHNSTONE, J., & SWENCIONIS, C. (1979). Differential right hemisphere involvement in two reading tasks. *Psychophysiology, 16*(4), 398–401.

ORNSTEIN, R., & SOBEL, D. S. (1987). *The healing brain.* New York: Simon & Schuster.

ORNSTEIN, R., & SOBEL, D. S. (1989). *Healthy pleasures.* Reading: Addison-Wesley.

ORNSTEIN, R., & SWENCIONIS, C. (1985). Analytic and synthetic problem-solving strategies in hemispheric asymmetry. *Neuropsychologia.*

ORNSTEIN, R., & SWENCIONIS, C. (Eds.). (1990). *Scientific papers about the healing brain.* New York: Guilford.

ORNSTEIN, R., THOMPSON, R., & MACAULAY, D. (1984). *The amazing brain.* Boston: Houghton Mifflin.

OSGOOD, C., SUCI, G.J., & TANNENBAUM, P.H. (1971). *The measurement of meaning.* Urbana: University of Illinois Press.

OSIS, K., & HANALOSEN, E. (1977). *At the hour of death.* New York: Avon Books.

OSWALD, I. (1962). *Sleeping and waking.* Amsterdam, NY: Elsevier.

OZER, D. J. (1986). *Consistency in personality: a methodological framework.* New York: Springer-Verlag.

PAFFENBERGER (1986). *The American way of life is dangerous to your health.* San Francisco: Freeman.

PALLER, K. A., KUTAS M., SHIMAMURA, A. P., & SQUIRE, L. R. (1987). Brain responses to concrete and abstract words reflect processes that correlate with later performance on a test of stem-completion priming. *Electroencephalography and Clinical Neurophysiology, 40,* 360–365.

PALMORE, E. (1979). Social factors in aging. In E. Busse & D. Blazer (Eds.), *Handbook of geriatric psychiatry.* New York: Van Nostrand Reinhold.

PALMORE, E. (1981). *Social patterns in normal aging.* Durham, NC: Duke University Press.

PAPERT, S. (1980). *Mindstorms: Children, computers, and powerful ideas.* New York: Basic Books.

PAPEZ, J. W. (1937). A proposed mechanism of emotion. *Archives of Neurology and Psychiatry, 38,* 725–743.

PARDES, H., KAUFMANN, C. A., PINCUS, H. A., & WEST, A. (1989). Genetics and psychiatry: Past discoveries, current dilemmas, and future directions. *American Journal of Psychiatry, 146,* 435–443.

PARKES, C. M. (1972). *Bereavement: Studies of grief in adult life.* New York: International Universities Press.

PARKES, C. M., BENJAMIN, B., & FITZGERALD, R. G. (1969). Broken heart: A statistical study of increased mortality among widows. *British Medical Journal, 1,* 740.

PASNAK, R., TYLER, Z. A., & ALLEN, J. A. (1985). Effect of distance instructions on size judgements. *American Journal of Psychology, 98,* 297–304.

PATTISON, E. M. (1977). The will to live and the expectation of death. In E. M. Pattison (Ed.), *The experience of dying* (pp. 61–74). Englewood Cliffs, NJ: Prentice-Hall.

PAUL, G. L. (1965). Effects of insight, desensitization, and attention-placebo treatment of anxiety: An approach to outcome research in psychotherapy. *Dissertation Abstracts, 25*(9), 5388–5389.

PAVLOV, I. P. (1927). *Conditioned reflexes.* London: Oxford University Press

PAVLOV, I. P. (1928). *Lectures on conditioned reflexes.* New York: International Publishers

PAVLOV, I. P. (1941). *Conditional reflexes and psychiatry* (W. H. Gantt, Ed. and Trans.). New York: International Publishers.

PAXTON, A. L., & TURNER, E. J. (1978). Self-actualization and sexual permissiveness, satisfaction, prudishness, and drive among female undergraduates. *Journal of Sex Research, 14*(2), 65–80.

PEA, R. D. & KURLAND, D. M. (1989). On the cognitive effects of learning computer programming: A critical look. *New Ideas on Psychology*. New York: Mc-Graw-Hill.

PEARCE, P.L. (1980). Strangers, travelers, and Greyhound terminals: A study of small-scale helping behaviors. *Journal of Personality and Social Psychology, 38*, 935–940.

PEARLIN, L. (1980). Life strains and psychological distress among adults. In N. J. Smelser & E. H. Erikson (Eds.), *Themes of work and love in adulthood*. Cambridge: Harvard University Press.

PEARLIN, L., & JOHNSON, J. (1977). Marital stress, life strains and depression. *American Sociological Review, 42*, 704–715.

PECK, M. A., & SCHRUT, A. (1971). Suicidal behavior among college students. *HSMHA Health Reports, 86*(2), 149–156.

PECK, R., & BERKOWITZ, H. (1964). Personality and adjustment in middle age. In B. L. Neugarten et al. (Eds.), *Personality in middle and late life*. New York: Atherton.

PEDERSON, A. M., BARRY, D. J., & BABIGIAN, H. M. (1972). Epidemiological considerations of psychotic depression. *Archives of General Psychiatry, 27*, 193–197.

PEDERSEN, N. L., GATZ, M., PLOMIN, R., NESSELROADE, J. R., & MCCLEARN, G.E. (1989). Individual differences in locus of control during the second half of the life span for identical and fraternal twins reared apart and reared together. *Journal of Gerontology, 44*(4), 100–105.

PEDERSEN, N. L., PLOMIN, R., MCCLEARN, G. E., & FRIBERG, L. (1988). Neuroticism, extraversion, and related traits in adult twins reared apart and reared together. *Journal of Personality and Social Psychology, 55*(6), 950–957.

PENFIELD, W. (1975). *The mystery of the mind*. Princeton: Princeton University Press.

PENNEBAKER, J. (1988). Confiding traumatic experiences and health. In S. Fisher & J. Reason (Eds.), *Handbook of life stress, cognitions, and health*. New York: Wiley.

PENNEBAKER, J. (1989). Confession, inhibition and disease. In L. Berkowitz (Ed.), *Advances in experimental social psychology* (Vol. 22). New York: Academic Press.

PENNEBAKER, J. (1990, June). Paper presented at Healthy Pleasures conference, New York ISHK.

PENNEBAKER, J. W., et al. (1979). Don't the girls get prettier at closing time? *Personality and Social Psychological Bulletin, 5*, 122–125

PETERSON, C. (1988). *Personality*. San Diego: Harcourt Brace Jovanovich.

PETERSON, C., & SELIGMAN, M. E. (1987). Explanatory style and illness. *Journal of Personality, 55*(2), 237–265.

PETERSON, C., SELIGMAN, M. E., & VAILLANT, G. E., (1988). Pessimistic explanatory style is a risk factor for physical illness.

Journal of Personality and Social Psychology, 55(1), 23–27.

PETTIGREW, J. (1961). Social psychology and desegregation research. *American Psychologist, 15*, 61–71.

PETTY, R. E., & CACIOPPO, J. T. (1981). *Attitudes and persuasion: Classic and contemporary approaches*. Dubuque, IA: Brown.

PHILLIPS, D. P. (1974). The influence of suggestion on suicide: Substantive and theoretical implications of the Werther effect. *American Sociological Review, 39*, 340–354.

PHILLIPS, D. P. (1979). Suicide, motor vehicle fatalities, and the mass media: Evidence toward a theory of suggestion. *American Journal of Sociology, 84*, 1150–1174.

PHILLIPS, D. P. (1980). Airplane accidents, murder, and the mass media: Towards a theory of imitation and suggestion. *Social Forces, 58*, 1001–1024.

PHILLIPS, D. P. (1983). The impact of mass media violence on U.S. homicides. *American Sociological Review, 48*, 560–568.

PHILLIPS, D. P., & FELDMAN, K. A. (1973). A dip in deaths before ceremonial occasions: Some new relationships between social integration and mortality. *American Sociological Review, 38*, 678–696.

PIAGET, J. (1952). *The origins of intelligence in children*. New York: International Universities Press.

PIAGET, J. (1960). *The moral judgment of the child*. Glencoe, IL: Free Press. (Original work published 1932)

PILBEAM, O. (1972). *The ascent of man*. New York: Macmillian.

PILISUK, M., & MINKLER, M. (1980). Supportive networks: Life ties for the elderly. *Journal of Social Issues, 36*(2), 95–116.

PINKER, S. (Ed.). (1985). *Visual cognition*. Cambridge: MIT Press/Bradford.

PIZZAMIGLIO, L., CALTAGIRONE, C., MAMMUCARI, A., EKMAN P., & FRIESEN, W. V. (1987). Imitation of facial movements in brain damaged patients. *Cortex, 23*(2), 207–221.

PLOMIN, R. (1989). Environment and genes: Determinants of behavior. *American Psychologist, 44*(2), 105–111.

PLOMIN R., & LOEHLIN, J. C., (1989). Direct and indirect IQ heritability estimates: A puzzle. *Behavior Genetics, 19*(3), 331–342.

PLOMIN, R., & ROWE, D.C. (1977). A twin study of temperament in young children. *Journal of Psychology, 97*, 107–113.

PLUTCHIK, R. (1980). *Emotion: A psychoevolutionary synthesis*. New York: Harper & Row.

PLUTCHIK, R. (1984). Emotions: A general psychoevolutionary theory. In K. Scherer & P. Ekman (Eds.), *Approaches to emotion*. Hillsdale, NJ: Erlbaum.

POINCARE, H. (1921). The value of science. In G. B. Halstead (Trans.), *The foundations of science*. New York: Science Press.

POLIVY, J., & HERMAN, P. (1983). *Breaking the diet habit: A natural weight alternative*. Boston: Houghton Mifflin.

POLYA, G. (1957). *How to solve it*. Garden City, NY: Doubleday/Anchor.

POMERLEAU, O. F. (1979). Behavioral factors in the establishment, maintenance, and cessation of smoking. In *Smoking and health: A report of the Surgeon General* (PHS79–50066). Washington, DC: US Government Printing Office.

POOL, I. DE S. (Ed.). (1977). *The social impact of the telephone*. Cambridge: MIT Press.

POON, L. W. (1985). Memory skill training for the elderly. *Psychological Reports, 45*, 345–349.

POON, L. W., et al. (1980). *New directions in memory and aging*. Hillsdale, NJ: Erlbaum.

PÖPPEL, E., HELD, R., & FROST, D., (1973). Residual brain function after wounds. *Nature, 243*, 295–296.

PORAC, C., & COREN, S., (1986). Sighting dominance and egocentric localization. *Vision Research, 6*(10), 1709–1713.

POST, F. (1980). Paranoid, schizophrenia-like and schizophrenic states in the aged. In J. E. Birren & R. B. Sloane (Eds.), *Handbook of mental health and aging*. Englewood Cliffs, NJ: Prentice Hall.

POTKAY, C. P., & ALLEN, B. P. (1986). *Personality theory, research, and application*. Monterey, CA: Brooks/Cole.

PREMACK, D. (1965). Reinforcement theory. *Nebraska symposium on motivation*. Lincoln: University of Nebraska Press.

PRENTICE, N. M. (1972). The influence of live and symbolic modeling on promoting moral judgment of adolescent delinquents. *Journal of Abnormal Psychology, 80*(2), 157–161.

PRETI, G., et al. (1986). Human axillary secretions influence women's menstrual cycles. *Hormones and Behavior, 20*(4), 414–452.

PREVOST, F. (1975). An indication of sexual and aggressive similarities through humour appreciation. *Journal of Psychology, 91*, 283–288.

PRICE, J. S. (1968). The genetics of depressive disorder. In A. Coppen & A. Walk (Eds.), *Recent developments in affective disorders. British Journal of Psychiatry*, Special Publication, 2.

PROSSER, H. A. (1978). Social factors affecting the timing of the first child. In W. Miller & L. Neuman (Eds.), *The first child and family formation*. Chapel Hill: Caroline Population Center.

PUSKA, P. (1984). Community based prevention of cardiovascular disease: The North Karelia Project. In J. D. Matarazzo, S. M. Weiss, et al. (Eds.), *Behavioral health*. New York: Wiley.

QUAY, H. C. (1965). Psychopathic personality as pathological stimulation-seeking. *American Journal of Psychiatry, 122*, 180–183.

RABKIN, J. G., GELB, L., & LAZAR, J. B. (Eds.). (1980). *Attitudes toward the mentally ill: Research perspectives.* Rockville, MD: National Institute of Mental Health.

RABKIN, S. W., MATHEWSON, F., & TATE, R. B. (1980). Chronobiological cardiac sudden death in men. *Journal of the American Medical Association, 244,* 1357–1358.

RACHMAN, S. (1978). *Fear and courage.* San Francisco: W. H. Freeman.

RADLOFF, L. (1975). Sex differences in depression: The effects of occupation and marital status. *Sex Roles, 1,* 249–265.

RAHE, R. H., & ARTHUR, R. J. (1978, March). Life change and illness studies: Past history and future directions. *Journal of Human Stress,* pp. 3-15.

RAHULA, W. (1969). *What the Buddha taught.* New York: Grove Press.

RANDI, J. (1975). *The magic of Uri Geller.* New York: Ballantine Books.

RAPOPORT, J. (1989). *The boy who couldn't stop washing: The experience and treatment of obsessive compulsive disorder.* New York: Dutton.

RAUDICH, A., & LOLORDO, V. M. (1979). Associative and nonassociative theories of the UCS preexposure phenomenon: Implications for Pavlovian conditioning. *Psychological Bulletin, 86,* 523–548.

RAY, O. (1983). *Drugs, society, and human behavior* (3rd ed.). St Louis: Mosby.

RAZRAN, G. (1939). A quantative study of meaning by conditioned salivary technique (semantic conditioning). *Science, 90,* 89–91.

REDMOND, D. E., HUANG, Y. H., BAULU, J., SNYDER, R. V., & MAAS, J. W. (1971). In R. A. Vigersky (Ed.), *Anorexia nervosa* (pp. 81–96). New York: Raven Press.

REES, W. D. (1971). The hallucinations of widowhood. *British Medical Journal, 4,* 37–41.

REICH, J., & ZAUTRA, A. (1981). Life events and personal causation: Some relationships with satisfaction and distress. *Journal of Personality and Social Psychology, 41,* 1002–1012.

REICHARD, S., LIVSON, F., & PETERSON, P. (1962). *Aging and personality: A study of eighty-seven older men.* New York: Wiley.

REID, D. K. (1977). *Early identification of children with learning disabilities.* Regional Access Project, Region 11, New York University.

REINSEL, R., WOLLMAN, M., & ANTROBUS, J. S. (1986). Effects of environmental context and cortical activation on thought. *Journal of Mind and Behavior, 7,* 259–276.

REISBERG, D., HEUER, F., O'SHAUGHNESSY, M., & McLEAN, J. (1984, November). *Memory vividness.* Paper presented at Psychonomic Society Conference, San Antonio, TX.

REISBERG, D., HEUER, F., O'SHAUGHNESSY, M., McLEAN, J., RICHMAN, H. B., & SIMON, H. A. (1989). Context effects in letter perception: Comparison of two theories. *Psychological Review, 96,* 417–432.

REISMAN, D., GLAZER, N., & DENNEY, R. (1950). *The lonely crowd: A study of the changing American character.* New Haven: Yale University Press.

REITE, M., & FIELDS, T. (Eds.). (1985). *The psychobiology of attachment and separation.* New York: Academic Press.

REST, J. R., DAVISON, M. L., & ROBBINS, S. (1978). Age trends in judging moral issues: A review of cross-sectional, longitudinal, and sequential studies of the defining issues test. *Child Development, 49,* 263–279.

REVENSON, T. A. (1984). Social demographic correlates of loneliness in late life. *American Journal of Community Psychology, 12,* 71–85.

REVUSKY, S., GARCIA, J., RICHARDS, M., & LIGHT, P. (1986). *Children of social worlds.* Cambridge: Harvard University Press.

RICCELLI, P. T., ANTILA, C. E., & DALE, J. A., Depressive and elative mood inductions as a function of exaggerated versus contradictory facial expressions. *Perceptual and Motor Skills, 68*(2), 443–452.

RICH, A. (1980). Compulsory heterosexuality and lesbian experience. *Signs: Journal of Women in Culture and Society, 5,* 631–660.

RICHARDS, M., & LIGHT, P. (1986). *Children of social worlds.* Cambridge: Harvard University Press.

RICHMAN, H. B., & SIMON, H. A. (1989). Context effects in letter perception: A comparison of two theories. *Psychological Review, 96*(3), 417–423.

RIEGEL, K. F., & RIEGEL, R. M. (1972). Development, drop, and death. *Developmental Psychology, 9,* 306–319.

RING, K. (1980). *Life at death: A scientific investigation of the near-death experience.* New York: Coward-McCann.

RING, K. (1984). *Heading toward Omega.* New York: Morrow.

ROAZIN, P. (1986). *Erik Erikson.* New York: Free Press.

ROBERTSON, P. W. (1967). Color words and color vision. *Biology and Human Affairs, 33,* 28–33.

ROBERTS, M. C. (1984) *Cancer today: Origins, prevention and treatment.* Washington, DC: Institute of Medicine/National Academy Press.

ROBEY, D. (1981). Computer information systems and organizational structure. *Communications of the ACM, 24,* 679–687.

ROBINSON, B., & THURNER, M. (1979). Taking care of aged parents: A family cycle. *Transition Gerontologist, 19*(6).

ROCK, I. (1985). *Perception.* New York: Scientific American.

RODEHEAVER, D. (1987). When old age became a social problem, women were left behind. *Gerontologist, 27,* 741–746.

RODIN, J. (1986). Aging and health: Effects of the sense of control. *Science, 233,* 1271–1276.

RODIN, J., & LANGER, E. (1977). Long-term effects of a control-relevant intervention with the institutional aged. *Journal of Personality and Social Psychology, 35*(12), 897–902.

ROEDIGER, H. L., & CRAIK, F. I. M. (Eds.). (1989). Varieties of memory and consciousness: Essays in honor of Ender Tulving. Hillsdale, NJ: Erlbaum.

ROGERS, C. R. (1951). *Client-centered therapy.* Boston: Houghton Mifflin.

ROGERS, C. R. (1959). A theory of therapy, personality and interpersonal relationships, as developed in the client-centered framework. In S. Koch (Ed.), *Psychology: A study of a science* (Vol. 3, pp. 184–256). New York: McGraw-Hill.

ROGERS, C. R. (1970). *On becoming a person: A therapist's view of psychotherapy.* Boston: Houghton Mifflin.

ROGERS, C. R. (1972). Some social issues which concern me. *Journal of Humanistic Psychology, 12*(2), 45–60.

ROGERS, C. R. (1974). In retrospect: Forty-six years. *American Psychologist, 29,* 115–123.

ROGERS, C. R. (1980). *A way of being.* Boston: Houghton Mifflin.

ROGERS, R. W. (1975). A protection motivation theory of fear appeals and attitude change. *Journal of Psychology, 91,* 93–114.

ROGERS, T. B., KULPER, N. A., & KIRKER, W. S. (1977). Self-reference and the encoding of personal information. *Journal of Personality and Social Psychology, 35,* 677–688.

ROKEACH, M. (1960). *The open and closed mind.* New York: Basic Books.

ROKEACH, M. (1973). *The nature of human values.* New York: Free Press.

ROOK, K. S. (1984). The negative side of social interaction: Impact on psychological well-being. *Journal of Personality and Social Psychology, 46,* 1097–1108.

ROSCH, E. (1973). Natural categories. *Cognitive Psychology, 4,* 328–350.

ROSCH, E. (1975). Cognitive representation of semantic categories. *Journal of Experimental Psychology, 104,* 192–233.

ROSCH, E., & MERVIS, C. (1975). Family resemblances: studies in the internal structure of categories. *Cognitive Psychology, 8,* 382–439.

ROSCH, E., MERVIS, C., GRAY, W., JOHNSON, D., & BOYES-BRAEM, P. (1976). Basic objects in natural categories. *Cognitive Psychology, 8,* 382–439.

ROSEKRANS, M. A., & HARTUP, W. W. (1967). Imitative influences of consistent and inconsistent response consequences to a model on aggressive behavior in children. *Journal of Personality and Social Psychology, 7,* 429–434.

ROSEN, B. C. (1959). Race, ethnicity, and the achievement syndrome. *American Sociological Review, 24,* 47–60.

791

ROSEN, G. (1946). Mesmerism and surgery: A strange chapter in the history of anaesthesia. *Journal of the History of Medicine, 1,* 527–550.

ROSENHAN, D. L. (1973). On being sane in insane places. *Science, 179,* 250–258.

ROSENHAN, D. L., & SELIGMAN, M. (1985). *Abnormal Psychology.* New York: Norton.

ROSENMAN, R. H., & FRIEDMAN, M. (1980). The relationship of Type A behavior pattern to coronary heart disease. In H. Selye (Ed.), *Selye's guide to stress research* (Vol. 1). New York: Van Nostrand Reinhold.

ROSENMAN, R. H., et al. (1975). Coronary heart disease in the Western Collaborative Study: Final follow-up experience of eight and one-half years. *Journal of the American Medical Association, 223,* 872–877.

ROSENSTOCK, I. M. (1966). Why people use health services. *Milbank Memorial Fund Quarterly, 44,* 94–127.

ROSENTHAL, D. (Ed.). (1963). *The Genain quadruplets.* New York: Basic Books.

ROSENTHAL, D., et al. (1970). *Genetic theory and abnormal behavior.* New York: McGraw-Hill.

ROSENTHAL, N. E. (1986, August). *Seasonal affective depression.* Paper delivered at American Psychological Association meeting.

ROSENTHAL, N. E., SACK, D. A., et al. (1984). Seasonal affective disorder: A description of the syndrome and preliminary findings with light therapy. *Archives of General Psychiatry, 41,* 72–80.

ROSENTHAL, R. (1966). *Experimenter effects in behavioral research.* New York: Appleton-Century-Crofts.

ROSENTHAL, R., & ROSNOW, R. (1985). *Contrast analysis: Focused comparisons in the analysis of variance.* New York: Cambridge University Press.

ROSS, A. O. (1987). *Personality: The scientific study of complex human behavior.* New York: Holt, Rinehart & Winston.

ROSS, L. (1969). *Cue- and cognition-controlled eating among obese and normal subjects.* Unpublished doctoral dissertation, Columbia University.

ROSS, L., AMABILE, T. M., & STEINMETZ, J. L. (1977). Social roles, social control, and biases in social-perception process. *Journal of Personality and Social Psychology, 35,* 485–494.

ROSS, L., GREENE, D., & HOUSE, P. (1977). The false consensus phenomenon: An attributional bias in self-perception and social perception processes. *Journal of Experimental Social Psychology, 13,* 279–301.

ROSS, L., & NISBETT, R. (in press). *The person and the situation.*

ROSS, M., & CONWAY, M. (1986). Remembering one's own past: The construction of personal histories. In R. Sorrentino & E. T. Higgins (Eds.), *Handbook of motivation and cognition* (pp. 122–144). New York: Guilford.

ROTHWELL, N. J., & STOCK, M. J. (1979). Regulation of energy balance in two models of reversible obesity in the rat. *Journal of Comparative and Physiological Psychology, 93*(6), 1024–1034.

ROTTER, J. B. (1966). Generalized expectancies of internal versus external control of reinforcement. *Psychological Monographs, 81*(1 Whole No. 609).

ROUTENBERG, A. (1976). The reward system of the brain. *Scientific American, 239,* 154–164.

ROWE, J. W., & KAHN, R. L. (1987). Human aging: Usual and successful. *Science, 237,* 143–149.

RUBIN, D. C. (1977). Very long term memory for prose and verse. *Journal of Verbal Learning and Verbal Behavior, 16,* 611–621.

RUBIN, J. Z., PROVENZANO, F. J., & LURIA, Z. (1974). The eye of the beholder: Parents' view on sex of newborns. *American Journal of Orthopsychiatry, 44,* 512–519.

RUBIN, L. B. (1976). *Worlds of pain.* New York: Basic Books.

RUBIN, Z. (1980). *Children's friendships.* Cambridge: Harvard University Press.

RUMBAUT, R. G., ANDERSON, J. P., & KAPLAN, R. M. (in press). Stress, health and the "sense of coherence." In M. J. Megenheim (Ed.), *Geriatric Medicine and the Social Sciences.* Philadelphia: Saunders.

RUMELHART, D. E., & McCLELLAND, J. L. (1986). *Parallel distributed processing: Explorations in the microstructure of cognition.* Cambridge: MIT Press.

RUNYAN, W. M. (1984). *Life histories and psychobiography: Explorations in theory and method.* New York: Oxford University Press.

RUSSELL, B. (1929). *Marriage and morals.* New York: Liveright.

RUSSELL, B. (1979). In D. Tennov, *Love and limerence* (p. 56). New York: Stein & Day.

RUSSELL, M. A. H., (1976). Tobacco smoking and nicotine dependence. In R. J. Gibbins (Ed.), *Research advances in alcohol and drug problems* (Vol. 3). New York: Wiley.

RUTTER, M., MAUGHAN, B., MORTIMER, P., OUSTON, J., & SMITH, A. (1979). *Fifteen thousand hours.* Cambridge: Harvard University Press.

SACKHEIM, H. A., GUR, R. C., & SAUCY, M. C. (1978). Emotions are expressed more intensely on the left side of the face. *Science, 202,* 434–436.

SACKS, O. (1985). *The man who mistook his wife for a hat.* New York: Simon & Schuster.

SAGAN, L. A. (1988). Family ties: The real reason people are living longer. *The Sciences, 28,* 20–29.

SAGI, A., & HOFFMAN, M. L. (1976). Empathic distress in newborns. *Developmental Psychology, 12,* 175–176.

SAHLINS, M. (1972). *Stone Age economics.* Chicago: Aldine.

SALAPATEK, O., & KESSEN, W. (1966). Visual scanning of triangles by the human newborn. *Journal of Experimental Child Psychology, 3,* 111–122.

SANDERS, M. D., WARRINGTON, E. K., & MARSHALL, J. (1974, April). 'Blind sight': Vision in a field defect. *Lancet,* 707–708.

SAPOLSKY, B. S., STOCKING, S. H., & ZILLMAN, D. (1977). Immediate versus delayed retaliation in male and female adults. *Psychological Reports, 40*(1), 197–198.

SARASON, I. G., & SARASON, B. G. (1984). *Abnormal psychology.* Englewood Cliffs, NJ: Prentice-Hall.

SARBIN, T. R., & COE, W. C. (1972). *Hypnosis: A social psychological analysis of infuence communication.* New York: Holt, Rinehart, & Winston.

SCARR, S. (1984). *Mother care/Other care.* New York: Basic Books.

SCARR, S., PHILLIPS, D., & McCARTNEY, K. (1989). Working mothers and their families, *American Psychologist, 44,* 1402–1409.

SCHACHTER, S. (1951). Deviation, rejection and communication. *Journal of Abnormal and Social Psychology, 46,* 190–207.

SCHAIE, K. W., & WILLIS, S. L. (1986). Can decline in adult intellectual functioning be reversed? *Developmental Psychology, 22,* 223–232.

SCHEIER, M. F., & CARVER, C. S., (1987). Dispositional optimism and physical well-being: The influence of generalized outcome expectancies on health. *Journal of Personality, 55*(2), 169–210.

SCHEIER, M. F., & CARVER, C. S., (1985). Optimism, coping, and health: Assessment and implications of generalized outcome expectancies. *Health Psychology, 4*(3), 219–247.

SCHEIER, M. F., WEINTRAUB, J. K., & CARVER, C. S., (1986). Coping with stress: divergent strategies of optimists and pessimists. *Journal of Personality and Social Psychology, 51*(6), 1257–1264.

SCHLEIFER, S. J. (1989). Bereavement, depression, and immunity: The role of age. In L. L. Carstensen & J. M. Neale (Eds.), *Mechanisms of psychological influence on physical health: With special attention to the elderly.* New York: Plenum.

SCHLEIFER, S. J., KELLER, S. E., CAMERINO, M., THORNTON, J. C. & STEIN, M. (1983). Suppression of lymphocyte stimulation following bereavement. *Journal of the American Medical Association, 250,* 374–377.

SCHMIDT, D. D., ZYZANSKI, S., ELLNER, J., KUMAR, M. L., & ARNO, J. (1985). Stress as a precipitating factor in subjects with recurrent herpes labialis. *Journal of Family Practice, 20,* 359–366.

SCHNEIDER, D. J. (1973). Implicit personality theory: A review. *Psychological Bulletin, 79,* 294–309.

SCHULSINGER, F. (1972). Psychopathy, heredity, and environment. *International Journal of Mental Health, 1,* 190–206.

SCHULZ, R., & BRENNER, G. F. (1977). Relocation of the aged: A review and theoretical analysis. *Journal of Gerontology, 32,* 323–333.

SCHWARTZ, G. E., DAVIDSON, R. J., & MAER, F.

(1975). Right hemispheric lateralization for emotion in the human brain: Interactions with cognition. *Science, 190*, 286–288.

SCHWARTZ, J. L., (1987). *Review and evaluation of smoking cessation methods: The United States and Canada, 1978–1985*. NIH Pub. No. 87-2940. Bethesda, MD: Division of Cancer Prevention and Control, NCI, US Dept. of HHS, PHS, NIH.

SCHWARTZ, S., & GRIFFIN, T. (1986). *Medical thinking: The psychology of medical judgment and decision making.* New York: Springer-Verlag.

SEARLE, J. (1984). *Minds, brains and science* Cambridge: Harvard University Press.

SEARLEMAN, A., PORAC, C., & COREN, S. (1989). Relationship between birth order, birth stress, and lateral preferences: A critical review. *Psychological Bulletin, 105*(3), 397–408

SEEMAN, T. (1985). *Social support and angiography.* Doctoral dissertation, University of California, Berkeley.

SEGAL, M. H., CAMPBELL, D. T., & HERSKOVITS, M. J. (1963). Cultural differences in the perception of geometric illusions. *Science, 139*, 769–771.

SEGAL, N. L. (1989). Origins and implications of handedness and relative birth weight for IQ in monozygotic twin pairs. *Neurologica, 27*(4), 549–561.

SEJNOWSKI, T. J., & ROSENBERG, C. R. (1987). Parallel networks that learn to pronounce English text. *Complex Systems,* 145–168.

SELFE, L. (1977). *Nadia, a case of extraordinary drawing ability in an autistic child.* London: Academic Press.

SELIGMAN, M. E. P. (1970). On the generality of the law of learning. *Psychological Review, 77*, 406–418.

SELIGMAN, M. E. P. (1973). Fall into hopelessness. *Psychology Today, 7*(1), 43–48.

SELIGMAN, M. E. P. (1975). *Helplessness: On depression, development and death.* San Francisco: W. H. Freeman.

SELIGMAN, M. E. P. et al. (1988). Explanatory style change during cognitive therapy for unipolar depression. *Journal of Abnormal Psychology, 97*(1), 13–18

SELIGMAN, M. E. P., & HAGER, J. (1972). *Biological boundaries of learning.* New York: Appleton-Century-Crofts.

SELYE, H. (1956). *The stress of life.* New York: McGraw-Hill.

SELYE, H. (1978). They all looked sick to me. *Human Nature, 1*(2), 58–63.

SHAH, I. (1970). *Tales of the dervishes.* New York: Dutton.

SHAH, I. (1971). *The pleasantries of the incredible Mulla Nasrudin.* New York: Dutton.

SHAH, I. (1982). *Seeker after truth.* San Francisco: Harper & Row.

SHAH, I. (1986). *The exploits and subtleties of Mulla Nasrudin.* London: Octagon Press.

SHANAS, E. (1979). Social myth as hypoth-

esis: The case of the family relations and old people. *Gerontologist, 19*(1), 3-9.

SHANAS, E., TOWNSEND, D., WEDDERBURN, D., FRIIS, H., MILHOJ, P., & STENOUWER, J. (1968). *Older people in three industrial societies.* New York: Atherton Press.

SHANON, B. (1979). Yesterday, today and tomorrow. *Acta Psychologica, 43*, 469–476.

SHAPIRO, D., & GOLDSTEIN, I. B. (1982). Biobehavioral perspectives on hypertension. *Journal of Consulting and Clinical Psychology, 50*(6), 841–858.

SHATAN, C. (1978). The emotional context of combat continues. In C. R. Figley (Ed.), *Stress disorders among Vietnam veterans.* New York: Brunner/Mazel.

SHEDLER, J., & MANIS, M. (1986). Can the availability heuristic explain vividness effects? *Journal of Personality and Social Psychology, 51*, 26–36.

SHELDON, W. (1942). *The varieties of temperament: A psychology of consitutional differences.* New York: Harper.

SHEPARD, R. (1967). Recognition memory for words, sentences, and pictures. *Journal of Verbal Learning and Verbal Behavior, 6*, 156–163.

SHEPARD, R. (1984). Ecological constraints in internal representation. *Psychological Review, 94*(4), 417–447.

SHEPARD, R., & SHEENAN, M. M. (1963). Immediate recall of numbers containing a familiar prefix or postfix. *Perceptual and Motor Skills, 21*, 263–273.

SHERIF, M., HARVEY, O. J., WHITE, B. J., HOOD, W., & SHERIF, C. (1961). *Intergroup conflict and cooperation: The robbers' cave experiment.* Norman: University of Oklahoma Institute of Intergroup Relations.

SHERMAN, J. (1982). Mathematics, the critical filter: A look at some residues. *Psychology of Women Quarterly, 6*, 28–44.

SHERMAN, S. (1973). Visual field deficits in monocularly and binocularly deprived cats. *Brain Research, 49*, 25–45.

SHIMAMURA, A. P., & SQUIRE, L. R. (1986). Memory and metamemory: A study of the feeling-of-knowing phenomenon in amnesic patients. *Journal of Experimental Psychology, 12*(3), 452–460

SHIMAMURA, A. P., & SQUIRE, L. R. (1987). A neuropsychological study of fact memory and source amnesia. *Journal of Experimental Psychology, 13*(3), 464–473

SHIMAMURA, A. P., & SQUIRE, L. R. (1988). Long-term memory in amnesia: Cued recall, recognition memory, and confidence ratings. *Journal of Experimental Psychology, 14*(4), 763–770

SHIRLEY, M. N. (1933). The first two years. *Institute of Child Welfare Monograph, 7.* Minneapolis: University of Minnesota Press.

SHNEIDERMAN, B. (1983). Direct manipulation: A step beyond programming languages. *IEEE Computer, 16*(8), 57–69.

SHORTRIDGE, K. (1984). Poverty is a woman's problem. In J. Freeman (Ed.), *Women: A feminist perspective* (3rd ed.). Palo Alto: Maxfield.

SIEGEL, R. K. (1980). The psychology of life after death. *American Psychologist, 35*, 911–931.

SIEGEL, R. K. (1981). Accounting for "afterlife experiences." *Psychology Today, 15*, 64–75.

SIEGEL, S. (1976). Morphine analgesic tolerance: Its situational specificity supports a Pavlovian conditioning model. *Science, 193*, 323–325.

SILVERMAN, L. H. (1983). The subliminal psychodynamic activation method. In J. Masling (Ed.). *Empirical studies of psychoanalytic theories.* Hillsdale, NJ: Erlbaum

SIMONTON, D. K. (1986). Aesthetic success in classical music: A computer analysis of 1,935 compositions. *Empirical Studies of the Arts, 4*, 1-17.

SIMONTON, D. K. (1989). The swan-song phenomenon: Last works effects for 172 classical composers. *Psychology and Aging, 4*, 42–47.

SIMON, W., BERGER, A. S., & GAGNON, J. S. (1972). Beyond anxiety and fantasy: The coital experiences of college youth. *Journal of Youth and Adolescence, 1*, 203–222.

SINCLAIR-GIEBEN, A. H. C., & CHALMERS, D. (1959). Evaluation of treatment of warts by hypnosis. *Lancet, 11*, 480–482.

SINGER, B., & LUBORSKY, L. (1975). Comparative studies of psychotherapies: Is it true that 'everyone has won and all must have prizes?' *Archives of General Psychiatry, 32*(8), 995–1008.

SINGER, J. L. (1976). *The inner world of daydreaming.* New York: Harper & Row.

SINGER, J. L. (1984). *The human personality.* San Diego: Harcourt Brace Jovanovich.

SINGER, J. L., & SINGER, D. G. (1981). *Television, imagination and aggression.* Hillsdale, NJ: Erlbaum.

SINGER, S., & HILGARD, H. (1978). *The biology of people.* San Francisco: W. H. Freeman.

SKEELS, H. M. (1966). Adult status of children with contrasting early life experience. *Monographs of the Society for Research in Child Development, 31*(3), 1-65.

SKEELS, H. M., & DYE, H. B. (1939). A study of the effects of differential stimulation of mentally retarded children. *Proceedings of the American Association on Mental Deficiency, 44*, 114–136.

SKEELS, J. M., & HAMS, I. (1948). Children with inferior social histories: Their mental development in adoptive homes. *Journal of Genetic Psychology, 72*, 283–294.

SKINNER, B. F. (1938). *The behavior of organisms.* New York: Appleton-Century-Crofts.

SKINNER, B. F. (1957). *Verbal behavior.* New York: Appleton-Century-Crofts.

SKINNER, B. F. (1972). *Cumulative record: A collection of papers* (3rd ed.). New York: Appleton-Century-Crofts.

SKINNER, B. F. (1981). Selection by consequences. *Science, 213,* 501–504.

SKINNER, B. F. (1982). *Notebooks.* (R. Epstein Ed.). Englewood Cliffs, NJ: Prentice-Hall.

SKINNER, B. F. (1986). What is wrong with behavior in the Western world? *American Psychologist, 41*(5), 568–574.

SKOLNICK, A. (1986). *The psychology of human development.* San Diego: Harcourt Brace Jovanovich.

SLATER, E., & COWIE, V. (1971). *The genetics of mental disorders.* London: Oxford University Press.

SLOBIN, D. I. (1970). Universals of grammatical development in children. In G. B. Flores d'Arcais & W. J. M. Levelt (Eds.), *Advances in psycholinguistics.* Amsterdam: North-Holland Publishing.

SMILANSKY, B. (1974). Paper presented at the meeting of the American Educational Research Association, Chicago.

SMITH, M. L., GLASS, G. V., & MILLER, T. I. (1980). *Benefits of psychotherapy.* Baltimore: Johns Hopkins University Press.

SMITH, R. N., DIENER, E. D., & WEDELL, D. H. (1989). Intrapersonal and social comparison determinants of happiness: Range frequency analysis. *Journal of Personality and Social Psychology, 56*(3), 317–325.

SNOW, R. E., & FARR, M. J. (Eds.). (in press) *Aptitude, learning, and instruction: Vol. 3. Conative and affective process analysis.* Hillsdale, NJ: Erlbaum.

SNOWMAN, M. K., & DIBBLE, M. V., (1979). Nutrition components and comprehensive development program. *Journal of the American Dietetic Association, 64*(2), 119–124.

SNYDER, M. (1979). Self-monitoring processes. In L. Berkowitz (Ed.), *Advances in experimental social psychology* (Vol. 12). New York: Academic Press.

SNYDER, M. (1983). The influence of individuals on situations: Implications for understanding the links between personality and social behavior. *Journal of Personality, 51,* 497–516.

SNYDER, M. (1984). When belief creates reality. In L. Berkowitz (Ed.), *Advances in experimental social psychology* (Vol. 18). New York: Academic Press.

SNYDER, M. (1987). *Public appearances/ private realities.* New York: W. H. Freeman.

SNYDER, M., & SWANN, W. (1978). Behavioral confirmation in social interaction: From social perception to social reality. *Journal of Experimental Social Psychiatry 14,* 148–162.

SNYDER, M., TANKE, E. D., & BERSCHEID, E. (1977). Social perception and interpersonal behavior: On the self-fulfilling nature of social stereotypes. *Journal of Personality and Social Psychology, 35,* 656–666.

SNYDER, S. H. (1980a). *Biological aspects of mental disorder.* New York: Oxford University Press.

SNYDER, S. H. (1980b). Brain peptides and neurotransmitters. *Science, 209,* 976–983.

SOLOMON, G. F., & AMKRAUT, A. A. (1981). Psychoneuroendocrinological effects on the immune response. *Annual Review of Microbiology, 35,* 155–184.

SOLOMON, G. F., TEMOSHOK, L., O'LEARY, A., & ZICH, J., (1987). An intensive psychoimmunologic study of long-surviving persons with AIDS. *Annals of the New York Academy of Science, 496,* 647–655.

SOLOMON, M. R., & SCHOPLER, J. (1978). The relationship of physical attractiveness and punitiveness: Is the linearity assumption out of line? *Personality and Social Psychology Bulletin, 4,* 483–486.

SOLOMON, R. L. (1980). The opponent-process theory of acquired motivation: The costs of pleasure and the benefits of pain. *American Psychologist, 35,* 691–712.

SOLOMON, R. L., & CORBIT, J. D. (1973). An opponent-process theory of motivation: Pt 1. Cigarette addiction. *Journal of Abnormal Psychology, 81,* 158–171.

SOLOMON, R. L., & CORBIT, J. D. (1974). An opponent-process theory of motivation: Pt. 2. Temporal dynamics of affect. *Psychological Review, 81,* 119–145.

SOLOMON, S., & SAXE, L. (1977). What is intelligent, as well as attractive, is good. *Personality and Social Psychology Bulletin, 3,* 670–673.

SPANIER, G. B., & GLICK, P. C. (1981). Marital instability in the U.S.: Some correlates and recent changes. *Family Relations, 31,* 329–338.

SPEARMAN, C. (1927). *The abilities of man.* New York: Macmillian.

SPEISMAN, J. C., LAZARUS, R. S., DAVIDSON, L., & MORDKOFF, A. M. (1964). Experimental analysis of a film used as a threatening stimulus. *Journal of Consulting Psychology, 28*(1), 23–33.

SPELKE, E. S. (in press). Principles of object perception. *Cognitive Science.*

SPENCE, D. P., (1982). Narrative truth and theoretical truth. *Psychoanalytical Quarterly, 51*(1), 43–69.

SPENCE, D. P. (1983). The paradox of denial. In Bresnitz, S. (Ed.). *The Denial of Stress.* New York: International Universities Press.

SPERRY, R. W. (1952). Neurology and the mind-brain problem. *American Scientist, 40,* 291–312.

SPERRY, R. W. (1982). Some effects of disconnecting the cerebral hemispheres. *Science, 217,* 1223–1226, 1250.

SPITZER, R. L., SKODOL, A. E., GIBBON, M., & WILLIAMS, J. B. (1980). *Diagnostic and statistical manual of mental disorders* (3rd ed.). Washington, DC: American Psychiatric Association.

SPITZER, R. L., SKODOL, A. E., GIBBON, M., & WILLIAMS, J. B. (1981). *DSM-III Casebook* (3rd ed.). Washington, DC: American Psychiatric Association.

SPRECHER, S., & HATFIELD, E. (1985). Interpersonal attraction. In G. Stricker & R. H. Keisner (Eds.), *From research to clinical practice.* New York: Plenum.

SPRINGER, S., & DEUTSCH, G. (1984). *Left brain, right brain* (2nd ed.). San Francisco: W. H. Freeman.

SQUIRE, L. R. (1986). Mechanisms of memory. *Science, 27,* 1612–1619.

SQUIRE, L. R. (1987). *Memory and the brain.* New York: Oxford.

SQUIRE, L. R. (1989). On the course of forgetting in very long-term memory. *Journal of Experimental Psychology, 15*(2), 241–245.

SQUIRE, L. R., AMARAL, D. G., ZOLA-MORGAN, S., KRITCHEVSKY, M., & PRESS, G. (1989). Description of brain injury in the amnesic patient N. A. based on magnetic resonance imaging. *Experiments in Neurology, 105*(1), 23–35.

SQUIRE, L. R., & COHEN, N. J. (1984). Human memory and amnesia. In G. Lynch et al. (Eds.). *Neurobiology of learning and memory.* New York: Guilford Press.

SQUIRE, L. R., ZOLA-MORGAN, S., & CHEN, K. S., (1988). Human amnesia and animal models of amnesia: Performance of amnesic patients on tests designed for the monkey. *Behavioral Neuroscience, 102*(2), 210–221.

SQUIRE, L. R., & ZOUZOUNIS, J. A., (1988). Self-ratings of memory dysfunction: Different findings in depression and amnesia. *Journal of Clinical and Experimental Neuropsychology, 10*(6), 727–738.

STAMPFL, T. G., & LEVIS, D. J. (1967). Essential of implosive therapy: A learning theory-based psychodynamic behavioral therapy. *Journal of Abnormal Psychology, 72,* 157–163.

STAUDENMAYER, H., KINSMAN, R. A., DIRKS, J. F., SPECTOR, S. L., & WANGAARD, C. (1979). Medical outcome in asthmatic patients: Effects of airways hyperreactivity and symptom-focused anxiety. *Psychosomatic Medicine, 41,* 109–118.

STEFFENS, A. B., MOGENSON, G. J., & STEVENSON, J. A. F. (1972). Blood glucose, insulin, and free fatty acids after stimulation and lesions of the hypothalamus. *American Journal of Physiology, 222,* 1446–1452.

STEFFENSMEIER, D. J., & TERRY, R. M. (1973). Deviance and respectability: An observational study of reactions to shoplifting. *Social Forces, 51,* 417–426.

STEIGLEDER, M. K., WEISS, R. F., BALLING, S. S., WENNINGER, V. L., & LOMBARDO, J. P. (1980). Drivelike motivational properties of competitive behavior. *Journal of Personality and Social Psychology, 38,* 93–104.

STEIL, J. M. (1984). Marital relationships and mental health: The psychic costs of inequality. In J. Freeman (Ed.), *Women: A feminist perspective* (3rd ed., pp. 113–123). Palo Alto: Mayfield.

STEIN, M., SCHLEIFLER, S. J., & KELLER, S. E. (1981). Hypothalamic influences on immune responses. In R. Ader (Ed.), *Psychoneuroimmunology.* New York: Academic Press.

STEPHAN, W. G. (1973). Parental relationships and early social experiences of activist male homosexuals and male heterosexuals. *Journal of Abnormal Psychology, 82,* 506–513.

STEPHENSON, W. (1953). *The study of behavior: Q-Technique and its methodology.* Chicago: University of Chicago Press.

STERMAN, M. B. (1978). Effects of sensorimotor EEG feedback training on sleep and clinical manifestations of epilepsy. In J. Beatty & H. Legewie (Eds.), *Biofeedback and behavior.* New York: Plenum.

STERNBACH, R. A. (1966). *Principles of psychophysiology.* New York: Academic Press.

STERNBERG, R. J. (1985). *Beyond IQ: A triarchic theory of human intelligence.* New York: Cambridge University Press.

STERNBERG, R. J. (1986). *Intelligence applied: Understanding and increasing your intellectual skills.* San Diego: Harcourt Brace Jovanovich.

STERNBERG, R. J. (1989). *The triarchic mind: A new theory of human intelligence.* New York: Penguin.

STEVENSON, J., GRAHAM, P., FREDMAN, G., & MCLOUGHLIN, V. A. (1987). Twin study of genetic influences on reading and spelling ability and disability. *Journal of Child Psychiatry, 28*(2), 229–247.

STEVENS, S. S. (1935). The relation of pitch to intensity. *Journal of the Acoustical Society of America, 6,* 150–154.

STEVENS, S. S. (1956). The direct estimation of sensory magnitudes-loudness. *American Journal of Psychology, 69,* 1–25.

STEVENS, S. S. (1957). On the psychophysical law. *Psychological Review, 64,* 153–181.

STEVENS, S. S. (1961). The psychophysics of sensory functions. In W. A. Rosenblith (Ed.), *Sensory communication.* Cambridge: MIT Press.

STEVENS, S. S., & WARSHOFSKY, F., (1965). *Sound and hearing.* New York: Time-Life Books.

STILES, W. B., SHAPIRO, D. A., & ELLIOTT, R. (1986). Are all psychotherapies equivalent? *American Psychologist, 41*(2), 165–180.

STOKOLS, D. (1972). On the distinction between density and crowding: Some implications for future research. *Psychological Review, 79,* 275–277.

STONE, A. A., COX, D. S., VALDIMARSDOTTIR, H., JANDORF, L. & NEALE, J. M. (1987). Evidence that secretory IgA antibody is associated with daily mood. *Journal of Personality and Social Psychology, 52*(5), 988–993.

STONE, A. A., COX, D. S., VALDIMARSDOTTIR, H., & NEALE, J. M. (1987). Secretory IgA as a measure of immunocompetence. *Journal of Human Stress, 13*(3), 136–140.

STORMS, M. S. (1981). A theory of erotic orientation development. *Psychological Review, 88,* 340–353.

STRATTON, G. M. (1896). Some preliminary experiments on vision without inversion of the retinal image. *Psychological Review, 3,* 611–617.

STRATTON, G. M. (1897). Vision without inversion of the retinal image. *Psychological Review, 4,* 341–360, 463–481.

STRUBLE, J. H., & STEFFENS, A. B. (1975). Rapid insulin release after ingestion of a meal in the unanesthetized rat. *American Journal of Physiology, 229,* 1019–1022.

STUNKARD, A. J. (1979). Behavioral medicine and beyond: The example of obesity. In O. F. Pomerleau & J. P. Brady (Eds.), *Behavioral medicine: Theory and practice.* Baltimore: Williams & Wilkins.

SUEDFIELD, P. (1980). Restricted environmental stimulation: Research and clinical applications. New York: Wiley.

SUNDSTROM, E. (with M. G. SUNDSTROM) (1986). *Work places.* New York: Cambridge University Press.

SUPPES, P., & MORNINGSTAR, M. (1969). Computer-assisted instruction. *Science, 166,* 343–350.

SURMAN, O. S., GOTTLIEB, S. K., HACKETT, T. P., & SILVERBERG, E. L. (1973). Hypnosis in the treatment of warts. *Archives of General Psychiatry, 28,* 439–441.

SWEENEY, P. D., ANDERSON, K., & BAILEY, S. (1986). Attributional style in depression: A meta-analytic review. *Journal of Personality and Social Psychology, 50,* 974–991.

SWENCIONIS, C. (1987). Unpublished research videotapes. BECHS 1303, Albert Einstein College of Medicine; Bronx, NY.

SWENCIONIS, C. (1990). Type A Behavior and the Brain. In R. Ornstein, & C. Swencionis (Eds.), *Scientific Papers on the Healing Brain.* New York: Guilford Press.

SYLVIA, W. H., CLARK, P. M., & MONROE, L. J. (1978). Dream reports in subjects high and low in creative ability. *Journal of General Physiology, 99,* 205–211.

SYME, S. L. (1984). Sociocultural factors and disease etiology. In W. Doyle Gentry (Ed.), *Handbook of Behavioral Medicine.* New York: Guilford Press.

SYMONS, D. (1980). Precis of the evolution of human sexuality. *Behavioral and Brain Sciences, 3,* 171–214.

SYMONS, D. (1989). A critique of Darwinian anthropology. *Ethology ond Sociobiology, 10,* 131–144.

SZASZ, T. (1961). *The myth of mental illness.* New York: Harper & Row.

TAKAHASHI, K. (1986). Examining the strange-situation procedure with Japanese mothers and 12-month-old infants. *Developmental Psychology, 22,* 256–270.

TALBERT, G. B. (1977). The aging of the reproductive system. In C. Finch & L. Hayflick (Eds.), *Handbook of the biology of aging.* New York: Van Nostrand Reinhold.

TANNER, J. M. (1955). *Growth at adolescence.* Springfield, IL: Thomas.

TANNER, J. M. (1962). *Growth at adolescence* (2nd ed.). Oxford: Blackwell Scientific.

TARG, R., & PUTHOFF, H. (1977). *Mind reach: Scientists look at psychic ability.* New York: Delacorte Press.

TART, C., PUTHOFF, H. E., & TARG, R. (Eds.). (1979). *Mind at large.* Institute of Electrical and Electronics Engineers Symposia on the Nature of Extra-sensory Perception. New York: Praeger.

TART, C. T. (1971). *On being stoned.* Palo Alto: Science and Behavior Books.

TASKIN, D. P., CALVERESE, B. M., SIMMONS, M. S., & SHAPIRO, B. J. (1978). *Respiratory status of 74 habitual marijuana smokers.* Presented at the annual meeting of the American Thoracic Society, Boston.

TAVRIS, C. (1982). Anger defused. *Psychology Today, 16,* 25–35.

TAYLOR, R. (1989). *Mind or body.* New York: McGraw-Hill.

TAYLOR, R. P. (Ed.). (1980). *The computer in the school: Tutor, tool, tutee.* New York: Teachers College Press.

TAYLOR, S. (1970). Aggressive behavior as a function of approval motivation and physical attack. *Psychonomic Science, 18,* 195–196.

TAYLOR, S. (1989) *Positive Illusions.* New York: Basic Books.

TAYLOR, S. E., & THOMPSON, S. C. (1982). Stalking the elusive "vividness" effect. *Psychological Review, 89,* 155–181.

TAYLOR, S. P., GAMMON, C. B., & CAPASSO, D. R. (1976). Aggression as a function of the interaction of alcohol and threat. *Journal of Personality and Social Psychology, 34*(5), 938–941.

TAYLOR, S. P., VARDARIS, R. M., RAWITCH, A. B., GAMMON, C. B., CRANSTON, J. W. , & LUBETKIN, A. I. (1976). The effects of alcohol and delta-9-tetra hydrocannabinal on human physical aggression. *Aggressive Behavior, 2,* 153–161.

TEITELBAUM, P. (1957). Random and food-directed activity in hyperphagic and normal rats. *Journal of Comparative and Physiological Psychology, 50,* 486–490.

TELLEGEN, A., LYKKEN, D. T., et al. (1988). Personality similarity in twins reared apart and together. *Journal of Personality and Social Psychology, 54*(6),1031–1039

TEMOSHOK, L. (1987). Personality, coping style, emotion and cancer: Towards an integrative model. *Cancer Survival, 6*(3), 545–567.

TEMOSHOK, L. (1988). Psychoimmunology and AIDS. *Advances in Biochemical Psychopharmacology, 44,*187–97.

TENNOV, D. (1979). *Love and limerence.* New York: Stein & Day.

TERMAN, L. M., BUTTENWEISER, P., FERGUSON, L. W., JOHNSON, W. B., & WILSON, D. P. (1938). *Psychological factors in marital happiness.* New York: McGraw-Hill.

TESSER, A., & CAMPBELL, J. (1983). Self-definition and self-evaluation maintenance. In J. Suls & A. G. Greenwald (Eds.), *Psychological perspectives on the self* (Vol. 2). Hillsdale, NJ: Erlbaum.

TEYLER, T. (1978). *A primer of psychobiology.* San Francisco: W. H. Freeman.

THELEN, E., KELSO, J. A., FOGEL, A. (1987). Self-organizing systems and infant motor development. *Developmental review, 7,* 39–65.

THOMAS, L. (1982). *The youngest science.* New York: Viking Press.

THOMAS, S. A., et al. (1984). Blood pressure and heart rate changes in children when they read aloud in school. *Public Health Reports, 99*(1), 77–84.

THOMPSON, R. A., LAMB, M. E., & ESTES, D. (1982). Stability of infant-mother attachment and its relationship to changing life circumstances in an unselected middle-class sample. *Child Development, 53,* 144–148.

THOMPSON, R. F. (1967). *Foundations of physiological psychology.* New York: Harper & Row.

THOMPSON, R. F. (1975). *Introduction to physiological psychology.* New York: Harper & Row.

THOMPSON, R. F. (1986). *The brain.* New York: W. H. Freeman.

THORNDIKE, E. L. (1911). *Animal intelligence.* New York: Macmillan.

THORNDIKE, R. L. (1954). The psychological value systems of psychologists. *American Psychologist, 9,* 787–789.

THURSTONE, L. L. (1938). Primary mental abilities. *Psychometrika Monographs, 1.*

TINBERGEN, N. (1951). *The study of instinct.* Oxford: Clarendon.

TJOSVOLD, D. (1986). *Working together to get things done: Managing for organization productivity.* Lexington, MA: Heath, Lexington Books.

TOATES, F. (1986). *Motivational behavior.* New York: Cambridge University Press.

TOCH, H. (1969). *Violent men.* Chicago: Aldine.

TOLMAN, E. C., & HONZIK, C. H. (1930). 'Insight' in rats. *University of California Publications in Psychology, 4,* 215–232.

TOMKINS, S. S. (1962). *Affect, imagery, consciousness: Vol. 1. The positive affects.* New York: Springer-Verlag.

TOMKINS, S. S. (1963). *Affect, imagery, consciousness: Vol. 2. The negative affects.* New York: Springer-Verlag.

TOMKINS, S. S. (1979). Script theory: Differential magnification of affects. In H. E. Howe & R. A. Dienstbier (Eds.), *Nebraska Symposium on Motivation, 1978, 26.* Lincoln: University of Nebraska Press.

TOMKINS, S. S. (1984). Affect theory. In K. Scherer & P. Ekman (Eds.), *Approaches to emotion.* Hillsdale: Erlbaum.

TOOBY, J., & COSMIDES, L., (1989). The innate versus the manifest: How universal does the universal have to be? *Behavioral and Brain Sciences, 12,* 36–37.

TORGERSEN, S. (1983). Genetic factors in anxiety disorders. *Archives of General Psychiatry, 40,* 1085–1089.

TREISMAN, A. (1986). Features and objects in visual processing. *Scientific American, 255,* 114–125.

TREVARTHEN, W. R. (1981). Maternal touch at first contact with the newborn infant. *Developmental Psychology, 14*(6), 549–558.

TRIPLETT, N. (1897). The dynamogenic factors in pace making and competition. *American Journal of Psychology, 9,* 507–533.

TRIVERS, R. L. (1978). The evolution of reciprocal altruism. *Quarterly Review of Biology, 46,* 35–57.

TROLIER, T. K., & HAMILTON, D. L. (1986). Variables influencing judgments of correlational relations. *Journal of Personality and Social Psychology, 50,* 879–888.

TROLL, L. (1971). The family of later life: A decade review. *Journal of Marriage and the Family, 44,* 263–290.

TULVING, E. (1972). Episodic and semantic memory. In E. Tulving & W. Donaldson (Eds.), *Organization and memory.* New York: Academic Press.

TULVING, E. (1984). Precis of elements of episodic memory. *The Behavioral and Brain Sciences, 7,* 223–228.

TURNBULL, C. (1961). Some observations regarding the experiences and behavior of the Bambuti pygmies. *American Journal of Psychology, 74,* 304–308.

TURNER, J. S., & HELMS, D. B. (1987). *Lifespan development* (3rd ed.). New York: Holt, Rinehart & Winston.

TURNER, P. (1986, May). The shrinking of George. *Science,* 23–37.

TURSKY, B., & STERNBACH, R. A. (1967) Further physiological correlates of ethnic differences in responses to shock. *Psychophysiology, 4,* 67–74.

TURVEY, M. T., & SHAW, R. (1979). The primacy of perceiving. In G. Nillson (Ed.), *Perspectives on memory research essays in honor of Uppsala University's 500th anniversary.* Hillsdale, NJ: Erlbaum.

TVERSKY, A. (1977). Features of similarity. *Psychological Review, 84,* 327–352.

TVERSKY, A. (1990). *Endowment and contrast in happiness.* Unpublished manuscript, Stanford University.

TVERSKY, A., & GATI, I. (1978). Studies of similarity. In E. Rosch & B. B. Lloyd (Eds.), *Cognition and categorization.* Hillsdale, NJ: Erlbaum.

TVERSKY, A., & KAHNEMAN, D. (1973). Availability: A heuristic for judging frequency and possibility. *Cognitive Psychology, 5,* 207–232.

TVERSKY, A., & KAHNEMAN, D. (1981). The framing of decisions and the psychology of choice. *Science, 211,* 453–458.

UHLARIK, J., & JOHNSON, R. (1978). Development of form perception in repeated brief exposures to visual stimuli. In R. Walk & L. Pick, Jr. (Eds.), *Perception and Experience.* New York: Plenum.

ULLMAN, L., & KRASNER, L. (1965). *Case studies in behavior modification* New York: Holt, Reinhart & Winston.

ULLMAN, M., KRIPPNER, S., & VAUGHN, A. (1973). *Dream telepathy.* New York: Macmillan.

ULLMAN, S. (1980). Against direct perception. *Behavioral and Brain Sciences, 3,* 373–381.

ULLRICH, R. S. (1984). View through a window may influence recovery from surgery. *Science, 224,* 420–421.

UNGERLEIDER, L. G., & MISHKIN, M. (1982). Two cortical visual systems. In D. J. Ingle, M. A. Goodale, & R. J. W. Mansfield (Eds.), *Analysis of visual behavior.* Cambridge: MIT Press.

U.S. DEPARTMENT OF COMMERCE, BUREAU OF THE CENSUS. (1982). *Statistical Abstract of the United States: 1982–1983* (103rd ed.). Washington, DC: U.S. Government Printing Office.

U.S. DEPARTMENT OF HEALTH, EDUCATION, & WELFARE. (1971). *Marihuana and health.* Washington DC: U.S. Government Printing Office.

U.S. SENATE SPECIAL COMMITTEE ON AGING. (1970). *Developments in aging.* Washington, DC: U.S. Government Printing Office.

U.S. SENATE SPECIAL COMMITTEE ON AGING. (1985). *America in transition: An aging society.* Washington, DC: U.S. Government Printing Office.

VALINS, S. (1966). Cognitive effects of false heart-rate feedback. *Journal of Personality and Social Psychology, 4,* 400–408.

VALLIANT, G. (1977). *Adaptation to life.* Boston: Little, Brown.

VALLIANT, G., & MILOFSKY, E. (1978). Natural history of male psychological health: Pt. 9. Empirical evidence for Erikson's model of the life cycle. *American Journal of Psychiatry, 137* (11).

VAN ESSEN, D. C. (1984). Functional organization of primate visual cortex. In A. Peters & E. G. Jones (Eds.), *Cerebral Cortex* (Vol. 3). New York: Plenum.

VANDELL, D., WILSON, K., & BUCHANAN, N. (1980). Peer interaction in the first year of life: An examination of its structure, content, and sensitivity to toys. *Child Development, 41,* 481–488.

VANDENBOS, G., A. (1986). Psychotherapy research: A special issue. *American Psychologist 41*(2), 111–112.

VAUGHN, B. E., GOVE, F. L., & EGELAND, B. (1980). The relationship between out-of-home care and the quality of infant-mother attachment in an economically disadvantaged population. *Child Development, 51,* 1203–1214.

VIERLING, J. S., & ROCK, J. (1967). Variations in olfactory sensitivity to Exaltolide during the menstrual cycle. *Journal of Applied Physiology, 22,* 311–315.

VOGEL, G. W. (1978). An alternative view of the biology of dreaming. *American Journal of Psychiatry, 135*(12), 1531–1535.

VON BEKESY, G. (1949). *Experiments in hearing.* New York: McGraw-Hill.

VYGOTSKY, L. (1978). *Mind in society.* Cambridge: Harvard University Press.

WADDEN, T. A., & ANDERSON, C. H. (1982). The clinical use of hypnosis. *Psychological Bulletin, 91,* 215–243.

WADDINGTON, C. H. (1957). *The strategy of the genes.* New York: Macmillan.

WALLERSTEIN, J. S., & KELLY, J. B. (1980). *Surviving the breakup: How children and parents cope with divorce.* New York: Basic Books.

WALSTER, E., ARONSON, V., ABRAHAMS, D., &

ROTTMANN, L. (1966). The importance of physical attractiveness in dating behavior. *Journal of Personality and Social Psychology, 4*, 508–516.

WALSTER, E., & WALSTER, G. W. (1978). *A new look at love.* Reading, MA: Addison-Wesley.

WALSTER, E., WALSTER, G. W., & TRAUPMANN, J. (1978). Equity and premarital sex. *Journal of Personality and Social Psychology, 37*, 82–92.

WARD, R. A. (1977). The impact of subjective age and stigma on older persons. *Journal of Gerontology, 32*, 227–232.

WARD, W. C., & JENKINS, H. M. (1965). The display of information and the judgment of contingency. *Canadian Journal of Psychology, 19*, 231–241.

WARREN, R. M., & WARREN, R. P. (1972). Auditory illusions and confusions. *Scientific American, 223*, 30–36.

WASHBURN, S. (1960). Tools and human evolution. *Scientific American, 203*(3), 67–73.

WATSON, J. B. (1914). *Behavior: An introduction to comparative psychology.* New York: Henry Holt.

WATSON, J. B. (1925). *Behaviorism.* New York: W. W. Norton.

WATSON, J. B., & RAYNOR, R. (1920). Conditioned emotional reactions. *Journal of Experimental Psychology, 3*, 1–14.

WEARY, G., JORDAN, J. S., & HILL, M. G. (1985). The attributional norm of internality and depressive sensitivity to social information. *Journal of Personality and Social Psychology, 49*, 1283–1293.

WEBER, E. H. (1834). *De pulsu, resorptione, auditu et tactu: Annotationes anatomical et physiological.* Leipzig: Koehler.

WEINBERGER, A. (1979). Stereotyping of the elderly: Elementary school children's responses. *Research on aging, 1*, 113–136.

WEINBERGER, L. E., & MILLHAM, J. (1975). A multi-dimensional, multiple method analysis of attitudes toward the elderly. *Journal of Gerontology, 30*, 343–348.

WEINER, H. (1977). *Psychobiology and human disease.* New York: Elsevier.

WEISKRANTZ, L., WARRINGTON, E. K., SANDERS, M. D., & MARSHALL, J. (1974). Visual capacity in the hemianopic field following a restricted occipital ablation. *Brain, 97*, 709–728.

WEISS, J. M. (1968). Effects of coping response on stress. *Journal of Comparative and Physiological Psychology, 65*, 251–260.

WEISS, J. M. (1971a). Effects of coping behavior in different warning signal conditions on stress pathology in rats. *Journal of Comparative and Physiological Psychology, 77*, 1, 13.

WEISS, J. M. (1971b). Effects of coping behavior with and without feedback signal on stress pathology in rats. *Journal of Comparative and Physiological Psychology, 77*, 22–30.

WEISSMAN, M. M., & KIERMAN, G. L. (1971). Sex differences in the epidemiology of depression. *Archives of General Psychiatry, 34*, 98–111.

WENEGRAT, B. (1984). *Sociobiology and mental disorder: A new view.* Menlo Park: Addison-Wesley.

WERNER, E. E., & SMITH, R. S. (1982). *Vulnerable, but Invincible: A Study of Resilient Children.* New York: McGraw-Hill.

WEST, S. G., & GRAZIANO, W. G. (1989). Long-term stability and change in personality: An introduction. *Journal of Personality, 57*(2), 175–193.

WESTHEIMER, G. (1979). Spatial sense of the eye. *Investigative Opthamology and Visual Science, 18*, 893–912.

WHITBOURNE, S. K. (1986). *The me I know: A study of adult identity.* New York: Springer-Verlag.

WHITBOURNE, S. K., & WEINSTOCK, C. S. (1979). *Adult development: The differentiation of experience.* New York: Holt, Rinehart & Winston.

WHITE, L., TURSKY, B., & SCHWARTZ, G. (1985). *Placebo.* New York: Guilford Press.

WHORF, B. (1942). *Language, thought, and reality: Selected writings of Benjamin Lee Whorf.* (J. B. Carroll, Ed.). New York: Wiley.

WHORF, B. L. (1956). Science and linguistics. In J. B. Carroll (Ed.), *Language, thought and reality: Selected writings of Benjamin Lee Whorf* (pp. 207–219). Cambridge: MIT Press.

WHYTE, W. H. (1956). *The organization man.* New York: Simon & Shuster.

WICKELGREN, W. (1979). *Cognitive psychology.* Englewood Cliffs, NJ: Prentice-Hall.

WICKELGREN, W. A. (1977). *Learning and memory.* Englewood Cliffs, NJ: Prentice-Hall.

WILDER, D. A., & ALLEN, V. L. (1973). *Veridical dissent, erroneous dissent, and conformity.* Unpublished master's thesis.

WILLEMSEN, E. (1979). *Understanding infancy.* San Francisco: W. H. Freeman.

WILLERMAN, L. (1979). *The psychology of individual and group differences.* San Francisco: W. H. Freeman.

WILLIAMS, R. B., JR. (1983). Hostility and hormones: New clues to why Type A's have more heart disease. Paper presented to American Heart Association's 10th Science Writers Forum, Tucson, AZ.

WILLIAMS, R. B., JR. (1989). *The trusting heart.* New York: Times Books.

WILLIS, S. L., & SCHAIE, W. (1986). Training the elderly on the ability factors of spatial orientation and inductive reasoning. *Psychology and Aging, 1*, 239–247.

WILL, J. A., SELF, P. A., & DATAN, N. (1976). Maternal behavior and perceived sex of infant. *Journal of Orthopsychiatry, 46*, 135–139.

WILLS, T. A. (1985). Supportive functions of interpersonal relationships. In S. Cohen & S. L. Syme (Eds.), *Social support and health.* Orlando: Academic Press.

WILSON, C. P. (1979). *Jokes: Form, content, use and function.* London: Academic Press.

WILSON, E. O. (1975). *Sociobiology.* Cambridge: Harvard University Press.

WILSON, H. R. (1986). Responses of spatial mechanisms can explain hyperacuity. *Vision Research, 26*, 453–469.

WILSON, J., & HERRNSTEIN, R. (1985). *Crime and human nature.* New York: Simon & Schuster.

WILSON, M. (1989). Marital conflict and homicide in evolutionary perspective. In R. W. Bell & N. J. Bell (Eds.). *Sociobiology and the social sciences.* Lubbock: Texas Tech University Press.

WINNICK, M. (1979). Starvation studies. *Human Nature Manuscript Series, 4.*

WINOGRAD, T. (1980, February). Face savings memory. *Psychology Today*, p. 81.

WINOKUR, G. (1981). *Depression: The facts.* New York: Oxford University Press.

WINOKUR, G., CLAYTON, P. J., & REICH, T. (1969). *Manic-depressive illness.* St. Louis: Mosby.

WINSTON, P. H. (1984). *Artificial Intelligence* (2nd ed.). Reading, MA: Addison-Wesley.

WINSTON, P. H., & BROWN, R. H. (1979). *Artificial Intelligence: A MIT perspective.* Cambridge: MIT Press.

WINSTON, P. H., & PRENDERGAST, K. A. (Eds.). (1984). *The AI Business: Commercial uses of artificial intelligence.* Cambridge: MIT Press.

WISDOM, C. S. (1977). A methodology for studying noninstitutionalized psychopaths. *Journal of Consulting and Clinical Psychology, 45*, 674–683.

WISHNER, J. (1960). Reanalysis of "Impressions of personality." *Psychological Review, 67*, 96–112.

WITELSON, S. F. (1976). Sex and the single hemisphere: Specialization of the right hemisphere for spatial processing. *Science, 193*, 425–427.

WOLFE, J. B. (1936). Effectiveness of token-rewards for chimpanzees. *Comparative Psychology Monograph, 12*, 5.

WOLMAN, B. (Ed.). (1982). *Handbook of developmental psychology.* Englewood Cliffs, NJ: Prentice-Hall.

WOLMAN, B. B., & ULLMAN, M. (Eds.). (1986). *Handbook of States of Consciousness.* New York: Van Nostrand Reinhold.

WOLPE, J. (1958). *Psychotherapy by reciprocal inhibition.* Stanford: Stanford University Press.

WOLPE, J. (1981). The experimental model and treatment of neurotic depression. *Behavior Research and Therapy, 17*(6), 555–565.

WOOD, R. E., & BANDURA, A. (1989). Impact of conceptions of ability on self-regulatory mechanisms and complex decision-making. *Journal of Personality and Social Psychology, 56*, 407–415.

WORCHEL, S., COOPER, J., & GOETHALS, G. R. (1987). *Understanding social psychology* (4th ed.). Chicago: Dorsey Press.

WORCHEL, S., LEE, J., & ADEWOLE, A. (1975). Effects of supply and demand on ratings of object value. *Journal of Personality and Social Psychology, 32*, 906–914.

WORKING GROUP ON SPEECH UNDERSTANDING AND AGING. (1988). *Speech understanding and aging. Journal of the Acoustical Society, 83,* 859–895.

WRIGHT, J. C., & VLEITSTRA, A. G. (1975). The development of selective attention: From perceptual exploration to logical search. In H. W. Reese (Ed.), *Advances in child development and behavior* (Vol. 10). New York: Academic Press.

WURTMAN, R., & WURTMAN, J. (1984). *Nutrition and the brain* (Vol. 7). New York: Raven.

WYNDER, E. L., HERTZBERG, S., & PARKER, E. (1981). *The book of health.* New York: Franklin Watts.

WYNN, E., CROMWELL, R. L., & MATTYSSE, S. (Eds). (1978). *The nature of schizophrenia: New approaches to research and treatment.* New York: Wiley.

YALOM, I. D. (1989). *Love's executioner and other tales of psychotherapy.* New York: Basic Books.

YAMAMOTO, J., OKONOGI, K., IWASAKI, T., & YOSHIMURA, S. (1969). Mourning in Japan. *American Journal of Psychiatry, 125*(12), 1660–1665.

YARROW, L. J., RUBENSTEIN, J. L., PEDERSEN, F. A., & JANKOWSKI, J. J. (1972). Dimensions of early stimulation and their differential effects on infant development. *Merrill-Palmer Quarterly, 18,* 205–218.

YATES, S., & ARONSON, E. (1983). A social-psychological perspective on energy conservation in residential buildings. *American Psychologist, 38,* 435–444.

YESAVAGE, J. A., ROSE, T. L., & SPIEGEL, D. (1982). Relaxation training and memory improve ment in elderly normals: Correlation of anxiety ratings and recall improvement. *Experimental Aging Research, 8,* 195–198.

ZAHN-WAXLER, C., et al. (Eds.). (1986). *Altruism and Aggression: Social and biological origins.* New York: Cambridge University Press.

ZAJONC, R. B. (1965). Social facilitation. *Science, 149,* 269–274.

ZAJONC, R. B. (1980). Feeling and thinking: Preferences need no interferences. *American Psychologist, 35*(2), 151–175.

ZAJONC, R. B. (1986). The decline and rise of Scholastic Aptitude scores. *American Psychologist, 41*(8), 862–867.

ZAJONC, R. B., MARKUS, H., & MARKUS, G. P. (1979). The birth order puzzle. *Journal of Personality and Social Psychology, 37,* 1325–1341.

ZANNA, M. P., & REMPLE, J. K. (1988). Attitudes: A new look at an old concept. In D. Bar-Tal & A. Kruglanski (Eds.), *The social psychology of knowledge.* New York: Cambridge University Press.

ZEGANS, L., & /TEMOSHOK, L. (Eds). (1985). *Emotions and Health.* San Diego: Grune & Stratton.

ZIHL, J., (1980). 'Blindsight': Improvement of visually guided eye movement by systematic practice in patients with cerebral blindness. *Neuropsychologica, 18,* 71–77.

ZILLMAN, D., JOHNSON, R. C., & DAY, K. D. (1974). Attribution of apparent arousal and proficiency of recovery from sympathetic activation affecting activation transfer to aggressive behavior. *Journal Experimental Social Psychology, 10,* 349–371.

ZIMBARDO, P. G. (1970). The human choice: Individuation, reason, and order versus deindividuation, impulse, and chaos. In W. J. Arnold & D. Levine (Eds.), *Nebraska Symposium on Motivation.* Lincoln: University of Nebraska Press.

ZIMBARDO, P. G. (1972). The tactics and ethics of persuasion. In B. T. King & E. McGinnis (Eds.), *Attitudes, conflict and social change.* New York: Academic Press.

ZIMBARDO, P. G. (1973a). A field experiment in auto-shaping. In C. Ward (Ed.), *Vandalism.* London: Architectural Press.

ZIMBARDO, P. G. (1973b). The psychological power and pathology of imprisonment. *Catalog of Selected Documents in Psychology, 30,* 45.

ZIMBARDO, P. G., ANDERSEN, S. M., & KABAT, L. G. (1981). Induced hearing deficit generates experimental paranoia. *Science, 212*(4502), 1529–1531.

ZIMBARDO, P. G., HANEY, C., BANKS, C., & JAFFE, R. (1973). The psychology of imprisonment: Privation, power and pathology. *Catalog of selected documents in psychology, 30,* 45.

ZOLA-MORGAN, S., SQUIRE, L. R., & AMARAL, D. G. (1986). Human amnesia and the medial temporal region: enduring memory impairment following a bilateral lesion limited to field CA1 of the hippocampus. *Journal of Neuroscience, 6*(10), 2950–2967.

ZOLA-MORGAN, S., SQUIRE, L. R., & AMARAL, D. G. (1989a). Lesions of the amygdala that spare adjacent cortical regions do not impair memory or exacerbate the impairment following lesions of the hippocampal formation. *Journal of Neuroscience 9*(6), 1922–1936.

ZOLA-MORGAN, S., SQUIRE, L. R., & AMARAL, D. G. (1989b). Lesions of the hippocampal formation but not lesions of the fornix or the mammillary nuclei produce long-lasting memory impairment in monkeys. *Journal of Neuroscience, 9*(3), 898–913.

ZUBOFF, S. (1988) *In the age of the smart machine: The future of work and power.* New York: Basic Books.

ZUCKERMAN, M. (1979). Attribution of success and failure revisited, or the motivational bias is alive and well in attribution theory. *Journal of Personality, 46,* 245–287.

ZUCKERMAN, M. (1984). Sensation-seeking: A comparative approach to a human trait. *Brain and Behavioral Sciences, 73,* 413–433.

COPYRIGHTS AND ACKNOWLEDGEMENTS

PHOTOS AND ILLUSTRATIONS

FIGURES

brary/Photo Researchers, Inc. **3-21:** Adapted from *Human Anatomy and Physiology* by Anthony J. Gaudin and Kenneth C. Jones, copyright © 1989 by Harcourt Brace Jovanovich, Inc., reprinted by permission of W. B. Saunders Company. **3-26:** Adapted from *The Amazing Brain,* 1984, by R. Ornstein, R. F. Thompson, and D. Macaulay, Redwood City, CA, The Scientific Press. **3-28:** McConnell, P. and Berry, M., 1978, "The effects of undernutrition on Purkinje cell dendrite growth in the rat," *Journal of Comparative Neurology,* 177: 159–171. Adapted by permission of Alan R. Liss, Inc., Publisher & Copyrights Holder.

CHAPTER 4 **4-3:** Cytogenics Laboratory, University of California, San Francisco. **4-4:** Cytogenics Laboratory, University of California, San Francisco. **4-5:** © Culver Pictures. **4-6:** Gottesman, I. I., *Developmental Genetics and Ontogentic Psychology,* Minnesota Symposia on Child Psychology, Vol. 8, edited by A. D. Pick, Copyright © 1974 University of Minnesota. Reprinted by the University of Minnesota Press. **4-7:** © Peter Jones. **4-10:** Adapted form "The Brain," by David Hubel. Copyright © 1979 by Scientific American, Inc. All rights reserved. **4-11:** CNMHS/Spadem/Art Resource, New York. **4-12:** The Affluence of Hunting and Gathering Societies, from "In Search of the Affluent Society" by Allen Johnson from *Human Nature* magazine, September 1978. Copyright © 1978 Human Nature, Inc. Reprinted by permission of the publisher. **4-15:** From *Human Emerging,* 2/E, by Bernard G. Campbell. Copyright © 1979 by Bernard G. Campbell. Reprinted by permission of Scott, Foresman and Company. **4-16:** Adapted from "Imprinting in Animals," by Eckhard H. Hess. Copyright © 1958 by Scientific American, Inc. All rights reserved. **4-17:** Nina Leen, *Life* Magazine, © Time, Inc. **4-18, top:** Courtesy of Fiona Anderson. **4-18, bottom:** © Frank Siteman/Stock, Boston. **4-19:** From *The Study of Instinct* by N. Tinbergen. Published by Oxford University Press, New York, 1951. **4-20:** Adapted from *Sociobiology and Mental Disorder* by Brant Wenegrat. Copyright © 1984, Addison Wesley Publishing Company, Menlo Park, California. Reprinted with permission.

CHAPTER 5 **5-3:** From Verheijen, F. J., 1961, "A simple after-image method demonstrating multidirectional eye movements during fixation," *Optica Acta,* 1961, 8: 309–311. Adapted by permission of the *Journal of Modern Optics,* Taylor and Francis, Ltd., publisher. **5-4:** S. Stevens, 1961, "The psychophysics of sensory fucntion," in W. A. Rosenblith, ed., *Sensory Communication,* MIT Press. Adapted by permission of MIT Press. **5-5:** From Bloom and Fawcett, 1968, *A Textbook of Histology,* W. B. Saunders Company, © D. W. Fawcett, MD. Adapted with permission of the author. **5-7:** © John Radcliff Infirmary/Science Photo Library/Photo Resarchers, Inc. **5-9:** © Lennart Nilsson. **5-12:** © Grant Heilman Photography. **5-13:** Hurvich, L. M., and Jameson, D., 1974, "Opponent processes as a model of neural organization," *American Psychologist,* 29: 88–102. Copyright © 1974 by the American Psychological Association. Adpated by permission. **5-15:** © Grant Heilman Photography. **5-18, left:** Oscar Claude Monet, *Rouen Cathedral, Façade.* Oil on canvas, 39⅝x26 in. (100.5 x 66.2 cm.). Juliana Cheney Edwards Collection. Courtesy, Museum of Fine Arts, Boston. **5-18, right:** Winslow Homer, *Hurricane, Bahamas,* Watercolor on paper. H. 14½ in., W. 21 in. The Metropolitan Museum of Art, Amelia B. Lazarus Fund, 1910. **5-20:** Figure from *Human Information Processing,* Second Edition, by Peter Lindsay, Donald A. Norman, copyright © 1977 by Harcourt Brace Jovanovich, Inc., reprinted by permission of the publisher. **5-23, 5-24, 5-25:** D. H. Hubel and T. N. Weisel, 1962. *Journal of Physiology,* 160: 106–154. Adapted with permission from The Physiological Society, Oxford. **5-26:** Gross, C. G., Rocha-Miranda, C. E., and Bender, D. B., 1972, "Visual properties of neurons in inferotemporal cortex of the macaque," *Journal of Neurophysiology,* 35, 96–111. Reprinted by permission of the author and the American Physiological Society. **5-27:** From L. Yarbus, 1967, in *Eye Movements and Vision.* Reprinted with permission of Plenum Publishing Corporation. **5-28:** Adapted form *Human Anatomy and Physiology* by Anthony J. Gaudin and Kenneth C. Jones, copyright © 1989 by Harcourt Brace Jovanovich, Inc., reprinted by permission of W. B. Saunders Company. **5-30:** Figure from *Human Information Processing,* Second Edition, by Peter Lindsay, Donald A. Norman, copyright © 1977 by Harcourt Brace Jovanovich, Inc., reprinted by permission of the publisher. **5-32:** © Lennart Nilsson. **5-33, 5-34, 5-35:** From *Introduction to Sensory Processes* by Jacqueline Ludel. Copyright © 1978 by W. H. Freeman and Company. Reprinted with permission. **5-36:** Adapted from "Opiate Receptors and Internal Opiates," by S. H. Snyder, *Scientific American,* 51, March 1977. **5-37:** © Daniel Ferro. **5-38:** © Susan Holtz.

CHAPTER 6 **6-1:** © Susan Holtz. **6-2, 6-3:** Carraher, R. G., & Thurston, J. B., 1968, *Optical Illusions and the Visual Arts* © 1966 Litten Educational Publishing. Reproduced by permission of Wadsworth, Inc. **6-4:** Kopfermann, H., 1930, "Psychologische Untersuchungen über die Wirkung Zweidimensionaler Darstellung Korperlicher Gebilde," *Psychologische Forschang,* 13: 293–364. Adapted with permission of Springer-Verlag, Publishers. **6-6, top:** Kaiser Porcelain, Ltd. **6-11:** Coren S., 1972, "Subjective contours and apparent depth," *Psychological Review,* 79: 359–367. Copyright © 1972 by the American Psychological Association. Adapted by permission. **6-12:** From Gregory, R., 1970, *The Intelligent Eye* Weidenfeld and Nicolson, London. Reprinted with permission of the publisher. **6-13:** © Norman Snyder. **6-18:** © Susan Holtz. **6-21:** © Robin Risque. **6-22:** Adapted from *Eye and Brain,* 1973, 1977 by R. L. Gregory. Copyright © 1977 by McGraw-Hill & Co. **6-23:** Ralph Crane, *Life* Magazine, © Time, Inc. **6-24:** British Information Services. **6-25:** Hudson, W., 1962, "Pictorial perception and education in Africa," *Psychologia Aficana,* 9: 226–239. **6-28:** © Susan Holtz. **6-29, left:** Vincent van Gogh, *Hospital Corridor at Saint-Rémy.* (1889). Gouache and watercolor on paper, 24⅛ x 18⅝". Collection, The Museum of Modern Art, New York. Abbey Aldrich Rockefeller Bequest. **6-29:** M. C. Escher, *Waterfall.* © 1990 M. C. Escher Heirs/Cordon Art-Baarn-Holland. **6-30:** Courtesy, Chase Manhattan Bank. **6-31:** © Grant Heilman Photography. **6-32:** From J. J. Gibson et al., 1969, "The change from visible to invisible: A study of optical transitions," *Perceptions and Psychophysics* v. 5, 113–116. Reprinted by permission of Psychonomic Society, Inc., and the author. **6-33:** From *Vision.* By David Marr. Copyright © 1982 by W. H. Freeman and Company. Reprinted with permission. **6-34:** Figure from *Sensation and Perception,* Second Edition, by Stanley Coren and Lawrence Ward, Copyright © 1984 by Harcourt Brace Jovanovich, Inc., reprinted by permission of the publisher.

CHAPTER 7 **7-1:** © UPI/Bettmann Newsphotos. **7-2:** © Judith Aron/Peter Arnold, Inc. **7-3:** © Robin Risque. **7-6:** Van de Castle, R., *The Psychology of Dreaming,* Morristown, N. J.: General Learning Corporation, 1971. Adapted with permission of the author. **7-7:** © Robert McElroy/Woodfin Camp & Associates. **7-8:** © Christopher Brown/Stock, Boston. **7-9:** Reprinted from *Triangle,* Sandoz Journal of Medical Science, Vol. II, No. 3, 1955. Copyright Sandoz, Ltd., Basel, Switzerland. **7-10:** The Hidden Observer, from "Hypnosis and Consciousness" by E. R. Hilgard from *Human Nature* magazine, Jaunary 1978. Copyright © 1978 by Human Nature, Inc. Reprinted by permission of the publisher.

CHAPTER 8 **8-4:** Courtesy, Dr. Skinner, Harvard University. **8-6:** Yerkes Regional Primate Center of Emory University. **8-7:** Yerkes Regional Primate Center of Emory University. **8-8:** Yerkes Regional Primate Center of Emory University. **8-9:** E. C. Tolman and C. H. Honzik, 1930, "Insight in rats," University of California Publications in Psychology, 4, 215–232. Adapted with permission of the University of California Press. **8-10:** Garcia, J., and Koelling, R. A., 1966, "Relation of cue to consequence in avoidance learning," *Psychometric Science* 4: 123–214.

CHAPTER 9 **9-1:** Nickerson, R. S., and Adams, M. J., 1979, "Long-term memory for a common object," *Cognitive Psychology,* 11: 297. Adapted with permission of the author and Academic Press. **9-3:** Shannon, B., 1979, "Yesterday, today and tomorrow," *Acta Psychologica,* 43, 469–476. Reprinted by permission of Elsevier Science Publishers. **9-5:** H. P. Bahrick et al., 1975, "Fifty years of memory for names and faces: A cross-sectional approach," *Journal of Experimental Psychology,* 104: 54–75. Copyright © 1975 by the American Psychological Association. Adapted by permission. **9-6:** Rubin, D. C., 1977, "Very long-term memory for prose and verse, *Journal of Verbal Learning and Verbal Behavior,* 16, 611–621. Adapted with permission of Academic Press. **9-7:** © AP/Wide World Photos. **9-8:** Shepard, R. N., 1967, "Recognition memory for words, sentences, and pictures." *Journal of Verbal Learning and Verbal Behavior,* 6, 156–163. Adapted with permission of Academic Press. **9-9, 9-10A, 9-10B:** From *On the Experience of Time* by Robert E. Ornstein (Penguin Books, 1969), copyright © Robert E. Ornstein, 1969. **9-11:** Bartlett, F. C., 1932, *Remembering: A study in experimental and social psychology,* Cambridge, Cambridge University Press, Publisher. Adapted with permission of the publisher. **9-14:** E. F. Loftus, 1979, *Eyewitness Testimony,* Harvard Univeristy Press, p. 79. Reproduced with permission of the author. **9-15:** T. B. Rogers et al., 1977, "Self-reference and the encoding of personal information," *Journal of Personality and Social Psychology,* 35: 677–688. Copyright © 1977 by the American Psychological Association. Adapted by permission.

CHAPTER 10 **10-2:** © Three Lions. **10-4:** N. Chomsky, 1966, *Aspects of the Theory of Syntax,* Cambridge, MIT Press. Adapted by permission of the publisher. **10-5:** McClelland, J. L., and Rumelhart, D. E., 1981, "An interactive activation model of context effects in latter perception, Part 1: An account of basic findings," *Psychological Review,* 88: 380. Copyright © 1981 by the American Psychological Association. Reprinted by permission. **10-6:** Rumelhart, D. E., and McClelland, J. L., 1986, *Parallel Distributed Processing, Explorations in the Microstructure of Cognition,* Vol. 1, Foundations, MIT Press, Cambridge.

CHAPTER 11 **11-1:** Adapted from "Development of Mental Abilities," by N. Bayley, 1970, in *Carmichael's Manual of Child Psychology,* Vol. 1, P. Mussen, ed., copyright © 1970 John Wiley & Sons Inc. **11-2:** © Dan McCoy/Rainbow. **11-3:** Adapted from Terman, L. M., and Merrill, M. A., *Manual for the Third Revision of the Stanford-Binet Intelligence Scale.* Boston: Houghton Mifflin Co., 1973. Reproduced with permission of the Riverside Publishing Company, 8420 W. Bryn Mawr Ave., Chicago, Il. 60631. **11-4:** © Elizabeth Crews. **11-5:** © Anthony Jalandoni/Monkmeyer Press Photos. **11-6:** From Feuerstein, R., 1979, *The Dynamic Assessment of Retarded Performers,* Baltimore, University Park Press.

CHAPTER 12 **12-1:** © 1986 James Sugar/Black Star. **12-2:** From Ekman, P. (Ed.), 1973, *Darwin and Facial Expression,* New York, Academic Press. Adapted with permission of Suzanne Chevalier-Skolnikoff and the publisher. **12-3:** Figure from *Emotion: A Psychorevolutionary Synthesis* by Robert Plutchik. Copyright © 1980 by Robert Plutchik. Reprinted by permission of Harper & Row, Publishers, Inc. **12-4:** Courtesy, Dr. Paul Eckman. **12-5:** Scala/Art Resource, NY. **12-6:** Dr. H. A. Sackheim, "Emotions are expressed more intensely on the left side of the face," *Science,* Figure 1, Vol. 202, Pages 434–436, 27 October 1978. Copyright 1978 by the AAAS. **12-7:** J. C. Spiesman et al., 1964, "Experimental reduction of stress based on ego-defense theory," *Journal of Abnormal and Social Psychology,* 68: 367–380. Copyright © 1964 by the American Psychological Association. Adapted by permission.

CHAPTER 13 **13-2:** "Hierarchy of Needs" from *Motivation and Personality* by Abraham H. Maslow. Copyright © 1954 by Harper & Row, Publishers, Inc. Copyright © 1970 by Abraham H. Maslow. Reprinted by permission of the publishers. **13-5:** I. L. Powley and R. E. Keesey, 1970, "Relationship of body weight to the lateral hypothalamic feeding syndrome," *Journal of Comparative and Physiological Psychology,* 70: 25–36. Copyright © 1970 by the American Psychological Association. Adapted by permission. **13-6:** Photo courtesy of Neal E. Miller. **13-7:** B. G. Hoebel and P. Teitelbaum, 1966, "Effects of force-feeding and starvation on food intake and body weight of a rat with ventromedial hypothalamic lesions," *Journal of Comparative and Physiological Psychology,* 61: 189–193.

TABLE CREDITS

TEXT CREDITS

INDEX

Page references in *italics* indicate figures, tables, or other illustrative material.

A   0
B   1
C   2
D   3
E   4
F   5
G   6
H   7
I   8
J   9